USING

Simply Accounting® by Sage

Premium 2008

M. PURBHOO

Covers both Simply Accounting Premium 2008 and Simply Accounting 2008

PEARSON

Addison
Wesley

Toronto

LIBRARY AND ARCHIVES CANADA CATALOGUING IN PUBLICATION

Purbhoo, Mary, 1949–
    Using Simply Accounting by Sage Premium 2008 / M. Purbhoo.

Includes index.

Issued also as trade ed. under title: Teach yourself Simply Accounting by Sage Premium 2008. The title of trade ed. is found on separate bellyband on monograph.

ISBN 978-0-321-54938-9 (college ed.).
ISBN 978-0-321-56913-4 (trade ed.)

1. Simply Accounting for Windows (Computer file). 2. Accounting—Computer programs.
I. Title. II. Title: Teach yourself Simply Accounting by Sage Premium 2008.

HF5679.P899 2009   657'.0285536   C2008-902012-X

This edition is also published as Teach Yourself Simply Accounting by Sage® Premium 2008.

ISBN-13: 978-0-321-54938-9 (college ed.)
ISBN-10: 0-321-54938-4 (college ed.)

ISBN-13: 978-0-321-56913-4 (trade ed.)
ISBN-10: 0-321-56913-X (trade ed.)

Vice President, Editorial Director: Gary Bennett
Executive Editor: Samantha Scully
Sponsoring Editor: Alexandra Dyer
Marketing Manager: Cas Shields
Developmental Editors: Rema Celio, John Lewis
Senior Production Editors: Jen Handel, Cheryl Jackson
Copy Editor: Nicole Mellow
Production Coordinators: Andrea Falkenberg, Sarah Lukaweski
Page Layout: Mary Purbhoo
Permissions and Photo Research: Sandy Cooke
Art Director: Julia Hall
Interior and Cover Design: Anthony Leung
Cover Image: Bill Frymire/Masterfile

Credits
Photo of the body fat scale used in the data files on the Student CD-ROM: Courtesy Tanita.
Page 473, screenshot from Canada Revenue Agency website: Canada Revenue Agency and the Minister of Public Works and Government Services Canada, 2008.

1 2 3 4 5   12 11 10 09 08

Printed and bound in the United States of America.

CONTENTS

PREFACE

Using Simply Accounting® by Sage Premium 2008 provides full coverage of the Simply Accounting program for the Premium and Simply version features. The Simply Accounting by Sage 2008 – Student Version is again included (Release B), so all users can learn the program using the same release the author used to create the data files, screens and keystrokes. Although we do not address the Enterprise version of Simply Accounting, the book is also compatible with this version.

In this edition, we have added coverage of inventory locations and more detail on customizing reports. Consistent with the new Enhanced view user interface for Simply Accounting, we work with module windows throughout the text. We create user-specific customized shortcuts to access journals in other modules and use the industry-specific terms for the different applications. For users already familiar with the program, we provide margin notes for the traditional Classic view.

Feedback from users encouraged us to keep the modified organization we introduced for our 2007 version text — separate setup for payroll, delayed introduction of advanced Accounts Receivable and Payable topics and realistic source documents that give you the "feel" of actual company transactions throughout the text.

We have, of course, maintained other aspects of the book that users have told us they value:
- the diversity of companies and business situations, including non-profit, service and inventory businesses
- comprehensive tax coverage for different provinces including remittances. All GST rates and amounts have been updated once again, to 5 percent.
- the realistic approach
- easy-to-follow, step-by-step keystroke instructions and screen illustrations, updated for Version 2008
- the currency of our information (although keeping up with currency rates proves challenging)

Our data files are presented as backup files for both Premium and Simply versions. The Simply Accounting database structure for 2008 results in significantly larger data sets (over 25 MB each), and all our data files would not fit on a CD-ROM. Rather than use DVDs, we chose the more standard CD-ROM with Simply Accounting backup files. Of course, we provide detailed instructions on restoring these backups. This decision has additional advantages — backup files can be restored to your hard disk directly from the CD, the same backup can be restored more than once and the smaller files can be copied very quickly.

The Student CD-ROM with Data Files has the following additional resources:
- review questions and cases for each chapter
- additional appendices with supplementary materials
- the interactive Accounting Cycle Tutorial that introduces basic accounting terms and concepts

The page-length bookmark is included again, with a mini index and a ruler-marked edge to help you refer to specific lines on a page. We hope that you will use the bookmark to manage the page-flipping that is inevitable with a keystroke text.

The basic organization of the text is unchanged. Part One provides an overview and introduction to Simply Accounting and sales taxes. Data applications that can be completed with both Simply and Premium versions are located in Part Two. We introduce the six ledgers of the Simply Accounting program (General, Payables, Receivables, Payroll, Inventory and Division) in separate applications. Budgeting and account reconciliation procedures are covered in two more applications. Advanced Receivables and Payables features (orders and quotes, tax remittances, sales to foreign customers and Internet linkages) are demonstrated in two separate chapters. Online banking is included again, too, with a simulation that allows you to download a bank statement that integrates with data from the text. The required data files for all these chapters are set up in advance, and for each new type of transaction we provide detailed keystrokes and matching screens.

Four applications cover setting up a computerized accounting system using Simply Accounting. Again, detailed instructions with screen illustrations are given for each setup as you learn to convert, design and implement a complete accounting system.

- In Chapter 4, you set up a non-profit organization that uses only the General Ledger.
- In Chapter 7, you set up a service organization using the General, Payables and Receivables Ledgers.
- In Chapter 9, you add payroll to a data file that already has the General, Payables and Receivables Ledgers.
- In Chapter 16, you set up a comprehensive retail organization that uses the General, Payables, Receivables, Payroll and Inventory Ledgers.

In the final application in Part Two (Stratford Country Inn, Chapter 17), you set up a computerized accounting system on your own. All source documents in this chapter are realistic and descriptive.

Time & Billing and Departmental Accounting, advanced features available only in the Premium version, are covered in Part Three. Separate chapters and data files are prepared for these. All Part Three pages are edged with a blue stripe so that you can find them quickly.

Eleven appendices are provided for reference or further study — four in Part Four of the text and seven on the Student CD-ROM. The text includes the following:
- A: Installing Simply Accounting
- B: Windows Basics, Shortcuts & Terms (includes chart of Simply Accounting keyboard shortcuts; accounting vs. non-accounting terms; terms used for different types of industries)
- C: Correcting Errors after Posting (descriptions and screen displays for reversing entries)
- D: Working in Multi-User Mode

The remaining appendices in PDF format on the Student CD-ROM are available for you to read or print:
- E: Review Questions and Cases
- F: Customizing Reports
- G: Customizing Sales Invoices
- H: Setting Security and Passwords (entering and removing users, access rights and passwords)
- I: Integration with Other Software (linking with MS Office documents, exporting GIFI financial reports and payroll T4s to Canada Revenue Agency, importing customer or vendor data, accounts and transactions)
- J: Online Banking
- K: Review of Basic Accounting

USING THIS BOOK

The accounting applications in this text were prepared using the Premium 2008 and Simply 2008 versions (Release B) of the Simply Accounting software published by The Sage Group PLC.

You must have a hard disk and CD-ROM drive, or a network system with Windows installed. If you do not have your own copy of the Simply Accounting program, you can use the Student Premium software included with this text. Network system users should work with the site administrator to ensure complete data access.

In addition, you should have a standard accounting text for reviewing accounting principles. The text provides some accounting principles and procedures, and the Review of Basic Accounting (Appendix K) and the Accounting Cycle Tutorial on the Student CD-ROM also provide an introduction. However, these are not intended to replace the breadth and depth of most standard accounting texts. You should also consult the built-in Help features and the Simply Accounting manuals on the program CD.

The text is as simple and straightforward as we could make it, but you will still need some familiarity with computers before you work through it. Your life will be easier still if you have acquired some of the fundamentals of troubleshooting.

Instructors can order an Instructor's Resource CD-ROM that includes Simply Accounting solutions for each application after all transactions are completed, an Instructor's Resource Manual with answers for all the cases in the text and a Test Item File. Instructor packages to accompany this text should be ordered from your Pearson Education Canada sales representative.

The Student CD-ROM with Data Files

Because the text is used with the Simply version as well as Premium, we have tried to make version differences, such as differences in features, terminology and labels, as clear as possible. Margin notes in the text for the Simply version and separate data sets should make it easy for all users to follow the text.

The Student CD-ROM has an autorun feature that should open the Student CD-ROM home window automatically when you insert the CD into your CD drive. From this home window you can choose to install data files, view the supplementary appendices in PDF format, run the Accounting Cycle Tutorial or browse the CD. The Student CD-ROM home window will remain open for you to make another selection until you close it.

If the Student CD-ROM does not start automatically,

> **Choose** the **Start menu** and click Run. In the filename window,
>
> **Type** d:\start.exe (where d: is the drive letter for your CD drive). **Click OK**.
>
> **Click** **Exit** to close the Student CD-ROM.

The separate installation programs will help you install the data set you need. To choose the correct data set, you must know what version you are using. You can get this information from the program package, from the program CD or from the Select Company window in the program. SIMPLY ACCOUNTING BY SAGE or SIMPLY ACCOUNTING BY SAGE PREMIUM appears in the Home window for all data files. If you accepted the default installation settings, the program folder name also matches the version.

Use the following chart to help you install the data set you need.

FOR PROGRAM VERSION	CLICK INSTALL BUTTON	DATA SET (FOLDER ON CD)
Simply Version 2008	Install Simply Version Data	Simply
Student Premium Version 2008	Install Premium Version Data	Premium
Premium Version 2008	Install Premium Version Data	Premium
Enterprise Version 2008	Install Premium Version Data	Premium

Both installation programs create a data folder named SimData on drive C. If you need to work with another location for your data files, refer to page 6 in this text. You can install the data as often as you need to.

You can restore files directly from the Student CD-ROM to your hard disk. However, we recommend installing the backup files to your hard disk and keeping the original CD safe for later use.

If you are using the Enterprise version, the Simply Accounting data conversion wizard will convert the Premium data files when you restore them. Because the backup files remain unchanged, you can restore the same files later using the Premium version.

Passwords

We have not added any passwords to any data files to ensure maximum accessibility. However, if you are using the Premium version in a multi-user or network environment that includes users and passwords, you will need to enter your user name and password before you can open the data files. Ask your instructor or site administrator for the user name and password that you should use. Refer to Appendix H on the Student CD-ROM for instructions on working with passwords.

Working with Different Versions of Simply Accounting

You can use the Student CD-ROM data files with the 2008 Simply, Premium, Enterprise and Premium Student versions of Simply Accounting, Release B or later.

The Student version is a fully functional Premium version that you can use for 14 months after installation, but you cannot restore or open data files from previous versions with it. You can install only one version of Simply Accounting 2008 on your computer. If you are using the Simply version and want to install the Student Premium version, you must first uninstall the Simply version.

If you try to restore the backup files with earlier versions of Simply Accounting (2007 and earlier), Simply Accounting displays an error message. If you use 2008, Release A, you will see a warning that the files have been used in a later version. You can continue. Users who have a different version can install the Student program accompanying the text.

Although the data files can be used with later versions of the software, you may see changes in screens, keystrokes and payroll tax amounts. Before you open a data file with a later version, the Simply Accounting conversion wizard will update the data file to match the program version you are using. Always refer to the manuals and update notices for later versions.

Working Through the Applications

Keystroke Instruction Style

We have incorporated different paragraph styles for different kinds of statements in the text to help you identify the instructions that you must follow to complete the transactions correctly and see the screens that we present. These different styles are illustrated below:

Press (enter) or **press** the **Add button** to start the Add Account wizard. (Keystroke command line — command word is in bold and the object of the command, what you press, is in colour. Lines are indented and spaced apart. Additional text or information for the line is shown in plain text.)

Type West Carbide Tools (net 30) (Command line with text you type in a special font.)

Or you can click the Comment field to advance the cursor. (Alternative keystroke sequence that you may want to use later. Paragraph is indented in block style and plain text style is used.)

Regular text is presented in normal paragraphs like this one. **Key words** are shown in colour to make it easy to identify the topics covered in the text. Names of icons, fields, text and tool buttons that you will see on-screen in the program have all initial letters capitalized in our text (for example, Adjust A Previously Posted Invoice tool or Display A Reminder If Exchange Rate Is One Day Old). Account names included in regular text paragraphs are italicized (for example, *Revenue from Sales* or *Cost of Goods Sold*).

The text also uses Notes and Warnings that contain additional important information and cautions.

Order of Applications

Setup applications are introduced early in the text. Advanced users should have no difficulty working through the applications in the order given and may even choose to skip some applications. However, at a minimum, we recommend working through all keystroke transactions (the ones with a ✓ beside them) so that you become familiar with all the journals before starting the more comprehensive applications.

There are alternatives if the text is used at an introductory level in one course and then at an advanced level for a different course. In this case, students can complete the General, basic Payables, basic Receivables, Payroll and Inventory transaction applications (Chapters 3, 5, 6, 8 and 10) in the introductory course and the remaining chapters later. Chapters 11 and 12 may be completed at any time after Chapter 6 and before Chapter 13 because these chapters do not have payroll or inventory transactions. Students can also complete the transactions for the four setup applications separately from setting up these data files because we provide data files for these setup chapters as well (except Stratford Country Inn, Chapter 17). Chapters may also be completed in a different sequence, outlined on the following page.

1. Read and work through the two Getting Started chapters in Part One.

2A. Complete the ledger applications in order: Missoni Marbleworks (General), Chai Tea Room (basic Payables), Air Care Services (basic Receivables), Helena's Academy (Payroll), Adrienne Aesthetics (Inventory), Andersson Chiropractic Clinic and Maple Leaf Rags (advanced features of the first three ledgers) and Truman Tires* (Division or Project).

2B. (Premium version only) Complete the Part Three applications in any order: Flabuless Fitness — Time & Billing and Able & Associates (Departmental Accounting).

3. Complete the account reconciliation (Tesses Tresses) and budgeting (Village Galleries) applications.

4. Complete the four setup applications in order: Toss for Tots (General), Dorfmann Design (three ledgers), Lime Light Laundry (adding the Payroll ledger) and Flabuless Fitness (six ledgers).

5. Complete the Stratford Country Inn setup application with realistic source documents. Users may want to attempt this setup with the help of the setup wizard from the Setup menu in the Home window.

* Truman Tires (Division Ledger, Chapter 13) may be completed after all other chapters because it does not introduce keystrokes required for any other application.

This order is shown graphically in the following chart:

AN ALTERNATIVE SEQUENCE FOR WORKING THROUGH THE APPLICATIONS

NOTES

Each box includes the chapter or application title, the chapter number and the topic being introduced.

Applications within the same box may be completed in any order.

ACKNOWLEDGMENTS

It has been said that the only constant is change, and it occurs on all fronts. Change can challenge and keep us motivated. Some changes make us happy, others do not.

Writing is very much a solitary job, but each project brings new contacts at Pearson and at Sage. And, sometimes we are fortunate to work with old friends.

It has been a pleasure to work closely with Jennifer Handel. Her dedication to her job and talent for organization meant that I could always count on her to remind me what I needed to focus on when I was feeling frazzled or overwhelmed by a multitude of details. Jen's constantly cheerful disposition meant that I always felt happier after our meetings than before. She will definitely be missed as she moves on to her new career at Pearson. The care she took with her job made the transition seamless though, even in the final weeks. I am thankful to Mary Ann Field and Cheryl Jackson for stepping in for the last few frantic weeks.

Several others at Pearson have also been instrumental in seeing this project to successful completion. Gary Bennett and Alexandra Dyer assumed the role of overseeing the entire project, usually played by Samantha Scully. I am thankful for their support as all were affected by Samantha's absence. Michael Kelley spent several hours helping me make the transition to working on the Mac. Rema Celio is another old friend who came back to work on the text briefly this year. And Anthony Leung provided another innovative cover design. All of them are busy with many projects, yet my involvement with them and other members of the team made me feel that mine was the most important project they had to work on.

My Sage contacts help me to stay connected. I am fortunate to be able to put a face to most of the phone calls I make as I have met most of them at Simply Partnership Conferences over the years. Jaclyn Ng comes through with timely delivery of the software — the multiplicity of versions I need to work with. Alec Loo has helped me navigate the new Simply Accounting data base at the raw data level, saving me hours of work in re-entering source documents to arrive at solution files. And Jim Collins has been as faithful as ever in coming to my rescue as I encountered inconsistencies in my data files. The only thing I can think of that would make these contacts even more perfect would be to have them work weekends — when I am most likely to encounter snags that I cannot resolve. (Is that Murphy's Law at work or a subtle reminder that I should take more time off on weekends?)

Some people thrive on detail work — that is a good thing because I am not one of them. Nicole Mellow, who has worked on my texts in the past, was available again this year for copy editing. She still managed to improve the text, even the parts that have been reworked countless times. Martin Tooke, a second editor, made even more improvements. And Efren Barrato, who completed the technical check of all the instructions and numbers, did an excellent job of finding the little things I missed. Simply Accounting's user interface changed quite dramatically this year. In addition, the federal government's decision to change the GST rate, once again, necessitated recalculating every number in the text yet again. (Am I the only one who lamented when the second GST rate reduction was implemented in January.) So, their ability to find my inconsistencies and suggest corrections was very important and I greatly appreciate their editorial contributions. All these extra eyes help to build the text's reputation for quality.

User surveys and feedback are an important source of information for me. Because I am no longer in the classroom myself, they help me maintain this link and I value their input. I hope that they will always feel free to tell me about mistakes I can correct and improvements I can make.

In particular, Les Barnhouse (Grant MacEwan College), Andrew Dykstra (Georgian College), Michael Malkoun (St. Clair College) and Hazel Matheson (NBCC – Moncton) provided invaluable feedback on the current edition.

Samantha Scully has been absent from this project for personal health reasons, and she has been sorely missed. We have worked together for almost a decade now, during which time I learned to trust her, depend on her as both advocate and advisor and value her judgment, positive outlook and friendship. This book is dedicated to her as she continues her battle to regain health.

In memory of Samantha Scully
July 6, 2008

Part 1
Getting Started

Getting Started

OBJECTIVES

After completing this chapter, you should be able to

- ■ **access** the Simply Accounting program
- ■ **restore** backup files and access data files for a business
- ■ **open** a working copy of the data files for a business
- ■ **understand** Simply Accounting's help features
- ■ **save** your work
- ■ **back up** your data files
- ■ **finish** your session
- ■ **change** default date format settings

NOTES

The instructions in this chapter for starting the program and copying files refer to Windows XP procedures. If you are using a different version of Windows, please refer to Windows and Simply Accounting Help and manuals for assistance with these procedures.

⚠ **WARNING!**

You will be unable to open the data files with Simply 2008 Release A or earlier versions.

The Student CD-ROM with Data Files will be referred to as the Student CD-ROM throughout the text.

GETTING STARTED

Data Files and Abbreviations

The applications in this workbook were prepared using Windows XP and the Simply Accounting Premium 2008 and Simply Accounting 2008 (Release B) software packages produced by Sage Software. You will be unable to open the data files with Simply 2008 Release A or earlier versions. Later releases and versions of the software use later income tax tables and may have changes in screens or keystrokes. If you have a version other than 2008 Release B, you can install the Simply Accounting by Sage 2008 – Student Version (Release B) that comes with this text to work through the applications.

The instructions in this workbook have been written for a stand-alone PC, with a hard disk drive and a CD-ROM disk drive. Windows should be correctly installed on your hard drive. Your printers should be installed and accessible through the Windows program. Refer to Windows Help and manuals for assistance with these procedures.

This workbook reflects the author's approach to working with Simply Accounting. There are alternative approaches to setting up company accounts and to working with the software. Refer to Simply Accounting and Windows Help and manuals for further details.

DATA APPLICATION FILES (All data files are located in C:\SimData\)

Company	Folder\File Name	Chapter
Getting started	start1.CAB	1
Missoni Marbleworks	missoni1.CAB	3
Toss for Tots	skeleton1.CAB (and Setup\toss1.CAB)	4
Chai Tea Room	chai1.CAB	5
Air Care Services	aircare1.CAB	6
Dorfmann Design	Setup\dorfman1.CAB	7
Helena's Academy	helena1.CAB	8
Lime Light Laundry	limelite1.CAB (and Setup\lime-pay1.CAB)	9
Adrienne Aesthetics	adrienne1.CAB	10
Andersson Chiropractic Clinic	anderson1.CAB	11
Maple Leaf Rags	maple1.CAB	12
Truman Tires	truman1.CAB	13
Village Galleries	village1.CAB	14
Tesses Tresses	tess1.CAB	15
Flabuless Fitness	Setup\flab-apr1.CAB	16
	Setup\flab-may1.CAB	16
	Setup\flab-jun1.CAB	16
Stratford Country Inn	user setup	17
Flabuless Fitness (Premium)	flab-time1.CAB	18
Able & Associates Inc. (Premium)	able1.CAB	19

The applications increase in complexity. Each one introduces new ledgers, setups or features as shown in the following chart.

DATA APPLICATION	LEDGER USED						OTHER
	GL	AP	AR	PAY	INV	PROJ	
Missoni Marbleworks	*						
Toss for Tots	*						2
Chai Tea Room	*	*					
Air Care Services	*	*	*				3
Dorfmann Design	*	*	*				2, 3
Helena's Academy	*	*	*	*			
Lime Light Laundry	*	*	*	*			2
Adrienne Aesthetics	*	*	*	*	*		3
Andersson Chiropractic Clinic	*	*	*				
Maple Leaf Rags	*	*	*				3, 4, 7
Truman Tires	*	*	*	*	*	*	3, 7
Village Galleries	*	*	*	*	*		3, 5, 7
Tesses Tresses	*	*	*		*		6
Flabuless Fitness (Chapter 16)	*	*	*	*	*		2, 3, 4, 7
Stratford Country Inn	*	*	*	*			1, 3, 8
Flabuless Fitness (Chapter 18)	*	*	*	*	*		PREMIUM 1
Able & Associates Inc.	*	*	*	*	*		PREMIUM 2

LEDGERS

GL	= General Ledger		PAY	= Payroll
AP	= Accounts Payable		INV	= Inventory
AR	= Accounts Receivable		PROJ	= Project (Allocations or jobcosting)

Other:

1 All realistic source documents (most chapters have some realistic source documents)

2 Setup application with keystrokes	5 Budgeting	7 Foreign currency transactions
3 Credit cards	6 Account reconciliation	8 Setup application without keystrokes
4 Internet links		

PREMIUM 1 Time & Billing; Build from Bill of Materials; Inventory locations (Premium version only)

PREMIUM 2 Departmental Accounting (Premium version only)

NOTES

The applications in Chapters 1 through 17 can be completed with both the Simply and the Premium versions. For the applications in Chapters 18 and 19, you must use the Premium version.

The Stratford Country Inn file is not set up in advance for you. You must create that file on your own.

The Student CD-ROM also includes data files for bank reconciliation for Chapter 15, Case 6 for Chapter 16 in Appendix E, and online banking in Appendix J. (Appendices E and J are also on the Student CD-ROM.)

NOTES
For an introduction to basic Windows terminology used in this text, refer to Appendix B. This appendix also includes charts of Simply Accounting keyboard shortcuts and terminology for different industry types.

NOTES
For assistance with installing the Simply Accounting program, refer to Appendix A.

NOTES
Access the business guides from the Start menu on the desktop (choose Start, then point to Programs and Simply Accounting and click New Business Guide). You can also access the business guides from Simply Accounting's Home window (choose the Business Assistant menu and click New Business Guide). Choose your province and type of business.

WARNING!
Unless you have experience working with Windows folders, we recommend using the autoinstall option on the Student CD-ROM to install your data set.

The Simply Accounting Program

Simply Accounting is an integrated accounting program with many features that are suitable for small- and medium-sized businesses. It includes several ledgers and journals that work together so that data entered in one part of the program will be linked and available in other parts of the program. Thus ledgers are automatically updated from journal entries, and reports always include the most recent transactions and ledger changes. A business can use one or more of the accounting modules: General, Payables, Receivables, Payroll, Inventory, Project and Time and Billing (Premium version or higher). Only the features used are set up for each application. Thus, if payroll is not used, there is no need to set up the Payroll module, and it can be hidden from view. A more complete description of the program and its features is presented in Chapter 16, pages 615–616.

Simply Accounting Program Components

When you select the Typical Installation option, several components will be installed:

- **Simply Accounting Program**: the Simply Accounting software you will need to perform the accounting transactions for your company. It will be placed in the main Simply Accounting Premium 2008 folder under the Program Files folder or the folder location you selected.
- **Samples**: complete company records for a sample company — Universal Construction. They will be placed in a folder under Documents and Settings called Samdata.
- **Templates**: predefined charts of accounts and settings for a large number of business types. These files will be stored in a folder called Template. Two starter files with only charts of accounts also appear in this folder.
- **Crystal Reports Print Engine**, **Forms** and **Management Reports**: a variety of commonly used business forms and reports that you can customize to suit your own business needs as well as the program to access and print them. They will be placed in a folder under Simply Accounting Premium 2008 called Forms.
- **Customizable Forms** and **Microsoft Office Documents**: a variety of documents designed for integrated use with Simply Accounting. They will be placed in a Reports folder under Simply Accounting Premium 2008.
- **New Business Guide**: a number of checklists showing the steps to follow when setting up a new business, customized for a variety of business types in different provinces. This guide includes addresses and phone numbers as well as Web addresses that you can access for further information.
- **Manuals**: documentation that will help you learn how to use Simply Accounting.

Backing Up Your Data Files

Before you begin the applications, you should copy the data to your hard disk drive. The data files on the Student CD-ROM are Simply Accounting backup files. The original files are very large and will not fit on one CD. Furthermore, you cannot work in Simply Accounting from a CD because Simply Accounting will not open read-only files, and all CD-ROM files are read-only files. Keep the CD in a safe place just in case you need to start over from the original files. The following instructions will copy all the files to your hard disk drive and create the necessary folders.

Installing Your Data

The Student CD-ROM contains Simply and Premium versions of the data files and several supplementary files for the book. It also has programs that will automatically copy the data to a new SimData folder on your hard drive (drive C:). If you want to use a different location for your data files, proceed to page 6.

You must work with the correct version of the data set. If you are working with the Simply version, install the Simply data files — you cannot open Premium version files. If you are working with the Premium (or Student) version, install the Premium data files.

If you are using the **Simply version**, refer to sidebar notes for the differences between the Simply 2008 and Premium 2008 versions.

Insert the **Student CD-ROM** into your CD drive. The home window appears:

Click   **Install Simply Version Data** to copy the data set for Simply 2008, or

Click   **Install Premium Version Data** for the Premium and Student versions.

When all the files have been copied, you will see the following message:

Click   **OK**. The data files have been copied to C:\SimData.

If the Student CD-ROM home window does not open automatically,

Choose the **Start menu** on the desktop and **click Run** to open the Run window.

Type   d:\start.exe (where D: is the drive letter for your CD drive.)

Click   **OK**.

You can also view the supplementary files on the CD, save these files to your hard drive or print them if you want.

Click   **Appendices E–K** and then **click** the **file** you want.

Close   the **PDF file** when you have finished viewing or printing it. **Click Exit** to close the Student CD-ROM window.

All the data files for the book are now located in the new SimData folder in drive C:. We will use the shorthand C: instead of Local Disk (C):. We will restore the backups from this folder and use it as our working data folder.

Working with Other File Locations

You can copy the files to a different location by copying the data from the CD just as you would copy other files to your hard disk drive. Choose the correct version of the data set (Simply or Premium).

You cannot open a Simply Accounting data file directly from a CD, but you can restore a Simply Accounting backup file from a CD. You must save the file on your hard drive before you can work with the data.

You can also work on a removeable USB drive in Simply Accounting because this is a rewritable medium.

Starting Simply Accounting and Accessing Data Files

From your Windows desktop,

Click **Start** (on the task bar) so the pop-up menu appears.

Point to **Programs**. Hold the mouse on Programs until the list of programs appears.

Point to **Simply Accounting Premium 2008**. Hold the mouse on Simply Accounting until its cascading menu list of programs appears.

Click **Simply Accounting Premium 2008**. You should follow the path illustrated in the Classic Windows view that follows:

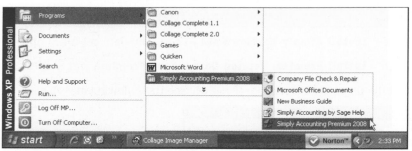

If you are using the Windows XP view,

Click **Start**. **Point to All Programs**, then **point to Simply Accounting Premium 2008** and **click Simply Accounting Premium 2008** as shown in the following screen:

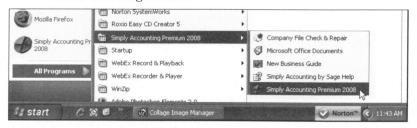

You will open the registration screen the first time you use the program. Otherwise, you will see the Simply Accounting Select Company screen on the following page.

NOTES
Alternative instructions or commands that you may need to use are shown in indented paragraphs without highlighting, like the paragraph beside this note, beginning with "You can copy the files to..."

NOTES
If you have already restored the backup file, refer to page 20 for instructions on accessing a working copy of a data set.

NOTES
If you added a desktop shortcut when you installed the program, you can double click to open the Simply Accounting program.

NOTES
If you used a different name for the program when you installed it, choose that name.

If you have not yet registered the program refer to Appendix A, page A-8 in the text. Until you register and activate the program, you will be allowed to use the program only for a limited time.

If you have already restored the backup file, refer to page 20 for instructions on accessing a working copy of a data set.

Opening a Data File from a Backup

You will now see the Simply Accounting Select Company Welcome screen:

The opening window gives you several options: working with the sample company files, creating new company files, restoring backup files or working with existing data files. If you have worked with the program before, the option to Open The Last Company You Worked On appears with the name of the file you used most recently (see page 20). We need to restore a backup file.

If your working files are lost or damaged, you will also need to restore backup files. You can also restore files from the File menu in the Home window of any data file, including the Sample Company file.

> **Click** **Restore From Backup**.

> **Click** **OK** to start the Simply Accounting Restore From Backup wizard:

> **Click** **Next** to begin:

The first time you restore a backup, no default location or backup files are entered.

> **Click** **Browse** to open the folder you worked in most recently.

The folder names in your Look In field and Browse windows may be different from the ones we show. Simply Accounting 2008 uses a folder under Documents and Settings as the default location for files, so you may see this as the selected folder initially. If you have opened another data file, you may see the folder where that file is stored. To ensure consistency in file names and locations for our instructions, we always work with the folder we created when installing the data files, that is, C:\SimData.

WARNING!
You will be allowed to use the program only for a limited time before entering the registration validation codes.

Remember to activate Payroll as well. Refer to Appendix A in this text. You must have a payroll ID code in order to use the Payroll features of the program.

You must register the Student version before you can use it, but you will not need to activate payroll.

NOTES
The Select Company window shows the version you are using. This window has Premium added to the screen.

In Chapter 4, we show the location of the Select Company option in the View menu.

WARNING!
Each application has many files containing different parts of the accounting information. All files must be contained in the same folder. If any file is missing, you will be unable to access the information. When you restore a backup, you will keep the necessary files together.

NOTES
Your screens may look different if you have selected different viewing options such as displaying the folders as lists or icons. The viewing options can be changed from the View menu for Windows.

Click the **Look In field list arrow** to change the folder you are searching and see all the drives on your computer:

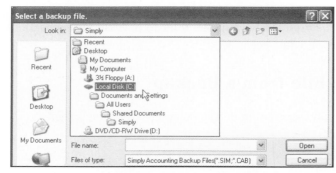

The backup files we need are in C:\SimData, if you used the automatic installation feature of the Student Data and CD-ROM.

Click **C:** to show the files and folders in this drive:

Click **SimData** to select it.

Click the SimData folder icon SimData if your viewing mode is icons.

Click **Open** to see the list of files you copied from the Student CD-ROM:

Only Simply Accounting format backup files and folders are listed because we are working with the Restore Backup wizard.

Click **start1.CAB** to select it. (Click **start1** if you are not showing file extensions.) Start1 is added to the File Name field.

If you are viewing the files in icon mode, click the start1.CAB icon start1.CAB .

Click **Open**.

You will return to the wizard with the backup files now listed in the Select A Backup File text box with start1.CAB selected as shown:

Click   **Next** to continue, showing the selections you have made:

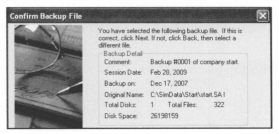

If the information is incorrect, click Back to return to the file selection screen.

Click   **Next** to continue if the information is correct:

At this stage, you should enter the name of the file you are restoring. If you have created the backup from your own file, the name and location of the original file from which you created the backup are shown as the default.

We will create a new folder for each data set in this text. We will continue to work in the SimData folder. If the name you see is different from the one shown above,

Type   C:\SimData\Start\start

Click   **Next**.

You can choose a different location and file name by clicking Browse to access your folders. Enter the location and file name you want to use.

You will see a screen advising you that you are using folder and file names that are new. Simply Accounting will create the new folders and files for you:

Click   **Yes** to confirm and continue.

If you are replacing a corrupt or unusable file, you will see a warning when you type the file name and location file. Click Yes to accept the replacement.

Simply Accounting now confirms that all the data required have been entered:

This is your last chance to change information by clicking Back.

Click   **Finish** to begin restoring the file. You should see the screen that prompts you to enter the session date:

Click   **OK** to open the Home window.

NOTES
We have not set passwords for any data files in this text, but your site administrator for the network may have done so.

NOTES
If your update is later than Release B, you can use the Student Premium Version Release B program that comes with the text.

SIMPLY VERSION
You will see an additional message about upgrading to the Premier version of Simply Accounting.

NOTES
You can download updates periodically (from the Help menu) when you have finished working through the applications in this text.

SIMPLY VERSION
The terms customers and vendors will replace clients and suppliers.

Simply Accounting restores the .SAI file that you use to access the data set and the .SAJ folder that contains the database files.

If passwords have been set up for the file, you will see this password entry screen before the Session date window:

Ask your instructor or site administrator for the name and password you should use (see Appendix H on the Student CD-ROM). Enter your user name and password. Click OK to open the session date screen.

If you see a screen advising that the data has been used in a newer version of the program, your program may be an earlier version of Release B. You will be asked if you wish to proceed; click Yes to open the file. If your version of the program is even earlier (2007), you will be unable to open the data file.

The first time you use the program, you will see a message about automatic program updates (see page A-10). **Do not update your program yet.** Later updates will download later versions and your answers may not match the screens we show.

Do not choose automatic updates.

Simply Accounting Window (Enhanced View)

The Simply Accounting Receivables Home window should be open:

Title bar
Menu bar
Tool/Search bar
Change View command
Open module
Modules pane
Ledger icon
Clients (Customers list)
Task panes
Journal activity icons
Reports pane
Shortcuts pane
General Journal shortcut
Recent reports list
Related tasks pane
Help pane
Status bar

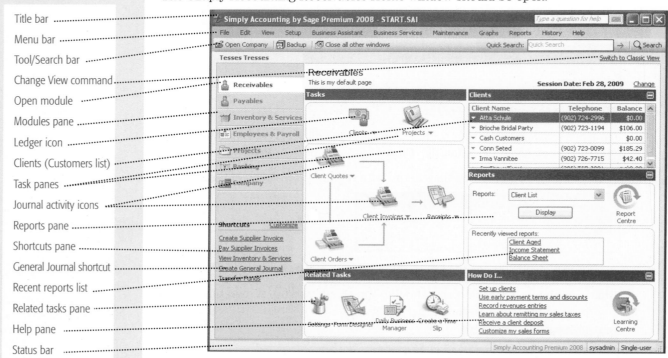

The **title bar** is at the top of the Home window, and it contains the program name, Simply Accounting By Sage Premium 2008, the file name, START.SAI, the Control Menu icon and the size buttons. The **main menu bar** comes next with the **tool bar** below. Tool buttons provide quick access to commonly used menu items and the **search** function. The Search field enables you to look up information in any journal or ledger. Different Simply Accounting windows have different buttons on the tool bar. Below the tool bar, you will find the command to **Switch To Classic View** (see page 13).

The Home window is divided into several panes. The **Modules pane** lists all the modules available for this company data set. The open module — Receivables in this illustration — has a lighter background. The Receivables module is the default Home window, but you can choose any module as the Home window. Activities for the module are represented by separate icons. To access a function or activity, click the related icon.

Below the list of modules, the **Shortcuts pane** allows one-click access to as many as ten different tasks and activities that you set up or customize for each user.

The next column has all the icons you need to complete the activities for the module. The upper **Tasks pane** has the **ledger icon** that allows you to create and modify customer records from the Customers (Clients) window and Projects in the Projects window. In the Premium version, the ledger icon labels change to suit the type of company. For the service company illustrated here, the ledger icon is labelled Clients.

The second Tasks pane has the icons for **journal activities** or **transactions**. Use these icons to enter the accounting transactions in this text. Clicking the icon opens the journal directly for that type of transaction.

Each ledger and journal icon has a **shortcuts list arrow**. Clicking an entry in a shortcuts list will access the activity directly and bypass the main task window. For example, you can begin adjusting an invoice to make a correction if an entry was posted in error, bypassing the first step of opening the journal.

> **Click**   the **shortcuts drop-down list arrow for Client Invoices** ▼ :

> **Click**   some **other shortcut list arrows** to see the choices.

Below the ledger and journal icons, you will find the **Related Tasks pane**. From the icons in this pane, you can perform other ledger-related activities such as entering settings for the open ledger.

The right-hand column also has three different panes. The first one has a **list of ledger accounts** for the selected module. For the Receivables module, the list shows clients or customers with the phone number and outstanding balance. The Payables ledger will show the list of suppliers or vendors.

Below the list of customers or clients, the **Reports pane** allows quick access to all reports for the ledger from the **Reports drop-down list** and to the **Report Centre**, from which you can access all reports. Reports that you displayed most recently are added to the list in the **Recently Viewed Reports** section. Clicking a report in this list will open the last report you viewed.

In the lower right-hand corner, the **Help pane** has a list of **How Do I ...** topics to help you get started using the module. Click a topic to see the steps for that activity. The Help window will stay open until you close it. You can keep it open to assist you while you are completing a task or transaction. You can also access the **Learning Centre**, another way of getting help, here.

> **Click**   **Set Up Clients (Customers)** on the How Do I list of topics.

> **Read**   the **instructions** and then **close** the **Help window**.

The **status bar** appears last. In the Enhanced View, the status bar shows the program name and version as well as the user's name.

SIMPLY VERSION
The program name in the title bar is Simply Accounting by Sage 2008. You will not see the Create A Time Slip icon (Related Tasks pane).

NOTES
Appendix B shows a complete chart of alternative terms used in Simply Accounting for different types of industries.

SIMPLY VERSION
Icon labels do not change. Customers will replace the Clients label for the ledger icon and list. Sales Invoices replaces Client Invoices.

NOTES
In other windows, the status bar describes the purpose of the icon or field that has the pointer.

To work with another module, you can click the module you want from the list in the modules pane.

> **Click**   **Employees & Payroll** in the modules pane.

This module now becomes the Home window, so its icons for ledger and journal activities are displayed. The Ledger icon is now labelled Employees as shown:

In this module, the quill pen symbol shows that the Payroll Ledger is not set up — the history is not finished. When ledgers are not finished, you can add and change historical data. When you create new company data files, all ledgers have this symbol.

Your Missoni Home window (in Chapter 3) will show the Company Module with access only to the General Ledger and journals — Chart of Accounts and General Journal. Icons for unused features and ledgers that are not set up will be hidden.

Open and close some of the other module windows to see their activity icons.

NOTES
Many Simply Accounting windows include a Home window tool that brings the Home window to the front without closing the other windows.

Simply Accounting on the Windows Desktop

> **Click**   **Receivables** in the modules pane list.

> **Click**   **Create General Journal** in the Shortcuts pane list. This will open the General Journal.

> **Click**   the **Edit menu**. Your desktop should now look like the one that follows:

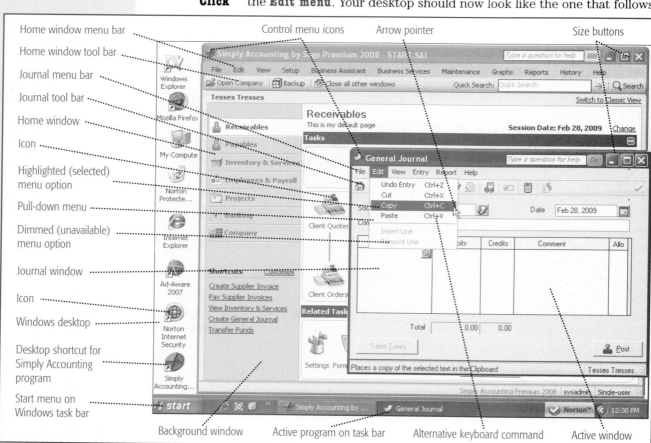

If you need an explanation of terms in this illustration, please refer to Appendix B.

Click   ☒ to close the journal window and return to the Home window.

Simply Accounting Classic View Home Window

Throughout this text, we will work from the Enhanced view Home window. However, we will provide alternate instructions for using the Classic view in sidebar notes.

Click   Switch To Classic View to change the Home window:

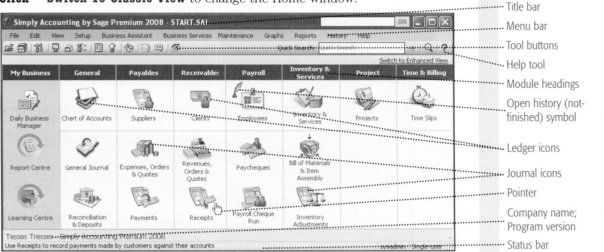

The tool bar in the Classic view has more items than in the Enhanced view. The **ledger** or module names come next with their respective icons filling up the major part of the window. The ledgers in the top row are below the ledger or module name, and the **journal icons** are under their respective ledgers in the last two icon rows of the window. All journals and ledgers can be accessed from the icons in this single Classic view Home window. Below the journal icons are two more information lines: the company name and the **status bar**. In this example, the status bar describes the purpose of the Receipts Journal because the pointer is on the Receipts icon.

The **My Business tab** allows quick access to the Daily Business Manager, Report Centre and Learning Centre.

Hold the mouse pointer on a tool button for a few seconds to see the name or function of the tool button and the keyboard shortcut if there is one. Hold the mouse over an icon to see its description or function in the status bar at the bottom of the window.

Click   Switch To Enhanced View to change Home window views again.

Simply Accounting Help Features

Simply Accounting provides program assistance in several different ways. You can display or print Help information on many topics. General accounting information, advice topics and Simply Accounting software assistance are included. You can access Help from the Home window at any time.

The most immediate form of help comes from the **status bar** at the bottom of many program windows. It offers a one-line description of the icon or field that the mouse is pointing to. As you move the mouse around the screen, the status bar information changes accordingly. The message in the status bar is connected to the mouse position only. This may not be the same as the position of the cursor or insertion point, which is located wherever the mouse was when you last clicked the mouse button.

We have already seen that each module window includes a **How Do I list** for activities related to that module. In addition, many settings or options windows include a **Help button** that offers context-sensitive help for the procedure you are using.

Simply Accounting general help can be accessed several ways:

Click the Learning Centre icon ,

Press $f1$,

Choose the Help menu and click Search Help, or

In the Classic view, click the Help tool ? on the tool bar.

Click   the **Learning Centre icon** :

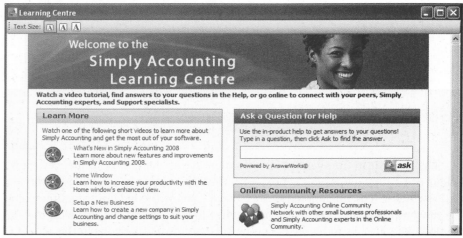

From this centre you can get different types of assistance: you can search for information, run one of the tutorials, find out about courses and training, contact a Simply Accounting expert or provide your feedback to Sage Software. We will demonstrate the Search option.

Click   the **Type In A Question field** in the Ask A Question For Help pane.

Type   purchase orders **Click** the **Ask button**:

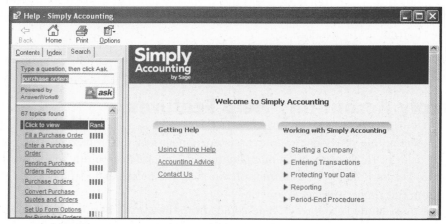

NOTES
You may see a warning about Internet security because many parts of the Learning Centre use Internet access. The Ask portion does not require an Internet connection.

The Help Welcome screen opens and several topics related to purchase orders are listed in the left-hand pane. The topics are shown in order of likely relevance — their **Rank**. Information can be displayed for the underlined topics.

Click   Enter A Purchase Order to display information for this topic:

Click any underlined topic in the topics list or in the information display pane to display the information for that newly selected topic.

Close   the **Help window** and the **Learning Centre window**.

Click   the **Help menu** in the Home window:

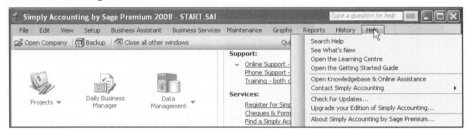

The options on this menu include all the ones we saw in the Learning Centre. In addition, you can update the program to a later release, upgrade the program to Premium from Simply, and see the version number and serial number for your program (About Simply Accounting by Sage Premium).

Choose   the **Help menu** and **click Search Help**. **Click** the **Contents tab**:

CLASSIC VIEW
In the Classic view, you can also click the Help tool [?] to access Help screens.

Major topics in the Contents menu have a book symbol beside them [book].

Click [+] beside a topic to see the list of subtopics under that heading (or double click the topic).

When a topic has a question mark beside it [?], there is detailed help on that subject. Click the topic or the question mark symbol to display information on that subject in the right-hand side of the Help window.

Welcome, with a question mark [?] beside it, is selected, so this topic is displayed. The Welcome screen has topics to help you get started in Simply Accounting. Clicking an arrow ▶ beside a topic in the right-hand side display pane expands the list of topics. Clicking underlined text provides further information on that topic.

Click a book title or click ⊟, the boxed minus sign beside it, to close the book and hide the list of subtopics.

Click **Vendors**. The list expands with several subtopics.

Click **Purchases** to view the second list of subtopics.

Click **Paying Vendors (Payments)** to view the next list of subtopics.

Click **Paying A Vendor** (with a question mark ? beside it) to see the help information on this topic:

Click the **Index tab** to see an alphabetic list of entries as shown here:

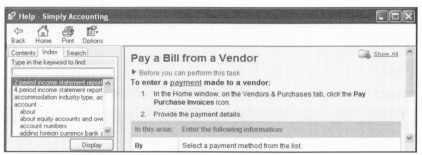

Notice that the previous topic remains on display until you select a new topic.

Click a topic and then click Display to open the help information. Type a letter in the field above the list to advance the alphabetic list quickly.

Click the **Search tab** to open the Search function.

This screen is the same one we accessed from the Learning Centre (page 14). Again, the previous topic remains displayed until you select a new one. The last item you searched for is listed in the Type In A Question field. Purchase orders is still entered.

You can search for a topic by typing it in the **Type A Question** field. Then click the **Ask** button to see the entries that include the topic you typed.

Click the **Type A Question field** and **type** `delete`

Click the **Ask button**.

Click **Vendors** to display the information. Vendors is underlined so the details are displayed directly. **Close** the **Help windows** when finished.

The Simply Accounting program also includes **Advice** on a number of topics.

Choose the **Business Assistant menu**, then **click Business Advice** and **All Modules** as shown:

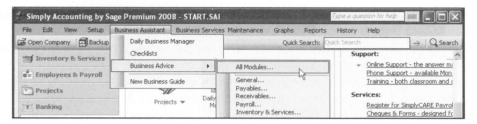

A list of topics opens:

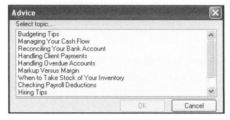

These topics provide general business information or accounting practices.

Management Reports, available from the Reports menu in the Home window, also provide advice, but the information is specific to the company data set that is open. Management reports are available only for ledgers that are not hidden, so the list you see is not always complete. These reports combine the company data with forms and reports provided through the Crystal Report Engine. Management Reports are covered with other reports for each module in the following chapters.

Click the **topic** you want and then **click OK**. **Close** the **advice report windows** when finished.

A final source of general assistance is available as **automatic advice**. This feature can be turned off from the Setup menu (User Preferences, View) in the Home window if it is not needed. We recommend leaving it on. When it is turned on, the Simply Accounting program will provide warning statements as, for example, when you choose a customer who has exceeded their credit limit:

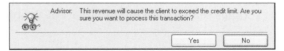

To proceed, you must close the advice screen. In the example shown here, you can click Yes if you want to proceed with the sale, or No if you want to make a change (perhaps by asking for a deposit).

The following warning about a customer appears when you choose a customer with a history of making late payments:

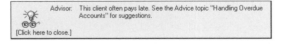

To close this message, click the advisor icon as indicated [Click Here To Close].

The program also warns when year-end is approaching and it is time to complete year-end adjustments, when your chequing account is overdrawn or when inventory items reach the reorder point.

Date Formats and Settings

Before closing the program we will review date format settings. Simply Accounting has date format control settings within each file that are independent of the display date settings for Windows. When you enter dates using a series of two digits for month, day and year, it is important to know how these will be interpreted. For example, when you type 08-06-05, this date may be June 8, August 6 or June 5 in the year 2005, 1905, 1908 or 2008, depending on whether month, day or year comes first and whether your computer defaults to 1900 dates or is preset for 2000 dates. We always use month, day and year as the order for presenting dates in this text.

Fortunately, Simply Accounting allows you to enter and display dates as text. Thus, you may type June 7, 2008, in a date field. And if you want, you can display this date as Jun 7, 2008, even if you enter numbers in the date field.

All date fields also have a **Calendar icon** ⊞ that you can click to access a month-by-month calendar from which you can select a date. These two options will help you avoid making date errors from incorrect orders. To access the date settings,

Click   the **Settings icon** ⬚ in the Related Tasks pane, or **choose** the **Setup menu**, then **click Settings**.

Click   **Company** in the list of modules on the left to open the Company settings:

Each entry in the list opens the settings screen for a different part of the program. We want the date format settings.

Click   **Date Format** (the entry under Company or from the list on the right) to open the Settings window for Dates:

Each field has a drop-down list of format options. The **Short Date Format** uses two digits each for month and day. For the year, you can choose a two-digit or four-digit format. You can choose to begin with month, day or year — the Short Date Format shows which comes first. The **Short Date Separator** character may be a slash, dash or period. This is the character that will appear on the screen regardless of how you entered the date. The sample shows the appearance that you can expect from your selections.

The **Long Date Format** shows the month as a three-letter text abbreviation. Either the month or the day can be the first character in the long date style. The sample shows the result of your selection.

The next section allows you to select the short or long date styles for your screen and reports. You can select different date styles for your reports and screen displays.

We will use the same date format settings for all files to avoid any confusion about dates when the numeric entry might be ambiguous. For reports you can use long or short date formats.

Click the **Short Date Format field list arrow**.

Click **MM dd yyyy**. Be sure that Month (MM) is the first part of the entry.

Click the **Long Date Format field list arrow**.

Click **MMM dd, yyyy**.

Click **Long Dates** beside the option On The Screen, Use.

Click **OK** to save the settings.

Saving and Backing Up Your Work

Simply Accounting saves your work automatically at various stages when you are working with the program. For example, when you display or print reports, Simply Accounting writes all the journal transactions to your file to compile the report you want. When you exit from the program properly, Simply Accounting also saves all your work.

On a regular basis, you should also make a backup copy of your files. The Backup command is described in detail in Chapter 3.

Click the **Backup tool** 🖫 or **choose** the **File menu** and **click Backup** to start the Backup wizard.

The wizard will create a separate backup folder inside your current working folder so that the backup will remain separate from your working copy.

While **Backup** creates a compressed copy of the files that must be restored with the Restore command before you can use them, the next two options create separate complete working copies of your data files that can be opened directly. Both save the file under a different file name so that you will have two working copies of the files, the original and the copy. You cannot create backups on a CD with the Backup command.

Save As makes a copy, closes the original file and lets you continue to work with the new copy. Because the new file becomes your working file, you can use Save As to copy to any medium that you can also work from in Simply Accounting — your hard disk drive or a removable memory stick, but not a CD. **Save A Copy** makes a copy of the file and then allows you to continue working with the original file. You can use Save A Copy to save your files to a CD. You must copy the CD files back to your hard disk drive and remove the read-only property before working with these files.

Because the data files are very large, we recommend using the Backup procedure described in Chapter 3 rather than Save As or Save A Copy for regular backups.

Choose the **File menu** and **click Save A Copy** to open the file name window.

You can save the copy in the same folder as the original or use a different folder. We recommend using different folders. To change to a different folder,

Click the **Save In field list arrow** and **choose** a different **folder**.

NOTES
Showing a four-digit year will ensure that you see whether you are using 1900 or 2000 year dates. Most programs now have 2000 as the default instead of 1900.

NOTES
A final date option allows you to indicate the normal first weekday for the business.

NOTES
You may want to use the Save A Copy or Save As command when you are unsure how a journal entry will be posted and you want to experiment with different methods of entering the same transactions.

NOTES

You can also use the Windows Copy command to make CD copies of your data, but you must close the Simply Accounting data file before you start to copy. Remember to copy the data folders when you copy from Windows to ensure that you keep all necessary files (the .SAI file and the SAJ folder) together.

You cannot open the data files from the CD. You must first copy them back to your hard disk drive and remove the read-only property.

Double click   the **folder** to open it. To create a new folder inside the one that you have open,

Click   the **New Folder icon** .

Type   a **new name** to replace New Folder, the selected text. **Click Open**.

Double click   the file name **NEW** or **NEW.SAI** if you show file extensions.

Type   the **new file name**. **Click Save**.

You will return to your original file and you can continue working.

To save the file under a different name and continue working with the new file, use the Save As command.

Choose   the **File menu** and **click Save As** to open the file name window.

The remaining steps are the same as Save A Copy, as shown above.

Change folders, create a new folder, rename the folder, open the new folder, type a file name for the copy and click Save. Remember to return to your original working copy before entering any transactions if you use the Save As command.

You can also back up all your data files at the same time by using Windows Copy and Paste commands. In this way, you can save the files to a different folder on your hard drive or on a CD.

Finishing a Session

Choose   the **Control Menu icon** and **click Close** or **click** ☒ to close the journal input form or display window you are working in.

You will return to the main Home window.

Choose   the **Control Menu icon** and **click Close**, or **click** ☒ or **choose** the **File menu** and **click Exit** to close the Home window.

Your work will be saved again automatically when you complete this step. You should now be in the Windows desktop.

Opening a Working Copy of a Data File

Start   the **Simply Accounting program** from the Start menu or **click** [Simply Accounting Premium 2008], the desktop icon, to open the Select Company Welcome window:

This time, because we have worked with the program before, the option to Open The Last Company You Worked On appears last with the name of the file you used. If

you use this option when you use the same data set for several work sessions, you will bypass the Open Company window (shown below).

Click   Select An Existing Company. Click OK.

The Simply Accounting Open Company window appears next:

The path shown will be for the file you used most recently, in this case, the Start file. The most recently used file will be selected for you to accept or to change. Therefore, the file name you see on your screen may be different from the ones we show.

Click   the **Look In field list arrow** to see the folder path for the file selected:

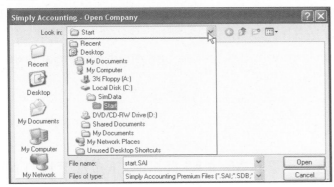

Click   Start or the **folder** you need to select it.

Click   Open to list the Simply Accounting data files contained in this folder and to display the selected folder name in the Look In field.

You can gain access to the company records through the *.SAI file. Simply Accounting recognizes this file extension as a Simply Accounting format file. The remaining data files for the company are in the SAJ folder. Both the SAI file and the SAJ folder that are part of the data set must be located in the same folder.

Click   start.SAI or the **SAI file** you want to select it and add its name to the File Name field as shown:

WARNING!
If you are not showing file extensions, you will click start. Do not click the start.SAJ folder.

Click   Open to see the session date screen shown on page 9. **Click OK** to open the Home window.

R E V I E W

The Student CD-ROM with Data Files includes Review Questions for this chapter.

The GST and PST

After completing this chapter, you should be able to

OBJECTIVES

- **understand** the terms relevant to the federal Goods and Services Tax
- **understand** the different methods of calculating the GST
- **understand** how to file for a remittance or refund
- **understand** Harmonized Sales Tax and other provincial taxes in relation to GST

GENERAL TAX INFORMATION

Definition of GST

The Goods and Services Tax is levied by the federal government at the rate of 5 percent on most goods and services in Canada. Retailers pay the GST to their wholesalers and vendors but are allowed to deduct any GST they pay from the GST they collect from customers. Retailers remit the difference, GST owing, to the Receiver General for Canada or claim a refund with monthly or quarterly returns.

GST Registration   Any business with annual sales exceeding $30 000 per year must register for GST collection and must collect GST on all applicable sales. Registration is optional for most smaller businesses. Businesses that are not registered for GST do not charge GST on sales to their customers, but they also cannot recover the GST they pay on business-related purchases.

Collecting the GST   The business must collect GST for those goods and services sold that are not zero rated or tax exempt. The business must remit GST at regular intervals, filing GST returns monthly, quarterly or annually and paying instalments, depending on annual income and GST owing.

Zero Rated Goods and Services   Zero rated goods and services are those on which the tax rate is zero. These goods include basic groceries, prescribed medical devices, prescribed drugs, exported goods and services, agricultural products and fish products. A business selling only zero rated goods and services does not collect GST on sales, but it can still claim a refund for GST it pays for purchases.

Tax Exempt Goods and Services   Tax exempt goods and services are those on which tax is not collected. These goods and services include health care, dental

 NOTES
Provinces may or may not include GST in the price on which they calculate Provincial Sales Tax (PST). Provincial tax rates vary from province to province. See page 25.

 NOTES
GST collected on sales is reduced by the GST on sales returns.

care, daycare services and rents on residences. Most educational and financial services are also included in this group. These businesses are not able to claim refunds for GST paid for business purchases related to selling tax exempt goods and services.

Paying the GST A business must pay GST for purchases made specifically for business purposes, unless the goods or services purchased are zero rated or tax exempt. The business can use the GST paid as an input tax credit by subtracting the amount of GST paid from the amount of GST collected and remitting GST owing or claiming a refund. GST paid on purchases for personal use do not qualify as input tax credits.

Bank and Financial Institution Services Most bank products and services are not taxable. Exceptions include safety deposit box rentals, custodial and safekeeping services, personalized cheques, self-administrated registered savings plan fees, payroll services, rentals of night depository, rentals of credit card imprinters and reconciliation of cheques. Banks remit the full amount of GST they collect from customers. Because most bank services are not taxable, banks cannot claim input tax credits for GST they pay on business-related purchases.

GST on Imported and Exported Goods GST is not charged on exported goods. Customers in other countries who import goods from Canada do not pay GST. However, businesses in Canada must pay GST on the items they import or purchase from other countries. The GST is collected by Canada Revenue Agency (CRA) when the goods enter Canada based on the purchase price (plus import duty) and current exchange rates. Businesses must pay this GST and other import duties before the goods are released to them.

Administering the GST

The federal government has approved different methods of administering the GST; the regular method is most commonly used.

The Regular Method

The regular method of administering the GST requires the business to keep track of GST paid for all goods and services purchased from vendors (less returns) and of GST collected for all goods and services sold to customers (less returns). It then deducts the GST paid from the GST collected and files for a refund or remits the balance owing to the Receiver General on a monthly or quarterly basis.

Accounting Examples Using the Regular Method (without PST)

SALES INVOICE Sold goods to customer for $200 plus $10 GST collected (5%). Invoice total, $210.

Date	Particulars	Debit	Credit
xx/xx	Accounts Receivable	210.00	
	GST Charged on Sales		10.00
	Revenue from Sales		200.00

PURCHASE INVOICE Purchased supplies from vendor for $300 plus $15 GST paid (5%). Invoice total, $315.

Date	Particulars	Debit	Credit
xx/xx	Supplies	300.00	
	GST Paid on Purchases	15.00	
	Accounts Payable		315.00

NOTES
The input tax credit is reduced by the amount of GST for purchases returned.

NOTES
Visitors to Canada can request a GST refund for GST paid on goods purchased in Canada that they are taking home with them. They cannot claim a refund for goods and services they consumed in Canada, such as entertainment and dining.

NOTES
GST Paid on Purchases is a contra-liability account because it normally has a debit balance while most liability accounts have a credit balance. Therefore, GST Paid on Purchases reduces the total GST liability to the Receiver General.

The GST owing is further reduced by any GST adjustments — for example, GST that applies to bad debts that are written off. If the debt is later recovered, the GST liability is also restored as an input tax credit adjustment.

Other Methods of Calculating GST

NOTES
Under the Quick Method, the GST remittance or refund amount is based on a flat rate percentage of total sales.
These alternative methods of calculating GST are not used in the applications in this workbook.

Certain small businesses may be eligible to use simpler methods of calculating their GST refunds and remittances that do not require them to keep a separate record for GST on each individual purchase or sale. The simplified accounting method, the streamlined accounting method and the quick method are examples of these alternatives.

Calculating GST Refunds or Remittances

The following example uses the regular method for a retailer who is filing quarterly.

Quarterly Total Sales (excluding GST)	$50 000.00	
Quarterly Total Purchases	29 700.00	
5% GST Charged on Sales		$2 500.00
Less: 5% GST Paid on Purchases		
Cash Register (cost $1 000)	50.00	
Inventory (cost $25 000)	1 250.00	
Supplies (cost $500)	25.00	
Payroll Services (cost $200)	10.00	
Store Lease (cost $3 000)	150.00	
Total GST Paid		− 1 485.00
GST Remittance		$1 015.00

GST Remittances and Refunds

The business must file returns that summarize the amount of GST it has collected and the amount of GST it has paid. CRA may require reports monthly, quarterly or yearly, depending on total sales. Yearly reports usually require quarterly instalments.

GST Collected on Sales	>	GST Paid on Purchases	=	GST Owing
GST Collected on Sales	<	GST Paid on Purchases	=	GST Refund

Accounting Examples for Remittances

NOTES
The rules concerning the GST may change periodically, as in the 2006 federal budget when the rate changed from 7 percent to 6 percent. In the 2007 budget, the rate was reduced again to 5 percent. Always refer to current guidelines.

Usually a business will make GST remittances since sales usually exceed expenses — the business operates at a profit. The following example shows how the GST accounts are cleared and a liability (*Accounts Payable*) is set up to remit GST owing to the Receiver General for Canada. In this case, the usual one, the Receiver General becomes a vendor for the business so that the liability can be entered and the payment made.

Date	Particulars	Debit	Credit
03/31	GST Charged on Sales	2 500.00	
	GST Paid on Purchases		1 485.00
	A/P - Receiver General		1 015.00
03/31	A/P - Receiver General	1 015.00	
	Cash in Bank		1 015.00

Accounting Examples for Refunds

The example below shows how the GST accounts are cleared and a current asset account (*Accounts Receivable*) is set up for a GST refund from the Receiver General for Canada. In this case, the Receiver General owes money to the business; that is, it acts like a customer, so a customer record is set up to record and collect the refund.

Date	Particulars	Debit	Credit
03/31	GST Charged on Sales	1 500.00	
	A/R - Receiver General	500.00	
	GST Paid on Purchases		2 000.00
04/15	Cash in Bank	500.00	
	A/R - Receiver General		500.00

GST and Provincial Sales Taxes

The rules governing provincial sales taxes vary from province to province in terms of the tax rate, the goods and services that are taxed and whether Provincial Sales Tax (PST) is applied to the GST as well as to the base purchase price (that is, whether GST is taxable). The following examples assume that the item sold has both GST and PST applied.

Although GST is applied at each level of sale, resale and manufacturing, PST is paid only by the final consumer of a product or service. Thus, a business purchasing inventory to sell to customers will not pay PST on these purchases. When the same business buys supplies or services for its use in conducting business, it must pay PST because it has become the final consumer of these goods or services.

PST applies only to sales within a province, not to sales to customers in a different province or in a different country.

Alberta has no Provincial Sales Tax. Thus, the examples provided earlier without PST illustrate the application of GST for Alberta.

PST in Ontario, Manitoba, Saskatchewan and British Columbia

The provinces west of Quebec apply PST to the base price of the sale, the amount without GST included. The following example illustrates the application in Ontario.

Ontario business sold goods on account for $500. GST charged is 5% and PST charged is 8%.

GST = (0.05 × 500) = $25
PST in Ontario = (0.08 × 500) = $40
Total amount of invoice = $500 + $25 + $40 = $565

Date	Particulars	Debit	Credit
xx/xx	Accounts Receivable	565.00	
	GST Charged on Sales		25.00
	PST Payable		40.00
	Revenue from Sales		500.00

The full amount of PST collected on sales is remitted to the provincial Minister of Finance (less any applicable sales tax compensation).

Harmonized Sales Tax — Nova Scotia, New Brunswick and Newfoundland and Labrador

In these Atlantic provinces, GST and PST are harmonized at a single rate of 13 percent. The full 13 percent Harmonized Sales Tax (HST) operates much like the

NOTES
If a business purchases inventory for resale but later uses the inventory within the business instead, it must remit PST on this internal transaction. The business has become the final consumer of the products.

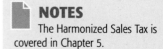
NOTES
The Harmonized Sales Tax is covered in Chapter 5.

basic GST, with HST remittances equal to HST collected on sales less HST paid on purchases. The following example illustrates the application in New Brunswick.

New Brunswick business sold goods on account for $565, including HST at 13% ($500 base price).

HST = (0.13 × 500) = $65
Total amount of invoice = $565

Date	Particulars	Debit	Credit
xx/xx	Accounts Receivable	565.00	
	HST Charged on Sales		65.00
	Revenue from Sales		500.00

A single remittance for the full 13 percent is made to the Receiver General; the provincial portion of the HST is not tracked or collected separately.

Quebec Sales Tax (QST)

Provincial sales tax in Quebec (QST) is also combined with the GST. The provincial tax rate is applied to a broader base of goods and services than PST in Ontario, like the base that has GST applied. The QST is calculated on the base amount of the sale plus the GST. That is, QST is applied to GST — a piggy-backed tax or a tax on a tax.

Quebec business sold goods on account for $500. GST charged is 5% and QST charged is 7.5%.

GST = (0.05 × 500) = $25
QST = (0.075 × 525) = $39.38
Total amount of invoice = $500.00 + $25.00 + $39.38 = $564.38

Date	Particulars	Debit	Credit
xx/xx	Accounts Receivable	564.38	
	GST Charged on Sales		25.00
	QST Charged on Sales		39.38
	Revenue from Sales		500.00

QST is remitted to the ministre du Revenu du Québec, separately from GST. However, the QST is refundable and businesses can deduct the QST they pay on their purchases from the QST they collect on sales. The QST paid on a few items or services — QST on some telecommunication services and insurance — is not refundable. Therefore, QST paid must be designated as refundable or non-refundable at the time of the purchase and when the purchase is recorded.

PST in Prince Edward Island

Provincial sales tax in PEI (PST) is applied to the base sale price plus GST. However, unlike Quebec, and like Ontario, some items have only GST applied, and some have both GST and PST applied.

PEI business sold goods on account for $500. GST charged is 5% and PST charged is 10%.

GST = (0.05 × 500) = $25
PST = (0.10 × 525) = $52.50
Total amount of invoice = $500.00 + $25.00 + $52.50 = $577.50

Date	Particulars	Debit	Credit
xx/xx	Accounts Receivable	577.50	
	GST Charged on Sales		25.00
	PST Payable		52.50
	Revenue from Sales		500.00

The full amount of PST collected on sales is remitted to the provincial Minister of Finance (less 3 percent sales tax compensation).

Part 2
Applications

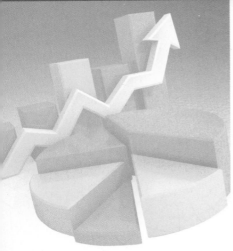

CHAPTER THREE

MissoniMarbleworks

OBJECTIVES

After completing this chapter, you should be able to

- **access** the data files for the business
- **open** the General Journal
- **enter** transactions in the General Journal
- **edit** and **review** General Journal transactions
- **post** transactions
- **create** new General Ledger accounts
- **adjust** journal entries after posting
- **display** and **print** General Ledger and General Journal reports
- **graph** General Ledger reports
- **display** and **print** comparative financial reports
- **customize** reports
- **back up** your data files
- **advance** the session date
- **finish** an accounting session

COMPANY INFORMATION

Company Profile

NOTES
Missoni Marbleworks
66 Allies Avenue
Edmonton, Alberta T3P 4C2
Tel 1: (403) 763-4127
Tel 2: (800) 455-4127
Fax: (403) 765-4842
Business No.: 743 647 397

Missoni **Marbleworks** in Edmonton, Alberta, is owned and operated by Maria Missoni, who opened the business after graduating from college and training in Italy with Renaissance Marble Works. She builds stone fireplaces and chimneys, stone porches, patios and stairs and installs ceramic and marble tile floors in homes and fountains in shopping malls. Her love of Italian architecture has led her to repairing old marble in museums, galleries and homes. She hopes to include more art restoration in her work in the future. Missoni also has considerable artistic and creative talents. The marble stands that she carves for statues, masks and vases are sold from her home studio, at local craft shows and to individual customers who commission special pieces.

Some of her customers have set up accounts with Missoni, and she has set up accounts with her regular vendors and suppliers.

To convert her accounting records to Simply Accounting in April, she has used:

- Chart of Accounts
- Trial Balance
- Accounting Procedures

CHART OF POSTABLE ACCOUNTS

MISSONI MARBLEWORKS

ASSETS
1080 Cash in Bank
1200 A/R - St. Albert Museum
1220 A/R - Jasper Gallery
1240 A/R - Stoney Plain Plaza
1320 Prepaid Insurance
1360 Marble Inventory
1540 Computer Equipment
1550 Power Marble Tools
1560 Power Marble Equipment
1570 Van ▶

▶LIABILITIES
2100 A/P - West Carbide Tools
2120 A/P - Marblehead Suppliers
2180 A/P - Chinook Promotions
2650 GST Charged on Sales
2670 GST Paid on Purchases

EQUITY
3100 Missoni, Capital
3150 Missoni, Drawings
3600 Net Income ▶

▶REVENUE
4100 Revenue from Contracts
4150 Revenue from Repairs
4200 Interest Revenue

EXPENSE
5020 Advertising & Promotion
5040 Bank Charges
5060 Hydro Expense
5080 Interest Expense
5100 Maintenance & Repairs ▶

▶5110 Marble Inventory Used
5120 Rental Expenses
5140 Telephone Expenses
5160 Wages Expenses

NOTES: The Chart of Accounts includes only postable accounts and the Net Income or Current Earnings account. Simply Accounting uses the Net Income account for the Income Statement to calculate the difference between revenue and expenses before closing the books.

TRIAL BALANCE

MISSONI MARBLEWORKS

April 1, 2010		Debits	Credits
1080	Cash in Bank	$ 24 000	
1200	A/R - St. Albert Museum	2 400	
1220	A/R - Jasper Gallery	3 600	
1320	Prepaid Insurance	1 000	
1360	Marble Inventory	2 050	
1540	Computer Equipment	2 500	
1550	Power Marble Tools	4 500	
1560	Power Marble Equipment	28 000	
1570	Van	32 000	
2100	A/P - West Carbide Tools		$ 1 200
2650	GST Charged on Sales		1 500
2670	GST Paid on Purchases	940	
3100	Missoni, Capital		85 110
3150	Missoni, Drawings	900	
4100	Revenue from Contracts		21 000
4150	Revenue from Repairs		4 000
5020	Advertising & Promotion	200	
5040	Bank Charges	60	
5060	Hydro Expense	300	
5100	Maintenance & Repairs	400	
5110	Marble Inventory Used	5 400	
5120	Rental Expenses	600	
5140	Telephone Expenses	360	
5160	Wages Expenses	3 600	
		$112 810	$112 810

Accounting Procedures

GST

NOTES
Most bank and financial institution services used in this text are exempt from GST charges. Alberta does not levy a provincial sales tax.

Missoni has chosen the regular method for remittance of the Goods and Services Tax (GST). She records the GST collected from customers as a liability (credit) in the *GST Charged on Sales* account. She records GST that she pays to vendors in the *GST Paid on Purchases* account as a decrease (debit) to her liability to Canada Revenue Agency. Her GST remittance or refund is calculated automatically in the *GST Owing (Refund)* subtotal. You can see these accounts when you display or print the Balance Sheet. Missoni files her GST remittances or requests for refunds with the Receiver General for Canada on the last day of each fiscal quarter. (For details, please read Chapter 2 on the Goods and Services Tax.)

INSTRUCTIONS

1. **Restore** the **data file for Missoni Marbleworks**. Instructions begin on page 34.

2. **Enter** the **source documents for April** in the General Journal in Simply Accounting using the Chart of Accounts and Trial Balance for Missoni Marbleworks. The procedures for entering each new type of transaction for this application are outlined step by step in the Keystrokes section following the source documents. These transactions have a ✓ in the check box and, immediately below the check box, the page number on which the relevant keystrokes begin. Put your own checkmark in each transaction box after you finish entering the transaction to show that you have completed it.

3. **Print** the **reports and graphs** indicated on the printing form below after you have completed your entries. Keystrokes for reports begin on page 48.

REPORTS

Accounts
- [ ] Chart of Accounts
- [ ] Account List
- [ ] General Journal Entries: Apr 1 to Apr 30

Financials
- [✓] Comparative Balance Sheet dates: Apr 1 and April 30 with difference in percentage
- [✓] Income Statement from Jan 1 to Apr 30
- [✓] Trial Balance date: Apr 30
- [✓] General Ledger accounts: 1080 2650 3100 4100 from Apr 1 to Apr 30

Management Reports
- [ ] General

GRAPHS
- [ ] Revenues by Account
- [ ] Expenses by Account
- [✓] Expenses and Net Profit as % of Revenue

SOURCE DOCUMENTS

NOTES
Remember that the ✓ in the check box and the number beneath it indicate that keystroke instructions for this entry begin on page 36.

NOTES
[✓] Create new Group
41   account 2300 Bank Loan. (See keystrokes on page 41.)

SESSION DATE – APRIL 7, 2010

[✓] **Purchase Invoice WCT-161**   **Dated April 2, 2010**

36   From West Carbide Tools, $885 plus $44.25 GST paid for diamond-tip drill and drill bits. Purchase invoice total $929.25. Terms: net 30 days.

[✓] **Bank Credit Memo #AT-C3104**   **Dated April 3, 2010**

41   From Alberta Trust Company, $10 000 bank loan secured for purchase of new marble equipment. Loan deposited into bank account. Create new Group account 2300 Bank Loan.

☐ **Sales Invoice #MM-40**   **Dated April 3, 2010**

To St. Albert Museum, $3 800 plus $190 GST charged to build marble display stands for statues as per contract. Sales invoice total $3 990. Terms: net 30 days.

☑ **Memo #1**   **Dated April 4, 2010**

43   From Owner: The invoice from West Carbide Tools was entered incorrectly. The cost of the drill was $900 plus $45 GST paid. The revised purchase invoice total is $945. Adjust the posted invoice to make the correction.

☐ **Cheque Copy #48**   **Dated April 5, 2010**

To West Carbide Tools, $1 200 in payment of invoice #WCT-129.

☐ **Cash Receipt #20**   **Dated April 5, 2010**

From St. Albert Museum, cheque #828 for $2 400 in payment of invoice #MM-37.

☐ **Cash Sales Invoice #MM-41**   **Dated April 6, 2010**

To Rolf Kleinje, $2 100 plus $105 GST charged for replacement of marble kitchen counter and other repair work. Sales invoice total $2 205. Received certified cheque #AT-603 in full payment of account.

☐ **Purchase Invoice #MS-611**   **Dated April 6, 2010**

From Marblehead Suppliers, $6 000 plus $300 GST paid for marble pieces (inventory) of different sizes to complete contracted work. Purchase invoice total $6 300 Terms: net 30 days.

SESSION DATE – APRIL 14, 2010

☐ **Bank Debit Memo #AT-D3691**   **Dated April 8, 2010**

From Alberta Trust Company, $24 for bank service charges.

☐ **Purchase Invoice #WMM-4499**   **Dated April 10, 2010**

From West Mall Mechanical, $300 plus $15 GST paid for repairs and maintenance work on equipment. Purchase invoice total $315. Terms: net 10 days. Create new Group account 2190 A/P - West Mall Mechanical.

☐ **Memo #2**   **Dated April 11, 2010**

Missoni paid her hydro and telephone bills from her personal chequing account. She wrote cheque #49 for $283.50 to reimburse herself for these expenses. The hydro bill was $150 plus $7.50 GST and the telephone bill was $120 plus $6.00 GST.

☐ **Bank Credit Memo #AT-C3421**   **Dated April 11, 2010**

From Alberta Trust Company, $500 semi-annual interest earned on bank account.

☐ **Cash Receipt #21**   **Dated April 12, 2010**

From Jasper Gallery, cheque #58821 for $3 600 in full payment of invoice #MM-38.

☐ **Sales Invoice #MM-42**   **Dated April 14, 2010**

To Jasper Gallery, $2 000 plus $100 GST charged for building of marble pedestals and base units as per contract. Sales invoice total $2 100. Terms: net 30 days.

NOTES
If you use MM-xx as the source for sales, you can apply the report filter we show in Appendix F.

NOTES
If you use Cheque #xx as the source for cheques, you can apply the report filter we show in Appendix F.

NOTES
 See keystrokes on
46   Advancing the Session Date, page 46.

SESSION DATE – APRIL 21, 2010

NOTES
Create new Group account:
2210 A/P - Devon Equipment

To: Missoni Marbleworks
      66 Allies Avenue
      Edmonton, AB
      T3P 4C2

DEVON
EQUIPMENT CO.

68 CUTTERS ROAD EDMONTON, AB T4C 3N6

TEL: 403-775-6116

Date: April 15, 2010

No: DE-1141

Description of item	
Marble Cutting Equipment	9,600.00

GST # 651 034 271	**Terms:** net 30 days	**Subtotal**	9,600.00
		GST	480.00
Signature *M. Missoni*		**Total**	$10,080.00

NOTES
Use the General Journal for
the payroll transaction in this
application.

Missoni Marbleworks

No: 50

66 Allies Avenue
Edmonton AB
T3P 4C2

Date 1 8 0 4 2 0 1 0
      D D M M Y Y Y Y

Pay to the order of   Giovanni Assuri $ 4,200.00

———————— Four Thousand, Two Hundred ———————— 00 /100 **Dollars**

AT **Alberta Trust**
121 Money Way
Edmonton, AB T3C 4N6

M. Missoni

⑈⑈⑈⑈ 40361⑈ 050

Re: Wages to assistant for contracted   **No: 50**
     work to date, $4,200.00   April 18, 2010

Sales Invoice #MM-43   **Dated April 19, 2010**

To Lindbrook Estates, $1 200 plus $60 GST charged for repairs to fireplace
mantle. Sales invoice total $1 260. Terms: net 10 days. Create new Group
account 1280 A/R - Lindbrook Estates

Cheque Copy #51   **Dated April 20, 2010**

To West Mall Mechanical, $315 in full payment of account. Reference invoice
#WMM-4499.

☐ **Sales Invoice #MM-44**   **Dated April 20, 2010**

To Sherwood Park Estates (new customer), $3 000 plus $150 GST charged for contracted new marble tile kitchen floor and walls. Sales invoice total $3 150. Terms: net 10 days. Create new Group account 1260 A/R - Sherwood Park Estates.

☐ **Cash Receipt #22**   **Dated April 21, 2010**

From Lindbrook Estates, cheque #189 for $1 260 in payment of invoice #MM-43.

SESSION DATE – APRIL 28, 2010

☐ **Purchase Invoice #BT-2194**   **Dated April 23, 2010**

From Beaumont Tekstore, $1 300 plus $65 GST paid for external hard drive for computer. Purchase invoice total $1 365. Terms: net 10 days. Create new Group account 2220 A/P - Beaumont Tekstore.

☐ **Sales Invoice #MM-45**   **Dated April 24, 2010**

To Stoney Plain Plaza, $3 600 plus $180 GST charged to install marble floors in public washroom as per contract. Sales invoice total $3 780. Terms: net 30 days.

☐ **Cash Purchase Invoice #BAA-719**   **Dated April 24, 2010**

From Bon Accord Advertising, $300 plus $15 GST paid for printing and copying advertising flyers. Purchase invoice total $315. Terms: cash on receipt. Invoice paid in full with cheque #52.

☐ **Cheque Copy #53**   **Dated April 28, 2010**

To Fonteyn Dance Studio, $390 for one session of dance lessons for daughter. Use Drawings account.

SESSION DATE – APRIL 30, 2010

☐ **Memo #3**   **Dated April 30, 2010**

Missoni used $3 800 of marble inventory to complete projects in April.

☐

Sherwood Park Estates
900 Sherwood Park Rd.
Edmonton, AB
T4J 4S6

No: 23

Date 3 0 0 4 2 0 1 0
      D D M M Y Y Y Y

Pay to the order of   Missoni Marbleworks $ 3,150.00

———————— Three Thousand one hundred and fifty ———— 00 /100 **Dollars**

Royal Bank
69 Royalty Avenue
Edmonton, AB T3P 7C6

Robin Sherwood
Signature

⑆⑈ 393214 ⑈ 023

- -

Re: Reference Invoice #MM-44, $3,150.00   No: 23
     In full payment of account. $3,150.00   April 30, 2010

<table>
<tr><td colspan="2"></td><td></td><td style="text-align:right">April 30, 2010</td></tr>
<tr><td>**Account No.**</td><td>40361</td><td rowspan="2">**ADVICE TO
ACCOUNT HOLDER**</td><td>**DEBIT MEMO**</td></tr>
<tr><td>**Code:**</td><td>15</td><td>AT-D4341</td></tr>
</table>

Account No. 40361   **ADVICE TO ACCOUNT HOLDER**   **DEBIT MEMO**

Code: 15   AT-D4341

Particulars:

| Interest charged on outstanding loan | $70.00 |

Issued by: *MP*   **Verified by:** *3R*

Missoni Marbleworks
66 Allies Avenue
Edmonton AB
T3P 4C2

AT
Alberta Trust
121 Money Way
Edmonton, AB T3C 4N6

KEYSTROKES

Opening Data Files

Double click the **Simply Accounting icon** on your desktop, or

Choose **Start** then **choose Programs** (or **All Programs**) and **Simply Accounting Premium 2008**. **Click Simply Accounting Premium 2008**.

Click **Restore From Backup** and **click OK**. **Click Next**.

Click **Browse**. **Locate** the folder **C:\SimData** where you installed the data.

Double click the **SimData folder** to open it.

Click **missoni.cab** to select the file you need. **Click Open**.

Click **Next** and confirm the details.

Click **Next**. You now need to enter the name for your restored file.

Click the **Enter The Name field**.

Type C:\SimData\Missoni\missoni

Click **Next** and **click Yes** to confirm the creation of the new folder and file.

Click **Finish**. Refer to Chapter 1, page 6 for detailed instructions on restoring data files.

The following screen appears, asking (prompting) you to enter the session date for this work session:

NOTES
In these instructions, our starting point for opening the file is the Start file in Chapter 1 as the last company you worked on.
If you have already restored the backup file, refer to page 20 for instructions on opening the data file.

NOTES
Many screens include a Cancel button. If you click Cancel, you will return to your previous screen without entering any changes.
The Advancing the Session Date section on page 46 will explain how to work with later dates.
Refer to Chapter 1, page 18, and Windows Help for further information on date formats.

The date format on your screen is controlled by the Dates Settings options in Simply Accounting, not by the format you use to enter the date. (Refer to page 18.)

The session date is the date of your work session, the date on which you are recording the accounting transactions on the computer. A business with a large number of transactions may record these transactions at the end of each day. One with fewer transactions may enter them once a week. In this workbook, transactions are entered once a week for most applications so the session date is updated by one week at a time. The session date may or may not be the same as the date on which the transaction actually took place.

The session date for your first session is April 7, 2010. Since this is not the default shown on the screen, you must change the date. Every date field has a Calendar icon.

> **Click**   the **Calendar icon** to open the calendar:

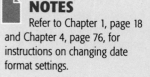

The calendar has the current session date highlighted with a blue background. The calendar for any date field also shows the range of dates that will be accepted based on the settings chosen for the company files. The arrows allow you to move forward to a later month ▶ or back to a previous month ◀. The calendar stops at the dates that indicate the range you may use. Click a date on the calendar to enter it or use one of the following alternative formats. Note that they use the same order of month, day and year. Entering the year is optional.

- use different characters to separate numbers: 04-07-10 or 04/07/10
- omit leading zeros: 4/7/10 or 4-7-10
- leave spaces between numbers: 04 07 10 or 4 7 10
- type lower- or upper-case text: April 7, 2010 or APRIL 7, 2010
- use three-letter abbreviations for the month: Apr 7 10 or apr 7 10
- use three-letter abbreviations for the month with the day first: 7 apr or 7 Apr
- other non-alpha or non-numeric separating characters may also be used
- you may also enter dates without the year

We will use a variety of date formats throughout this workbook but we always show the dates on-screen in the text format to minimize entering incorrect dates. Using the calendar to choose a date or using a text version to enter a date will also prevent an incorrect date entry.

> **Click**   **7** on the April date calendar or
>
> **Type**   april 7, 2010
>
> **Click**   **OK**.

NOTES
Company settings are discussed in Chapter 4.

NOTES
Refer to Chapter 1, page 18 and Chapter 4, page 76, for instructions on changing date format settings.

NOTES
When you enter the date using text, the date is not ambiguous, so you can enter the day first.

NOTES
Keystrokes that you must use are shown in command statements like these:
> **Type**   april 7 or
> **Click**   **OK**

Instruction lines are indented; command words are in boldface; text you type is shown in a special font (Courier); and things that you must click on or select are in colour and bold. This format makes it easy to find the instruction statements in the text.

SIMPLY VERSION
The program name in the title bar will be Simply Accounting by Sage 2008.

NOTES
Maximize the Home window if necessary. Refer to Chapter 1 for a more detailed description of the Home window.

NOTES
Although the Banking module is not used, it cannot be hidden if you want to use the General Journal.

NOTES
The Daily Business Manager is used in Chapter 11. The Learning Centre was introduced in Chapter 1.

Your screen shows the following Company module Home window:

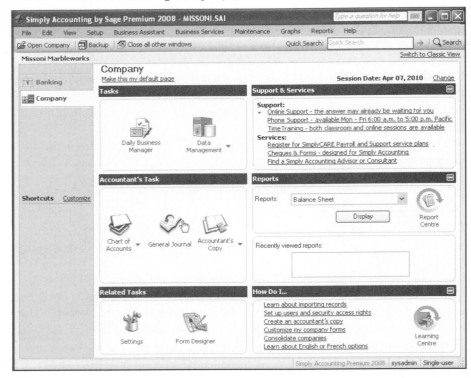

For Missoni Marbleworks, the Company module is the default Home page. Only the General Ledger and Journal can be accessed for this file. When ledger icons are hidden, all main menu options related to those ledgers are also hidden or unavailable. (Click ⬚ to maximize the window if necessary.) The Home window is divided as follows: the title bar is on top with the program and file names, control menu icon and size buttons; the main menu bar comes next; the tool bar follows. Tool buttons permit quick access to commonly used menu items. The Home window tools from left to right (with their alternative pull-down menu locations) are Open Company and Backup (File menu) and Close All Other Simply Accounting Windows (View menu). The Search function and tool (Edit menu) are located on the far right for easy access.

The major part of the window is divided into three columns of panes or sections — the modules and shortcuts panes on the left, the ledger and journal task panes in the middle and the Reports and Help pane on the right. For the Company module, the upper right pane has access to support services for Simply Accounting. For other modules, this pane has the ledger accounts. The session date and the change date command are located above the Support pane.

Below these panes is the status bar with the program name and version and the user name (sysadmin) and status (Single-user). In other windows, the status bar shows the purpose of the field or icon that has the pointer on it.

Entering General Journal Transactions

All transactions for Missoni Marbleworks are entered in the General Journal in the Accountant's Task pane, indicated by the pointer in the following screen:

Click   the **General Journal icon** in the Accountant's Task pane of the
Company module Home window to open the General Journal.

The General Journal input form that follows appears on your screen:

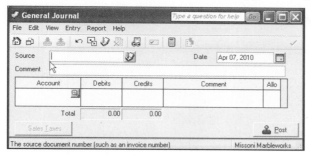

You are now ready to enter the first transaction in the General Journal input screen.
The cursor, a flashing vertical line, is blinking in the Source field, ready to receive
information. The Source field identifies the reference document from which you obtain
the information for a transaction, in this case, the invoice number.

Type   WCT-161

Press   ⌨(tab) to advance to the Adjust Journal Entry icon. **Press** ⌨(tab) again.

The cursor advances to the next field, the Date field. You should enter the
transaction date here. The program enters the session date by default. It is highlighted,
ready to be accepted or changed. Because the work was completed on April 2, 2010, the
session date of April 7 is incorrect and must be changed.

Type   04-02

Press   ⌨(tab) to move to the Calendar icon. Notice that the text form of the
date is displayed, even though we entered the date as numbers.

If you click the Calendar icon in the Date field now, the session date has a red
frame around it. The current transaction date has a solid blue background.

Press   ⌨(tab) again to accept the date and advance to the Comment field.

The year is added to the date. In the Comment field, you should enter a description
of the transaction to make the permanent record more meaningful. You may enter up to
75 characters, including spaces.

Type   West Carbide Tools

Press   ⌨(tab).

The cursor moves forward to the first line of the Account field, creating a dotted
box for the first account.

Simply Accounting organizes accounts into sections or categories using the
following boundaries for numbering:

- 1000–1999 Assets
- 2000–2999 Liabilities
- 3000–3999 Equity
- 4000–4999 Revenue
- 5000–5999 Expense

This system makes it easy to remember the first digit of an account. Double clicking
the Account field will display the list of accounts. If you type the first digit of an
account number then double click or press ⌨(enter) while the cursor is flashing in any
account field, the program will advance the list to accounts beginning with that digit.

NOTES
Many fields that allow you to select an account or other information from a list have the Select or List icon to provide quick access to the list. Showing the List icon is an option that you select as a user preference setting.
    Other fields have list arrows that provide a drop-down or pop-up list.

NOTES
If the cursor is in the Account field, you can also press (enter) to open the Select Account list.

NOTES
The statement beginning "You can also double click..." is another example of an alternative command statement.

Click   the **List icon** , or **double click** the dotted box in the **Account column** to list the accounts.

The following list of accounts appears on your journal screen:

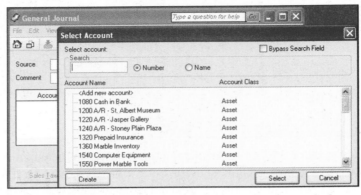

The beginning of the account list is displayed. The list includes only postable accounts, those that can be debited or credited in journal entries. The cursor is in the Search field. If you want to place the cursor in the account list directly from the Account field, you can choose the **Bypass Search Field** option. We will not select this option. Typing a number in the Search field also places the cursor directly in the list. Following usual accounting practice, we enter the account to be debited first.

Click   **1550 Power Marble Tools** to select this asset account.

Click   the **Select button**. (A darker frame or an inner dotted box shows that a button is selected.)

You can also double click a selected account or press (enter) to add it directly to your journal entry form. Instead of using the selection list, you can find the number in the Chart of Accounts, type it in and press (tab).

Notice that the account number and name have been added to your input form, so you can easily see whether you have selected the correct account. If the screen does not display the entire account title, you can see the rest of the account title by clicking anywhere on the part that is showing.

Your cursor is now positioned in the Debits field. The amount 0.00 is selected, ready to be changed. All journals include a **Windows Calculator tool** that opens the calculator directly for easy calculation of amounts if needed.

Click the Display The Windows Calculator tool [icon] to open the calculator. You can leave it open in the background for easy access.

Type amounts without dollar signs. You do not need to type decimals when you enter whole numbers. The Simply Accounting program ignores any non-numeric characters that you type in an amount field.

Type   885

Press   (tab).

The cursor moves to the Comment field. You can add a comment for each account line in the journal. Account line comments are optional. You can add a comment for each line, for some lines or for none of the lines, but the extra details can be included in the journal report and will give you more information about the transaction.

Type   diamond tip drill and drill bits

Press   (tab).

Your input form should now appear as follows:

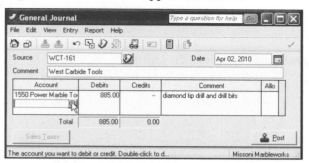

The cursor has advanced to the next line of the Account field, creating a new dotted box so you can enter the next account for this transaction — the liability account *GST Paid on Purchases*. Remember, liability accounts start with 2. However, we will type 3 to include the end of the 2000 level accounts.

Type   3

Click   the **List icon** to advance your list to the 3000 accounts as shown:

We have bypassed the Search field and selected the first account with the number we typed. This method quickly moves you to a later position in the list.

Click   **2670 GST Paid on Purchases** from the displayed list to highlight it. If necessary, click a scroll arrow (or) to move through the account list to include *2670* in the display.

Press   (enter).

Again, the account number and name have been added to your transaction form. The cursor has advanced to the Credits field, which shows 885.00 as the default amount because this amount will balance the entry. The amount is highlighted to indicate that you may edit it. This is a compound entry. You must change the amount to separate the GST, and you must delete the credit entry because the GST account is debited.

Press   (del) to delete the credit entry.

Click   the **Debits field** on the second journal line below 885.00 to move the cursor.

Type   44.25

Press   (tab) to advance to the optional Comment field.

Type   GST @ 5%

Press   (tab). The cursor moves to the next line in the Account field.

Press   (enter) to open the Select Account list. The cursor is in the Search field.

Type   2

The list advances to the 2000 accounts. The liability account, *2100 A/P - West Carbide Tools*, is selected because it is the first 2000-level account.

Click   **Select** to enter it and return to the journal.

The cursor advances to the Credits field again, where the amount that will now balance the entry is shown. The amount is correct, so you can accept it. The total for the Credits column is still displayed as zero.

Press   (tab) to update the totals and advance to the Comment field.

Type   `terms: net 30`

Your completed input form should appear as follows:

Until the debits and credits of a transaction are equal, you cannot post an entry. Once the entry is complete and balanced, it can be posted. The Store (⬇️) button, for recurring entries, is also darkened. Before you proceed either to store or post an entry, you should review the transaction.

Reviewing the General Journal Entry

Choose the **Report menu** and then **click Display General Journal Entry** as shown:

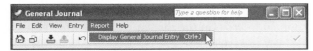

The journal entry for the transaction is displayed as follows:

Click the **Maximize button** ▢ to change your display to full screen size or use the scroll arrows to see more of the display if your transaction does not fit on the screen.

To return to your input form,

Click   ☒ or **choose** the **Control Menu icon** and **click Close**.

CORRECTING THE GENERAL JOURNAL ENTRY BEFORE POSTING

Press ⟨tab⟩ to advance to the field that has the error. To move to a previous field, **press** ⟨shift⟩ and ⟨tab⟩ together (that is, while holding down ⟨shift⟩, **press** ⟨tab⟩). The field will be highlighted, ready for editing. **Type** the **correct information** and **press** ⟨tab⟩ to enter it.

You can also use the mouse to **point** to a field and **drag** through the **incorrect information** to highlight it. You can highlight a single number or letter, or the entire field. **Type** the **correct information** and **press** ⟨tab⟩ to enter it.

To correct an account number, **click** the **incorrect account number** (or **name**) to select the field. **Press** ⟨enter⟩ to display the list of accounts. **Click** the **correct account**. **Click Select**. **Press** ⟨tab⟩ to advance to the next line and enter the correction.

Click an **incorrect amount** to highlight it. **Type** the **correct amount** and **press** ⟨tab⟩.

You can insert a line or remove a line by clicking the line that will be moved down or removed. Then **choose** the **Edit menu** and **click Insert Line** or **Remove Line**.

To discard the entry and begin again, **click** ☒ (Close) to close the journal or **click** ↺ (Undo on the tool bar) to open a blank Journal window. When Simply Accounting asks whether you want to discard the entry, **click Yes** to confirm your decision.

NOTES
Refer to page 43 for assistance with correcting errors after posting.

Posting

Once you are sure that all the information is correct, you are ready to post the entry.

Click the **Post button** in the lower right corner of the General Journal (the one that looks like a stamp) or **choose** the **Entry menu** and then **click Post**.

We have chosen the option to confirm when a transaction is posted successfully, so you will see a confirmation message each time you post or record a transaction:

Click OK.

A new General Journal input form appears for you to enter the next transaction for this session date.

WARNING!
Don't post the transaction until you make sure that it is correct. Always review a transaction before posting it.

Adding a New Account

The bank credit memo on April 3 uses an account that is not listed in your Chart of Accounts. Often a company will need to create new accounts as it expands or changes direction. These future needs are not always foreseen when the accounts are first set up. You must add the account *2300 Bank Loan* to enter the bank credit memo transaction. You can add accounts in the Accounts Ledger (Chart of Accounts icon). The Accounts Ledger is explained in Chapter 4. You can also add accounts directly from the Account field in any journal. First, enter the Source.

Type AT-C3104

Press ⟨tab⟩ **twice** to advance to the Date field. The date of the previous journal entry becomes the default date until you close the journal.

Click the **Calendar icon** and then **click 3**.

Press ⟨tab⟩ to advance to the Comment field.

NOTES
When you close the journal and open it later, the session date becomes the default again.

Type   Alberta Trust - new loan

Double click the **Account field**.

Double click the **Cash in Bank** account.

Type   10000   (the amount of the loan) as the debit part of the transaction.

Press   ⌨tab⌨ to advance to the Comment field for the account.

Type   loan for marble equipment

Press   ⌨tab⌨ to advance to the Account field on the second journal line.

Click   the **List icon** 🔍 or **press** ⌨enter⌨ to see the Select Account list.

Click   **Add New Account**, the first entry in the list, or **click** the **Create** button.

Click   **Select** to begin the wizard for adding a General Ledger account:

The first screen prompts you for the account number and name. The cursor is in the Number field.

Type   2300

Press   ⌨tab⌨.

Type   Bank Loan

Click   **Next** or **press** ⌨enter⌨ to continue.

The next screen asks for the **GIFI code**. This is the four-digit account number assigned by Canada Revenue Agency for this category of account for use with electronically filed business returns. GIFI codes are not used in this workbook. They are described in Appendix I.

Click   **Next** to skip this screen and continue.

The next screen asks whether this account is to be used as a **Heading** or **Total** in the financial statements. *Bank Loan* is an ordinary postable account that has a balance so the default selection, No, is correct. A partial balance sheet illustrates account types.

Click   **Next** to accept the default and continue.

The following screen deals with another aspect of the **account type**. Accounts may be **subtotalled** within their group of accounts. For example, if you have several bank accounts, you will want your Balance Sheet report to include the total cash deposited in all of them together. Different account types will be explained fully in the Toss for Tots application (Chapter 4), where you will set up the accounting records for a new company.

Bank Loan is a Group account. It is not subtotalled with any other account so the default selection, No, is correct.

Click   **Next** to continue.

NOTES
Next is selected so you can press ⌨enter⌨ repeatedly to advance through the wizard screens that you do not need to change.

⚠ WARNING!
Account types must be set correctly or you will get the error message that accounts are not in logical order when you display financial reports. If you see one of these messages, you can edit the account type. See Chapter 4, page 87, for help with creating and editing accounts.

The next wizard screen refers to the **account class**. Account classes are explained in Chapter 7. The default selection is the name of the section. Therefore, for account *2300*, Liability is the section and the default class. Generally, you can accept the default selection.

Click   **Next** to continue.

Now you are being asked whether you want to **allocate** the balance of the account to different projects or divisions. Projects are not set up for Missoni Marbleworks, so the default selection, set at No for Balance Sheet accounts, is correct.

Click   **Next** to continue.

The next setting screen asks whether you want to include or **omit** this account **from financial statements** when it has a zero balance. Choosing Yes means that if the balance in this account is zero, the account will not be included in your financial statements. If you choose No, the account will be printed even if it has a balance of zero. Some accounts, such as *Cash in Bank*, should always be printed in financial statements. In Chapter 4 we explain this setting. The default setting, to include accounts (not to omit), is never wrong.

Click   **Next** to continue to the final screen, like the one shown here:

This final screen shows the selections you have made.

Check   your **work**. **Click Back** until you reach the screen with the error. **Make** the **correction** and **click Next** until you reach this final screen again.

When all the information is correct, you must save the new account information.

Click   **Finish**.

You will return to the General Journal window with the new account added to the account field. Notice that the cursor has not yet advanced, so you can change your account selection if you need to.

Click   the **Credits field**.

Press   (tab) to accept the amount and advance to the Comment field.

Type   Alberta Trust loan

Display the **journal entry** to see whether it is correct.

Close   the **display**. **Make corrections** if you find errors.

Click   **Post** [Post] to save the information. **Click OK** to confirm.

Enter   the next sale transaction.

Adjusting a Posted Entry

Sometimes you discover after posting a journal entry that it had an error. You can make corrections directly in the General Journal by adjusting the previously posted transaction. Simply Accounting allows you to make the correction by adjusting the entry

NOTES
You can use the wizard in any account field to create a new account at any time. You do not need to use the account after creating it when you return to the journal.

without completing a reversing entry. The program creates the reversing and correcting journal entries after you post the correction so that the audit trail is complete. The purchase from West Carbide Tools on April 2 was posted with an incorrect amount.

The General Journal should still be open.

NOTES
Pressing *ctrl* + A will also start the adjust entry process in any journal when the option is available.

Click   the **Adjust A Previously Posted Entry tool** 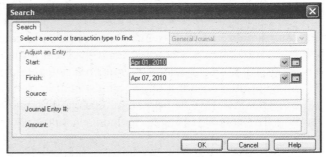 or **click** , the **Adjust An Entry button** beside the Source field, or **choose** the **Entry menu** and **click Adjusting Entry**.

The Search screen opens:

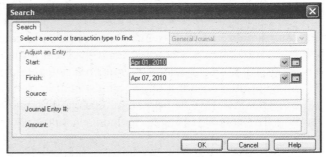

The Adjust Entry and Search functions are combined. Because we selected the Adjust option, the Search section of the screen is dimmed, but General Journal is indicated as the search area. If you begin from the Search option, the cursor will be placed in the Search part of the window. Finding a transaction is the same for both functions. You can select a range of journal entry dates to search. The date we converted the data files to Simply Accounting and the session date are the default start and finish dates for the list. If you know the Source number for the entry, you can enter it in the Source field and access the journal entry directly by clicking OK.

We can accept the default dates because they include the transaction we need.

Click   **OK** to list the journal entries:

All journal entries are listed with the most recent one at the top of the list (Z...A order). You can choose the way the journal entries are sorted.

Click   the **list arrow** beside the Date entry for **View Entries By**:

NOTES
You should choose the order that makes it easiest to find your entry. That will depend on what information you entered and what you remember as well as how many entries you have.

You can organize the list of entries by journal entry number, date, source number, comment or amount. The Z...A button lets you choose ascending or descending order.

Click   **Journal Entry #**.

Click   **Z...A** to change the order and place the one we want first in the list.

Click   **Journal Entry #1**, **WCT-161** to select it.

Click   **Select** or **press** *enter* to open the journal entry as it was posted:

You can also double click anywhere on the line for a journal entry to open the Adjusting General Journal screen.

All fields may now be edited, just as if you had not yet posted the transaction.

Click	**885.00**, the amount in the Debit column for *Power Marble Tools*, to select it for editing.
Type	900
Click	**44.25** or **press** ⬇ to select the Debit column amount for *GST Paid on Purchases*.
Type	45
Click	**929.25**, the Credit column amount for *AP - West Carbide Tools*.
Type	945
Press	(tab) to update the totals with the correct amounts.

We will also modify the source to show that this entry is the correction for the memo.

Click	the **Source field** before the current entry (**before W**).
Type	(COR)

You can change the date for the correcting entry to April 4 if you want. We have not changed the date for this correction.

Review	the **entry** to see the correct transaction and **close** the **display**. **Make corrections** if necessary.
Click	**Post** [Post]. **Click OK** to confirm the posting. Notice that the entry is JE #5. (JE #4 is the reversing entry created by the program.)
Continue	with the **journal entries**.

When you display the General Journal Report (refer to page 56) with Corrections selected, you will see three entries for the purchase invoice — the original incorrect entry, a reversing adjusting entry created by the program (ADJWCT-161) and the correct entry (COR) WCT-161 — providing a complete audit trail for the transaction and correction. See the General Journal Report display on page 56.

REVERSING A GENERAL JOURNAL ENTRY AFTER POSTING

If you need to reverse an entry instead of making changes to it, click the Reverse Entry tool [icon] in the tool bar of the General Journal – Adjusting window, or choose the Entry menu and click Reverse Entry. You will see a confirmation message before the action is taken. Click Yes to continue. Simply Accounting does not delete the original entry. Instead it adds the reversing entry to the journal report for a complete audit trail. You can hide reversing entries in journal reports by not showing corrections.

NOTES
Usually clicking a number in a field will select the entire number. Sometimes, however, depending on exactly where you click, only part of the number is selected or an insertion point is added. Double clicking will always select the entire number in the field so that you can edit it.

NOTES
The adjusting and correcting entries are posted with the same date – the date you used for the adjusting entry. If you want, you can change the date for the adjusting entry but not for the reversing entry.

Advancing the Session Date

When you have finished all the entries for the April 7 session date, the date for the next transaction is later than April 7. Therefore, you must advance the session date before you can continue. If you do not advance the date before posting the April 8 transaction, you will receive an error message.

Before advancing the date, however, save and back up your work because you have already completed one week of transactions.

Although Simply Accounting saves automatically each time you display a report or exit the program, it is important to know how to save and back up your work directly to a separate file and location or disk because your working files may become damaged and unusable.

Click   ☒ or **choose** the **File menu** for the journal and **click Close** to close the General Journal.

You can save a complete duplicate working copy of the file under a different file name. Choose the File menu and click Save A Copy to continue working with the original files or Save As to open a new working copy of the file. This option requires more disk storage space because the copy is not compressed.

The data files for this workbook have been prepared with the default warning to back up your work weekly. Since we also advance the session date by one week at a time, you will be reminded to back up each time you advance the session date. You are now ready to advance the session date to April 14.

Click   **Change** beside **Session Date: Apr 07, 2010** on the right-hand side of the Home window:

Or, **choose** the **Maintenance menu** and **click Change Session Date** as shown:

The Change Session Date window opens with the current session date highlighted:

Type   04-14-10 (or click the date calendar and click 14)

Click   **OK** to accept the new date.

The following message advises you that you have not yet backed up your work:

Click **Yes** to proceed with the backup. The next screen asks for a file name for the backup:

Simply Accounting will create a file named Backup1 inside a new Backup subfolder of the folder that contains your working data files. You can edit the file name and comment. The name Backup is selected so you can change the name.

Type `missoni`

If you want to change the location of the backup, click Browse, select a folder and file name and click OK.

Click **OK** to proceed.

When you name a new folder, you will see the following advisory message:

The program recognizes that the name is new and offers to create the folder. If you have typed the correct name and location,

Click **Yes** to accept the information and continue.

The backup file is different from the one you create by copying or using the Save A Copy or Save As command. The Save A Copy and Save As commands create a complete working copy of your data that you can access with the Simply Accounting program directly. Backup creates a compressed file that must first be restored before you can use it to enter transactions. This file has a .CAB file extension.

After a brief interval, you will see the message that the backup is complete:

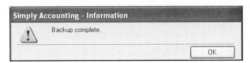

Click **OK** to proceed. You may now enter transactions for this session date.

If you have already created a backup for this data file, or when you change the session date again, you will be advised of the most recent backup date when you are prompted to back up again:

Click **Yes** to continue.

Simply Accounting will provide the same file name and location that you used for your most recent backup. The backup number in the Comment field will be updated.

Your backup information screen will look like the one we show, with different dates:

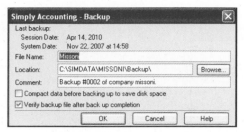

Click   **OK**, or **make** the **changes** you want and then **click OK**.

If you use the same backup file name, you will be asked to replace the previous file:

Click Yes to continue with the replacement or click No to enter a different name.

Enter   the **remaining transactions for April**.

Displaying General Reports

A key advantage to using Simply Accounting rather than a manual system is the ability to produce financial reports quickly for any date or time period. Simply Accounting allows you to enter accounting data accurately so you can prepare the reports you need for reporting to government and investors and for business analysis.

Reports that are provided for a specific date, such as the Balance Sheet, can be produced for any date from the time the accounting records were converted to the computerized system up to the latest journal entry. Reports that summarize a financial period, such as the Income Statement, can be produced for any period between the beginning of the fiscal period and the latest journal entry.

Reports are available from multiple locations: the Accounts window, the Home window Reports menu, the Display tool in the Classic View, and from the Reports list and the Report Centre in the Reports pane of the Home window.

Click the Chart of Accounts icon in the Home window (Classic View or Enhanced View) to open the Accounts window. All General Ledger reports will be available from the Reports menu in this window.

The Reports Menu

From the Home window Reports menu, most General Ledger Reports are located under the Financials option as shown:

The Display Tool in the Classic View

The Display tool 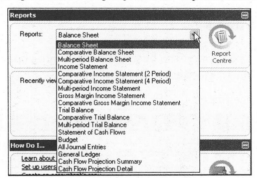 (on the Classic view Home window tool bar) provides a shortcut to displaying reports related directly to the ledger and journal icons. These include lists related to the ledgers such as the Chart of Accounts, supplier and employee lists as well as all journal reports. The Display tool works in three different ways.

1. If a ledger or journal icon is selected but not open, the options window for that report is displayed immediately when you click the Display tool. The label for the Display tool changes to name the report for a selected icon.

2. If no icon is highlighted, clicking the Display tool produces the Select Report window that lists all journal reports and ledger lists. Click the list arrow ☑ and choose a report from this list. Click Select to display the report options window.

3. When the Accounts window is open, clicking the Display tool provides a Select A Report window that lists all the reports for the General Ledger. Click the list arrow ☑, choose from this list and click Select to display the report or its options window. In other ledger windows, the report list will include the reports related to that ledger.

CLASSIC VIEW
Right-click a Classic view Home window icon to select it without opening the journal or ledger.

The Reports Pane and Report Centre

The Reports pane allows access to reports in three ways: from the Report Centre, from the list of recently viewed reports or from the drop-down list of reports for the module you have open. The Company module reports list is shown here:

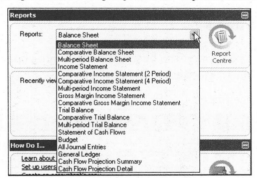

Clicking a report in this list will display it with the default report settings. Once you have displayed a report, it will be added to the Recently Viewed Reports list. Clicking the report in this list will display it with the settings you used most recently. If you have modified a report, using this list provides quick access to your modified report.

We will work from the Reports Centre. There are advantages to using the Report Centre: you can either display the report with the default settings immediately or display the options windows. Furthermore, before opening the report, you will see the purpose and a brief description of the report you want and a display of a sample report.

Click   the **Report Centre icon** in the Reports pane:

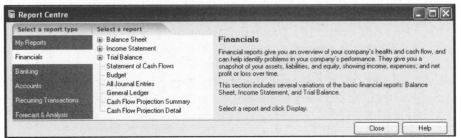

SIMPLY VERSION
The Simply version does not have Forecast & Analysis reports.

As from the Reports menu, reports for ledgers that are hidden are not available. Financial reports are selected because we started from the Company module Home window, and a list of the different financial reports is added. You can see that several of the reports have a ⊞ beside them indicating that there are different forms of the report. A brief explanation of Financial Reports appears.

Read   the **description**.

Click   each ⊞ beside each report type to expand the list.

Click   **Balance Sheet** to see a general description of balance sheets:

Because Balance Sheet is selected, the description now applies to that report. Standard (single-period) and comparative (two-period) reports are available. When you have data for more than two months, you can also display multi-period Balance Sheets, to compare reports for periods ranging from one to 12 months.

Displaying the Balance Sheet

The Balance Sheet shows the financial position of the business on the date you select for the report. You can display the Balance Sheet at any time.

Click   **Standard** below Balance Sheet:

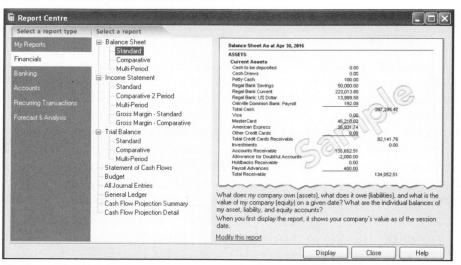

You now see a sample of a standard Balance Sheet with its description and purpose. If you click **Display** at this point, you will display the report with the default settings. The sample shows a report with these default settings. To change the settings or to see what the defaults are, you can use the **Modify This Report** option. We will use this approach so that we can learn to modify the settings to suit our specific needs.

Click   **Modify This Report** to open the Balance Sheet options window:

You can also choose the Reports menu, then choose Financials and click Balance Sheet. The report options window will open.

Default Report Options appears as the template the first time you view a report. The next time you open this window, the Last Used Report Options will display as the template. This selection allows you to see the same report the next time without re-entering dates and other options. At any time you can choose **Default Report Options** on the Template drop-down list to restore the program default settings. The default is to use the session date for the report — Today is selected in the **As At** field. You can choose a standard time period from the As At drop-down list, or you can enter a specific date in the Date field. In the **Date** field, you can also select from a list that includes the first day of the fiscal period, the first day of transactions entered in the program or the session date. The session date is entered in the Date field to match the selection in the As At field. You can also select a date from the **Calendar icon** 🗓 to the right of the Date field.

Click   the **As At field list arrow** to see the options:

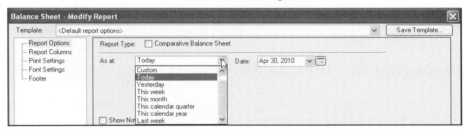

If you want to show the Balance Sheet for two different dates at the same time, you can use the Comparative Balance Sheet. Remember that this was also one of the options in the Report Centre window.

Click   **Comparative Balance Sheet** to select this style of report and open the
            second date field as follows:

Your most recent session date is displayed in the first date field. The second date is the date on which the files were converted to Simply Accounting, the earliest transaction date.

Press   `tab` to highlight the first date if you want to change it.

Click   the **Calendar icon** 🗓 to the right of the date (As At) field.

To enter a date, click 🗓 and choose a date, select a date from the list or type the date you want using one of the accepted formats given earlier.

Press   `tab` or **press** `tab` **twice** if you type the date.

NOTES
Later applications use comparative statements for analysis purposes.

NOTES
If you want a single Balance Sheet only, do not click Comparative Balance Sheet (the check box does not have a ✓ in it). Your most recent session date is displayed by default and highlighted. Choose from the calendar, choose from the date field list or type in the date you want. Click OK to display the Balance Sheet.

If you have accounting data for more than one fiscal period, you can display reports for the previous period as well as for the current period.

Type   the **second date** or choose from the calendar.

Click   the **Report On field** to display the report types in the drop-down list:

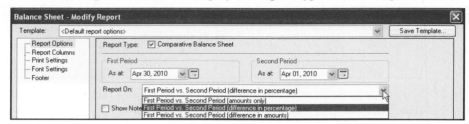

Choose **Amounts Only** if you want only the dollar balances for both dates. Choose **Difference In Percentage** if you want the dollar balances as well as the percentage increase from the second, earlier period amount to the first period amount. Choose **Difference In Amounts** if you want the dollar balances together with the difference between them in dollars. The second, earlier period amount is subtracted from the first to calculate the difference.

Click   the report **contents** you want.

Click   **OK** to display the Balance Sheet.

From any displayed report, you can change the report options to create a different report.

Click   the **Modify tool** or **choose** the **Options menu** and **click Modify Report** to access the report options screen again.

Click   ☒ when you have finished to return to the Report Centre.

Displaying the Income Statement

The Income Statement is a summary of how much a business has earned in the interval you select for the statement. You can view the Income Statement at any time from the Report Centre or the Reports menu. We will continue from the Report Centre. The Income Statement list should still be expanded. You can see that the options are to display a Standard (single-period), Comparative (two-period) or Multi-Period statement. If inventory costs are tracked, Gross Margin Statements that separate the cost of goods sold from other expenses can be displayed.

Click   **Standard** under Income Statement in the Select A Report list to see the report sample.

Click   **Modify This Report** to open the report options window:

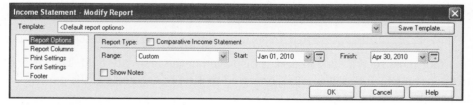

From the Home window, choose the Reports menu, then choose Financials and click Income Statement to open the Modify Report window.

As for the Balance Sheet, you can choose a range of dates from the Range field list or from the Start and Finish field lists. Or you can enter your own choices for the date range (Custom) by typing them in the Start and Finish fields or selecting other dates from the Calendar for those fields.

Click   the **Range field list arrow**:

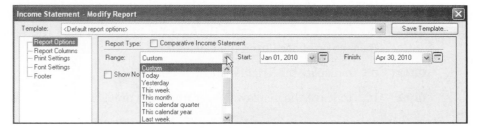

The Income Statement also has a comparative report option, allowing comparisons between two different periods. You might want to compare the income for two months, quarters or years. For the comparative report, you have the same amount and difference options as the Balance Sheet.

Click   **Comparative Income Statement** to select this option:

By default, the earliest transaction date is provided as the start date for the first period and the fiscal start is the start date for the second period. The session date is the finish date for both periods when you select the comparative report.

You must enter beginning and ending dates for the period (or periods) you want your Income Statement to cover. You may accept the defaults, choose a date from the calendar, choose from the date field list or type in the dates.

Click   the **Start date** and **enter** the **date** on which your Income Statement period begins.

Press   (tab) (**twice** if you type the date).

Enter   the **date** on which your Income Statement period ends.

Enter   the **Start** and **Finish dates** for the second period and **choose** the report **content** for comparative reports.

Click   **OK**.

Click   to close the display window when you have finished.

Displaying the Trial Balance

The Trial Balance shows account balances for all postable accounts in debit and credit columns. You can display the Trial Balance at any time while working with the software.

Click   **Standard** under Trial Balance in the Select A Report list to display the sample Trial Balance.

Click   **Modify This Report** to see the report options window:

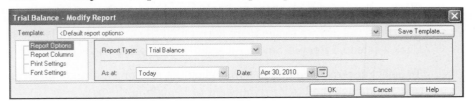

NOTES
If you have data for two fiscal periods, the dates for these two periods will be the defaults for comparative income statements.

NOTES
The Trial Balance is also available as a comparative report with the same options as the Balance Sheet. Click Comparative Trial Balance, enter the first and second dates, choose the report contents from the Report On list and click OK.

From the Home window choose the Reports menu, then choose Financials and click Trial Balance to open the report options window.

Click   the **default date** and **enter** the **date** for which you want the Trial Balance or choose from the calendar.

Click   **OK** to display the Trial Balance.

Click   ☒ to leave the display and return to the previous screen or window.

Displaying the General Ledger Report

The General Ledger Report lists all transactions for one or more accounts in the selected interval. You can display the General Ledger at any time.

Click   **General Ledger** in the Select A Report list to display the sample report.

Click   **Modify This Report** to see the report options window:

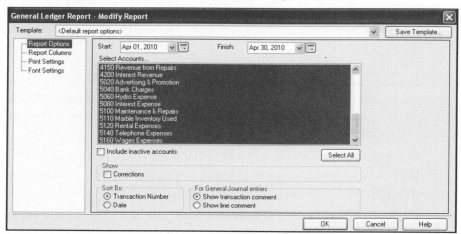

From the Home window choose the Reports menu, then choose Financials and click General Ledger to display the report options.

The General Ledger Report can be sorted in order of the transaction number (journal entry number) or the transaction date. The report includes account balances and transaction or account line comments. The earliest transaction and session dates are the default Start and Finish dates. All accounts are selected for the report.

Click   an **option** to select it or to change the default choices.

Enter   the **starting date** for your General Ledger Report, choose a date from the calendar or choose a date from the Start field drop-down list.

Press   (tab) (**twice** if you type the date).

Enter   the **ending date** for your General Ledger Report.

The **Select All** option works like a toggle switch. When all accounts are selected, clicking Select All will remove all selections. When one or more are selected, clicking Select All will include all accounts for the reports.

Click   the **account** or **press** and **hold** (ctrl) and **click** the **accounts** you want.

Use the scroll arrows to see more accounts if the one you want is not visible. Click a selected item or Select All again to turn off the selection.

To select several accounts in a row, click the first one and then press and hold (shift) and click the last one you want to include in the list.

You can choose to include the comment for the transaction or for individual account lines in your report. You can also choose to sort the report by date or transaction (journal entry) number.

Click   **OK** to view the report.

Click   ☒ to close the **display window** after viewing it.

Displaying the Chart of Accounts

The Chart of Accounts is a list of all accounts that shows the account number, name and account type and class.

Click   **Accounts** in the Select A Report Type list (the list on the left) to expand the Select A Report list:

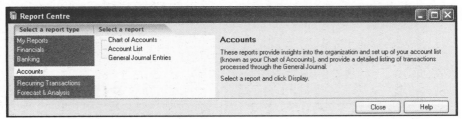

A brief description for the class of Accounts reports appears with the expanded list.

Click   **Chart of Accounts** in the Select A Report list to display the sample.

Click   **Modify This Report** to see the report options window:

Or, choose the Reports menu, then choose Lists and click Chart Of Accounts to display report options.

Choose   the **Template** and the **year** (in the Select Fields list).

Click   **OK** to see the chart. **Close** the **display** when you have finished.

Displaying the Account List

If you want to display the Chart of Accounts and include other selected details, you can use the Account List. For example, you could create an account list with only GIFI numbers or account balances as the additional information.

Click   **Account List** in the Select A Report list to display the sample.

Click   **Modify This Report** to see the report options window:

CLASSIC VIEW
From the Home window, right-click the Chart of Accounts icon

to select it. Click ▦, the Display tool on the tool bar.
Right-click an icon in the Home window (click the right mouse button) to select it without opening the ledger or journal. Clicking the left mouse button will open the journal or ledger.

NOTES
When you have data for more than one fiscal period, you can display the Chart of Accounts for any of these years. For Missoni, only the Current Year is available.

NOTES
GIFI numbers are used for reporting to Canada Revenue Agency.

From the Home window, choose the Reports menu, then choose Lists and click Accounts to see the report options.

Click   **OK** to view the report. The default report shows the account number and name, balance, account type and account class.

Click   ☒ to close the **display window** after viewing it.

Displaying the General Journal

Click   **General Journal Entries** in the Select A Report list to display the sample.

Click   **Modify This Report** to see the report options window:

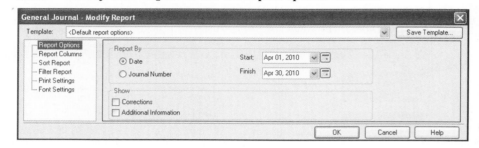

Or, choose the Reports menu. Then choose Journal Entries and click General to display the report options.

Journal reports may include correcting or adjusting entries or may omit them. You may select entries for the report either by the (posting) **Date** of the journal entries or by journal entry number. When you choose **Journal Number**, you must enter the first and last numbers for the entries you want to display. If you do not know the journal numbers, the date method is easier. Furthermore, your journal entry numbers might not match the ones we use if you have made any additional or correcting journal entries. Therefore, all reports in this workbook are requested by date — the default setting.

The earliest transaction and the latest session date are given by default for the period of the report.

Click   **Corrections** to include the adjusting entries.

You can choose any dates for the Journal Report between the fiscal start and the last journal entry, including postdated entries.

Accept   **April 1** and **April 30** as the dates for your journal report.

Click   **OK** to display the report. A partial report is included here:

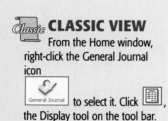

CLASSIC VIEW
From the Home window, right-click the General Journal icon to select it. Click 🗐, the Display tool on the tool bar.

NOTES
Since we have only General Journal entries for Missoni, this report will be the same as the one for All Journal Entries that you select from the Financials report list.

⚠ WARNING!
If you do not choose Show Corrections, the journal report will include only the latest corrected version of all entries. Showing the corrections will include the original incorrect entry, the reversing entry and the final correct one, thus providing a complete audit trail.

The reversing and the final corrected entry for Memo #1 on page 31 are in this report. J1 (not shown here) has the original incorrect entry. If corrections were not included, only J5, the final correct entry, would be shown. The complete report shows the audit trail.

NOTES
Sometimes, depending on who will see the report, you may want to omit the corrections.

Customizing Reports

When we selected dates, comparative options or reversing journal entries, we were customizing reports. Modify Report windows also include customization options in the pane on the left. You can change the columns or fields in the report, sort reports and filter them. Sorting reports changes the order in which data are presented, while filtering reports selects the records to include according to the data fields used as selection criteria. Printing options may also be modified.

Reports already on display may also be modified. You can choose the elements you want to change from the Modify tool drop-down list as shown:

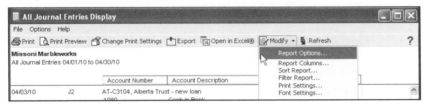

You can also modify columns directly in the display. For example, you can widen a column by dragging the header to the right or remove a column by dragging it to the left. Double clicking a column head will sort the report by the contents of that column, if the report can be sorted. Report modifications are covered further in Appendix F.

> **Close** the **displayed report** when finished.

Drill-Down Reports

Some reports can be accessed from other reports that you have opened or displayed. These are cross-referenced or drill-down reports.

Whenever the pointer changes to 🔍 (a magnifying glass icon with a plus sign inside it) the additional reports can be displayed. When the other ledgers are used, detailed customer, vendor and employee reports are also available from the General Ledger Report and from the General Journal.

> **Move** the **mouse pointer** over various items in the first report. The type of second report available may change. The name of the second report will appear in the status bar.

> **Double click** while the magnifying glass icon is visible to display the second report immediately. The first report stays open in the background.

The General Ledger Report for a specific account can be accessed from the Balance Sheet, Income Statement, Trial Balance, Chart of Accounts or General Journal when you double click an account number, name or balance amount. The General Ledger record for an account can be accessed from the General Ledger Report.

While you have the additional drill-down report displayed, you may print it or drill down to other reports. (See Printing General Reports on page 58.)

> **Close** the **second report** and then **close** the **first report** when you have finished viewing them. **Close** the **Report Centre**.

Displaying Management Reports

Management reports provide accounting information that is specific to the company data file. When the other ledgers are used, the menu also includes management reports for these ledgers. Management reports are not available from the Report Centre or the Reports drop-down lists in the Reports pane.

> **Choose** the **Reports menu**, then **choose Management Reports** and **click General** to see the display of available reports:

To see a report, click a topic to select it. The date field may de dimmed, depending on the topic selected. If it is not, type the date for the report in the Show Report As At field. The program will select a default report form from the ones you installed with the program. Generally, the default is the best choice. You can click Browse to see other report forms available and select the one you need. If you have the appropriate software program, you may customize the report form. Click OK to display the report.

For example, click the advice topic Accounts With A Negative Balance. Click OK. Your report should include *GST Paid on Purchases* and *Missoni, Drawings* because these contra-accounts normally have negative balances.

> **Close** the **display** when you have finished.

Printing General Reports

> **Display** the **report** you want to print by following the instructions in the preceding pages on displaying reports.

There are overall print settings for the company file. These are available from the Home window and from any open report. From the displayed report,

> **Click** the **Change Print Settings tool** 🖨 or **choose** the **File menu** and **click Reports & Forms** to open the Report & Form Options screen:

From the Home window, choose the Setup menu and click Reports & Forms.

These company settings become the defaults for individual reports.

From this window, you can select a printer, set the margins and choose the default style for different parts of the report. You can also add the computer system date to the report and indicate whether the report is filtered. The Default button will restore the original program default settings for the report.

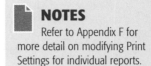

NOTES
Refer to Appendix F for more detail on modifying Print Settings for individual reports.

Choose your **printer** from the drop-down list in the Printer field.

Click   **OK** to save your changes and return to the display or **click Cancel** if you do not want to save the changes you made.

If you want to change the appearance only for the displayed report, you can modify the report. The Modify Report windows include Print Settings and Font Settings as elements that you can modify separately for each type of report.

Graphing General Reports

Graphs are available only from the main menu in any Home window.

Expenses and Net Profit as % of Revenue

Choose the **Graphs menu**, then **click Expenses And Net Profit As % Of Revenue** to display the following report options:

Double click the **default Start date** and **enter** the **beginning date** of the period for your graph.

Press   `tab` (**twice** if you type the date).

Type   the **ending date** of the period for your graph.

Press   and **hold** `ctrl` and **click each expense account you want** included in the graph or **click Select All** to include all accounts.

Click   **OK** to display the graph:

NOTES
The default dates for the graph are the fiscal start date and the session date.

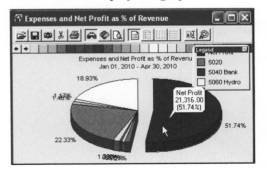

The pie chart shown on the previous page includes all expense accounts for the period from January 1 to April 30, and is a form of the Income Statement. You have several options regarding the graph at this stage. The tool bar options are the same for all graphs. By selecting the appropriate button on the tool bar, you can import a graph, export the displayed graph, copy it to the clipboard as a bitmap or a text file, print the graph, change the view from 3-D to 2-D, hide the legend, edit or add titles, etc. Hold the mouse pointer over a tool button for a few seconds to see a brief description of the tool's purpose. Most tool buttons lead to an additional option or control window requiring your input.

In addition, you can change colours by dragging the colour you want to the pie section you want to change; expand or shrink the legend by dragging its bottom border down or up respectively; or pull out a section of the pie chart by dragging it away from the rest of the chart. The graph displayed has the Net Profit portion pulled out for emphasis.

> Double click a portion of the graph to see the name of the account, the dollar amount and the percentage of the total.

> Double click the legend to make it larger and to add the account names. Double click the expanded legend to reduce it.

> Right-click the legend title to view a set of options for positioning the legend on the graph page. To move the legend to the new position, click the new legend position option. Double click the legend to restore the original size and position.

> **Close**   the **graph** when you have finished.

Revenues by Account

> **Choose**   the **Graphs menu**, then **click Revenues By Account** to display the following report options:

> **Enter**   the **beginning date** of the period for your graph.

> **Press**   `tab` (**twice** if you typed the date).

> **Enter**   the **ending date** of the period for your graph.

> **Press**   `ctrl` and **click each revenue account you want** included in the graph or **click Select All** to include all accounts in the graph.

> **Click**   **OK** to display the pie chart as shown:

The pie chart has each revenue account represented by a different piece of the pie. You can see that most of the revenue comes from contracts. If you double click a section of the pie, the amount and percentage for that account are shown in a bubble.

You have the same options for this graph as you do for the Expenses and Net Profit as % of Revenue graph.

> **Double click** a **pie section** to show its amount and percentage.

> **Close** the **graph** when you have finished.

Expenses by Account

> **Choose** the **Graphs menu** and **click Expenses By Account** to display the options:

> **Enter** the **beginning date** of the period for your graph.

> **Press** `tab` (**twice** if you typed the date).

> **Enter** the **ending date** of the period for your graph.

> **Press** `ctrl` and **click each expense account you want** included in the graph or **click Select All** to include all accounts in the graph. **Click OK**:

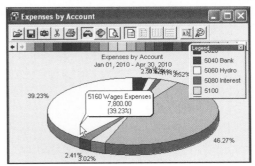

Each expense account that was selected is represented as a separate piece of the pie. The accounts not selected are grouped together in the **Other** category. The expenses graph makes it easy to identify at a glance the items that make up the largest share of expenses — marble inventory and wages in this example.

> **Close** the **graph** when finished.

Finishing a Session

Finish the last transaction you are working on for this session.

> **Click** ☒ to close the transaction window (such as journal input or display) to return to the Home window.

You can click the Close All Other Windows tool in the Home window if you have more than one open window. To restore the Home window,

Click   the **Home window tool** in an open journal window. Or,

Click   the **Simply Accounting by Sage button** on the desktop task bar.

Click   the **Close All Windows tool** in the Home window.

Click   ☒ to close the program. Alternatively, **choose** the **File menu** and **click Exit** to close the program.

You will see the following message about backing up the data file:

Simply Accounting - Backup

Do you want to back up this company before closing?
⦿ Yes   ○ No

☐ Do not ask me again.

OK   Cancel   Help

If you did not back up the file after the last set of transactions, you should do so now.

Click   **OK** to start the backup procedure. Follow the instructions on page 47 to complete the backup.

After the backup is complete, the file will close.

The Simply Accounting program will automatically save your work when you finish your session and exit properly. You can now turn off your computer.

R E V I E W

The Student CD-ROM with Data Files includes Review Questions and Supplementary Cases for this chapter.

Toss for Tots

OBJECTIVES

After completing this chapter, you should be able to

- **plan** and **design** an accounting system for a non-profit organization
- **prepare** a conversion procedure from manual records
- **understand** the objectives of a computerized accounting system
- **create** company files using the skeleton starter file
- **change** the default home window
- **set up** the organization's accounts
- **enter** historical account information
- **finish** entering accounting history to prepare for transactions
- **enter** fiscal end adjusting transactions
- **close** the books and start a new fiscal period
- **enter** transactions for a previous fiscal period

COMPANY INFORMATION

Company Profile

NOTES

Toss for Tots
North Toronto PO Box 42665
Toronto, Ontario M5N 3A8
Tel: (416) 489-2734
Fax: (416) 489-6277
Business No.: 127 362 644

Toss for Tots is a charitable organization created to raise awareness and to support research on cancer in children. One salaried event manager, assisted by a large group of volunteers, organizes a basketball free-throw tournament to raise money for children's cancer research and family support. The tournament uses a ladder-style elimination to determine the championship. During the first two weekends, a first round of 20 free throws determines the basic skill level of each participant for the initial pairing. The subsequent one-on-one free-throw elimination rounds take place over the next two weekends. Two basketball courts are rented, allowing eight participants to play at the same time for the early rounds — two at a time at each end of the two courts. One thousand people are expected to participate in the initial rounds. Professional basketball players are not permitted to compete.

Funds are raised in several ways during the event: each participant pays an entry fee of $50 and receives a $30 tax receipt; each participant is expected to get sponsors who can donate a fixed amount or an amount for each successful

NOTES

Spectators and players can pay $10 for a surprise bag that contains a variety of donated items such as gift certificates, magazines, books and games. The items are hidden from view, and the value of each package is never less than $10.

basketball throw; spectators pay an admission fee to watch the tournament — $10 for one day, $15 for one weekend or $25 for both weekends; snacks and drinks are sold to spectators and participants; surprise bags are sold for $10 each; and photos of participants on the court are sold for $10 each. Prizes, donated by various corporations, are offered to participants who collect large donation amounts, and a cash prize of $1 000 is awarded to the tournament champion.

Volunteers handle all the registrations, monitor the contest and determine placements or pairings for successive rounds on the ladder. Costs are also minimized by the large number of merchandise donations for the surprise packages and prizes. The organization does incur some expenses, including the event manager's salary, rental of the basketball courts, a computer to record all registrations, donations and ladder sequence, office supplies, promotional materials, telephones, drinks, snacks and so on.

At the start of the tournament, many of the participants have already paid their registration fees and most of the merchandise has been purchased or received. The organization has been operating for several months to prepare for the tournament.

The bank account has been set up for the early cash donations and registrations and to write cheques for pre-tournament expenses. Some cash is also kept on hand at the tournament to make change for on-site sales and for immediate purchases. Most of the cash and cheques received from registrations and admissions are deposited immediately for security purposes.

Toss for Tots has decided to use Simply Accounting to keep the accounting records for the tournament in July 2010, part way through its current fiscal year. The charity requires only General Ledger accounts. The following information is available to set up the accounts using the General Ledger:

- Chart of Accounts
- Income Statement
- Balance Sheet
- Trial Balance
- Accounting Procedures

CHART OF ACCOUNTS

TOSS FOR TOTS

ASSETS
1000 CURRENT ASSETS [H]
1020 Bank: Toss for Tots [A]
1100 Cash on Hand [A]
1150 Total Cash [S]
1200 Surprise Bag Supplies
1300 Food Supplies
1320 Office Supplies
1360 T-shirts
1390 TOTAL CURRENT ASSETS [T]

1400 FIXED ASSETS [H]
1420 Fax/Telephone
1450 Computer
1500 Digital Camera
1590 TOTAL FIXED ASSETS [T] ▶

▶**LIABILITIES**
2000 CURRENT LIABILITIES [H]
2100 Bank Loan
2200 A/P - Designs U Wear
2300 A/P - Quiq Kopy
2350 A/P - Central College
2400 A/P - Snack City
2670 GST Paid on Purchases
2690 TOTAL CURRENT LIABILITIES [T]

EQUITY
3000 EQUITY [H]
3560 Accumulated Surplus
3600 Net Income [X]
3690 TOTAL EQUITY [T] ▶

▶**REVENUE**
4000 REVENUE [H]
4020 Revenue: Registrations
4040 Revenue: Sponsors
4080 Revenue: Surprise Bags
4100 Revenue: Admissions
4120 Revenue: Food Sales
4390 TOTAL REVENUE [T]

EXPENSE
5000 ADMIN EXPENSES [H]
5020 Court Rental Expense
5200 Office Supplies Used
5220 Non-refundable GST
5240 Postage Expense
5280 Printing & Copying ▶

▶5300 Telephone Expense
5320 Publicity & Promotion
5400 Wages - Manager
5420 Miscellaneous Expenses
5440 TOTAL ADMIN EXPENSES [T]

5450 MERCHANDISE & FOOD EXPENSES [H]
5500 Cost of T-shirts
5520 Cost of Surprise Bags
5550 Cost of Food
5690 TOTAL MERCHANDISE & FOOD EXPENSES [T]

NOTES: The Chart of Accounts is based on the current expenses and accounts. Account types are marked in brackets for subgroup Accounts [A], Subgroup totals [S], Headings [H], Totals [T] and Current Earnings [X]. All unmarked accounts are postable Group [G] accounts. The explanation of account types begins on page 83.

INCOME STATEMENT

TOSS FOR TOTS

For the Nine Months Ending June 30, 2010

Revenue		
4000	REVENUE	
4020	Revenue: Registrations	$20 000.00
4040	Revenue: Sponsors	2 000.00
4390	TOTAL REVENUE	$22 000.00
	TOTAL REVENUE	$22 000.00
Expense		
5000	ADMIN EXPENSES	
5020	Court Rental Expense	$15 000.00
5200	Office Supplies Used	640.00
5240	Postage Expense	450.00
5280	Printing & Copying	2 000.00
5300	Telephone Expense	360.00
5320	Publicity & Promotion	4 000.00
5400	Wages - Manager	6 000.00
5440	TOTAL ADMIN EXPENSES	$28 450.00
	TOTAL EXPENSE	$28 450.00
	NET INCOME (LOSS)	($6 450.00)

NOTES: Because the event has not yet started, some expenses are still at zero. Because most of the funds have not yet come in, the Income Statement shows a net loss.

BALANCE SHEET

TOSS FOR TOTS

July 1, 2010

Assets			
1000	CURRENT ASSETS		
1020	Bank: Toss for Tots	$18 550.00	
1100	Cash on Hand	1 000.00	
1150	Total Cash		$19 550.00
1200	Surprise Bag Supplies		500.00
1300	Food Supplies		1 200.00
1320	Office Supplies		750.00
1360	T-shirts		800.00
1390	TOTAL CURRENT ASSETS		$22 800.00
1400	FIXED ASSETS		
1420	Fax/Telephone		500.00
1450	Computer		2 400.00
1500	Digital Camera		900.00
1590	TOTAL FIXED ASSETS		$ 3 800.00
	TOTAL ASSETS		$26 600.00 ▶

▶ Liabilities		
2000	CURRENT LIABILITIES	
2100	Bank Loan	$ 15 000.00
2200	A/P - Designs U Wear	800.00
2300	A/P - Quiq Kopy	150.00
2350	A/P - Central College	10 500.00
2400	A/P - Snack City	900.00
2670	GST Paid on Purchases	−1 850.00
2690	TOTAL CURRENT LIABILITIES	$25 500.00
	TOTAL LIABILITIES	$25 500.00
Equity		
3000	EQUITY	
3560	Accumulated Surplus	$ 7 550.00
3600	Net Income	−6 450.00
3690	TOTAL EQUITY	$ 1 100.00
	TOTAL EQUITY	$ 1 100.00
	LIABILITIES AND EQUITY	$26 600.00

TRIAL BALANCE

TOSS FOR TOTS

July 1, 2010	Debits	Credits
1020 Bank: Toss for Tots	$18 550.00	
1100 Cash on Hand	1 000.00	
1200 Surprise Bag Supplies	500.00	
1300 Food Supplies	1 200.00	
1320 Office Supplies	750.00	
1360 T-shirts	800.00	
1420 Fax/Telephone	500.00	
1450 Computer	2 400.00	
1500 Digital Camera	900.00	
2100 Bank Loan		$15 000.00
2200 A/P - Designs U Wear		800.00
2300 A/P - Quiq Kopy		150.00
2350 A/P - Central College		10 500.00
2400 A/P - Snack City		900.00
2670 GST Paid on Purchases	1 850.00	
3560 Accumulated Surplus		7 550.00
4020 Revenue: Registrations		20 000.00
4040 Revenue: Sponsors		2 000.00
5020 Court Rental Expense	15 000.00	
5200 Office Supplies Used	640.00	
5240 Postage Expense	450.00	
5280 Printing & Copying	2 000.00	
5300 Telephone Expense	360.00	
5320 Publicity & Promotion	4 000.00	
5400 Wages - Manager	6 000.00	
	$56 900.00	$56 900.00

Accounting Procedures

GST

Registered charities have two options with respect to the GST. Like regular for-profit businesses, they can register to apply the GST, charge GST on all sales and membership fees and claim all GST paid as input tax credits to reduce the liability to the Receiver General. The second option, used by Toss for Tots, does not require registration or collection of GST but permits a partial rebate of GST paid. Periodically, the charity submits an application for refunds, listing the total of all GST paid toward its operating expenses. Fifty percent of this amount is eligible for the rebate. Therefore, Toss for Tots records all purchases as compound General Journal entries, separating the amount paid for GST from the total and debiting this amount to *GST Paid on Purchases*. This account is cleared with a credit entry as the application for a rebate is submitted. The debit entries to the *GST Refund Receivable* and the *Non-refundable GST* expense accounts (50 percent each) will balance the journal entry.

Bank Accounts

The proceeds from the registrations and from the sale of merchandise are entered into the bank account. This account is used for all cheques to suppliers and to cover operating and administrative expenses and merchandise — drinks, snacks, T-shirts and surprise bag items. During the tournament, a *Cash on Hand* account is set up for day-to-day expenses incurred by the volunteer staff. Transfers are made from the *Bank: Toss for Tots* account to *Cash on Hand* by writing cheques to the Event Manager.

INSTRUCTIONS

1. **Set up** the **company accounts for Toss for Tots** in the General Ledger in Simply Accounting using all the information provided in this application. Detailed keystroke instructions follow the instructions.

2. **Back up your work frequently** when working through this application to keep your backups updated.

   You may finish your session at any time while completing the setup. Simply open the Toss for Tots data file again, accept the session date and continue from where you left off.

   If you are using a different location for your data files, substitute the appropriate data path, including the drive and folder for your data setup.

3. **Enter** the **source documents** that begin on page 93 in the General Journal in Simply Accounting using the Chart of Accounts and other information provided.

4. **Print** the **following reports** after you have completed your entries:

   a. General Journal from July 1 to September 30
   b. Comparative Balance Sheet at September 30 and October 1 (amounts)
   c. Income Statement for the period October 1, 2009, to September 30, 2010

KEYSTROKES FOR SETUP

The following are the five key stages in preparing the Simply Accounting program for use by a company:

1. creating company files
2. preparing the system
3. preparing the ledgers
4. printing reports to check your work
5. backing up your files and finishing the company history

   The following keystroke instructions are written for a stand-alone PC with a hard disk drive. The keystroke instructions provided in this application demonstrate one approach to setting up company accounts. Always refer to the Simply Accounting and Windows manuals and Help for further details.

Creating Company Files

The following instructions assume that you installed the Simply Accounting data files on your hard disk in drive C: in the SimData folder.

   Simply Accounting provides both templates and starter files to make it easier to create files for a new company. These files contain different sets of accounts that match the needs of different kinds of businesses. By starting with one of these files, you eliminate the need to create all the accounts for your business from scratch.

NOTES

We want to illustrate different ways of creating company files. Therefore, the method of creating your company files from scratch is described in the Dorfmann Design setup application, Chapter 7.

NOTES

If you prefer to enter the source documents before setting up the data files, you can restore the toss1.CAB file in the Setup folder inside your SimData folder. In this way, the setup may be easier to complete because you are already familiar with the account structure.

NOTES

If you use the Skeleton file located in C:\Program Files\ Simply Accounting Premium 2008\ Template\, you will be upgrading from Simply 2005 A to Premium (or Simply) 2008 Release B. Make a backup of this file before changing the settings and accounts. Use the File menu Save As command to create the new file C:\SimData\Toss\toss.SAI.

NOTES

Refer to page 7 for more detailed instructions on restoring backup files.

SIMPLY VERSION

The file will be converted from Release A to Release B. You will not see the Upgrade Company Wizard screens. The next screen you see will be the message about payroll tax changes (page 70).

There are many templates that work with the setup wizards to define not only accounts, but also a number of settings for the different ledgers. These settings and accounts are suited to the type of business named by the files.

In addition, Simply Accounting includes two starter files — inteplus.SAI (Integration Plus) and skeleton.SAI. The starter files contain only a set of basic accounts. Starter files are opened like any other company file. You should work with a copy of these files so that you can use the original files for future applications.

The Skeleton starter has only General Ledger accounts, whereas the Integration Plus starter is suitable for a variety of business types because it has the basic linked accounts for all the ledgers.

You will have to customize any of these starter files to your particular company. Rarely are accounts identical for any two businesses. The files that are best suited to the Chart of Accounts for Toss for Tots are the Skeleton starter files (skeleton.SAI). These files contain only a few General Ledger accounts, headings and totals. They contain no linked accounts that link General Ledger accounts to the subsidiary ledgers. This is appropriate for Toss for Tots, which uses only the General Ledger.

The starter files are located in the folder named Template in the Simply Accounting Premium 2008 folder — the folder that contains your Simply Accounting program.

This starter file is a Version 2005 Simply file so it must be upgraded before you can use it. The Student Premium Version of Simply Accounting cannot open files from previous version years, so we have created a backup file of the 2008 Simply Version of the Skeleton file. We will restore this backup (skeleton1.CAB) from the SimData folder.

Start   the **Simply Accounting program** to access the Select Company window.

Click   **Restore From Backup** to start the Restore Backup wizard.

Click   **Next** to open the screen for selecting the backup file. **Click Browse**.

Clicking Browse should place you in the folder you used to restore the previous backup, so this should be the SimData folder. If is not, click the list arrow beside the Look In field and click C: and then double click SimData.

Double click skeleton1.CAB to select it in the next screen as shown:

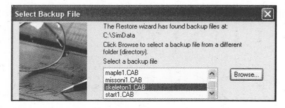

Click   **Next** to open the confirmation screen.

Click   **Next** to open the New File Name screen.

Click   the **Enter File Name field** and **Type** C:\SimData\Toss\toss

Click   **Next** to see the confirmation message about creating the new folder.

Click   **Yes** to continue.

Click   **Finish** to begin restoring the data file. The Upgrade Company Wizard now starts:

The Skeleton starter file is a Simply version file so it must be converted to Premium Release B.

Read   the **introduction** to the wizard and **click Next** to continue:

This screen shows the name and location of the working file and the version changes that will be made if you proceed.

Click   **Next**:

You can now back up the Skeleton file before proceeding. Simply Accounting will check your data file for problems and repair them if you choose this option.

Click   **Next** to see the final warning about converting files:

This final screen warns you of the changes you are making. After this step you cannot cancel the conversion. File conversions cannot be reversed — once you convert a file you will be unable to open it in the earlier version.

Click   **Finish** to begin the conversion.

Click   **OK** if you see a message about updating your employees' income tax claim amounts. Income tax tables are updated every six months.

You will now be asked to indicate the type of company you are working with. Different company types have different labels in the Premium version.

Click   the **list arrow beside Other**, the default entry, to see the types:

Click   **Non-Profit** and then **click OK**.

SIMPLY VERSION
Your data file will be updated to Release B, but you will not see the Upgrade Company Wizard or a message about the upgrade.

WARNING!
If you make a backup at this stage, it will be a Premium Version 2008 Release B backup.

SIMPLY VERSION
You will not see the Types of Company window. You can select the type on the Company Information Settings screen (page 72).

NOTES

The message about payroll tax changes appears because new releases of Simply Accounting are tied to tax table changes that occur every six months.

The GST rate message reminds users to update their sales tax rates and codes. In January 2008, the federal government reduced the GST rate to 5 percent and the HST rate to 13 percent.

SIMPLY VERSION

Simply Accounting by Sage 2008 is displayed as the program name in the title bar.

The ledger icon labels are Customers and Projects. Sales Invoices replaces Statements and Sales replaces Supporter for the journal labels.

SIMPLY VERSION

The Time & Billing module is not available in the Simply version, so the task icon for Create A Time Slip will not appear.

SIMPLY VERSION

The open history symbol appears with the Customers icon.

Click   OK if you see a messages about payroll tax legislation changes.

The Session Date window appears with January 1, 2000, as the session date.

Click   OK to accept the date. You may see a second message about GST rates.

Click   OK.

The Home window opens and all ledgers are available in the list of modules.

The file name TOSS.SAI (or TOSS) appears in the title bar. The Receivables module is the default for the Home window. We will change this default because this module is not used by Toss for Tots.

The ledger icon is labelled Supporters because we selected Non-Profit as the company type. For other types of companies, this icon may be labelled Customers or Clients. Projects are labelled Funds for non-profit companies.

The ledgers are not set up. An open history (quill pen) symbol appears beside Supporters, the ledger icon, indicating that you can enter historical data for the ledger. If you open the other modules, you will see the same symbol for each one. Although you can make journal entries at this stage, you should enter all the necessary company information and finish entering the history first.

Changing the Default Home Window

Toss for Tots uses only the General Ledger (Company module) so we will make this the Home window. The Receivables module has This Is My Default Page below the header.

Click   Company in the list of modules on the left to change the Home window.

Now we have the Chart of Accounts and the General Journal available. Notice that the message below Company has changed to Make This My Default Page. Clicking this option for any module will select the displayed module as the default Home window.

Click   Make This My Default Page.

The Company heading now has This Is My Default Page below it as shown:

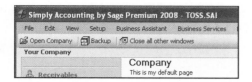

Preparing the System

Before entering financial records for a new company, you must prepare the system for operation. This involves changing the default settings to reflect the Toss for Tots company information such as the company name and address, fiscal dates, screen display preferences and the Chart of Accounts. Some initial defaults will not be suitable for Toss for Tots. You must also provide other information, such as the printer(s) that you will be using and the printing formats. This process of adding, deleting and modifying information is called customizing the system.

Changing Default Settings

Click the **Settings icon** in the Related Tasks pane, or **choose** the **Setup menu** and **click Settings**:

The Company Settings main menu window opens:

Most settings for a data file are entered from this central Settings screen. Some apply to features and modules not used by Toss for Tots. We will skip the screens that do not apply. They will be introduced in later chapters.

The modules are listed on the left. All have a ⊞ beside them indicating there are multiple settings. The larger right-hand side of the window begins with the same expanded list of entries for the selected module as the expanded list on the left.

Clicking a ⊞ beside an entry will expand the list. Clicking an entry in the list on the left without a ⊞ beside it or in the list on the right-hand side will open the options window for that entry.

Entering Company Information

Company settings apply to all modules of the company for all users of the data file.

NOTES
 Simply Accounting includes a Setup wizard that guides you through the company setup step by step with instructions. The wizard is not used in this application. To access the Setup wizard, choose the Setup menu, then choose Wizards and click Modify Accounts.

NOTES
 You cannot complete the setup in multi-user mode.

NOTES
 If another module is open when you choose Settings, you will see the settings for that ledger. Click Company and then click Information to see the Information screen.

Click   **Information** (in either the left-hand side or right-hand side list) to see the following information screen:

The Name field contains the information "Your Company" to let you know that this is where you should enter the name of your company.

Press   ⟨*tab*⟩ or **drag through Your Company** to select this text.

Type   Toss for Tots (add your own name)

Press   ⟨*tab*⟩.

The cursor moves to the Street 1 field, the first address field. You can enter the address immediately because the current contents are already highlighted.

Type   North Toronto

Press   ⟨*tab*⟩ to advance to the second street address line (Street 2 field).

Type   PO Box 42665

Press   ⟨*tab*⟩.

The cursor advances to and highlights the contents of the City field.

Type   Toronto **Press** ⟨*tab*⟩.

The cursor advances to the Province code field. It, too, is ready for editing.

Typing the first letter of the province name will enter the first province beginning with that letter. Typing the same letter again will advance the list to the next province starting with the same letter. You can also select a code from the drop-down list.

Type   O **Press** ⟨*tab*⟩ to advance to the province name field. ON and Ontario are entered as this is the only province beginning with "O."

Press   ⟨*tab*⟩ again to accept Ontario as the province.

The cursor is now placed in the highlighted Postal (postal code) field. You do not have to type the capitals or spaces in postal codes. The program automatically corrects the postal code format when you enter a Canadian postal code pattern.

Type   m5n3a8

In this case, all addresses will be in Canada, so we can leave the Country field blank. Now enter the telephone and fax numbers for the business. There is only one phone number so the Phone 2 field will remain blank. You do not need to type brackets or hyphens for phone numbers. Simply Accounting will correct the format when you enter a seven- or ten-digit phone number.

Click   the **Phone 1 field**. The postal code format is corrected.

Type   4164892734

Click   the **Fax field**. The telephone number format is corrected.

Type   4164896277

Press   (tab) to move to the Business No. field.

All companies must use a single Canada Revenue Agency business number that also serves as the GST registration number. All business numbers have an Rx extension that indicates the business area for tax purposes.

Type   127362644 RR0001 **Press** (tab).

There are a number of types of companies to choose from in the program. We selected the type when we restored and upgraded the data file. You can select from the **Industry Type** list to change the type. Changing the company type will also change the icon labels.

Simply Accounting will accept dates after January 1, 1900. You can store 100 years of accounting records.

The **Fiscal Start** field contains the date at which the current fiscal year begins. This date usually defines the beginning of the fiscal year for income tax purposes.

The **Fiscal End** is the date at which the company closes its books, usually one year after the fiscal start, and the end of the fiscal year used for income tax reporting purposes. For Toss for Tots, the fiscal end is two months after the tournament, when all the accounting information for the event has been entered.

The **Earliest Transaction** date is the date on which the company converts its manual accounting records to the computerized system. Entries before this date are historical entries. The earliest transaction date must not be earlier than the fiscal start and not later than the fiscal end. The earliest transaction date will be the first session date when you are ready to enter journal transactions. Simply Accounting automatically advances the earliest transaction date when you start a new fiscal year.

Notice that the **default date format** for this file is day-month-year. We will enter these dates in text form and then change the date format for the file. By entering text with four digits for the year initially, we will ensure that we enter the date correctly.

Press   (tab) to advance to the Fiscal Start field.

Type   oct 1 2009

Press   (tab) **twice**. The cursor moves to the Fiscal End field.

Type   sep 30 2010

Press   (tab) **twice**. The cursor is now in the Earliest Transaction field.

Type   jul 1 2010

The session date and the latest transaction date will change as you complete journal entries and advance the session date from the Home window. When the latest transaction date is later than the session date, it indicates there are postdated journal transactions.

You cannot change the earliest transaction date after finishing the history and making journal entries. The company name, address and fiscal end date can be edited at any time. Return to any field with errors to correct mistakes.

You will need to save the fiscal dates before completing the next step.

Click   **OK**.

Simply **SIMPLY VERSION**

You should select Non-profit from the Industry Type drop-down list. Icon labels do not change when you select a different company type.

You can store seven years of company data.

NOTES

Companies may use a fiscal period shorter than one year for reporting purposes and close their books more frequently, but the most common period is one year.

NOTES

When we entered various dates, the program accepted dates between 1900 and 2400 without an error message. There appear to be no practical restrictions on the dates you can use.

NOTES

Once you have entered the fiscal start, fiscal end and earliest transaction dates, the program will correctly fill in the year when you type only the last two digits or omit the year, because the date must fall between the earliest transaction and fiscal end dates.

NOTES

When you view the Company Information again, the session and latest transaction dates will have been updated to match the new fiscal dates.

SIMPLY VERSION
You will not see the warning about changing the industry type because the terminology does not change in the Simply version.

If you changed the type of company, you will see the following confirmation:

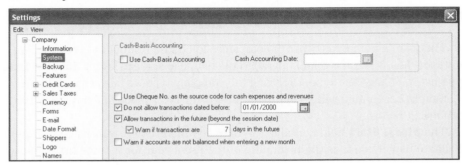

Click   Yes to accept the changes.

Click   the **Settings icon** , or **choose** the **Setup menu** and **click Settings** again to resume.

Setting System Defaults

Click   System in the list under Company to access the options:

The Company System settings apply to all modules of the program.

There are several important settings in this screen. The first refers to whether the business is using **cash-basis accounting** instead of the default, **accrual-basis accounting**. The cash basis of accounting records revenues and expenses on the date the money is paid or received. In the accrual method, revenues and expenses are recorded on the transaction date (matching principle). To change to the cash basis method, click the check box and enter the date on which the change is to take effect. This workbook uses the accrual basis. Do not change this setting.

The next option relates to the use of the **Cheque Number As The Source Code For Cash Purchases And Sales** in account reconciliation. Since Toss for Tots uses only the General Ledger, this option does not apply. When you are using the Payables and Receivables Ledgers, you should turn on the option.

The next option, **Do Not Allow Transactions Dated Before**, permits you to lock out any transactions for a previous period by entering the date. You can post transactions to earlier dates by removing the checkmark or entering an earlier date in this field. The feature should be turned off only for specific transactions and then turned on again so that you do not post in error with an incorrect date. Similarly, you should not generally allow posting to future periods, beyond the session date, unless you are entering a series of postdated transactions. You can activate the feature for specific transactions when needed so that you do not post with incorrect future dates. You can add a warning for dates beyond a certain period as well. We will restrict transactions before the starting date and not allow postdated transactions.

Remember that the date format is still day-month-year.

Double click the date **01/01/2000**.

Type   Jul 1

Click   Allow Transactions In The Future to remove the ✓ and not allow postdating.

Since Simply Accounting allows journal entries before the company setup details are completed, you can add a reminder **warning** as you continue to work with an

---

NOTES
Refer to Appendix K on the Student CD-ROM for more information on accrual- and cash-basis accounting.

WARNING!
The date you enter for Do Not Allow Transactions Dated Before must not be earlier than the Earliest Transaction Date on the Company Information screen.

If the check box is not checked, you can leave the date field blank. You can also enter the date later.

If you did not save the new fiscal dates, you will see an error message when you enter Jul 1 — the original fiscal dates will restrict the date allowed.

NOTES
Refer to page 101 for details on allowing transactions in a previous year.

incomplete and **unbalanced account history**. If you choose to post journal entries before completing the history, you should turn on the warning.

Setting Backup Options

Click **Backup**:

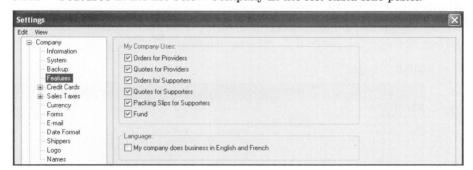

This screen has several options for backing up company files. You can select the **frequency** with which you **back up** your data. Since we usually advance the session date weekly, we will choose Weekly as the backup frequency as well. The program prompts you to back up according to this entry.

Click the **Display A Backup Reminder field list arrow** and **choose** Weekly.

If you want, you can choose a specific number of days as the interval between backups by choosing Other and typing the number in the Number Of Days field that opens with this choice.

The next option will show a **reminder** to back up the file each time you close the company file. Leave the option selected because you should back up data files regularly.

You can **compact** the backup files to further reduce the size. You should **verify** the backup files regularly to ensure there are no errors that will prevent you from restoring the data later.

You can also **schedule automatic backups**. You can choose the frequency, the backup file location and the number of old backup files that should be saved.

Choosing Company Features

Click **Features** in the list below Company in the left-hand side panel:

Most of these features (orders, quotes and packing slips) do not apply to General Ledger transactions. The final option refers to languages used. To create forms in both languages, you must choose the option to conduct business in French and English. The Settings option makes the language switch available for many name fields so you can enter names in both languages. The ability to work with the program in both languages is controlled from the View menu (see page 80), not from the Features setting.

(see page 80)

NOTES
In general, you do not need to compact the backup files as they are already reduced in size.

SIMPLY VERSION
Packing slips are not available in the Simply version.

> **Click**   **each line** to change all settings. This will remove all checkmarks and add one to **My Company Does Business In English And French**, the final option.

Credit cards, sales taxes, currency, e-mail, and form numbers, such as for invoices, and quotes, do not apply to the General Journal transactions entered by Toss for Tots. Toss for Tots does not use Shippers or the additional Names fields in the General Ledger, so you can skip these screens as well.

Changing Date Formats

The date formats for the starter file are different from the formats we used for other files. To avoid entering incorrect dates, we will choose the same format that we used for our other data files. We need to change the default setting so that month appears first. You can choose any separator character you want.

> **Click**   **Date Format** in the list below Company in the left-hand side panel:

> **Choose MM dd yyyy** from the Short Date Format drop-down list.

Choose another separator symbol from the Short Date Separator list, if you want.

On the screen we will show dates in the long form, text style, to make them as clear as possible. You can choose long or short dates for reports.

> **Click**   **Long Dates** beside the option for On The Screen, Use.

You can also enter the day that is normally the first day of the business week.

Adding a Company Logo

Next we will add the company Logo. This logo can be added to invoices or other company documents created in Simply Accounting.

> **Click**   **Logo**:

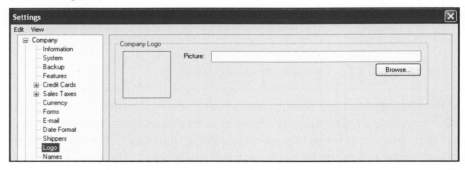

> **Click**   **Browse** and **click** the **Look In field list arrow. Click C:\.** Then **double click SimData**, **Setup** and **Logos** to locate the folder with company logos.

NOTES
Company logo files are located in the SimData\Setup\Logos folder. The default starting point for the Browse is the Forms folder under your Simply Program folder.

Click   **toss.bmp** and **click Open** to return to the Logo Settings window. The
image has been added.

Click   the ⊟ **beside Company** to close the Company list.

Setting General Defaults

To change the settings for the General Ledger for Toss for Tots,

Click   **General (Accounts)** in the list on the left:

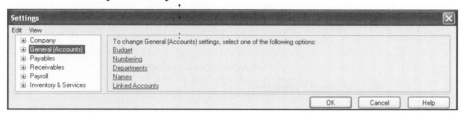

If you want the Simply Accounting program to prepare **budget** reports, click Budget
to open the Budget setup options. Then click Budget Revenue And Expense Accounts
and choose the budget period from the drop-down list. Each revenue and expense
ledger account window will include a Budget tab. Click this tab and then enter budget
amounts for the account to include the account automatically in budget reports. You
can activate budgeting at any time.

Toss for Tots does not have different **Departments** to track expenses, so we do not
need to turn on this option.

Click   **Numbering**:

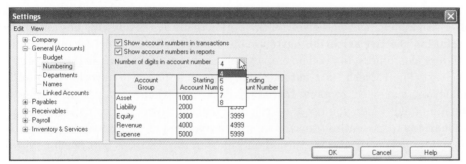

From the **Numbering** option, you can choose not to use account numbers in your
reports and journal transactions when the account names are unique; that is, there is no
duplication of names. We use account numbers in all the applications in this text.

You can also choose the **number of digits** for your account numbers. Each digit you
add to create five- to eight-digit numbers will add a zero to the starting and ending
number for the account group. When you use six-digit numbers, the Asset accounts will
range from 100 000 to 199 900, and the Liabilities accounts will range from 200 000 to
299 900. We use four-digit account numbers in this text.

Click   **OK** to save all the changes and return to the Home window. If you
changed the number of digits, you will see this warning:

Click OK to save the changes to account numbers.

Since the other ledgers are not used by Toss for Tots, you do not need to change
their settings.

SIMPLY VERSION
Departments are not
available in the Simply version.

CLASSIC VIEW
From the Home window
you can access the General
Settings window by clicking the
Setup tool bar button and
selecting Accounts. If the Accounts
icon in the Home window is
already selected, you will access
the General Settings directly when
you click the Setup button.

NOTES
The budgeting feature is
explained in the Village Galleries
application, Chapter 14.
Departments are illustrated
in Chapter 19.

SIMPLY VERSION
In the Simply version, you
cannot change the number of
digits for account numbers.

NOTES
In Part 2 of this text, we use
four-digit account numbers so that
the files can be used with the
Simply or Premium versions. We
introduce 5-digit account numbers
in Part 3, Chapter 19, for Premium
users.

Changing User Preference Settings

User preferences apply to individual users and indicate the way that person prefers to work with the data files. They do not affect the accounting processes. If you have multiple users who access the files, each user can set his or her own preferences.

Choose the **Setup menu**, then **click User Preferences** to see the options:

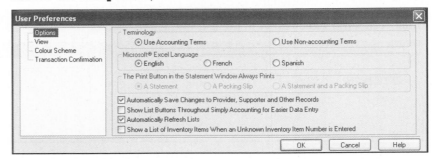

NOTES
An additional option, Always Apply Allocation To Entire Transaction, will be included when you use Funds (Projects or Divisions).

NOTES
Appendix B lists all equivalent accounting and non-accounting terms.

The first feature refers to the language used by the program. We use **accounting terms** throughout this workbook because most people who use accounting programs are familiar with that language. If you choose non-accounting terms, the Payables Ledger will be named Vendors and Purchases in menus and so on. To follow the instructions we provide, you should **Use Accounting Terms**. You can also choose the **language** of your **Excel** program.

NOTES
The Excel language option will apply only if you have installed a non–English-language version of the Excel program.

Some invoice windows include a **Print button**. If you print these invoices, you can set whether the invoice, packing slip or both will be printed as the default.

If you choose not to **automatically save changes** to ledger records when you close a record window, the program will prompt you to save if you close the ledger record after making changes and give you the option of always saving changes automatically. **Including the list selection button** in all account fields to select account numbers, vendors, customers, tax codes, employees, inventory items, etc., is the option we use in this text. The **refresh lists automatically** option applies when working in multi-user mode. You can select to **show inventory item lists** whenever a new item is entered in the item field. When you use the Project (Funds) feature, you can always **apply allocations** to the entire transaction. Inventory and allocations are covered in Chapters 10 and 13, respectively. (We turned off Funds in the Features Settings for this company (page 75).

NOTES
Many account input fields have list buttons or icons like the Account field that you saw in the General Journal in Chapter 3. Other fields have list arrows that provide a drop-down or pop-up list to select from.

NOTES
The Refresh Lists option applies only to the multi-user version of Simply Accounting Premium.

> **Click**   **Show List Buttons Throughout Simply Accounting For Easier Data Entry**.

The remaining default settings are correct. These settings can be changed at any time by clicking the option.

Changing the View Settings

Several important display or appearance options are controlled from the View option.

> **Click**   **View**:

You can **hide**, that is, not display, the icons for **modules** or **pages** that you are not using. We must hide the modules that are not used.

The **Icon Windows** check boxes allow you to hide the accounts icon window for one or more ledgers. If you select the Chart of Accounts icon (or other ledger icon) with this option turned on, account information for the first account will be displayed instead of the list of accounts. Icon windows can be hidden separately only if the module pages are not hidden.

> **Click**   the **Pages check box for Customers & Sales** to remove the ✓. The ✓ for Icon Windows is also removed.

> **Repeat** this step for **Vendors & Purchases, Inventory & Services, Employees & Payroll pages** and the **Time & Billing Feature** so that all these ✓ are removed.

> **Do not remove** the ✓ for **Banking**.

The next two options refer to the appearance of the **toolbar** in the Home window. You can display the tools with text or as icons only. The Classic view Home window toolbar never includes text. In our data files, we include the text with the icons.

Simply Accounting has reminders about upcoming activities such as payments that are due, discounts available and recurring entries. You can choose to be reminded of these activities through the **Checklists** and the **Daily Business Manager** each time you start the program, each time you advance the session date or both. Toss for Tots does not use these lists.

> **Click**   **After Changing Session Date** for **Daily Business Manager** to **remove** the ✓.

> **Click**   **After Changing Session Date** for **Checklists** to **remove** the ✓.

You can **Show the Company Name In the Status Bar** or omit this detail.

Automatic Advice shows advisory messages automatically while you are entering transactions, as, for example, when customers exceed credit limits or the chequing account is overdrawn. Clicking removes the ✓ and the feature. Leave Advice turned on.

We also select to **show the session date** each time we start a work session. If your company has several users who log on frequently during a single day, bypassing this step would be efficient. In that case, the system administrator would update the session day for all users at the start of each business day.

Showing the **Paid Stamp** on invoices and payments is another option. If you hide the Vendors & Purchases page, these options will be dimmed because they no longer apply.

You can change the design and colour of Simply Accounting windows from the **Colour Scheme** entry. You can choose backgrounds from a variety of colours and patterns for the different journal windows.

SIMPLY VERSION
There is no Time & Billing feature in the Simply version, so you will not need to hide it. The term Project replaces Fund.

CLASSIC VIEW
You will see two lists: Modules and Icon Windows. Time & Billing is added to the Modules list.

WARNING!
If you do not hide the remaining modules, you will be unable to complete the final setup step of finishing the history because essential information for those modules is missing.

NOTES
The ✓ for Fund is already removed because we turned off the feature.
The ✓ for Time & Billing is automatically removed when you remove Employees & Payroll.

WARNING!
Do not hide the Banking page. If you hide this page, you will be unable to access the General Journal.

NOTES
You can access Checklists and the Daily Business Manager any time, even if the automatic display for them is turned off.

NOTES

Remember that these are user preferences – each user can change these settings for personal preferences. User setup is described in Appendix H on the Student CD-ROM.

Confirming Posting of Transactions Settings

We will choose to have the program advise when transactions are successfully recorded.

Click **Transaction Confirmation**. You may see this warning:

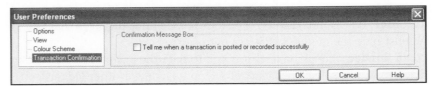

When you hide modules and icon windows, any information you had about icon positions is also removed.

Click **Yes** to continue to the transaction confirmation window:

Click the **check box** beside Tell Me When A Transaction Is Posted Or Recorded Successfully to add a ✓ and turn on the confirmation.

Click **OK** to save the settings and return to the Home window.

Your Home window now looks like this:

The unused modules (hidden pages) have been removed from the Modules pane list.

Changing View Menu Settings

The View menu controls some of the appearance options for the program:

Each journal has optional fields that can be hidden if they are not required by the program and the business. You can also change the order in which fields are accessed from the (tab) key, that is, which field is next when you press (tab). You can **customize all journals** from this menu or you can use the customize option within individual journals. To customize a journal,

> Choose the View menu and click Customize Journals. Click the journal you want. Click Columns or Tabbing Order and click the columns or details you want to change. Hidden fields may be restored at any time by clicking their names again.

> Click OK to save the changes and return to the Home window.

The Customize Journal tool 🖳 in each journal provides the same options as the View menu screen.

> You can also customize the order and size of journal columns. To change the order, drag a column heading to the location you want. To change the column size, point to the edge of the column heading; when the pointer changes to a double-headed arrow ⊞, drag the column margin to its new size.

The next choice on the main View menu refers to the **Select Company window** that appears when you first start Simply Accounting. There are advantages to showing this window. If you regularly use the same data file, you can bypass the Open Company file window, and open your data file with a single step by selecting Open The Last Company You Worked On. Similarly, you can restore a backup file from this window without first opening another data file. The View menu setting acts as a toggle switch, and you can change it at any time.

Simply Accounting is a fully bilingual program. You can **switch the program language** (choose to work in French or in English) from the View menu. When you are working in French, the View menu (now renamed *Vue*) option changes to *Passer A L'Anglais/* Switch To English.

The final View menu option allows you to **close all other Simply Accounting windows** in a single step, leaving only the Home window open. This menu choice is the same as the one in the toolbar.

You are now ready to make the necessary changes in the General Ledger.

Changing the Printer Defaults

You may select a different printer for customized forms or you may want to change the format of the printed reports. The following instructions should assist you.

> **Choose** the **Setup menu** and **click Reports & Forms** to see the settings screen:

NOTES
In Chapter 6, we customize journal columns and tabbing order.

NOTES
We have not hidden any fields in any journals used in the applications in this text, except by turning off features, so you can see the full range of input options for each journal.
We show how to customize journals in Chapter 6 and invoices in Appendix G on the Student CD-ROM.

SIMPLY VERSION
You will not see the Time Slips entry.

The printer selections apply to this data file and are saved with the file. If you use the file with a different computer system, they may be incorrect. Simply Accounting allows you to set up different printers and settings for reports, graphs, cheques, invoices, labels and so on. Many companies use one printer for their reports and another for various preprinted forms and invoices. Even if you use one printer, you may want to adjust fonts, margins and form selections for each type of printed report or statement.

Choose the printer you will use for reports from the list provided by the arrow beside the field. All printers installed on your computer should be on the list. Change the page margins if necessary. For each part of the report, choose font, type size and how to display positive and negative numbers by clicking the list arrows beside these fields. You can experiment to find the combination that will fit the reports neatly on the page. By default, reports include the computer system date and a message indicating whether filtering is applied.

To modify the printer setup for other outputs, click the relevant form in the list. You can modify printer setup information any time by returning to this screen.

Additional printer settings may be available for the source of the paper, the paper size and orientation. Additional control over your printed copy may be available from the Settings button screen. The screens and options will vary from printer to printer.

Click OK to leave each dialogue box and save the changes, or

Click   Cancel to exit without making changes and return to the Home window.

Preparing the Ledgers

The third stage in setting up an accounting system involves preparing each ledger for operation. For Toss for Tots, this stage involves the following steps:

1. organizing all accounting reports and records (this step has been completed)
2. modifying some existing accounts (you will not need to delete any accounts)
3. creating new accounts
4. entering historical account balance information

Defining the Skeleton Starter Files

When you created the company files for Toss for Tots in stage one, Creating Company Files (page 67), the preset startup accounts were provided.

Print the **Chart of Accounts** for the current year, as shown here:

No.	Description	Type	Account Class

Toss for Tots - Purbhoo
Chart of Accounts

Chart of Accounts - Current Year (2010)

ASSET
- 1000 CURRENT ASSETS .... H
- 1020 Bank .... G   Asset
- 1200 Accounts Receivable .... G   Asset
- 1390 TOTAL CURRENT ASSETS .... T

LIABILITY
- 2000 CURRENT LIABILITIES .... H
- 2200 Accounts Payable .... G   Liability
- 2690 TOTAL CURRENT LIABILITIES .... T

EQUITY
- 3000 EARNINGS .... H
- 3560 Retained Earnings .... G   Retained Earnings
- 3600 Current Earnings X   Current Earnings
- 3690 TOTAL EARNINGS .... T

REVENUE
- 4000 REVENUE .... H
- 4020 General Revenue .... G   Revenue
- 4390 TOTAL REVENUE .... T

EXPENSE
- 5000 EXPENSES .... H
- 5020 General Expense .... G   Expense
- 5390 TOTAL EXPENSES .... T

Accounts are organized by **section**: Assets, Liabilities, Equity, Revenue and Expense. The chart also shows the **account type** — such as Heading (H), Subgroup total (S), Total (T), subgroup Account (A), Group account (G) and Current Earnings (X) — and the Account Class. Account type is a method of classifying and organizing accounts within a section or subsection of a report.

Initial account numbers for each account are also shown on the Chart of Accounts. We are using only four digits for account numbers. The accounts in this chart follow the sectional boundaries we saw in Chapter 3 as follows:

- 1000–1999   Assets
- 2000–2999   Liabilities
- 3000–3999   Equity
- 4000–4999   Revenue
- 5000–5999   Expense

NOTES
Account classes will be explained in Chapter 7 when you set up the files for Dorfmann Design. For now you can accept the default class settings.

The Format of Financial Statements

When setting up the complete Chart of Accounts for Toss for Tots, it is important that you understand the composition and format of financial statements in Simply Accounting.

The Balance Sheet is divided into three sections, each with headings: Assets, Liabilities and Equity. The Income Statement is divided into two sections with headings: Revenue and Expense.

Each section of the financial statements can be subdivided into groups. Assets can be divided into groups such as CURRENT ASSETS, INVENTORY ASSETS and PLANT AND EQUIPMENT. Liabilities can be divided into groups titled CURRENT LIABILITIES and LONG TERM DEBT. Equity, Revenue and Expense sections can also be divided. Groups may be further divided by creating subgroups.

Simply Accounting requires that all accounts, including group headings, subgroup totals and group totals, be assigned numbers even if you do not use account numbers in transactions or reports. This is quite different from a manual accounting system, in which numbers are assigned only to postable accounts. Predefined section headings and section totals (e.g., ASSETS, TOTAL ASSETS and LIABILITIES), however, are not assigned numbers by the program.

The chart on the following page illustrates how Simply Accounting organizes accounts.

Financial Statement Sections

The following rules apply to financial statement sections in Simply Accounting:

1. Each financial statement section described above has a **section heading** and a **section total**. You cannot change the titles for these headings and totals.

2. A **section total** is the total of the individual group totals within that section. The program will calculate section totals automatically and print them in the financial statement reports. The five section totals are
    - TOTAL ASSETS
    - TOTAL LIABILITIES
    - TOTAL EQUITY
    - TOTAL REVENUE
    - TOTAL EXPENSE

3. The Liabilities and Equity section totals are also automatically added together. **LIABILITIES AND EQUITY** is the sum of TOTAL LIABILITIES and TOTAL EQUITY.

4. In the Income Statement, **NET INCOME**, the difference between TOTAL REVENUE and TOTAL EXPENSE, is automatically calculated and listed under TOTAL EXPENSE.

ORGANIZATION OF ACCOUNTS

BALANCE SHEET					INCOME STATEMENT			
Type	Account Description	Amount	Amount		Type	Account Description	Amount	Amount
ASSETS [section heading]					REVENUE [section heading]			
H	**CURRENT ASSETS**				**H**	**REVENUE**		
A	Bank: Toss for Tots	xxx			G	Revenue: Registrations		xxx
A	Cash on Hand	xxx			G	Revenue: Sponsors		xxx
S	Total Cash		xxx			—		
G	Surprise Bag Supplies		xxx			—		
G	Food Supplies		xxx		**T**	**TOTAL REVENUE**		**xxx**
	—				TOTAL REVENUE [section total]			xxx
T	**TOTAL CURRENT ASSETS**		**xxx**					
					EXPENSE [section heading]			
H	**FIXED ASSETS**				**H**	**ADMIN EXPENSES**		
G	Fax/Telephone		xxx		G	Court Rental Expense		xxx
G	Computer		xxx		G	Office Supplies Used		xxx
						—		
T	**TOTAL FIXED ASSETS**		**xxx**					
	TOTAL ASSETS [section total]		xxx		**T**	**TOTAL ADMIN EXPENSES**		**xxx**
LIABILITIES [section heading]					**H**	**MERCHANDISE & FOOD EXPENSES**		
H	**CURRENT LIABILITIES**				G	Cost of T-shirts		xxx
G	Bank Loan		xxx		G	Cost of Surprise Bags		xxx
G	A/P – Designs U Wear		xxx			—		
	—				**T**	**TOTAL MERCHANDISE**		
T	**TOTAL CURRENT LIABILITIES**		**xxx**			**& FOOD EXPENSES**		**xxx**
	TOTAL LIABILITIES [section total]		xxx			TOTAL EXPENSE [section total]		xxx
EQUITY [section heading]						NET INCOME		xxx
H	**EQUITY**							
G	Accumulated Surplus		xxx					
X	Net Income		xxx					
	—							
T	**TOTAL EQUITY**		**xxx**					
	TOTAL EQUITY [section total]		xxx					
	LIABILITIES & EQUITY		xxx					

Financial Statement Account Groups

Financial statement sections are further divided into account groups made up of different types of accounts. The following rules apply to account groups in Simply Accounting:

1. Each group must start with a **group Heading (H)**, which will be printed in boldface type. A heading is not considered a postable account, cannot be debited or credited through transaction entries and cannot have an amount assigned to it.

2. Each group must contain at least one **postable account** and can contain more. Postable accounts are those that can be debited or credited through journal transaction entries. Postable accounts may have an opening balance.

3. Postable accounts may be **subgroup Accounts (A)** or **Group accounts (G)**. Subgroup account balances appear in a separate column to the left of the group account balances, which are in the right column.

4. Postable subgroup accounts must be followed by a **Subgroup total (S)** account. A subgroup total is not a postable account and cannot be given an opening balance. The program automatically calculates a subgroup total by adding all preceding subgroup postable account balances that follow the last group, subgroup total or heading account. Subgroup total balances always appear in the right column. For

example, in the previous application, *GST Charged on Sales* and *GST Paid on Purchases* are subgroup accounts followed by the subgroup total *GST Owing (Refund)*. For Toss for Tots, the bank and cash accounts are subtotalled.

5. Each group must end with a **group Total (T)**. All amounts in the right column, for postable and subgroup total accounts, are added together to form the group total. A group total is not a postable account. The program automatically calculates this total and prints it in boldface type.

The Current Earnings (X) Account

There are two linked accounts for the General Ledger — **Retained Earnings** and **Current Earnings**. Both accounts are required and appear under the EQUITY section in the Balance Sheet. You do not need to change the links for these accounts.

The Current Earnings account is the only Type X account in the Chart of Accounts. This account is calculated as follows:

Current Earnings = Total Revenue – Total Expense

Current Earnings is not a postable account, but it appears in the right column with the group accounts. It cannot be removed, but its title and number can be modified (see Editing Accounts in the General Ledger, page 87). *Current Earnings* is updated from any transactions that change revenue and expense account balances. At the end of the fiscal period when closing routines are performed, the balance of this account is added to *Retained Earnings* (or its renamed account) and then reset to zero.

For Toss for Tots, a charitable organization, the *Retained Earnings* account will be renamed *Accumulated Surplus*. *Current Earnings* will be renamed *Net Income*.

Preparing the General Ledger

Compare the Skeleton Chart of Accounts you printed with the Toss for Tots Chart of Accounts, Balance Sheet and Income Statement provided in this application. You will see that some accounts are the same, and some accounts you need are not yet in the program. You have to customize the accounts for Toss for Tots.

Changing the Skeleton Accounts

The first step, that of identifying the changes needed in the Skeleton preset accounts to match the accounts needed for Toss for Tots, is a very important one. The changes that must be made to these preset accounts are outlined below:

1. Some starter accounts provided by the program require no changes. For the following accounts, the account title, the initial account number and the account type are the same as those in the financial statements:

CURRENT ASSETS	1000	Type H
TOTAL CURRENT ASSETS	1390	Type T
CURRENT LIABILITIES	2000	Type H
TOTAL CURRENT LIABILITIES	2690	Type T
REVENUE	4000	Type H
TOTAL REVENUE	4390	Type T

2. The following accounts have account titles that need to be changed. You must also change the account type for *Bank 1020*. (Account numbers are correct.)

NOTES
You will not need to delete any of the preset accounts for Toss for Tots.

FROM (SKELETON ACCOUNTS)			TO (TOSS FOR TOTS ACCOUNTS)
Account Name	Number	Type	Account Name (Type)
Bank	1020	Type G	Bank: Toss for Tots (Type A)
Accounts Receivable	1200	Type G	Surprise Bag Supplies
Accounts Payable	2200	Type G	A/P - Designs U Wear
EARNINGS	3000	Type H	EQUITY
Retained Earnings	3560	Type G	Accumulated Surplus
Current Earnings	3600	Type X	Net Income
TOTAL EARNINGS	3690	Type T	TOTAL EQUITY
General Revenue	4020	Type G	Revenue: Registrations
EXPENSES	5000	Type H	ADMIN EXPENSES
General Expense	5020	Type G	Court Rental Expense

3. The following account requires changes in both the account title and the number:

FROM (SKELETON ACCOUNTS)			TO (TOSS FOR TOTS ACCOUNTS)	
Account Name	Number	Type	Account Name	Number
TOTAL EXPENSES	5390	Type T	TOTAL ADMIN EXPENSES	5440

Creating the Chart of Accounts

After identifying the modifications that must be made to the Skeleton accounts, the next step is to identify the accounts that you need to create or add to the preset accounts. Again, you should refer to the company Chart of Accounts on page 64 to complete this step.

The chart that follows shows the accounts that you will need to create. The chart includes account titles, account numbers, account types and the option to omit printing zero balances. It lists both postable (group and subgroup) and non-postable accounts (subgroup totals, group headings and group totals).

CHART OF ACCOUNTS TO BE CREATED

Account: *Number	*Name	Type	Omit
1100	Cash on Hand	A	No
1150	Total Cash	S	
1300	Food Supplies	G	Yes
1320	Office Supplies	G	Yes
1360	T-shirts	G	Yes
1400	FIXED ASSETS	H	
1420	Fax/Telephone	G	Yes
1450	Computer	G	No
1500	Digital Camera	G	No
1590	TOTAL FIXED ASSETS	T	
2100	Bank Loan	G	Yes
2300	A/P - Quiq Kopy	G	Yes
2350	A/P - Central College	G	Yes
2400	A/P - Snack City	G	Yes
2670	GST Paid on Purchases	G	Yes
4040	Revenue: Sponsors	G	No
4080	Revenue: Surprise Bags	G	No
4100	Revenue: Admissions	G	No ▶

Account: *Number	*Name	Type	Omit
▶4120	Revenue: Food Sales	G	No
5200	Office Supplies Used	G	Yes
5220	Non-refundable GST	G	Yes
5240	Postage Expense	G	Yes
5280	Printing & Copying	G	Yes
5300	Telephone Expense	G	Yes
5320	Publicity & Promotion	G	Yes
5400	Wages - Manager	G	Yes
5420	Miscellaneous Expenses	G	Yes
5450	MERCHANDISE & FOOD EXPENSES	H	
5500	Cost of T-shirts	G	Yes
5520	Cost of Surprise Bags	G	Yes
5550	Cost of Food	G	Yes
5690	TOTAL MERCHANDISE & FOOD EXPENSES	T	

Account Types: A = Subgroup Account   S = Subgroup Total   G = Group Account   H = Heading   T = Group Total

* Account number and account name are required fields

You are now ready to enter the account information into the Toss for Tots files.

Entering General Ledger Accounts

From the Chart of Accounts icon 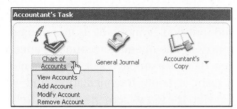 drop-down list you can make all ledger account record–related changes.

Click   the **Chart of Accounts shortcuts list arrow** as shown:

Editing Accounts in the General Ledger

We will change the first account that requires editing, *1020 Bank*. To modify accounts, use the Modify Account option.

Click   **Modify Account** in the Chart of Accounts shortcuts list to open the Search window:

This Search screen is like the one in the General Journal that opens the Adjust Entry feature. Accounts is selected as the search field area.

Click   **1020 Bank** to highlight or select it.

Click   **OK** or double click the account's name to open the account as shown:

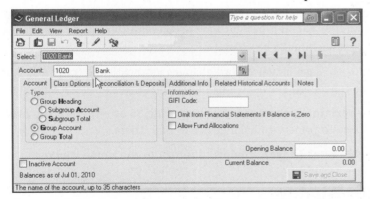

The Account information tab screen is displayed. We use this screen to edit the account name and type. For the bank account, the account number is correct.

Sometimes, it may be appropriate to print an account with a zero balance, although zero balance accounts usually do not need to be printed. In Simply Accounting, you have the option to omit accounts with zero balances from financial statements. You may select this option in the General Ledger.

The balance of bank accounts should always be displayed, so do not select Omit From Financial Statements If Balance Is Zero.

> **Press**   `tab`   **twice** to advance to the name of the account and highlight it.
>
> **Type**   `Bank: Toss for Tots`

NOTES
GIFI codes and exporting GIFI reports are covered in Appendix I.

NOTES
Account class is introduced in Chapter 7.

We are not using GIFI codes (Canada Revenue Agency's account numbering system for electronic report filing) or fund or project allocations, so we can leave these options unchecked. The current balance is displayed, but you cannot edit it. It is updated when you enter an opening balance and journal entries. The opening account balance will be added later (see Entering Historical Account Balances on page 91). There is no additional account information. We are not using Account Reconciliation, and we do not need to change the account class, so we can skip these tab screens. On the Related Historical Accounts tab screen, you can enter the relationship between different account numbers that are used for the same account in multiple fiscal periods. They do not apply here.

> **Click**   **Subgroup Account** to change the account type.

The bank and cash accounts together will be subtotalled. You can now advance to the next account for editing. There are different ways to do this.

> **Click**   the **Select field list arrow** to show the list of all accounts as shown:

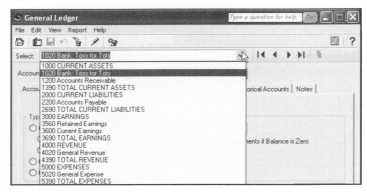

> **Click**   **1200 Accounts Receivable** to display the ledger record.

To open a different ledger record, you can also click the **Next Account tool** to open the ledger record for the next account in numerical sequence.

Or, you can close the bank account window to return to the Home window. Then click Modify Account in the Chart of Accounts shortcuts list again and select the next account to be changed.

Because you chose to save ledger record changes automatically (page 78) you do not need to save an account record (Save tool or File menu, Save) after each change.

> **Edit**   the **remaining accounts** shown on page 86 as required. You may choose to print zero balances or to omit them.
>
> **Close**   the **General Ledger window** to return to the Home window.

The Accounts Window

> **Click**   the **Chart of Accounts icon** in the Accountant's Task pane to open the Accounts window:

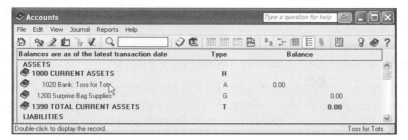

From this window, you can perform all ledger account–related activities as well. The tool buttons and menu options give access to the individual ledger records, and you can modify, delete, add records, display reports, access help and so on.

Click the Maximize button so that the Accounts window fills the screen. This will allow you to display more accounts and keep the Accounts window in view in the background while you are creating or editing accounts. To return the window to normal size, click ⬜, the Restore button.

Several tools control the appearance of the Accounts window. The preset accounts should be displayed in the **Type** format shown above. You can also show the Accounts window in the **Icon** format with icons representing each account. In the Icon view, you can rearrange icons by dragging so that frequently used accounts appear at the top for easier access. New accounts are automatically added at the bottom of the screen, but they can be moved to the desired location. In small icon viewing mode, more accounts can be displayed at the same time. You can rearrange the small icons too.

Another format is available with the **Name** view. Viewing accounts by name shows the account numbers, names and balances in debit and credit columns. Accounts remain in numerical order as new accounts are added.

For entering new accounts and editing a large number of existing accounts, it is easier to work with the accounts listed in numerical order. New accounts are inserted in their correct order, providing a better view of the progress during the setup phase. The addition of account type in the Type view is helpful for checking the logical order of accounts as they are created. You can change the Accounts window view at any time.

If your screen does not show the accounts by Type, you should change the way accounts are displayed.

Click   the **Display By Type tool** ▤ or **choose** the **View menu** and **click Type**.

When others are using the same data file, you can click the **Refresh tool** 🗍 to update your data file with changes that other users have made to accounts. In single-user mode, the tool is dimmed.

We can also check that the accounts are in proper sequence; that is, they follow the rules outlined on pages 83–85.

Click   the **Check Validity Of Accounts tool** ☑ or **choose** the **Edit menu** and **click Check The Validity Of Accounts** to see the message:

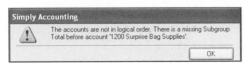

Without the second subgroup account and subgroup total, we have not followed the rules for Groups (page 84, rule 4). The accounts are not in logical order. You can periodically check the validity of accounts while you are adding accounts to see whether you have made errors in your account type sequence that will prevent you from finishing the account history.

Click   **OK** to return to the Accounts window.

NOTES
To edit an account from the Accounts window, double click the account you want to change; or click the account to select it and then either click the Edit tool or choose the Edit menu and click Edit.

SIMPLY VERSION
You will not see the Refresh tool.

NOTES
Only one error is listed, the first one encountered in checking the Chart of Accounts for validity of account order. After you correct the first error, the second error will be listed, if there is one.

When we add the remaining accounts, the accounts should be in logical order and the error will be corrected.

Creating New Accounts in the General Ledger

You are now ready to enter the information for the first new account, *Cash on Hand*, using the chart on page 86 as your reference. The following keystrokes will enter the account title, number, type and option to include or omit zero balance accounts.

We are entering new accounts from the Accounts window, and it should still be open.

Click   the **Create tool** 📇 on the Accounts window tool bar or **choose** the **File menu** and **click Create** to display the new account window:

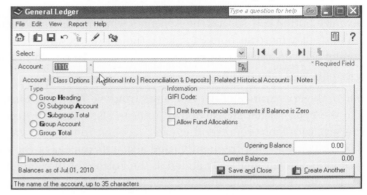

The tabs that appear in the ledger depend on the account section as defined by the account number. If no number is entered initially, only the tabs that apply to all accounts appear. We will create the first account that was not in the Skeleton Chart of Accounts, *Cash on Hand*. The account type is selected as the most likely option for logical account order. The default account type depends on the account record you used most recently. For example, group total accounts are often followed by a group account. The cursor is in the Account number field. The Simply Accounting program will not allow duplicate account numbers.

Two fields are required for accounts: the number and the name. An * appears beside a required field as long as it remains blank. Simply Accounting may enter an account number and type that is the most likely next entry based on the previous selection. If an account number is entered as a default, as in the screen we show, the * will be removed. After the error message, account 1200 is selected in the Accounts window so that you can correct the error. Its preceding account is a Subgroup account, so another Subgroup account most likely follows. The account number will be selected for editing.

Type   1100

Press   `tab` to advance to the Account name field.

Type   Cash on Hand

Click   **Subgroup Account** to change the account type if necessary.

Leave the option to Omit From Financial Statements turned off. Skip the GIFI field and the Fund (Project) Allocations check box.

Check   your work. **Make** any necessary **corrections** by pressing `tab` to return to the incorrect field, typing the correct information and pressing `tab` if necessary.

When the information has been entered correctly, save your work.

Click   **Create Another** 📇 Create Another to save the new account and to advance to another new account information window.

Both the number and name fields are now marked with an * .

Create   the **remaining accounts** from page 86.

Subgroup totals, group headings and group totals — the non-postable accounts — will have the Balance fields removed when you choose these account types.

Click   **Save And Close** to save the final account.

Display or **print** the **Chart of Accounts** to check the accuracy of your work.

If you find mistakes, edit the account information as described in the Editing Accounts in the General Ledger section on page 87.

If you want to end your session, close the General Ledger window and close the Accounts window to return to the Home window.

Entering Historical Account Balances

Before completing this step, we will create one more account to use as a test account for our Trial Balance. If you close the General Ledger before entering all the account balances, or if the total debits and credits are not equal, the program forces the Trial Balance to balance by adding the required debit or credit amount to another account.

This automatic adjustment may compensate for other errors that you have made in entering amounts, and you may be able to finish the history with errors in opening balances. You cannot change these balances after finishing the history. To detect this problem, we will create a test account and put all the adjustments into it. If all the balances are entered correctly, the test account will have a zero balance and we can remove the account.

Create   the new Group account **1005 Test Account**.

You are now ready to enter the opening historical account balances for all postable (type G or A) accounts. The opening balances for Toss for Tots can be found in the Trial Balance on page 66. Accounts with zero balances are not included in the Trial Balance. You should skip these accounts when entering account balances.

Click   the **Select field** list arrow and **choose 1020 Bank: Toss for Tots**. The ledger window opens:

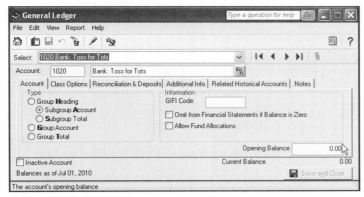

Click   the **Opening Balance field** to highlight it.

Type   18550

The Current Balance is updated but you cannot change it directly. Simply Accounting updates this balance automatically from journal entries.

Click   the **Next tool** to advance to the next ledger account window.

Enter   the **balances** for the remaining accounts.

> ⚠️ **WARNING!**
> Before you finish the history, the opening balance can be edited. The Current Balance has no data input field because you cannot edit it. Initially, it is the same as the opening balance but it changes when you add journal entries. Because you can enter journal transactions before finishing the history, this distinction is very important. The balance in the Accounts window is the current balance, which may not be the same as the opening balance.

WARNING!
Remember to enter the amount for GST Paid on Purchases with a minus sign to create a debit entry.

Remember that *GST Paid on Purchases* has a debit balance (add a minus sign). If you close the General Ledger window before entering all the account balances, you will see a screen like the following:

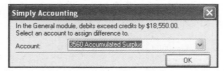

The message asks you to choose an account for the difference — an adjusting, balancing entry that will place the Trial Balance in balance. Choose *Test Account* from the drop-down list of accounts. You can choose any account from the drop-down list or accept the default. If you see this warning,

Choose account 1005 Test Account from the drop-down list.

Click   OK to continue.

After entering all the accounts and balances,

Close   the **Ledger window** to return to the Accounts window.

Display or **print** the **Trial Balance**, **Balance Sheet** and **Income Statement** to check the accuracy of your work.

Choose   the **Reports menu** in the Accounts window and **click Trial Balance** (or Balance Sheet or Income Statement).

Check   all your **opening balances** carefully before finishing the history.

Close   the **Accounts window** to return to the Home window.

Compare your reports with the information on pages 64–66 to be sure that all account numbers, names and balances are correct. The balance for *Test Account* should be zero. Make corrections if necessary.

Finishing the History

Making a Backup Copy

WARNING!
Back up the not-finished Toss for Tots files before proceeding. See Chapter 3 if you need further assistance.

WARNING!
You can change account numbers only after two fiscal periods have passed if the account was used in journal entries.

WARNING!
You can finish entering the history when the Trial Balance is in balance. Afterwards, you cannot change opening balances, even if they are incorrect. You will need to make adjusting entries. Simply Accounting always keeps the Trial Balance balanced. Therefore, checking for a zero balance in the Test Account can stop you from proceeding with incorrect account balances.

By having a backup copy of your files before finishing the history, you will be able to make changes easily, if you find an error, without having to repeat the entire setup from scratch. After the ledger history is finished, the program will not permit you to make certain changes, such as opening account balances and fiscal dates. You cannot change the account number for an account after making a journal entry to the account.

You should back up your unfinished open history files to a different folder so that they can be easily identified (e.g., NFTOSS).

Choose   the **File menu** and **click Backup**, or **click** the **Backup tool** ⬚.

Create   a **backup copy** by following the instructions. Refer to page 47 if you need help.

Finishing the General Ledger History

You should be in the Home window.

Choose   the **History menu** and **click Finish Entering History**.

The following caution appears:

If you have not made a backup copy yet, click Backup and do so before proceeding. If you have made your backup copy, you should continue.

Click   Proceed.

If you see a different screen at this stage, like the following one, you have errors that must be corrected before you can continue:

> Simply Accounting - Checking database
>
> Checking Accounts...
> The accounts are not in logical order. There is a missing Subgroup Total before account '1200 Surprise Bag Supplies'.
> This module cannot leave history mode because General module credits exceed debits by $19,550.00.
> Checking Providers...
> This module cannot leave history mode because the 'Payable Bank Account' linked account is not defined.
> This module cannot leave history mode because the 'Accounts Payable' linked account is not defined.
> This module cannot leave history mode because the 'Prepayments and Prepaid Orders' linked account is not defined.
> Checking Supporters...
> This module cannot leave history mode because the 'Receivable Bank Account' linked account is not defined.
> This module cannot leave history mode because the 'Accounts Receivable' linked account is not defined.
> This module cannot leave history mode because the 'Deposits and Prepaid Orders' linked account is not defined.
>
> Please correct the errors found before performing this action again.
>
> [OK]   [Print]

NOTES
The first error on this screen states that accounts are not in logical order. The remaining messages refer to missing linked accounts for modules that are not used but are also not hidden.

The message describes the mistakes you must correct. If your accounts are out of order, you cannot finish entering the history. If you did not hide the unused modules, you cannot finish entering the history because some essential linked accounts for these modules are not defined.

Read the error description carefully. Print the message for reference when you make corrections. Click OK to return to the Home window.

Make the necessary corrections. Remember to replace your previous unfinished history backup file. Then try again to finish the history.

Notice that the open or not-finished history symbol [quill pen icon], the quill pen, has been removed from the Chart of Accounts icon.

NOTES
You can now unhide the unused modules, but you do not need to do so. If you want to set them up later, you must first unhide them.

You can now exit the program or continue by entering the source documents. Remember to advance the Session Date. Enter all transactions for Toss for Tots in the General Journal.

SOURCE DOCUMENTS

SESSION DATE — JULY 7, 2010

☐ **Purchase Invoice #QK-2252**   **Dated July 2/10**
From Quiq Kopy, $216 (including PST) plus $10 GST for photocopying registration and donation forms. Invoice total $226. Terms: net 25 days.

☐ **Purchase Invoice #BC-10116**   **Dated July 2/10**
From Bell Canada, $324 (including PST) plus $15 GST for rental of cellular telephone equipment. Invoice total $339. Deposit required and balance due at end of month. Create new Group account 2140 A/P - Bell Canada.

NOTES
You do not enter PST paid as a separate amount because PST is not refundable. Therefore, we have already included it in the asset or expense amounts.

NOTES

In most businesses, the Cash on Hand balance is usually small and is used only for paying small amounts. In this application, we are using the Cash on Hand account to pay for any purchases that normally would require cash or credit card payments. The Event Manager receives cash advances to cover these costs.

☐ **Cheque Copy #167**   **Dated July 2/10**

To Bell Canada, $100 deposit on rental of telephone equipment. Reference invoice #BC-10116.

☐ **Memo #1**   **Dated July 2/10**

From Event Manager: Give T-shirts to volunteers. Cost of T-shirts given out is $120. Reduce T-shirt asset account and increase Cost of T-shirts expense account.

☐ **Memo #2**   **Dated July 4/10**

From Event Manager: Issue cheque #168 for $3 500 to transfer funds to Cash on Hand for snack purchases for the tournament.

☐ **Cash Purchase Invoice #SC-2168**   **Dated July 4/10**

From Snack City, $3 240 (including PST) plus $150 GST for drinks and snacks for participants and spectators. Invoice total $3 390 paid from Cash on Hand.

SESSION DATE — JULY 14, 2010

☐ **Purchase Invoice #DW-9493**   **Dated July 8/10**

From Designs U Wear, $1 188 (including PST) plus $55 GST for T-shirts to sell to spectators at tournament. Invoice total $1 243. Terms: net 20 days.

☐ **Cash Purchase Invoice #QAS-4632**   **Dated July 12/10**

From Quarts Arts Supplies, $108 (including PST) plus $5 GST for bristol board and paint supplies to make signs in gymnasiums. Invoice total $113. Paid from Cash on Hand. (Debit Office Supplies account.)

☐

Toss for Tots   No: 169

North Toronto
PO Box 42665
Toronto, ON M5N 3A8

Date [1][3][0][7][2][0][1][0]
     D D M M Y Y Y Y

Pay to the order of   Central College $ 10,500.00

———————————— Ten thousand five hundred dollars ———————— 00 /100 **Dollars**

TD-CT
2544 Yonge St.
Toronto, ON M4P 1A6

·— —03544·5499 388 169

Marcie Gilbert

Re: pay invoice # CC-47221 $10,500.00 **No: 169**

                                               July 13, 2010

☐ **Funds Raised Form #FR-10-7**   **Dated July 13/10**

Cash and cheques received on first two weekends of event. Create new revenue account 4160 Revenue: T-shirt Sales.

Participant registrations	$30 000
Sale of snack foods and drinks	3 500
Sale of T-shirts	1 000
Sale of surprise bags	560

Total $35 060 deposited in Bank: Toss for Tots.

SESSION DATE — JULY 21, 2010

☐ **Purchase Invoice #QK-5306** **Dated July 18/10**

From Quiq Kopy, $540 (including PST) plus $25 GST for printing cancer information leaflets for participants and spectators. Invoice total $565. Terms: net 25 days.

☐ **Cheque Copy #170** **Dated July 18/10**

To Designs U Wear, $800 in payment of account. Reference invoice #DW-6299.

☐ **Funds Raised Form #FR-10-8** **Dated July 20/10**

Record $30 200 in pledges to sponsor participants from sponsor forms submitted. Create new asset account 1180 Donations Receivable. (Credit Revenue: Sponsors.)

☐ **Cash Purchase Invoice #PH-34982** **Dated July 20/10**

From Pizza House, $270 (including PST) plus $12.50 GST for pizza and soft drinks for volunteers. Invoice total $282.50. Paid from Cash on Hand.

NOTES
Charge pizza expense to Miscellaneous Expenses.

SESSION DATE — JULY 28, 2010

☐

FUNDS RAISED FORM:	FR-10-9
Date:	July 27, 2010
Comment:	Cash & cheques received from third & fourth event weekend July 19-27

Description	Amount
T-shirt sales	$ 2 500
Admissions for spectators	11 160
Sale of snack foods and drinks	6 680
Surprise bag sales	1 750
Photo sales	3 900

Deposited to bank account July 27

Signature: *Marcie Gilbert*	Total	$25 990

NOTES
Create new revenue account 4180 Revenue: Photos.

☐ **Funds Raised Form #FR-10-10** **Dated July 27/10**

Record $80 500 in pledges to sponsor participants from sponsor forms submitted by participants. (Debit Donations Receivable.)

☐ **Cash Purchase Invoice #PH-39168** **Dated July 27/10**

From Pizza House, $345.60 (including PST) plus $16.00 GST for pizza and soft drinks for volunteers to celebrate successful tournament. Invoice total $361.60. Paid from Cash on Hand.

NOTES
Donated items are not included in these costs.

☐ **Cheque Copy #171**   **Dated July 27/10**

To Sunni Husein, $1 000 for winning tournament. Create new Group account 5430 Tournament Prizes.

☐

Toss for Tots

North Toronto
PO Box 42665
Toronto, ON M5N 3A8

M E M O #3

Date: July 27, 2010
From: Marcie Gilcrest
Re: Account adjustments required for event sales

Cost of t-shirts sold $1 750
Cost of food items sold   4 230
Cost of surprise bag items sold   500

Authorization: *MG*

☐ **Cheque Copy #172**   **Dated July 28/10**

To Marcie Gilcrest, manager, $2 000 for wages for month.

SESSION DATE – JULY 31, 2010

☐ **Cheque Copy #173**   **Dated July 29/10**

To Designs U Wear $1 243 in payment of account. Reference invoice #DW-9493.

☐ **Cheque Copy #174**   **Dated July 31/10**

To Quiq Kopy, $941 in full payment of account. Reference invoices #QK-5306, QK-2252 and previous balance owing.

☐ **Cheque Copy #175**   **Dated July 31/10**

To Bell Canada, $239 in full payment of account. Reference invoice #BC-10116 and cheque #167.

☐ **Cheque Copy #176**   **Dated July 31/10**

To Snack City, $900 in full payment of account. Reference invoice #SC-1005.

☐ **Memo #4**   **Dated July 31/10**

From Manager: Issue cheque #177 for $500 to transfer funds to Cash on Hand to purchase postage for mailing charitable donation receipts.

☐ **Bank Debit Memo #TDCT-3881**   **Dated July 31/10**

From TD-Canada Trust, $21.50 in bank charges for cheques and statement preparation. Create new Group account 5010 Bank Charges.

☐ **Memo #5**   **Dated July 31/10**

From Event Manager: Apply for GST rebate of $1 069.25. Record 50% of GST Paid on Purchases as GST Refund Receivable, and 50% as the Non-refundable GST expense. Create new Group account 1190 GST Refund Receivable. (Refer to Accounting Procedures on page 66.)

☐ **Funds Raised Form #FR-10-11**   **Dated July 31/10**

Received $92 300 from sponsors for pledges previously recorded. Amount deposited in bank account. (Credit 1180 Donations Receivable.)

SESSION DATE — AUGUST 31, 2010

☑ **Funds Received Form FR-10-12**   **Dated August 31/10**

98   Received $18 400 from sponsors for pledges previously recorded. Amount deposited in bank account.

☐ **Cash Purchase Invoice #CP-2**   **Dated August 31/10**

From Canada Post, $500 plus $25 GST for postage to mail receipts. Invoice total $525. Paid from Cash on Hand.

☐ **Memo #6**   **Dated August 31/10**

From Event Manager: Deposit $327.90, balance of Cash on Hand to bank.

☐ **Bank Debit Memo #TDCT-5218**   **Dated August 31/10**

From TD-Canada Trust, withdraw $15 400 from chequing account to repay loan for $15 000 plus $400 interest. Create new Group account 5100 Interest Expense.

SESSION DATE — SEPTEMBER 30, 2010

☑
98

Toss for Tots

North Toronto
PO Box 42665
Toronto, ON M5N 3A8   M E M O #7

Date: September 30, 2010
From: Marcie Gilcrest
Re: Final account adjustments required to clear inventory
         of supplies (donated)

Cost of all remaining t-shirts donated to shelters $118
Cost of all remaining food items donated to shelters   210
Cost of craft and office supplies not needed and
    donated to Campus Day Care Centre   580

Authorization: MG

☐   **Cash Purchase Invoice #BC-32423**   **Dated September 30/10**

From Bell Canada, $129.60 including PST plus $6.00 GST for telephone service for two months. Invoice total $135.60 paid in full by cheque #178.

☑   **Memo #8**   **Dated September 30/10**

99   All accounts for the event are settled so the books can be closed. Make a backup of the data files. Start a new fiscal period to close the books. (See Keystrokes following the next source document.)

☑   **Memo #9**   **Dated September 30/10**

101   Received cheque #488129 for $1 069.25 from the Receiver General for GST rebate. We forgot to make the entry before closing the books.

KEYSTROKES FOR CLOSING

Ending a Fiscal Period

Simply Accounting warns you as you approach the end of a fiscal period because important end of period adjusting entries are usually required.

When you change the session date to August 31, you will see the following warning:

Normally a business would advance the session date by a shorter period so the warning helps you to avoid entering the wrong session date.

Click   **OK** to confirm that you entered the date you intended.

You will see another warning that Simply Accounting displays about one month before the end of the fiscal period:

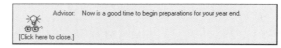

Close   the **advisor** to continue with the transactions for August 31.

Closing Adjusting Entries

When you advance the session date further to a date very close to the end of the fiscal period, September 30 in this case, you receive another warning about the types of adjusting entries required at the end of the year:

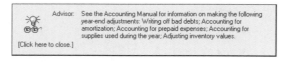

Close   the **advisor window**. Continue with the transactions for September 30.

The required adjusting entries are listed with the source documents for September 30. For Toss for Tots, these are the adjustments for remaining supplies. For other businesses, adjusting entries include depreciation entries, inventory adjustments, adjustments for prepaid expenses that have expired, accrued wages and so on. Most

WARNING!
You should advance to the new fiscal period in two steps. First advance to the last day of the current fiscal period and then advance to the first day of the new fiscal period. This control feature prevents you from advancing by mistake and losing important data or forgetting year-end adjusting entries.

NOTES
If the history is not finished when you choose to start a new fiscal year, the program will ask if you have finished entering the history and give you a chance to do so. You must finish the history before you can start a new fiscal period.

adjusting entries do not have an external source document that reminds you to complete them, and most of them are General Journal entries.

Print   all the **financial reports** for Toss for Tots for September 30, 2010.

Starting a New Fiscal Period

There are two methods for beginning a new fiscal year. The first is the method we have been using to change the session date.

Choose the **Maintenance menu** and **click Change Session Date**.

The first date of the new fiscal period is always on the drop-down list of dates in the Session Date window. The program will not accept any dates later than October 1, 2010.

Type   October 1, 2010 or choose this date from the date field list.

Click   OK. Because this step is not reversible, you will see a warning:

The expense and revenue amounts will be transferred to the capital account but historical data will be saved in the data file.

Read   the **warning** carefully.

The warning describes the changes about to take place in the data set. All revenue and expense accounts are reset to zero at the start of the new fiscal year. Their balances are closed out to the linked *Accumulated Surplus (Retained Earnings)* account, and the linked *Net Income (Current Earnings)* account is reset to zero to begin a new income statement. All previous year entries that are not cleared are stored as data for the previous year. The program also updates the fiscal date for the company by one year. The new fiscal end date becomes the final date allowed as a session date.

At this stage you can choose to back up the data files, continue with the date change or cancel the date change by clicking No.

Click   **Cancel** to return to the Session Date window and then **click Cancel** again to close the Change Session Date screen. We will use the second method to change to a new fiscal year.

Choose the **Maintenance menu** and **click Start New Year**.

Depending on when you are starting the new fiscal period, you may see a screen asking whether you want to start a new fiscal or calendar year:

The default will be the period that starts first. Make your choice and click OK to continue. Start New Fiscal Year is correctly selected.

Click   OK to continue.

NOTES
You cannot start a new fiscal period in multi-user mode.

WARNING!
Initially, from the last day of the fiscal period, you cannot advance the session date past October 1, the first day of the new fiscal period.

You will see a warning similar to the one on the previous page:

The default setting is to make a backup before continuing. If you have not yet made a backup, do so now. If you do not want to begin a new year, you can click Cancel and the old dates will remain in effect.

> **Click**   **No** because you have already backed up your files.

> **Click**   **OK** to begin the new fiscal period. You will now see another warning:

You have the option of retaining the old data or clearing it. Journal entries from the previous year are never cleared and Income Statement and Balance Sheet details for the previous year are also retained.

> **Click**   **Yes** because Toss for Tots has no other data. If in doubt, choose No.

Another message now appears:

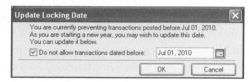

You must now change the earliest date that you will allow transactions for. We should not allow any transactions to the previous fiscal period so that the historical records cannot be altered in error.

> **Drag through**   **Jul 1, 2010**, the date entered.

> **Type**   10/01

> **Click**   **OK** to continue.

Journal reports are available for both periods, and other financial reports are now available as comparative reports for the two fiscal periods.

> **Print**   the **Comparative Trial Balance** and **Balance Sheet** for September 30 and October 1.

Notice the changes in the capital accounts on the Balance Sheet. The *Net Income* balance for September 30 has been added to the *Accumulated Surplus* account to create the October 1 balance in the *Accumulated Surplus* account.

> **Print**   the **Comparative Income Statement for the previous year** (Oct. 1, 2009, to Sep. 30, 2010) and the **current fiscal year to date** (Oct. 1, 2010, to Oct. 1, 2010).

The Income Statement for the current year shows no income or revenue. All accounts have a zero balance because you have not recorded any transactions for the new fiscal year.

NOTES
We describe how to clear data from company files in Chapter 15.

NOTES
Most reports offer comparisons with the previous year as an option.
A fiscal year of one year is assumed so the fiscal end will be advanced by 12 months.

WARNING!
If you have cleared paid invoices, these details will be unavailable for reports. Comparative Income Statements and Balance Sheets are always available for the two fiscal periods.

The files are now ready for transactions in the new fiscal period. When you check the Company Information, the fiscal dates are updated and you will see the additional information about last year's dates.

Choose the **Setup menu** and **click Settings**, or **click** the **Settings icon** .

Click **Company** if necessary and then **click Information** to see the changes:

The new Fiscal Start is October 1, 2010, and the new Fiscal End is September 30, 2011. Simply Accounting automatically updates the Fiscal End by 12 months but you can edit this date if the fiscal period is shorter. In fact, this is the only date that you can edit after you have made journal entries to a data file. The Earliest Transaction Date has also been updated to October 1, 2010. The dates for the previous fiscal period are provided for reference.

Click **Cancel** to close the Company Information window.

Entering Transactions for an Earlier Fiscal Period

Sometimes not all the information required is available before the books are closed for the fiscal period. However, it may be necessary to close the books (start a new fiscal period) so that transactions in the new year may be entered. The details of the adjusting entries may be calculated by an accountant who does not have the information until after a business has started entering transactions for a new year. Simply Accounting allows you to post transactions to the previous year so that the financial statements for both the previous year and the current year will be correct.

Enter **Memo #9**, the GST rebate receipt, with the **September 30** date, after starting the new fiscal period.

When you post the entry, you will see the following message:

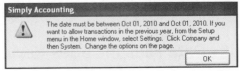

Before the program allows the entry, we must change the System Settings. We indicated that transactions earlier than Oct. 1, 2010, should not be allowed.

Click **OK** to close the message. **Close** the **journal** to discard the entry. **Click** **Yes** to confirm that you want to discard the entry.

Choose the **Setup menu** and **click Settings** or **click** the **Settings icon** .

NOTES
After you start a new fiscal period, you cannot change the fiscal start date.

NOTES
In Chapter 12, we show how to create a copy of your data for your accountant to update and how to import the transactions your accountant has completed for your company.

Click   **Company** if necessary and then **click System** to access the field we need:

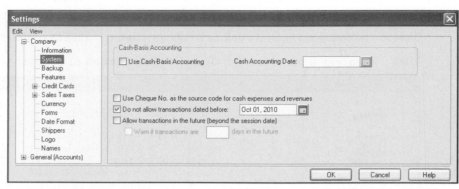

This is the same settings screen we saw earlier but now we must allow transactions in the previous period.

Click   **Do Not Allow Transactions Dated Before** to **remove** the ✓.

Click   **OK**.

Enter   the **transaction** again. **Review** and then **post** it. This time you will see a different warning:

Because the transaction date is in a previous month or period, you are advised that prior period reports may be affected by the transaction. The warning gives you a chance to correct the date if it was incorrect. But we want to proceed. After completing the transaction, we will change the System Settings option again to avoid mistakenly posting to the previous year.

Click   **Yes** to continue with posting.

Close   the **General Journal**.

Click   the **Settings icon** or **choose** the **Setup menu**, then **choose** **Settings** and **click Company** and **System**.

Click   **Do Not Allow Transactions Dated Before** to **add** the ✓.

Enter   **Oct 1** as the date and **click OK**.

Finish   your **session** by closing the files for Toss for Tots.

R E V I E W

The Student CD-ROM with Data Files includes Review Questions and Supplementary Cases for this chapter.

CHAI TEA ROOM

OBJECTIVES

- **open** the General and Payables journals
- **enter** supplier- or vendor-related purchase transactions
- **enter** supplier-related payment transactions
- **enter** partial payments to suppliers
- **enter** payments to suppliers with early payment discounts
- **enter** cash purchase transactions
- **enter** sales taxes in the General Journal
- **create** shortcuts in the Home window
- **store** recurring purchase transactions
- **add** new supplier accounts
- **edit** supplier accounts
- **edit** and **review** transactions in the journals
- **recall**, **use** and **edit** stored purchase transactions
- **adjust** and **reverse** purchase invoices and payments after posting
- **understand** Payables Ledger linked accounts
- **display** and **print** payables transactions and reports
- **graph** payables reports

After completing this chapter, you should be able to

COMPANY INFORMATION

Company Profile

Chai Tea Room, located in Fredericton, New Brunswick, is owned by Sarah Quinte. Originally, Quinte wanted to name her business Quintessentials but after an extended tour of the Far East, where she acquired a taste for exotic blends of tea, she chose the name Chai instead. Canadians are becoming more familiar with the name Chai, an East Indian word for tea that is often used for spiced Indian tea.

The downtown tea room, near the New Brunswick Parliament House, Art Gallery and other historic sites, with its scenic lookout over the Saint John River

NOTES
Chai Tea Room
125 King St.
Fredericton
New Brunswick E3B 2P4
Tel 1: (506) 454-6111
Tel 2: (800) 454-6000
Fax: (506) 454-6990
Business No.: 186 522 333

and railroad walking bridge, is very popular with professional women. Adjacent to a women's fitness and recreational centre, the tea room provides a comfortable atmosphere for customers to discuss finance, careers, or social or political issues after working out. The tea room boasts refinements such as a fireplace, comfortable living-room-styled cushioned sofas and chairs and very personal care and service from the owner and staff.

Chai Tea Room, essentially a tea room serving specialty teas from all around the world, also provides light lunches and superb desserts. Coffees and other beverages — both alcoholic and non-alcoholic — are available too. Quinte sells gift sets as well, packaged variety teas and tea service sets consisting of teacups, teaspoons, a teapot and a tea cozy. The tea service set items can also be purchased separately.

Sarah Quinte manages the day-to-day activities of the store. An assistant manager and kitchen staff handle business during her absence. The payroll is managed by the bank for a small fee. She has set up accounts with regular vendors or suppliers, such as the suppliers of food and beverages as well as the utility companies. Some of her suppliers offer discounts for early payment. Cleaning and maintenance of the premises is done professionally once a week by Sunbury Cleaning; they wash and wax floors and steam clean the carpets and furniture. They also clean and check all equipment and complete minor repairs. On a day-to-day basis, the tea room staff do the regular cleaning.

No HST (sales tax) is paid on food purchases but other purchases are subject to HST. HST at 13 percent is charged to customers on all food products consumed in the tea room and the gift sets.

Quinte currently manages all the accounting records for the tea room and has just finished converting the manual records to Simply Accounting using the following:

- Chart of Accounts
- Post-Closing Trial Balance
- Supplier Information
- Accounting Procedures

NOTES
HST, Harmonized Sales Tax, is charged instead of GST and PST in New Brunswick. HST at 13 percent includes both GST at 5 percent and PST at 8 percent. Refer to Accounting Procedures and Chapter 2 for further details.

CHART OF POSTABLE ACCOUNTS

CHAI TEA ROOM

ASSETS
1080 Cash in Bank
1300 Beverage Inventory
1320 Beer, Wine and Liquor
1340 Food Inventory
1360 Gift Set Inventory
1500 Cash Register and Computer
1520 Cutlery and Dishes
1540 Furniture and Fixtures
1560 Equipment
1580 Tea Room Premises ▶

▶LIABILITIES
2100 Bank Loan
2200 Accounts Payable
2650 HST Charged on Sales
2670 HST Paid on Purchases
2850 Mortgage Payable

EQUITY
3100 S. Quinte, Capital
3150 S. Quinte, Drawings
3600 Net Income ▶

▶REVENUE
4100 Customer Service and Sales

EXPENSE
5020 Advertising and Promotion
5040 Bank Charges
5060 Cleaning and Maintenance
5080 Cost of Goods Sold
5090 Purchase Discounts
5100 General Expense
5120 Hydro Expense ▶

▶5140 Interest Expense
5160 Licences and Permits
5180 Payroll Services
5220 Telephone Expense
5240 Wages

NOTES: The Chart of Accounts includes only postable accounts and the Net Income or Current Earnings account. Simply Accounting uses the Net Income account for the Income Statement to calculate the difference between revenue and expenses before closing the books.

POST-CLOSING TRIAL BALANCE

CHAI TEA ROOM

August 1, 2010		Debits	Credits
1080	Cash in Bank	$ 11 155	
1300	Beverage Inventory	1 500	
1320	Beer, Wine and Liquor	2 500	
1340	Food Inventory	500	
1360	Gift Set Inventory	4 000	
1500	Cash Register and Computer	5 000	
1520	Cutlery and Dishes	5 000	
1540	Furniture and Fixtures	15 000	
1560	Equipment	25 000	
1580	Tea Room Premises	150 000	
2100	Bank Loan		$ 12 000
2200	Accounts Payable		2 945
2650	HST Charged on Sales		4 845
2670	HST Paid on Purchases	345	
2850	Mortgage Payable		120 000
3100	S. Quinte, Capital		80 210
		$220 000	$220 000

SUPPLIER INFORMATION

CHAI TEA ROOM

Supplier Name (Contact)	Address	Phone No. Fax No.	E-mail Web Site	Terms Tax ID
Atlantic Tea Company (Boise Chai)	20 Oceanview Dr. Halifax, NS B3K 2L2	Tel 1: (902) 777-2346 Tel 2: (888) 337-4599	bchai@atcc.com www.atcc.com	net 10 288 411 755
Bathurst Food Supplies (C. Ricotte)	56 Cheddar St. Oromocto, NB E2V 1M8	Tel: (506) 544-6292 Fax: (506) 544-5217	cricotte@bfoods.com www.bfoods.com	1/10, n/30 385 345 865
Fundy Gift House (Red Rose)	71 Ridge Way Hopewell Cape, NB E0A 1Y0	Tel: (506) 499-3481 Fax: (506) 499-3482	rrose@fundygifts.com www.fundygifts.com	net 30 124 653 779
Minto Beverages (Earl Gray)	910 Lemone Ave. Bathurst, NB E2A 4X3	Tel 1: (506) 622-3188 Tel 2: (800) 622-2881	eg@mintobev.com www.mintobev.com	net 30 901 200 862
Moncton Kitchenwares (Tiff Flaun)	4 Pottery Rd. Moncton, NB E1C 8J6	Tel: (506) 721-5121 Fax: (506) 721-5522	tflaun@monctonkitchens.com www.monctonkitchens.com	1/10, n/30 567 321 447
NB Gas (N. Bridge)	355 Pipeline Road Fredericton, NB E3A 5B1	Tel: (506) 454-8110	nbridge@naturalgas.com www.naturalgas.com	net 7
NB Hydro (N. Ergie)	83 Water Street Fredericton, NB E3B 2M6	Tel: (506) 455-5120	n.ergie@nbhydro.nb.ca www.nbhydro.nb.ca	net 7
NB Liquor Control Board (Darke Beere)	4 Spirits Rd. Fredericton, NB E3B 1C5	Tel: (506) 456-1182	dbeere@lcb.gov.nb.ca www.lcb.gov.nb.ca	net 1
NB Tel (Les Chatter)	2 Communicate Rd. Fredericton, NB E3A 2K4	Tel: (506) 456-2355	chatter@nbtel.ca www.nbtel.ca	net 7
Sunbury Cleaning Company (Dee Tergent)	49 Scrub St. Gagetown, NB E0G 1V0	Tel: (506) 454-6611 Fax: (506) 454-3216	dtergent@sunburyclean.com www.sunburyclean.com	1/30, n/60 481 532 556
Vermont Coffee Wholesalers (Java Jean)	60 Columbia Lane Saint John, NB E2M 6R9	Tel 1: (506) 366-1551 Tel 2: (877) 366-1500	java@vermontcoffee.com www.vermontcoffee.com	net 1 345 667 211

OUTSTANDING SUPPLIER INVOICES					

CHAI TEA ROOM

Supplier Name	Terms	Date	Inv/Chq No.	Amount	Total
Bathurst Food Supplies	1/10, n/30	Jul. 26/10	BF-1044	$ 800	$ 800
Fundy Gift House	n/30	Jul. 6/10	FG-361	$ 920	$ 920
Moncton Kitchenwares	1/10, n/30	Jul. 25/10	MK-1341	$1 725	
		Jul. 25/10	Chq #167	500	
			Balance owing		$1 225
			Grand Total		$2 945

Accounting Procedures

The Harmonized Sales Tax (Provincial Sales Tax and Goods and Services Tax)

In New Brunswick, federal and provincial taxes are replaced by the Harmonized Sales Tax or HST, a single tax at the rate of 13 percent. The HST is applied to most goods and services. Like the GST, HST may be included in the price or added at the time of the sale. Chai Tea Room uses the regular method for calculating and remitting the HST. All items sold in the tea room have HST added to them. At the end of each quarter, the HST liability to the Receiver General is reduced by any HST paid to suppliers on purchases. Beverage and food supplies are zero rated for HST purposes. Chai's *HST Owing (Refund)* subgroup total account shows the amount of HST that is to be remitted to the Receiver General for Canada on the last day of each quarter. (For details please read Chapter 2 on the Goods and Services Tax.)

Open-Invoice Accounting for Payables

The open-invoice method of accounting for invoices allows a business to keep track of each individual invoice and partial payment made against the invoice. This is in contrast to methods that keep track only of the outstanding balance by combining all invoice balances owed to a supplier. Simply Accounting uses the open-invoice method. Fully paid invoices can be cleared (removed) periodically; outstanding invoices cannot be cleared.

Discounts

When discounts for early payment are offered by suppliers, Chai takes advantage of them by paying invoices before the discount period ends. When the payment terms are set up correctly for the supplier and invoice, and dates are entered correctly, discounts are calculated automatically by Simply Accounting and credited to *Purchase Discounts*, a contra-expense account that has a credit balance and reduces overall expenses.

Purchase of Inventory Items and Cost of Goods Sold

Inventory items purchased are recorded in the appropriate inventory or supplies asset account. Periodically, the food inventory on hand is counted to determine the value of items remaining and the cost price of inventory and food sold. The manager then issues a memo to reduce the inventory or supplies asset account and to charge the cost price to the corresponding expense account. For example, at the end of each month, the *Beverage Inventory* asset account (*1300*) is reduced (credited) and the *Cost of Goods Sold* expense account (*5080*) is increased (debited) by the cost price of the amount sold.

NOTES

Beverages and food items are zero rated goods; that is, the HST rate is 0 percent. Prepared food, as sold in restaurants, is taxed at 13 percent.

Most bank services and other financial institution services are exempt from HST charges. Bank payroll services are subject to HST charges.

Provincial sales tax is not levied as a separate tax in New Brunswick. It will be introduced in a later application.

NOTES

Discounts for early payment may be calculated on pretax amounts or on the full invoice amounts. This choice is entered in the ledger settings for the vendor or supplier.

INSTRUCTIONS

1. **Enter** the **source documents for August** in Simply Accounting using the Chart of Accounts, Trial Balance, Supplier Information and Accounting Procedures for Chai Tea Room. The procedures for entering each new type of transaction for this application are outlined step by step in the Keystrokes section following the source documents. These transactions have a ✓ in the check box, and below the box is the page number where the related keystrokes begin.

2. **Print** the **reports and graphs** indicated on the printing form below after you have completed your entries. Instructions for reports begin on page 142.

REPORTS

Accounts
- ☐ Chart of Accounts
- ☐ Account List
- ☐ General Journal Entries

Financials
- ☑ Comparative Balance Sheet dates: Aug. 1 and Aug. 31 with difference in percentage
- ☑ Income Statement from Aug. 1 to Aug. 31
- ☑ Trial Balance date: Aug. 31
- ☐ All Journal Entries
- ☑ General Ledger accounts: 1340 4100 5080 from Aug. 1 to Aug. 31

Banking
- ☐ Cheque Log Report

Payables
- ☐ Supplier List
- ☑ Supplier Aged Detail for all suppliers Aug. 31
- ☐ Aged Overdue Payables
- ☑ Purchase Journal Entries: Aug. 1 to Aug. 31
- ☑ Payment Journal Entries: Aug. 1 to Aug. 31

Mailing Labels
- ☐ Labels

Management Reports
- ☐ Ledger

GRAPHS
- ☐ Payables by Aging Period
- ☑ Payables by Supplier
- ☐ Revenues by Account
- ☐ Expenses by Account
- ☑ Expenses and Net Profit as % of Revenue

SOURCE DOCUMENTS

SESSION DATE – AUGUST 7, 2010

☑ **Purchase Invoice #FG-642**   **Dated Aug. 1/10**

112 From Fundy Gift House, $800 plus $104 HST for eight tea service sets. Invoice total, $904. Terms: net 30.

☑ **Purchase Invoice #BF-1243**   **Dated Aug. 1/10**

117 From Bathurst Food Supplies, $800 for pastries, breads, condiments and other foods. There is no HST on food products. Terms: 1/10, n/30. Store as weekly recurring entry.

☑ **Cheque Copy #171**   **Dated Aug. 2/10**

118 To Fundy Gift House, $700 in payment of account. Reference invoice #FG-361.

☑ **Cash Purchase Invoice #Fton-08**   **Dated Aug. 2/10**

121 From City Treasurer (use Quick Add for the new supplier), $250 for August licensing fees. Paid by cheque #172.

☑ **Cash Purchase Invoice #ACA-3492**   **Dated Aug. 3/10**

124 From All Campus Ads (add a complete record for the new supplier), $200 plus $26 HST for advertising brochures. Terms: cash on receipt. Invoice total $226 paid in full by cheque #173.

NOTES
All Campus Ads
☑ (contact Pierre Fullovit)
124 447 Slick St.
Fredericton, NB E3B 8J5
Tel: (506) 564-8907
E-mail: pfullovit@acads.ca
Terms: net 1
Expense account: 5020
Tax code: H - HST @ 13%

✓ **Memo #13**   Dated Aug. 4/10

129   From Owner: Adjust invoice #FG-642. The order received from Fundy Gift House was for 10 tea service sets for $900 plus $117 HST. The corrected invoice total is $1 017.

✓ **Cheque Copy #174**   Dated Aug. 4/10

131   To Bathurst Food Supplies, $792 in payment of account, including $8 discount for early payment. Reference invoice #BF-1044.

✓ **Cash Purchase Invoice #BT-100**   Dated Aug. 7/10

133   From Bette Tomailik (choose Continue for the new supplier), $25 as compensation to cover cost of dry cleaning for wine spilled by waiter. Issue cheque #175. Charge to General Expense account. No tax is applied on this transaction.

☐ **Purchase Invoice #SC-701**   Dated Aug. 7/10

From Sunbury Cleaning Company, $250 plus $32.50 HST for weekly cleaning of store premises. Purchase invoice total $282.50. Terms: 1/30, n/60. Store as weekly recurring transaction.

✓ **Cash Sales Receipt #34**   Dated Aug. 7/10

134   From tea room customers (tapes #5001–5380), $7 600 plus $988 HST for tea room sales and services. Total receipts $8 588 deposited in bank. Add a shortcut for the General Journal

SESSION DATE – AUGUST 14, 2010

✓ **Purchase Invoice #BF-2100**   Dated Aug. 8/10

137   From Bathurst Food Supplies, $800 (no HST) for pastries, breads, condiments and other foods. Terms: 1/10, n/30. Recall stored entry.

✓ **Memo #14**   Dated Aug. 9/10

138   From Owner: Edit the supplier record for NB Gas to include the default expense account. Create a new Group account 5110 Heating Expense.

☐ **Cash Purchase Invoice #NBG-559932**   Dated Aug. 9/10

From NB Gas, $200 plus $26 HST for monthly supply of natural gas on equal billing method. Invoice total $226 paid in full by cheque #176. Because equal billing applies, store as monthly recurring entry.

✓ **Memo #15**   Dated Aug. 9/10

139   From Owner: Adjust cheque #171 to Fundy Gift House. The cheque amount was $600 in partial payment of invoice #FG-361.

☐ **Cash Purchase Invoice #NBH-45321**   Dated Aug. 9/10

From NB Hydro, $120 plus $15.60 HST for one month of hydro service. Invoice total $135.60 paid in full by cheque #177.

☐ **Cheque Copy #178**   Dated Aug. 10/10

To Bathurst Food Supplies, $792 in payment of account, including $8 discount for early payment. Reference invoice #BF-1243.

☐ **Cash Purchase Invoice #SK-6110**   Dated Aug. 12/10

From Moncton Kitchenwares, $180 plus $23.40 HST for pots, pans and kitchen utensils. Invoice total $203.40 paid in full by cheque #179.

⚠ WARNING!
Remember to change the payment method for the Sunbury Cleaners invoice to Pay Later.

📄 NOTES
Use the General Journal for sales in this application.

☑ **Memo #16**   **Dated Aug. 13/10**

140   Cash Purchase Invoice #SK-6110 was entered for an incorrect supplier. The
purchase was from Sweeney's Kitchenwares, a new supplier. Reverse the original
entry and then enter the correct purchase (use Full Add for the new supplier)
for $180 plus $23.40 HST for pots, pans and kitchen utensils. Invoice total
$203.40 paid in full by cheque #180.

NOTES

Sweeney's Kitchenwares
(contact Tracey Potts)
44 Panning Ave.
Grand Sault, NB E3Y 1E1
Tel: (800) 566-7521
Web: www.sweeneys.com
Terms: net 1
Expense account: 1560
Tax code: H - HST @ 13%

		Invoice:	MB-6111
		Delivery Date:	Aug. 14, 2010
		Sold to:	Chai Tea Room 125 King St. Fredericton, NB E3B 2P4 (506) 454-6111

www.mintobev.com

910 Lemone Ave.
Bathurst, NB   E2A 4X3
Phone: (506) 622-3188   Toll free: (800) 622-2881

Date	Description	Tax Code	Amount
Aug 14/10	Bottled spring water (20 cases)	1	200.00
Aug 14/10	Natural fruit beverages (10 cases)	1	400.00

Thank you.

Signature

Payment Terms: Net 30 days	**HST**	0.00
Business No.: 901 200 862	**TOTAL**	600.00

Purchase Invoice #SC-1219   **Dated Aug. 14/10**

From Sunbury Cleaning Company, $250 plus $32.50 HST for weekly cleaning of
store premises. Purchase invoice total $282.50. Terms: 1/30, n/60. Recall stored
transaction.

Bank Debit Memo #AT-53186   **Dated Aug. 14/10**

From Atlantic Trust, withdrawals from bank account for bi-weekly payroll:

Wages, including payroll taxes	$3 200.00
Payroll services	40.00
HST Paid on Purchases (payroll services)	5.20

NOTES

   Use the General Journal for
the payroll transaction in this
application.
   Remember to enter the
sales tax code for the purchase.

Cash Sales Receipt #35   **Dated Aug. 14/10**

From tea room customers (tapes #5381–5750), $7 400 plus $962 HST for tea
room sales and services. Total receipts $8 362 deposited in bank.

SESSION DATE – AUGUST 21, 2010

Purchase Invoice #BF-2987   **Dated Aug. 15/10**

From Bathurst Food Supplies, $800 for pastries, breads, condiments and other
foods. Terms: 1/10, n/30. Recall stored entry.

NBTel

2 Communicate Rd.
Fredericton, NB
E3A 2K4
www.nbtel.ca
chatter@nbtel.ca

Account Inquiries: (506) 456-2355

Account Number
506-454-6111

Account Address

Chai Tea Room
125 King St.
Fredericton, NB
E3B 2P4

Billing Date: August 18, 2010

ACCOUNT SUMMARY

Current Charges	
Monthly Services (July 13–August 12)	60.00
Equipment Rentals	24.00
Chargeable Messages	16.00
HST (93436 8699)	13.00
Total Current Charges	113.00
Previous Charges	
Amount of last bill	93.00
Payment Received July 19 — thank you	93.00
Adjustments	0.00
Balance Forward	0.00

Paid in full by cheque #181
Sarah Quinto 08/18/10

Invoice:
NBT 557121

PLEASE PAY THIS AMOUNT UPON RECEIPT ➡

$113.00

Cheque Copy #182   **Dated Aug. 18/10**

To Bathurst Food Supplies, $792 in payment of account, including $8 discount for early payment. Reference invoice #BF-2100.

Cash Purchase Invoice #VCW-345   **Dated Aug. 19/10**

From Vermont Coffee Wholesalers, $400 for specialty coffees. Invoice paid in full by cheque #183.

Cash Purchase Invoice #NBLCB-776   **Dated Aug. 19/10**

From NB Liquor Control Board, $1 600 including HST and other taxes for beer, wine and liquor. Terms: COD. Invoice paid in full by cheque #184.

✓ **Purchase Invoice #SC-1790**   **Dated Aug. 21/10**

141   From Sunbury Cleaning Company, $300 plus $39 HST for weekly cleaning of store premises. Purchase invoice total $339. Terms: 1/30, n/60. Recall and edit the stored transaction. Store the changed entry.

Cash Sales Receipt #36   **Dated Aug. 21/10**

From tea room customers (tapes #5751–6149), $7 750 plus $1 007.50 HST for tea room sales and services. Total receipts $8 757.50 deposited in bank.

SESSION DATE – AUGUST 28, 2010

Purchase Invoice #BF-3778   **Dated Aug. 22/10**

From Bathurst Food Supplies, $850 for pastries, breads, condiments and other foods. Terms: 1/10, n/30. Recall and edit the stored entry. Store changed entry.

NOTES

Use HST code HI, taxes included, for purchases from the NB Liquor Control Board. This is the default tax code setting for this supplier.

```
                                                              No: 185
☕ CHAI TEA
   ROOM
125 King St
Fredericton, NB E3B 2P4                      Date  2 4 0 8 2 0 1 0
(506) 454-6111                                     D D M M Y Y Y Y

Pay to the order of   Bathurst Food Supplies              $ 792.00

──────────── Seven hundred ninety-two dollars ──────── 00  /₁₀₀ Dollars

Atlantic Trust
55 Freedom Ave.
Fredericton, NB  E3C 6S0
                                              Sarah Pointe
⑉──── 21292 ⑉ 60385 185                              Signature
```

Re: pay invoice #BF-2987	$792.00	No: 185
Includes $8 discount	Aug 24, 2010	

Purchase Invoice #ATC-3468   Dated Aug. 27/10

From Atlantic Tea Co., $500 for a variety of herbal, black and green teas as specified on order form. Terms: net 10 days.

Cash Purchase Invoice #Party   Dated Aug. 28/10

From The Little Party Shop (choose Continue), $30 plus $3.90 HST for party favours and decorations to decorate tea room for special event (General Expense). Invoice total $33.90 paid in full by cheque #186.

Purchase Invoice #SC-2987   Dated Aug. 28/10

From Sunbury Cleaning Company, $300 plus $39 HST for weekly cleaning of store premises. Purchase invoice total $339. Terms: 1/30, n/60. Recall stored transaction.

Bank Debit Memo #AT-99553   Dated Aug. 28/10

From Atlantic Trust, withdrawals from bank account for bi-weekly payroll:

Wages, including payroll taxes	$3 200.00
Salaries	8 000.00
Payroll services	70.00
HST Paid on Purchases (payroll services)	9.10

Create new Group account 5250 Salaries.

Cash Sales Receipt #37   Dated Aug. 28/10

From tea room customers (#6150–6499), $7 250 plus $942.50 HST for tea room sales and services. Total receipts $8 192.50 deposited in bank.

SESSION DATE – AUGUST 31, 2010

Purchase Invoice #BF-4633   Dated Aug. 29/10

From Bathurst Food Supplies, $850 for pastries, breads, condiments and other foods. Terms: 1/10, n/30. Recall stored entry.

Purchase Invoice #MK-8995   Dated Aug. 31/10

From Moncton Kitchenwares, $600 plus $78 HST for new gas burners for tea room kitchen. Invoice total $678. Terms: 1/10, n/30.

☕ **CHAI TEA ROOM**

125 King St
Fredericton, NB E3B 2P4
(506) 454-6111

No: 187

Date 3 1 0 8 2 0 1 0
D D M M Y Y Y Y

Pay to the order of Sunbury Cleaning Company $ 1,230.56

————————— One thousand, two hundred thirty dollars ————— 56 /100 **Dollars**

Atlantic Trust
55 Freedom Ave.
Fredericton, NB E3C 6S0

Sarah Quinte
Signature

⑈⎯⎯21292⎯⎯ 60385 187

Re: pay invoice #SC-701, 1219, 1790 and 2987 | $1,230.56 | **No: 187**
Includes $12.44 discount | Aug 31, 2010

◻ **Bank Debit Memo #AT-10023**   **Dated Aug. 31/10**

From Atlantic Trust, withdrawals for bank charges, and loan and mortgage payments:

Bank charges	$ 30
Mortgage payment	2 500
(including $2 250 interest and $250 principal)	
Loan payment	2 090
(including $90 interest and $2 000 principal)	

◻ **Memo #17**   **Dated Aug. 31/10**

From Owner: Make adjusting entries to reflect inventory used in the tea room during August. The end-of-month inventory count indicates the following inventory was used or sold:

Beverage inventory	$2 200
Beer, wine and liquor	1 700
Food inventory	3 100
Gift set inventory	1 000

All used inventory is charged to Cost of Goods Sold.

KEYSTROKES

Opening Data Files

NOTES
Refer to Chapter 1, page 6 if you need assistance with restoring files.

Restore SimData\chai1.CAB to SimData\Chai\Chai to open the data files for Chai Tea Room. (You should create the new folder.)

You are prompted to enter the session date, which is August 7, 2010, for the first group of transactions in this application.

Type Aug 7 10

Click OK to enter the first session date for this application.

The Payables module appears. This is the default Home page for Chai Tea Room.

Accounting for Purchases

All supplier-related transactions can be entered from the Payables module window. Purchases from suppliers are entered in the Purchases Journal, accessed from the Invoices icon as shown here:

The first transaction is a normal purchase invoice.

Click   the **Invoices icon** to open the Purchases Journal input form:

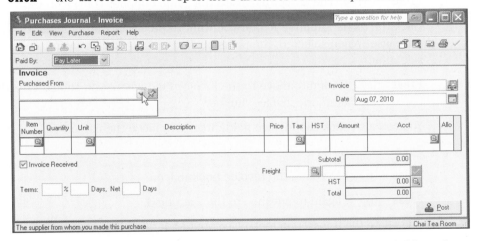

Move the mouse pointer across the various tool buttons and input fields and observe the status bar messages.

Invoice is indicated in the title bar and the option to Pay Later is correct because this is a credit purchase. Payment methods include cheque, cash and credit cards (when these are set up).

Most tool buttons should already be familiar. Notice that the Calculator button appears again in the tool bar. Several tool buttons have been added to the Purchases Journal window: Look Up An Invoice, Look Up Previous and Next Invoice, Track

NOTES
Access to the Receivables, Payroll, Inventory and Division ledgers is hidden because these ledgers are not set up or ready to use.

SIMPLY VERSION
The term Vendors will replace Suppliers for all icon labels and fields. Purchase Invoices is the label for the Purchase Journal icon.
Click the Purchase Invoices icon to open the journal.

CLASSIC VIEW
In the Classic View Home window, click the Purchases icon
to open the Purchases Journal. Invoice will be selected as the transaction type.

SIMPLY VERSION
The Refresh Lists tool applies to multi-user mode and does not appear in the Simply version.

NOTES
When the other features are not hidden, you will see a pull-down menu for Transaction types that includes quotes and purchase orders.
When more than one bank account is set up, a drop-down list of bank accounts is available for cheque transactions. These topics are covered in later chapters.

Shipments, Fill Backordered Quantities, Cancel Backordered Quantities, Printer Settings, Print Preview, E-mail and Print. Each tool will be discussed when used.

> **Click** the **Purchased From** (Supplier or Vendor) **field list arrow** to obtain the list of suppliers as shown:

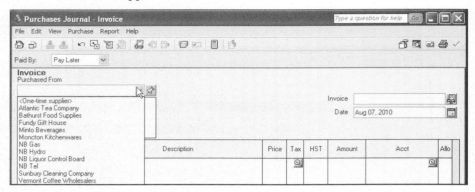

Whenever you see this arrow ☑ beside a field, you can make a selection from a drop-down list. Type the first letter of the supplier's name to advance to the names beginning with that letter. When you type in the Purchased From field, the program fills in a name from the supplier list by trying to match the letters you type.

> **Click** **Fundy Gift House**, the supplier for this purchase, to select and enter it.

Notice that the supplier's name and address have been added to your input form, making it easy to check whether you have selected the correct supplier. Many other details have also been added by default from the supplier's record. The tax code and the account number usually stay the same for a supplier so they are set up as defaults. The payment terms for the supplier are also included. Any of these details can be edited if required. If you have made an error in your selection, click the Purchased From field list arrow and start again. If you have selected correctly,

> **Press** (tab). The cursor moves to the Same Supplier (pin) icon 📌.

Click the **Same Supplier** icon if you want to preselect this supplier for the next purchase. When selected, the pin is pushed in 📌. Click it again to turn off the selection.

> **Press** (tab) again to move to the Invoice field where you should type the alphanumeric invoice number.

You can also click the Invoice field directly to move the cursor.

> **Type** FG-642

> **Press** (tab) to select the Invoice Lookup icon.

> **Press** (tab) again to advance to the Date field.

Enter the date the transaction took place, August 1, 2010. The session date appears by default. It is highlighted, ready to be accepted or changed. You need to change the date.

> **Type** aug 1

Many of the invoice fields (Item, Units, Description and Price) pertain mainly to inventory items. Because we are not using the Inventory Ledger for this application, you can skip the inventory-related fields. Any information you type in these fields does not appear in the journal report.

> You can click the Description field and type a description. Or add the quantity (8) in the Quantity field and the unit price in the Price field.

Click   the **Description field**.

Type   `tea service sets`

To select a different tax code, or to see the codes set up and available,

Click   the **Tax field List icon** to see the tax codes for Chai Tea Room:

The selected tax code is H, that is, HST is charged on the purchase at 13 percent, and the tax is not included in the price. You can select a different code if needed, but in this case, the tax code is correct.

Click   **Cancel** so that the selection remains unchanged.

Click   the **first line of the Amount field**, where you will enter the total amount for this purchase.

Type   800

Press   (tab).

The cursor moves to the Account field. The Account field for this purchase refers to the debit part of the journal entry, normally the acquisition of an asset or the incurring of an expense. It could also be used to decrease a liability or to decrease equity if the purchase were made for the owner's personal use. When you work in the subsidiary Payables journal, Simply Accounting will automatically credit your *Accounts Payable* control account in the General Ledger for the purchase. In fact, you cannot access *Accounts Payable* directly when the Payables Ledger is set up and linked.

In this example, the business has acquired an asset, and the correct account, *Gift Set Inventory,* is selected as the default for this supplier.

To select a different account, click the List icon for the Account field, double click the Account field or press (enter) to show the Select Account screen. You can also add a new account from the Select Account screen.

Press   (tab) to advance the cursor to the next invoice line. You can now enter additional purchases from this supplier if there are any.

Simply Accounting uses the tax code to calculate and enter the tax amount automatically in the HST field when you enter the amount.

Your screen should now resemble the following:

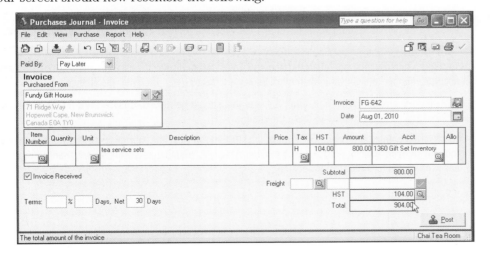

NOTES

For this application, the sales tax rate is set to 13 percent, the harmonized single tax rate for New Brunswick. For non-Atlantic provinces, the rate is 5 percent and tax codes will display as GST @ 5%.

Since the provincial and federal retail sales taxes are harmonized, there is no separate amount for PST. When PST is applicable and is set up in the defaults for the company, the program will calculate PST as well, based on the tax rates and codes entered for PST.

NOTES

Typing negative amounts will generate a credit entry with a debit for Accounts Payable.

NOTES

The account name may not fit in the account column if the column is very narrow. To change the width of a column, point to the line beside the column title. When the pointer changes to a double-sided arrow, drag the line to the new location. Make a journal window wider by dragging the side frame. You can also maximize a journal window to occupy the entire screen.

The payment terms have been set up as defaults for this supplier and are entered automatically. They can be edited if needed for specific purchases, but in this case they are correct. There is no discount and full payment is due in 30 days. The subtotal (amount owing before taxes) and the total amount are calculated and added automatically, so the entries for this transaction are complete and you are ready to review the transaction.

Reviewing the Purchases Journal Entry

Choose the Report menu and **click Display Purchases Journal Entry**:

NOTES
Pressing *ctrl* + J will also display the journal entry.

By reviewing the journal entry, you can check for mistakes. Note that the Simply Accounting program automatically updates the *Accounts Payable* control account because the Payables and General Ledgers are linked or fully integrated. Even though you did not enter account *2200*, Simply Accounting uses it because it is defined as the linked account to which all purchases should be credited. *HST Paid on Purchases*, the linked tax account, is also automatically updated. Using the Purchases Journal instead of the General Journal to enter purchases is faster because you need to enter only half the journal entry. The program provides a credit directly to the account of the selected supplier, and prevents you from choosing an incorrect payables account. The automatic selection of tax codes and accounts makes the transaction even simpler to enter.

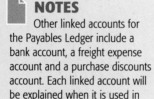

NOTES
Other linked accounts for the Payables Ledger include a bank account, a freight expense account and a purchase discounts account. Each linked account will be explained when it is used in this workbook.

Close the **display** to return to the Purchases Journal input screen.

NOTES
To correct a Purchases Journal entry after posting, refer to page 129 and Appendix C.

CORRECTING THE PURCHASES JOURNAL ENTRY BEFORE POSTING

Move to the field that has the error. Press *tab* to move forward through the fields or press *shift* and *tab* together to move back to a previous field. This will highlight the field information so you can change it. **Type** the **correct information** and **press** *tab* to enter it.

You can also use the mouse to **point** to a field and **drag through** the **incorrect information** to highlight it. **Type** the **correct information** and **press** *tab* to enter it.

If the supplier is incorrect, reselect from the supplier list by **clicking the Supplier (Purchased From) field list arrow. Click** the name of the **correct supplier**.

Click an **incorrect amount** to highlight it. Then **type** the **correct amount** and **press** *tab* to enter the change.

To select a different account, **click** the **Account List icon** to display the list of accounts. **Click** the **correct account** number to highlight it, then **click Select** and **press** *tab* to enter the change.

To insert a line or remove a line, **click** the **line** that should be moved. **Choose** the **Edit menu** and **click Insert Line** or **Remove Line** to make the change.

To discard the entry and begin again, **click** ☒ (Close) to close the Journal or **click** ↺ (Undo) on the tool bar to open a blank journal window. When Simply Accounting asks whether you want to discard the entry, **click Yes** to confirm your decision.

Posting

When you are certain that you have entered all the information correctly, you must post the transaction to save it.

Click   the **Post button** 🖊 Post or **choose** the **Purchase menu** and **click Post** to save your transaction. **Click OK** to confirm successful posting.

A new blank Purchases Journal form appears on the screen.

Storing a Recurring Journal Entry

The second transaction is the recurring purchase of food inventory. Businesses often have transactions that are repeated regularly. For example, loan payments, bank charges and rent payments usually occur on the same day each month; supplies may be ordered daily or weekly; insurance payments may occur less frequently but nonetheless regularly. Chai Tea Room has food supplies delivered weekly. By storing an entry, and indicating the frequency, it can be recalled when it is needed without re-entering all the information.

The Purchases Journal should still be open with payment method and date correct from the previous entry.

Choose   **Bathurst Food Supplies** from the supplier list, or

Click   the **Supplier field** and **type**   B

Press   (tab) **repeatedly** to move to the Invoice field.

Type   BF-1243

Enter   a **description** for the purchase.

The tax code is correct; no tax is charged on the purchase of food. The payment terms and account are also correct by default.

Click   the **Amount field**, **type** 800 and **press** (tab) to complete the transaction.

Choose   the **Report menu** and **click Display Purchases Journal Entry** to review the entry.

Close   the **display** and **make corrections** if necessary.

Click   the **Store tool** 📥 on the tool bar (or **choose** the **Purchase menu** and **click Store**) to open the following Store Recurring Transaction screen:

Simply Accounting enters the supplier and Monthly as the default name and frequency for the entry. The name is highlighted, so it can be changed by typing another descriptive name. Be sure to use one that you will recognize easily as belonging to this entry. The default frequency is incorrect since the food items are purchased weekly.

Click   **Monthly** to display the list of choices for the recurring frequency:

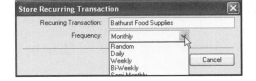

The frequency options are Random (for irregular purchases), Daily, Weekly, Bi-Weekly, Semi-Monthly, Monthly, 13-Period (13 times per year), Bi-Monthly, Quarterly, Semi-Annually and Annually.

> **Click** **Weekly**.

Simply Accounting will advance the default journal date when you recall the stored entry according to the frequency selected. The session date is entered if the Random frequency is chosen.

> **Click** **OK** to return to the Purchases Journal window.

Notice that 🔼 (the **Recall tool**) is now darkened and can be selected because you have stored a journal entry. The journal title bar label has also changed. It now shows Using Recurring Transaction Bathurst Food Supplies.

CORRECTING A STORED JOURNAL ENTRY

If you notice an error in the stored journal entry before posting, you must first **correct** the **journal entry** in the Purchases Journal window, then **click Store**. When asked to confirm that you want to overwrite or replace the previous version, **click Yes**.

If you edit the journal entry after storing it, Simply Accounting will warn you that the entry has changed. **Click Yes** to proceed.

Posting

When you are sure that you have entered all the information correctly, and you have stored the entry, you must post the transaction to save it.

> **Click** the **Post button** 🔨 Post or **choose** the **Purchase menu** and **click Post** to save your transaction. **Click OK** to confirm successful posting.

A new blank Purchases Journal form appears on the screen. The Recall tool is still available so we can recall the purchase we stored. Our next transaction is a payment, however, not a purchase.

> **Close** the **Purchases Journal window** to return to the Payables window.

Accounting for Payments

Payments are made in the Payments Journal in the Journals Tasks pane indicated by the hand pointer in the following screen:

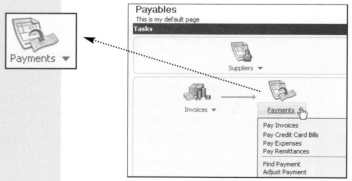

> **Click** the **Payments icon list arrow**, as shown above, to see a list of shortcuts for different payment types. When you click on one of these shortcuts, the journal will open and select the correct type of transaction.

Click   **Pay Invoices** to open the Payments Journal:

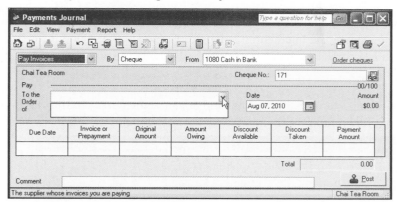

Pay Invoices is selected as the type of payment in the Pay field because we made this selection in the Home window. Pay Invoices is also the default transaction type when you click the Payments icon. Cheque appears as the method of payment in the By field and *1080 Cash in Bank* is the account the payment is made from. The defaults are correct.

Click   the **To The Order Of** (Supplier) **field list arrow** to see the familiar list of suppliers displayed in alphabetical order.

Click   **Fundy Gift House** (or **type**   F) to choose and enter the supplier to whom the payment is made.

The journal input form is updated with the supplier's name, address and outstanding invoice(s), making it easy to see whether you have selected correctly. The updated journal is shown here:

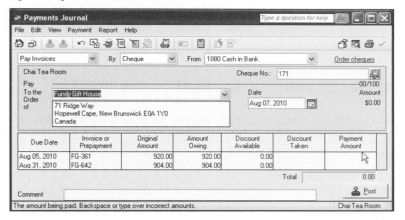

If you need to change the supplier, click the Supplier field list arrow again to select from the supplier list. The cheque number is entered in the Number field. The next cheque number appears according to the settings for the company. It is correct, so you can accept it. Normally the cheque number should be correct. It can be edited, if necessary, for reversing or correcting entries. When you have selected the correct supplier,

Click   the **Calendar icon** 📅 for the Date field.

Click   **2** in the August section. **Press** ⌨tab .

The cursor moves to the Due Date field. All outstanding invoices, including both the amount of the original invoice and the balance owing for the selected supplier, are listed on the screen.

Press   ⌨tab to advance to the Discount Taken field. Since there is no discount, skip this field.

Press   (tab).

The amount outstanding for the selected invoice is highlighted as the payment amount. You can accept the highlighted amount, or type another amount for partial payments. This is a partial payment so we need to change the amount.

Type   700

Press   (tab) to update the Total and advance the cursor to the Discount Taken field for the next invoice and complete the payment as shown:

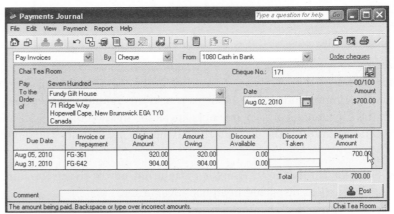

Notice that the upper cheque portion of the form is also complete. Notice too that there is no field for account numbers in the Payments Journal. You need to enter only the amount of the payment on the appropriate invoice line.

As you pay invoices in the subsidiary Payments Journal, you do not enter any accounts. Simply Accounting chooses the default linked accounts defined for the Payables Ledger to create the journal entry.

The entries for this transaction are complete, so you are ready to review and post your transaction.

Reviewing the Payments Journal Entry

Choose the Report menu and click Display Payments Journal Entry to display the transaction you have entered:

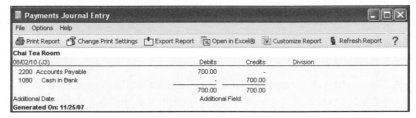

You can see that the Simply Accounting program automatically creates a related journal entry when you complete a Payments Journal entry. The program updates *Accounts Payable* and *Cash in Bank* because the Payables and General Ledgers are fully linked. *Cash in Bank* has been defined as the default Payables linked account to which payments are credited. The payment is also recorded to the supplier's account to reduce the balance owing.

Close   the **display** to return to the Payments Journal input screen.

You can also print the cheque but you should make corrections first, if necessary.

⚠ **WARNING!**
The amount for the next invoice should not be highlighted since this invoice is not being paid. If its amount is highlighted or entered, you must delete it by pressing (del) and then (tab) to correct the total cheque amount.

CORRECTING THE PAYMENTS JOURNAL ENTRY BEFORE POSTING

Move to the field that has the error. Press ⌨tab to move forward through the fields or press ⌨shift and ⌨tab together to move back to a previous field. This will highlight the field information so you can change it. **Type the correct information** and **press** ⌨tab to enter it.

You can also use the mouse to **point** to a field and **drag through** the **incorrect information** to highlight it. **Type the correct information** and **press** ⌨tab to enter it.

If the supplier is incorrect, **click** 🔙 to undo the entry or **reselect** from the **Supplier** list by **clicking** the **Supplier list arrow. Click** the name of the **correct supplier.** You will be asked to confirm that you want to discard the current transaction. **Click Yes** to discard the incorrect supplier entry and display the outstanding invoices for the correct supplier. **Re-enter** the **payment** information for this supplier.

NOTES
You can correct payment amounts after posting by clicking the Adjust Payment tool. Select the payment to adjust, just as you select a purchase invoice or General Journal entry for editing. Make the correction and post the revised payment.
To correct a payment after posting, refer to page 139 and to the section on NSF cheques on page 179.

If you print cheques, you should do so before posting the Payment. Be sure that the information is correct and that you have selected the correct printer and forms for printing cheques (see Chapter 4, page 81). You can check the printer settings by clicking the Change The Default Printer Settings tool 🖨 in the journal. Turn on the printer and click the Print tool 🖨 .

NOTES
When the batch printing option is selected in the settings for Forms, you can print cheques in batches after posting them. The Print Batches tool will be added to the tool bar. Batch printing is covered in Chapter 14.

Posting

When you are certain that you have entered all the information correctly, you must post the transaction to save it.

Click the **Post button** 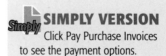 (or **choose** the **Payment menu** and **click Post**) to save your transaction and then **click OK** to confirm.

Entering Cash Purchases

The licence fees statement on August 2 is to be paid immediately on receipt of the invoice. Instead of recording the purchase and payment separately, you can record the payment with the purchase in the Payments Journal. This transaction also involves a company that is not listed as a supplier, so you must add the City Treasurer to the supplier list in order to record the transaction.

Suppliers can be added directly from the Payables Ledger or from the supplier field in the Purchases Journal or the Payments Journal. We will add the new supplier from the Payments Journal. The Payments Journal should still be open.

The date and the cheque number are correct. The date is unchanged from the previous Payments Journal transaction. The next available cheque number is entered by default, and the bank account is selected for the payment. Cheque numbers are updated in sequence for both payment journal entries and cash purchases.

Click   Pay Invoices to see the options for payment transactions:

Click   Make Other Payment from the drop-down list.

If you have closed the Payments Journal, you can open the form for cash purchases from the Home window. Click the Payments icon list arrow and click **Pay Expenses** (see page 118). In this case, you must enter August 2 as the date.

SIMPLY VERSION
Click Pay Purchase Invoices to see the payment options.

CLASSIC VIEW
From the Classic view Home window, click the Payments icon to open the Payments Journal. Click Pay Invoices and then click Make Other Payment as the type of transaction.

WARNING!
If you have closed the Payments Journal, the session date will be displayed and you must change it to August 2.

Journal input fields are added to the payment form:

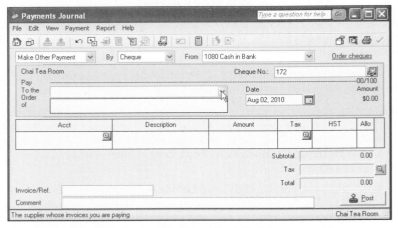

Click   the **To The Order Of (Supplier) field** to move the cursor.

Type   City Treasurer and then **press** (tab) to display the message:

SIMPLY VERSION
Remember that you will see the term vendors instead of suppliers in all journals.

The program recognizes that the name is new and gives you four options. **Continue** will add the name to the journal and the journal report and apply the default settings for the ledger. This option will not create a supplier record or include the name in the supplier list. **Quick Add** will create a partial record with only the supplier's name and will apply the default settings for the ledger. **Full Add** will open a new ledger record for the supplier and you can add complete details. **Cancel** will return you to the journal. You can then type or choose another name if the one you typed was incorrect.

If you are making a cash purchase and you will not be making additional purchases from this supplier, you can choose **One-time Supplier** from the Supplier list. Type the supplier's name and address in the text box area below the To The Order Of field. The default settings for the ledger will apply to the invoice. The transaction will be included in the GST/HST report but the supplier's name will not appear in supplier lists or in the journal reports.

NOTES
The Continue option will add the supplier's name to journal entries for purchase invoices entered in the Purchases Journal, but not for Other Payments entered in the Payments Journal.
If you create a partial supplier record with Quick Add, you can add more supplier details later by editing the record.

We want to add a partial record for the new supplier.

Click   **Quick Add** to return to the Payments Journal.

The Supplier name is added to the journal. Because an account is not set up for the supplier, you must enter the asset or expense account that is debited for the transaction.

Click   the **Account field List icon** to see the Select Account list.

Click   **Suggested Accounts** to modify the list as shown:

The list now shows only the expense accounts, the ones used most often for purchases. This list is easier to work with because it is shorter. When you enter sales in the Sales Journal, the suggested accounts will list only revenue accounts.

Scroll down and **click 5160 Licences and Permits**.

Click   **Select** to add the account and advance to the Description field.

Type   August licensing fees

Press   tab to advance to the Amount field.

Type   250 **Press** tab .

Since no tax is charged on the fees, the default entry of No Tax is correct.

Click   the **Invoice/Ref. field**.

Type   Fton-08 **Press** tab to advance to the Comment field.

The comment will become part of the journal record so you should include it.

Type   Fton-08, August licensing fees

The subtotal and total amounts are entered automatically. Your completed payment form should now look like the one shown here, and you are ready to review it:

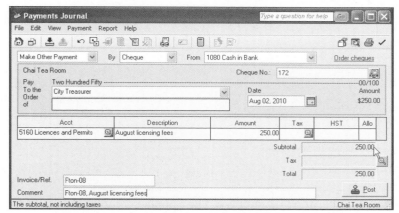

Choose the **Report menu** and **click Display Payments Journal Entry**. Your display should look like the following:

Notice that the program has automatically credited *Cash in Bank*, the Payables linked bank account, for the cash purchase instead of *Accounts Payable*.

Close   the **display** when you have finished.

Make   any **corrections** necessary. Double click an incorrect entry and type the correct details.

Click   the **Post button** 🔲 Post to save the **entry** when you are certain that it is correct. **Click OK**.

Close   the **Payments Journal**.

NOTES
When we tested the keystrokes, the Invoice/Ref. field contents were not included in journal reports and the Comment was included. Therefore, we repeat the invoice number in the Comment field to be sure that it will be included in the journal reports.

Adding a New Supplier Record

Cash purchases and new suppliers may be recorded in the Payments Journal or the Purchases Journal. We will record the next cash purchase in the Purchases Journal after we add a full record for the supplier. You can create a new supplier record on the fly, as in the previous transaction, by choosing Full Add, or you can open the Payables Ledger for a new supplier record from the Add Supplier option in the Suppliers shortcuts list. For this transaction, we will use the ledger option.

Click the **Suppliers icon shortcuts list arrow** as shown:

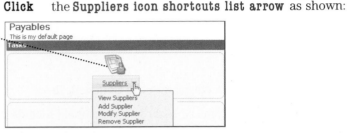

Click **Add Supplier** to open the Payables Ledger input form:

SIMPLY VERSION
Click Add Vendor in the Vendors shortcuts list.

CLASSIC VIEW
From the Classic view Home window, click the Suppliers icon to open the Suppliers window. Click the Create tool, or choose the File menu and click Create, or press ⌈ctrl⌋ + N.

SIMPLY VERSION
The Refresh tool does not appear in the Simply version.

NOTES
If you are missing any information for a supplier, you can leave the field blank and enter the details later by editing the record. See page 138.

You are ready to enter the new supplier. The Supplier Address tab information screen appears first. Note that required fields have an * beside them as they do in the General Ledger. The supplier name is the only required field. As soon as you begin to type in the field, the * is removed.

Type All Campus Ads **Press** ⌈tab⌋.

The cursor advances to the Contact field, where you enter the name of Chai Tea Room's contact person at All Campus Ads. This field can also be used to enter a third address line if two street lines are insufficient. This field or any other may be left blank by pressing ⌈tab⌋.

Type Pierre Fullovit

Press ⌈tab⌋. The cursor moves to the Street 1 field.

Type 447 Slick St.

The Street 2 field can be used for a second address line, if there is one. By default, the program has entered the name of the city, province and country from the Payables Ledger Address settings. You can accept the defaults because they are correct.

If the supplier is in a different city, province or country, type the correct information before continuing. Press ⌈tab⌋ to advance to a field and highlight the contents to prepare it for editing.

Click   the **Postal Code field** to move the cursor.

When you enter a Canadian postal code, you do not need to use capital letters, nor do you need to leave a space within the postal code. The program will make these adjustments for you.

Type   e3b8j5

Press   tab .

Notice that the format of the postal code has been corrected automatically. The cursor moves to the Country field and the entry is correct.

Press   tab .

The cursor moves to the Phone 1 field. You do not need to insert a dash, space or bracket when you enter a telephone number. Telephone and fax numbers may be entered with or without the area code.

Type   5065648907

Press   tab .

The format for the telephone number has been corrected automatically. The cursor advances to the Phone 2 field for the supplier's second phone number. We do not have additional phone or fax numbers at this time. They can be added later when they are obtained. The Tax ID number refers to the business federal tax or GST registration number. Adding e-mail and Web site information allows you to send purchase orders by e-mail and connect to the supplier's Web site directly from Simply Accounting. Type e-mail and Web addresses just as you enter them in your Internet program.

Click   the **E-mail field**.

Type   pfullovit@acads.ca

The date in the Supplier Since field is the session date or the date of the earliest transaction you enter for this supplier in Simply Accounting. You can enter a different date if this is appropriate. The Date Of Last Purchase is added automatically by the program, based on the transactions you enter for the supplier.

Click   the **Supplier Since date field**.

Type   Aug 3

The last two options concern the supplier's status. You can make a supplier inactive and remove the name from the selection lists and reports. Suppliers that you will not use again can be made inactive.

You can also designate the supplier as a Payroll Authority so that the supplier can be selected for payroll remittances. Payroll authorities who receive payroll remittances are explained in Chapter 8.

Click   the **Options tab** to open the next supplier information screen:

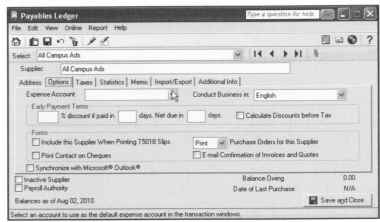

The Options screen has several important fields. In the first part of the Options screen, you can choose the default account and preferred language (English or French) for the supplier. Forms you send to that supplier will be in the selected language, although your own screens will not change. Usually an expense or asset account is the default account. Even though the field is named Expense Account, you may select any postable account. If you usually buy the same kinds of goods from a supplier, entering the account as the default saves time and prevents errors when completing journal entries. All Campus Ads provides promotional materials.

Click   the **Expense Account list arrow** to see the accounts available.

Scroll down   and **click 5020 Advertising and Promotion**.

In the Early Payment Terms section of the ledger, you can enter the discount for early settlement of accounts and the term for full payment. Discounts may be calculated on the amount before taxes or on the full invoice (after-tax) amount. Three fields are used to enter the discount. The first shows the discount rate as a percentage and the second holds the number of days over which the discount remains valid. In the final field, enter the number of days in which net payment is due. According to the source document, immediate payment is expected.

Click   the **Net Due In ____ Days field** (Early Payment Terms section).

Type   1

The next fields appear as check boxes. There are no discounts from this supplier. Leave the check box for Calculate Discounts Before Tax blank.

Include This Supplier When Printing T5018 Slips applies to amounts paid to subcontractors for construction services and does not apply to Chai Tea Room. Selecting Print Contact On Cheques will add the name of the contact person to the cheque written to the supplier. If the Contact field contains address information, check this box; otherwise, leave it unchecked.

The next option allows you to choose Print or E-mail Purchase Orders For This Supplier as the default setting, but you can change the selection for individual purchase orders if necessary. If you choose to e-mail the orders, you should check the E-mail Confirmation Of Purchase Invoices And Quotes option by clicking it.

If you want to synchronize lists in Simply Accounting with Microsoft Outlook, click the Synchronize With Microsoft Outlook check box.

The next input screen defines the tax options for this supplier.

Click   the **Taxes tab** to open the screen:

NOTES

Any account can be used as the default expense account, including capital accounts. This allows you to set up the owner as a supplier and link the transactions to the Drawings account.

NOTES

If you need to create a new account for this supplier, type the new account number in the Expense Account field and press `tab`. Click Add to confirm that you want to create the account. The Add An Account wizard will open.

NOTES

Typing 0 (zero) in the Net Days field will leave the payment terms fields on the invoice blank. Therefore, we enter net 1 (one) when payment is due immediately.

SIMPLY VERSION

The option to Synchronize With MS Outlook is not available in the Simply version.

[Payables Ledger window screenshot showing Taxes tab for supplier "All Campus Ads" with HST tax, Tax Exempt set to No, and "- No Tax" selected as the tax code. Balance Owing 0.00, Date of Last Purchase N/A, Balances as of Aug 02, 2010.]

All the taxes Chai Tea Room usually pays are set up for the company and appear on the list. HST is the only applicable tax. The default option is to pay the tax — the option under Tax Exempt is set at No — that is, Chai is not exempt from taxes on purchases from this supplier. Clicking No will change the tax exemption setting to Yes. This change would be appropriate for suppliers, such as the Receiver General, that do not supply goods or services. Refer to Chapter 2 for further information about taxes and discounts.

To enter a default tax code for purchases from the supplier, we can choose a code from the drop-down list in the next field. The default setting, No Tax, is incorrect.

> **Click   No Tax** to see the codes available:

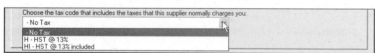

Three codes are defined for Chai Tea Room: **No Tax** for suppliers, such as Bathurst Foods, who do not charge any tax; **H** for suppliers of normal taxable goods or services when HST is not included in the price; and **HI** for suppliers of taxable goods such as gasoline or liquor when the tax is included in the purchase price.

All Campus Ads charges HST but does not include it in the price.

> **Click   H - HST @ 13%.**

The remaining input screens are not needed; they will be introduced in a later application. The Statistics tab screen stores cumulative historical purchases and payments, the Memo tab screen allows you to add messages to the Daily Business Manager and the Import/Export tab allows you to specify corresponding inventory item codes for your business and your suppliers. The Additional Info tab screen has other supplier information fields that can be customized for the company.

Check your work carefully before saving the information because the options you select will affect the invoices directly.

CORRECTING A NEW SUPPLIER ACCOUNT

Move to the field that has the error by **pressing** (tab) to move forward through the fields or **pressing** (shift) and (tab) together to move back to a previous field. **Type** the **correct information**.

You can also highlight the incorrect information by dragging the cursor through it. You can now type the correct information.

After a field has been corrected, **press** (tab) to enter the correction.

To open a different tab screen, **click** the **tab** you want.

When you are certain that all the information is correct,

> **Click   Save And Close** [Save and Close] to save the supplier information and return to the Home window.

Entering Cash Purchases

SIMPLY VERSION
Click the Purchase Invoices icon.

Click the **Invoices icon** to open the journal.

To create a full supplier record from the Supplier field:

Type the new supplier's name in the Purchased From field. Press `tab`. The program will recognize the name is new and give you the option to add a record.

Click Full Add to open a Payables Ledger record at the Address tab screen with the new supplier name already entered as you typed it in the Supplier field.

Enter all the details for the supplier as described above.

Click the Save And Close button to return to the invoice. The supplier's address, tax code and expense account will be added to the invoice form.

CLASSIC VIEW
From the Classic view Home window, click the Purchases icon to open the Purchases Journal.

Choose All Campus Ads from the Purchased From drop-down list. **Press** `tab`.

We can now enter the transaction details as we did for previous purchases. We need to change the payment method because this is a cash purchase.

NOTES
Remember that we use the term cash purchase for purchases with payment by cheque.

Click Pay Later in the Paid By field to see the payment options:

The payment options are the same as those in the Payments Journal for Other Payments, with the addition of Pay Later.

Click Cheque.

A cheque number field is added to the invoice with the next cheque number in the upper right corner of the journal. The cheque number is updated automatically. The account number and payment terms are added from the supplier record information we entered. You need to add the invoice number, transaction date and amount.

Click the **Invoice field** and **type** ACA-3492

Click the **Calendar icon** and **choose** August 3.

Click the **Amount field**.

Type 200 **Press** `tab`. You can add a description to complete the invoice:

NOTES
Sometimes a business uses more than one bank account. If multiple accounts are set up, all bank accounts will be listed in the Paid From drop-down list. You can choose the appropriate bank account from the list for purchases by cheque and for payments. Credit cards and multiple bank accounts are used in later applications.

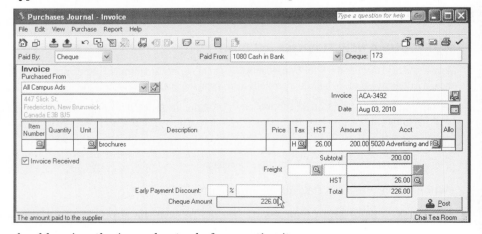

You should review the journal entry before posting it.

Choose the **Report menu** and **click Display Purchases Journal Entry**:

This journal entry is the same as the one from the Payments Journal when we chose Make Other Payment. *Cash in Bank* is credited instead of *Accounts Payable*. The supplier record is updated for the transaction by including both an invoice and a payment for the same date.

Close   the **display**.

Check   the **invoice** for errors and **make corrections** just as you would for regular purchases. When the information is correct,

Click   Post to save the transaction. **Click OK**.

Adjusting a Posted Invoice

In the same way that you can correct or adjust a previously posted entry in the General Journal, you can edit a Purchases Journal invoice after posting. Simply Accounting will create the necessary reversing entry when you post the revised invoice.

The Purchases Journal should still be open.

Click   the **Adjust Invoice tool** 🔳 or **choose** the **Purchase menu** and **click Adjust Invoice** to open the Search Purchase Invoices screen:

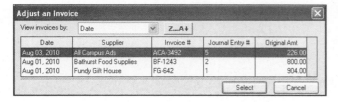

This is similar to the Search screen for the General Journal, but you have the additional option of searching for invoices by the name of the supplier. The program enters default start and finish dates. These dates can be edited like any other date fields or you can choose dates from the calendars. The default dates include all transactions for the journal, so we can accept them.

We will search all invoices by accepting the default to Search All Suppliers.

If you know the invoice or journal entry number, you can enter it in the Invoice Number or Journal Entry # field and click OK to select the invoice directly.

Click   OK to see the requested list of Purchases Journal invoices:

NOTES
You can also press ⌃ctrl + A to open the Adjust An Invoice window from any journal. See Appendix B for a list of keyboard shortcuts.

NOTES
From the Home window, click the Invoices shortcuts list arrow and click Adjust Invoice.

NOTES
Notice that cash purchases entered in the Payments Journal are not included in this list. You can adjust these transactions from the Payments Journal after you select Make Other Payment (see page 131).

Invoices are presented in order with the most recent one listed first and selected. The invoice that we need is Journal Entry #1, FG-642. You can change the order of the listed transactions by selecting from the **View Invoices By** drop-down list. You can list in order by date, supplier, invoice number, journal entry number or amount. And you can reverse the order by clicking the **Z...A** button.

Click   **FG-642**. (Click anywhere on the line to highlight the invoice.)

Click   **Select** or **press** ⟨enter⟩ to recall the selected transaction:

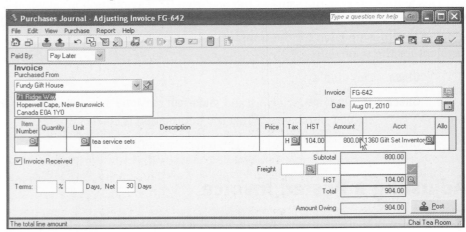

All fields are available for editing. We need to edit the amount.

Click   **800.00** in the Amount field.

Type   900

Press   ⟨tab⟩ to update the tax amount and totals.

You can add -R to the invoice number if you want to indicate that this is the revised invoice.

Your completed entry should now resemble the following:

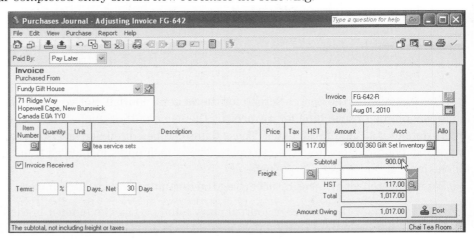

If you change the supplier, you will see a warning:

NOTES
When you change the supplier, the default settings for the previously selected supplier will still be used. Check your entry carefully before posting.

Before posting the revised transaction, review it for accuracy.

Choose the **Report menu** and **click** Display Purchases Journal Entry:

NOTES
If you edit the date, the correcting entry will be posted with the revised date. To see all three entries in the journal report, Corrections must be selected (see page 145).

Although you see only one journal entry at this stage, there are in fact three entries connected with this transaction — J1, the first one that was incorrect, J6, the second one created by Simply Accounting to reverse the incorrect entry and J7, the final correct one you see in this display. All use the original posting date unless you change the date for the adjustment.

Close   the **report display** when you have finished and **make** additional **corrections** if necessary.

Click   the Post button ⌷ Post , **click** OK and **close** the Purchases Journal.

CORRECTING CASH PURCHASES AND PAYMENTS FROM THE PAYMENTS JOURNAL

Purchases entered as Other Payments in the Payments Journal do not appear on the Search Purchase Invoices list from the Purchases Journal. You can, however, adjust these other payments from the Payments Journal as follows:

- **Click** the **Payments icon shortcuts list arrow** ⌷, and **click Adjust Payment**.

- **Select** your search parameters: the **date range**, supplier or cheque number. **Click OK**.

- **Click** the **cheque/invoice** you want to adjust. All cheques used to pay invoices and cash purchases will appear on this list.

- **Press** enter or **click Select** to open the cheque.

- **Make** the **corrections. Review** your **entry** and **post** the revised transaction.

- If the **Payments Journal** is already open, **click Make Other Payment** from the transaction list if you want to adjust a cash purchase payment.

- **Click Pay Invoices** from the transaction list if you want to adjust a cheque used to pay invoices.

- **Click** the **Adjust Payment** or **Adjust Other Payment tool** ⌷ or **choose** the **Payment menu** and **click Adjust Payment** or **Adjust Other Payment**.

- **Select** your search parameter. **Click OK** to open the list of cheques. Your list will include either payment cheques or cash purchase cheques, depending on the type of transaction you started from.

- **Make** the **corrections. Review** your **entry** and **post** the revised transaction.

Refer to page 139 for detailed instructions on correcting a payment cheque.

Entering Discounts for Early Payments

Entering discounts for early payments is very much like entering regular payments. The discounts show up automatically when the invoices and dates are correct.

Click   the **Payments icon** ⌷ to open the Payments Journal.

Choose `Bathurst Food Supplies` from the supplier list to display outstanding invoices:

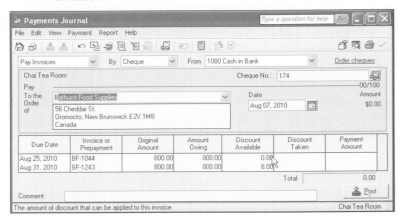

Initially, no discount is available for invoice #BF-1044 because the session date is beyond the discount period, that is, more than 10 days past the July 26 invoice date. The discount shows for the second invoice because the session date lies within its 10-day discount period.

Enter **August 4** as the date of the payment. **Press** (tab).

Both discounts are now available because the payment date falls within the 10-day discount period:

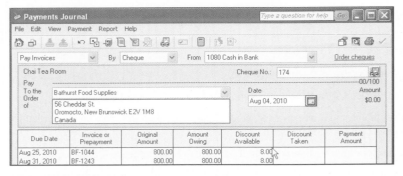

Press (tab) **twice** to advance to the Discount Taken field and enter the amount.

Press (tab) to advance to the Payment Amount field and accept the amount.

Notice that the discount has been subtracted from the invoice amount.

Press (tab) to accept the amount in the Payment Amount field and update the total and the cheque portion of the journal as shown:

At this stage, a discount amount is entered for the second invoice, but this invoice is not being paid. Therefore you must delete this entry to avoid adding it to the invoice.

Press   `ctrl` + **J** to see the payment as you have it entered so far:

Chai Tea Room		
08/04/10 (J8)	Debits	Credits
2200 Accounts Payable	808.00	-
1080 Cash in Bank	-	792.00
5090 Purchase Discounts	-	16.00
	808.00	808.00

If you do not delete this second discount, your entry will be posted as shown. Both discount amounts are included.

Close   the journal display.

Press   `del` to remove the highlighted second discount taken amount and complete the payment form as shown:

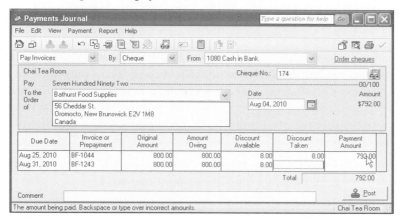

Choose the **Report menu** and **click** Display Payments Journal Entry to review the transaction before posting:

Payments Journal Entry			
File Options Help			
🖨 Print Report 📑 Change Print Settings 📤 Export Report 📊 Open in Excel® 📋 Customize Report 🔍 Refresh Report ?			
Chai Tea Room			
08/04/10 (J8)	Debits	Credits	Division
2200 Accounts Payable	800.00	-	
1080 Cash in Bank	-	792.00	
5090 Purchase Discounts	-	8.00	
	800.00	800.00	

In the related journal entry, the program has updated the General Ledger *Accounts Payable* control account for the full amount of the invoice and reduced the balance owing to the supplier by the same amount. The amount taken from *Cash in Bank* is the actual amount of the payment, taking the discount into consideration. The discount amount is automatically debited to the linked *Purchase Discounts* account. *Purchase Discounts* is a contra-expense account. It has a credit balance, so it reduces total expense and increases income.

Close   the **display** to return to the Payments Journal input screen and **correct** your **work** if necessary. (Refer to page 121 for assistance.)

Post   the **transaction. Click** OK. **Close** the **Payments Journal.**

Using Continue to Enter New Suppliers

Sometimes you may want to include the name of a supplier in the journal record without creating a supplier record. In these situations, you can use the Continue feature. For the cheque to Tomailik, a cash purchase, we will use this approach.

Click   the **Invoices icon** [Invoices ▾] to open the Purchases Journal.

Click   the **Purchased From field** and **type** Bette Tomailik

NOTES
Pay Later is not an option when you choose Continue or One-time Supplier. Only immediate payment is allowed — Cash and Cheque.

NOTES
When you choose Continue for a new supplier in the Make Other Payment journal, the name is not added to the journal entry.

CLASSIC VIEW
Users who are familiar with earlier versions of Simply Accounting may prefer to work from the Classic view. You can access all journals and ledgers from a single Home window.

Press   (tab) to open the message about a new supplier name.

Click   **Continue** to return to the journal.

Choose **Cheque** as the Paid By method and then **enter** the **remaining details** of the cash purchase as usual.

Review and **post** the **transaction**.

Enter   the **purchase** from **Sunbury Cleaning**. **Change** the Paid By entry to **Pay Later**. **Store** the **entry**, **post** it and then **close** the **Purchases Journal**.

Entering Sales Taxes in the General Journal

The sales summary on August 7 is entered in the General Journal because Chai does not use the Receivables Ledger. When you set up and link sales tax accounts, you can add General Journal sales tax entries to the tax reports. A Sales Taxes button becomes available when you use one of these linked tax accounts in the General Journal. Chai has two linked tax accounts, *HST Charged on Sales* and *HST Paid on Purchases*.

The General Journal is accessed from the Company module window that we used in the previous two chapters.

To open the Company module window, click Company in the list of modules in the upper left Modules pane. Click the General Journal icon.

Instead, we will create a shortcut to open the General Journal.

Creating Shortcuts

Click   **Customize** in the Shortcuts pane below the modules as shown:

The Customize Shortcuts window opens:

Click   the ⊞ beside **Company** to expand the list of Company tasks:

You can create up to 10 shortcuts for each user. The expanded list for each module shows the items for which you can create shortcuts. Once you create it, you can click the name in the Shortcuts pane to access that journal or task directly.

> **Click**   **Create General Journal** in the list of Company tasks.

> **Click**   **Add>** to move this task to the Shortcuts box as shown:

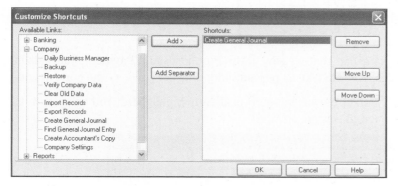

> **Click**   **OK** to return to the Home window.

Create General Journal now appears in the Home window Shortcuts pane as shown:

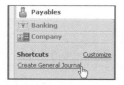

> **Click**   **Create General Journal** in the Shortcuts pane. The General Journal opens immediately. This shortcut will be available at all times.

> **Enter**   the **Source** and **Comment** for the sale. The session date is correct.

> **Choose**   **Cash in Bank** as the account to be debited and **type** 8588 as the amount. **Enter** an appropriate **Comment** for the account.

> **Choose**   **HST Charged on Sales** as the account. Advance to the credit column.

> **Type**   988 as the amount to be credited. **Press** (tab). Your screen should now resemble the one shown here:

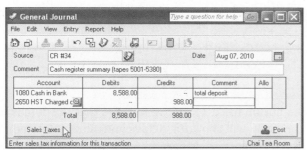

The Sales Taxes button became available as soon as you entered the tax amount.

> **Click**   the **Sales Taxes button** to open the tax detail screen:

NOTES
When you enter HST Paid on Purchases as the account, Purchase is selected as the default transaction type because this account is linked to the Payables module.

Because you entered *HST Charged on Sales* as the account, the transaction is recognized as a sale. You can change the transaction type if it is not correct. The account and tax amount are already entered on the form. We need to add the tax code.

Click   the **List icon** in the Tax Code field to open the tax code list:

This is the same list that we saw in the Purchases and Payments journals in the tax code fields. Sales have HST at 13 percent added to the price so the correct code is H.

Click   **Select** because code H is already highlighted. You will return to the tax detail screen:

Because the tax amount was already entered, the sales amount — the Amount Subject To Tax — is calculated as soon as you select the tax code. The sales amount is correct so we can continue. If the amount is not correct because there are other taxes included, you can edit the default amount and enter an amount for Other Taxes Charged.

Click   OK.

Enter   a **Comment** for the tax line and then add the final account line — **choose** account **4100**, accept the amount and **add** an appropriate **comment**.

Your completed journal entry should look like the one shown here:

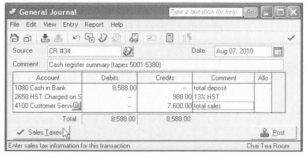

Notice that the Sales Taxes button has a ✔ on it to indicate that tax details have been added. Clicking the button again will show the details and allow you to edit them.

Review the **journal entry** and then **close** the **display**. When the entry is correct,

Click   the **Post button** . **Click** OK.

If you forgot to enter the tax codes for *HST Charged on Sales*, you will see the warning message to confirm you do not want to add tax details:

If you forgot to add the tax details, click No to open the Sales Taxes window. Add the missing details and then post the journal entry.

Close   the `General Journal` to return to the Home window.

Back up your `data file. Advance` the `session date` to `August 14.`

Recalling a Stored Entry

The first journal entry for the August 14 session date is the recurring purchase from Bathurst Food Supplies. Since we have stored this purchase, we do not need to re-enter all the information.

Click   the `Invoices icon` to open the Journal.

Click   the `Recall tool` 📤 in the tool bar (or **choose** the `Purchase menu` and **click** `Recall`) to display the Recall Recurring Transaction dialogue box as shown here:

NOTES
You can press `ctrl` + R to recall a stored entry.

The stored entries are listed in order according to the next date that they will be repeated. If you want, you can display the stored entries in a different order.

Click   the `View Recurring Transactions By list arrow` to see the options:

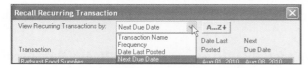

You can choose to view the stored entries in order by Transaction Name (which is the supplier's name if you did not change the default), by Frequency (how often the transaction is repeated), by the Date Last Posted or by the Next Due Date. If you have a large number of stored entries, it may be easier to find the one you need with a different order. You can also reverse the order for any of the order selections with the A...Z button. Since we have only two stored entries, the default order, Next Due Date, placed the one we want first. Do not change the default.

From the Recall Stored Entry dialogue box, you can remove an entry that is incorrect or no longer needed. Click an entry to select it. Click Remove and then click Yes to confirm that you want to delete the entry. (See page 445.)

Bathurst Food Supplies, the name of the entry we want to use, should be selected because it is the recurring entry that is due next.

Click   `Bathurst Food Supplies` if it is not already selected.

Click   `Select` or **press** `enter` to return to the Purchases Journal.

The entry we stored is displayed just as we entered it the first time, except that the date has been changed to one week past the previous posting date, as needed, and the Invoice field is blank so we can enter the new invoice number. Remember that Simply Accounting does not accept duplicate invoice numbers.

Click   the `Invoice field` to move the cursor.

Type   BF-2100

The entry is now complete. You should review it before posting.

> **Choose** the Report menu and **click** Display Purchases Journal Entry.
>
> **Close** the display when finished and **make** any necessary **corrections**.
>
> **Click** the Post button ⌹ Post . **Click** OK.
>
> **Close** the Purchases Journal.

Editing a Supplier Record

Sometimes a supplier record must be revised after it is saved because the initial information has changed or because information that was not available initially is now known. We need to edit the record for NB Gas to add the default expense account.

Supplier records are accessed from the Suppliers icon shortcuts list, or from the Suppliers list, or from the Suppliers window. Modify Supplier, as shown in the drop-down shortcuts list with the Suppliers icon, is one starting point for the edit. The other is the supplier's name in the list of suppliers on the right:

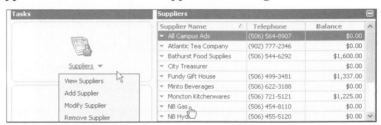

> **Click** NB Gas in the Suppliers list to open the Address tab information screen. Or, you can
>
> **Click** the Suppliers shortcuts list arrow and **click** Modify Supplier to open the Search Suppliers window:

NOTES
You can open the Suppliers window by clicking the Suppliers icon in the Home window in either the Classic or the Enhanced view. From the Suppliers window, double click the supplier you want to open the record at the Address tab screen.

Each supplier on record is listed on the Search Supplier selection window. Suppliers is entered as the search area. Notice that Bette Tomailik is not listed.

> **Double click** NB Gas to open the Address tab information screen.
>
> **Click** the Options tab to access the Expense Account field:

Click   the **Expense Account field**.

You can also choose an account from the list provided by the list arrow, or add a new account. We need to create an account.

Type   5110 **Press** (tab) and then **click Add** to start the Add Account wizard. **Enter Heating Expense** as the account name and accept the remaining default settings. **Click Finish** to return to the Ledger.

Click   **Save And Close** 💾 Save and Close to close the Payables Ledger (supplier record) window to return to the Payables module window.

Click   **Pay Expenses** from the Payments icon shortcuts list to open the Payments Journal.

Enter   the **cash purchase from NB Gas**; the account will appear automatically.

Adjusting a Posted Payment

Just as you can correct a purchase invoice after posting, you can correct a cheque that has been posted.

Choose   **Pay Invoices** from the Payments transaction list.

Click   the **Adjust Payment tool** 📝 or **choose** the **Payment menu** and **click Adjust Payment** to open the Search screen for Adjust Payments:

Again we see the familiar Search window for the selected journal.

Click   OK to see the list of cheques already posted for this date range:

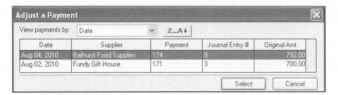

Only the two cheques used to pay invoices are listed because we started from the Pay Invoices window.

NOTES
Remember that although the field is named Expense Account, you can choose any postable account as the default for the supplier. You can also select a different account in the journal if necessary.

NOTES
Pressing (ctrl) + A will also open the Search window to begin the adjusting procedure.

NOTES
When you choose Adjust Payment from the Payments icon shortcuts list, you will see the list of all cheques, those used to pay invoices and those for other payments.

Double click `Fundy Gift House` to see the cheque we posted:

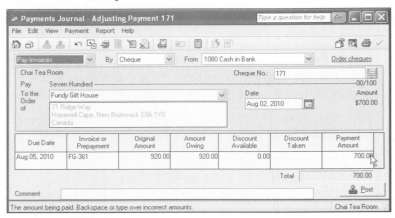

The cheque appears as it was completed. You can edit all the details.

Click   **700.00** in the Payment Amount field.

Type   600

Click   the **Comment field**.

Type   previous chq amount incorrectly entered

Check   your **work** carefully. **Click Post** to save the changes:

A message about the cheque number being out of sequence appears because we have already used this cheque number. The cheque number is correct so we should continue without changing it.

Click   **No** to accept the number and continue.

Simply Accounting will create an entry that reverses the original payment, and the original entry is also saved for a complete audit trail.

Enter   the next group of **transactions**.

Reversing a Posted Purchase Entry

The cash purchase for Moncton Kitchenwares selected an incorrect supplier. We will reverse this entry rather than adjust it because other details may also be incorrect. Any journal that has an Adjust option also has the option to reverse an entry.

The journal you used to enter the purchase should still be open, either the Payments Journal with Make Other Payment selected or the Purchases Journal. You can also use either the Adjust or the Lookup feature to begin. In each case, you can follow the steps below.

Click   the **Lookup Other Payment tool** 🔲 in the Payments Journal with Make Other Payment selected, or the **Lookup An Invoice tool** in the Purchases Journal. Or

Click   the **Adjust Other Payment (Adjust An Invoice) tool** 🔲 to open the Search screen.

Click   **OK** to see the list of cheques (or purchases) already posted.

Double click Moncton Kitchenwares to see the cash purchase.

The Reverse tool in the tool bar is now available.

Click the **Reverse tool** , or **choose** the **Payment** (or **Purchase**) **menu** and **click Reverse Other Payment** (or **Invoice**) to see the confirmation:

Click **Yes** to confirm.

Simply Accounting will create the entry that reverses the original one automatically. You can see both the original and the reversing entry in the journal report when you choose Show Corrections.

Enter the **transaction**, choosing the correct supplier this time.

When you change the supplier for a cash purchase transaction you will see the message stating that the supplier name will be changed (the remaining information on the invoice will be unchanged):

Enter the **next** group of **journal transactions** up to August 21.

Changing a Stored Entry

The first entry on August 21 is the weekly purchase from Sunbury Cleaning Supplies. The amount of the purchase has changed, however, and we need to update the stored entry. If the change is for a single purchase and will not be repeated, edit the entry after recalling it but do not store the entry again.

Click the **Invoices icon** in the Payables window to open the Journal.

Click the **Recall tool** on the tool bar, or **choose** the **Purchase menu** and **click Recall** to display the Recall Recurring Transaction dialogue box.

Double click Sunbury Cleaning Supplies, the entry we want to use to display the purchase entry with the new date.

Click the **Invoice field** so you can add the invoice number.

Type SC-1790

Click 250.00, the Amount, to highlight it so that you can edit it. Double click if necessary to select the amount.

Type 300

Press (tab) to enter the change.

Review the **journal entry** as usual to make sure that it is correct before proceeding.

Click the **Store button**, or **choose** the **Purchase menu** and **click Store**.

Click OK to accept the name and frequency without changes.

NOTES
The Receipts Journal Report in Chapter 6, page 181 shows the two entries that result when you reverse a transaction.

The following warning appears:

Click   Yes to confirm that you want to replace the previous stored version and return to the Purchases Journal.

Click   the Post button 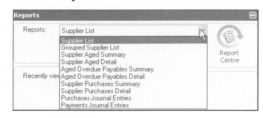 to save the entry. **Click** OK and **close** the Journal.

Enter   the remaining journal transactions for August.

Displaying Supplier Reports

Supplier-related reports can also be displayed and printed from the multiple starting points, including the Suppliers window.

Click the Suppliers icon to open the Suppliers window. The Reports menu now lists only supplier reports. You can select the report you want from this list to open the report options window.

Choose   the Reports menu in the Home window, then **choose** Payables and **click** the report you want to see the options window for the report.

Click   the Reports list arrow in the Reports pane to see the list of supplier reports:

We will work from the Report Centre again so that we can see the report samples, descriptions and options.

Click   the Report Centre icon in the Home window.

Click   Payables in the Select A Report Type list if necessary to open the list of available supplier reports:

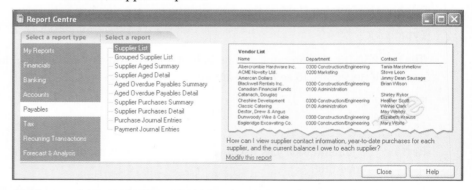

You should see a general description of the Supplier List, the first report in the Payables list.

SIMPLY VERSION
The term vendor will replace supplier in all report names and report fields.
    Grouped Supplier Lists are not available.

NOTES
The Supplier Purchases Report deals mainly with inventory. It will be introduced in a later application.

NOTES
The Report Centre can also be accessed from the Reports menu.

CLASSIC VIEW
Click the Report Centre icon in the My Business column or open the Report Centre from the Reports menu.

Displaying Supplier Lists

Click   Supplier List in the Select A Report list if necessary to see the sample report and description.

Click   Modify This Report to see the report options:

In any Home window, you can choose the Reports menu, then choose Lists and click Suppliers to see the report options.

To select supplier details, you can choose the supplier record fields from the Report Columns screen. And you can include suppliers marked as inactive if you want.

Click   OK to see the report.

Close   the display when you have finished viewing the report.

You will return to the starting point for the report.

Displaying Supplier Aged Reports

You can display Supplier Aged reports at any time.

Click   Supplier Aged Summary in the Select A Report list to see the sample report and description.

Click   Modify This Report to see the report options:

Or, from any Home window, choose the Reports menu, then choose Payables and click Supplier Aged to see this report options window.

If you chose either One-Time Supplier or Continue for Bette Tomailik, she will not be included by name in the list of suppliers for reports and graphs. If you used Quick Add, her name will be included.

The **Summary** option provides the total balance owing to each supplier. It displays an alphabetic list of suppliers with outstanding total balances organized into aged columns. By default, the program selects this option.

Select the **Detail** option if you want to see individual outstanding invoices and payments made to suppliers. This more descriptive report is also aged. Management can use it to make payment decisions. With the Detail option, you can also add supplier payment terms by clicking Include Terms.

 CLASSIC VIEW
From the Home window, right-click the Suppliers icon
. (Clicking the left mouse button will open the ledger.) The Display tool label changes to the name of the report for the selected icon.
Click the Display tool on the tool bar.

NOTES
You can drill down to the Supplier Aged Detail Report from the Supplier List.

NOTES
The Grouped Supplier List is similar to the Supplier List, but you can also group the suppliers by a number of criteria, such as their city.

NOTES
The Supplier Aged Summary and Detail reports are both available directly from the Report Centre.

NOTES
From the Supplier Aged Detail Report, you can drill down to look up invoices and supplier ledgers. From the Summary Report, you can drill down to the Detail Report.

You can sort and filter the reports by supplier name, balance owing or aging period. You can select or omit any of the columns to customize the report.

Click Detail if you want the Detail Report.

Click the **name** or **press** and **hold** ⌈ctrl⌉ and **click** the **names** in the Suppliers list to select the suppliers you want in the report. **Click Select All** to include all suppliers or to remove all when all are selected.

Enter the **date** you want for the report or accept the session date given by default. After you have indicated all the options,

Click OK to see the report.

Close the **displayed report** when you have finished.

Displaying Aged Overdue Payables Reports

You can display Aged Overdue Payables reports at any time.

Click Aged Overdue Payables Summary in the Select A Report list to see the sample report and description.

Click Modify This Report to see the report options:

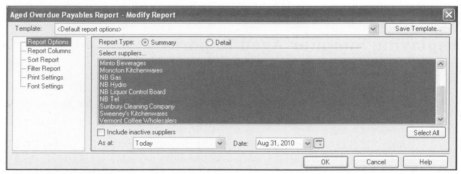

From the Home window, choose the Reports menu, then choose Payables and click Aged Overdue Payables to see the report options.

The Aged Overdue Payables Report includes the same information as the Supplier Aged Report but it adds a column for the invoice amounts that are overdue. Supplier name and balance owing may be selected as the criteria for sorting and filtering. The Summary Report shows totals for each supplier while the Detail Report includes details for each invoice.

You can sort and filter the reports by supplier name or by the balance owing. You can select or omit any of the columns to customize the report.

Choose Summary or Detail.

Press and **hold** ⌈ctrl⌉ and then **click** the **names** in the Suppliers list to select the suppliers that you want to see in the report. **Click Select All** to include all suppliers or to remove all when all are selected.

Enter the **date** you want for the report, or accept the session date given by default. After you have indicated all the options,

Click OK to see the report. One invoice from Moncton Kitchenwares and the balance on the first invoice from Fundy Gift House are overdue.

Close the **displayed report** when you have finished.

Displaying the Purchases Journal

Click   **Purchase Journal Entries** in the Select A Report list to see the sample report and description.

Click   **Modify This Report** to see the report options:

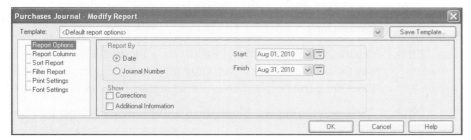

Or, choose the Reports menu, then choose Journal Entries and click Purchases.

Entries for the Purchases Journal can be selected by posting date or by journal entry number. By default, the Date option is selected, and the first transaction date and session date are the default dates for the report. All journal reports may be sorted and filtered by date, journal number, source or comment. You can choose the account name, number, debits and credits columns to customize the report column settings. Correcting or adjusting entries may be included or omitted from the report.

Type   the **beginning date** for the transactions you want to display.

Press   ⌜tab⌟ **twice**.

Type   the **ending date** for the transaction period you want to see.

Click   **Corrections** so that adjusting and reversing entries are included.

Click   **OK** to see the report.

Close   the **display** when you have finished.

Displaying the Payments Journal

Click   **Payment Journal Entries** in the Select A Report list to see the sample report and description.

Click   **Modify This Report** to see the report options:

Or choose the Reports menu, then choose Journal Entries and click Payments to see the report options.

For the Payments Journal, like other journal reports, you can select the transactions by posting date, the default setting, or by journal entry number. In addition, you can choose the type of payment for the report — invoice payments, credit card payments, other payments (cash purchases) and remittance payments. All types are selected

CLASSIC VIEW

From the Home window, right-click the Purchases icon to select it. Click the Display tool on the tool bar.

If no icons are selected in the Home window, Purchases and Payments Journal reports are available from the Select Report list when you click the Display tool.

NOTES

The dates August 1 and August 31 are available from drop-down list for both date fields.

NOTES

If you omit corrections, the journal reports will appear to be out of sequence because the journal entry numbers for the incorrect transactions and their reversing entries will be omitted from the report.

NOTES

You can drill down to look up invoices, to the Supplier Aged Report and to the General Ledger Report from the Purchases Journal or the Payments Journal Report.

CLASSIC VIEW

From the Home window, right-click the Payments icon to select it. Click the Display tool.

initially and clicking any one will remove it from the report. Corrections or adjustments may be included or omitted. Clicking will change your selections.

Type   the **beginning date** for the transactions you want to display.

Press   `tab` **twice**.

Type   the **ending date** for the transaction period you want to see.

Click   **Corrections**.

Click   **Credit Card Payments** and **Remittance Payments** because we did not use these transaction types. Only Invoice Payments and Other Payments, the transaction types we entered, should be included.

Click   OK to see the report. **Close** the **display** when you have finished.

Displaying All Journal Entries in a Single Report

To view the entries for all journals in a single report from a Home window, choose the Reports menu, then choose Journal Entries and click All.

From the Report Centre, click Financials in the Select A Report Type list and then click All Journal Entries in the Select A Report list. Click Display or choose Modify This Report if you want to change the default options.

Displaying Cheque Log Reports

If you regularly print cheques through Simply Accounting from the Payables journals or the Payroll journals, you can display and print a summary of these printed cheques in the Cheque Log Report.

Click   **Banking** in the Select A Report Type list to see the general description of banking reports and the list of available reports:

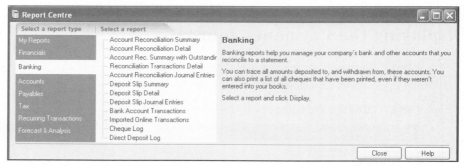

Click   **Cheque Log** in the Select A Report list to see the sample report and description.

Click   **Modify This Report** to see the report options:

From any Home window, choose the Reports menu, then choose Banking and click Cheque Log to open the report options window.

The report will include details for all cheques that you entered including whether or not the journal entry was posted and the number of times the cheque was printed. If you do not print cheques through the program, these payments are listed with a 0 (zero) for the number of times printed. Adjusted cheques are identified as Reversed.

To customize the report, you can choose any of the column headings to sort or filter the report and you can choose to include or omit any of these columns.

Choose the `bank account` from the Select Bank Account drop-down list.

Enter the `Start` and `Finish dates` for the report.

Click `OK` to see the report.

Close the `display` when you have finished.

Recurring Transactions Report

If you have stored transactions, you can generate a report of these transactions.

Click `Recurring Transactions` in the Select A Report Type list to see the general description of the report type and the list of available reports:

SIMPLY VERSION
Forecast & Analysis reports are not available in the Simply version.

The list now shows the different types of transactions that can be stored.

Click `All Transactions` in the Select A Report list to see the sample report and description.

Click `Modify This Report` to see the report options:

Again, the list shows the different types of transactions that can be stored and all are selected initially. Transactions without due dates are also included by default. You can restrict the report to include only those entries that are due within a specific time period by selecting `Only Show Transactions Due On Or Before`. The default date for this option is one week past the session date, but you can enter any date you want. You can `Group` the report `By Transaction Type`, or accept the default to show entries in order by the due date.

You can sort and filter this report by type of transaction, description, frequency, the date the entry was last processed or posted or by the due date.

NOTES
When you choose Random as the frequency for recurring transactions, they do not include a due date.

Choose the `options` you want and **click** `OK`.

Close the `Report Centre` when you have finished.

Displaying Management Reports

Management reports are available for each ledger. They can be displayed only from the Home window.

> **Choose** the **Reports menu**, then **choose Management Reports** and **click Payables** to open the report options window:

CLASSIC VIEW
You can also access Management Reports from the Advice tool in the Home window (see page 17).

Sometimes management reports can reveal patterns in the business more clearly than the regular financial reports. For example, the report for overdue accounts lists invoices that are outstanding, with supplier contact and invoice details and the number of days remaining until payment is due. The reports for increased or decreased monthly purchases show changes in purchase patterns over the previous year that an aged detail report may not.

> When you click a topic, the appropriate form will be selected from those installed with the program. Unless you have the programs required to customize forms, accept the default. If appropriate, enter a date for the report.
>
> **Click** **OK** to see the report. **Print** the **report** and then **close** the **display**.

⚠ **WARNING!**
Always check that the file location for the Form used for the report is correct for your program setup. The file should be in the Forms folder, a subfolder of your Simply Accounting Premium 2008 folder.

NOTES
In the management report for overdue payments, negative numbers indicate the number of days till payment is due (current invoices) and positive numbers show the number of days that the payment is overdue.

Printing Supplier Reports

Before printing supplier reports, make sure that the print options have been set correctly. To print a report,

> **Display** the **report** you want to print.
>
> **Click** the **Change Print Settings tool** 🖶 to open the Reports & Forms Settings screen. Check that you have the correct printer and form files selected for your report. **Close** the **Settings screen**.
>
> **Click** the **Print tool** 🖶 or **choose** the **File menu** and **click Print**.

Printing Mailing Labels

To print labels, you should first make sure that the print options have been set correctly and that your printer is turned on and has the correct labels paper. To set the program to use your printing labels,

> Choose the Setup menu in the Home window and click Reports & Forms.
> Click Labels in the list under Reports.
> Enter the appropriate margins, size and number across the page for your labels.
> Click OK to return to the Home window.
>
> **Choose** the **Reports menu** in the Home window, then **choose Mailing Labels** and **click Suppliers**:

NOTES
For practice, you can print the labels on plain paper.

Press and **hold** ⌜ctrl⌟ and then **click** the **names** of the suppliers for whom you want labels, or **click** Select All to include all suppliers.

Click OK.

Graphing Supplier Reports

Payables by Aging Period Charts

Choose the Graphs menu in the Home window, then **click** Payables By Aging Period to display the date entry screen:

Type the **date** for the graph or accept the default session date.

Click OK to display the pie chart:

Your graph provides a quick visual reference of amounts due to all suppliers combined in each of the aging periods selected in the company setup options. Most of the payments due are current but about 25 percent are overdue (over 31 days) — the amounts owing to Moncton Kitchenwares and Fundy Gift House.

Double click a portion of a graph to see the aging period, the dollar amount and the percentage of the total. Double click the legend to make it larger and add the aging periods if they are not included already. Double click the expanded legend to reduce it.

Close the **graph** when you have finished.

NOTES
The tool bar options, and the control of the colour and the legend, are the same for all graphs. Refer to page 60 for a review of these features.

Payables by Supplier Charts

> **Choose** the Graphs menu in the Home window, then **click Payables By Supplier** to display the pie chart options:

> **Press** and **hold** <kbd>ctrl</kbd> and then **click** the **names** of the suppliers to include in your pie chart, or **click Select All** to include all the suppliers.

> **Click** OK to display the pie chart:

The graph shows the proportion of the total payables that is owed to each selected supplier. The tool bar options, and the control of the colour and the legend, are the same as for the other graphs.

> **Close** the **graph** when you have finished.

> **Close** the **data file** to finish your Simply Accounting session.

REVIEW

The Student CD-ROM with Data Files includes Review Questions and Supplementary Cases for this chapter.

AirCare Services

OBJECTIVES

After completing this chapter, you should be able to

- **enter** transactions in the General, Payables and Receivables journals
- **enter** and **post** cash, credit card and account sale transactions
- **enter** and **post** customer payment transactions
- **customize** journals
- **enter** transactions including GST and PST
- **store** and **recall** recurring entries
- **enter** customer discounts and partial payments
- **add** and **edit** customer accounts
- **reverse** receipts to enter NSF cheques from customers
- **edit** and **review** customer-related transactions
- **create** shortcuts for General and Payables transactions
- **display**, **print** and **graph** customer reports
- **understand** linked accounts for the Receivables Ledger

COMPANY INFORMATION

Company Profile

NOTES
Air Care Services
100 Belair Avenue, Unit 25
Winnipeg, Manitoba R3T 0S3
Tel 1: (204) 456-1299
Tel 2: (888) 455-7194
Fax: (204) 456-3188
Business No.: 533 766 455

Air Care Services, located in Winnipeg, Manitoba, has been operating successfully for the past five years under the ownership and management of Simon Arturro. The company's range of services, related to heating equipment and air-conditioning units, draws on Arturro's experience with electrical wiring, boilers, plumbing and chimney work. He has two occasional assistants.

Revenue comes from four sources: installation, repairs, service contracts and subcontracting. Air Care installs air-conditioning and heating equipment, electronic thermostats and gas fireplaces in customers' homes. Installation work may include adding air-filtration and air-cleaning units to existing heating systems and installing gas fireplaces in private homes, offices and funeral homes. Upgrades for furnaces and fireplaces often require replacing chimney liners and installing direct venting. Product manufacturers pay Air Care for repairing equipment under warranty, and individual customers rely on Air Care for other repairs. Arturro also sells service contracts. And finally, Arturro handles installation subcontracts for large contractors.

Some customers — homeowners, owners of office buildings and companies that sell furnaces and air conditioners — have accounts with Air Care and receive a 1 percent discount if they pay within 10 days. They are asked to settle their accounts in 30 days, paying by cash or by cheque. PST and GST apply to all service work done by Air Care.

Accounts have been set up with a local hardware store, suppliers of chimney liners and parts for furnaces and air conditioners, and other regular suppliers.

After remitting all taxes before the end of April 2010, Arturro converted the accounts for Air Care using the following information:

- Chart of Accounts
- Post-Closing Trial Balance
- Supplier Information
- Customer Information
- Accounting Procedures

CHART OF POSTABLE ACCOUNTS

AIR CARE SERVICES

ASSETS
1080 Cash in Bank
1100 Credit Card Bank Account
1200 Accounts Receivable
1300 Air Conditioning Parts
1320 Furnace Parts
1340 Office Supplies
1420 Cash Register
1440 Computer System
1460 Service Equipment ▶

▶1480 Tools
1500 Van
1550 Shop

LIABILITIES
2100 Bank Loan
2200 Accounts Payable
2640 PST Payable
2650 GST Charged on Services
2670 GST Paid on Purchases ▶

▶2850 Mortgage Payable

EQUITY
3560 S. Arturro, Capital
3600 Net Income

REVENUE
4100 Installation Revenue
4120 Repairs Revenue
4140 Service Contract Revenue
4180 Sales Discounts ▶

▶EXPENSE
5100 Advertising and Promotion
5120 Bank Charges & Card Fees
5140 Interest Expense
5160 Hydro Expense
5180 Payroll Service Charges
5200 Purchase Discounts
5220 Telephone Expense
5240 Vehicle Expenses
5300 Wages

NOTES: The Chart of Accounts includes only postable accounts and the Net Income or Current Earnings account.

POST-CLOSING TRIAL BALANCE

AIR CARE SERVICES

April 30, 2010		Debits	Credits
1080	Cash in Bank	$ 14 660	
1100	Credit Card Bank Account	1 000	
1200	Accounts Receivable	4 140	
1300	Air Conditioning Parts	1 200	
1320	Furnace Parts	600	
1340	Office Supplies	400	
1420	Cash Register	500	
1440	Computer System	2 500	
1460	Service Equipment	10 000	
1480	Tools	3 000	
1500	Van	25 000	
1550	Shop	100 000	
2100	Bank Loan		$ 10 000
2200	Accounts Payable		4 200
2850	Mortgage Payable		80 000
3560	S. Arturro, Capital		68 800
		$163 000	$163 000

SUPPLIER INFORMATION

AIR CARE SERVICES

Supplier Name (Contact)	Address	Phone No. Fax No.	E-mail Web Site	Terms Tax ID
Beausejour Chimney Products (Janine Beausejour)	50 Fireplace Rd. Winnipeg, Manitoba R3F 2T2	Tel: (204) 476-5282 Fax: (204) 476-5110	jb@beausejour.com www.beausejour.com	1/15, n/30 444 276 534
Brandon Hardware (Nutley Bolter)	72 Hammer St. Winnipeg, Manitoba R4P 1B8	Tel: (204) 369-0808 Fax: (204) 369-6222	nbolter@yahoo.com	net 15 385 416 822
Killarney Furnace Equipment (Kieper Warme)	91 Radiator St. Winnipeg, Manitoba R1B 4F4	Tel: (204) 363-0210 Fax: (204) 363-2000	kwarme@heatexchange.com	1/5, n/30 571 277 631
Manitoba Hydro (Kira Strong)	1 Power Station Rd. Winnipeg, Manitoba R6G 2C1	Tel: (204) 479-2999	kira.strong@mnhydro.man.ca www.mnhydro.man.ca	net 1
Manitoba Telephone (Sotto Voce)	4 Speakers Corners Winnipeg, Manitoba R1E 2K2	Tel: (204) 361-3255	www.manitobatel.ca	net 1
Starbuck Advertising Agency (Pam Fletts)	300 Flyer St. Winnipeg, Manitoba R3V 6S3	Tel: (204) 361-1727 Fax: (204) 361-8229	pfletts@saa.com www.saa.com	net 1 610 728 365
Steinbach Airconditioning Inc. (Ezra Steinbach)	2 Ventilate St. Winnipeg, Manitoba R2H 9J9	Tel: (204) 475-6432 Fax: (204) 475-8600	esteinb@steinair.com www.steinair.com	1/10, n/30 177 235 441
UPS Delivery (Bea Carrier)	8 Freight St. Winnipeg, Manitoba R3A 7B2	Tel 1: (204) 479-1UPS (1877) Tel 2: (800) 477-1UPS Fax: (204) 477-6000	www.ups.com	net 1 522 534 677
Willow Garage (Axel Rodd)	699 Willow St. Winnipeg, Manitoba R2P 1B3	Tel: (204) 368-6444 Fax: (204) 368-6000	axel@wefixcars.com www.wefixcars.com	net 30 129 732 010

OUTSTANDING SUPPLIER INVOICES

AIR CARE SERVICES

Supplier Name	Terms	Date	Invoice No.	Amount	Total
Beausejour Chimney Products	1/15, n/30	Apr. 21/10	B-894	$1 600	$1 600
Steinbach Airconditioning Inc.	1/10, n/30	Apr. 27/10	SA-2141	$1 500	$1 500
Willow Garage	net 30	Apr. 10/10	W-1142	$1 100	$1 100
			Grand Total		$4 200

CUSTOMER INFORMATION

AIR CARE SERVICES

Customer Name (Contact)	Address	Phone No. Fax No.	E-mail Web Site	Terms Credit Limit
Brandon School Board (Ed Ducate)	49 Trainer St. Winnipeg, Manitoba R3P 2T5	Tel 1: (204) 466-5000 Tel 2: (204) 466-1123 Fax: (204) 466-2000	Ed.D@bsb.com www.bsb.com	1/10, n/30 $2 500
Grande Pointe Towers (Sophie Grande)	77 LaPointe Cr. Winnipeg, Manitoba R2G 4D1	Tel: (204) 322-7500 Fax: (204) 322-7436	sgrande@GPTowers.com www.GPTowers.com	1/10, n/30 $3 000
Midwestern Funeral Home (N. Mourning)	8 Quiet St. Winnipeg, Manitoba R7B 1E1	Tel: (204) 763-WAKE (9253) Fax: (204) 762-9301	nm@midwestfh.com www.midwestfh.com	C.O.D. (net 1) $2 000

Customer Name (Contact)	Address	Phone No. Fax No.	E-mail Web Site	Terms Credit Limit
Oak Bluff Banquet Hall (Ann Oakley)	4 Celebration Ave. Winnipeg, Manitoba R8V 3H7	Tel: (204) 622-7391 Fax: (204) 622-7900	annie@OBBH.com www.OBBH.com	1/10, n/30 $5 000
Selkirk Furnaces Inc. (Elsa Selkirk)	588 Heater St. Winnipeg, Manitoba R3T 8N1	Tel: (204) 368-4575 Fax: (204) 368-2198	elsas@selkirk.com www.selkirk.com	1/10, n/30 $5 000

OUTSTANDING CUSTOMER INVOICES

AIR CARE SERVICES

Customer Name	Terms	Date	Inv/Chq No.	Amount	Total
Grande Pointe Towers	1/10, n/30	Apr. 25/10	A-696	$1 380	
		Apr. 25/10	Chq #3166	700	
		Apr. 26/10	A-698	700	
			Balance owing		$1 380
Oak Bluff Banquet Hall	1/10, n/30	Apr. 28/10	A-700	$1 140	
		Apr. 30/10	A-702	1 620	
			Balance owing		$2 760
			Grand Total		$4 140

Accounting Procedures

Open-Invoice Accounting for Receivables

The open-invoice method of accounting for invoices issued by a business allows the business to keep track of each individual invoice and of any partial payments made against it. In contrast, other methods keep track only of the outstanding balance by combining all invoice balances owed by a customer. Simply Accounting uses the open-invoice method. Fully paid invoices can be removed (cleared) periodically.

Discounts for Early Payments

Air Care offers discounts to some regular customers if they pay their accounts within ten days. Full payment is expected in 30 days. Customers who pay by cheque or by credit card do not receive discounts. No discounts are allowed on partial payments.

Some suppliers with whom Air Care has accounts set up also offer discounts for early payments.

NSF Cheques

If a cheque is deposited from an account that does not have enough money to cover it, the bank may return it to the depositor as NSF (non-sufficient funds). The NSF cheque from a customer requires a reversing entry in the Receipts Journal. Simply Accounting can complete these reversals automatically. (See Keystrokes, page 179.) In most companies, the accounting department notifies the customer who wrote the NSF cheque to explain that the debt remains unpaid. Many companies charge an additional fee to the customer to recover their bank charges for the NSF cheque. A separate sales invoice should be prepared for the additional charge. NSF cheques to suppliers are handled in the same way, through reversing entries in the Payments Journal.

Taxes (GST and PST)

Air Care Services is a contracting service business using the regular method of calculating GST. GST, at the rate of 5 percent, charged and collected from customers will be recorded as a liability in *GST Charged on Services*. GST paid to suppliers will be recorded in *GST Paid on Purchases* as a decrease in tax liability. The balance owing, the difference between the GST charged and GST paid, or the request for a refund will be remitted to the Receiver General for Canada quarterly.

Air Care charges customers 7 percent PST on all sales and pays PST on some goods. Air Care is exempt from PST for purchases of items that are sold or used in service work because the customer pays PST on these products.

Cash and Credit Card Sales of Services

Cash and credit card transactions are a normal occurrence in most businesses. Simply Accounting has Paid By options to handle these transactions. When you choose the correct Paid By method, the program will debit *Cash in Bank* or *Credit Card Bank Account* instead of the *Accounts Receivable* control account. (See Keystrokes, page 172 and page 182.)

INSTRUCTIONS

1. **Record entries for the source documents** in Simply Accounting using all the information provided for Air Care Services. The procedures for entering each new type of transaction in this application are outlined step by step in the Keystrokes section following the source documents. These transactions are indicated with a ✓ in the completion box beside the source document. The page on which the relevant keystrokes begin is printed immediately below the check box.

2. **Print** the **reports and graphs** indicated on the following printing form after you have finished making your entries. Instructions for reports begin on page 187.

REPORTS

Accounts
- ☐ Chart of Accounts
- ☐ Account List
- ☐ General Journal Entries

Financials
- ✓ Balance Sheet: May 31
- ✓ Income Statement from May 1 to May 31
- ✓ Trial Balance date: May 31
- ✓ All Journal Entries: May 1 to May 31
- ✓ General Ledger accounts: 1300   4120   4140 from May 1 to May 31
- ☐ Statement of Cash Flows
- ✓ Cash Flow Projection Detail Report for account 1080 for 30 days

Taxes
- ✓ GST Report May 31
- ✓ PST Report May 31

Banking
- ☐ Cheque Log Report

Payables
- ☐ Supplier List
- ☐ Supplier Aged
- ☐ Aged Overdue Payables
- ☐ Purchase Journal Entries
- ☐ Payment Journal Entries

Receivables
- ☐ Customer List
- ✓ Customer Aged Detail for all customers
- ☐ Aged Overdue Receivables
- ✓ Sales Journal Entries: May 1 to May 31
- ✓ Receipt Journal Entries: May 1 to May 31
- ☐ Customer Statements

Mailing Labels
- ☐ Labels

Management Reports
- ☐ Ledger

GRAPHS
- ☐ Payables by Aging Period
- ☐ Payables by Supplier
- ☐ Receivables by Aging Period
- ☐ Receivables by Customer
- ✓ Sales vs Receivables
- ✓ Receivables Due vs Payables Due
- ✓ Revenues by Account
- ☐ Expenses by Account
- ✓ Expenses and Net Profit as % of Revenue

SOURCE DOCUMENTS

SESSION DATE — MAY 8, 2010

✓ **Sales Invoice #A-710**   **Dated May 1/10**

162   To Selkirk Furnaces Inc., $800 plus $40 GST and $56 PST for subcontracting work on apartment air-conditioning system. Invoice total, $896. Terms: 1/10, n/30. Create new Group account 4160 Subcontracting Revenue. Customize the sales invoice by removing the columns that are not used by Air Care Services.

✓ **Cash Receipt #20**   **Dated May 2/10**

168   From Grande Pointe Towers, cheque #3499 for $866.20, including $666.20 in full payment of invoice #A-696 and $200 in partial payment of invoice #A-698, including $13.80 discount for early payment. Customize the journal by changing the tabbing order.

✓ **Cash Sales Invoice #A-711**   **Dated May 3/10**

172   To Midwestern Funeral Home, $900 plus $45 GST and $63 PST for installation of air-conditioning equipment. Terms: Cash on completion of work. Received cheque #394 for $1 008 in full payment.

✓ **Sales Invoice #A-712**   **Dated May 3/10**

174   To Hazel Estates (use Full Add for the new customer), $1 600 plus $80 GST and $112 PST for installation of new furnace equipment. Invoice total $1 792. Terms: 1/10, n/30.

✓ **Bank Debit Memo #14321**   **Dated May 4/10**

179   From Flatlands Credit Union, cheque #3499 for $866.20 from Grand Pointe Towers has been returned because of non-sufficient funds. Reverse the payment and notify the customer of the outstanding charges.

✓ **Memo #1**   **Dated May 5/10**

181   From Owner: Edit the ledger record for Grande Pointe Towers to change the payment terms to net 1. Certified cheques will be requested in the future. Edit the records for all other customers to set the credit limit at $4 000.

✓ **Credit Card Sales Invoice #A-713**   **Dated May 5/10**

182   Sales Summary
To various one-time customers

Repairs Revenue	$ 600
Service Contract Revenue	800
GST charged	70
PST charged	98
Total deposited to credit card bank account	$1 568

✓ **Memo #2**   **Dated May 5/10**

184   From Owner: The work done for Hazel Estates included $800 plus $40 GST and $56 PST for repairs to the heating system. The revised and correct invoice total is $2 688. Adjust the posted entry (reference invoice #A-712).

✓ **Memo #3**   **Dated May 5/10**

186   Create shortcuts for tasks and transactions in other modules.

☐ **Cheque Copy #101**   **Dated May 5/10**

To Beausejour Chimney Products, $1 584 in payment of account, including $16 discount for early payment. Reference invoice #B-894.

☐ **Purchase Invoice #W-1993**   **Dated May 6/10**

From Willow Garage, $60 for gasoline, including taxes (use tax code IN) for weekly fill-up of van. Store the transaction as a weekly recurring entry. Terms: net 30.

☐ **Purchase Invoice #SA-2309**   **Dated May 6/10**

From Steinbach Airconditioning, $400 plus $20 GST. Invoice total $420 for air-conditioning parts, filters, coils, etc. Terms: 1/10, n/30. Store as bi-weekly recurring transaction.

☐ **Sales Invoice #A-714**   **Dated May 7/10**

To Brandon School Board, $500 plus $25 GST and $35 PST for installation of new pipes on school furnace. Invoice total $560. Terms: 1/10, n/30.

☐ **Cheque Copy #102**   **Dated May 7/10**

To Steinbach Airconditioning, $1 485 in payment of account, including $15 discount for early payment. Reference invoice #SA-2141.

☐ **Cheque Copy #103**   **Dated May 8/10**

To Willow Garage, $1 100 in payment of account. Reference invoice #W-1142.

☐ **Purchase Invoice #BH-42001**   **Dated May 8/10**

From Brandon Hardware, $500 plus $25 GST and $35 PST for new ladders and tools. Invoice total $560. Terms: net 15.

☐ **Sales Invoice #A-715**   **Dated May 8/10**

To Vinod Residence (use Full Add for the new customer), $400 plus $20 GST and $28 PST for repairs. Invoice total $448. Terms: 1/10, n/30.

SESSION DATE — MAY 15, 2010

☐ **Bank Credit Memo #21432**   **Dated May 9/10**

From Flatlands Credit Union, $3 000 loan for new service equipment approved and deposited to bank account. Principal of six-month loan and interest at 7.5% to be paid in full at the end of six months.

☐ **Cash Receipt #21**   **Dated May 9/10**

From Oak Bluff Banquet Hall, cheque #2995 for $1 900, including $1 140 in full payment of invoice #A-700 and $760 in partial payment of invoice #A-702.

☐ **Sales Invoice #A-716**   **Dated May 9/10**

To Selkirk Furnaces Inc., $1 200 plus $60 GST and $84 PST for subcontracting work. Invoice total $1 344. Terms: 1/10, n/30.

☐ **Cash Receipt #22**   **Dated May 10/10**

From Selkirk Furnaces Inc., cheque #533 for $887.04 in payment of account, including $8.96 discount for early payment. Reference invoice #A-710.

☐ **Cash Receipt #23**   **Dated May 11/10**

From Hazel Estates, cheque #230 for $2 661.12 in full payment of account, including $26.88 discount for early payment. Reference invoice #A-712.

☐ **Cash Receipt #24**   **Dated May 12/10**

From Vinod Residence, cheque #432 for $443.52 in payment of account, including $4.48 discount for early payment. Reference invoice #A-715.

⚠ **WARNING!**
Do not include the discount for the second invoice in the payment to Steinbach.

▌ **NOTES**
Vinod Residence
☐ (contact Viran Vinod)
56 House St.
Winnipeg, MB R2P 8K1
Tel: (204) 761-8114
E-mail: v.vinod@interlog.com
Terms: 1/10, n/30
Revenue account: 4120
Tax code: GP
Credit limit: $2 000

⚠ **WARNING!**
Do not include the discount for the second invoice in the receipt from Oak Bluffs Banquet Hall.

NOTES

Remember to change the amounts if you recall the sales summary.

✓ **Credit Card Sales Invoice #A-717**   **Dated May 12/10**

184   Sales Summary
To various one-time customers

Repairs Revenue	$ 500
Service Contracts	600
GST charged	55
PST charged	77
Total deposited to credit card bank account	$1 232

☐ **Purchase Invoice #W-2356**   **Dated May 13/10**

From Willow Garage, $60 for gasoline, including taxes (use tax code IN) for weekly fill-up of van. Terms: net 30 days. Recall stored entry.

☐ **Cash Purchase Invoice #UPS-3467**   **Dated May 14/10**

From UPS Delivery, $60 for special delivery of air-conditioner parts plus $3 GST. Invoice total $63. Issued cheque #104 in full payment. Create new Group account 5130 Delivery Expenses. Edit the supplier record to add the new expense account as the default expense account.

NOTES

Click the View Suppliers shortcut to open the Suppliers window. Double click UPS Delivery to open the ledger record. Refer to page 138 if you need help with editing a supplier record.

☐ **Cash Receipt #25**   **Dated May 15/10**

From Grande Pointe Towers, certified cheque #3682 for $1 380 in payment of account. Reference invoices #A-696 and A-698.

SESSION DATE — MAY 22, 2010

☐

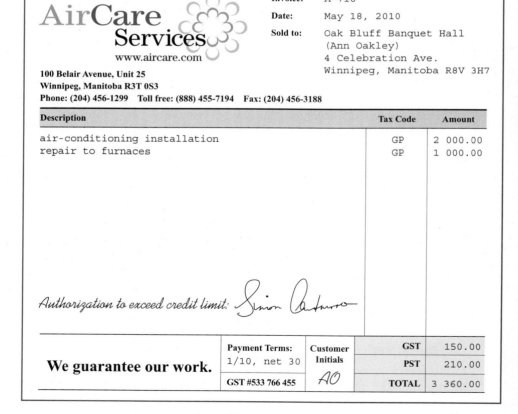

AirCare Services		
www.aircare.com		

100 Belair Avenue, Unit 25
Winnipeg, Manitoba R3T 0S3
Phone: (204) 456-1299   Toll free: (888) 455-7194   Fax: (204) 456-3188

Invoice:	A-718
Date:	May 18, 2010
Sold to:	Oak Bluff Banquet Hall (Ann Oakley) 4 Celebration Ave. Winnipeg, Manitoba R8V 3H7

Description	Tax Code	Amount
air-conditioning installation	GP	2 000.00
repair to furnaces	GP	1 000.00

Authorization to exceed credit limit: _____

We guarantee our work.

Payment Terms: 1/10, net 30	Customer Initials	GST	150.00
	AO	PST	210.00
GST #533 766 455		TOTAL	3 360.00

Bank Debit Memo #37191   **Dated May 18/10**

From Flatlands Credit Union, cheque #432 for $443.52 from Vinod Residence has been returned because of non-sufficient funds. Reverse the payment and notify the customer of the outstanding charges.

Memo #4   **Dated May 18/10**

Edit the ledger record for Vinod Residence to set the credit limit to zero and terms to net 1. The customer will be placed on cash-only terms.

Cash Receipt #26   **Dated May 19/10**

From Selkirk Furnaces Inc., cheque #586 for $1 330.56 in payment of account, including $13.44 discount for early payment. Reference invoice #A-716.

NOTES
Remember to change the account as well as the amounts if you recall the sales summary.

AirCare Services

www.aircare.com

Invoice:	A-719
Date:	May 19, 2010
Sold to:	Sales Summary

100 Belair Avenue, Unit 25
Winnipeg, Manitoba R3T 0S3
Phone: (204) 456-1299   Toll free: (888) 455-7194   Fax: (204) 456-3188

Description	Tax Code	Amount
Repairs	GP	600.00
Service Contracts	GP	400.00

Deposited to credit card bank account
May 19/10:

Thank you.

Payment Terms: Credit Card	Customer Initials	GST	50.00
		PST	70.00
Business No.: 533 766 455		**TOTAL**	1 120.00

Purchase Invoice #W-2893   **Dated May 20/10**

From Willow Garage, $75 for gasoline, including taxes for weekly fill-up of van. Terms: net 30 days. Recall the stored entry, edit the amount and save the changed entry.

Purchase Invoice #SA-2579   **Dated May 20/10**

From Steinbach Airconditioning, $400 plus $20 GST for air-conditioning parts and filters, etc. Invoice total $420. Terms: 1/10, n/30. Recall stored entry.

Cheque Copy #105   **Dated May 21/10**

To Brandon Hardware, $560 in payment of account. Reference invoice #BH-42001.

Cash Purchase Invoice #SAA-1098   **Dated May 22/10**

From Starbuck Advertising Agency, $1 100 plus $55 GST and $77 PST for brochures and flyers. Invoice total, $1 232. Paid by cheque #106.

```
┌─────────────────────────────────────────────────────────────────────┐
│  Vinod Residence                                   ┌──────────────┐   │
│  56 House St.                                      │   No: 432    │   │
│  Winnipeg, MN  R2P 8K1                             └──────────────┘   │
│                                                                       │
│                                          Date  2 2 0 5 2 0 1 0        │
│                                                D D M M Y Y Y Y        │
│                                                                       │
│  Pay to the order of   Air Care Services              $ 448.00       │
│                                                                       │
│  ─────────────── Four hundred forty-eight dollars ──── 00/100 Dollars │
│                                                                       │
│   F  Flatlands Credit Union                                           │
│      389 Prairie Blvd.                                                │
│      Winnipeg MN R2P 1B6                                              │
│                                                    Viren Vinod        │
│      ⑈⑈─── 92999⑈⑈16883 432                              Signature   │
│  ─ ─ ─ ─ ─ ─ ─ ─ ─ ─ ─ ─ ─ ─ ─ ─ ─ ─ ─ ─ ─ ─ ─ ─ ─ ─ ─ ─ ─ ─ ─ ─ ─  │
│  Re:  pay invoice #A-715              $448.00            No: 432      │
│       CERTIFIED Cheque replaces NSF cheque (receipt #27)  May 22, 2010│
└─────────────────────────────────────────────────────────────────────┘
```

NOTES

Staples Business Depot
Expense account: 1340
Tax code: GP
Leave the remaining fields blank.

Cash Purchase Invoice #BD-4821   Dated May 22/10

From Staples Business Depot (use Full Add for the new supplier), $140 plus $7.00 GST and $9.80 PST for stationery and office supplies. Invoice total, $156.80. Paid by cheque #107.

Sales Invoice #A-720   Dated May 22/10

To Grande Pointe Towers, $2 400 plus $120 GST and $168 PST for installation of new furnace and air-conditioning unit. Invoice total, $2 688. Terms: net 1.

Cash Purchase Invoice #MH-44371   Dated May 22/10

From Manitoba Hydro, $400 plus $20 GST for two months of hydro service. Invoice total, $420. Paid by cheque #108.

SESSION DATE — MAY 31, 2010

Purchase Invoice #KE-679   Dated May 24/10

From Killarney Furnace Equipment, $3 000 plus $150 GST and $210 PST for new service equipment. Invoice total, $3 360. Terms: 1/5, n/30.

Cash Purchase Invoice #BD-6113   Dated May 25/10

From Staples Business Depot, $40 plus $2.00 GST and $2.80 PST for stationery and other office supplies. Invoice total, $44.80. Paid by cheque #109.

Cash Purchase Invoice #MT-36128   Dated May 25/10

From Manitoba Telephone, $130 plus $6.50 GST and $9.10 PST for telephone and Internet service. Invoice total, $145.60. Paid by cheque #110.

Sales Invoice #A-721   Dated May 26/10

To Felicia Mountbatten (use Quick Add for the new customer), $1 600 plus $80 GST and $112 PST for installation services. Invoice total $1 792. Terms: net 1.

Sales Invoice #A-722   Dated May 26/10

To Midwestern Funeral Home, $1 000 plus $50 GST and $70 PST for repair work on furnace and heating system. Invoice total $1 120. Terms: 1/10, n/30. Remember to edit the terms for the invoice.

NOTES

When you use Quick Add, you can type the address in the Ship To field so that it will appear on the printed invoice. The new customer's name appears in the Sold To and Ship To fields.

Grande Pointe Towers
77 LaPointe Cr.
Winnipeg, MN R2G 4D1
Tel: (204) 322-7500

No: 4543

Date 2 6 0 5 2 0 1 0
D D M M Y Y Y Y

Pay to the order of   Air Care Services $ 2,688.00

————— Two Thousand Six Hundred Eighty-eight dollars ——— 00 /100 **Dollars**

F **Flatlands Credit Union**
389 Prairie Blvd.
Winnipeg MN R2P 1B6

⑈—— 92999–⑈46771 4543

Joplie Grande
Signature

Re: pay invoice #A-720 $2,688.00   No: 4543
     (receipt #28)   May 26, 2010

Credit Card Sales Invoice #A-723   **Dated May 26/10**

Sales Summary
To various one-time customers

Repairs Revenue	$400
Installation Revenue	400
GST charged	40
PST charged	56
Total deposited to credit card bank account	$896

Cheque Copy #111   **Dated May 28/10**

To Killarney Furnace Equipment, $3 326.40 in payment of account, including $33.60 discount for early payment. Reference invoice #KE-679.

Bank Debit Memo #55131   **Dated May 30/10**

From Flatlands Credit Union, pre-authorized monthly payroll for employees

Wages and payroll expenses	$4 000
Payroll services fee	100
GST paid on payroll service	5
Total withdrawal	$4 105

Memo #5   **Dated May 31/10**

From Owner: Create three new Group expense accounts for supplies used during the month: 5125 Air Conditioning Parts Used
       5135 Furnace Parts Used
       5165 Office Supplies Used
Enter adjustments for supplies used: Air Conditioning Parts $600
                         Furnace Parts   350
                         Office Supplies   200

Bank Debit Memo #56159   **Dated May 31/10**

From Flatlands Credit Union, pre-authorized withdrawals for service charges, mortgage and loan payments

Bank charges, including NSF cheques	$ 80
Interest expense	900
Loan principal repayment	1 000
Mortgage principal repayment	200

NOTES
Enter the payroll transaction in the General Journal.
Remember to add the sales tax details for GST Paid on Purchases.

KEYSTROKES

Opening Data Files

Restore the backup file **SimData\aircare1.CAB** to **SimData\Aircare\aircare** to open the data files for Air Care Services.

Type `May 8 2010` to enter the first session date.

Click **OK** to see the following warning statement:

This warning appears whenever you advance the session date by more than one week. Normally a business would update its accounting records more frequently. If you have entered the correct date,

Click **OK** to accept the date entered and display the Home window.

The Payroll, Inventory and Project ledger names do not appear in the Modules pane list. These ledgers are hidden because they are not set up.

Accounting for Sales

Sales are entered in the Sales Journal indicated by the Bills icon in the Receivables module Home window:

SIMPLY VERSION

Icon labels are the same for all company types.

Click the Sales Invoices icon

to open the Sales Journal. In the Simply Classic view, this icon is labelled Sales.

CLASSIC VIEW

Click the Sales icon

to open the Sales Journal.

You can enter sales from the Bills icon in the Receivables window. The Bills label is used for Construction/Contracting companies. For other company types, the label for this icon may be Sales, Invoices, Sales Invoices, Customer Invoices, Client Invoices, Statements or Charges. The icon itself does not change.

Click the **Bills icon** to open the The Sales Journal input form:

Most tool bar buttons in the Sales Journal are familiar from other journals — Home window, Daily Business Manager, Store, Recall, Undo, Customize Journal, Calculator and Allocate. Print and E-mail buttons allow you to print or e-mail the invoice before posting to provide a customer or store copy of the sales invoice. You can also use tool buttons to preview an invoice, change print settings and to adjust or reverse a posted invoice. The tools for Invoice Lookup, Additional Information, Track Shipments and Add Time Slip Activities will be explained in later applications.

Pay Later is correctly selected as the payment option for this regular sale.

Click   the **Sold To** (Customer) **field list arrow** to obtain the list of customers as shown on the following screen:

Click   **Selkirk Furnaces Inc.**, the customer in the first source document, to select and enter it.

Notice that the customer's name and address have been added to your input form. If you have made an error in your selection, click the customer list arrow and start again. By default, the Sold To and the Ship To fields are completed from the customer's ledger record. You can edit the shipping address if necessary. If you have selected the correct customer, you can skip over the shipping information.

The invoice number, 710, the numeric portion, is entered and correct. It is updated automatically by the program. The payment terms and tax code for the customer have also been entered. When a default revenue account is entered in the customer's record, it will also be included on the invoice form.

The session date appears by default so you need to change it. Enter the date on which the transaction took place, May 1, 2010.

Click   the **Date field Calendar icon** 🗓️ .

Click   **1**

If you want, you can enter a quantity (one for the service, in this case) and a price per unit in the Price field and let the program calculate the amount by multiplying the two together. You can use this method if you are selling more than one item that is not an inventory item.

Click   the **Description field** on the first line. The Description field is used to enter a description or comment concerning the sale.

Type   subcontracting - apartment building

Press   (tab) .

The cursor is now in the Price field. The Price field also refers to unit prices; it is not needed for the contract.

Press   (tab) .

The cursor should now be positioned in the Amount field, where you will enter the amount for this invoice before taxes.

Type   800 **Press** (tab) .

The cursor is now positioned in the Tax field. The default tax code for the customer, GP, is entered from the customer record details in the data files and it is correct. Customers pay both GST and PST on services. The invoice subtotal and total have been updated.

Press   (enter) to see the tax code descriptions set up for Air Care Services:

NOTES
You can also press (tab) repeatedly to move to any field you need.

NOTES
Entering a negative amount in the Amount field will generate a debit entry for the sale with a credit to Accounts Receivable.

The tax code options are: charge **No Tax** on the sale; code **G**, charge GST only; code **P**, charge PST only; code **GP**, charge both GST and PST; and code **IN**, both GST and PST are charged and included in the price. Notice that PST is described as non-refundable.

NOTES
When you select a tax code from the selection list, the cursor advances to the next invoice field. When you choose Cancel, the cursor does not move to the next field.

You can select a different tax code from this list if the default is incorrect. Click the correct code and then click Select. You will return to the Sales Journal with the cursor in the Account field.

Click   **Cancel** to return to the journal.

Press   (tab) to advance to the Account field.

The Account field in a sales invoice refers to the credit portion of the journal entry, usually a revenue account. Again, you cannot access *Accounts Receivable*, the linked account, directly. The software will automatically debit the *Accounts Receivable* control account in the General Ledger when you enter positive amounts.

You may set up a default revenue account for customers, just as you set up default expense accounts for suppliers. Because Air Care customers use more than one revenue account, we have not entered default accounts for them. In the Account field, you can choose an account from the list of accounts or create a new account, just like any other account field. We need to create a new revenue account for this sale.

NOTES
You can choose any postable account as the default revenue account for customers just as you can use any account as the default expense account for suppliers.

Type   4160

Press   (enter) .

Press   (enter) to open the Add An Account wizard (Add An Account is selected).

NOTES
Because Add An Account is already selected, pressing (enter) will choose it.

Press (tab) .

Type Subcontracting Revenue as the **account name** and **accept** the remaining **defaults**. **Click Finish** to return to the journal. The account number is added to the journal.

Press (tab) to advance the cursor to line 2 in the Item field, ready for additional sale items if necessary.

The Comments field can be used in two ways: you can set up a default comment for the business that appears on all invoices, or you can enter a comment at the time of the sale. You can add to or change a default comment if you want. We will add a comment.

Click the **Comments field**.

Type We guarantee our work.

The payment terms have been set up as defaults for customers as 1 percent discount in 10 days with net payment due in 30 days. You can change terms for individual customers or sales invoices.

Click the **List icon beside the PST amount field** to see the detailed summary of taxes included in the sale:

Close the **Tax Summary window** to return to the invoice.

The transaction is now complete, and your invoice should resemble the following:

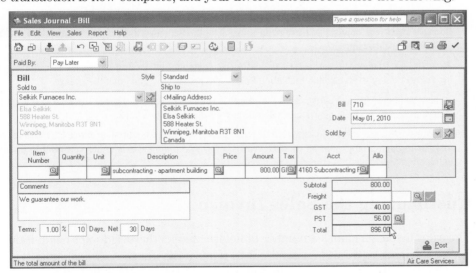

Before storing, posting or printing a sales journal entry, review it carefully.

Reviewing the Sales Journal Entry

Choose the **Report menu** and **click Display Sales Journal Entry**.

NOTES
Payment terms can be modified for individual customers in the Receivables Ledger. You can also edit the terms for individual sales in the Sales Journal.

NOTES
If necessary, such as for rounding errors, you can edit the tax amounts on the Tax Summary screen.

NOTES
You can also press (ctrl) + J to open the journal display.

You will display the transaction you have entered as shown:

Review the **journal entry** to check for mistakes.

You can see that *Accounts Receivable*, the control account, has been updated automatically by the Simply Accounting program because the Receivables and General ledgers are fully integrated. All credit sales are debited to *Accounts Receivable*, the default linked account for the Receivables Ledger. *GST Charged on Services* has also been updated correctly because of the tax code you entered and because *GST Charged on Services* was defined as the GST linked account for sales. Similarly, *PST Payable* is defined as the linked account for PST collected from customers and it too is updated correctly because of the tax code. You did not need to enter any of these accounts directly in the Sales Journal. The balance owing by this customer is also directly updated as a result of the Sales Journal entry.

Close   the **display** to return to the Sales Journal input screen.

CORRECTING THE SALES JOURNAL ENTRY BEFORE POSTING

Move to the field that has the error. **Press** (tab) to move forward through the fields or **press** (shift) and (tab) together to move back to a previous field. This will highlight the field information so you can change it. **Type** the **correct information** and **press** (tab) to enter it.

You can also use the mouse to **point** to a field and **drag** through the **incorrect information** to highlight it. **Type** the **correct information** and **press** (tab) to enter it.

If the customer is incorrect, **reselect** from the **Customer** list by **clicking** the **Customer list arrow**. **Click** the name of the **correct customer**.

Click an **incorrect amount** or description to highlight it. Then **type** the **correct information** and **press** (tab) to enter the change.

To correct an account number or tax code, **click** the **Account List icon** to display the selection list. **Click** the **correct entry** to highlight it, then **click Select** and **press** (tab) to enter the change.

To insert a line or remove a line, **click** the **line** that you need to move. **Choose** the **Edit menu** and **click Insert Line** and **type** the new line or **click Remove Line** to delete a line.

To discard the entry and begin again, **click** ☒ **(Close)** to close the journal or **click** ↰ **(Undo)** on the tool bar to open a blank journal window. When Simply Accounting asks whether you want to discard the entry, **click Yes** to confirm your decision.

Customizing the Sales Invoice

The sales invoice includes a number of fields/columns that we do not need. Before saving the invoice, we will customize it to remove the unnecessary columns.

The Premium Version has different invoice styles already built in.

Click   the **Style list arrow** as shown to see the predefined style options:

NOTES
Other Receivables Ledger linked accounts will be used and explained later. These are the Receivables bank account, freight revenue account and sales discount account.

NOTES
To correct Sales Journal entries after posting, refer to page 184 and Appendix C.

SIMPLY VERSION

Different invoice styles are not available in the Simply version, so you will skip this step. The Standard Style is the only one used. You can still hide or show any columns by customizing the invoice, as shown on page 167.

There are three predefined invoice styles for different business types. Each style displays a different combination of columns. The Standard Style, the default, includes all columns. We will select the Professional style because it more closely matches Air Care's needs. Both the Standard and Retail styles include columns for inventory and orders and Air Care does not use these features.

> **Click**   **Professional** to modify the columns that are displayed as shown:

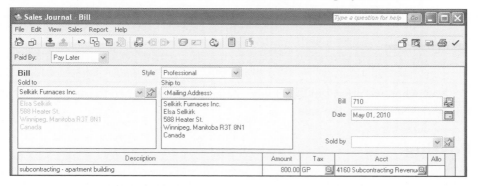

We can now continue to modify the journal. Air Care does not allocate to projects so we can also remove the Allocations column.

> **Click**   the **Customize Journal tool** or **choose** the **View menu** and **click** **Customize Journal** to open the Settings options for Sales Invoices:

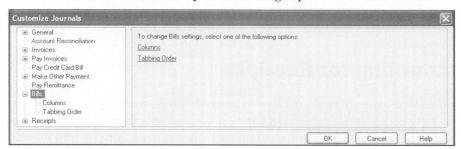

We can modify the selection of columns and the order in which the tab key advances you from one part of the invoice to another. For the Bills (Sales Invoices), we will modify the column selections. For Receipts, we will modify the tabbing order.

> **Click**   **Columns** to open the column selection window:

Most of the fields we want to hide are removed (checkmarks added) because the Professional Style has been selected. The columns we can remove are listed under the For Professional Style, Do Not Show These Columns heading. We can remove additional columns by clicking the check boxes. The Form Options button accesses printer setup options for the forms. Modifying printed forms is covered in Appendix G on the Student CD-ROM.

> **Click**   the **check box** for **Allocations**.

NOTES
You can also customize journals by dragging the column headings to change the size of columns. Point to the column heading margin. When the arrow changes to a double-headed arrow, drag the margin to its new location or size. Dragging the right column margin to the left until it overlaps the next column will remove that column. You can restore missing columns from the Customize Journal window.

NOTES
When Orders and Quotes are used (Company Settings, Features), they will appear on the list as well. You can customize orders and quotes differently from invoices if you want (in the Premium version).

SIMPLY VERSION
The settings for the Standard Style invoice are displayed so all check boxes will be blank. You must click the check boxes for Item Number, Quantity Shipped, Price, Unit, and Allocations to create the form we show here. Quantity On Order and Quantity On Back Order are dimmed because orders are not used by Air Care.
You cannot customize orders and quotes separately from invoices.

NOTES
Customizing the journal does not change the printed invoice. Refer to Appendix G on the Student CD-ROM to learn how to customize printed invoices and other forms.

Click **OK** to return to the modified journal:

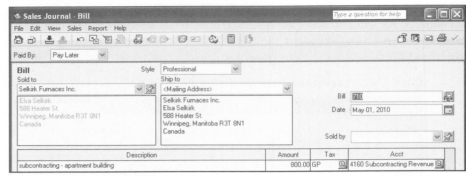

Now when we press the (tab) key, the cursor will advance to the next field, and it will be one we use for the sale.

Posting

NOTES
You can also choose the Sales menu and click Post or press (alt) + P to save your transaction.

When you are certain that you have entered the transaction correctly, you must post it.

Click the **Post button** [Post]. **Click OK** to confirm successful posting.

A new blank Sales Journal form appears on the screen.

Close the **Sales Journal** because the next transaction is a receipt.

Notice that the balance for Selkirk Furnaces in the Customers list has been updated.

Accounting for Receipts

NOTES
A discount of 1 percent for paying within 10 days is comparable to an interest penalty of 18 percent per year — it costs the customer 1 percent to borrow the money for the extra 20 days.

Receipts from customers are entered in much the same way as payments to suppliers. After you choose the customer, outstanding invoices appear automatically and you can enter the payment amounts without entering any accounts. Air Care offers early payment discounts as an incentive to customers to pay their accounts promptly.

Receipts are entered in the Receipts Journal indicated by the hand pointer:

CLASSIC VIEW
The Receipts icon is located below the Sales icon. It has no shortcuts list arrow.

Click the **Receipts icon** to open the Receipts Journal:

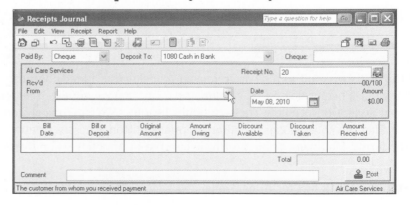

SIMPLY VERSION
The Refresh tools do not appear in the Simply version. Invoice replaces Bill in the journal column headings.

NOTES
The Refresh tools will update the journal with changes made by other users, such as the addition of new invoices.

As with payments to suppliers, you cannot enter account numbers in the Receipts Journal. You need to enter only the amount paid on the appropriate invoice line. The program automatically creates the journal entry.

As with the Sales Invoice, you can customize the journal.

Click   the **Customize Journal tool** 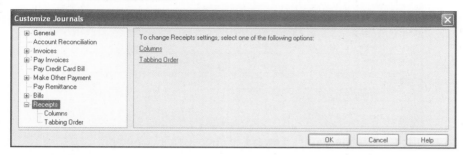 or **choose** the **View menu** and **click Customize Journal**:

Click   **Columns** to open the customization options for columns.

When they are not needed, you can remove the Invoice Date and the two Discount columns. Air Care offers customer discounts so we must include these columns.

Click   **Tabbing Order** to continue:

You can choose the default tabbing order or you can change the order. We will change the order so that after choosing the customer, the cursor will move to the cheque number field. This field is in the upper right corner. With the default tabbing order, the cursor reaches this field last, making it easy to forget to enter the number.

Click   **Custom Tabbing Order** to continue:

Notice that Cheque Number appears before Customer Name. However, when you open the Receipts Journal, the cursor starts in the Customer Name field, so the Cheque Number field is last. We want the next field to be the Cheque Number.

To move a field, select it and then click the Move Fields Up and Down arrows beside the list until you have the order you want.

Click   **Cheque Number**.

NOTES
You can customize the order further by making the date field follow the cheque number, and so on, until the customer address fields are last.
You can also choose to remove the Address fields from the tabbing order entirely. To access the address in that case, you can click the field.

Click the **Move Fields Down button** beside the Tabbing Order list. This will place Cheque Number after the Customer Name.

Click **OK** to return to the form.

Click the **Customer (Rcv'd From) list arrow** to display the Customer list:

NOTES
Simply Accounting allows you to set up more than one bank account. If more than one bank account is set up, choose the account from the Deposit To drop-down list.

Click **Grande Pointe Towers** to choose this customer:

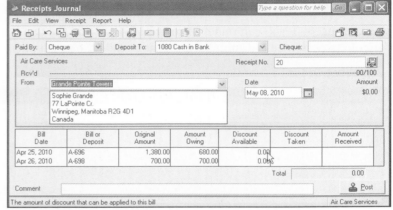

The customer's name and address have been added to your input form, together with all outstanding invoices for the customer. Notice that no discount appears in the Discount Available fields because the session date is past the ten-day discount period.

Air Care has a single bank account so it is correctly selected in the Deposit To field. If you have chosen the wrong customer, display the list again and click the correct customer. If you have selected correctly,

NOTES
You can use the Lookup button to review a receipt, or to reverse it (see page 179).

Press (tab) to move to the **Cheque field**.

Type 3499

The Receipt No. field records the receipt number that increases automatically. There is a Lookup icon beside the Receipt No. field.

We need to replace the session date with the date for this transaction.

SIMPLY VERSION
The cursor advances to the column labelled Invoice Date.

Choose May 2 from the Date field pop-up calendar. **Press** (tab) to move the cursor to the Bill Date field. The discounts are now available:

NOTES
For other company types, the Bill Date column may be labelled Statement Date, Invoice Date and so on.

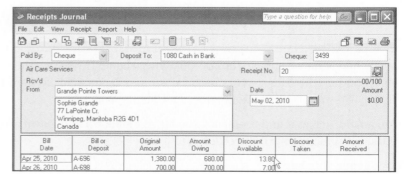

Notice that the discount is 1 percent of the original amount, not the amount owing. Until the discount period has passed, the full discount remains available.

Press (tab) to advance to the Discount Taken field.

Discount amounts can be changed or deleted. We will accept this discount.

Press (tab) to advance to the Amount Received field.

By default, the amount owing on the first invoice is shown and highlighted. All outstanding invoices are listed on the screen. For this invoice, the full amount is being paid so you can accept the default. Notice that the discount has been subtracted from the amount received.

Press (tab) to accept the amount in the Amount Received field.

The cursor will advance to the Discount Taken field for the next invoice:

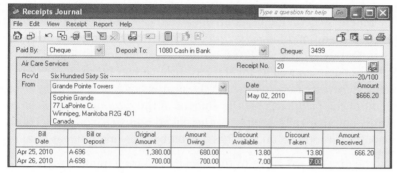

Because the payment for this invoice is only a partial payment, we need to remove the discount.

Press (del) to remove the discount for the second invoice.

Press (tab) to advance to the Amount Received field.

This time the full invoice amount is entered because the discount has been changed to zero. However, the full amount is not being paid, so we must edit the amount. To replace the highlighted default amount,

Type 200

Press (tab) to enter the new amount and complete the invoice as shown:

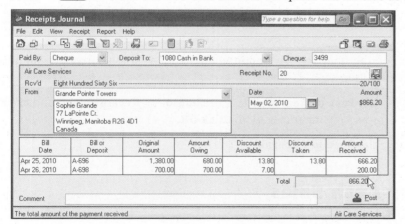

Notice that the upper cheque portion of the form has also been completed. In making Receipts Journal entries, you do not need to enter any accounts because Simply Accounting chooses the linked bank and receivable accounts defined for the Receivables Ledger to create the journal entry.

You have made all the entries for this transaction, so you are ready to review before posting your transaction.

Reviewing the Receipts Journal Entry

Choose the **Report menu** and **click Display Receipts Journal Entry** to display the transaction you have entered as follows:

Here you can see the related journal entry created for the Receipts Journal transaction. The Simply Accounting program updates the General Ledger *Accounts Receivable* control account and *Cash in Bank* because the Receivables and General ledgers are fully integrated. *Cash in Bank* is defined as the default linked bank account for the Receivables Ledger as well as for the Payables Ledger because Air Care has only one bank account. *Accounts Receivable* and the customer's balance owing are reduced by the full amount of the payment plus the amount of the discount taken ($880). The discount amount is automatically debited to the linked *Sales Discounts* account. *Sales Discounts* is a contra-revenue account. It has a debit balance and reduces total revenue.

Close the **display** to return to the Receipts Journal input screen.

CORRECTING THE RECEIPTS JOURNAL ENTRY BEFORE POSTING

Move to the field with the error. **Press** (tab) to move forward or (shift) and (tab) together to move back to a previous field. This will highlight the field contents. **Type** the **correct information** and **press** (tab) to enter it.

You can also use the mouse to **point** to a field and **drag** through the **incorrect information** to highlight it. **Type** the **correct information** and **press** (tab) to enter it.

If the customer is incorrect, **reselect** from the **Customer** list by **clicking** the **Customer list arrow**. **Click** the name of the correct **customer**. To confirm that you want to discard the current transaction, **click Yes** to display the outstanding invoices for the correct customer. **Type** the **correct** receipt **information**.

You can also discard the entry. **Click** ☒ or ↺ and then **click Yes** to confirm.

Posting

When you are certain that you have entered all the information correctly, you must post the transaction to save it.

Click the **Post button** 🔲 Post or **choose** the **Receipt menu** and **click Post** to save your transaction. **Click OK.**

Close the **Receipts Journal**.

Entering Cash Sales

To enter the cash sale on May 3,

Click the **Bills icon** 🔲 Bills to open the Sales Journal.

Simply SIMPLY VERSION
Click the Sales Invoices icon
🔲 Sales Invoices ▾ to open the Sales Journal.

Click   the **Paid By list arrow** to view the payment options — Pay Later, Cash, Cheque and Credit Card:

Click   **Cheque** as the method of payment to change the invoice screen as shown here:

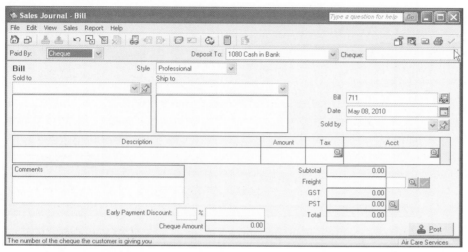

When you choose Cheque as the method of payment, a cheque number field is added in the upper right corner of the invoice so that you can add the customer's cheque number. When you choose Cash, the cheque number field is not included.

Notice that the invoice number has also been increased automatically.

In the payment terms section, the Net Days field has been removed and a Cheque Amount field has been added.

Press   ⌨(tab) **twice** to advance to the Cheque number field.

Type   394 **Press** ⌨(tab) to advance to the Sold To field.

Type   M

Midwestern Funeral Home is added to the Sold To field because it is the first customer entry beginning with M. The rest of the name is still highlighted in case you want to continue typing another name.

Enter   **May 3** in the Date field as the transaction date.

Enter   a **description**. **Press** ⌨(tab) to advance to the Amount field. **Type**   900

Double click the **Account field**.

Click   **Suggested Accounts** below the account list to modify the list:

The list of suggested accounts now includes only Revenue accounts because we are in the Sales Journal. This shorter list makes it easier to select the correct account. For purchases, only expense accounts will be listed. You can switch back to the complete account list at any time by selecting **All Accounts**. The Suggested Accounts button remains selected when we close the journal until we change the selection again.

Click **4100 Installation Revenue**. **Press** (enter).

Click the **Comments field**. **Type** Thank you to complete the sales entry:

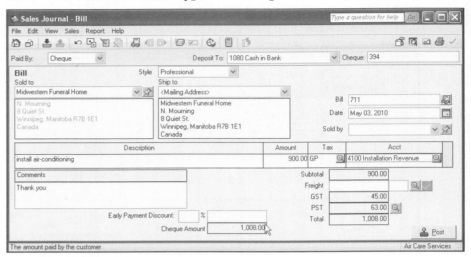

As usual you should review the entry.

Choose the **Report menu** and **click Display Sales Journal Entry**. Your display should look like the one shown here:

Notice that *Cash in Bank* is debited automatically instead of *Accounts Receivable* because we selected Cheque as the method of payment.

Close the **display** when you have finished. **Make corrections** if necessary.

Click Post ![Post] to save the entry. **Click OK**. Leave the journal open.

Adding a New Customer

The next sale is to a new customer who should be added to your files. We will add the customer directly from the Sales Journal.

Click the **Paid By field** and **choose Pay Later** as the method of payment. The date is correct.

Click the **Sold To** (Customer) **field**.

Type Hazel Estates

Press (tab) to display the warning that you have typed a name that is not on the list and the option to add a ledger record:

The options are the same as for new suppliers. If you typed an incorrect name, click **Cancel** to return to the journal and start again. If you typed the name correctly, you can choose to add the customer's name only — **Quick Add** — or to add a full customer record with the **Full Add** option. If you need to change any defaults, you must choose the Full Add option. You can still skip customer fields that you do not need. The remaining option, **Continue**, will add the customer's name to the journal entry but will not create a ledger record for the customer or add the customer to the other Receivables Ledger reports.

Click   **Full Add** to open the customer's Address information screen:

You are ready to enter your new customer. The Customer field is completed with the new name highlighted for editing if necessary. The Customer name is the only required field for new customer records. Because it is already entered, the * reminder symbol for required fields has been removed.

The field we need next is the Contact field. Enter the name of the particular individual Air Care normally deals with.

Click   the **Contact field**.

Type   Joelle Beausoleil

Press   (tab) to move the cursor to the Street 1 field.

Type   488 Sunshine St. **Press** (tab).

Type   Suite 1200 **Press** (tab) to move to and select the City field.

Notice that the city, province and country in which Air Care is located have been entered by default from the Address Settings. The province is correct but you must change the city.

Type   West St. Paul

Click   the **Postal Code field**.

You do not need to use capital letters or to leave a space within Canadian postal codes. The program will make these adjustments.

Type r4g5h3

Click the **Phone 1 field**. The postal code format is corrected automatically.

You do not need to add spaces, dashes or brackets for telephone numbers. Telephone and fax numbers may be entered with or without the area code.

Type 2043677611 **Press** (tab).

Type 8773679000 **Press** (tab) to move to the Fax field.

Type 2043692191 **Press** (tab) to advance to the E-mail field.

Notice that the format for telephone and fax numbers is corrected automatically.

E-mail and Web addresses are typed exactly as you would type them in your regular Internet and e-mail access programs. You can also add these details later when you actually want to use them. When you click the Web or E-mail buttons, you will be prompted to enter the addresses if they are not part of the customer's record already.

Type JB@hazelestates.com **Press** (tab).

Type www.hazelestates.com

When salespersons are set up, you can choose the name of the regular sales contact person for a customer from the drop-down list in the **Salesperson** field. Air Care does not have salespersons set up. Salespersons are covered in Chapter 9.

Hazel Estates is completing its first sale on May 3 but the session date is entered as the default date in the **Customer Since** field.

Choose May 3 from the Customer Since field calendar icon.

The **Internal Customer** option applies when one department supplies services to another and charges for these services. The option is available when time and billing is used. If the customer no longer buys from the company, but you still want to keep the record on file, mark the customer as **Inactive**. The **Balance Owing** and **Date Of Last Sale** will be entered automatically by the program based on the customer's transactions.

Click the **Ship-to Address tab**.

You can enter multiple customer addresses, and apply your own labels for these addresses. For example, you may have separate summer and winter addresses for residential customers or different store locations for retail customers.

You can also remove an address label that is not needed.

Click the **Address Name list arrow** to see the predefined names:

The program allows you to enter multiple addresses for customers. For example, the billing address may be different from the location where a service is provided or products are delivered. The mailing address is provided as the default ship-to address, as indicated by the ✓ for Default Ship-To Address. The address information is dimmed because you cannot remove the mailing address on this screen. You can enter complete address and contact information for the shipping address, add new address labels and information for them, edit the labels and remove address names.

To enter information for an address name, click the name from the drop-down list.

Click **Ship-To Address** to open the address fields for editing:

All the fields are now open for editing. You can make any address the Default Ship-to Address by clicking the check box when this label's information is displayed.

The shipping address is the same as the mailing address for this customer, so we can remove the ship-to address name for this customer.

Click **Remove** to see the confirmation warning message:

Click **Yes** to confirm the removal.

Click **Add New** to open the name field to add a new address:

Type a new name and then click OK to have the new name appear in the drop-down list. Then you can select it to add the address details.

Click **Cancel** to return to the Ship-To Address tab screen.

Click the **Options tab**:

The first option is to add a default revenue account for the customer.

Click the **Revenue Account list arrow**.

Click **4100**.

The Options tab screen contains payment terms details. The **Price List** — Regular, Preferred or Web Price — refers to the prices customers pay for inventory items and will be introduced in Chapter 10. For Air Care, all customers pay Regular prices. You can select French or English as the customer's preferred **language for conducting business**.

NOTES
You can add back an address name that you removed by clicking Add New and re-entering its name.

Sales invoices and other forms you prepare for customers will be printed in the language you select here. Your own program screens will not change.

The payment terms for Hazel Estates are the same as those for other customers and are entered by default.

You may also choose to **Produce Statements For This Customer**, and you may print or e-mail invoices and quotes. You should use the correct forms, but you can also print statements on ordinary printer paper.

If you use **Microsoft Outlook** to organize your contacts, you can synchronize the address list in Simply Accounting with Outlook.

You can change the Options tab settings at any time.

SIMPLY VERSION
The option to Synchronize With Microsoft Outlook is not available in the Simply version.

> **Click**   the **Taxes tab**:

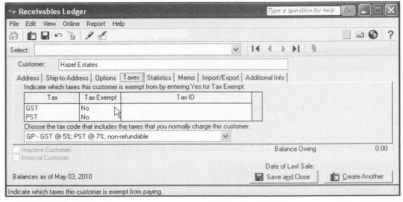

The customer is correctly described as not **Tax Exempt** for PST and GST by default, allowing accurate tax calculations for sales transactions to be included in Tax reports. The default tax code taken from the ledger settings is also correct.

WARNING!
Unless you have indicated that the customer is not exempt from taxes, the taxes will not be calculated in the Sales Journal for that customer, even if you select the correct tax code.

> **Click**   **GP - GST @5%; PST @7%, non-refundable** to see the codes available.

> **Click**   the **Statistics tab** to open the next screen we need:

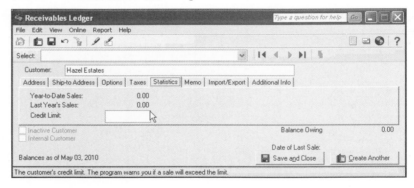

The Statistics screen has a summary of the sales to the customer for the current year and previous year. These fields are updated from sales transactions.

In the **Credit Limit** field, you can enter the customer's upper credit limit to help minimize bad debts. When a customer exceeds the credit limit, the program will warn you before you can post the sale. You can accept the over-the-limit sale, or ask for a deposit to avoid exceeding the credit limit. Customers should be notified of changes in credit policies. Customers who have previously defaulted on making their payments can be placed on a cash-only basis by setting their credit limits at zero. Air Care is presently analyzing customer payment trends to add this feature. The limit is set at $4 000 on a trial basis.

> **Click**   the **Credit Limit field** to position the cursor.

> **Type**   4000

Saving a New Customer Account

The remaining tab screens are not required. They serve the same purpose as they do for suppliers. When you are certain that all the information is correct, you must save the newly created customer account and add it to the current list.

> **Click**   **Save And Close** ⊟ Save and Close to save the new customer information and return to the Sales Journal.

Notice that the tax code, revenue account and payment terms are added to the journal. Any of these fields can be edited for an individual invoice.

> **Enter**   the **sale** for the new customer by following the procedures outlined earlier.

> **Review** the **journal entry**. **Close** the **display** and **make corrections**.

> **Click**   **Post** 🖳 Post . **Click OK** and then **close** the **Sales Journal**.

Reversing a Receipt (NSF Cheques)

When a cheque is returned by the bank as NSF, you need to record the fact that the invoice is still outstanding. You can do this in the Receipts Journal by reversing the cheque.

> **Click**   the **Receipts icon shortcuts list arrow** as shown:

> **Click**   **Adjust Receipt**. If the Receipts Journal is open,

You can click the **Adjust Receipt tool** 📧 , or **press** ⌷ctrl⌷ + **A**, or **choose** the **Receipt menu** and **click Adjust Receipt**.

You can also **click** the **Lookup tool** 📧 , or **press** ⌷ctrl⌷ + **L**, or **choose** the **Receipt menu** and **click Look Up Receipt**.

The familiar Search screen opens:

The Search window opens with Receipts as the search area.

NOTES
The Lookup and Adjust tools both open the Search window. The Reverse tool and menu option are available from the journal windows provided by both.
Find Receipt in the Receipts icon shortcuts list also opens the Search window.
From Lookup and Find Receipt, the search parameters will show Receipt Lookup as the heading.

Click   **OK** to see all the receipts we have entered:

The single cheque from Grande Pointe Towers we have entered is selected.

Press   (enter) or **click Select** to open the cheque we entered:

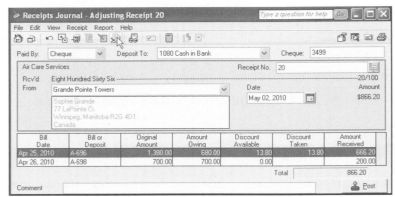

At this stage you can adjust the cheque by editing incorrectly entered information, just as you can edit a purchase invoice or payment cheque. We need to reverse the cheque because it has been returned as NSF.

Click   the **Reverse Receipt tool** [icon] or **choose** the **Receipt menu** and **click Reverse Receipt** to see the confirmation message:

Click   **Yes** to confirm the reversal. **Click OK** when Simply Accounting confirms the successful reversal. A blank Receipts Journal form opens.

If you change the customer for a receipt, Simply Accounting will automatically reverse the receipt and show you the confirmation:

We will look at the journal report generated by reversing this receipt.

Minimize   the **Receipts Journal** to return to the Home window.

Choose   the **Reports menu**, then **choose Journal Entries** and **click Receipts** to open the report options window:

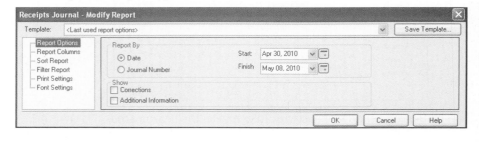

NOTES

If you recorded a receipt incorrectly, and do not need to reverse it, you can choose the Adjust Receipt tool to access the posted receipt and make the correction, just as you do for sales (page 184) or for payments (page 139).

NOTES

In Chapter 15, you will see that you cannot reverse the receipt if the cheque is not deposited directly to the bank account when you enter the receipt (that is, the bank deposit is recorded later as a separate transaction). Instead, you must enter a negative receipt.

CLASSIC VIEW

From the Home window, right-click the Receipts icon

[icon] Click the Display tool

[icon] to see the Receipts Journal report options.

WARNING!

If you display the Journal Report from the Home window Reports pane Reports list, you will use the default settings which do not show corrections. You will see the message that there is no data because there are no other Receipts Journal entries.

By default, corrections are not included in reports. In order to see adjustments, we must include them. The remaining defaults are correct.

Click **Corrections** under the Show heading.

Click **OK** to display the two journal entries:

NOTES
You can also click the Report Centre icon. Then click Receivables, Receipts Journal Entries and Modify This Report.

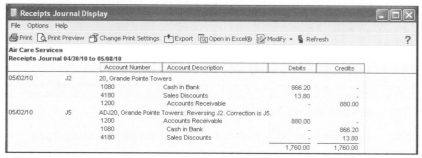

You can see that the two entries cancel each other — all amounts were reversed, including the discount. The debits to *Cash in Bank* and *Sales Discounts* were entered as credits in the reversing entry, and the credit to *Accounts Receivable* was entered as a debit. Simply Accounting created the reversing entry automatically when we reversed the receipt, adding ADJ to the receipt number so that you can link the two transactions.

When you adjust a receipt and post the corrected entry, Simply Accounting will create the reversing entry automatically. Three entries result — the original incorrect one, the reversing entry and the final corrected version. You can see the complete audit trail by including Corrections in the Journal Reports.

Close the **display** when you have finished.

Restore the **Receipts Journal**.

Choose Grande Pointe Towers from the Customer list.

Both invoices have been fully restored. When the replacement payment is received, you can enter it in the usual way.

Close the **Receipts Journal**.

Editing a Customer Record

Most fields in the customer record can be changed at any time. Only the current balance owing, which is updated from sale and payment transactions, cannot be changed.

Click the **Customers icon shortcuts list arrow** as shown:

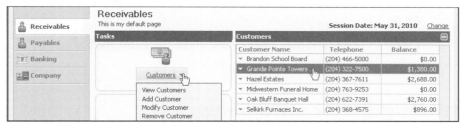

From the Customers shortcuts list, you can choose Modify Customer. When the Search screen opens, you can select the customer.

You can also click the customer's name in the right-hand Customers pane to open a record for a customer directly.

Click   the **Customers icon** 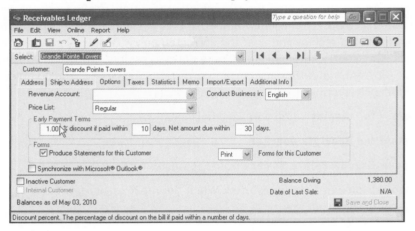 to open the Customers window:

Click   **Grande Pointe Towers** to select it.

Click   the **Edit tool** 🖉 or **choose** the **File menu** and **click Open**.

The Receivables Ledger record for Grande Pointe Towers opens at the Address screen. We need to modify the Terms, which appear on the Options tab.

Click   the **Options tab** to access the payment terms information:

Click   **1.00** in the % Discount field of the Early Payment Terms section.

Press   del to remove the entry. **Press** tab to advance to the Days field.

Press   del . **Press** tab to advance to the Net Days field.

Type   1

To modify other customer records, click Next ▶ or Previous ◀ to move to a different record or choose the customer you need from the Select drop-down list.

Click   the **Statistics tab** to change credit limits for the remaining customers.

Close   the **Receivables Ledger** and **close** the **Customers window**. You can now continue with the journal entries.

Entering Credit Card Sales

Most businesses accept credit cards from customers in lieu of cash and cheques. Customers expect this convenience, and although businesses benefit by avoiding NSF cheques, they do incur a cost for this service. Credit card companies charge the business a transaction fee: a percentage of each sale is withheld by the card company.

Credit card sales are entered like other sales, by selecting the correct payment method and then entering the invoice details.

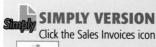 **SIMPLY VERSION**
Click the Sales Invoices icon
 to open the Sales Journal.

Click   the **Bills icon** .

Click   the **Paid By list arrow** and **click Credit Card** to modify the invoice.

As for cash sales, the Net Days field for early payment discounts is removed and a Credit Card Amount field is added. There is no cheque number field for credit cards.

Choose One-Time Customer from the Sold To drop-down list.

Type   Sales Summary in the Mailing Address text box.

Enter   **May 5** as the transaction date.

Click   the **Description field** and **type** the **description** for the first sale item.

Press   `tab` and **type** 600

Press   `tab` **twice** and **enter 4120** as the account.

Enter   the **second invoice line details** for the service contract revenue work to complete the invoice as shown:

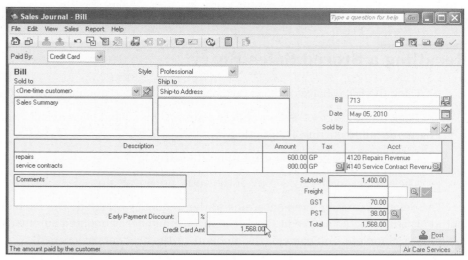

As usual, we will review the journal entry before posting.

Press   `ctrl` **+ J** or **choose** the **Report menu** and **click Display Sales Journal Entry**:

Air Care Services			
05/05/10 (J6)	Debits	Credits	Project
1100 Credit Card Bank Account	1,528.80	–	
5120 Bank Charges & Card Fees	39.20	–	
2640 PST Payable	–	98.00	
2650 GST Charged on Services	–	70.00	
4120 Repairs Revenue	–	600.00	
4140 Service Contract Revenue	–	800.00	
	1,568.00	1,568.00	

This entry differs somewhat from the standard cash sale entry. Instead of *Cash in Bank*, the linked *Credit Card Bank Account* is debited for the amount of the deposit, but this is less than the total amount of the sale. The deposit is reduced by the transaction fee that is charged to the linked expense account *Bank Charges & Card Fees*. In this case, the credit card company withholds 2.5 percent of each transaction as the fee for using the card. This fee includes the cost to the credit card company for assuming the risk of non-payment from customers.

Close   the **display** and **make corrections** to the invoice if necessary.

NOTES
The transaction fee varies from one card company to another, as well as from one retail customer to another. Stores that have a larger volume of credit card sales usually pay lower transaction fees.

Before posting the transaction, we will store it so that we will not need to re-enter all the details the next time we enter the sales summary transaction.

Storing a Recurring Sales Entry

Completing and storing a recurring entry in the Sales Journal is similar to storing a General or Purchases Journal entry.

Click the **Store tool** or **choose** the **Sales menu** and **click Store**.

The familiar Store Recurring Transaction window appears with the customer name as the entry name, and the default frequency, Monthly, selected. If you want, you can change the entry name to Sales Summary.

Click **Monthly** to display the frequency options.

Click **Weekly** to choose the frequency.

Click **OK** to save the entry and return to the Sales Journal. The Recall button will be available.

Click **Post** to save the journal entry. **Click OK**.

Recalling a Stored Sales Entry

Click the Bills (Sales or Sales Invoices) icon to open the Sales Journal.

Click the Recall tool or choose the Sales menu and click Recall to display the Recall Recurring Transaction window.

Click the transaction you want to use to select it.

Click Select to display a copy of the entry previously posted.

The default date is entered according to the frequency selected. The payment method is still selected as Credit Card. The invoice number is updated automatically so the entry is complete. You can edit the amounts or the accounts as needed.

Review the entry to be certain that it is correct.

Click the Post button to save the entry.

If you have made any changes to the entry, Simply Accounting may warn that posting the entry may affect the next due date. This warning will appear if you have made any changes to the entry before posting, although the message mentions only the date.

Click Yes to accept the change and post the entry. Click OK to confirm posting.

Adjusting a Posted Sales Journal Entry

If you discover an error in a Sales Journal entry after posting it, you can adjust or correct the posted transaction in the same way that you can adjust a purchase invoice after posting. You can edit any field in the invoice except the customer. If you need to change the customer, you can open the Adjust (or Lookup) window and click the Reverse tool, just as you do for purchases or receipts.

The entry for Hazel Estates was missing the second invoice line to record the revenue from repair work. The Sales Journal should still be open.

Click the **Adjust Invoice tool** to open the Search window:

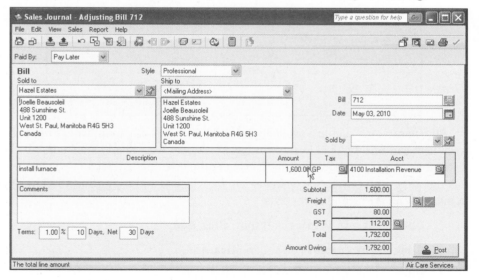

NOTES

Just as you can choose a specific supplier for purchase invoice adjustments, you can choose a specific customer and click OK to see a reduced list of invoices for the selected customer. You can also enter a specific invoice number and click OK to access the invoice directly.

The default date and customer selections will include all invoices.

Click   OK to open the Adjust A Bill screen:

All Sales Journal entries for the selected customers and within the selected date range are listed. You can **view** the list of transactions in order by date, the default selection, customer, invoice number, journal entry number or amount. For each view, you can switch between descending and ascending order with the **Z...A button**.

Journal Entry #4 for Hazel Estates is the one we need to edit.

Click   Hazel Estates.

To choose an invoice for adjusting, you can click on any part of the line for that invoice to highlight it, then press (enter), or click Select or you can double click the entry to open the journal immediately.

Click   Select or **press** (enter) to open the invoice. It is ready for editing:

NOTES

If the invoice has already been paid, the program will ask if you want to create a credit note for the customer — a negative invoice. The default source for this invoice will be CN plus the original invoice number, e.g., CN-712, but you can enter a different reference number if you want.

This credit amount can be applied (paid) to other outstanding invoices for the customer.

Click   the **Description field** on the second line, below the first description.

Type   repair work **Press** (tab) to advance to the Amount field.

Type   800 **Press** (tab).

The tax code GP should be entered. You can select or change the code if needed. Click the Tax code List icon to open the Tax Code screen. Double click GP.

Click   the **Account field List icon** .

Double click 4120 Repairs Revenue.

Click   the **Comments field** and **type** Revised invoice

As with other adjustments in other journals, this adjustment creates a reversing entry in addition to the corrected journal entry. You will see all three transactions in the journal reports when you include Corrections.

When you change the customer for an invoice, Simply Accounting will warn you that the name will be changed, but the remaining information (terms, tax codes and so on) will not.

Review the **entry**. **Close** the **display**. **Make corrections** if necessary and **Post**.

Adding Shortcuts for Other Transactions

Just as we added a shortcut for General Journal entries in Chapter 5, we can add shortcuts for the Payables journals and tasks we will use for Air Care. Refer to page 134 if you need help.

Click   **Customize** beside Shortcuts.

Click   the ⊞ beside **Company** to expand the list.

Click   **Create General Journal** and then **click Add**.

Click   the ⊞ beside **Payables** to expand this list as shown:

All transactions that are available from the Invoices, Payments and Suppliers drop-down lists can be added as Home window shortcuts. We will add shortcuts for the types of Payables transactions we use most frequently: creating and paying invoices and making other cash purchases (expenses). We will also add a shortcut to View Suppliers so that we can edit supplier records.

Click   **Create Invoice** and then **click Add**.

Click   **Pay Invoices** and then **click Add**.

Click   **Pay Expenses** and then **click Add**.

Click   **View Suppliers** and then **click Add**.

Click   **OK** to return to the Home window:

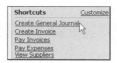

These five tasks/windows are now available from any module Home window by clicking the shortcut.

Enter the **remaining transactions** and then **restore** the **Home window**.

Displaying Customer Reports

Customer reports can be accessed any time from the Home or the Customers window, or from the Report Centre.

Click the Customers icon to open the Customers window.

The Reports menu now contains only customer reports. You can select the report you want from this list and follow the instructions below to choose report options. You can also obtain all customer reports from the Home window Reports menu.

In the Receivables module Home window, the Reports pane includes all the customer reports in the drop-down list. Opening the reports from this list will display them immediately with the default settings. This report list is shown here:

We will continue to work from the Report Centre, so we can see the sample reports, descriptions and report options.

Click the **Report Centre icon** in the Home window.

The Receivables reports are listed because we started from the Receivables window:

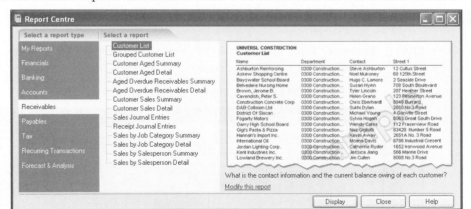

Displaying Customer Lists

Click **Customer List** in the Select A Report list to open the sample report.

NOTES
Management reports and graphs are not available from the Customers window or from the Report Centre. You can access these from the Home window.

SIMPLY VERSION
Grouped Customer Lists and Forecast & Analysis reports are not available in the Simply version.

NOTES
Forecast & Analysis reports use data for multiple fiscal periods. They are covered briefly in Chapter 10.

CLASSIC VIEW
From the Home window, right-click the Receipts icon. Click the Display tool to see the Receipts Journal report options.

Click   Modify This Report to open the report options:

Or, choose the Reports menu, then choose Lists and Customers to see the options.

You can include or omit inactive and internal customers, and shipping addresses. You can sort and filter Customer Lists by any of the fields selected for the report. You can select customer record fields by customizing the Report Columns.

Click   OK. Close the **display** when you have finished viewing it.

Displaying Grouped Customer Lists

You can also organize your customer list by a number of categories to make contacting them more efficient.

Click   Grouped Customer List in the Select A Report list to open the sample report and its description.

Click   Modify This Report to open the report options.

Click the **list arrow for the Group By field** to see the criteria you can use to sort your report:

Choose the **grouping criterion** you want. Click OK to display the report.

Close the **display** when you have finished viewing it.

Displaying Customer Aged Reports

Click   Customer Aged Summary in the Select A Report list to open the sample report and its description.

Click   Modify This Report to open the report options:

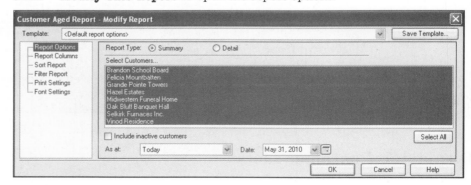

Or, choose the Reports menu, then choose Receivables and Customer Aged.

New customers you entered using Quick Add will appear on the list of customers in the report options windows. Sales for one-time customers and customers for whom you chose the Continue option will not appear because these cash transactions did not create an entry for Accounts Receivable.

The **Summary** option will display an alphabetic list of the selected customers with outstanding total balances owing, organized into the aging periods columns set up for the company. The **Detail** option shows all the invoices and payments made by customers and the balance owing. This more descriptive report is also aged. Management can use it to make credit decisions. You can add payment terms to the Detail Report.

You can customize the Customer Aged and Aged Overdue reports (that is, choose columns, sort and filter) by name, balance owing and aging periods.

Click   **Detail** to include details for individual transactions.

Enter   the **date** for the report, or accept the default session date.

Press   and **hold** ⌈ctrl⌋ and **click** the appropriate **names** in the customer list. **Click Select All** to include all customers, or remove them when they are all selected.

After you have indicated the options you want,

Click   **OK** to see the report. **Close** the **displayed report** when finished.

Displaying Aged Overdue Receivables Reports

Click   **Aged Overdue Receivables Summary** in the Select A Report list to open the sample report and its description.

Click   **Modify This Report** to open the report options:

From the Home window, choose the Reports menu in the Home window, then choose Receivables and click Aged Overdue Receivables to see the options.

Enter   the **date** for the report, or accept the default session date.

The **Summary** option will display an alphabetic list of the selected customers with outstanding total balances owing, organized into aging periods, with an additional column for the overdue amount. Individual invoices, due dates, payments, overdue amounts and the balance owing for the selected customers are added when you choose the **Detail** Report.

You can use name, balance owing and aging periods as the criteria for sorting and filtering the Aged Overdue Receivables reports and for choosing columns.

Click   **Detail** if you want to include the invoice details.

Enter   the **date** for the report, or accept the default session date.

NOTES
You can drill down to look up invoices and to the Customer Aged Report from the Aged Overdue Receivables Report. From the Summary Report, you can drill down to the Detail Report.

Press   and **hold** ⌈ctrl⌉ and **click** the appropriate **names** in the customer list. **Click Select All** to include all customers, or remove them all.

Click   **OK** to see the report. **Close** the **displayed report** when finished.

Displaying the Customer Sales Report

Click   **Customer Sales Summary** in the Select A Report list to open the sample report and its description.

Click   **Modify This Report** to open the report options:

From the Home window, choose the Reports menu in the Home window, then choose Receivables and click Customer Sales to see the options.

In this report, you can display the total number of transactions and the total sales for each customer (in the **Summary** Report) or the individual sales invoice amounts (in the **Detail** Report). The Detail Report also includes journal details (date, source, journal entry number and revenue amounts) for each transaction. Only the Other Amounts and Freight amounts are available when the inventory module is not set up. When inventory items are set up, you can display the sales for these items as well. This report will be discussed further when inventory is introduced in Chapter 10. The earliest transaction and session date provide the default date range.

You can select the customers to include and the date range for the report.

Press   and **hold** ⌈ctrl⌉ and **click** the appropriate **names** in the customer list. **Click Select All** to include all customers, or remove the entire selection.

Enter   the **Start** and **Finish dates** for the report.

Click   **OK** to see the report. **Close** the **displayed report** when finished.

Displaying the Sales Journal

Click   **Sales Journal Entries** in the Select A Report list to open the sample.

Click   **Modify This Report** to open the report options:

CLASSIC VIEW
From the Home window, right-click the Sales icon

. Click the Display tool

.

Sales and Receipts Journal reports are also available from the Select Report list when you click the Display tool button if no icon is selected in the Home window.

From the Home window, choose the Reports menu, then choose Journal Entries and click Sales to see the report options.

You can select Sales Journal entries by posting date or by journal entry number. We use the default setting, By Date, for all reports in this workbook, so leave the selection unchanged. You can include corrections (adjusting and reversing entries) or omit them.

You can sort and filter journal reports by Date, Journal No., Source and Comment. You can choose account, description, debits and credits columns for the reports.

Enter the **beginning date** for the journal transactions you want. Or choose a date from the list arrow selections.

Press (tab) **twice**. **Enter** the **ending date** for the transaction period.

Click **Corrections** to provide a complete audit trail.

Click **OK** to view the report. **Close** the **display** when you have finished.

Displaying the Receipts Journal

The Receipts Journal was covered earlier in this chapter. Refer to page 180.

Displaying Tax Reports

Tax reports show the taxable purchases and sales with and without tax amounts included and the taxes paid or charged on each transaction or the total.

Click **Tax** in the Select A Report Type list to open the list of tax reports:

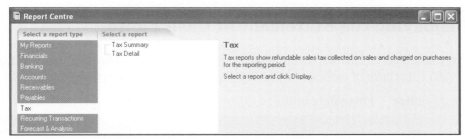

Click **Tax Summary** to display a sample report and description.

Click **Modify This Report** to display the Tax Report options window:

From the Home window, choose the Reports menu and click Tax to display the Tax Report options window.

All taxes that were defined for the company and included the option to report on them are listed in the Select Taxes field.

The earliest transaction and the session date are entered as the default date range for the report. You can include either sales or purchase transactions that include tax or both. Both purchases and sales are reported by default. In addition, the report can include taxable, exempt and non-taxable transactions. By default all are selected. You can also organize the report by tax codes.

The **Summary** Report has only the totals for each category selected while the **Detail** Report lists individual transactions for each category. You can include the total tax amounts by the tax rate as well.

Click **Detail** to select the more detailed level for the report.

Enter or **choose** the **dates** for which you want the report to start and finish.

Click a **tax name** in the Select Tax list to select it or **click Select All** to report on all the taxes listed.

Click the **transactions** (Purchases or Sales) to remove a ✓ or to add one if it is not there to include the transaction in the report.

Click a **transaction tax status** (Taxable, Exempt or Non-Taxable) to remove a ✓ or to add one if it is not there.

Click **Include Totals By Rate** if you have selected more than one tax.

Once you have selected the options you want,

Click **OK** to view the report. **Close** the **display** when you have finished.

Displaying Cash Flow Reports

Displaying the Statement of Cash Flows

The Statement of Cash Flows summarizes sources (income, investments, etc.) and uses of cash (purchase of assets, etc.) and changes in liabilities during the designated period.

Click **Financials** in the Select A Report Type list to open the list of reports:

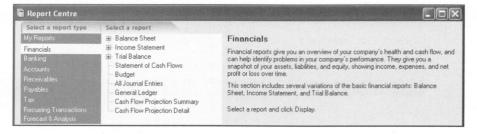

Click **Statement of Cash Flows** to display a sample report and description.

Click **Modify This Report** to display the Modify Report window:

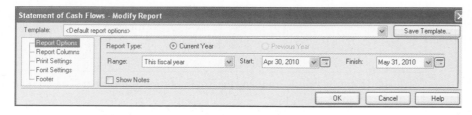

From the Home window, choose the Reports menu, then choose Financials and click Statement Of Cash Flows to see the report options.

Enter   the **Start** and **Finish dates** for the report. The fiscal start and session dates are the defaults.

Click   **OK** to view the report.

By organizing the transactions involving cash, net changes in cash positions, as well as changes in liabilities, the statement allows the owner to judge how efficiently cash is being used for the business. The owner can also see potential problems resulting from increases in liabilities or decreases in the collection of receivables.

Close   the **display** when you have finished.

Displaying Cash Flow Projection Reports

Cash Flow Projection reports predict the flow of cash in and out of an account — usually a bank account — over a specific future period based on current information.

Click   **Cash Flow Projection Summary** to display a sample report and description.

Click   **Modify This Report** to display the Modify Report window:

From the Home window, choose the Reports menu, then choose Financials and click Cash Flow Projection to see the report options.

Click   **1080 Cash in Bank** or the account for which you want the report.

Click   the **Date field**.

Type   the **date** at which you want the projection to start.

Press   ⌜tab⌝ **twice**.

Enter   the **number of days** in the future for which the report should project the cash flow.

Usually, you will include only the number of days for which you have reasonable information, such as the number of days in which net payment is due. The session date and 30 days are useful periods, so you can accept the defaults.

In the report, you may choose to include discounts in the amounts you expect to receive or pay, and you may include overdue transactions, or omit them if you expect them to remain unpaid. By default, all details are included. Clicking a detail will remove it from the report. The Projection Report assumes all amounts are paid on the invoice due date.

The report projects the account balance based on receivables and payables due and recurring transactions coming due within the time frame specified. The **Summary** Report shows the totals for the specified report period while the **Detail** Report shows, by date, the individual transactions that are expected.

NOTES
You might want to compare projection reports prepared with and without some of these extra details.

Select the **additional categories** for which you want details.

Click **Detail** to include individual transactions.

Click **OK** to view the report.

Close the **display**. **Close** the **Report Centre** to return to the Home window.

Displaying Management Reports

Management reports are displayed from the Home window Reports menu.

Choose the **Reports menu**, then **choose Management Reports** and **click Receivables** to see the reports and options:

You can produce four different reports for the Receivables Ledger: a list of all customers who have exceeded their credit limits, sales amounts for customers who have decreased their purchases since the previous year, amounts for customers who have increased purchases and customers with overdue payments. The Overdue Amounts Report is helpful for making a list of customers to remind about settling their accounts because it includes customer contact details.

Click the **topic** for the report.

The program will add a date, if appropriate, and a form for the report. Change the date if you need to, but leave the default report form unless you have the programs required to modify these forms.

Click **OK** to display the report and print it if you want. **Close** the **display**.

Printing Customer Reports

Display the **report**.

Click the **Change Print Settings tool** 📇 to check that you have the correct printer selected. **Click OK** to return to the report.

Click the **Print tool** 🖨 or **choose** the **File menu** in the report window, and then **click Print**.

Close the **display** when you have finished.

Printing Customer Statements

You can e-mail all customer statements or print them, or you can choose e-mail and print on a customer-by-customer basis according to the setting (preference) in the customer's ledger record.

Be sure your printer is set up with the correct forms before you begin because statements are printed immediately when you click OK after selecting your options.

CLASSIC VIEW
You can also access Management Reports from the Advice tool in the Home window.

WARNING!
If a form appears in the Form field, check that its location is correct for your program installation. It should be located in the Forms folder, under your Simply Accounting Premium 2008 folder.

NOTES
One customer account is currently overdue by more than 30 days. Two more customers have passed the 10-day discount window.

NOTES
Refer to Chapter 4, page 81, and to Chapter 5, page 148, for details on setting up printers for different forms, reports and labels.

NOTES
You can customize customer statements but not mailing labels.

Choose the **Reports menu** in the Home window, then **choose Receivables** and **click Customer Statements** to see the following options:

You should preview statements before printing them. To preview statements, you must select Custom Simply Form. Choose the Setup menu and click Reports & Forms. Click Statements. Choose Custom Form and then Custom Simply Form. If you also want to customize the statements, choose User Defined Form in the Printed Form Description field. Click the Customize button to open the Simply Form Designer. Save the new form when finished.

Press and **hold** ⌈ctrl⌉ and **click** the **customers** for whom you want to print statements, or **click Select All** to include all customers.

Click **Include Due Dates** if you want to add the payment due dates for invoices, and **click OK**.

Printing Customer Mailing Labels

You should turn on the printer, insert labels paper and set the program for printing labels before choosing the options for the labels because printing begins immediately.

Choose the Setup menu in the Home window and click Reports & Forms. Click Labels. Enter the details for the labels. Click OK.

Choose the **Reports menu** in the Home window, then **choose Mailing Labels** and **click Customers** to see the following options:

You can print labels for business mailing addresses, for shipping addresses or for any address list you created.

Press and **hold** ⌈ctrl⌉ and **click** the **customers** for whom you want to print the labels, or **click Select All** to include all customers. **Click OK**.

Graphing Customer Reports

The customer-related graphs are available from the Home window. You cannot view them from the Customers window or from the Report Centre.

Receivables by Aging Period Graph

Choose the **Graphs menu** in the Home window and **click Receivables By Aging Period** to see the options screen:

Enter a **date** for the graph and **click OK**.

The pie chart shows the total receivables divided according to the aging intervals set up in the company defaults. The chart is the customer equivalent of the Payables By Aging Period Graph and shows the timeliness of account collections. You have the same tool bar options and colour and legend control choices that you have for the other graphs. Refer to page 60 for a review of these features if you need further assistance.

Double click a portion of a graph to see the aging period, the dollar amount and the percentage of the total.

Double click the legend to make it larger. Double click the expanded legend to reduce it.

Close the **graph** when you have finished.

Receivables by Customer Graph

Choose the **Graphs menu** in the Home window and **click Receivables By Customer** to see the following options:

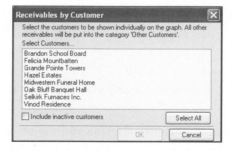

Press and **hold** ⎡ctrl⎤ and **click** the individual **customers** you want on the chart, or **click Select All** to include all customers.

Click   **OK** to see the pie chart graph:

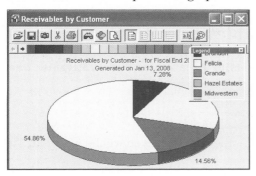

The amount owed by each customer, represented by different colours in the pie chart, is shown as a proportion of the total receivables. The options for displaying, editing, printing and exporting the graph are the same for all graphs.

> Double click a portion of a graph to see the customer, the dollar amount and the percentage of the total.

> Double click the legend to make it large and add the customer names. Double click the expanded legend to reduce it.

Close   the **graph** when you have finished.

Sales vs Receivables Graph

Choose the **Graphs menu** and **click Sales Vs Receivables** to see the options:

Press   and **hold** ⌐ctrl⌐ and **click** the **revenue accounts** that you want in the graph. **Click Select All** to include all revenue accounts.

Click   **OK** to display the following bar chart for the end of May:

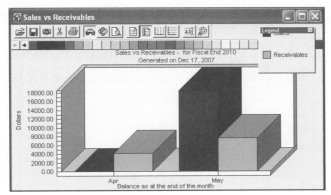

NOTES
The sales for April show as zero because we have not entered any transactions for April. The April receivables balance was the historical amount outstanding when we set up the data file.

Although this is not a pie chart, you have the same options for exporting, copying, changing the display and so on that you do for other graphs. The graph indicates cash flow by showing how much of the sales are not yet collected.

> Double click a portion of the chart to see the period, the category (Sales or Receivables) and the dollar amount.

Close   the **graph** when you have finished.

Receivables Due vs Payables Due Graph

Choose the **Graphs menu** and **click Receivables Due Vs Payables Due**:

All receivables and payables due by the date displayed will be included. The session date is the default.

Enter   the **date** that you want for the graph.

Click   **OK** to display the bar chart:

The graph shows the total amounts for receivables and payables due by June 30, 30 days beyond the session date, providing another indicator of cash flow. For this bar chart, you have the same options for exporting, copying, changing the display and so on that you do for other graphs.

Double click a portion of the graph to see the period, the category (Payables or Receivables) and the dollar amount.

Close   the **graph** when you have finished.

R E V I E W

The Student CD-ROM with Data Files includes Review Questions and Supplementary Cases for this chapter.

Dorfmann**Design**

OBJECTIVES

After completing this chapter, you should be able to

- *plan* and *design* an accounting system for a small business
- *prepare* procedures for converting from a manual system
- *understand* the objectives of a computerized system
- *create* company files
- *create* and *understand* linked accounts
- *set up* accounts in the General, Payables and Receivables ledgers
- *enter* historical information for suppliers and clients
- *correct* historical transactions after recording them
- *set up* credit cards for receipts and payments
- *set up* sales taxes and tax codes
- *finish* entering history after entering journal transactions
- *enter* postdated transactions

COMPANY INFORMATION

Company Profile

NOTES
Dorfmann Design
17 Tapestry Lane
Calgary, Alberta T3B 4U2
Tel: (403) 683-9145
Fax: (403) 685-8210
Business No.: 233 281 244

Dorfmann Design, owned by Desiree Dorfmann, has operated successfully in Calgary, Alberta, for several years. As a master of space management, Dorfmann is invited to take on many different work assignments. She has designed boutiques in department stores, cosmetic counters and coffee bars; office space in banks; offices for professionals; countertop display areas in stores; shelving for display items, books or journals; and classroom and auditorium arrangements in colleges, universities and schools. She is frequently asked to convert unpleasant or unused spaces into attractive, inviting places by maximizing the usable space and making it open and comfortable while respecting the need for privacy. Sometimes she uses rich, textured fabrics in classical designs as well as sleek and modern materials to enhance an office or sales area. The end result always attracts attention.

Some clients ask only for her consultation, preferring to do the work themselves. For those clients she generates reports on how to maximize the use of space, or how to create attractive environments that encourage clients to buy. Most clients employ her because they understand the value of good design.

Dorfmann has accounts set up with her regular suppliers, some of whom offer discounts for early payment on a before-tax basis. These suppliers provide office and computer supplies, specialized design software and materials for building scale models. She also has a maintenance contract with a local cleaning company. All purchases are subject to 5 percent GST.

Most of Dorfmann's clients are in the Calgary region. She is negotiating with businesses in Wyoming, but so far none of these leads has led to confirmed contracts. Canadian clients pay GST on all services provided and are offered an after-tax discount of 1 percent if they pay within five days. Overdue accounts are subject to interest charges at the rate of 1.5 percent after 30 days.

On March 31, she gathered the following business information to convert her accounting records to Simply Accounting:

- Business Information
- Chart of Accounts
- Income Statement
- Balance Sheet
- Trial Balance
- Supplier Information
- Client Information
- Accounting Procedures

BUSINESS INFORMATION

DORFMANN DESIGN

COMPANY INFORMATION

Address: 17 Tapestry Lane
             Calgary, Alberta T3B 4U2
Phone: (403) 683-9145
Fax: (403) 685-8210
Business No.: 233 281 244 RT0001
Fiscal Start: Jan. 1, 2010
Fiscal End: June 30, 2010
Earliest Transaction: March 31, 2010
Company Type: Service

REPORTS & FORMS
Choose settings for your printer and forms

USER PREFERENCES
Options
  Use Accounting Terms
  Automatically Save Changes to Records
  Show List Buttons
  Show Session Date at Startup
  Show Paid Stamp during Lookup
View Settings
  Hide: Inventory & Services, Employees &
         Payroll, Project, Time & Billing
  Daily Business Manager: turn off
  Checklists: turn off
  Transaction Confirmation: turned on

COMPANY SETTINGS
System
  Allow Future Transactions

  Warn if more than 7 days in future
  Warn if Accounts Not Balanced
Backup
  Backup Weekly
  Turn off scheduled backup
Features
  Do not use orders, quotes, packing slips, &
     projects
  Use both French and English
Credit Card Information
  Card Accepted: Visa
  Discount Fee: 2.9%
  Expense Account: 5020
  Asset Account: 1070

  Card Accepted: MasterCard
  Discount Fee: 2.7%
  Expense Account: 5020
  Asset Account: 1080

  Card Used: Visa
  Payable Account: 2160
  Expense Account: 5020
Sales Taxes
  Taxes: GST 5%
  Code: G - GST @ 5%

Date Format: Use long form on the screen
Logo: SimData\Setup\logos\dorfmann.bmp

Forms Settings (Next Number)
  Sales Invoices No. 44
  Receipts No. 25

GENERAL SETTINGS: No changes

PAYABLES SETTINGS
Address: Calgary, Alberta, Canada
Options
  Aging Periods: 15, 30, 45 days
  Discounts before Tax: Yes

RECEIVABLES SETTINGS
Address: Calgary, Alberta, Canada
Options
  Aging Periods: 5, 15, 30 days
  Interest Charges: 1.5% after 30 days
  Statements Include Invoices for 31 days
  New Client Tax Code: G
Discounts
  Payment Terms: 1/5, n/15 after tax
  Discounts before Tax: No
  Line Discounts: No
Comments
  Sales Invoice: Interest @ 1.5% per month
       charged on accounts over 30 days.

BANK ACCOUNTS: NEXT CHEQUE NO.
  Bank: Chequing 65

CHART OF ACCOUNTS

DORFMANN DESIGN

ASSETS

1000	CURRENT ASSETS [H]
1010	Test Balance Account
1060	Bank: Chequing [A]
1070	Bank: Visa [A]
1080	Bank: MasterCard [A]
1100	Net Bank [S]
1200	Accounts Receivable
1210	Prepaid Insurance
1220	Model Parts Inventory
1230	Computer Supplies
1240	Office Supplies
1250	Software
1290	TOTAL CURRENT ASSETS [T]
1400	OFFICE & EQUIPMENT [H]
1410	Computer Equipment
1420	Design Equipment
1430	Furniture & Fixtures ▶

▶ 1440	Motor Vehicle
1450	Office Condominium
1490	TOTAL OFFICE & EQUIPMENT [T]

LIABILITIES

2000	CURRENT LIABILITIES [H]
2100	Bank Loan
2160	Credit Card Payable
2200	Accounts Payable
2650	GST Charged on Services [A]
2670	GST Paid on Purchases [A]
2750	GST Owing (Refund) [S]
2790	TOTAL CURRENT LIABILITIES [T]
2800	LONG TERM LIABILITIES [H]
2850	Mortgage Payable
2890	TOTAL LONG TERM LIABILITIES [T] ▶

▶ EQUITY

3000	OWNER'S EQUITY [H]
3560	D. Dorfmann, Capital
3650	Current Earnings [X]
3690	UPDATED CAPITAL [T]

REVENUE

4000	GENERAL REVENUE [H]
4020	Revenue from Design
4040	Revenue from Consulting
4060	Sales Discounts
4100	Interest Revenue
4290	TOTAL REVENUE [T]

EXPENSE

5000	OPERATING EXPENSES [H]
5010	Bank Charges
5020	Credit Card Fees
5040	Purchase Discounts

5050	Delivery Expenses
5060	Hydro Expense
5070	Maintenance Services
5100	Model Parts Used
5110	Computer Supplies Used
5120	Office Supplies Used
5150	Insurance Expense
5160	Telephone Expense
5200	Loan Interest Expense
5210	Mortgage Interest Expense
5990	TOTAL OPERATING EXPENSES [T]

NOTES: The Chart of Accounts includes all accounts. Account types are marked for all subgroup Accounts [A], Subgroup totals [S], Heading accounts [H], Total accounts [T] and the type X account. All other unmarked accounts are postable Group accounts.

INCOME STATEMENT

DORFMANN DESIGN

January 1 to March 31, 2010

Revenue

4000	GENERAL REVENUE	
4020	Revenue from Design	$38 000
4040	Revenue from Consulting	7 400
4060	Sales Discounts	−400
4100	Interest Revenue	371
4290	TOTAL REVENUE	$45 371
	TOTAL REVENUE	$45 371 ▶

▶ Expenses

5000	OPERATING EXPENSES	
5010	Bank Charges	$ 225
5020	Credit Card Fees	590
5040	Purchase Discounts	−300
5050	Delivery Expenses	180
5060	Hydro Expense	750
5070	Maintenance Services	1 391
5100	Model Parts Used	1 600
5110	Computer Supplies Used	1 200
5120	Office Supplies Used	1 150
5150	Insurance Expense	600
5160	Telephone Expense	400
5200	Loan Interest Expense	625
5210	Mortgage Interest Expense	6 000
5990	TOTAL OPERATING EXPENSES	$ 14 411
	TOTAL EXPENSE	$ 14 411
	NET INCOME (LOSS)	$30 960

BALANCE SHEET

DORFMANN DESIGN

March 31, 2010

Assets

1000	CURRENT ASSETS		
1060	Bank: Chequing	$ 29 211	
1070	Bank: Visa	1 950	
1080	Bank: MasterCard	1 060	
1100	Net Bank		$ 32 221
1200	Accounts Receivable		3 860
1210	Prepaid Insurance		1 800
1220	Model Parts Inventory		4 000
1230	Computer Supplies		1 500
1240	Office Supplies		1 000
1250	Software		2 000
1290	TOTAL CURRENT ASSETS		$ 46 381
1400	OFFICE & EQUIPMENT		
1410	Computer Equipment		12 000
1420	Design Equipment		8 000
1430	Furniture & Fixtures		4 000
1440	Motor Vehicle		50 000
1450	Office Condominium		100 000
1490	TOTAL OFFICE & EQUIPMENT		$174 000
	TOTAL ASSETS		$220 381 ▶

▶ Liabilities

2000	CURRENT LIABILITIES		
2100	Bank Loan		$ 25 000
2160	Credit Card Payable		1 010
2200	Accounts Payable		9 174
2650	GST Charged on Services	$1 530	
2670	GST Paid on Purchases	−840	
2750	GST Owing (Refund)		690
2790	TOTAL CURRENT LIABILITIES		$ 35 874
2800	LONG TERM LIABILITIES		
2850	Mortgage Payable		75 000
2890	TOTAL LONG TERM LIABILITIES		$ 75 000
	TOTAL LIABILITIES		$ 110 874

Equity

3000	OWNER'S EQUITY		
3560	D. Dorfmann, Capital		$ 78 547
3650	Current Earnings		30 960
3690	UPDATED CAPITAL		$ 109 507
	TOTAL EQUITY		$ 109 507
	LIABILITIES AND EQUITY		$220 381

TRIAL BALANCE

DORFMANN DESIGN

March 31, 2010

		Debit	Credit
1060	Bank: Chequing	$ 29 211	
1070	Bank: Visa	1 950	
1080	Bank: MasterCard	1 060	
1200	Accounts Receivable	3 860	
1210	Prepaid Insurance	1 800	
1220	Model Parts Inventory	4 000	
1230	Computer Supplies	1 500	
1240	Office Supplies	1 000	
1250	Software	2 000	
1410	Computer Equipment	12 000	
1420	Design Equipment	8 000	
1430	Furniture & Fixtures	4 000	
1440	Motor Vehicle	50 000	
1450	Office Condominium	100 000	
2100	Bank Loan		$ 25 000
2160	Credit Card Payable		1 010
2200	Accounts Payable		9 174
2650	GST Charged on Services		1 530
2670	GST Paid on Purchases	840	
2850	Mortgage Payable		75 000 ▶

		Debit	Credit
▶ 3560	D. Dorfmann, Capital		78 547
4020	Revenue from Design		38 000
4040	Revenue from Consulting		7 400
4060	Sales Discounts	400	
4100	Interest Revenue		371
5010	Bank Charges	225	
5020	Credit Card Fees	590	
5040	Purchase Discounts		300
5050	Delivery Expenses	180	
5060	Hydro Expense	750	
5070	Maintenance Services	1 391	
5100	Model Parts Used	1 600	
5110	Computer Supplies Used	1 200	
5120	Office Supplies Used	1 150	
5150	Insurance Expense	600	
5160	Telephone Expense	400	
5200	Loan Interest Expense	625	
5210	Mortgage Interest Expense	6 000	
		$236 332	$236 332

SUPPLIER INFORMATION

DORFMANN DESIGN

Supplier Name (Contact)	Address	Phone No. Fax No.	E-mail Web Site Tax ID	Terms Account	YTD Expenses (YTD Payments) Tax Code
Alberta Energy Corp. (Con Edison)	50 Watts Rd. Suite 800 Calgary, Alberta T3G 5K8	Tel 1: (403) 755-6000 Tel 2: (403) 755-3997 Fax: (403) 754-7201	accounts@aeg.ca www.aeg.ca 459 021 643	net 10 5060	$802 ($802) G
Designers Den (Art Masters)	166 Blackfoot Trail Calgary, Alberta T3P 5P4	Tel: (403) 459-3917 Fax: (403) 459-6200	artm@artful.com www.artful.com 562 553 400	2/10, n/30 (before tax) 1420	G
DesignMaster Software (Dee Collage)	233 Crowchild Trail Mississauga, Ontario L4F 2B5	Tel: (905) 566-3754 Fax: (905) 566-5623	deecoll@dms.com www.dms.com 465 377 299	1/5, n/30 (before tax) 1250	G
Maintenance & More (Rehab Major)	51 Bragg Creek Rd. Calgary, Alberta T3C 4N3	Tel: (403) 762-7622 Fax: (403) 762-9888	RMajor@mandm.com www.mandm.com 712 300 807	net 15 5070	$1 155 ($1 155) G
Models to Scale (Bill Derr)	649 4th Street Calgary, Alberta T4P 5D6	Tel: (403) 477-5997 Fax: (403) 478-8103	billd@models.com www.models.com 923 488 561	2/10, n/30 (before tax)	G
Purolator Delivery (Cam Carter)	598 Bow River Rd. Calgary, Alberta T4T 2M1	Tel 1: (403) 458-2144 Tel 2: (888) 458-2144	www.purolator.com 822 012 906	net 1 5050	$193 ($193) G
Receiver General for Canada	Sudbury Tax Services Office PO Box 20004 Sudbury, Ontario P3A 6B4	Tel 1: (800) 561-7761 Tel 2: (800) 959-2221	www.cra-arc.gc.ca	net 1 2650	($790) No tax
Staples Business Depot (Joel)	60 Richmond Rd. Calgary, Alberta T4G 2T2	Tel: (403) 761-6288 Fax: (403) 769-5532	joel@businessdep.com www.businessdep.com	net 10 1240	$1 890 ($1 890) G
Western Bell (Sal Fone)	74 Sounder Ave. Calgary, Alberta T5L 4G2	Tel 1: (403) 755-3255 Tel 2: (403) 755-5721	accounts@bell.ca www.bell.ca 492 304 590	net 1 5160	$630 ($630) G

OUTSTANDING SUPPLIER INVOICES

DORFMANN DESIGN

Supplier Name	Terms	Date	Inv/Chq No.	Amount	Tax	Total
Designers Den	2/10, n/30 (before tax)	Mar. 26/10 Mar. 26/10	DD-4502 Chq 62	$2 500	$125	$2 625 2 180
	2/10, n/30 (before tax)	Mar. 28/10	DD-4630 Balance owing	500	25	525 $ 970
DesignMaster Software	1/5, n/30 (before tax)	Mar. 13/10	DMS-234	$1 900	95	$1 995
Maintenance & More	net 15 net 15	Mar. 24/10 Mar. 31/10	MM-211 MM-242 Balance owing	$105 105		$105 105 $210
Models to Scale	2/10, n/30 (before tax)	Mar. 25/10 Mar. 25/10	MS-376 Chq 59	$4 000	$200	$4 200 2 000
	2/10, n/30 (before tax)	Mar. 28/10	MS-453 Balance owing	2 000	100	2 100 $4 300
			Grand Total			$7 475

CLIENT INFORMATION

DORFMANN DESIGN

Client Name (Contact)	Address	Phone No. Fax No.	E-mail Web Site	Terms Revenue Acct Tax Code	YTD Sales (Credit Limit) Client Since
Alberta Heritage Bank (A. Spender)	306 Revenue Road Fourth Floor Okotoks, Alberta T0L 1T3	Tel 1: (403) 744-5900 Tel 2: (403) 744-6345 Fax: (403) 744-5821	spender@heritagebank.com www.heritagebank.com	1/5, n/15 (after tax) 4020 G	$3 150 ($5 000) Jan. 1/10
Banff Condominiums (R.T. House)	99 Main Street Banff, Alberta T0L 0C0	Tel: (403) 764-3884 Fax: (403) 764-3917	rthouse@banffcondos.ca www.banffcondos.ca	1/5, n/15 (after tax) 4020 G	($5 000) Jan. 1/10
Calgary Arms Hotel (Enda Lodge)	601 Regiment Road Calgary, Alberta T4G 5H4	Tel 1: (403) 622-4456 Tel 2: (877) 623-9100 Fax: (403) 622-5188	enda@calgarms.com www.calgarms.com	1/5, n/15 (after tax) 4020 G	$7 770 ($5 000) Apr. 1/08
Calgary District School Board (Seconde Grader)	88 Learnex Avenue 8th Floor Calgary, Alberta T3C 4B6	Tel 1: (403) 788-3000 Tel 2: (403) 788-7107 Fax: (403) 788-3327	sg@cdsb.ca www.cdsb.ca	1/5, n/15 (after tax) 4020 G	$8 400 ($5 000) Jul. 1/04
Glitter Jewellers (Di Monde)	60 Ruby Street Calgary, Alberta T4C 2G6	Tel: (403) 745-6181 Fax: (403) 745-6297	di@glitter.com www.glitter.com	1/5, n/15 (after tax) 4020 G	$5 250 ($5 000) Apr. 1/08
Lougheed, Klein & Assoc - Lawyers (Bill Bigger)	121 Advocate Ave. Suite 300 Calgary, Alberta T4D 2P7	Tel 1: (403) 398-4190 Tel 2: (403) 377-2534 Fax: (403) 377-3799	bbigger@LKlawyers.com www.LKlawyers.com	1/5, n/15 (after tax) 4020 G	$10 500 ($5 000) Jul. 1/06
Passions Dept Store (Mann E. Kinn)	44 Highlife Ave. Bragg Creek, Alberta T0L 0K0	Tel: (403) 762-8662 Fax: (403) 763-9115	www.passions.com	1/5, n/15 (after tax) 4020 G	$6 300 ($5 000) Jan. 1/05

OUTSTANDING CLIENT INVOICES

DORFMANN DESIGN

Client Name	Terms	Date	Inv/Chq No.	Amount	Total
Alberta Heritage Bank	1/5, n/15 (after tax)	Mar. 23/10	38	$3 150	
		Mar. 23/10	Chq 6754	1 400	
			Balance owing		$1 750
Banff Condominiums	1/5, n/15 (after tax)	Mar. 28/10	39	$2 100	
		Mar. 28/10	Chq 4388	1 040	
	1/5, n/15 (after tax)	Mar. 31/10	41	1 050	
			Balance owing		$2 110
				Grand Total	$3 860

Accounting Procedures

Open-Invoice Accounting for Payables and Receivables

The open-invoice method of accounting for invoices allows the business to keep track of each individual invoice and any partial payments made against it. This method is in contrast to methods that only keep track of the outstanding balance by combining all invoice balances owed to a supplier or by a client. Simply Accounting uses the open-

NOTES
Provincial sales taxes are not levied in Alberta.
Most bank services and other financial institution services are exempt from GST collection.

invoice method. When invoices are fully paid, they should be removed periodically after statements are received from the supplier or sent to the clients.

The Goods and Services Tax: Remittances

Dorfmann uses the regular method for GST remittances. GST collected from clients is recorded as a liability in *GST Charged on Services*. GST paid to suppliers is recorded in *GST Paid on Purchases* as a decrease in the liability. The balance, or request for refund, is remitted to the Receiver General for Canada by the last day of the month for the previous month.

Sales of Services

Accounts are set up for several clients. Other clients pay for their purchases immediately by cash, cheque or credit card. Separate bank accounts are set up for credit card deposits. You can enter transactions for cash and credit card clients by choosing One-Time Client/Customer and typing the name of the client in the Address field or by typing the client's name in the Name field and choosing the Quick Add or Continue option.

For cash sales, the program will debit *Bank: Chequing* (or *Bank: Visa* or *MasterCard* for credit card payments) instead of the *Accounts Receivable* control account.

Purchases

Most regular suppliers have given Dorfmann credit terms, including some discounts for early payment. Some purchases are accompanied by immediate payment, usually by cheque or credit card. Cheque payments are preferred because the cancelled cheques become part of the business records. Enter the cash transaction for purchases from new suppliers in the Payments Journal as an Other Payment. Choose the appropriate "paid by" option; choose One-Time Supplier from the Supplier list; type the supplier's name in the Address field. You can also type the name in the Supplier field and choose Quick Add or Continue.

For cash purchases paid by cash or cheque, the program will credit *Bank: Chequing* instead of the *Accounts Payable* control account. For credit card purchases, *Credit Card Payable* is credited. All other accounts for this transaction will be appropriately debited and credited.

Discounts

Dorfmann Design offers a 1 percent discount to account clients if they settle their accounts within five days. Full payment is requested within 15 days. These payment terms are set up as defaults. When the receipt is entered, if the discount is still available, the program will show the amount of the discount and the net amount owing automatically. Discounts are not allowed on partial payments or on cash purchases paid by cheque or credit card. All sales discounts are calculated on after-tax amounts.

Some suppliers also offer discounts, calculated on the amounts before taxes, for early settlement of accounts. Again, when the terms are entered for the supplier and full payment is made before the discount period expires, the program will display the pretax discount as available and automatically calculate a net balance owing. Payment terms vary from supplier to supplier.

NOTES
The terms customer and client are interchangeable. The Premium version uses client and the Simply version uses customer.

SIMPLY VERSION
When we use the term supplier for the Premium version, Simply version users should substitute the term vendor.

INSTRUCTIONS

NOTES

Source documents begin on page 251 after the setup instructions.

1. **Set up** the **company accounts** using the Business Information, Chart of Accounts, Balance Sheet, Income Statement, Trial Balance and Supplier and Client Information provided for March 31, 2010. Detailed instructions to assist you in setting up the company accounts follow.

2. If you prefer to enter the source documents before setting up the data files, you can restore the dorfmann1.CAB file in the SETUP folder (inside the SimData folder). In this way, you will become familiar with the account structure, and the setup may be easier to complete.

3. **Enter** the **transactions** beginning on page 251 in Simply Accounting using the Chart of Accounts, Supplier Information, Client Information and Accounting Procedures.

4. **Print** the **reports and graphs** indicated on the following printing form after you have completed your entries:

REPORTS

Accounts
- ☐ Chart of Accounts
- ☐ Account List
- ☐ General Journal Entries

Financials
- ☑ Comparative Balance Sheet: April 1 and April 30, difference in percentage
- ☑ Income Statement: January 1 to April 30
- ☑ Trial Balance: April 30
- ☑ All Journal Entries: April 1 to June 15
- ☑ General Ledger accounts: 1060 4020 4040 from April 1 to April 30
- ☑ Cash Flow Projection Detail Report for account 1060 for 30 days
- ☐ Statement of Cash Flows

Tax
- ☑ GST Report April 1 to April 30

Banking
- ☐ Cheque Log Report

Payables
- ☐ Supplier List
- ☐ Supplier Aged
- ☐ Aged Overdue Payables
- ☐ Expense Journal Entries
- ☐ Payment Journal Entries

Receivables
- ☐ Client List
- ☐ Client Aged
- ☐ Aged Overdue Receivables
- ☐ Revenues Journal Entries
- ☐ Receipt Journal Entries
- ☐ Client Statements

Mailing Labels
- ☐ Labels

Management Reports
- ☐ Ledger

GRAPHS
- ☐ Payables by Aging Period
- ☐ Payables by Supplier
- ☐ Receivables by Aging Period
- ☐ Receivables by Client
- ☐ Sales vs Receivables
- ☐ Receivables Due vs Payables Due
- ☐ Revenues by Account
- ☐ Expenses by Account
- ☑ Expenses and Net Profit as % of Revenue

KEYSTROKES FOR SETUP

Creating Company Files

For Dorfmann Design, we will create the company files from scratch rather than use one of the starter files. Once we create the files and define the defaults, we will add the accounts, define linked accounts for the General, Payables and Receivables ledgers and create supplier and client records.

Start the **Simply Accounting program**. You should see the Simply Accounting, Select Company window:

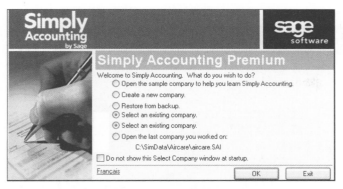

Click   Create A New Company. Click OK.

You will see the Setup wizard introduction screen:

This screen introduces the Setup wizard and some support options.

Click   Next to continue:

You must now enter company information for the business. The cursor is in the Name field. Alberta and its two-letter abbreviation — the first entry in the province list — are entered as defaults. Use the Business Information on page 200 to enter the company name and address details.

Type   Dorfmann Design **Press** (tab) to enter the name.

Type   17 Tapestry Lane **Press** (tab) to enter the street address.

Press   (tab) to skip the Street 2 field.

Type   Calgary and **click** the **Postal Code field**.

Type   t3b4u2 **Press** (tab) to enter the postal code.

Type   Canada **Press** (tab) to enter the country.

Type   4036839145 **Press** (tab) to enter the phone number.

Press   (tab) to skip the Phone 2 field and move to the Fax field.

Type   4036858210

NOTES
The initial date format for your new file is determined by your computer system settings, so your screen may show DD-MM-YYYY. The author's computer had MM-DD-YYYY as the setting so this format is shown for dates.

The Calendar icon shows the current month for your computer system. It is easier to type in the dates than it is to scroll through several months to find the one you need.

Remember that you should type a four-digit year the first time you enter a date in the year 2000 or later to be certain that the year will be 2010 and not 1910.

Typing the date in text format ensures that you will enter it correctly.

NOTES
To find out if you need to enter four digits for the year, try typing a date such as 6-5-1.

NOTES
The Earliest Transaction date is also the initial date before which you do not allow transactions.

Click   **Next** to open the company fiscal dates screen:

These company fiscal dates are like the ones you entered for Toss for Tots (Chapter 4) as part of the Company Information setup. The cursor is in the Fiscal Year Start field. This is the date on which the business begins its fiscal year. For Dorfmann Design, the fiscal start date is the beginning of the calendar year.

Type   jan 1 2010 **Press** (tab) to advance to the calendar.

The program enters the fiscal start as the **earliest transaction date**. This is the date on which the business is changing from a manual accounting system to a computerized accounting system — the earliest date for posting journal entries and the latest date for historical information. Dorfmann is converting her records on March 31.

Press   (tab) to advance to the Earliest Transaction date field.

Type   mar 31 2010

Press   (tab) **twice** to advance to the Fiscal Year End field — the date Dorfmann Design ends its fiscal period. The end of the year is the default fiscal end date. Dorfmann Design's fiscal period is six months.

Type   jun 30 2010

Click   **Next** to continue:

You can let Simply Accounting create a set of accounts that are suitable for the business type you selected, start from scratch to create the data files or copy data from another program. Because our setup is relatively small and we want to show all the stages of the setup, we will start from scratch. This approach allows us to show all the options available for each stage.

Click   **Let Me Build The List Of Accounts Myself After The Company Is Created**:

This message confirms your selection to create all the accounts on your own.

Click   **Yes** to continue with the setup options:

At this stage you should choose the type of business that best describes your company. This selection will determine some of the default settings and icon labels when you use the Setup wizard. You can scroll down the list to see the various types. Dorfmann Design is a service business.

Click   **Service** as the Industry type.

Click   **Next** to open the File Name screen:

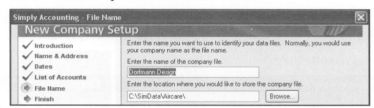

Now you must choose a file name and folder to store the new data set. The company name is entered as the default name for the data file, and it is selected.

Type   dorfmann

Press   [tab] to advance to the location field.

The last folder you used will be the default selection — that is, Aircare, if you last worked with the Air Care Services data set. Change folders if necessary to access the one with your other data files. If you have already created the folder you want to use,

Click   **Browse** to open the Browse For Folder screen to select a folder. Otherwise,

Drag through Aircare\ in the folder name or the last folder in the location field.

Type   DORFMANN\   to replace Aircare or the last folder in the name.

Click   **Next** to see the confirmation message:

Simply Accounting advises that you have named a new folder and asks if you want to create it.

SIMPLY VERSION
Remember that icon labels are the same for all company types — customer and vendor are the terms used throughout the Receivables and Payables modules respectively.

NOTES
Simply Accounting will automatically add the correct file extension. You do not need to type it when you are creating a new data set.

Click   Yes to create the new folder and file:

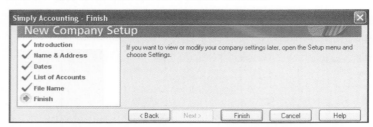

This screen reminds you that you can change this information from the Setup menu.

Click   Finish to see the final Setup screen:

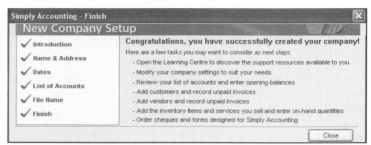

Click   Close to complete the file creation stage and start the Simply Accounting program.

If you see a message about the payroll plan, **close** the **advisor message**.

The Receivables module Home window is open:

The Home window is now open with the name Dorfmann in the title bar. However, non-accounting terms are selected, so the module names are different from the ones in previous applications. Clients & Revenues replaces Receivables and Suppliers & Expenses replaces Payables. We will change these terms as part of the setup.

The Clients ledger icon has the open history quill pen icon because the ledgers are still open for entering historical information. No ledgers are hidden.

Display the **Chart of Accounts** for the Current Year.

NOTES
Your session date may be shown as 31/03/2010 if you have selected to show the day before month in your computer system settings.

SIMPLY VERSION
Customer replaces Client for all labels in the Module window. The Client Invoices icon is named Sales Invoices.

In the Modules pane, the modules are labelled Customers & Sales and Vendors & Purchases. You will not see the Create A Time Slip icon.

NOTES
The list of equivalent accounting and non-accounting terms is shown in Appendix B.

The only account provided by default is the type X account, the General Ledger linked account, *Current Earnings*.

Close   the **Chart of Accounts**.

Preparing the System

The next step is to enter the company information that customizes the files for Dorfmann Design. You begin by preparing the system and changing the defaults.

> You should change the user preference and reports and forms defaults to suit your own work environment.

Use the Business Information on page 200 to enter defaults for Dorfmann Design.

Changing User Preferences

Choose   the **Setup menu**, then **click User Preferences**.

If you are working in multi-user mode, decide whether you want to refresh lists automatically so that changes other users make affect your file immediately. The option to Show List Buttons is already selected.

Choose Use Accounting Terms so that your on-screen terms will match the ones used in this workbook.

Choose Automatically Save Changes To Supplier, Client And Other Records.

Click   View.

Click   Inventory & Services, **Employees & Payroll**, **Project** and **Time & Billing** to hide the unused modules and features.

Click   After Changing Session Date to remove the ✓ for **Daily Business Manager** and **Checklists**.

Choose Show Change Session Date At Startup.

Choose Show Paid Stamp On Fully Paid Invoices for **Clients** and **Suppliers**.

Click   Transaction Confirmation. Confirm that the **Confirmation Message Box** is checked to activate this option.

Click   OK to save the preference changes and return to the Home window.

You should now see the familiar accounting term labels for the modules. At this stage your Home window should look like the following, with hidden modules removed:

NOTES
You may want to refer to the keystrokes in Chapter 4 to assist you in completing the setup and to the keystrokes in other chapters to assist you with the transactions for this application.

NOTES
Update your backup copy frequently as you work through the setup.

SIMPLY VERSION
The Automatically Refresh Lists option does not apply to the Simply version.

NOTES
When you automatically save changes to records, you will not be prompted to save information each time you close a ledger after making a change.

SIMPLY VERSION
The Time & Billing module is not available in Simply so you do not need to hide it.

NOTES
The option to show inventory lists does not apply to Dorfmann. You can remove this checkmark if you want.

WARNING!
You cannot complete many of the setup steps in multi-user mode.

CLASSIC VIEW
The Setup tool 🔧 is available. Clicking it when a ledger icon is selected will display the settings for that ledger.

If you click the Setup tool when no ledger or journal icon is selected, you must select a ledger from the list.

NOTES
The RT extension for the business number indicates the area of the business for reporting purposes to Canada Revenue Agency. For example, payroll has a different extension than income tax.

NOTES
If you click the calendar for the prior transactions field, you will see that the program does not allow you to choose a date before March. Entering a date prior to March 31 will generate an error with the advice that the date must be between March 31 and June 30.

Changing Default Settings

Many of the next steps for setting up company defaults and entering General Ledger accounts can be completed directly from the Company module Home window. We will start from that point.

> **Click**   **Company** in the Modules list to change the Home window.

You should now see the company window that we used for Missoni Marbleworks and Toss for Tots. You can open the Company Settings screen from the Settings icon, and you are able to create ledger accounts by clicking on the Chart of Accounts icon.

If you need help entering company settings, refer to page 71.

Changing Company Information

> **Click**   the **Settings icon** [Settings] in the Related Tasks pane.

> **Click**   **Information** to display the Company Information screen.

From any Home window, you can also choose the Setup menu, then click Settings, Company and Information.

Most of the fields on this screen are complete from the information we entered to create the company files. You can edit the information if you made a mistake. We still need to add the business number.

Notice that the earliest transaction date appears as the session date on the Company Information screen. If there are any postdated transactions in the file, the Latest Transaction Date will be later than the session date.

You can return to the Company Information screen at any time to make changes. The program will set up defaults for the session date based on this information.

> **Click**   the **Business Number field**.

> **Type**   233 281 244 RT0001

Changing System Defaults

> **Click**   **System** in the list of company options on the left.

Most of the default System Settings are correct. Dorfmann uses the accrual basis of accounting, so Use Cash-Basis Accounting should be unchecked. The option to Use Cheque No. as the source code can remain selected because Dorfmann uses cheques and may later choose to use account reconciliation.

Initially, we will not allow any transactions before March 31, the earliest transaction date. We want to allow posting to future transactions but receive a warning if the dates are more than seven days in the future. The defaults are correct. Since you can enter transactions before completing the history, you should activate the warning about unbalanced accounts to prevent mistakes. The warning makes you aware of errors or omissions before you proceed too far with transactions.

> **Click**   **Do Not Allow Transactions Dated Before** to add a ✓. **Press** (tab).

> **Type**   3-31-10

> **Click**   **Warn If Accounts Are Not Balanced When Entering A New Month**.

Changing the Backup Options

We will back up the files on a weekly basis and leave on the reminder to back up each time we close the data file.

Click   **Backup** in the list on the left.

Choose **Weekly** as the frequency for Backup Reminders.

Click   **Automatically Back Up This File** to remove the ✓.

Changing the Features Selections

Customizing the icons and features that appear can simplify journal entries.

Click   **Features** in the list on the left.

Click   **Packing Slips For Clients** and **My Company Does Business in English and French** to change the status.

This will remove the additional features and add Business in English and French to make bilingual data entry and forms available.

Since we need to choose linked accounts when we set up credit cards and sales taxes, we will create accounts before entering these settings. Since Dorfmann does not use other currencies, we will skip this setup screen.

Changing Forms Default Settings

Click   **Forms** to display the Settings for Forms:

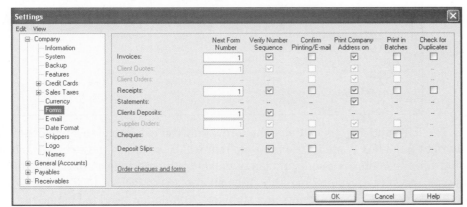

The Forms screen allows us to set up the automatic numbering sequences for business forms and to include warnings if the number you entered is a duplicate or out of sequence. You can set up the numbering sequence for all business forms that are generated internally or within the company.

Most forms that Dorfmann does not use are dimmed. The remaining one, for client deposits, we will leave blank. Cheque sequence numbers are added separately in the reports and forms settings for each bank account. (See page 219.)

Click   the **Invoices field**.

Type   44

Click   the **Receipts field**.

Type   25

The column checklists on the Forms Settings screen allow you to **verify sequence numbers** and add reminders if you print invoices, quotes, purchase orders and so forth. Verifying sequence numbers will warn you if you skip or duplicate a number and give you a chance to make a correction if necessary before posting. Choosing to **confirm** will set up the program to remind you to print or e-mail the form if you try to post before printing since posting removes the form from the screen. You should add the confirmation if you print or e-mail these forms regularly.

NOTES
If you choose to back up your file automatically, leave the option checked and choose the backup frequency and the backup file location.

Simply SIMPLY VERSION
Packing slips are not available in the Simply version.

NOTES
Form Numbers for features in the modules that are not used are hidden. For Payroll, the Direct Deposit Stubs are numbered, and for Time and Billing, the time slips are numbered. Form Number fields for unused features are dimmed.

NOTES
The additional options in the columns also apply to Cheques, even though we do not have sequence numbers for them on the Forms Settings screen. These should be set correctly for your own setup.

The third column allows you to add the **company address** to various forms. If you use preprinted forms that already include the address, remove the checkmarks to avoid double printing this information. If you have generic blank forms, leave the checkmarks so that the address is included. The next column refers to **batch printing**. If you want to print the forms on the list in batches (for example, print all the invoices for the day at the end of each day) you should check this option. Batch printing is covered in Chapter 14.

Click to add a ✓ to the check box and click again to remove a ✓.

The final column allows the program to check for duplicate invoice and receipt numbers. We should check for these duplicates as well.

Click   the **check box for Invoices** in the Check For Duplicates column.

Click   the **check box for Receipts** in the Check For Duplicates column.

Entering Default Comments for E-mail

The next step is to add a default message to e-mail communications.

Click   **E-mail** in the list of Company options to open the next Settings screen:

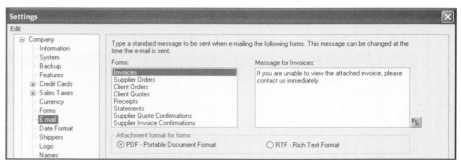

The left-hand list box contains the forms that you can e-mail to suppliers or clients. The right-hand box contains the message that will be added to the selected e-mails. You could add the company phone and fax numbers to the message so that the client or supplier can contact you more easily. You can also select PDF or RTF as the format for the file you e-mail to your clients and suppliers. You do not need to change the default messages for Dorfmann.

Click a form to select it and then type a message in the box beside it.

Entering Defaults for Date Formats

The default date formats use the short form on-screen. We want to use the long form so that the date will always be clear. Sunday is correct as the first day of the week.

Click   **Date Format** in the list of Company options:

Click   **Long Dates** beside On The Screen, Use to change the selection. **Choose MM dd yyyy** from the Short Date Format drop-down list if necessary.

Adding a Company Logo

We still need to add the company logo. The logo is located in the SimData\Setup\Logos folder (or the folder you chose) where you copied the other data files.

Click   **Logo** in the list on the left:

Click   **Browse**. **Click** the **Look In list arrow**. **Choose C:**, **SimData**, **Setup**, **Logos** and **dorfmann**.

Click   the **Open button** to add the image to the field as shown:

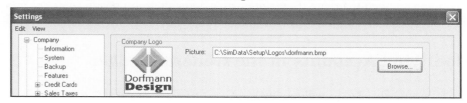

Check   the **information** you have just entered and **make** any necessary **corrections**, including corrections to the fiscal dates.

Click   **OK** to save the new information and return to the Home window.

Changing the Printer Defaults

Choose   the **Setup menu** and **click Reports & Forms**.

The printer setting options for reports are given. Notice that the defaults include adding the computer system (calendar) date to reports and information about whether the report is filtered. You can check to see if the report fits on the page to improve the appearance of your printed reports, and you can change Reports & Forms settings any time. When the settings are correct,

Click   **OK** to save the new information, or click Cancel if you have not made any changes, and return to the Home window.

Preparing the Ledgers

Before entering the remaining settings, we will create the Chart of Accounts because many of the settings require us to enter default or linked accounts.

The next stage in setting up an accounting system involves preparing each ledger beginning with the General Ledger. This stage involves the following steps:

1. organizing all accounting reports and records (this step has been completed)
2. modifying the *Current Earnings* account
3. creating new accounts
4. setting up credit cards, taxes and other features

NOTES
The Forms folder under the Simply Accounting Program folder is the default location for the logo when you click Browse.
    If you are showing file extensions, the picture file will be named dorfmann.bmp.

WARNING!
Verify that the Form location for the forms you will use are dimmed or valid for your program setup. If they are not, you will see an error message when you try to close the Reports & Forms window.

NOTES
Refer to Appendix F on the Student CD-ROM for more information about printing options and customizing reports.

5. defining linked accounts for the ledgers
6. inserting supplier and client information
7. entering historical account balances, invoices and payments

Preparing the General Ledger

Accounts are organized by section, including Assets, Liabilities, Equity, Revenue and Expense. **Account type** — such as **Heading** (H), **Subgroup total** (S), **Total** (T), **subgroup Account** (A), **Group account** (G) and **Current Earnings** (X) — is a method of classifying and organizing accounts within a section or subsection of a report.

The accounts follow the same pattern described previously:

- 1000–1999   Assets
- 2000–2999   Liabilities
- 3000–3999   Equity
- 4000–4999   Revenue
- 5000–5999   Expense

Use the Chart of Accounts, Income Statement and Balance Sheet to enter all the accounts you need to create. Remember to include all group headings, totals and subgroup totals in addition to the postable group and subgroup accounts.

Modifying Accounts in the General Ledger

The following keystrokes will modify the *Current Earnings* account in the General Ledger to match the account number defined in the Chart of Accounts.

In the Home window,

Click   the **Chart Of Accounts icon** in the Accountant's Task pane to open the Accounts window.

The accounts should be displayed in Type view — in numerical order, with names, account types and balances. There is only one predefined account.

Double click 3600 Current Earnings to display its ledger form.

You can also open the ledger by clicking the account to select it. Then click the Edit tool button or choose the Edit menu and click Edit.

Press   ⌨tab   to select the Account number field.

Type   3650

The account types are dimmed because the *Current Earnings* account type must remain as type X. Only the account number and account title can be edited. You cannot enter a balance because the program automatically calculates the amount as the net difference between the total revenue and expense account balances for the fiscal period.

Click   **Save And Close** .

Close the Accounts window to return to the Home window unless you want to continue to the next step, which also involves working in the General Ledger.

Creating New Accounts in the General Ledger

We will enter account balances as a separate step so that you can enter all balances in a single session. This may help you avoid leaving the data file with an incorrect Trial Balance.

Open the **Accounts window** or any **account ledger window**, if necessary.

Click the **Create tool** in the Accounts window or **choose** the **File menu** and **click Create**.

Enter **account information** for all accounts from the Chart of Accounts on page 201. Remember, you cannot use duplicate account numbers.

Type the **account number** and **press** (tab).

Type the **account name** or title.

Click the **account Type** for the account.

If this is a postable account, indicate whether you want to omit the account from financial statements if its balance is zero. You do not need to change the default setting for Allow Project Allocations. The option will be be checked when you enter 4000- and 5000-level accounts.

Skip the **Opening Balance field** for now. We will enter all account balances in the next stage.

When all the information is entered correctly, you must save your account.

Click **Create Another** [Create Another] to save the new account and advance to a new blank ledger account window.

Create the **remaining accounts** from the Chart of Accounts.

Click **Save And Close** [Save and Close] to close the General Ledger account window after entering the last account.

Display or **print** your updated **Chart of Accounts** to check for account type errors as well as incorrect numbers and misspelled names. **Make corrections**.

Click the **Check The Validity Of Accounts tool** [✓] for descriptions of errors in account type. **Make** the **corrections** required.

Check the **validity** again and repeat the process until you see the message that the accounts are in logical order.

Entering Opening Account Balances

The opening historical balances for Dorfmann Design can be found in the Trial Balance dated March 31, 2010, on page 202. Headings, totals and subgroup totals — the non-postable accounts — have no balances and the Balance field is removed.

Use the *Test Balance Account* for any adjustments that would leave the Trial Balance in a forced balance position before you are finished or if one of the remaining balances is incorrect. After entering all balances, the *Test Balance Account* should have a zero balance, and you can remove it.

The Accounts window should be open.

Open the **General Ledger** account information window for the first account that has a balance, **1060 Bank: Chequing**.

Click the **Opening Balance field** to highlight its contents.

Type the **balance**.

Balances for accounts that decrease the total in a group or section (i.e., *GST Paid on Purchases*, *Sales Discounts*, and *Purchase Discounts*) must be

---

NOTES
Pressing (ctrl) + N will also open a new ledger record form.

NOTES
Refer to page 90 for assistance with creating new account records and page 91 for assistance with entering historical account balances.

NOTES
The project allocation option will not apply until you choose to use projects. The default settings will then be appropriate.

WARNING!
Remember that Net Bank and GST Owing (Refund) are subgroup totals, following the subgroup bank and GST accounts respectively.

NOTES
To remove the Test Balance Account, click its icon or name in the Accounts window and click the Remove tool or choose the File menu and click Remove. Check that you have selected the right account. Click Yes to confirm that you want to remove the account.
If the Test Account balance is not zero, you cannot remove the account.

entered as negative numbers. The balances for these accounts have a (–) minus sign in the Balance Sheet or Income Statement.

Correct the **information** if necessary by repeating the above steps.

Click the **Next button** ▶ in the Ledger window to advance to the next account ledger record.

Enter the **remaining account balances** as indicated in the Trial Balance by repeating the above procedures.

Close the **General Ledger window** to return to the Accounts window. You can check your work from the Trial Balance.

Choose the **Reports menu** and **click Trial Balance** to display the Trial Balance. **Print** the **report**.

Close the **display**. **Correct** the account **balances** if necessary. Open the Ledger window, click the amount and type the correction.

Close the **Accounts window** if you want to save your work and finish your session.

Entering the Account Class: Bank Accounts

Before setting up the Payables and Receivables ledgers, we must change the account class for bank accounts and some other accounts. **Account class** is another way of organizing accounts into related groups. Each section may be divided into various classes. For example, assets may be subdivided into bank accounts, credit card accounts, receivables, inventory and so on. When you create a new account, the program assigns a default class (Asset, Liability, Equity, Operating Revenue or Cost of Goods Sold) according to the first digit of the account number. For most accounts, you can accept this setting and the program will prompt you to change the class for special purpose accounts as needed. Bank accounts are not automatically reassigned by the program. You should also change the class for expense accounts by choosing either Expense or Operating Expense as the account class. Dorfmann does not sell merchandise and has no Cost of Goods Sold accounts.

Chequing bank accounts have additional information that must be entered in the ledger and therefore require that you change the class. You cannot select bank accounts for payments and receipts unless the **Bank class** is assigned. Bank class accounts must also be defined as such before you can select them as the default linked accounts for the Payables, Receivables and Payroll ledgers. The chequing account, *Bank: Chequing* must be defined as a Bank class account.

Click the **Chart of Accounts icon**.

Double click 1060 Bank: Chequing to open its ledger window.

Click the **Class Options tab** to see the current class setting — Asset:

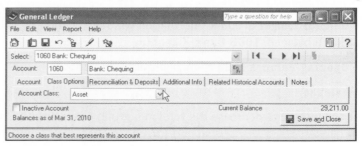

Click   the **Account Class list arrow** to see the asset account class options.

Click   **Bank** from the list to open the bank-related fields:

This screen allows you to define the type of bank account, and Chequing, the default, is correct. You can also enter a starting number for the deposit slip sequence and identify the bank for online banking access. We are not using deposit slips in this exercise, so you can skip this field. When different currencies are used, the currency for the bank account is also identified on the Class Options tab screen.

Click   **Change The Next Cheque Number** to open the cheque Form settings:

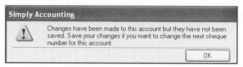

Before entering the cheque number, we need to save the account class change.

Click   **OK** to return to the ledger window.

Click   the **Save tool** 💾 or **choose** the **File menu** and **click Save**.

Click   **Change The Next Cheque Number** to open the cheque Form settings:

We need to enter only the cheque number. We do not need to change the printer settings for the cheques.

Click   the **Next Cheque No. field**.

Type   65

Click   **OK** to return to the account ledger window.

Defining the Class for Credit Card Accounts

Although credit card accounts are bank accounts, they are used as credit card linked accounts and are assigned the Credit Card class. Before setting up the cards with their linked accounts, we must change the account class for the accounts we need. We will change the linked asset accounts to the Credit Card Receivable class and the payable account to the Credit Card Payable class. If you also make payments from or deposits to these accounts, you should use the Bank class so they will be available in the bank account fields in the journals and in the Transfer Funds Journal.

Click   the **Next button** ▶ to advance to account 1070 Bank: Visa.

Click   the **Class Options tab**.

Choose **Credit Card Receivable** from the Account Class list to change the class.

Click   the **Next button** ▶ to open the ledger for 1080 Bank: MasterCard.

Choose **Credit Card Receivable** from the Account Class list.

Click   the **Select field list arrow** to see the list of accounts.

Click   **2160 Credit Card Payable** to open this account ledger.

Choose **Credit Card Payable** from the Account Class list.

Defining the Class for Expense Accounts

Expense accounts are defined as Cost of Goods Sold by default when you create them from the General Ledger new account window. These account classes should be changed unless they refer to inventory cost accounts. When you create expense accounts from an Account field using the Add An Account wizard, the default account class is Operating Expense, so you do not need to change it.

To create the Gross Margin Income Statement Report, you must correctly separate the Cost of Goods Sold accounts from other expenses.

Choose **account 5010** from the Select Account list to open the ledger.

Choose **Operating Expense** (or **Expense**) from the Account Class list.

Click   the **Next button** ▶. **Change** the **class** for all Group expense accounts.

Close   the **Ledger window**.

Close   the **Accounts window** to return to the Home window.

Setting Up Credit Cards

Now that all the ledger accounts have been created, we can enter the remaining company and ledger settings.

Since Dorfmann accepts credit card payments from clients and uses credit cards in payment for purchases, we must set up the credit cards by naming them and identifying the linked accounts for deposits, payments and fees associated with the cards. Dorfmann accepts Visa and MasterCard for sales, and uses Visa for credit card payments. You should be in the Company module Home window.

Click   **Company** in the Modules pane if necessary.

Entering the Credit Cards

Click   the **Settings icon** to open the Company Settings options list.

Click   Credit Cards:

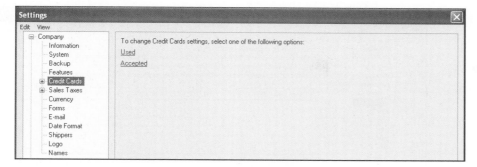

You can set up Credit Cards Used to make purchases from suppliers and Credit Cards Accepted from clients in payment.

Click   Used to open the screen for the cards that the business uses:

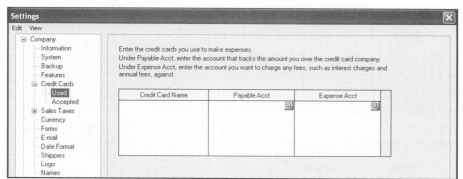

Each card named on this screen will appear in the Purchases Journal in the Paid By list. There is no discount fee associated with individual purchases, although there may be an annual or monthly fee attached to the card. Each card is listed on a separate line with its associated linked accounts.

Click   the Credit Card Name field.

Type   Visa Press tab.

The cursor moves to the **Payable Acct** field. This account is the liability account that records the balance owing to the card company.

Click   the Account List icon to see the list of available accounts.

Click   2160, the liability account for the card.

Click   Select to add the account and move to the Expense Acct field.

The **Expense Account** records any monthly or annual fees paid to the card company for the privilege of using the card and interest charges on cash advances or overdue amounts. Not all cards have user fees, but all cards charge interest on cash advances and balances not paid by the due date. These amounts are entered as additional fees when you pay credit cards in the Payments Journal (Chapter 12). Dorfmann uses one expense account for all credit card–related expenses.

Click   the Account List icon to see the account list.

Double click   5020

Cards accepted in payment from clients are set up in the same way. The business may use and accept the same cards or different cards.

Click   Accepted in the Company list on the left under Credit Cards.

NOTES
You can add a new account at this stage if necessary. Type the new account number and press tab. Click Add to start the Add An Account wizard. Remember to choose the correct Account Class when using the wizard.

WARNING!
You must choose a Bank, Cash or Credit Card Payable class account as the linked Payable account for credit cards used.

The cards clients can use to make payments are entered on this screen:

All the cards you name here will appear in the Paid By list for Sales Invoices. Each card accepted should be listed on a separate line.

Click   the **Credit Card Name field**.

Type   Visa **Press** (tab).

The cursor advances to the **Discount Fee %** field. The discount fee is the amount that the card company withholds as a merchant transaction fee for use of the card. This expense is withheld from the total invoice amount that the card company deposits to the business bank account for each sale. Fees vary from one credit card company to another and also for the type of business. For example, high-volume businesses pay a lower percentage than businesses with a smaller volume of sales.

Type   2.9 **Press** (tab).

The cursor advances to the **Expense Account** field. This is the linked account that will be debited automatically for the discount fee for a credit card sale. The expense amount or fee is the total invoice amount times the discount fee percentage.

Click   the **Account List icon** to see the accounts available for linking.

Click   **5020** to choose the account.

Click   **Select** to add the account to the Card Information screen.

The cursor is in the **Asset Account** field, the linked account for deposits from the card company. Normally a bank account is set up for credit card deposits.

Click   the **Account List icon** to see the list of accounts available for linking.

Click   **1070 Bank: Visa** to choose the account.

Click   **Select** to add the account and advance to the second line.

Enter   **MasterCard** in the Name field and **2.7** in the Discount Fee % field. **Choose** Expense Account **5020** and Asset Account **1080**.

You can enter information for additional credit cards the same way.

If you did not change the account class correctly, you will see the following warning message about incorrect account classes:

Click OK. Click Cancel to close the Credit Card Information window. Make the necessary account class changes and re-enter the credit card details.

Setting Up Sales Taxes

Setting up sales taxes before entering supplier and client records will allow us to choose default tax codes for clients and suppliers for automatic entry in journals.

> **Click   Sales Taxes** to see the options for sales tax settings:

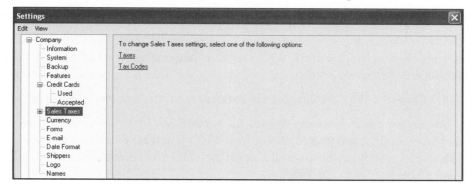

NOTES
Other taxes and tax codes can be added later if needed. The details for each tax and code can be modified if the tax legislation changes.

To set up sales taxes, we must identify the taxes that are charged and paid, and then define the codes that will be displayed in the journals.

> **Click   Taxes**:

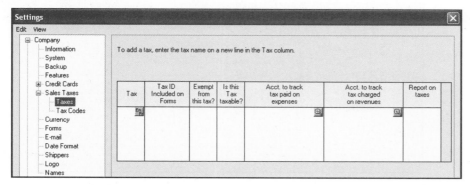

Simply Accounting has no preset tax information. You can customize the taxes to suit any business by entering all the taxes applied and paid by a business and by creating as many tax codes as needed to account for all the possible combinations of taxes. Taxes can be added later or edited if needed. For Dorfmann, the only tax that applies is the GST.

> **Click**   the **Tax field** or **press** (tab) so you can enter the name of the tax.

> **Type**   GST **Press** (tab) to advance to the Tax ID field.

If the tax number should be included on invoices, you can enter it in this field. For GST, this is the business number. For PST, it is the provincial registration number that indicates the supplier is licensed to charge PST. GST numbers are normally included on forms because GST is refundable. PST numbers are not normally included on invoices.

> **Type**   233 281 244 **Press** (tab).

The cursor moves to the **Exempt From This Tax?** column. Choose Yes only if your business — Dorfmann in this case — does not pay the tax. Dorfmann Design pays GST, so the default selection No is correct. The next field, **Is This Tax Taxable?** asks if another tax includes this tax in its base calculation. For example, in Quebec and Prince Edward Island, PST is charged on GST so the GST in those provinces is taxable. For Alberta, where Dorfmann is located, the correct answer is No.

The next two fields define the linked accounts that **track the taxes paid** and the **taxes charged**. The taxes paid account records the total of the amounts entered in the

NOTES
A PST registration number is required for businesses that charge PST on sales and do not pay PST on purchases of merchandise that they sell to clients (only the final client pays PST).

GST field in the Purchases Journal whenever a purchase is made. Although you may choose an asset or a liability account, we use liability accounts because there is normally a balance owing to the Receiver General. If the tax is not refundable, such as PST paid, you can leave the account field for tracking taxes paid blank.

Click   , the **List icon for Acct. To Track Tax Paid On Expenses**.

Double click 2670 GST Paid on Purchases.

The cursor advances to the field for the Account To Track Tax Charged On Revenues. This account records the total of the amounts entered in the GST field in the Sales Journal whenever a sale is made. You may use an asset or a liability account.

Choose 2650 GST Charged on Services from the List icon ▣ list of accounts.

The cursor advances to the **Report On Taxes** field. To generate tax reports from Simply Accounting, you should choose Yes. The Yes and No entries on the tax screens act as toggle switches. Clicking will change the entry from one to the other, and you can change these entries at any time.

Click   **No** to change the default entry to Yes.

Click   **Tax Codes** to open the next information screen:

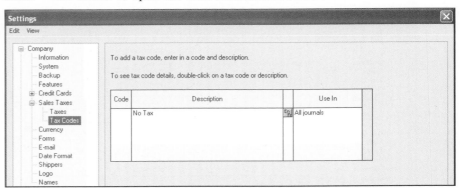

On this screen, you can create the tax codes required for all the different rates and combinations of taxes that apply to a business. No codes are entered initially so the only entry is the blank code when **No Tax** is applied.

Click   the **Code column** below the blank on the first line.

Type   G **Press** ⟮tab⟯ to move to the Description field.

Press   ⟮enter⟯ or **double click** to open the Tax Code Details screen:

On this screen, you define how the tax is calculated and reported.

Click   the **Tax field List icon** ▣ to see the list of taxes entered:

NOTES

Sales tax amounts entered in the General Journal are also tracked in these linked accounts.

NOTES

If at any time the tax regulations change, you can return to this screen and change the settings. For example, in 2004, BC decreased the PST rate from 7.5 percent to 7 percent. The federal government has changed the GST rate twice in the past two years. To make these changes in the data files, just edit the Rate in the Tax Code Details screen and the Description in the Tax Code screen. The description is not automatically updated when you change the tax rate.

NOTES

The Tax field List icon does not appear until you click the field.

Because only one tax was entered on the taxes list, only one is listed here. At this stage, you are asked to choose the taxes that should be applied (charged or paid) when this code is used in a journal entry.

Click   **Select** because GST is already selected and return to the Details.

Defaults are entered for the remaining fields. The tax **Status** is Taxable and this is correct — tax is calculated and charged. Other status options and their explanations can be viewed by clicking the List icon [icon]. The Non-taxable Status is used for items that are not taxed but for which the amounts are still included in reports to the Receiver General. Similarly, the Exempt Status is used for items that are exempt from the tax but the amounts are still included in the tax reports filed. For example, although food is zero rated (no tax is charged), suppliers may still claim a GST refund and must report their sales amounts.

The remaining fields are straightforward. **Rate** is the percentage rate for the tax. Taxes may be **included** in the sales and purchase prices or not included. If some suppliers include the tax and others do not, create two separate tax codes. And finally, is the tax **refundable** — that is, are the taxes paid on purchases refunded? GST is not included for any of Dorfmann's suppliers' or clients' prices and GST is refundable.

Click   the **Rate field**.

Type   5

Click   **No** in the Is Refundable column to change the entry to Yes.

Click   **OK** to return to the Tax Codes screen for additional codes.

The description GST @ 5% appears beside the code G. You can edit the description if you want. If the tax were not refundable, non-refundable would be added to the description automatically. However, if you change the details, you must also update the description. It is not updated automatically.

You can also choose in which journals you want to have the tax codes appear. The default is to have the codes available in all journals and is usually the correct choice.

Click   **All Journals** and then **click** the **List icon** [icon] to see the options:

You can choose to have the tax codes available for all revenues, all expenses, or for all transactions (Purchases Journal, the Sales Journal and General Journal).

Click   **Cancel** or **Select** to return to the Tax Codes screen because the default selection is correct.

Click   the [icon] **beside Company** to reduce the Settings list.

Linked Accounts

Linked accounts are accounts in the General Ledger that are affected by changes resulting from entries in journals for the other ledgers. We have seen some of these linked accounts at work in journal entries in previous chapters. For example, an entry to record a credit sale in the Sales Journal will cause automatic changes in several General Ledger accounts. In the General Ledger, the *Accounts Receivable* [+], *Revenue from Sales* [+], *GST Charged on Services* [+] and *PST Payable* [+] accounts will all be affected by the sale. The type of change, increase [+] or decrease [–], is indicated in the

NOTES
For charities that get 50 percent of the GST they pay refunded, you can set up two taxes: one for the refundable portion and one for the non-refundable portion, each at 2.5 percent. Then create a tax code that uses both the 2.5 percent refundable tax and the 2.5 percent non-refundable tax. For the non-refundable tax, you do not need to track taxes paid. They will then be added to the asset or expense portion of the entry, just like non-refundable PST.

NOTES
Charities that do not charge GST but are eligible for GST refunds may choose to show tax codes only in the Purchases Journal.

CLASSIC VIEW
The Setup tool 🔧 can be used to enter linked accounts. Select (right-click) a journal icon and click the Setup tool to see the Linked Accounts window for that ledger. If no icon is selected, choose the journal name from the Select Setup list to display the linked accounts for the ledger. If a ledger icon is selected, clicking the Setup tool displays ledger settings.

SIMPLY VERSION
Departmental Accounting and expanded Numbering are not included in the Simply version, so you will not see entries for them.

NOTES
Names are used to add labels for the additional fields in each ledger. Additional fields for the Payroll Ledger are named and used in Chapter 9 (see pages 316 and 333).

CLASSIC VIEW
In the Home window, right-click the General Journal icon 📖 . Click the Setup tool 🔧 to open the General Linked Accounts screen.
Do not click (i.e., click the left mouse button) the journal icons because you want to select the icon without opening the journal. Right-clicking will select the icon.

brackets. The program must know which account numbers are to be used for posting journal entries in any of the journals. Often you do not enter account numbers for linked accounts in the journals. It is this interconnection of account numbers and information between ledgers that makes Simply Accounting fully integrated.

Since the only linked account already defined is *Current Earnings*, the linked account for Current Earnings in the General Ledger, we must identify the remaining linked accounts for the General, Payables and Receivables ledgers. Dorfmann does not use the Payroll or Inventory ledgers and you do not need to define linked accounts for them. Linked accounts are entered from the Settings screens for the ledgers, so we will enter them with other default ledger settings.

Changing Ledger Settings and Linked Accounts

Changing General Ledger Settings and Linked Accounts

Click **General (Accounts)** in the list on the left

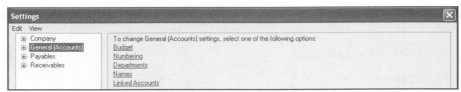

The General Ledger settings are correct for Dorfmann Design. The budget feature, departmental accounting and expanded account numbers are not used, but we need to add linked accounts.

Defining the General Linked Accounts

Click **Linked Accounts** to display the General Linked Accounts window:

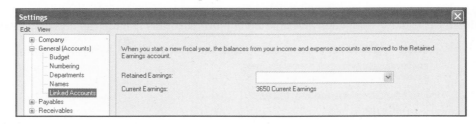

Press ⟨tab⟩ to place the cursor in the Retained Earnings field.

The Retained Earnings account is the capital (equity) account to which expense and revenue accounts are closed at the end of the fiscal period. You must choose a capital (3000 range) account.

Click the **list arrow** beside the field. All postable capital accounts are listed.

Click **3560 D. Dorfmann, Capital**.

You can also type account numbers directly in the linked account fields. Then press ⟨tab⟩ to complete the entry and advance to the next field. If you type a new account number, you can create the new account.

The Current Earnings account is correctly defined — the single type X account is always used. This linked setup cannot be changed, although you can modify the account number and account name.

Payables Default Settings

Click   **Payables** in the list on the left to expand the options list:

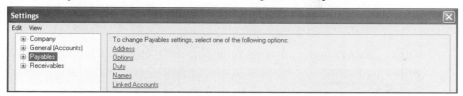

The Payables Ledger has address settings, general options, settings for imports (Duty), Names for icons and additional ledger fields, and Linked Accounts. Dorfmann does not import items that have duty applied and does not use the additional fields.

Click   **Address** to display the default address information for the suppliers:

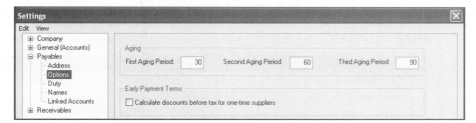

The information you enter here will be used in the ledger records as the defaults when you add suppliers. If most suppliers are in the same location, entering these locations here will save data entry time later. Most of the suppliers for Dorfmann are located in Calgary, Alberta. The cursor is in the City field.

Type   `Calgary` **Press** (*tab*) to advance to the Province field.

Type   `Alberta` **Press** (*tab*) to advance to the Country field.

Type   `Canada`

Click   **Options** to display the default settings for the Payables Ledger:

The option for the aging of accounts in the Payables Ledger is preset at 30, 60 and 90 days. We will change these options for Dorfmann to reflect the payment and discount terms most commonly used by Dorfmann's suppliers.

Double click 30 in the First Aging Period field.

Type   15 **Press** (*tab*) to advance to the Second Aging Period field.

Type   30 **Press** (*tab*) to advance to the Third Aging Period field.

Type   45

The second option determines how discounts are calculated. If the discount is taken only on the pretax total of the invoice, the discount is calculated before taxes. If the discount is applied to the entire invoice amount, including taxes, the discount is not calculated before taxes. Dorfmann's suppliers calculate discounts before taxes so you must change the setting.

Click   **Calculate Discounts Before Tax For One-Time Suppliers**.

NOTES
You can click the ⊟ beside General to reduce the Settings list.

Classic **CLASSIC VIEW**
In the Home window, you can right-click the Suppliers icon . Click the Setup tool 🔧 to open the Payables Ledger Settings screen.

Simply **SIMPLY VERSION**
The term Vendor will replace Supplier on all Settings screens.

NOTES
Usually clicking a number in a field will select the entire number. Sometimes, however, depending on exactly where you click, only part of the number is selected or an insertion point is added. Double clicking will always select the entire number in the field so that you can edit it.

NOTES
Refer to Chapter 2 for further information about taxes and discounts. We will add discount terms to individual supplier records when we set up the Payables Ledger.

Changing Payables Terminology

Simply Accounting has a set of default terms that it uses, based on the type of company you define. These are the terms we saw that changed for different company types in previous chapters. If you want, you can modify the default selections.

Click **Names** under Payables to display the Names and Terminology window:

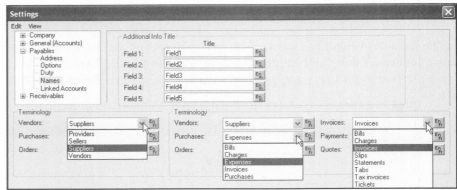

The Names window includes the Additional Information fields for the Payables Ledger. You can name five additional fields. These will appear on the Additional Information tab screen for ledger records and you have the option to include them in journal windows.

The second part of the screen has the terms used for icons and fields throughout the program. The drop-down lists for the three names you can change — the names for Vendors, Purchases and Invoices — are shown together in the screen above. You cannot modify the Payments label. The names you select will apply to icons, fields and reports.

If you want to use different names, click the field for the name you want and select a different name from the drop-down list.

Defining the Payables Linked Accounts

We will enter the Payables Ledger linked accounts next.

Click **Linked Accounts** under Payables to display the Linked Accounts window:

We need to identify the default General Ledger bank account used to make payments to suppliers. This is an essential linked account; it is required before you can finish the history for the company data file. Cash transactions in the Payments Journal will be posted to the bank account you select in the journal window. All Bank class accounts are available in the journals, and the principal linked account defined here will be selected as the default.

You can see the accounts available for linking by clicking the drop-down list arrow for any linked account field. Only Bank class (or Cash) accounts may be used in the bank fields. That is why we needed to define the Bank class accounts first.

When additional currencies are used, fields will be available for linked bank accounts for those currencies as well. Because we have not set up foreign currencies, their linked bank account fields are omitted. The chequing account is Dorfmann's principal bank account for supplier transactions.

Click   the **Principal Bank Account field list arrow**.

Click   **1060 Bank: Chequing** and **press** $\boxed{tab}$.

The cursor advances to the Accounts Payable field. This control account is also required and is used to record the amounts owing to suppliers whenever a credit (Pay Later) Purchases Journal entry is completed. The balance in this account reflects the total owing to all suppliers. You must use a liability account in this field.

Select   **2200 Accounts Payable** from the Account list.

Press $\boxed{tab}$ to enter the account number.

The cursor advances to the Freight Expense field, used to record the delivery or freight charges associated with purchases. Only freight charged by the supplier should be entered using this account. Since Dorfmann's suppliers do not charge for delivery, you should leave this field blank. You can add a linked account for freight later if you need it.

Press $\boxed{tab}$ to advance to the Early Payment Purchase Discount field. This account is used to record any supplier discounts taken for early payments.

Choose   **5040 Purchase Discounts** from the drop-down list.

Press $\boxed{tab}$ to advance to the Prepayments And Prepaid Orders field.

Choose   **2200 Accounts Payable** from the drop-down list.

Dorfmann's suppliers do not request prepayments at this time, but you cannot leave this field blank.

Check the linked accounts carefully. To delete a linked account, click it to highlight it and press $\boxed{del}$. You must complete this step of deleting the linked account before you can remove the account in the General Ledger from the Accounts window.

To select a different account, highlight the one that is incorrect and type the correct number, or select an account from the drop-down list.

Receivables Default Settings

Click   **Receivables** to display the Receivables Ledger choices:

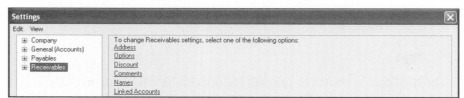

The Receivables Ledger has address settings, general settings (Options), Discount settings, settings for Comments, Names for icons and additional ledger fields, and Linked Accounts.

Click   **Address** to display the default address information for the Clients:

NOTES
The linked account for prepayments is also a required linked account. Because we are not using the feature, we can enter Accounts Payable.

NOTES
You can click the beside Payables to reduce the Settings list.

Classic **CLASSIC VIEW**
In the Home window, you can right-click the Clients icon . Click the Setup tool to open the Receivables Ledger Settings screen.

Simply **SIMPLY VERSION**
Remember that you will see the term Customers when we refer to Clients.

Just as you entered default address information for suppliers, the information you enter here will be used in the ledger records as the defaults when you add clients. Most of Dorfmann's clients are also located in Calgary. The cursor is in the City field.

Type   Calgary **Press** (tab) to advance to the Province field.

Type   Alberta **Press** (tab) to advance to the Country field.

Type   Canada

Click   **Options** to display the default settings for the Receivables Ledger:

Dorfmann Design offers a 1 percent discount if clients pay within 5 days and expects full payment within 15 days. After 30 days, clients are charged 1.5 percent interest per month on the overdue accounts. Therefore, the aging periods 5, 15 and 30 days will be used, and we must change the default settings.

Double click **30** in the First Aging Period field.

Type   5 **Press** (tab) to advance to the Second Aging Period field.

Type   15 **Press** (tab) to advance to the Third Aging Period field.

Type   30

Click   **Interest Charges** to add a ✓ and select this feature.

NOTES

You can use the statements to find the interest amount that you will enter on the invoice.

When interest charges are applied on overdue invoices, Simply Accounting calculates interest charges and prints them on the client statements and management reports. However, the program does not create an invoice for the interest. You must create a Sales Journal entry for the amount of interest charged.

Press   (tab) to advance to and highlight the contents of the Interest Rate field for editing.

Type   1.5 **Press** (tab) to advance to and highlight the contents of the Days field for editing.

Type   30

The next option relates to printing historical information on invoices. The maximum setting is 999 days. For Dorfmann Design, client statements are sent every month so the period should be 31 days. Any invoices paid in the past 31 days will be included in the statements and unpaid invoices are always included. The default setting is correct.

If all or most clients use the same sales tax code, you can choose a **default tax code** that will be entered when you create new clients or when you choose One-time Client or Quick Add in a sales invoice.

Click   the **Tax Code For New Clients list arrow**.

Click   **G GST @ 5%** as the default tax code.

When salespersons are set up, you can **print** the name of the **salesperson** on invoices, orders and quotes. Dorfmann does not have sales staff.

Entering Discount Settings

Next we must enter the payment terms for account clients.

Click   **Discount** in the list under Receivables on the left:

For all account clients, the payment terms are: 1 percent discount if the account is paid in the first 5 days and net payment is due in 15 days. All client discounts are calculated on after-tax amounts so the Calculate Discounts Before Tax selection is correctly turned off.

Click   the **% field** in the first Early Payment Terms field to advance the cursor.

Type   1.0 **Press** (*tab*) to advance to the Days field.

Type   5 **Press** (*tab*) to advance to the Net Days field.

Type   15

Simply Accounting adds the payment terms you just entered as a default for all clients. Individual client records or invoices can still be modified if needed.

The remaining discount option allows you to apply discounts to individual lines on an invoice. A % Discount column will be added to the invoice form. We will use this feature in Chapter 19.

SIMPLY VERSION
Line discounts are not available in the Simply version.

Click   **Calculate Line Item Discounts on Invoices, Orders And Quotes** to remove the ✓. You will see a warning:

Click   **Yes** to confirm the removal of line discounts.

Entering Default Comments

Simply Accounting allows you to add a default comment to all client forms. You can change the default message any time you want, and you can edit it for a particular form when you are completing the invoice, quote or order confirmation.

Click   **Comments** under Receivables to open the screen for default comments:

SIMPLY VERSION
The field label Sales Invoices replaces Client Invoices in the Simply version.

We want to add a comment that will appear on every client invoice. The comment may include payment terms, company motto, notice of an upcoming sale or a warning about interest charges.

> **Click** the **Client (Sales) Invoices field** to move the cursor.
>
> **Type** `Interest at 1.5% per month charged on accounts over 30 days.`

You can enter the same comment for all sales forms (invoices, orders and quotes), or you can add a unique comment for each. The comment fields for quotes and orders are dimmed because Dorfmann does not use these features.

Changing Receivables Terminology

The terms for the Receivables Ledger can also be customized.

> **Click** **Names** under Receivables to display the Names and Terminology window:

For Receivables, you can also name five additional fields to appear in ledger records and, if you choose, in journal windows.

The second part of the screen shows the terms used. The drop-down lists for the names you can change — Customers, Sales and Invoices — are shown together in the screen above. You cannot modify the Receipts label. The names you select will apply to icons, fields and reports.

> If you want to use different names, click the field for the name you want and select a different name from the drop-down list.

Defining the Receivables Linked Accounts

The Receivables Ledger linked accounts parallel those for the Payables Ledger.

> **Click** **Linked Accounts** under Receivables:

We need to identify the default General Ledger bank account used to receive payments from clients. Cash transactions in the Sales and Receipts journals will be posted to the bank account you select in the journals. The linked account will be the default account but any Bank class account may be selected.

Dorfmann uses *Bank Account: Chequing* as the principal bank account for client transactions. Although most linked accounts may be used only once, one bank account can be linked to the Payables, Receivables and Payroll ledgers.

> **Click** the **Principal Bank Account field list arrow**.

> **Click** **1060 Bank: Chequing** and **press** tab .

The cursor advances to the Accounts Receivable field. This control account records the amounts owed to Dorfmann by clients whenever a credit (Pay Later) Sales Journal entry is completed. The balance in this account reflects the total owed by all clients. You must use an asset account in this field.

> **Select** **1200 Accounts Receivable** from the drop-down list.

Dorfmann does not collect freight revenue because it does not charge for deliveries. Leave the Freight Revenue field blank.

> **Click** the **Early Payment Discount field list arrow**.

This field is used to record the discounts clients receive for early settlement of their accounts.

> **Choose 4060 Sales Discounts** from the drop-down list. **Press** tab .

The cursor advances to the Deposits And Prepaid Orders field. This account is linked to client deposits. Although Dorfmann does not request client deposits, this is an essential linked account so we cannot leave this field blank. Because we do not use it, we can use Accounts Receivable.

> **Choose 1200 Accounts Receivable** from the drop-down list.

> **Click** **OK** to see the program's message about account class changes:

Many linked accounts must have a specific account class to be used as linked accounts. Normally, you can accept the account class definitions and changes assigned by the program. The exception is the Bank class accounts, which you must define before you can use them as linked bank accounts.

> **Click** **Yes** to accept the change and save the linked account setting. You will see a second confirmation message for account 2200:

> **Click** **Yes** to accept the class change, save the linked accounts and see the final message about the account class change for account 1200:

> **Click** **Yes** to accept the change and return to the Home window.

NOTES
When additional currencies are used, fields will be available for linked bank accounts for them as well. You can choose a separate linked account for each currency, or you may use the Canadian dollar account for more than one currency. Because we have not set up foreign currencies, their linked bank account fields are omitted.

NOTES
You must choose Yes to confirm the account class changes and to continue. If you choose No, you will return to the Linked Accounts screen.

Entering Suppliers in the Payables Ledger

Use the Supplier Information for Dorfmann Design on page 203 to enter supplier details and historical invoices. The following keystrokes will enter the information for Alberta Energy Corp., the first supplier on Dorfmann Design's list.

You can open the ledger screen from the Payables module window Suppliers icon or from its shortcuts list. First we must open the Payables module window.

Click   **Payables** in the Modules pane to open the window we need.

Click   the **Suppliers icon** 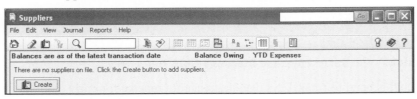 in the window to display the empty Suppliers window:

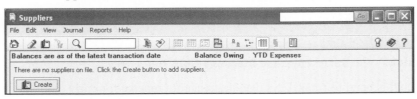

Or click the Suppliers shortcuts list arrow as shown and choose View Suppliers:

The Suppliers window is empty because no suppliers are on file. Once we add the supplier accounts, this window will contain a listing for each supplier that you can use to access the supplier's ledger record. The suppliers may be displayed in icon form or by name with balances and year-to-date amounts. The default is the listing by name.

If you prefer to list the suppliers by icon in the Suppliers window, choose the View menu and click Icon. New suppliers will be added at the end of the display but you can drag icons to any position you want so that frequently used icons appear together at the top of the window.

Click   the **Create button** 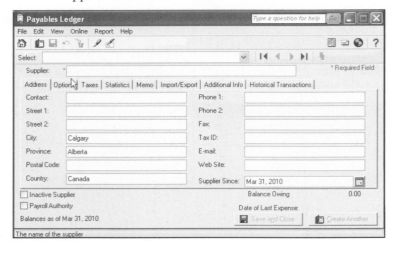 or the **Create tool** in the Suppliers window, or **choose** the **File menu** and **click Create** to display the supplier Address tab screen:

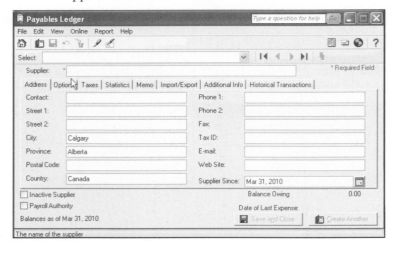

NOTES

If you click Add Supplier on the shortcuts list, you will open the New Supplier ledger window immediately.

NOTES

If you display the suppliers by icon, you can restore the alphabetic order for the icons by choosing the View menu and clicking Re-sort Icons.

NOTES

Pressing *ctrl* + N in the Suppliers window or in a ledger record window will also open a new supplier ledger record form.

NOTES

If you choose to skip the Suppliers icon window from the Home window Setup menu (User Preferences, View), you will see this Payables Ledger (supplier) Address tab window immediately when you click the Suppliers icon.

Most of the Supplier input screens should be familiar from entering records for new suppliers in previous chapters. The Address tab screen is displayed first and the cursor is in the Supplier name field, the only required field for the record.

Type   `Alberta Energy Corp.` **Press** `tab`.

The cursor advances to the Contact field. Here you should enter the name of the person (or department) at Alberta Energy Corp. with whom Dorfmann Design will be dealing. This information enables a company to make inquiries more professionally and effectively. For a small business, the owner's name may appear in this field.

Type   `Con Edison` **Press** `tab` to advance to the Street 1 field.

Type   `50 Watts Rd.` **Press** `tab` to move to the Street 2 field.

Type   `Suite 800`

The program uses the Payables Address Settings as the defaults for City, Province and Country fields. In this case, they are correct.

Click   the **Postal Code field**.

Type   `t3g5k8`

Click   the **Phone 1 field**.

The program corrects the format of the postal code. (Only Canadian postal codes are reformatted — those with the specific letter and number sequence.) You can enter phone and fax numbers with or without the area code.

Type   `4037556000` **Press** `tab` to advance to the Phone 2 field.

Type   `4037553997` **Press** `tab` to advance to the Fax field.

Type   `4037547201` **Press** `tab` to advance to the Tax ID field.

The program corrects the format of the phone numbers. The Tax ID field allows you to enter the supplier's tax ID or business number. The following two fields contain the e-mail and Web site addresses for the supplier. Enter them just as you would type them in your Internet and e-mail programs.

Type   `459 021 643` **Press** `tab`.

Type   `accounts@aeg.ca` **Press** `tab`.

Type   `www.aeg.ca` **Press** `tab`.

The cursor moves to the Supplier Since field. The program has entered the session date as the default, but we should change it to reflect the company's actual transaction history. All suppliers have been used by Dorfmann since she started her business in 2001.

Type   `July 1 2001`

Notice that the supplier's account balance appears at the bottom of the ledger. A supplier may also be marked as Inactive if there are currently no transactions. You have the option to include or omit inactive suppliers from reports. All Dorfmann's suppliers are active.

Payroll Authorities are suppliers to whom payroll remittances are made. Payroll remittances are covered in Chapter 8.

The remaining supplier details are entered from the other tab screens.

NOTES
You may skip any of the address tab fields if the information is missing for the supplier. Just click the next field for which you have information to move the cursor. To edit any field, drag to highlight the contents and type the correct information.

NOTES
Remember that the postal code sequence for Canada is letter, number, letter, number, letter and number.

Click the **Options tab** to open the next screen:

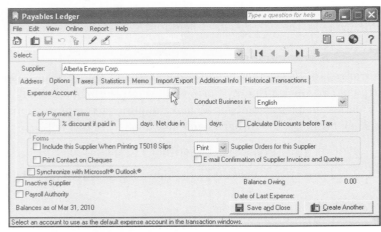

The supplier's name appears at the top of each tab screen for reference. We want to enter the default expense account so that it will automatically appear in journal entries.

Click the **Expense Account list arrow**. All postable accounts are listed.

Click **5060 Hydro Expense** (you will need to scroll down first).

When you use multiple currencies, the supplier's currency is also defined on the Options tab screen.

Regardless of the language you use to work in Simply Accounting, you can choose a language for the supplier so that all Simply Accounting forms you send to this supplier will be in the language selected on the Options tab screen.

If the supplier offers a discount for early payment or has a term for the net amount, enter these details in this screen. There is no discount, so start in the third Terms field.

Click the **Net Due In ____ Days field**.

Type 10

Skip the Discount Before (or after) Tax option because there is no discount.

Do not turn on the option to Print Contact On Cheques because the Contact field does not contain address information.

If you e-mail purchase orders to a supplier, choose this option from the drop-down list to replace the default option to print purchase orders. Click E-mail Confirmation if you e-mail purchase orders to be certain that the order is received. Even if you choose Print as the default, you can still e-mail the order from the Purchases Journal.

Click the **Taxes tab** to access the next input screen:

This screen allows you to indicate which taxes the supplier normally charges and the default tax code for journal entries. The codes are available from the drop-down list as shown in the screen above.

All suppliers for Dorfmann Design, except the Receiver General, charge GST so the correct entry for the Tax Exempt column is No. Suppliers such as the Receiver General for Canada, who do not supply goods or services eligible for input tax credits, should have Yes in the Tax Exempt column to indicate that Dorfmann does not pay tax to them. If you choose Yes, the tax will not be calculated in the Purchases Journal for that supplier, even if you choose a tax code that applies the tax.

Leave the Tax Exempt entry as No to indicate that this supplier charges GST and to make tax codes available for purchases. Clicking No changes the entry to Yes.

Click   the **list arrow beside No Tax** to choose a default tax code.

Click   **G - GST @ 5%** to select the code.

Click   the **Statistics tab** to open the next information screen:

The Statistics fields record the historical purchase and payment totals for two years and are updated automatically from journal entries.

Click   the **Year-To-Date Expenses field**.

Type   802

Click   **the Payments For 2010 field**.

Type   802

Click   the **Memo tab** to advance to the next screen:

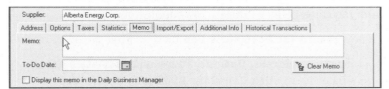

The Memo tab screen allows you to enter a message related to the supplier that is added to the Daily Business Manager lists, the automatic reminder system.

Click   the **Import/Export tab** to open the next information screen:

The Import/Export screen refers to inventory items. If the supplier also uses Simply Accounting, you can match the supplier's inventory item codes to your own for electronic transfers of information.

Click   the **Additional Info tab**:

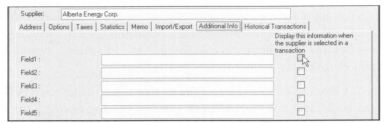

NOTES
The field names on this tab screen are taken from the Names settings for the ledger.
We will customize Payroll Ledger records by adding fields in Chapter 9.

You can customize the records for any ledger by adding up to five fields. The customized names you added from the Names Settings option for the ledger will appear on this Additional Info screen. This additional information can be included in journal transaction windows and in Supplier List reports. Dorfmann Design does not use any additional fields and there are no outstanding invoices for Alberta Energy Corp. so we are ready to check the supplier details.

Correct any **errors** by returning to the field with the mistake, **highlighting** the **errors** and **entering** the **correct information**. You can now save the record.

Click   **Create Another** [Create Another] to save the supplier information and display a blank New Supplier screen.

Click   the **Address tab** to prepare for entering the next supplier record.

When you return to the Suppliers window, you will see that Simply Accounting has created a Supplier icon and listing for Alberta Energy Corp. The default view for suppliers is to list them alphabetically by name with the balance owing and year-to-date purchases.

The Create button has been removed. The Create tool is still available.

WARNING!
Remember to click Calculate Discounts Before Tax for all suppliers who offer discounts.

NOTES
You can also display suppliers by icon. Choose the Icon tool or choose the View menu and click Icon. Supplier icons may be moved to a different position by dragging. New suppliers are added to the end of the display, regardless of order. To restore the alphabetic order for icons, choose the View menu and then Re-sort Icons.

Entering Historical Supplier Information

You can enter all the historical invoices and payments for the fiscal year to date, but you must enter all outstanding invoices and partial payments toward them. Designers Den has outstanding invoices so we must enter historical transaction details. The following keystrokes will enter the historical information from page 203 for Designers Den. You should have a blank Payables Ledger Address tab window on-screen.

Create a new **record for Designer's Den** by repeating the steps above.

Finish entering the **Address, Options, Taxes and Statistics details**, remembering to **click Calculate Discounts Before Tax**.

You can also enter these details for all suppliers and then open the ledger to add historical information by clicking the Historical Transactions tab. Open the ledger for any supplier by double clicking the supplier's name in the Suppliers window.

Click   the **Historical Transactions tab**:

NOTES
If you have already created the record, you will not see the Save Now option on the Historical Transactions tab screen. Instead, you will see the next screen asking you to choose Invoices or Payments.

You must save or create the supplier record before adding historical invoices.

Click   the **Save Now button** to modify the ledger screen:

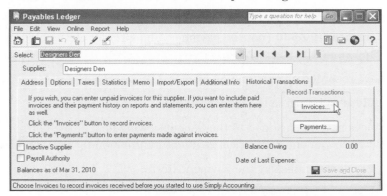

The Create Another button has been removed and the Save And Close button is dimmed. The screen now has two new buttons: Invoices and Payments. You should select Invoices to record outstanding invoices and Payments to record prior payments that you want to keep on record after entering invoices.

Click   **Invoices** to see the following input screen:

The cursor is in the Invoice No. field so you can enter the first invoice number.

Type   DD-4502   **Press** ⟮tab⟯ to advance to the Date field.

Enter the invoice date to replace the default earliest transaction date. The invoice date must not be later than the earliest transaction date — the date of the first journal transaction after the historical data in the setup.

Type   03-26-10

The Terms are entered from the Supplier record and are correct, although they can be edited if necessary. You should enter the amount for the first invoice. The amount is divided into pretax and tax amounts so that Simply Accounting can correctly calculate the discount on the before-tax amount. When the option to calculate discounts before tax is not selected, a single amount field appears on the invoice for the full amount of the invoice with taxes included.

Click   the **Pre-tax Amount field** to advance the cursor.

WARNING!
Enter invoice details carefully. To correct a historical invoice amount, you must pay the invoice and clear the paid transactions (Maintenance menu). Then reset the historical payments for the year to zero (Payables Ledger, Statistics tab screen) and re-enter the outstanding invoices. Refer to page 249.

Type   2500 **Press** (tab) to advance to the Tax amount field.

Type   125.50 **Press** (tab) to update the Invoice Total.

The totals of all outstanding invoice and payment amounts must match the opening balance in the *Accounts Payable* control account in the General Ledger.

Correct any **errors**. **Press** (tab) to return to the field with the error and **highlight** the **error**. Then **enter** the **correct information**.

Be sure that all the information is entered correctly before you save your supplier invoice. If you save incorrect invoice information and you want to change it, refer to page 249 for assistance.

Click   **Record** to save the information and to display another blank invoice for this supplier.

Enter   **invoice DD-4630** (not the payment, Chq #62) for Designers Den by repeating the steps above.

When you have recorded all outstanding invoices for a supplier,

Click   **Close** to return to the ledger.

The two invoices have been added to the Balance Owing field at the bottom of the ledger screen. Now you can enter historical payment information for this supplier.

Click   **Payments** to display the payments form:

All outstanding invoices that you entered are displayed. Notice that the discount amounts are 2 percent of the pretax amounts. Entering historical payments is very much like entering current payments in the Payments Journal. You should make separate payment entries for each cheque.

Click the Number field if necessary to move the cursor to the cheque number field.

Type   62 **Press** (tab) to advance to the Date field.

Enter the cheque date for the first payment toward invoice #DD-4502 to replace the default earliest transaction date.

Type   3-26

Click   the **Amount Paid column** on the line for Invoice #DD-4502.

Because the full amount is not being paid, the discount does not apply. The full amount of the discount will remain available until the 10 days have passed. If the balance is paid within that time, the full discount will be taken.

The full invoice amount, displayed as the default, is highlighted so you can edit it.

Type   2180 **Press** (tab). **Press** (del) to delete the Disc. Taken amount.

Check   the **information** carefully and **make corrections** before you proceed.

WARNING!
You must choose Record to save each invoice and payment and then Close the invoice form. If you close the input screen before selecting Record, the information is not saved.

NOTES
The View menu has the option to refresh the invoices from information added by other users. It applies only to the multi-user mode and is not available in the Simply version.

NOTES
The discount amounts are $50 (2 percent of $2 500) and $10 (2 percent of $500).

WARNING!
If an amount appears in the Disc. Taken field, delete it before recording the payment.

NOTES
Clicking the Amount Paid field directly ensures the discount amount is not entered.

Click   **Record** to save the information and display another payment form for this supplier in case there are additional payments to record.

The amount owing for invoice DD-4502 has been updated to include the payment you entered but the full discount amount remains available.

Repeat these procedures to enter any other payments to this supplier.

When you have recorded all outstanding payments to a supplier,

Click   **Close** to return to the supplier information form.

When you click the Statistics tab, you will see that the invoices and payment you entered have been included to increase the totals for 2010.

Click   the **Create tool** or **press** ⌨ctrl + **N** to enter the next supplier.

Click   the **Address tab** to prepare for entering the next supplier record.

Enter   the **remaining suppliers** and historical transactions. After entering the last supplier record,

Click   **Save And Close** 🖫 Save and Close to close the Supplier Ledger. **Close** the **Suppliers window** to return to the Home window.

Display or **print** your **Supplier List** to check the address details.

Display or **print** a **Supplier Aged Detail Report**. Include terms and historical differences to check the historical transactions.

Entering Clients in the Receivables Ledger

Use the Client Information chart for Dorfmann Design on page 204 to complete this step. The following keystrokes will enter the information for Alberta Heritage Bank, the first client on the list for Dorfmann Design. You should open the Receivables window.

Click   **Receivables** in the Modules pane list to open the window we need.

Click   the **Clients icon** 📇 to display the Clients (Customers) window. The Clients window is empty because there are no clients on file yet.

Click   the **Create button** 🗐 Create or **tool** 📖 in the Clients window, or **choose** the **File menu** and **click Create**:

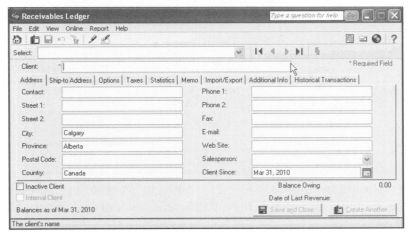

The client information screen opens at the Address tab screen. The cursor is in the Client field, the only required field. The default Province and Country entered from the Receivables Address settings are correct, but we need to change the city name.

NOTES
Even though the historical invoices and payments were entered correctly, you will notice that there is an outstanding historical difference. This is addressed on page 249.

SIMPLY VERSION
Customer replaces Client on all Receivables Ledger screens.

NOTES
If you choose not to view the Customers icon window from the Home window Setup menu (User Preferences, View), you will see this Receivables Ledger window immediately when you click the Clients icon.

You may skip any of the address tab fields if information is missing. Just click the next field for which you have information to move the cursor.

Type   Alberta Heritage Bank **Press** (tab).

Dorfmann's primary contact about a sale should be entered in the Contact field.

Type   A. Spender **Press** (tab) to advance to the Street 1 field.

Type   306 Revenue Road **Press** (tab) to move to the Street 2 field.

Type   Fourth Floor **Press** (tab) to advance to the City field.

Type   Okotoks

Click   the **Postal Code field**.

Type   t0l1t3

Click   the **Phone 1 field**. The postal code format is corrected.

Type   4037445900 **Press** (tab). The format is corrected automatically.

Type   4037446345 **Press** (tab).

Type   4037445821 **Press** (tab) to advance to the E-mail field.

Type   spender@heritagebank.com **Press** (tab) to move to the Web Site field.

Type   www.heritagebank.com

Press   (tab) **twice** to move to the Client Since date field.

Type   Jan 1 10

The current balance is noted at the bottom of the Ledger window. Like suppliers and accounts, clients may be marked as inactive and omitted from reports if they have not bought merchandise or services for some time.

Click   the **Ship-To Address tab**:

The Ship-To Address screen allows you to enter multiple addresses for clients who want merchandise to be shipped to different addresses. You can apply labels to each address. The default setting is to use the mailing address as the shipping address.

Click   the **Options tab** to see the payment and invoice options for the client:

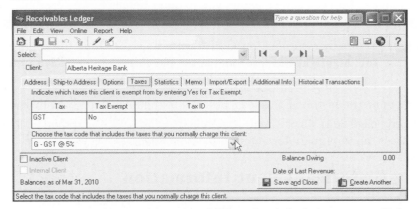

All the default settings are correct. You can select English or French as the client's language — all forms you send to the client will be prepared in the selected language. The Price List field applies to inventory and services prices that can be set at different rates for different clients. Dorfmann supplies customized services and does not use the Inventory module. The payment terms are entered automatically from the Receivables Settings. Terms can be edited if necessary for individual clients and invoices in the Sales Journal. Dorfmann charges interest on overdue accounts so we need to be able to produce statements.

You need to add only a default revenue account for the client. Although there are two revenue accounts that apply to clients, most clients use Dorfmann's design services, so we can choose this as the default. Remember that you can choose a different account in the Sales Journal for any invoice. You may prefer to leave the Revenue Account field blank so that you do not select an incorrect revenue account.

Click   the **Revenue Account field list arrow**.

Click   **4020 Revenue from Design**.

Click   the **Taxes tab**:

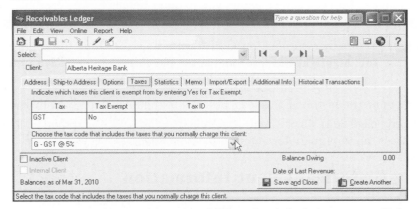

The client is not exempt from paying GST so the default is correct. If the client does not pay the tax, enter the tax ID number so that it appears on invoices. For example, retail stores do not pay PST on inventory that they will sell. They must have a tax number to permit the exemption. Some clients are also exempt from GST payments. Taxes will be calculated only if the client is marked as not tax exempt. The default tax code, G - GST @ 5%, should be entered.

Click   the **Statistics tab** to view the next set of client details:

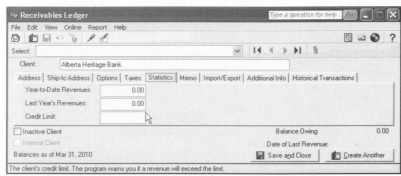

Balances will be included automatically once you provide the outstanding invoice information. **Year-To-Date Revenues** are updated from journal entries, but you can add a historical balance as well. When you have two years of data, there will be an amount for last year's sales too. Records for foreign clients will have sales summary amounts and balances in both currencies.

The **Credit Limit** is the amount that the client can purchase on account before payments are required. If the client goes beyond this credit limit, the program will issue a warning when you attempt to post the invoice.

Click   the **Year-To-Date Revenues field**.

Type   3150 **Press** ⟨tab⟩ **twice** to advance to the Credit Limit field.

Type   5000

The **Memo tab** screen for clients is just like the Memo tab screen for suppliers. It allows you to enter messages related to the client. If you enter a reminder date, the program will display the message on the date you provide.

If the client also uses Simply Accounting, you can match the client's inventory codes to your own on the **Import/Export tab** screen to allow for electronic data transfers.

The **Additional Info tab** screen allows you to enter details for the custom-defined fields you created for clients, similar to the Additional Info tab fields for suppliers.

Correct errors by returning to the field with the error. **Click** the appropriate **tab**, **highlight** the **error** and **enter** the **correct information**. You can correct address and options details any time.

If there are no historical invoices, proceed to the final step of saving the client record (page 204). Click Create Another [🗐 Create Another] and then click the Address tab to prepare for entering the next client.

Entering Historical Client Information

As for suppliers, you can enter all historical invoices and payments for the year-to-date, but you must enter outstanding invoice amounts. The following keystrokes will enter historical information for Alberta Heritage Bank from page 204.

Click   the **Historical Transactions tab**:

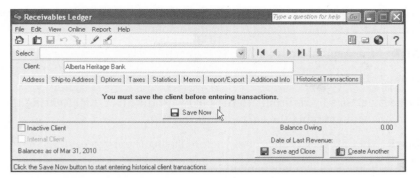

You must save or create the client record before adding historical invoices.

Click   the **Save Now button** to access the invoice and payment buttons:

Again, the Create Another button has been removed and the Save And Close button is dimmed because you have already saved the record.

If you prefer, you can enter address, options and credit limit details for all clients and then add the historical invoices and payments from the Historical Transactions tab screen. You can open a client ledger record by double clicking the client's name in the Clients window. Then click the Historical Transactions tab.

Just as in the Payables Ledger, you enter invoices and payments separately. You can use the Payments option to record any payments against previous invoices that you want to keep on record. The totals of all outstanding invoices, after payments, must match the opening balance in the *Accounts Receivable* control account in the General Ledger.

Click   **Invoices** to display the following input form:

There is a single Amount field because client discounts are calculated on after-tax amounts. When discounts are calculated before tax, there is an additional input field so that the sale and the tax amounts can be entered separately as we saw in the Payables Historical Invoices screen. The earliest transaction date is the default invoice date. The cursor is in the Invoice No. field so you can enter the first invoice number.

Type   38 **Press** (tab) to advance to the Date field.

Type   mar 23

Because the payment terms are correctly entered, we can skip them. Discounts are calculated after taxes so only the single after-tax amount is needed.

Click   the **Amount field**.

Type   3150

Correct   errors by returning to the field with the error, **highlighting** the **error** and **entering** the **correct information**.

Check   the **information** carefully before saving the invoice.

Incorrect invoices can be changed only by paying the outstanding invoices, clearing paid transactions (Home window, Maintenance menu, Clear Data, Clear Paid Transactions, Clear Paid Client/Customer Transactions) and then re-entering the invoices (see page 249).

Click   **Record** to save the invoice and to display a new blank invoice form for this client.

Repeat   these **procedures** to enter the remaining invoices for this client, if there are any.

Click   **Close** to return to the Historical Transactions window after entering all invoices for a client.

Notice that the program has added the client's balance to the Ledger window. You are now ready to record the payment made by Alberta Heritage Bank against this invoice.

Click   **Payments** to display the client payments form:

All outstanding invoices that you entered are displayed. Entering historical client payments is much like entering current receipts in the Receipts Journal. As usual, the earliest transaction date is the default. The default March 31 transaction date is more than five days after the invoice date so no discount is available.

Click the Number field to move the cursor to the cheque number field if necessary.

Type   6754 **Press** to advance to the Date field.

Type   03-23

The discount is now available. Discounts can be taken only when the full payment is made before the due date, so we must skip the Discount fields. The full discount remains available until the discount period has ended.

Click   the Amount Paid column on the line for invoice #38.

The full invoice amount is displayed as the default and highlighted so you can edit it.

Type   1400 **Press** tab .

Check   your **information** carefully before you proceed and **make corrections** if necessary.

NOTES
This invoice amount will be added to the Year-To-Date Revenues amount on the Statistics tab screen.

WARNING!
If an amount appears in the Disc. Taken field, delete it before recording the payment.

Click   **Record** to save the information and to display another payment form for this client in case there are additional payments to record.

Notice that the full discount remains available after the payment — its amount is not reduced although the balance owing has been reduced.

Repeat these procedures to enter other payments by this client if there are any.

When you have recorded all outstanding payments by a client,

Click   **Close** to return to the client information form.

Notice that the balance owing in the ledger has been updated to include the payment entry just completed.

Click   the **Address tab** to prepare for entering the next client.

Click   the **Create tool** 🗒 to open another new client input screen.

Saving the Client Record

When all the information is entered correctly, you must save the client information. If you have not added historical information,

Click   **Create Another** [Create Another] to save the information and advance to the next new client input screen.

Click   the **Address tab** to prepare for entering the next client.

Simply Accounting created a listing for Alberta Heritage Bank in the Clients window.

Repeat these **procedures** to enter the remaining clients and historical transactions. After entering the last client,

Click   **Save And Close** [Save and Close] to close the Client Ledger window.
         Close the **Clients icon window** to return to the Home window.

Display or **print** the **Client List** to check the accuracy of your address information.

Display or **print** a **Client Aged Detail Report** including terms and historical differences to check the historical information.

Preparing for Journal Entries

The last stage in setting up the accounting system involves closing off the historical entries. This step indicates that all historical data have been entered and cannot be changed. You can proceed with journalizing before finishing the history, but you must complete this step before beginning the next fiscal period. Finishing history involves changing the status of each ledger from an open to a finished history state. In the open history state the ledgers are not integrated, so you can add or change historical information in one ledger without affecting any other ledger. It is easier to correct mistakes.

Making a Backup of the Company Files

To make a backup of the not-finished files, you can use Save A Copy from the File menu or use the Backup command. Both methods allow you to keep working in your original working data file.

WARNING!
Make a backup copy before proceeding. If you finish entering history and discover an incorrect amount, you can correct the error without re-entering all the information.

WARNING!
You cannot use Backup or Save As with CDs in Simply Accounting. You can use Save A Copy to make CD backups.
Refer to page 19 for more information on backup methods and storage media.

NOTES

Substitute the appropriate drive and folders for the location of your files.

Choose the **File menu** and **click Backup**. **Click Browse**.

Create a **new folder** called **NF-DORF** in your data folder to store the not-finished version of your data files. **Select** this **new folder**. **Click OK**.

Double click **Backup** in the File Name field. **Type** nf-dorf

Click **OK**.

The "NF" designates files as not finished or open to distinguish them from the ones you will work with to enter journal transactions. Continue by following the backup instructions on-screen. You can use another name and location for your backup if you want. This will create a backup copy of the files for Dorfmann Design.

Click **OK** when the backup is complete.

Working with Unfinished History

Simply Accounting allows you to enter current journal transactions before the history is finished and balanced. In this way, you can keep the journal records current and enter the historical details later when there is time available to do so, or the setup may be completed later by a different individual.

There are, however, a number of elements that you must complete before you can make journal entries. You must create the General Ledger accounts and define the essential linked accounts before you can use the journals. You must enter historical client and supplier invoices before you can enter payments for them, and invoices must have the correct payment terms and dates.

You do not need to enter General Ledger opening account balances. These balances may be added later in the Opening Balance field on the Account tab screen. The General Ledger also shows the current balance that changes as you post new journal entries. Without the opening balances, the current balance is also not correct and you cannot get accurate reports. The Trial Balance and the Accounts window display only current balances, making it more difficult to trace the correct historical amounts.

Some errors may be corrected at any time. For example, after entering journal transactions and after finishing the history, you can correct account, supplier and client names and address details, but you cannot change historical amounts because their dates precede the earliest transaction date.

From a control point of view, it is preferable to enter all historical information first so that you do not confuse the historical and current data or work with accounts that are not correct in some way. You cannot change account numbers after the accounts are used in journal entries so some corrections may be difficult to make later. After you start journalizing, the balances for *Accounts Receivable* and *Accounts Payable* reflect all the entries made to date. There may be mistakes in current journal entries as well as in the history, making it more difficult to find the historical errors later.

There are a number of checks that you can perform to increase the accuracy of your work. You should compare your reports carefully with the charts given at the beginning of this application and make corrections. Pay particular attention to correct account numbers and historical invoices. Printing Supplier and Client Aged Detail reports with historical differences can reveal errors in invoices or payments. The Accounts window has an option to check the validity of accounts from the Edit menu or the tool button. The Home window Maintenance menu has an option to check data integrity that looks for differences in balances between the subsidiary ledgers and the corresponding General Ledger control accounts. All these checks help point to mistakes that should be corrected before proceeding.

Choose the **Maintenance menu** and **click Check Data Integrity**:

WARNING!
Read this section carefully before proceeding.

NOTES
You can create new accounts "on the fly" while making journal entries by using the Add An Account wizard. You will also be prompted to add the essential linked accounts when you try to open the journals. Some linked accounts, such as Sales Discounts, are not essential and you can access the journals without them. However, the journal entry will not be correct without the linked account, so there are some accounts that you must create before you can use the journals.

The summary shows that the supplier history is not correct. This error will prevent us from finishing the history, as we will see in the following step.

Click   **OK** to return to the Home window.

Choose the **History menu** and **click Finish Entering History**:

When all your essential linked accounts are defined and all historical amounts balance, you will see the warning that this step cannot be reversed, as in Chapter 4, page 93. Otherwise, Simply Accounting warns you about errors that prevent you from finishing the history. For example, the accounts may be out of order if a subgroup total is missing after a set of subgroup accounts, or the Receivables Ledger balances may not equal the *Accounts Receivable* control account balance. If you have omitted an essential linked account, that information will also be included on this screen.

We see the message that the Suppliers or Accounts Payable history is not balanced. Since the Trial Balance is correct, we may be missing a historical Payables Ledger invoice.

Click   **Print** to print the message for reference to help you correct mistakes.

Click   **OK** to return to the Home window.

We can proceed with entering the source documents. When the missing invoice surfaces, we can enter it and finish the history. You can proceed with journal entries until you start the next fiscal period. At that point, you must finish the history.

Correcting Historical Invoices

In reviewing all the records for the year to date, Dorfmann discovered part of the discrepancy between the *Accounts Payable* balance and the supplier ledger balances. Invoice #DD-4650 from Designers Den was incorrectly entered. The correct amount was $1 500 plus $75 tax, not $500 and $25. We will correct this error before making journal entries. The first step is to pay the invoices already entered.

Click   **Payables** in the Modules pane list.

Click   **Designers Den** in the Suppliers list pane to open the ledger.

Click   the **Historical Transactions tab**.

NOTES
If you printed the Supplier Aged Detail Report with historical difference, you would also see that the supplier history was not correct.

NOTES
Notice that the unused, hidden ledgers are balanced. If you view these ledgers and finish the history, you will be unable to add historical information for them later.
If you finish the history when the unused ledgers are hidden, they remain in the unfinished state and you can add historical information later. (See Chapter 9.)

WARNING!
Make sure that the Test Account balance is zero. An error in this amount will not prevent you from finishing the history.

Click   **Payments** to open the Historical Payments form:

Type   5 5 in the Number field.

Type   3–28 in the Date field.

Click   the **Amount Paid column for Invoice DD-4502**.

Click   the **Amount Paid column for Invoice DD-4630** and **press** tab to update the total.

Click   **Record** and then **click Close**.

Close   the **supplier ledger record** and the **Suppliers window**.

The next step is to clear the paid transactions for Designers Den so that these invoices and payments will be removed from the records.

Choose   the **Maintenance menu** and then **choose Clear Data** and **Clear Paid Transactions**. **Click Clear Paid Supplier Transactions** as shown:

You will see the list of suppliers:

Click   **Designers Den** to select the supplier.

Accept   the **default date** and the other **settings** and **click OK**:

Click   **Yes** to confirm that you want to clear the data.

Open   the ledger **record** for **Designers Den**.

Click   the **Statistics tab**.

Delete   the **year-to-date** expense and payment **amounts** to restore the balance amounts to zero. **Click** the **Save tool** .

Click   the **Historical Transactions tab**.

Enter   the **correct invoices** and **payments** shown below:

Supplier Name	Terms	Date	Inv/Chq No.	Amount	Tax	Total
Designers Den	2/10, n/30 (before tax)	Mar. 26/10	DD-4502	$2 500	$125	$2 625
		Mar. 26/10	Chq 62			2 180
	2/10, n/30 (before tax)	Mar. 28/10	DD-4630	1 500	75	1 575
			Balance Owing			$2 020

Close   the **supplier ledger record** and the **Suppliers window**.

When we change the session date to April 7, Simply Accounting will show a warning because we are entering a new month and we turned on the warning.

We see the following data check message:

Simply Accounting - Checking database   [X]

Checking Suppliers...
The sum of your Suppliers' information does not equal the current balance of account 2200 Accounts Payable.

  $8,525.00   Total Outstanding Invoices and Prepaid Order
  $9,174.00   Current Balance of 2200 Accounts Payable
  -$649.00   Difference
Either your Suppliers' historical information or the opening balance of account 2200 Accounts Payable, or both, is incorrect.
Checking Clients...
No error detected.

Please correct the errors found before performing this action again.

                                    [OK]   [Print]

There are still invoices outstanding. They will be entered in Memo #6 on May 1.

You should update (replace) the not-finished backup file. You can now exit the program or continue by entering the transactions that follow. Remember to advance the session date.

SOURCE DOCUMENTS

SESSION DATE – APRIL 7, 2010

☐ **Sales Invoice #44**   **Dated Apr. 4/10**

To Glitter Jewellers, $2 000 plus $100 GST for designing a "welcoming" space for shopping. Sales invoice total, $2 100. Terms: 1/5, n/15.

☐ **Cash Receipt #25**   **Dated Apr. 4/10**

From Alberta Heritage Bank, cheque #7110 for $1 750 in full payment of account. Reference invoice #38. Customize the tabbing order so that Cheque Number follows the client (refer to page 169).

☐ **Cheque Copy #65**   **Dated Apr. 4/10**

To Models to Scale, $4 180 in payment of account including $120 discount for early payment. Reference invoices #MS-376 and MS-453.

☐ **Cheque Copy #66**   **Dated Apr. 4/10**

To Designers Den, $1 940 in payment of account including $80 discount for early payment. Reference invoices #DD-4502 and DD-4630.

NOTES
You will see this reminder again when you advance the session date to May 1.

NOTES
Create shortcuts for General Journal entries (Company module) and for purchase invoices, other payments and invoice payments (Payables module). Refer to pages 134 and 186 if you need assistance with creating these shortcuts.

WARNING!
Be sure to select the correct revenue account for sales. You may need to change the default selection.

DorfmannDesign

No: 067

17 Tapestry Lane
Calgary, Alberta
T3B 4U2

Date 0 5 0 4 2 0 1 0
      D D M M Y Y Y Y

Pay to the order of   Maintenance & More $ 210.00

——————————— Two hundred and ten dollars ——————————— 00 /100 **Dollars**

MT Midwestern Trust
2596 Eighth Avenue
Calgary AB T1D 1P3

Desiree Dorfmann

⋯⋯⋯ 044 21876 ⋯ 133774 - 067

Re: Pay invoices #MM-211 & MM-242 $210.00 **No: 067**
                                                          April 5, 2010

Purchase Invoice #DMS-596   **Dated Apr. 5/10**

From DesignMaster Software, $750 plus $37.50 GST for new design software.
Purchase invoice total, $787.50. Change the payment terms to net 30 days.

Purchase Invoice #SBD-643   **Dated Apr. 7/10**

From Staples Business Depot, $200 for office supplies and $300 for computer
supplies, plus $25 GST. Purchase invoice total, $525. Terms: net 10 days.

Visa Purchase Invoice #P-61142   **Dated Apr. 7/10**

From Purolator Delivery, $30 plus $1.50 GST for delivery charges for express
shipment of designs and reports. Purchase invoice total, $31.50 charged to Visa
credit card.

Purchase Invoice #MM-263   **Dated Apr. 7/10**

From Maintenance & More, $100 plus $5 GST for regular maintenance of
premises. Purchase invoice total, $105. Terms: net 15 days. Store as weekly
recurring entry.

Memo #1   **Dated Apr. 7/10**

From Owner: Withdrew $250 from the business to pay for daughter's birthday
presents. Issued cheque #68. Use Full Add for the Owner's supplier record.
Create new Group account 3580 Dorfmann, Drawings.

Cash Receipt #26   **Dated Apr. 7/10**

From Glitter Jewellers, cheque #342 for $2 079 in full payment of account
including $21 discount for early payment. Reference sales invoice #44.

SESSION DATE – APRIL 14, 2010

Memo #3   **Dated Apr. 8/10**

From Owner: A model of store interior was accidentally dropped and destroyed.
It was worth $400 in model parts. Charge to new Group account 5025 Damaged
Model Parts.

NOTES
Although the owner's
withdrawal is a cash purchase, you
should create a supplier record for
the owner because she will make
further withdrawals. Leave the
address tab fields blank. Enter Yes
in the Tax Exempt column and
enter 3580 Dorfmann, Drawings
as the default expense account.
Record the withdrawal as a cash
purchase in the Payments Journal
or the Purchases Journal.

MEMO #2

Dorfmann**Design**

www.dorfmann.design.com

creating wide open spaces

17 Tapestry Lane, Calgary, Alberta T3B 4U2

Tel: (403) 683-9145   Fax: (403) 685-8210

Date: April 8, 2010
From: Desiree Dorfmann
Re: Change in purchase price

Design software purchased from DesignMaster Software (invoice #DMS-596)
was upgraded with new features by the software company. New price
for product is $800, plus GST.
Edit purchase invoice -- revised invoice total, $840. Terms unchanged.

Authorization for upgrade   *DD April 8*

Purchase Invoice #DD-6431   **Dated Apr. 11/10**

From Designers Den, $800 for Artograph vertical projector and $450 for tracer projector, plus $62.50 GST paid. Purchase invoice $1 312.50. Terms: 2/10, n/30.

Bank Debit Memo #642067   **Dated Apr. 13/10**

From Midwestern Trust, $1 500 for reduction of bank loan principal. Since this is a fixed payment, store it as a recurring monthly entry. Interest on the loan was $200. The bank withdrew $1 700 from the chequing account.

Cheque Copy #69   **Dated Apr. 14/10**

To Staples Business Depot, $525 in full payment of account. Reference invoice #SBD-643.

Sales Invoice #45   **Dated Apr. 14/10**

To Passions Department Store, $3 000 for designing display cabinets for cosmetic department and $800 for consultation work and reports, plus $190 GST. Sales invoice total, $3 990. Terms: 1/5, n/15.

Purchase Invoice #MM-314   **Dated Apr. 14/10**

From Maintenance & More, $100 plus $5 GST for regular maintenance of premises. Purchase invoice total, $105. Terms: net 15 days. Recall stored entry.

SESSION DATE — APRIL 21, 2010

Purchase Invoice #MS-850   **Dated Apr. 15/10**

From Models to Scale Co., $500 plus $25 GST for outsourcing on a design. Purchase invoice total, $525. Terms: 2/10, n/30. Create new Group account 5015 Contracted Labour Costs.

DorfmannDesign

17 Tapestry Lane
Calgary, Alberta
T3B 4U2

Invoice:	46
Date:	April 15, 2010
Sold to:	Calgary District School Board 88 Learnex Avenue 8th Floor Calgary, AB T3C 4B6
Phone:	(403) 788-3000

Service Provided	Amount
Consultation and reports on redesign To refurbish atrium at Board's central office	1 200.00

Payment: 1/5, n/15	1.5% interest on accounts over 30 days	GST	60.00
GST #233 281 244	Customer Initials *SG*	Invoice Total	1 260.00

creating wide open spaces
Tel: (403) 683-9145   Toll free: (888) 455-7194   www. dorfmann.design.com   Fax: (403) 685-8210

NOTES
Use Full Add for the new suppliers if you want to add the default expense account (Insurance Expense). GST is not charged on insurance so you do not need to add a tax code.

NOTES
Add B and C to the original purchase invoice numbers for the postdated payment entries.

Cash Purchase Invoice #WI-6913   **Dated Apr. 15/10**

From Westrock Insurance (use Quick Add), $185 per month for a one-year car insurance policy with $2 000 000 liability coverage and $4 000 deductible. Terms: first month payable in advance on acceptance of quote followed by monthly instalments at the end of each month. Pay first month's premium of $185 in advance. Issue cheque #70. Store as recurring monthly transaction.

Memo #4   **Dated Apr. 15/10**

Recall the stored entry for car insurance from Westrock Insurance to pay next month's premium of $185. Issue cheque #71 postdated for May 15. After posting, recall the entry again to pay the premium due June 15 with cheque #72. Choose Yes to confirm that the future date is correct.

Cheque Copy #73   **Dated Apr. 16/10**

To DesignMaster Software, $1 995 in payment of account. Reference invoice #DM-234.

Cash Receipt #27   **Dated Apr. 18/10**

From Calgary District School Board, cheque #1437 for $1 247.40 in full payment of account including $12.60 discount for early payment. Reference sales invoice #46.

Sales Invoice #47   **Dated Apr. 18/10**

To Banff Condominiums, $2 500 for designing foyer with water fountain for condominium complex and $800 for consultation work and reports, plus $165 GST. Sales invoice total, $3 465. Terms: 1/5, n/15. Reports and designs to be shipped by Purolator Delivery. Allow client to exceed credit limit.

Sales Invoice #48   **Dated Apr. 18/10**

To Lougheed, Klein and Associates, $800 plus $40 GST for consultation on future design work on law office building. Sales invoice total, $840. Terms: 1/5, n/15.

Cheque Copy #74   **Dated Apr. 20/10**

To Designers Den, $1 287.50 in payment of account including $25 discount for early payment. Reference invoice #DD-6431.

Purchase Invoice #DD-6896   **Dated Apr. 20/10**

From Designers Den, $1 200 plus $60 GST for new Designtek aluminum drawing table. Purchase invoice total $1 260. Terms: 2/10, n/30.

Purchase Invoice #MM-399   **Dated Apr. 21/10**

From Maintenance & More, $120 plus $6 GST for regular maintenance of premises. Purchase invoice total, $126. Terms: net 15 days. Recall and edit the stored entry to enter the increased price. Store the entry to save the changes.

Cash Receipt #28   **Dated Apr. 21/10**

From Lougheed, Klein and Associates, cheque #444 for $831.60 in full payment of account including $8.40 discount for early payment. Reference sales invoice #48.

Dorfmann Design

17 Tapestry Lane
Calgary, Alberta
T3B 4U2

Invoice:	49
Date:	April 21, 2010
Sold to:	Alliance Party Headquarters
Phone:	

Service Provided	Amount
Consultation fee Re: Redesign and refurbish party headquarters	500.00

| Payment: Visa | | GST | 25.00 |
| GST #233 281 244 | Customer Initials RK | Invoice Total | 525.00 |

creating wide open spaces
Tel: (403) 683-9145   Toll free: (888) 455-7194   **www. dorfmann.design.com**   Fax: (403) 685-8210

Cheque Copy #75   **Dated Apr. 21/10**

To Maintenance & More, $210 in payment of account. Reference invoices #MM-263 and MM-314.

NOTES

Remember to change the default revenue account for invoice #48.

SESSION DATE – APRIL 28, 2010

☐ **Sales Invoice #50**   **Dated Apr. 27/10**

To Calgary Arms Hotel, $3 200 for design work and $800 consultation fee, plus $200 GST charged. Sales invoice total, $4 200. Terms: 1/5, n/15.

☐ **Cash Receipt #29**   **Dated Apr. 28/10**

From Passions Department Store, cheque #614 for $3 990 in full payment of account. Reference sales invoice #45.

☐ **Cash Purchase Invoice #WB-669943**   **Dated Apr. 28/10**

From Western Bell, $125 plus $6.25 GST for telephone services. Purchase invoice total, $131.25. Issue cheque #76 in full payment.

☐ **Cash Purchase Invoice #AE-43214**   **Dated Apr. 28/10**

From Alberta Energy Corp., $120 plus $6 GST for hydro services. Purchase invoice total, $126. Issue cheque #77 in full payment.

☐ **Visa Purchase Invoice #P-70431**   **Dated Apr. 28/10**

From Purolator Delivery, $30 plus $1.50 GST for delivery charges for sending reports to Banff Condominiums. Purchase invoice total, $31.50. Full amount charged to Visa credit card.

☐ **Purchase Invoice #MM-464**   **Dated Apr. 28/10**

From Maintenance & More, $120 plus $6 GST for regular maintenance. Purchase invoice total, $126. Terms: net 15 days. Recall the stored entry.

SESSION DATE – APRIL 30, 2010

☐ **Memo #5**   **Dated Apr. 30/10**

From Owner: Prepare adjusting entries for the following

Model Parts used	$450
Computer Supplies used	240
Office Supplies used	220
Prepaid Insurance expired	208

☐ **Bank Debit Memo #643214**   **Dated Apr. 30/10**

From Midwestern Trust, $30 for monthly bank service charges and $1 320 for monthly mortgage payment withdrawn from chequing account. The mortgage payment includes $1 200 for interest and $120 for reduction of principal.

SESSION DATE – MAY 1, 2010

☐ **Memo #6**   **Dated May 1/10**

From Owner: Received monthly statements showing missing historical information. The statement from Staples Business Depot included an overdue amount of $166 from invoice #SBD-201 dated March 24, 2010. The statement from Models to Scale included an overdue amount of $460 plus $23 GST from invoice #MS-287 dated March 14, 2010.

> Add the historical invoices for these two transactions in the supplier ledger records as historical transactions. Refer to page 238. You can open the Payables module window or add a Payables shortcut to modify supplier to access the records for these suppliers.
>
> Pay these two invoices in the Payments Journal as current transactions dated May 1 using cheques #78 and #79.

⚠ WARNING!
You must enter these outstanding invoices as historical invoices and the payments as current payments or you will be unable to finish the history.

☐ **Memo #7**   **Dated May 1/10S**

Check the data integrity (Maintenance menu) after entering the historical invoices. Make a backup copy of the data files and finish entering the history. Choose the History menu in the Home window and click Finish Entering History.

☐ **Memo #8**   **Dated May 1/10**

From Owner: Print or preview client statements. Two invoices for Banff Condominiums are overdue. Complete sales invoice #51 for Banff Condominiums for $31.65, the interest charges on the overdue amount. Terms: net 15 days. Use the No Tax code for the interest charges and choose Interest Revenue as the account. Remember to remove the discount.

R E V I E W

The Student CD-ROM with Data Files includes Review Questions and Supplementary Cases for this chapter.

HELENA'S ACADEMY

OBJECTIVES

After completing this chapter, you should be able to

- **open** the Payroll Journal
- **enter** employee-related payroll transactions
- **understand** automatic payroll deductions
- **understand** Payroll Ledger linked accounts
- **edit** and **review** payroll transactions
- **adjust** Payroll Journal invoices after posting
- **enter** employee benefits and entitlements
- **complete** payroll runs for a group of employees
- **release** vacation pay to employees
- **remit** payroll taxes
- **display** and **print** payroll reports
- **prepare** record of employment and T4 slips

COMPANY INFORMATION

Company Profile

NOTES
Helena's Academy
250 Satchel Lane
Edmonton, Alberta T7F 3B2
Tel: (780) 633-8201
Fax: (780) 633-8396
Business No.: 188 255 345

Helena's Academy was opened in Edmonton, Alberta, in 2001 by Helena Teutor as a small private junior elementary school. The school has maintained its small size in order to offer individualized programming with high academic standards for students with artistic interests and abilities. Helena works as principal and also teaches the upper grades. Two other teachers handle the kindergarten and junior primary grades. Although all teachers have a background in fine arts and are trained music teachers, an additional half-time art and music specialist rotates among all the classes. A full-time office administrator, caretaker and classroom assistant make up the rest of the staff. The classroom assistant also runs the after-school program.

Parents pay tuition fees in two instalments, one before the start of the school year in August and the second at the beginning of January. They pay additional fees to participate in the after-school programs. Three teachers offer private half-hour weekly music lessons that parents also pay for separately.

All classes are split-grade classes, an arrangement required by the small school enrolment, but desired because of the opportunities for students to help each other. Older students in each class, even in kindergarten, are expected to help their younger classmates. All parents are also required to volunteer in the classroom and library, and the kindergarten parents provide the healthy daily snacks for the kindergarten classes. The volunteer expectations are viewed favourably by the families at the school because they enable parents to understand and reinforce the learning philosophy of the school.

The school closes for the month of July each year, but all teachers and staff return to work in August to plan their programs for the coming year. The caretaker uses this month before students return to catch up on repairs and maintenance.

Individual client accounts are not set up for this exercise and all regular tuition fees have been paid. Fees for the after-school program and private lessons are paid on the first of each month. No taxes are charged on any of the school's fees, and as an educational institution providing only tax-exempt services, the academy is not eligible for GST refunds on the taxes it pays. The school has accounts set up with a few regular suppliers and some of these offer discounts.

On October 1, 2010, Helena's Academy converted its accounts, using the following information:

- Chart of Accounts
- Trial Balance
- Supplier Information
- Client Information
- Employee Profiles and Information Sheet
- Accounting Procedures

CHART OF POSTABLE ACCOUNTS

HELENA'S ACADEMY

ASSETS
1080	Bank: Chequing Account
1090	Bank: Savings Account
1100	Investments: Restricted Use Funds
1200	Fees Receivable
1240	Advances Receivable
1260	Prepaid Taxes
1280	Office Supplies
1300	Arts Supplies
1320	Library Material
1340	Textbooks
1520	Classroom Computers
1540	Office Equipment
1560	Furniture
1580	School Vehicle
1620	School Premises ▶

▶**LIABILITIES**
2100	Bank Loan
2200	Accounts Payable
2300	Vacation Payable
2310	EI Payable
2320	CPP Payable
2330	Income Tax Payable
2400	RRSP Payable
2410	Family Support Payable
2430	Medical Payable - Employee
2440	Medical Payable - Employer
2460	WCB Payable
2920	Mortgage Payable

EQUITY
3560	Academy, Invested Capital
3580	Retained Surplus
3600	Net Income ▶

▶**REVENUE**
4020	Revenue from School Fees
4040	Revenue from Lessons
4060	Revenue from Programs
4100	Revenue from Interest

EXPENSE
5020	Purchase Discounts
5040	Bank Charges
5060	Hydro Expenses
5080	Insurance Expense
5100	Office Supplies Used
5110	Textbook Expenses
5120	Art Supplies Used
5140	Interest Expense
5180	Promotional Expenses
5190	Property Taxes
5200	Telephone Expenses ▶

▶
5210	Vehicle Expenses
5250	Wages: Teaching Staff
5260	Wages: Support Staff
5280	Wages: Music Lessons
5310	EI Expense
5320	CPP Expense
5330	WCB Expense
5380	Tuition Fees Expense
5400	Medical Premium Expense

NOTES: The Chart of Accounts includes only postable accounts and Net Income.

TRIAL BALANCE

HELENA'S ACADEMY

October 1, 2010

		Debits	Credits				Debits	Credits
1080	Bank: Chequing Account	$ 90 000.00			▶ 3560	Academy, Invested Capital		540 000.00
1090	Bank: Savings Account	160 000.00			3580	Retained Surplus		57 604.02
1100	Investments: Restricted				4020	Revenue from School Fees		680 000.00
	Use Funds	540 000.00			4040	Revenue from Lessons		500.00
1260	Prepaid Taxes	2 700.00			4060	Revenue from Programs		3 000.00
1280	Office Supplies	4 100.00			4100	Revenue from Interest		2 150.00
1300	Arts Supplies	3 850.00			5040	Bank Charges	66.00	
1320	Library Material	14 500.00			5060	Hydro Expenses	1 220.00	
1340	Textbooks	5 300.00			5080	Insurance Expense	3 680.00	
1520	Classroom Computers	6 800.00			5100	Office Supplies Used	240.00	
1540	Office Equipment	4 900.00			5110	Textbook Expenses	800.00	
1560	Furniture	16 000.00			5120	Art Supplies Used	280.00	
1580	School Vehicle	23 000.00			5140	Interest Expense	4 600.00	
1620	School Premises	840 000.00			5180	Promotional Expenses	2 800.00	
2100	Bank Loan		65 000.00		5190	Property Taxes	1 800.00	
2200	Accounts Payable		1 880.00		5200	Telephone Expenses	350.00	
2300	Vacation Payable		2 320.50		5210	Vehicle Expenses	600.00	
2310	EI Payable		948.58		5250	Wages: Teaching Staff	31 838.00	
2320	CPP Payable		2 044.60		5260	Wages: Support Staff	16 917.60	
2330	Income Tax Payable		3 841.06		5280	Wages: Music Lessons	750.00	
2400	RRSP Payable		300.00		5310	EI Expense	1 095.93	
2410	Family Support Payable		1 000.00		5320	CPP Expense	2 033.31	
2430	Medical Payable - Employee		187.00		5330	WCB Expense	504.87	
2440	Medical Payable - Employer		187.00		5380	Tuition Fees Expense	180.00	
2460	WCB Payable		299.95		5400	Medical Premium Expense	357.00	
2920	Mortgage Payable		420 000.00 ▶				$1 781 262.71	$1 781 262.71

SUPPLIER INFORMATION

HELENA'S ACADEMY

Supplier Name (Contact)	Address	Phone No. Fax No.	E-mail Web Site	Terms Tax ID
Alberta Minister of Finance (A.M. Weller)	280 Wellness Blvd. Edmonton, AB T6G 2B7	Tel: (780) 427-7164 Fax: (780) 427-8109	www.health.gov.ab.ca	net 1
Alberta Workers' Compensation Board	55 Payout Cr. Edmonton, AB T5J 2S5	Tel: (780) 498-3999 Fax: (780) 498-7999	www.wcb.ab.ca	net 1
Energy Supply Services (N.U. Cleer)	690 Service Ave. Edmonton, AB T6T 4G4	Tel: (780) 456-3293 Fax: (780) 456-1229	nucleer@ess.ca www.ess.ca	net 1
Loomis Art Supplies (Dee Ziner)	64 Canvas St. Edmonton, AB T5Z 2S4	Tel: (780) 462-1706 Fax: (780) 452-1700	dz@loomis.com www.loomis.com	1/10, n/30 186 519 184
Maintenance Enforcement Program (Al I. Mony)	43 Brownlee St. Edmonton, AB T5J 3W7	Tel: (780) 422-5555 Fax: (780) 401-7575	alberta.mep@gov.ab.ca www.justice.gov.ab.ca/mep	net 1
Receiver General for Canada	56 Heron Rd. Ottawa, Ontario K3A 6B4	Tel 1: (800) 561-7761 Tel 2: (800) 959-2221	www.cra-arc.gc.ca	net 1
Rocky Mountain Trust (Rocky)	59 High St. Edmonton, AB T4P 1M3	Tel: (780) 388-1825 Fax: (780) 388-2663	www.rockymtntrust.ca	net 1
Telus Alberta (Toks Lotts)	499 Cellular Rd. Edmonton, AB T8F 2B5	Tel: (780) 348-5999 www.telus.com		net 1

OUTSTANDING SUPPLIER INVOICES

HELENA'S ACADEMY

Supplier Name	Terms	Date	Invoice No.	Amount	Total
Loomis Art Supplies	1/10, n/30	Sep. 29/10	LT-438	$1 880	$1 880

CLIENT INFORMATION

HELENA'S ACADEMY

Client Name	Address
Parents of Students	Edmonton
(individual client records are not set up for this application)	

EMPLOYEE INFORMATION SHEET

HELENA'S ACADEMY

	Helena Teutor	Marina Booker	Lars Teicher	Arte Tiste	Neela Nerture	Morty Filer	Jerome Handie
Position	Principal	Teacher	Teacher	Specialist	Assistant	Office Admin	Caretaker
Social Insurance No.	699 344 578	277 639 118	403 401 599	513 288 191	129 495 768	374 588 127	813 402 302
Address	21 Socratic Blvd. Edmonton, AB T5H 2L2	49 Dewey Pl. Edmonton, AB T6K 4K2	15 Practicum St. Edmonton, AB T5B 4C1	2 Creative Way Edmonton, AB T6H 1X3	93 Formula Cr. Edmonton, AB T5E 2L2	10 Basics Lane Edmonton, AB T5A 4K2	4 Repairal Cr. Edmonton, AB T5B 4C1
Telephone	(780) 466-7736	(780) 436-9015	(780) 463-4870	(780) 429-5656	(780) 488-8554	(780) 440-3301	(780) 461-1328
Date of Birth (mm-dd-yy)	7-28-76	9-14-79	10-5-80	7-18-77	5-19-75	4-3-72	3-3-69
Federal (Alberta) Tax Exemption – TD1							
Basic Personal	$9 600 (16 161)	$9 600 (16 161)	$9 600 (16 161)	$9 600 (16 161)	$9 600 (16 161)	$9 600 (16 161)	$9 600 (16 161)
Spouse	–	$9 600 (16 161)	–	$9 600 (16 161)	$9 600 (16 161)	$9 600 (16 161)	–
Other	–	$1 460 (1 652)	–	$4 095 (4 355)	–	$3 720 (4 104)	–
Total Exemptions	$9 600 (16 161)	$20 660 (33 974)	$9 600 (16 161)	$23 295 (36 677)	$19 200 (32 322)	$22 920 (36 426)	$9 600 (16 161)
Employee Earnings							
Regular Wage Rate	–	–	–	$30.00	$18.00	$20.00	$20.00
Overtime Wage Rate	–	–	–	–	$27.00	$30.00	$30.00
Regular Salary	$5 000	$4 200	$3 800	–	–	–	–
Pay Period	monthly	monthly	monthly	semi-monthly	semi-monthly	semi-monthly	semi-monthly
Hours per Period	160	160	160	40	82.5	82.5	82.5
Lessons (#/period)	–	$25.00 (16)	$25.00 (12)	$25.00 (22)	–	–	–
Vacation	4 weeks	4 weeks	4 weeks	6% retained	6% retained	6% retained	6% retained
Vacation Pay Owed	–	–	–	$1 152.00	$345.60	398.40	424.50
WCB Rate	0.89	0.89	0.89	0.89	1.15	0.89	2.44
Employee Deductions							
Medical	$22.00	$44.00	$22.00	$22.00	$22.00	$22.00	$11.00
RRSP	$100.00	$50	$50	–	$25.00	–	$25.00
Family Support	–	–	$500.00	–	–	–	$250.00
Additional Tax				$200.00			
EI, CPP & Income Tax	Calculations built into Simply Accounting program						
Direct Deposit	No	Yes	Yes	No	Yes	No	Yes

NOTES: Medical premiums are deducted every pay period. The amounts are adjusted for the monthly rates.

Employee Profiles and TD1 Information

Employee Benefits and Entitlements   All employees are entitled to 10 days per year as sick leave. If the days are not needed, employees can carry these days forward to a new year, to a maximum of 90 days. Currently, all employees have some unused sick leave days accrued from previous years. Most employees take their vacations in July when the school is closed, with salaried employees receiving their regular salary and the full-time hourly workers receiving the retained vacation pay at the end of June with their regular paycheque. Vacation pay cannot be accumulated or carried forward beyond the calendar year. Tiste has not yet collected any vacation pay this year.

In keeping with the educational goals, the Academy encourages all employees to continue their education by paying 50 percent of the tuition fees for college or university programs. Booker and Filer are currently taking courses and receiving the tuition fee benefit. A second benefit applies to all employees — the Academy pays 50 percent of the medical premiums for the Alberta Health Care Insurance Plan. Both benefits are taxable income for the employee and expenses for Helena's Academy.

Music Lessons   Booker, Teicher and Tiste give private music lessons at lunchtime and after school. Parents pay the school $30 per half-hour lesson and the school pays the teachers. These fees are set up on a "piece rate" basis at $25 per lesson and added to each paycheque.

Employer Expenses   In addition to the expenses for the tuition fees and medical premium benefits, Helena's Academy pays the compulsory CPP, EI and WCB.

Helena Teutor   As the principal and founder of the school, Teutor frequently speaks to parent groups in order to promote the school. She also teaches the senior class of grade 4, 5 and 6 students and hires new staff when needed. She is married and has no children. Since her husband is also fully employed, she uses the single federal and provincial tax claim and medical premium amounts. At the end of each month, she receives her salary of $5 000 per month by cheque. She makes monthly contributions to her RRSP plan as well.

Marina Booker   is the regular teacher for the primary class of grade 1, 2 and 3 students. She supplements her monthly salary of $4 200 with income from private music lessons offered through the school. She earns $25 for each half-hour lesson taught in the previous month. Booker is married and claims the basic and spousal amounts for income tax purposes. She also has a claim for her RRSP contributions and her tuition fees of $900 for a university course and the $140 per month federal ($188 provincial) education deduction for the part-time course. She pays medical premiums at the family rate. Her pay is deposited directly to her bank account every month.

Lars Teicher   teaches the two junior and senior kindergarten classes. He too supplements his monthly salary of $3 800 with income from private music lessons at $25 per lesson. Teicher is separated from his wife and is required to make family support payments. For this, $500 is deducted from each paycheque. As a single employee, he claims only the basic federal and provincial amounts for income tax purposes, but he does have an additional deduction for his RRSP contributions. He also pays the single rate towards the provincial medical plan. He too has his paycheque deposited directly to his bank account.

Arte Tiste   is the half-time art teacher who works four hours in the school every afternoon, dividing his time among the three classes but concentrating on the senior class. He spends the mornings painting in his home art studio. Although he is single, he can claim the spousal equivalent plus caregiver amounts because he looks after his infirm brother. These claims significantly reduce the income tax he pays on his wages of

NOTES
The Academy pays $450 of her tuition fees at the rate of $45 per pay period for 10 months.

$30 per hour. He teaches music lessons after school at the per-lesson rate of $25. His medical premium is deducted from his semi-monthly paycheque at the family rate to cover himself and his brother. His 6 percent vacation pay is retained. Instead of receiving his vacation pay in June like the other hourly workers, Tiste takes his vacation pay sometime in the fall to pay for his December travels. Because Tiste has additional income from the sale of his paintings, he has elected to pay additional federal taxes each month instead of making extra quarterly tax remittances on this extra income. Tiste is paid by cheque twice each month.

Neela Nerture   works full-time in the school as a classroom assistant and also runs the after-school program for children who require daycare. She divides her time among the three classes as needed by the teachers and program schedules. Nerture is married and fully supports her child and her husband while he is finishing his studies. Therefore, she pays the family medical premiums and has the basic and spousal claim amounts for income taxes. She is paid twice a month at the hourly rate of $18 per hour. When she works more than 7.5 hours in a day, she earns $27 per hour for the extra time. This time is sometimes required for extended daycare and can be charged back to the parents. This fee encourages parents to pick up their children on time. On top of her pay, she earns 6 percent vacation pay that is retained until the end of June. Nerture has her paycheques deposited directly to her bank account.

Morty Filer   runs the school office, handling the routine phone calls to and from parents, arranging lessons, scheduling parent volunteers, collecting fees and doing the bookkeeping. For these duties he earns $20 per hour for the first 7.5 hours each day in each half-month pay period and is paid by cheque. For additional hours, he earns $30 per hour. The 6 percent vacation pay he earns on his regular and overtime wages is retained until the end of June. Filer supports his wife and claims both the basic and spousal federal and provincial amounts for tax purposes. His medical premium is at the family rate. He has an additional claim for his university tuition of $2 600 and the $140 per month federal education deduction ($188 provincial) for the eight-month school year.

Jerome Handie   is the caretaker for the school and grounds. He works year-round, except for his vacation time in July, cleaning the school's rooms and providing general maintenance. During August, he paints the classrooms and steam-cleans all carpets. From each semi-monthly paycheque that is deposited to his bank account, $250 is withheld to support his ex-wife and two children. He claims only the basic federal and provincial amounts for tax purposes, and the single medial premium. He also makes contributions to his RRSP program with regular payroll deductions. His hourly pay rate is $20 for the first 7.5 hours per day and $30 per hour for any additional time. His vacation pay is calculated and retained at the rate of 6 percent.

Accounting Procedures

Taxes: GST and PST

As an educational institution that offers only tax-exempt services, Helena's Academy is not eligible for any refunds on the GST it pays for products and services. Therefore, no sales taxes are set up in this application and the prices in the source documents include all taxes. Provincial sales tax is not charged in Alberta.

Discounts

Some suppliers offer discounts on after-tax purchase amounts. These discount terms are set up in the supplier records so that Simply Accounting will automatically calculate the discount when full payment is made within the discount period. No discounts are offered on school fees.

> **NOTES**
> Because hourly employees are paid twice a month, the pay period may include 10 or 11 days. The number of regular hours is therefore either 75 or 82.5 hours, based on working 7.5 hours per day.

> **NOTES**
> The Academy pays $1 300 of Filer's tuition at the rate of $130 per pay period for five months (10 pay periods).

> **NOTES**
> The sales tax amounts are included with the asset or expense portion of the purchase.

Direct Payroll Deposits

The Academy allows employees to have their regular pay deposited directly to their bank accounts or to be paid by cheque. Four employees have selected direct payroll deposits.

Payroll Remittances

Some suppliers are identified as payroll authorities with the following remittances: EI, CPP and income tax are remitted to the Receiver General for Canada; medical premiums are remitted to the Alberta Minister of Finance; Workers' Compensation Board premiums are remitted to the Alberta Workers' Compensation Board; RRSP contributions are remitted to Rocky Mountain Trust; family support payments are remitted to Maintenance Enforcement Program. All payments are remitted monthly for the pay period ending the previous month.

Tuition fees are paid directly to the employee.

INSTRUCTIONS

SIMPLY VERSION
In the Simply version, customer replaces the term client, vendor replaces the term supplier, Sales Invoices replaces the icon label Statements and Sales Journal replaces the term Fees Journal.

1. **Enter** the **transactions** in Simply Accounting using the Chart of Accounts and Supplier, Client and Employee Information. The procedures for entering new transactions for this application are outlined step by step in the Keystrokes section following the source documents. These transactions have a ✓ in the check box, and the page number where the keystrokes begin appears immediately below the check box.

2. **Print** the **reports and graphs** marked on the following printing form after you have finished making your entries. Keystrokes for payroll reports begin on page 297.

REPORTS

Accounts
- ☐ Chart of Accounts
- ☐ Account List
- ☐ General Journal Entries

Financials
- ☑ Balance Sheet: Dec. 31
- ☑ Income Statement: Aug. 1 to Dec. 31
- ☑ Trial Balance date: Dec. 31
- ☑ All Journal Entries: Oct. 1 to Dec. 31
- ☑ General Ledger accounts: Oct. 1 to Dec. 31
  5250 5260 5280
- ☐ Statement of Cash Flows
- ☑ Cash Flow Projection Detail Report: for 1080 for next 30 days

Banking
- ☐ Cheque Log Report

Payables
- ☐ Supplier List
- ☐ Supplier Aged

- ☐ Aged Overdue Payables
- ☐ Purchase Journal Entries
- ☐ Payment Journal Entries

Receivables
- ☐ Client List
- ☐ Client Aged
- ☐ Aged Overdue Receivables
- ☐ Fees Journal Entries
- ☐ Receipt Journal Entries
- ☐ Client Statements

Employees & Payroll
- ☐ Employee List
- ☑ Summary for all employees
- ☐ Deductions & Expenses
- ☑ Remittances Summary Report: for all payroll authorities Dec. 31
- ☑ Payroll Journal Entries: Oct. 1 to Dec. 31
- ☑ T4 Slip for Tiste
- ☑ Record of Employment for Tiste

Mailing Labels
- ☐ Labels

Management Reports
- ☐ Ledger

GRAPHS
- ☐ Payables by Aging Period
- ☐ Payables by Supplier
- ☐ Receivables by Aging Period
- ☐ Receivables by Client
- ☐ Fees vs Receivables
- ☐ Receivables Due vs Payables Due
- ☐ Revenues by Account
- ☐ Expenses by Account
- ☐ Expenses and Net Profit as % of Revenue

SOURCE DOCUMENTS

SESSION DATE – OCTOBER 15, 2010

☐ **Cash Sales Invoice #1036** **Dated Oct. 1/10**

To parents of students, $3 200, total monthly fees for after-school programs and $2 130, total monthly fees for individual music lessons. Deposited $5 330 to chequing account.

☐ **Cash Purchase Invoice #GL-38827** **Dated Oct 2/10**

From Global Liability Inc. (use Full Add for new supplier), $1 800 for monthly premium on a one-year insurance policy for school and staff. Paid by cheque #211. Store as a recurring monthly entry.

☐ **Cheque Copy #212** **Dated Oct. 5/10**

To Loomis Art Supplies, $1 861.20 in payment of account, including $18.80 discount for early payment. Reference invoice #LT-438.

EMPLOYEE TIME SUMMARY SHEET #19

(Dated October 15, 2010, for the pay period ending October 15, 2010)

Name of Employee	Regular Hours	Overtime Hours	Lessons	Tuition	Advance (Repaid)	Sick Days	Direct Deposit
☑ Filer, Morty	82.5	4	–	$130	$200	–	No
271							
☑ Handie, Jerome	82.5	2	–	–	–	1	Yes
276							
☐ Nerture, Neela	82.5	–	–	–	–	–	Yes
☑ Tiste, Arte	44.0	–	20	–	–	–	No
278							

a. Using Employee Time Summary Sheet #19 and the Employee Information Sheet, complete payroll for weekly paid employees. Handie has taken one sick day.

b. Issue $200 advance to Morty Filer and recover $50 from each of the following four paycheques.

c. Issue cheques #213 and #214 and Direct Deposit (DD) slips #55 and 56.

SESSION DATE – OCTOBER 31, 2010

☑ **Memo #1** **Dated Oct. 17/10**

279 From Manager: Morty Filer returned his paycheque for adjustment. He worked 6 hours of overtime during the week but was paid for only 4 hours. Adjust his paycheque and re-issue cheque #213 to make the correction.

☑ **Memo #2** **Dated Oct. 17/10**

282 Tiste has booked his vacation and will receive his retained vacation pay to pay for the holiday. Release the accrued retained vacation pay for Arte Tiste and issue cheque #215.

☑ **Memo #3** **Dated Oct. 17/10**

285 Make payroll remittances for the pay period ending October 1.
Receiver General for Canada: EI, CPP and income tax
Alberta Minister of Finance: Medical premiums from employee and employer
Alberta Workers' Compensation Board: WCB
Rocky Mountain Trust: RRSP
Maintenance Enforcement Program: Family support payments
Issue cheques # 216 to #220.

NOTES
You should create shortcuts for the non-payroll transactions.

NOTES
For the educational service company, the customers icon is labelled clients, sales invoices are labelled as statements and sales or revenues are renamed fees.

NOTES
Global Liability Inc.
Terms: net 1
Expense account: 5080

NOTES
The pay period for hourly paid employees included 11 days.

☐ **Cash Purchase Invoice #ESS-4689**　　　　**Dated Oct. 18/10**

From Energy Supply Services, $610 including taxes for heat and hydro on equal monthly billing plan. Store as recurring monthly entry. Paid by cheque #221.

☐ **Cash Purchase #TA-113368**　　　　**Dated Oct. 20/10**

From Telus Alberta, $220 including all taxes for one month of telephone services. Invoice total paid in full with cheque #222.

NOTES
The pay period for hourly paid employees included 11 days.

EMPLOYEE TIME SUMMARY SHEET #20

(Dated October 31, 2010, for the pay period ending October 31, 2010)

Name of Employee	Regular Hours	Overtime Hours	Lessons	Tuition	Advance (Repaid)	Sick Days	Direct Deposit
✓ Filer, Morty	82.5	2	–	$130.00	–$50	–	No
✓ Handie, Jerome	82.5	2	–	–	–	–	Yes
✓ Nerture, Neela	82.5	–	–	–	–	–	Yes
✓ Tiste, Arte	44.0	–	22	–	$100	–	No
✓ Booker, Marina	160	–	16	$45.00		1	Yes
✓ Teicher, Lars	160	–	12				Yes
✓ Teutor, Helena	160	–	–				No

290

a. Using Employee Time Summary Sheet #20 and the Employee Information Sheet, complete payroll for all employees.
b. Recover $50 advanced to Morty Filer.
c. Issue $100 advance to Tiste and recover $25 from each of the next four paycheques.
d. Issue cheques #223, #224 and #225 and DD slips #57, #58, #59 and #60.

☐ **Bank Debit Memo #277581**　　　　**Dated Oct. 31/10**

From Scholar Heights Bank, $4 025 was withdrawn from chequing account for the following pre-authorized transactions:

Bank Charges	$ 25
Interest on Bank Loan	320
Reduction of Principal on Bank Loan	880
Interest on Mortgage	2 500
Reduction of Principal on Mortgage	300

Store as a recurring monthly entry.

☐ **Bank Credit Memo #467116**　　　　**Dated Oct. 31/10**

From Scholar Heights Bank, $1 890 interest on investments and bank account was deposited to chequing account. Store as a recurring monthly entry.

☐ **Memo #4**　　　　**Dated Oct. 31/10**

Complete end-of-month adjusting entries for the following:

Office supplies used	$180
Art supplies used	335
Textbooks used	85
Prepaid property taxes	900

You can store this as a recurring monthly entry if you want.

SESSION DATE – NOVEMBER 15, 2010

☐ **Cash Sales Invoice #1037**　　　　**Dated Nov. 1/10**

To parents of students, $3 200 total monthly fees for after-school programs, and $2 280 total monthly fees for individual music lessons. Deposited $5 480 to chequing account.

Cash Purchase Invoice #GL-38827-B   **Dated Nov. 2/10**

To Global Liability Inc., $1 800 for monthly insurance premium as stated on policy #GL-38827. Paid by cheque #226. Recall stored entry.

Cash Purchase Invoice #ES-1446   **Dated Nov. 15/10**

From Engine Services (use Quick Add), $220 including taxes for gasoline, tire repairs, oil change and lubrication on school vehicle. Invoice total paid in full with cheque #227.

Aim higher!

HELENA'S ACADEMY

Employee Time Summary Sheet
Business No.: 188 255 345 RT 0003

#21
Cheque Date: November 15, 2010   Last day of pay period end: November 15, 2010

Employee SIN	M. Filer 374 588 127	J. Handie 813 402 302	N. Nerture 129 495 768	A. Tiste 513 288 191	H. Teutor 699 344 578	M. Booker 277 639 118	L. Teicher 403 401 599
Nov 2-6	37.5	41.5	37.5	20			
Nov 9-13	37.5	37.5	37.5	20			

Reg. hrs	75	75	75	40			
Overtime	--	4	--	--			
Lessons	--	--	--	22			
Tuition	130.00	--	--	--			
Advance	-50.00	--	--	-25.00			
Sick leave	--	--	1	--			
Chq/DD #	Chq 228	DD61	DD62	Chq 229			

Payroll Prepared by: Morty Filer Nov 15/10

NOTES
Type –50 in the Advance Amount field for Filer and –25 for Tiste to recover these amounts.

⚠ **WARNING!**
Remember to change the number of regular hours from 82.5 to 75 for Income (Regular hours) and Entitlements. This pay period included 10 days for hourly paid employees.

SESSION DATE – NOVEMBER 30, 2010

Memo #5   **Dated Nov. 17/10**

Make payroll remittances for the pay period ending October 31.
   Receiver General for Canada: EI, CPP and income tax
   Alberta Minister of Finance: Medical premiums from employee and employer
   Alberta Workers' Compensation Board: WCB
   Rocky Mountain Trust: RRSP
   Maintenance Enforcement Program: Family support payments
Issue cheques #230 to #234.

Cash Purchase Invoice #ESS-5568   **Dated Nov. 18/10**

From Energy Supply Services, $610 including taxes for heat and hydro on equal monthly billing plan. Recall stored entry. Paid by cheque #235.

Cash Purchase #TA-193245   **Dated Nov. 20/10**

From Telus Alberta, $165 including all taxes for one month of telephone services. Invoice total paid in full with cheque #236.

NOTES
You will see the message that the date precedes the session date because October 31 is in the previous month. You can click Yes to confirm that this is correct or you can enter November 1 as the ending date for the pay period.

NOTES
Type –50 in the Advance Amount field for Filer and –25 for Tiste to recover these amounts.

NOTES
The pay period for hourly paid employees included 11 days.

HELENA'S ACADEMY

Aim higher!

Employee Time Summary Sheet
Business No.: 188 255 345 RT 0003

#22
Cheque Date: November 30, 2010   Last day of pay period end: November 30, 2010

Employee SIN	M. Filer 374 588 127	J. Handie 813 402 302	N. Nerture 129 495 768	A. Tiste 513 288 191	H. Teutor 699 344 578	M. Booker 277 639 118	L. Teicher 403 401 599
Nov 2-6	pd	pd	pd	pd	➤➤	➤➤	➤➤
Nov 9-13	pd	pd	pd	pd	➤➤	➤➤	➤➤
Nov 16-20	37.5	37.5	39.5	20	➤➤	➤➤	➤➤
Nov 23-27	37.5	39.5	41.5	20	➤➤	➤➤	➤➤
Nov 30	7.5	7.5	7.5	4	➤➤	➤➤	➤➤
Reg. hrs	82.5	82.5	82.5	44	160	160	160
Overtime	--	2	6	--	--	--	--
Lessons	--	--	--	22	--	16	12
Tuition	130.00	--	--	--		45.00	
Advance	-50.00	--	--	-25.00			
Sick leave	--	--	1	--			
Chq/DD #	Chq 237	DD64	DD65	Chq 239	Chq 238	DD63	DD66

Payroll Prepared by: Morty Filer Nov 30/10

Bank Debit Memo #422344   Dated Nov. 30/10

From Scholar Heights Bank, $4 025 was withdrawn from chequing account for the following pre-authorized transactions:

Bank Charges	$ 25
Interest on Bank Loan	320
Reduction of Principal on Bank Loan	880
Interest on Mortgage	2 500
Reduction of Principal on Mortgage	300

Recall stored entry.

Bank Credit Memo #64567   Dated Nov. 30/10

From Scholar Heights Bank, $1 890 interest on investments and bank account was deposited to chequing account. Recall stored entry.

Memo #6   Dated Nov. 30/10

Complete end-of-month adjusting entries for the following:

Office supplies used	$275
Art supplies used	180
Textbooks used	110
Prepaid property taxes	900

SESSION DATE – DECEMBER 15, 2010

Cash Sales Invoice #1038   Dated Dec. 1/10

To parents of students, $2 400 total monthly fees for after-school programs, and $1 580 total monthly fees for individual music lessons. Deposited $3 980 to chequing account.

Cash Purchase Invoice #GL-38827-C   Dated Dec. 2/10

To Global Liability Inc., $1 800 for monthly insurance premium as stated on policy #GL-38827. Paid by cheque #240. Recall stored entry.

Aim higher!

Employee Time Summary Sheet
Business No.: 188 255 345 RT 0003

#23
Cheque Date: December 15, 2010   Last day of pay period end: December 15, 2010

Employee SIN	M. Filer 374 588 127	J. Handie 813 402 302	N. Nerture 129 495 768	A. Tiste 513 288 191	H. Teutor 699 344 578	M. Booker 277 639 118	L. Teicher 403 401 599
Dec 1-4	30.0	30.0	30.0	16			
Dec 7-11	37.5	38.5	41.5	20			
Dec 14-15	15.0	16.0	16.0	8			
- - - -							
Reg. hrs	82.5	82.5	82.5	44			
Overtime	--	2	5	--			
Lessons	--	--	--	22			
Tuition	130.00	--	--	--			
Advance	-50.00	--	--	-25.00			
Sick leave	--	--	--	--			
Chq/DD #	Chq 241	DD67	DD68	Chq 242			

Payroll Prepared by: Morty Filer Dec 15/10

NOTES
Type −50 in the Advance Amount field for Filer and −25 for Tiste to recover these amounts.

NOTES
The pay period for hourly paid employees included 11 days.

SESSION DATE – DECEMBER 31, 2010

Aim higher!

MEMO   #7

From the desk of Morty Filer
Dated: Dec. 17, 2010

RE: Payroll remittances
Made payroll remittances for the pay period ending November 30 to

      Receiver General for Canada for EI, CPP and
        income tax cheque #243
      Alberta Minister of Finance for medical premiums
        from employee and employer cheque #244
      Alberta Workers' Compensation Board for WCB cheque #245
      Rocky Mountain Trust for RRSP cheque #246
      Maintenance Enforcement Program for
        Family support payments cheque #247

Payments submitted *Dec 17 Morty Filer*

NOTES
You will see the message that the date precedes the session date because November 30 is in the previous month. You can click Yes to confirm that this is correct or you can enter December 1 as the ending date for the pay period.

✓ **Memo #8**   **Dated Dec. 17/10**

294   Adjust the Dec. 15 paycheque for Tiste — he is leaving and should have the full advance recovered from his paycheque. (Increase the advance recovered to $50.) Create an additional paycheque #248 to release his accrued vacation pay.

☐ **Cash Purchase Invoice #ESS-7889**   **Dated Dec. 18/10**

From Energy Supply Services, $610 including taxes for heat and hydro on equal monthly billing plan. Recall stored entry. Paid by cheque #249.

☐ **Cash Purchase #TA-266778**   **Dated Dec. 20/10**

From Telus Alberta, $170 including all taxes for one month of telephone services. Invoice total paid in full with cheque #250.

EMPLOYEE TIME SUMMARY SHEET #24

(Dated December 31, 2010, for the pay period ending December 31, 2010)

Name of Employee	Regular Hours	Overtime Hours	Lessons	Tuition	Advance (Repaid)	Sick Days	Direct Deposit
☐ Filer, Morty	75	–	–	$130.00	–	–	No
☐ Handie, Jerome	75	4	–	–	–	–	Yes
☐ Nerture, Neela	75	–	–	–	–	1	Yes
☐ Booker, Marina	160	–	10	$45.00			No
☐ Teicher, Lars	160	–	8		$200		Yes
☐ Teutor, Helena	160	–	–				No

  a. Using Employee Time Summary Sheet #2 and the Employee Information Sheet, complete payroll for all employees. Hourly paid employees are paid for their regular hours during the Christmas holiday break.
  c. Issue $200 advance to Teicher and recover $50 from each of the next four paycheques.
  d. Issue cheques #251 and #252 and DD slips #69, #70, #71 and #72.

☐ **Bank Credit Memo #69886**   **Dated Dec. 31/10**

From Scholar Heights Bank, $1 890 interest on investments and bank account was deposited to chequing account. Recall stored entry.

☐ **Bank Debit Memo #532281**   **Dated Dec. 31/10**

From Scholar Heights Bank, $4 025 was withdrawn from chequing account for the following pre-authorized transactions:

Bank Charges	$ 25
Interest on Bank Loan	320
Reduction of Principal on Bank Loan	880
Interest on Mortgage	2 500
Reduction of Principal on Mortgage	300

Recall stored entry.

☐ **Memo #9**   **Dated Dec. 31/10**

Complete end-of-month adjusting entries for the following:

Office supplies used	$230
Art supplies used	250
Textbooks used	150
Prepaid property taxes	900

☐ **Memo #10**   **Dated Dec. 31/10**

Transfer $30 000 from the savings account to the chequing account.

✓ **Memo #11**   **Dated Dec. 31/10**

296   Prepare a Record of Employment and T4 slip for Tiste.

KEYSTROKES

Entering Payroll Transactions

Payroll transactions may be entered in the Payroll Journal or in the Payroll Run Journal. We will show both methods. If you are preparing paycheques for more than one employee, the Payroll Run Journal is usually faster. For this application, we made the Employees & Payroll module the Home window.

> **Restore** **SimData\helena1.CAB**, the backup file, for Helena's Academy to **SimData\Helena\helena**. **Enter October 15** as the session date.

> **Create** **shortcuts** for **Create General Journal** (Company), **Create Statement** (Receivables) and **Pay Expenses** (Payables). **Enter** the **cash sale** and the **two cash purchase transactions**.

Individual paycheques are entered in the Payroll Journal indicated by the pointer on the Paycheques icon on the following screen:

NOTES
Remember that you must have a valid Payroll ID code from Sage Software in order to use the payroll features of the program. The Student version does not require a payroll ID.
Choose the Business Services menu in the Home window and click Simply CARE Service for more information.

NOTES
If you choose not to create shortcuts, you can change modules each time you need to access a journal in a different module.

Click the **Paycheques icon** to open and display the Payroll Journal:

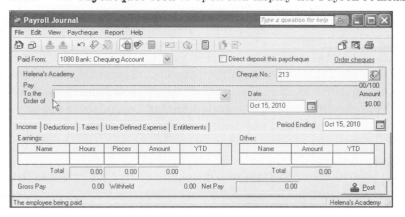

SIMPLY VERSION
The Refresh and Time Slips tools do not appear in the Simply version.

Three tool buttons on the tool bar relate specifically to the Payroll Journal: Calculate Taxes Automatically, Enter Taxes Manually and Recalculate Taxes. The Time Slips tool is used to enter time and billing information for the employee and will be covered in Chapter 18. The remaining tools — Home window, Daily Business Manager, Store, Recall, Undo, Adjust Cheque, Reverse Cheque, Enter Additional Information, Windows Calculator, Refresh and Print — are the same as those found in other journals. You can also change report form options and preview the paycheque before printing. Adjust Cheque is the Payroll equivalent of the Adjust tool in other Journals.

The cursor is in the Employee (To The Order Of) field.

Click   the **To The Order Of (Employee) field arrow** to see the employee list:

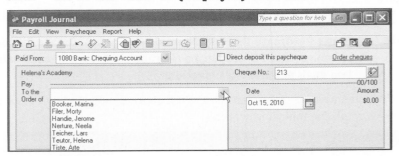

Click   **Filer, Morty** to select this employee and add his name to the form. If you have not chosen correctly, return to the employee list and select again.

To add new employees from the Payroll Journal, type the new name in the Name field. Press (*tab*) and click Add. There is no Quick Add option for employees because additional details are required for income tax purposes.

Press   (*tab*) to add the payroll details for the selected employee:

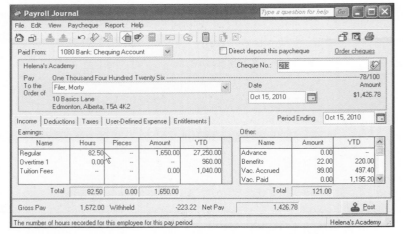

Most of the payroll form is completed automatically based on the ledger details for the employee. The cursor is now in the Cheque (No.) field. The employee's address has been added. The cheque number, 213, should be correct because we have set up automatic numbering. If the number is incorrect, you can change it.

There are two date fields. In the **Date** field, you should enter the date of payment. As usual, the session date, October 15, has been entered by default. Since this session date is correct, you should accept it. The **Period Ending** field refers to the last day of the pay period for the employee. It may be later or earlier than the cheque date. In this case, the session date is also the same as the pay period ending date, so you can accept the default date again.

The Payroll Journal information is divided among different tab screens. The Income tab screen has all the sources of income for the employee divided into two categories:

NOTES
Helena's Academy uses a single chequing account for Payables and Payroll cheques, so there is a single sequence of cheque numbers.

NOTES
The Period Ending date is usually earlier than the cheque date for hourly paid employees who must complete the hours and have this summary submitted to the payroll department before a cheque is prepared.

For salaried workers, the Period Ending date may be later than the cheque date because they are paid at the same rate each period. If they are not paid for missed work days, they may have those amounts deducted from later paycheques.

Earnings and Other. **Earnings** include the regular income sources such as Regular and Overtime wages for the hourly paid employees and tuition fees repaid. We have set up the employee records so that only their own sources of income appear on the form. **Other** has all the other sources of income, including payroll advances, taxable benefits and vacation pay accrued and paid out. Year-to-date amounts are added for all fields.

The **Regular Hours** field contains the number of hours an employee has worked for the regular pay rate during the pay period. You can edit the default entry. The **Overtime** field contains the number of overtime hours an employee has worked during the pay period. No default number of overtime hours is entered because the time varies from week to week. If there are different overtime rates, you can set up a second overtime field and rate. For example, pay for evening overtime work may be less than the pay for Sundays or holidays. You can define 20 different sources of income.

The **Gross Pay** amount (the pay rate times number of hours worked) is calculated and added to the bottom portion of the journal window. The total amount **Withheld** for taxes and other deductions and the **Net Pay** also appear at the bottom of the journal.

For salaried employees, the Salary field will replace the Regular and Overtime fields and salary amounts are entered automatically from the employee record.

Click the **Taxes tab**. Tax amounts are calculated automatically:

Income	Deductions	Taxes	User-Defined Expense	Entitlements		Period Ending	Oct 15, 2010	
EI		28.55		QPIP				
CPP/QPP		75.55						
Tax		97.12						
Tax (Que)								

Because we have chosen to let the program complete the tax calculations, the tax fields are not available for editing.

If you need to edit the tax amounts, click the **Enter Taxes Manually tool** to open the tax fields for editing.

Click the **Income tab** to continue with the payroll entry.

Click the **Overtime 1 Hours field** to continue.

Type 4 **Press** ⟨tab⟩.

Notice that the Gross Pay and Vacation pay are updated to include the additional pay. Notice, too, that the upper cheque portion of your Input Form window is updated continually as you add information. Year-to-date (YTD) amounts are also updated continually as you add information.

If amounts are not updated, click the **Calculate Taxes Automatically tool** on the tool bar. The option to enter taxes manually may be selected, an option that allows you to edit tax amounts but will not update these amounts automatically.

The cursor has advanced to the **Tuition Fees** Amount field. Helena's Academy pays 50 percent of eligible tuition fees and the amount refunded to employees — a taxable benefit — is entered in this income field. Because the amount is paid directly to the employee, and it is taxable, it is set up as an income amount. Filer is currently taking a course and will receive $130 per pay period as the refund for his tuition until the entire amount has been repaid.

Type 130 **Press** ⟨tab⟩ to enter the Amount paid for tuition fees.

The cursor now moves to the Advance Name field in the Other income column. The **Advance** fields are used to enter amounts advanced to an employee in addition to his or her normal pay from wages or salary. Advances are approved by management for emergencies or other personal reasons. An advance offered to an employee is shown as a positive amount. An advance recovered is indicated as a negative amount in this same

NOTES
If sales commissions are paid to employees, they must be calculated separately and added manually.

NOTES
To verify that tax amounts have also changed, click the Taxes tab. Click the Income tab again to continue with the payroll entry, and click the Tuition Fees Amount field to position the cursor.

NOTES
The tuition fee benefit could also be set up in the employee ledger so that it is added automatically until the entire amount is paid. Then you would remove it from the ledger. Instead, we will edit the amount in the journal.

NOTES
By dividing the tuition fee benefit among several pay periods, the income tax burden will also be spread out over several paycheques.

field. An advance of $200 for Morty Filer has been approved. Advance amounts owing will appear in the YTD column for Advance.

> **Press**   ⸤tab⸥   again to move to the Amount field for Advances.
>
> **Type**   2 0 0   **Press** ⸤tab⸥.

The cheque portion of the journal and the gross pay are updated again. Advances do not affect the tax amounts or vacation pay.

The **Benefits** field under Other Earnings is used to enter the total amount of taxable benefits a business offers to its employees, such as health insurance or dental plans when the payments are made to a third party. Half of Filer's medical premium is paid by Helena's Academy. Benefit amounts are included in the pretax total income to arrive at the amount of income tax and then subtracted again to determine the net pay amount. The employer contribution to medical premiums (an employer expense) is also set up as an automatic entry that appears on the User-Defined Expense tab screen.

> **Click**   the **User-Defined Expense tab**:

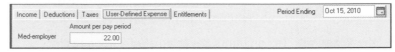

> **Click**   the **Income tab** to continue.

Simply Accounting automatically calculates an amount in the **Vac. Accrued Amount** field and displays it as a default. Filer's default amount is calculated at the vacation pay rate of 6 percent and will be retained by the business (*Vacation Payable* account) until he takes a vacation in July or leaves the employ of the business. Therefore, the Vacation Paid Amount on this cheque is zero. (See the Employee Information Sheet on page 261 for each employee's vacation pay rate.) The Vacation Paid amount in the YTD (Year-To-Date) column shows the amount of vacation pay that has been paid to the employee already this year.

The total accumulated vacation pay owing (withheld since vacation pay was last paid and including this pay) shows as the YTD amount for the Vac. Accrued. This amount appears in the **Vac. Paid** field when you release the accumulated vacation pay retained for an employee. The amount retained and available for release appears as a default when you turn off the option to retain vacation in the Employee Ledger. (See page 283.)

> **Click**   the **Deductions tab**:

The **Deductions tab screen** has the employee medical deduction entered automatically from the amounts stored in the ledger record. For other employees, the RRSP contributions and/or family support payments also appear on this screen. These amounts can be edited.

We will use the Entitlements tab screen for Handie's payroll entry.

> **Click**   the **Income tab** again to see the complete payroll form as shown in the following screen:

NOTES

Medical benefits are not paid in cash to the employee. They are added to gross pay to determine income tax and then subtracted again to determine the net pay.

You can see the tax implications of benefits by deleting the amount and then re-entering it while observing the changes in gross pay and amounts withheld.

NOTES

If the User-Defined Expense amount is omitted from the record, it can be entered in the paycheques journal as needed.

NOTES

Salaried employees receive their regular pay during their vacations instead of receiving vacation pay. They receive vacation days as an entitlement.

NOTES

If the amount of a deduction is incorrect, and it is not a one-time change, you should edit the employee record in the Payroll Ledger. The next time you open the Payroll Journal for the employee, the edited amount will be entered.

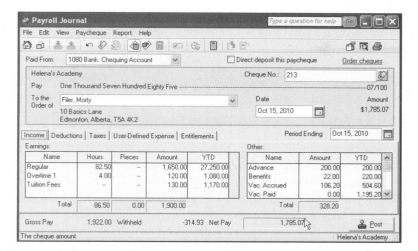

NOTES
If you are using a later version of the Simply Accounting program than 2008 Release B, your tax amounts and amount withheld may be different from those shown because different tax tables are used. Your Gross Pay and Vacation amounts should always be the same as the ones we show.

Reviewing the Payroll Journal Transaction

When you have entered all the information, you should review the completed transaction before posting.

> **Choose** the **Report menu** and **click Display Payroll Journal Entry**. The transaction you have just completed appears as follows:

Payroll Journal Entry Display

Helena's Academy
10/15/2010 (J4)

	Debits	Credits	Division
1240 Advances Receivable	200.00	-	
5260 Wages: Support Staff	1,876.20	-	
5310 EI Expense	42.87	-	
5320 CPP Expense	87.92	-	
5330 WCB Expense	17.12	-	
5380 Tuition Fees Expense	130.00	-	
5400 Medical Premium Expense	22.00	-	
1080 Bank: Chequing Account	-	1,785.07	
2300 Vacation Payable	-	106.20	
2310 EI Payable	-	73.49	
2320 CPP Payable	-	175.84	
2330 Income Tax Payable	-	174.39	
2430 Medical Payable - Employee	-	22.00	
2440 Medical Payable - Employer	-	22.00	
2460 WCB Payable	-	17.12	
	2,376.11	2,376.11	

Notice that all the relevant wage expense accounts have been debited. The hourly wages and tuition fee benefit are tracked in separate wage expense accounts. In addition, all the wage-related liability accounts and *Bank: Chequing Account* have been updated automatically because the Payroll Ledger is linked to the General Ledger. All accounts in the journal entry have been defined as linked accounts for the Payroll Ledger so you do not enter any account numbers directly.

Simply Accounting uses the Canada Revenue Agency tax formulas to calculate the deduction amounts for CPP, EI and income tax. These formulas are updated every six months. The remaining deductions are determined from Employee Ledger entries when different rates apply to different employees (WCB, vacation pay rate and Medical), or from Payroll Ledger settings when the same rate applies to all employees (EI factor of 1.4). These rates can be modified for individual employees in their ledger records.

Payroll expense accounts reflect the employer's share of payroll tax obligations. The liabilities reflect the amounts that the owner must remit to the appropriate agencies and include both the employer's share of these tax liabilities and the employee's share (deductions withheld). For example, CPP contributions by the employee are matched by the employer. Therefore, the *CPP Expense* (employer's share) is one-half of the *CPP Payable* amount (employee and employer's share). WCB is paid entirely by the employer, so the expense amount is the same as the liability amount. Medical

NOTES
Separate linked wage accounts are set up for the wages of teaching staff and for support staff and for music lesson wages. Vacation pay can also be linked to a separate account if you want to track this amount separately from other wage expenses.

NOTES
Both the employer's and the employee's share of the medical premiums are payable to the provincial Minister of Finance.

NOTES

If you see an error message about a missing file or form when you preview the cheque, click OK. In the Journal, click the Change The Default Printer Settings tool to access the form settings. Choose Custom Forms and Custom Simply Form. In the Description fields, choose the generic forms Payment Cheque for payments and Payroll Cheque With YTD Payments for paycheques. If you are previewing direct deposit stubs, choose Direct Deposit Stubs as the description. The file location reference should be dimmed. Click OK.

You should now be able to preview the payment.

NOTES

Of course, a real business should always work with the current payroll tax tables. Sage Software provides payroll updates every six months when you sign up for the payroll update service. We cannot change the source dates in the text after publishing, and using fixed dates and program (tax table) versions assures that you can obtain the same results we show.

NOTES

Payroll Journal entries may be stored as recurring entries before posting. Follow the same steps as you do for recurring sales or purchases.

NOTES

We have turned on the option to confirm successful posting of transactions, so you should click OK each time you see this message.

contributions by employer and employee are equal but they are represented in different accounts — the employer's share is shown in expense and payable accounts, *Medical Premium Expense* and *Medical Payable - Employer*, while the employee's share appears only in the payable account, *Medical Payable - Employee*. For EI, the employer's share is 1.4 times the employee's share. Vacation pay is part of the Wages expense. The tuition benefit is entered as a debit to *Tuition Fees Expense*.

Close   the **display** to return to the Payroll Journal input screen.

You can preview the paycheque before printing it if you want. You can also modify the reports and forms settings from the journal. Tool buttons are included for both these functions. You must have selected Custom Forms and Custom Simply Form as the Form Type in the Reports and Forms settings screen. The default form locations should be dimmed; otherwise, they may refer to incorrect file locations because these settings are saved with the data file that was created with different default settings.

Click   the **Print Preview tool** . (See margin Notes.)

You will see a warning about payroll formulas:

The caution is displayed whenever the dates of the transaction are different from the dates of the tax tables in your Simply Accounting program.

Click   **Yes** to continue to the preview. At this point, you have not yet posted the transaction, so you can still make changes if needed.

The preview shows the cheque and cheque stub with payroll summary details.

Click   **OK** to close the preview when finished to return to the journal.

CORRECTING THE PAYROLL JOURNAL ENTRY BEFORE POSTING

Move the cursor to the field that contains the error. If you need to change screens to access the field you want, **click** the appropriate **tab**. **Press** (tab) to move forward through the fields or **press** (shift) and (tab) together to move back to a previous field. This will highlight the field information so that you can change it. **Type** the **correct information** and **press** (tab) to enter it.

You can also use the mouse to **point** to a field and **drag** through the **incorrect information** to highlight it. You can highlight a single number or letter or the entire field. **Type** the **correct information** and **press** (tab) to enter it.

Click an **incorrect amount** to highlight it. **Type** the **correct amount** and **press** (tab).

You can discard the entry by **clicking** ☒ (Close) or ↶ (Undo) or by returning to the Employee list and **clicking** a **different employee** name. **Click** the name of the **correct employee** and **press** (tab). When prompted, confirm that you want to discard the incorrect entry. **Click Yes**, and start again.

Posting

When all the information in your journal entry is correct,

Click   **Post** to see the caution about dates and tax tables again.

Click   **Yes** to continue. **Click OK**. A blank Payroll Journal input screen appears.

Entering Payroll Entitlements

Jerome Handie has taken a sick leave day during the two-week pay period.

Choose Handie, Jerome from the employee list. **Press** ⟨tab⟩:

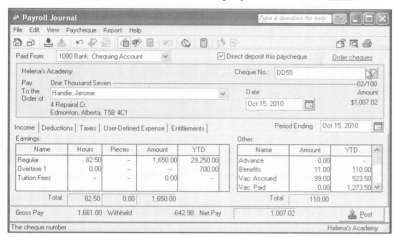

Handie's payroll details are added to the form. You will notice that instead of a cheque number, the entry DD55 appears on the form because the check box for Direct Deposit This Paycheque is selected. Handie has chosen to have his pay deposited directly to his account. The bank account deposit details are added to the employee's ledger record.

Handie has overtime hours for this pay period.

Click   **0.00** in the **Hours field** beside Overtime 1.

Type   2

Click   the **Deductions tab** to open these fields.

Handie has two deductions in addition to the medical premium: one for his RRSP contribution and one for his family support payment.

Click   the **Entitlements tab** to open these fields:

Income	Deductions	Taxes	User-Defined Expense	Entitlements			Period Ending	Oct 15, 2010	
The number of hours worked in this pay period:					82.50				
		Days Earned		Days Released					
Vacation									
Sick Leave		0.52							

Two entitlements are defined for Helena's Academy: vacation days (for salaried employees only) and sick leave days for all full-time employees. The amounts entered in the Days Earned fields show only the number of days earned for this pay period — two weeks. Sick leave is accrued at the rate of 5 percent per hour worked. The total number of days accrued from prior work periods will be recorded and updated in the ledger record. If the number of days released exceeds the number of days accrued, you will see a warning message that asks you if a negative balance is allowed.

Handie has taken one day of sick leave in this pay period.

Click   the **Days Released column beside Sick Leave**.

Type   1   **Press** ⟨tab⟩ to save the entry and update the form:

Income	Deductions	Taxes	User-Defined Expense	Entitlements			Period Ending	Oct 15, 2010	
The number of hours worked in this pay period:					82.50				
		Days Earned		Days Released					
Vacation									
Sick Leave		0.52		1.00					
Gross Pay	1,721.00	Withheld	-665.18	Net Pay		1,044.82		Post	

The number of days released for Sick Leave during the pay period   Helena's Academy

Entitlements do not affect gross pay, net pay or taxes. You are now ready to review the journal entry.

NOTES

For every 20 days of work, the employee is entitled to one day of sick leave (the rate is 5 percent).

For some entitlements, such as vacation days, employers may require the employee to work a minimum number of months before taking any time off.

The total number of days accrued appears only in the ledger record for the employee and does does not appear in the journal.

NOTES
To preview a direct deposit stub, click the Preview tool [icon]. If you see an error message about missing forms, click OK. In the Journal, click the Change The Default Printer Settings tool [icon] to access the form settings. Choose Custom Forms and Custom Simply Form. In the Description fields, choose the generic form Direct Deposit Stubs as the description. The file location reference should be dimmed. Click OK.

You should now be able to preview the payment.

NOTES
We will not continue the reminder to click OK each time you see the confirmation message when you post a transaction.

Choose the **Report menu** and **click Display Payroll Journal Entry**:

Helena's Academy			
10/15/2010 (J5)	Debits	Credits	Division
5260 Wages: Support Staff	1,812.60	-	
5310 EI Expense	41.41	-	
5320 CPP Expense	77.97	-	
5330 WCB Expense	41.99	-	
5400 Medical Premium Expense	11.00	-	
1080 Bank: Chequing Account	-	1,044.82	
2300 Vacation Payable	-	102.60	
2310 EI Payable	-	70.99	
2320 CPP Payable	-	155.94	
2330 Income Tax Payable	-	271.63	
2400 RRSP Payable	-	25.00	
2410 Family Support Payable	-	250.00	
2430 Medical Payable - Employee	-	11.00	
2440 Medical Payable - Employer	-	11.00	
2460 WCB Payable	-	41.99	
	1,984.97	1,984.97	

This entry is similar to the previous one, with the additional payable entries for RRSP and family support. Entitlements taken do not appear in the payroll journal entry, but the days accrued are recorded on the cheque stub and in the employee's ledger record.

Close   the **journal entry display** to return to the journal.

Make   **corrections** to the journal entry if necessary.

Click   Post [Post icon] to save your work.

Click   **Yes** to bypass the warning about payroll dates. **Click** the **Income tab**.

Select   **Nerture, Neela** for the next payroll transaction. **Press** (tab).

Nerture has no additional income, deductions or entitlements, so you can accept all the default amounts.

Click   Post [Post icon]. **Click Yes** to bypass the warning about payroll dates.

Select   **Tiste, Arte** for the next payroll transaction. **Press** (tab) to add his default payroll amounts:

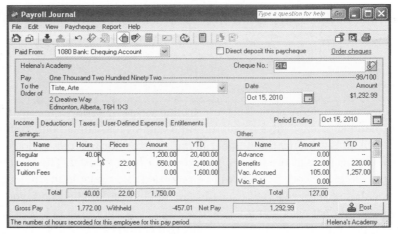

Tiste has 40 entered as the regular number of hours per period. Because this half month has 11 days and he works 4 hours per day, we need to change the hours. Tiste does not receive overtime pay.

Click   **40.00** in the Hours field for Regular.

Type   44 **Press** (tab) to update the gross pay and taxes.

Lesson rates and a default number of lessons per period are entered for teachers in their ledger records. Simply Accounting calculates the total dollar amount by multiplying the per lesson piece rate times the number of lessons. You can define a different rate for each employee. If different rates are paid for different kinds of work, you can define additional piece rate fields. Tiste has given 20 individual lessons in the past two weeks, so we need to change the default entry, 22.00. This amount should be highlighted.

Type   20   **Press** (tab) to enter the Amount for lessons and complete the entry as shown:

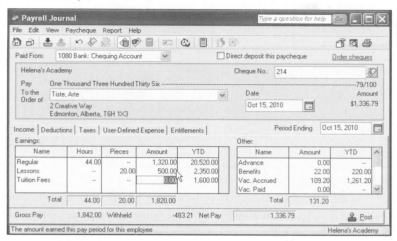

Press (ctrl) **+ J** to open the journal entry display:

Helena's Academy			
10/15/2010 (J7)	Debits	Credits	Division
5250 Wages: Teaching Staff	1,929.20	-	
5310 EI Expense	44.09	-	
5320 CPP Expense	83.96	-	
5330 WCB Expense	16.40	-	
5400 Medical Premium Expense	22.00	-	
1080 Bank: Chequing Account	-	1,336.79	
2300 Vacation Payable	-	109.20	
2310 EI Payable	-	75.58	
2320 CPP Payable	-	167.92	
2330 Income Tax Payable	-	345.76	
2430 Medical Payable - Employee	-	22.00	
2440 Medical Payable - Employer	-	22.00	
2460 WCB Payable	-	16.40	
	2,095.65	2,095.65	

Again, we see a similar journal entry. For each employee, you can define one overall linked income account, or you can choose the default linked accounts for each income. For Tiste, a teacher, we have linked his hourly wages to *Wages: Teaching Staff* rather than to the *Wages: Support Staff* account used for other hourly employees. Therefore, his wages for lessons are included with the expense for teaching wages. For salaried teachers, lesson wages are linked to a separate expense account.

Close   the **display** when finished and make corrections if necessary.

Post   the **entry** and **click Yes** to bypass the warning about payroll formulas.

Close   the **Payroll Journal window** to return to the Home window. **Advance** the **session date** to October 31.

Adjusting Payroll Entries

On October 17, Filer returned his paycheque because he worked six hours of overtime instead of the four he was paid for. Simply Accounting does not require reversing and correcting entries for these situations. Instead, you can complete a paycheque adjustment in the Payroll Journal, just as you do in the other journals. You can access the Adjust Journal screen in different ways.

Click   the **Paycheques icon** to open the Payroll Journal.

Click   the **Adjust Paycheque tool** or **choose** the **Paycheque menu** and **click Adjust Cheque** to open the familiar Search window. Or,

Click   the **Pancheques icon shortcuts list arrow** and **click**
Adjust Paycheque to open the Search window:

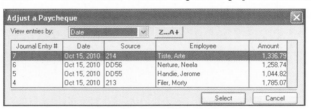

Pancheques is selected as the search area.

You can select beginning and ending dates to create the list. You can also enter the source (cheque or direct deposit number) or journal entry number and click OK to access the paycheque immediately.

The default dates are the earliest transaction date and the session date for the data file. We can accept the default dates to have all payroll transactions listed.

Click   **OK** to access the list of posted payroll entries:

Click   **Journal Entry #4 Filer, Morty** to select Filer's journal entry.

Click   **Select** to display the entry that was posted.

First, Simply Accounting reminds you about recalculating taxes:

The program is advising you that the tax recalculation will not be automatic if you change an amount on the payroll entry.

Click   the **Advisor icon** to close the warning and display the journal:

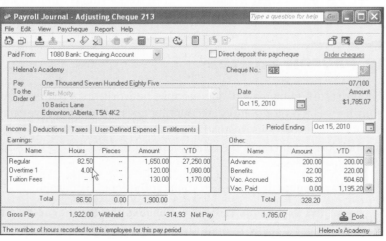

This is a duplicate of the payroll entry. All the fields can be edited with the exception of the employee name. If you want, you may change the date for the new cheque to October 17. The reversing entry will retain the original posting date. The cheque number is highlighted because normally you would prepare a new cheque. However, Filer has returned the cheque so we can use the same number. We need to change the number of overtime hours.

Click   **4.00** in the **Hours column for Overtime 1** to select the current entry.

Type   6   **Press** ⌐tab⌐ to enter the change and update the gross pay.

The Vacation pay and Withheld amounts have not been updated for the new amount of gross pay. Compare the amounts with those in the journal screen display on page 275.

Click   the **Taxes tab**. Tax amounts have not changed and they can be edited:

Income	Deductions	Taxes	User-Defined Expense	Entitlements		Period Ending	Oct 15, 2010	
EI		30.62		QPIP				
CPP/QPP		87.92						
Tax		174.39						
Tax (Que)								
Gross Pay	1,982.00	Withheld	-314.93	Net Pay	1,845.07			👤 Post

Click   the **Recalculate Taxes button** 🔲 on the Payroll Journal tool bar or **choose** the **Paycheque menu** and **click Recalculate Taxes**:

Income	Deductions	Taxes	User-Defined Expense	Entitlements		Period Ending	Oct 15, 2010	
EI		31.66		QPIP				
CPP/QPP		90.89						
Tax		193.59						
Tax (Que)								
Gross Pay	1,982.00	Withheld	-338.14	Net Pay	1,821.86			👤 Post

All the tax deduction and vacation pay amounts are updated for the extra overtime hours worked.

Click   the **Income tab** to see that the Vacation amount has increased from $106.20 to $109.80.

Review the Payroll Journal **entry**. **Close** the **display** when you have finished. **Make corrections** if necessary.

Click   the **Post button** to save the adjustment.

Simply Accounting displays the following warning when you do not change the cheque number:

Read the question in the warning carefully. To change the cheque number to the next number in the automatic sequence, click Yes. In this case, you can use the duplicate cheque number because Filer returned the original cheque.

Click   **No** to continue. **Click OK** to confirm posting.

Close   the **Payroll Journal** to return to the Home window.

When you display the Payroll Journal and include corrections, you will see three journal entries for Filer: the original entry, the reversing adjusting entry and the final correct entry.

All three journal entries are posted with the original date, unless you changed it.

NOTES
If you need to change the employee or to reverse a cheque for other reasons, you can reverse the payroll transaction. See page 282.

NOTES
The total amount Withheld is still $314.93 and the Vacation Accrued is still $106.20.

⚠ WARNING!
Do not confuse the Recalculate Taxes tool with the Windows Calculator tool. The Calculator tool is the last one on the left side of the tool bar before the Refresh tools.

NOTES
The program provides a warning about the cheque sequence because we selected to verify number sequences in the Forms Settings window (see page 213).

Reversing a Paycheque

You should reverse an entry to correct it when you have selected the wrong employee, or because you need to delete it. The Reverse tool performs this in a single step.

Click the Adjust Paycheque tool ✎ or press (*ctrl*) + A.

Define your search parameters and click OK to access the list of posted entries.

Double click the entry you want to reverse to open the journal entry.

Click the Reverse Paycheque tool ▧ or choose the Paycheque menu and click Reverse Paycheque.

Click Yes to confirm that the entry will be reversed.

Simply Accounting saves both the original and the reversing entry. When you show corrections for journal reports, you have a complete audit trail.

Releasing Vacation Pay

Tiste needs to pay for the vacation he has booked and should receive the retained vacation pay. Before releasing the vacation pay, you must change the setting in the employee ledger so that the vacation pay is not retained. There are several ways to open the employee record.

Click the **Employees icon** 🪪 to open the Employees window:

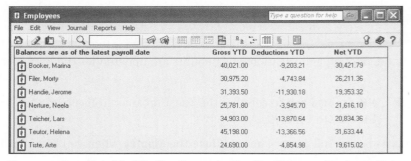

You can also click Modify Employee in the Employees shortcuts list as shown:

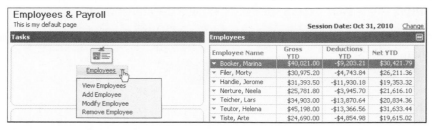

The Search window for employees will open for you to select the employee:

Double click the listing for **Arte Tiste** to open his ledger record:

However, the most direct way to open the record is to click Tiste, Arte in the Home window Employees pane list.

Click the **Income tab** to access the vacation pay settings:

> **NOTES**
> The ✓'s in the Use column show which items will appear in the journal for this employee. There is no ✓ for Overtime 1, so Overtime does not appear in the Income column for Tiste (see the Payroll Journal screen for Tiste on this page).

Click **Retain Vacation** near the bottom of the screen to remove the ✓.

Close the **Ledger window** to return to your starting point.

If you started from the Employees window, Tiste's name should still be selected.

Click the **Payroll Journal icon** [icon] in the Employees window or **choose** the **Type menu** and **click Payroll Journal** to access the journal for Tiste:

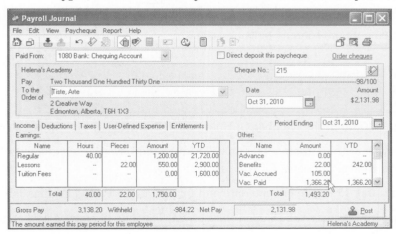

> **NOTES**
> The Vac. Accrued amount ($105.00) is the vacation pay on the wages for this pay period and is included in the Vac. Paid amount.
> When you remove the regular hours, the accrued vacation is reduced to zero and the vacation paid is also reduced by $105.00.

If you are in the Home window, (the Employees window is not open),

Click   the **Paycheques icon** 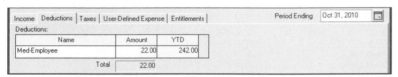.

Choose Tiste from the employee list and press (tab) to continue.

The accumulated vacation pay now appears in the Vac. Paid Amount field. However, amounts also appear for regular wages and benefits so we must edit the default entries. No regular hours should be included and benefits do not apply to vacation pay.

Click   **40.00** in the Regular Hours field. (Double click if the entire amount is not selected.)

Press   (del). **Press** (tab) to select entry for the number of lessons (Pieces).

Press   (del) to remove the entry and update the amounts again. Notice that the accrued vacation amount is reduced to zero.

Click   **22.00** in the Benefits Amount field.

Press   (del). **Press** (tab) to update the amounts.

Since deductions should not be taken from vacation pay, Tiste's medical premium amount should also be deleted before printing the cheque and recording the entry. This is a one-time change, and it should be made directly in the journal.

Click   the **Deductions tab** to open this screen:

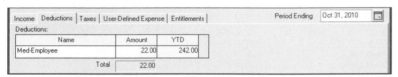

Click   the **Med-Employee Amount field entry** to select it.

Press   (del) to remove the amount. **Press** (tab) to update the net pay. The Taxes tab screen opens.

Click   the **User-Defined Expense tab**:

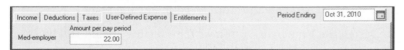

Click   the **Med-employer Amount field entry** to select it.

Press   (del) to remove the amount. **Press** (tab) to update the journal.

The Entitlements tab screen opens.

NOTES
Tiste, a part-time employee, does not receive entitlements — his entries for days earned are blank. For other employees, delete the number of hours in the Entitlements tab screen because entitlements are not earned on vacation pay.

Click   **40.00** in the Number Of Hours field. **Press** (del) to remove the entry.

For employees with entitlements, this will reduce the Days Earned amounts to zero. We still need to change the dates for the paycheque.

Enter   **Oct 17** as the cheque date and **Oct 15** as the Period Ending date.

Click   the **Income tab** to open this screen. The journal entry is now complete as shown here:

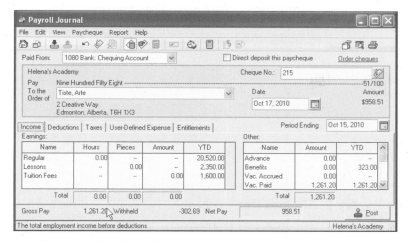

You should review the journal entry before posting.

Choose the **Report menu** and **click Display Payroll Journal Entry**:

Helena's Academy			
10/17/2010 (J10)	Debits	Credits	Division
2300 Vacation Payable	1,261.20	-	
5310 EI Expense	30.55	-	
5320 CPP Expense	55.21	-	
5330 WCB Expense	11.22	-	
1080 Bank: Chequing Account	-	958.51	
2310 EI Payable	-	52.37	
2320 CPP Payable	-	110.42	
2330 Income Tax Payable	-	225.66	
2460 WCB Payable	-	11.22	
	1,358.18	1,358.18	

The released vacation pay shows as a debit (decrease) to *Vacation Payable*. Payroll taxes are charged on the vacation pay, as they are charged on other wages, because they have not yet been paid on this income, that is, on retained vacation pay. The employer's expense for vacation pay, a debit to the wages expense account, was recognized when the original paycheque was prepared. At that time Vacation Payable was credited to create the liability.

Close the **display** to return to the journal and **make corrections** if necessary.

Click Post . **Click Yes** to skip the payroll formula warning.

Close the **Payroll Journal**.

Open the **Ledger** for **Tiste** and **click** the **Income tab**.

Click **Retain Vacation** so that his future paycheques will be entered correctly with vacation pay retained.

Close the **Ledger window** and then **close** the **Employees window** to return to the Home window.

Making Payroll Tax Remittances

Simply Accounting tracks payroll remittances when the suppliers are designated as payroll authorities and the taxes are linked to these suppliers.

You cannot adjust these remittances once they are posted; therefore, you should make a backup copy of your data file before making the payments.

Back up your **data file**.

Taxes are remitted from the Payments Journal. You can open this journal from the Payables module Payments Journal, or from its shortcuts list arrow or from the Employees & Payroll module. We will demonstrate the access from the Payroll window first.

WARNING!
Remember to turn the Retain setting back on.

WARNING!
Because you cannot adjust payroll remittances once they are posted, you should back up your data file before making the payments. Corrections must be entered as Adjustments in the Payments Journal Pay Remittance form, but it may be difficult to sort out the exact amounts that you need to enter for the correction.

NOTES

The Pay Remittance icon has no shortcuts list.

CLASSIC VIEW

Click the Payments icon

to open the Payments Journal. Then select Pay Remittances from the Pay transaction list to open the journal form we need.

Click the **Pay Remittance icon** to open the Payments Journal form we need.

Click the **Pay To The Order Of list arrow** to see the payroll authorities:

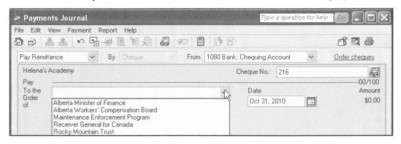

Notice that the Adjust tool button is dimmed and unavailable.

Five suppliers who collect payroll deductions and taxes have been identified as payroll authorities in the supplier records so their names appear on the list of suppliers.

The first remittance will be to the Receiver General for EI, CPP and income tax.

Click **Receiver General for Canada** to select the supplier.

The Payments Journal is updated with the taxes collected for this supplier:

NOTES

Your tax amounts may be different if your program uses later payroll tax tables.

Accept the default amounts in your data file, unless you know that you have made an error in the paycheque.

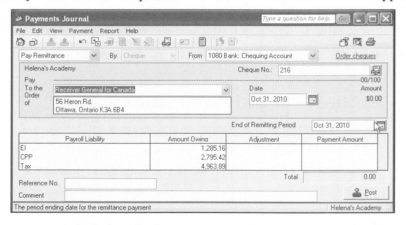

These amounts include only the taxes entered through Payroll Journal entries and any opening balance adjustments. If taxes were not remitted immediately before the files were converted to Simply Accounting, the payroll tax liability accounts will have outstanding balances. For Helena's Academy, these opening balances were entered as part of the Payroll Ledger setup. These amounts are shown here:

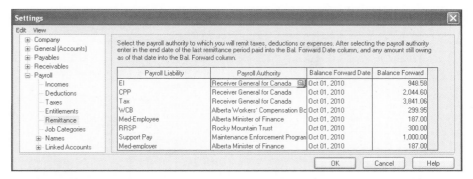

NOTES
In Chapter 9, we show how to enter these opening balances as Payroll Ledger settings.
The Medical liability has two entries, one for the employee's share and one for the employer's share.

You can see that these balances match the amounts in the Trial Balance for October 1 on page 260.

The Remittance journal has two date fields: one for the date of the cheque and a second below the cheque section for the payroll period covered by the remittance. The session date is the default for both. When you change the **End Of Remitting Period date**, the amounts will be updated to show the General Ledger amounts at that date. Remittances are usually due one month after the pay period they cover, so we are paying the taxes that were withheld to the end of September.

The Adjustment field should be used for any tax expenses that are not already included in the payable account balances. A positive entry will increase the tax expense and the total amount submitted. Negative adjustment amounts will decrease the tax expense amount and the total amount submitted.

Enter   **Oct 17** as the date of the cheque. **Press** (tab) **twice**.

Enter   **October 1** in the End Of Remitting Period date field and **press** (tab) to update the amounts owing:

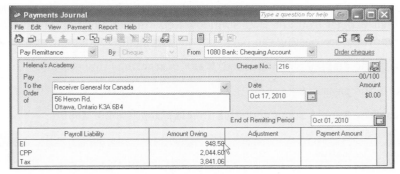

NOTES
Because the earliest transaction date allowed is October 1, we cannot enter September 30 as the date for the end of the remitting period. The amounts for October 1 are the same as the amounts for September 30.

Notice that all the tax amounts have been reduced to match the opening balance amounts. The full amount is being paid for each tax.

Click   the **Payment Amount column for EI** to enter the amount owing as the payment amount.

Press   (↓) to enter the payment amount for CPP.

Press   (↓) to enter the payment amount for Tax.

Press   (tab) to accept the final payment and update the cheque amount.

Click   the **Reference field**.

Type   Memo 3A **Press** (tab) to advance to the comment field.

Type   Memo 3A, Payroll Tax remittance for September

NOTES
The Reference No. is not added to the journal so we repeat it in the Comment, just as we did for Other Payment entries in this journal.

This completes the form as shown:

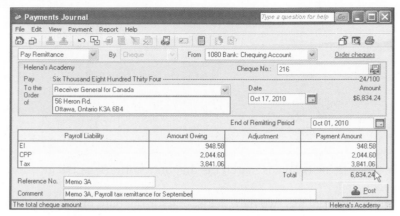

We can now review the journal entry.

Choose the **Report menu** and **click Display Payments Journal Entry**:

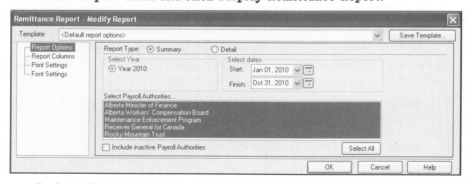

The three liability accounts have been debited to reduce the liability, and the bank account is credited. If you had entered adjustments, those amounts would be debited (for positive adjustments) to the corresponding tax expense account.

From the journal Report menu you can also display the Remittance Report, the same report that you get from the Home window Reports menu or Report Centre. If you display this report before posting the payment, the payment amount will still be zero.

Close   the **display** when finished. **Make corrections** if necessary.

Post   the **payment**.

Choose the **Report menu** and **click Display Remittance Report**:

You can display a **Summary Report** with total amounts for each tax, or a **Detail Report** with a line entry for each tax for each payroll transaction in the report period. You can prepare the report for one or more payroll authority, and you can choose a remittance period for the report. We can accept the default dates — we want the report for October — and we will view the Summary Report for the Receiver General to see the remittance we just completed.

Click   **Receiver General For Canada** and then **click OK** to see the report:

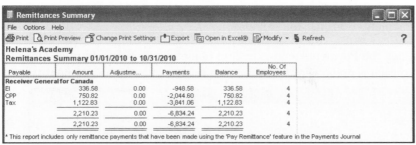

The report shows the total of Payroll Journal entry amounts for each tax, adjustments, payments and final balances. The new balances are the total amounts for the October paycheques for the four employees and the vacation pay for Tiste.

Close the **report** when finished to return to the Payments Journal.

Choose **Alberta Minister of Finance** as the supplier for the next remittance.

Pay the **two Medical tax amounts**.

Enter **Memo 3B** in the Reference field and **enter** an appropriate **comment**.

Review and then **post** the **payment**.

Choose **Alberta Workers' Compensation Board** as the supplier.

Pay the **WCB amount**.

Enter **Memo 3C** in the Reference field and **enter** an appropriate **comment**.

Review and then **post** the **payment**.

Choose **Rocky Mountain Trust** as the supplier for the next remittance.

Pay the **RRSP contributions** withheld.

Enter **Memo 3D** in the Reference field and **enter** an appropriate **comment**.

Review and then **post** the **payment**. Leave the journal open.

Choose **Maintenance Enforcement Program** as the supplier.

Pay the **Family Support payments** withheld.

Enter **Memo 3E** in the Reference field and **enter** an appropriate **comment**.

Review and then **post** the **payment**.

Enter the **next two cash purchase transactions** and then close the journal.

Entering Remittances from the Payables Module Window

Click Payables in the Modules pane list to open the Payables window. Click the Payments icon shortcuts list arrow:

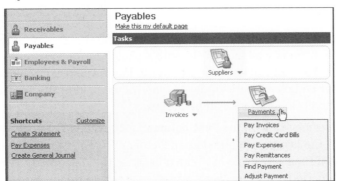

NOTES

The Amount column entries reflect only the amounts from Payroll Journal entries for the four paycheques on Oct. 15 and Tiste's vacation pay. They do not include the opening balance forward amounts.

The note reminds us that the report accounts only for transactions completed with the Pay Remittance feature.

NOTES

You can enter the cash purchases as Other Payments in the Payments Journal or as Purchases Paid By Cheque in the Purchases Journal.

The shortcuts include Pay Remittances. Click Pay Remittances to modify the Payments Journal. You can also

Click the Payments icon to open the Payments Journal. Once the Journal is open, click Pay Purchase Invoices to see the payment types:

Click Pay Remittance to modify the Payments Journal. Choose the payroll authority and continue with the remittance entry as outlined above.

Completing a Payroll Cheque Run

When several employees are paid at the same time, you can complete a payroll cheque run to prepare all the cheques and journal entries in a single transaction. All employees are being paid on October 31, so we will pay them from the Payroll Run Journal, shown with the pointer in the following screen:

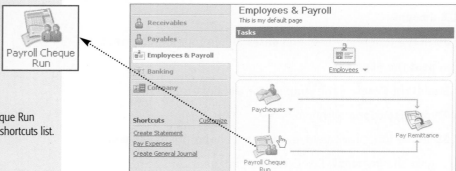

NOTES
The Payroll Cheque Run icon does not have a shortcuts list.

 SIMPLY VERSION
The Refresh tool applies to multi-user operation of the program. It does not apply in the single-user Simply version. The Time Slips tool also does not appear in the Simply version.

NOTES
You cannot adjust paycheques from the Payroll Run Journal, although paycheques prepared here can be adjusted in the Paycheques Journal. See page 294.

Click the **Payroll Cheque Run** icon to open the Payroll Run Journal:

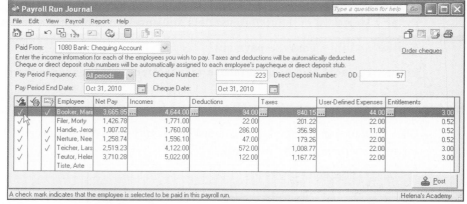

From this screen, you can pay all employees with a single transaction, and you can enter or edit any details that you can enter or edit in the Payroll Journal. Employees are listed in alphabetic order and checkmarks indicate who will be paid in this payroll run and who has selected direct deposits instead of cheques.

Initially, all employees have a ✓ in the **Post column** 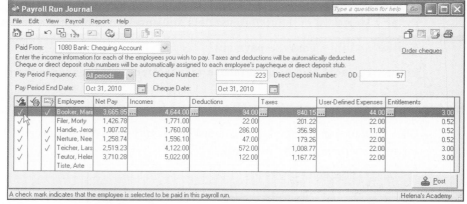 except Tiste because he received a cheque since the last paycheque date of October 15. The program selects all employees for inclusion if their pay cycle has ended because the default **Pay Period Frequency** option is All Periods. You can select a single pay period frequency for the cheque run from the Pay Period Frequency list or you can choose All Periods to include more than one period. If we chose 24 (semi-monthly pay) as the Pay Period Frequency, only the four hourly paid employees would be marked with a ✓ in the Post column.

The form also includes deposit information in the **Direct Deposit column** . A ✓ in this column indicates that the paycheque will be deposited to the employee's bank account. Both the next Cheque and Direct Deposit Numbers are on the form.

The pay period ending date and initial cheque number can also be edited if necessary.

The columns mirror the tabs in the Payroll Journal and contain total amounts for all fields in that tab screen, using the default ledger entries. If you do not need to change any details, you can post the transaction directly. To change some of the details, you can access the individual fields for a column heading by selecting an employee and clicking the **Detail button** beside an amount.

Click   the **✓ beside Tiste** in the Post column to select the employee and add his ✓ and default paycheque amounts.

You can remove an employee from the payroll run by clicking the ✓ in the Post column to remove it. You can change the direct deposit status for an employee by clicking the ✓ in the Direct Deposit column to remove it. A cheque will then be created instead.

Click   **Filer** to select this employee. Detail buttons are added to his amounts.

Click   the **Incomes Detail button** ⋯ to open the Earnings fields:

Payroll Detail								
View								
Income	Deductions	Taxes	User-Defined Expense	Entitlements				
Earnings:					Other:			
Name	Hours	Pieces	Amount	YTD	Name	Amount	YTD	
Regular	82.50	--	1,650.00	28,900.00	Advance	0.00	200.00	
Overtime 1	0.00	--	--	1,140.00	Benefits	22.00	242.00	
Tuition Fees	--	--	0.00	1,170.00	Vac. Accrued	99.00	607.20	
					Vac. Paid	0.00	1,195.20	
Total	82.50	0.00	1,650.00		Total	121.00		
Gross Pay	1,672.00	Withheld	-223.22	Net Pay	1,426.78	OK	Cancel	

This screen is just like the Income tab screen in the Payroll Journal as shown on page 272, and we can enter or edit all the amounts in the same way as in that journal. For Filer, we need to add the overtime hours, tuition fee amount and the advances repayment. All these details are entered in the Income Detail screen.

Click   **0.00** in the **Hours column beside Overtime 1**.

Type   2

Press   ⟨tab⟩ to select the Tuition Fees amount.

Type   130

Press   ⟨tab⟩ **twice** to select the Advance amount.

By default, –200.00, the entire amount owing, is entered. Filer is repaying $50 each week so we must change the amount.

Type   –50

Click   the **Deductions tab**:

Payroll Detail			
View			
Income	Deductions	Taxes	User-Defined Expense	Entitlements
Deductions:			
Name	Amount	YTD	
Med-Employee	22.00	242.00	
Total	22.00		
Gross Pay	1,862.00	Withheld	-291.84	Net Pay	1,498.16	OK	Cancel

We do not need to change these amounts, but you can see that the deduction amounts are available for editing.

Click   the **Taxes tab**:

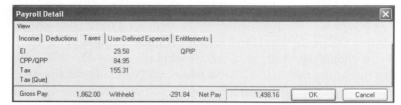

Taxes cannot be edited in the Payroll Run Journal. If you need to change tax amounts, you must use the Payroll Journal and choose to calculate taxes manually.

Click   the **User-Defined Expense tab**:

The employer's expense for the medical premium is included here and can be edited if required. Entitlements can also be edited (see page 293).

Click   **OK** to return to the Payroll Run Journal summary screen.

Click   **Handie** to prepare for entering his additional details.

We need to add the overtime hours.

Click   the **Incomes Detail button** ⚏ to open the Earnings fields.

Click   **0.00** in the **Hours column beside Overtime 1**.

Type   2   **Press** (tab) to update all amounts.

Click   **OK** to return to the Payroll Run Journal summary screen.

No changes are needed for Nerture's pay, so we can enter the information for Tiste next. We need to change the number of regular hours and include the advance. The default entry for number of lessons is correct.

Click   **Tiste** to prepare for entering his additional details.

Click   the **Incomes Detail button** ⚏ to open the Earnings fields.

Click   **40.00** in the **Hours column beside Regular**.

Type   44

Click   **0.00** beside Advances in the Amount column.

Type   100   **Press** (tab) to update all amounts.

Click   **OK** to return to the Payroll Run Journal summary screen.

Click   **Booker** to prepare for entering the additional details for her.

Click   the **Incomes Detail button** ⚏ to open her Earnings fields:

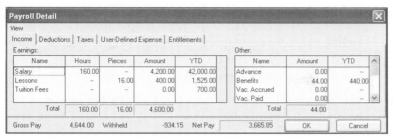

Booker is a salaried employee who also teaches music lessons after school. Her regular salary is entered as the default but the amount can be edited if necessary. We need to add her tuition fees benefit and enter one day of sick leave.

Click   **0.00** in the Tuition Fees Amount column.

Type   4 5   **Press** ⌞tab⌟ to update all amounts.

Click   the **Entitlements tab** to open the entitlements fields:

Once again, the fields we see are the same as those in the Payroll Journal Entitlements tab screen (see page 277).

Click   the **Days Released field beside Sick Leave**.

Type   1

Click   **OK** to return to the Payroll Run Journal summary screen.

No changes are required for Teicher or Teutor's salaried paycheques, so the transaction is complete and should look like the one we show here:

You are now ready to review the journal entry.

Choose the **Report menu** and **click Display Payroll Run Journal Entry** to review the journal entry.

There are seven journal entries, one for each employee in the payroll run.

Close   the **display** when finished.

You cannot preview a paycheque from the Payroll Run Journal. You can modify the reports and forms setting from the journal by using the tool button.

Turn on your **printer**.

NOTES
Remember that the entry for Days Earned reflects only the amount earned for this pay period based on the number of hours worked in this pay period.

> **Choose** the **Report menu** and **click Print Payroll Cheque Run Summary** to provide a printed record of the payroll run transactions paid by cheque or **click Print Direct Deposit Stub Summary** to provide a printed record of the payroll run transactions paid by direct deposit. You cannot display these summaries.
>
> **Click**   Post   Post   to save the transaction. **Click Yes** to bypass the warning about payroll formula dates.

The confirmation message advises that seven journal entries were posted. The Payroll Run Journal remains open with the direct deposit and cheque numbers updated after the payroll run cheques and direct deposits as shown:

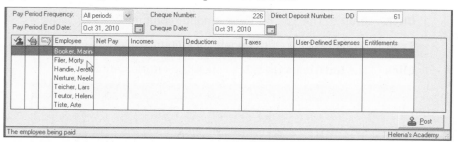

No employees are selected because they have all been paid. There are no ✓ in the Post column.

> **Close**   the **Journal** to return to the Home window.

When you open the Payroll Run Journal for the November 15 pay period, the four hourly paid employees will be selected, as shown:

Pay Period Frequency:	All periods		Cheque Number:	228	Direct Deposit Number:	DD	61
Pay Period End Date:	Nov 15, 2010		Cheque Date:	Nov 15, 2010			

			Employee	Net Pay	Incomes	Deductions	Taxes	User-Defined Expenses	Entitlements
			Booker, Marin						
✓			Filer, Morty	1,426.78	1,771.00	22.00	201.22	22.00	0.52
	✓		Handie, Jerom	1,007.02	1,760.00	286.00	356.98	11.00	0.52
	✓		Nerture, Neela	1,258.74	1,596.10	47.00	179.26	22.00	0.52
			Teicher, Lars						
			Teutor, Helena						
✓			Tiste, Arte	1,292.99	1,877.00	22.00	435.01	22.00	

A check mark indicates that the employee is selected to be paid in this payroll run.   Helena's Academy

NOTES
You will see this screen after you change the session date to November 15.

The salaried employees are not selected. They are not due to be paid again until November 30.

> **Continue**   entering **transactions** up to the payroll adjustment for Dec. 17.

Adjusting a Payroll Run Entry

We can adjust a Payroll Run Journal entry from the Payroll Journal, just as we edited the transaction for Filer. Tiste has handed in his resignation and should repay the remainder of the amount he received as an advance. He should also receive his final vacation pay.

First, we will change his retained vacation pay option as we did before. Refer to page 282 if you need assistance.

> **Click**   **Tiste, Arte** in the Employees List pane in the Home window to open his ledger record.
>
> **Click**   the **Income tab**.
>
> **Click**   the ✓ **for Retain Vacation** to change the setting.

Close   the **ledger record**.

Click   the **Paycheques icon** .

Click   the **Adjust Paycheque tool** or **press** `ctrl` + **A**.

Click   **OK** to see the list of posted payroll entries. Notice that all the entries from both payroll journals are included.

Double click the **Dec. 15 entry for Tiste** to open the journal. You will see the following message:

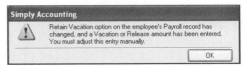

We cannot add vacation pay as a paycheque adjustment unless we enter all the amounts and taxes manually. Instead, we will prepare a separate paycheque for the vacation pay amount.

Click   **OK** to close the message. **Close** the **Paycheques Journal**.

Click   **Tiste, Arte** in the Employees List pane of the Home window to open his ledger record. **Click** the **Income tab**. **Click Retain Vacation** to change the option again so that his vacation pay is retained.

Close   the **ledger record** and the **Employees window**.

Click   the **Paycheques icon** to open the Payroll Journal.

Click   the **Adjust Paycheque tool**, or **choose Adjust Paycheque** from the Paycheques icon shortcuts list.

Click   **OK** to access the list of posted payroll entries.

Double click the **Dec. 15 entry for Tiste**.

Click   the **Advisor icon** to close the warning and display the Payroll Journal:

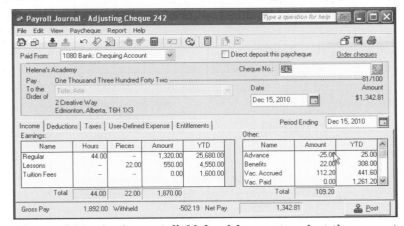

Click   **-25** in the **Amount field for Advance** to select the current entry.

Type   −50 **Press** `tab` to enter the change and update the gross pay. The YTD amount for Advance is reduced to zero.

Click   the **Recalculate Taxes tool** on the Payroll Journal tool bar or **choose** the **Paycheque menu** and **click Recalculate Taxes**.

Review the Payroll Journal **entry**. **Close** the **display** when you have finished. **Make corrections** if necessary.

NOTES
The tax amounts do not change this time because advances are not taxed.

Click   the **Post button** 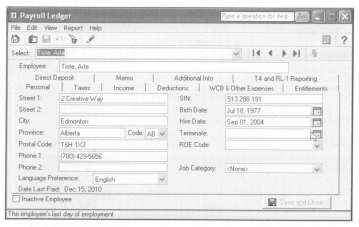 Post to save the adjustment.

Click   **No** to bypass the cheque number warning.

Change   the **Retain Vacation** settings for Tiste so you can issue the vacation pay.

Release   the **remaining accrued vacation for Tiste**. Remember to delete all amounts that do not apply. Refer to page 283.

Close   the **Paycheques Journal**. **Enter** the **remaining transactions**.

Terminating an Employee

When an employee leaves the company, his or her ledger record should be updated with the date of termination and the reason for leaving. Then a record of employment can be issued that indicates the number of hours worked and the total income. This form is used to determine eligibility for employment insurance.

Tiste will be going back to school full time in January and he has received his last paycheque, so we should modify his record. We will work from the Employees window, so that we can also print reports.

Click   the **Employees icon** Employees to open the Employees window.

Double click   **Tiste, Arte** to open his ledger record at the Address tab screen:

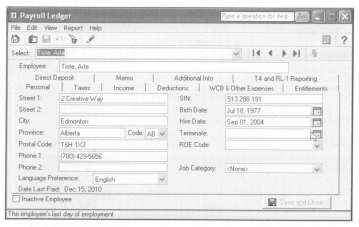

The two fields we need are on this screen: the Terminate date field and the ROE (Record of Employment) Code field.

Click   the **Terminate field**.

Type   12 15

Click   the **ROE Code list arrow** to see the codes available:

Click   **C - Return To School**.

Click **Save And Close** to open the following message:

Normally, an employee's status is changed to inactive when he or she has left the company. In this way, the employee's name will no longer appear in the employee lists in the journals. Data for the individual can still be included in any reports by including inactive employees.

Click **Yes** to change the status and close the ledger.

We will now be able to print a record of employment for Tiste. We will print this report from the Employees window.

Printing Payroll Reports

You can access all payroll reports from the Reports menu in the Employees window and from the Home window. In addition, most payroll reports can also be accessed from the Report Centre. Some payroll reports cannot be displayed; they are printed directly.

Printing Record of Employment Reports

The Record of Employment Report provides information about employees who have terminated their employment to determine their eligibility for Employment Insurance benefits. The report includes the length of employment, the earnings, the total number of hours worked and the reason (code) for the termination. You can print the report only for employees who have been terminated, and you must have the correct preprinted forms. You should still be in the Employees window.

NOTES
You cannot access the Record of Employment from the Report Centre.

Choose the **Reports menu**, then **click Print Record Of Employment**:

From the Home window, choose the Reports menu, then choose Payroll and click Print Record Of Employment.

Tiste is the only employee listed in this option window because he is the only one with a termination date. The date range includes the fiscal year to date. If you have data for a different time period, you can change these dates and then click Display to update the list of employees. For this report, you need to provide the company payroll contact's name and telephone number.

Click **Tiste, Arte** to select the employee for the report.

If there are more employees with termination dates, you can click Select All to create reports for all the listed employees.

Click the **Payroll Contact Person field**.

Type Morty Filer

Click   **OK** to continue:

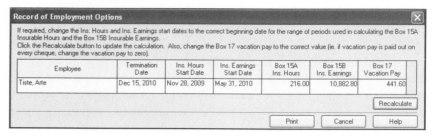

You now have the summary details for the selected employee. They include only the amounts entered in the payroll journals; they do not include the year-to-date opening balance amounts. You can edit the fields in this window. If you have payroll data for a longer period, you can enter those dates and recalculate the amounts. However, only the three months of payroll data we entered in Simply Accounting are tracked in this form, so we must update the details. The year-to-date insurable earnings amount is tracked in the employee ledger on the T4 and RL-1 Reporting tab screen as shown here:

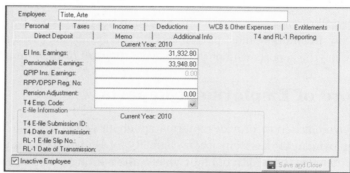

We can see that Tiste has $31 932.80 in EI insurable earnings this year. He has also worked additional hours before October — 20 hours per week for 34 weeks, or 680 hours, so his total number of hours is 896 (680 + 216). And finally, he has received all his vacation pay, so this amount should be changed to zero. You can also edit the start dates for EI insurable hours and earnings.

Enter   **Jan 1** in the Ins. Hours Start Date field and also in the Ins. Earnings Start Date field.

Click   **216.00** in the Box 15A Ins. Hours field.

Type   896

Press   (tab) to select the Ins. Earnings amount.

Type   31932.80

Press   (tab) to select the Vacation Pay amount.

Press   (del). Check your entries.

Click   **Print** to see an additional warning:

You may need to add missing details on the form manually if the final printed form is not complete.

Click   **OK** to begin printing.

Close   the **Employees window**.

Printing T4s

NOTES
You cannot access the T4 Slips from the Report Centre.

T4 Slips and Relevé 1 Slips are also not available for display but they be can be printed. Relevé 1 slips are used only in Quebec, and the Print Relevé 1 Slips Report options screen will list only employees for whom Quebec is the province of taxation. Relevé 1 options are similar to those for T4 slips. You can print T4 slips, which are compulsory for employees filing income tax returns, using either the tax statement forms from Canada Revenue Agency (CRA) or plain paper. You should retain payroll information for employees who leave during the year so that you can prepare T4 slips to mail to them.

Before printing T4s, you should check your printer and forms selections.

Choose   the **Setup menu**, then **choose Reports & Forms** and **click Government Forms** and **click Federal Payroll** to display the following options:

Select   **Plain Paper** as the Form Type for T4 Slips and T4 Summary.

Click   **OK** to save the selections and return to the Home window.

Choose   the **Reports menu**, then **choose Payroll** and **click Print T4 Slips and Summary** (or Print Relevé 1 Slips) to display the following options:

NOTES
You can also print T4s and Summary from the Employees window. Choose the Reports menu and click Print T4s and Summary to open the options window.

You need to select the employees in order to prepare their T4 slips. Inactive employees are not listed by default. You can print copies of the T4s for the employees and the company, or for Canada Revenue Agency (CRA). You can also print the summary for CRA. All are selected as the default.

Click   **Include Inactive Employees** to add Tiste to the list.

Click   **Tiste, Arte**.

Press and hold ⟨ctrl⟩ and click the names of the employees for whom you want the report printed or click Select All to prepare T4s for all employees.

Enter the type of business. For sole proprietorship, partnership or private companies, enter the Social Insurance Number of the owners or partners. You must also enter the contact details for the person completing the forms.

Click   the **T4 Summary Contact Information tab** to open the contact fields:

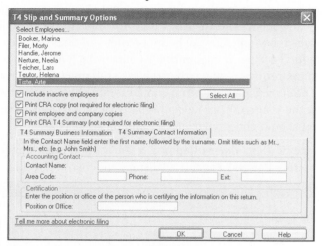

Enter   the **contact details** for the person completing the forms. You can use Morty Filer's name and Social Insurance Number (see page 261).

Click   **OK** to open the warning:

The warning appears when you do not select all employees because the remittance amounts apply to all employees. Thus, reported amounts for employer contributions may be incorrect.

Click   **OK** to open the T4 Box Options screen:

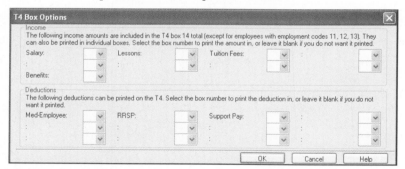

Each box on the T4 slip is numbered and can be designated for a specific deduction or income. You can choose a form box number for these amounts if they are related to income tax and should be included on the T4s. Each item has a list of box numbers that you can select. Income and tax items that are standard for T4s are not listed because their boxes are already assigned. If you do not change the box selections, the income amounts are all combined and the deductions listed are not reported. You can check with CRA to see what each box number is used for. The defaults are correct for Tiste.

Choose   appropriate **box numbers** for the items that should appear on the T4.

Click   **OK** to begin printing. After the T4s are printed, the T4 Summary report is displayed:

These amounts do not include the year-to-date remittances made before Simply Accounting was used for payroll. The remittance amounts shown are those for all employees for three months. The employee contribution amounts are the year-to-date totals for the individual, and the employer contribution amounts are those related to this employee for three months. The employer contribution and remittance year-to-date totals are not included in the payroll history when you do not set up the program at the start of the calendar year. You should edit the amounts.

Click   Print when the amounts are correct to continue.

After printing, you should see a summary of the items printed:

Click   Print Log to print the report printing summary or **click OK** to close the summary.

Printing Employee Mailing Labels

We will continue with the payroll reports that are not available from the Report Centre. You can print labels for employees (like labels for suppliers and clients). Set up the printer for printing labels (Setup menu, Reports and Forms, Labels) before starting.

Choose the **Reports menu**, then **choose Mailing Labels** and **click Employees** to display the list of employee names:

Press and **hold** ⌈ctrl⌉ and **click** the employees' **names** or **click Select All**.

Click   OK to start printing.

Displaying Payroll Reports

Most payroll reports can be accessed from the Employees window Reports menu, from the Home window Reports menu, from the Reports drop-down list in the Reports pane, or from the Report Centre. As usual, we will work from the Report Centre so that you can see sample reports and the report description and purpose.

Click   the **Report Centre icon** in the Reports pane.

Click   **Employees & Payroll** in the Select A Report Type list to see the list of payroll reports:

Displaying Employee Lists

Lists of employees are available, just like lists for other ledgers.

Click   **Employee List** in the Select A Report list to see the report sample.

Click   **Modify This Report** to see the report options:

Or choose the Reports menu, then choose Lists and click Employees to see the report options.

To select employee fields, you can customize the Report Columns. Choose Custom Report Columns and select the ones you want.

The report will display a list of all current employees, together with data for all the details you chose.

Close   the **display** when you have finished.

Displaying Employee Reports

Click   **Employee Summary** in the Select A Report list.

Click   **Modify This Report** to see the report options:

Or, choose the Reports menu, then choose Payroll and click Employee.

The **Summary** option allows you to see the accumulated totals for all deductions and payments, which are updated each pay period. Summary reports are available only for the session date.

You can include or omit inactive employees from the report. You can also omit details that have no amounts or have not been used.

If you use job categories, you can prepare a report for a specific category by choosing it from the drop-down list of categories.

You cannot customize the Employee Summary Report. You can use the **Detail** Report to see individual amounts for each paycheque. To prepare a report for specific deductions or payments, you can customize the column selection for the Detail Report.

> **Click**   **Include Inactive Employees** if you want to report on them as well.
>
> **Press**   and **hold** `ctrl` and **click** the **employees** you want in the report, or **click Select All** to include all employees in the report.
>
> **Click**   **Detail** to include individual transaction details.
>
> **Click**   **Report Columns** in the left-hand pane.
>
> **Click**   **Custom Report Column Settings** to see the information that is included by default and the details that you can add to the report:

> **Select**   the **columns** you want to include or remove and **click OK** to save your new column selections and return to the Report Options screen.

The amount for each detail you choose will be listed for each payroll period in the selected date range for the selected employees, together with the totals for the period selected. The earliest transaction and session dates are the defaults for the Detail Report.

> **Enter**   the **beginning date** for the report you want in the Start field.
>
> **Enter**   the **ending date** for the report in the Finish field.
>
> **Click**   **OK** to see the report. **Close** the **display** when you have finished.

Displaying Deductions and Expenses Reports

Click   **Deductions & Expenses Summary** in the Select A Report list.

Click   **Modify This Report** to see the report options:

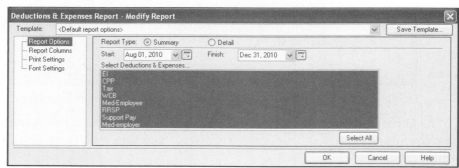

From the Home window, choose the Reports menu, then choose Payroll and click Deductions & Expenses.

This report provides details for all payroll deductions and expenses. The **Summary Report** shows the total amounts and the number of employees the deduction or expense applied to for each payroll item in the selected date range. The **Detail Report** shows individual entries for each selected item, including the date, cheque or deposit number, employee, job category, amount, period totals and number of employees.

You can customize the report by selecting the columns you want to include.

Select the details you want in the report and the date range for the report. The earliest transaction and session dates are the default selections.

Press   and **hold** `ctrl` and **click** the **deductions** and **expenses** you want in the report, or **click Select All** to include all details in the report.

Enter   the **Start date** and the **Finish date** for the report.

Click   **OK** to see the report and **close** the **display** when you have finished.

Displaying the Payroll Remittance Report

The Payroll Remittance Report is described on page 288. To access this report from the Report Centre,

Click   **Remittances Summary** in the Select A Report list.

Click   **Modify This Report** to see the report options.

Displaying the Payroll Journal

The Payroll Journal Report includes all transactions from the Payroll Journal and the Payroll Run Journal.

Click   **Payroll Journal Entries** in the Select A Report list.

Click   **Modify This Report** to see the report options:

CLASSIC VIEW
From the Home window, right-click either the Paycheques or the Payroll Cheque Run icon

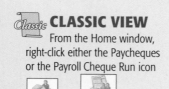

Then click the Display tool to open the Modify Report window.

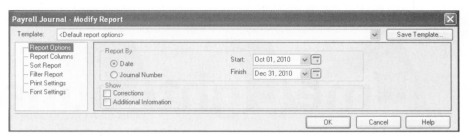

Or, choose the Reports menu, then choose Journal Entries and click Payroll to display the Options window.

The usual sort and filter journal options are available for the Payroll Journal Report. By default, the Date option we use for selecting transactions is the default. Your earliest transaction and latest session dates appear as the default Start and Finish dates.

Type	**the beginning** and **ending date** for the report.
Click	**Corrections** to include the original and reversing entries for the paycheques you adjusted or reversed.
Click	**OK**. **Close** the **display** when you have finished.
Close	the **Report Centre** to return to the Home window.

Management Reports for Payroll

Management reports can be displayed only from the Home window Reports menu.

Choose the **Reports menu**, then **choose Management Reports** and **click Payroll**:

Click	the **topic** you want to see. For the report on Employees With Overtime Hours This Month,
Choose	a **month** from the list for Show Report As At. Choose a form, if appropriate.
Click	**OK** to see the report. **Close** the **display** when you have finished.

Printing Other Payroll Reports

Display the **report** you want to print. **Choose** the **File menu** from the report window and **click Print**. **Choose** your **printer**. **Click OK**. **Close** the **display** when finished.

R E V I E W

The Student CD-ROM with Data Files includes Review Questions and Supplementary Cases for this chapter.

NOTES

Remember that you can see the journal entries for all journals in a single report. From the Report Centre, choose the Financials list of reports and then click All Journal Entries. From the Home window, choose the Reports menu, then choose Journal Entries and click All. You will open the report options window.

NOTES

You can drill down to the Employee Detail Report and the General Ledger Report from the Payroll Journal.

NOTES

You should verify that the form location for the Management Report is correct for your program setup.

NOTES

Remember to check that you have selected the correct printer for your setup. If you click the Print tool, printing will start immediately and you cannot change the selected printer.

CHAPTER NINE

Lime Light Laundry
Laundry Services • Pickup & Deliver

OBJECTIVES

After completing this chapter, you should be able to

- **add** the Payroll Ledger to a company data file
- **enter** Payroll Ledger settings
- **enter** Payroll Ledger linked accounts
- **define** payroll authorities
- **create** employee ledger records
- **enter** employee historical information
- **set up** payroll remittances
- **set up** taxes for income, benefits and deductions
- **create** job categories
- **assign** employees to job categories
- **enter** salespersons on invoices
- **display** and **print** job category and salesperson reports

COMPANY INFORMATION

Company Profile

NOTES
Lime Light Laundry
25 Snow White Lane
Vancouver, British Columbia
V8G 3B2
Tel: (604) 633-8201
Fax: (604) 633-8396
Business No.: 324 732 911

Lime Light Laundry started in Vancouver, British Columbia, in 1994 with a single employee assisting the owner, Charles Chaplin. They provided laundry services to one hotel as a regular client and to a few individual clients. Now Lime Light provides complete laundry services for a number of large hotels in the Vancouver area and has seven full-time employees. Chaplin himself is no longer involved in daily business operations, and the laundry serves only hotels and no individual clients. Chaplin's goal as entrepreneur is business growth. In fact, two employees have recently been hired. Chaplin is negotiating new contracts with a major hotel chain and considering expansion into adjacent premises that are for sale.

Lime Light's business success has enabled it to establish favourable account terms with regular suppliers, including some discounts for early payments. The discount terms for clients also encourage timely payment of accounts. All discounts are calculated on after-tax amounts. Because there are no individual clients, only hotels, Lime Light does not accept credit card payments. Similarly, most regular suppliers do not accept credit cards and Chaplin does not use them in his business.

All laundry services provided by Lime Light are subject to 5 percent GST. Cleaning services are exempt from provincial sales taxes. Lime Light pays the 7 percent PST on non-exempt purchases as well as the 5 percent GST.

On February 1, 2010, Chaplin closed his books so he could begin using the payroll feature in Simply Accounting. The following information summarizes his data:

- Chart of Accounts
- Post-Closing Trial Balance
- Supplier Information
- Client Information
- Employee Profiles and Information Sheet
- Accounting Procedures

Simply SIMPLY VERSION
The terms vendor and customer will replace supplier and client. Sales and Purchases replace the terms Revenues and Expenses in the program for journals and reports.

CHART OF POSTABLE ACCOUNTS

LIME LIGHT LAUNDRY

ASSETS
1080	Cash in Bank
1200	Accounts Receivable
1240	Advances Receivable
1260	Prepaid Insurance
1280	Cleaning Supplies
1300	Clothes Hangers
1320	Packaging Supplies
1520	Computer System
1540	Delivery Vehicle
1560	Laundry and Cleaning Equipment
1580	Pressing Equipment
1600	Railings and Belts
1620	Laundry Premises ▶

▶LIABILITIES
2100	Bank Loan
2200	Accounts Payable
2250	Accrued Wages
2300	Vacation Payable
2310	EI Payable
2320	CPP Payable
2330	Income Tax Payable
2400	MSP Payable - Employee
2410	RRSP Payable
2420	Travel Allowances Payable
2430	Tuition Fees Payable
2440	MSP Payable - Employer
2460	WCB Payable
2640	PST Payable
2650	GST Charged on Services ▶

▶2670	GST Paid on Purchases
2920	Mortgage Payable

EQUITY
3560	C. Chaplin, Capital
3600	Current Earnings

REVENUE
4020	Revenue from Services
4040	Sales Discounts

EXPENSE
5020	Advertising Expenses
5040	Bank Charges
5060	Hydro Expenses
5080	Insurance Expense ▶

▶5100	Cleaning Supplies Used
5120	Clothes Hangers Used
5140	Packaging Supplies Used
5150	Purchase Discounts
5160	Telephone Expenses
5180	Vehicle Expenses
5300	Wages: General
5305	Wages: Cleaning Staff
5310	EI Expense
5320	CPP Expense
5330	WCB Expense
5340	Commissions
5350	Piece Rate Bonuses
5360	Travel Allowances
5380	Tuition Fees Expense
5400	MSP Premium Expense

NOTES: The Chart of Accounts includes only postable accounts and Current Earnings.

POST-CLOSING TRIAL BALANCE

LIME LIGHT LAUNDRY

February 1, 2010

		Debits	Credits				Debits	Credits
1080	Cash in Bank	$52 640.30		▶	2250	Accrued Wages		1 150.00
1200	Accounts Receivable	4 305.00			2300	Vacation Payable		1 098.00
1240	Advances Receivable	200.00			2310	EI Payable		1 022.80
1260	Prepaid Insurance	2 200.00			2320	CPP Payable		2 090.94
1280	Cleaning Supplies	2 000.00			2330	Income Tax Payable		3 054.53
1300	Clothes Hangers	800.00			2400	MSP Payable - Employee		296.28
1320	Packaging Supplies	1 200.00			2410	RRSP Payable		200.00
1520	Computer System	3 000.00			2430	Tuition Fees Payable	325.00	
1540	Delivery Vehicle	35 000.00			2440	MSP Payable - Employer		296.28
1560	Laundry and Cleaning Equipment	15 000.00			2460	WCB Payable		678.97
1580	Pressing Equipment	25 000.00			2650	GST Charged on Services		1 955.00
1600	Railings and Belts	10 000.00			2670	GST Paid on Purchases	585.00	
1620	Laundry Premises	250 000.00			2920	Mortgage Payable		200 000.00
2100	Bank Loan		$12 000.00		3560	C. Chaplin, Capital		173 372.50
2200	Accounts Payable		5 040.00 ▶				$402 255.30	$402 255.30

SUPPLIER INFORMATION

LIME LIGHT LAUNDRY

Supplier Name (Contact)	Address	Phone No. Fax No.	E-mail Web Site	Terms Tax ID
BC Energy Group (Sol R. Heater)	33 Windmill Rd. Vancouver, BC V8K 3C3	Tel: (604) 388-1298	srh@bceg.ca www.bceg.ca	net 1
BC Minister of Finance (M.T. Handed)	7 Fiscal Way Victoria, BC V8V 2K4	Tel: (250) 887-3488 Fax: (250) 887-8109	www.fin.gov.bc.ca	net 1
BC Telephone (Kommue Nicate)	91 Cellular Way Vancouver, BC V8G 8B5	Tel: (604) 348-2355	www.bell.ca	net 1
BC Workers' Compensation Board (N. Jured)	55 Accidental Cr. Victoria, BC V8W 3X6	Tel: (250) 887-7199 Fax: (250) 887-9211	www.worksafebc.com	net 1
Ferndale Paper Products (T. Issue)	43 Ferndale Ave. Vancouver, BC V8F 2S6	Tel: (604) 466-3929 Fax: (604) 466-3935	tissue@ferndalepaper.com www.ferndalepaper.com	1/10, n/30 (after tax) 445 668 714
Langley Service Centre (Otto Fixer)	64 Mechanic St. Langley, BC V2Z 2S4	Tel: (604) 556-7106 Fax: (604) 556-7188	otto@lss.com www.lss.com	net 1 672 910 186
Pacific Laundry Suppliers (Al Washindon)	29 Spotless Dr. Vancouver, BC V8K 1N6	Tel: (604) 782-1618 Fax: (604) 781-5127	aw@pacificlaundry.com www.pacificlaundry.com	net 30 129 554 377
Receiver General for Canada	PO Box 20004 Sudbury, Ontario P3A 6B4	Tel 1: (800) 561-7761 Tel 2: (800) 959-2221	www.cra-arc.gc.ca	net 1
Richmond Equipment Co. (N.U. Dryer)	78 Richmond St. Richmond, BC V7C 3V2	Tel: (604) 699-3601 Fax: (604) 699-1577	Dryer@REC.com www.REC.com	1/10, n/30 (after tax) 366 455 281
Surrey Printers (H.P.L. Jett)	690 Surrey Ave. Surrey, BC V3H 6T1	Tel: (604) 286-9193 Fax: (604) 286-9100	jett@surreyprinters.com www.surreyprinters.com	net 1 125 481 262
Victoria Trust (Victoria Royale)	59 Queen St. Vancouver, BC V8U 1M6	Tel: (604) 388-1825 Fax: (604) 388-2663	www.victoriatrust.ca	net 1

OUTSTANDING SUPPLIER INVOICES

LIME LIGHT LAUNDRY

Supplier Name	Terms	Date	Invoice No.	Amount	Total
Ferndale Paper Products	1/10, n/30	Jan. 29/10	FP-901	$560	$560
Pacific Laundry Suppliers	net 30	Jan. 3/10	PL-644	$1 120	$1 120
Richmond Equipment Co.	1/10, n/30	Jan. 27/10	RE-4111	$3 360	$3 360
			Grand Total		$5 040

CLIENT INFORMATION

LIME LIGHT LAUNDRY

Client Name (Contact)	Address	Phone No. Fax No.	E-mail Web Site	Terms Credit Limit
Capilano Centre Hotel (Lotte Reste)	3 Stopover Cr. North Vancouver, BC V7H 5D3	Tel 1: (604) 587-2563 Tel 2: (888) 587-3882	lreste@cch.com www.cch.com	1/15, n/30 (after tax) $5 000
Coquitlam Motel (B. & B. Roadside)	56 Sliepers Rd. Vancouver, BC V8K 6F3	Tel 1: (604) 366-7155 Tel 2: (800) 366-9175	bbr@coquitlammotel.com www.coquitlammotel.com	1/15, n/30 (after tax) $5 000

Client Name (Contact)	Address	Phone No. Fax No.	E-mail Web Site	Terms Credit Limit
Delta Hotel (A. Good-Knight)	86 Holiday St. Richmond, BC V7R 4D9	Tel: (604) 782-5431 Fax: (604) 781-7528	goodknight@deltahotel.com www.deltahotel.com	1/15, n/30 (after tax) $5 000
Kingsway Inn (Abel Traveller)	77 Roomie Dr. Vancouver, BC V8E 2W2	Tel: (604) 566-7188 Fax: (604) 565-4281	at@kingsway.com www.kingsway.com	1/15, n/30 (after tax) $5 000
Port Moody Resort (Kat Napper)	425 Vacation Ave. Port Moody, BC V3H 4S3	Tel: (604) 369-5826 Fax: (604) 369-7993	knapper@pmresort.com www.pmresort.com	1/15, n/30 (after tax) $5 000

OUTSTANDING CLIENT INVOICES

LIME LIGHT LAUNDRY

Client Name	Terms	Date	Invoice No.	Amount	Total
Delta Hotel	1/15, n/30	Jan. 28/10	69	$2 940	$2 940
Kingsway Inn	1/15, n/30	Jan. 30/10	72	$1 365	$1 365
			Grand Total		$4 305

EMPLOYEE INFORMATION SHEET

LIME LIGHT LAUNDRY

	Clyne Fretton	Mouver Durtee	Soffte Landings	Iean Sissler	Claire Brumes	S. Pott Tran	Cryper Houseman
Position	Senior Cleaner	Cleaner	Senior Presser	Presser	Manager	Delivery	Maintenance
Social Insurance No.	218 738 631	552 846 826	422 946 541	931 771 620	726 911 134	638 912 634	822 546 859
Address	21 Spotter St. Vancouver, BC V3K 4K2	34 Wash Ave. Vancouver, BC V9B 4C1	92 Flat St. Vancouver, BC V8U 1X3	63 Iron Blvd., #2 Vancouver, BC V7N 2L2	11 Sweeper St. Vancouver, BC V7N 2L2	2 Kerry St. Richmond, BC V8K 4K2	4 Fixall Cr. Vancouver, BC V9B 4C1
Telephone	(604) 693-7595	(604) 381-8138	(604) 488-6353	(604) 389-2291	(604) 829-6291	(604) 693-7995	(604) 381-2238
Date of Birth (mm-dd-yy)	8-15-78	11-3-75	8-6-65	7-31-72	7-31-72	8-15-78	11-3-75
Date of Hire (mm-dd-yy)	2-7-03	12-4-09	4-6-03	11-6-09	1-1-04	8-5-04	6-6-00
Federal (BC) Tax Exemption – TD1							
Basic Personal	$9 600 (9 189)	$9 600 (9 189)	$9 600 (9 189)	$9 600 (9 189)	$9 600 (9 189)	$9 600 (9 189)	$9 600 (9 189)
Spouse	$9 600 (7 868)	–	$9 600 (7 868)	–	–	$9 600 (7 868)	$9 600 (7 868)
Other	–	–	$9 371 (8 142)	$1 970 (1 330)	–	–	–
Total Exemptions	$19 200 (17 057)	$9 600 (9 189)	$28 571 (25 199)	$11 570 (10 519)	$9 600 (9 189)	$19 200 (17 057)	$19 200 (17 057)
Additional Fed Taxes	$100	–	–	–	–	–	–
Employee Taxes							
Historical Income tax	$398.92	$375.68	$172.72	$328.64	$869.49	$423.90	$485.18
Historical EI	$68.97	$48.40	$52.29	$47.00	$82.34	$59.84	$67.32
Historical CPP	$164.75	$116.01	$127.27	$117.28	$206.18	$147.54	$166.44
Deduct EI; EI Rate	Yes; 1.4	Yes; 1.4	Yes; 1.4	Yes; 1.4	Yes; 1.4	Yes; 1.4	Yes; 1.4
Deduct CPP	Yes	Yes	Yes	Yes	Yes	Yes	Yes
Employee Income							
Advances: Hist Amt	$200.00	(use) ✓	(use) ✓	(use) ✓	(use) ✓	(use) ✓	(use) ✓
Benefits Per Period	$22.15	$6.23	$22.15	$6.23	$54.00	$24.92	$54.00
Benefits: Hist Amt	$44.30	$24.92	$44.30	$124.92	$54.00	$49.84	$54.00
Vacation Pay Owed	$564.98	$170.06	$295.76	$67.20	–	–	–
Vacation Paid	–	–	–	–	–	–	–
Regular Wage Rate	$18.00	$14.00	$16.00	$14.00	(do not use)	(do not use)	(do not use)
(Hours per Period)	(80 hours)	(40 hours)	(80 hours)	(40 hours)	–	–	–
Reg. Wages: Hist Amt	$2 880.00	$2 240.00	$2 560.00	$2 240.00	–	–	–

▶

EMPLOYEE INFORMATION SHEET CONTINUED

LIME LIGHT LAUNDRY

	Clyne Fretton	Mouver Durtee	Soffte Landings	Iean Sissler	Claire Brumes	S. Pott Tran	Cryper Houseman
Employee Income Continued							
Overtime 1 Rate	$27.00	$21.00	$24.00	$21.00	(do not use)	(do not use)	(do not use)
Overtime 1: Hist Amt	$54.00	$168.00	$48.00	$84.00	–	–	–
Salary	(do not use)	(do not use)	(do not use)	(do not use)	$4 000.00	$1 600.00	$3 600.00
(Hours Per Period)	–	–	–	–	(150 hours)	(80 hours)	(150 hours)
Salary: Hist Amt		––	–	–	$4 000	$3 200	$3 600
Commission	(do not use)	(do not use)	(do not use)	(do not use)	1% net sales	(do not use)	(do not use)
Commission: Hist Amt	–	–	–	–	$390.00	–	–
Piece Rate/Set	$0.10	$0.10	$0.10	$0.10	(do not use)	(do not use)	(do not use)
Piece Rate: Hist Amt	$189.00	$180.00	$188.00	$190.00	–	–	–
Pay Periods	26 (bi-weekly)	52 (weekly)	26 (bi-weekly)	52 (weekly)	12 (monthly)	26 (bi-weekly)	12 (monthly)
Vacation Rate	6% retained	4% retained	6% retained	4% retained	0% (3 weeks)	0% (3 weeks)	0% (3 weeks)
Record Wage Exp in	Linked Accts	Linked Accts	Linked Accts	Linked Accts	Linked Accts	Linked Accts	Linked Accts
Employee Deductions							
RRSP	(use) ✓	(use) ✓	(use) ✓	$25.00	$50.00	(use) ✓	$50.00
RRSP: Hist Amt	–	–	–	$100.00	$50.00	–	$50.00
MSP-Employee	$22.15	$6.23	$22.15	$6.23	$54.00	$24.92	$54.00
MSP-Hist Amt	$44.30	$24.92	$44.30	$24.92	$54.00	$49.84	$54.00
WCB and Other Expenses							
WCB Rate	3.02	3.02	3.02	3.02	3.02	5.00	3.02
Travel Allow	–	–	–	–	$300.00	–	–
Travel Allow: Hist Amt	–	–	–	–	$300.00	–	–
Tuition Fee	–	–	–	$25.00	–	–	–
Tuition Fee: Hist Amt	–	–	–	$100.00	–	–	–
MSP-Employer	$22.15	$6.23	$22.15	$6.23	$54.00	$24.92	$54.00
MSP-Employer: Hist Amt	$44.30	$24.92	$44.30	$24.92	$54.00	$49.84	$54.00
Entitlements: Rate, Maximum Days, Clear? (Historical Amount)							
Vacation: Rate: Max	–	–	–	–	8%, 25 days	8%, 25 days	8%, 25 days
Clear? (Days Accrued)	–	–	–	–	No (10 days)	No (5 days)	No (15 days)
Sick Leave: Rate: Max	5%, 20 days	5%, 20 days	5%, 20 days	5%, 20 days	5%, 20 days	5%, 20 days	5%, 20 days
Clear? (Days Accrued)	No (7 days)	No (5 days)	No (9 days)	No (8 days)	No (8 days)	No (8 days)	No (10 days)
Personal Days: Rate: Max	2.5%, 10 days	2.5%, 10 days	2.5%, 10 days	2.5%, 10 days	2.5%, 10 days	2.5%, 10 days	2.5%, 10 days
Clear? (Days Accrued)	No (3 days)	No (4 days)	No (1 day)	No (2 days)	No (3 days)	No (2 days)	No (2 days)
Direct Deposit							
Yes/No	Yes	No	No	Yes	Yes	No	Yes
Bank, Transit No.	300, 49921	–	–	180, 06722	103, 30099	–	285, 12084
Account No.	2883912	–	–	4556221	2009123	–	2399012
Percent	100%	–	–	100%	100%	–	100%
Additional Information							
Emergency Contact	Aidan Fretton	Alex Durtee	Petra Landings	Kierin Safta	Jay Brumes	Sima Tran	Pedro Perez
Contact Number	(604) 497-1469	(604) 477-4573	(604) 488-6353	(604) 364-1892	(604) 899-2197	(604) 693-7995	(604) 447-5602
T4 and RL-1 Reporting							
EI Insurable Earnings	$3 123.00	$2 588.00	$2 796.00	$2 614.00	$4 390.00	$3 200.00	$3 600.00
Pensionable Earnings	$3 167.30	$2 612.92	$2 840.30	$2 638.92	$4 444.00	$3 249.84	$3 654.00
Withheld	$676.94	$565.01	$396.58	$617.84	$1 262.01	$681.12	$822.94
Net Pay	$2 646.06	$2 022.99	$2 399.42	$1 896.16	$3 127.99	$2 518.88	$2 777.06

EI, CPP & Income Tax Calculations built into Simply Accounting program

NOTES: Medical (MSP) premiums are deducted every pay period. The amounts are adjusted for the monthly rates.

Employee Profiles and TD1 Information

Employee Benefits and Entitlements   All employees are entitled to 10 days per year as sick leave and five days' leave for personal reasons. If the days are not needed, employees can carry these days forward to a new year, to a maximum of 20 and 10 days respectively. Currently, all employees have some unused sick leave and personal leave days accrued from the previous year. Salaried employees are allowed to carry forward two of their three weeks' vacation entitlement. That is, they are allowed to accumulate a maximum of 25 unused vacation days at any one time.

To encourage personal development, Lime Light offers to pay 50 percent of the tuition fees for any employee enrolled in college or university programs. Currently, only Iean Sissler is taking courses and receiving the tuition fee benefit. This benefit for Sissler is considered an expense for Lime Light Laundry. A second benefit applies to all employees — Lime Light Laundry pays 50 percent of the medical premiums.

Piece Rate Bonuses   Lime Light Laundry pays the cleaning staff — the cleaners and pressers — a piece rate bonus of 10 cents per sheet set in excess of the first 500 sets each week. This bonus is added to each paycheque.

Employer Expenses   Lime Light Laundry currently has three employer payroll expenses beyond the compulsory CPP, EI and WCB: 50 percent of the employee's medical premiums for the BC Medical Services Plan (MSP), 50 percent of eligible tuition fees and a travel allowance for Brumes as compensation for using her car for business travel.

Claire Brumes   As the manager of the laundry, Brumes negotiates deals with clients, schedules work, hires new staff and discusses problems with the owner, who does not participate in the day-to-day affairs of the business. She is married and has no children. Since her husband is also fully employed, she uses the single federal and provincial tax claim amounts but she pays the family medical premiums. At the end of each month, her salary of $4 000 per month plus a commission of 1 percent of revenue from services, net of taxes, is deposited to her account. She is recorded as salesperson for all sales for the purpose of calculating her commission. In addition, she receives $300 per month in a separate cheque as a travel allowance to cover the expense of her regular client visits and business promotion. This amount is an employer expense, not an employee benefit. She makes monthly contributions to her RRSP plan as well. In lieu of vacation pay, she is entitled to take three weeks of paid vacation each year.

Clyne Fretton   As the senior cleaner, Fretton performs regular laundry duties, such as cleaning the incoming bed sheets and table linens. She has several years of experience with Lime Light and is helping to train Durtee, the junior cleaner who was recently hired. Her regular pay of $18 per hour is supplemented by the piece rate bonus and by overtime wages at the rate of $27 per hour when she works more than 40 hours per week. In addition, she receives vacation pay at the rate of 6 percent of her total wages, equivalent to about three weeks of pay, but this amount is retained until she chooses to take a vacation. Because she is married and fully supports her husband, she claims a spousal amount for income tax purposes and she also pays medical premiums at the family rate. To offset the tax from her additional income, she chooses to have an additional $100 in taxes withheld each month. She has received an advance of $200 which she will repay over the next four pay periods. She has her pay deposited directly to her bank account every two weeks.

Mouver Durtee   is the second and junior cleaner. For sharing all the cleaning duties with Fretton, he earns $14 per hour, $21 per hour overtime when he works more than 40 hours in a week and the piece rate bonus. He is paid weekly by cheque and his 4 percent vacation pay is retained. As a single self-supporting person, Durtee claims the

NOTES
Taxable benefits are not paid in cash to the employee. However, they are added to gross pay to determine income tax and then subtracted again to determine the net pay.

basic single amount for income tax and pays single medical premiums.

Soffte Landings   is the senior presser. She operates the clothes pressing equipment, assisted by Sissler. Landings is single but supports her invalid aged mother so she is able to claim the spousal equivalent TD1 amount, the caregiver amounts and her mother's age amount. These claims significantly reduce the income tax she pays on her wages of $16 per hour, $24 for overtime hours and her piece rate bonus. Her medical premium is deducted from her bi-weekly paycheque at the family rate to cover herself and her mother. Her 6 percent vacation pay is retained.

lean Sissler   assists Landings with operating the equipment to press the laundry. She is single with no dependents, so she pays single medical premiums and has only the basic single TD1 claim amounts, plus her tuition of $850 and the education allowances ($140 per month federal and $60 provincial). From her weekly deposited pay, she contributes $50 to an RRSP program. Her pay at $14 per hour and $21 for overtime hours with 4 percent vacation pay, is less than Landings' pay because she has less experience. She also receives the piece rate bonus. Sissler is enrolled in a business program at the local community college. She pays 50 percent of her tuition herself and Lime Light Laundry pays an equal amount. This taxable benefit, entered on Sissler's paycheque at the rate of $25 per week, has already been paid for one month.

S. Pott Tran   Tran's main responsibility with Lime Light is delivery. He picks up the dirty laundry from hotels throughout the city and drops off the clean linens. Tran is married and fully supports his wife and one child, so he pays the family medical premiums and has the basic and spousal claim amounts for income taxes. He is paid his bi-weekly salary of $1 600 by cheque, and he can take three weeks of vacation yearly.

Cryper Houseman   is responsible for general maintenance at Lime Light — he keeps the machines running and cleans the premises. As a single parent who supports two children, he can claim the spousal amount for income tax purposes. He has worked for Lime Light since the business started. At the end of each month, Houseman has his monthly salary of $3 600 deposited to his bank account. He also makes contributions to his RRSP program with regular payroll deductions. As a salaried employee, he is entitled to take three weeks of paid vacation per year.

Accounting Procedures

Taxes: GST and PST

Lime Light Laundry uses the regular method for remittance of the Goods and Services Tax. It records the GST collected from clients as a liability in *GST Charged on Services*. GST paid by suppliers is recorded in *GST Paid on Purchases* as a decrease in the liability to Canada Revenue Agency. The GST quarterly refund or remittance is calculated automatically in the *GST Owing (Refund)* subgroup total account. Lime Light files for a refund or remits the balance owing to the Receiver General for Canada by the last day of the month for the previous quarter.

Provincial Sales Tax is not charged on laundry services in British Columbia. Lime Light does pay PST on most purchases. Tax codes are set up in the defaults for the company so that Simply Accounting will automatically calculate the tax when it is paid.

Discounts

All clients are offered a discount of 1 percent on the after-tax amount of the sale if they pay their accounts in full within 15 days. Full payment is requested in 30 days. Discount terms are set up as the default in the client records. Some suppliers also offer discounts on after-tax purchase amounts. These discount terms are set up in the supplier records so that Simply Accounting will automatically calculate the discount when full payment is made within the discount period.

Direct Payroll Deposits

Chaplin allows employees to have their regular pay deposited directly to their bank accounts or to be paid by cheque. Four employees have selected direct payroll deposits.

Payroll Remittances

Four suppliers are identified as payroll authorities with the following remittances: EI, CPP and income tax are remitted to the Receiver General for Canada; medical premiums are remitted to the BC Minister of Finance; Workers' Compensation Board premiums are remitted to the BC Workers' Compensation Board; and RRSP contributions are remitted to Victoria Trust.

INSTRUCTIONS

1. **Set up** the **Payroll Ledger** using the employee information, employee profiles and TD1 information. Detailed keystroke instructions for setting up payroll follow.

2. **Enter** the **transactions** in Simply Accounting using the Chart of Accounts and Supplier, Client and Employee Information. Source documents begin on page 341 following the payroll setup instructions.

2. **Print** the **reports and graphs** marked on the following printing form after you have finished making your entries.

NOTES
If you want to enter the source documents before attempting the payroll setup, or you if do not want to complete the payroll setup, you can restore the backup file SimData\Setup\lime-pay1.CAB.

REPORTS

Accounts
- ☐ Chart of Accounts
- ☐ Account List
- ☐ General Journal Entries

Financials
- ☑ Comparative Balance Sheet: Feb. 1 and Feb. 28 with difference in percentage
- ☑ Income Statement: Feb. 1 to Feb. 28
- ☑ Trial Balance date: Feb. 28
- ☑ All Journal Entries: Feb. 1 to Feb. 28
- ☑ General Ledger accounts: Feb. 1 to Feb. 28
  4020 5300 5305 5350
- ☐ Statement of Cash Flows
- ☑ Cash Flow Projection Detail Report: for 1080 for next 30 days

Tax
- ☐ GST Report

Banking
- ☐ Cheque Log Report

Payables
- ☐ Supplier List
- ☐ Supplier Aged
- ☐ Aged Overdue Payables
- ☐ Expense Journal Entries
- ☐ Payment Journal Entries

Receivables
- ☐ Client List
- ☐ Client Aged
- ☐ Aged Overdue Receivables
- ☐ Revenues Journal Entries
- ☐ Receipt Journal Entries
- ☑ Revenues by Salesperson Feb. 1 to Feb. 28
- ☐ Revenues by Job Category
- ☐ Client Statements

Employees & Payroll
- ☐ Employee List
- ☐ Summary
- ☐ Deductions & Expense
- ☐ Job Category

- ☐ Remittances
- ☑ Payroll Journal Entries: Feb. 1 to Feb. 28
- ☐ T4 Slips
- ☐ Record of Employment

Mailing Labels
- ☐ Labels

Management Reports
- ☐ Ledger

GRAPHS

- ☐ Payables by Aging Period
- ☐ Payables by Supplier
- ☐ Receivables by Aging Period
- ☐ Receivables by Client
- ☐ Revenues vs Receivables
- ☐ Receivables Due vs Payables Due
- ☐ Revenues by Account
- ☐ Expenses by Account
- ☑ Expenses and Net Profit as % of Revenue

PAYROLL SETUP KEYSTROKES

Adding the Payroll Module

Restore SimData\limelite1.CAB to SimData\Limelite\limelite to open the data file for **Lime Light**. **Accept** Feb. 1 as the **session date**.

The Payroll module is hidden because it was not used. Before we can set it up, we need to unhide it. We will then work from this module to enter settings and employees.

Choose the **Setup menu** and **click User Preferences** to open the Options screen.

Click View to access the screen we need:

Click the **Pages check box for Employees & Payroll** to add ✓'s.

Click OK to save the settings and return to the Home window.

Click Employees & Payroll in the Modules pane list:

The Payroll ledger and its icons have been added. The Employees icon has the not finished symbol to indicate that the module history is not finished. From this window we can enter ledger settings and records.

Setting Up the Payroll Ledger

Before you can enter payroll journal transactions, you must set up the payroll module. This involves the same steps as setting up other ledgers:

1. Change the settings for the ledger.
2. Create employee ledger records.
3. Add historical employee data.
4. Back up the data file and finish the history.

Changing Payroll Ledger Settings

Click the **Settings icon** to open the Payroll Settings screen:

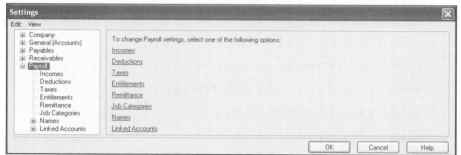

You can also choose the Setup menu and click Settings. Click Payroll if necessary.

Because the Employees & Payroll window is open, the Settings window opens with the Payroll Settings list. For payroll, we need to define the types of income paid to employees, the payroll deductions, payroll taxes, employee entitlements, remittances, job categories, names for income, deductions and additional fields and linked accounts for all these functions. We will begin by entering names and deleting the ones we do not need. The reduced list will be easier to work with.

Click the ⊞ **beside Names** and the ⊞ **beside Linked Accounts**.

This will expand the list, so that labels for all the settings will be available with a single click.

Changing Payroll Names

Click **Income & Deductions** under the Names subheading:

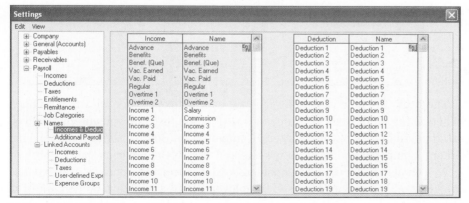

The first screen we need to modify has all the names for incomes and deductions used. Many of the standard income types are mandatory and cannot be changed. These fields are shown on a shaded background. Some of the other default names are also

CLASSIC VIEW
From the Home window, right-click the Employees icon
. Then click the Setup tool
. You can also click the Setup tool and select Employees from the drop-down list.

NOTES
In any module window, click the Settings icon and then click Payroll to open the Payroll Settings screen.

NOTES
By modifying the names first, only the ones we need to set up will appear on later screens.

NOTES
You can enter names for any of these fields later if you need to add more incomes or deductions.

SIMPLY VERSION
You will not see the Expense Groups entry.

NOTES
Lime Light Laundry does not use Expense Groups (under Linked Accounts).

correct so you do not need to redefine them. You can leave Income 1 and Income 2, labelled "Salary" and "Commission," unchanged because Lime Light Laundry has salaried employees and pays a sales commission to Brumes. There is allowance for 20 different kinds of income in addition to the compulsory fields and 20 different payroll deductions. Each income and deduction label may have up to 12 characters.

Lime Light uses an additional income field for the piece rate bonus that is based on the number of sets of bedding the employees launder. The travel allowance for Brumes will be set up as a user-defined expense. The remaining income fields are not used.

Lime Light also has two payroll deductions at this time: RRSP, the Registered Retirement Savings Plan, and the employee share of provincial medical plan premiums (MSP-Employee). The remaining deduction fields are not used.

Click   **Income 3 in the Name column** to highlight the contents.

Type   Piece Rate **Press** (tab) to advance to the Income 4 field.

Click the **En/Fr language icon** to open the extra fields if you want to enter labels or names in both French and English.

Press   (del). **Press** (tab) to advance to the Income 5 field.

Press   (del) to remove the entry. **Press** (tab) to select the next field.

Delete   the **remaining Income names** until they are all removed.

Press   (tab) **twice** after deleting Income 20 to select Deduction 1 in the Name column.

Type   RRSP **Press** (tab) to advance to the second deduction Name field.

Type   MSP-Employee **Press** (tab) to highlight the next field.

Press   (del). You can delete the remaining Deduction fields because Lime Light Laundry does not have other payroll deductions.

Press   (tab) to select the next field. **Delete** the **remaining deductions**.

Click   **Additional Payroll** under the Names subheading:

The Prov. Tax field is used for Quebec payroll taxes. Since we will not choose Quebec as the employees' province of taxation, the program will automatically skip the related payroll fields. WCB (Workers' Compensation Board) is entered as the name for Workers' Compensation because we selected British Columbia as the business province.

We can also name the additional ledger fields, the additional payroll expenses for Lime Light and the entitlements for employees. Lime Light pays 50 percent of the employee's provincial health care plan medical premiums and eligible tuition fees. It also pays a travel allowance to Brumes and offers sick leave and personal leave days for all employees as well as vacation days for salaried employees. First, we will name the ledger

---

NOTES
We are not setting up travel allowances as income because separate cheques are issued for this. If it were set up as an income (reimbursement), it would be added to the paycheque as non-taxable income.

NOTES
If clicking does not highlight the field contents, drag through an entry to select it. Double clicking will select only one word, either Income or 3.

WARNING!
If you later change the province in the Company Information screen, the WCB name entered does not change. You must enter the correction manually by choosing from the drop-down list.

fields. We will use these fields to store the name and phone number of each employee's emergency contact.

Double click `Field1`.

Type   `Emergency Contact`

Press   ⌨tab **twice** to skip the language label icon and highlight the next field.

Type   `Contact Number`

Press   ⌨tab **twice**. **Press** ⌨del to delete the name for Field 3.

Delete   the **names** for Field 4 and Field 5.

Benefits and expenses can be handled in different ways.

The medical premium payment is a taxable benefit for employees. It is also entered as a user-defined expense because the premiums are paid to a third party rather than to the employee. Tuition, the other taxable benefit and user-defined expense, is also paid to a third party — the educational institution. Benefits paid directly to the employee on the payroll cheque should be set up as income. Reimbursements for expenses may be entered as non-taxable income or as user-defined expenses. If we repay the expenses on the payroll cheque, we define them as reimbursements — an income type that is not taxable — and link them to an expense account. If we enter them as user-defined expenses, we create both a linked payable and expense account and issue a separate payment to the employee. Brumes' travel allowance is set up as a user-defined expense.

Drag through   `User Exp 1`, the Expense 1 field, to highlight the contents.

Type   `Travel Allow` **Press** ⌨tab **twice** to select the next expense name.

Type   `Tuition Fees` **Press** ⌨tab **twice**.

Type   `MSP-Employer` **Press** ⌨tab **twice**.

Press   ⌨del. **Press** ⌨tab **twice** to select the final expense. **Press** ⌨del.

Drag through   `Days 1`, the Entitlement 1 field, to highlight the contents.

Type   `Vacation` **Press** ⌨tab **twice** to select the next entitlement name.

Type   `Sick Leave` **Press** ⌨tab **twice**.

Type   `PersonalDays` **Press** ⌨tab **twice**.

Press   ⌨del. **Press** ⌨tab **twice** to select the final name. **Press** ⌨del.

Setting Defaults for Payroll

Click   **Incomes** under the Payroll subheading to display the income setup:

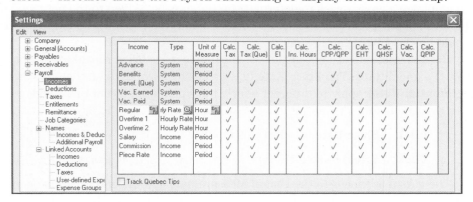

At this stage, we will change the tax settings for Incomes and Deductions.

NOTES

For Lime Light Laundry, we use the generic Benefits field to enter all employee benefits.

NOTES

In Chapter 16, we create Travel Expenses as an income (reimbursement type) that is added to the paycheque. Here it is a user-defined expense and we issue separate cheques to the employee for them.

NOTES

You can use up to 12 characters for User-Defined Expense and Entitlement names including spaces — that is why we omitted the space for the Personal Days entitlement name.

We will first modify this screen by hiding the columns that do not apply to British Columbia so that only the columns we need are on-screen at the same time.

> **Point to** the **right column heading margin for Calc. Tax (Que.)** until the pointer changes to a two-sided arrow .
>
> **Drag**   the **margin to the left** until the column is hidden.
>
> **Point to** the **right column heading margin for Calc. QHSF** until the pointer changes to a two-sided arrow. **Drag** the **margin to the left** until the column is hidden.
>
> **Point to** the **right column heading margin for Calc. QPIP** until the pointer changes to a two-sided arrow. **Drag** the **margin to the left**.
>
> **Point to** the **right column heading margin for Calc. EHT** until the pointer changes to a two-sided arrow. **Drag** the **margin to the left**.

Notice that only the income names you did not delete (page 316) appear on this screen. For each type of income you must indicate what taxes are applied and whether vacation pay is calculated on the income. Most of the information is correct. Regular and overtime hours are paid on an hourly basis, while salary and commissions are paid at designated income amounts per period. All taxes apply to these types of income in British Columbia so these default settings are correct. Vacation pay, however, is paid only to the hourly paid employees, so some of these checkmarks should be removed. In addition, we should designate the type of income for Piece Rate, the income we added, and the taxes that apply to it. Choosing the type of income will change the defaults that are applied.

> **Click**   **Piece Rate** to place the cursor on the correct line.
>
> **Press**   (tab) to move to the Type column. A List icon is added.
>
> **Click**   the **List icon** to see the types we can select:

By default, all new income entries are assigned to the Income type. This assignment is correct for Salary. Taxable benefits paid directly to the employee instead of a third party should also be classified as Income. The Benefit type is used for items such as medical or life insurance premiums that the employer pays directly to a third party on behalf of the employee. The monetary value of the premiums is added as a benefit to the employee's gross wages to determine taxes but is not added to the net pay. The employee does not receive the actual dollar amount. If a benefit is added to net pay, it should be classified as an Income.

Reimbursements are not taxable — the employee is being repaid for company-related expenditures. The **Piece Rate** type calculates pay based on the number of units. **Differential Rates** apply to different hourly rates paid at different times and are not used by Lime Light.

> **Click**   **Piece Rate** to select this type for Piece Rate.
>
> **Click**   **Select** to add the Type to the Settings screen. **Press** (tab).

The cursor advances to the Unit of Measure field and the entry has changed to Item. The amount paid to employees is based on the number of sheet sets laundered. Notice that the Insurable Hours checkmark was removed when we changed the type.

Type   Sets

We need to modify the other Insurable Hours settings. The number of hours worked determines eligibility for Employment Insurance benefits. Regular, overtime and salary paid hours are entered but commissions are not — no time can be reasonably attached to commissions so they are not counted. The checkmark for it should be removed. The ✓ for Piece Rate was automatically removed when we changed the income type.

Click   **Commission** to select this income line.

Press   (tab) **repeatedly** until the cursor is in the **Calc. Ins. Hours field**.

Click   to remove the ✓, or **press** the **space bar**.

We also need to modify the entries for vacation pay. In British Columbia, vacation pay is calculated on all performance-based wages. This includes the regular wages, overtime wages and piece rate pay. We need to remove the remaining ✓. Salaried workers receive paid time off rather than a percentage of their wages as vacation pay. We do not need to remove the ✓ for Overtime 2. If it is used later, vacation pay will be calculated on it as well.

Click   **Salary** in the Income column.

Press   (tab) **repeatedly** until the cursor is in the **Calc. Vac. column**.

Click   to remove the ✓, or **press** the **space bar**.

Press   ⬇ to place the cursor in the **Calc. Vac. field for Commission**.

Click   to remove the ✓, or **press** the **space bar**.

The completed Settings screen is shown below:

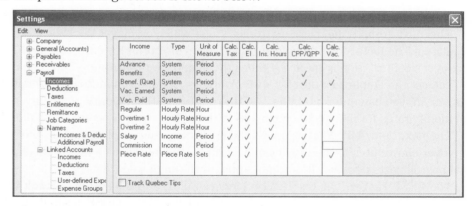

Click   **Deductions** under the Payroll subheading:

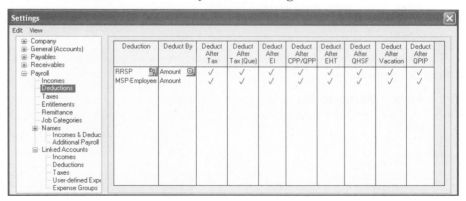

You can hide the columns you do not need — those for Quebec taxes and EHT.

NOTES
Vacation pay is also paid for statutory holidays. Lime Light pays workers their regular pay for these days, as if they had worked. For occasional workers, this pay may be calculated as a percentage of wages.

In Quebec, vacation pay is also paid on benefits.

NOTES
Vacation pay is calculated on all wages. This calculation includes the piece rate pay — number of sheet sets — because it is a performance-based wage or income. Vacation pay is not applied to benefits.

The regulations governing vacation pay are set provincially.

NOTES
You can modify the Deductions screen as you modified the Incomes Settings screen so that only the columns you need are on-screen. You can remove the Deduct After Tax (Que.), EHT, QHSF and QPIP columns.

Only the two deduction names you entered earlier appear on this screen. You can calculate deductions as a percentage of the gross pay or as a fixed amount. Some deductions, like union dues, are usually calculated as a percentage of income. The Amount settings are correct for Lime Light Laundry.

All deductions are set by default to be calculated after all taxes (Deduct After Tax is checked). For MSP-Employee, this is correct — it is subtracted from income after income tax and other payroll taxes have been deducted. However, RRSP contributions qualify as tax deductions and will be subtracted from gross income before income tax is calculated, but not before EI, CPP and so on, so you must change only this setting.

> **Click**   the **Deduct After Tax column** for RRSP to remove only the one ✓ and change the setting to before tax.

The remaining settings are correct. RRSP is deducted after the other payroll taxes and vacation pay because these deductions are based on gross wages.

> **Click**   **Taxes** under the Payroll subheading:

This next group of fields refers to the rate at which employer tax obligations are calculated. The factor for Employment Insurance (**EI Factor**) is correct at 1.4. The employer's contribution is set at 1.4 times the employee's contribution. In the next field, you can set the employer's rate for **WCB** (Workers' Compensation Board) premiums. On this screen, you can enter 3.02, the rate that applies to the majority of employees. You can modify rates for individual employees in the ledger records, as we will do for Tran.

The next field, **EHT Factor**, shows the percentage of payroll costs that the employer contributes to the provincial health plan in Ontario. The rate is based on the total payroll costs per year. It does not apply to BC employees.

The **QHSF Factor** (Quebec Health Services Fund) and the option to **track tips** apply to payroll in Quebec, so we do not need to enter them. QHSF is similar to EHT.

> **Click**   the **WCB Rate field**.
>
> **Type**   3.02

The Quebec tax fields will not be available when we select British Columbia as the province for employees.

> **Click**   **Entitlements** (the Payroll subheading):

NOTES

EHT in Ontario applies if the total payroll is greater than $400 000.

QHSF is used for Village Galleries in Chapter 14.

NOTES

The WCB rate is based on the injury history and risk factors for the job and for the industry. Tran's rate is higher than the others' because his work — driving a delivery truck — is considered more dangerous.

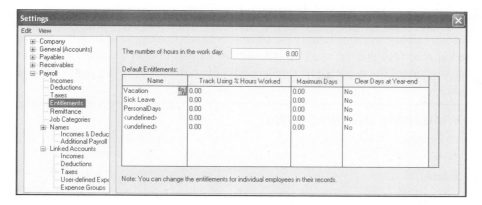

On this screen you can enter the rules for entitlements that apply to all or most employees. When we enter the rules here, they will be added to each employee's record. You can change entitlement amounts for individual employees in their ledger records.

Entitlements may be given directly or may be linked to the number of hours worked. For example, usually employees are not entitled to take vacation time until they have worked for a certain period of time. Or they may not be allowed to take paid sick leave immediately after being hired. You can use the **Track Using % Hours Worked** to determine how quickly vacation or sick days accumulate. For example, 5 percent of hours worked yields about one day per month. Thus, you would enter 5 percent if the employee is entitled to 12 days of leave per year. You can also indicate the **Maximum** number of **Days** per year that an employee can take or accumulate. And finally, you must indicate whether the unused days are **cleared at the end of a year** or can be carried forward. If the days earned, but not used, at the end of a year are carried forward, then the Maximum will still place a limit on the number of days available. The number of days of entitlement is based on an eight-hour day, but this can be changed.

Lime Light Laundry gives salaried workers three weeks of vacation (tracked at 8 percent) and allows a maximum of 25 days. Sick leave at 10 days per year is earned at the rate of 5 percent to the maximum of 20 days. Personal leave days (5 days) accrue at the rate of 2.5 percent for a maximum of 10 days. None are cleared at year-end.

Lime Light Laundry allows two weeks of vacation time and sick leave and one week of personal days to be carried over to the following year.

Click   the **Track Using % Hours Worked field for Vacation**.

Type   8 **Press** ⟨tab⟩ to advance to the Maximum Days field.

Type   25 **Press** ⟨tab⟩.

Click   the **Track Using % Hours Worked field for Sick Leave**.

Type   5 **Press** ⟨tab⟩ to advance to the Maximum Days field.

Type   20 **Press** ⟨tab⟩.

Click   the **Track Using % Hours Worked field for PersonalDays**.

Type   2.5 **Press** ⟨tab⟩ to advance to the Maximum Days field.

Type   10 **Press** ⟨tab⟩.

Until we modify the supplier records and create the employee records, we will not have all the information we need to set up Remittances and Job Categories. Therefore, we will add Payroll Remittance and Job Category settings later.

NOTES
Three weeks' vacation is equivalent to about 6 percent when paid as a percentage of wages. When tracked as a percentage of hours worked, 8 percent will yield about three weeks of time off.

SIMPLY VERSION
Remember that you will see Vendor when we use the term Supplier.

Identifying the Payroll Linked Accounts

There are many linked accounts for payroll because each type of income, tax, deduction and expense that is used must be linked to a General Ledger account. You do not need to create any of these accounts; they are already in the Chart of Accounts. The following income linked accounts are used by Lime Light Laundry for the Payroll Ledger.

PAYROLL LINKED ACCOUNTS: INCOMES					
Principal Bank	1080	Cash in Bank			
Vacation Owed	2300	Vacation Payable	Advances	1240	Advances Receivable
Income					
Vac. Earned	5305	Wages: Cleaning Staff	Salary	5300	Wages: General
Regular	5305	Wages: Cleaning Staff	Commission	5340	Commissions
Overtime 1	5305	Wages: Cleaning Staff	Piece Rate	5350	Piece Rate Bonuses
Not used		Overtime 2			

Click **Incomes** under Linked Accounts to display the income accounts:

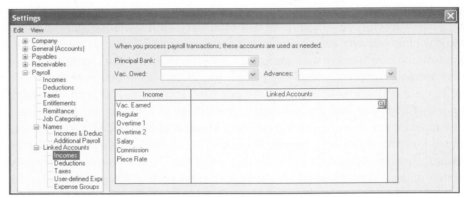

The linked accounts for all types of income appear together on this first screen. You must identify a wage account for each type of employee payment used by the company, even if the same account is used for all of them. Once the Payroll bank account is identified as the same one used for Payables, the program will apply a single sequence of cheque numbers for all cheques prepared from the Payables and Payroll journals.

Accounts you can use for more than one link will be available in the drop-down list. Otherwise, once an account is selected as a linked account, it is removed from the list.

To enter accounts, you can **type** the **account number** or **select** the **account** from the drop-down list and **press** (tab) to advance to the next linked account field, just as you did to enter the linked accounts for Dorfmann.

Choose 1080 Cash in Bank for the Principal Bank field.

Choose 2300 Vacation Payable for the Vacation field.

Choose 1240 Advances Receivable for the Advances field.

Choose 5305 Wages: Cleaning Staff for Vacation Earned, Regular and Overtime 1.

Choose 5300 Wages: General for Salary.

Choose 5340 Commissions for Commission.

Choose 5350 Piece Rate Bonuses for Piece Rate.

PAYROLL LINKED ACCOUNTS: DEDUCTIONS				
RRSP	2410	RRSP Payable	MSP-Employee 2400	MSP Payable - Employee

CLASSIC VIEW
You can add the Payroll Ledger linked accounts by right-clicking the Paycheques or the Payroll Cheque Run Journal icon in the Home window to select it.

Click the Setup tool or choose the Setup menu, then click Settings, Payroll, Linked Accounts and Income.

If no Home window icon is selected, you can use the Setup tool pop-up list, choose Payroll and click Select.

NOTES
You can access the Payroll Linked Accounts screens from the Setup menu. Choose Settings and click Payroll and Linked Accounts.

NOTES
The deleted income and deduction names do not appear on the screens for linked accounts. Deleting the unused names also simplifies the data entry for linked accounts.

Click   **Deductions** under Linked Accounts to see the next set of accounts:

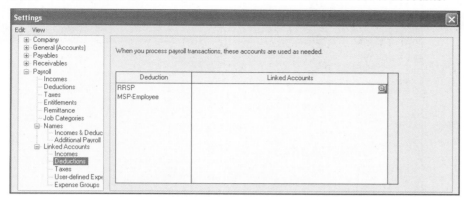

NOTES
You can add accounts from the Linked Accounts windows. Type a new number, press *enter* and choose to add the account.

The names here are the ones you entered in the Names: Incomes & Deductions screen. If you deleted a name, it will not appear here.

Enter   the **linked** payable **accounts** for **RRSP** and **MSP-Employee** from the chart on page 322.

PAYROLL LINKED ACCOUNTS: TAXES

Payables			**Expenses**		
EI	2310	EI Payable	EI	5310	EI Expense
CPP	2320	CPP Payable	CPP	5320	CPP Expense
Tax	2330	Income Tax Payable	WCB	5330	WCB Expense
WCB	2460	WCB Payable			
Not used	EHT, Tax (Que.), QPP, QHSF, QPIP		**Not used**	EHT, QPP, QHSF, QPIP	

Click   **Taxes** under Linked Accounts to see the next set of linked accounts:

When the employer pays the tax, linked payable and expense accounts are needed. Only the employee pays the income tax, so only the payable linked account is needed. This tax does not create an employer expense. For EI and CPP, employee contributions are added to those of the employer to calculate the total amount payable.

Enter   the **linked payables accounts** for **EI**, **CPP**, **Tax** and **WCB** in the Payables section and the **linked expense accounts** for **EI**, **CPP** and **WCB** in the Expenses section from the chart on this page.

PAYROLL LINKED ACCOUNTS: USER-DEFINED EXPENSES

Payables			**Expenses**		
Travel Allow	2420	Travel Allowances Payable	Travel Allow	5360	Travel Allowances
Tuition Fees	2430	Tuition Fees Payable	Tuition Fees	5380	Tuition Fees Expense
MSP-Employer	2440	MSP Payable - Employer	MSP-Employer	5400	MSP Premium Expense

Click **User-Defined Expenses** under the Linked Accounts subheading to see the final Payroll accounts:

Enter the **linked payable accounts** for **Travel Allow**, **Tuition Fees** and **MSP-Employer** from the chart on page 323.

Enter the **linked expense accounts** for **Travel Allow**, **Tuition Fees** and **MSP-Employer** from the chart on page 323.

Check the **linked** payroll **accounts** against the charts on pages 322–323 before proceeding. **Click** each **heading** under Linked Accounts to see the different screens.

Click **OK** to save the Settings changes and return to the Payroll Home window:

Because we deleted some income and deduction names, we are being warned that any accounts linked to these deleted fields will also be removed. We can proceed.

Click **Yes** to open a second confirmation message:

Again, we are warned because of the additional field names we deleted.

Click **Yes** to continue and return to the Payroll Home window.

Entering Employee Ledger Records

Use the Lime Light Laundry Employee Information Sheet, Employee Profiles and Additional Payroll Information on pages 309–312 to create the employee records and add historical information.

We will enter the information for Lime Light Laundry employee Clyne Fretton.

Click the **Employees icon** [Employees] in the Home window.

The Employees icon window opens:

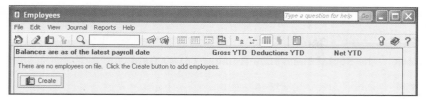

The Employees icon window is blank because no employees are on file at this stage.

Click the **Create button** 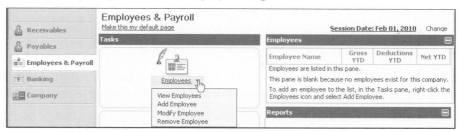 or **choose** the **File menu** and **click Create**.

You can also choose Add Employee from the Employees icon shortcuts list, as shown below, to open the new employee ledger window:

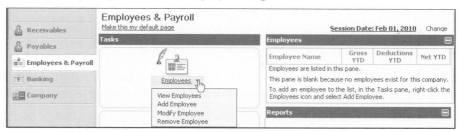

Entering Personal Details

The following Payroll Ledger new employee information form will open at the Personal information tab screen so you can begin to enter the employee record:

The Payroll Ledger has a large number of tabs for the different kinds of payroll information. The cursor is in the Employee field, ready for you to enter information. By entering the surname first, your employee lists will be in correct alphabetic order.

Type Fretton, Clyne **Press** (tab).

The cursor advances to the Street 1 field.

Type 21 Spotter St.

The default city, province and province code, those for the business, are correct.

Click the **Postal Code field**.

Type v3k4k2 **Press** (tab).

The program corrects the postal code format and advances the cursor to the Phone 1 field.

NOTES
If you skip the Employees icon window (Setup menu, User Preferences, View screen) you will see the Payroll Ledger window immediately when you click the Employees icon.
You will also skip the Employees window if you use the Add Employee shortcut.

NOTES
As in other ledgers, required fields that you cannot leave blank are marked with *.
On the Address tab screen, the employee name and the date of birth are essential. All other fields can be completed later.

NOTES
The Set Field Names tool in the ledger window will open the Payroll Settings Additional Names screen.

> **Type** 6046937595 **Press** (tab) to see the corrected phone number format.

The default **Language Preference** is correctly set as English.

> **Click** the **Social Insurance Number (SIN) field**. You must use a valid SIN.

> **Type** 218738631 **Press** (tab).

The cursor advances to the Birth Date field. Enter the month, day and year using any accepted date format.

> **Type** 8-15-78 **Press** (tab) **twice**.

The cursor moves to the Hire Date field, which should contain the date when the employee began working for Lime Light Laundry.

> **Type** 2-7-03 **Press** (tab).

The next two fields will be used when the employee leaves the job — the date of termination and the reason for leaving that you can select from the drop-down list. The final option designates employees as active or inactive. All employees at Lime Light Laundry are active, so the default selection is correct.

Job Categories are used to identify salespersons who can be linked to specific sales so that their sales revenue is tracked and used to calculate commissions. The employee's Job Category can be selected here if categories are already set up, or you can place employees in categories when you create the categories. We will create categories later and assign employees to them at that stage.

When you use Simply Accounting to pay employees, the Date Last Paid will be entered automatically by the program.

The remaining details for the employee are entered on the other tab screens.

Entering Tax Information

> **Click** the **Taxes tab** to advance to the next set of employee details:

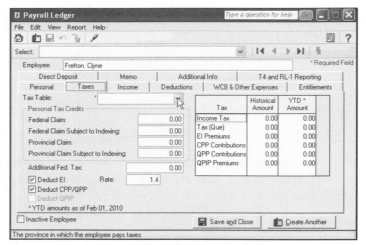

This screen allows you to enter income tax–related information for an employee, including the historical amounts for the year to date.

> **Click** the **Tax Table list arrow**. A list of provinces and territories appears on the screen. This is a required field.

> **Click** **British Columbia**, the province of taxation for Lime Light Laundry for income tax purposes.

NOTES

The program will allow you to omit the Social Insurance Number but you must enter the employee's date of birth. The SIN can be added later.

NOTES

The termination date and reason for leaving a job will determine the employee's eligibility to collect Employment Insurance. Refer to page 296.

NOTES

You should drag the column margins so that all amounts and headings are on-screen. The YTD column may be hidden initially.

NOTES

The Tax Table (Province) is the only required field on this screen. Taxes will be based on the minimum basic claim amounts if no claim amounts are entered. Tax Table is a required field because different provinces have different income tax rates.

Press (tab) to advance to the **Federal Claim** field, which holds the total claim for personal tax credits.

Type 19200 **Press** (tab) to advance to the next field

The **Federal Claim Subject To Indexing** is the amount of personal claim minus pension and tuition/education amounts.

For **Sissler**, enter **9600** in this field.

Type 19200 **Press** (tab) to advance to the Provincial Claim field.

Since 2001, provincial personal income taxes have not been linked to the rates for federal income taxes so separate **provincial claim** amounts are needed.

Type 17057 **Press** (tab).

Type 17057 **Press** (tab) to enter the Provincial Claim Amount Subject To Indexing.

For **Sissler**, enter **9189** in this field.

The cursor advances to the **Additional Federal Tax** field.

When an employee has chosen to have additional federal income tax deducted from each paycheque, you enter the amount of the deduction in the **Additional Fed. Tax** field. Employees might make this choice if they receive regular additional income from which no tax is deducted. By making this choice, they avoid paying a large amount of tax at the end of the year and possible interest penalties. Fretton is the only employee with other income who chooses to have additional taxes withheld.

Type 100

If an employee is insurable by EI, you must leave the box for **Deduct EI** checked. The default EI contribution factor, 1.4, for Lime Light Laundry is correct. We entered it in the Payroll Taxes Settings window (page 320).

All employees at Lime Light make CPP contributions so this check box should remain selected. Employees under 18 or over 70 years of age do not contribute to CPP, so clicking the option for these employees (to remove the ✓) will ensure that CPP is not deducted from their paycheques. Employees who elect to receive their CPP payments earlier also do not pay CPP while they collect the pension.

We will enter the historical income tax amounts next. You can drag the column margins so that all amounts and headings are on-screen.

Click the **Historical Amount field** for **Income Tax**.

Type 398.92 **Press** (tab) to advance to the EI Premiums Historical Amount field. Enter the amount of EI paid to date.

Type 68.97 **Press** (tab) to move to the CPP Contributions Historical Amount field.

Type 164.75

Entering Income Amounts

We defined all the types of income for Lime Light Laundry when we set up Names (see page 315). All the details you need to complete the Income tab chart are on pages 309–312. The list on the following page summarizes the types of income, used by each employee. Not all will be used on all paycheques.

NOTES
For all employees except Sissler, the total federal and provincial claim amounts are subject to indexing. Governments raise these claim amounts based on inflation and budget decisions.
    Sissler's total claim includes $1 970 federal and $1 320 provincial for tuition and education deductions.

NOTES
These historical details are needed because there are yearly maximum amounts for CPP and EI contributions. Totals for optional deductions are also retained in the employee record.

NOTES
The program skips the Quebec tax fields because British Columbia was selected as the province of taxation.

- Advance and Benefits: all employees (see Notes)
- Vac. Owed and Vac. Paid: all hourly paid employees (see Notes)
- Regular: four hourly paid employees — Fretton, Durtee, Landings, Sissler
- Overtime 1: four hourly paid employees — Fretton, Durtee, Landings, Sissler
- Piece Rate: four hourly paid employees — Fretton, Durtee, Landings, Sissler
- Salary: three salaried employees — Brumes, Tran, Houseman
- Commission: Brumes

Click the **Income tab** to open the next screen of employee details:

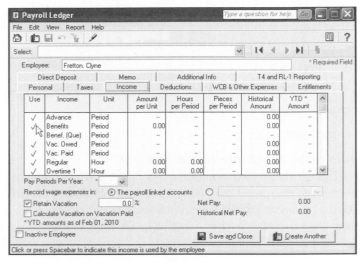

On the Income chart you can indicate the types of income that each employee receives (the **Use** column), the usual rate of pay for that type of income (**Amount Per Unit**), the usual number of hours worked (**Hours Per Period**), the usual number of units for a piece rate pay base (**Pieces Per Period**) and the amounts received this year before the earliest transaction date or the date used for the first paycheque (**Historical Amount**). The **Year-To-Date (YTD) Amount** is added automatically by the program based on the historical amounts you enter and the paycheques entered in the program.

Checkmarks should be entered in the Use column so that the fields are available in the payroll journals, even if they will not be used on all paycheques.

We need to add the historical advances, benefits and vacation amounts for Fretton. Fretton has $200 in advances not yet repaid, and she has not used all the vacation pay she has earned.

No employees have received vacation pay this year. If they have, you enter the amount in the **Vac. Paid** field. Vacation pay not yet received is entered in the **Vac. Owed** field. Any advances paid to the employees and not yet repaid are recorded in the **Advance Historical Amount** field. There is no record of advance amounts recovered.

Click the **Historical Amount column beside Advance** to move the cursor.

Type 200 **Press** (tab) to move to the Benefits Amount Per Period column.

The provincial medical premiums paid by the employer are employee benefits.

Type 22.15 **Press** (tab) to move to the Historical Amount for Benefits.

Type 44.30 **Press** (tab) to advance to the Vac. Owed Historical Amount.

Type 564.98 **Press** (tab) to advance to the Historical Vac. Paid Amount.

Press (tab) **twice** to advance to the **Use column for Regular**.

Press (tab) to advance to the Amount Per Unit field where we need to enter the regular hourly wage rate.

Type 18

Press (tab) to advance the Hours Per Period field.

Bi-weekly paid employees usually work 80 hours per period. You can change the amount in the Payroll journals. Salaried workers normally work 150 hours each month.

Type 80 **Press** (tab) to advance to the Historical Amount field.

Historical income and deduction amounts for the year to date are necessary so that taxes and deductions can be calculated correctly and T4 statements will be accurate.

Type 2880 **Press** (tab).

The amount is entered automatically in the YTD column and the cursor advances to the Use column for Overtime 1.

Press (tab) so you can enter the overtime hourly rate.

Type 27

Press (tab) **twice** to advance to the Historical Amount field. There is no regular number of overtime hours.

Type 54 **Press** (tab) to advance to the Overtime 2 Use column.

The next three income types do not apply to Fretton so they should not be checked. The next income that applies is Piece Rate, the piece rate method of pay. We need to enter the rate or amount per unit (set) and the historical amount. There is no fixed amount per unit or period for Piece Rate.

If no linked account is entered for an income, the Use column will be blank.

Click the **Use column beside Salary** to remove the ✓.

Click the **Use column beside Commission** to remove the ✓.

Click **Piece Rate** in the Income column to select the line. **Press** (tab).

Type 0.10 to enter the amount received for each set. **Press** (tab) **twice**.

Type 189 to enter the historical amount.

For **Tran** and **Houseman**, click the Use column for Regular, Overtime 1, Commission and Piece Rate to remove the ✓. Enter the monthly salary and press (tab). Enter 150 as the number of hours worked in the pay period for Houseman and 80 for Tran. Press (tab) and enter the historical amount. You cannot remove the ✓ for Vac. Owed and Vac. Paid, even if they are not used.

For **Brumes**, repeat these steps but leave Commission checked and enter $390 as the historical amount.

Pay Periods Per Year refers to the number of times the employee is paid, or the pay cycle. This is a required field. Fretton is paid every two weeks, 26 times per year.

Click the **list arrow** beside the field **for Pay Periods Per Year**:

Click 26.

NOTES
When an amount varies from one pay to another, you should leave its amount field blank in the ledger and enter the amount in the journal.

NOTES
No linked account was entered for Overtime 2, so no checkmark appears beside it.

NOTES
Pressing the space bar when you are in the Use column will also add a ✓ or remove one if it is there.
Pressing ⏎ will move you to the next line in the same column.

NOTES
Remember that commissions must be calculated manually and entered in the Payroll journals. The Commission field in the Payroll Ledger allows only a fixed amount, not a percentage of sales, as the entry.

NOTES
Employees may be paid yearly (1), semi-annually (2), monthly for 10 months (10), monthly (12), every four weeks (13), every two weeks for a 10-month year (22), twice a month (24), every two weeks (26) or weekly (52).

Retaining Vacation pay is normal for full-time hourly paid employees. Part-time and casual workers often receive their vacation pay with each paycheque because their work schedule is irregular. You will turn the option to retain vacation off when an employee receives the vacation pay, either when taking a vacation or when leaving the company (see page 282). If the employee is salaried and does not receive vacation pay, the option should also be turned off. For employees who receive vacation pay, leave the option to Retain Vacation checked and type the vacation pay rate in the % field.

Double click the **% field beside Retain Vacation**.

Type 6

For **Brumes**, **Tran** and **Houseman**, click Retain Vacation to remove the ✓.

Employee wages may be linked to the default expense account or to another expense account that you can select from the drop-down list. Wage expenses for all Lime Light Laundry employees are linked to the default accounts entered on pages 322–324.

> **NOTES**
> When you select a specific account, all payroll expenses for that employee will be linked to the same account — the one you identify in this field. If you want to use different accounts for different wage expenses, you must use the linked accounts.

> **NOTES**
> For one-time changes, you can edit deduction amounts in the payroll journals on the Deductions tab screen.

Entering Payroll Deduction Amounts

Click the **Deductions tab** to open the screen for payroll deductions:

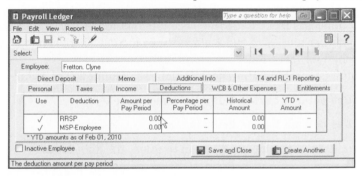

On this screen, you can indicate which deductions apply to the employee (Use column), the amount normally deducted and the historical amount — the amount deducted to date this year. Both deductions are correctly selected in the Use column (a ✓ is entered).

By entering deductions here, they will be included automatically on the Payroll Journal input forms. Otherwise, you must enter them manually in the Journal for each pay period. Not all employees make RRSP contributions at this time, but they have done so in the past, so we will leave this field available. When you enter the amounts here, the deductions are made automatically, but changes can still be made in the journals. You should make permanent changes by editing the employee ledger record. Fretton does not currently have RRSP contributions withheld from her pay.

If you choose to calculate deductions as a percentage of gross pay in the Payroll Settings, the Percentage Per Pay Period fields will be available.

Click **MSP-Employee** in the Deduction column to select the line.

Press (tab). You should enter the amount that is withheld in each pay period.

Type 22.15 **Press** (tab) to advance to the Historical Amount field.

Type 44.30 **Press** (tab) to update the YTD Amount.

The remaining deductions are not used by Lime Light Laundry. The names were deleted so they do not appear on the chart.

Entering WCB and Other Expenses

In other provinces, the tab label will be changed to match the name used for WCB in that province. Ontario uses the name WSIB — Workplace Safety and Insurance Board — instead of WCB, so the tab label is WSIB & Other Expenses.

Click   the **WCB & Other Expenses tab**:

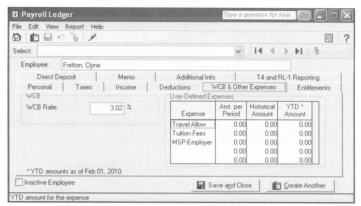

The user-defined expenses we created in the Additional Payroll Names screen (page 316) and the default WCB rate (page 320) are entered on this screen. The default WCB rate is entered from our setup information, but you can enter a different rate for an individual employee in this field. The rate is correct for Fretton.

For **Tran**, enter 5.0 as the WCB rate.

Other user-defined expenses are also added on this screen. Lime Light Laundry has three user-defined expenses, but only MSP-Employer applies to Fretton now.

Click   the **MSP-Employer Amt. Per Period**. Enter the amount that the
employer contributes in each pay period.

Type   22.15 **Press** (tab) to advance to the Historical Amount field.

Type   44.30

For **Sissler**, enter **25** as the Tuition Fees Amt. Per Period and **100** as the Historical Amount.

For **Brumes**, enter **300** as the Travel Allow Amt. Per Period and **300** as the Historical Amount.

The remaining expenses are not used by Lime Light Laundry.

Entering Entitlements

We entered the default rates and amounts for entitlements as Payroll Settings (page 321), but they can be modified in the ledger records for individual employees.

We must also enter the historical information for entitlements. This historical number will include any days carried forward from the previous periods. The number of days accrued cannot be greater than the maximum number of days defined for the entitlement for an employee. The number of Net Days Accrued, the amount unused and available for carrying forward, is updated automatically from the historical information and current payroll journal entries.

NOTES
You should drag the column margins so that you can see all the columns and amounts.

Click   the **Entitlements tab**:

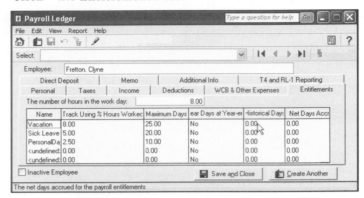

You cannot enter information directly in the Net Days Accrued field.

Fretton receives vacation pay instead of paid time off so the vacation entitlements details should be removed. The defaults for sick leave and personal days are correct.

Click   the **Track Using % Hours Worked field for Vacation**.

Press   del   to remove the entry 8.00.

Press   tab   to advance to the Maximum Days field.

Press   del   to remove the entry.

Click   the **Historical Days field for Sick Leave**.

Type   7

Press   ↓ to advance to the Historical Days field for PersonalDays. The number of days is added to the Net Days Accrued.

Type   3 **Press** tab to enter the amount.

For Brumes, Tran and Houseman, the default entries for tracking and maximum days are correct, but you must enter the Historical Days for each entitlement.

NOTES
If employees take days before the sufficient number of hours worked have been accrued, the program will warn you. Then you can allow the entry for entitlements or not. This entry is similar to allowing clients to exceed their credit limits.

Entering Direct Deposit Information

Click   the **Direct Deposit tab**:

Four employees have elected to have their paycheques deposited directly to their bank accounts. On this screen, we need to enter the bank account details. For each employee who has elected the Direct Deposit option, you must turn on the selection in the Direct Deposit Paycheques For This Employee check box. Then you must add the three-digit **Bank Number**, five-digit **Transit Number**, the bank **Account Number** and finally the amount that is deposited, or the percentage of the cheque. Fretton has chosen the direct deposit option.

Click   the **Direct Deposit Paycheques For This Employee check box** to add a ✓.

Click   the **Bank Number field**.

Type   300 **Press** (tab) to advance to the Transit Number field.

Type   49921 **Press** (tab) to advance to the Account Number field.

Type   2883912 **Press** (tab) **twice** to advance to the Percentage field.

Type   100

Click   the **Memo tab**:

The Memo tab will not be used at this time. You could enter a note with a reminder date to appear in the Daily Business Manager, for example, a reminder to issue vacation paycheques on a specific date or to recover advances.

Entering Additional Information

Lime Light Laundry enters emergency contacts for each employee.

Click   the **Additional Info tab** to access the additional fields:

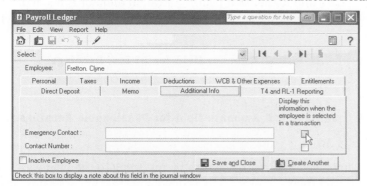

You can indicate whether you want to display any of the additional information when the employee is selected in a transaction. We do not need to display the contact information in the Payroll Journal.

Click   the **Emergency Contact field**.

Type   Aidan Fretton **Press** (tab) **twice**.

Type   (604) 497-1469 to enter the contact's phone number.

Entering T4 and RL-1 Reporting Amounts

The next information screen allows you to enter the year-to-date EI insurable and pensionable earnings. By adding the historical amounts, the T4 slips prepared for

NOTES
All banks in Canada are assigned a three-digit bank number and each branch has a unique five-digit transit number. Account numbers may vary from five to twelve digits.

NOTES
The paycheque deposit may be split among more than one bank account by entering different percentages for the accounts.
To delete bank account details, change the employee's status to Inactive and then delete the bank information. Click Inactive Employee to reset the employee status to Active.

NOTES
The Daily Business Manager is covered in Chapter 11.

NOTES
Additional information for other ledgers may also be displayed or hidden in journal transactions.

WARNING!
The Contact Number field is not predefined as a telephone number. The format will not be corrected automatically by the program.

income taxes at the end of the year and the record of employment termination reports will also be correct.

Click the **T4 and RL-1 Reporting tab** to open the final screen:

In the **Historical Amounts field for EI Ins. Earnings**, you should enter the total earned income received to date that is EI insurable. The program will update this total every time you make payroll entries until the maximum salary on which EI is calculated has been reached. At that time, no further EI premiums will be deducted.

Pensionable Earnings — the total of all income plus benefits — are also tracked by the program. This amount determines the total income that is eligible for Canada Pension Plan. The Pension Adjustment amount is used when the employee has a workplace pension program that will affect the allowable contributions for personal registered pension plans and will be linked with the Canada Pension Plan. Workplace pension income is reduced when the employee also has income from the Canada Pension Plan. Since Lime Light Laundry has no company pension plan, the Pension Adjustment amount is zero and no pension plan registration number is needed.

The T4 Employee Code applies to a small number of job types that have special income tax rules.

Double click the **Historical Amounts field for EI Ins. Earnings**.

Type 3123

Double click the **Historical Amounts field for Pensionable Earnings field**.

Type 3167.30

Correct any employee information **errors** by returning to the field with the error. **Highlight** the **error** and **enter** the **correct information**. **Click each tab** in turn so that you can check all the information.

When all the information is entered correctly, you must save the employee record.

Click **Create Another** to save the record and to open a new blank employee information form.

Click the **Personal tab** so that you can enter address information.

Repeat these procedures to **enter** other employee **records**.

Click **Save And Close** after entering the last record to save the record and close the Payroll Ledger.

Do not finish the **history** if you are prompted to do so at this stage.

Close   the **Employees window** to return to the Home window.

Display or **print** the **Employee List** and the **Employee Summary Report** to check the accuracy of your work.

Setting Up Payroll Remittances

Because we have entered all payroll settings and all suppliers, we can enter the final settings — for payroll remittances and job categories. Entering remittance settings involves three steps: identifying the suppliers who receive payroll remittance amounts, linking the suppliers to the taxes or deductions they receive, and entering opening dates and balances. First, we should designate the suppliers that are payroll authorities.

Identifying Payroll Authorities

The chart on the following page identifies the payroll authorities and the balances owing as at February 1. Balances are those shown in the Trial Balance on page 307.

PAYROLL AUTHORITIES

Supplier	Payroll Liability	Balance Date	Balance Forward
BC Minister of Finance	MSP-Employee	Feb. 1, 2010	296.28
	MSP-Employer	Feb. 1, 2010	296.28
BC Workers' Compensation Board	WCB	Feb. 1, 2010	678.97
Receiver General for Canada	EI	Feb. 1, 2010	1 022.80
	CPP	Feb. 1, 2010	2 090.94
	Tax	Feb. 1, 2010	3 054.53
Victoria Trust	RRSP	Feb. 1, 2010	200.00

Click   **Payables** in the Modules pane list.

Click   **BC Minister of Finance** in the Suppliers pane list in the Payables window to open this supplier's record:

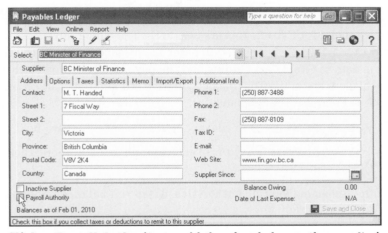

Click   **Payroll Authority** to add the ✓ and change the supplier's payroll status.

Click   the **Next Supplier tool** ▶ **twice** to access the record for the BC Workers' Compensation Board, the next payroll authority. Or,

Click   the **Select list arrow** and **click BC Workers' Compensation Board**.

Click   **Payroll Authority** to add the ✓ and change the supplier's payroll status.

Repeat these **steps** for the remaining payroll authorities: **Receiver General for Canada** and **Victoria Trust**.

Close the **Payables Ledger** to return to the Payables Home window.

Linking Remittances to Suppliers

Click the **Settings icon** 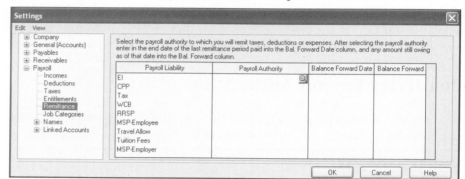 to open the Payables Settings screen.

Click **Payroll** and then **click Remittance** to open the screen we need:

All the payroll items that are linked to liability (remittance) accounts are listed: taxes, deductions and user-defined expenses. For each liability, we can select a supplier and enter the balance forward date and amount.

Click the **List icon** in the Payroll Authority column on the line for EI to see the list of suppliers we marked as Payroll Authorities:

Click **Receiver General for Canada**.

Click **Select** or **press** enter to return to the Remittance Settings screen.

The Receiver General for Canada appears beside EI. The cursor advances to the Balance Forward Date field for EI. We need to enter the balances owing at the time we are converting the data to Simply Accounting and the pay period covered by those amounts. These balances are in the Trial Balance on page 307 and the chart on page 335. The effective date is February 1 for all liabilities.

Type Feb 1 **Press** tab to advance to the Balance Forward field.

Type 1022.80 **Press** tab to advance to the Payroll Authority field for CPP.

Enter the remaining **Payroll Authorities**, **dates** and **balances** from page 335.

Entering Job Categories

Job categories can be used to identify salespersons and to organize reports.

Click **Job Categories**:

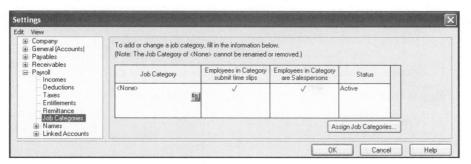

SIMPLY VERSION
The column for Submit Time Slips is not available in the Simply version. It applies to Time and Billing, a Premium feature.

On the Job Categories screen, you enter the names of the categories and indicate whether the employees in each category submit time slips and whether they are salespersons. Categories may be active or inactive. We need a new category called Sales.

Notice that if you do not create categories, the employees in the default selection <None> are salespersons so they can be selected in the Sales Journal.

Click   the **Job Category field below <None>**.

Type   Sales **Press** ⌨tab to add checkmarks to the next two columns and set the status to Active.

Click   the **Job Category field below Sales**.

Type   Other **Press** ⌨tab to add the checkmarks

The Other category does not apply to sales or time slips so we need to change the settings. Employees in the Other category will not appear in the Salesperson field on sales invoices.

Click   the ✓ in the column Employees In Category Submit Time Slips.

Click   the ✓ in the column Employees In Category Are Salespersons.

Click   **Sales** in the Job Category list.

Click   **Assign Job Categories** to change the screen:

The screen is updated with employee names. Initially all are Employees Not In This Job Category.

You can add employee names to the category by choosing an employee and clicking **Select** or by choosing **Select All**. Once employees are in a category (the column on the right), you can remove them by selecting an employee and clicking **Remove** or clicking **Remove All** to move all names at the same time.

Click   **Brumes** and then **click Select** to place her in the Sales category:

> **Choose**   **Other** from the Job Category drop-down list:

Notice that <None> is one of the category list choices.

> **Press**   ⌈ tab ⌉ to add the employee names.

All employees are listed as Not In This Category.

> **Click**   **Select All** to place all names on the In This Category list. Now we need to remove Brumes' name from this list.
>
> **Click**   **Brumes** and then **click Remove** to remove her from the Other category:
>
> **Click**   **OK** to save the information and return to the Settings screen.

Changing Payroll Form Settings

Before closing the setting screens, we still need to enter the form number to set up the automatic numbering of direct deposit slips.

> **Click**   **Company** and then **click Forms** to see the number setup screen:

> **Click**   the **Direct Deposit Stubs Next Form Number field**.
>
> **Type**   48
>
> **Click**   **OK** to save the change and return to the Home window.

Finishing Payroll History

Once the setup is complete, we can back up the data file and finish the payroll history. Like the other modules, you can use the payroll journals before finishing the history. However, the automatic payroll calculation feature will be turned off. Therefore, we should finish the history first. We can also check the data integrity as we did for Dorfmann to see if there are any data inconsistencies that we need to correct.

> **Choose** the **Maintenance menu** and **click Check Data Integrity**.

Two control accounts are used for the Payroll Ledger. The *Advances Receivable* General Ledger account balance must equal the advances paid (the total of all historical employee amounts) and the *Vacation Payable* balance must equal the total of all vacation owed amounts in the ledgers. Employees Historical Information should be Balanced.

Click   **OK** to close the Data Integrity window.

If corrections are necessary, compare your amounts with the ones on pages 309–312 and modify the employee ledger records.

Once we finish the history, we cannot change any historical amounts. Therefore, we should prepare a backup first.

Back up the **data file**.

Choose the **History menu** and **click Finish Entering History** as shown:

 NOTES
The remaining modules on the Finish History menu are dimmed because the history for them is already finished.

When we added the Payroll module, the History menu became available again. When you finish, the Home window has all modules in the finished history state. You are now ready to enter transactions.

The first transaction on page 341 adds the salesperson to an invoice, applying the job category we set up to track sales for commissions.

Adding Salespersons to Sales Invoices

When employees receive sales commissions, you can add the salesperson's name to the sales invoice. You can then use the Sales By Salesperson Report to determine the sales revenue amount for calculating the commission. After creating job categories, we indicated for each category whether its employees were salespersons and then identified the employees in the category.

Advance the session date to **February 7**.

Click   **Receivables** in the Modules pane list.

Click   the **Client Invoices icon** to open the Revenues (Sales) Journal.

Choose Capilano Centre Hotel as the client.

Enter   **Feb 2** as the invoice date.

Enter   a **Description** for the sale.

Enter   **2900** as the invoice amount.

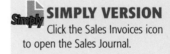 **SIMPLY VERSION**
Click the Sales Invoices icon to open the Sales Journal.

Click   the **Sold By list arrow** to see the list of salespersons as shown:

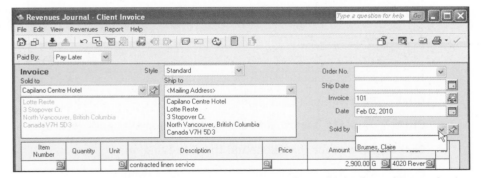

Brumes is the only employee responsible for sales at Lime Light Laundry, so she is the only one on the list. Brumes is the only employee we placed in the Sales job category. All other employees are in the second category labelled "Other," which does not have any salespersons.

> **Click**   **Brumes** to add her name to the invoice.
>
> **Click**   the **Use The Same Salesperson pin icon** .

This will lock in the salesperson's name on the invoice form until we close the journal. The pin has changed position 🖉 — it now looks like it has been pushed in:

Sold by   Brumes, Claire

If you leave the journal open in the background, the salesperson remains selected. If you close the journal, you must re-select the salesperson for each invoice. You must close the journal before advancing the session date.

> **Review**   the **journal display**. The salesperson is not added to the journal report.
>
> **Close**   the **display** when finished.
>
> **Check**   your **work** and **make corrections** if necessary.
>
> **Store**   the **transaction** to recur **weekly**. Brumes will be entered as the salesperson in the stored transaction.
>
> **Post**   the **invoice** and **minimize** (or close) the **Sales Journal**.
>
> **Enter**   the **remaining transactions** for February.

NOTES
The Use The Same Salesperson pin icon is the same as the Use The Same Client Next Time and works the same way.

Adding Salespersons to Client Records

Because Brumes is the only salesperson, we can add her name to all client records.

> **Click**   **Capilano Centre Hotel** in the Clients pane list of clients to open the ledger.
>
> **Click**   the **Salesperson field list arrow** as shown:

> **Click**   **Brumes** to add her name.
>
> **Click**   the **Next Record tool** ▶ to open the next client's record.
>
> **Choose**   **Brumes** for this client and the remaining ones.
>
> **Click**   **Save And Close** to return to the Home window.

When you open the sales journal and choose any client on record, Brumes will be entered automatically in the Salesperson field.

SOURCE DOCUMENTS

SESSION DATE – FEBRUARY 7, 2010

☑ **Sales Invoice #101**   **Dated Feb. 2/10**

339   To Capilano Centre Hotel, $2 900 plus $145 GST for weekly contracted linen laundry service. Invoice total $3 045. Terms: 1/15, n/30. Enter Brumes as the salesperson. Store as recurring weekly transaction.

☐ **Memo #1**   **Dated Feb. 2/10**

Add shortcuts for Create General Journal (Company), Create Supplier Invoice and Pay Supplier Invoices (Payables), Payroll Cheque Run and Create Paycheque (Employees & Payroll).

☐ **Cash Purchase Invoice #LS-504**   **Dated Feb. 2/10**

From Langley Service Centre, $400 plus $20 GST and $28 PST for maintenance service and repairs to delivery truck. Invoice total $448. Paid by cheque #74.

☐ **Purchase Invoice #FP-1297**   **Dated Feb. 2/10**

From Ferndale Paper Products, $200 plus $10 GST and $14 PST for bags and wrapping paper for clean laundry. Invoice total $224. Terms: 1/10, n/30. Store as bi-weekly recurring entry.

☐ **Cash Receipt #31**   **Dated Feb. 3/10**

From Delta Hotel, cheque #4123 for $2 910.60 in payment of account, including $29.40 discount for early payment. Reference invoice #69.

☐ **Cheque Copy #75**   **Dated Feb. 5/10**

To Ferndale Paper Products, $554.40 in payment of account, including $5.60 discount for early payment. Reference invoice #FP-901.

☐ **Sales Invoice #102**   **Dated Feb. 6/10**

To Coquitlam Motel, $3 400 plus $170 GST for contracted laundry services. Invoice total $3 570. Terms: 1/15, n/30. Enter Brumes as the salesperson. Store as recurring bi-weekly transaction.

☐ **Purchase Invoice #PL-903**   **Dated Feb. 6/10**

From Pacific Laundry Suppliers, $300 plus $15 GST and $21 PST for weekly supply of cleaning products. Invoice total $336. Terms: net 30. Store as weekly recurring transaction.

☐ **Sales Invoice #103**   **Dated Feb. 7/10**

To Port Moody Resort, $2 600 plus $130 GST for contracted laundry services for two weeks. Invoice total $2 730. Terms: 1/15, n/30. Enter Brumes as the salesperson. Store as recurring bi-weekly transaction.

☐ **Cash Purchase Invoice #SP-2991**   **Dated Feb. 7/10**

From Surrey Printers, $600 plus $30 GST and $42 PST for copying and mailing advertising brochures outlining new prices to clients. Invoice total $672 paid in full with cheque #76.

☐ **Cheque Copy #77**   **Dated Feb. 7/10**

To Pacific Laundry Suppliers, $1 120 in partial payment of account. Reference invoice #PL-644.

NOTES
Enter Brumes as the salesperson for all sales, either in the journal (see page 339) or by adding her to the client records (see page 340).

 SIMPLY VERSION
Purchase will replace Supplier for the shortcut labels.

NOTES
You can Pay Remittances and Make Other Payments from the Pay Supplier Invoices transaction drop-down list. You can adjust paycheques from the Payroll Journal

WARNING!
Remember not to include the discount for the second invoice in payments and receipts.

NOTES
You can use the Paycheques or the Payroll Run Journal to complete the payroll transactions.

WARNING!
Remember to edit the Benefit amount for Sissler so that the tuition amount is included — type 31.23 in the Benefits Amount field.

Or, you can edit her ledger record and enter 31.23 as the Amount Per Unit for Benefits.

Lime Light Laundry
Employee Time Summary Sheet #5

Cheque Date: Feb 7, 2010   Pay period end: Feb 7, 2010

Employee SIN	M. Durtee 552 846 826	I. Sissler 931 771 620	C. Fretton 218 738 631	S. Landings 422 946 541	S. Pott Tran 638 912 634	C. Houseman 822 546 859	C. Brumes 726 911 134
Week 1	40	40					
Regular hrs	40	40					
Overtime hrs	2	—					
#sheet sets	480	395					
Benefits	6.23	31.23					
Advance	100.00*	—					
Sick leave days	—	—					
Personal days	—	1**					
Chq/DD #	Chq 78	DD48					

* to be repaid at $25 per pay
** personal day to enroll in university course

Completed by: *Brumes* 2/7/10

SESSION DATE – FEBRUARY 14, 2010

Memo #2
From Manager's Desk

Dated Feb. 8/10
Corrected Feb 7 paycheque for Mouver Durtee to include
6 hours of overtime.
He was paid for only 2 hours.
Re-issued cheque #78 -- original cheque returned

Claire Brumes

NOTES
Brumes will be entered as the salesperson in the stored transaction.
Allow clients to exceed the credit limit.

Sales Invoice #104   **Dated Feb. 9/10**

To Capilano Centre Hotel, $2 900 plus $145 GST for weekly contracted linen laundry service. Invoice total $3 045. Terms: 1/15, n/30. Recall stored transaction.

Cheque Copy #79 Dated Feb. 12/10

To Richmond Equipment, $3 360 in payment of invoice #RE-4111.

Cash Receipt #32 Dated Feb. 13/10

From Capilano Centre Hotel, cheque #2314 for $3 014.55 in partial payment of account, including $30.45 discount for early payment. Reference invoice #101.

Purchase Invoice #PL-1213 Dated Feb. 13/10

From Pacific Laundry Suppliers, $300 plus $15 GST and $21 PST for weekly supply of cleaning products. Invoice total $336. Terms: net 30. Recall stored transaction.

Sales Invoice #105 Dated Feb. 13/10

To Kingsley Inn (use Full Add for the new client), $2 800 plus $140 GST for new contract for daily laundry service with bi-weekly invoices. Invoice total $2 940. Terms: 1/15, n/30. Brumes is the salesperson. Store as recurring bi-weekly entry.

Sales Invoice #106 Dated Feb. 13/10

To Delta Hotel, $2 900 plus $145 GST for bi-weekly invoice for contracted laundry services. Invoice total $3 045. Terms: 1/15, n/30. Enter Brumes as the salesperson. Store as bi-weekly recurring transaction.

Lime Light Laundry
Employee Time Summary Sheet #6

Cheque Date: Feb 14, 2010   Pay period end: Feb 14, 2010

Employee SIN	M. Durtee 552 846 826	I. Sissler 931 771 620	C. Fretton 218 738 631	S. Landings 422 946 541	S. Pott Tran 638 912 634	C. Houseman 822 546 859	C. Brumes 726 911 134
Week 1	pd	pd	40	40	40		
Week 2	40	40	40	42	40		
Regular hrs	40	40	80	80			
Overtime hrs	—	—	—	2			
#sheet sets	370	470	860	950			
Benefits	6.23	31.23	22.15	22.15	24.92		
Advance	-25.00	200.00*	-50.00	—	—		
Sick leave days	1	—	1	—	—		
Personal days	—	—	—	—	—		
Chq/DD #	Chq 80	DD50	DD49	Chq 81	Chq 82		

* to be repaid at $50 per pay

Completed by: *Brumes* 2/14/10

Cash Purchase Invoice #BCEG-78522 Dated Feb. 14/10

From BC Energy Group, $600 plus $30 GST for one month of hydro services. Invoice total $630 due within five days to avoid interest penalty. Paid in full with cheque #83.

NOTES

Kingsley Inn
(contact Rume Kingsley)
302 Sandman Dr.
Vancouver, BC V8H 1P1
Tel: (604) 259-1881
Fax: (604) 259-1893
Terms: 1/15, n/30
Revenue account: 4020
Tax code: G - GST @ 5%
Credit limit: $5 000
Salesperson: Brumes

NOTES

Type –25 in the Advance Amount field for Durtee and –50 for Fretton to recover the advances.

Type 31.23 in the Benefits Amount field for Sissler.

☐ **Cash Purchase #BCT-11229**   **Dated Feb. 14/10**

From BC Telephone, $100 plus $5 GST and $7 PST for one month of telephone services. Invoice total $112. Paid in full with cheque #84.

SESSION DATE – FEBRUARY 21, 2010

☐ **Purchase Invoice #FP-2635**   **Dated Feb. 16/10**

From Ferndale Paper Products, $200 plus $10 GST and $14 PST for wrapping paper and bags. Invoice total $224. Terms: 1/10, n/30. Recall stored entry.

☐ **Sales Invoice #107**   **Dated Feb. 16/10**

To Capilano Centre Hotel, $2 900 plus $145 GST for weekly contracted linen laundry service. Invoice total $3 045. Terms: 1/15, n/30. Recall stored transaction.

☐ **Cash Receipt #33**   **Dated Feb. 18/10**

From Port Moody Resort, cheque #5120 for $2 702.70 in payment of account, including $27.30 discount for early payment. Reference invoice #103.

☐ **Cash Receipt #34**   **Dated Feb. 18/10**

From Capilano Centre Hotel, cheque #2692 for $3 014.55 in partial payment of account, including $30.45 discount for early payment. Reference invoice #104.

☐ **Purchase Invoice #PL-1634**   **Dated Feb. 20/10**

From Pacific Laundry Suppliers, $300 plus $15 GST and $21 PST for weekly supply of cleaning products. Invoice total $336. Terms: net 30. Recall stored entry.

☐ **Sales Invoice #108**   **Dated Feb. 20/10**

To Coquitlam Motel, $3 400 plus $170 GST for contracted bi-weekly laundry services. Invoice total $3 570. Terms: 1/15, n/30. Recall stored transaction. Allow client to exceed credit limit.

☐ **Cash Sales Invoice #109**   **Dated Feb. 20/10**

To Burnaby Private Hospital (use Quick Add), $1 200 plus $60 GST for emergency linen and laundry service. Invoice total $1 260. Terms: C.O.D. Received cheque #561 for $1 260 in full payment. There is no discount.

NOTES
Use Quick Add for new cash clients. Remember to enter Brumes as the salesperson.

NOTES
Type –25 in the Advance Amount field for Durtee and –50 for Sissler to recover these amounts.
Type 31.23 in the Benefits Amount field for Sissler.

EMPLOYEE TIME SUMMARY SHEET #7

(pay period ending February 21, 2010)

Name of Employee	Regular Hours	Overtime Hours	Piece Rate Quantity	Benefits	Advance (Repaid)	Sick Days	Personal Days	Direct Deposit
☐ Durtee, Mouver	40	2	440	$ 6.23	–$25	1	–	No
☐ Sissler, Iean	40	2	520	$31.23	–$50	–	–	Yes

a. Using Employee Time Summary Sheet #7 and the Employee Information Sheet, complete payroll for the weekly paid employees. Use the Payroll Journal or the Payroll Run Journal.
b. Recover $25 advanced to Mouver Durtee and recover $50 advanced to Iean Sissler.
c. Issue cheque #85 and DD slip #51.

☐ **Sales Invoice #110**   **Dated Feb. 21/10**

To Port Moody Resort, $2 600 plus $130 GST for contracted laundry services for two weeks. Invoice total $2 730. Terms: 1/15, n/30. Recall stored transaction.

☐ **Cash Receipt #35**   **Dated Feb. 21/10**

From Delta Hotel, cheque #4439 for $3 014.55 in payment of account, including
$30.45 discount for early payment. Reference invoice #106.

☐ **Purchase Invoice #RE-6998**   **Dated Feb. 21/10**

From Richmond Equipment, $2 000 plus $100 GST and $140 PST for new
presser. Invoice total $2 240. Terms: 1/10, n/30.

SESSION DATE – FEBRUARY 28, 2010

☐ **Sales Invoice #111**   **Dated Feb. 23/10**

To Capilano Centre Hotel, $2 900 plus $145 GST for weekly laundry service.
Invoice total $3 045. Terms: 1/15, n/30. Recall stored entry.

☐ **Cash Receipt #36**   **Dated Feb. 25/10**

From Capilano Centre Hotel, cheque #2974 for $3 014.55 in payment of account,
including $30.45 discount for early payment. Reference invoice #107.

☐ **Cash Receipt #37**   **Dated Feb. 25/10**

From Kingsley Inn, cheque #439 for $1 966 in partial payment of account.
Reference invoice #105.

☐ **Cash Receipt #38**   **Dated Feb. 25/10**

From Coquitlam Motel, cheque #276 for $3 570 in payment of account. Reference
invoice #102.

☐ **Cheque Copy #86**   **Dated Feb. 26/10**

To Ferndale Paper Products, cheque #86 for $445.76 in payment of account,
including $2.24 discount for early payment. Reference invoices #FP-1297 and
#FP-2635.

☐ **Purchase Invoice #PL-2098**   **Dated Feb. 27/10**

From Pacific Laundry Suppliers, for $300 plus $15 GST and $21 PST for weekly
supply of cleaning products. Invoice total $336. Terms: net 30. Recall stored entry.

☐ **Sales Invoice #112**   **Dated Feb. 27/10**

To Delta Hotel, sales invoice #112 for $2 900 plus $145 GST for bi-weekly invoice
for linen service. Invoice total $3 045. Terms: 1/15, n/30. Recall stored entry.

☐ **Sales Invoice #113**   **Dated Feb. 27/10**

To Kingsley Inn, sales invoice #113 for $2 800 plus $140 GST for bi-weekly billing
for laundry service. Invoice total $2 940. Terms: 1/15, n/30. Recall stored entry.

☐ **Memo #3**   **Dated Feb. 28/10**

From Manager: Receipt #37 from Kingsley Inn for $1 966 was entered incorrectly.
On Feb. 25, cheque #439 for $2 910.60 was received from Kingsley Inn in full
payment of invoice #105, including $29.40 for early payment. Adjust the original
receipt to make the correction.

☐ **Memo #4**   **Dated Feb. 28/10**

Complete month-end adjusting entries for supplies used in February.

Cleaning supplies used	$680
Clothes hangers used	250
Packaging supplies used	350

> **NOTES**
> Use the Adjust Receipt tool
> to correct the receipt. Simply
> Accounting will automatically
> make the reversing entry. Delete
> the original Payment Amount. You
> will need to enter the amount of
> discount taken manually. It may
> be easier to reverse the receipt
> (refer to page 179) and then enter
> the client's payment correctly.

☐ **Memo #5**   **Dated Feb. 28/10**

Complete an adjusting entry for one month of prepaid insurance expired. The one-year insurance policy was purchased on December 31, 2008, for $2 400.

NOTES
Type –25 in the Advance Amount field for Durtee and –50 for Sissler and Fretton to recover these amounts.
Type 31.23 in the Benefits Amount field for Sissler.

EMPLOYEE TIME SUMMARY SHEET #8

(pay period ending February 28, 2010)

Name of Employee	Regular Hours	Overtime Hours	Piece Rate Quantity	Benefits	Advance (Repaid)	Sick Days	Personal Days	Direct Deposit
☐ Durtee, Mouver	40	–	510	$ 6.23	–$25	–	–	No
☐ Sissler, Iean	40	2	510	31.23	–$50	–	–	Yes
☐ Fretton, Clyne	80	2	1 030	22.15	–$50	–	–	Yes
☐ Landings, Soffte	80	–	930	22.15		1	–	No
☐ Tran, S. Pott	80	–		24.92		–	–	No
☐ Brumes, Claire	150	–		54.00		–	–	Yes
☐ Houseman, Cryper	150	–		54.00		–	–	Yes

a. Using Employee Time Summary Sheet #8 and the Employee Information Sheet, complete payroll for all employees. Use the Payroll Journal or the Payroll Run Journal.
b. Recover $25 advanced to Mouver Durtee, $50 from Clyne Fretton and $50 advanced to Iean Sissler.
c. Claire Brumes earned a sales commission of $258 for the month of February and took five days' vacation (use the Vacation Days Released field, Entitlements tab).
d. Issue cheques #87, #88 and #89, and DD #52 to #55.

NOTES
The travel allowance for Brumes is set up in her ledger record so that the amount is included automatically as an employer expense that debits Travel Allowance Expenses and credits Travel Allowances Payable just as tuition fees were set up for Sissler. You do not need to enter the expense separately.
This is not a taxable benefit.
In Chapter 16, we set up travel expenses as non-taxable reimbursement income.

☐

imeLight Laundry
Laundry Services • Pickup & Deliver

Memo #6
From Manager's Desk

Dated Feb. 28/10
Paid Claire Brumes' travel allowance for February 2010.
Issued cheque #90 for $300 to Brumes as other payment in Payments
Journal.(Added Brumes as vendor and used Travel Allowances
Payable account.)

Claire Brumes

☐ **Memo #7**   **Dated Feb. 28/10**

Clyne Fretton is taking some vacation time. Clyne asked to receive her vacation pay by cheque. Release her retained vacation pay and issue cheque #91. Refer to page 282.

☑ **Memo #8**   **Dated Feb. 28/10**

347   Adjust the paycheque for Brumes. She has returned her deposit pay stub because her earned commission was incorrect. Use the Revenues By Salesperson Report to verify that the correct amount was $362, not $258.

☐ **Bank Debit Memo #532281**   **Dated Feb. 28/10**

From Mountain Heights Bank, $2 045 was withdrawn from the chequing account for the following pre-authorized transactions:

Bank Charges	$ 45
Interest on Bank Loan	120
Reduction of Principal on Bank Loan	880
Interest on Mortgage	900
Reduction of Principal on Mortgage	100

Create new Group account: 5110 Interest Expense

☐ **Memo #9**   **Dated Feb. 28/10**

Using the payroll remittance option, remit the following payroll taxes for the pay period ending February 28, including the balance owing from January:

To Receiver General: EI Payable, CPP Payable and Income Tax Payable
To BC Minister of Finance: MSP Payable and MSP Payable - Employer
To BC Workers' Compensation Board: WCB Payable
To Victoria Trust: RRSP Payable
Issue cheques #92 through #95 in payment.

☐ **Memo #10**   **Dated Feb. 28/10**

Complete an adjusting entry to reverse the year-end accrued wages entry for $1 150. (Debit 2250 Accrued Wages and credit 5305 Wages: Cleaning Staff.)

Displaying Salesperson Reports

Two reports become available when we add salespersons to journal entries.

Displaying the Sales by Salesperson Report

Click   the **Report Centre icon** in the Home window.

Click   **Receivables** to open the list of client reports that you can display from the Report Centre.

Click   **Revenues By Salesperson Summary** in the Select A Report list.

Click   **Modify This Report** to open the report options:

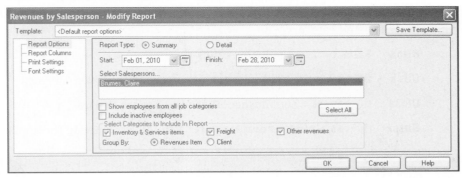

Or, choose the Reports menu, then choose Receivables and click Revenues By Salesperson to open the report options screen.

    Brumes is the only employee designated as a salesperson so only her name appears on the list, and she is already selected. You have the option to show all employees, but we do not need them all — we want Brumes' February sales data. The default dates for Start and Finish cover the period we want. You can group the sales information by client

> **SIMPLY VERSION**
> The terms Customer and Sales will replace Client and Revenues in the Report Centre. Click Sales By Salesperson Summary to select the report.

or by sales item. You can also include information for freight and other non-inventory sales. For Lime Light, we need to show only the Other sales because inventory and freight do not apply. The ✓ for Inventory & Services items is already dimmed because the module is hidden. You can also show the report in detail with a line item for each sale, or in summary form with totals only for each item or client.

You can exclude Freight amounts from the report by clicking Freight to remove the ✓.

Click   **OK** to see the report.

The total sales revenue for January was $36 200, so Brumes' commission amount should be changed to $362.

Close   the displayed **report**.

Displaying the Sales by Job Category Report

This next report is similar except that it combines the information for all employees in each category. Because we have only one person in the Sales category, reporting by this category should give us the same information as the Revenues By Salesperson Report. The list of Receivables reports should still be open in the report centre.

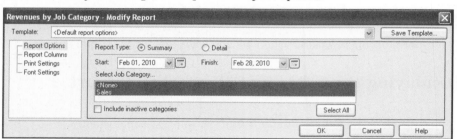

> **SIMPLY VERSION**
> Click Sales By Job Category
> Summary to select the report.

Click   **Revenues By Job Category Summary** in the Select A Report list.

Click   **Modify This Report** to open the report options:

Or, choose the Reports menu, then choose Receivables and click Revenues By Job Categories to open the report options screen.

Again the default dates give us the report for the month we need. Categories that do not have salespersons in them are not included in this report. You can create a Detail Report with a listing for each individual invoice or a Summary Report that provides the total for each selected category.

Click   **Sales** to select only this category.

Click   **OK** to see the total sales for all persons in the Sales category.

Close   the **report** when finished. **Close** the **Report Centre**.

Enter   the **remaining transactions for Feb. 28** to complete the application.

R E V I E W

The Student CD-ROM with Data Files includes Review Questions and Supplementary Cases for this chapter.

OBJECTIVES

- ■ *enter* inventory-related purchase transactions
- ■ *enter* inventory-related sale transactions of goods and services
- ■ *make* inventory adjustments
- ■ *assemble* new inventory items from other inventory
- ■ *enter* returns on sales and purchases
- ■ *enter* sales to preferred customers
- ■ *enter* freight on purchases
- ■ *understand* the integration of the Inventory Ledger with the Payables, Receivables and General ledgers
- ■ *create* new inventory items
- ■ *display* and *print* inventory reports

After completing this chapter, you should be able to

COMPANY INFORMATION

Company Profile

NOTES
Adrienne Aesthetics
65 Bytown Ave.
Ottawa, Ontario K2C 4R1
Tel 1: (613) 722-9876
Tel 2: (613) 722-8701
Fax: (613) 722-8000
Business No.: 567 643 778

Adrienne Aesthetics Beauty Salon and Spa is located in the Byward Market area in the heart of downtown Ottawa. Nearby are the Parliament Buildings, galleries, museums and the downtown shopping district. Adrienne Aesthetics caters to professional women and the well-to-do clientele of the upwardly mobile community.

Regular products for sale include high-quality cosmetic and beauty products but the salon also provides a variety of services and consultation for clients. For Valentine's Day, the salon offers special packages, which have been popular gifts.

Adrienne Kosh, the owner, is active in the day-to-day sales and management of the salon, assisted by two employees who provide all the services. All are trained cosmeticians. Among the repeat customers, Adrienne serves a local television show and a film studio. All customers rely on the honest and professional advice and service provided by the staff. The on-site service is also appreciated by the regular customers who receive a 2 percent discount when they settle their accounts within five days. Full payment is requested in 30 days.

Preferred price list customers receive an additional discount of about 10 percent off the regular prices and are eligible for the early payment discount for 15 days.

Adrienne has accounts with most of her regular suppliers, including beauty product manufacturers.

At the end of January, Adrienne converted all her business records to Simply Accounting using the following information:

- Chart of Postable Accounts
- Post-Closing Trial Balance
- Supplier Information
- Customer Information
- Employee Profiles and TD1 Information
- Inventory Information
- Accounting Procedures

CHART OF POSTABLE ACCOUNTS

ADRIENNE AESTHETICS

ASSETS
Current Assets
1080 Bank Account: Chequing
1090 Bank Account: Credit Cards
1150 Investments
1200 Accounts Receivable
1250 Clinical Supplies
1260 Packaging Supplies
1270 Prepaid Insurance
1280 Towels and Capes

Inventory Assets
1310 Creams and Lotions
1320 Face Care Products
1330 Sun Care Products
1380 Miscellaneous Inventory
        Products

Fixed Assets
1420 Cash Register ▶

▶1440 Computer Equipment
1480 Display Cabinets
1500 Clinical Equipment
1520 Aesthetics Salon

LIABILITIES
Current Liabilities
2100 Bank Loan
2200 Accounts Payable
2220 Credit Card Payable
2300 EI Payable
2310 CPP Payable
2320 Income Tax Payable
2390 EHT Payable
2400 Group Insurance Payable
2420 WSIB Payable
2640 PST Payable
2650 GST Charged on Sales
2670 GST Paid on Purchases ▶

▶Long Term Liabilities
2940 Mortgage Payable

▶EQUITY
Equity
3560 Share Capital
3600 Current Earnings

REVENUE
Revenue
4020 Revenue from Sales
4030 Sales Allowances and
        Discounts
4040 Revenue from Services
4050 Sales Returns
4080 Freight Revenue
4100 Sales Tax Compensation

EXPENSE
Operating Expenses
5020 Advertising & Promotion ▶

▶5030 Bank Charges
5040 Credit Card Fees
5060 Cost of Goods Sold
5065 Cost of Services
5070 Variance Costs
5080 Item Assembly Costs
5090 Purchases Returns
5100 Inventory Losses
5200 Freight Expense
5220 Interest Expense
5240 Hydro Expense
5250 Telephone Expense

Payroll Expenses
5300 Salaries
5310 EI Expense
5320 CPP Expense
5330 WSIB Expense
5360 EHT Expense

NOTES: The Chart of Accounts includes only postable accounts and Current Earnings. WSIB (Workplace Safety and Insurance Board) is the name for WCB (Workers' Compensation Board) in Ontario.

POST-CLOSING TRIAL BALANCE

ADRIENNE AESTHETICS

February 1, 2010

		Debits	Credits				Debits	Credits
1080	Bank Account: Chequing	$51 743.52		▶	1520	Aesthetics Salon	100 000.00	
1090	Bank Account: Credit Cards	2 100.00			2100	Bank Loan		$5 000.00
1150	Investments	90 000.00			2200	Accounts Payable		3 150.00
1200	Accounts Receivable	4 095.00			2220	Credit Card Payable		255.00
1250	Clinical Supplies	600.00			2300	EI Payable		270.00
1260	Packaging Supplies	700.00			2310	CPP Payable		481.26
1270	Prepaid Insurance	2 200.00			2320	Income Tax Payable		2 605.26
1280	Towels and Capes	1 200.00			2390	EHT Payable		117.60
1310	Creams and Lotions	2 660.00			2400	Group Insurance Payable		30.00
1320	Face Care Products	5 810.00			2420	WSIB Payable		284.40
1330	Sun Care Products	5 240.00			2640	PST Payable		2 400.00
1420	Cash Register	1 500.00			2650	GST Charged on Sales		2 100.00
1440	Computer Equipment	2 500.00			2670	GST Paid on Purchases	875.00	
1480	Display Cabinets	4 500.00			2940	Mortgage Payable		80 000.00
1500	Clinical Equipment	8 400.00 ▶			3560	Share Capital		187 430.00
							$284 123.52	$284 123.52

SUPPLIER INFORMATION

ADRIENNE AESTHETICS

Supplier Name (Contact)	Address	Phone No. Fax No.	E-mail Web Site	Terms Tax ID
Acqua Viva Cosmetics (Tomi Hillfinger)	466 Ralf Loren Dr. Montreal, Quebec H3B 4C4	Tel: (888) 448-7274 Fax: (514) 447-3726	thill@acquaviva.com www.acquaviva.com	net 10 438 456 120
Bell Canada (Annie Heard)	82 Wireless Alley Ottawa, Ontario K3B 5R9	Tel: (613) 781-2355	heard@bell.ca www.bell.ca	net 1
Biotech Laboratories (Avivah Rubenstein)	75 Klinique St. Markham, Ontario L3K 1P1	Tel: (800) 466-2991 Fax: (905) 471-2494	avivah@biotech.com www.biotech.com	net 10 297 382 266
Derma Laboratories (Masc Karah)	34 Makeover Way Mississauga, Ontario L8H 7V1	Tel: (877) 374-8107 Fax: (905) 722-5491	mk@skindeep.com www.skindeep.com	net 5 178 629 718
Esthetica Incorporated (Ellis Arden)	61 Pumice Rd. Toronto, Ontario M4P 2R1	Tel: (416) 556-4997 Fax: (416) 558-1900	ea@superficial.com www.superficial.com	net 30 364 139 617
Minister of Finance, Ontario	49 Pecuniary Rd. Toronto, Ontario M5G 4T1	Tel: (800) 622-5100	www.fin.gov.on.ca	net 1
Ottawa Hydro (Kohl Genrater)	77 Voltage St. Orleans, Ontario K4B 3N7	Tel: (613) 785-9113	www.otthydro.ca	net 1
Sun Lab Products, Inc. (Maxine Factor)	59 Botox Cr. Kanata, Ontario K2F 3M8	Tel: (613) 620-5388 Fax: (613) 621-7392	maxine@sunlab.com www.sunlab.com	net 15 724 527 455

OUTSTANDING SUPPLIER INVOICES

ADRIENNE AESTHETICS

Supplier Name	Terms	Date	Invoice No.	Pretax Amount	Tax	Total
Esthetica Incorporated	net 30	Jan. 8/10	EI-641	$3 000.00	$150.00	$3 150.00

CUSTOMER INFORMATION

ADRIENNE AESTHETICS

Customer Name (Contact)	Address	Phone No. Fax No.	E-mail Web Site	Terms Credit Limit
Ariandanos Residence (Arianne Ariandanos)	29 Revlon Blvd. Ottawa, Ontario K1P 2M2	Tel: (613) 762-8664	arianne@radiantway.com www.radiantway.com	2/5, n/30 $1 500
Botelli & Giroux, Lawyers (Gina Botelli)	30 Court St. Orleans, Ontario K4R 1C7	Tel: (613) 699-2911 Fax: (613) 697-2735	gina@botelli.giroux.com www.botelli.giroux.com	2/5, n/30 $1 500
Lavender Estates (Katherine Harris)	9 Lavender Ct. Ottawa, Ontario K1X 3J6	Tel: (613) 782-7300 Fax: (613) 782-8190	harris@lavender.com www.lavender.com	2/5, n/30 $3 000
Montreal Fashions (Leontyne Coutumier)	85 Haute Couture Ave. Kanata, Ontario K2N 5F9	Tel: (613) 622-1711 Fax: (613) 623-8118	leontyne@lookpretty.com www.lookpretty.com	2/5, n/30 $3 000
*Star Film Corporation (Francine Despardieu)	6 Royal Road Ottawa, Ontario K1P 2M2	Tel: (613) 787-1226	fdes@stars.com www.estars.com	2/15, n/30 $3 000
*Valley TV (CKOV) (Celeb Brittie)	17 Broadcast Ave. Ottawa, Ontario K6B 7F3	Tel: (613) 784-6000 Fax: (613) 784-5234	celebrit@valleystars.com www.valleystars.com	2/15, n/30 $4 000

NOTES: The asterisk (*) indicates preferred price list customers. A record is also set up for Cash Customers.

OUTSTANDING CUSTOMER INVOICES

ADRIENNE AESTHETICS

Customer Name	Terms	Date	Invoice No.	Pretax Amount	Tax	Total
*Star Film Corporation	2/15, n/30	Jan. 20/10	AA-11	$2 150.00	$107.50	$2 257.50
*Valley TV (CKOV)	2/15, n/30	Jan. 24/10	AA-16	$1 750.00	$87.50	$1 837.50
			Grand Total			$4 095.00

EMPLOYEE INFORMATION SHEET

ADRIENNE AESTHETICS

	Blossom, Lysis	Hydra, Collagen
Position	Beautician	Beautician
Social Insurance No.	459 562 344	562 391 888
Address	522 Colvin Cline Ct., #22 Ottawa, Ontario K6B 2L8	71 Lipogone St. Ottawa, Ontario K3V 5F2
Telephone	(613) 729-1991	(613) 753-7994
Date of Birth (mm-dd-yy)	02-02-69	02-14-72
Federal (Ontario) Tax Exemption - TD1 Total Exemptions	$9 600 (8 681)	$9 600 (8 681)
Employee Earnings Regular Salary Commission	$2 000 bi-weekly (75 hours) 2% (sales less returns)	$2 000 bi-weekly (75 hours) 2% (sales less returns)
WSIB Rate	2.37	2.37
Employee Deductions Group Insurance EI, CPP & Income Tax	$5 Calculations built into Simply Accounting program	$5

Employee Profiles and TD1 Information

Lysis Blossom and **Collagen Hydra** both assist with sales in the salon and provide the services to customers. Blossom specializes in facials, pedicures and massages while Hydra handles the waxing and electrolysis services. Both are salaried employees who receive their $2 000 bi-weekly pay by cheque and contribute $5 each period to a group insurance plan. Blossom and Hydra are single and self-supporting with no dependants and no other deductions, so they have the basic claim amounts for income tax. Instead of vacation pay, they take three weeks of vacation with regular pay each year. Neither has received any payroll advances.

Both employees are listed as salespersons. They receive a sales commission of 2 percent of their net sales (sales less returns) with each paycheque. Their names are entered as salespersons on invoices so that the commissions can be tracked for the Sales by Salesperson Report.

INVENTORY INFORMATION

ADRIENNE AESTHETICS

Code	Description	Min Stock	Selling Price Reg	Selling Price (Pref)	Unit	Qty on Hand	Total (Cost)
Creams and Lotions (asset account 1310)							
CL01	Cleansing Lotion 225 ml	2	$15	($13)	tube	20	$ 120
CL02	Cleansing Milk 225 ml	2	25	(22)	tube	20	240
CL03	Eye Contour Smoothing Cream 30 ml	2	35	(32)	jar	20	320
CL04	Eye Contour Smoothing Gel 30 ml	2	40	(36)	jar	20	360
CL05	Masks: herb 100 ml	2	40	(36)	jar	20	360
CL06	Masks: sea 100 ml	2	35	(32)	jar	20	320
CL07	Night Cream 200 ml	2	45	(41)	jar	20	420
CL08	Protection Cream: dbl action 60 ml	2	25	(22)	tube	20	240
CL09	Protection Cream: moisturizer 60 ml	2	30	(27)	tube	20	280
	Total Creams and Lotions						$2 660
Face Care Products (asset account 1320)							
FC01	Blush 8 g	3	10	(9)	each	30	$120
FC02	Concealer 15 ml	3	20	(18)	tube	30	240
FC03	Epidermal Cleanser: face+ 300 ml	3	60	(55)	jar	30	750
FC04	Epidermal Cleanser: phytogel 300 ml	3	50	(45)	jar	30	660
FC05	Eye Shadow duo-pack	3	15	(13)	pair	30	120
FC06	Foundation 35 ml	3	25	(22)	jar	30	360
FC07	Lipstick 5 g	20	15	(13)	tube	400	2 400
FC08	Kohl Pencil	10	15	(13)	each	60	180
FC09	Mascara 9 ml	12	10	(9)	tube	80	320
FC10	Powder: loose 15 g	3	20	(18)	jar	30	240
FC11	Powder: pressed 15 g	3	30	(27)	each	30	420
	Total Face Care Products						$5 810
Sun Care Products (asset account 1330)							
SC01	Sun Care Cream SPF#15 125 ml	4	30	(27)	tube	40	560
SC02	Sun Care Cream SPF#30 125 ml	4	45	(41)	tube	40	840
SC03	Sun Tan Milk SPF#4 200 ml	4	40	(36)	jar	40	720
SC04	Sun Tan Milk SPF#15 200 ml	4	50	(45)	jar	40	840
SC05	UV #15 Total Cream 125 ml	4	50	(45)	tube	40	880
SC06	UV #30 Total Cream 125 ml	4	75	(68)	tube	40	1 400
	Total Sun Care Products						$5 240
	Total Inventory						$13 710

NOTES: All inventory products use the same linked Revenue, COGS and Variance accounts: 4020 Revenue from Sales, 5060 Cost of Goods Sold and 5070 Variance Costs. Linked asset accounts are shown in the inventory list with the heading line for each inventory group.

▶

Code	Description	Selling Price Reg	(Pref)	Unit	Taxes
Aesthetic Services					
AS01	Bridal Makeup/Styling	$ 70	($63)	job	no PST
AS02	Cellulite Treatment	80	(72)	job	no PST
AS03	Electrolysis: 45 min treatment	60	(54)	session	no PST
AS04	Electrolysis: 60 min treatment	75	(68)	session	no PST
AS05	European Deep Cleansing Facial	60	(54)	job	no PST
AS06	Hydroptimate Treatment	120	(108)	job	no PST
AS07	Makeup	40	(36)	job	no PST
AS08	Massage: Swedish	75	(68)	job	no PST
AS09	Promotional Pkg: spa treatment	100	(90)	job	no PST
AS10	Package: Super 5 spa treatments	600	(540)	series	no PST
AS11	Package: Deluxe 5 spa treatments	800	(720)	series	no PST
AS12	Skin Treatment	100	(90)	job	no PST
AS13	Manicure/Pedicure	25	(22)	job	no PST
AS14	Waxing: full leg	50	(45)	job	no PST
AS15	Waxing: half leg or bikini	20	(18)	job	no PST

NOTES: All Services are linked to 4040 Revenue from Services for revenue and to the expense account 5065 Cost of Services.

Accounting Procedures

The Goods and Services Tax (GST): Remittances

NOTES
Refer to Chapter 2 for further information about GST and PST remittances.

Adrienne Aesthetics uses the regular method for remittance of the Goods and Services Tax. GST collected is recorded as a liability in *GST Charged on Sales*. GST paid, recorded in *GST Paid on Purchases,* decreases the liability. The salon files its return with the Canada Revenue Agency (CRA) quarterly, either requesting a refund or remitting the balance owing.

Provincial Sales Tax (PST)

Provincial Sales Tax of 8 percent is applied to all cash and credit sales of goods in Ontario. Customers do not pay PST on the services provided by Adrienne Aesthetics. PST on goods is remitted monthly to the Minister of Finance. A 5 percent sales tax compensation for prompt payment reduces the liability to the Minister of Finance.

PST at the rate of 8 percent is also paid on purchases that are not inventory items for resale. Since PST paid is not refundable, it is charged to the asset or expense account associated with the purchase, not to a separate account.

Sales Invoices

NOTES
Printing of invoices will begin immediately, so be sure you have selected the correct printer and forms before you begin.
Remember that to preview invoices, you should select Custom Form and Custom Simply Form on the Reports & Forms Settings screen for Invoices.

Adrienne allows customers to pay on account, or by cash, cheque or credit card. The keystrokes for cash and credit card inventory transactions are similar to those for account sales, except for the method of payment. The program will automatically debit the appropriate bank account instead of *Accounts Receivable*.

Source documents for cash and credit card sales are presented as weekly summaries to avoid a large number of small revenue transactions. Cash Customer and Credit Card Customer records are set up so these sales can be tracked.

You can print and e-mail sales invoices through the program. Before posting the Sales Journal transaction, preview the invoice. Then click the Print button or the E-mail button.

Credit Card Sales and Purchases

Adrienne has set up its accounts for credit card sales and purchase transactions.

Freight Expenses and Charges

When a business purchases inventory items, the cost of any freight that cannot be directly allocated to a specific item must be charged to *Freight Expense*. This amount is regarded as an expense rather than a charge to an inventory asset account. Freight or delivery charges to customers are allocated to *Freight Revenue*.

Discounts

To encourage customers to settle their accounts early, Adrienne Aesthetics offers its account customers a 2 percent discount on before-tax amounts if they pay their accounts within five days. For preferred customers, the discount period is 15 days. Discounts are calculated automatically when the payment terms are set up and the customer is eligible for the discount. There are no discounts on cash or credit card sales.

In addition, some customers have preferred price list status that entitles them to reduced prices. Regular and preferred prices are set up in the Inventory Ledger so the prices are entered automatically.

Valentine's Day Packages

Each February, Adrienne Aesthetics offers special promotional gift packages that include a variety of popular beauty products and services. When assembled, these packages require some special packaging materials such as boxes, wrappings, foils and ribbons, which incur additional costs.

Returns

Returned goods are a normal part of retail businesses. Customers may not be satisfied with the product for a number of reasons. Adrienne Aesthetics provides full refunds on unopened items returned within 14 days. Some items such as lipstick cannot be returned for hygienic reasons. Returned items are debited to the contra-revenue account, *Sales Returns*, so that the returns can be tracked. Refer to page 384.

Returns on purchases also occur for a variety of reasons; for example, the goods may be damaged or the wrong items may have been shipped. Refer to page 386.

INSTRUCTIONS

1. **Record entries** for the source documents in Simply Accounting using the Chart of Accounts, Trial Balance, and Supplier, Customer, Employee and Inventory Information provided. The procedures for entering each new type of transaction are outlined step by step in the Keystrokes section that follows the source documents. These transactions have a ✓ in the check box, and the page number where the keystrokes begin is printed below the check box.

2. **Print** the **reports** indicated on the following printing form after finishing your entries. Instructions for printing inventory reports begin on page 386.

NOTES
We use the term cash sales and purchases to apply to payments by cash and by cheque.

REPORTS

Accounts
- ☐ Chart of Accounts
- ☐ Account List
- ☐ General Journal Entries

Financial
- ☑ Balance Sheet date: Feb. 14
- ☑ Income Statement: Feb. 1 to Feb. 14
- ☑ Trial Balance date: Feb. 14
- ☑ All Journal Journal Entries: Feb. 1 to Feb. 14
- ☑ General Ledger accounts: 1310 1320 1330 4020 4040 from Feb. 1 to Feb. 14
- ☐ Statement of Cash Flows
- ☐ Cash Flow Projection Detail Report
- ☑ Gross Margin Income Statement: Feb. 1 to Feb. 14

Tax
- ☐ Report on

Banking
- ☐ Cheque Log Report

Payables
- ☐ Supplier List
- ☐ Supplier Aged
- ☐ Aged Overdue Payables
- ☐ Purchase Journal Entries
- ☐ Payment Journal Entries
- ☐ Supplier Purchases

Receivables
- ☐ Customer List
- ☐ Customer Aged
- ☐ Aged Overdue Receivables
- ☐ Sales Journal Entries
- ☐ Receipt Journal Entries
- ☐ Customer Sales
- ☑ Sales by Salesperson: Feb. 1 to Feb. 14
- ☐ Customer Statements

Payroll & Employees
- ☐ Employee List
- ☑ Summary: All employees
- ☐ Deductions & Expenses
- ☐ Remittances
- ☐ Payroll Journal Entries
- ☐ T4 Slips
- ☐ Record of Employment

Inventory & Services
- ☐ Inventory & Services List
- ☑ Summary
- ☐ Quantity
- ☐ Inventory Statistics
- ☑ Sales Summary for all Services: from Feb. 1 to Feb. 14
- ☑ Transaction Summary for FC07 Lipstick, all journals: Feb. 1 to Feb. 14
- ☐ Price Lists

- ☑ Item Assembly Journal Entries: Feb. 1 to Feb. 14
- ☑ Adjustments Journal Entries: Feb. 1 to Feb. 14

Forecast & Analysis
- ☐ Labels

Mailing Labels
- ☐ Forecast
- ☐ Customer Analysis
- ☐ Product Analysis
- ☐ Sales Synopsis

Management Reports
- ☐ Ledger

GRAPHS
- ☐ Payables by Aging Period
- ☐ Payables by Supplier
- ☐ Receivables by Aging Period
- ☐ Receivables by Customer
- ☐ Sales vs Receivables
- ☐ Receivables Due vs Payables Due
- ☐ Revenues by Account
- ☐ Expenses by Account
- ☑ Expenses and Net Profit as % of Revenue

SOURCE DOCUMENTS

SESSION DATE – FEBRUARY 7, 2010

☑ **Sales Invoice #20**   Dated Feb. 1/10

363   Sold by Hydra to Montreal Fashions

8	CL04	Eye Contour Smoothing Gel 30 ml	$40 /jar
8	FC02	Concealer 15 ml	20 /tube
4	FC03	Epidermal Cleanser: face+ 300 ml	60 /jar
4	FC04	Epidermal Cleanser: phytogel 300 ml	50 /jar
8	FC05	Eye Shadow duo-pack	15 /pair
5	AS02	Cellulite Treatment	80 /job
8	AS07	Makeup	40 /job
		Goods and Services Tax	5%
		Provincial Sales Tax	8%

Terms: 2/5, n/30.

☐ **Cash Receipt #11**   Dated Feb. 1/10

From Star Film Corporation, cheque #6732 for $2 214.50 in payment of account including $43 discount for early payment. Reference invoice #AA-11.

✓ **Purchase Invoice #AC-1124**   **Dated Feb. 1/10**

368   From Acqua Viva Cosmetics

5	SC03 Sun Tan Milk SPF#4 200 ml	$ 90.00
5	SC04 Sun Tan Milk SPF#15 200 ml	105.00
	Freight	10.00
	GST Paid	10.25
	Invoice Total	$215.25

Terms: net 10 days.

✓ **Memo #1**   **Dated Feb. 2/10**

371   From Owner: Adjust inventory records for Eye Contour Smoothing Gel, item
CL04. One jar was dropped and broken. Charge to Inventory Losses.

✓ **Memo #2**   **Dated Feb. 3/10**

373   From Owner: Two new inventory items are required for special Valentine's Day
gift packages. Create new asset Group account 1350 Gift Packages. Create two
new inventory records.

Number Description	Min.	Reg (Pref) Selling Price	/Unit	Picture
VP01 Valentine Gift: super pkg	1	$100 (95)	/pkg	VP01.bmp
VP02 Valentine Gift: deluxe pkg	1	$150 (140)	/pkg	VP02.bmp

Linked accounts: Asset 1350
Revenue 4020
Expense 5060
Variance not required

> **NOTES**
> Notice that only inventory items appear on the list for adjustments because service items do not have quantities in stock.

✓ **Item Assembly #ItA-1**   **Dated Feb. 3/10**

379   Assemble 10 VP01 Valentine Gift: super packages. Transfer 10 of each
component item as follows:

10 CL01	Cleansing Lotion 225 ml	$ 6 each tube
10 CL07	Night Cream 200 ml	21 each jar
10 FC01	Blush 8 g	4 each
10 FC07	Lipstick 5 g	6 each tube
10 SC01	Sun Care Cream SPF#15 125 ml	14 each tube
Additional Costs		$50

Assembled Items:

10 VP01	Valentine Gift: super pkg	$56 each pkg

☐ **Item Assembly #ItA-2**   **Dated Feb. 3/10**

Assemble 10 VP02 Valentine Deluxe Gift Packages. Transfer 10 of each
component item as follows:

10 CL02	Cleansing Milk 225 ml	$12 each tube
10 CL07	Night Cream 200 ml	21 each jar
10 FC07	Lipstick 5 g	6 each tube
10 FC11	Powder: pressed 15 g	14 each
10 SC06	UV #30 Total Cream 125 ml	35 each tube
Additional Costs		$50

Assembled Items:

10 VP02	Valentine Gift: deluxe pkg	$93 each pkg

> **NOTES**
> You will see the advisor message that one or more inventory items has dropped below the reorder point. Read and then close the message.

☐ **Memo #3**   **Dated Feb. 3/10**

From Owner: Adjust purchase invoice #AC-1124 from Acqua Viva Cosmetics.
Change the quantity for both items to 10. The unit cost price and freight are
unchanged. The revised invoice total is $420.

✓ **Sales Invoice #21**   **Dated Feb. 4/10**

383   Sold by Hydra to Valley TV (CKOV) preferred customer

5	CL03	Eye Contour Smoothing Cream 30 ml	$ 32.00 /jar
5	CL05	Masks: herb 100 ml	36.00 /jar
5	FC02	Concealer 15 ml	18.00 /tube
5	AS06	Hydroptimate Treatment	108.00 /job
5	AS07	Makeup	36.00 /job
		Goods and Services Tax	5%
		Provincial Sales Tax	8%

Terms: 2/15, n/30.

NOTES
To change a purchase price, click the number in the Amount field to select it. Type the new total amount to replace it, and press [tab] to update the unit price and totals.

☐ **Purchase Invoice #DL-518**   **Dated Feb. 4/10**

From Derma Laboratories

10	CL01	Cleansing Lotion 225 ml	$ 60.00
10	CL02	Cleansing Milk 225 ml	120.00
20	CL07	Night Cream 200 ml	440.00
		Freight	20.00
		GST Paid	32.00
		Invoice Total	$672.00

Terms: net 5 days. Note price increase for CL07.

☐

	To:
	Customer: **Adrienne Aesthetics**
	Address: 65 Bytown Ave.
	Ottawa, ON K2C 4R1
	PST Reg # 29977336

SUN LAB PRODUCTS, INC.
59 Botox Cr. Kanata, Ontario K2F 3M8
Tel: (613) 620-5388 Fax: (613) 621-7392
www.sunlab.com

Invoice #: SL-4100
GST # 724 527 455

Feb. 4, 2010

qty	code	item	total
10	SC01	Sun Care Cream SPF#15 125 ml @ $14	140.00
15	SC06	UV #30 Total Cream 125 ml @ $35	525.00
		Freight	10.00
		GST	33.75
		Invoice Total	708.75

Terms: n/15   *MF*

☐ **Cheque Copy #205**   **Dated Feb. 5/10**

To Esthetica Incorporated, $3 150 in full payment of account. Reference invoice #EI-641.

WARNING!
Do not include the discount for the second invoice in the amount received from Valley TV.

☐ **Cash Receipt #12**   **Dated Feb. 5/10**

From Valley TV (CKOV), cheque #29975 for $1 802.50 in payment of account, including $35 discount taken. Reference invoice #AA-16.

Cheque Copy #206   **Dated Feb. 6/10**

To Derma Laboratories, $672 in full payment of account. Reference invoice
#DL-518.

Adrienne Aesthetics

INVOICE # 22   **Sold to:** Visa Sales Summary
Adrienne Aesthetics   **Address:** One-time customers
65 Bytown Ave.
Ottawa, ON K2C 4R1
567 643 778

Salesperson: Blossom   **Date:**   Feb. 6/10

QTY	CODE	DESCRIPTION	PRICE/UNIT	TAX CODE	TOTAL
5	CL08	Protection Cream:			
		dbl action 60 ml	25 /tube	1	125.00
3	FC05	Eye Shadow duo-pack	15 /pair	1	45.00
5	FC10	Powder: loose 15 g	20 /jar	1	100.00
3	SC05	UV #15 Total Cream 125 ml	50 /tube	1	150.00
2	AS08	Massage: Swedish	75 /job	2	150.00
4	AS13	Manicure/Pedicure	25 /job	2	100.00
4	AS14	Waxing: full leg	50 /job	2	200.00
2	VP02	Valentine Gift: deluxe pkg	150/pkg	1	300.00

Direct deposit to Visa account   LB

Terms:	Visa		
		GST 5%	58.50
		PST 8%	57.60
		Total	1 286.10

Tel 1: (613) 722-9876   or   (613) 722-8701   Fax: (613) 722-8000
www.adrienneaesthetics.com
look good, feel good

MasterCard Sales Summary Invoice #23   **Dated Feb. 6/10**

Sold by Blossom to various one-time Cash Customers

20	FC08	Kohl Pencil	$ 15 each	$ 300.00
10	FC09	Mascara 9 ml	10 /tube	100.00
2	SC03	Sun Tan Milk SPF#4 200 ml	40 /jar	80.00
2	AS12	Skin Treatment	100 /job	200.00
4	AS15	Waxing: half leg or bikini	20 /job	80.00
3	VP02	Valentine Gift: deluxe pkg	150 /pkg	450.00
		Goods and Services Tax	5%	60.50
		Provincial Sales Tax	8%	74.40

Total paid by MasterCard $1 344.90

Item Assembly #ItA-3   **Dated Feb. 7/10**

Assemble five VP02 Valentine Deluxe Gift Packages. Transfer five of each item as
follows:

5	CL02	Cleansing Milk 225 ml	$12	each tube
5	CL07	Night Cream 200 ml	22	each jar
5	FC07	Lipstick 5 g	6	each tube
5	FC11	Powder: pressed 15 g	14	each
5	SC06	UV #30 Total Cream 125 ml	35	each tube

Additional Costs $25

Assembled Items:
5	VP02	Valentine Gift: deluxe pkg	$94	each pkg

NOTES
  Choose Cash Customers for
the Visa and MasterCard sales
summaries.

NOTES
  If you recall the stored item
assembly transaction, change the
total amount for the Assembled
Items to $470. Notice that the
assembly component price for
CL07 is updated from $21 to $22
automatically for the new costs.
(See Item Assembly #ItA-2 on
page 357.)

NOTES
Choose Cash Customers for the cash sales summary.

Cash Sales Summary Invoice #24   **Dated Feb. 7/10**

Sold by Hydra to various one-time Cash Customers

2	CL04	Eye Contour Smoothing Gel 30 ml	$ 40 /jar	$ 80.00
5	CL06	Masks: sea 100 ml	35 /jar	175.00
15	FC07	Lipstick 5 g	15 /tube	225.00
3	SC02	Sun Care Cream SPF#30 125 ml	45 /tube	135.00
2	AS01	Bridal Makeup/Styling	70 /job	140.00
5	AS03	Electrolysis: 45 min treatment	60 /session	300.00
2	AS06	Hydroptimate Treatment	120 /job	240.00
2	VP01	Valentine Gift: super pkg	100 /pkg	200.00
		Goods and Services Tax	5%	74.75
		Provincial Sales Tax	8%	65.20
		Total cash received		$1 634.95

Cheque Copy #207   **Dated Feb. 7/10**

To Sun Lab Products, $708.75 in full payment of account. Reference invoice #SL-4100.

SESSION DATE – FEBRUARY 14, 2010

Purchase Invoice #BL-669   **Dated Feb. 8/10**

From Biotech Laboratories

5	FC10	Powder: loose 15 g	$ 40.00
15	FC11	Powder: pressed 15 g	210.00
		Freight	10.00
		GST Paid	13.00
	Invoice Total		$273.00

Terms: net 10 days.

Adrienne Aesthetics

INVOICE # 25
Adrienne Aesthetics
65 Bytown Ave.
Ottawa, ON K2C 4R1
567 643 778

Sold to: Star Film Corporation
Address: 6 Royal Road
Ottawa, Ont. K1P 2M2
ATTN: Francine Despardieu

Salesperson: Blossom   **Date:**   Feb. 8/10

QTY	CODE	DESCRIPTION	PRICE/UNIT	TAX CODE	TOTAL
4	CL05	Masks: herb 100 ml	36 /jar**	1	144.00
4	CL06	Masks: sea 100 ml	32 /jar	1	128.00
8	FC03	Epidermal Cleanser: face+ 300 ml	55 /jar	1	440.00
8	FC04	Epidermal Cleanser: phytogel 300 ml	45 /jar	1	360.00
3	FC06	Foundation 35 ml	22 /jar	1	66.00
5	SC06	UV #30 Total Cream 125 ml	68 /tube	1	340.00

** *preferred customer discounts applied LB*

Terms: 2/15, n/30	**GST** 5%	73.90
	PST 8%	118.24
	Invoice Total	1,670.14

Tel 1: (613) 722-9876   or   (613) 722-8701   Fax: (613) 722-8000
www.adrienneaesthetics.com
look good, feel good

☑ **Visa Sales Return #22-R**   **Dated Feb. 8/10**

384   Returned to Blossom by Cash Customer

–1	CL08 Protection Cream: dbl action 60 ml	$25.00
–1	SC05 UV #15 Total Cream 125 ml	50.00
	Goods and Services Tax	3.75
	Provincial Sales Tax	6.00
	Total credited to Visa account	$84.75

☑ **Purchase Return #BL-669R**   **Dated Feb. 8/10**

386   Return to Biotech Laboratories because package safety seal was broken.

–5	FC10 Powder: loose 15 g	$40.00
	GST Paid	2.00
	Total Credit	$42.00

Terms: net 60 days.

☐ **Purchase Invoice #EI-933**   **Dated Feb. 9/10**

From Esthetica Incorporated

	Manicure and pedicure preparation products	$ 90.00
5	FC02 Concealer 15 ml	45.00
5	CL03 Eye Contour Smoothing Cream 30 ml	65.00
5	CL04 Eye Contour Smoothing Gel 30 ml	95.00
	Freight	20.00
	GST Paid	15.75
	Invoice Total	$330.75

Terms: net 30 days. Note the price increases.

NOTES

Remember to edit the purchase prices by changing the numbers in the Amount field.

Use account 1380 Miscellaneous Inventory Products for the manicure and pedicure products.

☐ **Cheque Copy #208**   **Dated Feb. 9/10**

To Acqua Viva Cosmetics, $420 in full payment of account. Reference invoice #AC-1124.

☐

INVOICE # 26			**Sold to:**	Lavender Estates	
Adrienne Aesthetics			**Address:**	9 Lavender Ct.	
65 Bytown Ave.				Ottawa, Ont. K1X 3J6	
Ottawa, ON K2C 4R1			**ATTN:**	Katherine Harris	
# 567 643 778					

Salesperson: Blossom   **Date:**   Feb. 10/10

QTY	CODE	DESCRIPTION	PRICE/UNIT	TAX CODE	TOTAL
3	CL09	Protection Cream: moisturizer 60 ml	30 /tube	1	90.00
3	SC04	Sun Tan Milk SPF#15 200 ml	50 /jar	1	150.00
2	AS11	Package: Deluxe 5 spa treatments	800 /series	2	1,600.00
2	VP02	Valentine Gift: deluxe pkg	150 /pkg	1	300.00

LB

Terms: 2/5, n/30	**GST** 5%	107.00
	PST 8%	43.20
	Invoice Total	**2,290.20**

Tel 1: (613) 722-9876   or   (613) 722-8701   Fax: (613) 722-8000
www.adrienneaesthetics.com
look good, feel good

☐ **Sales Invoice #27**   **Dated Feb. 11/10**

Sold by Hydra to Botelli & Giroux, Lawyers

3	AS09	Promotional Pkg: spa treatment	$100 /job
3	VP01	Valentine Gift: super pkg	100 /pkg
3	VP02	Valentine Gift: deluxe pkg	150 /pkg
		Goods and Services Tax	5%
		Provincial Sales Tax	8%

Terms: 2/5, n/30.

☐ **Cash Purchase Invoice #HP-125**   **Dated Feb. 11/10**

From Hull Promotions (use Quick Add for the new supplier), $200 plus $10 GST and $16 PST for business cards and flyers for promotion. Purchase invoice total $226 paid by cheque #209.

☐ **Purchase Invoice #EI-1303**   **Dated Feb. 12/10**

From Esthetica Incorporated

		Manicure and pedicure preparation products	$ 90.00
5	CL05	Masks: herb 100 ml	90.00
5	CL06	Masks: sea 100 ml	80.00
5	FC03	Epidermal Cleanser: face+ 300 ml	125.00
5	FC04	Epidermal Cleanser: phytogel 300 ml	110.00
		Freight	20.00
		GST Paid	25.75
		Invoice Total	$540.75

Terms: net 30 days.

☐ **Cash Purchase Invoice #OH-42455**   **Dated Feb. 13/10**

From Ottawa Hydro, $200 plus $10 GST for hydro services. Purchase invoice total $210 paid by cheque #210.

☐ **Cash Purchase Invoice #BC-16721**   **Dated Feb. 13/10**

From Bell Canada, $80 plus $4.00 GST and $6.40 PST for telephone services. Purchase invoice total $90.40 paid by cheque #211.

NOTES

Only GST applies to the sales invoice from Ariandanos Residence because it includes only services.

☐ **Sales Invoice #28**   **Dated Feb. 13/10**

Sold by Blossom to Ariandanos Residence

1	AS01	Bridal Makeup/Styling	$ 70 /job
1	AS04	Electrolysis: 60 min treatment	75 /session
1	AS05	European Deep Cleansing Facial	60 /job
1	AS06	Hydroptimate Treatment	120 /job
1	AS12	Skin Treatment	100 /job
		Goods and Services Tax	5%

Terms: 2/5, n/30.

☐ **Visa Sales Summary Invoice #29**   **Dated Feb. 13/10**

Sold by Hydra to various one-time Cash Customers

3	CL02	Cleansing Milk 225 ml	$ 25 /tube	$ 75.00
2	CL07	Night Cream 200 ml	45 /jar	90.00
5	AS09	Promotional Pkg: spa treatment	100 /job	500.00
2	VP01	Valentine Gift: super pkg	100 /pkg	200.00
1	VP02	Valentine Gift: deluxe pkg	150 /pkg	150.00
		Goods and Services Tax	5%	50.75
		Provincial Sales Tax	8%	41.20
		Total paid by Visa		$1 106.95

☐ **MasterCard Sales Summary Invoice #30**   **Dated Feb. 13/10**

Sold by Blossom to various one-time Cash Customers

2	CL01	Cleansing Lotion 225 ml	$ 15 /tube	$	30.00
2	CL02	Cleansing Milk 225 ml	25 /tube		50.00
1	AS05	European Deep Cleansing Facial	60 /job		60.00
2	AS11	Package: Deluxe 5 spa treatments	800 /series	1	600.00
2	VP01	Valentine Gift: super pkg	100 /pkg		200.00
		Goods and Services Tax	5%		97.00
		Provincial Sales Tax	8%		22.40
		Total paid by MasterCard		$2	059.40

☐ **Cash Sales Summary Invoice #31**   **Dated Feb. 14/10**

Sold by Hydra to various one-time Cash Customers

1	CL06	Masks: sea 100 ml	$ 35 /jar	$	35.00
2	FC01	Blush 8 g	10 each		20.00
2	AS01	Bridal Makeup/Styling	70 /job		140.00
3	AS10	Package: Super 5 spa treatments	600 /series	1	800.00
2	VP02	Valentine Gift: deluxe pkg	150 /pkg		300.00
		Goods and Services Tax	5%		114.75
		Provincial Sales Tax	8%		28.40
		Total cash received		$2	438.15

☐ **Cash Receipt #13**   **Dated Feb. 14/10**

From Star Film Corporation, cheque #8091 for $1 640.58 in payment of account including $29.56 discount for early payment. Reference invoice #25.

☐ **Memo #4**   **Dated Feb. 14/10**

From Owner: Complete payroll run to pay salaried employees Blossom and Hydra. Issue cheques #212 and #213. Add the 2 percent sales commissions based on the net sales for each employee from Feb. 1 to Feb. 14.

KEYSTROKES

Accounting for Inventory Sales

The first transaction involves the sale of inventory items. Many of the steps are identical to those you used for sales in previous applications. You will be using the inventory database and all the Sales Invoice fields to complete this transaction.

> **Restore** **SimData\adrienne1.CAB** to **SimData\Adrienne\adrienne** to open the data files for Adrienne Aesthetics.

> **Type**   2 7 10 or **choose Feb. 7** from the calendar and **click OK**.

This will enter the session date February 7, 2010. The familiar Receivables module window appears. Inventory & Services has been added to the Modules pane list. Inventory sales are entered in the Sales Journal.

> **Click**   the **Sales Invoices icon** to open the Sales Journal.

NOTES
Use the Sales by Salesperson Summary Report (by Customer) to find the net sales for each employee. Do not include freight or other sales in the report.

NOTES
Refer to to the instructions in Chapter 1, page 7, if you need assistance with restoring files from backups.

NOTES
We have selected Retail as the type of industry for Adrienne Aesthetics because they sell inventory items.

Classic **CLASSIC VIEW**
Click the Sales icon to open the Sales Journal.

You will open and display the familiar Sales Journal input screen:

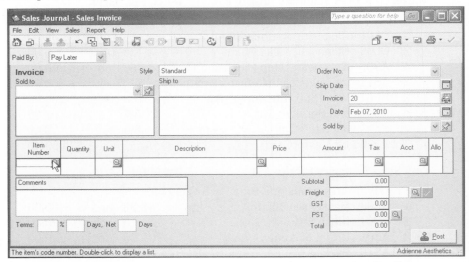

SIMPLY VERSION
The invoice does not include Order No. or Ship Date fields.

The Sales Journal looks the same as in earlier data files, except for the Sales Journal we customized for Air Care Services in Chapter 6. All the invoice fields are used when we sell inventory. Pay Later is correctly selected as the payment method.

Click   the **Sold To** (Customer) **field list arrow** to display the list of customers.

Click   **Montreal Fashions** to enter the customer's name and address on the form. If you selected an incorrect customer, return to the customer list and select again.

You can skip the Ship To fields because the default information is correct, and the Order No. is not used for invoices. The Invoice number is correct because the numeric invoice sequence has been set up in the defaults. If necessary, you can edit the invoice number. The payment terms, tax code and revenue account are also added from the default settings and can be edited if necessary.

Click   the **Date field Calendar icon** to advance the cursor. The default session date is incorrect.

Click   **1** on the February calendar and **press** (tab) to advance the cursor to the Sold By field.

Choose Hydra as the salesperson.

Press   (tab) twice to skip the Use Same Salesperson icon.

The cursor advances to the first line of the Item field. One line is used for each inventory item or service sold by the business. A separate line would also be used to enter returns and allowances made.

Click   the **Item field List icon**, or **press** (enter) or **double click** the **field** to access the inventory list:

You can type C, the first letter or number of the code, in the journal's Item field and press (enter) to advance to the part of the list beginning with that letter or number, just as you do for account, supplier and customer lists.

Notice that you can add new inventory items from the Select Inventory/Service screen. The inventory items are listed in order by number or code, but you can change the order and sort by description or name. Sorting inventory items by number or description is an option in the Inventory Settings. For inventory items, the quantities available are also included in this display for reference.

The cursor is in the Search field. We will bypass the search field so that future references to this list will place the cursor in the list rather than in the Search field.

Click   **Bypass Search Field** so that the next time the cursor will start in the item list.

Click   ☑ to scroll down the list. **Click** in the **list** and **type** c if you want to advance the list to the codes beginning with C.

Click   **CL04 Eye Contour Smoothing Gel 30 ml** from the list.

Click   **Select** to add the inventory item to your form. If you have made an incorrect selection, return to the Item field and reselect from the inventory list.

You can also type the code number in the Item field and press (tab), but you must match the case of the code number in the ledger.

The cursor moves to the Quantity field. Notice that the program adds information in each field automatically, based on the inventory record information. All the information except quantity and amount is added by default as soon as you enter the inventory item number. If you select a preferred customer, the default price is the preferred customer price instead of the regular selling price (see page 383).

You should enter the number of units of this item sold in the Quantity field.

Type   8   **Press** (tab).

If your company settings do not allow inventory levels to go below zero, the program prevents you from continuing if you enter a quantity greater than the available stock. You will see this warning:

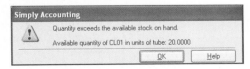

Click   **OK** to return to the journal so you can reduce the quantity.

Since the remaining default information is correct, you do not need to change it. The default tax code — GP — is the code entered for the customer because the

NOTES

Inventory items can be oversold, but you must change the Inventory Ledger settings to allow the quantity on hand to go below zero. This setting is explained in the setup for Flabuless Fitness (Chapter 16).

No quantities are shown for services because they are not held in stock.

NOTES

If you want to type in the item codes instead of using the selection list for each item, turn on Caps Lock for your keyboard. This will speed up your data entry and ensure you are using the correct case.

NOTES

If your company settings allow, you may want to continue with an order to oversell the items if the customer is purchasing backordered inventory stock.

NOTES
If you have entered a default revenue account for the customer that is different from the one for the item, the account for the item replaces the customer's revenue account.

WARNING!
If you click the second line and it is used for part of the description for the first item, you will select and replace the first item instead.

customer pays both GST at 5 percent and PST at 8 percent. Services have been set up in the Inventory Ledger so that by default PST is not applied.

The program automatically calculates an amount based on the selling price per unit. This figure appears in the Amount field.

The default revenue account for the item appears but can be accepted or changed. You would change the account for returns and allowances or unusual entries. Accept the default revenue account for this sale.

You can select another tax code from the Tax Code list if necessary. You can also edit the price to change the selling price for a particular item or customer. To change the account, click the Account field List icon 🔍, press *enter* or double click in the Account field to obtain a list of accounts.

Press *tab* **repeatedly** to advance to the next invoice line and update the first line because all the default information based on the records is correct.

Or you can click the Item field on the second line, or the third line, if the item description wraps around to the second invoice line.

Press *tab* in the Account field to add a new invoice line in the viewing space of the journal when you reach the last invoice line of the journal.

Enter the **remaining sale items** using the same steps that you used to enter the first item.

As you complete each line and advance to the next, the totals and tax amounts at the bottom of the form are updated to include the last item entered.

The tax code shown on the screen for the service items is GP, the one for the customer, but only GST is added to the invoice total.

To include more invoice lines on your screen, drag the lower frame of the Sales Journal window or maximize the window.

There are no freight charges for these items.

After entering the final service item for the customer, your completed invoice should look like the one shown here:

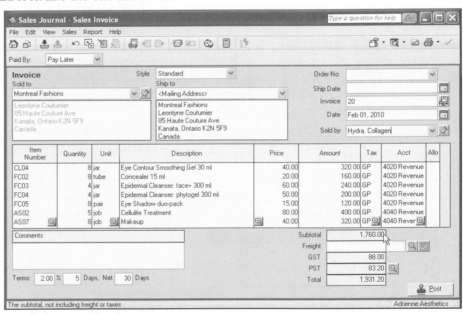

You should review the journal entry before posting it.

Reviewing the Inventory Sales Journal Transaction

Choose the **Report menu** and **click Display Sales Journal Entry**:

Adrienne Aesthetics 02/01/2010 (J1)	Debits	Credits	Division
1200 Accounts Receivable	1,931.20	-	
5060 Cost of Goods Sold	428.00	-	
1310 Creams and Lotions	-	144.00	
1320 Face Care Products	-	284.00	
2640 PST Payable	-	83.20	
2650 GST Charged on Sales	-	88.00	
4020 Revenue from Sales	-	1,040.00	
4040 Revenue from Services	-	720.00	
	2,359.20	2,359.20	

From the tax amounts, you can see that PST is charged only on the *Revenue from Sales* amount — 8% × \$1 040 = \$83.20 — while GST is charged on both sales and services — 5% × (\$1 040 + \$720) = \$88. Both taxes are calculated correctly because of the tax codes assigned in the Inventory Ledger records.

Notice that all relevant accounts have been updated automatically because the Inventory and Receivables ledgers are linked to the General Ledger. Therefore, the linked asset, revenue and expense accounts defined for each inventory item have been debited or credited as required. In addition, the linked Receivables accounts we saw earlier are used — *PST Payable*, *GST Charged on Sales* and *Accounts Receivable*. The inventory database and customer record are also updated.

Simply Accounting uses the average cost method to determine the cost of goods sold. If the stock for an inventory item were purchased at different times and prices, the average of these prices would be used as the cost of goods sold.

Close the **display** to return to the journal input screen.

CORRECTING THE INVENTORY SALES ENTRY BEFORE POSTING

To **correct** an **item** on the inventory line, **click** the **incorrect field** to move the cursor and highlight the field contents. **Press** (enter) to display the list of inventory items, tax codes or accounts. **Click** the **correct selection** to highlight it, then **click Select**, or for the remaining fields, **type** the **correct information**. **Press** (tab) to enter the change.

If you **change** the **inventory** item, you must **re-enter** the **quantity sold** in the Quantity field and **press** (tab). The totals will be updated correctly if you follow this procedure.

To **insert** a new **line**, if you have forgotten a complete line of the invoice, **click** the **line below** the one you have forgotten. **Choose** the **Edit menu** and **click Insert Line** to add a blank invoice line to your form. To **remove** a line, **click** the **line** you want to delete and **choose** the **Edit menu** and **click Remove Line**.

For corrections of other invoice details, refer to page 166.

To correct errors after posting, click the Adjust Invoice tool or choose the Sales menu and click Adjust Invoice. Or choose Adjust Invoice from the Sales Invoices shortcuts list. Refer to page 184.

If this is a recurring inventory sale, you can store it just like other sales.

Posting

When all the information in your journal entry is correct, you must post the transaction to save your work.

Click   **Post** 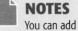 to save the transaction. **Click OK**.

Close   the **Sales Journal** to exit to the Home window.

Enter   the **sales receipt** as the next transaction.

Create   **shortcuts** for transactions in other modules (Create Purchase Invoice, Pay Purchase Invoices, Create General Journal and Payroll Cheque Run.)

Accounting for Inventory Purchases

The third transaction involves the purchase of inventory items. Inventory purchases are entered in the Purchases Journal, and many of the steps are the same as those for other credit purchases. Now the inventory database will provide the additional information.

Click   Create Purchase Invoice in the Shortcuts pane to display the familiar Purchases Journal input form window:

Pay Later is correctly selected as the method of payment.

Click   the **Purchased From field list arrow** to display the list of suppliers.

Click   Acqua Viva Cosmetics from the list to add it to your input form.

Check your selection. If you have selected an incorrect supplier, select again from the supplier list. If you have selected correctly, proceed by entering the invoice number.

Click   the **Invoice field** to skip the Order/Quote No.

Type   AC-1124 **Press** (tab) **twice**.

The cursor advances to the Date field, where you should enter the invoice date.

Type   February 1

Press   (tab) **twice** to advance the cursor to the Item field. **Press** (tab) **once** if you choose the date from the Date field calendar.

Press   (enter) or **click** the **List icon** to see the list of inventory items.

Notice that you can add new inventory from the Select Inventory/Service window.

Scroll down   and **click SC03 Sun Tan Milk SPF#4 200 ml** from the list to highlight it.

Press   (enter). If you have made an incorrect selection, return to the Item field and select again.

The cursor advances to the Quantity received field. The Description field should now show the name, Sun Tan Milk SPF#4 200 ml. The default price is the most recent purchase price. Now enter the quantity for this item.

Type   5 **Press** (tab).

The cursor advances to the Unit field. The Unit and Description are correct based on Inventory Ledger records.

The Price field records the unit price paid for the purchase of the inventory items. This amount should not include any GST paid that can be used as an input tax credit. The default information, based on previous purchases, is correct so do not change it.

The correct tax code — code G — is entered by default from the supplier record. Adrienne pays only GST on purchases of inventory items that will be resold.

> If a price is incorrect because it has changed, you can edit the default amount. If the code is incorrect, you can change it by selecting from the tax code list.

> When purchasing new inventory, no price is recorded. You should enter the quantity and, in the Amount field, enter the total purchase amount. Press (tab) to advance the cursor. Simply Accounting will calculate the price per unit.

> **Press** (tab) **repeatedly** to advance to the next line, with the cursor blinking in the Item field again, or **click** the **Item field** in the next line.

Notice that the cursor skips the PST amount field because the supplier tax code does not include PST. The Account field was also skipped over, because you cannot change the entry for inventory purchases. The Asset account for the inventory purchase is defined in the Inventory Ledger as the linked account for purchases and sales. To change the account, you must edit the Inventory Ledger record. The default account for the supplier does not apply to the inventory purchase.

> **Enter** **the second item** from the source document, using the same steps that you used to record the first item.

Your journal looks like the following when you are ready to enter the freight charge:

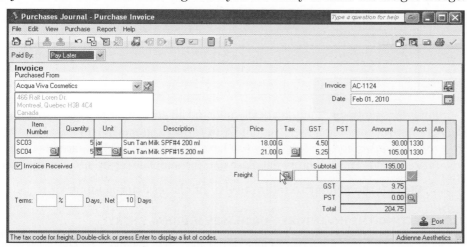

The Freight fields are used to enter any freight charges that cannot be allocated to the purchase of a specific item and to enter the taxes paid on the freight charges. There are four Freight fields: tax code, GST amount, PST amount and finally the base amount of the freight charge. Because GST is paid on freight you must enter a tax code if the supplier charges freight.

> **Click** the **first Freight field**. The tax code for the supplier, code G, should be entered by default.

> If the tax code is not entered automatically, press (enter) to see the familiar list of tax codes. Click G and then click Select.

You do not need to enter amounts for the taxes on freight; they are calculated as soon as you enter the amount of freight charged.

> **Click** the **final Freight field**, the amount field, below the Subtotal.

NOTES
PST is not paid on items that are purchased for resale because the store is not the final customer.

NOTES
PST is not charged on freight in Ontario. The correct tax code for freight is code G - GST @ 5%.

> **Type** 10 **Press** (tab).

Simply Accounting calculates the amount of GST (and PST if it is paid) and updates all the totals. Your input form is complete and should appear as follows:

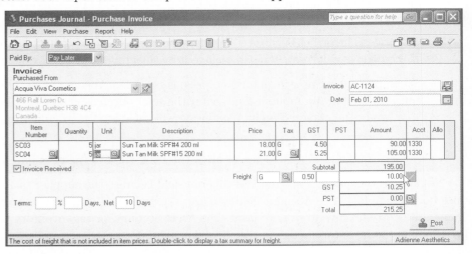

The Subtotal includes all items purchased but does not include freight or taxes.

Reviewing the Inventory Purchase Transaction

NOTES

Pressing (ctrl) + J will also open the journal display.

Choose the **Report menu** and **click Display Purchases Journal Entry** to display the transaction you have entered, as shown:

Simply Accounting has automatically updated all accounts relevant to this transaction. The appropriate inventory asset account (*Sun Care Products*), *Accounts Payable, GST Paid on Purchases* and *Freight Expense* have been updated as required because the ledgers are linked. The inventory database and the supplier record are also updated.

Close the **display** to return to the Purchases Journal input screen.

CORRECTING THE INVENTORY PURCHASES JOURNAL ENTRY

If the inventory item is incorrect, **reselect** from the **inventory** list by **pressing** (enter) while in this field. **Click Select** to add the item to your form. **Type** the **quantity** purchased and **press** (tab) to update the totals.

Account numbers cannot be changed for inventory items on the purchase invoice. They must be edited in the Inventory Ledger.

To **insert** a new **line**, if you have forgotten a complete line of the invoice, **click** the **line below** the one you have forgotten. **Choose** the **Edit menu** and **click Insert Line** to add a blank invoice line to your form. To **remove** a complete **line, click** the **line** you want to delete, **choose** the **Edit menu** and **click Remove Line**.

For assistance with correcting other invoice details, refer to page 116.

To correct an inventory purchase after posting, use the **Adjust Invoice tool** or **choose** the **Purchase Menu** and **click Adjust Invoice**. Refer to page 129. If you selected the wrong supplier, you can reverse the purchase transaction (page 140).

If this is a recurring purchase, you can store it, just like other recurring purchases.

Posting

When all the information in your journal entry is correct, you must post the transaction.

Click   **Post** 🖧 Post . **Close** the **Purchases Journal**.

Making Inventory Adjustments

Sometimes inventory is lost, stolen or damaged and adjusting entries are required to reflect the expenses. These inventory adjustments are made in the Inventory Adjustments Journal in the Inventory & Services window. This journal is also used to record lost inventory that is recovered and inventory that is used by the business instead of being sold to customers.

Click   **Inventory & Services** in the Modules pane list. The Adjustments Journal is indicated in the Home window shown here:

The Inventory module has icons for the ledger records and for journal entries. The records are listed as they are for other modules so you can access them directly. The Reports pane includes all inventory reports in the Reports list.

Click   the **Adjust Inventory icon** to open the blank Adjustments Journal:

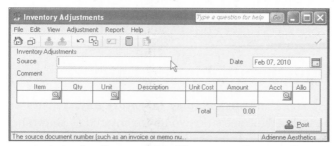

The cursor is in the Source field. The source for an adjustment will normally be a memo from a manager or owner.

> **Type**   Memo 1 **Press** (tab).

The cursor is in the Date field, with the session date entered and highlighted.

> **Type**   02-02-10 **Press** (tab) **twice**.

The cursor is now in the Comment field, where you can enter a brief explanation for this transaction.

> **Type**   Jar dropped and broken **Press** (tab).

The cursor advances to the Item field.

> **Press**   (enter) or **click** to display the familiar inventory list.

Notice that the quantities on the list have been updated to include the previous sale and purchase. Services are not included in the list because they have no quantities in stock and cannot be lost or damaged.

> **Double click CL04 Eye Contour Smoothing Gel** from the list to select it and enter it onto the form.

The item description, Eye Contour Smoothing Gel, the unit, the unit cost and the account have been added automatically. The cursor advances to the Quantity field. You need to indicate that the inventory has been reduced because of the damaged item. You do this by typing a **negative** number in the field. Remember always to enter a negative quantity when there is an inventory loss. If lost inventory is recovered later, enter the adjustment with a positive quantity.

> **Type**   -1 **Press** (tab).

The cursor advances to the Unit field. The rest of the journal line is completed automatically. In the Amount field, a negative amount, reflecting the inventory loss, automatically appears as a default based on the average cost. In the Account field, *Inventory Losses*, the default linked account for inventory losses appears for this entry. This is the correct account.

> If you need to choose another account, press (enter) to display the list of accounts and select the account as usual. You can also edit the amount if you know that the price of the unit was different from the default price, the average of all inventory in stock. You can store Adjustments Journal entries just as you store entries in other journals.

Your entry is complete as shown and you are ready to review it:

Item	Qty	Unit	Description	Unit Cost	Amount	Acct	Allo
CL04	-1		Eye Contour Smoothing	18.00	-18.00	5100 Invent	
				Total	-18.00		

Reviewing the Adjustments Journal Entry

> **Choose** the **Report menu** and **click Display Inventory Adjustments Journal Entry** to display the transaction you have entered as shown here:

NOTES
Stores that sell inventory frequently use some inventory stock in the store. Use the Adjustments Journal to record these transfers by choosing the appropriate asset or expense account to replace the default linked account. Enter negative quantities because the inventory stock is reduced. Because the store has become the final customer — it has bought the items from itself — it is responsible for reporting the purchase and paying PST on the cost price of these internal sales.

NOTES
The Allo (allocation) field for project allocations is not used by Adrienne Aesthetics. We will discuss it in a later application.

NOTES
Pressing (ctrl) + J will also open the journal display.

NOTES
The second Inventory Ledger linked account is used for item assembly costs in the Item Assembly Journal. Item assembly is introduced in the next transaction.

You can see that Simply Accounting has automatically updated all relevant accounts for this transaction. The appropriate inventory asset defined for this inventory item, *Creams and Lotions*, and the inventory database have been reduced to reflect the loss at the average cost price. *Inventory Losses*, the Inventory linked expense account that was defined for inventory losses or adjustments, has been debited or increased.

> **Close**   the **display** to return to the Adjustments Journal input screen.

CORRECTING THE ADJUSTMENTS JOURNAL ENTRY

Move to the field that has the error. **Press** *(tab)* to move forward or **press** *(shift)* and *(tab)* together to move back to a previous field. This will highlight the field information so you can change it. **Type** the **correct information** and **press** *(tab)* to enter it.

You can also use the mouse to **point** to a field and **drag** through the **incorrect information** to highlight it. **Type** the **correct information** and **press** *(tab)* to enter it.

If the inventory item is incorrect, **reselect** from the **inventory** list by **pressing** *(enter)* while in this field. **Click Select** to add it to the form. **Type** the **quantity** and **press** *(tab)*. After changing any information on an inventory item line, **press** *(tab)* to update the totals.

To start over, **click** ☒ or ↶ (or **choose** the **Edit menu** and **click Undo Entry**). **Click Yes** when asked to confirm that you want to discard the transaction.

Posting

When all the information in your journal entry is correct, you must save the transaction.

> **Click**   **Post** [⚏ Post].

> **Close**   the **Adjustments Journal** to return to the Inventory window. The next keystroke transaction creates and assembles new inventory items.

Adding a New Inventory Item

Before entering the item assembly transaction, we will create the necessary new inventory items. Refer to Memo #2 (page 357) for the inventory item details. Inventory items can be added from any inventory item field in a journal, from the Inventory & Services icon or from its shortcuts list as shown:

NOTES

You can add inventory items from any journal inventory field when the selection list is available, that is, in the Sales and Purchases journals and the two inventory journals, Adjustments and Item Assembly. Click the List icon in the Item field to open the selection list. Click Add New Inventory/ Service and press (enter) to open the Inventory Ledger window.

Click   the **Inventory & Services icon** to open the Inventory & Services window:

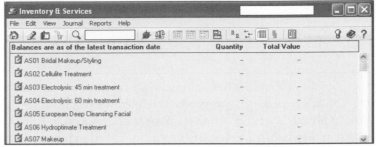

This window is like the Accounts, Suppliers, Customers and Employees windows in other modules and it lists all inventory items and services. If you chose the Add Inventory shortcut, you will skip this Inventory & Services window.

Click   the **Create tool** ▣, **choose** the **File menu** and **click Create**, or **press** (ctrl) **+ N** to open the the Inventory Ledger:

SIMPLY VERSION

The Simply version does not have the Build tab. It applies to the Build From Bill Of Materials option in the Bill of Materials & Item Assembly Journal. This feature is not available in the Simply version.

The Inventory & Services Ledger record has many of the tools that are available in other ledgers, including the Refresh tool. The Show tool icons allow you to limit the Select field list to inventory items, services or activities (for time and billing). If all three tools are selected, the list includes all three kinds of items. All Show tools are selected for Adrienne Aesthetics, so all records are included in the Select list.

You can enter both inventory and service items in the Inventory Ledger. When you enter a service item, you can designate it as an activity with time and billing information attached. Activities are available for the time and billing features and for selection as internal services — services that are provided by one department to another within the company and can be tracked as expenses. The Time and Billing function will be covered in Chapter 18.

SIMPLY VERSION

The Time & Billing function is not available in the Simply version. The Simply version has only two Show tools — one for inventory items and one for service items. The Refresh tool is also not on the Simply version tool bar.

The gift packages are inventory, so as a result the type selection is correct and the fields we need are included. The Quantity tab information is displayed because it is the first tab screen.

The setup option we selected for inventory sorts the items by code or number. Therefore, the Number field is the first item field. When you choose to sort by description, the longer Description field will come first. (See Chapter 16, page 657.)

From your source document information, you must enter the item code and description. The first Item field contains the code or number of the inventory item — the only required field on this screen; the second Item field contains the description or item name.

NOTES

As in other ledgers and journals, the Refresh tool applies when you work in multi-user mode. Clicking the tool will update the record with changes made by other users who are accessing the data file at the same time.

Click   the **Item Number field**.

Type   VP01 **Press** (tab) to advance to the Item Description field.

Type   Valentine Gift: super pkg

Click   the **Minimum Level field** in the Reorder Quantities section.

Here you must enter the stock level at which you want to reorder the item in question, or in this case, assemble more packages. When you print inventory reports, items that have fallen below the minimum level will be flagged.

Type   1

The Quantity On Hand, Value, and Order fields are updated from journal entries. Before the Inventory Ledger history is finished, you can add this information as historical data.

Click   the **Units tab**:

Units show the way in which goods are stored, bought and sold (e.g., by the dozen, by the tonne or by the item). These units may be different if, for example, merchandise is purchased in bulk packages and sold in individual units. When a store buys or stocks inventory in different units from those it sells, you also enter the relationship between the sets of units, for example, 12 units per carton.

Adrienne Aesthetics measures all units the same way so only one entry is needed.

Double click   **Each** in the Stocking Unit Of Measure field.

Type   pkg

Click   the **Pricing tab**:

Each item may be assigned a regular price, a selling price for preferred customers and a Web price. Adrienne Aesthetics has two customers with preferred customer status. Regular, preferred and Web selling prices can also be entered in foreign currencies when other currencies are used.

Click   the **Price Per Selling Unit column** beside Regular.

Type   100

Press   ⌨tab⌨ to advance to the Price Per Selling Unit field for preferred prices.

The regular price is entered as the default Preferred and Web Price.

> **Type**   95
>
> **Click**   the **Linked tab** to access the linked accounts for the inventory item:

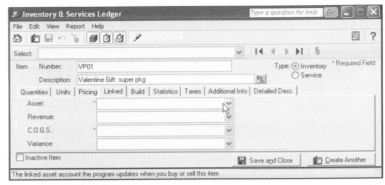

There are two sets of linked accounts for inventory: those that apply to the entire ledger — the default accounts for inventory adjustments and item assembly costs — and those that apply to specific inventory items. The ones in the ledger are item specific and are used as the default accounts whenever inventory items are sold or purchased. Linked accounts are defined for each item in the Inventory Ledger because each inventory item can be related to separate asset, revenue, expense and variance accounts.

In the **Asset** field, you must enter the number of the linked asset account affected by purchases and sales of this item. A list of accounts is available from the drop-down list arrow in the Asset field. Only asset accounts are available in the list for the Asset field. Because the account does not yet exist, we cannot choose it from the account list for the field, so we will create it here. The linked asset account is a required field.

> **Click**   the **Asset field**.
>
> **Type**   1350 **Press** (tab).

You will see the screen that allows you to create the new account:

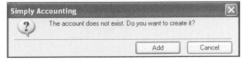

> **Click**   **Add** to proceed to the Add An Account wizard. **Press** (tab) and **type** Gift Packages
>
> **Accept** the **remaining** account **settings** and **finish** creating the account.

After you click Finish, you will see another message advising you of an account class change for the linked account:

> **Click**   **Yes** to accept the change. Clicking No will return you to the Linked Accounts screen so you can select a different account.

In the **Revenue** field, you must enter the linked revenue account that will be credited when this inventory item is sold. You can type the account number or select from the list. Only revenue accounts are available for the Revenue field.

> **Click**   the **Revenue field list arrow** to see the revenue accounts available.
>
> **Click**   **4020 Revenue from Sales** to enter it on your form.

NOTES

For other ledgers, the linked accounts are defined for the entire ledger. For example, there is only one Accounts Receivable account.

NOTES

You can type the account name in the field at the same time and then press (tab). The wizard will add both the number and the name for the account.

NOTES

The linked revenue account is not a required account – you can choose an account in the Sales Journal when you sell inventory.

Click   the **C.O.G.S. field list arrow** (Cost of Goods Sold expense) to see the expense accounts available.

In the **C.O.G.S.** field, you must enter the linked expense account that will be debited when this inventory item is sold. Only expense accounts are available for the C.O.G.S. field and the Variance field. Adrienne uses the single *Cost of Goods Sold* account for all inventory items. The linked C.O.G.S. account is also required.

Click   **5060 Cost of Goods Sold** from the list.

The **Variance** field contains the linked variance expense account used when the inventory sold is on order, before the goods are in stock. At the time of the sale, *Cost of Goods Sold* is debited for the average cost of the inventory on hand, based on previous purchases. When the goods are received, the actual purchase price may be different from this historical average cost. The price difference is charged to the variance account. Adrienne Aesthetics does not allow inventory to be oversold so you can leave the Variance account field blank.

Click   the **Build tab**:

On the Build tab screen, you enter the inventory components that are needed to make the item. You identify the number of items you are building at one time and the required component items. This process is similar to the one found in the Components section of the Item Assembly Journal (see page 380). When it is time to build the item (in the Bill of Materials & Item Assembly Journal), you indicate how may items you are building and the rest of the details are taken from the Build screen of the ledger record. We will use the Build feature in Chapter 18.

Click   the **Statistics tab**:

This screen applies to historical data. Since this is a new inventory item, there are no previous sales, and you should leave all entries at zero. The **Date Of Last Sale** shows the most recent date that this item was sold. The **Year To Date** section refers to historical information for the current fiscal period, and the **Last Year** fields apply to the

NOTES
If necessary, you can create new linked revenue and expense accounts in the same way you created the new asset account.

WARNING!
Check the linked account numbers carefully. If they are incorrect, corresponding journal entries will be posted incorrectly. If you discover the error when you are reviewing the journal entry, you should delete the journal entry line and then edit the Inventory Ledger record before posting.

NOTES
Variance accounts are used in the Truman Tires application in Chapter 13.

SIMPLY VERSION
Simply Click the Statistics tab at this stage.
The Simply version does not have a Build tab because this screen applies to Build From Bill Of Materials, a function not available in the Simply version.

NOTES
You can define multiple levels of building — one item may be made from other items that in turn are made from multiple inventory items.

NOTES
You can enter the historical dates using any of the usual date formats.
Simply Accounting continually updates the Statistics tab fields from journal entries.

previous year because Simply Accounting stores two years of transactions. Inventory Statistics are added to inventory tracking reports.

The **No. (number) Of Transactions** refers to the total number of times the item was sold. For example, if one customer bought the item on three separate dates, there would be three transactions. If four customers bought the item on one day, there would be four transactions. If one customer bought four of the same item at one time, there would be one transaction. The **Units Sold** counts the total number of items that were sold on all occasions to all customers in the relevant period. In the **Amount Sold** field you would enter the total sale price of all items sold in the period, and in the **Cost Of Goods Sold** field, you would enter the total purchase price of all items sold.

Click   the **Taxes tab**:

All taxes set up for the company will appear on this screen. PST and GST may be charged or omitted by default. Because most goods have these taxes applied to the sale, the default is to charge them — No is entered in the Tax Exempt column. The **Tax Exempt** entry is a toggle switch. Clicking the current entry changes it. The default settings are correct. The services provided by Adrienne Aesthetics were designated as tax exempt for PST.

When inventory items are imported and duty is charged, you can enter the duty rate on this screen as well.

The **Additional Info** tab allows for custom-defined information fields relating to the item, just like the Additional Info tabs in other ledgers. It is not used by Adrienne.

Click   the **Detailed Desc. tab**:

On this screen you can enter a detailed description of the inventory item and the name of a file where an image of the item is stored. The bitmap file for this item is located in the Setup\Logos folder in the SimData folder that has your other data files.

NOTES
Notice when you click Browse that the default location is Documents and Settings. Because we do not know how you have organized your files and folders, we continue to use C:\SimData as the location for all the files for this text. This allows us to give clear file path instructions.

Click   **Browse** beside the Picture field to open the file location window.

Locate   the **SimData folder**.

Double click   **Setup** and then **double click Logos** to open these folders.

Double click   **VP01** (or **VP01.bmp**) to add the image and file name:

CORRECTING THE INVENTORY ITEM BEFORE CREATING THE RECORD

Correct the information if necessary by **clicking** the field that contains the **error**. **Click** the appropriate **tab** to change information screens if necessary. **Highlight** the **error** and **type** the **correct information**. **Press** `tab` to enter the correction.

When all the information is correct, you must save your information.

Click   **Create Another** `Create Another` to save the new record. The ledger remains open so you can add the second new item.

Click   the **Quantities tab**.

Enter   all the details for item **VP02**.

Click   **Save And Close** `Save and Close` to save the new record. Both items are added to your ledger list of inventory items.

Close   the **Inventory & Services window** to return to the Home window.

EDITING AN INVENTORY ITEM AFTER CREATING THE RECORD

You cannot edit an Inventory Ledger record while you are using the item in a journal. You must first **delete** the **journal line containing the item**. **Click** the **journal line**, **choose** the **Edit menu** and **click Remove Line**. Then **click** the journal's **Home window tool** 🏠 to return to the Home window. **Click Inventory & Services** in the Modules pane list. **Click** the name of the **inventory item** that you need to change in the Inventory pane Item list to open the item's record. **Click** the **tab** you need. **Highlight** the **information** that is incorrect, and then **type** the **correct information**. **Close** the **Ledger window** and then **close** the **Inventory & Services window**. **Click Minimize** ⎯ to minimize the Home window and return to the journal.

Assembling Inventory Items

Inventory item assembly can be used to build new inventory from other inventory items, to create package offers of two or more regular items for sale at a special price or to reserve inventory for a special project or contract. Adrienne's new inventory items, the special packages, are offered at reduced prices, and the cost is the sum of the original component costs. Adrienne Aesthetics uses the inventory Bill of Materials & Item Assembly Journal to create the special Valentine's Day gift packages. The journal can be used to build from Item Assembly or from the Bill of Materials.

The journal's two methods are shown by separate icons. We will use the Item Assembly approach:

SIMPLY VERSION
In the Simply version, only the Item Assembly approach is available.

CLASSIC VIEW

Click the Bill of Materials & Item Assembly icon

to open the journal.

NOTES

We will use Item Assembly Journal to refer to the Bill of Materials & Item Assembly Journal.

Click the **Build From Item Assembly icon** to open the Journal:

There are two ways to assemble items in the Premium version of Simply Accounting: Item Assembly or Build From The Bill Of Materials defined in the ledger on the Build tab screen (see page 377). The build method will be covered in Chapter 18. We will use the Item Assembly method now. You can access both methods from the Build drop-down list in the journal as shown:

SIMPLY VERSION

The drop-down list is not available. The cursor will be in the Source field.

CLASSIC VIEW

Click Build From Item Assembly in the Build drop-down list if necessary to open the journal form we need.

When you build items from the bill of materials, the journal has only the assembled items part — the components information is drawn from the ledger record.

We are using the item assembly method, so you do not need to modify the journal.

Press ⬚ tab ⬚ to place the cursor in the Source field, where you should enter the reference or form number.

Type ItA-1

Press ⬚ tab ⬚ to advance to the Date field. Enter the date of the transfer.

Type 02-03-10

Press ⬚ tab ⬚ **twice** to advance to the Comment field.

Type Assemble Super gift packages

Press ⬚ tab ⬚ to advance to the first line in the Item field.

You are in the **Assembly Components** section. This first section refers to the items that are being removed from inventory, the "from" part of the transfer or assembly. These items will form the gift package.

NOTES

You could also add the new inventory items, the gift packages, and the new asset account, 1350 Gift Packages, directly from the journal while entering the assembly transaction.

Press ⬚ enter ⬚ or **click** the **List icon** 🔍 to display the familiar inventory selection list.

Notice that you can add new inventory items from the Select Inventory list in the Item Assembly Journal. Services are not on this list because they cannot be assembled.

Click **CL01 Cleansing Lotion 225 ml** to select the first item needed.

Click **Select** to add the item to the item assembly form and advance to the Quantity (Qty) field. You must enter the quantity.

Type 10 **Press** ⬚ tab ⬚ to advance the cursor to the Unit field and to update the amount.

The unit cost is correct but it can be edited if you know it is incorrect.

Drag   the **lower frame of the journal window** to have more input lines on the screen and see your entire entry on the screen at once.

Click   the **next line** in the Item column.

Select   the next **inventory item** to be transferred, **enter** the **quantity** and then continue to **enter** the **remaining inventory** for the package.

At this stage, your screen should look like the one shown here:

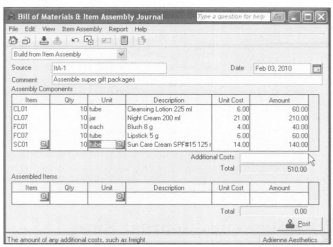

NOTES
The unit cost may be different when the cost of transferred items is lower than the default because older stock is being transferred and it was purchased at a lower price. If you change the unit cost, press `tab` to update the amount.

The middle part of the item assembly form contains two fields, Additional Costs and Total. **Additional costs** may come from shipping or packaging involved with assembling, moving or transferring the inventory. Services involved in the package may also be entered as additional costs. The extra costs for all items transferred should be entered into the Additional Costs field. The **Total** is calculated automatically by Simply Accounting to include the individual costs of all items transferred or assembly components plus any additional costs. Adrienne Aesthetics has additional costs of $50 ($5 per package) for wrapping materials and gift boxes.

Click   the **Additional Costs field**.

Type   50   **Press** `tab` to update the total.

The cursor advances to the first line in the Item column of the **Assembled Items** section. This section refers to the new or reserved inventory, the item being assembled or the "to" part of the transfer.

Press   `enter` or **click** the **List icon** to display the familiar inventory selection list.

Click   **VP01 Valentine Gift: super pkg** to select the item we created.

Click   **Select** or **press** `enter` to add the item to the item assembly form and advance to the Quantity (Qty) field.

Type   10

The unit cost of the assembled items is the total cost of the assembly components, plus additional costs, divided by the quantity or number of units assembled. When a single type of item is assembled and the quantity is greater than one, it is simpler to enter the quantity and the amount (the Total in the assembly components portion in the top half of the form) and let Simply Accounting calculate the unit cost. You can also enter the individual item cost in the Unit Cost field and allow the program to calculate the Amount (Qty times Unit Cost). We will enter the total from the upper portion of the journal.

Click the **Amount field**.

Type 560 **Press** (tab) to enter the cost and update the unit cost and total.

The totals in the two parts of the assembly form should be the same. If they are not, you will be unable to post the entry.

Your completed form should now resemble the following:

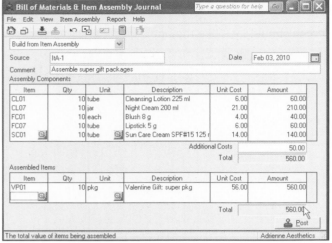

Reviewing the Item Assembly Journal Entry

Choose the **Report menu**, then **click Display Bill Of Materials & Item Assembly Journal Entry** to display the transaction you have entered:

Notice that Simply Accounting has moved the inventory items from their original asset accounts (credit entries) to the newly created inventory account (debit entry). When you display inventory selection lists or quantity reports, you will see that the quantities for all items involved have been updated. The necessary items are taken out of their regular individual item inventory account and transferred to the new account. Thus the quantities of the original items are reduced because they have been transferred to the new account. Additional Costs are assigned to *Item Assembly Costs*, the linked account defined for these costs. This is a contra-expense account because it adds to the inventory value of the assembled inventory asset.

Close the **display** to return to the Item Assembly Journal input screen.

CORRECTING THE ITEM ASSEMBLY JOURNAL ENTRY

Move to the field that has the error. **Press** (tab) to move forward through the fields or **press** (shift) and (tab) together to move back to a previous field. This will highlight the field information so you can change it. **Type** the **correct information** and **press** (tab) to enter it. You must advance the cursor to the next invoice field to enter a change.

You can also use the mouse to **point** to a field and **drag** through the **incorrect information** to highlight it. **Type** the **correct information** and **press** (tab) to enter it.

If an inventory item is incorrect, **press** (enter) while the cursor is in the Item field to **display** the appropriate list. **Double click** the **correct inventory item**. **Re-enter** the **quantity** and **press** (tab) to update the totals.

Because the item assembly is a complex transaction, it is very easy to make a mistake, so check your work carefully. You may also want to store the original entry. If you discover later that you have made an error, you can recall the entry and add a minus sign to each quantity and to the Additional Costs amount to create a reversing entry.

Click   the **Store button** to display the familiar Store Recurring Transaction screen:

Because this is not a regular recurring transaction, we will use the Random frequency. Choosing the Random frequency for recurring entries enters the session date as the default transaction date when you recall the journal entry.

Click   **Monthly** to display the Frequency options.

Click   **Random** to select this frequency.

Click   **OK** to save the entry and return to the Item Assembly Journal. Notice that the Recall button is now active.

Posting

Click   **Post** when you are certain that all the information is correct.

Enter   the next **assembly transaction**. When you post it, you will see the message about low inventory:

> Advisor: Entries just processed caused one or more inventory items to drop below the reorder point. Print the Inventory Item Quantity report to see which items to reorder.
> [Click here to close.]

Click   the **Advisor message** to close it.

Close   the **Journal** to return to the Inventory & Services module window.

Click   **Receivables** in the Modules pane list to restore this window.

Add   shortcuts for **Item Assembly** and **Inventory Adjustments** from the Inventory & Services list in the Customize Shortcuts window.

Enter   the **purchase invoice adjustment**. (Open the journal and click the Adjust tool.)

Selling to Preferred Customers

Simply Accounting allows you to record different inventory prices and to identify customers by the prices they will pay (preferred or regular). Sales for both groups of customers are entered the same way since the program automatically enters the correct price depending on the customer selected. Valley TV is a preferred customer — Preferred is entered as the Price List on the customer's Options tab screen.

Click   the **Sales Invoices icon** 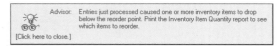 to open the Sales Journal.

Pay Later is the correct selection for this sale to Valley TV. The Invoice number is also correct by default.

Choose Valley TV (CKOV) from the customer list.

WARNING!
When you recall an Item Assembly transaction, the unit costs and amounts for assembly components may be different from the original entry. The average cost may have changed since you posted the entry if you purchased new components at different prices. The new average cost price will be displayed. The quantities will be correct.

NOTES
Customers may also be identified as using Web prices or another user-defined price list.

> **Enter**   **Feb. 4** in the Date field.
>
> **Choose**   **Hydra** as the salesperson in the Sold By field.
>
> **Double click**   the **Item field** to see the inventory list.
>
> **Scroll down**   and then **double click CL03 Eye Contour Smoothing Cream 30 ml** to add it and advance to the Quantity field.

This adds the first item sold to the customer at the preferred customer price of $32.00 instead of $35.00, the regular price.

> **Type**   5   **Press** (tab).
>
> **Enter**   the **remaining items** sold to this customer to complete the journal entry as shown:

You should review the entry as usual.

> **Choose** the **Report menu** and **click Display Sales Journal Entry**:

Adrienne Aesthetics			
02/04/2010 (J9)	Debits	Credits	Division
1200 Accounts Receivable	1,241.90	-	
5060 Cost of Goods Sold	210.00	-	
1310 Creams and Lotions	-	170.00	
1320 Face Care Products	-	40.00	
2640 PST Payable	-	34.40	
2650 GST Charged on Sales	-	57.50	
4020 Revenue from Sales	-	430.00	
4040 Revenue from Services	-	720.00	
	1,451.90	1,451.90	

This entry is the same as a regular non-discounted sale. Revenue is reduced because of the change in selling price but this change is not recorded as a discount.

> **Close**   the **display** when finished and **make corrections** if necessary.
>
> **Post**   the **entry** and **close** the **Sales Journal**.
>
> **Continue**   with the **journal entries** up to the sales return on February 8.

Entering Sales Returns

Customers may return purchases for many different reasons. For example, the size, colour or quality may have been other than expected. Stores have different policies with respect to accepting and refunding returns. Most stores place reasonable time limits on the period in which they will give refunds. Some stores offer credit only and some

WARNING!
If the Price List is not entered in the customer's record, you must manually change all the prices in the journal. You cannot choose the price list in the journal.

charge a handling fee on goods returned. Adrienne Aesthetics will provide full refunds for purchases within two weeks of the sale if the items have not been opened. Sales returns are entered in the Sales Journal and are very similar to sales, but the quantity is entered with a minus sign — a negative quantity is sold. Different accounts may be used.

Open　the **Sales Journal** if it is not open from the previous transactions.

The return must use the same customer and payment method as the original sale.

Choose Visa from the Paid By list.

Choose Cash Customers from the Customer list.

You should use a different invoice number so that the return can be differentiated from a normal sale.

Click　the **Invoice field** and **type** 22-R

Enter　**Feb. 8** in the Date field if this is not the date shown already.

Enter　**Blossom** as the salesperson.

Double click　the **Item field** to see the inventory list.

Scroll down　and **double click CL08 Protection Cream: dbl action 60 ml** to enter it and move the cursor to the Quantity field.

This adds the first item returned by the customer at the regular price.

Type　-1　**Press** ⟨_tab_⟩.

Notice that a positive amount appears in the Price field and a negative amount is added to the Amount field — a positive price times the negative quantity. We should also change the default account so that returns can be tracked separately.

Click　the **Account field List icon** 🔍 and **choose 4050 Sales Returns**.

Enter　the **second item** returned by this customer. Your finished journal entry should look like the following one:

NOTES
Most stores have separate forms for returns with their own separate number sequences.

NOTES
The salesperson should be entered for sales returns because commissions are calculated on total sales less returns.

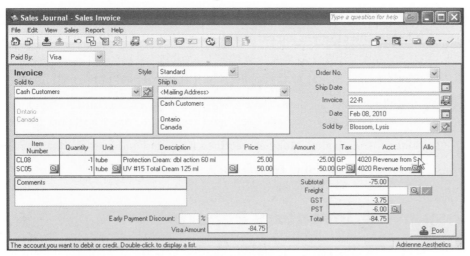

Choose the **Report menu** and **click Display Sales Journal Entry** to review it:

Adrienne Aesthetics			
02/08/2010 (J22)	Debits	Credits	Division
1310 Creams and Lotions	12.00	-	
1330 Sun Care Products	22.00	-	
2640 PST Payable	6.00	-	
2650 GST Charged on Sales	3.75	-	
4050 Sales Returns	75.00	-	
1090 Bank Account: Credit Cards	-	82.42	
5040 Credit Card Fees	-	2.33	
5060 Cost of Goods Sold	-	34.00	
	118.75	118.75	

NOTES
When you reverse an invoice that has been paid, Simply Accounting will create a credit note for the customer and assign a number (CN#) for reference.

Notice that the entry is the reversal of a regular sale. The two asset accounts are debited because inventory is added back. *Sales Returns* — a contra-revenue account — is debited, and *Bank Account: Credit Cards* is credited because money has been returned to the customer's credit card account. Similarly, *PST Payable* and *GST Charged on Sales* are debited because the tax liabilities have decreased and finally, the expense accounts, *Credit Card Fees* and *Cost of Goods Sold* are credited because these expenses have gone down.

If the sale was a Pay Later invoice, the sales return entry will add a negative invoice amount to the Receipts Journal for the customer — a credit balance is created.

Close   the **display** when finished to return to the journal. **Make corrections** if necessary.

In the Comment field, you could add the reason for the return. The customer's name and address could be added to the Ship To field or the Comment field.

Post   the **entry** and **close** the **Sales Journal**.

Entering Purchase Returns

Purchase returns are entered in the same way as sales returns — by adding a minus sign to the quantity so that all the amounts become negative. The supplier and payment method must be the same as the original purchase.

Open   the **Purchases Journal**. Pay Later is correct.

Choose   **Biotech Laboratories** as the supplier.

Enter   **BL-669R** as the invoice number and **Feb. 8** as the date.

Choose   **FC10 Powder: loose 15 g** from the inventory selection list and advance to the Quantity field.

Type   −5 (the quantity with a minus sign).

You cannot change the default asset account for inventory purchases or returns.

Change   the **payment terms** to **net 60** so that the credit does not show as overdue.

Review   the **journal entry** to see that it is a reversed purchase entry.

The inventory asset account, *Face Care Products*, and *Accounts Payable* have decreased. *GST Paid on Purchases* has been credited to restore the tax liability.

NOTES
If you open the Payments Journal for Biotech Laboratories, you will see that the return is entered as a negative amount. When you pay the supplier, click the amount field for the return to reduce the amount of the payment.

Close   the **display**. **Make corrections** if needed and **post** the **transaction**.

Enter   the **remaining transactions**.

Displaying Inventory Reports

Most inventory reports can be displayed from the Reports menu in the Inventory & Services window, from the Home window Reports menu, from the Inventory & Services module window Reports pane drop-down list and from the Report Centre. We will access the reports from the Report Centre.

Click   the **Report Centre icon** in any window.

Click   **Inventory & Services** to open the list of inventory reports:

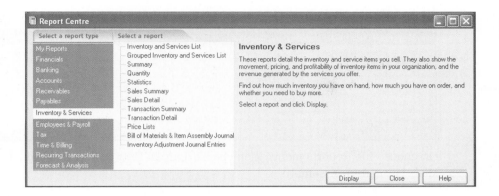

Displaying Inventory Lists

Click   **Inventory And Services List**. **Click Modify This Report**:

Or, you can choose the Reports menu and choose Lists; then click Inventory & Services to see the report options.

To select the fields for the report, choose Report Columns.

Click   **OK** to see the list. **Close** the **display** when you have finished.

Displaying Grouped Inventory Lists

Click   **Grouped Inventory And Services List**. **Click Modify This Report**.

Click   **Type** in the Group By field:

From this list, choose the way you want to sort the list. You can organize by Type (inventory and services are separated) or by any of the additional information fields you created for the ledger. To select the fields for the report, choose Report Columns.

Click   **OK** to see the list. **Close** the **display** when you have finished.

Displaying the Item Assembly Journal

Click   **Bill Of Materials & Item Assembly Journal Entries** to see the report sample and description.

NOTES
If you click the Report Centre icon in the Inventory & Services window, you will open the list of Inventory & Services reports with the first report selected and its sample displayed.

SIMPLY VERSION
Item Assembly Journal Entries replaces Bill of Materials & Item Assembly Journal Entries in the Select A Report Type list.

CLASSIC VIEW
Right-click the Inventory & Services icon . Click the Display tool to open the Modify Report window.

SIMPLY VERSION
The Simply version does not have the option to Include Internal Service Activities.

SIMPLY VERSION
Grouped lists are not available in the Simply version.

NOTES
You can drill down to the Inventory Transaction Detail Report from the Inventory List and from the Grouped Inventory List.

CLASSIC VIEW
Right-click the Bill of Materials & Item Assembly icon . Click the Display tool .

SIMPLY VERSION
In the Report Centre list, click Item Assembly Journal Entries. Or, choose the Report menu, then choose Journal Entries and click Item Assembly.

NOTES
Additional Information for journal entries is covered in Chapter 11.

NOTES
You can drill down to the General Ledger reports from the from the Item Assembly Journal and from the Adjustments Journal.

CLASSIC VIEW
Right-click the Inventory Adjustments icon
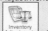. Click the Display tool
.

Click   Modify This Report to open the report options window:

Or, choose the Reports menu, then choose Journal Entries and click Bill of Materials & Item Assembly.

As usual, the earliest transaction date, session date and the Report By Date options are provided by default. The sorting, filtering and column options are the same for all journal reports.

Enter   the **beginning date** for the report you want.

Press   (tab) (**twice** if you type the date).

Enter   the **ending date** for the report.

Click   **OK. Close** the **display** when you have finished.

Displaying the Adjustments Journal

Click   Inventory Adjustment Journal Entries to see the sample.

Click   Modify This Report to open the report options window:

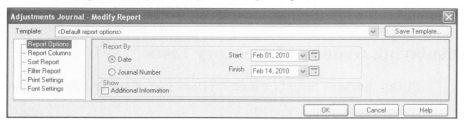

Or, you can choose the Reports menu, then choose Journal Entries and click Inventory Adjustments.

As usual, the earliest transaction date, session date and the Report By Date options are provided by default.

Enter   the **beginning date** for the report you want.

Press   (tab) (**twice** if you type the date).

Enter   the **ending date** for the report.

Click   **OK. Close** the **display** when you have finished.

Displaying Inventory Summary Reports

Click   Summary from the Select A Report list to see the sample.

Click   Modify This Report to open the report options window:

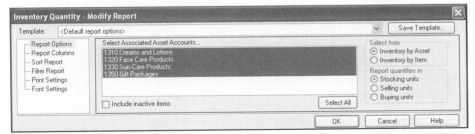

You can also choose the Reports menu, then choose Inventory & Services and click Summary to display the report options.

Selecting **Inventory By Asset** will provide information for all inventory items in the asset group(s) chosen. The **Inventory By Item** option will provide information for all the items selected. When you click Inventory By Item, the box lists all inventory items. Services are not included because there is no quantity or cost information for them.

Click a single asset or item to change selections or provide a report for that item only. To select multiple items, press and hold ⌷ctrl⌷ and then click the items you want in the report. To obtain information for all items, choose Select All.

The **Summary** Report lists the quantity on hand, the unit cost of the inventory and the total value or cost of inventory on hand for the items requested. The total value of the inventory in an asset group is also provided when you select one asset group. You can view the Summary Report for the Latest Transaction Date or for another date by entering a date in the **As At** date field.

You can prepare the report with quantities in any of the units you use for the item if these are different, that is, the stocking, buying or selling units (see page 375).

Choose the **options** you need for your report.

Press and **hold** ⌷ctrl⌷ and **click** the **items** or **assets** you want included.

Click **OK**. **Close** the **display** when you have finished.

Displaying Inventory Quantity Reports

Click **Quantity** from the Select A Report list. **Click Modify This Report**:

Or, choose the Reports menu, then choose Inventory & Services and click Quantity to display the report options.

The **Quantity** Report provides current information for selected items about the quantity on hand, the minimum stock levels and outstanding purchase and sales orders. This report enters the minimum level number in the To Order column when an item has fallen below the minimum level and needs to be re-ordered.

You can select the items for the report in the same way as you did for the Inventory Summary Report. Selecting **Inventory By Asset** will provide information for all inventory items in the asset group(s) chosen. The **Inventory By Item** option will

NOTES
You can customize summary reports by selecting any of the columns usually included in the report. You can sort and filter by item or description.

NOTES
You can drill down to the Inventory Transaction Report from the Inventory Summary or Quantity reports.

NOTES
Select All acts as a toggle switch. When all items are selected, clicking Select All will remove all selections. When one or a few items are selected, clicking Select All will select all the entries on the list.

NOTES
You can customize Quantity Reports by selecting any of the columns usually included in the report. You can sort and filter by most of the columns usually included in the report.

provide information for all the items selected. When you click Inventory By Item, the box lists all inventory items. Services are not included in the Quantity Report because there is no quantity or cost information for them.

> Click a single asset or item to change selections or provide a report for that item only. To select multiple items, press and hold ⌐ctrl⌐ and then click the items you want in the report. To obtain information for all items, choose Select All.

You can prepare the report with quantities in any of the units you use for the item if they are different, that is, the stocking, buying or selling units (see page 375).

> **Choose** the **options** you need for your report.
>
> **Press** and **hold** ⌐ctrl⌐ and **click** the **names** of all the items or asset groups you want to include in the report.
>
> **Click** OK and **close** the **display** when you have finished.

Displaying Inventory Price Lists

The different inventory prices — regular, preferred, Web and customized prices — are not available in the other inventory reports, but you can see all of these prices together on the Price Lists Report.

> **Click** **Price Lists** from the Select A Report list. **Click Modify This Report**:

You can also choose the Reports menu, then choose Inventory & Services and click Price Lists to display the report options.

You can choose the item or items that you want on the price list by selecting them from the list, just as you select items for other inventory reports. You can include Regular, Preferred, Web prices and any customized price lists you created.

> **Click** the **Price List** you want to report on.
>
> **Click** OK to see the price lists and **close** the **display** when you have finished.

Displaying Inventory Tracking Reports

Several reports provide information about the turnover of inventory products. These reports show whether items are selling well and are profitable and how the sales are distributed over time and customers.

Inventory Statistics Reports

Click   **Statistics** from the Select A Report list. **Click Modify This Report**:

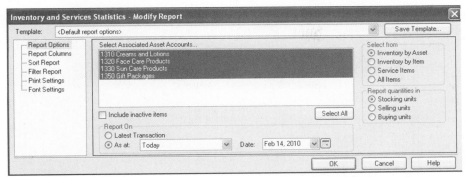

Or, choose the Reports menu, then choose Inventory & Services and click
Statistics to display the report options.

The Statistics Report summarizes transactions for the year to date and the previous
year, the same historical information that is contained in the Inventory Ledger record
(see page 377). You can use the report to determine whether a large volume of sales of
an item resulted from a single sale for a large quantity or from a large number of smaller
sales.

You can prepare the report for the session date (**Latest Transaction**) or for another
date (**As At Date**). When you choose As At, the Date field is available. The report will
show the statistics you request as at the date you enter.

The report shows: the **Number Of Transactions** (the number of separate sales
invoices that included the inventory item); **Units Sold** (the total number of individual
items of a kind that were sold in the period); the **Amount Sold** (the total sale price for
all items sold); and the **Cost Of Goods Sold** (the total purchase cost of all the items that
were sold). Simply Accounting uses the average cost method to calculate the cost of
goods sold.

Press and hold ⌜ctrl⌟ and click one or more asset groups to include them in the
report, or click Select All to include all asset groups in the report. Selecting an
asset group will include all the inventory items in that group in the report. To
select multiple assets or items, press ⌜ctrl⌟ and then click the items you want.

Click **Inventory By Item** to list individual inventory items. Select one or more
items for the report, or click Select All to include all inventory items.

Click **Service Items** to list individual services. Press ⌜ctrl⌟ and hold and click
services to include them, or click Select All to include all services.

Click **All Items** to include both individual inventory items and individual
services in the report. Press ⌜ctrl⌟ and hold and click the items and services to
include them in the report, or click Select All to include all items and services.

The list of items will expand according to your selection, and you can choose single
or multiple items for inclusion. **Quantities** can be reported in any of the units on record
— the units for stocking the inventory, for buying and for selling — if these are different.

Choose the **items** you want in the report.

Choose the **date** for the report (Latest Transaction or As At Date). **Enter** a
         date in the Date field if you chose the As At option.

Click   **OK** to display the report. **Close** the **display** when you have finished.

Inventory Sales Reports

Click   **Sales Summary** from the Select A Report list. **Click Modify This Report**:

Or, choose the Reports menu, then choose Inventory & Services and click Sales.

The reports include the number of transactions (Summary option), the quantity of items sold, the revenue per item, the cost of goods sold and the profit for each item. Non-inventory sales are not included. The **Summary** option, selected by default, shows the total for each detail for the selected inventory items organized by item. The **Detail** option provides the same information listed by individual journal entry, including the source document numbers and journal entry numbers. Click Detail to choose the Detail option. **Quantities** may be reported for stocking, buying or selling units.

As usual, you can choose to report on inventory items, services or both. To report only on all services, click **Service Items** and then Select All. Click **All Items** to include both inventory and services. The list of items will expand accordingly, and you can choose single or multiple items for inclusion. Select All at this stage will provide a report on all inventory and service items.

Again, quantities may be reported in stocking, buying or selling units.

Type   the **starting date** for the report in the Start field and the **ending date** for the report in the Finish field.

Choose   the **items** to include in the report.

Choose   the **Summary** or **Detail** option.

Click   **OK**. **Close** the **display** when you have finished.

Inventory Transaction Reports

The Transaction Report summarizes inventory activity according to the journal used to record the transaction.

Click   **Transaction Summary**. **Click Modify This Report**:

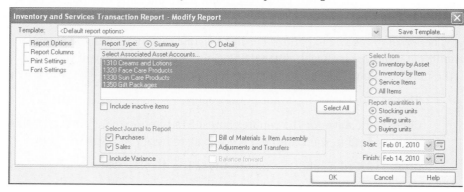

> **NOTES**
> You cannot sort or filter the Sales Report but you can customize the report by selecting the columns you want to include.

> **NOTES**
> To see the Inventory Sales Summary Report on Services, you must click Select From Service Items or choose All Items. The Inventory By Item and Inventory By Asset selections include only inventory items.

> **NOTES**
> You can drill down to the Inventory Detail Report from the Inventory Sales Summary Report. You can display the Customer Aged, Inventory Ledger, Journal Report and Invoice Lookup from the Inventory Sales Detail Report.

> **SIMPLY VERSION**
> Item Assembly is the Journal name in the Simply version instead of Bill of Materials & Item Assembly.

Or, choose the Reports menu, then choose Inventory & Services and click Transaction to display the report options.

The report includes details on the number of transactions (Summary option only), the **Quantity In** (increases to inventory from purchases, sales returns, recovery of lost items or assembled items) and **Out** (decreases in inventory from sales, purchase returns, losses and adjustments or assembly components used) and the **Amount In** and **Out** (cost price) for each item chosen in each of the selected journals. The **Summary** option, selected by default, includes totals for the selected inventory items organized by item. The **Detail** option provides the same information listed by individual journal entry, including the source document numbers and journal entry numbers.

As in the Sales Report, you can prepare a report for one or more asset groups, one or more inventory items, one or more service items or a combination of services and items (All Items). Clicking the appropriate entry in the Select From list will expand the item list accordingly.

Quantities may be reported in stocking, buying or selling units. Variances can also be added to the report when they are used.

You can choose to show the Balance Forward to include opening balances or to Include Variance to add cost variances for each item.

Click   **Detail** to include individual transaction details.

Type   the **starting date** for the report in the Start field and the **ending date** for the report in the Finish field. By default, the earliest transaction and session date appear.

Click   the **journals** to include in the report.

Click   **OK**. **Close** the **display** when you have finished.

Supplier Purchases Reports

The next two reports combine inventory information with supplier or customer details to show how purchases are spread among suppliers and how sales are divided among customers. The Supplier Purchases and Customer Sales reports also allow you to include information for non-inventory purchases or sales.

Click   **Payables** in the Select A Report Type list.

Click   **Supplier Purchases Summary**. **Click Modify This Report**:

Or, choose the Reports menu and choose Payables and click Supplier Purchases.

The Supplier Purchases report includes details on the number of transactions (Summary option only), the quantity purchased, the unit cost and the total cost of the purchase. Non-inventory purchases, such as telephone services, are listed as **Other**.

NOTES
You can drill down to the Transaction Detail Report from the Transaction Summary Report. You can display the Inventory Ledger and Journal Report from the Transaction Detail Report. You can also look up invoices from the Detail Report.

SIMPLY VERSION
This report is named the Vendor Purchases Report.

NOTES
Inventory & Services Amounts will be automatically selected whenever you select an item.

NOTES
You cannot sort or filter the Supplier Purchases Report, but you can select the columns you want in the report.

The **Summary** option organizes the report by supplier and includes totals for the selected categories and items or asset group. The **Detail** option provides the same information by individual journal entry, including the source document numbers and journal entry numbers. Click Detail to choose the Detail option.

The selection of inventory, services or asset groups is the same as for the other inventory reports. Reports can be prepared for either stocking, buying or selling units if these are different.

All items and suppliers are selected initially.

Click   a **supplier name** or item to begin a new selection.

Enter   the **starting date** for the report in the Start field and the **ending date** for the report in the Finish field.

Click a purchase category — Inventory & Services, non-inventory (Other) and Freight charges — to remove the ✓ and deselect it for the selected supplier and item transactions. Click it again to select it.

Click   **OK**. **Close** the **display** when you have finished.

Customer Sales Reports

The Customer Sales Report provides the same details as the Inventory Sales Report, but the Customer Sales Report has the details organized by customer as well as by item. Customer Sales reports also have the option to include non-inventory sales.

Click   **Receivables** in the Select A Report Type list.

Click   **Customer Sales Summary**. **Click Modify This Report**:

Or, choose the Reports menu and choose Receivables and click Customer Sales.

The report includes the number of transactions (Summary option only), the quantity of items sold, the revenue per item, the cost of goods sold and the profit on each sale transaction. Non-inventory sales, such as sales allowances or non-inventory services, are listed as **Other**.

The **Summary** option organizes the report by customer and includes totals for the selected categories and items or asset groups. The **Detail** option provides the same information listed by individual journal entry, including the source document numbers and journal entry numbers. Click Detail to choose the Detail option. Reports can be prepared for stocking, buying or selling units if these are different. All customers and items are selected initially.

Select   **assets**, **inventory** or **services**, **customers**, **dates** and **categories** as you do for Supplier Purchases reports.

Click   **OK**. **Close** the **display** when you have finished.

Gross Margin Income Statement

This financial report becomes relevant when a business sells inventory. The report shows the income after inventory costs have been deducted from revenue and before operating expenses are included. To see this report,

Click **Financials** in the Select A Report Type list.

Click the ⊞ for **Income Statement** to expand the list.

Click **Gross Margin - Standard (under Income Statement)**.

Click **Modify This Report** to open the report options window:

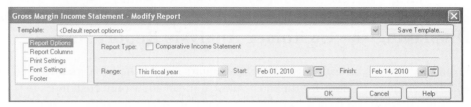

Or, choose the Reports menu, then choose Financial and click Gross Margin Income Statement to display the report options.

The report will include different income amounts: gross margin (revenue minus cost of goods sold, before taking into account the other operating expenses), income from operations (operating expenses are deducted from the gross margin) and net income (non-operating revenue and expenses are entered).

The options for this Income Statement are the same as for regular Income Statements, including the option to generate a Comparative Income Statement.

Type the **starting date** for the report in the Start field and the **ending date** for the report in the Finish field.

Click **OK**. **Close** the **display** when you have finished.

Displaying Forecast and Analysis Reports

This group of reports provides more detailed information about performance and trends.

Click **Forecast & Analysis** in the Select A Report Type list:

Displaying the Forecast Report

The report will provide monthly forecasts for revenues and expenses, based on the same month in the previous year. This report requires data for more than one year.

 WARNING!
You must assign the correct account classes to expense accounts to generate the Gross Margin Income Statement. Cost of Goods Sold Accounts must be correctly identified and separated from other types of expenses.

 NOTES
Refer to page 53 for details on the Comparative Income Statement.

 SIMPLY VERSION
Forecast and Analysis Reports are not available in the Simply version.

Click   **Forecast Summary** and then **click Modify This Report**:

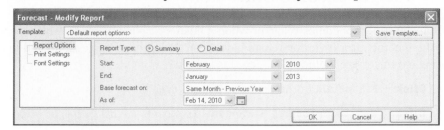

Choose the **months** for which you want the forecast.

Click   **OK**. **Close** the **display** when you have finished.

Displaying the Customer Analysis Report

From this report, you can observe the customer sales for the fiscal year to date to see which customers account for the most sales. You can show only customers in the top or bottom x percent, rank them according to revenue, profit, quantity or return on investment (ROI), and you can select the items you want to report on.

Click   **Customer Analysis** and then **click Modify This Report**:

The Detail Report will show individual journal entries while the summary will give total amounts.

Choose the **reporting period**, **ranking criteria**, **percentage** and **items**.

Click   **OK**. **Close** the **display** when you have finished.

Displaying the Product Analysis Report

The Product Analysis Report, similar to the Customer Analysis Report, is organized primarily by product (items and services). You can select the customers to include. Again, you can rank the sales according to revenues, quantity sold, profit and return on investment. You can choose whether to report on the top x percent or the bottom x percent of items.

Click   **Product Analysis** and then **click Modify This Report**:

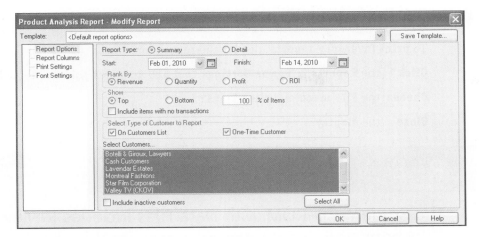

Choose the **reporting period**, **ranking criteria**, **percentage** and **customers**.

Click   **OK**. **Close** the **display** when you have finished.

Displaying the Sales Synopsis Report

The Sales Synopsis Report summarizes sales and receipts. The report includes the items sold, gross sales per item and the methods of payments used.

Click   **Sales Synopsis** and then **click Modify This Report**:

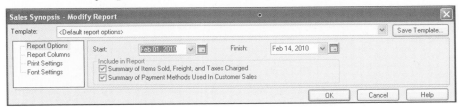

Choose the **reporting period** and the **details** you want in the report.

Click   **OK**. **Close** the **display** when you have finished. **Close** the **Report Centre**.

Displaying Inventory Management Reports

The management reports for the Inventory Ledger focus on potential problem items, inventory items with low markups or items that are not profitable. Management reports are displayed from the Home window Reports menu.

Choose the **Reports menu**, then **choose Management Reports** and **click Inventory & Services**:

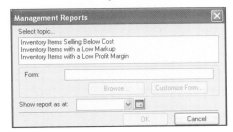

Select   a **report** from the list and choose the report form if necessary.

Click   **OK** to view the report. **Close** the **display** when you have finished.

NOTES
You cannot access Management Reports from the Report Centre.

NOTES
Adrienne currently has no products that meet the Inventory Management Reports' criteria so there will be no data included in these reports.

Printing Inventory Reports

To **print inventory reports**, display the report you want.

Click   the **Reports & Forms Settings tool** to check your printer settings.

Choose the **File menu** and **click Print**.

Close   the **display**.

R E V I E W

The Student CD-ROM with Data Files includes Review
Questions and Supplementary Cases for this chapter.

Andersson Chiropractic Clinic

OBJECTIVES

- **track** additional information for receipts, sales and purchases
- **place** and **fill** supplier orders and quotes
- **enter** and **fill** sales quotes and orders
- **convert** sales and purchase quotes to orders
- **adjust** orders and quotes
- **enter** debit card sale transactions
- **make** payments and deposits using multiple bank accounts and a line of credit
- **enter** deposits from customers and prepayments to suppliers
- **enter** deposits and prepayments on orders
- **delete** stored transactions
- **remove** quotes
- **enter** transactions from the Daily Business Manager

After completing this chapter, you should be able to

COMPANY INFORMATION

Company Profile

Andersson Chiropractic Clinic is a private clinic owned by Maria Andersson, who practises her profession in Regina, Saskatchewan. This is her second year in private practice after graduating as D.C. (Doctor of Chiropractic) and D.Ac. (Doctor of Acupuncture). She used some bank loans and her line of credit to consolidate her student loans and set up the clinic.

Andersson specializes in sports injuries and has some sports teams as clients. To treat patients, she uses chiropractic treatments and adjustments for back pain, and physiotherapy, massage, ultrasound, laser treatments, electrical stimulation and acupuncture for other joint and soft tissue injuries. Individual regular patients usually come two or three times per week, although some come daily. These patients settle their accounts bi-weekly. Sports teams have contracts and are billed monthly. Contract customers are offered a discount if they settle their accounts within 10 days. Cash, cheques and debit cards are accepted in payment.

A single assistant in the clinic divides her time between reception, administration and some basic treatments such as laser and ultrasound under the chiropractor's supervision. Andersson designates the precise area to be treated and the time and intensity settings for the equipment.

The office space that Andersson rents has a reception area and four treatment rooms with tables. The monthly rent includes heat but not hydro or telephone. One of the four treatment rooms doubles as Andersson's office and another room has the potential to accommodate a whirlpool. She is considering adding a whirlpool for hydrotherapy and deep water massage treatments because some sports injuries respond well to hydrotherapy.

For new sports team contracts, Andersson prepares sales quotes. When new customers accept a contract, they pay a deposit that is applied to the first month's payment.

Andersson has two bank accounts and a line of credit she uses to pay her bills. The limit on her line of credit is $50 000, and she has already borrowed $15 000 against it. A third bank account is used exclusively for debit card transactions.

Accounts for regular suppliers of treatment equipment, linens, laundry services, office maintenance and so on, are set up. Some of these suppliers also offer discounts for early payments and some require Andersson to make prepayments with purchase orders.

No taxes are charged for medical treatment and supplies. Because GST is not charged to customers, the business is not eligible for a GST refund. Therefore tax amounts are not tracked — they are included with the expense or asset amounts. Andersson pays both PST and GST for other goods and services.

To convert her accounting records to Simply Accounting on October 1, 2010, she used the following information:

- Chart of Accounts
- Trial Balance
- Supplier Information
- Patient/Customer Information
- Accounting Procedures

CHART OF POSTABLE ACCOUNTS

ANDERSSON CHIROPRACTIC CLINIC

ASSETS
1060 Bank: Regina Chequing
1080 Bank: Eastside Chequing
1100 Bank: Interac
1200 Accounts Receivable
1220 Prepaid Insurance
1240 Prepaid Subscriptions
1280 Purchase Prepayments
1300 Linen Supplies
1320 Office Supplies
1340 Other Supplies
1420 Computer Equipment
1430 Accum Deprec: Computers
1450 Treatment Equipment
1460 Accum Deprec: Equipment
1520 Office Furniture ▶

▶1530 Accum Deprec: Furniture
1550 Treatment Tables
1560 Accum Deprec: Tables
1580 Vehicle
1590 Accum Deprec: Vehicle

LIABILITIES
2100 Loans Payable
2200 Accounts Payable
2250 Prepaid Sales and Deposits
2300 Line of Credit Payable

EQUITY
3400 M.A. Capital
3450 M.A. Drawings
3600 Net Income ▶

▶**REVENUE**
4100 Revenue from Services
4150 Sales Discounts
4200 Interest Income

EXPENSE
5010 Bank Charges and Interac Fees
5030 Purchase Discounts
5050 Office Supplies Used
5060 Other Supplies Used
5080 Subscriptions and Books
5090 Insurance Expense
5100 Interest Expense
5110 Freight Expense
5120 Clinic Maintenance ▶

▶5140 Laundry Services
5150 Professional Dues
5180 Depreciation Expenses
5200 Hydro Expense
5240 Telephone Expense
5260 Rent
5300 Vehicle Expenses
5500 Wages Expense
5520 Payroll Services

NOTES: The Chart of Accounts includes only postable accounts and the Net Income or Current Earnings account.

TRIAL BALANCE

ANDERSSON CHIROPRACTIC CLINIC

September 30, 2010

		Debits	Credits				Debits	Credits
1060	Bank: Regina Chequing	$33 530		▶ 3450	M.A. Drawings		18 000	
1080	Bank: Eastside Chequing	19 100		4100	Revenue from Services			114 000
1100	Bank: Interac	3 430		4150	Sales Discounts		140	
1200	Accounts Receivable	12 500		4200	Interest Income			160
1220	Prepaid Insurance	1 600		5010	Bank Charges and Interac Fees		390	
1240	Prepaid Subscriptions	480		5030	Purchase Discounts			210
1300	Linen Supplies	1 300		5050	Office Supplies Used		350	
1320	Office Supplies	270		5060	Other Supplies Used		1 130	
1340	Other Supplies	530		5080	Subscriptions and Books		2 400	
1420	Computer Equipment	4 200		5090	Insurance Expense		8 000	
1430	Accum Deprec: Computers		$ 1 050	5100	Interest Expense		2 500	
1450	Treatment Equipment	12 600		5110	Freight Expense		120	
1460	Accum Deprec: Equipment		2 100	5120	Clinic Maintenance		2 100	
1520	Office Furniture	9 600		5140	Laundry Services		1 800	
1530	Accum Deprec: Furniture		800	5150	Professional Dues		495	
1550	Treatment Tables	8 400		5180	Depreciation Expenses		10 850	
1560	Accum Deprec: Tables		1 400	5200	Hydro Expense		1 200	
1580	Vehicle	22 000		5240	Telephone Expense		1 100	
1590	Accum Deprec: Vehicle		5 500	5260	Rent		23 000	
2100	Loans Payable		45 000	5300	Vehicle Expenses		1 300	
2200	Accounts Payable		7 290	5500	Wages Expense		21 000	
2300	Line of Credit Payable		15 000	5520	Payroll Services		450	
3400	M.A. Capital		33 355 ▶				$225 865	$225 865

SUPPLIER INFORMATION

ANDERSSON CHIROPRACTIC CLINIC

Supplier Name (Contact)	Address	Phone No. Fax No.	E-mail Web Site	Terms
Canadian Chiropractic Association (O. Fisshal)	33 Backer Road Toronto, Ontario M4T 5B2	Tel 1: (416) 488-3713 Tel 2: (888) 488-3713	www.cca.ca	net 10
Cleanol and Laundry Services (Bessie Sweeps)	19 Duster Road Regina, Saskatchewan S4R 4L4	Tel: (306) 398-0908 Fax: (306) 398-8211	bsweeps@cls.com www.cls.com	net 30
Grasslands Fuel				net 1 (cash)
Medical Linen Supplies (Oll Whyte)	500 Agar St. Saskatoon, Saskatchewan S7L 6B9	Tel: (306) 662-6192 Fax: (306) 662-4399	owhyte@medsupplies.com www.medsupplies.com	2/10, n/30
OnLine Books			www.onlinebooks.com	net 1 (cheque)
Prairie Power Corp. (M. Jouls)	48 Powers Bay Regina, Saskatchewan S4X 1N2	Tel: (306) 395-1125	www.prairiepower.ca	net 1
Pro Suites Inc. (Kendra Walls)	19 Tenant Cr. Regina, Saskatchewan S4N 2B1	Tel: (306) 396-6646 Fax: (306) 396-5397	walls@prosuites.com www.prosuites.com	net 1 (first of month)
Sonartek Ltd. (T. Waver)	390 Retallack St. Regina, Saskatchewan S4R 3N3	Tel: (306) 579-7923 Fax: (306) 579-8003	twaver@sonartek.com www.sonartek.com	2/15, n/30
The Papery				net 15
Thera-Tables Inc. (Li Flatte)	60 Flatlands Cr. Saskatoon, Saskatchewan S7K 5B1	Tel: (306) 662-6486 Fax: (306) 662-7910	www.theratables.com	2/5, n/30
Western Communications (V. Du Parler)	99 Listener St. Regina, Saskatchewan S4R 5C9	Tel: (306) 395-5533	www.westcom.ca	net 1

OUTSTANDING SUPPLIER INVOICES

ANDERSSON CHIROPRACTIC CLINIC

Supplier Name	Terms	Date	Invoice No.	Amount	Total
Cleanol and Laundry Services	net 30 net 30	Sep. 14/10 Sep. 28/10	CLS-2419 CLS-2683 Balance owing	$90 90	 $180
Medical Linen Supplies	2/10, n/30	Sep. 26/10	MLS-102		$690
Sonartek Ltd.	2/15, n/30	Sep. 22/10	SL-3456		$6 420
			Grand Total		$7 290

PATIENT INFORMATION

ANDERSSON CHIROPRACTIC CLINIC

Patient Name (Contact)	Address	Phone No. Fax No.	E-mail Web Site	Terms Credit Limit
Albert Blackfoot	16 Prairie Bay Regina, Saskatchewan S4N 6V3	Tel: (306) 582-1919	ablackfoot@shaw.ca	net 15 $500
Canadian Royals (K. Player)	1910 Buckingham St. Regina, Saskatchewan S4S 2P3	Tel: (306) 578-4567 Fax: (306) 578-7382	kplayer@canroyals.com www.canroyals.com	1/10, n/30 $5 000
Interplay Ballet School (S. Lightly)	2755 Flamenco St. Regina, Saskatchewan S4V 8C1	Tel: (306) 396-6190 Fax: (306) 396-8186	lightly@lighterthanair.com www.lighterthanair.com	1/10, n/30 $5 000
Roughrider Argos (B. Ball)	2935 Fowler St. Regina, Saskatchewan S4V 1N5	Tel: (306) 399-8000 Fax: (306) 399-8115	 www.proball.com/ra	1/10, n/30 $5 000
Suzanne Lejeune	301 Pasqua St. Regina, Saskatchewan S4R 4M8	Tel: (306) 573-6296	slejeune@hotmail.com	net 15 $500

OUTSTANDING PATIENT INVOICES

ANDERSSON CHIROPRACTIC CLINIC

Patient Name	Terms	Date	Invoice No.	Amount	Total
Canadian Royals	1/10, n/30	Sep. 29/10	#638	$4 500	$4 500
Interplay Ballet School	1/10, n/30	Sep. 26/10	#632	$3 100	$3 100
Roughrider Argos	1/10, n/30	Sep. 29/10	#639	$4 900	$4 900
			Grand Total		$12 500

Accounting Procedures

Taxes

Since medical services are not taxable, patients do not pay GST or PST on the treatments and GST paid is not refundable. Therefore, no taxes have been set up in the data files, and no tax options are available in the journal Tax fields. Andersson pays provincial tax at the rate of 6 percent and GST at 5 percent on normal purchases — medical equipment is not taxed. All prices are shown with taxes included but taxes are not recorded separately — they are included with the expense or asset part of purchases.

Cash and Debit Card Sales

Andersson's individual patients frequently pay by Interac or debit card. Sales invoice amounts are deposited directly to the linked bank account. For this service, Andersson pays a small fee to the bank for each transaction, as well as a monthly rental fee for the terminal. These fees are deducted from the account periodically and are not deducted from deposits for individual transactions. Rather than create a large number of small invoices, debit card transactions are summarized every two weeks.

Payroll

Andersson's assistant is paid a monthly salary through arrangements with the bank. In lieu of a salary, Andersson draws $2 500 per month.

Discounts

Customers (sports teams) who have contracts with Andersson are offered a 1 percent discount if they pay their accounts in full within 10 days. Full payment is requested within 30 days. Individual patients are asked to pay their accounts every two weeks. Some suppliers also offer discounts for early payments.

    All discount terms are set up in the customer and supplier records.

Deposits

When sports team managers sign new contracts for regular monthly billing for treating the team members, they pay a deposit to Andersson. Similarly, some suppliers ask for a deposit or prepayment when Andersson places a large order.

Revenue and Expense Accounts

The customer records for Andersson Chiropractic Clinic are set up with *Revenue from Services* as the default account. For suppliers, the account most often associated with purchases for a supplier has been entered as the default for that supplier.

Bank Accounts and Line of Credit

Andersson has two chequing accounts for deposits and payments. A third bank account is used for all Interac or debit card payments.

    Andersson also uses her line of credit when making payments by cheque. At the end of each month Andersson makes a payment for the interest owing on the line of credit used. When she has the funds, she also pays down the principal owing.

    All cheque numbers are updated automatically when the correct account is selected.

INSTRUCTIONS

1. **Record entries for the source documents** in Simply Accounting using the Chart of Accounts, Supplier Information, Patient Information and Accounting Procedures for Andersson Chiropractic Clinic. The procedures for entering each new type of transaction in this application are outlined step by step in the Keystrokes section following the source documents. These transactions are indicated with a ✓ in the completion box beside the source document. The page on which the relevant keystrokes begin is printed immediately below the check box.

2. **Print** the **reports and graphs** indicated on the following printing form after you have finished making your entries.

REPORTS

Accounts

- [ ] Chart of Accounts
- [ ] Account List
- [ ] General Journal Entries

Financials

- [x] Comparative Balance Sheet: amounts only for Oct. 31, 2010, and Nov. 30, 2010
- [x] Income Statement from Dec. 1, 2009, to Nov. 30, 2010
- [x] Comparative Trial Balance: amounts only for Nov. 30 and Dec. 1, 2010
- [x] All Journal Entries: Oct. 1 to Nov. 30
- [ ] General Ledger
- [x] Statement of Cash Flows from Oct. 1 to Nov. 30
- [x] Cash Flow Projection Detail Report for accounts 1060 and 1080 for 30 days

Taxes

- [ ] Tax

Banking

- [ ] Cheque Log Report

Payables

- [ ] Supplier List
- [x] Supplier Aged Detail for all suppliers
- [ ] Aged Overdue Payables
- [ ] Expenses Journal Entries
- [ ] Payments Journal Entries
- [x] Pending Supplier Orders as at Jan. 15, 2010

Receivables

- [ ] Patient List
- [x] Patient Aged Detail for all customers
- [ ] Aged Overdue Receivables
- [ ] Patient Statements
- [ ] Fees Journal Entries
- [ ] Receipts Journal Entries
- [x] Pending Patient Orders as at Jan. 15, 2010

Mailing Labels

- [ ] Labels

Management Reports

- [ ] Ledger

GRAPHS

- [ ] Payables by Aging Period
- [ ] Payables by Supplier
- [ ] Receivables by Aging Period
- [ ] Receivables by Patient
- [x] Fees vs Receivables
- [x] Receivables Due vs Payables Due
- [ ] Revenues by Account
- [ ] Expenses by Account
- [x] Expenses and Net Profit as % of Revenue

SIMPLY VERSION

In the Simply version, the terms Purchases and Vendors will replace Expenses and Suppliers.

Sales, Customer and Invoice will replace Fees, Patient and Statement.

WARNING!

Two bank accounts and the line of credit are available for receipts and payments. Before posting a transaction, check carefully that you have selected the right account.

SOURCE DOCUMENTS

SESSION DATE – OCTOBER 7, 2010

[x] **Purchase Quote #TT-44**   **Dated October 1, 2010**

413   Delivery date October 10, 2010
From Thera-Tables Inc., $4 000 including taxes for custom-built adjustable height treatment table with drop ends. Terms: 2/5, n/30. Deposit of 10 percent required on accepting quote.

[ ] **Purchase Quote #MT-511**   **Dated October 1, 2010**

Delivery date October 20, 2010
From Medi-Tables (use Quick Add for the new supplier), $4 550 including all taxes for custom-built treatment table. Terms: net 20. Deposit of 20 percent required on accepting quote.

[x] **Purchase Order #TT-44**   **Dated October 2, 2010**

415   Delivery date October 10, 2010
To Thera-Tables Inc., $4 000 including taxes for custom-built treatment table. Terms: 2/5, n/30. Convert quote #TT-44 to purchase order #TT-44.

[x] **Cheque Copy #567**   **Dated October 3, 2010**

417   To Thera-Tables Inc., $400 from Regina Chequing account as prepayment in acceptance of quote #TT-44 and to confirm order #TT-44.

[x] **Cheque Copy #103**   **Dated October 3, 2010**

419   To Sonartek Ltd., $6 291.60 from the line of credit in payment of account including $128.40 discount for early payment. Reference invoice #SL-3456.

☐ **Cash Purchase R2010-10**   **Dated October 3, 2010**

To Pro Suites Inc., cheque #121 for $2 300 to pay rent for October. Store the transaction as a monthly recurring entry. Pay from Eastside Chequing account.

☐ **Cheque Copy #568**   **Dated October 4, 2010**

To Medical Linen Supplies, $676.20 from Regina Chequing account in payment of account including $13.80 discount for early payment. Reference invoice #MLS-102.

☑ **Cash Receipt #58**   **Dated October 4, 2010**

419   From Interplay Ballet, cheque #447 for $3 069 in payment of account including $31 discount for early payment. Reference invoice #632. Deposited to Eastside Chequing account.

☑ **Sales Quote #51**   **Dated October 4, 2010**

420   Starting date October 15, 2010
To Giant Raptors (use Full Add for the new customer), a local basketball team, $3 500 per month for unlimited chiropractic services during the regular six-month training and playing season. Andersson will attend or be on call for all home games. If the team enters the playoffs, the contract may be extended for $1 200 per week. Terms: 1/10, n/30. A deposit of $2 000 will be required on acceptance of the contract. Enter 6 as the number ordered.

☑ **Memo #1**   **Dated October 5, 2010**

422   After some negotiations with the Giant Raptors, Andersson agreed to reduce the contract price to $3 300 per month for the playing season. Playoff games will be billed at $1 100 per week. Adjust the sales quote to change the price.

☑ **Sales Order #51**   **Dated October 5, 2010**

423   Starting date October 15, 2010
The Giant Raptors have accepted the modified sales quote #51. Convert the quote to a sales order. All terms and dates are unchanged from the revised quote for $3 300 per month.

☑ **Cash Receipt #59**   **Dated October 6, 2010**

424   From the Giant Raptors, cheque #838 for $2 000 as deposit #14 to confirm sales order #51. Deposited to Regina Chequing account.

SESSION DATE – OCTOBER 14, 2010

☐ **Cash Receipt #60**   **Dated October 8, 2010**

From Roughrider Argos, cheque #1122 for $4 851 in payment of account including $49 discount for early payment. Reference sales invoice #639. Deposited to Eastside Chequing account.

☐ **Cash Receipt #61**   **Dated October 8, 2010**

From Canadian Royals, cheque #3822 for $4 455 in payment of account including $45 discount for early payment. Reference sales invoice #638. Deposited to Regina Chequing account.

☑ **Purchase Order #44 and Cheque #104**   **Dated October 9, 2010**

426   Delivery date October 19, 2010
From Sonartek Ltd., $6 000 including taxes for ultrasound machine with multiple frequencies and interchangeable wands. Terms: 2/15, n/30. Deposit of $1 500 paid with cheque #104 from Line of Credit Payable account to confirm order.

NOTES
Each month, the sales invoice for Giant Raptors will be entered as partially filling the order.

NOTES
Giant Raptors
☐ (contact Rex Saurus)
550 Tyrannus Dr.,
Regina, SK S4R 5T1
Tel 1: (306) 398-8753
Tel 2: (306) 398-5339
Fax: (306) 398-5339
E-mail: rex@raptors.com
Web: www.raptors.com
Terms: 1/10, n/30
Revenue account: 4100
Credit limit: $5 000

✓ **Purchase Invoice #TT-4599**   **Dated October 10, 2010**

428   From Thera-Tables Inc., to fill purchase order #TT-44 for $4 000 including taxes for custom-built treatment table. Terms: 2/5, n/30.

✓ **Sales Invoice #649**   **Dated October 10, 2010**

430   To Giant Raptors, to fill the first month of the contract on sales order #51 for $3 300. Terms: 1/10, n/30.

✓ **Cash Receipt #62**   **Dated October 13, 2010**

431   From the Giant Raptors, cheque #939 for $1 267 in full payment of account including $33 discount for early payment. Reference sales invoice #649 and deposit #14. Deposited to Eastside Chequing account.

Quote:	52
Date:	Oct 13, 2010
Starting date:	Oct 25, 2010
Customer:	Veronica Kain
	Veronica Kain School of Dance
	35 Lady Slipper Rd.
Address:	Regina, SK S3V 4H7
Phone No:	(306) 376-3218

Andersson Chiropractic Clinic
www.betterbacks.com
4500 Rae St.
Regina, Saskatchewan S4S 3B4
Tel 1: (306) 577-1900
Tel 2: (306) 577-2199   Fax: (306) 577-1925

QUOTE

Treatment description	Amount
Chiropractic services for the school year (Sep-Jun) Monthly contract rate $1 000 deposit when contract accepted Contract may be extended for summer months	2 500.00

Terms: 1/10, n/30
Signed: *Maria Andersson* | Customer Initials: *VK* | TOTAL | 2 500.00

✓ **Sales Order #52 and Deposit #15**   **Dated October 14, 2010**

432   Starting date October 25, 2010
From Veronica Kain School of Dance, acceptance of quote #52. Convert the quote to a sales order leaving all terms and amounts unchanged. Received cheque #865 for $1 000 as deposit #15 to confirm sales order #52. Deposited to Eastside Chequing account.

✓ **Debit Card Sales Summary Invoice #650**   **Dated October 14, 2010**

433   To various one-time patients, $260 for initial assessments for new patients and $450 for follow-up treatment sessions. Total amount deposited in Interac bank account, $710. Store as a recurring bi-weekly transaction.

☐ **Cheque Copy #122**   **Dated October 14, 2010**

To Cleanol and Laundry Services, $90 from Eastside Chequing account in payment of account. Reference invoice #CLS-2419.

☐ **Cheque Copy #123**　　　　　**Dated October 14, 2010**

To Thera-Tables Inc., $3 520 from Eastside Chequing account in full payment of account including $80 discount for early payment. Reference invoice #TT-4599 and cheque #567. Remember to "pay" the prepayment.

☐ **Purchase Invoice #CLS-3926**　　　　　**Dated October 14, 2010**

From Cleanol and Laundry Services, $90 for contracted twice weekly laundry service. Terms: net 30. Store the transaction as a bi-weekly recurring entry.

SESSION DATE – OCTOBER 21, 2010

☑ **Purchase Invoice #SL-4622**　　　　　**Dated October 17, 2010**

435　From Sonartek Ltd., to fill purchase order #44, $6 000 including taxes for multi-frequency ultrasound machine. Terms: 2/15, n/30.

☐ **Cash Purchase GF-2641**　　　　　**Dated October 18, 2010**

From Grasslands Fuel, $62 for gasoline for business vehicle. Invoice total $62 paid in full by cheque #569 from Regina Chequing account. Store as bi-weekly recurring entry.

☐ **Cash Sales Invoice #651**　　　　　**Dated October 20, 2010**

To Albert Blackfoot, $315 for seven treatment sessions. Invoice total paid in full by cheque #315 and deposited to Regina Chequing account. Store as monthly recurring entry.

SESSION DATE – OCTOBER 31, 2010

☑ **Sales Invoice #652**　　　　　**Dated October 25, 2010**

437　To Veronica Kain School of Dance, to fill sales order #52, $2 500 for contracted services for one month. Terms: 1/10, n/30. Store as recurring monthly entry.

☐ **Sales Invoice #653**　　　　　**Dated October 25, 2010**

To Interplay Ballet School, $2 500 for contracted services for one month. Terms: 1/10, n/30. Store transaction as recurring monthly entry.

☐ **Purchase Invoice #CLS-4723**　　　　　**Dated October 28, 2010**

From Cleanol and Laundry Services, $90 for contracted laundry service. Terms: net 30. Recall stored transaction.

☐ **Cash Purchase Invoice #WC-83825**　　　　　**Dated October 28, 2010**

From Western Communications, $125 including taxes for one month of telephone and Internet service. Invoice total paid by cheque #124 from Eastside Chequing account. Store as monthly recurring entry.

☐ **Sales Invoice #654**　　　　　**Dated October 28, 2010**

To Canadian Royals, $4 500 for contracted services for one month. Terms: 1/10, n/30. Store transaction as recurring monthly entry.

☐ **Sales Invoice #655**　　　　　**Dated October 28, 2010**

To Roughrider Argos, $4 900 for contracted services for one month. Terms: 1/10, n/30. Store transaction as recurring monthly entry.

NOTES

When you advance the session date to Oct. 31, you will see an advice statement that it is time to prepare for year-end. Read and then close the advisory statement to proceed.

NOTES
Recall the stored transaction but do not store the changed transaction. When you post the transaction, you will see the message that the transaction has changed and the next posting date will be updated. Click Yes to continue. Refer to page 184.

Sales Invoice: 656		
Date: Oct 28, 2010		

Andersson Chiropractic Clinic
www.betterbacks.com

4500 Rae St.
Regina, Saskatchewan S4S 3B4
Tel 1: (306) 577-1900
Tel 2: (306) 577-2199   Fax: (306) 577-1925

Customer: Debit card sales summary

Address:

Phone No:

Treatment description	Amount
Initial assessments	130.00
Follow-up treatments	630.00

Terms: paid by Interac
Direct deposit to Interac account
Signed: *Maria Andersson*   Customer Initials: **INVOICE TOTAL**   760.00

Cash Receipt #63   **Dated October 29, 2010**

From Interplay Ballet, cheque #501 for $2 475 in payment of account including $25 discount for early payment. Reference sales invoice #653. Deposited to Regina Chequing account.

Cheque Copy #570   **Dated October 29, 2010**

To Cleanol and Laundry Services, $180 from Regina Chequing account in payment of account. Reference invoices #CLS-2683 and #CLS-3926.

Bank Debit Memo #477211   **Dated October 29, 2010**

From Eastside Trust, $2 100 for monthly payroll and $45 payroll service fee withdrawn from chequing account. Store payroll transaction as monthly recurring entry.

☑ **Cash Receipt #64**   **Dated October 29, 2010**

438 From Veronica Kain School of Dance, cheque #878 for $1 475 in payment of account including $25 discount for early payment. Reference sales invoice #652. Deposited to Regina Chequing account.

Purchase Quote #45   **Dated October 29, 2010**

Starting date November 1, 2010
From Cleanol and Laundry Services, $210 every two weeks to increase service from twice per week to daily laundry service. Terms: net 30.

Purchase Quote #FS-644   **Dated October 29, 2010**

Starting date November 1, 2010
From Fresh Spaces (use Quick Add for the new supplier), $125 per week for daily laundry service. Terms: net 30.

PO#:   45
Date: Oct 29, 2010
Starting date: Nov 1, 2010

**Andersson
Chiropractic Clinic**
www.betterbacks.com

Ordered from: Cleanol and Laundry Services
Address: 19 Duster Road
               Regina, SK S4R 4L4
Phone No: (306) 398-0908
Fax No:
Contact: Bessie Sweeps

4500 Rae St.
Regina, Saskatchewan S4S 3B4
Tel 1: (306) 577-1900
Tel 2: (306) 577-2199   Fax: (306) 577-1925

PURCHASE ORDER

Order description	Amount
Contract for daily laundry service bi-weekly rate including GST terms: net 30 days	210.00
Ref: quote #45	
Order Total	210.00
Deposit	——
Balance Owing	210.00

Authorization: *Maria Andersson*

Memo #2   **Dated October 31, 2010**

Transfer $1 060 from the Regina Trust Chequing account to pay down the line of credit. This amount includes $60 for one month of interest on the amount of credit used. Store as monthly recurring entry. (Use the General Journal.)

SESSION DATE – NOVEMBER 7, 2010

✓ **Memo #3**   **Dated November 1, 2010**
439 Review memos and enter the next transactions from the Daily Business Manager.

✓ **Cheque Copy #571**   **Dated November 1, 2010**
440 To Sonartek Ltd., $4 380 from Regina Chequing account in full payment of account including $120 discount for early payment. Reference purchase invoice #SL-4622 and cheque #568 (prepayment).

✓ **Cash Purchase Invoice #GF-3677** **Dated November 1, 2010**
442 From Grasslands Fuel, $62 for gasoline for business vehicle. Invoice total paid in full from Regina Chequing account by cheque #572. Recall stored entry.

✓ **Cash Purchase R2010-11**   **Dated November 3, 2010**
442 To Pro Suites Inc., cheque #125 for $2 300 from Eastside Chequing account to pay rent for November. Recall stored entry.

✓ **Cash Receipt #65**   **Dated November 5, 2010**
443 From Canadian Royals, cheque #4011 for $4 455 in payment of account including $45 discount for early payment. Reference sales invoice #654. Deposited to Regina Chequing account.

NOTES
To transfer the funds, you should debit the Line of Credit Payable and Interest Expense accounts and credit the bank account.

Cash Receipt #66   **Dated November 7, 2010**

From Roughrider Argos, cheque #1636 for $4 851 in payment of account including $49 discount for early payment. Reference sales invoice #655. Deposited to Eastside Chequing account.

PO#:	46
Date:	Nov 7, 2010
Starting date:	Dec 28, 2010

ANDERSSON Chiropractic Clinic

www.betterbacks.com

Ordered from:	Get Better Whirlpools
Address:	35 Eddy Circle
	Saskatoon, SK S7K 6E3
Phone No:	(306) 665-7210 or
	(877) 699-1270
Fax No:	(306) 663-6281
Contact:	Ira Spinner

4500 Rae St.

Regina, Saskatchewan S4S 3B4

Tel 1: (306) 577-1900

Tel 2: (306) 577-2199   Fax: (306) 577-1925

PURCHASE ORDER

Order description	Amount
therapeutic whirlpool (Model WP-299X) including GST and PST terms: net 20 days	24 000.00
Deposit: $2 000 paid by cheque #573 (Regina Chequing Account)	
Order Total	24 000.00
Deposit	2 000.00
Balance Owing	22 000.00

Authorization: *Maria Andersson*

SESSION DATE – NOVEMBER 14, 2010

Sales Invoice #657   **Dated November 9, 2010**

444   To Giant Raptors, to fill one month of the contract in sales order #51 for $3 300. Terms: 1/10, n/30.

Purchase Invoice #CLS-5884   **Dated November 11, 2010**

445   From Cleanol and Laundry Services, to fill purchase order #45, $210 for contracted daily laundry service. Terms: net 30. Store as bi-weekly recurring entry. (Remove the old stored entry then store new one.)

Debit Card Sales Summary Invoice #658   **Dated November 11, 2010**

To various one-time patients, $260 for initial assessments and $450 for follow-up treatment sessions. Total amount deposited in Interac bank account, $710. Recall the stored transaction.

Cash Purchase Invoice #TP-1188   **Dated November 12, 2010**

From The Papery, $230 for paper supplies for treatment rooms and $60 for office supplies. Invoice total $290 paid in full from Eastside Chequing account by cheque #126.

SESSION DATE – NOVEMBER 21, 2010

☐ **Cash Receipt #67**   **Dated November 18, 2010**

From the Giant Raptors, cheque #1334 for $3 267 in full payment of account including $33 discount for early payment. Reference sales invoice #657. Deposited to Eastside Chequing account.

☐ **Purchase Order #47**   **Dated November 19, 2010**

Starting date January 1, 2011
From HydraTub Care (use Full Add for new supplier), $200 per month, including taxes for one-year service contract. The contract includes weekly maintenance of whirlpool and repairs. Parts required for repairs will be billed separately. Terms: net 20. Create new Group account 5220 Whirlpool Maintenance. Use this as the default expense account for the supplier. You must enter the year for the starting date because it is different from the default entry of 2010.

☐ **Purchase Quote #SU-5532**   **Dated November 19, 2010**

Starting date December 1, 2010
From Space Unlimited (use Quick Add), $2 250 per month for rent of office space for the next 12 months. Rent does not include heat or hydro. Terms: net 1. Rent payment is due on the first of each month. Security deposit of one month's rent required in advance. Postdated cheques will be accepted.

☐ **Purchase Quote #48**   **Dated November 19, 2010**

Starting date December 1, 2010
From Pro Suites Inc., $2 350 per month for rent of office space for the next 12 months. Rent includes heat but does not include hydro. Rent payment is due on the first of each month. A series of postdated cheques will be accepted.

☐ **Purchase Order #48**   **Dated November 20, 2010**

Starting date December 1, 2010
From Pro Suites Inc., $2 350 per month for rent of office space for the next 12 months. Convert purchase quote #48 to a purchase order.

SESSION DATE – NOVEMBER 28, 2010

☐ **Debit Card Sales Summary Invoice #659**   **Dated November 25, 2010**

To various one-time customers, $260 for initial assessments and $630 for follow-up treatment sessions. Total amount deposited in Interac bank account, $890. Recall the stored transaction and edit the amounts. Do not save the changes.

☐ **Purchase Invoice #CLS-6543**   **Dated November 25, 2010**

From Cleanol and Laundry Services, $210 for contracted laundry service. Terms: net 30. Recall stored transaction.

☑ **Sales Invoice #660**   **Dated November 25, 2010**

446   To Interplay Ballet School, $2 500 for contracted services for one month. Terms: 1/10, n/30. Recall stored transaction.

☐ **Sales Invoice #661**   **Dated November 25, 2010**

To Veronica Kain School of Dance, $2 500 for contracted services for one month. Terms: 1/10, n/30. Recall stored transaction.

☐ **Sales Invoice #662**   **Dated November 28, 2010**

To Canadian Royals, $4 500 for contracted services for one month. Terms: 1/10, n/30. Recall stored transaction.

NOTES
HydraTub Care
☐ 550 Splash St.
Regina, SK S4T 7H5
Tel: (306) 578-2996
Terms: net 20
Expense acct: 5220 (Start the Add Account wizard by typing the new account number in the Expense Account field.)

NOTES
The year-end advisor appears when you advance the session date. Read the message and close the advisor.

NOTES
Enter the recurring transactions from the Daily Business Manager.

☐ **Sales Invoice #663**   **Dated November 28, 2010**

To Roughrider Argos, $4 900 for contracted services for one month. Terms: 1/10, n/30. Recall stored transaction.

☐ **Cash Purchase Invoice #WC-122002**   **Dated November 28, 2010**

From Western Communications, $125 including taxes for telephone and Internet service. Invoice total paid from Eastside Chequing account by cheque #127. Recall stored transaction.

☑ **Cheque Copy #128**   **Dated November 28, 2010**

447   To Cleanol and Laundry Services, $300 from Eastside Chequing account in payment of account. Reference invoices #CLS-4723 and CLS-5884.

☐ **Cash Purchase Invoice #PPC-76511**   **Dated November 28, 2010**

From Prairie Power Corp., $380 including taxes for two months of hydro service. Invoice total paid from Regina Chequing account by cheque #574.

SESSION DATE – NOVEMBER 30, 2010

NOTES
Enter the recurring transactions from the Daily Business Manager.

☐ **Cash Receipt #68**   **Dated November 29, 2010**

From Interplay Ballet, cheque #553 for $2 475 in payment of account including $25 discount for early payment. Reference invoice #660. Deposited to Eastside Chequing account.

☐ **Bank Debit Memo #747721**   **Dated November 29, 2010**

From Eastside Trust, $2 100 for monthly payroll and $45 payroll service fee withdrawn from chequing account 1080. Recall stored transaction.

☐ **Memo #3**   **Dated November 30, 2010**

Transfer $1 060 from the Regina Trust Chequing account to pay down the line of credit. This amount includes $60 for one month of interest on the amount of credit used. Recall stored transaction.

☐ **Bank Debit Memo #747937**   **Dated November 30, 2010**

From Eastside Trust, pre-authorized withdrawals from chequing account:
     For bi-monthly loan repayment, $1 370 principal and $230 interest
     For bank service charges and debit card fees, $108

☐ **Bank Debit Memo #120022**   **Dated November 30, 2010**

From Regina Trust, $36 withdrawn from account for service charges.

☐ **Memo #4**   **Dated November 30, 2010**

From Manager: Record the accumulated depreciation for the two-month period for all fixed assets as follows:

Computer Equipment	$ 230
Treatment Equipment	420
Office Furniture	160
Treatment Tables	280
Vehicle	1 100

☐ **Memo #5**   **Dated November 30, 2010**

From Manager: Record the adjusting entries for supplies used in the previous two months:

Office Supplies	$105
Paper and Other Supplies	260

☐ **Cheque Copy #129**   **Dated November 30, 2010**

To M. Andersson (use Quick Add), $5 000 from Eastside Chequing account for drawings to cover personal expenses.

☑ **Memo #6**   **Dated November 30, 2010**

448   From Manager: Three purchase quotes that are on file are no longer valid. Remove quote #MT-511 from Medi-Tables, quote #FS-644 from Fresh Spaces and quote #SU-5532 from Space Unlimited.
Remove recurring transactions for Grasslands Fuel (cash purchase) and Albert Blackfoot (sale) because they will no longer be used.

☐ **Memo #7**   **Dated November 30, 2010**

From Manager: Close out the M.A. Drawings account by transferring the balance to M.A. Capital.

☐ **Memo #8**   **Dated November 30, 2010**

From Manager: Print all financial reports. Back up the data files and start a new fiscal period on December 1, 2010.

KEYSTROKES

Opening Data Files

Restore `SimData\anderson1.CAB` to `SimData\Anderson\anderson` to open the data files for Andersson. **Enter Oct. 7, 2010** as the Session date.

Entering a Purchase Quote

On October 1, Andersson received two quotes for a treatment table that will be delivered later in the month. A quote usually provides a fixed price for some work or products. The offer is often limited to a stated time period. If the business chooses to accept the offer, the quote may be filled as a purchase for immediate delivery or converted to a purchase order for future delivery. When the goods are received, or the work is completed, the quote is filled and the purchase is completed. Supplier quotes are entered and filled in the Expenses or Purchases Journal.

Click   **Payables** in the Modules pane list. Icons are added for quotes and orders.

Click   the **Supplier Quotes icon** shown in the following screen:

Supplier Quotes ▾

NOTES
Enter the drawings cheque as an Other Payment in the Payments Journal. You can add a memo number as the source if you want.

NOTES
To close the Drawings account, credit Drawings and debit Capital. You can find the amount in the Trial Balance, Balance Sheet or General Ledger.

NOTES
Refer to page 99 for assistance with starting a new fiscal period if needed.

NOTES
The Payroll, Inventory and Project modules are not included in the Modules pane — they are hidden because these ledgers are not used and are not set up.

Simply **SIMPLY VERSION**
Purchase replaces the term Supplier. Purchase Quotes, Purchase Orders and Purchase Invoices are used as the Home window icon labels.

Simply **CLASSIC VIEW**
Click the Expenses, Orders & Quotes icon to open the journal. Choose Quote from the journal's Transaction drop-down list.

NOTES
For Medical companies, Simply Accounting uses the term Expenses Journal instead of Purchases Journal.

SIMPLY VERSION
Purchases Journal — Quote will appear in the journal's title bar.

NOTES
Notice that Andersson's address is in the Ship To field for the quote.

NOTES
You must choose the supplier before entering the quote number because the supplier issues the quote number.

NOTES
You cannot enter a quantity for quotes.

NOTES
In a purchase order, the B/O (backordered quantity) field is filled in automatically with the order quantity. In a quote, this field remains blank.

NOTES
If you want, you can customize the journal by removing the columns that are not required. Refer to page 166.
You can remove (do not show) the Item, Unit and Allo fields because they are not needed.

The Expenses Journal — Quote window opens.

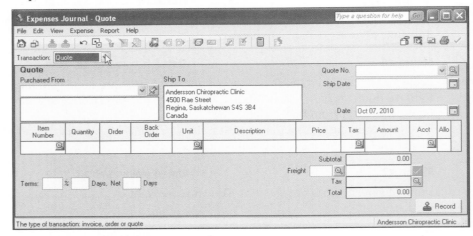

Quote is selected in the Transaction field.

Click   the **Purchased From field** and **select Thera-Tables Inc.**

Click   the **Quote No. field** to advance the cursor and skip the address fields.

Type   TT-44

Press   (tab) **twice** to advance to the Ship Date field and skip the Lookup icon.

This is the date on which the order is to be received or the work is to be completed. Sometimes, instead of shipping date, we use the term delivery date for services or starting date for a contract because these terms are more appropriate for quotes and orders for services.

Type   10-10

Press   (tab) **twice** to advance to the Date field where you should enter the date that the quote was received.

Type   10-1

The Item field refers to the code for inventory items. The Quantity (quantity received with this purchase) field will remain blank because this is not a purchase and no goods are received. However, you must enter the number of units that are ordered. You cannot leave the Order field blank. One table is being ordered.

Click   the **Order field**.

Type   1

Press   (tab) to advance to the Unit field that also applies to inventory.

Press   (tab) to advance to the Description field.

Type   custom-built treatment table

Press   (tab) to advance to the Price field. This field refers to the unit price of the items.

Type   4000

Press   (tab) to advance to the Tax field.

Because taxes are not used in this data set, we can skip the tax fields. The amount is entered automatically as the quantity on order times the unit price.

The account is also entered automatically from the supplier's ledger record, so the quote is complete as shown:

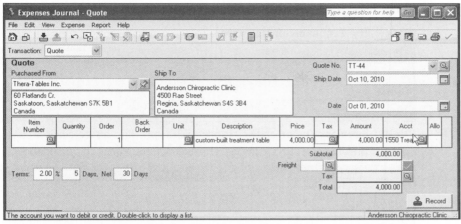

Check your **work** carefully and **make** any **corrections** necessary just as you do for other Purchases Journal entries. Refer to page 116 if you need help correcting the entry.

If you try to display the Expenses Journal entry, you will see that there is no journal entry associated with the quote. The related journal entry will be completed when the quote is filled and the purchase is completed. When you are sure that the entry is correct,

Click the **Record button** 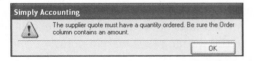 or **choose** the **Expense menu** and **click Record** to save your transaction.

If you forgot to enter the quantity ordered, you will see the following warning:

Simply Accounting
⚠ The supplier quote must have a quantity ordered. Be sure the Order column contains an amount.
OK

Click OK and enter the quantity in the Order field and try again to record.

Enter the **second purchase quote** from a new supplier. Remember to add the account number and payment terms to the quote.

Placing a Purchase Order from a Quote

Sometimes purchase orders are entered without a quote and sometimes they are converted from a purchase quote. Entering a purchase order directly, without the quote, is the same as entering a purchase quote except that you choose Supplier Order as the type of transaction instead of Quote.

The purchase order to Thera-Tables Inc. is a quote converted to an order. The Expenses Journal should still be open and Quote is selected as the Transaction type.

Click the **Quote No. field list arrow** as shown:

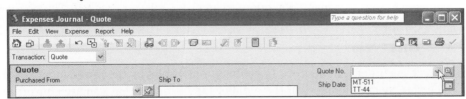

The drop-down list includes all unfilled purchase quotes and purchase orders. The two quotes entered above are listed.

Click **TT-44** to select it.

NOTES
The Post button label changes to Record for quotes and orders because no journal entry is posted.
You should click OK to confirm successful posting or recording of transactions. We will not continue to include this instruction.

NOTES
We will use the terms purchase order and supplier order interchangeably, unless the term appears in the Simply Accounting screen.

Press   tab to select the quote and place it on-screen.

Click   the **Transaction list arrow** to see the transaction types as shown:

Click   **Supplier Order** as the transaction type. The quote screen changes to a purchase order. Order No. replaces Quote No. as the field label:

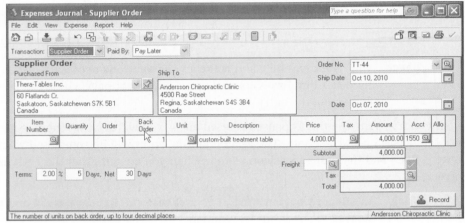

Notice that the purchase order includes a Paid By field. You can enter prepayments with the order. We show this method of entering prepayments on page 426.

The Order quantity has been copied to the Back Order field.

The session date is entered on the revised form so we need to change it. If you try to change the quote number, you will see the warning (see margin note):

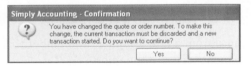

Click No to save the quote information.

Click   the **Date field Calendar icon** .

Choose October 2. Press tab .

Click   the **Record button** 🗍 Record .

The program displays the warning message:

Since we want to convert the quote to an order, we can proceed. The order will replace the quote.

Click   Yes.

Purchase order numbers are updated automatically by the program, just like sales invoice and cheque numbers. If the number for the quote that you are converting is larger than the next purchase order sequence number, a second warning will appear when you record the order because the number is out of sequence. When the number is larger than the next automatic sequence number for purchase orders, Simply Accounting asks if you want to update your sequence starting number:

This does not apply to the alphanumeric number we used.

Click Yes if you want to reset the numbering sequence for future purchase orders. Click No to avoid resetting the automatic sequence to the higher number. The higher purchase order number will still be recorded but the automatic counter will not be changed.

Close   the **Supplier Order window**.

Making a Prepayment to a Supplier

Businesses frequently request a deposit — down payment or prepayment — when an order is placed, especially for customized orders. Deposits may be refundable or not. A deposit may be used to pay for materials that are ordered specifically for a project; it may ensure that the purchaser will follow through with the order or it may provide the supplier with some revenue if the order is cancelled and part of the deposit is not refundable.

Prepayments can be made in the Payments Journal or in the Supplier Order Journal window. If the prepayment accompanies the order, you should enter it on the Order form. This prepayment is made later, so we will enter it in the Payments Journal.

Click   the **Payments icon** to open the Payments Journal.

Click   the **Enter Supplier Prepayments tool** or **choose** the **Payment menu** and **click Enter Prepayments**.

SIMPLY VERSION
Click the Enter Vendor Prepayments tool.

NOTES
Entering a prepayment on the Supplier Order form is shown on page 426.

This tool button/menu option acts as a switch that opens the fields for deposits:

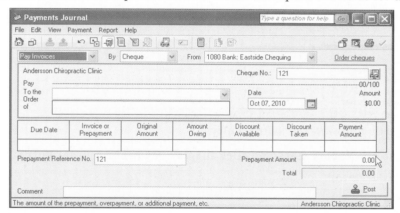

Two new fields are added to the journal: one for the prepayment reference number and one for the amount. The reference number is the next cheque number in sequence for the selected bank account and is updated automatically by the program. The rest of the journal is the same as before, but the invoice payment lines are not used. Outstanding invoices, if there are any, will be included in the journal. When the payment is made by cheque, the From field has the list of bank accounts you can choose. The default bank account and cheque number are not correct. We must change them.

Click   the **From field list arrow** to see the list of available bank accounts:

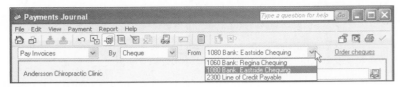

Click   Bank: Regina Chequing.

When you select a different bank account, the cheque number is updated for the new account. Each bank account has its own cheque number sequence, and these numbers are updated as you make payments from each account.

If an outstanding invoice is paid with the same cheque, enter the invoice payment in the usual way in addition to the deposit amount.

Choose   Thera-Tables Inc. as the supplier from the drop-down list.

Enter   October 3 as the date of the cheque.

Click   the **Prepayment Amount field**.

Type   400

Click   the **Comment field**. Advancing the cursor updates the Total.

Type   Prepayment for order #TT-44

The entry is complete and the journal looks like the one shown here:

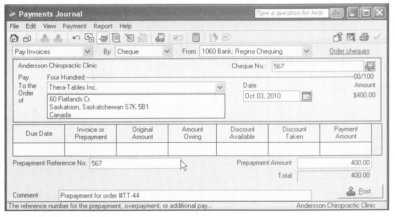

You are ready to review the journal entry.

Choose the **Report menu** and **click Display Payments Journal Entry**:

Andersson Chiropractic Clinic			
10/03/10 (J1)	Debits	Credits	Partner
1280 Purchase Prepayments	400.00	-	
1060 Bank: Regina Chequing	-	400.00	
	400.00	400.00	

As for other payments, the bank account is credited. However, the prepayment creates an asset until the order is filled, so *Purchase Prepayments*, the linked asset account, is debited. If there is no previous balance owing to the supplier, the prepayment creates a debit balance for the account. After the purchase, when you pay the supplier, the prepayment will be displayed in red under the heading "Prepayments" and you "pay" it by accepting the amount, just as you do to pay the invoice itself.

Close   the **display** when you have finished and **make corrections** to the
        journal entry if necessary.

Click   Post [Post] to save the transaction.

> ### NOTES
> Notice that the journal entry number (J1) has not increased because of the quotes and orders.

> ### NOTES
> For corrections to deposits or prepayments after posting, use the Adjust tool or refer to Appendix C. They can also be reversed, just like receipts. (See page 179.)

Click   the **Enter Supplier Prepayments tool** again to close the prepayment fields.

Entering Payments from a Line of Credit

Choose **Sonartek** from the Supplier list to enter the next payment.

This payment is made from Andersson's line of credit. However, *Bank: Regina Chequing* is still selected as the bank account in the From field.

Click   the **From list arrow** to select a different account as shown:

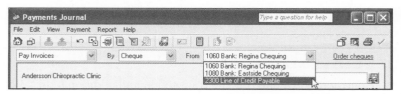

The line of credit is a liability account that operates like a bank account, but it has a credit balance. By defining it as a Bank class account, it can be used to write cheques in the Payments Journal.

Choose **Line of Credit Payable** to select this account and to update the cheque number for the new account.

Enter   the cheque **date**, the **discount** amount and the **payment amount**.

Press   `ctrl` **+ J** to open the journal display:

Andersson Chiropractic Clinic			
10/03/10 (J2)	Debits	Credits	Partner
2200 Accounts Payable	6,420.00	-	
2300 Line of Credit Payable	-	6,291.60	
5030 Purchase Discounts	-	128.40	
	6,420.00	6,420.00	

The only difference between this entry and the earlier payment entries is the use of *Line of Credit Payable* as the account that is credited. This increases the business liability — more money has been borrowed against the line of credit available.

Close   the **journal display**. **Check** your transaction **details** carefully.

Post   the **payment** when you are certain the details are correct.

Choose **Make Other Payment** from the transaction drop-down list.

Enter   the **cash purchase** from Pro Suites. Remember to change the selected bank account and to store the transaction.

Choose **Pay Invoices** from the transaction drop-down list.

Enter   the **payment** to Medical Linen Supplies on October 4. Remember to change the selected bank account.

Close   the **Payments Journal**.

Entering Additional Information for Transactions

The tool bar in journals has an icon for the option of adding information to a journal report. This Additional Information tool allows tracking of one additional date and one other field for transactions in all journals. Andersson has chosen to enter the number of the invoice paid as additional information so it can be included in journal reports.

Click   **Receivables** in the Modules pane list.

NOTES
The Credit Card account class is assigned to Bank: Interac so it does not appear with the list of banks.
The Bank account class is available for all Balance Sheet accounts from the Options tab in the General Ledger. Account classes were introduced in Chapter 7, page 218.

NOTES
You can click the Invoice/Prepayment field and press `tab` to accept the discount and payment amounts.

SIMPLY VERSION
Choose Pay Purchase Invoices from the transaction list.

NOTES
You can name the additional fields in the Company Settings Names window.

Click   the **Receipts icon** to open the Receipts Journal.

Customize the **tabbing order** for the journal so that the cheque number follows the customer. Refer to page 169.

Choose **Interplay Ballet**. The default bank account is correct.

Enter   the **cheque number**, **date**, **discount** and **amount received**.

Click   the **Enter Additional Information tool** [✓] or **choose** the **Receipt menu** and **click Enter Additional Information**:

You can enter one additional date for the transaction and additional text. Both will be available for journal reports when you show the Additional Information (page 451). You can rename these fields as part of the company setup.

Click   the **Additional Field** text box.

Type   `Ref: inv #632`

Click   **OK** to return to the journal.

Adding the additional details does not change the appearance of the journal. You are ready to review the transaction before posting it.

Choose the **Report menu** and **click Display Receipts Journal Entry** to display the transaction you have entered as follows:

Andersson Chiropractic Clinic		Debits	Credits	Partner
10/04/10 (J5)				
1080 Bank: Eastside Chequing		3,069.00	-	
4150 Sales Discounts		31.00	-	
1200 Accounts Receivable		-	3,100.00	
		3,100.00	3,100.00	
Additional Date:			Additional Field: Ref: inv #632	

In addition to the usual debit and credit details, the invoice number entered as additional information is included in the display so that you can check it as well.

Close   the **display** to return to the Receipts Journal input screen and **correct** your **work** if necessary. (Refer to page 172 for assistance.)

Click   **Post** [Post] .

Close   the **Receipts Journal** to return to the Home window.

Entering a Sales (Patient) Quote

Sales quotes are like purchase quotes. They offer a customer a guaranteed price for a limited time for merchandise or for work to be completed. The customer may choose to accept or reject the offer.

Quotes are entered from the Patient Quotes icon shown in the expanded view Receivables window:

NOTES
You can also use the Comment field to enter the additional information for the journal report.

WARNING!
Because the additional field information is optional, the program does not warn you if you forget to enter it. Therefore, you should make reviewing the journal entry routine practice.

Separate icons are added for orders and quotes, just as they are for the suppliers.

Click the **Patient Quotes icon** 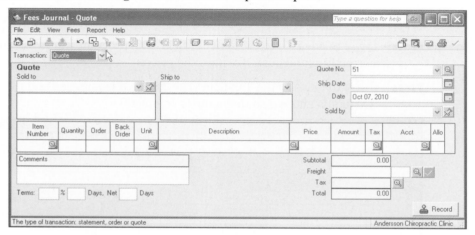 to open the Fees Journal.

The invoice screen changes to the form for a patient quote:

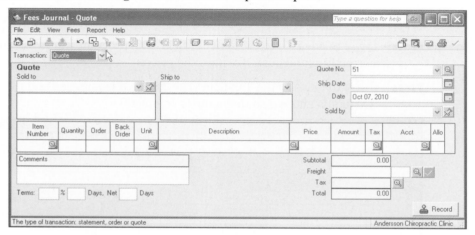

The quote is completed in much the same way as the sales invoice. However, you must enter a quantity in the Order field, just as you did for purchase quotes and orders. The quote number is entered and updated automatically from the defaults for the Receivables Ledger.

Additional fields are not available for quotes and orders. The tool is dimmed.

Click the **Sold To field**.

Type `Giant Raptors` in the Sold To field and **press** `tab`.

Notice that you cannot choose Continue for new customers when entering quotes.

Choose Full Add and add the customer/patient record.

Patient Name (Contact)	Address	Phone No. Fax No.	E-mail Web Site	Revenue Account	Terms Credit Limit
Giant Raptors (Rex Saurus)	550 Tyrannus Dr. Regina, Saskatchewan S4R 5T1	Tel 1: (306) 398-8753 Tel 2: (306) 398-5339 Fax: (306) 398-5339	rex@raptors.com www.raptors.com	4100	1/10, n/30 (change default terms) $5 000

Click **Save And Close** 🖫 Save and Close after entering all the customer details.

You will return to the quote screen with the account and payment terms added.

Side notes:

SIMPLY VERSION
Sales Quotes, Sales Orders and Sales Invoices will replace the icon labels Patient Quotes, Patient Orders and Statements.
Click the Sales Quotes icon to open the form you need.

CLASSIC VIEW
Click the Fees, Orders & Quotes icon to open the journal, and choose Quote from the journal's Transaction drop-down list.

SIMPLY VERSION
Sales Journal — Quote will appear in the journal's title bar instead of Fees Journal — Quote.

WARNING!
You must choose Quote as the Transaction type before entering the customer. Otherwise, a blank quote screen replaces the previous one and you must re-enter the customer.

NOTES

For services such as those provided by Andersson, the term Shipping Date is not appropriate. In the source documents, we use Starting Date instead.

Click   the **Ship Date field** to move the cursor because the shipping address and quote number are correct.

Type   10 15

Drag through   the **date in the Date field**.

Type   10 4

Click   the **Order field**.

Instead of entering the quote as the monthly rate and filling it in the first month, we will enter it as a six-month contract with monthly unit prices. After each month of service, the quote will be partially filled with one month of service.

Type   6

Click   the **Description field**.

Type   6 months of service

Press   `tab` to move to the Price field. You must complete the Price field.

Type   3500

Press   `tab` to advance to the Amount field. The program enters the amount correctly as the quantity times the price.

Press   `tab` to move to the Tax field. The Tax field is not used and the account is entered so the quote is complete:

WARNING!

If you do not enter a price in the Price field, you cannot fill the quote or order. When you choose this option, the form will remain incomplete.

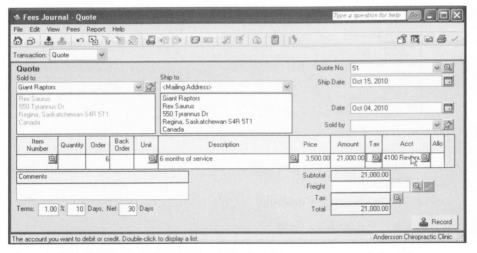

Check   the **quote** carefully and **correct mistakes** just as you do in sales invoices. Refer to page 166 for assistance if needed.

There is no journal entry to display. When a quote is filled by making a sale, the journal entry will be created.

Click   **Record** [Record] to save the quote.

Leave   the **Fees Journal open** to adjust the quote.

Adjusting a Sales Quote

Sometimes a quote contains an error or must be changed if prices are renegotiated. You can adjust sales and purchase quotes and orders after recording them just as you can adjust sales and purchase invoices after posting.

The Fees Journal — Quote screen should still be open.

Click   the **Quote No. field list arrow** to see the list of quotes on file.

Click   **51** to select the quote you just entered.

Press   ⟨tab⟩ to add the quote to the screen:

At this stage, you cannot edit the quote.

Click   the **Adjust Quote tool** 🗒 or **choose** the **Fees menu** and **click Adjust Quote** to open the fields for editing.

Click   **3,500.00** in the Price field.

Type   3300 **Press** ⟨tab⟩ to update the subtotal and total amount to $19 800.

Drag through the **date in the Date field**.

Type   10-5 to enter the date for the revised quote.

Click   the **Comments field** and **type** Revised quote

Check   your **work** carefully.

Click   **Record** ⬜ Record to save the revised quote. Keep the journal open.

Converting a Sales Quote to a Sales Order

Sales quotes can be converted to orders just as purchase quotes can be converted to purchase orders.

The Fees Journal should be open with Quote selected as the transaction type.

Click   **Quote** in the Transaction field and then **click Patient Order** as shown:

Click   the **Order No. field list arrow** and **click 51**, the quote number we want.

⚠ WARNING!
If Quote is not selected as the Transaction type, you will convert the quote to a sales order, or fill the quote when you bring the quote on to the screen.

📝 NOTES
To view and adjust orders and quotes, you do not need to use the lookup or search features we used to adjust purchase and sales invoices after posting. Orders and quotes are available directly from the Order/Quote No. field.

📝 NOTES
Pressing ⟨ctrl⟩ + A will open the quote fields for editing. In other journals, pressing ⟨ctrl⟩ + A opens the Adjust An Invoice Search window.

📝 NOTES
All fields in a quote can be edited, except the name and address details. To change the name, you must remove the quote and re-enter it for the correct customer. However, you cannot use the same quote number twice.

Simply SIMPLY VERSION
Choose Sales Order in the Transaction field.
The term Invoice will replace Statement in the Transaction list.

SIMPLY VERSION
You will see Sales Journal –
Sales Order in the journal title bar.

NOTES
The Quote No. field is
labelled Order No. as soon as you
modify the form.

Press (tab) to place the revised quote on-screen as a patient order:

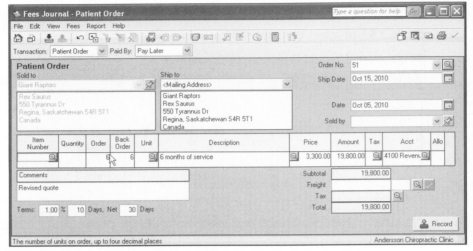

The order quantity — 6 — has been added to the Back Order field.

> **Enter**   **October 5** as the sales order date if necessary.

> **Check**   all the **details** carefully because there is no journal entry to review.

All other details should be correct for the order because they have not changed.
The order can be edited at this stage if needed. We will revise the comment.

> **Click**   the **Comments field**. **Type** Order based on revised quote

> **Click**   **Record** to save the sales order and see the warning:

Since we want to change the quote to an order, we should proceed.

> **Click**   **Yes**.

> **Close**   the **Fees Journal** so that you can enter the customer's deposit.

Entering Customer Deposits

NOTES
We will enter the next
customer deposit directly in the
sales order (page 432).

Andersson also requests deposits from her customers when they place orders. Deposits
are entered in the Receipts Journal in the same way as supplier prepayments are
entered in the Payments Journal. The customer deposit tool opens fields for a reference
number and an amount.

> **Click**   the **Receipts icon** to open the Receipts Journal.

SIMPLY VERSION
Click the Enter Customer
Deposits tool – Customer
replaces the term Patient in the
Simply version.

> **Click**   the **Enter Patient Deposits tool** 🗗 or **choose** the **Receipt menu** and
> **click Enter Deposits**.

This tool button/menu option acts as a switch that opens the fields for deposits:

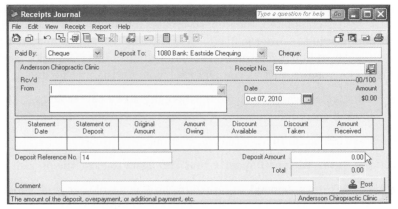

The two new fields added to the journal for the reference number and for the amount serve the same purpose as they do for supplier prepayments. The reference number is the deposit number and is updated automatically by the program. The invoice lines are not used for the deposit. Outstanding invoices, if there are any, will be included in the journal. If they are being paid with the same customer cheque, enter the receipt in the usual way in addition to the deposit amount.

The receipt number is updated and correct, but we need to change the bank account.

Choose Giant Raptors from the Rcv'd From drop-down list.

Click the **Cheque field**.

Type 838

Enter **October 6** as the date of the cheque.

Click the **Deposit To list arrow** to see the list of bank accounts:

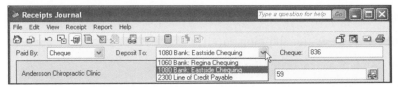

Just as we can pay from any of the accounts that we identify as Bank class accounts, we can deposit to any bank account.

Choose Bank: Regina Chequing to change the account selection.

Click the **Deposit Amount field** at the bottom of the journal.

Type 2000 **Press** (tab).

Click the **Enter Additional Information tool** ⌨️ , or **choose** the **Receipt menu** and **click Enter Additional Information**.

Click the **Additional Field** text box.

Type Deposit for SO #51

Click **OK** to return to the journal so you can review the transaction.

Choose the **Report menu** and **click Display Receipts Journal Entry**:

Andersson Chiropractic Clinic			
10/06/10 (J6)	Debits	Credits	Partner
1060 Bank: Regina Chequing	2,000.00	-	
2250 Prepaid Sales and Deposits	-	2,000.00	
	2,000.00	2,000.00	
Additional Date:		Additional Field: Deposit for SO #51	

As for other receipts, the bank account is debited. The account credited is *Prepaid Sales and Deposits*, a liability account linked to the customer deposits field. If the customer has no previous outstanding balance, the deposit creates a credit entry for the account. Until the sale is completed, the deposit creates a liability — we owe the customer this amount until the order is filled. After the sale, when the customer pays the invoice, the deposit will be displayed in red under the heading "Deposits" and it is "paid" by accepting its amount, just as you enter receipts for the invoice itself.

Close   the **display** when you have finished and **make corrections** to the journal entry if necessary.

Click   Post ![Post] to save the transaction.

Click   the **Enter Patient Deposits tool** ![icon] again to close the deposit fields.

Close   the **Receipts Journal** to return to the Receivables module window.

Change   the **session date** and **enter** the **next two receipts**. Remember to **change** the selected **bank account** when necessary.

Placing a Purchase Order with Prepayment

Placing a purchase order directly without the quote is similar to entering a purchase quote. For this order, a prepayment is included so we will enter it directly on the order.

Click   **Payables** in the Modules pane list to open the Payables window.

Click   the **Supplier Orders icon** 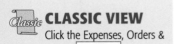 to open the Expenses Journal with Supplier Order selected as the transaction type.

The Order No. is entered automatically (Forms Settings), and it will be incremented automatically because purchase orders are generated in the business.

Choose   **Sonartek Ltd.** from the supplier list.

Enter   **Oct. 19** as the shipping date.

Enter   **Oct. 9** as the order date.

Click   the **Order field**.

Type   1 **Press** (tab).

The program automatically completes the Back Order field with the quantity on order. The entire order quantity is considered as backordered.

Click   the **Description field**.

Type   ultrasound machine **Press** (tab) to move to the Price field.

Type   6000 **Press** (tab).

If the account number is not entered by default, or if it is incorrect for this order, choose the correct account from the Account field selection list.

We will now enter the prepayment details.

Click   the **Paid By field list arrow** to see the payment options:

The options are the same as they are for other payments.

CLASSIC VIEW

Click the Expenses, Orders & Quotes icon ![Expenses, Orders & Quotes] to open the journal, and choose Purchase Order from the journal's Transaction drop-down list.

SIMPLY VERSION

Click the Purchase Orders icon to open the Purchases Journal with Purchase Order selected as the transaction type.

NOTES

You must choose the type of transaction before selecting the supplier or customer. If you do not, the supplier or customer field will be cleared when you select a different type of transaction.

Click   **Cheque** to open the Paid From bank account field. *Bank: Eastside Chequing*, the default bank account, is entered.

Click   the **Paid From list arrow** to see the familiar list of Bank class accounts:

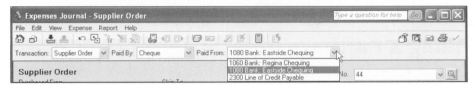

Choose **Line of Credit Payable** to open the cheque number field with the next cheque number for this account.

A Prepayment Paid field has also been added at the bottom of the order form. By default the entire order amount is entered so we need to change it. $1 500 is being paid at this time.

Click   the **Prepayment Paid field** to select the default amount.

Type   1500 **Press** (tab).

The order form is now complete as shown:

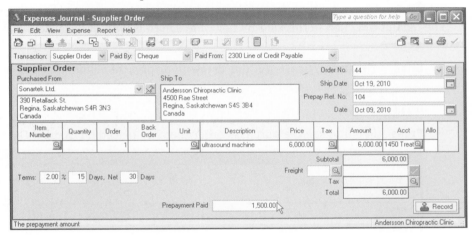

Check   the **order** details carefully.

Because we have now actually entered a transaction that affects our account balances, there is a journal entry to review.

Choose the **Report menu** and **click Display Expenses Journal Entry**:

Andersson Chiropractic Clinic			
10/09/10 (J9)	Debits	Credits	Partner
1280 Purchase Prepayments	1,500.00	-	
2300 Line of Credit Payable	-	1,500.00	
	1,500.00	1,500.00	

This prepayment journal entry is the same as the one we made earlier from the Payments Journal (page 418).

Close   the **journal display** to return to the order.

Make   **corrections** if necessary. **Click Record** [Record] to save the order. Leave the journal open for the next transaction.

Entering a Sales Order

Sales orders are entered in the same way as sales quotes, except that you start with the Patient or Sales Order form instead of the Patient or Sales Quote form.

SIMPLY VERSION
Choose Display Purchases Journal Entry from the Report menu.

Click Receivables in the Modules pane and click the Patient Orders icon. Then
choose the customer and complete the order details. The Order field cannot be
left blank. Sales order numbers are generated by the customer; they are not
entered or updated by the program. Enter the customer's sales order number.

Filling a Purchase Order

When an ordered item is received, or work is completed, you must complete a purchase
invoice entry to record the transaction. Andersson will record the purchase order
number in the Additional Field for the journal reports.

The Expenses Journal should still be open. Supplier Order is selected as the
Transaction type and must be changed.

Choose Invoice from the Transaction list as shown:

The default selection in the Paid By field, Pay Later, is correct because this is a
credit purchase.

> **Click**   the **Order/Quote No. list arrow** to display the numbers for all unfilled
> quotes and orders.

> **Click**   **TT-44**.

> **Press**   ⌞tab⌟ to see the purchase order that was placed on October 3:

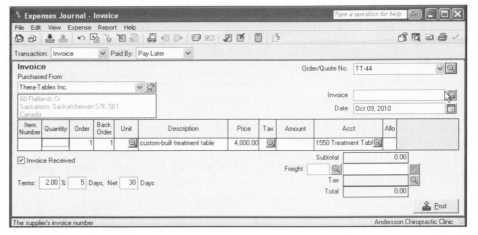

Notice that the prepayment made in the Payments Journal does not show on the
invoice and that the full amount is invoiced. When the prepayment is added to the order
form, it does appear on the invoice (page 436).

The cursor is in the Invoice field.

> **Type**   TT-4599

> **Press**   ⌞tab⌟ **twice** to advance to the Date field.

> **Type**   10-10

The invoice is still incomplete because the quantity displays as backordered and the
invoice amount is zero. We need to "fill" the order.

Click   the **Fill Backordered Quantities tool** in the tool bar or **choose** the
Expense menu and **click Fill Supplier Order**.

Simply **SIMPLY VERSION**
Choose the Purchase menu
and click Fill Purchase Order.

If you did not enter the price for the order, you must edit the invoice to add the
missing details. Your invoice should now look like the one shown below:

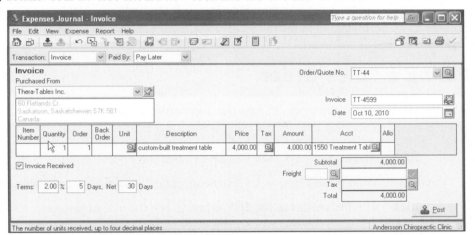

The Back Order quantity has been moved to the Quantity column to reflect the
completion of the order.

NOTES
If the order is partially filled,
the backordered quantity will be
reduced.

Click   the **Enter Additional Information tool** or **choose** the **Expense
menu** and **click Enter Additional Information**:

Simply **SIMPLY VERSION**
Choose the Purchase menu
and click Enter Additional
Information.

This data entry screen is the same for all journals.

Click   the **Additional Field** text box.

Type   Ref: fill P.O. #TT-44

Click   **OK** to return to the journal.

Check   the **entry** carefully to be sure that it is correct.

Choose   the **Report menu** and **click Display Expenses Journal Entry**. You can
see that this is a normal journal entry with the order number as
additional information. Prepayment amounts are not included.

Close   the **display**. When the information is correct,

Click   the **Post button** or **choose** the **Expense menu** and **click Post**
to see the following message:

Filled orders and quotes are not saved, but their numbers cannot be used again.

Click   **OK** to display a new Expenses Journal invoice form.

Close   the **Expenses Journal**.

Click   **Receivables** in the Modules pane list to open the Receivables window
for the next group of transactions.

Filling a Purchase Quote

Filling a purchase quote is similar to filling an order. Choose Invoice, select the quote number and press (tab) to place the quote on-screen as an invoice. The quantity automatically moves to the Quantity column and the total Amount is added. You do not need to choose Fill Backordered Quantities for quotes. Again, you can record the quote number as an additional field for the journal.

Filling a Sales Order

Filling a sales order is similar to filling a purchase order. Sometimes only part of the order is received and the order is not completely filled at once.

Click   the **Statements icon** [Statements ▾] to open the Fees Journal.

Pay Later should be selected as the payment option for the Statement transaction.

Click   the **Order/Quote No. list arrow** to see the available quotes.

Click   **51. Press** (tab) to display the sales order on the invoice screen:

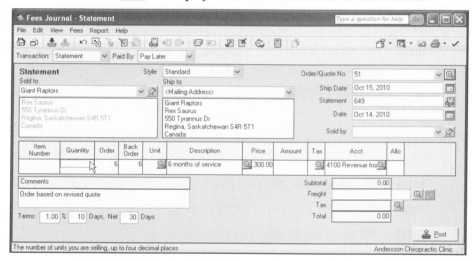

Enter   **October 10** as the transaction date.

Click   the **Quantity field**. Only one month is being billed at this time.

Type   **1** **Press** (tab) to update the invoice as shown:

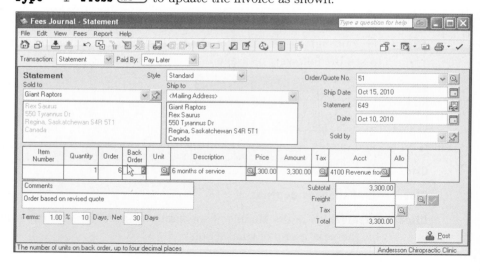

The Amount entered is the fee for one month of service and the Back Order quantity is reduced to five. When the sixth and final month is completed, the order will be filled and removed.

Click   the **Enter Additional Information tool** or **choose** the **Fees menu** and **click Enter Additional Information**.

Click   the **Additional Field** text box.

Type   Ref: S.O. #51

Click   **OK** to return to the journal. We should also modify the comment.

Click   the **Comments field**.

Type   Invoice based on revised quote

Review the **journal entry** and **check** your **work** carefully.

Choose   the **Report menu** and **click Display Sales Journal Entry**.

Close   the **display** to return to the invoice. **Make corrections** if necessary.

Click   **Post**   Post   to record the invoice. The order is not filled, so you do not see the message that the order will be removed.

Close   the **Fees Journal**.

Filling a Sales Quote

Filling a sales quote is similar to filling an order. Choose Statement (or Invoice), select the quote number and press (tab) to place the quote on-screen as an invoice. The quantity automatically moves to the Quantity column and the total Amount is added. You do not need to choose Fill Backordered Quantities for quotes.

Entering Receipts on Accounts with Deposits

The next receipt pays the balance of an account for a customer who has made a deposit.

Click   the **Receipts icon**   Receipts ▾   to open the Receipts Journal.

Choose **Giant Raptors** from the Received From customer drop-down list:

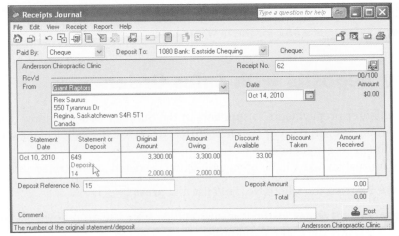

Customer deposits are displayed in red below the outstanding invoices. The colour indicates that they are negative invoices that reduce the balance owing. The invoice is shown with the full amount.

SIMPLY VERSION
Choose the Sales menu and click Enter Additional Information.

NOTES
You can double click the single word Order in the Comment field and type Invoice to replace it.

NOTES
If necessary, drag the lower frame of the journal to include the deposit on the screen or maximize the window.

> **Enter**   **939** as the Cheque number field and **enter Oct 13** in the Date field.
>
> **Click**   the **Discount Taken field** for invoice #649 to accept the discount.
>
> **Press**   (tab) to accept the Amount Received.
>
> **Press**   (tab) **twice** to accept the Deposit amount and update the receipt.
>
> **Enter**   the **invoice number** as additional information to complete the receipt:

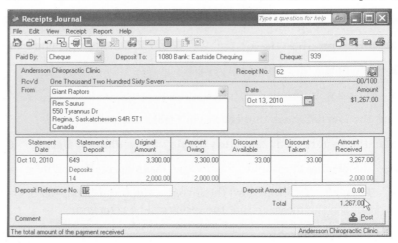

The discount and deposit are subtracted from the full invoice amount so that the total amount now matches the cheque amount.

> **Choose**   the **Report menu** and **click Display Receipts Journal Entry**:

Andersson Chiropractic Clinic			
10/13/10 (J12)	Debits	Credits	Partner
1080 Bank: Eastside Chequing	1,267.00	-	
2250 Prepaid Sales and Deposits	2,000.00	-	
4150 Sales Discounts	33.00	-	
1200 Accounts Receivable	-	3,300.00	
	3,300.00	3,300.00	
Additional Date:		Additional Field: Ref invoice #649 & deposit #14	

Accounts Receivable has been credited for the full invoice amount to clear the invoice. The *Sales Discounts* contra-revenue account has been debited to record the reduction to sales revenue. The *Prepaid Sales and Deposits* account has been debited for the full deposit amount to clear the receivable credit balance, and the bank account is debited for the amount of the cheque.

> **Close**   the **journal display window**. **Make corrections** if necessary.
>
> **Post**   the **receipt** and then **close** the **Receipts Journal**.
>
> **Enter**   **sales quote #52** for the new customer.

Entering Deposits with Sales Orders

Just as you can enter prepayments to suppliers in the Supplier Order window, you can enter customer deposits on the Patient Order form. When the deposit accompanies the order, this method is recommended.

The Fees Journal should still be open with Quote selected as the transaction type.

> **Choose**   **52** from the Quote No. field list and **press** (tab).
>
> **Choose**   **Patient Order** as the transaction type from the drop-down list to convert the quote to an order.
>
> **Click**   the **Paid By list arrow** to see the payment options:

NOTES
The initial deposit creates a liability. The customer has paid us and we have not provided anything yet. When the order is filled, the liability is removed, so the Accounts Receivable balance debit is offset by the initial liability. When the customer pays the invoice for the balance owing, the initial credit entry must be removed from the record.

SIMPLY VERSION
Choose Sales Order from the Transaction list in the Sales Journal.

SIMPLY VERSION
Your screen's title bar will
show Sales Journal — Sales Order.

The same customer payment types are available here as in the Receipts Journal.

Click   Cheque in the Paid By list to open the payment fields we need:

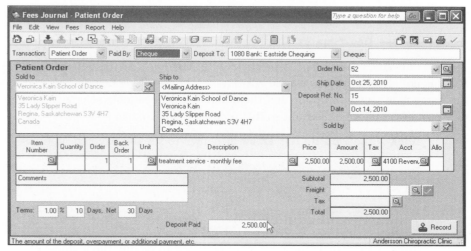

The default bank account is selected for the Deposit To field at the top of the order form. A Cheque number field has also been added to the top of the form and a Deposit Paid field has been added to the bottom of the order form, just like other cash sales.

The session date and bank account are correct so we can add the payment details.

Click   the **Cheque field**.

Type   865

Double click   the **Deposit Paid field**. The full amount of the order is entered as the default amount and we need to change it.

Type   1000

Press   ⎡tab⎤ to update and complete the form.

Choose the **Report menu** and **click Display Fees Journal Entry**:

SIMPLY VERSION
Choose the Report menu
and click Display Sales Journal
Entry.

Andersson Chiropractic Clinic			
10/14/10 (J13)	Debits	Credits	Partner
1080 Bank: Eastside Chequing	1,000.00	-	
2250 Prepaid Sales and Deposits	-	1,000.00	
	1,000.00	1,000.00	

You can see that this journal entry is identical to the journal entry for deposits entered in the Receipts Journal (page 425). The prepayment or deposit with the sales order creates a journal entry although the sales order itself does not.

Close   the **display** and **click Record** [Record] to save the transaction.

Click   **Yes** to confirm that you are changing the quote to an order.

Entering Debit Card Sale Transactions

Customers pay for purchases using cash, cheques, credit cards or debit cards. Debit and credit card purchases are similar for a store — the payment is deposited immediately to the linked bank account. The difference is that debit card transactions withdraw the

NOTES

Fees for debit cards can be lower than credit card fees because the risk of non-payment is eliminated. Debit card payments require the customer's bank balance to cover the amount before the payments are approved.

SIMPLY VERSION

Choose Invoice from the Transaction list. Choose One-Time Customer from the Sold To list.

NOTES

Pay Later is not an option for one-time customers so the Cash Amount (amount received) field is added automatically.

SIMPLY VERSION

You will see Sales Journal – Sales Invoice in the journal's title bar.

money from the customer's bank account immediately while credit cards advance a loan that the customer repays on receipt of the credit card bill. The store pays a percentage discount or transaction fee to credit card companies for the service. For debit card transactions, the store pays a flat fee for each transaction. Both involve a setup fee and a monthly rental charge for the terminal that communicates electronically with the card-issuing company. Andersson uses the name Interac for all debit card transactions.

The Fees Journal should be open from the previous transaction. If it is not, open it by clicking the Statements icon. The session date is correct as the invoice date.

> **Choose** **Statement** from the Transaction list.

> **Choose** **One-Time Patient** from the Sold To list and **press** (tab).

For one-time customers, Cash replaces the Pay Later as the default option — Pay Later is not an option for one-time customers. The Net Days field is removed to match the immediate payment option and the default bank account is selected. The terms for new customers offer no discount so the discount fields are blank.

> **Click** the **Paid By list arrow** as shown to see the payment options:

> **Click** **Interac** as the method of payment to modify the invoice.

There is no bank account field or cheque number field as there is when the payment is made by cheque. Interac is linked automatically to a dedicated bank account as part of the company file setup, just like credit cards. Interac Amount replaces Cash Amount as the label for the amount received.

> **Type** Debit Card Sales Summary (in the Address field).

> **Complete** the rest of the **invoice** in the same way as account or cash sales.

> **Click** the **Description field** and **type** initial assessments

> **Click** the **Amount field** and **type** 260

> **Click** the **List icon** in the Account field to display the Account list.

> **Double click** **4100 Revenue from Services** to add it to the invoice.

> **Click** the **Description field** on the second line of the invoice.

> **Type** follow-up treatments

> **Click** the **Amount field**.

> **Type** 450

> **Click** the **List icon** in the Account field to display the Account list.

> **Double click** **4100 Revenue from Services** to complete the invoice:

[Screenshot: Fees Journal - Statement window]

Choose the **Report menu** and **click Display Fees Journal Entry** to review the entry before posting:

```
Andersson Chiropractic Clinic
10/14/10 (J14)                          Debits        Credits      Partner
  1100  Bank: Interac                   710.00           -
  4100    Revenue from Services            -          710.00
                                        710.00        710.00
```

Notice the new linked account for this transaction. The debit card account — *Bank: Interac* — replaces the usual bank account for other cash sales and *Accounts Receivable* for account sales.

Close   the **display** to return to the Fees Journal input screen.

Make   **corrections** if necessary, referring to page 166 for assistance.

We can store the entry and use it to enter the debit card summaries each week. When you recall the transaction, you can edit the amounts. You will not need to save the changes and store the transaction again.

Click   the **Store tool** 🖫 to save the transaction for repeated entries.

Choose Biweekly as the frequency and **click OK** to save the stored entry.

Click   the **Post button** 🔖 Post .

Close   the **Fees Journal**. **Click Payables** in the Modules pane list.

Enter   the **next three transactions** for October 14.

Advance   the **session date** to October 21.

Filling Purchase Orders with Prepayments

When a prepayment is added directly to the purchase order, the payment details remain on the invoice when you fill the order.

Click   the **Invoices icon** to open the Expenses Journal.

Click   the **Order/Quote No. field list arrow**.

Choose   **order #44** from the Order/Quote No. field drop-down list.

SIMPLY VERSION
Choose the Report menu and click Display Sales Journal.

SIMPLY VERSION
Click the Purchase Invoices icon to open the Purchases Journal.

CLASSIC VIEW
Click the Expenses, Orders & Quotes icon

Press (tab) to add the order details to the invoice form:

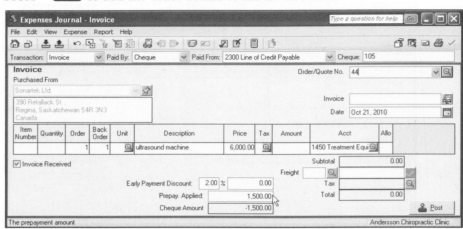

Notice that Cheque is still selected as the Paid By method. The prepayment information from the order is entered as the amount in the **Prepay Applied** field. The cheque amount is negative because no invoice amount has been added yet.

Click the **Fill Backordered Quantities tool** in the tool bar or **choose** the **Expense menu** and **click Fill Supplier Order**.

Now the cheque amount is 4 380.00 — the total invoice amount minus the prepayment and 2 percent discount. This is not a cash purchase, so we need to change the payment method.

Choose Pay Later from the Paid By drop-down list to update the form. The amount owing changes to $4 500 ($6 000 minus the $1 500 prepayment.)

Enter the **invoice number** and **purchase date** to complete the form:

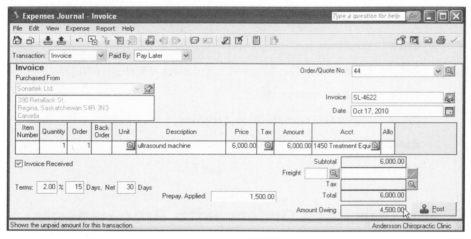

Click the **Additional Information tool** . **Click** the **Additional Information field**.

Type Ref: fill PO #44 **Click OK** to return to the journal.

Press (ctrl) + **J** to open the journal display:

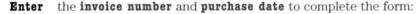

Andersson Chiropractic Clinic			
10/17/10 (J18)	Debits	Credits	Partner
1450 Treatment Equipment	6,000.00	-	
1280 Purchase Prepayments	-	1,500.00	
2200 Accounts Payable	-	4,500.00	
	6,000.00	6,000.00	
Additional Date:		Additional Field: Fill P.O # 44	

The entry is different from the standard journal entry because of the amount for *Purchase Prepayments*. Because the purchase is complete, the credit with the supplier is removed and the prepayment is treated like a partial payment toward the invoice. Thus, *Purchase Prepayments* has been credited to reduce this account's balance to zero. *Treatment Equipment* is debited for the full purchase invoice amount and *Accounts Payable* is credited for the balance owing after the prepayment is subtracted.

When you enter a prepayment in the Payments Journal, Simply Accounting does not know which purchase it is related to, so the prepayment shows later in the Payments Journal for that supplier. It can be applied to any purchase. Entering the prepayment on the order establishes a link to this purchase. When the prepayment is made at the same time as the order, it should be entered on the order. When it is made at a different time, either prior to or later than the order, it should be entered in the Payments Journal.

Close   the **Journal display**.

Make   **corrections** to the invoice if necessary and then **post** the **purchase**.

Click   **OK** to confirm that the order has been filled.

Enter   the **next two transactions**. **Change** modules as needed.

Filling Sales Orders with Deposits

When you advance the session date to October 31, you will see an advisor message:

Click   to close the message about year-end preparation.

Open   the **Fees Journal**. Statement should be selected as the transaction.

Select   **Sales Order #52** from the Order/Quote No. list and **press** (tab) to recall the order:

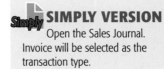**SIMPLY VERSION**
Open the Sales Journal. Invoice will be selected as the transaction type.

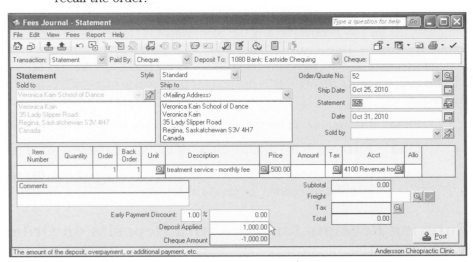

Information about the deposit is included in the invoice. Since the deposit was paid by cheque, this is the default payment method, and we need to change it.

Click   the **Paid By list arrow** and **choose Pay Later** to modify the form.

Click   the **Fill Backordered Quantities tool** 🗐 in the tool bar or **choose** the **Fees menu** and **click Fill Patient Order**.

SIMPLY VERSION
Choose the Sales menu and click Fill Sales Order.

This will update update the amounts on the form:

The Cheque Amount field has been removed but the Deposit Applied details remain. The Amount Owing is reduced by the $1 000 deposit.

Enter   **Oct 25** as the date for the sale.

Click   the **Enter Additional Information tool** 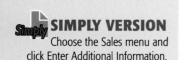 or **choose** the **Fees menu** and **click Enter Additional Information**.

Enter   `Ref SO #52 & deposit #15` in the Additional Field.

Click   **OK** to return to the journal.

Choose   the **Report menu** and **click Display Sales Journal Entry**:

Andersson Chiropractic Clinic

10/25/10 (J21)	Debits	Credits	Partner
1200 Accounts Receivable	1,500.00	-	
2250 Prepaid Sales and Deposits	1,000.00	-	
4100 Revenue from Services	-	2,500.00	
	2,500.00	2,500.00	
Additional Date:		Additional Field: Ref SO #52 and deposit 15	

The entry is similar to the Expenses Journal entry on page 436. Because the sale is complete, the liability is removed and the prepayment is treated like a partial payment toward the invoice. Thus *Prepaid Sales and Deposits* has been debited to reduce this account's balance to zero, *Revenue from Services* is credited for the full sales invoice amount and *Accounts Receivable* is debited for the balance owing after the deposit is subtracted.

Close   the **display**. **Store** the **entry** as a monthly recurring transaction.

Click   **Post** to save the invoice. **Click OK** to confirm the removal of the order.

Enter   the **next group of transactions** up to Cash Receipt #64. **Change modules** as needed, or **create shortcuts**.

Entering Receipts for Sales with Deposits on Orders

When a customer makes the final payment toward an invoice that had a deposit with the sales order, the journal entry is different from an entry with a separate deposit.

Open   the **Receivables module window**.

Open   the **Receipts Journal** and **select Veronica Kain School of Dance**:

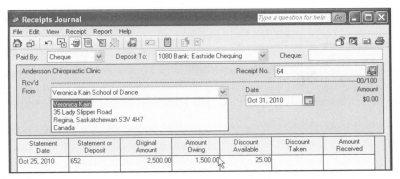

Because the prepayment was cleared at the time of the sale, it does not appear in the Receipts Journal. Instead, the Amount Owing has been reduced so this is a standard receipt entry. The discount is based on the full invoice amount, or 1 percent of $2 500.

Enter   the **remaining transaction details** to complete the entry. Remember to change the bank account.

Review the **transaction** and then **post** it.

Enter   the **remaining transactions** for the Oct. 31 session date and then **advance** the **session date**. **Change modules** as needed.

Working from the Daily Business Manager

Simply Accounting helps a business monitor its performance and cash flow by generating several of the reports that you have seen so far. It also keeps track of recurring transactions, payments and receipts with the Daily Business Manager lists. These lists offer an additional method of internal control. In addition to these lists, the Daily Business Manager can compile financial performance data for the company.

You should be in the Home window after changing the session date to November 7. We will enter most of the transactions for November from the Daily Business Manager.

There are several ways to open the Daily Business Manager.

Each module window has a Daily Business Manager icon in the Related Tasks pane:

Click   the **Daily Business Manager icon**, or **choose** the **Business Assistant menu** and **click Daily Business Manager**:

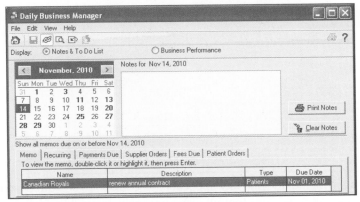

You can also access the Daily Business Manager from any journal by clicking the Daily Business Manager tool icon .

Or choose the View menu in any journal and click Daily Business Manager.

You can show Daily Business Manager lists automatically each time you advance the session date, each time you start the program or both. Choose the Setup menu, then choose User Preferences and click View. Click At Startup and After Changing Session Date below Daily Business Manager to select these options. Menu and tool bar access to the lists are always available from the Home window.

By default, Simply Accounting chooses a date that is one week past the current session date for its Daily Business Manager. The date can be changed by clicking a new date on the calendar. Lists will be updated to reflect the change in date.

Each tab screen includes instructions for accessing journals or selecting an entry.

You can also type notes for a date directly into the Notes box. They will remain on-screen for that date until you choose Clear Notes. You can print these notes and clear them when they are no longer needed.

The Memo tab screen opens with a note for one of the customers about renewing the contract. This memo was entered in the customer's ledger Memo tab screen with a due date and the option to display in the Daily Business Manager.

Double click **Canadian Royals** to open the ledger record:

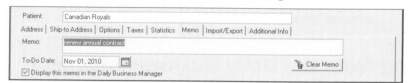

The customer's record opens at the Memo tab screen. You now have the option to remove the memo, if it no longer applies, or to change the date for its appearance in the Daily Business Manager. You can see that we have checked the option to display the memo.

Close   the **ledger window** to return to the Daily Business Manager.

Payments Due

The first entry for November is a cheque issued for an outstanding invoice. To be certain that all outstanding invoices are paid in a timely fashion, we can enter payments from the Daily Business Manager.

Click   the **Payments Due tab**:

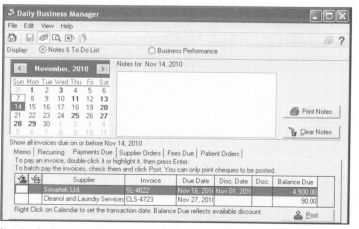

The list includes payments due and any applicable discounts. To see the payments due in a longer period, and to be sure that all discounts available will be included, you can select a later date on the calendar. You might use this list to plan a payment schedule. We want to be able to take advantage of purchase discounts, so we will leave the list selection date unchanged — it shows payments due in the next month.

The list includes the Supplier name, Invoice number, payment Due Date, Discount Date, Discount availability and the Balance Due (owing). The Disc. Date shows when the discount period ends. You can pay the invoices directly from this screen when no changes are needed. You can also open the Payments Journal by double clicking an invoice line or by clicking an invoice and pressing (enter).

If you pay from the Daily Business Manager, the session date is the default. To change the cheque date, right-click the date you want in the calendar. The default amount and bank account are also selected but you cannot change these fields.

Right-click Nov 1 on the calendar. The discount for Sonartek is now available.

In the November calendar section, 1 now has a red box framing it to indicate it will be the transaction posting date. The Disc. column now has a ✓ and the Balance Due for invoice #SL-4622 has been updated to include the discount:

Memo	Recurring	Payments Due	Supplier Orders	Fees Due	Patient Orders

To pay an invoice, double-click it or highlight it, then press Enter.
To batch pay the invoices, check them and click Post. You can only print cheques to be posted.

✓	✓	Supplier	Invoice	Due Date	Disc. Date	Disc.	Balance Due
		Sonartek Ltd.	SL-4622	Nov 16, 2010	Nov 01, 2010	✓	4,380.00
		Cleanol and Laundry Services	CLS-4723	Nov 27, 2010			90.00

If we post from the business manager now, the date and discount will be correct, but the bank account not. Therefore, we must open the journal to pay the invoice.

Double click the **entry for Sonartek** to open the Payments Journal:

The session date is now entered again as the default, but you can change it. The full amount owing is also entered by default without the discount, so we must also make this change. First we will delete the payment amount because it is already selected.

Press (del) to remove the amount.

Enter **Nov 1** as the date for the payment. **Press** (tab) to make the discount available.

Choose **Bank Regina Chequing** in the From field to update the cheque number.

Click the **Discount Taken field** and then the **Payment Amount field.**

Press (tab) to complete the cheque.

Click the **Post button** [Post] to save the entry.

Close the **Payments Journal** to return to the Daily Business Manager.

The Sonartek Paper Products entry has been removed from the list.

Right-click Nov 7 on the calendar to reset the session date as the posting date.

Recurring Transactions Due

The next transaction is the recurring cash purchase.

An advantage to using the Daily Business Manager is that the recurring entries for all journals are listed together. You can open a journal and recall a stored transaction in a single step. You can also post and print sales invoices, individually or in batches, directly from this screen, but you cannot preview them.

Click   the **Recurring tab**:

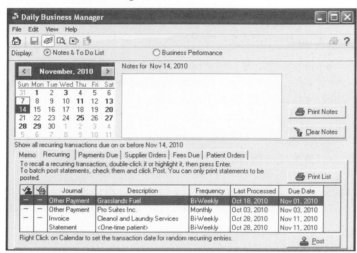

All recurring entries due on or before November 14 (the date marked on the calendar) are listed, together with the Journal used for the original entry, the entry name (Description) and its recurring Frequency. The most recent posting date (Last Processed) and the Due Date are also included. The entries are listed according to the Due Date, with the earliest date at the top of the list.

You can see that the first entry — the fuel purchase from Grasslands Fuel — is due Nov. 1. Recurring purchases require an invoice number as additional information so we need to open the journal first. This payment does not use the default bank account selection.

> **Double click Grasslands Fuel**, the Other Payment entry, to open the Payments
> Journal with this transaction on-screen.

You may need to scroll up in the transaction section of the journal to see the original entry if this area appears empty.

Bank: Regina Chequing is preselected as the bank account in the From field because we stored the transaction with this selection. This is another advantage to storing a transaction.

> **Enter   GF-3677** in the Invoice/Ref. field. Copy this number to the Comment
> line as well.

> **Post**   the **transaction**.

> **Close**   the **Payments Journal** to return to the Daily Business Manager. The
> entry for Grasslands Fuel has been removed.

> **Double click Pro Suites**, the Other Payment entry, to open the journal.

> **Enter   R-2010-11** in the Invoice/Ref. field. Copy this number to the Comment
> line as well.

> **Post**   the **transaction**. **Close** the **Payments Journal**.

The Recurring Transactions list has been updated again — the Pro Suites transaction has been removed.

The remaining list items are not due today, so we can proceed to another list in the Daily Business Manager. We want to process some receipts next.

Fees (Sales) Due

Click the **Fees Due tab** to see the list of Invoices due within the week:

SIMPLY VERSION

Click the Sales Due tab. Customer, Invoice and Invoice Date replace Patient, Statement and Statement Date as the column headings.

The Fees Due list is easy to use as well. It can be used to locate customers with outstanding debts. The list shows the Patient's name, Statement number and Date, payment Due Date and Balance Due (owing) on the due date without the discount. Invoices displayed can be matched against receipts on hand, and you can open the Receipts Journal directly from this window. No invoices are listed because they are not due in the next week. However, most of Andersson's customers take advantage of sales discounts, so we should look at sales due over a longer span than one week. Payments were received from Canadian Royals and Roughrider Argos. These payments are not due until late November, but the customers are paying early to take the discounts.

We cannot post receipts from the Daily Business Manager because customer cheque numbers cannot be added automatically.

Click **30** on the November calendar to see the sales invoices due this month:

Show all statements due on or before Nov 30, 2010

| Memo | Recurring | Payments Due | Supplier Orders | Fees Due | Patient Orders |

To record payment of a statement, double-click it or highlight it, then press Enter.

Patient	Statement	Statement Date	Due Date	Balance Due
Canadian Royals	654	Oct 28, 2010	Nov 27, 2010	4,500.00
Roughrider Argos	655	Oct 28, 2010	Nov 27, 2010	4,900.00

The invoices we need now appear on the list so we can enter receipts for them.

To open the journal, you can double click any part of the line for the entry you want or click the line and press (enter).

Double click the **Canadian Royals** (Invoice #654) to open the Receipts Journal for the selected customer.

Press (tab) to accept the discount and amount for the first invoice. The amount should appear in the Total field and the upper cheque portion.

Choose Bank: Regina Chequing as the bank account in the Deposit To field.

Add the customer's **cheque number** (#4011) in the Cheque field.

Change the **date** of the cheque to November 5.

Display the **journal entry** to review your work. **Close** the **display** and **make corrections** if necessary.

WARNING!

If the discount had expired by November 7, the session date, you would change the date first. Then delete the default amount and re-enter the discount taken and payment amount.

NOTES
If you return to the Daily Business Manager, the default date and bank account are correct for the receipt from Roughrider Argos. If you remain in the Receipts Journal, you must change the date and the bank account.

SIMPLY VERSION
Enter the purchase order from the Purchases Journal, Purchase Order screen.

SIMPLY VERSION
Click the Sales Orders tab. Customer replaces Patient as the column heading.

Click   Post ⌐ Post ⌐ to record the transaction.

Enter   the next **receipt (from Roughrider Argos)** from the Receipts Journal. Or close the Receipts Journal and return to the Daily Business Manager window.

Close   the **Receipts Journal** after entering the two receipts to return to the Daily Business Manager.

Close   the **Daily Business Manager window** so you can enter the purchase order and then advance the session date.

Enter   the **purchase order with prepayment** from the Expenses Journal, Supplier Order screen.

Advance the **session date** to November 14.

Open   the **Daily Business Manager window**.

Patient (Sales) Orders Due

Two more lists are available, Supplier Orders and Patient Orders. To see outstanding items, click the corresponding tab. Lists for orders show unfilled orders due within the next week. You can access the journal windows for items on these lists just as you did for payments and fees due. We can enter the sale from order #51 on November 9 from the Daily Business Manager.

Click   the **Patient Orders tab** to see the list:

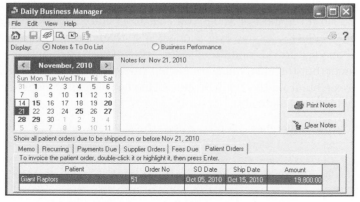

The list displays the patient, order number, order date (SO Date), shipping date and amount. The order we want is listed. You can turn the order into an invoice from the Daily Business Manager by opening the journal with the order on-screen. As usual, double clicking will open the transaction window we need.

Double click **Giant Raptors** (Order #51).

The Fees Journal opens with the order. Notice that the backordered amount is 5. One month of the contract has been completed.

Enter   **Nov 9** in the Date field.

Click   the **Quantity field** and **type** 1

Press   ⌐ tab ⌐ to update the amount. The backordered amount changes to 4.

Check   your **entry** and when it is correct, **click Post**.

Close   the **Fees Journal** to return to the Daily Business Manager. The order remains on the list because it has not been completely filled.

Purchase Orders Due

The next transaction fills the order from Cleanol and Laundry Services.

Click the **Supplier Orders tab** to see the list:

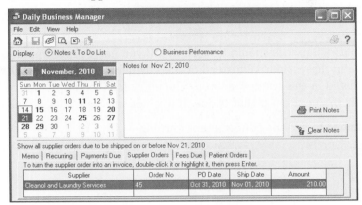

SIMPLY VERSION
Click the Purchase Orders tab. Vendor replaces Supplier as the column heading.

The list displays the supplier, order number, order date, shipping date and amount, making it easy to find orders that you need to track or follow up with the supplier.

Again, we can turn the order from Cleanol and Laundry Services into an invoice from the Daily Business Manager by opening the journal with the order on-screen.

Press (enter) to open the journal entry — Cleanol and Laundry Services is already selected.

Enter **CLS-5884** as the invoice number.

Enter **Nov 11** as the invoice date.

Click the **Fill Backordered Quantities tool**.

Enter the **order number** as additional information.

Do not post the **transaction** yet because we want to store it.

Removing Recurring Transactions

Sometimes a recurring transaction is no longer required, or it needs to be replaced. If you try to store the new purchase invoice from Cleanol and Laundry Services before removing the old entry, Simply Accounting will not allow you to continue because the name duplicates the entry on file.

Click the **Store tool**. **Choose Biweekly** as the frequency for the transaction and **click OK**.

You will see the Duplicate Entry warning:

Click **OK** to return to the Store Recurring Transaction screen.

Click **Cancel** to return to the journal. We need to remove the old stored transaction first.

Click the **Recall tool** to open the Recall Recurring Transaction list:

Cleanol and Laundry Services should be selected. If you entered the rental payment to Pro Suites in the Purchases Journal instead of the Payments Journal as an Other Payment, it will be listed in this window as well. The entry for Cleanol should still be selected because it is the next entry that is due. If it is not selected, click to select it.

Click **Remove** to see the confirmation warning:

![Simply Accounting - Confirmation dialog: Are you sure you want to remove the recurring transaction Cleanol and Laundry Services? Yes / No]

Click **Yes** to confirm the removal if you have selected the correct entry.

Click **Cancel** if the Recall Transaction window is still open. (See Notes.)

Click the **Store tool** .

Choose **Biweekly** as the frequency for the new recurring invoice. **Click OK**.

Post the **purchase transaction**.

Click **OK** to confirm that the filled order has been removed.

Close the **Expenses Journal** to return to the Daily Business Manager.

Enter the **cash sales summary** transaction from the Recurring tab screen.

Close the **Fees Journal** and the **Daily Business Manager**.

Enter the **cash purchase transaction** and **advance** the **session date**.

Enter the **transactions** for the November 21 session date.

Advance the **session date** to November 28. **Close** the **year-end message**.

Posting Directly from the Daily Business Manager

All the Daily Business Manager transactions we have shown so far have been posted after opening the journals. Cheques (payments) and recurring sales invoices can also be posted directly from the Daily Business Manager, if you can accept the default information, that is, the bank account used. The cheque to Cleanol can be posted directly without opening the journal because it uses the default account.

Open the **Daily Business Manager** and **click** the **Recurring tab**.

Enter the **recurring cash sale** and **purchase invoice** from the respective journals.

We will post the next four sales transactions directly without opening the journal. They are due on two different days, so we will enter the sales for each day separately. We set the posting (Payment) date on the November calendar, not December.

If you need to print the invoices, click the Print column beside the invoice.

NOTES
If you have only one recurring transaction, the window closes after you remove it. If there are more transactions, the window stays open and you must click Cancel to close it.

⚠ WARNING!
When you post directly from the Daily Business Manager, you cannot review the journal entry or make other changes.

NOTES
If you set the dates correctly, November 25 on the calendar should have a red box framing it and November 28 will appear in a solid coloured box.

Click   the **left arrow** at the top of the December calendar to access the November calendar.

Right-click 25 in the November calendar to select this as the posting date.

Click   (left-click) **28** to reset the session date.

Click   the **Post column** [icon] (the first column) **beside** the sale for **Interplay Ballet** to add a ✓.

Click   the **Post column** [icon] **beside Veronica Kain School of Dance**.

Click   **Post** [Post].

A message appears asking if there is additional information to enter before posting:

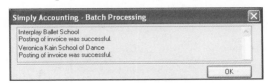

If you want to add details, click Yes to open the Additional Information screen. This screen will not open the journal itself for any other changes. There are no details to add to the Sales Journal entry. We can continue.

Click   **No** to see a message naming the invoices that are currently being processed. When posting is completed, you will see the confirmation:

> **Simply Accounting - Batch Processing**
> Interplay Ballet School
> Posting of invoice was successful.
> Veronica Kain School of Dance
> Posting of invoice was successful.
>
> OK

All invoices that were processed will be listed.

Click   **OK** to return to the list of recurring entries. The two sales invoices have been removed from the list. Their next occurrence is after December 5.

If the entry did not post successfully, check the journal report for the transaction. If it is not included, repeat the transaction.

Right-click Nov 28 on the calendar to select this as the posting date for the next two invoices.

Click   the **Post column** [icon] **beside** the sale for **Canadian Royals**.

Click   the **Post column** [icon] **beside** the sale for **Roughrider Argos**.

Click   **Post** [Post].

A message appears asking if there is additional information to enter before posting.

Click   **No** to see the message naming the invoices being processed. **Click OK** when you see the confirmation screen.

Enter   the **recurring cash purchase** for telephone services. **Close** the **Journal**.

Click   the **Payments Due tab**. The cheque is posted on the session date.

Click   the **Post column** [icon] **beside Inv #CLS-4723 and CLS-5884 (Cleanol and Laundry Services)** to add two ✓.

Click   **Post** [Post].

You will be asked if you want to enter additional information for the cheque.

WARNING!
Remember that when you pay from the Daily Business Manager, the default amount and bank account are selected. You cannot change them.

Click Yes to open the additional information window or click No to continue.

After a brief period, you will see the successful posting confirmation:

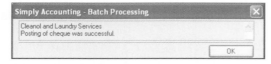

Click   OK.

Business Performance

Before closing the Business Manager, we will look at the key performance indicators.

Click   Business Performance:

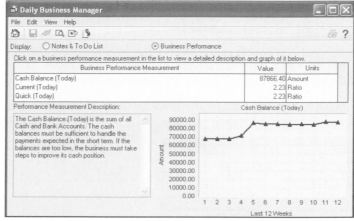

Performance information includes the current bank account balance, the current ratio and the quick ratio at the session date. The information is provided numerically and graphically. Detailed descriptions explain the indicators and guidelines for these financials. Clicking an indicator will display the results.

Click   [X] to close the Daily Business Manager and return to the Home window.

Enter   the **cash purchase transaction**.

Advance the **session date** to November 30.

Open   the **Daily Business Manager**. **Click Notes & To Do List** to restore the lists.

Enter   the next **receipt** and the **two recurring transactions**.

Close   the **Daily Business Manager**.

Enter   the **transactions** for November 30 up to Cheque #129.

Removing Quotes and Orders

Quotes and orders that will not be filled should be removed so that they are not confused with active quotes and orders. To remove purchase quotes,

Click   the **Invoices icon** to open the Expenses Journal.

Choose **Quote** from the Transaction list.

Choose **quote #MT-511** and **press** (tab) to place the quote on-screen.

Click   the **Remove Quote tool** 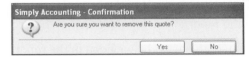 or **choose** the **Expense menu** and **click Remove Quote**.

As usual, Simply Accounting warns you before making the deletion:

Click   **Yes** to confirm.

Remove the **other two quotes** that are not needed and then **close** the **journal**.

To remove purchase orders,

Open the Expenses (Purchases) Journal.

Choose Supplier Order from the Transaction list. Choose the order number and press ⌈tab⌋ to put the order on-screen.

Click the Remove Supplier Order tool ▦ or choose the Expense menu and click Remove Supplier Order to see the warning.

Click Yes to confirm.

To remove sales quotes or sales orders,

Open the Fees (Sales) Journal.

Choose Quote (or Patient Order) as the transaction and then select the Quote or Order No. from the list. Press ⌈tab⌋ to bring the quote or order onto the screen.

Click the Remove Quote (or Patient Order) tool ▦ or choose the Fees menu and click Remove Quote (or Patient Order).

Click Yes to confirm that you want to delete the quote or order.

Enter   **Memo #7**. **Make** a **backup** and then **start** a **new fiscal period**.

Displaying Reports

Displaying Pending Supplier (Purchase) Orders

Any purchase orders that are not yet filled can be displayed in a report. You can also use this report to check for orders that are delayed or should be removed.

Open   the **Report Centre**.

Click   **Payables** in the Select A Type Of Report list.

Click   **Pending Supplier Orders Summary by Supplier** to open the sample.

Click   **Modify This Report** to open the report options window:

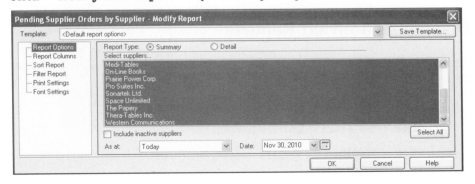

Simply SIMPLY VERSION
The labels/terms Purchase Journal, Purchase menu and Purchase Order will be used.
The labels/terms Sales Journal, Sales menu and Sales Order will be used.

Simply SIMPLY VERSION
The report is named Pending Purchase Orders By Vendor.

NOTES
The Pending Supplier/Patient Orders reports can be sorted and filtered by Order No., Order Date, Ship Date and Amount.

NOTES
From the Pending Orders reports, you can drill down to the Supplier/Patient Aged Report and to the order form.
If you drill down to the order, you can fill the order directly by choosing Invoice as the type of transaction and then filling the order as usual. Confirm your intention to change the order to an invoice.

From the Home window, choose the Reports menu, then choose Payables and Pending Supplier Orders and click By Supplier to see the report options.

Press   and **hold** `ctrl` and **click** the appropriate **names** in the supplier list.

Enter   **Dec. 31** as the date for the report.

Click   **OK** to view the report.

All orders due in the next month should be included in the report. The purchase order with HydraTub Care is not included because its starting date is January 1.

Click   the **Modify Report tool** .

Display the **report** again using January 15 as the date to see all outstanding orders.

Close   the **display** when you have finished.

Displaying Pending Patient (Sales) Orders

Any sales orders that are not yet filled can be displayed in the Pending Sales Orders Report. You can also use this report to check for orders that should be removed.

Click   **Receivables** in the Select A Type Of Report list.

Click   **Pending Patient Orders Summary by Patient** to open the sample.

Click   **Modify This Report** to open the report options window:

You can also choose the Reports menu, then choose Receivables and Pending Patient Orders and click By Patient to view the report options.

Press   and **hold** `ctrl` and **click** the appropriate **names** in the customer list.

Enter   **Dec. 31** as the report date to see orders for the next month.

Click   **OK** to view the report. One sales order is listed, the partially filled order for the Giant Raptors' contract.

Close   the **display** when you have finished.

Displaying Journal Reports

When you choose to include additional fields in the journal entries, you can also include these details in the journal reports.

Click   **Financials** in the Select A Type Of Report list.

Click   **All Journal Entries** to open the sample.

Click   **Modify This Report** to open the report options window:

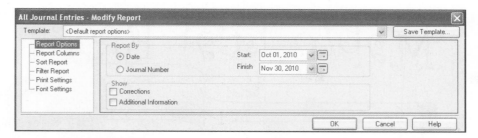

Or, choose the Reports menu, then choose Journal Entries and click All to see the report options.

A check box is used for the Additional Information. If you do not want to include these details in the report, you can leave the check box blank.

Click	**Additional Information** to add a ✓.
Click	**Corrections**.
Enter	the **Start date** for the report. You can type the date or choose from the list or the calendar.
Enter	the **Finish date** for the report.
Click	**OK** to see the Journal Report.
Close	the **display** when you have finished.
Close	the **Report Centre**.

R E V I E W

The Student CD-ROM with Data Files includes Review Questions and Supplementary Cases for this chapter.

CHAPTER TWELVE

Maple Leaf Rags

OBJECTIVES

- **make** payments toward credit card accounts
- **make** GST and PST remittances
- **apply** sales taxes to interprovincial sales
- **enter** sales and receipts for foreign customers
- **enter** purchases and payments for foreign suppliers
- **access** supplier or customer Web sites
- **e-mail** invoices to customers
- **look up** invoices after posting them
- **track** shipments to customers
- **transfer** funds between different currency bank accounts
- **monitor** business routines with Checklists
- **create** an Accountant's Copy of data for adjustments
- **import** Accountant's Copy journal entries

After completing this chapter, you should be able to

COMPANY INFORMATION

Company Profile

Maple Leaf Rags Inc. is a privately held corporation operated by Jaz Bands out of a small office in Victoria, British Columbia. While studying fine arts at Concordia University, Bands worked part time in local music stores. Customers frequently asked about Canadian performing artists in general and were sometimes frustrated that they had to look in every department to find a variety of types of music by Canadians. After completing an MBA at Queen's University, and based on his knowledge of and contacts in the music industry and some careful business research, Bands opened his own business, Maple Leaf Rags Inc., a store specializing in Canadian recording artists.

Maple Leaf Rags Inc. sells CDs by Canadian artists over the Internet to individuals. It also sells to music stores throughout Canada and the United States, usually to American stores that serve a large Canadian resident and tourist

NOTES

Maple Leaf Rags Inc.
2642 Goldstream Avenue
Victoria, British Columbia
V9B 2X2
Tel 1: (250) 63M-USIC
Tel 2: (888) 63M-USIC
Fax: (250) 633-4888
Business No.: 128 488 632
Rag is a style of music set in ragtime. Many of Scott Joplin's tunes, including "Maple Leaf Rag," are examples of ragtime music.

clientele. These stores rely on Bands as a convenient source of Canadian artists' recordings, including native and ethnic music produced by A.B. Original Sounds, which is Bands' recording company. Bands hopes to expand the business to other countries where pockets of Canadian populations can be found, such as countries with Canadian Armed Forces bases.

Bands is fortunate to be able to rely on the advice of his friend Dave Manga, whose Outset Media board-game business distributes its products in a similar way to Maple Leaf Rags. His friend also shares information about suppliers who might be able to provide some of Bands' supplies.

Maple Leaf Rags has expanded rapidly, though Bands is still able to operate out of his own home because the demands for inventory storage space are small. He pays himself rent for use of his home office space.

Bands buys CDs from various recording studios. He buys CD masters from A.B. Original Sounds, and suppliers across Canada copy and package the CDs for his company at competitive prices. He has accounts set up for all his regular suppliers, many of whom offer discounts for early payments. Bands also has set up accounts for his wholesale customers, with discounts for early payment.

At the end of each fiscal year, Bands creates a copy of the data files for the accountant who checks the accuracy of the accounting records and adds the outstanding adjusting entries.

Bands converted his accounting records to Simply Accounting after completing a brief course at the community college. The following company information summarizes the conversion after the first nine months of the current fiscal period:

- Chart of Accounts
- Trial Balance
- Supplier Information
- Customer Information
- Accounting Procedures

CHART OF POSTABLE ACCOUNTS

MAPLE LEAF RAGS INC.

ASSETS
1020 Bank: Savings Account
1040 Bank: Chequing Account
1060 Bank: Visa
1080 Bank: MasterCard
1100 Bank: Amex
1140 Bank: USD
1200 Accounts Receivable
1240 Purchase Prepayments
1280 Office Supplies
1300 CD Inventory
1340 Prepaid Expenses
1410 Computers
1420 Accum Deprec: Computers
1450 Furniture & Equipment
1480 Accum Deprec: Furn & Equip ▶

▶1500 Automobile
1520 Accum Deprec: Automobile

LIABILITIES
2100 Bank Loan
2180 Prepaid Sales and Deposits
2200 Accounts Payable
2250 Amex Payable
2260 Visa Payable
2460 PST Payable
2650 GST Charged on Sales
2660 HST Charged on Sales
2670 GST Paid on Purchases
2680 HST Paid on Purchases
2850 Long Term Loan ▶

▶**EQUITY**
3560 Common Stock
3600 Retained Earnings
3800 Current Earnings

REVENUE
4100 Revenue from Sales
4180 Sales Discounts
4200 Freight Revenue
4250 Interest Revenue
4280 Sales Tax Compensation
4300 Exchange Rate Differences

EXPENSE
5100 Advertising & Publicity
5150 Bank Charges & Card Fees
5200 Depreciation Expense ▶

▶5220 Freight & Shipping Expenses
5260 Purchase Discounts
5280 Interest Expense
5300 Internet & Web Site Expenses
5360 CD Assembly Materials Costs
5380 Cost of CDs Sold
5400 Office Rent
5500 Office Supplies Used
5520 Research Expenses
5560 Telephone Expenses
5580 Travel Expenses

NOTES: The Chart of Accounts includes only postable accounts and the Net Income or Current Earnings account.

TRIAL BALANCE

MAPLE LEAF RAGS INC.

June 30, 2010		Debits	Credits			Debits	Credits
1020	Bank: Savings Account	$ 46 640		▶ 2670	GST Paid on Purchases	2 300	
1040	Bank: Chequing Account	31 000		2850	Long Term Loan		60 000
1060	Bank: Visa	1 800		3560	Common Stock		160 000
1080	Bank: MasterCard	2 350		3600	Retained Earnings		12 014
1100	Bank: Amex	840		4100	Revenue from Sales		321 000
1140	Bank: USD ($730 USD)	760		4180	Sales Discounts	6 840	
1200	Accounts Receivable	67 200		4200	Freight Revenue		5 460
1280	Office Supplies	600		4250	Interest Revenue		2 150
1300	CD Inventory	194 350		4280	Sales Tax Compensation		45
1340	Prepaid Expenses	3 900		5100	Advertising & Publicity	18 800	
1410	Computers	8 200		5150	Bank Charges & Card Fees	1 980	
1420	Accum Deprec: Computers		$ 1 100	5220	Freight & Shipping Expenses	4 810	
1450	Furniture & Equipment	9 100		5260	Purchase Discounts		850
1480	Accum Deprec: Furn & Equip		1 500	5280	Interest Expense	9 960	
1500	Automobile	16 800		5300	Internet & Web Site Expenses	540	
1520	Accum Deprec: Automobile		9 800	5360	CD Assembly Materials Costs	1 800	
2100	Bank Loan		12 000	5380	Cost of CDs Sold	150 650	
2200	Accounts Payable		1 572	5400	Office Rent	7 200	
2250	Amex Payable		390	5500	Office Supplies Used	800	
2260	Visa Payable		860	5520	Research Expenses	1 200	
2460	PST Payable		450	5560	Telephone Expenses	905	
2650	GST Charged on Sales		3 650	5580	Travel Expenses	1 950	
2660	HST Charged on Sales		434 ▶			$593 275	$593 275

SUPPLIER INFORMATION

MAPLE LEAF RAGS INC.

Supplier Name (Contact)	Address	Phone No. Fax No.	E-mail Web Site	Terms Tax ID
A.B. Original Sounds (Marie Raven)	380 Abbey Rd. Vancouver, BC V3P 5N6	Tel: (604) 882-6252 Fax: (604) 882-1100		1/10, n/30 (before tax) 129 646 733
BC Tel (Manny Voyses)	45 Nexus Ave. Victoria, BC V7R 3D1	Tel: (250) 679-1011 Fax: (250) 679-1000	www.bell.ca	n/1
Federal Express (DayLee Runner)	59 Effex Road Victoria, BC V7F 6X2	Tel: (800) 488-9000 Fax: (250) 488-1230	www.fedex.com	n/1
Grandeur Graphics (Kathy Grandeur)	26 Drawing Way Halifax, NS B5T 3D1	Tel: (902) 665-3998 Fax: (902) 665-3900	www.wedesignit.com	2/20, n/30 (before tax) 459 112 341
Let 'm Know (Jabber Jaws Lowder)	599 Broadcast Rd. Vancouver, BC V2F 7J8	Tel: (604) 604-6040 Fax: (604) 604-4660	www.wetellit.com	2/20, n/30 (before tax) 453 925 376
Miles 'R on Us (N. Gins)	522 Drivers St. Victoria, BC V6T 5E3	Tel: (800) 592-5239 Fax: (250) 591-4929		n/1
Minister of Finance	55 Munificence St. Victoria, BC V7P 2B5	Tel: (250) 529-7292	www.fin.gov.bc.ca	n/1
Purolator (Speedy Carriere)	46 Shipping Mews Victoria, BC V7H 6S2	Tel: (800) 355-7447 Fax: (250) 355-7000	www.purolator.com	n/1
Receiver General for Canada	Summerside Tax Centre Summerside, PE C1N 6L2	Tel: (902) 821-8186	www.cra-arc.gc.ca	n/1
Wrap It (Able Boxer)	80 Cubit Road Richmond Hill, ON L5R 6B2	Tel: (905) 881-7739 Fax: (905) 881-7000		1/5, n/30 (before tax) 634 529 125

OUTSTANDING SUPPLIER INVOICES

MAPLE LEAF RAGS INC.

Supplier Name	Terms	Date	Invoice No.	Amount	Tax	Total
Grandeur Graphics	2/20, n/30 (before tax)	6/28/10	GG-1304	$ 400	$ 52	$ 452
Let 'm Know	2/20, n/30 (before tax)	6/29/10	LK-692	$1 000	$120	$1 120
			Grand Total			$1 572

CUSTOMER INFORMATION

MAPLE LEAF RAGS INC.

Customer Name (Contact)	Address	Phone No. Fax No.	E-mail Web Site	Terms Credit Limit
Canadian Sounds (X. Pats)	46 Ontario St. Tampa, Florida 33607 USA	Tel: (813) 930-4589 Fax: (813) 930-7330	XPats@cansounds.com www.cansounds.com	3/30, n/60 (before tax) $20 000 USD
CDN Music (Michelle Strings)	230 Nightingale Pl. Scarborough, ON M2R 9K4	Tel: (416) 288-6189 Fax: (416) 288-6000	mstrings@upbeat.com www.cdn.music.ca	3/30, n/60 (before tax) $20 000
Entertainment House (Rob Blinde)	101 Booker St. Toronto, ON M4F 3J8	Tel: (416) 484-9123 Fax: (416) 488-8182	www.ent.house.com	3/30, n/60 (before tax) $150 000
It's All Canadian (Leaf Mapleston)	39 Federation Ave. Victoria, BC V8W 7T7	Tel: (250) 598-1123 Fax: (250) 598-1000	www.canstuff.com	3/30, n/60 (before tax) $20 000
Music Music Music (M. Porter)	10 Red Rock Canyon Sedona, Arizona 86336 USA	Tel: (520) 678-4523 Fax: (520) 678-4500	mporter@music3.com www.music3.com	3/30, n/60 (before tax) $10 000 USD
Total Music (Goode Sounds)	93 Waterside Rd. Fredericton, NB E3B 4F4	Tel: (506) 455-7746 Fax: (506) 455-7000	goode@totalmusic.com www.totalmusic.com	3/30, n/60 (before tax) $50 000
Treble & Bass (Bea Flatte)	399 Chord Blvd. Vancouver, BC V4E 5T6	Tel: (604) 557-5438 Fax: (604) 557-5550	bflatte@t&b.com www.t&b.com	3/30, n/60 (before tax) $30 000
Web Store Customers				Prepaid by Credit Card

OUTSTANDING CUSTOMER INVOICES

MAPLE LEAF RAGS INC.

Customer Name	Terms	Date	Invoice No.	Amount	Tax	Total
CDN Music	3/30, n/60 (before tax)	6/25/10	591	$ 4 500	$ 225	$ 4 725
Entertainment House	3/30, n/60 (before tax)	1/4/10	233	$56 000	$2 800	$58 800
It's All Canadian	3/30, n/60 (before tax)	6/6/10	589	$ 3 500	$ 175	$ 3 675
			Grand Total			$67 200

Accounting Procedures

GST

Maple Leaf Rags Inc. uses the regular method of calculating GST. The GST charged and collected from customers is recorded as a liability in *GST Charged on Sales*. Customers in Nova Scotia, New Brunswick, and Newfoundland and Labrador (participating provinces) pay HST at the rate of 13 percent instead of GST, and these amounts are recorded in *HST Charged on Sales*. Bands has set up both GST and HST as taxes with appropriate codes. GST paid to suppliers is recorded in *GST Paid on Purchases* (or *HST Paid on Purchases* if the supplier is in a participating province) as a decrease in tax liability. The balance owing is the difference between the GST plus HST charged and GST plus HST paid.

Cash Sales of Services

Cash transactions for Bands are limited to credit card sales since most of his business is with wholesale customers who have accounts. He has merchant Visa, MasterCard and American Express (Amex) arrangements with three different financial institutions. Maple Leaf Rags pays a percentage of each sale directly to the credit card companies (the fee is withheld from the sale amount). To simplify the transaction entries, we provide summaries of these credit card sales as if they were to a single customer called Web Store Customers.

Bands uses a Visa gold card and an American Express card for some business purchases and pays annual user fees for these cards.

Discounts

Discounts are calculated automatically by the program when the discount terms are entered as part of the invoices. If the payments are made before the discount terms have expired, the discount appears in the Payments and Receipts journals automatically. All discounts are calculated on before-tax amounts. Bands offers a 3 percent discount to wholesale customers to encourage them to pay their accounts on time. Web store customers pay by credit card and do not receive discounts.

Some suppliers offer before-tax discounts to Maple Leaf Rags as well. These discount terms are set up in the supplier and customer records.

PST

Wholesale customers do not pay PST on merchandise they buy for resale. Thus, when Bands sells directly to stores, he charges only GST. He does not charge PST to stores because they are not the final consumers of the product. When individual customers buy directly from Bands, he charges PST at 7 percent to customers in British Columbia but not to customers in other provinces. All customers pay GST at 5 percent or HST at 13 percent. PST and GST are also paid on all freight or shipping charges in British Columbia. When Maple Leaf Rags makes the PST remittance, it reduces the amount of the remittance by 3.3 percent, the amount of the sales tax compensation.

Freight

Customers who order through the Internet pay a shipping rate of $5 for the first CD and $2 for each additional CD. Wholesale customers pay the actual shipping costs. GST and PST are charged on freight in British Columbia. Bands has accounts set up with his three regular shippers so that he can track shipments online. Their Web site addresses are included in the shipping setup data.

Sales Orders and Deposits

When a customer places a sales order, Bands requests a deposit as confirmation of the order. Deposits are entered on the Sales Order form (see page 432) or in the Receipts Journal (see page 424).

Foreign Customers and Suppliers

Customers outside Canada do not pay GST or PST on goods imported from Canada. Therefore, sales outside the country do not have taxes applied to them. These customers also do not pay GST or PST on shipping charges.

Purchases from suppliers outside of Canada are subject to GST when the goods are used in Canada. No import duties are charged on goods coming from the United States.

INSTRUCTIONS

1. **Record entries for the source documents** in Simply Accounting using the Chart of Accounts, Supplier Information, Customer Information and Accounting Procedures for Maple Leaf Rags. The procedures for entering each new type of transaction in this application are outlined step by step in the Keystrokes section following the source documents. These transactions are indicated with a ✓ in the completion box beside the source document. The number for the page on which the relevant keystrokes begin is printed immediately below the check box.

   Change module windows as needed, or create shortcuts for journals in other modules.

2. **Print** the **reports for the end of the fiscal period** suggested by the Simply Accounting checklists after you have finished making your entries. Refer to the Keystrokes section, page 490. If you have started a new fiscal period, choose **Previous Year** to see the reports you need.

SOURCE DOCUMENTS

SESSION DATE – JULY 15, 2010

☑ **Visa Credit Card Sales Invoice #593**   **Dated July 2/10**

466   To various Web Store customers, for CDs sold during previous three months

Sales to BC customers	$1 200	plus 5% GST and 7% PST
Sales to Ontario customers	1 400	plus 5% GST
Sales to HST provinces	600	plus 13% HST
Shipping	480	plus 5% GST and 7% PST

(Shipped by Purolator #PCU773XT)
Invoice total $4 029.60. Paid by Visa.

☐ **MasterCard Credit Card Sales Invoice #594   Dated July 2/10**

To various Web Store customers, for CDs sold during previous three months

Sales to BC customers	$2 300	plus 5% GST and 7% PST
Sales to HST provinces	900	plus 13% HST
Sales to other provinces	2 800	plus 5% GST
Shipping	780	plus 5% GST and 7% PST

Invoice total $7 406.60. Paid by MasterCard.

NOTES
For Maple Leaf Rags's retail business type, the terms Customer and Supplier are used. Sales and Purchases are used as icon labels, in journal names and in reports.

Simply SIMPLY VERSION
Vendors will replace Suppliers for icon, field and report names.

NOTES
In the data files, PBC is the tax name we use for PST in BC (British Columbia) so that it can be distinguished from PST applied in other provinces. PST applied in Ontario is named PO in the data files.

NOTES
Remember to select the correct credit card name.
You do not need to enter shipping information for the remaining Web store sales.

☐ **Amex Credit Card Sales Invoice #595**   **Dated July 2/10**

To various Web Store customers, for CDs sold during previous three months
Sales to BC customers $ 700   plus 5% GST and 7% PST
Sales to HST provinces   200   plus 13% HST
Sales to other provinces   1 300   plus 5% GST
Shipping   280   plus 5% GST and 7% PST
Invoice total $2 688.60. Paid by Amex.

☐ **Visa Purchase Invoice #MR-1699**   **Dated July 2/10**

To Miles 'R on Us, $520 plus 5% GST and 8% PST for two-week car rental while
attending Trade Show in Toronto. Invoice total $587.60. Paid by Visa.

☑ **Cheque #761**   **Dated July 2/10**

469   To Visa, $723.50 in payment of credit card account, including $609 for purchases
charged from May 16 to June 15, $105 for annual renewal fee and $9.50 in
interest charges on the unpaid balance from a previous statement.

☑ **Memo #43**   **Dated July 3/10**

472   From J. Bands: Access the Web site for Canada Revenue Agency to see whether
any recent announcements about GST affect the business.

☑ **Memo #44**   **Dated July 5/10**

474   From J. Bands: Refer to June 30 General Ledger balances to remit GST and HST
to the Receiver General. Issue cheque #762 for $1 784 from Chequing Account.

☑ **Memo #45**   **Dated July 5/10**

476   From J. Bands: Refer to the June 30 General Ledger balance to remit PST
Payable to the Minister of Finance. Reduce the payment by the sales tax
compensation of 3.3% of the balance owing. Issue cheque #763 for $435.15 from
Chequing Account.

☑ **Sales Invoice #596**   **Dated July 5/10**

477   To Canadian Sounds, $2 190 USD for CDs. Shipped by Federal Express
(#F19YTR563) for $120. Invoice total $2 310 USD. Terms 3/30, n/60. The
exchange rate is 1.0255.

☐ **Cash Receipt #125**   **Dated July 5/10**

From It's All Canadian, cheque #884 for $3 570 in payment of account including
$105 discount taken for early payment. Reference invoice #589.

☐ **Sales Order #TB-04 & Deposit #14**   **Dated July 5/10**

Shipping date July 10/10
From Treble & Bass, $10 300 plus 5% GST for CDs. Enter one (1) as the order
quantity. Shipping by Purolator for $110 plus GST and PST. Invoice total
$10 938.20. Terms 3/30, n/60. Received cheque #911 for $2 000 as deposit #14 to
confirm the order. Refer to page 432.

☐ **Sales Invoice #597**   **Dated July 10/10**

To Treble & Bass, to fill sales order #TB-04, $10 300 plus 5% GST for CDs.
Shipped by Purolator (#PCU899XT) for $110 plus GST and PST. Invoice total
$10 938.20. Terms 3/30, n/60. Enter the shipper so you can track the shipment.

☐ **Sales Invoice #598**   **Dated July 11/10**

To Music Music Music, $1 630 USD for CDs. Shipped by Federal Express
(#F27CGB786) for $100. Invoice total $1 730 USD. Terms 3/30, n/60. The
exchange rate is 1.0001.

NOTES
Because the car rental is purchased and used in Ontario, the Ontario Provincial Sales Tax rate applies. Use tax code GO (GST plus Ontario PST).

NOTES
You can use the Additional Field for the invoice number.
Use the bank account 1040 for receipts from Canadian customers.

NOTES
Wholesale customers who will be selling the product to their own customers do not pay PST, except on shipping charges.

⚠ WARNING!
Remember to change the payment method to Pay Later for invoice #597. Cheque remains selected from the Sales Order. Refer to page 437. The balance owing is $8 938.20.

☑ **Cash Receipt #126**   **Dated July 15/10**

478   From Canadian Sounds, cheque #2397 for $2 240.70 USD in payment of account less $69.30 discount for early payment. Reference invoice #596. The exchange rate for July 15 is 0.995.

☑ **Memo #46**   **Dated July 15/10**

480   From J. Bands: Treble & Bass called to inform you that they have not received their shipment of CDs. Look up invoice #597, e-mail a copy of the invoice to the customer and check the delivery status.

SESSION DATE — JULY 31, 2010

☑ **Purchase Invoice #DA-722**   **Dated July 16/10**

484   From Design Anything (use Full Add for new USD supplier), $3 000 plus 5% GST for design of labels and CD case inserts for new CDs. Invoice total $3 150 USD. Terms: net 30. The exchange rate is 0.999.

☐ **Cheque Copy #764**   **Dated July 16/10**

To Amex, $335 in payment of credit card account, including $290 for purchases charged from May 25 to June 25 and $45 for annual renewal fee.

☐ **Cheque Copy #765**   **Dated July 18/10**

To Grandeur Graphics, $444 in full payment of account, including $8 discount for early payment. Reference invoice #GG-1304.

☐ **Cheque Copy #766**   **Dated July 18/10**

To Let 'm Know, $1 100 in full payment of account, including $20 discount for early payment. Reference invoice #LK-692.

☐ **Cash Receipt #127**   **Dated July 20/10**

From CDN Music, cheque #28563 for $4 590 in payment of account including $135 discount taken for early payment. Reference invoice #591.

☑ **Cheque Copy #284**   **Dated July 30/10**

486   To Design Anything, $3 150 USD in full payment of account. Reference invoice #DA-722. The exchange rate is 0.982.

☑ **Memo #47**   **Dated July 30/10**

487   From J. Bands, transfer $1 000 USD from Bank: Chequing Account to Bank: USD. The exchange rate is 0.982.

☐ **Purchase Order #204 & Cheque #767**   **Dated July 31/10**

Shipping date Aug. 15/10
To A.B. Original Sounds, $50 000 plus 5% GST for master copies of new CDs. Invoice total $52 500. Enter 1 as the order quantity. Terms: 1/10, n/30. Use CD Assembly Materials Costs account.
Paid $10 000 as prepayment on order with cheque #767.

☐ **Purchase Order #205 & Cheque #768**   **Dated July 31/10**

Shipping date Aug. 15/10
To Super Dupers (use Full Add for the new supplier), $12 000 plus 5% GST for duplicating CDs, labels and case inserts. Invoice total $12 600. Terms: 1/10, n/30. Use CD Assembly Materials Costs account.
Paid $2 000 as prepayment on order with cheque #768.

NOTES

Use Full Add so you can enter the correct currency.

☐ Design Anything
(contact Joy Pikchur)
900 Park St., Unit 5
Seattle, Washington 98195
USA
Tel: (800) 639-8710
Fax: (206) 755-8852
Currency: USD
Terms: net 30
Expense account: 5360
Tax code: G

NOTES

Super Dupers
☐ 777 Copiers Ave.
Richmond Hill, ON L4T 6V2
Terms: 1/10, n/30 before tax
(Remember to click Calculate Discount Before Tax.)
Expense account: 5360
Tax code: G (PST is not charged on freight in Ontario.)

Maple Leaf Rags

www.mapleleafrags.com

2642 Goldstream Avenue
Victoria, British Columbia V9B 2X2
Tel 1: (250) 63M-USIC
Tel 2: (888) 63M-USIC   Fax: (250) 633-4888

PO#:	206
Date:	July 31, 2010
Shipping date:	Aug 15, 2010
Ordered from:	Wrap It
Address:	80 Cubit Road
	Richmond Hill, ON L5R 6B2
Phone No:	(905) 881-7739
Fax No:	(905) 881-7000
Contact:	Able Boxer

PURCHASE ORDER

Order description	Amount
Provide CD cases add labels and inserts terms: 1/5, n/30	6 300.00

Freight (Canada Post)	120.00
GST	321.00
PST	—
Order Total	6 741.00
Deposit	2 000.00
Balance Owing	4 741.00

Deposit: chq #769 for $2 000

Approved by: *Jaz Bands*

NOTES
Change the default account to Prepaid Expenses for the invoice from Let 'm Know.

Purchase Invoice #LK-2303   Dated July 31/10

From Let 'm Know, $1 500 plus 5% GST and 7% PST for series of ads to run for the next five months (prepaid expense). Invoice total $1 680. Terms: 2/20, n/30.

Cash Purchase Invoice #BCT-6632   Dated July 31/10

From BC Tel, $165 plus 5% GST and 7% PST for telephone services for two months. Invoice total $184.80. Terms: payment on receipt of invoice. Paid by cheque #770.

Cash Purchase Invoice #PE-49006   Dated July 31/10

From Purolator, $1 400 plus 5% GST and 7% PST for shipping services used from May 25 to July 25. Invoice total $1 568. Terms: payment on receipt of invoice. Paid by cheque #771.

Visa Purchase Invoice #PC-34992   Dated July 31/10

From Petro-Canada (use Quick Add), $50 plus 5% GST and 7% PST for gasoline for business use. Invoice total $56 paid by Visa.

NOTES
Use Quick Add for the new supplier. Include gasoline costs with Travel Expenses. Use tax code GP – GST and PBC (PST in BC) apply.

SESSION DATE – AUGUST 15, 2010

Cheque Copy #772   Dated Aug. 2/10

To Visa, $838.60 in payment of balance shown on Visa account statement for purchases before July 15, 2010.

Cash Receipt #128   Dated Aug. 7/10

From Music Music Music, cheque #8531 for $1 678.10 USD in payment of account less $51.90 discount for early payment. Reference invoice #598. The exchange rate for Aug. 7 is 0.989 Deposit to Bank: USD account.

Cheque Copy #773   **Dated Aug. 8/10**

To Let 'm Know, $1 650 in full payment of account, including $30 discount for early payment. Reference invoice #LK-2303.

Cash Receipt #129   **Dated Aug. 9/10**

From Treble & Bass, cheque #1144 for $8 625.90 in payment of account including $312.30 discount taken for early payment. Reference invoice #597 and deposit #14. Deposit to Bank: Chequing Account.

Sales Invoice #599   **Dated Aug. 9/10**

To Total Music, $4 000 plus 13% HST for CDs. Shipping charges $210 plus GST and PST. Invoice total $4 755.20. Terms 3/30, n/60.

Sales Order #FA-05   **Dated Aug. 9/10**

Shipping date Aug. 22/10
To Fiddler & Associates (use Full Add for the new customer), $24 000 plus 5% GST for CDs purchased by major music store chains. Shipping charges $200 plus GST and PST. Invoice total $25 424. Terms 3/30, n/60.

NOTES

Fiddler & Associates
(contact Ken Fiddler)
50 Rue des Bagatelles
Montreal, QC H4S 9B3
Tel: (514) 487-2936
Fax: (514) 488-1500
E-mail: kfiddler@istar.ca
Terms: 3/30, n/60
Revenue account: 4100
Tax code: G - GST @ 5%
Credit limit: $70 000

Maple Leaf Rags

No: 774

2642 Goldstream Avenue
Victoria, British Columbia V9B 2X2

Date 1 0 0 8 2 0 1 0
      D D M M Y Y Y Y

Pay to the order of   Amex $ 100.00

——————— One hundred dollars ——————— 00 /100 **Dollars**

WT Western Trust
3598 First Avenue
Victoria BC V3B 1K1

Jaz Bands

⑈⑆⑈— 029 17643 ⑆ 988652 774

- -

Re: pay Amex bill for June 26-July 25 purchases $100.00 **No: 774**

Aug. 10, 2010

Cash Receipt #130   **Dated Aug. 11/10**

From Fiddler & Associates, cheque #502 for $5 000 as down payment, deposit #15, to confirm sales order #FA-05.

Purchase Invoice #CA-7998   **Dated Aug. 12/10**

To Cars for All (use Quick Add for new supplier), $20 000 plus 5% GST and 7% PST for new automobile less $5 000 as a trade-in allowance on old car. Invoice total $16 800. The entry to write off the old car will be made by the accountant at year-end.

Purchase Invoice #ABO-8823   **Dated Aug. 13/10**

From A.B. Original Sounds, to fill purchase order #204, $50 000 plus 5% GST for CD masters. Invoice total $52 500. Terms: 1/10, n/30. (Balance owing is $42 500.)

 WARNING!

Remember to change the payment method to Pay Later for invoices that fill purchase orders with prepayments.

SESSION DATE — AUGUST 31, 2010

NOTES

When you advance the session date to Aug. 31, you should see an advice statement that it is time to prepare for year-end. Read and then close the advisory statement to proceed.

NOTES

The order from Wrap It is shipped from Ontario where PST is not charged on shipping.

NOTES

Close the advisor warnings about the overdrawn chequing account. The funds transfer in Memo #49 will cover the cheques.

☐ **Purchase Invoice #SD-9124**   **Dated Aug. 18/10**

From Super Dupers, to fill purchase order #205, $12 000 plus 5% GST for duplicating CDs, labels and case inserts. Invoice total $12 600. Terms: 1/10, n/30. (Balance owing is $10 600.)

☐ **Purchase Invoice #WI-3719**   **Dated Aug. 18/10**

From Wrap It, to fill purchase order #206, $6 300 plus 5% GST to prepare CDs for sales. Shipped by Canada Post (#75 553 789 249) for $120 plus 5% GST (tax code G). Invoice total $6 741. Terms: 1/5, n/30. (Balance owing is $4 741.)

☐ **Memo #48**   **Dated Aug. 20/10**

From J. Bands: Owner invests $50 000 personal capital to finance production of new CDs. Amount deposited to Bank: Savings Account and credited to Common Stock.

☐ **Sales Invoice #600**   **Dated Aug. 21/10**

To Fiddler & Associates, to fill sales order #FA-05, $24 000 plus 5% GST for CDs purchased by major music store chains. Shipping charges $200 plus GST and PST. Invoice total $25 424. Terms 3/30, n/60.

☐ **Cheque Copy #775**   **Dated Aug. 23/10**

To A.B. Original Sounds, $42 000 in full payment of account, including $500 discount for early payment. Reference invoice #ABO-8823 and prepayment by cheque #767.

☐ **Cheque Copy #776**   **Dated Aug. 23/10**

To Wrap It, $4 676.80 in full payment of account, including $64.20 discount for early payment. Reference invoice #WI-3719 and prepayment by cheque #769.

☐ **Cheque Copy #777**   **Dated Aug. 23/10**

To Super Dupers, $10 480 in full payment of account, including $120 discount for early payment. Reference invoice #SD-9124 and prepayment by cheque #768.

☐ **Memo #49**   **Dated Aug. 23/10**

From J. Bands: Transfer $60 000 CAD from Bank: Savings Account to Bank: Chequing Account to cover cheques because the chequing account is overdrawn.

☐ **Purchase Invoice #JH-0875**   **Dated Aug. 23/10**

To J. Henry & Associates (use Quick Add), $1 500 plus $75 GST for legal fees to recover money owed by Entertainment House. Invoice total $1 575. Terms: net 30. Create new Group account 5240 Legal Fees.

☐ **Visa Purchase Invoice #PC-49986**   **Dated Aug. 30/10**

From Petro-Canada, $50 plus 5% GST and 7% PST for gasoline for business use. Invoice total $56 paid by Visa.

SESSION DATE — SEPTEMBER 15, 2010

NOTES

If you do not change the date for the purchase invoice adjustment, you will see a warning that the transaction date precedes the session date because the transaction was dated in a previous month. Click Yes to proceed.

☐ **Memo #50**   **Dated Sep. 2/10**

When his Visa bill arrived, Bands realized that he had entered the purchase from Cars for All as a Pay Later invoice instead of a Visa payment. Adjust invoice #CA-7998 from Cars for All. Change the method of payment to Visa.

Cheque Copy #778   **Dated Sep. 2/10**

To Visa, $16 856 in payment of account for purchases from July 16 to
August 15, 2010.

Sales Invoice #601   **Dated Sep. 5/10**

To Canadian Sounds, $4 500 USD for CDs. Shipped by Federal Express
(#F36FYT863) for $220. Invoice total $4 720 USD. Terms 3/30, n/60. The
exchange rate is 1.005.

Cash Receipt #131   **Dated Sep. 5/10**

From Total Music, cheque #2491 for $4 628.90 in payment of account including
$126.30 discount taken for early payment. Reference invoice #599. Deposit to
Bank: Chequing Account.

Maple Leaf Rags

www.mapleleafrags.com

2642 Goldstream Avenue
Victoria, British Columbia V9B 2X2
Tel 1: (250) 63M-USIC
Tel 2: (888) 63M-USIC   Fax: (250) 633-4888
GST # 128 488 632

I N V O I C E

| Sales Invoice: | #602 |
| Date: | September 10, 2010 |

Customer:	Music Music Music
Address:	10 Red Rock Canyon
	Sedona, Arizona 86336 USA
Phone No:	(520) 678-4523
Fax No:	
Contact:	M. Porter

Item description	Amount
150 CDs	1 500.00 USD

Freight	120.00 USD
GST	—
PST	—
HST	—
Invoice Total	1 620.00 USD

Shipped by: Federal Express

Payment: 3/30, n/60
Exchange rate for Sep 10 was 0.9990 — JB

Sold by: *Jaz Bands*

SESSION DATE — SEPTEMBER 29, 2010

Cash Receipt #132   **Dated Sep. 18/10**

From Fiddler & Associates, cheque #574 for $19 698 in payment of account
including $726 discount taken for early payment. Reference invoice #600 and
deposit #15. Deposit to Bank: Chequing Account.

Visa Purchase Invoice #PC-59128   **Dated Sep. 29/10**

From Petro-Canada, $50 plus 5% GST and 7% PST for gasoline for business use.
Invoice total $56 paid by Visa.

NOTES
When you advance the
session date to Sep. 29, you may
see an advice statement about the
year-end adjustments required.
Read and then close the advisory
statement to proceed.

Maple Leaf Rags

www.mapleleafrags.com

2642 Goldstream Avenue
Victoria, British Columbia V9B 2X2
Tel 1: (250) 63M-USIC
Tel 2: (888) 63M-USIC   Fax: (250) 633-4888
GST # 128 488 632

Sales Invoice: #603
Date: September 29, 2010

Customer: Web Store customers
Address:

Phone No:
Fax No:
Contact:

INVOICE

Description	Amount
Sales summary for 3 months	
CDs sold to BC customers (add GST and PST)	1 100.00
CDs sold to HST province customers (add HST)	200.00
CDs sold to customers in other provinces (add GST)	2 100.00

Freight (add GST and PST)	350.00
GST	177.50
PST	101.50
HST	26.00
Invoice Total	4 055.00

Shipped by: Purolator

Payment: Visa
Direct deposit to Visa bank account *JB*

☐ **Amex Credit Card Sales Invoice #604**   **Dated Sep. 29/10**

To various Web Store customers, for CDs sold during previous three months
BC	$600	plus 5% GST and 7% PST
HST provinces	150	plus 13% HST
Other provinces	880	plus 5% GST
Shipping charges	210	plus 5% GST and 7% PST

Invoice total $2 000.70. Paid by Amex.

☐ **MasterCard Credit Card Sales Invoice #605   Dated Sep. 29/10**

To various Web Store customers, for CDs sold during previous three months
BC	$1 400	plus 5% GST and 7% PST
HST provinces	500	plus 13% HST
Other provinces	1 900	plus 5% GST
Shipping charges	360	plus 5% GST and 7% PST

Invoice total $4 531.20. Paid by MasterCard.

☐ **Cash Purchase Invoice #BCT-9810**   **Dated Sep. 29/10**

From BC Tel, $180 plus 5% GST and 7% PST for telephone services for two
months. Invoice total $201.60. Terms: payment on receipt of invoice. Paid by
cheque #779.

☐ **Cash Purchase Invoice #PE-62331**   **Dated Sep. 29/10**

From Purolator, $1 200 plus 5% GST and 7% PST for shipping services. Invoice
total $1 344. Terms: payment on receipt of invoice. Paid by cheque #780.

☐ **Cash Purchase Invoice #FE-46678**   **Dated Sep. 29/10**

From Federal Express, $2 100 plus 5% GST and 7% PST for shipping services.
Invoice total $2 352. Terms: payment on receipt of invoice. Paid by cheque #781.

SESSION DATE — SEPTEMBER 30, 2010

☐ **Memo #51**   **Dated Sep. 30/10**

From J. Bands: Refer to the Sep. 30 General Ledger balance to remit PST
Payable to the Minister of Finance. Reduce the $719.60 payment by the sales tax
compensation of 3.3% of the balance owing. Issue cheque #782 for $695.85 from
Bank: Chequing Account.

☐ **Memo #52**   **Dated Sep. 30/10**

From J. Bands: Prepare for closing the books by completing adjusting entries for
prepaid expenses and supplies used:

Office Supplies	$ 280
Prepaid Internet Expenses (3 months)	135
Prepaid Rent (3 months of 6)	2 400
Prepaid Advertising (2 months of 5)	642

☐ **Memo #53**   **Dated Sep. 30/10**

From J. Bands: Complete an adjusting entry for $36 500 of inventory sold during
the quarter. Reduce the CD Inventory asset account and increase Cost of CDs
Sold expense.

☐ **Memo #54**   **Dated Sep. 30/10**

From J. Bands: Complete an adjusting entry to transfer $73 097 in completed
CDs from production and assembly to CDs inventory. Debit CD Inventory and
credit CD Assembly Materials Costs.

☐ **Memo #55**   **Dated Sep. 30/10**

From J. Bands: Received debit memo from Western Trust regarding pre-authorized
withdrawals from Bank: Chequing Account for quarterly interest payments on
loans. Complete adjusting entries for interest paid during the quarter:

On bank loan	$ 200
On long term loan	4 000

> **NOTES**
> Bands pays only interest
> on the loans. Both amounts are
> deducted from the Bank:
> Chequing Account.

☐ **Memo #56**   **Dated Sep. 30/10**

From J. Bands: The following transfers of funds were completed.
  $15 000 from Bank: Chequing Account to Bank: Savings Account
  $7 000 from Bank: Visa to Bank: Savings Account
  $12 000 from Bank: MasterCard to Bank: Savings Account
  $3 000 from Bank: Amex to Bank: Savings Account

> **NOTES**
> You can use the Transfer
> Funds Journal for the first transfer,
> but the Credit Card class accounts
> will not be available. To complete
> the funds transfer entry as a
> single journal entry, you must use
> the General Journal.

☐ **Memo #57**   **Dated Sep. 30/10**

From J. Bands: Record Interest Revenue as follows:

Bank: Savings Account	$300
Bank: Chequing Account	70

☑ **Memo #58**   **Dated Sep. 30/10**

489   From J. Bands: Create an Accountant's Copy of the data files so the accountant
can review the accounting entries and add the final adjustments for depreciation
and the trade-in on the automobiles.

☑ **Memo #59**   **Dated Sep. 30/10**

490   From J. Bands: Review the year-end checklists. Print all reports for the fiscal
period ended. Back up the data files. Check data integrity. Advance the session
date to October 1, the first day of the next fiscal period.

☑ **Memo #60**   **Dated Oct. 1/10**

492   From J. Bands: Import the adjusting entries completed by the accountant.

KEYSTROKES

Opening Data Files

NOTES
Refer to Chapter 1, page 7 if you need assistance with restoring backup files.

Restore SimData\maple1.CAB to SimData\Maple\maple to open the data files.

Enter **July 15, 2010** as the session date for this application.

Click **OK** and then **click OK** to bypass the session date warning.

Session dates are advanced two weeks at a time for Maple Leaf Rags, and the backup frequency is set at two-week intervals. The Receivables Home window opens.

> **NOTES**
> Payroll, Inventory and Project do not appear in the Modules pane list because these ledgers are not set up.

Tracking Sales

Businesses that ship goods to customers usually have accounts set up with shipping companies so they can track shipments.

Click the **Sales Invoices icon** to open the Sales Journal.

Choose **Web Store Customers** from the Sold To list. Leave the transaction type as Invoice.

Web store purchases are usually paid by credit card.

Click the **Paid By list arrow**:

Internet customers have been set up without discounts so the discount fields are blank. Three different credit cards are set up for the methods of payment accepted.

Click **Visa** as the method of payment.

Type July 2 (as the transaction date).

Click the **Description field** and **type** BC sales

Click the **Amount field** and **type** 1200

Press (tab) to advance to the Tax field and **press** (enter) to see the Tax codes:

> **NOTES**
> We have used the tax name PBC for provincial sales tax in BC and PO for the Ontario sales tax.
> Goods and services consumed in a province are subject to the PST for that province. Goods shipped to other provinces are exempt from the PST.

We have created tax codes to accommodate interprovincial sales to customers in the participating Atlantic provinces who pay HST (**code H**) and to customers in other provinces who do not pay PST (**code G**). The **code GO** is used for purchases in Ontario because Bands has suppliers in Ontario. He pays the Ontario PST rate at 8 percent on these purchases. The first sale is to BC customers, so the **code GP** is used — the GST rate is 5 percent and the PST rate is 7 percent.

Click   **GP - GST @ 5%, PBC @ 7% non-refundable**.

Click   **Select** to return to the sales invoice and advance to the Account field. Account 4100 is correctly entered as the default revenue account.

Click   the **Description field** on the second invoice line.

Type   Ontario sales

Click   the **Amount field** and **type** 1400 **Press** (tab).

The tax code GP is entered as the default from the previous invoice line. PST is charged only to BC customers. Customers outside the province do not pay this tax. These customers pay only GST so code G is needed.

Press   (enter) or **click** the **List icon** 🔍 to see the Tax Code list.

Double click **G - GST @ 5%** to add the code and advance to the Account field. The default account is entered only for the first invoice line.

Type   4100

Click   the **Description field** on the next invoice line.

Type   HST province sales

Click   the **Amount field** and **type** 600 **Press** (tab).

Tax code G is now entered as the default from the previous line. Again PST is not applied to these sales because it is harmonized with the GST. The HST rate at 13 percent applies to these sales.

Press   (enter) or **click** the **List icon** 🔍 to see the Tax Code list.

Double click **H - HST @ 13%** to add the code and advance to the Account field.

Type   4100

There are two freight fields in the Sales Journal, directly below the subtotal amount:

Subtotal	3,200.00
Freight	
Tax	292.00
Total	3,492.00

The first field is for the freight amount and the second is for the tax code. Because taxes are paid on freight you must enter a tax code if the customer pays freight. In British Columbia, both PST and GST apply to freight so code GP is required.

Click   the **first Freight field**.

Type   480 **Press** (tab) to advance to the tax code field for Freight.

Tax code H, the last code used, is entered as the default.

Press   (enter) or **click** the **List icon** 🔍 to display the list of tax codes.

Double click **GP - GST @ 5%, PBC @ 7% non-refundable** to add the tax code.

The tax amount is calculated as soon as you enter the amount of freight charged and the tax code. This amount is added to the Tax total.

We will now enter the shipping information so that the shipments can be traced if they are not delivered within the expected time. To track a shipment, you must have the tracking number for the package. To arrange for tracking shipments online, a business must have an account with the shipper and a PIN (personal identification number) to access the account. When an invoice for these shipments is received from the shipper, it will be entered as a purchase to record the expense to Maple Leaf Rags.

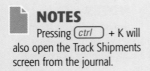

NOTES
Pressing ⌷ctrl⌷ + K will also open the Track Shipments screen from the journal.

Click   the **Track Shipments tool** or **choose** the **Sales menu** and **click Track Shipments** to open the shipping data entry window:

Click   the **Shipper field list arrow** to see the list of shippers:

Click   **Purolator**.

Press   ⌷tab⌷ to advance to the Tracking Number field.

Type   PCU773XT

Click   **OK** to return to the completed invoice. The tracking details do not appear on the invoice form.

All taxes are combined on the invoice as a single entry in the Tax field. To see the breakdown of individual taxes paid by the customer,

Click   the **List icon** beside the Tax field to see the detailed list:

NOTES
Tax amounts may be incorrect because rounded off amounts are added together. If the tax is calculated for each line, the total may be different from the tax calculated on a single subtotal amount.

You can edit these tax amounts if they are incorrect.

Click   **OK** to return to the Sales Journal.

Before posting the entry, you should review it.

Choose the **Report menu** and **click Display Sales Journal Entry**:

Maple Leaf Rags Inc.		Debits	Credits	Division
07/02/10 (J1)				
1060	Bank: Visa	3,888.56	-	
5150	Bank Charges & Card Fees	141.04	-	
2460	PST Payable	-	117.60	
2650	GST Charged on Sales	-	154.00	
2660	HST Charged on Sales	-	78.00	
4100	Revenue from Sales	-	3,200.00	
4200	Freight Revenue	-	480.00	
		4,029.60	4,029.60	

Several linked accounts are used for this transaction. The credit card account — *Bank: Visa* — is debited for the total invoice amount minus the transaction discount fees withheld by the credit card company. These fees are debited to the linked fees expense account — *Bank Charges & Card Fees*. Both the *GST* and *HST Charged on Sales* accounts are credited to show the increase in the tax liability to the Receiver General. PST collected from customers is credited to the *PST Payable* account to show the increased liability to the Minister of Finance for British Columbia. Freight charged to customers is credited automatically to the linked *Freight Revenue* account.

Close   the **display** to return to the Sales Journal input screen. **Make corrections** if necessary, referring to page 166 for assistance.

The next two transactions are also summary sales to Web Store customers. We can choose to use the same customer next time so that the customer is selected automatically.

Click   the **Use The Same Customer Next Time tool** ⊠ beside the customer name.

The Use The Same Customer Next Time tool 🔘 has changed shape to indicate it is selected. Clicking the tool again will turn off the selection.

Click   the **Post button** [⊞ Post].

Enter   the next two credit card sale transactions. Remember to select the correct credit card from the Paid By list.

Close   the **Sales Journal** to return to the Home window.

Click   **Payables** in the Modules pane list to open the Payables module.

Enter   the **Visa purchase** for the car rental.

Entering Credit Card Bill Payments

Credit card payments are entered in the Payments Journal. You can access the bill payment window from the Pay Credit Card Bills shortcut in the Payments icon drop-down shortcuts list as shown:

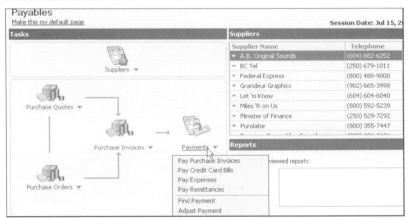

Click   **Pay Credit Card Bills** in the Payments icon shortcuts list:

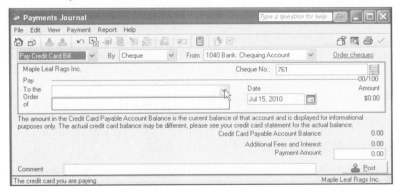

Pay Credit Card Bill is selected as the transaction type in the Pay field.

The Pay list in the journal allows you to choose between paying suppliers, paying credit card bills, making cash purchases (other payments) and making payroll remittances.

NOTES
When you close the Sales Journal, the Use The Same Customer Next Time tool is automatically turned off or deselected.

NOTES
We will not include the reminder to click OK each time you see the successful posting message.

You can also access this form by clicking the Payments icon and selecting Pay Credit Card Bill from the transaction (Pay) drop-down list as shown:

The **By** field (method of payment) has the same options as other journals — payment by cash, cheque or by any of the credit cards set up. The **From** field allows you to select a bank account from which to pay because more than one bank account is defined as a Bank class account. The default payment is by cheque. The bank account and the cheque number — the next one in the sequence for this account — are correct. The From list has three bank accounts. The default account is correct for this payment.

> **Click**   the **To The Order Of field list arrow** to access the list of credit cards set up for purchases:

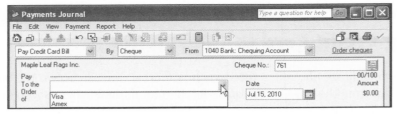

Credit card accounts are set up for Visa and Amex (American Express).

> **Click**   **Visa** to update the journal with the Visa account information:

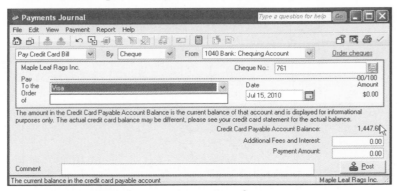

The Account Balance shows the accumulation of all unpaid purchases to date according to the General Ledger *Visa Payable* account balance. This amount is not usually the same as the balance that appears on the credit card statement. Purchases after the statement date will not appear on the statement, and interest charges or renewal fees are not included in the General Ledger account balance.

> **Drag through** the **date in the Date field**.
>
> **Type**   Jul 2
>
> **Click**   the **Additional Fees And Interest field**.

This field is used to record interest charges on previous unpaid amounts as well as other fees associated with the use of the card. These amounts usually appear on the statement. You must add these amounts together and enter the total in the Additional Fees And Interest field. Maple Leaf Rags owes $105 for the annual card renewal fee and $9.50 in accumulated interest for a total of $114.50.

> **Type**   114.50 **Press** (tab) to advance to the Payment Amount field.

In this field you should enter the total amount of the cheque that is written in payment, including interest, fees and purchases. This will match the balance owing on the statement if the full amount is being paid, or some other amount if this is a partial payment. The remaining balance in the General Ledger *Visa Payable* account reflects current charges or purchases that will be included in the balance owing on the next statement and paid at that time.

NOTES
When a partial payment is made to a credit card bill, the payment is applied first to interest and additional fees before reducing the outstanding balance from current purchases.

Type   `723.50`

Press   `tab` to update the journal and complete the cheque amount in the upper portion of the journal.

You can add a comment to the journal entry in the Comment field.

The journal is now complete and should look like the following:

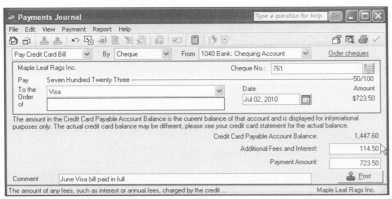

You should review the journal entry before proceeding.

Choose the **Report menu** and **click Display Payments Journal Entry** to display the transaction:

Maple Leaf Rags Inc.				
07/02/10 (J5)	Debits	Credits	Division	
2260 Visa Payable	609.00	-		
5150 Bank Charges & Card Fees	114.50	-		
1040 Bank: Chequing Account	-	723.50		
	723.50	723.50		

Notice that the linked Payables bank account is credited for the full amount of the payment. The payment amount is divided between the debit to *Visa Payable* to reduce the liability and the debit to *Bank Charges & Card Fees*, the linked expense account for credit card expenses.

Close the **display** when you have finished reviewing it to return to the Payments Journal.

Make **corrections** by reselecting from a drop-down list or by highlighting an incorrect entry and typing the correct amount. Press `tab` after changing an amount to update the totals.

Click the **Post button** 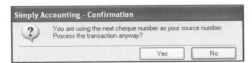. A message appears about the cheque number:

NOTES
Remember that you will click OK after posting because transaction confirmation is activated.

NOTES
This message appears only for credit card bill payments.

> **Simply Accounting - Confirmation**
>
> ?   You are using the next cheque number as your source number. Process the transaction anyway?
>
>   Yes   No

Click **Yes** to continue processing the payment.

Close the **Payments Journal** to return to the Payables window.

Accessing a Supplier's Web Site

SIMPLY VERSION
Remember that the term vendor will replace supplier.

NOTES
The results from the Search field entry will display all uses of the text you entered in the data file. The Search tool allows you to choose the search area, either records or transactions.

Before making the GST remittance, we will search the Canada Revenue Agency Web site to see whether there are any recent tax changes that affect this business.

There are a number of ways to access a supplier record. Because the principles are the same for finding records in all ledgers, we will illustrate different methods.

> **Click** **Receiver General** in the Suppliers pane list in the Payables module window to open the record directly. **Close** the **ledger record**.

You can type text in the Search field or use the Search tool (or Search menu option).

> **Click** the **Search field** in the upper-right section of the Home window.

> **Type** `rec` and **press** —>:

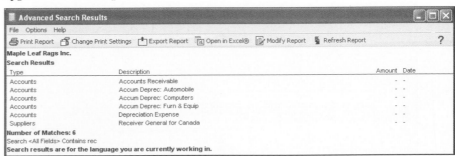

Several account names include this text as well as the supplier record we want.

> **Double click** the supplier, **Receiver General for Canada** to open the record. **Close** the **ledger record** and **Search window**.

> **Click** the **Search tool** 🔍 , or **choose** the **Edit menu** and **click Search** or **press** `ctrl` + **F** to begin:

SIMPLY VERSION
The Advanced Search tab and option are not available in the Simply version.

NOTES
You can type a letter in the Search field to advance the list if you have many suppliers.
The Advanced Search feature allows you to define additional search parameters.

NOTES
If you click the Search tool after entering a transaction, you will open the search for a transaction screen. If you click the Search tool after viewing a ledger record, you will list the records for that module.

The Search window opens. The default list depends on your starting point. In any Search window, you can select the search area from the Select A Record Or Transaction Type To Find drop-down list as shown:

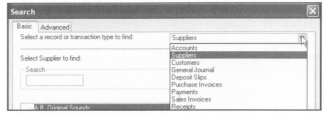

Clicking Suppliers will display the list of suppliers. Click the Search field and type R to advance to that part of the list. Receiver General for Canada will be selected because it is the first record beginning with R.

> **Double click** **Receiver General** to open the record. **Close** the **ledger record**.

You can start from the Suppliers icon shortcuts list.

> **Choose** **Modify Supplier** from the Suppliers (Payables window) drop-down shortcuts list to open the Search window:

This Search screen looks the same, but Select Supplier To **Modify** replaces Find.

> **Double click** **Receiver General** to open the record. **Close** the **ledger record**.

You can also access the record from the Suppliers window.

> **Click** the **Suppliers icon** to open the Suppliers window:

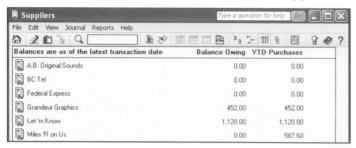

All suppliers are listed with their balances and total year-to-date purchases.

> **Double click** **Receiver General for Canada** to open the supplier's ledger:

You can access the Web site directly from this supplier ledger page.

> **Click** the **Web tool** or **choose** the **Online menu** and **click Web Site**:

Depending on how your Internet connection is set up, you may access the Web site directly or you may see a screen asking you to connect at this stage. You may need to enter the user ID and password for your Internet provider (if they are not set up to be saved and allow automatic connection). Again, your setup may be different.

You should see the homepage for the Canada Revenue Agency.

> **Choose** your language preference.
>
> **Click** the **Forms And Publications** option.
>
> **Click** the **Listed By Document Type** option.

You should see a list of types of publications. Several types of GST publications are listed. Select one to list the items for that type.

> You can also click Search, enter "GST publications" in the Search For field and click the Search button.
>
> **Close** your **Internet connection** when you have found the information you need or when you have finished. You will return to the supplier's ledger.
>
> **Close** the **Ledger window**. **Close** the **Suppliers window** if it is open.

Tax Remittances

NOTES
The Pay Remittances shortcut for the Payments icon is used only to remit payroll taxes.

NOTES
Tax amounts that you enter on the Sales Taxes screen in the General Journal are included in the tax reports.

Tax remittances are entered in the Purchases Journal as non-taxable purchase invoices with payment by cheque, or as Other Payments in the Payments Journal. There are two parts to a GST remittance — accounting for the GST (and HST) collected from customers and accounting for the GST (and HST) paid for purchases. The first is owed to the Receiver General while the second part — the input tax credit — is refunded or used to reduce the amount owing. Refer to Chapter 2 for further details. The GST Report can be used to help prepare the GST return, but the ledger account balances for the date of the filing period should be used as a final check in case there are amounts that were not entered in the journals. For Maple Leaf Rags, the opening or historical balance is needed. These amounts were not entered through journal transactions so we cannot use the GST or the PST Report.

PST remittances also have two parts — accounting for the PST collected from customers and reducing the tax remitted by the sales tax compensation for filing the return on time. Again, you can refer to the PST Report to help you.

> **Display** or **print** the **General Ledger Report** for the following tax accounts for June 30, 2010, to see the amounts you must enter. (See page 54 if you need assistance.)

- 2460 PST Payable
- 2650 GST Charged on Sales
- 2660 HST Charged on Sales
- 2670 GST Paid on Purchases
- 2680 HST Paid on Purchases

The General Ledger balances you need are the GST and PST amounts in the Trial Balance on page 454. You can also display or print the Trial Balance or Balance Sheet for June 30 to see the amounts for the tax accounts.

Making GST Remittances

CLASSIC VIEW
Click the Payments icon to open the journal and select Make Other Payment from the Pay drop-down list.

> **Choose** **Pay Expenses** from the Payments icon shortcuts list.
>
> **Choose** **Receiver General for Canada** as the supplier.

Choose July 5 from the pop-up calendar as the transaction date.

Click the **Account field List icon** 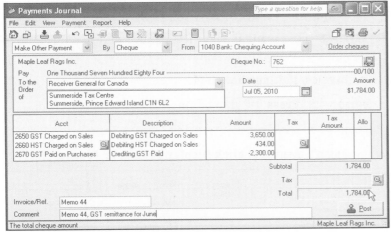 to display the account list.

Choose 2650 GST Charged on Sales to advance to the Description field.

Type   `Debiting GST Charged on Sales`

Press [tab] to advance to the Amount field. **Type** `3650`

No Tax is correctly selected as the default tax code.

Click the **Account field List icon** on the next journal line.

Choose 2660 HST Charged on Sales and advance to the Description field.

Type   `Debiting HST Charged on Sales`

Press [tab] to advance to the Amount field. **Type** `434`

Click the **Account field List icon** on the next journal line.

Choose 2670 GST Paid on Purchases. In the Description field,

Type   `Crediting GST Paid`

Press [tab] to advance to the Amount field.

Type   `-2300` (Use a **minus sign** or hyphen. The minus sign is necessary to create a credit for the liability account.)

The balance in the *HST Paid on Purchases* account is zero; therefore, we do not need to include an invoice line for it.

Click the **Invoice/Ref. field**.

Type   `Memo 44` **Press** [tab].

Type   `Memo 44, GST remittance for June`

This completes your entry as shown here:

NOTES
If the Payment Journal is already open, choose Make Other Payment from the Pay transactions drop-down list.

NOTES
No default account was entered for the Receiver General because four different accounts are required.

A review of the journal entry will help to clarify the transaction.

Choose the **Report menu** and **click Display Payments Journal Entry**:

Maple Leaf Rags Inc.				
07/05/10 (J6)	Debits	Credits	Division	
2650 GST Charged on Sales	3,650.00	-		
2660 HST Charged on Sales	434.00	-		
1040 Bank: Chequing Account	-	1,784.00		
2670 GST Paid on Purchases	-	2,300.00		
	4,084.00	4,084.00		

Normally, a positive amount will create a debit entry in the Payments Journal for an expense or an asset purchase. *GST/HST Charged on Sales* are GST payable accounts with a credit balance. Therefore, entering a positive amount will reduce the GST payable balance by debiting the accounts, as we did for the GST and HST collected from customers. The negative entry or credit for *GST Paid on Purchases* will offset the debit balance in the ledger and will reduce the total amount that is paid to the Receiver General. *HST Paid on Purchases* would also be entered as a negative amount because this amount is refundable. The net cheque amount is credited to the bank account.

> **Close**   the **display** window when you have finished. **Make corrections** if necessary.
>
> **Click**   **Post** ⌨ Post . You are now ready to make the PST remittance.

Making PST Remittances

You should still be in the Payments Journal with Make Other Payment selected as the type of transaction.

> **Choose**   **Minister of Finance** as the supplier. Accept the default bank account.
>
> **Accept**   **July 5** as the date and **accept** the default **account**, *2460 PST Payable*.
>
> **Click**   the **Description field**.
>
> **Type**   Debiting PST Payable
>
> **Press**   (tab) to move the cursor to the Amount field. **Type**   450

You are now ready to enter the revenue from sales tax compensation, 3.3 percent of the *PST Payable* amount.

> **Click**   the **Account field List icon** 🔍 on the second journal line.
>
> **Choose**   **4280 Sales Tax Compensation**. The cursor advances to the Description field.
>
> **Type**   Sales Tax Compensation **Press** (tab).
>
> **Type**   -14.85 (Use a **minus sign**. The minus sign will reduce the total amount that is paid to the Minister of Finance.)
>
> **Click**   the **Invoice/Ref. number field**.
>
> **Type**   Memo 45 **Press** (tab) to advance to the Comment field.
>
> **Type**   Memo 45, PST remittance for June
>
> **Choose** the **Report menu** and **click Display Payments Journal Entry**:

Maple Leaf Rags Inc.				
07/05/10 (J7)		Debits	Credits	Division
2460	PST Payable	450.00	-	
1040	Bank: Chequing Account	-	435.15	
4280	Sales Tax Compensation	-	14.85	
		450.00	450.00	

The full *PST Payable* amount is debited to reduce the entire liability by crediting the bank account for the amount of the cheque and the *Sales Tax Compensation* revenue account for the amount of the tax reduction.

> **Close**   the **display** when you have finished. **Make corrections** if needed.
>
> **Click**   **Post** ⌨ Post . **Close** the **Payments Journal**.

Entering Sales to Foreign Customers

Click   **Receivables** in the Modules pane list to open the Receivables window.

Click   the **Sales Invoices icon** 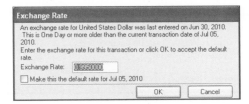 to open the Sales Journal. Invoice and Pay Later, the default selections, are correct.

Choose **Canadian Sounds** as the customer from the Sold To drop-down list:

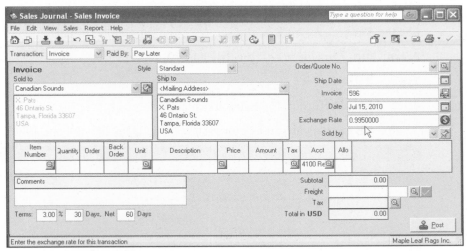

The invoice is modified for the foreign customer. A field for the exchange rate appears below the Date, and the Total is expressed in USD (United States dollars) rather than in Canadian dollars. An exchange rate button provides a list of exchange rates already entered for various dates. There is no rate for July 5.

Choose **July 5** from the Date field calendar.

The Exchange Rate screen opens because the exchange rate on record is more than one day old and no rate has been recorded for this date:

Exchange Rate

An exchange rate for United States Dollar was last entered on Jun 30, 2010. This is One Day or more older than the current transaction date of Jul 05, 2010.
Enter the exchange rate for this transaction or click OK to accept the default rate.

Exchange Rate: 0.9950000

☐ Make this the default rate for Jul 05, 2010

[OK]   [Cancel]

The Exchange Rate setting for the company file warns when the exchange rate on record is more than one day old so that an incorrect old rate is not accepted in error. The most recent exchange rate is entered and selected for editing. You can also edit the exchange rate directly in the journal screen just as you enter information in other fields.

Type   1.0255

Click   **Make This The Default Rate For Jul 05, 2010**.

Click   **OK** to return to the Sales Journal.

Click   the **Description field**.

Type   CDs

Click   the **Amount field**.

Type   2190

⚠ WARNING!

If you click the Date field before clicking the calendar, the Exchange Rate screen pops up with July 15 (the session date) as the date for which you are entering the rate. Then when you enter the transaction date, the Exchange Rate screen pops up again.

If you click the calendar first, the Exchange Rate screen will not open until after you choose the date.

Exported goods are not taxable because they are "consumed" outside of Canada. The No Tax code (blank) is entered as the default and it is correct. The default revenue account is also correct.

Click   the **Freight field**.

Type   120 **Press** (tab) to update the amounts.

No taxes are applied to freight on exported goods.

Click   the **Track Shipments tool** 📇.

Choose **Federal Express** as the shipper from the Shipped By list.

Press   (tab) to advance to the Tracking Number field.

Type   F19YTR563

Click   **OK** to return to the Sales Journal.

Your completed journal entry, ready for review, should look like the one shown:

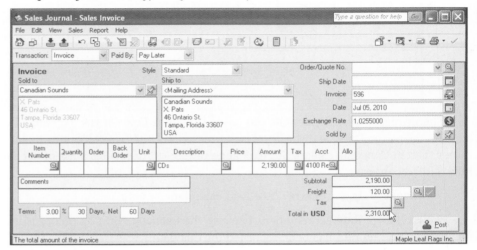

Choose the **Report menu** and **click Display Sales Journal Entry**:

Maple Leaf Rags Inc.					
07/05/10 (J8)		Foreign Amt.	Debits	Credits	Division
1200	Accounts Receivable	US$2,310.00	2,368.91	-	
4100	Revenue from Sales	US$2,190.00	-	2,245.85	
4200	Freight Revenue	US$120.00	-	123.06	
			2,368.91	2,368.91	
1 United States Dollar equals 1.0255000 Canadian Dollars					

Although the journal itself shows the amounts only in US dollars, the journal entry has both the Canadian amounts and the US amounts as well as the exchange rate applied to the transaction. The remainder of the entry is the same as it would be for sales to Canadian customers.

Close   the **display** when finished and **make corrections** if necessary.

Click   Post 📇 Post to save the transaction. **Close** the **Sales Journal**.

Enter   the **next group of transactions** up to the receipt from Canadian Sounds.

Entering Foreign Customer Receipts

Click   the **Receipts icon** 📇 Receipts ▾ to open the Receipts Journal.

Choose **Canadian Sounds** from the customer list:

SIMPLY VERSION

In the Simply version, the USD amounts are shown under the heading USD Amount because this version allows only two currencies, the home currency and one foreign currency.

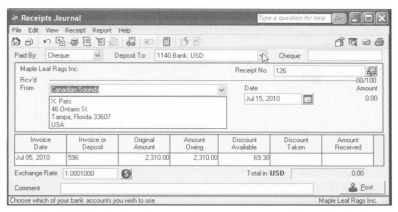

The journal is modified for the foreign customer. The outstanding invoice appears on the screen and the currency is marked as USD. An Exchange Rate field also becomes available.

Deposits from US customers are made to the USD bank account. This account is set up as the default bank account for foreign currency transactions.

Click   the **Cheque field**.

Type   2397

Click   the **Date field**. The session date is correct as the transaction date.

Press   (tab) to open the Exchange Rate screen.

If the rate has not changed, you can accept it by clicking Make This The Default Rate For Jul 15, 2010 and click OK.

Again, because the last exchange rate we entered was for July 10, the rate is out of date, and we must enter a new one. The previous rate is highlighted.

Type   0.995

Click   **Make This The Default Rate For Jul 15, 2010**.

Click   **OK** to return to the Receipts Journal. The cursor is on the calendar icon.

Click   the **Discount Taken field**.

Press   (tab) to accept the discount because the full invoice is being paid. The cursor advances to the Amount Received field.

Press   (tab) to accept the amount and update the cheque portion of the form.

Click   the **Enter Additional Information tool** 🗹.

The Total and cheque amount fields are updated in the background journal window.

Click   the **Additional Field text box** to move the cursor.

Type   Ref: inv #596

NOTES
If the correct bank account is not selected by default, you can choose it from the Deposit To drop-down list of bank accounts.

NOTES
If the Exchange Rate screen does not open when you enter a date, you can type the exchange rate directly in the Exchange Rate field.

Click   OK to return to the completed journal entry:

| Receipts Journal | | | | | | |

Paid By: Cheque   Deposit To: 1140 Bank: USD   Cheque: 2397

Maple Leaf Rags Inc.   Receipt No. 126

Rcv'd   Two Thousand Two Hundred Forty --70/100

From   Canadian Sounds   Date   Amount
X. Pats   Jul 15, 2010   2,240.70
46 Ontario St.
Tampa, Florida 33607
USA

Invoice Date	Invoice or Deposit	Original Amount	Amount Owing	Discount Available	Discount Taken	Amount Received
Jul 05, 2010	596	2,310.00	2,310.00	69.30	69.30	2,240.70

Exchange Rate 0.9950000   Total in USD   2,240.70

Comment   Post

Enter the exchange rate for this transaction   Maple Leaf Rags Inc.

You should review the journal entry.

Choose the **Report menu** and **click Display Receipts Journal Entry**:

Maple Leaf Rags Inc.					
07/15/10 (J13)		Foreign Amt.	Debits	Credits	Division
1140	Bank: USD	US$2,240.70	2,229.50	-	
4180	Sales Discounts	US$69.30	68.95	-	
4300	Exchange Rate Differences	-	70.46	-	
1200	Accounts Receivable	US$2,310.00	-	2,368.91	
			2,368.91	2,368.91	
1 United States Dollar equals 0.9950000 Canadian Dollars					

In addition to the usual linked accounts for receipts, an entry for *Exchange Rate Differences* appears. Because the exchange rate was higher on the day of the sale, the date the revenue was recorded, than on the day of the receipt, there has been a debit to the account. Maple Leaf Rags has lost money on the delay in payment — fewer Canadian dollars are received for the same US dollar amount than when the exchange rate is higher. When the rate increases, there is a gain. As for foreign customer sales, amounts are given in both currencies along with the exchange rate.

NOTES

The gain/loss situation is reversed for payments to foreign suppliers. When the rate increases, the purchased goods cost more and money is lost. A decrease in exchange rate creates a gain.

Close the **display** to return to the journal and **make corrections** if necessary.

Click Post   to save the transaction.

Close the **Receipts Journal**.

Looking Up Invoices to Track Shipments

Lookup provides an exact copy of the posted invoice that you can store, print or e-mail if you have forgotten to do so before posting. This feature can be useful if a customer has an inquiry about a purchase or needs a copy of the invoice. Once a sales or purchase invoice is posted with details about the shipping company, you can look up the invoice to track the shipment to see when delivery is expected. You can use the Find Invoice approach or the Search feature (see Notes).

NOTES

You can also type Treble in the Search field and press —>.

The result will list the record for the customer and the sales invoice. Double click the sales invoice entry to open the lookup screen for this transaction.

The Next and Previous tools will not be available because this sales invoice is the only one that meets the criterion.

Choose Find Invoice from the Sales Invoices shortcuts list as shown:

You will open the Search dialogue window:

If the Sales Journal is open, you can click the Look Up An Invoice tool ▨ on the tool bar or beside the Invoice field, or choose the Sales menu and click Look Up Invoice, to open this Search window.

The Lookup screen options are like those for adjusting an invoice. You can search through all invoices for the fiscal year to date (or for the previous year if you have not cleared the transactions and lookup data) or enter a narrower range of dates; you can search through invoices for all customers or for a specific customer; or you can search for a specific invoice number. Your search strategy will depend on how much information you have before you begin the search and how many invoices there are altogether.

The default displayed Start date may be the start of the fiscal period, the calendar date or the date you created the company files. The Finish date is the most recent session date. You can change these dates to narrow the search, just as you would edit any other date fields, or you can choose dates from the drop-down list or calendar. We want to include all invoices in the search, beginning with the earliest transaction date in the data file, the fiscal start date.

Click   the **Start date**.

Type   7 1

The Customer Name option allows you to Search All Customers, the default setting, or a specific customer's invoices. You can also look up the invoices for one-time customers.

> To display the list of customers, click the Customer Name field or its drop-down list arrow and click the name you need to select a specific customer.

> If you know the invoice number, enter it in the Invoice Number field and click OK.

In this case we will look at all invoices by choosing the default to Search All Customers.

Click   **OK** to display the list of invoices that meet the search conditions of date and customers:

You can sort the list by order of posting date, customer, journal entry number, invoice number and amount. You can also reverse the order of the entries in the list by clicking the A...Z button.

Click   **Treble & Bass, Invoice Number 597** for $10 938.20 to select it. Click anywhere on the line.

Click   Select. The requested invoice will be displayed as follows:

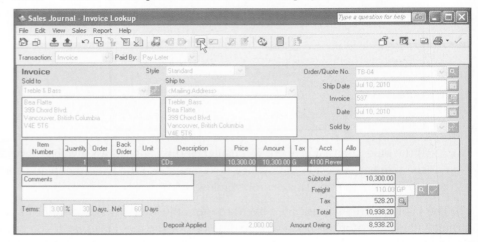

Notice that this is an exact copy of the original invoice, except that you cannot edit or post it. You can, however, store, e-mail or print it. Although you cannot adjust an invoice from the Lookup window directly, the Adjust Invoice tool is available. When you click Adjust Invoice, the journal screen changes to the Adjust Invoice form. You can use the lookup method to locate the invoice you need to adjust. You can also reverse a transaction directly from the Lookup screen.

If you have selected the wrong invoice, or if you want to view other invoices from this one, you can access them from any Lookup window. If there are no invoices in one or both directions, the corresponding button or tools will be dimmed.

Click Look Up Next Invoice ▣▶ or Look Up Previous Invoice ◀▣ or choose Previous or Next Invoice from the Sales menu to display other invoices. You can browse through the invoices in this way until you find the one you need. You should practise viewing other invoices by clicking the Look Up Next and Previous Invoice tools.

Click   the **Track Shipments tool** 📷 or **choose** the **Sales menu** and **click Track Shipments** to see the shipping details for the sale.

If you need to add or edit the information, click Cancel to close the tracking details window. Click the Adjust Invoice tool in the journal and then Track Shipments.

Click   the Web icon 📷 to close the shipping details screen and continue:

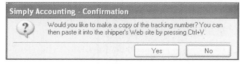

If you have set up a shipping account and have entered the actual number, you can choose Yes and save the number for entering on the Web site tracking page. However, we do not have an account with Purolator.

Click   No to continue to the Internet connection.

Your screen at this stage will depend on your Internet setup — you may connect and access the Web site directly, or you may need to enter your account and password first.

Continue as you would for your usual Internet connection.

NOTES

If you entered other Search parameters, the Next and Previous tools will show you all invoices that meet those criteria.

WARNING!

If you have a network connection, such as high-speed access, you must start the Internet connection before clicking the Track Shipments tool.

NOTES

Web sites are continually updated so the screens and sequence of steps may be different from the ones we provide.

You will access the Web site for Purolator.

Click the **Track Shipment field**, **enter** the **PIN Number**, **press** --> and follow the instructions provided to proceed with tracking the shipment.

Close the **Web Site screen** when finished to return to the Lookup screen.

Click **OK** to close the Track Shipments screen.

We are now ready to e-mail a copy of the invoice to the customer as notice of the shipping date and carrier. (Read the Warning margin note.)

Click the **E-mail tool** 📧 or **choose** the **File menu** and **click E-mail**.

Since printing invoices is the default setting in the customer's ledger record, you are asked if you want to continue, just in case you clicked the wrong button.

Click **E-mail** to continue to the E-mail Information screen:

If there is no e-mail address in the ledger record, you can enter it here. You could also edit the default ledger record entry if needed. The E-mail Address field should be selected. You can replace it with your own address to test the e-mail feature.

Type (Type your own e-mail address in this field, or that of a classmate.)

You can add a message in the Message field about the shipment tracking details to inform the customer of the expected delivery date.

Click **Send**.

You will see another advisory screen asking whether you want to update the e-mail address in the ledger record.

Click **Yes** to proceed.

At this stage, your screens will depend on your e-mail and Internet setups. You should be connected to your Internet provider. Depending on the e-mail program you are using, you may see a message that the program is trying to send a message:

Click **Send**.

You may have to enter your ID and password before your e-mail program starts.

Close your **e-mail** and **Internet connections** to return to the Sales Journal – Invoice Lookup window.

Close the **Lookup window** to return to the Receivables window.

Looking Up and Tracking Purchases

You can look up purchase invoices in the same way as you look up sales invoices. You can look up purchase invoices from the Purchases Journal and from the Payments Journal.

NOTES
You can also look up Purchases Journal invoices from the Payments Journal, Pay Purchase Invoices screen.

Open the Purchases or Payments Journal, click Look Up An Invoice 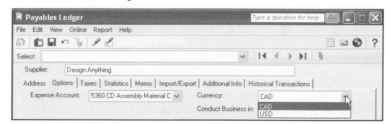, decide whether you want to restrict the search dates or suppliers and click OK. Choose an invoice from the displayed list and click Select. If you know the invoice number, you can enter it directly, click OK to display the requested invoice.

From the Payments Journal, choose Make Other Payment then click ▦ (Look Up An Invoice) to see cash invoices posted in the Purchases Journal.

Once you look up a purchase invoice, you can track shipments and look up other invoices in the same way as you do for sales. You can also adjust the invoice. Tracking is not available for cash purchases entered as Other Payments in the Payments Journal.

Entering Purchases from Foreign Suppliers

Purchases from foreign suppliers are entered in much the same way as purchases from other suppliers. Once you choose a supplier who uses a different currency, the Purchases Journal changes to add the appropriate fields.

Advance the **session date** to July 31.

Open the **Payables module window**.

WARNING!
You must choose Full Add for the new supplier so that you can choose USD as the currency.

Click the **Purchase Invoices icon** [Purchase Invoices ▾] to open the Purchases Journal. Invoice and Pay Later are correctly selected.

Click the **Supplier field**.

Type Design Anything **Press** ⟨tab⟩.

Entering a Foreign Supplier Record

Click **Full Add** to open the Payables Ledger supplier input screen.

Type the supplier address details from the source documents (page 459).

Enter **July 16** as the date for the Supplier Since field.

Click the **Options tab**. Notice the additional field for currency.

Choose **5360 CD Assembly Materials Costs** as the default expense account.

Click the **Currency list arrow** as shown:

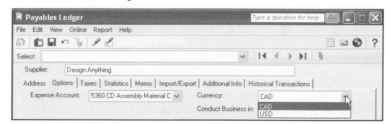

Choose **USD**. A Balance Owing in USD amount is added to the record.

Enter **net 30 days** as the payment terms.

Click   the **Taxes tab** to see the default settings.

Click   the **Tax Code list arrow** to see the options:

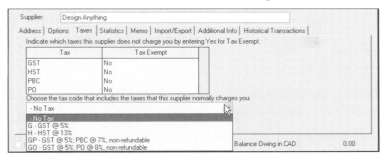

Maple Leaf Rags is not exempt from paying taxes on purchases from Design Anything, and that is the default selection. All tax codes will be available. Most purchases from US suppliers are subject to GST so we should choose G - GST @ 5% as the default tax code. Maple pays GST on imported goods.

Click   **Code G - GST @ 5%**.

Click   **Save And Close** 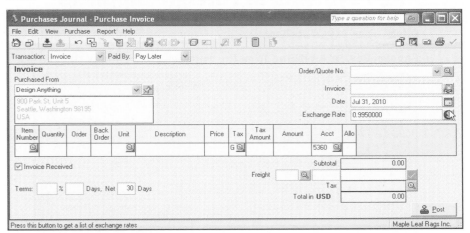 to return to the modified invoice:

The invoice currency is now shown as USD and exchange rate fields are added. The default terms, expense account and tax code are also on the invoice.

If you have entered several different exchange rates, you can click 💲, the exchange rate tool, to access them and select one for the current transaction.

Enter   the **Invoice number**, **Date**, **Exchange Rate** and **Amount** to complete the invoice as shown:

Review the entry before posting.

> **Choose** the **Report menu** and **click Display Purchases Journal Entry**:

Maple Leaf Rags Inc.					
07/16/10 (J14)		Foreign Amt.	Debits	Credits	Division
2670	GST Paid on Purchases	US$150.00	149.85	-	
5360	CD Assembly Material Costs	US$3,000.00	2,997.00	-	
2200	Accounts Payable	US$3,150.00	-	3,146.85	
			3,146.85	3,146.85	
1 United States Dollar equals 0.9990000 Canadian Dollars					

The only difference between this and other purchase entries is the addition of the USD currency amounts and exchange rate.

> **Close** the **display** to return to the journal and **make corrections** if necessary.
>
> **Click** Post [Post] . **Close** the **Purchases Journal**.

Return to the source documents and **enter** the **next group of transactions**, until Cheque #284.

> **Change** module windows as needed.

Entering Payments to Foreign Suppliers

> **Click** the **Payments icon** [Payments] to open the Payments Journal.
>
> **Choose Design Anything** from the Supplier list to modify the journal:

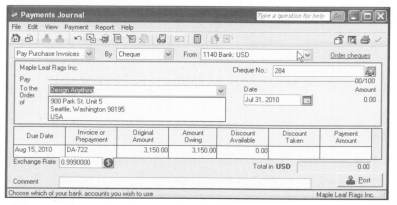

The outstanding invoice appears on the screen and the currency is marked as USD. An Exchange Rate field also becomes available.

Payments to US suppliers are made from the USD bank account. This account is set up as the default bank account for foreign currency transactions. The cheque number is the next in sequence for this account.

> **Click** the **Calendar icon** [calendar] and **choose July 30** as the transaction date.

The Exchange Rate screen should open automatically because the exchange rate is out of date.

> **Type** `0.982`
>
> **Click** **Make This The Default Rate For Jul 30, 2010**.
>
> **Click** **OK** to return to the Payments Journal. The cursor is on the calendar icon.
>
> **Click** the **Payment Amount field**. There is no discount.
>
> **Press** (*tab*) to accept the amount and complete the entry as shown:

Press (ctrl) **+ J** so you can review the journal entry:

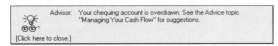

Maple Leaf Rags Inc.				
07/30/10 (J19)	Foreign Amt.	Debits	Credits	Division
2200 Accounts Payable	US$3,150.00	3,146.85	-	
1140 Bank: USD	US$3,150.00	-	3,093.30	
4300 Exchange Rate Differences	-	-	53.55	
		3,146.85	3,146.85	
1 United States Dollar equals 0.9820000 Canadian Dollars				

A credit entry for *Exchange Rate Differences* appears because the exchange rate was higher on the day of the purchase, the date the purchase was recorded, than on the day of the payment. However, because this is a payment, Maple Leaf Rags has gained on the payment delay as shown by the credit entry — fewer Canadian dollars are needed to pay the same US dollar amount. As for other foreign currency transactions, amounts are given in both currencies, and the exchange rate is included.

Close the **display** to return to the journal. **Make corrections** if necessary.

Click **Post** [Post] to see this message:

> Advisor: Your chequing account is overdrawn. See the Advice topic
> "Managing Your Cash Flow" for suggestions.
>
> [Click here to close.]

The message indicates that the bank account is overdrawn. We will transfer funds to the USD account to cover the cheque before the supplier has a chance to cash it.

Click the **Advisor icon** to close the message. **Close** the **Payments Journal**.

Transferring Foreign Funds

Click **Banking** in the Modules pane list to open this module window:

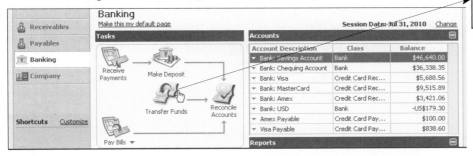

The Banking module window has no ledger icons although it does allow direct access to the ledger records for all accounts involved in making or receiving payments. Three journal icons — Make Deposits, Transfer Funds, Reconcile Accounts — are for bank account transactions. The Receive Payments and Pay Bills icons open the Receipts and Payments journals and are duplicated from Receivables and Payables modules.

NOTES

Access to the Payments and Receipts journals from the Banking module allows all bank-related activities to be completed from this screen.

Deposits and account reconciliation are covered in Chapter 15.

Make Other Payment is the default type of transaction from the Pay Bills icon.

We use the Transfer Funds Journal to move money from one bank account to another.

Click the **Transfer Funds icon** to open the journal we need:

Type July 30 (as the Date).

Click the **Currency list arrow** to see the currency options as shown:

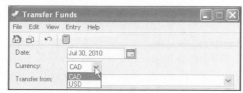

Both currencies are available for Transfer Funds transactions.

Click **USD**. The exchange rate is entered correctly for this date.

Click the **Transfer From list arrow** to see the available accounts:

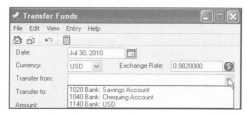

Choose 1040 Bank: Chequing Account in the Account field. **Press** (tab).

Click the **Transfer To list arrow** to see the available accounts.

Choose 1140 Bank: USD and **press** (tab) to advance to the Amount field.

Type 1000 **Press** (tab) to advance to the comment field.

Type Transfer funds to cover cheques

The journal entry is complete as shown here:

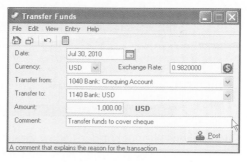

Check your transaction carefully because you cannot display the journal entry before posting. To make corrections after posting, you can adjust or reverse the transfer in the General Journal.

When you display the Journal Entries Report, the transfer is entered as a typical debit and credit entry, with the exchange rate added and amounts given in both currencies as for other foreign currency transactions.

Click   **Post** ![Post] to save the transaction.

Close   the **Transfer Funds Journal**.

Enter   the **remaining transactions**, including those for September 30. Change module windows as needed.

Creating an Accountant's Copy

Many businesses rely on professional accountants to assist them with their accounting. The accountants will check the data entered by the business for errors and make corrections. They also may add the adjusting entries required at the end of a fiscal period to bring the books up to date and to prepare for filing tax returns. The business then begins the new year with a complete and accurate data file.

Simply Accounting allows a data file to be saved as an accountant's copy. This backup data file can only be restored and opened in the Accountants' Edition of Simply Accounting. The accountant can add journal entries to the file that can be added back to the original business data file. The business may continue with day-to-day journal entry and even start a new fiscal period while the accountant is preparing the additional entries.

To create an accountant's copy,

Choose the **File menu**, then **choose Accountant's Copy** and **click Create Accountant's Copy** as shown:

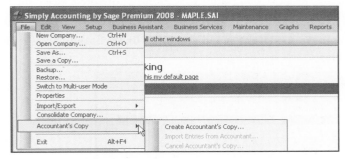

You can also create the copy from the Company module window Accountant's Task Pane.

Choose **Create Accountant's Copy** from the Accountant's Copy icon shortcuts drop-down list as shown:

You will be asked to choose a location for the new backup file:

The default name for the file adds Accountant's_Copy_ to the original name so it will not be confused with your other backup files. The default location is a new ACCOUNTANT folder inside the Data folder (in the Simply Accounting program folder).

To choose another folder, click Browse and click the folder you want to use. Enter a different name for the file if you want.

Click   OK to begin making the specialized backup.

When the copy is complete, you will see the following information window:

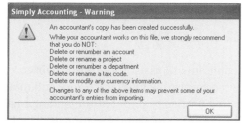

Read this message carefully as it warns you of the things you can and cannot do in your working file while the accountant is working with the accountant's copy of your file.

Click   OK to return to your data file.

Monitoring Routine Activities

The end of September is the end of Bands' fiscal year. There are a number of steps to complete before beginning the new year. Simply Accounting provides assistance with these steps in its checklists.

CLASSIC VIEW

Click [ ] (the Checklists tool) to open the Checklists window.

Choose the **Business Assistant menu** and **click Checklists** to see the lists available:

Checklists are available for different periods — end of a fiscal period, end of a business day, end of a month and end of a calendar year for payroll.

You can also create your own checklists, add procedures to one of the predefined checklists and print the checklists for reference.

Before checking the fiscal year-end procedures, we will add a reminder to the daily tasks checklist.

Click   Day-End Procedures and then **click Modify** to open the list:

NOTES

You cannot edit checklists in multi-user mode.

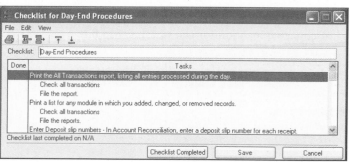

Each checklist can be customized for a company by using the tool buttons or the Edit menu items to insert activities, delete them or rearrange them.

Click   the **Insert Item tool** or **choose** the **Edit menu** and **click Insert** to add a blank line at the top of the task list.

Press   `tab` to advance to the Tasks field.

Type   `Check bank balances for possible overdrafts`

Click   **Save** to return to the Checklists window.

Double click   **Fiscal Year-End Procedures** to see the checklist we need:

Maple Leaf Rags does not use the budgeting feature of the program so we can remove these tasks from the checklist.

     Scroll down and **click Printing Budget Reports**.

Click   the **Remove Item tool** or **choose** the **Edit menu** and **click Remove**.

Click   **Yes** to confirm that you want to continue with the deletion.

Click   the **Print tool** 🖨 to print the checklist for reference.

Back up the **data files** and **print reports**. These are the most important elements on this list. Do not print reports for Payroll, Inventory or Projects. You can remove these reports from the list if you want.

Click   the **Done column** after completing a task — a ✓ will be added to the Done column.

Click Save if you want to leave the list and return later. A ✓ will appear in the Task In Progress column on the Checklists screen.

Complete all the **tasks** listed, except printing the reports for the modules that are not used. After finishing all the activities,

Click   **Checklist Completed**. The session date will be added to the Date Last Completed column on the Checklists screen.

Open the remaining checklists to see the tasks to be completed at the end of each month and at end of a calendar year. Print these lists for reference.

Click   **Close** to leave the Checklists window when you have finished.

Start   the **new fiscal year** on October 1, 2010.

NOTES
Reconciling Accounts will be explained in Chapter 15 and Budgeting is covered in Chapter 14.

NOTES
In Chapter 15, we describe how to clear data from company files.

NOTES
Refer to page 99 for assistance with starting a new fiscal period.

The Accountant Works with Your Data

When the accountant opens the file you sent, it will be restored in the same version of Simply Accounting that you used. Only the General Journal, the one used for adjusting entries, is available to the accountant.

The Classic view Home window for the Accountant's Copy file is shown here:

The No Edit symbol appears with all the ledger and journal icons except for the General Journal. The accountant can view, but not change, the information in the other journals and ledgers.

After adding the required adjustments, the accountant exports the new journal entries to a text file. This option is available from the Accountants' Edition menu by choosing Accountant's Copy and then Export Entries for Client as shown:

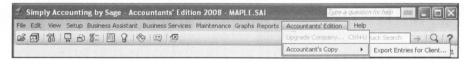

The exported text file of journal entries is sent back to you, the client.

Importing the Accountant's Journal Entries

When you receive the file from the accountant, you must import the journal entries to add them to your working file.

> **Restore** the data file **SimData\ACCOUNTANT\AE-maple** for this step.
>
> **Choose** the **File menu**, then **choose Accountant's Copy** and **click Import Entries from Accountant**. Or **choose Import Entries from Accountant** from the Accountant's Copy icon shortcuts list:

Both the file menu options and the shortcuts list for Accountant's Tasks in the Company module window have changed. Once you create an accountant's copy, the other submenu options become available. The program stores the information that there is an outstanding accountant's copy for the file so you can import the journal entries later. This menu option remains available until the entries have been imported. You cannot create another accountant's copy while there is one outstanding. If you discover an error after you create the accountant's copy, you can cancel that version and then create a new accountant's copy. The option to Cancel Accountant's Copy is used for this purpose. After cancelling, the option to create becomes available again.

The Import Entries wizard begins:

Click   Next:

NOTES
The procedure for importing entries from the accountant is similar to importing other General Journal entries. Refer to Appendix I.

You are asked to make a backup before proceeding. Since the step of importing entries cannot be reversed, you should back up the data file first.

Click   Backup and follow the steps for creating a backup of the data file. **Click Next** to continue:

Now you must locate the file the accountant sent. We have added the file you need to the SimData\ACCOUNTANT folder where the AE-Maple backup is stored.

Click   Browse.

Locate   SimData\ACCOUNTANT\Accountant's_Entries_maple-AE.TXT and **click** to select it.

Click   Open and then **click Next**.

NOTES
The file you need is Accountant's_Entries_maple-AE.TXT. It is located in the SimData\ACCOUNTANT folder.

If you try to import the journal entries to a your own Maple Leaf Rags data file, or any other file that is different from the one used to create the accountant's copy, you will see the following error message:

Click   OK. You must use the data file in the Accountant folder for this step.

If you are using the correct matching data file, you will see this screen:

NOTES

If your system settings do not allow transactions in the previous year, you must first change this setting. Refer to page 101.

This warning appears because the entries are dated in the previous fiscal year. We want to accept the dates the accountant used because they are correct and the entries should be added to the financial reports for the previous year. We need to allow all these entries and do not want the message to appear for each one.

Click   **Do Not Show This Message Again**.

Click   **Yes**:

This summary of the imported transactions shows the entries added to your file.

Click   **OK**:

Click   **Finish**. The process is now complete.

The General Journal report for September 30 will include the accountant's entries:

NOTES

For this report, we selected to Show Only Entries Posted After Year End.

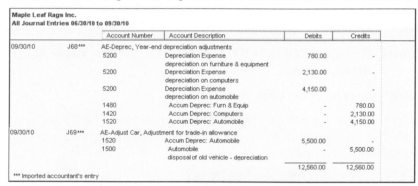

The journal entry numbers are marked *** to show that they were created outside the regular file by the accountant. The numbers may be out of sequence if you have added transactions while the accountant was working with the file.

Displaying Exchange Rate Reports

When a business has foreign currency transactions, Simply Accounting will generate reports related to exchange rate gains and losses.

Open   the **Report Centre** and **click Financials**:

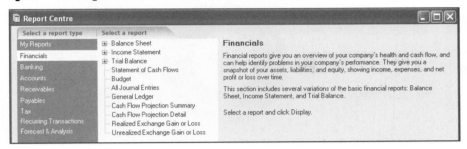

Click   **Realized Exchange Gain or Loss**. **Click Modify This Report**:

This first exchange rate report includes the gains or losses already realized or recorded because the payment has been made or received and the exchange rate difference is known.

Click   **Previous Year** to see reports for this application.

Enter   the **dates** for the report and **click OK**.

Close   the **display** when finished.

To access the second exchange rate report,

Click   **Unrealized Exchange Gain or Loss**. **Click Modify This Report**:

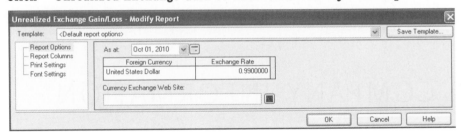

The second report includes the gains or losses that have not yet been realized or recorded — the payment has not been made but the exchange rate is known to have changed. When the payment is made or received, the actual gain may be different if the rate has changed again.

The report also revalues existing account balances and previous payments and receipts for the new exchange rate.

Enter   the **date** for the report and an **Exchange Rate** for that date. **Click OK**.

Close   the **display** when finished. **Close** the **Report Centre**.

NOTES
From the Home window, choose the Reports menu, then choose Financials and click Realized Exchange Gain/Loss to see the report options.

NOTES
You cannot sort or filter the Exchange Rate reports. You can choose the columns for the Realized Exchange Rate Report.

NOTES
From the Home window, choose the Reports menu, then choose Financials and click Unrealized Exchange Gain/Loss to see the report options.

R E V I E W

The Student CD-ROM with Data Files includes Review Questions and Supplementary Cases for this chapter, including a case with stock transactions that can be completed in the General Journal.

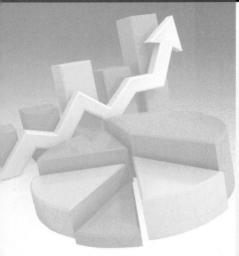

OBJECTIVES

After completing this chapter, you should be able to

- **enter** transactions in all journals
- **allocate** revenues and expenses in the General, Sales, Purchases, Payroll and Inventory journals
- **create** new divisions
- **change** the Division Ledger name
- **enter** import duty on purchases from foreign suppliers
- **make** import duty remittances
- **enter** purchases with cost variances
- **display** and **print** transactions with division details
- **display** and **print** division reports

COMPANY INFORMATION

Company Profile

NOTES
Truman Tires
600 Westminster St.
London, Ontario N6P 3B1
Tel: (519) 729-3733
Fax: (519) 729-7301
Business No.: 230 192 821

Truman Tires, located in London, Ontario, sells tires and wheels for all types of passenger cars, including taxis and service fleets for other businesses. Tyrone Truman completed an auto mechanics program at the local community college and then worked for an auto repair shop in Windsor for several years. He studied business administration part time to prepare him for starting his own business, which he now has operated for several years.

Although he sells all kinds of tires, throughout the year most people buy all-season radial tires. In December, the month in this application, Truman Tires sells mainly winter tires. All tire sales include free installation. The service centre, with its four service bays, also provides a limited range of services for automobiles, including oil changes, brake repairs and replacements, shocks replacements and wheel alignments. Four employees work on the cars while a manager and assistant manager handle all customer contacts and schedule appointments.

Truman Tires has a number of regular suppliers of inventory and other parts and supplies. Truman has accounts with most of these suppliers and some offer discounts for early payment. Some of the tires and wheels are imported from Japan and Truman pays import duties on these items.

Regular customers also have accounts with Truman Tires and are offered a 2 percent discount if they settle their accounts within 10 days. Some customers receive additional discounts through the preferred pricing schedule for all inventory sales and services.

In preparation for expanding his business, Tyrone Truman has decided to apply project costing for his two divisions, Sales and Service. He hopes to determine which aspect of the company is more profitable.

At the end of November 2010, Truman remitted all the company payroll taxes and deductions and closed his books. To convert his accounting records to Simply Accounting, he used the following:

- Chart of Accounts
- Post-Closing Trial Balance
- Supplier Information
- Customer Information
- Employee Information
- Employee Profiles and TD1 Information
- Inventory Information
- Division Information
- Accounting Procedures

SIMPLY VERSION
The term Vendors will be used instead of Suppliers throughout the program.

CHART OF ACCOUNTS

TRUMAN TIRES

ASSETS
Current Assets
1050 Bank: Chequing CAD
1060 Bank: Foreign Currency
1070 Bank: Visa
1080 Bank: MasterCard
1090 Bank: Interac
1200 Accounts Receivable
1220 Purchase Prepayments
1240 Brakes & Shocks Parts
1250 Supplies: Garage
1260 Supplies: Office

Inventory Assets
1360 Wheels
1380 Wheel Nuts & Locks
1400 Winter Tires

Plant & Equipment
1650 Cash Register
1660 Computer Equipment
1670 Garage Equipment
1680 Machinery & Tools
1690 Shop & Garage Bays ▶

▶1700 Tow Truck
1710 Yard

LIABILITIES
Current Liabilities
2100 Bank Loan
2150 Prepaid Sales and Deposits
2200 Accounts Payable
2220 Import Duty Payable
2250 Credit Card Payable
2300 Vacation Payable
2310 EI Payable
2320 CPP Payable
2330 Income Tax Payable
2390 EHT Payable
2400 CSB Payable
2410 Union Dues
2460 WSIB Payable
2640 PST Payable
2650 GST Charged on Sales
2670 GST Paid on Purchases

Long Term Liabilities
2850 Mortgage Payable ▶

▶**EQUITY**
Owner's Equity
3560 T. Truman, Capital
3580 T. Truman, Drawings
3600 Net Income

REVENUE
Revenue
4020 Revenue from Sales
4040 Revenue from Services
4100 Other Revenue
4150 Sales Discounts
4160 Sales Tax Compensation

EXPENSE
Operating Expenses
5020 Advertising & Promotion
5030 Bank Charges
5035 Exchange Rate Differences
5040 Credit Card Fees
5045 Assembly Costs
5050 Cost of Goods Sold
5055 Variance Costs ▶

▶5060 Cost of Services
5065 Freight Expense
5070 Hydro Expense
5080 Interest Expense - Loan
5090 Interest Expense - Mortgage
5100 Inventory Adjustment
5110 Tool Rentals
5120 Inventory Parts Used
5130 Purchase Discounts
5140 Repairs & Maintenance
5150 Telephone Expense

Payroll Expenses
5300 Management Wages
5310 General Wages
5320 Piece Rate Wage Expense
5330 Commissions and Bonuses
5410 EI Expense
5420 CPP Expense
5430 WSIB Expense
5460 EHT Expense

NOTES: The Chart of Accounts includes only postable accounts and Net Income. WSIB (Workplace Safety and Insurance Board) is the name for WCB (Workers' Compensation Board) in Ontario.

POST-CLOSING TRIAL BALANCE

TRUMAN TIRES

November 30, 2010

		Debits	Credits				Debits	Credits
1050	Bank: Chequing CAD	$20 765		▶	1670	Garage Equipment	75 000	
1060	Bank: Foreign Currency (¥215 280)	2 000			1680	Machinery & Tools	25 000	
1070	Bank: Visa	8 000			1690	Shop & Garage Bays	175 000	
1080	Bank: MasterCard	5 000			1700	Tow Truck	40 000	
1090	Bank: Interac	2 500			1710	Yard	25 000	
1200	Accounts Receivable	4 181			2100	Bank Loan		$ 12 000
1240	Brakes & Shocks Parts	6 800			2200	Accounts Payable		5 920
1250	Supplies: Garage	2 400			2250	Credit Card Payable		235
1260	Supplies: Office	600			2300	Vacation Payable		6 943
1360	Wheels	9 136			2640	PST Payable		3 360
1380	Wheel Nuts & Locks	738			2650	GST Charged on Sales		2 940
1400	Winter Tires	15 480			2670	GST Paid on Purchases	1 400	
1650	Cash Register	2 500			2850	Mortgage Payable		140 000
1660	Computer Equipment	2 500 ▶			3560	T. Truman, Capital		252 602
							$424 000	$424 000

SUPPLIER INFORMATION

TRUMAN TIRES

Supplier Name (Contact)	Address	Phone No. Fax No.	E-mail Web Site	Terms Tax ID
Bell Canada (Louis Gossip)	100 Ring Road London, Ontario N5W 2M3	Tel: (519) 387-2355	www.bell.ca	n/10
CAW Union				n/30
Equity Life				n/30
Gulf Oil Company (Petro Crewd)	30 Refinery Cr. London, Ontario N4R 6F1	Tel: (519) 641-6277	pc@gulfoil.com www.gulfoil.com	n/30
London Hydro (Les Current)	755 Ohm Blvd. London, Ontario N6C 1P9	Tel: (519) 649-8100	lesc@londonhydro.on.ca www.londonhydro.on.ca	n/10
London Tool Rentals (Roto Tiller)	239 Pneumatics Rd. London, Ontario N5X 2S4	Tel: (519) 633-7102 Fax: (519) 635-8191	roto@getitfromus.com www.getitfromus.com	n/20 325 622 934
Minister of Finance	Box 620, 33 King St. W Oshawa, Ontario L1H 8H5	Tel: (905) 443-8200	www.gov.on.ca/fin	n/30
MoTech Auto Parts (Moe Torrs)	2 Revving Parkway Windsor, Ontario N7T 7C2	Tel: (519) 722-1973 Fax: (519) 725-3664	moe@motech.com www.motech.com	2/10, n/30 (after tax) 163 482 977
Receiver General for Canada	PO Box 20004, Station A Sudbury, Ontario P3A 6B4	Tel: (705) 821-8186	www.cra-arc.gc.ca	n/30
Snowmaster Tire Company (I.C. Winters)	86 Sleet St. Tokyo, Japan 162-0829	Tel: (81-3) 5249 7331 Fax: (81-3) 5261 5492	icw@snowmaster.com www.snowmaster.com	net 15
Sylverado Wheels (Roy Rimmer)	100 Round Rd., Unit 2 Tokyo, Japan 100-7227	Tel: (81-3) 3643 8459 Fax: (81-3) 3663 5188	royrimmer@sylverado.com www.sylverado.com	n/30
TuffArm Shocks (Sally Shockley)	489 Spring St. Toronto, Ontario M4Z 3G3	Tel: (416) 699-2019 Fax: (416) 699-3854	Sal@tuffarm.shocks.com www.tuffarm.shocks.com	n/30 263 495 687
Western Hydraulic Repairs (Otto Raizer)	109 Lift St. London, Ontario N6F 8A5	Tel: (519) 645-6722 Fax: (519) 646-1145	o_raizer@whydraulics.com www.whydraulics.com	n/30 466 345 291
Workplace Safety & Insurance Board				n/30

OUTSTANDING SUPPLIER INVOICES

TRUMAN TIRES

Supplier Name	Terms	Date	Invoice No.	Amount CAD	Amount JPY
MoTech Auto Parts	2/10, n/30 (after tax)	Nov. 27/10	MT-1142	$630	
Snowmaster Tire Company	net 15	Nov. 26/10	ST-842	$2 544	¥274 138
Sylverado Wheels	n/30	Nov. 10/10	SW-724	$1 696	¥182 759
TuffArm Shocks	n/30	Nov. 4/10	TS-699	$1 050	
		Grand Total		$5 920	

CUSTOMER INFORMATION

TRUMAN TIRES

Customer Name (Contact)	Address	Phone No. Fax No.	E-mail Web Site	Terms Credit Limit
*Airport Taxi Service (Jett Plane)	100 Runway Rd. London, Ontario N5G 3J7	Tel: (519) 643-6182 Fax: (519) 645-1772	jett@gofly.com www.gofly.com	2/10, n/30 $4 000
Cash Customers				n/1
City Cab Company (Able Driver)	890 Transport St. London, Ontario N5W 1B3	Tel: (519) 641-7999 Fax: (519) 641-2539	driver@wetakeyou.com www.wetakeyou.com	2/10, n/30 $4 000
*London Car Leasing (Nick Borrow)	44 Fleet St. London, Ontario N6T 7V2	Tel: (519) 788-2538 Fax: (519) 789-3264	borrow@whybuy.com www.whybuy.com	2/10, n/30 $4 000
Lovely U Cosmetics (N.O. Blemish)	450 Phare Skinn Cr. London, Ontario N6B 3H3	Tel: (519) 782-4477 Fax: (519) 781-4372	blemish@lovelyU.com www.lovelyU.com	2/10, n/30 $4 000
*Polly Maid Services (Polly Mayden)	92 Scouring St. London, Ontario N6T 2K6	Tel: (519) 648-3645 Fax: (519) 648-2774	polly@pollymaid.com www.pollymaid.com	2/10, n/30 $4 000
Pronto Pizza & Delivery (Wayte Nott)	52 Marguerite St. London, Ontario N5B 2R5	Tel: (519) 784-7287 Fax: (519) 785-8220	waytenott@pronto.com www.pronto.com	2/10, n/30 $4 000

NOTES: Preferred price list customers are marked with an asterisk (*) beside their names. All discounts are after tax.

OUTSTANDING CUSTOMER INVOICES

TRUMAN TIRES

Customer Name	Terms	Date	Invoice No.	Amount	Total
City Cab Company	2/10, n/30 (after tax)	Nov. 26/10	120	$1 808	$1 808
Lovely U Cosmetics	2/10, n/30 (after tax)	Nov. 24/10	116	$1 356	$1 356
Polly Maid Services	2/10, n/30 (after tax)	Nov. 29/10	124	$1 017	$1 017
		Grand Total			$4 181

EMPLOYEE INFORMATION SHEET

TRUMAN TIRES

	Trish Tridon	Joy Fram	Shockley Monroe	Karlby Holley	Troy Niehoff	Albert C. Delco
Position	Manager	Asst Manager	Auto Worker	Auto Worker	Auto Worker	Auto Worker
Social Insurance No.	464 375 286	572 351 559	398 577 619	821 887 114	618 524 664	404 535 601
Address	59 Pond Mills Rd. London, Ontario N5Z 3X3	8 Rington Cres. London, Ontario N6J 1Y7	36 Artisans Cres. London, Ontario N5V 4S3	44 Lockyer St. London, Ontario N6C 3E5	98 Novello Ave. London, Ontario N6J 2A5	18 Ravenglass Cres. London, Ontario N6G 4K1
Telephone	(519) 645-6238	(519) 738-5188	(519) 784-7195	(519) 648-1916	(519) 641-6773	(519) 788-2826
Date of Birth (mm-dd-yy)	09-28-67	02-03-79	05-21-78	08-08-76	05-28-74	08-19-80
Federal (Ontario) Tax Exemption - TD1						
Basic Personal	$9 600 (8 681)	$9 600 (8 681)	$9 600 (8 681)	$9 600 (8 681)	$9 600 (8 681)	$9 600 (8 681)
Spouse	$9 600 (7 371)	–	–	–	$9 600 (7 371)	–
Other	–	–	–	$7 720 (7 744)	–	–
Total Exemptions	$19 200 (16 052)	$9 600 (8 681)	$9 600 (8 681)	$17 320 (16 425)	$19 200 (16 052)	$9 600 (8 681)
Employee Earnings						
Regular Wage Rate	–	–	$16.00	$16.00	$16.00	$16.00
Overtime Wage Rate	–	–	$24.00	$24.00	$24.00	$24.00
Regular Salary	$3 500/mo	$2 500/mo	–	–	–	–
Pay Period	monthly	monthly	bi-weekly	bi-weekly	bi-weekly	bi-weekly
Hours per Period	150	150	80	80	80	80
Piece Rate	–	–	$10/job	$10/job	$5/job	$5/job
Commission	1% (Sales – Returns)	–	–	–	–	–
Vacation	4 weeks	3 weeks	4% retained	4% retained	4% retained	4% retained
Vacation Pay Owed	–	–	$1 793	$1 486	$1 811	$1 853
WSIB Rate	3.40	3.40	3.40	3.40	3.40	3.40
Employee Deductions						
CSB	$200	$100	$50	$50	–	–
Union Dues	–	–	1%	1%	1%	1%
EI, CPP & Income Tax	Calculations built into Simply Accounting program.					

Employee Profiles and TD1 Information

All Employees   All employees are allowed ten days per year for illness and five for personal reasons. All employees have their paycheques deposited directly into their bank accounts. There are no other company benefits. All payroll remittances are due at the end of each month.

Trish Tridon   As the manager at Truman Tires, Tridon supervises the other employees, resolves customer problems and assists with sales. Her salary of $3 500 per month is supplemented by a commission of 1 percent of sales, less returns. Tridon is entered as the salesperson on all sales invoices to calculate the commission. She is paid at the end of each month and is allowed four weeks of vacation with pay. Tridon is married with two children under 12, and claims the basic and spousal tax claim amounts. She has $200 deducted from each paycheque to buy Canada Savings Bonds.

Joy Fram   As assistant manager, Fram helps Tridon with all her duties and also manages the accounting records for the business. She is paid a monthly salary of $2 500 and is allowed three weeks of vacation with pay. She has only the basic tax claim amount because she is single and self-supporting. She has chosen to buy Canada Savings Bonds by having $100 deducted from each paycheque.

Hourly Paid Employees   The four hourly paid employees — Monroe, Holley, Niehoff and Delco — share the work of servicing vehicles. Every two weeks, they are paid $16 per hour for the first 40 hours each week and $24 per hour for additional time for performing the full range of services provided by Truman Tires: installing, repairing and rotating tires, brake work, shocks and oil service. However, each hourly employee has one area of specialization and the piece-rate supplement is based on the number of jobs in this area. All receive 4 percent vacation pay that is retained until they take time off. All are union members and pay 1 percent of their wages as union dues.

Shockley Monroe   specializes in brake work. He is single and pays $50 from each paycheque toward the purchase of Canada Savings Bonds.

Karlby Holley   also buys Canada Savings Bonds through payroll deductions. Her specialty is shocks. As a recent graduate, she has $4 000 tuition and eight months of full-time study to increase her basic single tax claim amount.

Troy Niehoff   is married with one child under 12 years of age, so he has the basic and spousal tax claim amounts. He is not enrolled in the Canada Savings Bonds plan. His area of specialization is tire installation and wheel alignment.

Albert C. Delco   is single and does not purchase Canada Savings Bonds through payroll. His area of specialization is oil service and winter preparation.

INVENTORY INFORMATION

TRUMAN TIRES

Code	Description	Min Stock	Selling Price Reg	Selling Price (Pref)	Unit	Qty on Hand	Total (Cost)	Duty	Taxes
Winter Tires (Linked Accounts: Asset 1400; Revenue: 4020; COGS: 5050; Var: 5055)									
T101	P155/80R14 Tires	4	$ 70	($ 65)	each	20	$ 560	7.0%	GST & PST
T102	P175/70R14 Tires	4	85	(80)	each	20	680	7.0%	GST & PST
T103	P195/75R15 Tires	4	95	(88)	each	20	760	7.0%	GST & PST
T104	P205/75R15 Tires	8	100	(92)	each	28	1 120	7.0%	GST & PST
T105	P185/70R15 Tires	4	105	(96)	each	20	840	7.0%	GST & PST
T106	P195/65R15 Tires	4	110	(100)	each	20	880	7.0%	GST & PST
T107	P185/65R15 Tires	4	115	(105)	each	20	920	7.0%	GST & PST
T108	P185/60R15 Tires	4	120	(110)	each	20	960	7.0%	GST & PST
T109	P195/60R16 Tires	8	125	(115)	each	28	1 400	7.0%	GST & PST
T110	P195/65R16 Tires	8	130	(120)	each	28	1 456	7.0%	GST & PST
T111	P205/65R16 Tires	8	135	(124)	each	28	1 512	7.0%	GST & PST
T112	P205/60R16 Tires	8	140	(127)	each	28	1 568	7.0%	GST & PST
T113	P215/60R16 Tires	8	145	(132)	each	28	1 624	7.0%	GST & PST
T114	P225/60R17 Tires	4	150	(136)	each	20	1 200	7.0%	GST & PST
							$15 480		
Wheels (Linked Accounts: Asset 1360; Revenue: 4020; COGS: 5050; Var: 5055)									
W101	Aluminum R14 Wheels	4	180	(165)	each	16	$1 152	6.0%	GST & PST
W102	Aluminum R15 Wheels	4	195	(187)	each	16	1 248	6.0%	GST & PST
W103	Aluminum R16 Wheels	8	210	(190)	each	20	1 680	6.0%	GST & PST
W104	Aluminum R17 Wheels	4	225	(207)	each	16	1 440	6.0%	GST & PST
W105	Chrome-Steel R14 Wheels	4	70	(65)	each	16	448	6.0%	GST & PST
W106	Chrome-Steel R15 Wheels	4	80	(75)	each	16	512	6.0%	GST & PST
W107	Chrome-Steel R16 Wheels	8	90	(83)	each	20	720	6.0%	GST & PST
W108	Chrome-Steel R17 Wheels	4	100	(92)	each	16	640	6.0%	GST & PST
W109	Steel R14 Wheels	4	40	(38)	each	16	256	6.0%	GST & PST
W110	Steel R15 Wheels	4	45	(42)	each	16	288	6.0%	GST & PST
W111	Steel R16 Wheels	8	50	(46)	each	20	400	6.0%	GST & PST
W112	Steel R17 Wheels	4	55	(50)	each	16	352	6.0%	GST & PST
							$9 136		

INVENTORY INFORMATION

TRUMAN TIRES

Code	Description	Min Stock	Selling Price Reg	(Pref)	Unit	Qty on Hand	Total (Cost)	Duty	Taxes
Wheel Nuts & Locks (Linked Accounts: Asset 1380; Revenue: 4020; COGS: 5050; Var: 5055)									
WN01	Chrome Wheel Nuts	4	$ 10	($ 10)	pkg	24	$ 96	6.0%	GST & PST
WN02	Chrome Wheel Locks	4	25	(23)	pkg	24	240	6.0%	GST & PST
WN03	Nickel/Chrome Wheel Nuts	4	10	(10)	pkg	24	114	6.0%	GST & PST
WN04	Nickel/Chrome Wheel Locks	4	30	(28)	pkg	24	288	6.0%	GST & PST
							$738		
Services (Linked Accounts: Revenue: 4040; COGS: 5060)									
SRV01	Alignment - standard		75	(70)	job				GST & PST
SRV02	Alignment - w caster replacement		130	(120)	job				GST & PST
SRV03	Brake Service - standard pkg		140	(130)	job				GST & PST
SRV04	Brake Service - complete pkg		175	(163)	job				GST & PST
SRV05	Oil Service - standard pkg		30	(28)	job				GST & PST
SRV06	Oil Service - premium pkg		40	(37)	job				GST & PST
SRV07	Shocks - economy gas-charged		100	(92)	job				GST & PST
SRV08	Shocks - premium gas-matic		140	(130)	job				GST & PST
SRV09	Tire Repairs		30	(28)	job				GST & PST
SRV10	Tire Rotation		10	(10)	job				GST & PST
SRV11	Winter Prep. Service		60	(55)	job				GST & PST

Division Information

Truman Tires uses two divisions — one for sales of tires and wheels and their installation and one for services. Fram will set up these divisions at the beginning of December and Tridon will keep track of the percentage of time each employee works in each division. Because these times vary from one vehicle to another, the percentage allocation is included with each source document. Allocation details for other expenses and revenues are also included with the source documents. Amounts for assets, liabilities and equity accounts are not allocated.

Accounting Procedures

The Employer Health Tax (EHT)

The Employer Health Tax (EHT) is paid by employers in Ontario to cover the costs of health care for all eligible residents in the province. The EHT rate depends on the total annual remuneration paid to employees (gross wage expense). Employers with total payroll less than $400 000 are exempt from paying EHT. For those with higher annual payrolls, the EHT rate is 1.95 percent. Simply Accounting will calculate the employer's liability to the Ontario Minister of Finance automatically once the information is set up correctly in the payroll defaults and linked accounts. In Chapter 16, we will show the keystrokes necessary for setting up the EHT information. The EHT can be remitted monthly or annually, depending on the total payroll amount.

Taxes: GST and PST

Truman Tires pays GST on all goods and services that it buys, including the imported products, and charges GST on all sales and services. It uses the regular method for remittance of the Goods and Services Tax. GST collected from customers is recorded as a liability in *GST Charged on Sales*. GST paid to suppliers is recorded in *GST Paid on*

Purchases as a decrease in liability to Canada Revenue Agency. The report is filed with the Receiver General for Canada by the last day of the month for the previous quarter, either including the balance owing or requesting a refund.

In Ontario, PST is calculated on the base amount of the invoice, which does not include the GST. In this application, Provincial Sales Tax of 8 percent is applied to all sales and services offered by Truman Tires.

NSF Cheques

When a bank returns a customer's cheque because there were insufficient funds in the customer's bank account to cover the cheque, the payment must be reversed. If the payment was processed through the Receipts Journal, the reversal should also be processed through the Receipts Journal (see page 179). If the sale was a cash sale, the reversal must be processed through the Sales Journal. Create a customer record for the customer and process a credit (Pay Later) sale for the full amount of the NSF cheque. Enter No Tax in the Tax Code field to show that the amount is non-taxable because taxes for the sale were recorded at the time of the original sale. Enter the amount as a **positive** amount in the Amount field and enter *Bank: Chequing CAD* in the Account field. On a separate invoice line, enter the amount of the handling charge for the NSF cheque in the Amount field with *Other Revenue* in the Account field. Again, the handling charge is non-taxable.

Returns

When customers return merchandise, they are charged a 20 percent handling charge. In the Sales Journal, enter the quantity returned with a **minus** sign at the regular sale price, add the tax code and enter *Sales Returns & Allowances* in the Account field. The amounts will automatically be negative because of the minus sign in the quantity field, so that *Accounts Receivable* will be credited automatically as well. On a separate invoice line, enter the amount withheld — the handling charge — as a positive amount and credit *Other Revenue*. *Accounts Receivable* will be debited automatically for the amount of the handling charge.

If the original sale was a credit sale, and the account is not yet paid, the return should also be entered as a credit sale so that *Accounts Receivable* will be credited. If the original sale was paid in cash or by credit card, or the account has been paid, the return should be entered as a cash sale or credit card sale so that the appropriate bank account will be credited. (See page 384.)

Reserved Inventory for Divisions

When customers sign a contract, the inventory items needed to complete the work are set aside or reserved by transferring them through the Item Assembly Journal to a designated account. (Refer to page 379.) In this way, these items cannot be sold to other customers because the inventory quantities are already reduced. The minimum stock level for reserved inventory will be zero.

Cash, Credit Card and Debit Card Sales

Cash and credit card transactions for goods and services occur normally in most types of businesses. The Simply Accounting program handles these transactions automatically through the Sales Journal when you choose the appropriate method of payment. Choose Cash Customers from the Customer list, and add the new customer's name in the Ship To or Address fields if this is not a regular customer. If payment is by cheque, a Cheque Number field opens. Truman Tires accepts Visa, MasterCard and Interac Debit Cards from customers for store sales.

NOTES
The Sales Journal entry will credit Bank: Chequing CAD for the full amount of the sale including taxes and debit Accounts Receivable for the customer.

NOTES
If you created a customer record by using Quick Add, or used an existing record (e.g., Cash Customers), you can adjust the sales invoice by changing the method of payment from Cheque to Pay Later. You cannot choose Pay Later as the payment method for one-time customers.

NOTES
We use the term Cash Sales and Purchases for cash and cheque transactions.
You can also enter the name in the customer field and choose Continue when prompted. The name is then added to the journal report without creating a customer record.

The program will debit the appropriate bank account instead of the *Accounts Receivable* control account. All other accounts for this transaction will be appropriately debited or credited.

Cash Purchases

Similarly, for cash purchases, choose the supplier from the Supplier list or add the supplier using Quick Add. Cash purchases may be entered in the Payments Journal as Other Payments or in the Purchases Journal. Choose the appropriate method of payment from the Paid By list. For cheque payments, a Cheque Number field opens with the next cheque number entered. Complete the remainder of the cash transaction in the same way you would enter other transactions.

The program will debit *Bank: Chequing CAD* instead of *Accounts Payable*, the control account. All other accounts for the transaction will be appropriately debited or credited.

Freight Expense

When a business purchases inventory items, the cost of any freight that cannot be directly allocated to a specific item must be charged to *Freight Expense*. This amount will be regarded as an expense rather than charged to an inventory asset account.

Printing Invoices, Orders and Quotes

If you want to print the invoices, purchase orders or sales quotes through the program, complete the journal transaction as you would otherwise. Before posting the transaction, preview the invoice. If the invoice is correct, you can print it from the preview window, from the invoice by choosing the File menu and then Print or by clicking the Print tool on the tool bar for the invoice form. Printing will begin immediately, so be sure you have the correct forms for your printer before you begin. If you and the customer or supplier have e-mail, click the E-mail tool to send the invoice or order.

Foreign Purchases

Truman Tires imports some inventory items from companies in Japan. The currency for these transactions is Japanese yen (JPY) and the currency symbol is ¥. Truman Tires pays GST and import duties on these purchases. Duty rates are set up in the Inventory Ledger for the individual items and the amounts are calculated automatically by the program.

INSTRUCTIONS

1. **Record entries** for the source documents for December 2010 in Simply Accounting using the Chart of Accounts, Trial Balance and other information. The procedures for entering each new type of transaction are outlined step by step in the Keystrokes section that follows the source documents. A ✓ in the source document completion check box indicates that keystrokes are provided. The page number immediately below the check box indicates where these specific keystroke instructions begin. Keystroke instructions begin on page 517, after the source documents.

2. **Print** the **reports** and **graphs** indicated on the following printing form after you have finished making your entries.

SIMPLY VERSION
Remember that you will see the term vendors when we use the term suppliers.

NOTES
To preview, print or e-mail invoices, you must have the correct forms selected for invoices in the Reports & Forms Settings. You can access these settings from the Sales Journal tool bar.

NOTES
The transactions in this exercise provide a comprehensive practice set. If you want to use it only for review, you can complete the transactions without entering allocations.

REPORTS

Accounts
- [ ] Chart of Accounts
- [ ] Account List
- [ ] General Journal Entries

Financials
- [✓] Comparative Balance Sheet: Dec. 1 and Dec. 31, difference in percentage
- [✓] Income Statement from Dec. 1 to Dec. 31
- [✓] Trial Balance date: Dec. 31
- [✓] All Journals Entries: Dec. 1 to Dec. 31 with division allocations
- [✓] General Ledger accounts: 1400 4020 4040 from Dec. 1 to Dec. 31
- [ ] Statement of Cash Flows
- [✓] Cash Flow Projection Detail Report for account 1050 for 30 days
- [✓] Gross Margin Income Statement from Dec. 1 to Dec. 31

Tax
- [ ] Report on

Banking
- [ ] Cheque Log Report

Payables
- [ ] Supplier List
- [ ] Supplier Aged
- [ ] Aged Overdue Payables

- [ ] Purchase Journal Entries
- [ ] Payment Journal Entries
- [ ] Supplier Purchases

Receivables
- [ ] Customer List
- [ ] Customer Aged
- [ ] Aged Overdue Receivables
- [ ] Sales Journal Entries
- [ ] Receipt Journal Entries
- [ ] Customer Sales
- [✓] Sales by Salesperson
- [ ] Customer Statements

Payroll
- [ ] Employee List
- [✓] Employee Summary for all employees
- [ ] Deductions & Expenses
- [ ] Remittance
- [ ] Payroll Journal Entries
- [✓] T4 Slips for all employees
- [ ] Record of Employment

Inventory & Services
- [ ] Inventory & Services List
- [ ] Inventory Summary
- [ ] Inventory Quantity
- [ ] Inventory Statistics
- [✓] Inventory Sales Summary for Winter Tires from Dec. 1 to Dec. 31

- [✓] Inventory Transaction Summary for Wheels, all journals from Dec. 1 to Dec. 31
- [ ] Item Assembly Journal Entries
- [ ] Adjustment Journal Entries
- [ ] Inventory Price Lists

Division
- [ ] Division List
- [✓] Division Income Summary: all divisions, all accounts from Dec. 1 to Dec. 31
- [ ] Division Allocation Report

Mailing Labels
- [ ] Labels

Management Reports
- [ ] Ledger

GRAPHS
- [ ] Payables by Aging Period
- [ ] Payables by Supplier
- [ ] Receivables by Aging Period
- [ ] Receivables by Customer
- [ ] Sales vs Receivables
- [ ] Receivables Due vs Payables Due
- [ ] Revenues by Account
- [ ] Expenses by Account
- [✓] Expenses and Net Profit as % of Revenue

SOURCE DOCUMENTS

SESSION DATE – DECEMBER 7, 2010

- [✓] **Memo #1**   **Dated Dec. 1/10**

517   From Owner: Create the following new divisions for the shop to begin on December 1, 2010:
        Sales Division
        Service Division

- [✓] **Purchase Invoice #L-4441**   **Dated Dec. 1/10**

521   From London Tool Rentals, $280 plus $14.00 GST and $22.40 PST for monthly rental fee for specialty tools according to contract. Purchase invoice total $316.40. Terms: net 20 days. Charge 20% of the expenses to Sales Division and 80% to Service Division. Store as a monthly recurring entry.

- [ ] **Cheque Copy #200**   **Dated Dec. 2/10**

        To TuffArm Shocks, $1 050 in payment of account. Reference invoice #TS-699.

NOTES
There is no allocation in the Payments or the Receipts journals.

NOTES
Edit the purchase amounts. Amounts for Balance Sheet accounts are not allocated so there is no allocation for inventory purchases.
Allocate freight expenses for purchases by clicking the Allocate tool beside the Freight fields.
Remember that GST is charged on freight expenses.

☑ **Purchase Invoice #ST-916**   **Dated Dec. 2/10**

525   From Snowmaster Tire Company

	Miscellaneous parts	¥ 60 000	6% Duty
20	T110 P195/65R16 Tires	112 000	7% Duty
20	T111 P205/65R16 Tires	116 000	7% Duty
	Freight	7 500	
	GST Paid	14 775	
Invoice Total		¥310 275	
Import Duty	CAD $181.91	¥ 19 560	

The exchange rate is 0.0093.
Terms: net 15. Allocate 100% of the freight expense to the Sales Division.

☐ **Purchase Invoice #SW-876**   **Dated Dec. 2/10**

From Sylverado Wheels

20	W103 Aluminum R16 Wheels	¥181 000	
20	W107 Chrome-Steel R16 Wheels	77 500	
	Freight	5 600	
	GST Paid	13 205	
Invoice Total		¥277 305	
Import Duty	CAD $144.25	¥15 510	

The exchange rate is 0.0093.
Terms: net 30. Allocate 100% of the freight expense to the Sales Division.

NOTES
Duty rates already assigned to inventory items in the ledger records will not be listed separately in source documents.

☐ **Cash Receipt #80**   **Dated Dec. 3/10**

From Lovely U Cosmetics, cheque #4887 for $1 328.88 in payment of account including $27.12 discount for early payment. Reference invoice #116.

☐ **Cash Receipt #81**   **Dated Dec. 4/10**

From City Cab Company, cheque #855 for $1 771.84 in payment of account including $36.16 discount for early payment. Reference invoice #120.

NOTES
You can add Tridon as the Salesperson in all customer records.
For all cash, credit card or debit card sales, you can type the new customer name and choose Continue or choose Cash Customers and use the Additional Field for the customer name or credit card number.
There is no discount for cash, credit card or debit card sales (Visa, MasterCard and Interac).

☑ **Visa Sales Invoice #125**   **Dated Dec. 4/10**

527   Sold by Tridon to Bruno Scinto

4	T104	P205/75R15 Tires	$100 each	$ 400.00
4	T105	P185/70R15 Tires	105 each	420.00
4	W102	Aluminum R15 Wheels	195 each	780.00
1	SRV06	Oil Service - premium pkg	40 /job	40.00
		Goods and Services Tax	5%	82.00
		Provincial Sales Tax	8%	131.20
	Total paid by Visa #4205 5921 7456 3010			$1 853.20

Allocate 100% of revenue and expenses for inventory items to Sales Division and for service item to Service Division.

☐ **MasterCard Sales Invoice #126**   **Dated Dec. 5/10**

Sold by Tridon to Alice Ferante

4	T114	P225/60R17 Tires	$150 each	$ 600.00
4	W104	Aluminum R17 Wheels	225 each	900.00
		Goods and Services Tax	5%	75.00
		Provincial Sales Tax	8%	120.00
	Total paid by MasterCard #5901 8223 6558 6201			$1 695.00

Allocate 100% of revenue to Sales Division.

☐ **Cheque Copy #201**   **Dated Dec. 6/10**

To MoTech Auto Parts, $617.40 in payment of account, including $12.60 discount for early payment. Reference invoice #MT-1142.

Sales Invoice #127   **Dated Dec. 6/10**

Sold by Tridon to London Car Leasing (preferred customer)

12	T101	P155/80R14 Tires	$ 65 each
12	T106	P195/65R15 Tires	100 each
12	W106	Chrome-Steel R15 Wheels	75 each
12	W109	Steel R14 Wheels	38 each
		Goods and Services Tax	5%
		Provincial Sales Tax	8%

Terms: 2/10, n/30.

Allocate 100% of revenue and expenses to Sales Division.

Cash Sales Invoice #128   **Dated Dec. 7/10**

Tridon's Sales Summary for one-time Cash Customers

12	T101	P155/80R14 Tires	$ 70 each	$ 840.00
8	T103	P195/75R15 Tires	95 each	760.00
2	W103	Aluminum R16 Wheels	210 each	420.00
6	SRV02	Alignment - w caster replacement	130 /job	780.00
2	SRV03	Brake Service - standard pkg	140 /job	280.00
8	SRV06	Oil Service - premium pkg	40 /job	320.00
3	SRV08	Shocks - premium gas-matic	140 /job	420.00
		Goods and Services Tax	5%	191.00
		Provincial Sales Tax	8%	305.60
		Total cash received and deposited to bank account		$4 316.60

Allocate 100% of revenue and expenses for inventory items to Sales Division and for service items to Service Division.

Memo #2   **Dated Dec. 7/10**

From Owner: Two winter specials will be offered. Both packages include four tires and wheels and a winter preparation service. Alignments are included in WHP2.

Create new asset Group account 1420 Winter-Holiday Tire Packages.

Create two new inventory records:

No.	Description	Min.	Selling Price/Unit	
			Regular	(Preferred)
WHP1	Tires/Wheels/Winter Pkg	0	$900 /pkg	($850)
WHP2	Tires/Wheels/Alignment/Winter Pkg	0	$1 400 /pkg	($1 300)

Linked accounts: Asset   1420
                     Revenue   4020
                     Expense   5050
                     Variance   not required

Taxes: Not exempt for GST and PST
             Import Duty Rate: not applicable

Item Assembly #IA-1   **Dated Dec. 7/10**

Assemble five WHP1 Tires/Wheels/Winter Pkg. Transfer 20 of each component as follows:

20	T110	P195/65R16 Tires	$53.5523 each	$1 071.05
20	W107	Chrome-Steel R16 Wheels	37.100 each	742.00
		Additional Costs (for services)		$250.00

Assembled Items:

5	WHP1	Tires/Wheels/Winter Pkg	$412.61 each	$2 063.05

Accept the default prices for assembly components and copy the total to the assembled items total. The totals for assembly components (including additional costs) and assembled items must be exactly the same.

☐ **Item Assembly #IA-2**   **Dated Dec. 7/10**

Assemble five WHP2 Tires/Wheels/Alignment/Winter Pkg. Transfer 20 of each component as follows:

20	T111	P205/65R16 Tires	$55.5483 each	$1 110.97
20	W103	Aluminum R16 Wheels	86.6074 each	1 732.15
Additional Costs				$500.00

Assembled Items:

5	WHP2	Tires/Wheels/Alignment/Winter Pkg		
			$668.624 each	$3 343.12

Accept the default prices for assembly components and copy the total to the assembled items total to ensure the totals are exactly the same.

SESSION DATE – DECEMBER 14, 2010

☐ **Purchase Order #21**   **Dated Dec. 8/10**

Delivery date Dec. 13/10
From Snowmaster Tire Company

16	T101	P155/80R14 Tires	¥ 48 160
16	T103	P195/75R15 Tires	65 440
8	T106	P195/65R15 Tires	36 160
8	T107	P185/65R15 Tires	39 600
	Freight		7 500
	GST Paid		9 843
	Invoice Total		¥206 703

Terms: net 15. The exchange rate is 0.00929.

☐ **Purchase Order #22**   **Dated Dec. 8/10**

Delivery date Dec. 13/10
From Sylverado Wheels

16	W106	Chrome-Steel R15 Wheels	¥54 560
8	W109	Steel R14 Wheels	13 760
8	W110	Steel R15 Wheels	15 520
	Freight		5 600
	GST Paid		4 472
	Invoice Total		¥93 912

Terms: net 30. The exchange rate is 0.00929.

☐ **Cash Receipt #82**   **Dated Dec. 8/10**

From Polly Maid Service, cheque #2189 for $996.66 in payment of account including $20.34 discount for early payment. Reference invoice #124.

☐ **Cheque Copy #330**   **Dated Dec. 9/10**

To Snowmaster Tire Company, ¥274 138 in payment of account. Reference invoice #ST-842. The exchange rate is 0.00928.

☐ **Cheque Copy #331**   **Dated Dec. 9/10**

To Sylverado Wheels, ¥182 759 in payment of account. Reference invoice #SW-724. The exchange rate is 0.00928.

☐ **Memo #3**   **Dated Dec. 9/10**

From Owner: Transfer ¥400 000 from Chequing account to Foreign Currency account to cover cheques. The exchange rate is 0.00928. Remember to change the currency setting to JPY.

NOTES
Close the advisor message about the overdrawn account. The transaction, Memo #3, will transfer funds to cover the overdraft.

Sales Invoice #129   **Dated Dec. 11/10**

Sold by Tridon to Pronto Pizza & Delivery
   12 T108   P185/60R15 Tires $120 each
   12 W106 Chrome-Steel R15 Wheels   80 each
   4   SRV03 Brake Service - standard pkg   140 /job
   4   SRV07 Shocks - economy gas-charged   100 /job
              Goods and Services Tax   5%
              Provincial Sales Tax   8%
Terms: 2/10, n/30.
Allocate 100% of revenue and expenses for inventory items to Sales Division and for service items to Service Division.

NOTES
You will see the advisor message that inventory items have dropped below the re-order point. Close the advisor to continue.

Sales Invoice #130   **Dated Dec. 13/10**

Sold by Tridon to Airport Taxi Service (preferred customer)
   8   T103   P195/75R15 Tires $ 88 each
   8   W102 Aluminum R15 Wheels   187 each
   8   WN04 Nickel/Chrome Wheel Locks   28 /pkg
   6   SRV04 Brake Service - complete pkg   163 /pkg
   6   SRV08 Shocks - premium gas-matic   130 /job
              Goods and Services Tax   5%
              Provincial Sales Tax   8%
Terms: 2/10, n/30.
Allocate 100% of revenue and expenses for inventory items to Sales Division and for service items to Service Division.

NOTES
Allow the customer to exceed the credit limit.

Sales Order #12-1   **Dated Dec. 13/10**

Starting date for contract Dec. 21/10
From Lovely U Cosmetics, $5 100 plus $255 GST and $408 PST for tire and wheel contract for five vehicles. Invoice total $5 763. Terms: 2/10, n/30.
Sold by Tridon. Received cheque #9754 for $1 020 as deposit #13 with order.

NOTES
This is a non-inventory sales order. Credit Revenue from Sales.

✓ **Purchase Invoice #ST-1141**   **Dated Dec. 13/10**

530

From Snowmaster Tire Company, to fill purchase order #21
   16 T101 P155/80R14 Tires   ¥ 48 160
   16 T103 P195/75R15 Tires   65 440
   8   T106 P195/65R15 Tires   36 160
   8   T107 P185/65R15 Tires   39 600
           Freight   7 500
           GST Paid   9 843
   Invoice Total   ¥206 703
     Import Duty   CAD $123.21   ¥13 255
Terms: net 15. The exchange rate is 0.009295. Allocate the freight to Sales.

Purchase Invoice #SW-1024   **Dated Dec. 13/10**

From Sylverado Wheels, to fill purchase order #22
   16 W106 Chrome-Steel R15 Wheels   ¥54 560
   8   W109 Steel R14 Wheels   13 760
   8   W110 Steel R15 Wheels   15 520
           Freight   5 600
           GST Paid   4 472
   Invoice Total   ¥93 912
     Import Duty   CAD $46.76   ¥5 031
Terms: net 30. The exchange rate is 0.009295. Allocate the freight to Sales.

NOTES
Enter 2 as the quantity for the purchases from MoTech Auto Parts and edit the amount if necessary.

The wheel locks and nuts have different buying and selling units. They are purchased in boxes of one dozen packages and sold as individual packages.

Cash Receipt #83 **Dated Dec. 13/10**

From London Car Leasing, cheque #111 for $3 694.29 in payment of account including $75.39 discount. Reference invoice #127.

Purchase Invoice #MT-1521 **Dated Dec. 13/10**

From MoTech Auto Parts

2 dozen	WN01	Chrome Wheel Nuts	$ 96.00
2 dozen	WN02	Chrome Wheel Locks	240.00
2 dozen	WN03	Nickel/Chrome Wheel Nuts	114.00
2 dozen	WN04	Nickel/Chrome Wheel Locks	288.00
		Freight	20.00
		GST Paid	37.90
Invoice Total			$795.90

Terms: 2/10, n/30. Allocate the freight to Sales.

✓ 530 **Memo #4** **Dated Dec. 14/10**

From Owner: Pay import duty charged on purchases to date to Receiver General. Issue cheque #202 for $496.13 to pay account balance in full. Reference sales invoices #ST-916, ST-1141, SW-876 and SW-1024.

Item Assembly: **Dated Dec. 14/10**
Reserve Inventory Form #RIF-1001

Reserve inventory required for Lovely U Cosmetics contract.
Create new inventory asset Group account 1440 Reserved Inventory for Workorders.
Create new inventory record in the Inventory Ledger for the contract as follows:

NOTES
Accept the default costs and enter total assembly components cost for assembled items total cost.

No.	Description	Min.	Regular Selling Price/unit
LC1	Lovely U Cosmetics Inventory	0	$5 100/contract

Linked accounts: Asset 1440   Revenue 4020   COGS 5050
Taxes: Not exempt for GST and PST. Duty does not apply.

Assemble the following as reserved inventory at cost price for the contract:

20	T111	P205/65R16 Tires	$55.5482 each	$1 110.96
20	W107	Chrome-Steel R16 Wheels	37.10 each	742.00
20	WN04	Nickel/Chrome Wheel Locks	12 /pkg	240.00

Package includes free installation.

Assembled Items:

1	LC1	Lovely U Cosmetics Inventory $2 092.96 each	$2 092.96

Cash Sales Invoice #131 **Dated Dec. 14/10**

Tridon's Sales Summary for one-time Cash Customers

6	SRV01	Alignment - standard	$ 75 /job	$ 450.00
8	SRV03	Brake Service - standard pkg	140 /job	1 120.00
6	SRV05	Oil Service - standard pkg	30 /job	180.00
7	SRV06	Oil Service - premium pkg	40 /job	280.00
12	SRV11	Winter Prep. Service	60 /job	720.00
1	WHP1	Tires/Wheels/Winter Pkg	900 /pkg	900.00
1	WHP2	Tires/Wheels/Alignment/Winter Pkg	1 400 /pkg	1 400.00
		Goods and Services Tax	5%	252.50
		Provincial Sales Tax	8%	404.00

Total cash received and deposited to bank account $5 706.50
Allocate 100% of revenue for service items to Service Division.
Allocate 95% of revenue for WHP1 to Sales and 5% to Service.
Allocate 90% of revenue for WHP2 to Sales and 10% to Service.

EMPLOYEE TIME SUMMARY SHEET #51   DATED DEC. 14/10

(pay period ending December 14, 2010)

	Name of Employee	Week 1	Week 2	Regular Hours	Overtime Hours	No. of Piece Rate Jobs	Sick Days	Personal Days
☑	Delco	40	40	80	0	34	1	–
531								
☐	Holley	40	42	80	2	13	–	1
☐	Monroe	42	40	80	2	20	–	–
☐	Niehoff	40	42	80	2	12	–	–

a. Use Employee Time Summary Sheet #51 and the Employee Information Sheet to complete the payroll run for hourly paid employees.
b. Allocate 100% of the payroll expenses to Service for all employees.
c. Issue deposit slips #112 to #115.

SESSION DATE – DECEMBER 21, 2010

Visa Sales Invoice #132   **Dated Dec. 16/10**

Sold by Tridon to Peter Manga

1	SRV08	Shocks - premium gas-matic		$ 140.00
1	WHP2	Tires/Wheels/Alignment/Winter Pkg		1 400.00
		Goods and Services Tax	5%	77.00
		Provincial Sales Tax	8%	123.20
		Total paid by Visa #4500 4678 1274 5630		$1 740.20

Allocate 100% of revenue for SRV08 to Service Division.
Allocate 90% of revenue for WHP2 to Sales and 10% to Service Division.

Cheque Copy #332   **Dated Dec. 16/10**

To Snowmaster Tire Company, ¥310 275 in payment of account. Reference invoice #ST-916. The exchange rate is 0.00929

Memo #5   **Dated Dec. 16/10**

From Owner: Transfer ¥400 000 (JPY) from Chequing account to Foreign Currency account to cover cheques. The exchange rate is 0.00929.

Cash Purchase Invoice #LH-31421   **Dated Dec. 17/10**

From London Hydro, $260 plus $13 GST for hydro services. Invoice total $273 paid in full with cheque #203. Allocate 30% of expense to Sales and 70% to Service Division.

Cash Purchase Invoice #BC-64261   **Dated Dec. 17/10**

From Bell Canada, $90 plus $4.50 GST and $7.20 PST for telephone services. Invoice total $101.70 paid in full with cheque #204. Allocate 40% of expense to Sales and 60% to Service Division.

Cash Purchase Invoice #WH-690   **Dated Dec. 17/10**

From Western Hydraulic Repairs, $400 plus $20 GST and $32 PST for repairs to hydraulic lift in service bay and maintenance of other lifts. Invoice total $452 paid in full with cheque #205. Allocate 10% of expense to Sales and 90% to Service Division.

Cash Receipt #84   **Dated Dec. 19/10**

From Pronto Pizza & Delivery, cheque #399 for $3 720.86 in payment of account including $75.94 discount for early payment. Reference invoice #129.

NOTES
If you have difficulty accessing the Allo column, you can click an employee name and then click the Allo tool button.
    You can apply the allocation to the entire transaction in the Payroll Cheque Run Journal.

NOTES
Remember that the amounts in the Entitlements fields reflect only the time earned during this pay period. All employees have accrued time from previous periods. These times are recorded in the employee's ledger record.

☐ **MasterCard Sales Invoice #133**　　　　**Dated Dec. 20/10**

Sold by Tridon to Daniel BenDavid

4	WN01	Chrome Wheel Nuts	$ 10 /pkg	$ 40.00
1	SRV04	Brake Service - complete pkg		175.00
5	SRV05	Oil Service - standard pkg	30 /job	150.00
5	SRV06	Oil Service - premium pkg	40 /job	200.00
1	SRV08	Shocks - premium gas-matic		140.00
1	WHP1	Tires/Wheels/Winter Pkg		900.00
1	WHP2	Tires/Wheels/Alignment/Winter Pkg		1 400.00
		Goods and Services Tax	5%	150.25
		Provincial Sales Tax	8%	240.40
		Total paid by MasterCard #5809 8213 6238 1601		$3 395.65

Allocate 100% of the revenue and expenses for inventory items to Sales Division.
Allocate 100% of revenue for service items to Service Division.
Allocate 95% of revenue for WHP1 to Sales and 5% to Service Division.
Allocate 90% of revenue for WHP2 to Sales and 10% to Service.

☐ **Cash Purchase Invoice #MS-40002**　　　　**Dated Dec. 21/10**

From Motor Supply Company (use Quick Add for the new supplier), $500 plus $25 GST and $40 PST for cleaning fluids, cleaning cloths and other garage supplies. Invoice total $565 paid in full with cheque #206.

☐ **Sales Return #R-133**　　　　**Dated Dec. 21/10**

From one-time Cash Customer (sold by Tridon), wheel nuts were not required.

−4	WN01	Chrome Wheel Nuts	$10 /pkg	−$40.00
		Handling charge (20% of total sales price)		9.04
		Goods and Services Tax	5%	−1.55
		Provincial Sales Tax	8%	−2.48
		Total cash paid to customer		−$34.99

Create new Group revenue account: 4130 Sales Returns & Allowances.
The handling charge is credited to Other Revenue. Allocate 100% of the returns and the revenue to Sales.

☐ **Memo #6**　　　　**Dated Dec. 21/10**

Edit sales order #12-1 from Lovely U Cosmetics. Change the contract item ordered to the reserved inventory LC1. The quantity ordered remains as one.

☐ **Sales Invoice #134**　　　　**Dated Dec. 21/10**

Sold by Tridon to Lovely U Cosmetics, to fill sales order #12-1

1	LC1	Lovely U Cosmetics Inventory	$5 100	
		Goods and Services Tax	5%	
		Provincial Sales Tax	8%	

Terms: 2/10, n/30. The balance owing is $4 743.
Allocate 100% of sale to Sales Division.

SESSION DATE – DECEMBER 28, 2010

☐ **Interac Sales Invoice #135**　　　　**Dated Dec. 22/10**

Sold by Tridon to Cedric Ng

4	T111	P205/65R16 Tires	$135 each	$ 540.00
4	W103	Aluminum R16 Wheels	210 each	840.00
		Goods and Services Tax	5%	69.00
		Provincial Sales Tax	8%	110.40
		Total paid in full by debit card #5300 5291 6730 8161		$1 559.40

Allocate 100% of the sale to the Sales Division.

Memo #7   **Dated Dec. 22/10**

From Owner: Use the balance for November 30 to record PST payable for
November as a liability to the Minister of Finance. Reduce PST payable by 5% for
PST compensation. Issue cheque #207 for $3 192. Do not allocate the revenue
amount because it applies to the previous month.

NOTES
Use the Trial Balance on
page 498 for the November 30
PST Payable balance.

Purchase Invoice #SW-1159   **Dated Dec. 22/10**

From Sylverado Wheels

8	W107 Chrome-Steel R16 Wheels	¥31 000
	Freight	1 200
	GST Paid	1 610
Invoice Total		¥33 810
Import Duty	CAD $17.26	¥1 860

Terms: net 30. The exchange rate is 0.00928. Allocate the freight to Sales.

Purchase Invoice #TS-817   **Dated Dec. 22/10**

From TuffArm Shocks, $2 000 plus $100 GST for shocks and parts for services.
Invoice total $2 100. Terms: net 30.

Cash Receipt #85   **Dated Dec. 23/10**

From Airport Taxi Company, cheque #9902 for $4 631.15 in payment of account
including $94.51 discount for early payment. Reference invoice #130.

Cheque Copy #208   **Dated Dec. 23/10**

To MoTech Auto Parts, $779.98 in payment of account, including $15.92 discount
for early payment. Reference invoice #MT-1521.

Purchase Invoice #MT-1894   **Dated Dec. 26/10**

From MoTech Auto Parts, $800 plus $40 GST for brake hoses, cables, pads and
other brake parts and hardware. Invoice total $840. Terms: 2/10, n/30.

Cheque Copy #333   **Dated Dec. 26/10**

To Snowmaster Tire Company, ¥206 703 in payment of account. Reference
invoice #ST-1141. The exchange rate is 0.00927.

Interac Sales Invoice #136   **Dated Dec. 27/10**

Sold by Tridon to Federica Yuen

2	WHP1 Tires/Wheels/Winter Pkg	900	$1 800.00
2	SRV03 Brake Service - standard pkg	140	280.00
	Goods and Services Tax	5%	104.00
	Provincial Sales Tax	8%	166.40
Total paid by Debit Card #2816 3238 6010 1291			$2 350.40

Allocate 100% of revenue for service item to Service Division and allocate 95% of
revenue for WHP1 to Sales and 5% to Service Division.

Sales Invoice #137   **Dated Dec. 27/10**

Sold by Tridon to City Cab Company

1	WHP1 Tires/Wheels/Winter Pkg	$ 900 /pkg
2	WHP2 Tires/Wheels/Alignment/Winter Pkg	1 400 /pkg
	Goods and Services Tax	5%
	Provincial Sales Tax	8%

Terms: 2/10, n/30.
Allocate 95% of revenue for WHP1 to Sales and 5% to Service Division.
Allocate 90% of revenue for WHP2 to Sales and 10% to Service Division.

NOTES
Allow the customer to
exceed the credit limit.

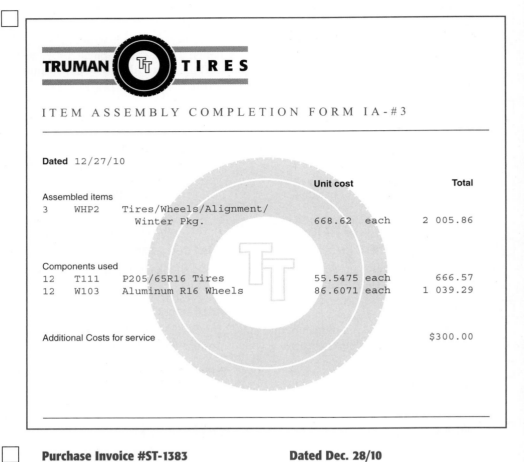

TRUMAN TIRES

ITEM ASSEMBLY COMPLETION FORM IA-#3

Dated 12/27/10

				Unit cost		Total
Assembled items						
3	WHP2	Tires/Wheels/Alignment/				
		Winter Pkg.		668.62	each	2 005.86
Components used						
12	T111	P205/65R16 Tires		55.5475	each	666.57
12	W103	Aluminum R16 Wheels		86.6071	each	1 039.29
Additional Costs for service						$300.00

Purchase Invoice #ST-1383   **Dated Dec. 28/10**

From Snowmaster Tire Company

12	T108	P185/60R15 Tires	¥ 62 160
20	T111	P205/65R16 Tires	116 000
8	T112	P205/60R16 Tires	48 320
8	T114	P225/60R17 Tires	51 840
	Freight		7 500
	GST Paid		14 291
	Invoice Total		¥300 111
Import Duty		CAD $180.59	¥19 482

Terms: net 15. The exchange rate is 0.00927.
Edit prices to match those in the invoice. Allocate the freight to Sales.

Bank Debit Memo #92564   **Dated Dec. 28/10**

From Universal Bank, authorized withdrawals were made from the chequing account.

Loan payment principal	$1 000
Loan payment interest	200
Mortgage payment interest	910
Mortgage payment principal	90
Bank charges	30

Allocate 50% of the expenses to Sales and 50% to the Service Division.

Memo #8   **Dated Dec. 28/10**

From Owner: Write off one Chrome-Steel R17 Wheel (W108) that was dented beyond repair by machinery. Allocate 100% of the write-off to Sales.

Truman Tires
600 Westminster St. London, Ontario N6P 3B1
Tel: (519) 729-3733 Fax: (519) 729-7301

Date of sale: Dec. 28/10

To: Summary
One-time cash customers

I N V O I C E   1 3 8

No.	Item			Price	Total	Division*
8	T112	P205/60R16 Tires		140	1 120.00	Sales
4	W101	Aluminum R14 Wheels		180	720.00	Sales
4	W103	Aluminum R16 Wheels		210	840.00	Sales
4	W105	Chrome-Steel R14 Wheels		70	280.00	Sales
4	WN02	Chrome Wheel Locks		25	100.00	Sales
5	SRV01	Alignment - standard		75	375.00	Service
3	SRV03	Brake Service - standard pkg		140	420.00	Service
3	SRV07	Shocks - economy gas-charged		100	300.00	Service

Terms: Cash		GST# 230 192 821	5%	207.75
* Internal use only	Salesperson: Tridon	PST	8%	332.40
Total cash deposited to bank 12/28/10	*T Tridon*			**4 695.15**

Truman Tires
600 Westminster St. London, Ontario N6P 3B1
Tel: (519) 729-3733 Fax: (519) 729-7301

Date of sale: Dec. 28/10

To: Louise Binder
One-time customer

I N V O I C E   1 3 9

No.	Item			Price	Total	Division*
4	T114	P225/60R17 Tires		150	600.00	Sales
4	W104	Aluminum R17 Wheels		225	900.00	Sales
4	WN04	Nickel/Chrome Wheel Locks		30	120.00	Sales

Terms: Visa (4515 7827 4563 8900)		GST# 230 192 821	5%	81.00
* Internal use only	Salesperson: Tridon	PST	8%	129.60
Total cash deposited to bank 12/28/10	*T Tridon*			**1 830.60**

NOTES
If you have difficulty accessing the Allo column, you can click an employee name and then click the Allo tool button.

EMPLOYEE TIME SUMMARY SHEET #52 **DATED DEC. 28/10**

(pay period ending December 28, 2010)

Name of Employee	Week 1	Week 2	Regular Hours	Overtime Hours	No. of Piece Rate Jobs	Sick Days	Personal Days
Delco	40	42	80	2	10	–	–
Holley	42	40	80	2	5	–	–
Monroe	42	40	80	2	6	1	–
Niehoff	40	44	80	4	5	–	2

a. Use Employee Time Summary Sheet #52 and the Employee Information Sheet to complete the payroll run for hourly paid employees.
b. Add a holiday bonus of $200 to each employee's paycheque. Use the Bonus field for the bonus.
c. Allocate 100% of the payroll expenses to Service for all employees.
d. Issue deposit slips #116 to #119.

SESSION DATE – DECEMBER 31, 2010

Purchase Invoice #SW-1419 **Dated Dec. 29/10**

From Sylverado Wheels

8	W102 Aluminum R15 Wheels	¥ 67 200
16	W103 Aluminum R16 Wheels	144 960
8	W104 Aluminum R17 Wheels	77 600
8	W106 Chrome-Steel R15 Wheels	27 200
20	W107 Chrome-Steel R16 Wheels	78 000
	Freight	7 000
	GST Paid	20 098
	Invoice Total	¥422 058
	Import Duty	CAD $219.92	¥23 698

Terms: net 30. The exchange rate is 0.00928. Allocate the freight to Sales.

NOTES
You may see the message about incomplete allocations. Rounding off dollar amounts in the currency conversion can lead to this warning. Check that you have allocated the amount correctly and then accept the incomplete allocation.

```
M E M O  # 9
Date   12/30/2010
From:  T. Tridon
To:    T. Truman

Paid import duty charged to Receiver General on all outstanding
purchases (#SW-1159, ST-1383, SW-1419).

Wrote cheque #209 for $417.77 to pay balance in full.


Trish Tridon
```

Bank Credit Memo #65925   **Dated Dec. 31/10**

From Universal Bank, $215 interest deposited to chequing account. Create new Group account 4200 Revenue from Interest and remember to allow allocation for this account. Allocate 50% of the interest revenue to Sales and 50% to the Service Division.

Memo #10   **Dated Dec. 31/10**

From Owner: Complete payroll run to pay salaried employees Fram and Tridon. Add a holiday bonus of $300 to Fram's cheque and $500 to Tridon's cheque. Issue deposit slips #120 and 121. Allocate 50% of Tridon's pay to Sales and 50% to Service. Allocate 60% of Fram's pay to Sales and 40% to Service.

Issue cheque #210 to Tridon for $359.40, her sales commission (1% of sales less returns). Allocate 100% of the commission to Sales. Include 10% income tax for the commission. Use the Income Statement. (Refer to margin notes.)

Memo #11   **Dated Dec. 31/10**

From Owner: Make payroll remittances for the December pay period as follows:
To Receiver General for Canada: EI, CPP and Income Tax
To Minister of Finance: EHT
To Equity Life: CSB Payable
To CAW Union: Union Dues
To Workplace Safety & Insurance Board: WSIB
Issue cheques #211 to #215 in payment. Use Memo 11a, 11b, etc., as the source.

Memo #12   **Dated Dec. 31/10**

From Owner: Prepare an adjusting entry for supplies used.
Create new Group accounts: 5160 Brakes & Shocks Parts Used
                          5170 Supplies Used: Garage
                          5180 Supplies Used: Office
Supplies Used: Brakes and Shocks Parts $4 900
      Supplies: Garage   1 820
      Supplies: Office   430
Allocate 90% of the Parts and Garage supplies to Service and 10% to Sales.
Allocate 50% of the Office Supplies to Service and 50% to Sales.

KEYSTROKES

Creating New Divisions

Simply Accounting allows allocations for all accounts. Each account ledger record has a check box to allow division allocations for the account (refer to page 90). If this box is checked, the allocation option is available for that account in any journal entry. If it is not checked, you cannot allocate an amount for that account. If you are unable to allocate an amount, check the ledger record for the account you are using to be sure that the option to Allow Division Allocations is selected. Truman Tires will allocate amounts for all revenue and expense accounts. The option to allow allocations is already turned on for all these accounts in your file.

Before entering any transactions with cost or revenue allocations, you should create the divisions.

> **Restore** SimData\truman1.CAB to SimData\Truman\truman. **Enter** Dec. 7, 2010 as the session date.

NOTES
Use the Bonus field for the bonus amounts.

Issue a separate cheque for Tridon's sales commission. Use the Paycheques Journal so that you can change the tax amounts. Remove the salary hours and amounts. Click the Taxes tab. Choose the Enter Taxes Manually tool to open the tax fields for editing. Enter 35.94 in the Income Tax field. Do not remove the CPP amount. Remove the CSB deduction on the Deductions tab screen and the number of hours worked on the Entitlements tab screen.

The Sales by Salesperson Report includes revenue from services. The sales commission is based only on the sales revenue.

NOTES
Assign the Expense or Operating Expense account class to the new accounts. Operating Expense is the default when you use the Add Account wizard.

NOTES
The option to allow allocations for Balance Sheet accounts is not selected in the files for Truman Tires.

SIMPLY VERSION
The ledger record option is to Allow Project Allocations.

Click   **OK** to enter the session date. The Receivables Home window appears.

Click   **Divisions** in the Modules pane list to change the Home window:

The Divisions module window has access to the Divisions ledger records, as well as to four journals that most often have allocated amounts. Divisions are created from the Divisions icon that open the ledger windows. The Divisions window can be also be accessed from the Company, Receivables, Payables and Employees & Payroll modules:

These four modules, as shown above, include the Divisions icon with the module ledger icon. These ledgers have journals that use allocations.

Click   the **Divisions icon** to open the Divisions window:

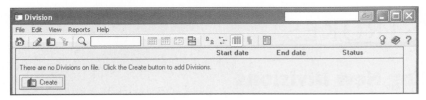

Click   **Create**. The new Division Ledger screen appears:

The cursor is in the Division name field. You must enter the name of the first division.

Type   Sales Division **Press** (tab) **twice** to skip the language button.

The cursor moves to the Start Date field. Enter the date on which you want to begin recording division information, December 1, 2010. The session date appears automatically as the default, ready to be edited. You need to change the date.

Type   12-01

You can enter an **Ending Date** for the division if this is appropriate. The ledger also has a **Balance Forward** field for **Revenue** and **Expense**. These fields can be used to enter historical information — the amount of revenue and expense generated by the division before the records were converted to Simply Accounting or before the Division Ledger was used. The balances are zero for Truman Tires because a new fiscal period is just beginning.

The next field shows the Status for the division.

Click   the **Status field** or list arrow to see the status options:

The division may be Pending (not yet started), In Progress or ongoing, Cancelled or Completed. The two divisions at Truman Tires are In Progress or active.

Click   **In Progress** from the Status drop-down list.

Click   **Create Another** [Create Another] to save the new division.

Enter   the **Service Division** division, using the steps described above for the Sales Division, **use Dec. 1, 2010** as the starting date and **select In Progress** as the Status.

Click   **Save And Close** [Save and Close] to save the second division.

You will return to the Divisions window. Notice that Simply Accounting has created a listing for each division including the name, starting and ending dates and status.

Close   the **Divisions window** to return to the module window.

Click   the **Settings icon** to display the Settings window as shown:

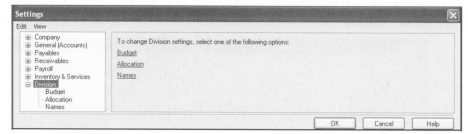

Or choose the Setup menu, then choose Settings and click Division. If the Divisions window is open, the Division Settings screen should open directly.

The Division Ledger has settings for budgeting, allocation and names. Budgeting is covered in Chapter 14. We need to view the setting for allocations.

Click   **Allocation** either in the list under Division or in the list on the right:

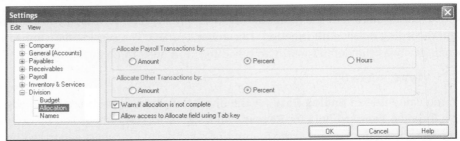

You can enter the allocation in different ways — by Amount, by Percent or by Hours. The option to Allocate By Amount requires you to enter the exact dollar amount for each division. Division work for payroll purposes is often recorded by time spent on the division. This is the third option for payroll allocations.

Simply Accounting includes a warning for incomplete allocations. It is easy to miss an allocation because you must complete the allocation procedure even if 100 percent of the costs are allocated to a single division, and you must allocate each account line in the journals. You will receive the warning if you try to post an entry that has not been fully allocated. If you are using divisions, you should always turn on the warning. The warning should be selected by default.

> If this option is not selected, click Warn If Allocation Is Not Complete. The default settings to allocate expenses by percentage, are correct.

You can also choose to access Allocation fields in journals with the ⟨tab⟩ key. Without this option, you must click the Allo field or tool to open the Allocation window. Using the ⟨tab⟩ key allows you to use the keyboard to enter the transaction and allocation. You can still click the field to move the cursor if you want.

Click   **Allow Access To Allocate Field Using Tab Key**.

Changing Division Names

In any version, you can change the name of the Ledger to Project, Department, Profit Centre, Cost Centre or something that is more appropriate for a business. The new name will replace Division in all windows and reports. Division as the ledger name for Truman Tires' Sales and Service Departments is appropriate.

Simply version users should change the name from Project to Division.

Click   **Names** under the Division heading:

Double click the Project Title field to select the default name.

Type Division (or the name you want to use).

The remaining input fields allow you to add your own user-defined fields for the ledger. The new fields will appear on the Additional Info tab screen. The ledger name can be changed at any time by repeating this step.

NOTES
If you are not using the allocation feature, do not select the option to Allow Access To Allocate Field Using Tab Key so that the cursor will skip the unused Allo field.

SIMPLY VERSION
These steps are included so that Simply version users will see the same names as the Premium version users.

NOTES
We are not renaming Divisions as Departments because Simply Accounting has a feature called departmental accounting that is different from division allocation (see Chapter 19).

NOTES
Once the project name is changed, by selecting an industry or by changing the Names setting, the terms will not change automatically when you change the industry type. You must change the name on the Settings screen if you want to use a different term.

Click   **OK** to save the Division settings.

A confirmation message is displayed when you change the name:

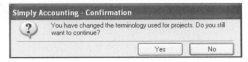

We are warned to ensure that we want the name change — all labels for the ledger icons, field names and report names will be changed.

Click   **Yes** to confirm the change in name.

Most of the journals we need for Truman are accessible from the Divisions module window; therefore, we will work from here. We can create shortcuts for the other journals used.

Create   **shortcuts** for **Pay Purchase Invoices** (Payables), **Create Receipt** (Receivables), **Transfer Funds** (Banking), **Item Assembly** and **Inventory Adjustments** (Inventory & Services), **Payroll Cheque Run** (Employees & Payroll), and **Create General Journal** (Company).

Entering Cost Allocations

Costs (or expenses) and revenues are allocated after the regular journal entry is completed but before it is posted. In a journal entry, whenever you use an account for which you have allowed division allocations in the General Ledger, the allocation option is available. For Truman Tires, all revenue and expense accounts allow division allocations.

Click   the **Purchase Invoices icon** [Purchase Invoices ▼] to open the Purchases Journal.

The journal has not changed with the setup of allocations, and we enter the purchase details the same way.

The first transaction does not involve the purchase of inventory items, so you will not use the inventory database to complete this transaction. Invoice is correct as the transaction type, and Pay Later is the correct payment method.

From the list of suppliers,

Click   **London Tool Rentals**.

Click   the **Invoice field**.

Type   L-4441 **Press** (tab) **twice**.

The cursor moves to the Date field. Replace the default session date with the transaction date.

Type   dec 1

The tax code GP and the account number 5110 should be added as the default. If they are not, you can add them or edit them as needed.

Enter   a **description**.

Click   the **Amount field** or press (tab) repeatedly to advance the cursor.

Type   280

Press   (tab) **twice** to enter the amount of the invoice and the tax amounts, and to advance to the Allo column.

NOTES
All transactions can be completed from these shortcuts and journal windows. For example, other payments and payroll remittances are completed from the Payments Journal. Orders and Quotes are entered from the Sales Invoices or Purchase Invoices windows by selecting from the transactions drop-down list in the journal.

NOTES
You can allow allocations for Balance Sheet accounts, but we have not done so for Truman Tires.

The journal now looks like a regular completed purchase transaction:

Notice that the Allocate tool ✓ is no longer dimmed. The cursor must be on an invoice line with an account that allows allocation. If the account does not allow allocation or if the cursor has advanced to an invoice line without an account, the Allocate tool and menu option will be dimmed and unavailable.

Click the invoice line for the amount you want to allocate to activate the Allocate option. Only accounts that have selected the option to Allow Division Allocations will activate the Allocate tool.

Click the **Allocate tool** ✓, or **press** (enter), or **click** the **Allo column** beside the account or **choose** the **Purchase menu** and **click Allocate**.

You will see the Division Allocation window for the Purchases Journal:

The cursor is in the Division field. The full amount to be allocated, $302.40 (the expense amount plus PST), is shown at the top for reference together with the proportion remaining to be allocated, 100.00%. Amounts can be allocated by percentage or by actual amount. This choice is made in the Division Settings window shown on page 520. (Choose the Setup menu, click Settings and then click Division and Allocation). The setting can be changed as needed. Truman Tires uses the Percentage allocation method as indicated in the Division Information.

You must complete the allocation process even if 100 percent of the revenue or expense is assigned to a single division. You must complete the allocation process for each account or invoice line on your input form.

Click the **Division List icon** 🔍 to display the Divisions in alphabetic order:

The first division is Sales, which incurs 20 percent of the total rental expense according to the source document information. Notice that you can add a new division from the Select Division window.

Choose Add to open the Division Ledger for creating a new division.

Click **Sales Division**, the first one we need.

Click **Select** to enter it on your form.

The cursor advances to the Percentage field because we selected this method of allocation. By default the unallocated portion (100%) is indicated in this field and selected for editing.

Type 20 **Press** (tab).

The program calculates the dollar amount for this division automatically based on the percentage entered. The percentage remaining at the top of the input form has been updated to 80.00%. The cursor moves to the next line in the Division field. Now you are ready to enter the amount for the remaining division, 80 percent. You need to repeat the steps above to allocate the remainder of the expense.

Press (enter).

Double click **Service Division**.

The cursor is in the Percentage field again, with 80.00 as the default amount because this was the unallocated percentage remaining. Since this amount is correct, we can accept it.

Press (tab) to enter it and complete the allocation as shown here:

Click **OK** to return to the Purchases Journal.

Your form is now complete as shown, and you are ready to review your work:

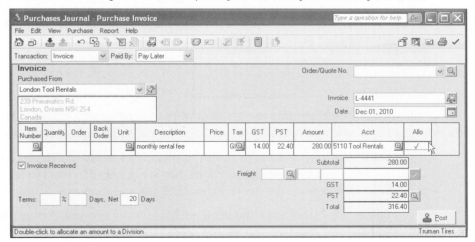

The journal appears unchanged, except for the ✓ in the Allo column indicating that the amount has been allocated.

Reviewing the Purchases Journal Allocation

Choose the **Report menu** and **click Display Purchases Journal Entry**:

Truman Tires		Debits	Credits	Division
12/01/10 (J1)				
2670	GST Paid on Purchases	14.00	-	
5110	Tool Rentals	302.40	-	
	- Sales Division			60.48
	- Service Division			241.92
2200	Accounts Payable	-	316.40	
		316.40	316.40	

Simply Accounting has automatically updated the *Accounts Payable* control account because the Payables and General ledgers are fully integrated. Notice also that the rental expense has been allocated to the two divisions. Only the amount for the expense account *Tool Rentals* is allocated because the other accounts are Balance Sheet accounts that are not set up to allow allocations.

Close   the **display** to return to the Purchases Journal input screen.

Click   the **Store tool** ⊟ . Accept the supplier name and **choose Monthly** as the frequency. **Click OK** to return to the journal.

To see the allocation again, click the Allocate tool ☑ when the cursor is on the relevant line or click the ✓ in the Allo column.

CORRECTING THE PURCHASES JOURNAL ENTRY ALLOCATION

Correct the Purchases Journal part of the entry as you would correct any other purchase invoice. Refer to page 116 if you need assistance.

If you have made an error in the allocation, **click** the Allocate tool ☑ to return to the Allocation window. Click the line for the amount being allocated to activate the Allocate tool if necessary. Click an incorrect division to highlight it. Press (enter) to access the Division list. Click the correct division and click Select to enter the change. Click an incorrect percentage and type the correct information. Press (tab) to save the correction. Click OK to return to the Journal window.

Posting

When you are certain that you have entered all the information correctly,

Click   **Post** 🖳 Post   to save the entry. **Click OK** to confirm posting.

If you have not allocated 100 percent of the amounts, you may see the warning:

Simply Accounting - Confirmation

? The following accounts have not been fully allocated:
5110 Tool Rentals
Process the transaction anyway?

[Yes]   [No]   [Help]

You will see a message like this one if you have not fully allocated a journal amount. If the warning is not selected (page 520) you may post the transaction incorrectly.

If you made an error, click No to return to the invoice in the Purchases Journal. Click the Allo column beside the account that is not fully allocated to return to the Allocation screen. Make the changes, click OK and then post.

If you do not want to allocate the full amount, or if the account that was not fully allocated was one that you cannot access the allocation procedure for, such as *Variance Costs* (see page 530), you should click Yes to continue.

Close   the **Purchases Journal** and **enter** the **payment transaction**.

Entering Import Duties

Governments may apply import duties that raise the price of imported goods to encourage the local economy. Duty rates or tariffs vary from one type of item to another, and from one country to another. The duty is collected by Canada Revenue Agency when the goods enter Canada before they are released to the buyer.

In Simply Accounting, before you can enter duty amounts with the purchase, you must change the Payables settings to charge and track import duties (see page 646). You must also indicate in the foreign supplier's record (Options tab screen) that duty is applied to purchases from that supplier (see page 661). In the Inventory Ledger records (Taxes tab screen), you can enter the duty applied as a percentage (see page 678), or you can enter the rates in the Purchases Journal. For non-inventory purchases, you must enter the rate directly in the Purchases Journal.

The purchase invoice from Snowmaster Tire Company has import duties applied because Canada does not have a free trade agreement with Japan. The company settings and the Supplier and Inventory Ledger records for Truman Tires are set up to apply duty.

Open   the **Purchases Journal**.

Choose Snowmaster Tire Company as the supplier and **press** (_tab_):

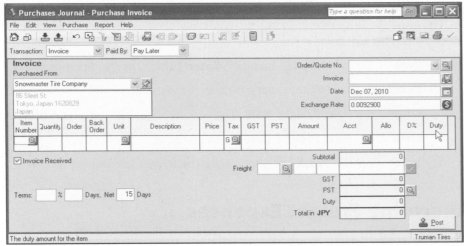

NOTES
You may need to scroll to see all the columns. You can also maximize the journal window or resize the columns.

In addition to the Exchange Rate field and the indication that Japanese yen (JPY) is the currency for this supplier, the duty fields are added because we selected a supplier for whom duty applies. The fields are used for the duty percentage and for the duty amount. Duty is charged on all items purchased from Snowmaster Tire Company.

Click   the **Invoice field** and **type** ST-916

Enter   **Dec 2** in the Date field and **press** (_tab_) to open the Exchange Rate screen with the most recent rate highlighted.

Type   .0093 **Click Make This The Default Rate For Dec. 2, 2010**.

Click   **OK** to return to the journal.

Click   the **Description field**. **Type** miscellaneous parts

Click   the **Amount field**. **Type** 60000 **Press** (_tab_).

Choose 1240 Brakes & Shocks Parts from the Account list. **Press** (_tab_) **twice**.

You will advance the cursor to the D% (duty rate) field where you should enter the rate that the government applies to this type of product.

Type   6 **Press** (_tab_) to enter the duty amount.

Press (tab) again to advance to the next line in the Item field. You can now add the inventory item purchases.

Double click the **Item field** to open the Inventory Selection screen.

Double click **T110** to add this item to the invoice:

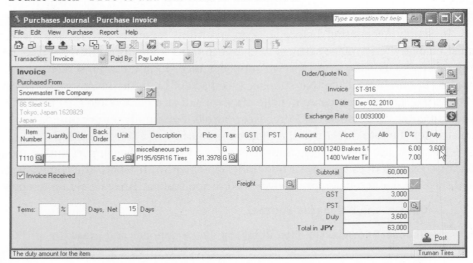

This time the duty rate is added automatically because the rate is recorded in the ledger record for the item.

Type 20 to enter the quantity. **Enter 112000** as the Amount.

Enter the **second inventory item** in the same way.

Click the **first Freight field**. The code G should be entered as the default.

Click the **final Freight field** for the amount.

Type 7500 **Press** (tab) to update the freight tax amount and total.

Allocating Freight Expenses

When you purchase inventory items, the Allocate tool and menu option are not available because the asset accounts were not set up to allow allocations. However, the freight expense for these purchases can be allocated.

The Freight field **Allocate button** ☑ (to the right of the freight amount field), indicated with the pointer in the following screen, is used for this purpose:

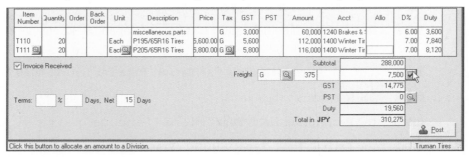

Click the **Allocate button** ☑ to the right of the Freight fields.

The Division Allocation screen opens. It is the same as the one we saw earlier. The Freight amount, ¥7 500, is entered as the amount to be allocated.

NOTES

Freight is allocated by amount – the cursor advances to the Amount field on the Allocation screen after you select the Division. You cannot change this setting.

Choose the **Sales Division** and **accept** the **amount** and percentage allocation.

Click OK to return to the journal. The journal has not changed in appearance.

Choose the **Report menu** and **click Display Purchases Journal Entry**:

Truman Tires 12/02/10 (J3)	Foreign Amt.		Debits	Credits	Division
1240 Brakes & Shocks Parts	¥63,600		591.48	-	
1400 Winter Tires	¥243,960		2,268.83	-	
2670 GST Paid on Purchases	¥14,775		137.41	-	
5065 Freight Expense	¥7,500		69.75	-	
- Sales Division		¥7,500			69.75
2200 Accounts Payable	¥310,275		-	2,885.56	
2220 Import Duty Payable	¥19,560		-	181.91	
			3,067.47	3,067.47	
1 Japanese Yen equals 0.0093000 Canadian Dollars					

Only the Freight Expense amount has a division allocation in the journal entry because it was the only amount allocated for the transaction.

Close the **Journal Entry** to return to the journal.

To correct the freight expense allocation, click the Allocate button ☑ beside the field to open the Division Allocation screen and make the needed changes.

Click **Post** 👤 Post to save the entry.

If you have not allocated the freight amount, you will see the warning about incomplete allocations on page 524.

Enter the next **three transactions**.

Allocating in the Sales Journal

Amounts for revenue accounts in the Sales Journal are allocated in the same way as amounts for expense accounts in the Purchases Journal. Each revenue amount in the journal must be allocated completely, but you can assign the same allocation percentages to all accounts in the journal rather than repeating the allocation entry for each invoice line. We will demonstrate this method by showing the steps involved in the Visa sale to Scinto on December 4.

Click the **Sales icon** Sales Invoices▾ to open the Sales Journal.

Enter **Bruno Scinto** in the Sold To field.

Press ⎢tab⎥ and **click Continue**.

Choose **Visa** as the method in the Paid By field.

Enter **Dec. 4** as the invoice date.

Choose **Tridon** as the salesperson in the Sold By field.

Click the **Use The Same Salesperson tool** 🖾.

Choose **T104** as the first inventory item for the sale.

Press ⎢tab⎥ to advance to the Quantity field.

Type 4

Press ⎢tab⎥ repeatedly to advance to the Allo field.

Click the **Allo field** to open the Division Allocation window.

As long as the cursor is on the invoice line you are allocating, the allocate function is available. Click the Allocate tool button or choose the Sales menu and click Allocate to open the Division Allocation screen.

SIMPLY VERSION
In the Simply version, you will see foreign amounts in a column with the heading JPY Amount.

NOTES
You can allocate freight revenue amounts in the same way. Simply click the Allocate tool beside the Freight fields.

NOTES
You can leave the Sales Journal open in the background while you complete transactions in other journals. The salesperson will remain selected until you change the session date. If you use this approach, ensure that you update the dates and payment methods for each sale.
You can also add Tridon as the salesperson in customer records. Remember to add the salesperson for new customers.

NOTES
You can also press ⎢ctrl⎥ + ⎢shift⎥ + A to open the Division Allocation window.

Choose the **Sales Division** for 100% of the revenue amount.

The allocation screen has a check box for the option Apply This Allocation To Entire Transaction as shown:

This option allows you to enter one allocation and let the program apply the same percentages for all other amounts automatically. Otherwise you will need to repeat the allocation procedure for each account in the journal.

Click   **Apply This Allocation To Entire Transaction** to open the message about this selection:

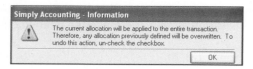

Read   the **message** and then **click OK** to return to the allocation screen.

If you do not want to continue with this selection, click the check box again.

The Division Allocation screen has changed as shown:

No amounts are entered at this time because the same percentages will be applied and the amounts will be different.

Click   **OK** to save the allocation and return to the journal.

Enter   the **remaining inventory** and **service items** for the sale.

The ✓ is added to the Allo field automatically as you complete the invoice:

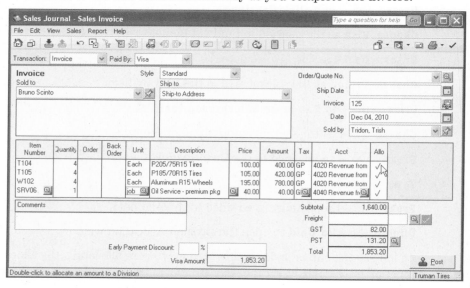

The invoice has been completely allocated, but the allocation is not correct, as you will see when you review the journal entry for the transaction.

Press   ⌈ctrl⌉ + **J** to open the journal display:

Truman Tires		Debits	Credits	Division
12/04/10 (J7)				
1070	Bank: Visa	1,801.31	-	
5040	Credit Card Fees	51.89	-	
	- Sales Division			51.89
5050	Cost of Goods Sold	640.00	-	
	- Sales Division			640.00
1360	Wheels	-	312.00	
1400	Winter Tires	-	328.00	
2640	PST Payable	-	131.20	
2650	GST Charged on Sales	-	82.00	
4020	Revenue from Sales	-	1,600.00	
	- Sales Division			1,600.00
4040	Revenue from Services	-	40.00	
	- Sales Division			40.00
		2,493.20	2,493.20	

The service revenue should not be allocated to Sales so we must change it.

Close   the displayed **report** to return to the journal.

Click   anywhere on the line for **item SRV06**.

Click   the **Allo tool** ☑, **click** the **Allo field** or **choose** the **Sales menu** and **click Allocate** to open the Division Allocation screen.

Click   **Apply This Allocation To Entire Transaction** to open the message about this change in selection:

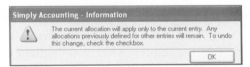

Simply Accounting - Information

⚠ The current allocation will apply only to the current entry. Any allocations previously defined for other entries will remain. To undo this change, check the checkbox.

[OK]

We can change the allocation for this invoice line without changing any other line.

Click   **OK** to return to the Division Allocation screen. Sales Division is selected.

Press   ⌈enter⌉ to open the list of divisions.

Double click   **Service Division** to add it to the Division Allocation screen.

Click   **OK** to save the change and return to the journal.

Choose the **Sales menu** and **click Display Sales Journal Entry**:

Truman Tires		Debits	Credits	Division
12/04/10 (J7)				
1070	Bank: Visa	1,801.31	-	
5040	Credit Card Fees	51.89	-	
	- Sales Division			50.62
	- Service Division			1.27
5050	Cost of Goods Sold	640.00	-	
	- Sales Division			640.00
1360	Wheels	-	312.00	
1400	Winter Tires	-	328.00	
2640	PST Payable	-	131.20	
2650	GST Charged on Sales	-	82.00	
4020	Revenue from Sales	-	1,600.00	
	- Sales Division			1,600.00
4040	Revenue from Services	-	40.00	
	- Service Division			40.00
		2,493.20	2,493.20	

The allocation is now correct. The allocation for Credit Card Fees is automatically split in the correct proportion. Cost of Goods Sold is also allocated. We can post the entry.

Close   the **Journal Entry** to return to the journal.

Click   **Post** ⊞ Post to save the entry.

Continue   entering the **transactions** to purchase invoice #ST-1141.

NOTES
You can also click or press ⌈enter⌉ in the Allo field, or press ⌈ctrl⌉ + ⌈shift⌉ + A for the selected item to open the Division Allocation screen.

Creating Cost Variances

If inventory is sold to a customer when the inventory stock is too low to fill the sale completely, the levels in inventory fall below zero and the outstanding items are backordered. The estimated cost of goods for the sale is based on the average cost for the items in stock at the time of the sale. When the items are received, the price may have changed, and the items that are used to fill the rest of the customer's order will have a different cost price from that recorded. The difference is the cost variance and is assigned to the linked variance account for the inventory item. The amount of the variance shows in the journal entry for the purchase. Thus two conditions are required for a variance to occur — the inventory is oversold and the cost has changed.

Normally, you do not have to do anything to record a cost variance because the program makes the calculations automatically and assigns the amount to the linked variance account for the inventory item.

After entering the purchase from Snowmaster Tire Company on Dec. 13, display the journal entry. It should match the one shown here:

Truman Tires					
12/14/10 (J21)		Foreign Amt.	Debits	Credits	Division
1400	Winter Tires	¥201,783	1,875.57	-	
2670	GST Paid on Purchases	¥9,843	91.49	-	
5055	Variance Costs	¥833	7.74	-	
5065	Freight Expense	¥7,500	69.71	-	
	- Sales Division	¥7,500			69.71
2200	Accounts Payable	¥206,703	-	1,921.30	
2220	Import Duty Payable	¥13,255	-	123.21	
			2,044.51	2,044.51	
1 Japanese Yen equals 0.0092950 Canadian Dollars					

There was insufficient stock left for item T101 on Dec. 7 when the cash summary sale was recorded, so the average historic cost for 12 tires, $336, was credited to *Cost of Goods Sold*. Only eight tires were in stock at the time of the sale, with an average cost of $28 ($112 for four tires). When the purchase of item T101 was recorded, the total cost for 16 tires was $478.98, or $119.74 for four. The difference, $7.74, between the new cost and the cost in the sales transaction is the cost variance.

When you post the transaction, you will see the following warning:

Variance costs cannot be allocated, so you must accept the incomplete allocation.

Click   **Yes** to continue posting the purchase.

Enter   the next group of **transactions** up to Memo #4.

Making Import Duty Remittances

Paying the import duty owing on imported merchandise is like paying other taxes. Normally duty must be paid before the package is released by Customs.

Open   the **Payments Journal**. The cheque number, bank account and date are correct.

Choose   **Make Other Payment**.

Choose   **Receiver General for Canada** as the supplier.

Choose   **2220 Import Duty Payable** as the account from the Selection list.

You should record the corresponding purchase invoice numbers in the journal as well.

Type   Duty re ST916, ST1141, SW876, SW1024

Press   tab to move to the Amount field.

Type   496.13

Click   the **Invoice/Ref. field** and **type** Memo 4 **Press** tab .

Type   Memo 4, Import duty remittance

Review the **journal entry**. **Close** the **display**. **Make corrections** if needed and then **post** the **transaction**. **Enter** the remaining **transactions**.

Allocating in Other Journals

Use the same principles outlined above to allocate revenues and expenses in the General Journal, Adjustments Journal or the Payroll journals to divisions or profit centres. You can change the setup to make allocations by dollar amounts or by percentage.

Once you have entered the journal information for an account that allows allocation, the Allocate tool ☑ will be available. You can use it to enter the allocation information.

In the Paycheques Journal, click the Allo tool ☑.

To correct allocations, click ☑ to re-open the allocation screen.

In the setup for Payroll allocations, you can choose to allocate expenses according to the number of hours worked on each division.

In the Payroll Cheque Run Journal, use the Allo column for the employee who is selected from the list. You can allocate for one employee at a time. Click the employee's name. Then click the Allo column or choose the Payroll menu and click Allocate to begin the allocation. You can also apply the same allocation to the entire transaction, just as we did in the Sales Journal.

In the Payroll journals, the total payroll expense, not the net pay, is allocated. This includes employer contributions such as EI, CPP, WSIB/WCB and EHT. When you review the journal entry, you will see that all the payroll-related expenses are divided among the divisions according to the percentages you entered. They are shown under the Division column. You may have to scroll to see all the information.

Displaying Division Reports

Division reports can be displayed from the Divisions window, from the Division module window Reports pane drop-down list, from the Home window Reports menu and from the Report Centre. We will continue to show reports from the Report Centre.

To print division reports, display the report you want using the instructions that follow. Click the Print tool 🖨 or choose the File menu and click Print.

To display the reports,

Click   the **Report Centre icon** [Report Centre] in the Home window.

Click   **Division**, if necessary, to open the list of division reports.

NOTES
The Paycheques Journal does not have an Allo column, so you must use the tool or the menu approach.

Simply SIMPLY VERSION
Remember that if you have not changed the ledger name, you will see Project instead of Division throughout the report menus and options.

For other company types, you can replace Division by a name that is appropriate for that type of company.

NOTES
The terms used for other types of industries will replace Division in all report titles and fields.

The division reports you can display from the Report Centre are listed:

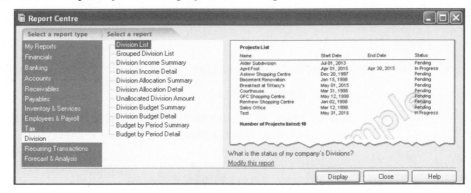

Displaying the Division List

CLASSIC VIEW
Right-click the Divisions icon

 to select it. Click the

Display tool .

Click   **Division List**. **Click Modify This Report** to open the report options:

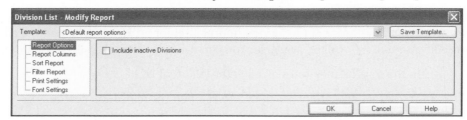

Or, choose the Reports menu, then choose Lists and click Division.

Click Report Columns to customize the fields shown on the report.

Click   **OK**. **Close** the **display** when you have finished viewing the report.

NOTES
You can display the Division Allocation Detail Report from the Division List.

Displaying the Grouped Division List

Click   **Grouped Division List**. **Click Modify This Report** to see the options.

Click   the **Grouped By drop-down list arrow** to see the ways you can organize the report:

SIMPLY VERSION
The Simply version does not have Grouped Division Lists.

You can group the divisions by division status (e.g., pending, in progress and so on), or by any of the additional fields you added for the ledger.

Choose the criterion for grouping.

Click   **OK**. **Close** the **display** when you have finished viewing the report.

Displaying Division Income Reports

The Division Income Report provides an income statement with revenue, expenses and net income for each division you select for the report.

Click   **Division Income Summary**. **Click Modify This Report**:

Or, choose the Reports menu, then choose Division and click Income to display the Options window.

You can sort and filter Division Income Detail reports by date, comment, source, journal number and amount per transaction. As usual, the fiscal start and session dates are the defaults. All divisions and accounts are selected initially.

Enter   the **beginning date** and **ending date** for the report.

Click   a **division** to change the selection. **Press** and **hold** `ctrl` and **click** the **divisions** you want to include in the report. **Click Select All** to include all divisions in the report.

Leave the **Summary** option, the one selected by default, if you want your report to show summary information (i.e., totals) for each account selected for each division. The **Detail** option provides complete journal information for each account for each division selected, including the names of all customers, suppliers and employees, as well as the reference document number, journal entry number and date. Both options provide a calculation for revenue minus expense.

Next you should select the revenue and expense accounts you want in the report.

Click   an **account** to change the selection. **Press** and **hold** `ctrl` and **click** the **accounts** you want to include in the report or **click Select All** to include them all.

Click   **OK** to display the report. **Close** the **display** when finished.

Displaying Division Allocation Reports

When you allow allocation for Balance Sheet accounts, they are reported in the Division Allocation Report together with Income Statement accounts. The Division Income Report has only revenue and expense accounts.

Click   **Division Allocation Summary**. **Click Modify This Report**:

From any Home window, choose the Reports menu, then choose Division and click Allocation to display the Division Allocation Report Options window.

The Division Allocation Report shows the breakdown of amounts for each division by account. It is similar to the Division Income Report, but the total revenue and expense and the net division income are omitted. Instead, a single total for all accounts is provided for each division.

Although the report options look the same as for the Income Report, if you scroll up the list of accounts, you will see that Balance Sheet accounts are included. All reports for which you have allowed allocation will be on the list.

Enter the **start** and **end dates** for the report.

Click a **division** to change the selection. **Press** and **hold** (ctrl) and **click** the **divisions** you want to include in the report or **click Select All**.

Like the Income Report, the Summary option will show totals and the Detail option provides complete journal information for each account for each division.

After you have indicated which options you want, choose the accounts.

Press and **hold** (ctrl) and **click** the **accounts** you want or **click Select All**.

Click **OK** to display the report. **Close** the **display** when you have finished.

Adding Division Details to Journal Reports

When you have entered division information in a journal, you can include the allocation details to any journal report.

Click **Financials** in the Select A Report Type list.

Click **All Journal Entries**. **Click Modify This Report**:

The Journal Report Options window includes a check box for division allocations.

Click **Division Allocations** to include division information in journal reports. By default, journal reports do not include division details.

Enter the **dates** for the report and **click OK**.

Close the **display** when finished. **Close** the **Report Centre**.

Displaying Division Management Reports

There are management reports for the Division Ledger, just as there are for other ledgers in Simply Accounting. Management Reports can be displayed only from the Home window Reports menu.

Choose the **Reports menu**, then **choose Management Reports** and **click Division** to see the list of management reports:

Click   the **topic** for the report. **Click OK** to display the report. **Close** the **display** when you have finished.

REVIEW

The Student CD-ROM with Data Files includes Review Questions and Supplementary Cases for this chapter.

NOTES
The Service Division is operating at a loss according to the Management Report.

WARNING!
Check that the file location for the form used by the report is correct for your program settings.

CHAPTER FOURTEEN

Village Galleries

OBJECTIVES

- ■ **turn on** the budgeting feature in Simply Accounting
- ■ **determine** budgeting periods and amounts
- ■ **allocate** budget amounts to revenue and expense accounts
- ■ **enter** transactions involving Quebec Sales Tax
- ■ **display** and **print** income statements with budget comparisons
- ■ **graph** budget reports
- ■ **analyze** budget reports
- ■ **print** invoices in batches

After completing this chapter, you should be able to

COMPANY INFORMATION

Company Profile

NOTES
Village Galleries
509 Boul. Rouin
Montreal, Quebec H3F 5G5
Tel: (514) 529-6391
Fax: (514) 529-7622
Business No.: 236 412 540

Village Galleries, located in Outremont, an upscale area of Montreal, is owned and operated by Renée and Gilles Montand, a husband-and-wife partnership. The small family-run business recently hired one employee, who will earn a commission on sales. She works in the store several days a week but the Montands maintain the regular operation of the business. Renée performs the accounting duties for the business. Other jobs are occasionally subcontracted.

The store, more like a furniture boutique, carries a limited range of high-quality inventory, selling to clients who are selective in their furniture and accessory preferences. Accessories and furniture for living rooms, bedrooms, dining rooms and kitchens comprise the major inventory items in the boutique. The brass furniture pieces are imported from Italy, and some items are high-quality reproductions of antiques made in small Quebec furniture factories by respected artisans. Most of the furniture is made of wood or wood frames covered with fine fabrics. The choice of wood includes mahogany, oak, cherry, ash and, of course, pine. Rich select woods of the highest quality are used to create solid wood pieces, but sometimes expensive veneers are used to complement the designs. In addition, the furniture boutique sells home accessories such as lamps, a small selection of handmade Persian and Oriental rugs made of wool and silk, mirrors and original framed numbered prints imported from Italy.

Most customers are local but, occasionally, customers from abroad who visit Montreal ask for furniture to be shipped to them. Delivery (shipping or freight) is charged on most orders and exported items. Preferred price list customers do not pay for delivery, and they receive discounted inventory prices. All account customers are entitled to a before-tax 2 percent discount if they settle their accounts within 10 days. After 30 days, interest charges accrue at the rate of 1.5 percent per month. Customer deposits from 20 to 25 percent of the total sale are required on all orders. Customers may pay by cheque, cash or credit card.

Some suppliers with whom Village Galleries has accounts require deposits to accompany purchase orders, and some suppliers offer after-tax purchase discounts for early payments. The store has a business credit card account with American Express.

The currency for all foreign transactions, the purchases from Italy and the sales to European customers, is the euro (€). Foreign prices for inventory are calculated from the exchange rate at the time of sale. No foreign prices are entered in the inventory ledger. Village Galleries pays import duties on the imported furniture but not on original art work such as the numbered prints.

Renée Montand used the following to set up the accounting files for Village Galleries in Simply Accounting:

- Chart of Accounts
- Post-Closing Trial Balance
- Supplier Information
- Customer Information
- Employee Information
- Inventory Information
- Accounting Procedures

CHART OF ACCOUNTS

VILLAGE GALLERIES

ASSETS
Current Assets
1060 Chequing Bank Account
1070 Visa Bank Account
1080 MasterCard Bank Account
1090 Bank Account - Euro
1100 Investment Portfolio
1150 Purchase Prepayments
1200 Accounts Receivable
1220 Office Supplies
1240 Furniture Supplies
1260 Prepaid Insurance

Inventory Assets
1320 Bedroom Furniture
1340 Home Accessories
1360 Kitchen & Dining Room
     Furniture
1380 Living Room Furniture

Fixed Assets
1420 Cash Register ▶

▶1440 Computer Equipment
1460 Equipment & Tools
1480 Gallery Fixtures
1500 Gallery

LIABILITIES
Current Liabilities
2200 Accounts Payable
2220 Prepaid Sales and Deposits
2250 Credit Card Payable
2260 Import Duty Payable
2330 Income Tax Payable
2350 QPP Payable
2360 Quebec Income Tax Payable
2370 QHSF Payable
2460 CSST Payable
2650 GST Charged on Sales
2670 GST Paid on Purchases
2800 Refundable QST Paid
2810 QST Charged on Sales ▶

▶Long Term Liabilities
2950 Mortgage Payable - Gallery

EQUITY
Owner's Equity
3560 Montand, Capital
3580 Montand, Drawings
3600 Current Earnings

REVENUE
4020 Revenue from Sales
4040 Sales Discount
4060 Freight Revenue
4100 Investment Revenue
4120 Interest Revenue

EXPENSE
Operating Expenses
5020 Advertising & Promotion
5030 Exchange Rate Differences
5040 Bank Charges
5050 Credit Card Fees ▶

▶5060 Cost of Goods Sold
5070 Variance Costs
5080 Furniture Supplies Used
5100 Damaged Inventory
5120 Purchase Discounts
5130 Freight Expense
5140 Delivery Expense
5160 Hydro Expense
5180 Insurance Expense
5190 Mortgage Interest Expense
5200 Office Supplies Used
5220 Telephone Expenses

Payroll Expenses
5300 Commissions
5330 CSST Expense
5340 QPP Expense
5350 QHSF Expense
5380 Subcontractor Fees

NOTES: The Chart of Accounts includes only postable accounts and Current Earnings. QPP (Quebec Pension Plan) replaces CPP in Quebec. QHSF (Quebec Health Services Fund) is an employer-funded provincial health and services tax program.
Linked payable and expense accounts for EI, CPP and QPIP (Quebec Parental Insurance Plan) are also included because they are essential linked accounts, but they are not used in this example.

POST-CLOSING TRIAL BALANCE

VILLAGE GALLERIES

June 30, 2010

		Debits	Credits				Debits	Credits
1060	Chequing Bank Account	$ 51 897.25		▶ 1440	Computer Equipment		2 800.00	
1070	Visa Bank Account	5 445.00		1460	Equipment & Tools		1 500.00	
1080	MasterCard Bank Account	3 555.00		1480	Gallery Fixtures		1 000.00	
1090	Bank Account - Euro (€ 1 410)	2 100.00		1500	Gallery		150 000.00	
1100	Investment Portfolio	50 000.00		2200	Accounts Payable			$ 11 395.00
1200	Accounts Receivable	5 643.75		2250	Credit Card Payable			240.00
1220	Office Supplies	400.00		2260	Import Duty Payable			240.00
1240	Furniture Supplies	600.00		2650	GST Charged on Sales			1 680.00
1260	Prepaid Insurance	250.00		2670	GST Paid on Purchases		980.00	
1320	Bedroom Furniture	35 200.00		2800	Refundable QST Paid		90.00	
1340	Home Accessories	30 900.00		2810	QST Charged on Sales			1 926.00
1360	Kitchen & Dining Room Furniture	24 995.00		2950	Mortgage Payable - Gallery			145 000.00
1380	Living Room Furniture	41 925.00		3560	Montand, Capital			250 000.00
1420	Cash Register	1 200.00 ▶					$410 481.00	$410 481.00

SUPPLIER INFORMATION

VILLAGE GALLERIES

Supplier Name (Contact)	Address	Phone No. Fax No.	E-mail Web Site	Terms Tax ID
Domo Carvaggio (Arturo Dessini)	8 Via Artistes Forli, 47100 Italy	Tel: (39-0543) 457 882 Fax: (39-0543) 457 113	www.domocarvaggio.com	net 30
Énergie Québec (Marie Nuclaire)	5010 Ave. Atomique Montreal, Quebec H2B 6C9	Tel: (514) 782-6101	www.energie.quebec.ca	net 1
L'Ascension Mobiliers (Suzie LaChaise)	RR #2 Jonquière, Quebec G7S 4L2	Tel: (450) 821-1029 Fax: (450) 822-1927	suzie@lascension.com www.lascension.com	1/5, n/30 (after tax) 322 749 610
Montreal Persia Emporium (Perse Moquette)	40 Rue de Tapis Longueuil, Quebec J4K 2L7	Tel: (450) 288-4334 Fax: (450) 288-8201	moquette@MPE.com www.MPE.com	2/5, n/30 (after tax) 473 540 911
Normandin Meubles (Normand Armoire)	RR #3 Nicolet, Quebec J3T 1H5	Tel: (450) 371-7273 Fax: (450) 371-7229	na@normand.meubles.com www.normand.meubles.com	2/10, n/30 (after tax) 136 492 446
Papineau Delivery (Martin Camion)	56 Papineau Ave. Outremont, Quebec H1M 3B3	Tel: (514) 690-2810 Fax: (514) 691-7283	martin@papineau.com www.papineau.com	net 10 288 344 566
Receiver General for Canada	Sudbury Tax Services Office PO Box 20004 Sudbury, Ontario P3A 6B4	Tel 1: (800) 561-7761 Tel 2: (800) 959-2221	www.cra-arc.gc.ca	net 1
Staples (Hélène Magazinier)	777 Ave. de Bureau Montreal, Quebec H4K 1V5	Tel: (514) 759-3488 Fax: (514) 758- 3910	www.staples.com	net 15 128 634 772
Telébec (Robert Bavarde)	84 Rue Causerie Montreal, Quebec H3C 7S2	Tel: (514) 488-2355	www.bell.ca	net 1

NOTES: All supplier discounts are calculated on after-tax amounts.

OUTSTANDING SUPPLIER INVOICES

VILLAGE GALLERIES

Supplier Name	Terms	Date	Invoice	Amount CAD	Total
L'Ascension Mobiliers	1/5, n/30 (after tax)	June 29/10	LM-2114	$4 558.00	$4 558.00
Normandin Meubles	2/10, n/30 (after tax)	June 28/10	NM-192	$6 837.00	$6 837.00
			Grand Total		$11 395.00

CUSTOMER INFORMATION

VILLAGE GALLERIES

Customer Name (Contact)	Address	Phone No. Fax No.	E-mail Web Site	Terms Credit Limit
Caisse Metropolitain (Tomas Monaire)	50 Rue Berri Montreal, Quebec H1B 6F4	Tel: (514) 466-2991 Fax: (514) 468-1826	tmonaire@caissemetro.ca www.caissemetro.ca	2/10, n/30 $5 000
Cash Customers				cash or credit card
Deon Estates (Kaline Deon)	600 Rue St. Denis Montreal, Quebec H2K 7C9	Tel: (514) 729-8217 Fax: (514) 729-9283	kaline.deon@istar.com	2/10, n/30 $5 000
*St. Leonard's Homebuilders (Félice Charpentier)	31 Boul. St. Joseph Montreal, Quebec H4N 2M1	Tel: (514) 788-3645 Fax: (514) 787-7114	felice@stleonards.com www.stleonards.com	2/10, n/30 $10 000
*Westmount Primrose Condos (M.T. Sweets)	121 Rue Notre Dame Montreal, Quebec H3K 4G5	Tel: (514) 499-7117 Fax: (514) 498-2889	sweets@wpcondos.com www.wpcondos.com	2/10, n/30 $10 000

NOTES: All customer discounts are calculated on amounts before tax. Customers pay 1.5% interest on accounts over 30 days. Asterisk (*) indicates preferred price list customer.

OUTSTANDING CUSTOMER INVOICES

VILLAGE GALLERIES

Customer Name	Terms	Date	Invoice	Amount	Tax	Total
Deon Estates	2/10, n/30 (before tax)	June 24/10	168	$5 000	$643.75	$5 643.75

Employee Profile and TD1 Information

Lianne Décor   started working for the boutique on July 1, 2010. Using her interior decorating and design skills, she visits homes for consultations to assess needs and suggest furniture from the store that matches the home style and customer taste. She is paid a commission of 20 percent of her monthly sales and takes four weeks of vacation each year. Décor is single and self-supporting. Her tax claim amounts are $11 600 federal and $11 215 provincial for basic and education amounts. She works for the store part time and supplements her sales commission with her independent business as an interior design consultant.

Other employee details:
SIN:	566 811 014	Address:	45 Rue Collage
Date of birth:	August 26, 1976		Montreal, Quebec
CSST (WCB) rate:	2.04		H2G 4R5
		Tel:	(514) 639-9202

NOTES

As an employer, Village Galleries makes contributions to the Quebec Health Services Fund equal to 2.7 percent of the total payroll amount for the provincial health care plan. This amount is entered in the Payroll Settings.

CSST (La Commission de la Santé et de la Sécurité du Travail) is the Workplace Compensation Board agency in Quebec.

Employer and employee deductions for the new Quebec Parental Insurance Plan are not required because Décor is not EI-insurable.

INVENTORY INFORMATION

VILLAGE GALLERIES

Code	Description	Unit	Min Qty	Selling Price Reg	(Pref)	Qty on Hand	Total (Cost)	Duty (Taxes)

Bedroom Furniture: Total asset value $35 200 (Linked accounts: Asset 1320; Revenue 4020; COGS 5060; Variance 5070)

Code	Description	Unit	Min Qty	Reg	(Pref)	Qty on Hand	Total (Cost)	Duty (Taxes)
BF-01	Armoire: dark oak	1-pc	0	$3 100	$3 000	2	$4 400	9.5%
BF-02	Armoire: light ash	1-pc	0	3 000	2 900	2	4 000	9.5%
BF-03	Bed: 3 piece oak	set	0	2 000	1 900	2	2 400	9.5%
BF-04	Bed: 5 piece light ash/oak	set	0	3 000	2 900	2	3 600	9.5%
BF-05	Bed: brass/silver	1-pc	0	1 800	1 700	3	3 300	8.0%
BF-06	Chest: cherry	1-pc	0	1 000	950	3	1 800	9.5%
BF-07	Dresser: cashmere, burl-maple	1-pc	0	1 600	1 500	5	4 500	9.5%
BF-08	Dresser: highboy - dark oak	1-pc	0	1 900	1 800	5	5 500	9.5%
BF-09	Wardrobe: light ash	1-pc	0	2 800	2 700	2	3 600	9.5%
BF-10	Wardrobe: pine	1-pc	0	1 750	1 650	2	2 100	9.5%

Home Accessories: Total asset value $30 900 (Linked accounts: Asset 1340; Revenue 4020; COGS 5060; Variance 5070)

Code	Description	Unit	Min Qty	Reg	(Pref)	Qty on Hand	Total (Cost)	Duty (Taxes)
HA-01	Framed Art: prints 45 x 60cm	each	0	200	180	40	4 000	0.0%
HA-02	Framed Art: prints 75 x 100cm	each	0	300	270	30	4 500	0.0%
HA-03	Lamp: floor solid brass	1-pc	0	400	360	10	2 200	7.0%
HA-04	Lamp: table solid brass	1-pc	0	600	550	10	3 500	7.0%
HA-05	Mirror: oval dark oak	1-pc	0	500	450	5	1 500	9.5%
HA-06	Mirror: square ash/mahogany	1-pc	0	550	500	5	1 900	9.5%
HA-07	Rugs: Persian Isfahan 185 x 275cm	each	0	1 250	1 150	10	6 000	n/a
HA-08	Rugs: Persian Kashan 185 x 275cm	each	0	990	950	10	4 500	n/a
HA-09	Rugs: Persian Tabriz 90 x 160cm	each	0	650	600	10	2 800	n/a

Kitchen & Dining Room Furniture: Total asset value $24 995 (Linked accounts: Asset 1360; Revenue 4020; COGS 5060; Variance 5070)

Code	Description	Unit	Min Qty	Reg	(Pref)	Qty on Hand	Total (Cost)	Duty (Taxes)
KD-01	Buffet: oak	1-pc	0	1 750	1 650	2	2 000	9.5%
KD-02	Buffet: cherry	1-pc	0	2 250	2 150	2	2 200	9.5%
KD-03	Chairs: 4 piece cherry	set	0	1 100	1 000	5	3 000	9.5%
KD-04	Chairs: 4 piece oak	set	0	975	950	5	2 375	9.5%
KD-05	China Cabinet: walnut	1-pc	0	2 100	2 000	2	2 100	9.5%
KD-06	China Cabinet: cherry	1-pc	0	850	800	2	800	9.5%
KD-07	Credenza: maple	1-pc	0	1 675	1 575	2	1 950	9.5%
KD-08	Extension Table: oak	1-pc	0	1 825	1 725	2	2 050	9.5%
KD-09	Huntboard: white pine	1-pc	0	725	650	2	850	9.5%
KD-10	Server: fruitwood	1-pc	0	980	950	2	1 000	9.5%
KD-11	Sideboard: cherry	1-pc	0	1 625	1 525	2	1 850	9.5%
KD-12	Table: brass with glass	1-pc	0	1 780	1 680	4	3 520	8.0%
KD-13	Table: ivory lacquer/pine	1-pc	0	625	550	4	1 300	9.5%

Living Room Furniture: Total asset value $41 925 (Linked accounts: Asset 1380; Revenue 4020; COGS 5060; Variance 5070)

Code	Description	Unit	Min Qty	Reg	(Pref)	Qty on Hand	Total (Cost)	Duty (Taxes)
LR-01	Bookcase: oak/walnut solid	1-pc	0	1 150	1 050	3	1 950	9.5%
LR-02	Chair: various patterns cotton	1-pc	0	525	500	10	2 750	9.5%
LR-03	Cocktail Table: cherry	1-pc	0	925	850	5	2 375	9.5%
LR-04	Console Table: oak	1-pc	0	950	900	5	2 500	9.5%
LR-05	Curio Cabinet: walnut/oak	1-pc	0	1 450	1 350	3	2 400	9.5%
LR-06	Desk: mahogany	1-pc	0	1 840	1 740	5	4 400	9.5%
LR-07	End Table: brass with glass	1-pc	0	610	550	5	1 400	8.0%
LR-08	Lamp Table: ash/oak solid	1-pc	0	825	750	5	2 625	9.5%
LR-09	Loveseat: chenille	1-pc	0	1 325	1 225	5	3 625	9.5%
LR-10	Ottoman & Slipcover: grey leather	2-pc	0	380	350	5	1 000	9.5%
LR-11	Recliner & Ottoman: brown leather	2-pc set	0	1 020	950	5	3 100	9.5%
LR-12	Sectional Sofa: charcoal linen	3-pc	0	2 300	2 200	3	4 200	9.5%
LR-17	Settee: light ash	1-pc	0	850	800	3	1 650	9.5%
LR-18	Sofa & Slipcover: celadon	2-pc	0	1 475	1 375	5	4 375	9.5%
LR-19	Swivel Chair & Slipcover: cotton	2-pc	0	640	600	5	1 950	9.5%
LR-20	Wing Chair: pastel	1-pc	0	575	525	5	1 625	9.5%

Total Inventory Value							$133 020	

Accounting Procedures

The Goods and Services Tax (GST): Remittances

Village Galleries uses the regular method for remittance of the Goods and Services Tax. GST collected from customers is recorded as a liability in *GST Charged on Sales*. GST paid to suppliers is recorded in *GST Paid on Purchases* as a decrease in the liability to Canada Revenue Agency. Montand files returns to the Receiver General for Canada by the last day of the month for the previous quarterly period, either requesting a refund or remitting the balance owing.

Quebec Sales Tax (QST)

Provincial sales tax (Quebec Sales Tax or QST) of 7.5 percent is applied to all cash and credit sales of goods and services in the province of Quebec. The Quebec Sales Tax is applied to the amount of the invoice with GST included (i.e., GST is taxable). This is often referred to as a "tax on a tax." The defaults for this application are set so that the program will automatically calculate the QST on the amount with GST included. Accounting examples for sales taxes in different provinces are provided in Chapter 2.

QST owing (*QST Charged on Sales* less *Refundable QST Paid*) must be remitted quarterly to the ministre du Revenu du Québec.

Refundable and Non-refundable QST

Most business purchases qualify for refundable QST credits to reduce the QST owing in much the same way as the GST owing is calculated. Some exceptions are the QST on insurance and on some telecommunication services. The tax codes for GST and QST are included in the ledgers for customers and suppliers, therefore, include both refundable and non-refundable codes as follows:

G - GST @ 5%
GQ - GST @ 5%, QST @ 7.5%
Q - QST @ 7.5%, included, non-refundable

Deposits on Custom Orders

When customers place a sales order for furniture, they pay an advance of 20 percent to 25 percent of the price. The deposit may be entered in the Receipts Journal or on the Sales Order form. The Accounts Receivable Ledger for the selected customer will be credited for the advance and *Chequing Bank Account* will be debited. When the work is complete, fill the sales order to make a Sales Journal entry for the full amount of the contract, including relevant taxes. When the customer settles the account, mark the invoice amount and the deposit (if you used the Receipts Journal) as paid. The balance in the Receipts Journal should then match the amount of the customer's cheque.

Freight Expenses

When a business purchases inventory items, the cost of freight that cannot be directly allocated to a specific item purchased must be charged to *Freight Expense*. This amount will be regarded as an expense and will not be part of the costs of any inventory asset account.

Printing Sales Invoices

If you want to print sales invoices through the program, complete the Sales Journal transaction as you would otherwise. Preview the transaction before posting it. You can print from the preview window or from the journal (click Print or choose the File menu and then Print). Printing will begin immediately, so be sure you have selected the correct printer and forms before you begin. To e-mail an invoice, click the E-mail tool.

Foreign Purchases and Import Duty

Goods imported from Italy are subject to GST and to import duties at various rates. These taxes are collected at the time the goods are received and are usually paid directly to the Receiver General. To simplify the transactions in Simply Accounting, we have set up the foreign supplier record so that the supplier collects GST, just like suppliers in Canada.

Import duties are handled separately in the program. Duty is calculated automatically because the rates are entered in the Inventory Ledger records. The amount is credited to the linked *Import Duty Payable* account instead of *Accounts Payable* so the duty is not added to the balance owing to the supplier. The linked asset account is debited.

On receiving the merchandise, the business writes a cheque to the Receiver General to pay the import duties on the purchase. This payment is just like any other tax remittance — enter the duty payable as a positive amount for a cash purchase from the Receiver General and choose *Import Duty Payable* as the account. The amount is the current General Ledger account balance.

INSTRUCTIONS

1. **Set up** the **budget** for Village Galleries on July 1, 2010, using Simply Accounting. Detailed keystroke instructions to assist you begin on page 549 following the source documents.

2. **Enter** the **source documents** for July 2010 in Simply Accounting using the Chart of Accounts, Trial Balance, Supplier, Customer, Payroll and Inventory information provided.

3. **Print** the following **reports** and **graphs**. Instructions for budget reports and graphs begin on page 557.

   - Balance Sheet as at July 31
   - Journal Entries for all journals from July 1 to July 31
   - Inventory Sales Detail Report for Bedroom Furniture
   - Inventory Quantity Report for all items to check re-order requirements
   - Income Statement, Budget Report with Difference in Percentage for July 1 to July 31
   - Sales vs Budget graph for accounts 4020 and 4040
   - Expenses vs Budget graph for accounts 5060, 5120 and 5300

SOURCE DOCUMENTS

SESSION DATE – JULY 7, 2010

☐ **Memo #1**   **Dated July 2/10**

From Owner: Pay import duties owing to the Receiver General on June 30. Issue cheque #125 for $240 in full payment of duty owing.

Village Galleries

509 Boul. Rouin
Montreal, Quebec
H3F 5G5

Telephone:
(514) 529-6391
Fax:
(514) 529-7622

Date: July 2/10
To be delivered: July 14/10
For: Caisse Metropolitain
(Tomas Monaire)
50 Rue Berri
Montreal, Quebec H1B 6F4

QUOTE #71

Description	Qty	Price	Total
HA-03 Lamp: floor solid brass	1	400	400.00
HA-09 Rugs: Persian Tabriz 90 x 160cm	1	650	650.00
LR-01 Bookcase: oak/walnut solid	1	1150	1150.00
LR-12 Sectional Sofa: charcoal linen	1	2300	2300.00

Sale Terms: 2/10, n/30	Delivery	N/C
GST # 236 412 540	GST 5.0%	225.00
QST # 3344992	QST 7.5%	354.38
Prices quoted will remain valid for 15 days	Total	5079.38

NOTES
Create shortcuts for the journals from other modules, or change module windows as needed.

Memo #2 **Dated July 2/10**

From Owner: Convert sales quote #71 to sales order #71. All amounts, dates and terms are unchanged.

Purchase Quote #224 **Dated July 2/10**

Policy Start date July 5/10
From Quebecor Insurance Co. (use Quick Add), $3 600 for a one-year extension of business insurance policy. Terms: first two months' premium required as deposit on acceptance of quote. Balance is payable in 10 equal monthly payments. Enter 1 (one) as the quantity ordered and debit Prepaid Insurance.

Purchase Order #224 & Cheque #126 **Dated July 2/10**

Convert purchase quote #224 from Quebecor Insurance Co., $3 600 for a one-year extension of business insurance policy to a purchase order. Issued cheque #126 for $600 as deposit to confirm the order.

Purchase Invoice #QI-7711 **Dated July 3/10**

From Quebecor Insurance Co., to fill purchase order #224, $3 600 for a one-year extension of business insurance policy. The premium balance is due in 10 equal monthly payments. Change the payment method to Pay Later.

Cash Receipt #43 **Dated July 3/10**

From Deon Estates, cheque #118 for $5 543.75 in payment of account, including $100 discount for early payment. Reference invoice #168.

Cheque Copy #127 **Dated July 4/10**

To L'Ascension Mobiliers, $4 512.42 in payment of account, including $45.58 discount for early payment. Reference invoice #LM-2114.

WARNING!
You must update the cheque number to 127 for this payment. Click Yes to confirm the new numbering.

NOTES

Edit the sales prices. Prices for foreign transactions are taken from the exchange rate rather than from the Inventory Ledger records.

☐ Vasco Cardigos
Rua Mariella 36
1207 Lisbon, Portugal
Tel: (351-21) 347 6273
Terms: COD
Currency: EUR
Revenue account: 4020
Tax code: no tax

☐ **Cash Sales Invoice #170**   **Dated July 4/10**

To Vasco Cardigos (use Full Add for the new Portuguese customer)

1	BF-02	Armoire: light ash	€2 005.00
1	HA-06	Mirror: square ash/mahogany	365.00
		Shipping	200.00
		Invoice total deposited to bank account	€2 570.00

Paid by Cheque #4322. The exchange rate is 1.510.

☐ **Credit Card Purchase Invoice #A-1141**   **Dated July 4/10**

From Antoine's Hardware Store (use Quick Add for the new supplier), $50 plus $2.50 GST and $3.94 QST for computer screen cleaning kit (office supplies). Purchase invoice total $56.44 paid in full by Amex credit card.

☐ **Credit Card Purchase Invoice #PD-211**   **Dated July 5/10**

From Papineau Delivery, $180 plus $9.00 GST and $14.18 QST for contracted delivery of furniture. Purchase invoice total $203.18. Paid in full by Amex.

☐ **Interac Sales Invoice #171**   **Dated July 6/10**

To Catherine Geneve (choose Continue)

1	LR-04	Console Table: oak		$ 950.00
1	LR-05	Curio Cabinet: walnut/oak		1 450.00
		Delivery		100.00
		Goods and Services Tax	5.0%	125.00
		Quebec Sales Tax	7.5%	196.88
		Invoice total		$2 821.88

Paid by debit card #7695 4559 0062 0103.

☐ **Cheque Copy #128**   **Dated July 7/10**

To Normandin Meubles, $6 700.26 in payment of account including $136.74 discount for early payment. Reference invoice #NM-192.

SESSION DATE – JULY 14, 2010

☐ **Memo #3**   **Dated July 8/10**

From Owner: Adjust inventory for one HA-02 Framed Art Print dropped and damaged beyond repair. Charge to Damaged Inventory account.

☐ **MasterCard Sales Invoice #172**   **Dated July 8/10**

To Pierre Boudin

1	HA-07	Rugs: Persian Isfahan 185 x 275cm		$1 250.00
1	KD-07	Credenza: maple		1 675.00
1	LR-02	Chair: various patterns cotton		525.00
		Delivery		100.00
		Goods and Services Tax	5.0%	177.50
		Quebec Sales Tax	7.5%	279.57
		Invoice total		$4 000.07

Paid by MasterCard #5450 5590 0620 1036.

☐ **Credit Card Purchase Invoice #S-34689**   **Dated July 9/10**

From Staples, $150 plus $7.50 GST and $11.81 QST for sales invoice forms and other office supplies. Purchase invoice total $169.31 paid in full by Amex.

Credit Card Purchase Invoice #QA-197   Dated July 10/10

From Quik-Ads (use Quick Add), $200 plus $10.00 GST and $15.75 QST for promotional cards and flyers to advertise home design gallery. Purchase invoice total $225.75 paid in full by Amex credit card.

Cash Purchase Invoice #EQ-979764   Dated July 13/10

From Énergie Québec, $100 plus $5.00 GST and $7.88 QST for hydro service for one month. Purchase invoice total $112.88 paid in full by cheque #129.

Cash Sales Invoice #173   Dated July 13/10

To Marie Broussard

1	LR-18 Sofa & Slipcover: celadon		$1 475.00
	Goods and Services Tax	5.0%	73.75
	Quebec Sales Tax	7.5%	116.16
	Invoice total		$1 664.91

Received cheque #339 in full payment. Customer to arrange own delivery.

Visa Sales Invoice #174   Dated July 14/10

To Allysa Morel

1	KD-10 Server: fruitwood		$ 980.00
1	KD-12 Table: brass with glass		1 780.00
1	LR-09 Loveseat: chenille		1 325.00
	Goods and Services Tax	5.0%	204.25
	Quebec Sales Tax	7.5%	321.70
	Invoice total		$4 610.95

Paid by Visa #4185 4458 6712 8405.

Village Galleries

509 Boul. Rouin
Montreal, Quebec
H3F 5G5

Telephone:
(514) 529-6391
Fax:
(514) 529-7622

Date: July 14/10

To: Caisse Metropolitain
(Tomas Monaire)
50 Rue Berri
Montreal, Quebec H1B 6F4

#175

Description	Qty	Price	Total
HA-03 Lamp: floor solid brass	1	400	400.00
HA-09 Rugs: Persian Tabriz 90 x 160cm	1	650	650.00
LR-01 Bookcase: oak/walnut solid	1	1150	1150.00
LR-12 Sectional Sofa: charcoal linen	1	2300	2300.00

Ref: quote/order #71

GM

Sale Terms: 2/10, n/30	**Delivery**	N/C
GST # 236 412 540	**GST 5.0%**	225.00
QST # 3344992	**QST 7.5%**	354.38
	Sales Total	5079.38

☐ **Sales Invoice #176**   **Dated July 14/10**

To Marie Broussard (use Quick Add), $50 plus $2.50 GST and $3.94 QST for delivery of sofa. Sales invoice total $56.44. Terms: net 10. (Credit Freight Revenue.)

☐ **Credit Card Purchase Invoice #QD-980**   **Dated July 14/10**

From Quickie Delivery Service (use Quick Add), $50 plus $2.50 GST and $3.94 QST for emergency delivery of sofa to Marie Broussard. Purchase invoice total $56.44 paid in full by Amex. (Charge to Freight Expense.)

SESSION DATE – JULY 21, 2010

☐

Village Galleries

509 Boul. Rouin
Montreal, Quebec
H3F 5G5

Telephone:
(514) 529-6391
Fax:
(514) 529-7622

Date: July 16/10
To be delivered: July 20/10
From: St. Leonard's Homebuilders
(Félice Charpentier)
31 Boul. St. Joseph
Montreal, Quebec H4N 2M1

O R D E R # 7 2

Description	Qty	Price	Total
BF-01 Armoire: dark oak	1	3000	3000.00
BF-05 Bed: brass/silver	1	1700	1700.00
HA-08 Rugs: Persian Kashan 185 x 275cm	1	950	950.00
LR-09 Loveseat: chenille	1	1225	1225.00

Telephone order 7/16/10 *GM*

Sale Terms: 2/10, n/30	**Delivery**	N/C
GST # 236 412 540	**GST 5.0%**	343.75
QST # 3344992	**QST 7.5%**	541.41
	Total	7760.16

☐ **Purchase Invoice #MPE-664**   **Dated July 17/10**

From Montreal Persia Emporium (Create new inventory)

2	HA-10	Rugs: Mashad 170 x 240cm	$1 000.00
2	HA-11	Rugs: Qum silk 80 x 150cm	1 600.00
		Goods and Services Tax	130.00
		Quebec Sales Tax	204.75
	Invoice total		$2 934.75

Terms: 2/5, n/30.

New inventory items   **Prices**

Number	Description	Unit	Min	Reg.	(Pref.)
HA-10	Rugs: Mashad 170 x 240cm	1-pc	1	$ 800	($ 750)
HA-11	Rugs: Qum silk 80 x 150cm	1-pc	1	1 500	(1 400)

Linked Accounts: Asset 1340 **Revenue** 4020 **Cost of Goods Sold** 5060 **Variance** 5070
Taxes: GST exempt No **PST exempt** No **Duty Rate** Not applicable

☐ **Credit Card Purchase Invoice #PD-274   Dated July 17/10**

From Papineau Delivery, $300 plus $15 GST and $23.63 QST for contracted delivery of furniture. Purchase invoice total $338.63 paid in full by Amex.

☐ **Cash Purchase Invoice #T-55612   Dated July 18/10**

From Telébec, $75 plus $3.75 GST and $5.91 QST for telephone service. Purchase invoice total $84.66 paid in full by cheque #130.

☐ **Memo #4   Dated July 18/10**

From Owner: Adjust purchase invoice #MPE-664. Montreal Persia Emporium sent a revised invoice for MPE-664 that included a freight charge of $50 plus $2.50 GST and $3.94 QST. New purchase invoice total $2 991.19.

☐ **MasterCard Sales Invoice #177   Dated July 20/10**

To Jacques Altain

1	LR-06 Desk: mahogany		$1 840.00
1	LR-11 Recliner & Ottoman: brown leather		1 020.00
	Delivery		100.00
	Goods and Services Tax	5.0%	148.00
	Quebec Sales Tax	7.5%	233.11
	Invoice total		$3 341.11

Paid by MasterCard #5145 0559 0062 3612.

☐

Village Galleries

509 Boul. Rouin
Montreal, Quebec
H3F 5G5

Telephone:
(514) 529-6391
Fax:
(514) 529-7622

Date: July 20/10

To: St. Leonard's Homebuilders
(Félice Charpentier)
31 Boul. St. Joseph
Montreal, Quebec H4N 2M1

#178

Description	Qty	Price	Total
BF-01 Armoire: dark oak	1	3000	3000.00
BF-05 Bed: brass/silver	1	1700	1700.00
HA-08 Rugs: Persian Kashan 185 x 275cm	1	950	950.00
LR-09 Loveseat: chenille	1	1225	1225.00

Ref: sales order #72 *GM*

Sale Terms: 2/10, n/30	**Delivery**	N/C
GST # 236 412 540	**GST 5.0%**	343.75
QST # 3344992	**QST 7.5%**	541.41
	Total	7760.16

☐ **Credit Card Bill #AM-07020   Dated July 20/10**

From American Express (Amex), $894.68 for new purchases before the billing date, July 14, plus $10.50 monthly fee. Total payment required to avoid interest charges is $905.18. Issue cheque #131 for $905.18 to pay Amex balance in full.

☐   **Cheque Copy #132**   **Dated July 21/10**

To Montreal Persia Emporium, $2 931.37 in payment of account including $59.82 discount for early payment. Reference invoice #MPE-664A.

☐   **Interac Sales Invoice #179**   **Dated July 21/10**

To Julie Marie Delpy

1	LR-20	Wing Chair: pastel		$375.00
		Goods and Services Tax	5.0%	18.75
		Quebec Sales Tax	7.5%	29.53
		Invoice total		$423.28

Paid by debit card #7855 5867 1284 0505.

Edit the selling price. The price was reduced because the chair legs were scratched. Enter "Final sale" as the Comment.

☐   **Cash Receipt #44**   **Dated July 21/10**

From Caisse Metropolitain, cheque #967 for $4 989.38 in payment of account including $90 discount for early payment. Reference invoice #175.

SESSION DATE – JULY 28, 2010

☐   **Sales Invoice #180**   **Dated July 23/10**

To Westmount Primrose Condos (preferred customer)

1	LR-12	Sectional Sofa: charcoal linen	$2 200
2	LR-19	Swivel Chairs & Slipcovers: cotton	600 each
		Goods and Services Tax	5.0%
		Quebec Sales Tax	7.5%

Terms: 2/10, n/30.

☐   **Visa Sales Invoice #181**   **Dated July 27/10**

To Juliette Servais

1	KD-02	Buffet: cherry		$2 250.00
		Delivery		100.00
		Goods and Services Tax	5.0%	117.50
		Quebec Sales Tax	7.5%	185.07
		Invoice total		$2 652.57

Paid by Visa #4150 8671 2840 5052.

☐   **MasterCard Sales Invoice #182**   **Dated July 28/10**

To Pierre Binoche

1	KD-08	Extension Table: oak		$1 825.00
		Delivery		100.00
		Goods and Services Tax	5.0%	96.25
		Quebec Sales Tax	7.5%	151.60
		Invoice total		$2 172.85

Paid by MasterCard #5555 8445 5900 6236.

☐   **Cash Receipt #45**   **Dated July 28/10**

From Marie Broussard, cheque #357 for $56.44 in payment of account. Reference invoice #176.

SESSION DATE – JULY 31, 2010

☐   **Credit Card Purchase Invoice #PD-304**   **Dated July 30/10**

From Papineau Delivery, $400 plus $20 GST and $31.50 QST for contracted delivery of furniture. Purchase invoice total $451.50 paid in full by Amex.

☐ **Bank Debit Memo #643177**   **Dated July 30/10**

From Bank of Montreal, $30 for bank service charges for one month and
$1 700 for mortgage payment, that included $1 525 interest and $175 principal.

☐ **Bank Credit Memo #46234**   **Dated July 30/10**

From Bank of Montreal, $638 interest earned on investment securities deposited
to chequing account.

☐ **Cash Receipt #46**   **Dated July 30/10**

From St. Leonard's Homebuilders, cheque #3199 for $7 622.66 in payment of
account including $137.50 discount for early payment. Reference invoice #178.

☐ **Memo #5**   **Dated July 31/10**

From Owner: Issue cheque #133 for $300 to pay the premium for one month to
Quebecor Insurance Co. Reference invoice #QI-7711. Repeat the entry five times
to prepare the remaining payments for the year as postdated cheques. Issue
cheques #134 to 138, dated August 31, September 30, October 31, November 30
and December 31.

☐ **Memo #6**   **Dated July 31/10**

From Owner: Make adjusting entries for July.
    Office Supplies used $75
    Furniture Supplies used   50

☐ **Memo #7**   **Dated July 31/10**

From Owner: Lianne Décor earned $5 200 in commissions on her share of sales
in July. Issue cheque #139 to pay Décor's commissions.

☑ **Memo #8**   **Dated July 31/10**

554   From Owner: Decrease all revenue and expense budget amounts by 10%.

☑ **Memo #9**   **Dated July 31/10**

560   From Owner: Print all sales invoices for July.

KEYSTROKES

Setting Up Budgets

It is important for a business to gauge its performance against some standards. These
standards can be provided through comparisons with other companies that are in the
same kind of business or by comparing the same company over several time periods. It
is common for a business to set goals for the future based on past performance. For
example, there may be an expectation that profits will increase by 10 percent over the
previous year or that expenses will be reduced because of the introduction of new cost-
reduction methods. If a business waits until the end of the year to assess its progress
toward its goals, it may be too late to make necessary corrections if things are not
proceeding according to plan. Budgets offer a realistic financial plan for the future that
can be used to assess performance.

Before analyzing a budget report, you must turn on the option and enter the budget
amounts for the relevant accounts.

Turning On the Budgeting Feature

Restore `SimData\village1.CAB` to `SimData\Village\village`. Do not advance the session date until you have finished the budget setup.

Click the **Settings icon** 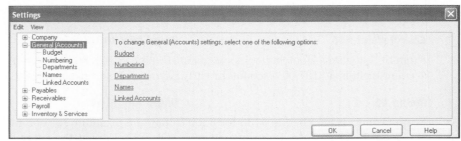. **Click General** to open the General Settings list:

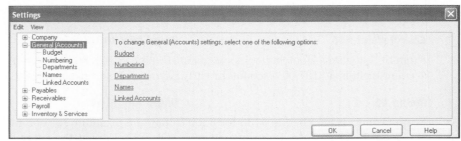

NOTES
You cannot activate the budget feature in multi-user mode, but you can add and change budget amounts.

Click **Budget** to open the budgeting options:

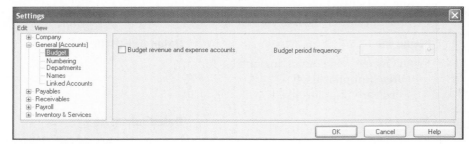

Click **Budget Revenue And Expense Accounts** to turn on the budget feature.

The first decision after choosing the budgeting feature involves a budget period. Whether a business chooses to budget amounts on a yearly, quarterly or monthly basis depends on the needs and nature of the business. Monthly budget reports will be appropriate if the business cycle of buying and selling is short but not appropriate if long-term projects are involved. The period chosen must provide meaningful feedback about performance. If the periods are too short, there may be insufficient information to judge performance; if the periods are too long, there may be no opportunity to correct problems because they will not be detected soon enough. Village Galleries will use monthly budget periods initially because the Montands want frequent progress reports.

Click the **Budget Period Frequency field** to see the period options:

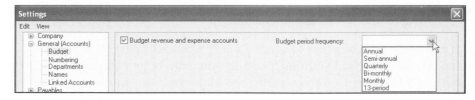

Click **Monthly**.

Click **OK** to return to the Home window and save the settings.

Setting a Budget

The next step is to enter the budget amounts for all expense and revenue accounts.

Budgets can be determined in several different ways. The most common methods are zero-based and incremental budgeting. With the zero-based method, a forecast is made for each revenue and expense account based on expectations about specific planned activities and expenditures. Each budget item must be justified. More commonly, last year's budgets and income statements are used as the starting point and a specific percentage change is applied. Thus, a company might expect to improve its performance over last year by 10 percent, either by increasing sales or by decreasing expenses. Planned special events such as annual month-long sales, new customer drives, and peak or slow periods can be built into the changes in budgeted amounts from one period to the next. Whatever method is used, it is important that the budget be realistic.

Renée Montand examined previous income statements and business practices to see where they could make improvements and to get a realistic forecast. The business has been growing by about 10 percent per year. The corresponding expenses, sales discounts, cost of goods sold and so on, also increased by about the same amount. Sales are not divided evenly throughout the 12-month period. Most customers purchase new furniture in the spring and summer, also the busiest home purchasing and moving seasons. Sales are slowest in the winter months and store sales are planned for those months.

This pattern has led Montand to expect 12 percent of the year's sales to occur each month from April to August, 10 percent in January during the store sales and 5 percent in each of the remaining months. The recent hiring of an interior consultant should also boost sales over last year's results.

Renée Montand's detailed budget forecast is presented in the following item-by-item budget chart and rationale:

MONTHLY BUDGET FORECAST FOR 2010

VILLAGE GALLERIES

Account	Jul–Aug	Sep–Dec	Jan	Feb–Mar	Apr–Jun	Total for 12 months
REVENUE						
Revenue from Sales	$50 454	$21 023	$42 042	$21 023	$50 454	$420 450
Sales Discount	−504	−210	−420	−210	−504	−4 200
Freight Revenue	1 010	420	830	420	1 010	8 400
Investment Revenue	638	638	638	638	638	7 656
Interest Revenue	22	22	22	22	22	264
TOTAL REVENUE	$51 620	$21 893	$43 112	$21 893	$51 620	$432 570
EXPENSES						
Advertising & Promotion	$ 288	$ 120	$ 240	$ 120	$ 288	$ 2 400
Exchange Rate Differences	0	0	0	0	0	0
Bank Charges	29	12	23	12	29	240
Credit Card Fees	252	105	210	105	252	2 100
Cost of Goods Sold	30 720	12 800	25 600	12 800	30 720	256 000
Variance Costs	144	60	120	60	144	1 200
Furniture Supplies Used	50	50	50	50	50	600
Damaged Inventory	307	128	257	128	307	2 560
Purchase Discounts	−307	−128	−257	−128	−307	−2 560
Freight Expense	307	128	257	128	307	2 560
Delivery Expense	1 010	420	830	420	1 010	8 400
Hydro Expense	90	90	90	90	90	1 080
Insurance Expense	300	300	300	300	300	3 600
Mortgage Interest Expense	1 270	1 270	1 270	1 270	1 270	15 240
Office Supplies Used	65	65	65	65	65	780
Telephone Expenses	80	80	80	80	80	960
Commissions	3 000	1 250	2 500	1 250	3 000	25 000
CSST Expense	61	26	49	26	61	510
QPP Expense	125	52	103	52	125	1 040
QHSF Expense	144	60	120	60	144	1 200
Subcontractor Fees	600	250	500	250	600	5 000
TOTAL EXPENSES	$38 535	$17 138	$32 407	$17 138	$38 535	$327 910
NET INCOME	$13 085	$ 4 755	$10 705	$ 4 755	$13 085	$104 660

BUDGET RATIONALE FOR 2010

VILLAGE GALLERIES

Estimates used to create budget forecasts

Revenue from Sales: increase by 10% over previous year. January, 10% of annual sales; February and March 5%;
April, May, June, July and August, 12%; September, October, November and December, 5% each

Sales Discount: expect about 1% of sales on average; most sales are not discounted

Freight Revenue: this has averaged around 2% of sales; most customers request delivery

Interest and Investment Revenue: constant monthly income; same as previous year

Cost of Goods Sold: 60% of net sales (based on markup)

Variance Costs: estimated from price variations in previous years

Damaged Inventory: 1% of Cost of Goods Sold

Purchase Discounts: average 1% of Cost of Goods Sold

Delivery: same amount as Freight Revenue

Freight Expense: average at about 1% of sales

Insurance and Mortgage Interest: same amount each month; small decrease from previous year

Furniture Supplies Used: for maintaining store inventory; constant amount each month

Commissions: estimate, will pay 20% of direct contributions to sales

EI, CPP and QPIP: these do not apply. Do not choose Budget This Account

QPP, CSST (WCB) and QHSF: straight percentage of commissions (QPP replaces CPP for Quebec)

Subcontractors' Fees: estimated additional assistance needed for peak periods

Bank Charges & Credit Card Fees: increase over last year for increased credit card usage

Exchange Rate Differences: zero — these are expected to cancel each other over time

Other Expenses: constant each month; no change over last year

---

Entering Budget Amounts in the General Ledger

NOTES
You can also click the Chart of Accounts icon and then double click the account to open the ledger record.

Click   **Company** in the Modules pane list to change windows.

Click   the **Chart of Accounts shortcuts list arrow** and **click Modify Account** to open the Search window. Accounts is selected as the record type:

Click   the **Search field**.

Type   4   to advance the cursor and **scroll down** the list to see the 4000-level Revenue accounts.

Click   **4020 Revenue from Sales** to highlight the first postable revenue account.

Click   **OK** to open the Account Ledger window as shown:

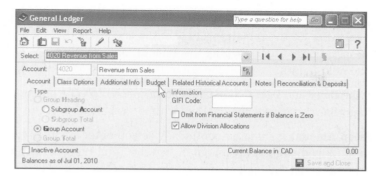

Because we turned on the Budgeting feature in the General Settings window, the Budget tab has been added. This tab will appear only for Income Statement accounts.

Click   the **Budget tab** to open the budget activation window as shown:

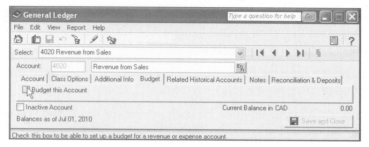

Click   **Budget This Account** to open the Budget amount fields as shown:

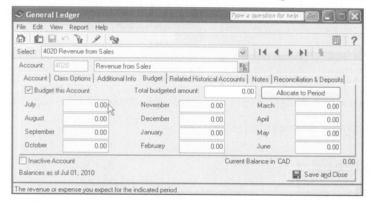

The budget periods displayed at this stage match the period frequency selected in the setup stage. Because we selected Monthly, a 12-month calendar is given, beginning with July, the first month of the fiscal year as entered in the Company Information window. If we had selected Quarterly, four input fields would be provided. You can enter the budget amounts for one period or for more, if the information is available. For Village Galleries, we will enter the amounts determined earlier for each month.

> You can change the budget frequency at any time in the General Settings Budget option window. The program will reallocate the previously budgeted amounts proportionately for the new periods after warning you that this will be done and giving you a chance to confirm that you want to proceed.

> Refer to the chart on page 551 for budget amounts.

For each revenue and expense, you can add or omit budget amounts. Including budget details for all accounts will, of course, provide the most meaningful budget reports.

Click   the **July field** to select the amount.

Type   50454   **Press**   ⌨ *tab* .

The cursor advances to the August field and highlights the entry for editing.

Enter the **amounts** for the **remaining 11 months** according to the budget forecast on page 551 by **typing** the **amount** and **pressing** ⌐tab⌐ to move to the next month.

You can use the **Copy** and **Paste** commands (Edit menu) to copy amounts from one field to another and save some data entry time.

The **Total Budgeted Amount** is updated continually as you enter amounts for each period. When you enter individual monthly amounts, use the Total Budgeted Amount to check your work. It should equal the budget amount for 12 months.

When you have entered the amounts for each month,

Click the **Next button** ▶ to advance to the next revenue account in the budget tab screen.

Enter budget information for the **remaining** revenue and expense **accounts** by following the steps outlined above. Use the amounts determined for each account in the chart on page 551.

Remember to enter **negative** budget amounts for accounts that decrease the total in a Group or Section (e.g., *Sales Discount*).

For some accounts, the budget amounts for each month are equal, and you can use a shortcut to enter the amounts. For example, for *4100 Investment Revenue*,

Click the **Total Budgeted Amount field**.

Type 7 656 **Click Allocate To Period** to divide the amount evenly among all budget periods (638 is entered for each month, 7 656/12).

After entering the budget amounts for all accounts,

Close the **account's General Ledger window**.

Display or **print** the **Budget Report** to check your amounts (see page 557).

Enter the **source documents** for July.

> **NOTES**
> Non-postable accounts, such as subtotals, headings and totals, do not have budget fields.
>   Do not enter budget amounts for CPP Expense, QPIP Expense and EI Expense. These accounts are not used by Village Galleries but they are required as essential linked accounts by the program.

> **NOTES**
> Because we accessed the ledger record from the Modify Account shortcut Search window, we bypassed the Accounts window. Closing the ledger record therefore returns you directly to the Home window.

Updating Budgets

Changing Budget Amounts

Budget amounts can be updated if needed based on feedback from earlier budget reports. They should not, of course, be changed without good reason.

If you discover that your budget forecasts are incorrect, you can update the amounts for each account individually by repeating the process described above for entering initial budget amounts. Or you can globally update all amounts by a fixed percentage. To update the amounts globally,

Choose the **Maintenance menu** in the Home window and **click Update Budget Amounts** to see the Update Budget window:

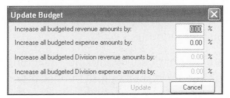

You can change the budgets for revenue and expense accounts separately. You can change division revenue and expense amounts by a different percentage.

Type the percentage change that you want to apply, and type a negative number for decreases. Click Update to apply the change. The screen that follows will ask you to confirm that you want to update the budget.

Click Yes to apply the changes and return to the Home window.

When you review the account's budget information in the account ledger, you will see that the change has been applied.

Changing Budget Frequencies

You can also change the budget frequency. This change is made in the General Ledger Settings screen. For example, to change the period from monthly to quarterly, choose the Setup menu, then click Settings. Click General (Accounts). Then choose Quarterly from the Budget Period Frequency drop-down list and click OK.

When you have a quarterly budget with different amounts for each quarter and you change the frequency to monthly, each month will have the same budget amount — the total for the four quarters divided by 12. You must edit the amounts if they are incorrect.

For example, a quarterly budget of $1 000, $3 000, $2 000 and $6 000 for the four quarters becomes $1 000 each month if the frequency is changed to monthly ($12 000/12).

Before applying the new budget settings, Simply Accounting generates the following warning each time you change a budget frequency:

The statement warns that previous budget amounts will be reallocated evenly among the new number of periods. If you change a monthly budget to quarterly, each quarter will have the same budget amount. You can accept or cancel the change.

Adding Budget Amounts to Divisions

If you are using division allocations, you can also enter budget amounts for each division. You must first turn on the budgeting feature and then choose a budget period or frequency. The following steps will illustrate this procedure.

Click the Settings icon and click Division to open the Division Settings:

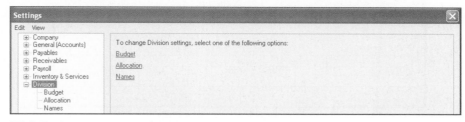

Click Budget to see the division activation screen:

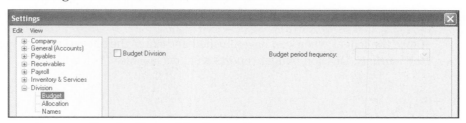

These options are like the General Ledger options.

Click Budget Division.

Choose a frequency from the Budget Period Frequency drop-down list.

Click OK to save the settings.

Click the Division icon to open the Divisions window.

Create the divisions if you have not already done so.

The Division Ledger window includes a Budget tab.

Click the Budget tab to open the budget activation window:

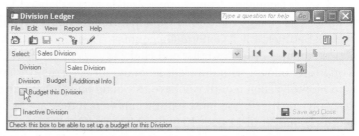

Click Budget This Division to open the budget amount fields. Quarterly periods have been selected for this illustration:

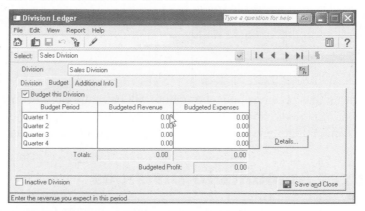

Enter the budgeted Revenue and Expense amounts for each period for this division.

Click Details to enter division budget amounts for individual accounts:

Click OK to save the details and return to the ledger record.

Open the ledger for the next division, and enter the budget amounts.

Close the ledger when you have finished and enter the allocations as usual in the journals. Division budget reports will be available.

Budget Reports

Effective use of budget reports involves more than merely observing whether budgeted targets were met or not. Sometimes more information is gained when targets are not met, because the differences can lead to important questions:

- Were the targets realistic? What items were not on target and why?
- If performance exceeds the targets, how can we repeat the success?
- If performance did not meet the targets, were there factors that we failed to anticipate?
- Should we revise future budgets based on the new information?

The problem-solving cycle is set in motion. Even an Income Statement that is on target should be reviewed carefully. There may be room for improvement if the budget was a conservative estimate. Or, you may want to include new information that will affect future performance and was unknown when the budget was drawn up.

Displaying Budget Reports

You can check the budget amounts you entered for accounts from the Budget Report. Budget reports are available from the Financials report list in the Report Centre.

Open   the **Report Centre** and **click Financials** in the Select A Report Type list.

Click   **Budget** and then **click Modify This Report**:

Select   the **accounts** you want in the report. **Choose** the **budget periods** in the Start and Finish fields and **click OK** to see the amounts.

Close   the **display** when you have finished.

Displaying Budget Income Statements

Click   the ⊞ beside **Income Statement** to expand the list.

Click   **Comparative 2 Period** and then **click Modify This Report**:

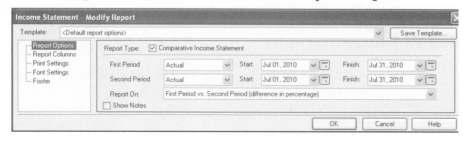

NOTES
You can also choose the Reports menu, then choose Financials and click Budget to open the report options screen.

NOTES
From the Budget Report, you can drill down to the General Ledger for the account so you can edit the budget amounts if necessary.
You can select report columns for the Budget Report, but you cannot sort or filter the report.

NOTES
You can also choose the Reports menu, then choose Financials and click Income Statement to display the Income Statement options. Click the Report Type field and click Comparative Income Statement (2 Periods).

Click   **Actual** in the Second Period field to see the budget-related option:

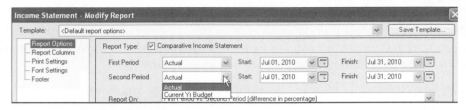

Click   **Current Yr Budget** to change the option.

Budget income statements compare budget to actual amounts.

The **Report On** options are the same as the options for regular comparative income statements, but now the Second Period refers to budget amounts. Three types of reports are available. The first, **First Period Vs. Second Period (Amounts Only)**, lists the amounts that were budgeted for the revenue and expense accounts for the period indicated and the revenues and expenses actually obtained for the same period. The second, **First Period Vs. Second Period (Difference In Percentage)**, gives these two amounts as well as the percentage that the actual amount is above or below the budgeted amount. The third option, **First Period Vs. Second Period (Difference In Amounts)** provides budget and actual as base amounts, plus the difference between them as a dollar amount.

For the dollar difference and the percentage difference reports, a positive difference means that the budget was exceeded, a negative difference indicates that the results came in under budget. Remember that for revenues, a positive difference means results were better than expected, but for expenses, a positive difference means that results were poorer than expected (expenses were higher than budgeted). Cost of goods sold will increase directly with sales, so positive differences can mean either improved sales or higher costs, or both.

Click   the **budget report** you want. **Close** the **display** when finished.

When you add budget details for divisions, you can also create **division budget reports**. Choose the Reports menu, then choose Division and click Budget. Choose the Report Type, dates and divisions and click OK.

To **print budget reports**,

Display the **report** you want to print. **Click** the **Print button** 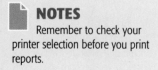 or **choose** the **File menu** in the report window and **click Print**.

Close   the **displayed report** when you have finished. **Close** the **Report Centre**.

Graphing Budget Reports

When the Budgeting option is activated and set up, two budget-related graphs are added to the Graphs menu: Sales vs Budget and Expenses vs Budget. Graphs are available only from the Home window.

Sales vs Budget Graphs

Choose   the **Graphs menu** in the Home window and **click Sales Vs Budget** to display the set of revenue accounts:

NOTES
You can choose to show the budget amounts in either the first or the second period.

NOTES
Remember to check your printer selection before you print reports.

Press   and **hold** (*ctrl*) and **click** the **accounts** you want to include in the
graph or **click Select All**.

Click   **OK** to display the graph as a bar chart:

The options for displaying, editing, printing and copying budget graphs, and so on,
are the same as those for other graphs.

The displayed graph includes all revenue accounts **before** the 10 percent budget
decrease at the end of July. The amounts for the selected revenue accounts are added
together in the single bar labelled Actual. The other bar represents the budgeted
amount for the same accounts together. Revenue was much lower than expected,
indicating a decline in performance.

Close   the **displayed graph** when you have finished.

Expenses vs Budget Graphs

Choose   the **Graphs menu** in the Home window and **click Expenses Vs Budget**
to display the set of expense accounts:

Press   and **hold** (*ctrl*) and **click** the **accounts** you want to include in the
graph or **click Select All**.

NOTES
Budget amounts are shown
for the remaining months of the
fiscal period. There are no actual
amounts after July.

Click   **OK** to display the bar chart:

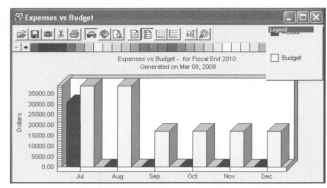

Budget amounts are shown for the remaining months of the fiscal period. There are no actual amounts after July.

    The displayed graph includes all expense accounts at the end of July, before changing the budget amounts. The amounts for the selected expense accounts are added together in the bar labelled Actual. The second bar represents the budgeted amount for the same accounts. The graph shows that expenses were also lower than expected, supporting the trend in the revenue graph for decreased sales because cost of goods sold, the largest expense, is directly proportional to sales. Net income for July was also significantly below the budget forecast.

Close   the **displayed graph** when you have finished.

Printing in Batches

In addition to printing invoices, orders, quotes and cheques at the time of a transaction, you can print them in batches at the end of a period, such as the end of a business day. This batch printing makes it easier to share printers. Any forms that can be printed individually can be printed in batches. First you need to allow batch printing for the data file.

Choose   the **Setup menu** and **click Settings**.

To set up for printing in batches, you must work in single-user mode.

Click   **Company** and then **click Forms** to open the Settings screen for Forms:

Click   the **Print In Batches check box for Invoices**, the first form listed.

Click   the **check box for the other forms** that you want to be able to print in batches.

Click   **OK** to save the changes.

    Now, the Reports menu in the Home window has a Print Batches menu option.

Choose the **Reports menu** then **choose** **Print Batches** and **click** **Sales Invoices** to see the printing options:

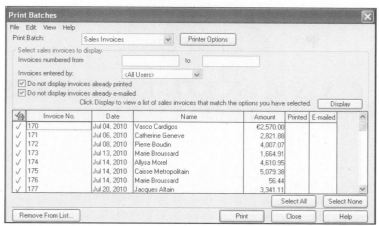

From this screen, you can choose other forms to print in batches. These are available from the **Print Batch** drop-down list. If some invoices have already been **Printed** or **E-mailed**, you can remove them from the display by clicking the appropriate check boxes. You can choose a **range of Invoice Numbers** or a specific **User** as selection criteria. After making these selections, click **Display** to show only the requested invoices. Initially all invoices are selected for printing as indicated by the ✓ in the Print column. Clicking **Select None** will remove all the ✓ and clicking **Select All** will select all listed invoices. You can also select invoices individually by clicking Select None and then clicking the invoices you want to print.

> **Choose** the **invoices** you want to print so that only those invoices have a ✓.
>
> **Click** **Print**. Printing begins immediately, so be sure that you have loaded the forms you need (or use plain paper for practice).
>
> **Click** **Close** or select another form from the Print Batch list to print other forms.

NOTES
To print the invoices, you must choose Custom Simply Form in the Reports & Forms settings on the Invoices screen. Choose Invoice in the Description field for invoices and e-mail.

NOTES
Remember that you can customize the invoices before printing them. Refer to Appendix G on the Student CD-ROM.
You cannot preview the invoices from the Print Batches window.

Printing in Batches from Journals

When you allow batch printing from the Forms Settings screen, you can print these forms in batches directly from the related journal.

All the journals that have a Print tool will have a **Print Batches tool** added to the tool bar for this purpose, that is, the Sales, Purchases, Payments and Paycheques journals.

R E V I E W

The Student CD-ROM with Data Files includes Review Questions and Supplementary Cases for this chapter.

CHAPTER FIFTEEN

OBJECTIVES

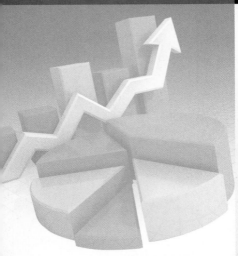

After completing this chapter, you should be able to

- **prepare** bank deposit slips
- **print** Transaction Reports for bank accounts
- **compare** bank statements with Transaction Reports
- **turn on** the account reconciliation feature
- **create** new linked accounts for reconciliation
- **set up** the account reconciliation information
- **reconcile** the bank account statement with the General Ledger
- **display** and **print** account reconciliation reports
- **clear** paid invoices and **remove** accounts

COMPANY INFORMATION

Company Profile

NOTES
Tesses Tresses
55 Salon Rd.
Charlottetown, PE C1A 6D3
Tel: (902) 729-6211
Fax: (902) 728-4821
Business No.: 136 422 374

Tesses Tresses, a hair salon in Charlottetown, Prince Edward Island, is a family business owned by Tess Dubois, her husband Ian and her daughter Felicia. All three had both professional and business management training to prepare them for running the salon. Together they provide a full range of hair care services to clients, most of whom return regularly. Unlike many salons where the price depends on the stylist and client, Tesses Tresses charges one price for each service regardless of client gender or stylist. They also sell a limited range of high-quality hair care products.

The salon building that they own includes two apartments that are rented to students. These tenants provided postdated cheques for three months at the beginning of January.

Instead of hiring a maintenance, cleaning and laundry company to take care of the premises, the Dubois family share this responsibility to reduce expenses. Cleaning is required almost continually to meet hygiene standards for health and safety.

The salon's regular suppliers provide inventory products including those used in the salon for regular client services; office supplies; cleaning supplies for the salon; linens such as towels, capes and gowns; and hair dressing equipment.

Supplier records are set up for all of these suppliers as well as for utility service companies and government agencies to which Tesses Tresses remits taxes. The salon pays GST on all purchases and PST on taxable goods and services except inventory.

Although most clients are one-time clients who pay by cash and credit card, some repeat clients have accounts and are entitled to a 2 percent discount if they pay within five days. Net payment is due in 15 days. The cash clients do not receive a discount. A record called Cash Customers is set up for the weekly summaries of cash and credit card sales. Clients pay both GST at 5 percent and PST at the rate of 10 percent on merchandise they buy from the salon and GST only on all services. The PST in Prince Edward Island is calculated on the base price of goods plus GST. The tax rates and codes are entered into client and inventory records, so the program automatically calculates taxes.

Tesses Tresses also provides hair styling services to local theatre companies, cutting and styling hair for cast members before performances, re-styling throughout the show for cast character changes and styling wigs. These evening commitments do not conflict with the usual daytime salon business hours. The theatre companies pay preferred prices at about 20 percent off regular prices in addition to the discount for early payment.

At the beginning of February, some unfilled purchase orders will provide the inventory for the additional purchases anticipated for Valentine's Day.

The accounting records for Tesses Tresses were converted to Simply Accounting at the beginning of January, and the transactions for January have been completed. The files are ready for January bank account transactions (deposits and account reconciliation) and February transactions. The current accounting records include:

- Chart of Accounts
- Trial Balance as at January 31, 2010
- Supplier Information
- Client Information
- Inventory Information
- Accounting Procedures

CHART OF ACCOUNTS

TESSES TRESSES

ASSETS
- 1030 Undeposited Cash and Cheques
- 1060 Bank: Chequing Account
- 1080 Bank: Credit Cards
- 1200 Accounts Receivable
- 1240 Prepaid Insurance
- 1260 Prepaid Subscriptions
- 1300 Towels and Capes
- 1320 Office Supplies
- 1340 Washroom & Cleaning Supplies
- 1360 Salon Supplies
- 1420 Hair Care Products ▶

- ▶1520 Computer and Cash Register
- 1540 Furniture and Fixtures
- 1560 Salon Equipment
- 1580 Salon and Building

LIABILITIES
- 2100 Bank Loan
- 2150 Credit Card Payable
- 2200 Accounts Payable
- 2640 PST Payable
- 2750 GST Charged on Sales
- 2760 GST Paid on Purchases
- 2850 Mortgage Payable ▶

▶EQUITY
- 3100 TT Capital
- 3150 TT Drawings
- 3600 Net Income

REVENUE
- 4100 Revenue from Sales
- 4120 Revenue from Services
- 4140 Rental Income
- 4160 Sales Discounts
- 4200 Sales Tax Compensation
- 4220 Interest Revenue
- 4240 Other Revenue ▶

▶EXPENSE
- 5020 Advertising and Promotion
- 5040 Bank Charges
- 5060 Credit Card Fees
- 5080 Cost of Services
- 5180 Inventory Losses
- 5200 Cost of Goods Sold
- 5220 Purchase Discounts
- 5240 Insurance Expense
- 5260 Subscriptions Expense
- 5300 Supplies Used
- 5320 Utilities
- 5340 Interest Expense

NOTES: The Chart of Accounts includes only postable accounts and Net Income.

TRIAL BALANCE

TESSES TRESSES

January 31, 2010

		Debits	Credits				Debits	Credits
1030	Undeposited Cash and Cheques	$ 13 677.19		▶	2750	GST Charged on Sales		1 079.40
1060	Bank: Chequing Account	33 463.35			2760	GST Paid on Purchases	172.90	
1080	Bank: Credit Cards	7 958.63			2850	Mortgage Payable		149 750.00
1200	Accounts Receivable	21.00			3100	TT Capital		101 749.00
1240	Prepaid Insurance	750.00			4100	Revenue from Sales		4 699.00
1260	Prepaid Subscriptions	270.00			4120	Revenue from Services		16 889.00
1300	Towels and Capes	530.00			4140	Rental Income		945.00
1320	Office Supplies	130.00			4160	Sales Discounts	52.04	
1340	Washroom & Cleaning Supplies	572.35			4200	Sales Tax Compensation		62.70
1360	Salon Supplies	259.00			5060	Credit Card Fees	298.55	
1420	Hair Care Products	1 963.50			5200	Cost of Goods Sold	1 860.50	
1520	Computer and Cash Register	4 200.00			5220	Purchase Discounts		57.08
1540	Furniture and Fixtures	7 600.00			5240	Insurance Expense	150.00	
1560	Salon Equipment	4 684.80			5260	Subscriptions Expense	30.00	
1580	Salon and Building	220 000.00			5300	Supplies Used	440.00	
2100	Bank Loan		$23 520.00		5320	Utilities	300.50	
2150	Credit Card Payable		80.85		5340	Interest Expense	1 370.00	
2200	Accounts Payable		1 428.00				$300 753.51	$300 753.51
2640	PST Payable		493.48 ▶					

SUPPLIER INFORMATION

TESSES TRESSES

Supplier Name (Contact)	Address	Phone No. Fax No.	E-mail Web Site	Terms Tax ID
Air Pro (Curly Locks)	390 Brows Lane Charlottetown, PE C1A 6M3	Tel: (902) 722-0217 Fax: (902) 723-8100	curly@airpro.com www.airpro.com	net 15 137 456 199
All U Need	Maypoint Plaza #64 Charlottetown, PE C1E 1E2	Tel: (902) 728-4314	www.alluneed.com	net 1 382 732 162
Atlantic Power Corp.	16 Lektrik Rd. Charlottetown, PE C1C 6G1	Tel: (902) 726-1615	www.apc.ca	net 1
Charlottetown City Treasurer	78 Fitzroy St. Charlottetown, PE C1A 1R5	Tel: (902) 725-9173	www.charlottetown.ca/fin	net 1
Eastern Tel (I.D. Caller)	36 Nassau St. Charlottetown, PE C1A 7V9	Tel: (902) 723-2355	www.bell.ca	net 1
Fine Brushes (Harry Bristle)	13 Ave. Costey Dorval, QC H9S 4C7	Tel: (514) 457-1826 Fax: (514) 457-1883	bristle@finebrushes.com www.finebrushes.com	net 20 188 462 457
Lookin' Good (N. Vayne)	18 Vivanle Cr. Summerside, PE C1N 6C4	Tel: (902) 829-4763 Fax: (902) 829-7392	vayne@lookingood.com www.lookingood.com	net 10 192 721 214
Pro-Line Inc. (Awl Fluff)	190 Rue Mutchmore Hull, QC J8Y 3S9	Tel: (819) 658-7227 Fax: (819) 658-7192	awl.fluff@proline.com www.proline.com	2/10, n/30 (after tax) 621 372 611
Provincial Treasurer	95 Rochford St., PO Box 2000 Charlottetown, PE C1A 7N8	Tel: (902) 368-4070 Fax: (902) 368-6164	www.gov.pe.ca/pt	net 1
Receiver General for Canada	Summerside Tax Centre Summerside, PE C1N 6L2	Tel: (902) 821-8186	www.cca-arc.gc.ca	net 1
Seaside Papers (Fyne Pulp)	40 Harbour View Dr. Charlottetown, PE C1A 7A8	Tel: (902) 720-1623 Fax: (902) 720-1639	pulp@seasidepapers.com www.seasidepapers.com	net 1 810 721 011

▶

Supplier Name (Contact)	Address	Phone No. / Fax No.	E-mail / Web Site	Terms / Tax ID
Sharp Scissors (S. Cutter)	22 Bellevue Ave. Summerside, PE C1N 2C7	Tel: (902) 923-1995 Fax: (902) 923-1726	cutter@sharp.com www.sharp.com	net 10 138 221 100
Zines Inc. (Buetee Tipps)	344 Lepage Ave. Summerside, PE C1N 3E6	Tel: (902) 553- 6291 Fax: (902) 553-7155	tipps@zines.com www.zines.com	net 10 205 602 301

OUTSTANDING SUPPLIER INVOICES

TESSES TRESSES

Supplier Name	Terms	Date	Inv/Chq No.	Amount	Discount	Total
Fine Brushes	net 20	Dec. 20/09	FB-4321	$330.00		$330.00
		Jan. 09/10	CHQ 411	330.00		330.00
	net 20	Jan. 17/10	FB-6219	504.00		504.00
			Balance owing			$504.00
Pro-Line Inc.	2/10, n/30	Dec. 28/09	PL-1002	$ 945.00		$ 945.00
		Jan. 4/10	CHQ 410	926.10	$18.90	945.00
	2/10, n/30	Jan. 4/10	PL-1012	1 908.90		1 908.90
		Jan. 14/10	CHQ 413	1 870.72	38.18	1 908.90
Sharp Scissors	net 10	Jan. 24/10	SS-432	$924.00		$924.00
			Grand Total			$1 428.00

NOTES: Cash and Credit Card Purchases are not included in the chart of supplier invoices.

CLIENT INFORMATION

TESSES TRESSES

Client Name (Contact)	Address	Phone No. / Fax No.	E-mail / Web Site	Terms / Credit Limit
Atta Schule (tenant)		Tel: (902) 724-2996	atta.schule@undergrad.upei.ca	first of month
Brioche Bridal Party (Bonnie Brioche)	75 Marital Way Charlottetown, PE C1E 4A2	Tel: (902) 723-1194 Fax: (902) 726-1921	brioche@weddingbells.com	2/5, n/15 $1 000
Cash Customers				cash/credit card
Conn Seted	14 Hi Brow St. Charlottetown, PE C1E 3X1	Tel: (902) 723-0099	conn.seted@aol.com	net 15 $1 000
Irma Vannitee	77 Makeover Cr. Charlottetown, PE C1B 1J5	Tel: (902) 726-7715	irma.van@skindeep.com	2/5, n/15 $1 000
*On Stage Theatre Company (Marvelle Stage)	100 Marquee Blvd. Charlottetown, PE C1A 2M1	Tel: (902) 727-8201 Fax: (902) 727-0663	marvelle@onstage.com www.onstage.com	2/5, n/15 $2 000
Proud Family	98 Proud St. Charlottetown, PE C1B 3C1	Tel: (902) 721-1113	theprouds@shaw.ca	net 15 $1 000
Stu Dents (tenant)		Tel: (902) 724-7103	stu.dents@undergrad.upei.ca	first of month
*Twilight Theatre (Ona Roll)	55 Footlights Dr. Charlottetown, PE C1B 6V2	Tel: (902) 728-4661 Fax: (902) 724-1556	ona.roll@twilight.com www.twilight.com	2/5, n/15 $2 000

NOTES: All client discounts are calculated on after-tax amounts.
* Indicates preferred customer.

OUTSTANDING CLIENT INVOICES

TESSES TRESSES

Client Name	Terms	Date	Inv/Chq No.	Amount	Discount	Total
Atta Schule	rent payment	Jan. 2/10	CHQ 415			$395.00
	rent payment	Feb. 1/10	CHQ 416 (postdated rent payment)			395.00
	rent payment	Mar. 1/10	CHQ 417 (postdated rent payment)			395.00
Brioche Bridal Party	2/5, n/15	Jan. 9/10	468	$119.39		$119.39
		Jan. 14/10	CHQ 206	$117.00	$2.39	119.39
Conn Seted	net 15	Jan. 24/10	477			$42.00
		Jan. 29/10	CHQ 238			42.00
Irma Vannitee	2/5, n/15	Dec. 28/09	452	$120.00		$120.00
		Jan. 2/10	CHQ 46	117.60	$2.40	120.00
	2/5, n/15	Jan. 2/10	464	89.36		89.36
		Jan. 7/10	CHQ 918	87.57	1.79	89.36
	2/5, n/15	Jan. 4/10	467	124.01		124.01
		Jan. 17/10	CHQ CC-61	124.01		124.01
	2/5, n/15	Jan. 16/10	471	66.05		66.05
		Jan. 20/10	CHQ 74	64.73	1.32	66.05
	2/5, n/15	Jan. 27/10	478	21.00		21.00
			Balance owing			$21.00
On Stage Theatre Company	2/5, n/15	Dec. 29/09	455	$250.00		$250.00
		Jan. 3/10	CHQ 382	245.00	$ 5.00	250.00
	2/5, n/15	Jan. 20/10	474	873.60		873.60
		Jan. 24/10	CHQ 429	856.13	17.47	873.60
	2/5, n/15	Jan. 28/10	479	873.60		873.60
		Jan. 31/10	CHQ 498	856.13	17.47	873.60
Stu Dents	rent payment	Jan. 2/10	CHQ 161			$550.00
	rent payment	Feb. 1/10	CHQ 162 (postdated rent payment)			550.00
	rent payment	Mar. 1/10	CHQ 163 (postdated rent payment)			550.00
Twilight Theatre	2/5, n/15	Dec. 28/09	453	$210.00		$210.00
		Jan. 2/10	CHQ 5121	205.80	$4.20	210.00
			Grand Total			$21.00

INVENTORY INFORMATION

TESSES TRESSES

Code	Description	Unit	Min Qty	Selling Price Reg	(Pref)	Qty on Hand	Total (Cost)
Hair Products: Total asset value $1 886.50 (Asset account: 1420, Revenue account: 4100, Expense account: 5200)							
BRS1	Hair Brush: natural bristle	each	2	$28	(24)	16	$ 192.00
BRS2	Hair Brush: styling	each	2	24	(21)	28	224.00
CN1	Pro-Line Conditioner: 150 ml	bottle	3	26	(22)	22	242.00
CN2	Pro-Line Hot Oil Treatment 75 ml	tube	3	29	(25)	37	351.50
FRZ1	Pro-Line Defrizzer: cream 100 ml	jar	3	14	(12)	33	198.00
GEL1	Pro-Line Spray Gel: shaper 150 ml	can	5	22	(18)	27	243.00
SHM1	Pro-Line Shampoo: 225 ml	bottle	5	21	(17)	33	297.00
SPR1	Pro-Line Hair Spray: gentle 150 ml	can	5	17	(14)	36	216.00
							$1 963.50

▶

Code	Description	Unit	Selling Price Reg	(Pref)	Tax PST	Tax GST
Salon Services (Revenue account: 4120, Expense account: 5080)						
SRV1	Colour	each	$ 45	($36)	No PST	Yes
SRV2	Conditioning Treatment	each	20	(16)	No PST	Yes
SRV3	Cut and Style	each	40	(32)	No PST	Yes
SRV4	Highlights	each	100	(80)	No PST	Yes
SRV5	Perm	each	80	(64)	No PST	Yes
SRV6	Wash and Style	each	20	(16)	No PST	Yes
SRV7	Wig Wash, Set and Style	each	30	(24)	No PST	Yes

NOTES: Brushes are purchased and sold individually. All other hair care products are purchased in cartons of 12 units and sold in individual units.

Accounting Procedures

Taxes

GST at 5 percent is charged on all goods and services sold by the salon. Tesses Tresses remits the GST owing — *GST Charged on Sales* less *GST Paid on Purchases* to the Receiver General by the last day of each month for the previous month.

PST at 10 percent for Prince Edward Island is charged on all inventory items sold by the salon. PST is calculated on the sale price plus the GST Charged (i.e., GST is taxable). Personal services, such as those provided by the salon, are exempt from PST. The inventory ledger records contain this information so that the correct taxes will be applied automatically. When PST is remitted, 3 percent of the PST collected is withheld as sales tax compensation, to an annual maximum compensation of $500.

Sales Summaries

Most salon sales are to one-time clients who do not have accounts. These sales are summarized weekly according to payment — by cash or by credit card — and entered for the client named Cash Customers. By choosing Cash Customers as the client for these sales, the default tax codes and terms should be correct.

Receipts and Bank Deposits

Cash and cheques received in payment are held for weekly deposits. Upon receipt, they are debited to the *Undeposited Cash and Cheques*.

NSF Cheques

If a cheque is deposited from an account that does not have enough money to cover it, the bank returns it to the depositor as NSF (non-sufficient funds). To record the NSF cheque, enter a negative receipt in the Receipts Journal. Select *Bank: Chequing Account* as the Deposit To account. Turn on the option to Include Fully Paid Invoices and enter a negative payment amount. Enter the bank debit number as the receipt and add NSF to the original cheque number in the Cheque field. If a discount was taken for early payment, reverse this amount as well. Then enter a Sales Journal invoice for the amount of the handling charge. Refer to page 577 and A–23 if you need more help.

Cost of Supplies

Instead of buying separate salon supplies for regular client services, Tesses Tresses uses its inventory stock of shampoos, conditioners, gels and so on. Inventory Adjustment entries are completed to make these transfers at cost from the inventory asset account to the supplies account.

 WARNING!

You need to enter a negative receipt for these NSF cheques. You cannot reverse the receipt because different accounts are involved. The original receipt was deposited to Undeposited Cash and Cheques but the NSF cheque credits the Bank: Chequing Account, after the deposit was entered.

NOTES

The store is liable for the PST on the cost of these transferred inventory items – the store sells the merchandise to itself at cost.

INSTRUCTIONS

1. **Enter** the **deposit slips** and **set up** and **complete** the **account reconciliation** for January using the Chart of Accounts, Trial Balance, Supplier, Client and Inventory information provided and using the keystrokes that start on page 581 as a guide. The journal transactions for January have been completed for you.

2. **Enter** the **source documents** for February, including the account reconciliation.

3. **Print** the **reports** indicated on the chart below after completing your entries.

REPORTS

Accounts
- ☐ Chart of Accounts
- ☐ Account List
- ☐ General Journal Entries

Financials
- ☑ Comparative Balance Sheet dates: Feb. 1 and Feb. 28 with difference in percentage
- ☑ Income Statement from Jan. 1 to Feb. 28
- ☑ Trial Balance date: Feb. 28
- ☑ All Journals Entries: Feb. 1 to Feb. 28
- ☑ General Ledger: for accounts 1060 and 1080 from Jan. 1 to Feb. 28
- ☐ Statement of Cash Flows
- ☑ Cash Flow Projection Detail Report for account 1060 for 30 days
- ☐ Gross Margin Income Statement

Tax
- ☐ Report on

Banking
- ☑ Account Reconciliation Summary Report: for 1060 and 1080 from Jan. 1 to Feb. 28
- ☐ Bank Transaction Report
- ☐ Reconciliation Transaction Report
- ☑ Deposit Slip Detail Report for account 1060 from Jan. 1 to Feb. 28

- ☑ Account Reconciliation Journal Entries: Jan. 1 to Feb. 28
- ☑ Deposit Slip Journal Entries: Jan. 1 to Feb. 28
- ☐ Cheque Log Report

Payables
- ☐ Supplier List
- ☐ Supplier Aged
- ☐ Aged Overdue Payables
- ☐ Expense Journal Entries
- ☐ Payment Journal Entries
- ☐ Supplier Expenses

Receivables
- ☐ Client List
- ☐ Client Aged
- ☐ Aged Overdue Receivables
- ☐ Revenues Journal Entries
- ☐ Receipt Journal Entries
- ☐ Client Revenues
- ☐ Revenues by Salesperson
- ☐ Client Statements

Inventory & Services
- ☐ Inventory & Services List
- ☐ Inventory Summary
- ☐ Inventory Quantity

- ☑ Inventory Statistics: all items and all details
- ☐ Inventory Sales Summary
- ☐ Inventory Transaction Summary
- ☐ Item Assembly Journal Entries
- ☐ Adjustment Journal Entries
- ☐ Inventory Price Lists

Mailing Labels
- ☐ Labels

Management Reports
- ☐ Ledger

GRAPHS
- ☐ Payables by Aging Period
- ☐ Payables by Supplier
- ☐ Receivables by Aging Period
- ☐ Receivables by Client
- ☐ Sales vs Receivables
- ☐ Receivables Due vs Payables Due
- ☐ Revenues by Account
- ☐ Expenses by Account
- ☐ Expenses and Net Profit as % of Revenue

SOURCE DOCUMENTS

SESSION DATE – JANUARY 31, 2010

☑   **Memo #7**   **Dated Jan. 31/10**

581   Use the following deposit information slips to prepare deposit slips #1 to #5. All amounts were deposited to Bank: Chequing Account.

DEPOSIT SLIP # 1   **JANUARY 7, 2010**

Date	Cheque #	Client	Amount
Jan 2	46	Irma Vannitee	$ 117.60
Jan 2	5121	Twilight Theatre	205.80
Jan 2	161	Stu Dents	550.00
Jan 2	415	Atta Schule	395.00
Jan 3	382	On Stage Theatre Company	245.00
Jan 7	918	Irma Vannitee	87.57
		Total Cheques	$1 600.97
		Cash	$2 170.04

(Consisting of   7 × $10;   35 × $20;   10 × $50;   9 × $100;   Coin $0.04)

| | | Total Deposit | $3 771.01 |

DEPOSIT SLIP # 2   **JANUARY 14, 2010**

Date	Cheque #	Client	Amount
Jan 9	61	Irma Vannitee	$121.53
Jan 14	206	Brioche Bridal Party	117.00
		Total Cheques	$238.53
		Cash	$1 733.34

(Consisting of   6 × $5;   10 × $10;   10 × $20;   8 × $50;   10 × $100;   Coin $3.34)

| | | Total Deposit | $1 971.87 |

DEPOSIT SLIP # 3   **JANUARY 21, 2010**

Date	Cheque #	Client	Amount
Jan 17	CC-61	Irma Vannitee	$124.01
Jan 20	74	Irma Vannitee	64.73
		Total Cheques	$188.74
		Cash	$1 961.30

(Consisting of   6 × $5;   7 × $10;   18 × $20;   12× $50;   9 × $100;   Coin $1.30)

| | | Total Deposit | $2 150.04 |

DEPOSIT SLIP # 4   **JANUARY 28, 2010**

Date	Cheque #	Client	Amount
Jan 24	429	On Stage Theatre Company	$856.13
		Total Cheques	$856.13
		Cash	$1 750.14

(Consisting of   20 × $5;   15 × $10;   20 × $20;   8 × $50;   7 × $100;   Coin $0.14)

| | | Total Deposit | $2 606.27 |

DEPOSIT SLIP # 5   **JANUARY 31, 2010**

Date	Cheque #	Client	Amount
Jan 29	238	Conn Seted	$ 42.00
Jan 31	498	On Stage Theatre Company	856.13
		Total Cheques	$898.13
		Cash	$2 279.87

(Consisting of   9 × $5;   12 × $10;   18 × $20;   13 × $50;   11 × $100;   Coin $4.87)

| | | Total Deposit | $3 178.00 |

   Memo #8   **Dated Jan. 31/10**

588   Set up account reconciliation for Bank: Chequing Account and Bank: Credit Cards.

✓ **Memo #9**   **Dated Jan. 31/10**

591   Use the following bank statement to reconcile Bank: Chequing Account.

SAVERS TRUST					
321 Queen St., Charlottetown, PE C1A 6D3				www.saverstrust.com	

Tesses Tresses
55 Salon Road
Charlottetown, PE C1A 6D3

ACCOUNT STATEMENT
CHEQUING

Transit / Account No
0290   003 433 38-2

Statement period
Jan 1, 2010 to Jan 31, 2010

Date	Note #	Description	Deposits	Withdrawals	Balance
		Balance Fwd			37,238.00
2 Jan	1	Deposit	1,177.00		38,415.00
7 Jan		Cheque #410		926.10	37,488.90
7 Jan	2	Deposit	3,771.01		41,259.91
9 Jan		Cheque #411		330.00	40,929.91
14 Jan	2	Deposit	1,971.87		42,901.78
14 Jan		Cheque #412		199.50	42,702.28
14 Jan		Cheque #413		1,870.72	40,831.56
14 Jan		Transfer 0290 004 123 22-8	5,000.00		45,831.56
15 Jan		NSF Cheque #61		121.53	45,710.03
15 Jan	3	Service Charge – NSF cheque		30.00	45,680.03
17 Jan		Cheque #414		1,830.00	43,850.03
20 Jan		Cheque #415		115.50	43,734.53
21 Jan	2	Deposit	2,150.04		45,884.57
27 Jan		Cheque #416		431.00	45,453.57
27 Jan	5	Scheduled payment: loan		600.00	44,853.57
27 Jan	5	Scheduled payment: mortgage		1,500.00	43,353.57
28 Jan	2	Deposit	2,606.27		45,959.84
31 Jan	3	Service Charges		23.50	45,936.34
31 Jan	4	Interest	52.25		45,988.59
31 Jan		Closing balance			45,988.59

Total Deposits	# 7	$16,728.44	
Total Withdrawals	# 12	$7,977.85	

NOTES
These numbers correspond to the Note # column of the statement.
1 Deposit recorded in December (outstanding prior transaction)
2 Deposit Slips: total amounts from deposit slips
3 Service charges
4 Interest received
5 Scheduled loan payments $2 100 (1 500 + 600)

✓ **Memo #10**   **Dated Jan. 31/10**

602   Use the bank statement on the following page to reconcile Bank: Credit Cards.
There is one outstanding prior transaction:
Sales invoice #457 dated Dec. 31, 2009 to Cash Sales for $230.

SAVERS TRUST

321 Queen St., Charlottetown, PE C1A 6D3   www.saverstrust.com

Tesses Tresses
55 Salon Road   ACCOUNT STATEMENT
Charlottetown, PE C1A 6D3   CREDIT CARD

Transit / Account No   Statement period
0290   004 123 22-8   Jan 1, 2010 to Jan 31, 2010

Date	Description	Deposits	Withdrawals	Balance
	Balance Fwd			1,970.00
2 Jan	Deposit	230.00		2,200.00
2 Jan	Deposit	2,094.39		4,294.39
9 Jan	Deposit	2,350.31		6,644.70
14 Jan	Transfer to 0290 003 433 38-2		5,000.00	1,644.70
16 Jan	Deposit	2,234.67		3,879.37
23 Jan	Deposit	2,135.77		6,015.14
30 Jan	Deposit	1,943.49		7,958.63
31 Jan	Service Charges		11.50	7,947.13
31 Jan	Interest	6.50		7,953.63
31 Jan	Closing balance			7,953.63

Total Deposits   #   7 $10,995.13
Total Withdrawals   #   2 $5,011.50

SESSION DATE — FEBRUARY 7, 2010

☐ **Cheque Copy #418**   **Dated Feb. 2/10**

To Sharp Scissors, $924.00 in payment of account. Reference invoice #SS-432.

☐ **Sales Invoice #482**   **Dated Feb. 2/10**

To Irma Vannitee

1	BRS1	Hair Brush: natural bristle	$28
1	CN2	Pro-Line Hot Oil Treatment 75 ml	29
1	SRV3	Cut and Style	40
1	SRV5	Perm	80
	GST		5%
	PST		10%

Terms: 2/5, n/15.

☐ **Purchase Invoice #PL-1988**   **Dated Feb. 4/10**

From Pro-Line Inc., to fill purchase order #52

2	CN1	Pro-Line Conditioner: 150 ml	264.00
2	CN2	Pro-Line Hot Oil Treatment 75 ml	228.00
2	GEL1	Pro-Line Spray Gel: shaper 150 ml	216.00
2	FRZ1	Pro-Line Defrizzer: cream 100 ml	144.00
2	SHM1	Pro-Line Shampoo: 225 ml	216.00
2	SPR1	Pro-Line Hair Spray: gentle 150 ml	144.00
	GST	5%	60.60
	Invoice total		$1 272.60

Terms: 2/10, n/30.

☐ **Cash Purchase Invoice #CCT-10-2**   **Dated Feb. 4/10**

From Charlottetown City Treasurer, $220 plus $11 GST for water and sewage treatment for three months. Purchase invoice total $231 paid by cheque #419 (Utilities account).

NOTES
Both PST and GST apply to the merchandise sold by the salon, while only GST applies to the salon services.

NOTES
Remember that all these inventory items are purchased in units of dozens.

☐ **Sales Invoice #483**   **Dated Feb. 4/10**

To Conn Seted

1	FRZ1	Pro-Line Defrizzer: cream 100 ml	$ 14
1	GEL1	Pro-Line Spray Gel: shaper 150 ml	22
1	SRV1	Colour	45
1	SRV3	Cut and Style	40
	GST		5%
	PST		10%

Terms: net 15.

☐ **Sales Invoice #484**   **Dated Feb. 5/10**

To Twilight Theatre to partially fill sales order #102

6	SRV3	Cut and Style	$32 each
18	SRV6	Wash and Style	16 each
	GST		5%

Terms: 2/5, n/15.

☐ **Cash Purchase Invoice CCT-299392**   **Dated Feb. 6/10**

From Charlottetown City Treasurer, $4 800 for annual property tax assessment, payable in three equal instalments of $1 600. First instalment is due on receipt of invoice. Remaining two instalments are due May 6 and August 6. Issue cheques #420, 421 and 422 dated Feb. 6, May 6 and August 6 in payment of account. Create new Group account 5380 Property Taxes. Store as quarterly recurring entry and recall for postdated series.

☐ **Credit Card Sales Invoice #485**   **Dated Feb. 6/10**

Sales Summary for credit card sales (to Cash Customers)

4	BRS1	Hair Brush: natural bristle	$ 28 each	$ 112.00
6	CN1	Pro-Line Conditioner: 150 ml	26 /bottle	156.00
3	FRZ1	Pro-Line Defrizzer: cream 100 ml	14 /jar	42.00
3	GEL1	Pro-Line Spray Gel: shaper 150 ml	22 /can	66.00
8	SHM1	Pro-Line Shampoo: 225 ml	21 /bottle	168.00
26	SRV3	Cut and Style	40 each	1 040.00
5	SRV4	Highlights	100 each	500.00
6	SRV6	Wash and Style	20 each	120.00
	GST		5%	110.20
	PST		10%	57.12
	Invoice total paid by credit cards			$2 371.32

Deposited to credit card bank account.

☐ **Credit Card Purchase Invoice #AUN-344**   **Dated Feb. 7/10**

From All U Need department store, $300 plus $15.00 GST and $31.50 PST for 100 white hand towels for use in the salon. Purchase invoice total $346.50 paid in full by credit card. Change the default account entry.

☐ **Cash Sales Invoice #486**   **Dated Feb. 7/10**

Sales Summary for cash sales (to Cash Customers)

4	BRS2	Hair Brush: styling	$24 each	$96.00
3	CN2	Pro-Line Hot Oil Treatment 75 ml	29 /tube	87.00
5	GEL1	Pro-Line Spray Gel: shaper 150 ml	22 /can	110.00
5	SPR1	Pro-Line Hair Spray: gentle 150 ml	17 /can	85.00
2	SRV1	Colour	45 each	90.00
16	SRV3	Cut and Style	40 each	640.00
	GST		5%	55.40
	PST		10%	39.70
	Invoice total paid by cash			$1 203.10

Deposited to Undeposited Cash and Cheques.

DEPOSIT SLIP # 6			FEB. 7, 2010	
Date	Cheque #	Client		Amount
Feb 1	416	Atta Schule		$395.00
Feb 1	162	Stu Dents		550.00
		Total Cheques		$945.00
Feb 7		Cash		$1 203.10
		(Consisting of 4 × $5; 10 × $10; 4 × $20; 4 × $50; 8 × $100; Coin $3.10)		
		Total Deposit		$2 148.10

SESSION DATE – FEBRUARY 14, 2010

☐ **Cash Purchase Invoice #AP-63322**   **Dated Feb. 8/10**

From Atlantic Power Corp., $220 plus $11 GST for hydro services for one month. Purchase invoice total $231 paid by cheque #423.

☐ **Sales Invoice #487**   **Dated Feb. 8/10**

To Brioche Bridal Party to partially fill sales order #101
    3 SRV3   Cut and Style $40 each
         GST   5%
Terms: 2/5, n/15.

☐ **Sales Invoice #488**   **Dated Feb. 9/10**

To Irma Vannitee
    1 SRV6   Wash and Style $20
         GST   5%
Terms: 2/5, n/15. Store as weekly recurring entry.

☐ **Credit Card Purchase Invoice #Z-6775**   **Dated Feb. 10/10**

From Zines Inc., $110 plus $5.50 GST and $11.55 PST to renew subscriptions for one year to hair and fashion magazines. Purchase invoice total $127.05 paid in full by credit card (Prepaid Subscriptions account).

☐ **Cash Receipt #144**   **Dated Feb. 10/10**

From Irma Vannitee, cheque #93 for $233.42 in payment of account including $0.42 discount for early payment. Reference sales invoices #478, 482 and 488.

☐ **Purchase Order #55**   **Dated Feb. 10/10**

Delivery date Feb. 22/10
From Air Pro, $300 for two large hair dryers and $50 for two small hair dryers plus $17.50 GST and $36.75 PST. Purchase invoice total $404.25. Terms: net 15.

☐ **Purchase Invoice #FB-27731**   **Dated Feb. 10/10**

From Fine Brushes, to fill purchase order #53
To Fine Brushes (stocking up for Valentine's gifts)
    30 BRS1   Hair Brush: natural bristle   360.00
    20 BRS2   Hair Brush: styling   160.00
      GST   5%   26.00
   Invoice total $546.00
Terms: net 20.

☐ **Cheque Copy #424**   **Dated Feb. 10/10**

To Pro-Line Inc., $1 247.15 in full payment of account including $25.45 discount for early payment. Reference invoice #PL-1988.

NOTES
Ignore the message about late payments for Vannitee because her cheque is on hand.

☐ **Sales Invoice #489**   **Dated Feb. 10/10**

To Proud Family

2	BRS1	Hair Brush: natural bristle	$ 28 each
2	BRS2	Hair Brush: styling	24 each
2	SHM1	Pro-Line Shampoo: 225 ml	21 each
4	SRV3	Cut and Style	40 each
1	SRV4	Highlights	100
1	SRV5	Perm	80
	GST		5%
	PST		10%

Terms: net 15.

☐ **Credit Card Sales Invoice #490**   **Dated Feb. 13/10**

Sales Summary for credit card sales (to Cash Customers)

8	BRS1	Hair Brush: natural bristle	$28 each	$ 224.00
6	BRS2	Hair Brush: styling	24 each	144.00
8	CN1	Pro-Line Conditioner: 150 ml	26 /bottle	208.00
8	SHM1	Pro-Line Shampoo: 225 ml	21 /bottle	168.00
30	SRV3	Cut and Style	40 each	1 200.00
7	SRV4	Highlights	100 each	700.00
3	SRV5	Perm	80 each	240.00
4	SRV6	Wash and Style	20 each	80.00
	GST		5%	148.20
	PST		10%	78.12
	Invoice total paid by credit cards			$3 190.32

Deposited to credit card bank account.

☐ **Purchase Order #56**   **Dated Feb. 13/10**

Delivery date Feb. 21/10
From Pro-Line Inc.

1	CN1	Pro-Line Conditioner: 150 ml	$ 132.00
1	GEL1	Pro-Line Spray Gel: shaper 150 ml	108.00
2	SHM1	Pro-Line Shampoo: 225 ml	216.00
1	SPR1	Pro-Line Hair Spray: gentle 150 ml	72.00
	GST	5%	26.40
	Invoice total		$554.40

Terms: 2/10, n/30.

☐ **Cash Sales Invoice #491**   **Dated Feb. 14/10**

Sales Summary for cash sales (to Cash Customers)

6	BRS2	Hair Brush: styling	$24 each	$ 144.00
8	GEL1	Pro-Line Spray Gel: shaper 150 ml	22 /can	176.00
3	FRZ1	Pro-Line Defrizzer: cream 100 ml	14 /jar	42.00
7	SPR1	Pro-Line Hair Spray: gentle 150 ml	17 /can	119.00
6	SRV1	Colour	45 each	270.00
24	SRV3	Cut and Style	40 each	960.00
1	SRV4	Highlights:	100 each	100.00
	GST		5%	90.55
	PST		10%	50.51
	Invoice total paid by cash			$1 952.06

Deposited to Undeposited Cash and Cheques.

☐ **Purchase Invoice #SS-555**   **Dated Feb. 14/10**

From Sharp Scissors, to fill purchase order #54, $600 plus $30 GST and $63 PST for professional high-grade stainless steel stylist scissors. Purchase invoice total $693. Terms: net 10.

DEPOSIT SLIP # 7			FEBRUARY 14, 2010	
Date	Cheque #	Client		Amount
Feb 10	93	Irma Vannitee		$233.42
		Total Cheques		$233.42
		Cash		$1 952.06
		(Consisting of 6 × $5; 7 × $10; 15 × $20; 13× $50; 9 × $100; Coin $2.06)		
		Total Deposit		$2 185.48

SESSION DATE – FEBRUARY 21, 2010

☐ **Sales Invoice #492** Dated Feb. 16/10

To Irma Vannitee

	1	SRV6	Wash and Style	$20
		GST		5%

Terms: 2/5, n/15. Recall stored transaction.

☐ **Memo #11** Dated Feb. 16/10

From Owners: Transfer $10 000 from credit card account to chequing account. Use the General Journal for this transfer.

☐ **Memo #12** Dated Feb. 17/10

From Owners: Pay GST owing to the Receiver General for the period ending January 31, 2010. Issue cheque #425 in payment.

☐ **Cash Purchase Invoice #ET-4588** Dated Feb. 18/10

From Eastern Tel, $110 plus $5.50 GST and $11.55 PST for telephone service. Purchase invoice total $127.05 paid in full by cheque #426.

☐ **Sales Quote #103** Dated Feb. 19/10

First performance date Mar. 1/10
To On Stage Theatre Company (for 12 theatre performances for three cast members) at preferred customer prices

3	SRV3	Cut and Style	$32 each
36	SRV6	Wash and Style	16 each
9	SRV7	Wig Wash, Set and Style	24 each
	GST		5%

Terms: 2/5, n/15.

☐ **Cash Receipt #145** Dated Feb. 19/10

From Conn Seted, cheque #269 for $130.83 in payment of account. Reference invoice #483.

☐ **Cash Receipt #146** Dated Feb. 20/10

From Twilight Theatre, cheque #5635 for $504 in payment of account. Reference invoice #484.

☐ **Credit Card Purchase Invoice #SP-399** Dated Feb. 20/10

From Seaside Papers, $200 plus $10 GST and $21 PST for office supplies for salon. Purchase invoice total $231 paid in full by credit card.

☐ **Credit Card Purchase Invoice #AUN-478** Dated Feb. 20/10

From All U Need department store, $90 plus $4.50 GST and $9.45 PST for cleaning supplies. Purchase invoice total $103.95 paid in full by credit card.

NOTES
To use the Transfer Funds Journal for the transfer, Bank must be selected as the account class for the credit card account.

NOTES
You can use the Tax Report for GST for January to obtain the GST amounts for the remittance, or you can refer to the General Ledger Report for the two GST accounts.

☐ **Purchase Invoice #AP-7111** **Dated Feb. 20/10**

From Air Pro, to fill purchase order #55, $350 plus $17.50 and $36.75 PST for two bonnet-style hair dryers and two handheld hair dryers. Purchase invoice total $404.25. Terms: net 15.

☐ **Purchase Invoice #PL-3488** **Dated Feb. 20/10**

From Pro-Line Inc., to fill purchase order #56

1	CN1	Pro-Line Conditioner: 150 ml	$ 132.00
1	GEL1	Pro-Line Spray Gel: shaper 150 ml	108.00
2	SHM1	Pro-Line Shampoo: 225 ml	216.00
1	SPR1	Pro-Line Hair Spray: gentle 150 ml	72.00
	GST	5%	26.40
	Invoice total		$554.40

Terms: 2/10, n/30.

☐ **Cash Receipt #147** **Dated Feb. 20/10**

From Brioche Bridal Party, cheque #986 for $126 in payment of account. Reference invoice #487.

☐ **Credit Card Sales Invoice #493** **Dated Feb. 20/10**

Sales Summary for credit card sales (to Cash Customers)

3	BRS1	Hair Brush: natural bristle	$28 each	$ 84.00
2	CN2	Pro-Line Hot Oil Treatment 75 ml	29 /tube	58.00
2	FRZ1	Pro-Line Defrizzer: cream 100 ml	14 /jar	28.00
4	SHM1	Pro-Line Shampoo: 225 ml	21 /bottle	84.00
6	SRV1	Colour	45 each	270.00
16	SRV3	Cut and Style	40 each	640.00
	GST		5%	58.20
	PST		10%	26.67
	Invoice total paid by credit cards			$1 248.87

Deposited to credit card bank account.

☐ **Purchase Order #57** **Dated Feb. 21/10**

Shipping date Mar. 3/10
From Lookin' Good, $400 plus $20 GST and $42 PST for 25 polyester and nylon water-resistant monogrammed capes for salon client use. Unit price is $16. Purchase invoice total $462. Terms: net 10.

☐ **Cash Sales Invoice #494** **Dated Feb. 21/10**

Sales Summary for cash sales (to Cash Customers)

5	BRS2	Hair Brush: styling	24 each	$ 120.00
4	CN1	Pro-Line Conditioner: 150 ml	26 /bottle	104.00
6	GEL1	Pro-Line Spray Gel: shaper 150 ml	22 /can	132.00
7	SPR1	Pro-Line Hair Spray: gentle 150 ml	17 /can	119.00
3	SRV1	Colour	45 each	135.00
22	SRV3	Cut and Style	40 each	880.00
10	SRV6	Wash and Style	20 each	200.00
	GST		5%	84.50
	PST		10%	49.88
	Invoice total paid by cash			$1 824.38

Deposited to Undeposited Cash and Cheques.

☐ **Cheque Copy #427** **Dated Feb. 21/10**

To Sharp Scissors, $693 in payment of account. Reference invoice #SS-555.

```
DEPOSIT SLIP #8                                  Date: Feb 21, 2010
Tesses Tresses
55 Salon Rd.
Charlottetown PE  C1A 6D3

Account No:  0290 3433382
```

Cheques						Amount	
269	Conn Seted	130.83	8	× 5	40	00
5635	Twilight Theatre	504.00	17	× 10	170	00
986	Brioche Bridal Party	126.00	28	× 20	560	00
			5	× 50	250	00
			8	× 100	800	00
				coin	4	38
			Total cash		1824	38
			Total cheque		760	83
			Subtotal		2585	21
			Cash received			
			Net Deposit		2585	21

Signature *Tess Dubois*

02/21/10   PW

SESSION DATE — FEBRUARY 28, 2010

Sales Invoice #495   Dated Feb. 23/10

To Irma Vannitee

    1   SRV6   Wash and Style $20

         GST   5%

Terms: 2/5, n/15. Recall stored transaction.

Sales Invoice #496   Dated Feb. 23/10

To Brioche Bridal Party to fill remainder of sales order #101

    5   SRV6   Wash and Style $20 each

         GST   5%

Terms: 2/5, n/15.

Credit Card Bill Payment #2-10   Dated Feb. 24/10

From credit card company, $554.40 for purchases made before Feb. 11 and $24 annual card fee. Total payment due to avoid interest penalty $578.40. Issued cheque #428 for $578.40 in full payment.

Bank Debit Memo #983321   Dated Feb. 25/10

From Savers Trust Co., cheque #986 from Brioche Bridal Party was returned because of insufficient funds. The cheque amount, $126, was withdrawn from the chequing account. Enter receipt #DM983321 to reverse the receipt from Brioche Bridal Party and restore the balance owing. Reference invoice #487. Enter NSF-986 as the client cheque number. (You cannot reverse this receipt because it was deposited to Undeposited Cash and Cheques and withdrawn from Bank: Chequing Account after the deposit slip entry. See the margin notes on this page for assistance.)

> **NOTES**
>
> Enter the NSF cheque in the Receipts Journal as a negative receipt. Choose Bank: Chequing Account in the Deposit To field. Show fully paid invoices (choose the Receipt menu and click Show Fully Paid Invoices or click the Include Fully Paid Invoices tool 🖹) so that invoice #487 appears in the journal with zero as the amount owing. Click the Amount Received field for invoice #487 and enter −126 as the amount. Delete the discount taken amount for the remaining invoice if it is entered. This entry will credit Bank: Chequing Account and debit Accounts Receivable so the original invoice is restored.

> ⚠ **WARNING!**
>
> Do not reverse the receipt to record this NSF cheque. You must change the Deposit To account.

☐ **Memo #13**   **Dated Feb. 25/10**

Prepare sales invoice #497 for $30 to charge Brioche Bridal Party for the NSF fee. Credit Other Revenue. Terms: net 15. (Do not charge tax or allow discount.)

☐ **Sales Invoice #498**   **Dated Feb. 25/10**

To Conn Seted

1	CN1	Pro-Line Conditioner: 150 ml	$ 26
2	SHM1	Pro-Line Shampoo: 225 ml	21 each
1	SRV4	Highlights	100
	GST		5%
	PST		10%

Terms: net 15.

☐ **Cash Receipt #148**   **Dated Feb. 27/10**

From Brioche Bridal Party, certified cheque #RBC7333 for $156 in payment of account. Reference invoices #487 and 497 and bank debit memo #983321.

☐ **Credit Card Sales Invoice #499**   **Dated Feb. 27/10**

Sales Summary for credit card sales (to Cash Customers)

6	BRS2	Hair Brush: styling	$24 each	$ 144.00
6	CN1	Pro-Line Conditioner: 150 ml	26 /bottle	156.00
3	FRZ1	Pro-Line Defrizzer: cream 100 ml	14 /jar	42.00
8	SPR1	Pro-Line Hair Spray: gentle 150 ml	17 /can	136.00
3	SRV1	Colour	45 each	135.00
26	SRV3	Cut and Style	40 each	1 040.00
2	SRV5	Perm	80 each	160.00
2	SRV6	Wash and Style	20 each	40.00
	GST		5%	92.65
	PST		10%	50.19
	Invoice total paid by credit cards			$1 995.84

Deposited to credit card bank account.

☐ **Sales Invoice #500**   **Dated Feb. 27/10**

To Twilight Theatre to fill the remainder of sales order #102 (for five nights of theatre performances for four cast members) at preferred customer prices

4	SRV3	Cut and Style	$32 each
16	SRV6	Wash and Style	16 each
4	SRV7	Wig Wash, Set and Style	24 each
	GST		5%

Terms: 2/5, n/15.

☐ **Cash Sales Invoice #501**   **Dated Feb. 28/10**

Sales Summary for cash sales (to Cash Customers)

3	BRS2	Hair Brush: styling	$ 24 each	$ 72.00
6	CN1	Pro-Line Conditioner: 150 ml	26 /bottle	156.00
5	GEL1	Pro-Line Spray Gel: shaper 150 ml	22 /can	110.00
6	SHM1	Pro-Line Shampoo: 225 ml	21 /bottle	126.00
1	SRV1	Colour	45 each	45.00
25	SRV3	Cut and Style	40 each	1 000.00
1	SRV5	Perm	80 each	80.00
2	SRV6	Wash and Style	20 each	40.00
	GST		5%	81.45
	PST		10%	48.72
	Invoice total paid by cash			$1 759.17

Deposited to Undeposited Cash and Cheques.

DEPOSIT SLIP #9			Date: Feb 28, 2010	
Tesses Tresses				
55 Salon Rd.				
Charlottetown PE C1A 6D3				

Account No: 0290 3433382

Cheques			Amount	
RBC-7333 Brioche Bridal Party 156.00	3	× 5	15	00
	16	× 10	160	00
	14	× 20	280	00
	12	× 50	600	00
	7	× 100	700	00
		coin	4	17
	Total cash		1759	17
	Total cheque		156	00
	Subtotal		1915	17
	Cash received			
	Net Deposit		1915	17

Signature *Tess Dubois*

02/28/10   PW

Memo #14   **Dated Feb. 28/10**

Enter the adjustments for expired prepaid expenses. $150 of the prepaid insurance and $40 of the subscriptions have expired.

Memo #15   **Dated Feb. 28/10**

Enter adjustments for supplies used:

Office Supplies	$ 60
Salon Supplies	285
Washroom & Cleaning Supplies	75

Memo #16   **Dated Feb. 28/10**

From Owners: The following items were transferred from inventory for use in the salon. Transfer all items at cost to Salon Supplies.

1	CN1	Pro-Line Conditioner: 150 ml
1	CN2	Pro-Line Hot Oil Treatment 75 ml
3	GEL1	Pro-Line Spray Gel: shaper 150 ml
5	SHM1	Pro-Line Shampoo: 225 ml
3	SPR1	Pro-Line Hair Spray: gentle 150 ml

Bank Debit Memo #10012   **Dated Feb. 28/10**

From Savers Trust Co. pre-authorized withdrawals

	Interest	Principal	Total
Mortgage	$1 240	$260	$1 500
Loan	115	485	600

Memo #18   **Dated Feb. 28/10**

Use the following bank statements to reconcile the bank and credit card accounts for February.

NOTES
Use the Inventory Adjustments Journal to transfer the inventory to the supplies account. Enter **negative** quantities and change the default Inventory Losses account to Salon Supplies for all items. Refer to Accounting Procedures, page 567.

> **NOTES**
> The backup data file **Bank\tess1** has all the journal entries completed except the bank reconciliation for February. If you prefer, you can use this file to complete the bank reconciliation for February.

> **NOTES**
> You do not need to add linked accounts or prior transactions. Enter the statement ending balance and then mark journal entries as cleared (keystrokes on page 596) to complete the reconciliation.
> Enter Feb 28 as the Statement End and Reconciliation dates.
> There are four deposit slips for group deposits.
> The loan and mortgage payments were entered together: 1 500 + 600 = 2 100
> Remember to change the status of the NSF cheque from Brioche Bridal Party for $126 (in deposit slip #8) to NSF and the status of its reversing entry to Adjustment.
> At the end of February, a cheque for $578.40 and one deposit for $1 915.17 are outstanding.

		SAVERS TRUST			

321 Queen St., Charlottetown, PE C1A 6D3   www.saverstrust.com

Tesses Tresses
55 Salon Road
Charlottetown, PE C1A 6D3

ACCOUNT STATEMENT
CHEQUING

Transit / Account No
0290   003 433 38-2

Statement period
Feb 1, 2010 to Feb 28, 2010

Date	Deposit #	Description	Deposits	Withdrawals	Balance
		Balance Fwd			45,988.59
1 Feb	5	Deposit	3,178.00		49,166.59
2 Feb		Cheque #417		2,027.30	47,139.29
5 Feb		Cheque #418		924.00	46,215.29
5 Feb		Cheque #419		231.00	45,984.29
7 Feb	6	Deposit	2,148.10		48,132.39
8 Feb		Cheque #420		1,600.00	46,532.39
10 Feb		Cheque #423		231.00	46,301.39
14 Feb	7	Deposit	2,185.48		48,486.87
16 Feb		Cheque #424		1,247.15	47,239.72
18 Feb		Transfer funds from 004 123 22-8	10,000.00		57,239.72
19 Feb		Cheque #426		127.05	57,112.67
21 Feb	8	Deposit	2,585.21		59,697.88
21 Feb		Cheque #425		906.50	58,791.38
25 Feb		NSF Cheque #986		126.00	58,665.38
25 Feb		Service Charge - NSF cheque		30.00	58,635.38
26 Feb		Cheque #427		693.00	57,942.38
28 Feb		Scheduled loan payment		600.00	57,342.38
28 Feb		Scheduled mortgage payment		1,500.00	55,842.38
28 Feb		Service Charges - chequing acct		23.50	55,818.88
28 Feb		Interest	57.75		55,876.63
28 Feb		Closing balance			55,876.63

Total Deposits   #   6 $20,149.54
Total Withdrawals   # 14 $10,266.50

		SAVERS TRUST			

321 Queen St., Charlottetown, PE C1A 6D3   www.saverstrust.com

Tesses Tresses
55 Salon Road
Charlottetown, PE C1A 6D3

ACCOUNT STATEMENT
CREDIT CARD

Transit / Account No
0290   004 123 22-8

Statement period
Feb 1, 2010 to Feb 28, 2010

Date	Description	Deposits	Withdrawals	Balance
	Balance Fwd			7,953.63
6 Feb	Deposit	2,307.29		10,260.92
13 Feb	Deposit	3,104.18		13,365.10
18 Feb	Transfer funds to 003 433 38-2		10,000.00	3,365.10
20 Feb	Deposit	1,215.15		4,580.25
28 Feb	Service charges		11.50	4,568.75
28 Feb	Interest	8.25		4,577.00
28 Feb	Closing balance			4,577.00

Total Deposits   #   4 $6,634.87
Total Withdrawals   #   2 $10,011.50

Memo #19   **Dated Feb. 28/10**

606   Back up the data files. Clear journal entries and paid transactions that are no longer needed using January 31 as the date for clearing. Do not clear data for February.

KEYSTROKES

Entering Bank Deposit Slips

Previously, we recorded receipts directly as deposits to the linked bank accounts. In this chapter, we show the procedure for recording receipts and deposits separately. The deposits for the cash and cheques received in January have not yet been recorded.

> **Restore** `SimData\tess1.CAB` to `SimData\Tess\tess`. **Accept January 31** as the session date.

> **Click**   **Banking** in the Modules pane list.

Deposits are made using the Make Deposit icon marked with the pointer:

> **Click**   the **Make Deposit icon** to open the Reconciliation & Deposits journal:

WARNING!
You cannot adjust deposit slips or account reconciliation after posting. Back up your data files before beginning the banking transactions.

NOTES
Remember that Make Other Payment is the default type of transaction from the Pay Bills icon in the Banking module window.

CLASSIC VIEW
Click the Reconciliation & Deposits icon to open the journal and choose Deposit Slip from the Transaction drop-down list.

The journal is named Reconciliation & Deposits because both types of transactions are entered here. You can choose from the Transaction drop-down list to change the type. Deposit Slip is selected in the Transaction field because we selected this icon.

The deposit transaction has two parts: the Deposit To component that we see here and the Deposit From portion. All cash and cheques were debited to *Undeposited Cash and Cheques*, a Cash class clearing account that is the default account for all receipts. Now we need to transfer these receipts to the *Bank: Chequing Account* as deposits.

First we choose the bank account receiving the deposit.

Click   the **Account list arrow** as shown:

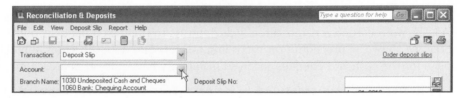

Both banking accounts are listed: *Undeposited Cash and Cheques* (the default linked Receivables Cash class account) and the Bank class *Bank: Chequing Account*. We must select *Bank: Chequing Account*, the account that is receiving the deposit.

Click   **Bank: Chequing Account**.

The deposit slip number is entered and will be updated automatically like the other forms in Simply Accounting.

Tesses Tresses makes weekly deposits to the bank account of all cash and cheques received during the week. We need to enter the date of the first deposit.

Enter   **January 7, 2010** in the Date field for the first deposit.

Next, we must select the outstanding cheques and cash that will be deposited. The Deposit Slip has cheques on the left and cash on the right. There are separate Select buttons for these two types of currency. We will add the cheques first by using the Select button in the centre of the journal, above the field for listing the cheques.

The Select button we need is shown with the arrow pointer on it:

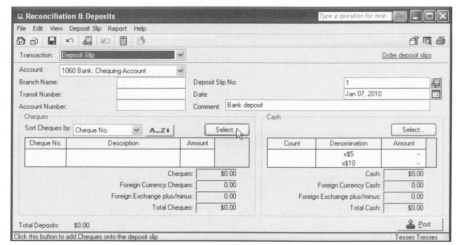

You can drag the column heading margins to change column sizes if you are unable to see all the information. Or you can maximize the journal.

Click   the **Select button** for Cheques to open the list of outstanding cheques:

NOTES

Undeposited Cash and Cheques is set up as a Cash class account so that we can use it as the default linked principal bank account for the Receivables Ledger. You could also choose Bank as the class for this account. Both Bank and Cash class accounts can be selected as the default Receivables Bank account.

NOTES

When the bank account is set up for online reconciliation, the bank transit and account number are also required in the ledger record and will be added to the Deposit Slip Journal. Online banking is illustrated in Appendix J on the Student CD-ROM.

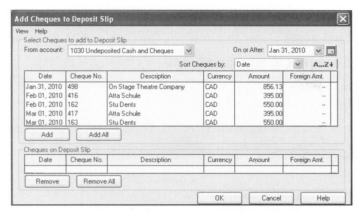

The first banking account, *Undeposited Cash and Cheques*, is selected as the default From Account and this is the one we want. Cheques are listed by date in ascending order, but you can choose a different order from the Sort Cheques By drop-down list. Cheques may also be sorted by any of the column headings for the list of cheques (cheque number, currency, amount, description, foreign amount or foreign exchange amount). You can use the A...Z button to sort in descending order.

The session date, January 31, is entered in the On Or After date field, so only the cheques for January 31 and the postdated rent cheques are listed. We need to show all cheques that are dated on or after January 1, so this is the date we should enter.

Click   the **On Or After field Calendar icon** and **click Jan 1** as the date to list all the outstanding cheques:

The next step is to select the cheques we want and add them to the deposit. Deposit slip #1 from page 569 is repeated here for reference:

DEPOSIT SLIP # 1			JANUARY 7, 2010
Date	Cheque #	Name	Amount
Jan 2	46	Irma Vannitee	$ 117.60
Jan 2	5121	Twilight Theatre	205.80
Jan 2	161	Stu Dents	550.00
Jan 2	415	Atta Schule	395.00
Jan 3	382	On Stage Theatre Company	245.00
Jan 7	918	Irma Vannitee	87.57
		Total Cheques	$1 600.97
		Cash	$2 170.04
		(Consisting of 7 × $10; 35 × $20; 10 × $50; 9 × $100; Coin $0.04)	
		Total Deposit	$3 771.01

We should select the six cheques that are dated on or before January 7, cheques from Vannitee, Twilight Theatre, Stu Dents, Atta Schule and On Stage Theatre Company.

Click to select a single cheque. To select multiple cheques, press and hold (ctrl) and click each cheque you want. To select several cheques in a row, click the first cheque you want, then press (shift) and click the last cheque you need.

NOTES
Once the list is in descending order, the order button label changes to Z...A. Clicking this button again restores the list to ascending order.

NOTES
You can also choose Jan 1 from the On Or After date field drop-down list.

>**Click**   **cheque number 46 from Irma Vannitee**, the first cheque on the list.
>
>**Click**   the **down scroll arrow** until you see cheque #918 from Vannitee.
>
>**Press**   (*shift*) and **click cheque number 918**.

All six cheques should now be selected. We should add them to the list of Cheques On Deposit Slip in the lower half of the form.

>**Click**   the **Add button** to place the selected six cheques on the deposit slip:

You can also add the cheques one at a time. Click a cheque and then click the Add button to move the cheque. Then click the next cheque and click Add. Repeat until all the cheques you want are in the Cheques On Deposit Slip list. If all cheques are deposited together, you can click Add All.

To change a selection, click a cheque in the Cheques On Deposit Slip list and click Remove. To start again, click Remove All to clear the list.

>**Click**   **OK** to return to the updated Reconciliation & Deposits Journal:

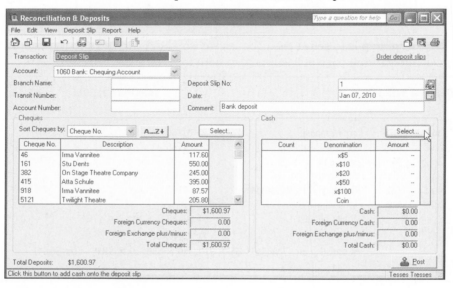

The total of the cheques should match the amount on the Deposit Slip source document. If it does not, click the Select button again to correct the cheque selection. If a cheque amount is incorrect, close the journal without saving the changes and correct the original receipt transaction.

The next step is to add the cash portion of the deposit. Tesses Tresses has one cash sale summary amount to deposit, $2 170.04.

NOTES

The cheques on the deposit slip are sorted by cheque number. You can reverse the order (A...Z button) or sort the cheques by description or amount.

Click   the **Select button** for Cash to open the deposit form for cash:

Cash receipts are not listed individually because they are usually combined in the store and held in the cash drawers or safe. When the deposits are made, some cash may be kept in the store to make change for future clients. This balance may be transferred from *Undeposited Cash and Cheques* to a *Cash on Hand* account by completing a General Journal or Transfer Funds transaction. Similarly, the denomination of notes and coins that are received from clients may not be the same as the ones that are deposited. To keep the exercise simple, we will deposit the full amount of cash received each week.

Since there isn't an account selected by default, we first need to select the account that we are depositing from.

Choose   Undeposited Cash and Cheques from the From Account drop-down list
        to modify the deposit form:

The Cash Deposit form is completed in the same way as a deposit slip at the bank. You enter the number of notes of each denomination or amount and the total amount of coins. Simply Accounting calculates and totals the amounts as soon as you enter the number of bills in the Count field. The $2 170.04 in deposited cash consists of 7 × $10; 35 × $20; 10 × $50; 9 × $100; and $0.04 in coins. There are no $5 notes.

Click   the **Count field beside** ×**$10** (on the second line).

Type   7   **Press** (tab) to enter $70 as the Amount.

Press   (tab) **again** to move to the Count field for $20 notes.

Type   35

Press   (tab) **twice** to advance to the Count field for $50 notes.

Type   10

Press   (tab) **twice** to advance to the Count field for $100 notes.

Type   9

NOTES
Instead of pressing (tab) twice, you can press (↓) to move the cursor to the next Count line on the form.

Instead of entering the count for each denomination, you can enter the amount and Simply Accounting will enter the corresponding count.

Press ⟨tab⟩ **twice** to advance to the Count field for coins.

The amount for coins is entered as a total amount in the Amount field. You cannot type in the Count field for Coin.

Press ⟨tab⟩ to advance to the Amount field for coins.

Type .04 (You must enter the decimal.)

Press ⟨tab⟩ to update the total as shown:

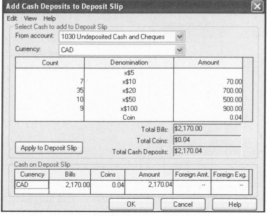

The total amounts for bills and coins remain separated, and the total for the cash deposit is calculated.

The next step is to apply the amount to the deposit slip.

Click the **Apply To Deposit Slip button** to update the form:

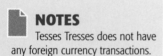

The total cash deposit amount is added to the Cash On Deposit Slip section. The currency for the amount is also included.

> To make changes, edit an amount in the Count field and press ⟨tab⟩. Click Apply To Deposit Slip to update the Cash On Deposit Slip.

We are now ready to add this deposit information to the journal form.

Click **OK** to return to the Reconciliation & Deposits journal:

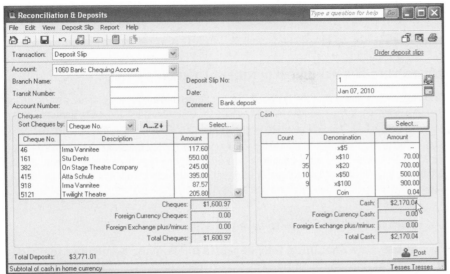

The form is complete. We can accept the default comment "Bank deposit" or change it. The comment will become part of the journal record.

Reviewing the Deposit Slip Entry

Before posting, we should review the journal entry created by the deposit.

Choose the **Report menu** and **click Display Deposit Slip Journal Entry**:

In the journal, each cheque and cash amount is listed separately. The payer for each cheque is also included. Each deposit item is shown as a debit to the *Bank: Chequing Account* and a credit to *Undeposited Cash and Cheques*. This detailed reporting makes it easier to find mistakes if any have been made.

Close the **Journal Entry Display** to return to the journal.

Check your **work** and **make corrections** if necessary.

You should also preview and print the deposit slip before posting it.

Click the **Print Preview tool** to open the deposit slip preview window.

NOTES
To preview the deposit slip, you must choose Custom Simply Form in the Reports & Forms settings on the Deposit Slips screen. Choose Deposit Slip in the Description field.

You can check and change the print settings from the Change The Default Printer Settings tool in the journal.

Click   the **Print tool** 🖨 to print the deposit slip.

Click   **OK** to close the Preview window and return to the journal.

CORRECTING THE DEPOSIT SLIP JOURNAL ENTRY

To change the cheque part of the deposit, **click** the **Select button** for the Cheque part of the journal. To change a selection, **click** a **cheque** in the Cheques On Deposit Slip list and **click Remove**. To start again, **click Remove All** to clear the list. **Click Cancel** to close the Cheques Deposits form and begin again.

If you need to make changes to the Cash part of the deposit, **click** the **Select button** on the Cash side of the Journal. **Click** the **incorrect amount** in the Count field and **type** the **correct amount**. **Press** ⬚tab⬚ to update the total. **Click Apply To Deposit Slip** to update the deposit amount that will be recorded. **Click Cancel** to close the Cash Deposits form and begin again.

Click   Post ⬚ **Post** ⬚ to save the transaction.

Enter   the **remaining four deposits** for January. Remember to change the date for each deposit.

Only the four postdated rent cheques remain for future deposits.

Close   the **Reconciliation & Deposits Journal**.

You should return to the Banking module window. We are now ready to set up the bank accounts for reconciliation.

Account Reconciliation

For any bank account, the timing of monthly statements is usually not perfectly matched with the accounting entries of the corresponding transactions. Usually some of the cheques written do not appear on the statement, and interest earned on the account or bank charges are not yet recorded because they may be unknown until receipt of the statement. Thus the balance of the bank statement usually does not match the General Ledger balance for the bank account. The process of identifying the differences to achieve a match is the process of account reconciliation.

You can apply account reconciliation to any Balance Sheet account for which you have regular statements, including credit card payable accounts. For each account you want to reconcile, you must complete the setup procedure.

The keystrokes that follow will set up account reconciliation for *Bank: Chequing Account* for Tesses Tresses.

Turning On the Account Reconciliation Feature

Before completing the reconciliation procedure, the General Ledger accounts that will be reconciled must be identified and modified. For the next stage, you will also need a report of all bank account transactions to compare with the bank statement. We will continue to work from the Banking module window to modify the account.

Click   **1060 Bank: Chequing Account** in the Banking module Home window Accounts list:

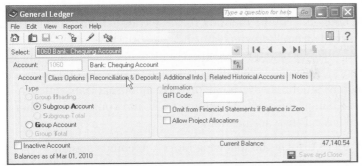

All Balance Sheet accounts have a Reconciliation & Deposits tab. You can reconcile any account for which you have regular statements. Usually these are the bank accounts or credit card accounts.

Click   the **Reconciliation & Deposits tab**:

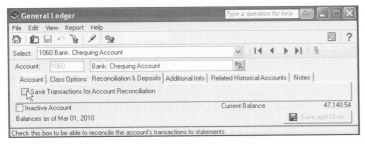

Click   **Save Transactions For Account Reconciliation** to display the Set Up button shown in the following screen:

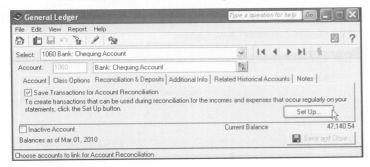

Naming and Linking Reconciliation Accounts

Most bank statements include monthly bank charges, loan or mortgage payments and interest on deposits. That is, there are usually some regular sources of income and expense. Normally the only source document for these bank account transactions is the bank statement. To use Simply Accounting's account reconciliation feature, you must first create the accounts that link to these regular bank account transactions. When you examine the January Bank Statement for Tesses Tresses on page 570, you can see that there is an interest deposit and a withdrawal for service charges. The salon already has accounts for both of these items. In addition, you will need an account to enter adjustments related to the reconciliation. The exact role of these accounts will become clearer as we proceed with the account reconciliation setup.

> You can save your work and exit at any time. Any changes you have made will be saved and you can continue from where you left off when you are ready.

The next step is to name bank statement–related transactions and identify the appropriate General Ledger accounts that link to these transactions. Tesses Tresses has income (interest received) from bank deposits and expenses associated with the bank account, such as bank charges or interest paid on bank loans. A third account will be needed for adjustments — small discrepancies between the accounting entries and the bank statements, such as amounts entered incorrectly in journal transactions.

You can edit these names and accounts at any time, and you can add other sources of income or expense later if they are needed.

Click **Set Up** to display the following Linked Accounts screen:

On this Account Reconciliation Linked Accounts form, you can identify up to three regular sources of income, three types of expenses and one adjustment account for each account you want to reconcile.

The name fields on this form cannot be left blank. You can leave the default names or enter "n/a" for not applicable if they are not needed.

The first Income Name field is highlighted, ready for editing. The only source of income for this account that is not accounted for elsewhere is interest income. This name is already entered so we can accept it.

Click the **list arrow for the Income 1 Account field** to list the revenue accounts that are available.

Click **4220 Interest Revenue**. **Press** (tab) to advance to the second Income field.

This field and the third Income field are not needed, so we will indicate that they are not applicable.

Type n/a

Press (tab) **twice** to skip the Account field and advance to the third Income field. Indicate that it too is not applicable.

Leave the default name for adjustments unchanged.

Click the **Adjustment Account field list arrow**.

Either an expense or a revenue account can be used for adjustments. Tesses Tresses will create an expense account for this purpose.

Type 5050 **Press** (tab). **Click Add** to start the Add An Account wizard.

Type Reconciliation Adjustments

Accept the **remaining defaults** and **click Finish** to add the account to the Linked Accounts form. **Press** (tab) to advance the cursor.

The first Expense 1 Name field is highlighted. The salon has one automatic bank account–related expense, bank charges. NSF fee, the second expense, is also used but we do not expect this to be a regular expense. These names are already entered as the default, so we can accept them. Tesses Tresses uses the same account for both expenses.

Click the **Account field list arrow for Expense 1** to display the list of expense accounts.

Select **5040 Bank Charges** for this expense account.

Click the **Account field list arrow for Expense 2**.

Select **5040 Bank Charges** for this expense account.

Press `tab` to advance to the third Expense field.

Type n/a to indicate that it is not needed.

Check your **work** carefully. When you are certain that all the names and accounts are correct,

Click **OK** to save the new information. The Set Up button remains available because you can add and change linked accounts.

While the General Ledger is still open, we will set up the linked accounts for *Bank: Credit Cards*.

Click the **Next Account button** ▶ to open the ledger we need.

Click the **Reconciliation & Deposits tab** if necessary.

Click **Save Transactions For Account Reconciliation**.

Click **Set Up**.

Choose **4220** as the linked account for Interest Income.

Choose **5050** as the linked account for Adjustment. **Press** `tab` to advance to the Expense 1 Name field.

Type Card Fees **Press** `tab`.

Choose **5060** as the linked account for Card Fees.

Click **OK** to save the reconciliation accounts.

Close the **Ledger window** to return to the Banking module window.

Reconciling the Bank Statement

Comparing the Bank Statement and Transaction Report

We are now ready to compare the Bank Transaction Report with the bank statement. The Bank Account Transaction Report will show all transactions for the account, similar to the General Ledger Report.

Choose the **Reports menu**, then **choose Banking** and **click Bank Account Transactions Report**.

NOTES
You can enter n/a or leave the default names unchanged for the unused incomes and expenses.

Simply SIMPLY VERSION
The Bank Account Transactions Report is not available in the Simply version.

Use the General Ledger Report for account 1060 for this step. (Choose the Reports Menu, Financials and General Ledger.) You will see the deposit slip total amounts instead of details in the General Ledger Report.

NOTES

You can also compare the General Ledger Report with the bank statement, but you will not have the option to show individual deposit items on the deposit slips.

You can change the account class for Bank: Credit Cards to Bank. As a result of this change, you can use it in the Transfer Funds Journal and you can print the Bank Account Transaction Report for it.

The Modify Report window opens:

Only Bank and Cash class accounts are listed because the report is available only for bank accounts. The credit card bank account is not shown because it is classified as a Credit Card Receivable account. In order to reconcile the credit card account, you can display or print the General Ledger Report for the period covering the bank statement.

For bank account reports, you can include corrections and deposit slip details or omit them. By default both items are omitted from the report. Since it is easier to work from a report that most closely matches the bank statement, you should omit corrections for this step. The deposit slip details do not appear on the bank statement, but they can be viewed or omitted in the Transactions Report. Because they can help us locate errors, we will include them at this stage.

You can report by date or transaction number and include transaction or line comments.

Click   **1060 Bank: Chequing Account** to select the account.

The default report dates are correct. In an ongoing business, include the date of the oldest outstanding item from your previous bank statement up to the date of the most recent statement.

Click   **Deposit Slip Details** to add the ✓.

Click   **OK** to view the report:

SIMPLY VERSION

Remember that the General Ledger Report will show the deposit slip total amounts instead of details.

Bank Account Transactions Report

File   Options   Help

Print   Print Preview   Change Print Settings   Export   Open in Excel®   Modify ▾   Refresh   ?

Tesses Tresses
Bank Account Transactions Report 01/01/10 to 01/31/10
Sorted by: Transaction Number

Date	Comment	Source #	JE#	Debits	Credits	Balance
1060	**Bank: Chequing Account**					38,415.00 Dr
01/04/10	Pro-Line Inc.	410	J14	-	926.10	37,488.90 Dr
01/09/10	Fine Brushes	411	J17	-	330.00	37,158.90 Dr
01/10/10	Atlantic Power Corp.: AP-57321, hyd...	412	J22	-	199.50	36,959.40 Dr
01/14/10	Pro-Line Inc.	413	J24	-	1,870.72	35,088.68 Dr
01/14/10	Transfer funds	Memo 1	J25	5,000.00	-	40,088.68 Dr
01/14/10	Receiver General for Canada: Memo...	414	J26	-	1,830.00	38,258.68 Dr
01/15/10	Irma Vannitee	DM-61899	J27	-	121.53	38,137.15 Dr
01/18/10	Eastern Tel: ET-4003, telephone ser...	415	J34	-	115.50	38,021.65 Dr
01/24/10	Credit Card	416	J42	-	431.00	37,590.65 Dr
01/27/10	Savers Trust - preauthorized withdra...	DM-792218	J44	-	2,100.00	35,490.65 Dr
01/31/10	Provincial Treasurer: Memo 6, PST r...	417	J53	-	2,027.30	33,463.35 Dr
01/07/10	Bank deposit	1	J54	117.60	-	33,580.95 Dr
01/07/10	Bank deposit	1	J54	205.80	-	33,786.75 Dr
01/07/10	Bank deposit	1	J54	395.00	-	34,181.75 Dr
01/07/10	Bank deposit	1	J54	550.00	-	34,731.75 Dr
01/07/10	Bank deposit	1	J54	245.00	-	34,976.75 Dr
01/07/10	Bank deposit	1	J54	87.57	-	35,064.32 Dr
01/07/10	Bank deposit	1	J54	2,170.04	-	37,234.36 Dr
01/14/10	Bank deposit	2	J55	121.53	-	37,355.89 Dr
01/14/10	Bank deposit	2	J55	117.00	-	37,472.89 Dr
01/14/10	Bank deposit	2	J55	1,733.34	-	39,206.23 Dr
01/21/10	Bank deposit	3	J56	124.01	-	39,330.24 Dr
01/21/10	Bank deposit	3	J56	64.73	-	39,394.97 Dr
01/21/10	Bank deposit	3	J56	1,961.30	-	41,356.27 Dr
01/28/10	Bank deposit	4	J57	856.13	-	42,212.40 Dr
01/28/10	Bank deposit	4	J57	1,750.14	-	43,962.54 Dr
01/31/10	Bank deposit	5	J58	42.00	-	44,004.54 Dr
01/31/10	Bank deposit	5	J58	856.13	-	44,860.67 Dr
01/31/10	Bank deposit	5	J58	2,279.87	-	47,140.54 Dr
				18,677.19	9,951.65	

The transactions part of the January bank statement is repeated here for comparison with the Transaction Report above:

	Note #	Balance Fwd			37,238.00
2 Jan	1	Deposit	1,177.00		38,415.00
7 Jan		Cheque #410		926.10	37,488.90
7 Jan	2	Deposit	3,771.01		41,259.91
9 Jan		Cheque #411		330.00	40,929.91
14 Jan	2	Deposit	1,971.87		42,901.78
14 Jan		Cheque #412		199.50	42,702.28
14 Jan		Cheque #413		1,870.72	40,831.56
14 Jan		Transfer 0290 004 123 22-8	5,000.00		45,831.56
15 Jan		NSF Cheque #61		121.53	45,710.03
15 Jan	3	Service Charge – NSF cheque		30.00	45,680.03
17 Jan		Cheque #414		1,830.00	43,850.03
20 Jan		Cheque #415		115.50	43,734.53
21 Jan	2	Deposit	2,150.04		45,884.57
27 Jan		Cheque #416		431.00	45,453.57
27 Jan	5	Scheduled payment: loan		600.00	44,853.57
27 Jan	5	Scheduled payment: mortgage		1,500.00	43,353.57
28 Jan	2	Deposit	2,606.27		45,959.84
31 Jan	3	Service Charges		23.50	45,936.34
31 Jan	4	Interest	52.25		45,988.59

NOTES
You may want to print the Transaction Report with and without deposit slip details to compare with the the bank statement that has only the total deposit amounts.

When you compare the statement with the Transaction Report, you will notice the following differences. (The numbers below correspond to the numbers in the margin notes and the bank statement Note # column.)

1 One deposit on January 2 appears on the bank statement and not in the Bank Transaction Report because the deposit was entered late in December.
2 Four deposits on the bank statement were multiple deposits entered on deposit slips and do not match any single entry in the Transactions Report.
3 Monthly bank charges of $23.50 and NSF charges of $30.00 have not been recorded in the Transactions Report.
4 Interest of $52.25 received on the deposit account does not appear in the Transactions Report.
5 A single General Journal entry combined the loan and mortgage payments.

In addition,

- Deposit slip #5 for $3 178.00 and cheque #417 for $2 027.30 in the Report are not listed on the bank statement, and the order of transactions is different.

All these items must be accounted for in order to have the bank statement match the bank balance in the account's General Ledger or on the Balance Sheet.

NOTES
These numbers correspond to the Note # column of the statement.
1 Deposit recorded in December
2 Deposit Slips: total amounts from deposit slips
3 Service charges
4 Interest received
5 Scheduled loan payments $2 100 (1 500 + 600)

Reconciling the Account

After entering the linked accounts, you can begin the reconciliation. The account reconciliation procedure consists of the following steps to update the General Ledger.

1. Record the opening and ending balances from the bank statement for the account.
2. Add outstanding transactions from prior periods that were not resolved in the previous bank statement.
3. Identify all the deposits and withdrawals that have been processed by the bank.
4. Complete journal entries for any transactions for which the bank statement is the source document.

The result should be a match between the bank balances in the two statements. All these steps are completed in the Account Reconciliation Journal.

The Banking module window should still be open.

Click the **Reconcile Accounts icon** shown with the hand pointer:

The Reconciliation Journal opens:

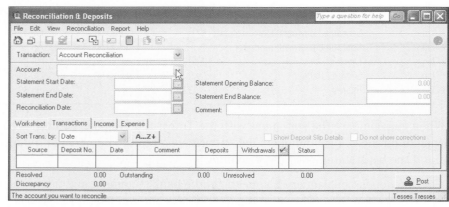

Click the **Account field list arrow** to display the available accounts for reconciliation. The list displays the bank and credit card accounts that we set up for account reconciliation.

Select **1060 Bank: Chequing Account** to display the reconciliation information for this bank account:

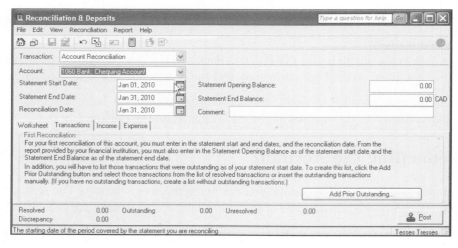

The account is entered in the Account field. The first transaction date is entered as the Statement Start Date and the session date is entered automatically in the Statement End Date field and the Reconciliation Date field. These dates will advance by one month when you have finished reconciling the bank account for the current month. The dates are correct, so do not change them.

We need to add the opening and closing bank statement balances.

Click the **Statement Opening Balance field**.

Type 37238 **Press** (tab) to advance to the Statement End Balance field.

Type   45988.59 **Press** to advance to the Comment field.

Type   January Bank Reconciliation

For the first reconciliation, we need to add the outstanding transaction from the previous period. A deposit of $1 177 appears on the bank statement but not in the ledger report. The deposit was made at the end of December, too late to be included in the December bank statement, so we need to add it now. Adding prior transactions in the Account Reconciliation Journal does not create a journal entry and does not affect the ledger balance. The step is necessary only to create a match between the bank statement and the current ledger.

Click   **Add Prior Outstanding** to see the confirmation message:

You must save the changes to the journal to continue. If you have not yet entered the account balances and dates, you will not see this message.

Click   **Yes** to continue and open the Add Outstanding Transactions window:

If there are no prior transactions that you need to insert, click OK at this stage to return to the journal.

If you have transactions in Simply Accounting that precede the bank statement starting date, they will appear in the upper portion of the screen, in the Resolved Transactions section. If they have been resolved, you can leave them there. If, however, some of them were outstanding, not included in the previous bank statement, you can add them to the lower Outstanding Transactions section by selecting them and choosing Add.

If we had entered February 1 as the statement starting date, all the January transactions would appear in the Resolved Transactions section. We would then include them all as outstanding transactions by clicking Add All.

We need to add a transaction as outstanding. It preceded the first entry in Simply Accounting on January 1 so it will not be in the transactions list automatically. We can add these types of items directly to the Outstanding Transactions section.

Click   **Insert Outstanding** to place the cursor in the Source field for Outstanding Transactions.

Type   5117 to enter the client's cheque number as the Source.

Press   <tab> to move to the Comment field. We will enter the client's name.

Type   Twilight Theatre **Press** <tab> to move to the Date field.

December 31, 2009, is entered as the default date, the last date from the previous statement period. This date is correct, so you do not need to change it. You can enter a different date if necessary.

WARNING!
The first time you complete a reconciliation for any account, you must complete this step (click Add Prior Outstanding) even if there are no outstanding prior transactions. If there are no prior transactions to add, click OK from the Add Outstanding Transactions screen.

WARNING!
You cannot access the Outstanding Transactions input fields until you choose Insert Outstanding.

Press (tab) to move to the Deposits column.

Type 1177 **Press** (tab).

If there are other outstanding prior transactions, enter them in the same way.

If there are no prior transactions, click OK to return to the journal.

Click **OK** to return to the journal window.

Marking Journal Entries as Cleared

You are now ready to begin processing individual journal entries to indicate whether they have been cleared in this bank statement. That is, you must indicate whether the bank has processed the items and the amounts have been withdrawn from or deposited to the account.

The updated journal window now looks like the following:

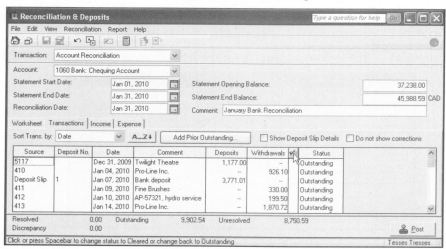

The Transactions tab is selected and all January bank account transactions are now listed, including the one we just added. The bottom section of the screen contains a summary of the transactions. Our goal is to reduce the unresolved amount to zero with no discrepancy. At this stage, a discrepancy may indicate an incorrect account balance.

The Statement End Balance should be correct because we entered it in the previous step. You can add or change it at this stage if necessary.

Showing Corrections

You can hide or show correcting journal entries in the list of transactions by clicking **Do Not Show Corrections**. Removing incorrect and reversing entries can make the reconciliation easier by increasing the match with the statement. When you hide the corrections and then clear transactions, Simply Accounting automatically applies the Reversed and Adjustment status to the original incorrect entry (Reversed status) and the reversing entry created by Simply Accounting (Adjustment status).

Group Deposits

Sometimes several cheques are deposited as a group, as they were on the weekly deposit slips. Each of these group deposits can now be cleared as a group. If you have not used the deposit slip journal to record deposits, you can define a group deposit by entering the deposit slip number for each item in the Deposit No. field beside the Source. When you clear one item in the group, the others will be cleared at the same time.

You may want to drag the lower frame of the journal window or maximize the journal window to include more transactions on your screen at the same time.

You are now ready to mark the transactions that have been cleared, that is, the ones that appear on the bank statement.

Click   the Clear column 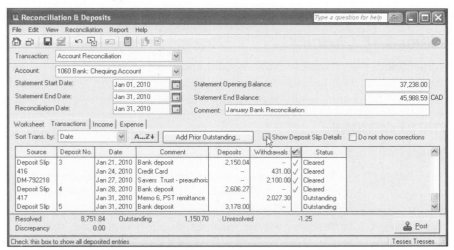 for Cheque #5117 (click in the column), the first transaction on the list.

A checkmark appears in the Clear column ☑, the Status has changed from Outstanding to Cleared and the Resolved Amount has increased to $1 177. As you clear each item, the Resolved and Unresolved amounts are updated.

Clear   the **remaining journal entries** that appear on the bank statement and scroll as necessary to display additional items.

Do not clear deposit slip #5 for $3 178.00 or the final cheque for $2 027.30.

If you mark an item as Cleared by mistake, click the ☑ column again to return the status to Outstanding.

Your transactions list appears as follows:

![Reconciliation & Deposits screen showing Account Reconciliation transaction for 1060 Bank: Chequing Account. Statement Start Date Jan 01, 2010, Statement End Date Jan 31, 2010, Reconciliation Date Jan 31, 2010. Statement Opening Balance 37,238.00, Statement End Balance 45,988.59 CAD. Comment: January Bank Reconciliation.]

Source	Deposit No.	Date	Comment	Deposits	Withdrawals	☑	Status
Deposit Slip	3	Jan 21, 2010	Bank deposit	2,150.04	--	✓	Cleared
416		Jan 24, 2010	Credit Card		431.00	✓	Cleared
DM-792218		Jan 27, 2010	Savers Trust - preauthori:	--	2,100.00	✓	Cleared
Deposit Slip	4	Jan 28, 2010	Bank deposit	2,606.27	--	✓	Cleared
417		Jan 31, 2010	Memo 6, PST remittance	--	2,027.30		Outstanding
Deposit Slip	5	Jan 31, 2010	Bank deposit	3,178.00			Outstanding

| Resolved | 8,751.84 | Outstanding | 1,150.70 | Unresolved | -1.25 |
| Discrepancy | 0.00 | | | | |

Check this box to show all deposited entries   Tesses Tresses

After clearing all transactions from the bank statement, the unresolved amount should be –1.25. This is the net difference for the three unmatched bank statement items: the NSF charge, the service charge and the interest. Journal entries for these items will be added later (page 599).

The next section describes the procedure for clearing transactions that are different in some way, like NSF cheques. By marking their status correctly, you will have a more accurate picture of your business transactions. Cheque #61 for $121.53 was returned as NSF and should be marked as such.

Showing Deposit Slip Details

The NSF cheque we need to mark was part of a group deposit (deposit slip #2), so it does not appear individually on the Transactions list. First we need to show the details of the deposit slips. Above the Transactions list is the **Show Deposit Slip Details** check box. This box is a toggle switch; you can hide the details when they are not required or show them if you need to change the status of a single item in the deposit group.

Click   **Show Deposit Slip Details** to add a ✓.

Press the **down scroll arrow** ☑ until you see the items for deposit slip #2:

All three details, the two cheques and the cash amount on the deposit slip, are marked as Cleared when we clear the deposit.

Marking NSF Cheques

For some items — for example, NSF cheques and their reversing entries — you should add further information because they have not cleared the account in the usual way. The available status alternatives are explained in the Status Options chart that follows.

STATUS OPTIONS

Cleared (C)	for deposits and cheques that have been processed correctly.
Deposit Error (D)	for the adjusting journal entry that records the difference between the amount of a deposit that was recorded incorrectly and the bank statement amount for that deposit. Assign the Cleared status to the original entry for the deposit.
Payment Error (P)	for the adjusting entry that records the difference between the amount of a cheque recorded incorrectly and the bank statement amount for that cheque. Assign the Cleared status to the original entry for the cheque.
NSF (N)	for client cheques returned by the bank because there was not enough money in the client's account. Assign the Adjustment status to the adjusting entry that reverses the NSF cheque.
Reversed (R)	for cheques that are cancelled by posting a reversing transaction entry to the bank account or the Sales or Purchases journals, that is, journal entries that are corrected. Assign the Adjustment status to the reversing entry that cancels the cheque.
Void (V)	for cheques that are cancelled because of damage during printing. Assign the Adjustment status to the reversing entry that voids the cheque.
Adjustment (A)	for the adjusting or reversing entries that are made to cancel NSF, void or reversed cheques. (See the explanations for NSF, Void and Reversed above.)

To mark a cheque as NSF,

Click **Cleared** in the Status column for Irma Vannitee's cheque for $121.53 in deposit slip #2, the NSF cheque.

Press (enter) to display the alternatives for the Status of a journal entry:

Click   **NSF** to highlight this alternative.

Click   **Select** to enter it. The Cleared status changes to NSF for this item.

The final step is to change the status of the entry that reverses the payment or NSF cheque to Adjustment. The final certified cheque received in payment has been cleared normally so its status as Cleared is already correct. Changing the status does not affect the resolved and unresolved amounts. The amounts are just cleared in different ways.

> **Double click** **Cleared in the Status column for Bank Debit Memo #61899**, the reversing entry.

> **Double click** **Adjustment** to select this as the status.

Your updated transactions list now looks like the one shown here:

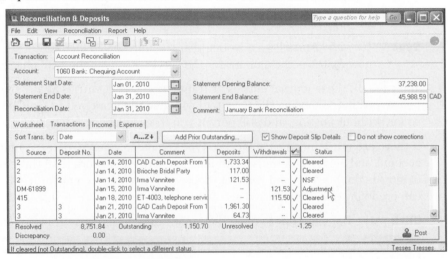

Click   **Show Deposit Slip Details** to restore the summary version for deposits.

The resolved, unresolved and outstanding amounts, the net of deposit and withdrawal amounts, are continually updated as you work through the reconciliation procedure. If you display your journal entry from the Report menu at this stage, you will see a credit to *Bank: Chequing Account* and a debit to the expense account *Reconciliation Adjustments* for $1.25, the unresolved amount at this stage — the net amount of interest and all bank charges. The expense amount total is greater than the interest amount. The journal entries for these items will remove the unresolved amount.

Adding Account Statement Journal Entries

You are now ready to begin entering the journal information for income to this account.

Click   the **Income tab**.

The Account Reconciliation Journal now includes journal entry fields as shown:

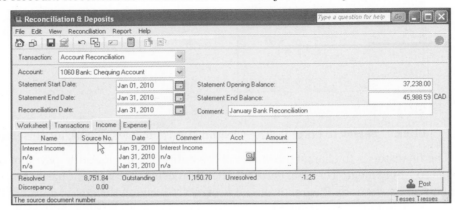

The first entry for Interest Income, the income source we named earlier, is partially completed with the correct default entries for date, comment and account. You can change any of these entries by editing the contents or selecting a different account.

Click   the **Source No. field** beside Interest Revenue to advance the cursor.

Type   Bk-Stmt

Click   the **Amount field**.

Type   52.25 **Press** ⌨tab . Notice that the unresolved amount — 53.50 — now matches the amount for the service fee plus the NSF charge.

You can edit these journal entries or transaction status entries at any time before posting. Choosing the Save tool will save the work you have completed so far, without posting, and still permit you to make changes later.

If there are other income categories, type the name, source, date, comment, account and amount on the second line. You can enter more than three sources of income on this form and you can choose any revenue account, although you can predefine only three linked accounts.

Click   the **Expense tab** to open the input fields for expense transactions:

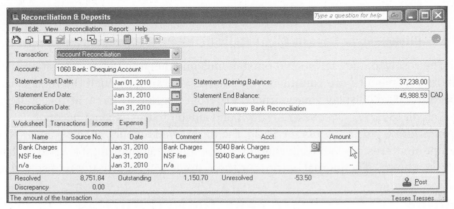

The expense transactions are also partially completed. We need to add the Source No. and the Amount. For the NSF fee, we need to change the date.

You can combine regular service charges with charges for other one-time or unusual services such as stopping a payment on a cheque or NSF fees. We have created a separate category for the NSF charge in order to track this expense. The bank statement contains the amounts for the expenses.

NOTES
You can drag the column heading margins if necessary to see all the input columns.

NOTES
You can select a different revenue account in the reconciliation journal for these predefined incomes if this is appropriate.

NOTES
You can drag the column heading margins if necessary to see all the input columns.

Click   the **Source No. field**. Duplicate source document codes are allowed in this journal.

Type   Bk-Stmt

Click   the **Amount field**.

Type   23.50 **Press** (tab) to advance to the next journal line.

We can now enter the NSF service charges. You can use the same account for more than one journal entry, but you cannot choose the same expense or income category twice. The date for this charge was January 15, so we must also change the default date.

Click   the **Source field**. We will enter the debit memo number as the source.

Type   DM#61899 **Press** (tab).

Type   Jan 15

Click   the **Amount field**.

Type   30 **Press** (tab).

If there are other expenses, enter the information in the same way. You can enter additional expenses and choose any expense account, although you can predefine only three linked accounts.

At this stage, your unresolved amount and discrepancy should be zero if everything is reconciled. We will look at the Worksheet to see a summary of the changes we made.

NOTES
You can select a different expense account in the reconciliation journal for these predefined expenses if this is appropriate.

Click   the **Worksheet tab**:

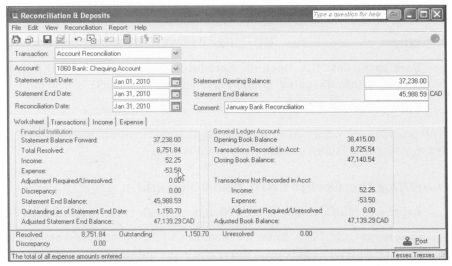

This summary shows the amounts for the bank statement and Simply Accounting records that have been entered to reconcile the differences. Both lists show the opening and closing balances and net total transaction amounts. The Account Reconciliation Journal transactions for income and expenses that were not recorded elsewhere are added to the General Ledger balance (Transactions Not Recorded In Acct), and outstanding amounts that were in the General Ledger but not on the bank statement (amount Outstanding As Of Statement End Date) are added to the Bank Statement balance. The result is a match between the two adjusted balance amounts.

You should also review the reconciliation journal entry before proceeding.

Choose the **Report menu** and **click Display Account Reconciliation Journal Entry**.

Your journal entry should appear as follows:

Account Reconciliation Journal Entry			
File Options Help			
Print Report Change Print Settings Export Report Open in Excel® Customize Report Refresh Report ?			
Tesses Tresses			
01/31/10		Debits	Credits
01/31/10	Bk-Stmt, Interest Income		
	1060 Bank: Chequing Account	52.25	-
	4220 Interest Revenue	-	52.25
01/31/10	Bk-Stmt, Bank Charges		
	1060 Bank: Chequing Account	-	23.50
	5040 Bank Charges	23.50	-
01/15/10	DM- 61899, NSF fee		
	1060 Bank: Chequing Account	-	30.00
	5040 Bank Charges	30.00	-
		105.75	105.75

The income and expense journal entries are listed. In addition, an adjustment entry will be displayed if there is any unresolved amount.

> **Close** the **Report window** when you have finished.

If the unreconciled amount is not zero, check your journal entries to see whether you have made an error. Click each option in the Display group to show your work for the corresponding part of the reconciliation procedure. Make corrections if necessary.

If you still have an unresolved amount, you can save the entry without posting and return later to try to determine whether you made a mistake or whether there was an error on the bank statement.

Any discrepancy or unresolved amount will be posted as an adjustment to the reconciliation adjustments expense account created earlier. This account should be used only for small amounts not significant enough to warrant a separate journal entry, such as differences from payroll tax rates in this text.

> **Click** the **Save button** ⊟ . **Click** ⊠ to close the journal without posting.

> **Back up** the **data file. Open** the **Account Reconciliation Journal**, **select 1060 Bank: Chequing Account** and resume your work.

> **Click** Post ⎶ Post . A blank journal window appears.

The program will warn you before posting an unresolved amount, allowing you to correct any mistakes before posting the journal entries.

Reconciling the Credit Card Bank Account

> **Refer** to **Memo #10 on page 570** and the **bank statement on page 571**.

> **Choose** account 1080. **Enter** a **comment** and the **opening** and **closing bank statement balances. Enter** the **prior outstanding transaction. Clear all journal entries** to process the statement items. **Add** journal **entries** for **service charges** and **interest. Refer** to **keystrokes** beginning on **page 593**.

> **Add** **Shortcuts** for transactions in other modules, or change modules as needed. **Enter** the **transactions for February**, including the account reconciliation.

Displaying Banking Reports

> **Click** the **Report Centre icon** ⟳ Report Centre in the Home window.

NOTES
The confirmation message shows that three journal entries were posted – the interest and expense transactions.

NOTES
There is one outstanding item from the previous month. There are no deposit slips.

Click **Banking** to open the list of banking reports that you can display from the Report Centre:

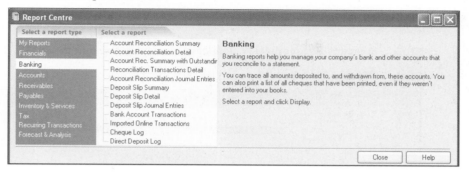

Account Reconciliation Journal

Click **Account Reconciliation Journal Entries**. **Click** **Modify This Report**:

Or choose the Reports menu, choose Journal Entries and click Account Reconciliation to see the report options screen.

The journal can be prepared by selecting journal entry numbers or dates. By default, the report uses posting dates. The usual journal report customizing, sorting and filtering options are available.

Enter the **starting** and **ending dates** or journal numbers for the report.

Click **OK**. **Close** the **display** when you have finished.

Deposit Slip Journal

Click **Deposit Slip Journal Entries** and **click** **Modify This Report**:

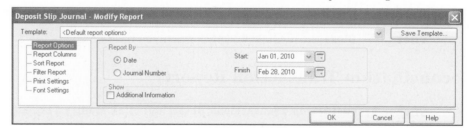

Or, from the Home window, choose the Reports menu, choose Journal Entries and click Deposit Slip to see the report options screen.

The journal can be prepared by selecting journal entry numbers or dates. By default, the report uses posting dates. The usual journal report customizing, sorting and filtering options are available.

Enter the **starting** and **ending dates** or journal numbers for the report.

Click   **OK**. **Close** the **display** when you have finished.

Account Reconciliation Report

Click   **Account Reconciliation Summary** to display the report sample.

Click   **Modify This Report** to see the report options:

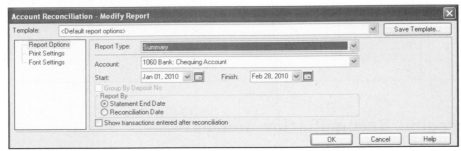

From the Home window, choose the Reports menu, then choose Banking and click Account Reconciliation Report to display the options.

Accept   **1060**   as the bank account or choose another account from the drop-down list for the Account field.

Enter   the **start** and **end dates**. Usually these dates will coincide with the bank statement period.

Click   the **Report Type list arrow**:

From the Report Type drop-down list, you can choose the **Summary** Report to provide totals for each reconciliation Status, totals for income and expense categories and outstanding amounts that will reconcile the bank statement with the General Ledger account balance. The **Detail** Report lists all journal entries with their status. You can group the Detail Report by Deposit Number. Choose **Summary Report With Outstanding Transaction Detail** if you want to add the list of General Ledger transactions that have not been reported on bank statements. You can choose either the bank **Statement End Date** or the **Reconciliation Date** recorded in the journal for the report.

Choose   the **report type** and **date options**.

Click   **OK**. **Close** the **displayed report** when you have finished.

Reconciliation Transaction Report

Click   **Reconciliation Transactions Detail** and **click Modify This Report** to see the report options window:

From the Home window, choose the Reports menu, then choose Banking and click Account Reconciliation Transaction Report.

Choose the **account** for the report from the drop-down list.

Enter **Start** and **Finish** dates for the report.

Choose the **Status categories** to include in your reports. By default, all are included, so clicking a category will remove the ✓ from the check box and omit this category from your report.

Click **OK** and **close** the **displayed report** when you have finished.

Deposit Slip Report

Click **Deposit Slip Summary** and **click Modify This Report**.

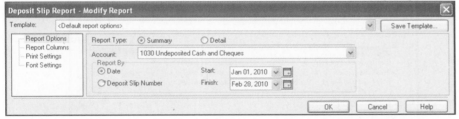

From the Home window, choose the Reports menu, then choose Banking and click Deposit Slip Report to display the options.

Choose the **account** for the report from the drop-down list.

You can display the report for a range of dates or deposit slip numbers. Choose the **Summary** option to see a list of totals for cash and cheques for each deposit slip. Choose **Detail** to see each item on each deposit slip and the totals.

Enter **Start** and **Finish** dates for the report.

Click **OK**. **Close** the **displayed report** and the **Report Centre** when finished.

Printing Account Reconciliation Reports

Display the **report** you want to print. **Click** or **choose** the **File menu** and **click Print** to print the report. **Close** the **Report window** when finished.

NOTES
You can customize the Deposit Slip and Reconciliation Transaction reports by selecting the columns to include but you cannot sort or filter the reports.
You cannot drill down to other reports from the Deposit Slip Report.

NOTES
Remember to check your printer selection before you begin printing.

End-of-Month Procedures

There are accounting activities that should be completed at the end of regular accounting periods. Earlier we used the checklists to review fiscal year-end accounting procedures. As we saw in Chapter 12, there are also checklists for the end of each business day and month. Normally, a business will print all journal transactions at the end of each business day. Statements and financial reports will be printed at the end of each month, and all reports should be printed at the end of the fiscal period. T4s should be printed at the end of the calendar year.

Periodically, a business will clear old information from its accounting files to make space. In the manual system, it might store the details in archives or on microfiche to keep the current files manageable in size. Computerized systems should be similarly maintained by making backups of the data files and then clearing the information that is not required. These periodic procedures include clearing journal entries for prior periods, removing paid invoices from client and supplier records and removing suppliers and clients who no longer do business with the company.

Simply Accounting's checklists can assist with these routine procedures. You should be in the Home window.

> **Choose** the **Business Assistant menu** and **click Checklists** to see the available lists.

> **Click**   **Month-End Procedures** to select it and then **click Modify**.

You will see the list of routines that should be completed at the end of a month:

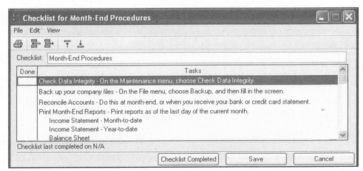

Read the task list. You have already completed some tasks on this list.

> **Click**   the **Done column beside** the two tasks that are completed — **Back Up** and **Reconcile Accounts**. We will complete the remaining tasks before marking them.

> **Click**   the **Home window** if part is showing or click the Simply Accounting button on the task bar to bring it to the front.

> **Choose** the **Maintenance menu** and **click Check Data Integrity**.

If you do not see the message "Data OK," make a note of any data inconsistencies and return to your most recent backup copy of the file.

> **Click**   **OK** to close the Integrity Summary window.

> **Click**   the **Done column beside Check Data Integrity**.

> **Click**   **Save** to return to the main checklists window. A ✓ appears in the Task In Progress column beside Month-End Procedures.

> **Click**   **Close** to leave the checklists window and return to the Home window.

CLASSIC VIEW
You can also click the Checklists button.

NOTES
Remember that you can print the task list for reference. Choose the File menu and click Print, click the Print tool or press *ctrl* + P to print the task list.

Clearing Paid Supplier Transactions

Choose the **Maintenance menu**, then **choose** **Clear Data** and **Clear Paid Transactions** and **click** **Clear Paid Supplier Transactions**:

NOTES

You cannot clear data when you are working in multi-user mode.

SIMPLY VERSION

You will choose Clear Paid Vendor Transactions. The term Vendor replaces Supplier.

You can clear invoices for one or more suppliers at the same time. Unpaid invoices are always retained.

Enter   **Jan 31** as the last date for which you want to remove invoices.

Click   **Select All**. (To select individual suppliers, **press** `ctrl` and **click** their **names**.) We also have stored lookup details that we no longer need.

Click   **Clear Lookup Data For All Paid Transactions**.

Click   **OK**. Simply Accounting presents the warning shown here:

If you have selected correctly and are ready to proceed,

Click   **Yes**. When you choose to clear lookup data, you will see this warning:

NOTES

After clearing data, display the relevant reports to see that the information has been cleared. You will be unable to look up and adjust posted invoices if you have removed lookup details for cleared paid transactions.

Again, if you are certain that you should continue,

Click   **Yes**.

Clearing Paid Client Transactions

Choose the **Maintenance menu**, then **choose** **Clear Data** and **Clear Paid Transactions** and **click** **Clear Paid Client Transactions**:

SIMPLY VERSION

You will choose Clear Paid Customer Transactions. The term Customer replaces Client.

Enter   **Jan 31** as the last date for which you want to remove invoices.

Clearing client invoices is similar to clearing supplier invoices.

We will keep all transactions for February. We can clear the invoices and lookup data for Cash Customers and Atta Schule because these are not needed. You can clear paid invoices for all clients by clicking Select All.

> **Click**   **Atta Schule**. **Press** $\boxed{ctrl}$ and **click Cash Customers**.

> **Click**   **Clear Lookup Data For All Paid Transactions**. **Click OK**.

The next warning is the same as the one we saw for removing supplier invoices. If you are ready, you should proceed.

> **Click**   **Yes**. Again, the additional warning for lookup data is shown. If you are certain that you want to continue,

> **Click**   **Yes** to remove the lookup data and return to the Home window.

Clearing Tax Reports

You should clear tax reports after filing the tax returns for the period covered by the return so that the next report will include only the current reporting period.

> **Choose** the **Maintenance menu**, then **choose Clear Data** and **click Clear Tax Report** to display the options:

Select the tax or taxes for which you want to clear the reports or click Select All. Then enter the date. Entries on and before the date you enter will be removed.

> **Click**   **OK** to see the familiar warning:

We do not want to remove any tax data because we have not submitted the returns.

> **Click**   **No** to cancel and return to the Home window.

Clearing Account Reconciliation Data

> **Choose** the **Maintenance menu**, then **choose Clear Data** and **Clear Account Rec.** and **click Clear Account Rec. Data** to display the options:

Select the account for which you want to remove the data. Then enter the date. Entries on and before the date you enter will be removed.

We do not want to remove the data at this time. If you choose to continue, you will see the familiar warning before any information is removed.

> **Click**   **Cancel** to return to the Home window.

Clearing Inventory Tracking Data

Choose the **Maintenance menu**, then **choose Clear Data** and **click Clear Inventory Tracking Data** to display the following dialogue box:

Enter   **Jan 31** as the date. Entries on and before Jan 31 will be removed.

Click   **OK**. Again, you see the warning before any data is removed.

If you are certain that you want to proceed,

Click   **Yes** to delete the requested information and return to the Home window.

Clearing Lookup Data

You can clear invoice lookup data for both purchase and sales invoices together in a single step or you can clear purchase and sales invoices in separate steps. You can also clear lookup data for Remittances from this menu.

Choose the **Maintenance menu**, then **choose Clear Data** and **Clear Invoice Lookup Data** and **click Clear Supplier Invoice & Client Invoice Lookup Data** to display the clearing options:

Enter   **Jan 31** as the date. Entries on and before Jan 31 will be removed.

Click   **OK**.

Once again, you see the warning before any data is removed. If you are certain that you want to proceed,

Click   **Yes** to continue.

If you cleared the lookup data with the paid transactions, you will see the message stating that there is no invoice lookup data to clear. Click OK to continue.

The requested information is deleted and you will return to the Home window.

If you want to clear only purchase invoice data, choose the Maintenance menu, then choose Clear Data and Clear Invoice Lookup Data and click Clear Supplier Invoice Lookup Data to display the list of suppliers. Choose the suppliers for which you want to clear the invoices, enter the data and click OK to see the familiar warning. Click Yes to continue with clearing the data.

To remove only sales invoice data, choose the Maintenance menu, then choose Clear Data and Clear Invoice Lookup Data and click Clear Client Invoice Lookup Data. Select clients for which you want to clear the invoices, enter the date and click OK. Click Yes to continue with clearing the data.

NOTES

If you choose to clear invoice lookup data for purchases or sales separately, you can choose to clear the data for one or more suppliers (or clients) or for all of them.

 SIMPLY VERSION

You will choose Clear Purchase Invoice and Sales Invoice Lookup Data to clear data for both sets of invoices.

SIMPLY VERSION

You will choose Clear Purchase Invoice Lookup Data to clear data for purchase invoices.

You will choose Clear Sales Invoice Lookup Data to clear data for sales invoices.

Clearing Deposit Slip Lookup Data

Choose the **Maintenance menu**, then **choose Clear Data** and **click Clear Lookup Data For Deposit Slips** to display the options:

Select the account for which you want to remove the data. Then enter the date. Entries on and before the date you enter will be removed.

We do not want to remove the data at this time. If you choose to continue, you will see the familiar warning before any information is removed.

Click **Cancel** to return to the Home window.

Clearing Lookup Data for Other Payments

Lookup data for other payments are cleared separately from Purchases Journal invoices.

Choose the **Maintenance menu**, then **choose Clear Data** and **click Clear Lookup Data For Other Payments** to display the clearing options:

Enter **Jan 31** as the date for the data you want to remove.

Choose the **suppliers**. **Click Select All** to select all suppliers.

Click **OK**.

You will see the warning before any data is removed. If you want to proceed,

Click **Yes** to continue.

The requested information is deleted, and you will return to the Home window.

Automatically Clearing Data

Simply Accounting can also clear data automatically when you start a new fiscal period. Data are automatically retained for seven years.

Choose the **Maintenance menu**, then **choose Clear Data** and **click Automatically Clear Data**.

The options screen shows the types of data you can clear automatically:

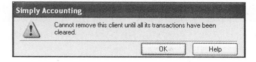

From this screen you can choose what data to clear and how many months of each type of data should be kept when the clearing occurs at the end of the fiscal period.

Click   **Cancel** to return to the Home window.

Removing Supplier and Client Records

Sometimes you know that you will not be doing business with a client or supplier again. Removing their records reduces the length of the lists to scroll through for journal entries and saves on mailing costs. Suppliers are removed from the Suppliers window. Clients are removed from the Clients window. We will remove the client (tenant) Stu Dents because he will be moving out of the apartment after March, the date of his final cheque. First we must clear all paid transactions.

Choose   the **Maintenance menu**, then **choose Clear Data** and **Clear Paid Transactions** and **click Clear Paid Client Transactions**.

Click   **Stu Dents** on the client list.

Enter   **Jan. 31, 2010** as the date.

Click   **OK**. When you see the warning,

Click   **Yes** to confirm. **Click Yes** to confirm removing lookup data if asked.

Click   **Receivables** in the Modules pane list.

Click   **Stu Dents** in the Home window Clients list to open the ledger record.

Click   the **Remove Client tool** in the ledger window, or **choose** the **File menu** and **click Remove** to see the warning:

You can also choose Remove Client from the Clients icon shortcuts list in the Receivables window. This will open the Search window with the option to Remove Client selected. Click Stu Dents in the Search window to select the client and click OK.

We have selected a client for which the invoices have not been cleared. Simply Accounting will not permit you to remove a client, or supplier, with uncleared transactions.

SIMPLY VERSION
The option to clear time slips data is not available in the Simply version.

NOTES
Another option is to mark clients or suppliers as Inactive and not include them in reports. Inactive clients and suppliers also do not appear in the drop-down lists in journals.

NOTES
In the ledger window, you can also press `ctrl` + R to remove the record.

NOTES
There are postdated rent cheques for Stu Dents, so not all the paid transactions were cleared when January 31 was selected as the date.

NOTES
You can select March 1 from the Date field drop-down list. (The latest transaction date is usually on the Date field drop-down lists.)

Click   **OK** to return to the Receivables module window. Clear the details using March 1 as the date and then remove the client's record. If all transactions are cleared, you will see the familiar warning.

Check that you have selected the client you want before continuing.

Click   **Yes** if you have selected correctly.

Click Yes to continue if you see the message about removing lookup data. If you see the message stating that there is no lookup data, click OK to continue.

Close   the **Receivables module window** to return to the Home window.

Completing the Month-End Checklist

We will now return to the month-end checklist by marking the remaining tasks as done. The tasks relating to budgeting do not apply so we can delete them from the list and customize the list for Tesses Tresses.

Choose   the **Business Assistant menu** and **click Checklists** to see the lists.

Double click **Month-End Procedures** to open this list.

NOTES
Refer to page 490 for more information on removing or adding tasks in checklists.

You can also add tasks to customize the list even further. Just click on the list where you want to add a task, choose the Edit menu and click Insert (or click the Insert Item tool). Then type the task description.

Scroll down the **list** to the budget-related tasks.

Click   **Check Your Budget** to select this line.

Click   the **Remove Item tool** or **choose** the **Edit menu** and **click Remove**.

Click   **Yes** to confirm and select the next task. Remove it and the following one relating to budgets.

Click   the **Done column** for the remaining tasks.

Click   **Checklist Completed** to return to the opening Checklist window.

The session date appears as the Date Last Completed beside Month-End Procedures.

Click   **Close** to return to the Home window.

REVIEW

The Student CD-ROM with Data Files includes Review Questions and Supplementary Cases for this chapter.

OBJECTIVES

After completing this chapter, you should be able to

- **plan** and **design** an accounting system for a small business
- **prepare** procedures for converting from a manual system
- **understand** the objectives of a computerized system
- **create** company files
- **set up** company accounts
- **enter** settings for foreign currency transactions
- **prepare** files for foreign currency transactions and importing goods
- **identify** preferred customers for reduced prices
- **enter** preferred customer prices and import duty rates for inventory
- **finish** entering the accounting history for all modules
- **insert** new accounts, suppliers, customers and employees as required
- **export** reports
- **use** spreadsheets for analyzing, planning and decision making
- **enter** end-of-accounting-period adjustments
- **perform** end-of-accounting-period closing routines
- **analyze** and **interpret** comparative reports
- **develop** further group interpersonal skills

INTRODUCTION

This application provides a complete accounting cycle for a merchandising business. It is a comprehensive application covering a three-month fiscal period. You will use Simply Accounting to convert a manual accounting system to a computerized accounting system and then enter transactions. The routines in this application are common to many small businesses, so they should be useful. The information in this chapter reflects the business realities in Ontario in 2008.

You may substitute information relevant to other provinces or the latest payroll and tax regulations wherever it is appropriate to do so.

Because of the length of the setup, instructions for working with the source documents are presented with those documents on page 683.

> **NOTES**
> If you change the province, remember that rules for the application of the federal Goods and Services Tax (GST), provincial sales taxes and payroll may vary from one province to another, and amounts in the source documents will change.

COMPANY INFORMATION

Company Profile

Flabuless Fitness, in Hamilton, Ontario, sells a wide range of fitness equipment and accessories for home and light commercial use. Stephen Reeves, the owner, opened his business a few years ago after retiring as a professional athlete, gaining business experience with another store and completing some business courses. Reeves has three employees to assist with the work in the store. They also perform other duties. One employee does the accounting, one teaches yoga classes and one delivers equipment and provides personal training services to clients. Reeves works mostly outside the store, promoting the business.

Several of the equipment suppliers offer discounts to the store for early payment. Two suppliers are located in the United States. Accounts are also set up for other supplies and services that are provided locally. The store uses a credit card for some of these purchases.

Most customers are situated in the Hamilton region, but Reeves has recently added two new customers in New York State. Prices in US dollars are entered in the ledger records so that all prices will be entered automatically in the correct amount and currency when the customer is selected. With the Canadian dollar approximately on par with the US dollar in 2008, Reeves has set all US dollar prices equal to Canadian dollar prices.

All account customers are given discounts for early payment and some preferred customers receive additional discounts. Individual customers usually pay by cash, debit or credit card and do not receive any discounts. Delivery is provided at a small charge and includes equipment setup and a brief demonstration on equipment use.

All items and services sold by the store are set up as inventory so that sales can be monitored. GST is charged on all sales and services, except to foreign customers. PST is charged on sales of inventory items but not on services. The store pays GST and PST on all taxable purchases, but inventory purchased for resale in the store is exempt from PST.

The owner decided to use Simply Accounting for record keeping after a consultant prepared the report on the following pages. Reeves found an application called Hearth House in an older Simply Accounting textbook. It appeared similar in complexity and structure to Flabuless Fitness and even included complete instructions for creating the data files. Before converting the books for the store, he asked his assistant to work through this application for practice. Next she printed all the relevant business guide information and prepared the following reports to assist with the conversion on April 1, 2010:

- Income Statement
- Business Information
- Chart of Accounts
- Balance Sheet
- Post-Closing Trial Balance

- Supplier Information
- Customer Information
- Employee Information
- Inventory Information
- Accounting Procedures

MANAGER'S REPORT ON SIMPLY ACCOUNTING

PREPARED FOR FLABULESS FITNESS

1. Simply Accounting allows a business to process all source documents in a timely fashion. It can automatically prepare both single-period and comparative accounting reports for planning, decision making and controlling operations within the business.
2. The software eliminates some of the time-consuming manual clerical functions. For example, it can automatically prepare invoices, cheques and statements, and it can perform all the necessary mathematical calculations. Being freed from these chores, the accountant can extend her role to assume a much higher level of responsibility. For example, the accountant will have more time to spend analyzing reports with the owner and can work directly with the owner in making business decisions.
3. Simply Accounting can easily export reports to spreadsheets for further analysis, or link with the Internet, with other software programs and with suppliers and customers for interactive data exchange. When combined with the graphing, account reconciliation and budgeting features, these reports permit the owner to analyze past trends and to make better predictions about the future behaviour of the business.
4. As the business grows, the manager can divide work more meaningfully among new accounting personnel. Since Simply Accounting provides subsidiary ledgers that are linked to control accounts in the General Ledger, it automatically coordinates accounting work performed by different individuals. Customizable window backgrounds can even accommodate mood changes of the different users.
5. Simply Accounting allows the owner to exercise business controls in a number of areas.

IN GENERAL

*   Access to confidential accounting records and editing capability can be restricted to authorized personnel by using passwords.
*   Mechanical errors can be virtually eliminated, since journal transactions with unequal debits and credits cannot be posted. Customer, supplier, employee, inventory and jobcost names appear in full on the journal entry input forms, making errors less likely.
*   The ability to preview forms, store recurring entries and look up posted invoices makes it possible to avoid errors in repeated information and to double check invoices in response to customer and supplier inquiries.
*   Errors in General, Sales, Receipts, Purchases, Payments and Payroll journal entries can be corrected as adjustments or reversed. The software automatically creates and posts the reversing entries.
*   Simply Accounting provides an audit trail for all journals.
*   Bank account, customer, supplier and inventory records can be set up to calculate many foreign currency transactions automatically, including import duties.
*   Daily Business Manager lists and checklists provide reminders of upcoming discounts, recurring entries and routine tasks.
*   Business guides, accounting advice and management reports and advice all provide helpful information for running the business.
*   Simply Accounting provides a directory of customers, suppliers and employees, and can create mailing labels for them.

GENERAL LEDGER

*   The software provides a directory of accounts used by the business, including all linked accounts for the other ledgers in Simply Accounting.
*   The information in these accounts can be used to prepare and analyze financial reports such as the Balance Sheet and Income Statement.

RECEIVABLES LEDGER

*   Credit limit entries for each customer should reduce the losses from non-payment of accounts. Customers with poor payment histories can have their credit limits reduced or their credit purchase privileges removed.
*   Preferred customers can be identified so that they automatically receive lower prices.
*   Sales quote and order entries result in automatic Sales Journal entries when the quotes or orders are filled.
*   Tax codes and accounts can be entered in the customer record so that they are automatically entered for sales when the customer is selected.
*   Accounts receivable can be aged, and each customer's payment behaviour can be analyzed. This feature allows for the accurate calculation of provisions for bad debts.

PAYABLES LEDGER

*   The information from the review of transactions with suppliers and from the accounts payable aged analysis can be combined with detailed cash flow reports to make payment decisions. Simply Accounting helps to predict short-term cash needs in order to establish priorities for making payments and to schedule payments to suppliers.
*   The GST remittance or refund is calculated automatically because of the linked GST accounts in the Payables and Receivables ledgers.
*   Simply Accounting purchase quote and order entries result in automatic Purchases Journal entries when quotes or orders are filled.
*   The usual tax code and expense account for a supplier can be entered in the supplier record so that they are entered automatically for purchases when the supplier is selected.

PAYROLL LEDGER

*   Simply Accounting maintains employee records with both personal and payment information for personnel files.
*   Paycheques for several employees can be processed in a single entry with direct payroll deposit.
*   Once records are set up, the program automatically withholds employee deductions including income tax, CPP (Canada Pension Plan) and EI (Employment Insurance) and is therefore less prone to error. Updated tax tables can be obtained from Sage Software, Inc.

▶

▶ <u>Manager's Report on Simply Accounting</u>   <u>Page 2</u>

PAYROLL LEDGER CONTINUED

•   Payroll summaries permit easy analysis of compulsory and optional payroll expenses and benefits, employee contributions and entitlements.
•   Different kinds of income can be linked to different expense accounts. In addition, the wages for different employees can be linked to different expense accounts, again permitting better tracking of payroll expenses.
•   Simply Accounting automatically links payroll with control accounts in the General Ledger. Remittance amounts are tracked and linked with the corresponding payroll authorities for monthly or quarterly remittance.

INVENTORY LEDGER

•   The software provides an inventory summary or database of all inventory items.
•   Services can be set up as inventory and tracked the same way as inventory items.
•   Inventory reports flag items that need to be re-ordered, and the reports can be used to make purchase decisions.
•   Import duty rates and different prices in home and foreign currencies can be set up in the ledger so they appear automatically in the journals. Additional price lists can be added.
•   Inventory codes can be matched to the supplier and customer item codes so that common order forms are created automatically.
•   The software calculates inventory variance costs when the items sold are out of stock and later purchased at different prices.
•   Simply Accounting automatically updates inventory records for multiple locations when inventory is purchased, sold, transferred, lost, recovered or returned. It warns when you try to oversell inventory.
•   Different units for stocking, selling and buying items can be saved for inventory items so that prices are automatically entered correctly for both sales and purchases. Reports can be prepared for any of the units on record.
•   Inventory tracking reports can monitor sales and purchase activity on individual inventory items to see which ones are selling well and which are not. These reports can be used to determine optimum inventory buying patterns to reduce storage costs.

6.   In summation, Simply Accounting provides an integrated management accounting information system with extensive built-in controls.

INCOME STATEMENT

FLABULESS FITNESS

January 1 to March 31, 2010

Revenue			
4000	GENERAL REVENUE		
4020	Revenue from Sales	$78 450.00	
4040	Revenue from Services	8 335.00	
4060	Sales Discounts	−965.00	
4100	Net Sales		$85 820.00
4120	Exchange Rate Differences		−12.00
4150	Interest Revenue		1 980.00
4180	Sales Tax Compensation		248.00
4200	Freight Revenue		379.00
4390	TOTAL GENERAL REVENUE		$88 415.00
TOTAL REVENUE			$88 415.00
Expense			
5000	OPERATING EXPENSES		
5010	Advertising and Promotion		$ 530.00
5020	Bank Charges		128.00
5030	Credit Card Fees		1 480.00
5040	Damaged Inventory	$ 80.00	
5050	Cost of Goods Sold: Accessories	5 395.00	
5060	Cost of Goods Sold: Equipment	3 149.00	
5070	Cost Variance	64.00	
5080	Freight Expense	432.00	
5090	Purchase Discounts	−524.00	
5100	Purchases Returns & Allowances	−367.00	
5110	Net Cost of Goods Sold		8 229.00
5120	Depreciation: Cash Registers	300.00	
5130	Depreciation: Computer Equipment	150.00 ▶	

▶ 5140	Depreciation: Furniture & Fixtures	80.00	
5150	Depreciation: Retail Premises	2 440.00	
5160	Depreciation: Van	190.00	
5180	Net Depreciation		3 160.00
5190	Delivery Expense		63.00
5200	Hydro Expense		528.00
5210	Insurance Expense		1 200.00
5220	Interest on Loan		1 240.00
5230	Interest on Mortgage		5 600.00
5240	Maintenance of Premises		1 055.00
5250	Supplies Used		165.00
5260	Property Taxes		2 700.00
5270	Uncollectable Accounts Expense		500.00
5280	Telephone Expense		295.00
5285	Van Maintenance & Operating Expense		638.00
5290	TOTAL OPERATING EXPENSES		$27 511.00
5295	PAYROLL EXPENSES		
5300	Wages		8 295.20
5305	Salaries		22 800.00
5310	Commissions & Bonuses		284.80
5320	EI Expense		998.00
5330	CPP Expense		1 201.00
5340	WSIB Expense		379.00
5360	EHT Expense		309.00
5370	Gp Insurance Expense		105.00
5490	TOTAL PAYROLL EXPENSES		$34 372.00
TOTAL EXPENSE			$61 883.00
NET INCOME			$26 532.00

BUSINESS INFORMATION

FLABULESS FITNESS

USER PREFERENCES: Options
Use Accounting Terms
Automatically save changes to records
Show   Paid stamp, Company name in status
        bar and Session date at startup

View
Daily Business Manager   Turned off
Checklists   Turned off
Transaction Confirmation   Turned on

COMPANY SETTINGS: Information
Address   199 Warmup Rd., Unit 500
             Hamilton, Ontario L8T 3B7
Tel 1   (905) 642-2348 (B-FIT)
Tel 2   (800) 448-2348 (B-FIT)
Fax   (905) 642-9100
Industry   Retail
Business No. 245 138 121 RT0001
Business Province Ontario
Fiscal Start   04-01-2010
Earliest Transaction 04-01-2010
Fiscal End   06-30-2010

System
Warn if accounts not balanced

Backup
Backup Semi-monthly
Display a backup reminder

Features All used
Forms Settings (Next Number)
Sales Invoices No. 3000
Sales Quotes No. 41
Receipts No. 39
Customer Deposits No. 15
Purchase Orders No. 25
Direct Deposits No. 19

Date Format
Use Long Dates on the screen

Logo
SimData\Setup\logos\flab.bmp

Names
Additional Field Ref. Number

Credit Card Information
Used: Visa
Payable 2250 Expense 5030

Accept:	Visa	Interac
Fee	2.5%	0%
Expense	5030	5030
Asset	1120	1120

Sales Taxes

Tax	ID on forms	Track:	Purch	Sales
GST	245 138 121		2670	2650
PST				2640

	Taxable?	Exempt?	Report?
GST	No	No	Yes
PST	No	No	Yes

Tax Codes
G: GST, taxable, 5%, not included, refundable
GP: GST, taxable, 5%, not included, refundable
    PST, taxable, 8% not included,
        not refundable
IN: GST, taxable, 5%, included, refundable
    PST, taxable, 8%, included, not refundable

Foreign Currency
USD   United States Dollars
Tracking Account   4120
Exchange Rate on 04/01/10   1.015

GENERAL SETTINGS No changes

PAYABLES SETTINGS
Address Hamilton, Ontario, Canada
Options: Aging periods 15, 30, 60 days
Discounts before tax Yes

Import Duty
Track import duty
Linked account 2220

RECEIVABLES SETTINGS
Address Hamilton, Ontario, Canada
Options: Aging periods 10, 30, 60 days
Interest charges 1.5% after 30 days
Statements include invoices for 31 days
Use code GP for new customers

Discount: Payment terms 2/10, n/30
Discounts before tax No
Line Discounts Not used

Comments
On Sales Invoice   Interest @ 1.5% per month
    charged on accounts over 30 days.

PAYROLL SETTINGS
Names: Income and Deduction
Income 1   Salary
Income 2   Commission
Income 3   No. Clients
Income 4   Bonus
Income 5   Tuition
Income 6   Travel Exp
Deduction 1   RRSP
Deduction 2   CSB Plan
Deduction 3   Garnishee

Names: Additional Payroll
Field 1   Emergency Contact
Field 2   Contact Number
User Expense 1   Gp Insurance
Entitlement 1   Vacation
Entitlement 2   Sick Leave
Entitlement 3   PersonalDays

Incomes

Income	Type	Taxable	Vac. Pay
Regular	Income	Yes	Yes
Overtime 1	Income	Yes	Yes
Salary	Income	Yes	No
Commission	Income	Yes	No
Bonus	Income	Yes	No
No. Clients	Piece Rate	Yes	Yes
Tuition	Income	Yes	No
Travel Exp	Reimburse	No	No

Deductions
RRSP Before tax, after other deductions
CSB Plan After tax and other deductions
Garnishee After tax and other deductions

Taxes
EI factor 1.4
EHT factor 0.98
WSIB rate 1.29
Prov. Tax Not applicable

Entitlements

Name	Track %	Max Days	Clear
Vacation	8.0%	25	No
Sick Leave	5.0%	15	No
PersonalDays	2.5%	5	No

Remittance

Payroll Liability	Payroll Authority
EI, CPP, Income Tax	Receiver General
EHT, PST	Minister of Finance
WSIB	Workplace Safety & Insurance Board
Gp Insurance, RRSP	Ancaster Insurance
CSB	Mt. Hope Investment
Garnishee	Receiver General

Opening balance amounts: see Trial Balance

Job Categories
Sales: employees are salespersons
All employees are in Sales category

INVENTORY SETTINGS
Profit evaluation by markup
Sort inventory by number
Allow inventory levels to go below zero
Foreign prices from inventory records

ACCOUNT CLASS SETTINGS
Bank
    1060 Bank: Hamilton Trust Chequing (CAD)
        Next cheque no. 101
        Next deposit no. 14
    1080 Bank: Hamilton Trust Savings (CAD)
    1120 Bank: Visa and Interac
    1140 Bank: USD Chequing (USD)
        Next cheque no. 346
Cash
    1030 Undeposited Cash and Cheques
Credit Card Payable
    2250 Credit Card Payable
All Postable Expense Accounts
    Expense or Operating Expense class

LINKED ACCOUNTS FOR LEDGERS
See pages 645–650, 656–658

CHART OF ACCOUNTS

FLABULESS FITNESS

ASSETS

1000	CURRENT ASSETS [H]
1010	Test Balance Account
1030	Undeposited Cash and Cheques [A]
1060	Bank: Hamilton Trust Chequing [A]
1080	Bank: Hamilton Trust Savings [A]
1120	Bank: Visa and Interac [A]
1140	Bank: USD Chequing [A]
1150	Net Bank [S]
1200	Accounts Receivable [A]
1210	Allowance for Doubtful Accounts [A]
1220	Advances Receivable [A]
1230	Interest Receivable [A]
1240	Net Receivables [S]
1250	Purchase Prepayments
1260	Office Supplies
1265	Linen Supplies
1270	Prepaid Advertising
1280	Prepaid Insurance
1300	TOTAL CURRENT ASSETS [T]
1500	INVENTORY ASSETS [H]
1520	Accessories
1540	Fitness Equipment
1580	TOTAL INVENTORY ASSETS [T]
1600	CENTRE & EQUIPMENT [H]
1610	Cash Registers [A]
1620	Accum Deprec: Cash Registers [A]
1630	Net Cash Registers [S]
1640	Computer Equipment [A]
1650	Accum Deprec: Computer Equipment [A]
1660	Net Computer Equipment [S]
1670	Furniture & Fixtures [A]
1680	Accum Deprec: Furniture & Fixtures [A]
1690	Net Furniture & Fixtures [S]
1700	Retail Premises [A]
1710	Accum Deprec: Retail Premises [A]
1720	Net Retail Premises [S]
1730	Van [A]
1740	Accum Deprec: Van [A]
1750	Net Van [S]
1890	TOTAL CENTRE & EQUIPMENT [T] ▶

▶LIABILITIES

2000	CURRENT LIABILITIES [H]
2100	Bank Loan
2200	Accounts Payable
2210	Prepaid Sales and Deposits
2220	Import Duty Payable
2250	Credit Card Payable
2300	Vacation Payable
2310	EI Payable [A]
2320	CPP Payable [A]
2330	Income Tax Payable [A]
2350	Receiver General Payable [S]
2380	EHT Payable
2400	RRSP Payable
2410	CSB Plan Payable
2420	Group Insurance Payable
2430	Garnisheed Wages Payable
2460	WSIB Payable
2500	Business Income Tax Payable
2640	PST Payable
2650	GST Charged on Sales [A]
2670	GST Paid on Purchases [A]
2750	GST Owing (Refund) [S]
2790	TOTAL CURRENT LIABILITIES [T]
2800	LONG TERM LIABILITIES [H]
2820	Mortgage Payable
2890	TOTAL LONG TERM LIABILITIES [T]

EQUITY

3000	OWNER'S EQUITY [H]
3560	S. Reeves, Capital
3600	Current Earnings [X]
3690	TOTAL OWNER'S EQUITY [T]

REVENUE

4000	GENERAL REVENUE [H]
4020	Revenue from Sales [A]
4040	Revenue from Services [A]
4060	Sales Discounts [A]
4100	Net Sales [S]
4120	Exchange Rate Differences
4150	Interest Revenue
4180	Sales Tax Compensation
4200	Freight Revenue
4390	TOTAL GENERAL REVENUE [T] ▶

▶EXPENSE

5000	OPERATING EXPENSES [H]
5010	Advertising and Promotion
5020	Bank Charges
5030	Credit Card Fees
5040	Damaged Inventory [A]
5050	Cost of Goods Sold: Accessories [A]
5060	Cost of Goods Sold: Equipment [A]
5065	Cost of Services [A]
5070	Cost Variance [A]
5080	Freight Expense [A]
5090	Purchase Discounts [A]
5100	Purchases Returns & Allowances [A]
5110	Net Cost of Goods Sold [S]
5120	Depreciation: Cash Registers [A]
5130	Depreciation: Computer Equipment [A]
5140	Depreciation: Furniture & Fixtures [A]
5150	Depreciation: Retail Premises [A]
5160	Depreciation: Van [A]
5180	Net Depreciation [S]
5190	Delivery Expense
5200	Hydro Expense
5210	Insurance Expense
5220	Interest on Loan
5230	Interest on Mortgage
5240	Maintenance of Premises
5250	Supplies Used
5260	Property Taxes
5270	Uncollectable Accounts Expense
5280	Telephone Expense
5285	Van Maintenance & Operating Expense
5290	TOTAL OPERATING EXPENSES [T]
5295	PAYROLL EXPENSES [H]
5300	Wages
5305	Salaries
5310	Commissions & Bonuses
5320	Travel Expenses
5330	EI Expense
5340	CPP Expense
5350	WSIB Expense
5360	EHT Expense
5370	Gp Insurance Expense
5380	Employee Benefits
5490	TOTAL PAYROLL EXPENSES [T]

NOTES: The Chart of Accounts includes all accounts and Net Income. Group account types are not marked. Other account types are marked as follows: [H] Heading, [A] subgroup Account, [S] Subgroup total, [T] Total, [X] Current Earnings.

BALANCE SHEET

FLABULESS FITNESS

March 31, 2010

Assets

1000	CURRENT ASSETS		
1060	Bank: Hamilton Trust Chequing	$ 77 988.00	
1080	Bank: Hamilton Trust Savings	108 250.00	
1120	Bank: Visa and Interac	8 635.00	
1140	Bank: USD (9 350 USD)	9 500.00	
1150	Net Bank		$204 373.00
1200	Accounts Receivable	17 110.00	
1210	Allowance for Doubtful Accounts	−800.00	
1220	Advances Receivable	100.00	
1230	Interest Receivable	420.00	
1240	Net Receivables		16 830.00
1260	Office Supplies		300.00
1265	Linen Supplies		450.00
1270	Prepaid Advertising		180.00
1280	Prepaid Insurance		4 800.00
1300	TOTAL CURRENT ASSETS		$226 933.00
1500	INVENTORY ASSETS		
1520	Accessories		15 270.00
1540	Fitness Equipment		78 616.00
1580	TOTAL INVENTORY ASSETS		$93 886.00
1600	CENTRE & EQUIPMENT		
1610	Cash Registers	5 000.00	
1620	Accum Deprec: Cash Registers	−1 000.00	
1630	Net Cash Registers		4 000.00
1640	Computer Equipment	3 000.00	
1650	Accum Deprec: Computer Equip	−1 000.00	
1660	Net Computer Equipment		2 000.00
1670	Furniture & Fixtures	2 000.00	
1680	Accum Deprec: Furn & Fixtures	−400.00	
1690	Net Furniture & Fixtures		1 600.00
1700	Retail Premises	200 000.00	
1710	Accum Deprec: Retail Premises	−5 000.00	
1720	Net Retail Premises		195 000.00
1730	Van	30 000.00	
1740	Accum Deprec: Van	−5 000.00	
1750	Net Van		25 000.00
1890	TOTAL CENTRE & EQUIPMENT		$227 600.00
	TOTAL ASSETS		$548 419.00 ▶

Liabilities

▶ 2000	CURRENT LIABILITIES		
2100	Bank Loan		$ 50 000.00
2200	Accounts Payable		16 780.00
2250	Credit Card Payable		220.00
2300	Vacation Payable		371.84
2310	EI Payable	$ 563.28	
2320	CPP Payable	824.77	
2330	Income Tax Payable	1 755.60	
2350	Receiver General Payable		3 143.65
2380	EHT Payable		320.50
2400	RRSP Payable		350.00
2410	CSB Plan Payable		350.00
2420	Group Insurance Payable		39.00
2430	Garnisheed Wages Payable		200.00
2460	WSIB Payable		392.51
2500	Business Income Tax Payable		3 600.00
2640	PST Payable		2 470.00
2650	GST Charged on Sales	2 450.00	
2670	GST Paid on Purchases	−1 050.00	
2750	GST Owing (Refund)		1 400.00
2790	TOTAL CURRENT LIABILITIES		$79 637.50
2800	LONG TERM LIABILITIES		
2820	Mortgage Payable		180 000.00
2890	TOTAL LONG TERM LIABILITIES		$180 000.00
	TOTAL LIABILITIES		$259 637.50

Equity

3000	OWNER'S EQUITY		
3560	S. Reeves, Capital		$262 249.50
3600	Current Earnings		26 532.00
3690	TOTAL OWNER'S EQUITY		$288 781.50
	TOTAL EQUITY		$288 781.50
	LIABILITIES AND EQUITY		$548 419.00

POST-CLOSING TRIAL BALANCE

FLABULESS FITNESS

March 31, 2010

		Debits	Credits				Debits	Credits
1060	Bank: Hamilton Trust Chequing	$ 77 988.00		▶	1730	Van	30 000.00	
1080	Bank: Hamilton Trust Savings	108 250.00			1740	Accum Deprec: Van		5 000.00
1120	Bank: Visa and Interac	8 635.00			2100	Bank Loan		50 000.00
1140	Bank: USD Chequing (9 350 USD)	9 500.00			2200	Accounts Payable		16 780.00
1200	Accounts Receivable	17 110.00			2250	Credit Card Payable		220.00
1210	Allowance for Doubtful Accounts		$ 800.00		2300	Vacation Payable		371.84
1220	Advances Receivable	100.00			2310	EI Payable		563.28
1230	Interest Receivable	420.00			2320	CPP Payable		824.77
1260	Office Supplies	300.00			2330	Income Tax Payable		1 755.60
1265	Linen Supplies	450.00			2380	EHT Payable		320.50
1270	Prepaid Advertising	180.00			2400	RRSP Payable		350.00
1280	Prepaid Insurance	4 800.00			2410	CSB Plan Payable		350.00
1520	Accessories	15 270.00			2420	Group Insurance Payable		39.00
1540	Fitness Equipment	78 616.00			2430	Garnisheed Wages Payable		200.00
1610	Cash Registers	5 000.00			2460	WSIB Payable		392.51
1620	Accum Deprec: Cash Registers		1 000.00		2500	Business Income Tax Payable		3 600.00
1640	Computer Equipment	3 000.00			2640	PST Payable		2 470.00
1650	Accum Deprec: Computer Equipment		1 000.00		2650	GST Charged on Sales		2 450.00
1670	Furniture & Fixtures	2 000.00			2670	GST Paid on Purchases	1 050.00	
1680	Accum Deprec: Furniture & Fixtures		400.00		2820	Mortgage Payable		180 000.00
1700	Retail Premises	200 000.00			3560	S. Reeves, Capital		288 781.50
1710	Accum Deprec: Retail Premises		5 000.00 ▶				$562 669.00	$562 669.00

SUPPLIER INFORMATION

FLABULESS FITNESS

Supplier Name (Contact)	Address	Phone No. Fax No.	E-mail Web Site	Terms Tax ID	Expense Acct Tax Code
Ancaster Insurance (Feulle Cuvver)	718 Montgomery Dr. Ancaster, ON L9G 3H5	Tel: (905) 588-1773 Fax: (905) 588-1624	fc@ancaster.insur.ca www.ancaster.insur.ca	net 1	no tax (not exempt)
Bell Canada (Noel Coller)	100 James St. N. Hamilton, ON L8R 2K5	Tel: (905) 525-2355	www.bell.ca	net 1	5280 GP
City of Hamilton Treasurer (Budd Jett)	53 Main St. W. Hamilton, ON L8P 2Z3	Tel: (905) 461-0063 Fax: (905) 461-9204	www.hamilton.city.ca	net 1	5260 no tax (exempt)
Energy Source (Manny Watts)	91 NacNab St. Hamilton, ON L8R 2L9	Tel: (905) 463-2664	watts@energysource.ca www.energysource.ca	net 1	5200 G
Feelyte Gym Accessories (Stretch Theraband)	7 Onondaga Dr. Ancaster, ON L9G 4S5	Tel: (905) 588-3846 Fax: (905) 588-7126	stretch@feelyte.com www.feelyte.com	2/10, n/30 (before tax) 466 254 108	G
Footlink Corporation (Onna Treadmill)	39 Treadwell St. Oakville, ON L6M 3K9	Tel: (905) 777-8133 Fax: (905) 777-8109	onna@footlink.com www.footlink.com	1/15, n/30 (before tax) 274 309 481	G
Hamilton Spectator (Dawn Newsman)	15 Wentworth St. N. Hamilton, ON L8L 5T8	Tel: (905) 525-1800 Fax: (905) 525-1816	newsman@spectator.ca www.spectator.ca	net 10	1270 GP
Minister of Finance (N.O. Money)	631 Queenston Rd. Hamilton, ON L8K 6R5	Tel: (905) 462-5555	www.gov.on.ca/fin	net 1	no tax (exempt)
Mt. Hope Investment Corp. (P. Cuniary)	122 King St. W. Hamilton, ON L8P 4V2	Tel: (905) 462-3338 Fax: (905) 461-2116	pc@mt.hope.invest.ca www.mt.hope.invest.ca	net 15	2410 no tax (exempt)

▶

Supplier Name (Contact)	Address	Phone No. Fax No.	E-mail Web Site	Terms Tax ID	Expense Acct Tax Code
Prolife Exercisers Inc. (C. Glider) (USD supplier)	1500 Redmond Road Suite 100, Woodinville Washington 98072 USA	Tel: (509) 628-9163 Fax: (509) 629-7164	glider@prolife.ex.com www.prolife.ex.com	2/10, n/30 (before tax)	G
Receiver General for Canada	Sudbury Tax Services Office PO Box 20004 Sudbury, ON P3A 6B4	Tel 1: (800) 561-7761 Tel 2: (800) 959-2221	www.cra-arc.gc.ca	net 1	no tax (exempt)
Redux Home Gym Wholesalers (Bi Sepps) (USD supplier)	4900 Columbia St., #650 El Cerrito, California 94533 USA	Tel 1: (510) 525-4327 Tel 2: (800) 567-9152 Fax: (510) 526-1135	bisepps@redux.com www.redux.com	2/10, n/30 (before tax)	G
Scandia Weights Co. (B. Fitt)	82 Nordica Lane Hamilton, ON L8P 2G6	Tel: (905) 465-6247 Fax: (905) 466-3554	fitt@scandiawts.com www.scandiawts.com	net 30 372 640 813	G
Trufit Depot (Varry Shapely)	43 Paling Ave. Hamilton, ON L8H 5J5	Tel: (905) 529-7235 Fax: (905) 529-2995	shapely@trufitdepot.ca www.trufitdepot.ca	2/5, n/30 (before tax) 244 573 650	G
Waterdown Sunoco (Mick Annick)	101 Niska Dr. Waterdown, ON L0R 2H3	Tel: (905) 622-6181 Fax: (905) 622-4777	mick@goodforcars.com www.goodforcars.com	net 1	5285 IN
Westdale Office Supplies (Clip Papers)	26 Dalewood Ave. Hamilton, ON L8S 1Y7	Tel: (905) 528-8199 Fax: (905) 528-8221	papers@wos.com www.wos.com	net 30 259 491 820	1260 GP
Workplace Safety & Insurance Board (I.M. Hurt)	PO Box 2099 Hamilton, ON L8N 4C5	Tel: (800) 525-9100 Fax: (905) 523-1824	www.wsib.on.ca	net 1	2460 no tax (exempt)

NOTES: Year-to-date purchases and payments are not recorded because this is a new fiscal period.

OUTSTANDING SUPPLIER INVOICES

FLABULESS FITNESS

Supplier Name	Terms	Date	Inv/Chq No.	Amount	Tax	Total
Feelyte Gym Accessories	2/10, n/30 (before tax)	Mar. 30/10	FG-1611	$1 000	$50	$1 050
Footlink Corporation	1/15, n/30 (before tax)	Mar. 20/10 Mar. 21/10	FC-618 Chq 96 Balance Owing	$10 000 2 120	$500	$10 500 2 120 $8 380
Redux Home Gym Wholesalers	2/10, n/30 (before tax)	Mar. 28/10	R-914	$6 900 USD	345 USD	$7 350 CAD
				Grand Total		$16 780

CUSTOMER INFORMATION

FLABULESS FITNESS

Customer Name (Contact)	Address	Phone No. Fax No.	E-mail Web Site	Terms Tax Code	Credit Limit
*Buffalo Health Clinic (Minnie Mussle)	75 Brawn Ave. Buffalo, New York 14202 USA	Tel: (716) 367-7346 Fax: (716) 367-8258	mmussle@buffalohealth.com www.buffalohealth.com Currency: USD	2/10, n/30 no tax	$12 000 ($12 000 USD)
*Chedoke Health Care (Wade Less)	13 Wellspring Dr. Hamilton, ON L8T 3B8	Tel: (905) 526-3344 Fax: (905) 525-1166	less@chedoke.healthcare.ca www.chedoke.healthcare.ca	2/10, n/30 GP	$12 000
Dundas Recreational Centre (X.S. Wayte)	190 Playtime Circle Dundas, ON L8C 2V8	Tel: (905) 466-5576 Fax: (905) 466-7284	xswayte@dundas.reccentre.ca www.dundas.reccentre.ca	2/10, n/30 GP	$12 000
Hamilton District Bd of Education (Nott Skinny)	10 James St. S. Hamilton, ON L8K 4G2	Tel: (905) 461-5997 Fax: (905) 461-6936	nskinny@hdsb.ca www.hdsb.ca	2/10, n/30 GP	$12 000

Customer Name (Contact)	Address	Phone No. Fax No.	E-mail Web Site	Terms Tax Code	Credit Limit
Lockport Gymnasium (B. Phatt)	62 Sweats St. Niagara Falls, New York 14301 USA	Tel: (716) 399-1489 Fax: (716) 399-2735	phatt@lockportgym.com www.lockportgym.com Currency: USD	2/10, n/30 no tax	$12 000 ($12 000 USD)
*McMaster University (Outov Shape)	Kinesiology Dept. McMaster University Hamilton, ON L8V 3M9	Tel 1: (905) 529-3000 Tel 2: (905) 529-3198 Fax: (905) 529- 3477	oshape@mcmasteru.ca www.mcmasteru.ca	2/10, n/30 GP	$12 000
*Mohawk College (Phat Nomore)	Physical Education Dept. Mohawk College Hamilton, ON L8F 7F2	Tel 1: (905) 622-9250 Tel 2: (905) 622-9238 Fax: (905) 622-9729	nomore@mohawkcoll.ca www.mohawkcoll.ca	2/10, n/30 GP	$12 000
*Stelco Health Club (Les Pound)	1 Stelco Rd. Hamilton, ON L8P 6N6	Tel: (905) 524-1000 Fax: (905) 524-1924	pound@stelco.health.com www.stelco.health.com	2/10, n/30 GP	$12 000
Stoney Creek Sports Arena (B. Thin)	93 Workout Rd. Stoney Creek, ON L7M 5C7	Tel: (905) 838-1800 Fax: (905) 838-1278	bthin@scsa.com www.scsa.com	2/10, n/30 GP	$12 000
Cash and Interac Customers Visa Sales (for Visa customers)				net 1 net 1	GP GP

NOTES: Preferred price list customers are marked with an asterisk (*). The ship-to address is the same as the mailing address for all customers.

OUTSTANDING CUSTOMER INVOICES

FLABULESS FITNESS

Customer Name	Terms	Date	Inv/Chq No.	Amount	Total
Chedoke Health Care	2/10, n/30 (after tax)	Mar. 30/10 Mar. 30/10	2199 Chq 488 Balance Owing	$9 040 2 100	$6 940
Mohawk College	2/10, n/30 (after tax)	Mar. 26/10	2194	$5 650	$5 650
Stoney Creek Sports Arena	2/10, n/30 (after tax)	Mar. 23/10	2191	$4 520	$4 520
				Grand Total	$17 110

EMPLOYEE INFORMATION SHEET

FLABULESS FITNESS

Employee	George Schwinn	Nieve Prekor	Assumpta Kisangel
Position	Shipping/Trainer	Sales/Yoga Instructor	Sales/Accounting
Address	55 Carter St. Hamilton, ON L8B 2V7	2 Meditation Circle Hamilton, ON L8B 7C1	300 Track Rd. Hamilton, ON L9G 4K8
Telephone	(905) 426-1817	(905) 527-4412	(905) 688-5778
Social Insurance No.	532 548 625	783 455 611	488 655 333
Date of Birth (mm-dd-yy) Date of Hire (mm-dd-yy)	09/18/69 01/06/03	03/15/72 02/15/00	05/24/75 08/25/03
Federal (Ontario) Tax Exemption - TD1 Basic Personal Spousal Other Total Exemptions	$9 600 (8 681) – – $9 600 (8 681)	$9 600 (8 681) – – $9 600 (8 681)	$9 600 (8 681) $9 600 (7 371) $4 095 (4 092) $23 295 (20 144)
Additional Federal Tax	–	$50.00	–

Employee	George Schwinn	Nieve Prekor	Assumpta Kisangel
Employee Taxes			
Historical Income tax	$1 562.21	$2 392.08	$1 537.85
Historical EI	$217.54	$270.00	$248.96
Historical CPP	$375.20	$478.38	$438.16
Deduct EI; EI Factor	Yes; 1.4	Yes; 1.4	Yes; 1.4
Deduct CPP	Yes	Yes	Yes
Employee Income			
Advances: Historical Amount	$100.00	(use) ✓	(use) ✓
Benefits Per Period	$5.00	$12.00	$12.00
Benefits: Historical Amount	$35.00	$36.00	$36.00
Vacation Pay Owed	$371.84	(do not use)	(do not use)
Vacation Paid	$385.92	(do not use)	(do not use)
Regular Wage Rate (Hours per Period)	$16.00/hr (80 hours)	(do not use)	(do not use)
Regular Wages: Historical Amount	$8 960.00	(do not use)	(do not use)
Overtime 1 Wage Rate	$24.00/hr	(do not use)	(do not use)
Overtime 1 Wages: Historical Amount	$336.00	(do not use)	(do not use)
Salary (Hours Per Period)	(do not use)	$4 000.00 (150 Hours)	$3 600.00 (150 hours)
Salary: Historical Amount	(do not use)	$12 000.00	$10 800.00
Commission	(do not use)	(do not use)	(use) ✓ 2% (service revenue)
Commissions: Historical Amount	(do not use)	(do not use)	$285.00
No. Clients (piece rate)	$10	$10	$10
Bonus:	(use) ✓	(use) ✓	(use) ✓
Tuition: Historical Amount	(use) ✓	(use) ✓	$440
Travel Exp.: Historical Amount	(use) ✓	$120.00	(use) ✓
Pay Periods	26	12	12
Vacation Rate	6% retained	0% not retained	0% not retained
Record Wage Expenses in	Linked Accounts	Linked Accounts	Linked Accounts
Deductions			
RRSP (Historical Amount)	$50.00 ($350.00)	$100.00 ($300.00)	$100.00 ($300.00)
CSB Plan (Historical Amount)	$50.00 ($350.00)	$100.00 ($300.00)	$100.00 ($300.00)
Garnishee (Historical Amount)	(do not use)	$200.00 ($400.00)	(do not use)
WSIB and Other Expenses			
WSIB Rate	1.29	1.29	1.02
Group Insurance (Historical Amount)	$5.00 ($35.00)	$12.00 ($36.00)	$12.00 ($36.00)
Entitlements: Rate, Maximum Days, Clear? (Historical Amount)			
Vacation	–	8%, 25 days, No (15)	8%, 25 days, No (15)
Sick Leave	5%, 15 days, No (12)	5%, 15 days, No (10)	5%, 15 days, No (8)
Personal Days	2.5%, 5 days, No (4)	2.5%, 5 days, No (2)	2.5%, 5 days, No (3)
Direct Deposit			
Yes/No	Yes	Yes	Yes
Bank, Transit, Account No.	102, 89008, 2998187	102, 89008, 3829110	102, 89008, 2309982
Percent	100%	100%	100%
Additional Information			
Emergency Contact & Number	Adrian Ingles (905) 722-0301	Alex Prekor (905) 548-2973	Martha Kisangel (905) 688-5778
T4 and RL-1 Reporting			
EI Insurable Earnings	$9 681.92	$12 000.00	$11 085.00
Pensionable Earnings	$9 716.92	$12 036.00	$11 561.00
Withheld	$2 854.95	$4 140.46	$2 824.97
Net Pay	$6 926.97	$7 979.54	$8 700.03

Employee Profiles and TD1 Information

All Employees   Flabuless Fitness pays group insurance premiums for all employees. They also are reimbursed for tuition fees when they successfully complete a university or college course. These two benefits are taxable. In addition, when they use their personal vehicles for company business, they are reimbursed for car expenses.

All employees are entitled to three weeks' vacation, ten days' sick leave and five personal days of leave per year. All three employees have sick leave and personal days that they can carry forward from the previous year. The two salaried employees take three weeks' vacation as paid time and the hourly employee receives 6 percent of his wages as vacation pay when he takes his vacation.

Starting in April, as an incentive to provide excellent customer service, all employees will receive a quarterly bonus of $10 for every completed satisfactory customer survey.

George Schwinn   is responsible for shipping, receiving, delivery and equipment setup for customers. He also works as the personal trainer in the store. He is single, so he uses only the basic tax claim amount. Every two weeks his pay, at the rate of $16 per hour, is deposited to his account. For the hours beyond 40 hours in a week, he receives an overtime rate of $24 per hour. He is owed two months of vacation pay. He contributes to his RRSP and Canada Savings Bond plan through payroll deductions. He still owes $100 from an advance of $200 and will pay back $50 of the advance in each of the next two pay periods.

NOTES
Wages may be garnisheed by any creditor, but the most common one is the Receiver General to pay back-taxes owing.

Nieve Prekor   is the store manager and yoga instructor for Flabuless Fitness, and she assists with store sales. Her monthly salary of $4 000 is deposited directly into her bank account. Prekor is married with one child but uses the basic single claim amount because her husband is also employed. Her payroll deductions include additional federal income tax for other income, wages garnisheed to pay for prior taxes owing and regular contributions to her Registered Retirement Savings Plan and Canada Savings Bonds.

Assumpta Kisangel   does the accounting and manages the Payables, Receivables and Payroll in addition to sales in the store. Although she is single, she supports her infirm mother so she has the spousal equivalent claim and a caregiver amount in addition to the basic single claim amount. A commission of 2 percent of revenue from services supplements her monthly salary of $3 600 that is deposited directly into her bank account. She has RRSP and CSB contributions withheld from her paycheques.

INVENTORY INFORMATION

FLABULESS FITNESS

Code	Description	Min Stock	CAD Prices Reg	(Pref)	USD Prices Reg	(Pref)	Stock/Sell Unit	Buying Unit	Relationship	Qty on Hand	Total (Cost)
Accessories: Total asset value $15 270 (Linked Accounts: Asset 1520; Revenue 4020, COGS 5050, Variance 5070)											
A010	Body Fat Scale	2	$ 100	($ 90)	$ 100	($ 90)	unit	carton	12/carton	10	$ 400
A020	Yoga Mats	3	30	(27)	30	(27)	unit	box	10/box	40	480
A030	Dumbbells: pair	25	1.50	(1.40)	1.50	(1.40)	kg	100kg	100/100kg	400	300
A040	Dumbbells: 5kg set	5	15	(13)	15	(13)	set		same	25	150
A050	Dumbbells: 10kg set	5	25	(22)	25	(22)	set		same	25	250
A060	Dumbbells: 15kg set	5	40	(36)	40	(36)	set		same	25	400
A070	Glide Slidetrak	3	50	(45)	50	(45)	each		same	20	500
A080	Heart Rate Monitor	2	75	(68)	75	(68)	unit	carton	12/carton	10	300
A090	Power Blocks up to 100 kg	3	160	(144)	160	(144)	set		same	10	800
A100	Power Blocks up to 200 kg	3	300	(270)	300	(270)	set		same	10	1500

▶

Code	Description	Min Stock	CAD Prices Reg	(Pref)	USD Prices Reg.	(Pref)	Stock/Sell Unit	Buying Unit	Relationship	Qty on Hand	Total (Cost)
Accessories: Continued											
A110	Stability Balls	5	$ 10	($ 9)	$ 10	($ 9)	each		same	25	100
A120	Wavemaster	2	150	(135)	150	(135)	unit		same	10	750
A130	Weight Plates	25	1.20	(1.10)	1.20	(1.10)	kg	100kg	100/100kg	400	240
A140	Weights: Olympic 75 kg	5	150	(135)	150	(135)	set		same	20	1 500
A150	Weights: Olympic 100 kg	5	200	(180)	200	(180)	set		same	20	2 000
A160	Weights: Olympic 125 kg	5	250	(225)	250	(225)	set		same	20	$ 2 500
A170	Weights: Olympic 150 kg	5	300	(270)	300	(270)	set		same	20	3 000
A180	Workout Gloves: all sizes	5	10	(9)	10	(9)	pair	box	10/box	25	100

Fitness Equipment: Total asset value $78 616 (Linked Accounts: Asset 1540; Revenue 4020, COGS 5060, Variance 5070)

Code	Description	Min Stock	CAD Prices Reg	(Pref)	USD Prices Reg.	(Pref)	Stock/Sell Unit	Buying Unit	Relationship	Qty on Hand	Total (Cost)
Elliptical Exercisers											
E010	Elliptical Exerciser: ME-100	2	1 100	(1 000)	1 100	(1 000)	unit		same	5	2 200
E020	Elliptical Exerciser: AE-200	2	1 700	(1 550)	1 700	(1 550)	unit		same	5	3 400
E030	Elliptical Exerciser: DE-300	2	2 000	(1 875)	2 000	(1 875)	unit		same	5	4 000
E040	Elliptical Exerciser: LE-400	2	2 200	(2 000)	2 200	(2 000)	unit		same	5	4 400
Exercise Bicycles											
E050	Bicycle: Calorie Counter CC-60	2	400	(360)	400	(360)	unit		same	10	1 600
E060	Bicycle: Dual Action DA-70	2	600	(540)	600	(540)	unit		same	10	2 400
E070	Bicycle: Recumbent R-80	2	750	(680)	750	(680)	unit		same	10	3 000
Exercise Equipment: Home Gyms											
E080	Home Gym: Basic HG-1400	2	1 000	(900)	1 000	(900)	set		same	5	$2 000
E090	Home Gym: Deluxe HG-1401	2	1 500	(1 400)	1 500	(1 400)	set		same	5	3 000
E100	Home Gym: Multi HG-1402	2	2 000	(1 875)	2 000	(1 875)	set		same	5	4 000
Riders, Walkers and Rowing Machines											
E110	Rider: Airwalker RA-900	3	300	(270)	300	(270)	unit		same	8	960
E120	Rider: Powerglider RP-1500	3	350	(315)	350	(315)	unit		same	8	1 120
E130	Rowing Machine: RM-1000	3	480	(435)	480	(435)	unit		same	8	1 536
Ski Exercisers											
E140	Ski Exerciser: Skitrek SE-680	3	400	(360)	400	(360)	unit		same	10	1 600
E150	Ski Exerciser: Linked SE-780	3	450	(410)	450	(410)	unit		same	10	1 800
E160	Ski Exerciser: Independent SE-880	3	600	(550)	600	(550)	unit		same	10	2 400
Stair Climbers											
E170	Stair Climber: Adjustable SC-A60	2	1 500	(1 375)	1 500	(1 375)	unit		same	5	3 000
E180	Stair Climber: Unlinked SC-U75	2	2 100	(1 925)	2 100	(1 925)	unit		same	5	4 200
Treadmills											
E190	Treadmill: Basic T-800B	3	1 200	(1 100)	1 200	(1 100)	unit		same	10	4 800
E200	Treadmill: Basic Plus T-910P	3	1 600	(1 450)	1 600	(1 450)	unit		same	10	6 400
E210	Treadmill: Deluxe T-1100D	3	2 400	(2 200)	2 400	(2 200)	unit		same	10	9 600
E220	Treadmill: Deluxe Plus T-1200P	3	2 800	(2 600)	2 800	(2 600)	unit		same	10	11 200
Services (Linked Accounts: Revenue 4040, COGS 5065)											
S010	Personal Trainer: 1 hour		75	(70)			hour		PST Tax Exempt		
S020	Personal Trainer: 1/2 day		200	(190)			1/2 day		PST Tax Exempt		
S030	Personal Trainer: full day		400	(380)			day		PST Tax Exempt		
S040	Yoga Instructor: 1 hour		100	(95)			hour		PST Tax Exempt		
S050	Yoga Instructor: 1/2 day		200	(190)			1/2 day		PST Tax Exempt		

NOTES: No duty is charged on items imported from the United States. The duty rate is 0%.
Stocking and selling units are the same for all items.
Buying units and the relationship to stocking units are entered only when these are different from the stocking/selling units.
"Same" is entered in the relationship column when the same unit is used for all measures.

Accounting Procedures

The Goods and Services Tax (GST)

GST at the rate of 5 percent is applied to all goods and services offered by Flabuless Fitness. Flabuless Fitness uses the regular method for remittance of the Goods and Services Tax. GST collected from customers is recorded as a liability in *GST Charged on Sales*. GST paid to suppliers is recorded in *GST Paid on Purchases* as a decrease in liability to Canada Revenue Agency (CRA). These two postable accounts are added together in the subgroup total account *GST Owing (Refund)*. The balance of GST to be remitted or the request for a refund is sent to the Receiver General for Canada by the last day of the current month for the previous month.

Tax calculations will be correct only for customers and suppliers for whom the tax exempt option was set as No. The GST Report available from the Reports menu will include transactions completed in the Sales, Purchases and General journals, but the opening historical balances will not be included. Therefore, the amounts shown in the GST Report may differ from the balances in the General Ledger GST accounts. You should use the General Ledger accounts to verify the balance owing (or refund due) and make adjustments to the report manually as necessary.

After the report is filed, clear the GST Report (choose the Maintenance menu, then Clear Data and click Clear Tax Report and select GST). Enter the last day of the previous month as the date for clearing. Always back up your files before clearing the GST Report.

Provincial Sales Tax (PST)

Provincial sales tax of 8 percent is applied to the sales of all goods but not services provided by Flabuless Fitness. It is applied to the amount of the sale without GST included and is not applied to freight. The PST collected must be remitted monthly to the Minister of Finance. Provincial sales taxes to be remitted must be set up as a liability owing to the supplier, Minister of Finance, in the Purchases Journal. The General Ledger balance for *PST Payable* for the last day of the previous month will provide the total owing. You may display or print this account for reference. A 5 percent sales tax compensation is earned if the remittance is made before the due date assigned to the business.

Business Income Tax

Flabuless Fitness pays income tax in quarterly instalments to the Receiver General based on its previous year's net income.

The Employer Health Tax (EHT)

The Employer Health Tax (EHT) is paid by employers in Ontario to provide Ontario Health Insurance Plan (OHIP) coverage for all eligible Ontario residents. The EHT is based on the total annual remuneration paid to employees. Employers whose total payroll exceeds $400 000 must pay EHT. Although the payroll for Flabuless Fitness is less than this amount, we show the application of EHT so that you can learn how to set up the expense and make the remittances. In this application, EHT will be remitted quarterly. *EHT Payable* is set up as a liability owing to the supplier, Minister of Finance. The Remittance Payments Journal will provide you with the balance owing to the Minister of Finance when the liability is linked to this supplier.

SIMPLY VERSION

The term Vendors replaces Suppliers throughout the program.

Aging of Accounts

Flabuless Fitness uses aging periods that reflect the payment terms it provides to customers and receives from suppliers. For customers, this will be 10, 30 and 60 days, and for suppliers, 15, 30 and 60 days. Interest at 1.5 percent is charged on customer accounts that are not paid within 30 days. Regular customer statements show interest amounts, and invoices are then prepared to add the interest to the amount owing in the ledger record.

Discounts

Flabuless Fitness offers a 2 percent discount to regular account customers if they settle their accounts within 10 days. Full payment is requested within 30 days. These payment terms are set up as defaults. When the receipt is entered and the discount is still available, the program shows the amount of the discount and the net amount owing. No discounts are given on cash or credit card sales. Customer discounts are calculated on after-tax amounts.

Some customers receive preferred customer prices, approximately 10 percent below the regular prices. These customers are identified in the ledger records and the preferred prices are set up in the inventory ledger records.

Some suppliers also offer discounts for early settlement of accounts. Again, when the terms are entered for the supplier and payment is made before the discount period expires, the program displays the discount as available and automatically calculates a net balance owing. Payment terms vary from supplier to supplier. Most supplier discounts are calculated on before-tax amounts but some are based on after-tax amounts.

Freight

When a business purchases inventory items, the cost of any freight that cannot be directly allocated to a specific item must be charged to *Freight Expense*. This amount will be regarded as a general expense rather than being charged to the costs of any inventory asset account. Customers also pay for delivery and setup. GST is charged on freight for both sales and purchases but there is no PST on freight. The tax code for all freight charges is code G.

Bank Deposits

Deposit slips are prepared weekly when cash and cheques are received. Receipts are debited to *Undeposited Cash and Cheques* and transferred weekly to *Bank: Hamilton Trust Chequing*.

Imported Inventory

Some inventory items are imported from the United States. The bank accounts, supplier records and inventory records are modified to accommodate the foreign currency transactions and import duties automatically.

Purchase Returns and Allowances

A business will sometimes return inventory items to suppliers because of damage, poor quality or shipment of the wrong items. Usually a business records these returns after it receives a credit note from a supplier. The return of inventory is entered in the Purchases Journal as an inventory purchase:

- Select the item in the Item field and enter the quantity returned as a **negative** amount in the Quantity field. The program will automatically calculate a negative amount as a default in the Amount field. You cannot change the account number.
- Accept the default amount and enter other items returned to the supplier.

NOTES
Daily Business Manager lists are helpful for making sure that you take advantage of available discounts.

NOTES
Although import duties are not charged on the items imported by Flabuless Fitness from the United States, we show the setup of import duties and set the rates at zero so that no tax will be charged.

- Enter the appropriate tax code for each item returned.

The program will create a negative invoice to reduce the balance owing to the supplier and will reduce the applicable inventory asset accounts, the freight accounts, *GST Paid on Purchases* and the quantity of items in the Inventory Ledger database.

Purchase allowances for damaged merchandise that is not returned are entered as non-inventory negative purchase invoices. Enter the amount of the allowance as a **negative** amount in the Amount field and leave the tax fields blank (i.e., treat it as non-taxable). Enter *Purchases Returns and Allowances* in the Account field.

Sales Returns and Allowances

NOTES

The sales tax rules for credits, allowances and discounts are complex. They may be different for provincial and federal taxes and they may differ from one province to another. Adjusting General Journal entries may be required to adjust the amount of tax owing and calculate the tax remittance. We have chosen to leave out the tax component for transactions of this type. Refer to Chapter 2 for more information about sales taxes.

Sometimes customers will return inventory items. Usually, a business records the return after it has issued a credit note. The return is entered in the Sales Journal as a negative inventory sale for the customer:

- Select the appropriate item in the Item field.
- Enter the quantity returned with a **negative** number in the Quantity field.
- The price of the item appears as a positive number in the Price field, and the Amount field is calculated automatically as a negative amount that should be correct. If it is not, you can change it.
- Enter the tax code for the sale and the account number for *Sales Returns & Allowances*.

The program will create a negative invoice to reduce the balance owing by the customer, and *Cost of Goods Sold*, *GST Charged on Sales* and *PST Payable*. The applicable inventory asset accounts and the quantity of items in the Inventory Ledger database will be increased.

Sales allowances are entered as non-taxable, non-inventory negative sales invoices, creating a debit entry for *Sales Returns & Allowances* and a credit for *Accounts Receivable*. If the allowance is paid by cheque, enter the allowance in the Payments Journal as an Other Payment paid by cheque.

NSF Cheques

NOTES

The Sales Journal entry will credit the bank account and debit Accounts Receivable.

If a cheque is deposited from an account that does not have enough money to cover it, the bank returns it to the depositor as NSF (non-sufficient funds). If the cheque was in payment for a cash sale, you must process the NSF cheque through the Sales Journal because there was no Receipts Journal entry. Create a customer record if necessary and enter a positive amount for the amount of the cheque. Choose *Bank: Hamilton Trust Chequing* as the account. Choose Pay Later as the method of payment. If the customer is expected to pay the bank charges, enter these on the second invoice line as a positive amount and select the appropriate revenue account.

If the NSF cheque was deposited to a different account than the one used in the Receipts Journal, create a negative receipt to reverse the cheque. Choose Include Fully Paid Invoices. Click the invoice line that this cheque was applied to. Enter the discount taken as a negative amount. Enter the Payment Amount as a negative amount. Choose the correct Bank Account from the Deposit To field.

Adjustments for Bad Debt

NOTES

Allowance for Doubtful Accounts is a contra-asset account that normally has a credit balance. Therefore, a debit entry will reduce this credit balance.

Most businesses set up an allowance for doubtful accounts or bad debts, knowing that some customers will fail to pay. When the allowance is set up, a bad debts or uncollectable accounts expense account is debited. When a business is certain that a customer will not pay its account, the debt should be written off by crediting *Accounts Receivable* and debiting *Allowance for Doubtful Accounts*. When taxes apply, an extra step is required. Part of the original sales invoice was entered as a credit (increase) to *GST Charged on Sales* and to *PST Payable*. By entering the full amount and the tax code for taxes included, the GST and PST payable amounts will automatically be reduced. In Simply Accounting, record the write-off of the debt in the Sales Journal using the following steps:

- Select the customer whose debt will not be paid.
- Enter a source document number to identify the transaction (e.g., memo).
- Enter a **negative** amount for the total unpaid invoice in the Amount field.
- Enter *Allowance for Doubtful Accounts* in the Account field.
- Enter the tax code **IN** (taxes included).

If the customer was also charged for the NSF fees, enter this information on the next invoice line:

- Enter a **negative** amount for the total NSF charge in the Amount field.
- Enter *Allowance for Doubtful Accounts* in the Account field.
- Enter the tax code **No tax**.

Review the transaction. *Accounts Receivable* is credited (reduced) by the full amount of the invoice to remove the balance owing by this customer. *Allowance for Doubtful Accounts* has been debited (reduced) by the amount of the invoice minus taxes. *GST Charged on Sales* and *PST Payable* have been debited for the tax portion of the invoice to reduce the tax liabilities.

After recording the write-off, "pay" both the original invoice and the write-off in the Receipts Journal. The balance will be zero and there will be no journal entry. This step removes the items from the Receipts Journal for the customer so that you can clear the paid transactions and later remove the customer's record.

Manually you would complete the entry as follows:

---

1. Set up the Allowance for Bad Debts.

Date	Particulars	Debit	Credit
xx/xx	Uncollectable Accounts Expense	1 000.00	
	Allowance for Doubtful Accounts		1 000.00

2. Customer G. Bell declares bankruptcy. Write off outstanding balance, $226, including GST and PST.

Date	Particulars	Debit	Credit
xx/xx	Allowance for Doubtful Accounts	200.00	
	GST Charged on Sales	10.00	
	PST Payable	16.00	
	Accounts Receivable, G. Bell		226.00

Occasionally, a bad debt is recovered after it has been written off. When this occurs, the above procedure is reversed and the GST and PST liabilities must also be restored. The recovery is entered as a non-inventory sale in the Sales Journal using the following steps:

- Select the customer and enter the date and source document number.
- Type an appropriate comment such as "Debt recovered" as the Description.
- Enter a **positive** amount for the total invoice amount in the Amount field.
- Enter the tax code **IN** (taxes included).
- Enter *Allowance for Doubtful Accounts* in the Account field.

Review the transaction. You will see that *Accounts Receivable* has been debited for the full amount of the invoice. *Allowance for Doubtful Accounts* has been credited for the amount of the invoice minus taxes. *GST Charged on Sales* and *PST Payable* have been credited for the tax portion of the invoice to restore the tax liabilities.

As the final step, record the customer's payment in the Receipts Journal as you would record any other customer payment.

NOTES

In practice, a business would make these four federal tax remittances to different federal offices and the two provincial remittances to different provincial tax offices. Separate supplier accounts would be needed for each remittance. For this application, one supplier account and address has been used for the Receiver General and one for the Minister of Finance to reduce the length of the supplier list.

Remittances

The Receiver General for Canada:
- Monthly EI, CPP and income tax deductions withheld from employees must be paid by the 15th of each month for the previous month.
- Monthly GST owing or requests for refunds must be filed by the end of each month for the previous month.
- Business income tax is paid in quarterly instalments.
- Garnisheed wages are submitted by the 15th of each month for the previous month. A separate cheque is issued for this remittance.

The Minister of Finance:
- Quarterly Employer Health Tax (EHT) deductions must be paid by the 15th of April, July, October and January for the previous quarter.
- Monthly Provincial Sales Taxes (PST) on revenue from sales must be paid by the 23rd of the month for the previous month. A 5 percent sales tax compensation is earned for prompt payment of PST.

Ancaster Insurance:
- Monthly Registered Retirement Savings Plan (RRSP) deductions withheld from employees must be paid by the 15th of the month for the previous month.
- Group insurance contributions paid by the employer must be paid by the 15th of the month for the previous month.

The Mt. Hope Investment Corporation:
- Monthly Canada Savings Bond Plan (CSB Plan) deductions withheld from employees must be paid by the 15th of the month for the previous month.

The Workplace Safety and Insurance Board:
- Quarterly Workplace Safety and Insurance Board (WSIB) assessment for employees must be paid by the 15th of the month for the previous quarter.

SPECIAL DATA FILES FOR FLABULESS FITNESS

Detailed keystroke instructions are included for you to set up the Flabuless Fitness application files. However, the Student CD-ROM also includes files so that you can complete segments of the application rather than having to work through it entirely. Each file stands alone so you can work through any month at your discretion.

To Enter	For (Period Covered)	Use (Backup File Name on Data CD)
Transactions:	April 1–April 30	setup\flab-apr1.cab
Transactions:	May 1–May 31	setup\flab-may1.cab
Transactions:	June 1–June 30	setup\flab-jun1.cab

INSTRUCTIONS FOR SETUP

Set up the **company accounts** in Simply Accounting using the Business Information, Chart of Accounts, Balance Sheet, Income Statement, Post-Closing Trial Balance and Supplier, Customer, Employee and Inventory Information provided above for March 31, 2010. Instructions to assist you in setting up the company accounts follow. The setup of the Inventory Ledger is given in detail. Abbreviated instructions are included for the remaining steps. Refer to the Toss for Tots (Chapter 4), Dorfmann Design (Chapter 7) and Lime Light Laundry (Chapter 9) applications if you need more detailed explanations for other ledgers. Page references for individual topics are included in this chapter.

KEYSTROKES FOR SETUP

Creating Company Files

We will create the company files from scratch. Once we create the files and define the defaults, we will add the accounts, define linked accounts for all ledgers, set up additional features, create supplier, customer, employee and inventory records and add historical data.

> Save your work and update your backup file frequently as you work through the setup.

Start   the **Simply Accounting program**. You should see the Select Company window.

Click   **Create A New Company**.

Click   **OK**. You will see the Setup wizard welcome screen.

Click   **Next** to open the Company Name and Address screen. The cursor is in the Name field.

Type   Flabuless Fitness (and your own name)   **Press** (tab) to advance to the Street 1 address field.

Type   199 Warmup Rd. **Press** (tab).

Type   Unit 500 **Press** (tab).

Type   Hamilton **Press** (tab).

Type   o to enter the province code (ON) and province (Ontario).

Click   the Postal Code field.

Type   l8t3b7 **Press** (tab).

Type   Canada **Press** (tab).

Type   9056422348 **Press** (tab) to enter the first phone number.

Type   8004482348 **Press** (tab) to enter the second phone number.

Type   9056429100 to enter the fax number.

Click   **Next** to open the company Dates window.

The cursor is in the Fiscal Year Start field, the date on which the business begins its fiscal year. Flabuless Fitness closes its books quarterly and is beginning a new quarter in April. To be certain that you have the correct year, type the date in text style using four digits for the year. Until we change the date format, they are displayed in the short form.

Enter   the **fiscal dates** as follows:

- Fiscal Start: April 1, 2010
- Earliest Transaction date: April 1, 2010
- Fiscal End: June 30, 2010

Remember that you can edit the company information and fiscal dates later from the Setup menu, Settings option (choose Company and Information). If you later change the province, you may have to change some settings linked to the province selection.

Click   **Next**.

NOTES
Refer to page 206 for detailed instructions on creating company files.

NOTES
You cannot complete the company setup in multi-user mode. Many of the settings options are dimmed and unavailable when you are working in multi-user mode.

NOTES
Add your own name to the company name to personalize your data files.

NOTES
Because we select Ontario as the province, some defaults will be added to the data file. WCB will be renamed WSIB.

NOTES
The default date format for new companies is determined by your own computer system settings. This may be day, month year or month, day year. Entering the date as text will result in correct fiscal dates.

Click   **Let Me Build The List Of Accounts Myself…. Click** Next.

Click   **Yes** to confirm your selection and continue to the industry type list.

Choose **Retail** as the Industry for the business. **Click Next**.

Type   `flabless` to replace the default entry for the file name.

Drag through **Tess** in the folder name field (or the folder you last worked with).

Type   `Flabless\`

If you are using an alternative location for your company files, substitute the appropriate path, folder or drive in the example.

Click Browse to locate the folder you want or type the complete path in the File Location field (e.g., Type c:\SimData\Flabless\).

Click   **Next**.

Click   **Yes** to confirm that you are creating a new folder.

Click   **Finish** to save the information. **Be patient**, wait for Simply Accounting to finish creating the data files.

Click   **Close** to advance to the Receivables Home window.

The Home window has the name Flabless in the title bar and non-accounting term labels for the modules in the Modules pane list. The program will automatically set up defaults based on the information you have just entered.

Preparing the System

The next step involves changing the defaults. Change the defaults to suit your own work environment, such as selecting your printer or choosing forms for cheques, invoices or statements. The keystroke instructions are given for computer-generated cheques, invoices and statements. Refer to the Business Information Chart on page 617 for the company default settings.

Changing the User Preference Settings

You should make the following changes to the User Preferences from the Setup menu. Refer to Chapter 4, page 78, for assistance if necessary.

Choose   the **Setup menu** and **click User Preferences** to open the Options screen.

Click   **Use Accounting Terms**.

Click   **Automatically Save Changes To Supplier…**.

Click   **View**.

Click   **After Changing Session Date** for **Daily Business Manager** and for **Checklists** to turn off these features and remove the ✓'s.

Click   **Show Change Session Date At Startup**.

The remaining settings you need, including Transaction Confirmation, are already selected. You can hide Division and Time & Billing. You do not need to hide them to finish the history because they have no linked accounts.

Click   **Division** in the **Pages column** to hide the module.

NOTES

You can select another folder by clicking Browse to open the folder path screen and then clicking the folder you want to use. Click OK to return to the File Name screen.

If the folder you want does not yet exist, click the folder you want to place the new folder in and click OK. Type Flabless\ at the end of the path in the Location field.

NOTES

Use the Backup feature frequently while setting up your files to update your backup copy.

You will save your work by finishing your session properly. You may finish your session at any time while completing the setup. Simply open the data file, accept the session date and continue from where you left off.

Simply **SIMPLY VERSION**

You will see the term Project instead of Division, and you will not see the Time & Billing feature.

Click   **Time & Billing** in the **Features column** to hide the module.

Click   **OK** to save the settings and return to the Home window.

Notice that modules now have accounting term names after changing these settings. The user preference settings can be modified at any time by repeating these steps.

Changing Company Defaults

Correcting Company Information

The first steps in setting up the company data files apply to the Company module. We will work from that window.

> Click OK at any time to save the settings and close the Settings window. To continue later, you can use the Settings icon to access Settings.

Click   **Company** in the Modules pane list to change the Home window.

Click   the **Settings icon** , or **choose** the **Setup menu** and **click Settings**.

Click   **Information**.

Click   the **Business No. field**. **Type** `245 138 121 RT0001`

Changing System Settings

Click   **System**. Use the following System settings:

- Use Cheque No. As The Source Code For Cash Purchases And Sales
- Do Not Allow Transactions Dated Before April 1, 2010
- Allow Transactions In The Future (Beyond The Session Date)
- Warn If Transactions Are More Than 7 Days In The Future
- Warn If Accounts Are Not Balanced When Entering A New Month

Changing Backup Settings

Click   **Backup**. Use the following Backup settings:

- Semi-monthly Backup Frequency
- Display a Backup Reminder When Closing This Company

Click   **Automatically Back Up This File** to remove the ✓. We do not want to schedule automatic backups for instructional files.

Changing Features Settings

Flabuless uses all features of the program except Divisions — orders, quotes and language options should be selected. Division and Packing Slips may be left unselected.

Click   **Features**.

Click   **each feature** to change its setting.

Changing Default Settings for Forms

Click   **Forms** to display the defaults.

Use the Forms options to set up the automatic numbering and printing of all cheques and invoices. They apply only to numerical invoices.

If you want to use automatic invoice numbering, type the next number from the source documents so the automatic numbering system can take over from the manual system. Using automatic numbering reduces the risk of typing and recording an incorrect invoice or cheque number even when you are not printing cheques and invoices through the program. For Flabuless Fitness, the next invoice is #3000.

Click   1 in the **Invoices Number field**.

Type   3000

Click   the **Sales Quotes Number field**. **Type**   41

Click   the **Receipts Number field**. **Type**   39

Click   the **Customer Deposits Number field**. **Type**   15

Click   the **Purchase Orders Number field**. **Type**   25

Click   the **Direct Deposit Stubs Number field**. **Type**   19

Leave selected the option to verify number sequences for all forms so that the program will warn you if you skip or duplicate a number.

Click a check box to add other features or to turn off an option once it is selected. The ✓ in the appropriate boxes indicates a feature is being used.

The option to Confirm Printing/E-mail will warn you to print before posting a transaction. When printing invoices, statements or cheques, you should include the company address, unless it is already printed on your forms.

If you print or e-mail invoices and cheques through the computer, you should turn on the option to Confirm Printing/E-mail.

We want to allow batch printing, printing several forms at once after posting, instead of one at a time while entering a transaction.

Click   the **Print In Batches check box** for each form to add a ✓ to each box.

We should also check for duplicate numbers. This control is not selected by default.

Click   the **Check For Duplicates check box for Invoices and Receipts**.

Changing Date Format Settings

Click   **Date Format**.

We want to use the long date form for all dates on the screen to verify that we are entering dates correctly. For the reports, you may use either the long or short form. MM (month) should be the first entry in the Short Date Format field.

Click   **Long Dates** as the setting for On The Screen, Use.

Adding the Company Logo

Click   **Logo**.

Click   **Browse**. **Click** the **Look In field drop-down list arrow**.

Click   **C:**.

Double click **SimData** to open this folder

Double click the **Setup folder** and **double click** the **Logos folder**.

Double click **Flab.bmp** to enter this file name. The logo should be added to the Logos Settings screen.

NOTES

Many invoices include the alpha or letter portion of the invoice number on the preprinted invoice form. You could then enter the next number from the numeric portion in the Invoices Number field. Alphanumeric invoice numbers, such as FF-399, cannot be increased automatically by the computer.

NOTES

If you hide Time & Billing, the next number for time slips will not be included on the Forms screen. You can leave the field blank if you are not hiding the feature.

WARNING!

Check that the short date format begins with month (MM).

NOTES

The Forms folder under your Simply Accounting Program folder is the default location when you click Browse.

Changing Default Names

Flabuless uses the additional information fields in journals. You can label these fields. However, you must use the same names for all journals. We will therefore enter a generic label for the Additional Information Field.

> **Click** **Names**:

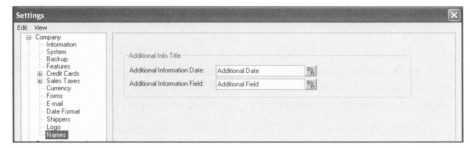

> **Drag through** **Additional Field**.
>
> **Type** Ref. Number
>
> **Click** **OK** to save the new information and return to the Home window.

Many of the other settings require linked accounts. Therefore, we will create all the General Ledger accounts before entering the remaining settings.

Preparing the General Ledger

This stage in setting up an accounting system involves preparing the General Ledger for operation. This stage involves

1. organizing all accounting reports and records (this step has been completed)
2. creating new accounts and adding opening balances
3. printing reports to check the accuracy of your records

Creating New Accounts

The next step is to create the accounts, including the non-postable accounts. Remember to enter the correct type of account. For postable accounts you should also indicate whether you want to omit accounts with zero balances from financial statements. You need to refer to the company Chart of Accounts on page 618 to complete this step. When we create the accounts, we will keep the Accounts window open in the background for reference.

Current Earnings is the only predefined account, and you do not need to edit it.

> Refer to Format of Financial Statements (page 83) for a review of these topics if needed. Refer to the instructions in the Toss for Tots application, page 90, if you need help with creating accounts.
>
> **Click** the **Chart of Accounts icon** to open the Accounts window.
>
> Maximize the Accounts window.
>
> If the accounts are not displayed by name or by type, you should change the view. Click the Display By Type tool or choose the View menu and click Type.
>
> **Click** the **Create tool** in the Accounts window tool bar or **choose** the **File menu** and **click Create**.

NOTES
Remember that you can finish your session any time. To continue, just open the file, accept the session date and start again from where you left off.

NOTES
Maximizing the Accounts window allows you to see the list of accounts as well as the new ones you are creating.

NOTES
You can also press *ctrl* + N to open a New Account ledger window and create a new account.

Drag the Ledger window so that both the Accounts window and Ledger window are visible. This will make it easier to monitor your progress.

Type   the **account number**. **Press** (tab) and **type** the **account name**.

Click   the correct **account type**. Remember subgroup accounts (A) must be followed by a subgroup total (S).

Click   **Omit From Financial Statements If Balance Is Zero** to select this option.

Allow Division Allocations will be selected by default for all postable revenue and expense accounts, so you do not need to change this option, even if you use divisions. You will enter the account balances in the next stage.
When all the information is correct, you must save your account.

Click   **Create Another** [🗐 Create Another] to save the new account and advance to a blank ledger account window.

Create   the **other accounts** by repeating these procedures.

Close   the **General Ledger window** when you have entered all the accounts on page 618, or when you want to end your session.

After entering all the accounts, you should check for mistakes in account number, name, type and order.

Display or **print** your updated **Chart of Accounts** at this stage to check for accuracy of account names and numbers. **Choose** the **Reports menu** and **click Chart of Accounts.**

Click   [✓] or **choose** the **File menu** and **click Check The Validity Of Accounts** to check for errors in account sequence such as missing subgroup totals, headings or totals. The first error is reported.

Correct   the **error** and **check** the **validity** again. Repeat this step until the accounts are in logical order.

Entering Historical Account Balances

The opening historical balances for Flabuless Fitness can be found in the Post-Closing Trial Balance dated March 31, 2010 (page 620). All Income Statement accounts have zero balances because the books were closed at the end of the first quarter. Headings, totals and subgroup totals (i.e., the non-postable accounts) do not have balances. Remember to put any forced balance amounts into the *Test Balance Account*.

Open   the account information window for **1060 Bank: Hamilton Trust Chequing**, the first account requiring a balance.

Click   the **Opening Balance field**.

Type   the **balance**.

Correct the **information** if necessary by repeating the above steps.

Click   the **Next button** [▶] to advance to the next ledger account window.

Enter   **negative numbers for accounts that decrease the total** in a group or section (e.g., *Allowance for Doubtful Accounts*, *Accum Deprec*, *GST Paid on Purchases*). These account balances are indicated with a minus sign (–) in the Balance Sheet on page 619.

NOTES
We will change the account class for expense accounts when we change the class for other accounts that are used as linked accounts.

WARNING!
It is important to have the accounts in logical order at this stage. You will be unable to display some reports when the accounts are not in logical order, so you will not be able to check some of your work. You cannot finish the history if accounts are not in logical order.

NOTES
For account 1140 Bank: USD Chequing, enter $9 500, the balance in Canadian dollars. The USD balance will be added after we set up currencies.

Repeat   these **procedures** to **enter** the **balances** for the remaining accounts in the Post-Closing Trial Balance on page 620. *Test Balance Account* should have a zero balance.

Close   the **Ledger window**.

After entering all account balances, you should display the Trial Balance to check the account balances. You can do this from the Accounts window.

Choose   the **Reports menu** and **click Trial Balance. Click** the **Print tool.**

Close   the **display** when finished. Leave the Accounts window open.

Check   all **accounts** and **amounts** and **make corrections** if necessary.

Defining Account Classes

Defining bank accounts involves changing the account class to Bank and indicating the currency for the accounts and the cheque and deposit number sequences. If you use online banking, you must also enter the bank name, account numbers and Web site. We must also change the class for *Undeposited Cash and Cheques* to either Bank or Cash to use it as the linked account for receipts. Cash is the appropriate selection. Remember that the bank account class changes must be saved before we can enter the next cheque numbers. Changes are saved automatically when we open the next ledger record.

We must also define the account class for the credit card asset and the credit card payable accounts. We will make all these changes before continuing the setup.

Double click   **1030 Undeposited Cash and Cheques** to open the ledger.

Click   the **Class Options tab**.

Choose   **Cash** from the drop-down list of account classes.

Click   the **Next Account button** ▶ to open the ledger for account **1060**.

Choose   **Bank** from the list of account classes.

Click   the **Next Deposit Number field**.

Type   14

Click   the **Next Account button** ▶.

Choose   **Bank** as the account class for *1080 Bank: Hamilton Trust Savings*.

Click   **Chequing** (Account Type field). **Click Savings** from the list.

Click   the **Next Account button** ▶ to **open** the ledger for **1120 Bank: Visa and Interac**.

Choose   **Bank** as the account class. This will allow us to use the account both for credit cards and bank transfers.

Click   the **Next Account button** ▶ to **open** the ledger for **1140 Bank: USD Chequing**.

Choose   **Bank** as the account class.

Click   the **Select Account list arrow**.

Click   **2250 Credit Card Payable** to open its ledger screen at the Class Options tab screen.

Choose   **Credit Card Payable** as the account class. Notice that Credit Card Receivable is not available as a class option for the liability account.

NOTES
Refer to the chart on page 617 for bank information and to page 218 for review of Bank class accounts.

NOTES
We must define 1030 Undeposited Cash and Cheques as a Bank or Cash class account in order to enter it as the linked bank account for Receivables. Cash is the most appropriate selection.
    Both Bank and Cash class accounts are available in the Deposit To field for cash sales and receipts.
    Both Bank and Credit Card Receivable class accounts can be selected as credit card asset accounts. Choosing Bank allows us to access the account in the Transfer Funds Journal.

NOTES
To open the ledger for Credit Card Payable, you can click the Next Account button repeatedly or choose the account from the Select Account list arrow.

NOTES
Remember that you can finish your session at any time. To continue, just open the file, accept the session date and start again from where you left off.

NOTES
Refer to the Business Information Chart on page 617 for credit card details. To review credit card setup, refer to page 220 for additional information.

NOTES
You must choose a Credit Card Payable or Bank class account as the Payable Account for cards used.

WARNING!
Although accounts in other classes appear on the Select Account list, selecting them will generate an error message when you save the entries.

NOTES
You must choose a Credit Card Receivable or Bank class account as the Asset Account for cards accepted.

NOTES
Refer to the Business Information Chart on page 617 for sales tax information. Refer to page 223 for a review of sales taxes.

Click the **Select Account list arrow** again and **choose 5010 Advertising and Promotion**.

Select **Operating Expense** or **Expense** as the account class.

Click the **Next Account button** ▶. **Select Operating Expense** or **Expense** as the account class for the remaining postable expense accounts.

Close the **General Ledger window** and the **Accounts window**.

Entering Company Default Settings

Setting Up Credit Cards

Flabuless Fitness accepts Visa credit card payments from customers as well as debit cards (Interac). The store also uses a Visa card to pay for some purchases. Setting up credit cards includes naming them, identifying the linked accounts and entering fees associated with the cards. You should be in the Company module Home window.

Click the **Settings icon** 🛠 and **click Credit Cards** under Company. Click Company first if necessary.

Click **Used** to open the Credit Card Information screen for the cards that the business uses.

Click the **Credit Card Name field**.

Type Visa **Press** (tab) to move to the Payable Account field.

Press (enter) to see the list of available accounts.

Double click **2250** to add the account and move to the Expense Account field.

Press (enter) to see the account list.

Double click **5030**.

Click **Accepted** to open the Credit Card Information screen for the cards that the business accepts from customers.

Click the **Credit Card Name field**.

Type Visa **Press** (tab) to advance to the Discount Fee % field.

Type 2.5 **Press** (tab) to advance to the Expense Account field.

Press (enter) to see the list of accounts available for linking.

Double click **5030** to choose and enter the account. The cursor advances to the Asset Account field.

Press (enter) to see the list of accounts available for linking.

Double click **1120** to choose and add the credit card bank account.

Enter **Interac** as the name, **0** as the %, **5030** as the Expense account and **1120** as the Asset account to set up the debit card.

Setting Up Sales Taxes

Flabuless Fitness charges and pays GST and PST, so we need to set up default codes for these two taxes. We want to generate reports on both taxes.

Click   **Sales Taxes** under Company. There are settings for tax names and codes.

Click   **Taxes** to access the Sales Tax Information screen:

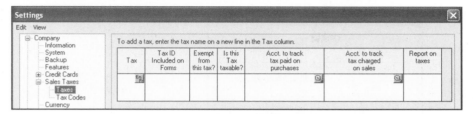

The cursor is in the Tax field on the Taxes screen where you should enter the name of the tax. We will enter the information for GST first.

Type   GST **Press** (tab) to advance to the Tax ID field where we enter the business number.

Type   245 138 121 **Press** (tab) to advance to the **Exempt From This Tax?** column.

Flabuless Fitness is not tax exempt for GST, so the default, No, is correct. GST is not taxable in Ontario (no other tax is charged on GST as it is in PEI and Quebec).

Click   🔍, the **List icon for Acct To Track Tax Paid On Purchases**.

Choose   **2670 GST Paid on Purchases**. The cursor advances to the field for the Account To Track Taxes Charged On Sales.

Choose   **2650 GST Charged on Sales** from the List icon 🔍 list of accounts. The cursor advances to the Report On Taxes field.

Click   **No** to change the default entry to Yes.

Press   (tab) so you can enter the information for PST.

Type   PST

Flabuless Fitness is not exempt for PST. The ID number is not required, PST is not taxable and the tax is not refundable, so PST paid on purchases is not tracked.

Click   🔍, the **List icon for Acct To Track Tax Charged On Sales**.

Double click   **2640 PST Payable**.

Click   **No** in the Report On Taxes column to change the entry to Yes.

Entering Tax Codes

Click   **Tax Codes** to open the next information screen:

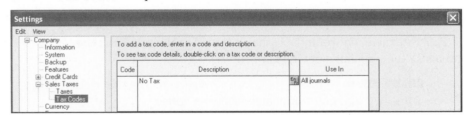

A single code, No Tax, is created as a default.

We need to create tax codes for sales and purchases when GST alone is charged and when both PST and GST apply. There are currently no situations where Flabuless Fitness charges or pays only PST, but there are purchases with both taxes included. We need a code for this situation as well (e.g., gasoline is priced with all taxes included).

Click   the **Code column** below the blank on the first line.

NOTES
In the Tesses Tresses application (Chapter 15) and the Village Galleries application (Chapter 14), we entered Yes for GST for Is This Tax Taxable? because PST is charged on GST in PEI and Quebec. (GST is taxable.) When you click Yes in the Is This Tax Taxable? column for GST, a list of taxes opens, and you can select the taxes that are to be charged on GST.

NOTES
Flabuless Fitness is exempt from PST on purchases of inventory items for sale in the store. These exemptions are handled through the supplier tax codes.

Type   G   **Press** (tab) to move to the Description field.

Press   (enter) or **double click** to open the Tax Code Details screen:

Click   the **Tax field List icon** to see the list of taxes entered.

Both taxes from the Taxes screen appear on the list.

Click   **Select** because GST is already selected and return to the Details.

Defaults are entered for the remaining fields. The **Status** is **Taxable** and the tax is **not included** — these are correct — tax is calculated and charged and is not included in the price.

Click   the **Rate field**.

Type   5

Click   **No** in the Is Refundable column to change the entry to Yes.

Click   **OK** to return to the Tax Codes screen for additional codes.

The description GST @ 5% appears beside the code G and the tax is used in all journals. You can edit the description if you want. If the tax were not refundable, non-refundable would be added to the description automatically. We are ready to enter the second code, to apply both GST and PST.

Press   (tab) until you advance to the next line in the Code column.

Type   GP   **Press** (tab) to move to the Description field.

Press   (enter) to open the Tax Code Details screen.

Click   the **Tax field List icon** .

Select   **GST**. Taxable and not included are correct.

Type   5   in the **Rate field**.

Click   **No** in the Is Refundable column to change the entry to Yes.

Press   (tab) to return to the Tax field again.

Press   (enter) and then **select PST**. **Type**   8   in the **Rate field**.

PST is taxable, not refundable, not included in the price and the tax is used in all journals so the remaining defaults are correct.

Click   **OK** to return to the Tax Codes screen. The description GST @ 5%; PST @ 8%, non-refundable has been added.

Press   (tab) until you advance to the next line in the Code column, below GP.

Type   IN   **Press** (tab) to move to the Description field.

Press   (enter) or **double click** to open the Tax Code Details screen.

Enter   **GST** as the tax, **5%** as the rate. Taxable status is correct.

Click   **No** in the Included In Price column to change the entry to Yes.

Click   **No** in the Is Refundable column to change the entry to Yes.

Press   `tab` to return to the Tax field again. PST at 8% is taxable, included in the price and not refundable.

Enter   **PST** as the tax and **8%** as the rate.

Click   **No** in the Included In Price column to change the entry to Yes.

Click   **OK** to return to the Tax Codes screen.

No description appears beside the code IN so we must add it. The cursor is in the Description field beside IN.

Type   `GST @ 5%, included; PST @ 8%, included`

Adding a Foreign Currency

Flabuless Fitness purchases some inventory items from suppliers in the United States and must set up the company files to allow transactions in USD, United States dollars. We will set up the foreign currency now because we need this information for bank account and supplier settings.

Click   **Currency** under Company to see the Currency Information window:

Canadian Dollars is the default in the Home Currency field, and its code, symbol, format and so on are added. You enter the currencies in the columns in the lower half of the screen, but first you must turn on the option to use other currencies.

Click   **Allow Transactions In A Foreign Currency**.

Exchange rates vary from day to day and even within the day. When purchases and payments are made at different times, they are subject to different exchange rates. We have seen these differences in the Maple Leaf Rags application (Chapter 12). Exchange rate differences may result in a gain — if the exchange rate drops before a payment is made or if the rate increases before a payment is received from a customer — or a loss — if the rate increases before a payment is made or if the rate drops before a customer makes a payment. These differences are tracked in the linked account designated on this screen. Rounding differences may also result in gains and losses because the amounts are recorded with two decimal places and exchange rates usually have several significant digits. The account for these differences may be an expense account or a revenue account. Flabuless Fitness uses a revenue account.

Click   the **list arrow** for **Track Exchange And Rounding Differences In**.

Both revenue and expense accounts are available for linking.

SIMPLY VERSION

The currency selection section and the Exchange Rate button will appear after you choose Allow Transactions In A Foreign Currency.

NOTES

The Premium version of Simply Accounting accepts more than one foreign currency. The Simply version of Simply Accounting is a dual currency version, with one home currency and one foreign currency.

NOTES

After allowing transactions in a foreign currency, you can change the column sizes by dragging the heading margins to allow all headings to appear clearly.

NOTES

You can add a new account at this stage if necessary. Type the new account number and press `tab`. Click Add to start the Add An Account wizard.

NOTES

If you have a Web site that you use for exchange rate information, you can enter it here as well. Then click the Web tool to access the Web site directly and obtain current rates. The Web tool appears on the Exchange Rate list screen that you access by clicking the Exchange Rate tool beside the Exchange Rate field.

Click   **4120 Exchange Rate Differences** to enter the linked account.

The next step is to identify the foreign currency or currencies.

Click   the **Foreign Currency field**.

Click   the **List icon** 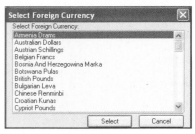 for the field to open the list of currencies:

Type   U   (We want to advance to currencies beginning with U in the list.)

Scroll down   and **double click United States Dollars** to add it to the Currency Information screen. The currency code, symbol and format are added for the selected currency. Accept the defaults.

Click   the **Exchange Rate button**:

On this screen, we enter the exchange rates for various dates for each currency. The selected currency is listed in the Select A Foreign Currency field. All currencies you created will be listed in the drop-down list for this field.

Click   the **Date field**.

Type   04 01 **Press** ⌨(tab) to advance to the Exchange Rate field.

Type   1.015

If you know the rates for other dates, you can enter them as well. Otherwise, you can enter current rates in the journals as we did in the previous chapters. These rates will be added to the list on this screen.

To ensure that you do not use an old exchange rate that is no longer accurate, you should turn on the reminder that warns if the rate is out of date. A one-day period for updating should be sufficient.

Click   **Display A Reminder If The Exchange Rate Is**.

Accept   **One Day Old** as the time interval.

Now every time you change the transaction date to one day past the rate previously used, the program will warn you and give you an opportunity to change the rate. If the rate has not changed, you can accept the old rate.

Click   **OK** to return to the Currency Settings screen.

Currency settings affect other settings — they require additional linked accounts — so they must be saved before continuing. And, now that we have added the foreign currency, we can identify the currency for the USD bank account. We must complete this step before we can choose it as the linked bank account for United States dollar transactions. At the same time we will add cheque numbers.

Click   **OK** to return to the Company module Home window.

Updating Bank Account Settings

Adding Currency to a Bank Account

We need to complete one more step for bank accounts — identifying the currency for the account. By default, the home currency is selected. We need to change this setting for the USD chequing account.

Click   the **Search tool** 🔍. Accounts should be selected.

Click   **1140 Bank: USD Chequing. Click OK** to open the ledger.

Click   the **Class Options tab** to see the current class setting — Bank.

Click   the **Currency list arrow**:

Once we identify an account as a bank account and allow foreign currency transactions, we identify the currency for the account on the Class Options tab screen.

Click   **USD**. Zero now appears as the balance amount for the USD currency.

Click   **Change The Next Cheque Number**:

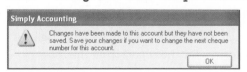

Click   **OK** to return to the ledger window so we can save the changes.

Click   the **Save tool** 💾 or **choose** the **File menu** and **click Save**:

Because we have entered the balance in only the Home currency, we are asked to confirm that this is correct. It is not.

Click   **No** to return to the ledger window so we can add the USD balance.

Click   the **Account tab** to return to the Opening Balance fields. A second field has been added for the balance in USD.

> **Click**   the **Opening Balance In USD field. Type** 9350
>
> **Click**   the **Save tool** .

Adding Cheque Numbers

> **Click**   the **Class Options tab**.
>
> **Click**   **Change The Next Cheque Number** to open the cheque Form settings:

The account we started from is selected, so the cheque number field is available.

> **Click**   the **Next Cheque No. field. Type** 346
>
> **Click**   **1060 Bank: Hamilton Trust Chequing** in the left panel under Cheques.
>
> **Click**   the **Next Cheque No. field. Type** 101

We will make additional printer setting changes before proceeding, while the Reports & Forms window is open.

Changing Other Printer Settings

Reports and forms settings apply only to the data file that you are using. They must be set for each data file separately and the settings are saved with each file.

> Click Reports or click the form for which you want to enter settings.
>
> Choose the printer you will be using for reports. Change the margins if necessary. Choose fonts and type sizes for the report from the lists.
>
> Click Setup to set the options for your particular printer if you need to change the paper size and location.
>
> Click OK to save your settings and return to the previous Printer setting screen.

Each type of form — cheques, invoices and so on — has its own setup.

> **Click**   **Invoices** to see the settings for printing invoices.
>
> **Check**   that the **file locations** for the forms are correct or dimmed.

For **E-mail** and **Printed Forms**, choose generic forms such as Invoice and Purchase Order to avoid a file location error message from an incorrect file path in the Form File field. The file name field will be dimmed when you change the selection.

> As you did for reports, select the printer, set the margins, font and type size to match the forms you are using. Preprinted forms were included as part of the

program installation and are located in the Forms folder under the main Simply Accounting program folder. You should Show Subtotals In Invoices.

To preview invoices, you must select the **Custom Forms** and **Custom Simply Form** options.

If you want to customize and preview the invoice form, choose **User-Defined Form** as the Printed Form Description and then click Customize Form.

To print labels, click Labels and enter the size of the labels and the number that are placed across the page.

To set the printer options for cheques or other forms, click the form you want and make the necessary changes.

Click   **OK** to save the information when all the settings are correct. You can change printer settings at any time.

Close   the **Ledger window** to return to the Home window.

Entering Ledger Default Settings

General Ledger Settings

Most of the settings for the General Ledger are already correct. Flabuless is not setting up budgets or departments yet, and it does not use the additional ledger record fields. Using and showing numbers for accounts, the default setting, is also correct. Flabuless Fitness used four-digit account numbers. We need to add linked accounts.

Choose the **Setup menu** and **click Settings** to continue entering the settings.

Defining Linked Accounts

Linked accounts are General Ledger accounts that are affected by entries in other journals. For example, recording an inventory purchase will update the Inventory Ledger, several General Ledger accounts and the balance owing to the supplier. Refer to page 225 for a review of linked accounts. Refer to page 85 for a review of the Current Earnings Account. Linked accounts are also needed for other features.

Identifying General Linked Accounts

The *Current Earnings* capital account records the changes in net income resulting from sales and expenses. At the end of the fiscal period, the net income, the balance from *Current Earnings*, is transferred to the Retained Earnings capital account — *S. Reeves, Capital* is the Retained Earnings account for Flabuless Fitness — and income and expense accounts are reset to zero to prepare for the new fiscal period.

Click   **General (Accounts)**.

If you have not yet saved the Currency settings, you will see a warning message:

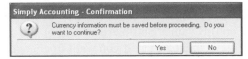

Click   **Yes** to continue if you see this message.

Click   **Linked Accounts under General (Accounts)**.

The General Ledger has two linked accounts. Both must be capital accounts.

NOTES
Refer to Appendix G on the Student CD-ROM if you want to customize printed invoices.

CLASSIC VIEW
   You can access the linked accounts screens for any ledger directly. Right-click a journal icon to select it for the ledger you want and then click the Setup tool.
   For example, to access General Linked Accounts, right-click the General Journal or the Reconciliation & Deposits icon

 or

   Click the Setup tool [icon]. Or choose the Setup menu, then Settings. The General linked accounts screen opens. If no icon is selected, click General from the Select drop-down list.
   Follow the same steps for other ledgers. Start with the Sales or Receipts icon to open the linked accounts screen for the Receivables Ledger, and so on.

NOTES
Refer to page 226 to review
General Linked accounts.

NOTES
You can create new accounts
from any Linked Accounts screen
by typing a new account number
in the Account field and pressing
`tab` to start the Add An Account
wizard.

⚠ **WARNING!**
Simply Accounting will not
allow you to remove an account
while it is being used as a linked
account. When you try to remove
an account, click OK in the
Warning window to return to the
Accounts window. First, turn the
linking function off by deleting the
account in the Linked Accounts
window. Then remove the
account in the Accounts window.
You cannot remove an account if
it has a balance or if journal
entries have been posted to it.

SIMPLY VERSION
Remember that the term
Vendors will replace Suppliers.

NOTES
You can change the
terminology used for Vendors,
Purchases, Invoices, Orders and
Quotes from the Names Settings
screen if you want.

GENERAL LINKED ACCOUNTS			
Retained Earnings		3560	S. Reeves, Capital
Current Earnings		3600	Current Earnings

> **Type**   the **account number** or **select** the **account** from the drop-down list.

Payables Ledger Settings

> **Click**   **Payables** and then **click Address**.
>
> **Enter**   **Hamilton**, **Ontario** and **Canada** as the default city, province and country for suppliers.
>
> **Click**   **Options**.

You should change the intervals for the aging of accounts. Some suppliers offer discounts for payment within 5, 10 or 15 days. Discounts from one-time suppliers are calculated on before-tax amounts.

> **Set**   the **aging** intervals at **15**, **30** and **60** days.
>
> **Click**   **Calculate Discounts Before Tax For One-Time Suppliers**.

Setting Up Import Duties

Although most goods imported from the United States are not subject to tariffs or import duties because of NAFTA (the North American Free Trade Agreement), you should know how to set up this feature. We will set up the program to charge duty but set the rates at zero so that no duty will be applied on purchases. You must activate the Duty option before creating supplier records so that you can indicate in the supplier records those suppliers that supply goods on which duty is charged. Without these two steps, the duty fields in the Purchases Journal will be unavailable.

> **Click**   **Duty** to access the settings we need:

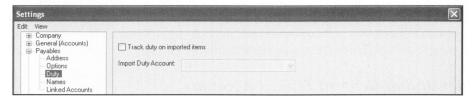

> **Click**   **Track Duty On Imported Items** to use the feature and open the linked account field.

A Payables account is linked to import duties for the liability to the Receiver General.

> **Click**   **2220 Import Duty Payable** from the Import Duty Account drop-down list.

Changing Payables Terminology

Simply Accounting chooses a set of terms that is appropriate for the type of business. These terms can be modified by the user on the Names Settings screen. For the companies in this text, we have accepted the default terms. If you want to change the terms and labels, use the following steps.

> Click Names to open the settings:

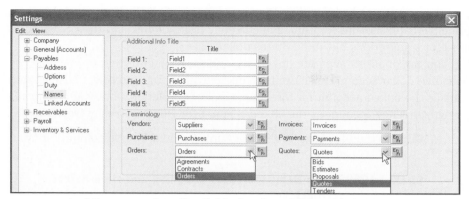

The upper part of the screen has five fields for the additional information you can add to the Payroll Ledger records. You can rename these fields if you want to use them.

The lower part of the screen has drop-down lists of terms for the various icons in the module. The names you select here will appear throughout the program as the names for icons, fields and reports. We have shown the drop-down lists of terms for Orders and Quotes. To see the terms you can choose for Vendors, Purchases and Invoices, refer to Chapter 7, page 228.

> To change the terms, click the term you want to change and click a different
> term from the drop-down list.

Identifying the Payables Linked Accounts

Flabuless Fitness uses *Bank: Hamilton Trust Chequing* as its principal linked bank account for the subsidiary Payables and Payroll ledgers — for all home currency cheque transactions.

PAYABLES

Bank Account to use for Canadian Dollars	1060	Bank: Hamilton Trust Chequing
Bank Account to use for United States Dollars	1140	Bank: USD Chequing
Accounts Payable	2200	Accounts Payable
Freight Expense	5080	Freight Expense
Early Payment Purchase Discount	5090	Purchase Discounts
Prepayments and Prepaid Orders	1250	Purchase Prepayments

To enter the Payables Ledger linked accounts,

> **Click** **Linked Accounts** to display the Linked Accounts window:

We need to identify the default General Ledger bank accounts used for payments to suppliers. Cash transactions in the Payments Journal will be posted to the bank account you select in the journal window. Bank and Cash class accounts are available in the journals, and the principal linked account defined here will be selected as the default.

You can see the list of accounts available for linking by clicking the drop-down list arrow for any linked account field. Only Bank and Cash class accounts may be used in the bank fields. That is why we needed to classify the bank accounts first.

Flabuless has two bank accounts for payments. The chequing account is the principal bank account for Canadian currency transactions, and the USD account is used for transactions in United States dollars.

You can choose a separate linked account for each currency, or you may use the Canadian dollar account for more than one currency. You can select a Home currency bank as the linked account for foreign currency transactions, but you cannot select a foreign currency account as the linked account for Home currency transactions.

Click the **List icon** 🔍 in the Bank Account To Use column for Canadian Dollars.

Click **1060 Bank: Hamilton Trust Chequing** and **click Select**.

Click List icon 🔍 in the Bank Account To Use column for United States Dollars.

Click **1140 Bank: USD Chequing** and **click Select**.

Enter the **remaining linked accounts** in the chart on the previous page. **Type** the **account number** or **select** the **account** from the drop-down list.

Check the linked accounts carefully. To delete a linked account, click it to highlight it and press (del). You must complete this step of deleting the linked account before you can remove the account in the General Ledger from the Accounts window.

Receivables Ledger Settings

Click **Receivables** and then **click Address**.

Enter **Hamilton**, **Ontario** and **Canada** as the default addresses for customers.

Click **Options**.

Flabuless Fitness prints the salesperson's name on all customer forms for the customer's reference in case a follow-up is required. Most customers use the tax code GP, so we will use this as the default for new customers. The default tax code will be selected when we enter the customer records.

Flabuless charges 1.5 percent interest on overdue accounts after 30 days, includes paid invoices on customer statements for 31 days — this is appropriate for the monthly statements — and uses the payment terms to set the aging intervals.

Enter **10**, **30** and **60** days as the **aging** periods.

Click **Interest Charges** to turn on the calculation.

Click the **% field** for **Interest Charges**.

Type 1.5 **Press** (tab).

Type 30

Click the **Tax Code For New Customers field** to see the list of tax codes.

Click **GP GST @ 5%; PST @ 8%, non-refundable**.

Click **Print Salesperson On Invoices Orders & Quotes**.

Entering Discount Settings

Flabuless Fitness offers its account customers a 2 percent after-tax discount for 10 days; full payment is due in 30 days. Flabuless does not use the line discount feature.

Click **Discount** to open the next Receivables settings screen.

Click the **% field** of the **Early Payment Terms** section.

Type 2 **Press** ⌐tab⌐.

Type 10 **Press** ⌐tab⌐.

Type 30

Click **Calculate Line Discounts On Invoices ...** to turn off the feature. You will see the warning:

Click **Yes** to confirm your selection.

Changing Default Comments

Click **Comments** under Receivables.

You may add a comment or notice to all your invoices, quotes and order confirmations. You could use this feature to include payment terms, a company motto or notice of an upcoming sale. Remember that you can change the default message any time you want. You can also edit it for a particular sale or quote when you are completing the invoice. The cursor is in the Sales Invoices field.

Type Interest @ 1.5% per month on accounts over 30 days.

Repeat this procedure to enter comments for the other forms.

Changing Receivables Terminology

Click **Names** under Receivables:

This screen has the same structure as the one for Payables additional information field names and ledger terminology.

In the screen above, we have shown the drop-down lists of terms for Orders and Quotes. The names you select here will appear throughout the program as the names for icons, fields and reports. To see the terms you can choose for Customers, Sales and Invoices, refer to Chapter 7, page 232.

To change the terms, click the term you want to change and click a different term from the drop-down list.

NOTES
You can change the terminology used for Customers, Invoices, Sales, Orders and Quotes from the Names Settings screen if you want.

CLASSIC VIEW
To add the Receivables Ledger linked accounts from the Home window, right-click the Sales, Orders & Quotes or the Receipts Journal icon in the Home window to select it.

Click the Setup tool. Or choose the Setup menu, then choose Settings, Receivables and Linked Accounts.

NOTES
Notice that this screen has changed because of the second currency. You can compare it with the one on page 232 for Dorfmann Design.

Defining the Receivables Linked Accounts

The Receivables Ledger linked accounts parallel those for the Payables Ledger.

Click   Linked Accounts under Receivables:

We need to identify the default General Ledger bank account used to receive payments from customers. Cash transactions in the Sales and Receipts journals will be posted to the bank account you select in the journals. The linked account will be the default account but any Bank or Cash class account may be selected.

Flabuless has several bank accounts. Cheques and cash receipts are held in the *Undeposited Cash and Cheques* account and then deposited weekly to the *Bank: Hamilton Trust Chequing* account. Therefore, the default principal Canadian bank account for receipts is *Undeposited Cash and Cheques. Bank: USD Chequing* is the default account for foreign currency customer transactions. Although most linked accounts may be used only once, one bank account can be linked to the Payables, Receivables and Payroll ledgers.

The following accounts are required as linked accounts for the Receivables Ledger.

NOTES
The remaining accounts were introduced in Chapter 7. Refer to page 232 if you need to review these accounts.

RECEIVABLES LINKED ACCOUNTS

Bank Account to use for Canadian Dollars	1030	Undeposited Cash and Cheques
Bank Account to use for United States Dollars	1140	Bank: USD Chequing
Accounts Receivable	1200	Accounts Receivable
Freight Revenue	4200	Freight Revenue
Early Payment Sales Discount	4060	Sales Discounts
Deposits and Prepaid Orders	2210	Prepaid Sales and Deposits

Click   the **List icon** in the Bank Account To Use column for Canadian Dollars.

Click   1030 Undeposited Cash and Cheques and **click Select**.

Click   List icon in the Bank Account To Use column for United States Dollars.

Click   1140 Bank: USD Chequing and **click Select**.

Enter   the **remaining linked accounts** from the chart on this page. **Type** the **account number** or **select** the **account** from the drop-down list.

Payroll Ledger Settings

NOTES
Refer to pages 315–324 to review payroll settings if necessary.

At this stage, we will change the settings for Payroll Names, Income, Deductions, Taxes and Entitlements. After creating supplier and employee records, we can change the Remittance and Job Category settings.

Entering Payroll Names

Because the names we use will appear on the remaining payroll setting screen, we will define them first.

Click   **Payroll** and then **click Names** in the list of Payroll options.

Click   **Incomes & Deductions** to access the first group of payroll names.

Many of the standard income types are mandatory and cannot be changed. These fields are shown in colour on a shaded background. Some of the other default names are also correct so you do not need to redefine them. You can leave Income 1 and Income 2, labelled "Salary" and "Commission," unchanged because Flabuless Fitness has two salaried employees and pays a sales commission to one employee. There is allowance for 20 different kinds of income in addition to the compulsory fields and 20 different payroll deductions. Each income and deduction label may have up to 12 characters.

Flabuless Fitness uses the additional income fields for bonuses, piece rate pay and taxable benefits (tuition fee payments) so that these incomes can be identified by name on the paycheque. The piece rate pay is based on completed favourable client surveys for the employees. Travel expenses repaid directly to employees are also entered as income but they will not be taxed.

Flabuless also has three payroll deductions at this time: RRSP — the Registered Retirement Savings Plan; CSB Plan — the Canada Savings Bond plan; and Garnishee — the wages that are withheld and submitted to the Receiver General for prior years' taxes.

Click   **Income 3 in the Name Column** to highlight the contents.

Type   No. Clients **Press** ⟨tab⟩ to advance to the Income 4 field.

Type   Bonus **Press** ⟨tab⟩ to advance to the Income 5 field.

Type   Tuition **Press** ⟨tab⟩ to advance to the Income 6 field.

Type   Travel Exp. **Press** ⟨tab⟩ to advance to the Income 7 field.

Press   ⟨del⟩ to remove the entry. **Press** ⟨tab⟩ to select the next field.

Delete   the **remaining Income names** until they are all removed.

Press   ⟨tab⟩ after deleting Income 20 to select Deduction 1 in the Deductions column.

Press   ⟨tab⟩ again if necessary to select Deduction 1 in the Name column.

Type   RRSP **Press** ⟨tab⟩ to advance to the second deduction Name field.

Type   CSB Plan **Press** ⟨tab⟩ to highlight the next field.

Type   Garnishee **Press** ⟨tab⟩ to highlight the next field.

Press   ⟨del⟩. Flabuless Fitness does not have other payroll deductions.

Press   ⟨tab⟩ to select the next field. **Delete** the **remaining deductions**.

Entering Additional Payroll Names

Flabuless Fitness keeps an emergency contact name and phone number for each employee in the personnel files. We will name these extra fields for the Payroll Ledger.

On this next screen, we also name the additional payroll expenses for Flabuless and the entitlements for employees. Flabuless has group insurance as a user-defined expense and offers sick leave and personal leave days for all employees as well as vacation days for salaried employees.

NOTES
If clicking does not highlight the field contents, drag through an entry to select it. Double clicking will select only one word, either Income or 3.

NOTES
In Chapter 9, we created Travel Expenses as a user-defined expense and issued separate cheques to the employee for them.

NOTES
For Lime Light Laundry, we used the generic Benefits field to enter all employee benefits.

NOTES
You can add names to any of these fields later if you need to.

We will briefly review income, benefits and user-defined expenses.

Group insurance is classified as a benefit for employees because the premiums are paid to a third party rather than to the employee. The employer's expense for the benefit is entered as a user-defined expense. Tuition is classified as an income because it is paid to the employee through regular paycheques. The employer's expense for this benefit is recorded in the expense account linked to the income, just like wage expenses. Reimbursements may also be entered as income or as user-defined expenses, depending on how the payment is made. If we entered travel expenses as a user-defined expense, we would create a linked payable account and then issue a separate cheque to the employee to provide the reimbursement. If we repay the expense on the payroll cheque, we defined it as an income — reimbursement — that is not taxable.

NOTES
Reimbursements are added to net pay (the amount of the paycheque), but are not added to gross pay to calculate taxes.
For Lime Light Laundry, travel expenses were set up as a user-defined expense — separate cheques were issued to the employee.

Click   **Additional Payroll**.

Double click   **Field1**.

Type   Emergency Contact **Press** (tab) **twice** to highlight the next field.

Type   Contact Number

Delete   the **names for fields 3 to 5**.

Drag through   **User Exp 1**, the Expense 1 field, to highlight the contents.

Type   Gp Insurance

Delete   the **remaining expenses**.

Drag through   **Days 1**, the Entitlement 1 field, to highlight the contents.

Type   Vacation **Press** (tab) **twice** to highlight the next entitlement name.

Type   Sick Leave **Press** (tab) **twice** to highlight the next name.

Type   PersonalDays

Delete   the **remaining entitlement names**.

NOTES
On the Additional Payroll screen, you need to press (tab) twice to skip the Fr/Eng language button. On the Incomes & Deductions screen, the language button is automatically skipped.

NOTES
You can use up to 12 characters for User-Defined Expense and Entitlement names including spaces — that is why we omitted the space for the Personal Days entitlement name.
You can use the language button to enter labels in the second language.

The Prov. Tax field is used for Quebec payroll taxes. Since we will not choose Quebec as the employees' province of taxation, the program will automatically skip the related payroll fields. WSIB is entered as the name for WCB (Workers' Compensation Board) because we selected Ontario as the business province. The field has a drop-down list of alternative names.

Entering Settings for Incomes

Click   **Incomes** under Payroll.

This screen designates the types of income and the taxes that apply. By deleting the names we do not need, this list is easier to work with. As we did for Lime Light (Chapter 9), we can modify this screen by deleting the columns that apply to Quebec so that only the columns we need are on-screen at the same time.

NOTES
If necessary, scroll to the right to see the column margin you need.

Point to   the **right column heading margin for Calc. Tax (Que.)** until the pointer changes to a two-sided arrow [+].

Drag   the **margin to the left** until the column is hidden.

Point to   the **right column heading margin for Calc. QHSF** until the pointer changes to a two-sided arrow. **Drag** the **margin to the left** until the column is hidden.

Point to   the **right column heading margin for Calc. QPIP** until the pointer changes to a two-sided arrow. **Drag** the **margin to the left**.

NOTES
When you close and re-open the Payroll Settings screen, the hidden and resized columns will be restored.
QPIP (Quebec Parental Insurance Plan) provides parental leave benefits to EI-insurable employees. Both employers and employees pay into the plan.

For each type of income, you must indicate what taxes are applied and whether vacation pay is calculated on the income. Most of the information is correct. Regular and overtime hours are paid on an hourly basis, while salary and commissions are paid at designated income amounts per period. All taxes apply to these types of income at Flabuless Fitness, so these default settings are correct. Vacation pay and EI, however, are not calculated on all incomes so some of these checkmarks should be removed. In addition, we should designate the type of income for the income names that we created and the taxes that apply to them. First, we should choose the type of income because that will change the defaults that are applied.

Click   **No. Clients** to place the cursor on the correct line.

Press   ⎝tab⎠ to move to the Type column. A List icon is added.

Click   the **List icon** 🔍 to see the income types.

By default, all new incomes are assigned to the Income type. This assignment is correct for Bonus, the extra annual holiday payment. The tuition fee payment is a taxable benefit paid directly to the employee, so it is classified as income. The Benefit type is used only for items such as medical or life insurance premiums that the employer pays directly to a third party on behalf of the employee. The monetary value of the premiums is added as a benefit to the employee's gross wages to determine taxes and then subtracted again to determine the net pay. The employee does not receive the actual dollar amount. If a benefit is added to net pay, it should be classified as an Income. Therefore, tuition is an Income.

Travel Expenses are **Reimbursements** and No. Clients is the name for the **Piece Rate** basis of paying bonuses. **Differential Rates** apply to different hourly rates paid at different times and are not used by Flabuless.

Click   **Piece Rate** to select this type for No. Clients.

Click   **Select** to add the Type to the Settings screen. **Press** ⎝tab⎠.

The cursor advances to the Unit of Measure field and the entry has changed to Item. The amount paid to employees is based on the number of completed surveys. Notice that the Insurable Hours checkmark was removed when we changed the type.

Type   Surveys

Click   **Travel Exp** to select this income line. **Press** ⎝tab⎠.

Click   the **List icon** to see the types we can select.

Double click Reimbursement to enter this type on the Settings screen. All taxes are removed because this type of payment is not taxable.

We need to make some other modifications. Insurable Hours, the number of work hours, is used to determine eligibility for Employment Insurance benefits. Regular, overtime and salary paid hours are counted but commissions, bonuses and benefits are not. No work time can be reasonably attached to commissions and bonuses so they are not counted. EI is not calculated on taxable benefit income. The checkmarks for these should be removed.

Click   **Commission** to select this income line.

Press   ⎝tab⎠ **repeatedly** until the cursor is in the **Calc. Ins. Hours field**.

Click   to remove the ✓, or **press** the **space bar**.

Press   ⬇ **twice** to place the cursor in the **Calc. Ins. Hours field for Bonus**.

Click   to remove the ✓, or **press** the **space bar**.

NOTES

Vacation pay is calculated on all wages. This calculation includes the piece rate pay – number of client evaluations – because it is a performance-based wage or income. Bonuses are not based on measurable performance; therefore, vacation pay is not applied to these amounts or to the other benefits.

The regulations governing vacation pay are set provincially.

Press ⬇ to place the cursor in the **Calc. Ins. Hours field for Tuition**.

Click to remove the ✓, or **press** the **space bar**.

Press (shift) and (tab) together to return to the Calc. EI field for Tuition.

Click to remove the ✓, or **press** the **space bar**.

We still need to modify the entries for vacation pay. In Ontario, vacation pay is calculated on all performance-based wages. This includes the regular wages, overtime wages and piece rate pay. We need to remove the remaining ✓. The ✓ for Travel Exp has already been removed. Salaried workers receive paid time off rather than a percentage of their wages as vacation pay. We do not need to remove the ✓ for Overtime 2. If it is used later, vacation pay will be calculated on it as well.

Click **Salary** in the Income column.

Press (tab) **repeatedly** until the cursor is in the **Calc. Vac. column**.

Click to remove the ✓, or **press** the **space bar**.

Press ⬇ to place the cursor in the **Calc. Vac. field for Commission**.

Click to remove the ✓, or **press** the **space bar**.

Press ⬇ to place the cursor in the **Calc. Vac. field for No. Clients**.

Press ⬇ to place the cursor in the **Calc. Vac. field for Bonus**.

Click to remove the ✓, or **press** the **space bar**.

Press ⬇ to place the cursor in the **Calc. Vac. field for Tuition**.

Click to remove the ✓, or **press** the **space bar**.

We do not need to change the Quebec tax settings. They will not be applied when we select Ontario as the province for employees. The option to **track tips** applies to payroll in Quebec, so we do not need to choose this option.

The completed Income Settings screen is shown below:

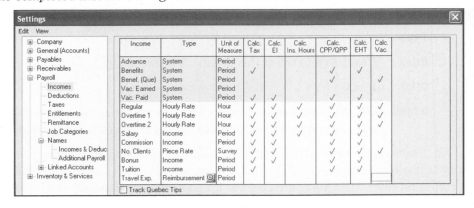

Entering Tax Settings for Deductions

Click **Deductions** under Payroll.

Only the deduction names you entered earlier appear on this screen. You can calculate deductions as a percentage of the gross pay or as a fixed amount. Some deductions, like union dues, are usually calculated as a percentage of income. The Amount settings are correct for Flabuless Fitness.

All deductions are set by default to be calculated after all taxes (Deduct After Tax is checked). For CSB Plan and Garnishee, this is correct — they are subtracted from

NOTES

You can modify this screen as we modified the Incomes Settings screen so that only the columns we need are on-screen. You can remove the Deduct After Tax (Que.), QHSF and QPIP columns.

income after income tax and other payroll taxes have been deducted. However, RRSP contributions qualify as tax deductions and will be subtracted from gross income before income tax is calculated, but not before EI, CPP and so on, so you must change its setting.

> **Click**   the **Deduct After Tax column** for RRSP to remove the ✓ and change the setting to Before Tax.

The remaining settings are correct. RRSP is deducted after the other payroll taxes and vacation pay because these deductions are based on gross wages.

Defining Default Tax Rates

> **Click**   **Taxes** under Payroll.

This group of fields refers to the rate at which employer tax obligations are calculated. The factor for Employment Insurance (**EI Factor**) is correct at 1.4. The employer's contribution is set at 1.4 times the employee's contribution. In the next field, you can set the employer's rate for **WSIB** (Workplace Safety and Insurance Board) premiums. On this screen, you can enter 1.29, the rate that applies to the majority of employees. You can modify rates for individual employees in the ledger records.

The next field, **EHT Factor**, shows the percentage of payroll costs that the employer contributes to the provincial health plan. The rate is based on the total payroll costs per year; the percentage for Flabuless Fitness is 0.98 percent.

The **QHSF Factor** (Quebec Health Services Fund) applies to Quebec employees so we do not need to enter a rate for it. QHSF is similar to EHT.

> **Click**   the **WSIB Rate field**.
>
> **Type**   1.29
>
> **Press**   ⟨tab⟩ to advance to the EHT Factor field.
>
> **Type**   .98

We do not need to change the Quebec tax settings. They will not be applied when we select Ontario as the province for employees.

Defining Entitlements

> **Click**   **Entitlements** under Payroll.

On this screen you can enter the rules for entitlements that apply to all or most employees. These will be added to new employee records as defaults.

Entitlements are linked to the number of hours worked. Employees at Flabuless Fitness are not entitled to take vacation time until they have worked for a certain period of time or to take paid sick leave immediately after being hired. The **Track Using % Hours Worked** determines how quickly entitlements accumulate. For example, 5 percent of hours worked yields about one day per month or 12 days of leave per year. Flabuless Fitness has **Maximums** for the number of Days per year that an employee can take or accumulate. And finally, the days unused are not **cleared at the end of a year**. The number of days carried forward is still limited by the Maximum number of days available. The calculations are based on an eight-hour day.

Flabuless Fitness gives salaried workers three weeks of vacation (8 percent) and allows a maximum of 25 days. Sick leave at 10 days per year is earned at the rate of 5 percent to the maximum of 15 days. Personal leave days (5 days) accrue at the rate of 2.5 percent for a maximum of 5 days per year. Flabuless Fitness allows two of the three weeks of vacation time and five of the ten days of sick leave to be carried over to the following year; that is, they are not cleared at the end of the year. Personal leave days cannot be carried forward — the maximum is the same as the yearly allotment.

Click   the **Track Using % Hours Worked field for Vacation**.

Type   8 **Press** (tab) to advance to the Maximum Days field.

Type   25 **Press** (tab).

Click   the **Track Using % Hours Worked field for Sick Leave**.

Type   5 **Press** (tab) to advance to the Maximum Days field.

Type   15 **Press** (tab).

Click   the **Track Using % Hours Worked field for PersonalDays**.

Type   2.5 **Press** (tab) to advance to the Maximum Days field.

Type   5 **Press** (tab).

Entering Payroll Linked Accounts

NOTES
Refer to page 322 to review payroll linked accounts if necessary.

There are many linked accounts for payroll because each type of income, tax, deduction and expense that is used must be linked to a General Ledger account. The following linked accounts are used by Flabuless Fitness for the Payroll Ledger.

WARNING!
Simply Accounting will not allow you to remove an account while it is being used as a linked account. When you try to remove an account, click OK in the Warning window to return to the Accounts window. First, turn the linking function off by deleting the account in the Linked Accounts window. Then remove the account in the Accounts window. You cannot remove an account if it has a balance or if journal entries have been posted to it.

PAYROLL LINKED ACCOUNTS

INCOMES

Principal Bank	1060	Bank: Hamilton Trust Chequing			
Vac. Owed	2300	Vacation Payable	Advances	1220	Advances Receivable

Income

Vac. Earned	5300	Wages	Commission	5310	Commissions & Bonuses
Regular	5300	Wages	No. Clients	5310	Commissions & Bonuses
Overtime 1	5300	Wages	Bonus	5310	Commissions & Bonuses
Overtime 2	Not used		Tuition	5380	Employee Benefits
Salary	5305	Salaries	Travel Exp.	5320	Travel Expenses

DEDUCTIONS

RRSP	2400	RRSP Payable	Garnishee	2430	Garnisheed Wages Payable
CSB Plan	2410	CSB Plan Payable			

TAXES

Payables			**Expenses**		
EI	2310	EI Payable	EI	5330	EI Expense
CPP	2320	CPP Payable	CPP	5340	CPP Expense
Tax	2330	Income Tax Payable	WSIB	5350	WSIB Expense
WSIB	2460	WSIB Payable	EHT	5360	EHT Expense
EHT	2380	EHT Payable			
Not used	Tax (Que.), QPP, QHSF, QPIP		**Not used**	QPP, QHSF, QPIP	

USER-DEFINED EXPENSES

Payables			**Expenses**		
Gp Insurance	2420	Group Insurance Payable	Gp Insurance	5370	Gp Insurance Expense

Click   **Linked Accounts** under Payroll then **click Incomes**.

The names here are the ones you entered in the Names windows. If you deleted a name, it will not appear here.

The linked accounts for all types of income appear together on this first screen. You must identify a wage account for each type of employee payment used by the company, even if the same account is used for all of them. Once the Payroll bank account is identified as the same one used for Payables, the program will apply a single sequence of cheque numbers for all cheques prepared from the Payables and Payroll journals.

Type   the **account number** or **select** the **account** from the drop-down list.

CLASSIC VIEW
To add payroll linked accounts, you can right-click the Paycheques or the Payroll Cheque Run Journal icon in the Home window to select it.
Click the Setup tool.
Or choose the Setup menu, and then choose Settings, Payroll and Linked Accounts.
If no Home window icon is selected, you can use the Setup tool icon pop-up list, choose Paycheques and click Select.

Choose **1060 Bank: Hamilton Trust Chequing** for the Principal Bank field.

Press (tab) to advance to the next linked account field.

Choose **2300 Vacation Payable** for the Vac. Owed field.

Choose **1220 Advances Receivable** for the Advances field.

Choose **5300 Wages** for Vacation Earned, Regular and Overtime 1.

Choose **5305 Salaries** for Salaries.

Choose **5310 Commissions & Bonuses** for Commission, No. Clients and Bonus.

Choose **5380 Employee Benefits** for Tuition.

Choose **5320 Travel Expenses** for Travel Exp.

Click   **Deductions** to see the next set of Payroll accounts.

Enter   the **linked** payable **accounts** for **RRSP**, **CSB Plan** and **Garnishee** from the chart on page 656.

Click   **Taxes** to see the next set of Payroll linked accounts.

Enter   the **linked payables accounts** for **EI**, **CPP**, **Tax**, **WSIB** and **EHT** in the Payables section and the **linked expense accounts** for **EI**, **CPP**, **WSIB** and **EHT** in the Expenses section from the chart on page 656.

Click   **User-Defined Expenses** to see the final Payroll accounts.

Enter   the **linked** payable **accounts** for **Gp Insurance Payable** and **Gp Insurance Expense** from the chart on page 656.

Check   the **linked** payroll **accounts** against the chart on page 656.

Inventory & Services Ledger Settings

Click   **Inventory & Services** to see the options for this ledger:

Click   **Options**:

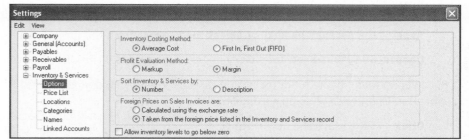

Profits may be calculated on the basis of margin or markup. You can change the setting at any time, so you can prepare reports using both evaluation methods. The formulas for profit evaluation by Margin and Markup are as follows:

Margin = (Selling Price – Cost Price) x 100%/Selling Price

Markup = (Selling Price – Cost Price) x 100%/Cost Price

Flabuless Fitness uses the markup method of evaluating the profit on inventory sales, so we need to change the default setting.

Click   **Markup** to change the calculation method.

If you choose to sort Inventory Ledger items by description, the product name field will appear before the product number in the Inventory Ledger input forms, and inventory selection lists will be sorted alphabetically by name. When item numbers are not used, sorting by description will make it easier to find the item you want.

Because we added a foreign currency, the option to take foreign prices for sales from the Inventory Ledger or from the exchange rate is added. The default setting to use the foreign price in the Inventory Ledger Record is correct for Flabuless Fitness. With this option, you can switch pricing methods for individual items. If you choose the exchange rate method, you cannot choose different methods for different items.

The final option is to Allow Inventory Levels To Go Below Zero. Flabuless Fitness will choose this option to permit customer sales for inventory that is backordered.

Click   **Allow Inventory Levels To Go Below Zero** to select the option.

In the Premium version, you can create additional price lists and modify price lists from this settings screen. You can also set up the locations for inventory if you have more than one place where inventory is stored or sold.

 NOTES
Price lists are used in Chapter 18 to update prices. You can change one price relative to another for all items in a single step. Inventory locations are also covered in Chapter 18.

Inventory Items Linked Accounts

Flabuless Fitness currently uses only one linked account for inventory, the one for inventory adjustments or damaged merchandise. The linked accounts for the Inventory Ledger are listed here:

INVENTORY
Item Assembly Costs	Not used
Adjustment Write-off	5040 Damaged Inventory

Click   the **Linked Accounts** under Inventory & Services:

CLASSIC VIEW
To add inventory linked accounts, you can also right-click the Item Assembly or the Inventory Adjustments Journal icon in the Home window to select it.
Click the Setup tool. Or choose the Setup menu, and then choose Settings, Inventory & Services and Linked Accounts.

Type   the **account number** or **select** the **account** from the drop-down list.

Choose 5040 Damaged Inventory as the Adjustment Write-off linked account.

Settings options for the hidden Division module are also hidden. Time and Billing, introduced in Chapter 18, has no settings options.

NOTES
To see the Division module options, refer to page 520.

Click   **OK** to save the new settings.

You will see several warnings. Because we deleted some payroll names, we are being warned that any accounts linked to these deleted fields will also be removed. The next message refers to the additional payroll names, and we are again being warned that their linked accounts will be removed. Refer to Chapter 9, page 324.

A second group of three warnings relates to required account class changes for linked accounts. Refer to Chapter 7, page 233.

WARNING!
Check your work carefully. Although you can change the designated linked accounts at any time, journal entries will be posted incorrectly if you do not have the correct linked accounts.

Read **each message carefully** and **click Yes** in response to return to the Home window.

Entering Users and Security Passwords

Simply Accounting allows you to set up passwords for different users. The password for the system administrator (sysadmin) controls access to the system or program. Passwords for other users control viewing and editing privileges for different ledgers, journals and reports. For example, if different employees work with different accounting records, they should use different passwords.

We strongly advise you not to set passwords for applications used for tutorial purposes. If you set them and forget them, you will be locked out of your data files.

If you want to set passwords, refer to Appendix H on the Student CD-ROM and your Simply Accounting manuals before you begin.

NOTES
Passwords have not been added to any data files for this text.

Preparing the Subsidiary Ledgers

We have now completed the General Ledger setup including:

1. organizing all accounting reports and records
2. creating new accounts
3. identifying linked accounts for all ledgers
4. activating additional features and entering their linked accounts

The remaining steps involve setting up the records in the subsidiary ledgers:

5. inserting supplier, customer, employee and inventory information
6. entering historical startup information
7. printing reports to check the accuracy of your records

Preparing the Payables Ledger

Use Flabuless Fitness' Supplier Information on pages 620–621 to create the supplier records and add the outstanding historical invoices. If any information is missing for a supplier, leave that field blank.

NOTES
For a review of the Payables Ledger setup, refer to page 234.

Entering Supplier Accounts

Click **Payables** in the Modules pane list.

Click the **Suppliers icon** to open the Suppliers window.

Click the **Create button** or **choose** the **File menu** and **click Create** or **press** ctrl + **N**. The cursor is in the Supplier field.

Enter the supplier's **name**. On the Address tab screen, enter the **contact**, **address**, **phone**, **fax** and **tax ID** numbers, and the **e-mail** and **Web site** addresses from pages 620–621.

Click the **Options tab**.

Enter the **discounts**, if there are any, in the Terms fields, and the number of days in which the net amount is due. **Click Calculate Discounts Before Tax** if the discounts are before tax. Otherwise, leave the box unchecked.

You can print the contact on cheques if this is appropriate for the supplier.

SIMPLY VERSION
Remember that the term Vendors will replace Suppliers.

> **Enter** the **default expense account** for the supplier if there is one.
>
> **Click** the **Taxes tab** to open the tax information screen for the supplier.
>
> **Click** the **Tax Code field list arrow** to see the codes.

For Ancaster Insurance, the selection No Tax is correct because some transactions are taxable and others are not. GST is not applied to insurance.

> **Click** **No** in the Tax Exempt column for GST to change the setting to Yes.

Do not change the tax exempt setting for PST because PST is charged on insurance in Ontario.

It is not necessary to change Tax Exempt entries. Leaving the setting at No will make all tax codes available for a supplier. As long as the tax code in the journal is correct, taxes will be calculated correctly. You can change the tax settings at any time. You do not need to enter any details on the Statistics, Memo and Import/Export tab screens.

> **Correct** any **errors** by returning to the field with the mistake, highlighting the errors and entering the correct information.
>
> **Enter** **historical transactions** using the keystroke instructions in the following section if the supplier has historical transactions.
>
> **Click** **Create Another** [Create Another] to save the record and open a blank Payables Ledger window.
>
> **Click** the **Address tab** to begin entering the next supplier record.

Entering Historical Supplier Transactions

The chart on page 621 provides the information you need to complete this stage.

> **Enter** the supplier's **name**, **address tab information**, **options** and **taxes**.
>
> **Click** the **Historical Transactions tab**.
>
> **Click** **Save Now**.
>
> **Click** **Invoices**.
>
> **Enter** the **Invoice Number**, **Date**, **Pre-Tax Amount** and **Tax** for the first invoice. The default terms should be correct.
>
> **Press** (tab) to advance to the next field after entering each piece of information.

When all the information is entered correctly, you must save your supplier invoice.

> **Click** **Record** to save the invoice and to display another blank invoice for this supplier.
>
> **Repeat** these steps to **enter other invoices** for this supplier.
>
> **Click** **Close** to return to the Payables Ledger when you have recorded all outstanding invoices for the supplier.

Historical Payments

> **Click** **Payments**.
>
> **Click** the **Number field**.

NOTES
Leaving the code as No Tax and leaving the exempt status set at No will permit you to charge taxes if needed. PST is applied to insurance in Ontario.
If taxes are not calculated correctly for a supplier or customer, check that the Ledger entries for Tax Exempt are set to No.

NOTES
Feelyte Gym Accessories is the first supplier with historical invoices.

WARNING!
If you save an incorrect invoice amount, you must pay the invoice, clear paid invoices for the supplier (Home window, Maintenance menu), reset the payments for the year to zero (supplier's ledger, Statistics tab) and re-enter the outstanding invoices. Refer to page 249.

Enter   the **cheque number** for the first payment.

Press   ⟨tab⟩ and **enter** the **payment date** for the first payment. Skip the Discount fields because discounts are taken only when the early payment is a full payment.

Click   the **Amount Paid column** (on the line for the invoice being paid).

Enter   the **payment amount**.

Press   ⟨tab⟩ to advance to the next invoice if there is one. Delete any amounts or discounts that are not included in the payment.

Click   **Record** to save the information and to display an updated statement for this supplier.

Repeat   these steps to **enter other payments** to this supplier.

When you have recorded all outstanding payments for a supplier,

Click   **Close** to return to the Payables Ledger for the supplier. Notice that the payments you have just entered have been added to the Balance field.

Click   the **Create tool** to display a new blank Payables Ledger screen.

Click   the **Address tab**.

Repeat   these procedures to **enter** the **remaining suppliers** and their **historical transactions**.

Identifying Foreign Suppliers

In order to identify Prolife Exercisers Inc. and Redux Home Gym Wholesalers as foreign suppliers, the Options tab screen requires additional information.

Enter   the supplier's **name** and **address tab information**.

Click   the **Options tab**:

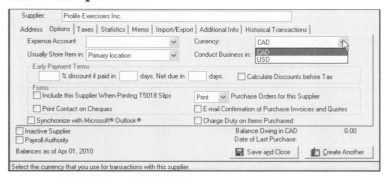

Enter   **2**% in **10** days, net **30** days as the Early Payment Terms for the supplier.

Click   **Calculate Discounts Before Tax**.

Click   the **Currency field list arrow**.

Click   **USD**.

Click   **Charge Duty On Items Purchased**.

You must change this Duty setting to make the duty fields in the Purchases Journal available for this supplier.

Do not enter a default expense account for inventory purchases — the linked asset account from the Inventory Ledger record is selected automatically by the program.

⚠ WARNING!
Remember not to include any discounts taken in the historical payments. If you do include them, the Payables Ledger will not be balanced and you will be unable to finish the history.

📄 NOTES
The historical invoices and payments will be entered on the Statistics tab screen as Last Year's Purchases and Payments because we are starting a new fiscal period.

📄 NOTES
Prolife Exercisers Inc. is the first foreign supplier you will enter, so we show the screens for this supplier.

⚠ WARNING!
You cannot change the currency for a supplier or customer after entering historical invoices, so you must set up the currencies first. After you enter historical invoices for a foreign supplier or customer, you cannot change the currency setting for the company. You must pay the invoices, clear paid transactions, remove the supplier and then re-create the supplier record from scratch.

You cannot access the duty fields in the Purchases Journal unless Charge Duty On Items Purchased is checked in the supplier's ledger.

The Balance Owing will be entered automatically by the program once you have entered historical invoices.

Click the **Taxes tab** and **choose code G** for the foreign supplier.

Correct any **errors** by returning to the field with the mistake, highlighting the errors and entering the correct information.

Enter **historical transactions** using the keystroke instructions in the following section if the supplier has historical transactions.

Click **Create Another** to save the record and open a blank Payables Ledger window.

Click the **Address tab** to begin entering the next supplier record.

Invoices for Foreign Suppliers

Enter the supplier's **name**, **address tab information**, **options** and **taxes**.

Click the **Historical Transactions tab**. **Click Save Now**.

Click **Invoices** on the Historical Transactions tab screen for Redux Home Gym Wholesalers:

The Historical Invoices input screen for foreign suppliers has additional fields for the second currency information.

You can edit the payment terms for individual invoices if needed.

Because Redux discounts are calculated before taxes, there are separate fields for pretax and tax invoice amounts.

Enter **R-914** as the **Invoice Number** and **Mar 28** as the invoice **Date**.

Press (tab).

If the Exchange Rate screen opens, **click Cancel**. We will enter the amounts in both currencies and allow the program to calculate the exchange rate.

Click the **Pretax Amount field for USD**.

Type 6900 **Press** (tab) to advance to the Tax amount field for USD.

Type 345

Click the **Home Amount field for CAD**.

Type 7350 **Press** (tab).

The exchange rate is determined automatically from these amounts.

Click **Record**.

 NOTES
The Exchange Rate screen opens as soon as you enter the date. If you press (tab) after entering the date, it will open immediately. If you do not press (tab) and click the USD Amount field, it will open at that point. Click Cancel when it appears.

⚠ WARNING!
You must enter this information in the correct order for the exchange rate calculation to be made correctly.

NOTES
The Statistics tab screen shows the summary amounts in both Canadian and United States dollars.

When you have recorded all outstanding invoices for a supplier,

Click   **Close** to save the invoice and return to the Historical Transactions tab screen.

The invoices you entered have been added to the Balance fields. Balances are displayed in both currencies. Continue by entering historical payments to this supplier if there are any, or proceed to enter the next supplier.

Click   the **Create tool** . **Click** the **Address tab**. **Enter** the **remaining suppliers**.

Click   **Save And Close** [Save and Close] after adding the last supplier and then **close** the **Suppliers window**.

Display or **print** the **Supplier List** and the **Supplier Aged Detail Report**, including terms, historical differences and foreign amounts, to check the accuracy of your work.

Preparing the Receivables Ledger

Use Flabuless Fitness' Customer Information on pages 621–622 to create the customer records and add the outstanding historical invoices. Revenue accounts are added from the inventory records so they are not needed in the customers' records. If any information is missing for a customer, leave that field blank.

Entering Customer Accounts

Click   **Receivables** in the Modules pane list.

Click   the **Customers icon** [Customers] to open the Customers window.

Click   the **Create button** or **choose** the **File menu** and then **click Create**. The cursor is in the Customer field.

Enter   the customer's **name**. On the Address tab screen, enter the **contact**, **address**, **phone** and **fax numbers**, and the **e-mail** and **Web site addresses** according to pages 621–622.

You can edit the default payment terms for individual customers or for individual historical invoices if necessary.

Click   the **Ship-To Address tab**.

The Mailing Address is already selected as the default ship-to address, so the same address will apply to both fields on invoices, orders and quotes.

Click   the **Options tab**.

Most entries on the Options tab screen are correct. Terms are entered from the default Receivables settings. Customer statements should be printed. Buffalo Health Clinic and Lockport Gymnasium are USD customers. All other customers are Canadian and use the Home currency (CAD).

Choose **USD** from the Currency list for Buffalo Health Clinic (and for Lockport Gymnasium).

Choose **Preferred** from the Price List field list for **Buffalo Health Clinic** and for other preferred customers (the ones marked with * in the customer information chart) to change the price list for these customers.

NOTES
For a review of the Receivables Ledger setup, refer to page 241.

NOTES
The preferred customers are:
Buffalo Health Clinic
Chedoke Health Care
McMaster University
Mohawk College
Stelco Health Club

⚠ WARNING!
Do not forget to remove the discount for cash and credit card customer sales. Changing the ledger records will make the sales invoice terms correct automatically.

Change the payment **terms** to **net 1** for **Cash and Interac**, and **Visa Sales customers**.

Click the **Taxes tab**. For most customers, the default code GP is correct.

Buffalo Health Clinic and Lockport Gymnasium, the foreign currency customers, do not pay taxes.

Select **No Tax** as the **tax code** from the drop-down list for the US customers.

Click the **Statistics tab**.

Enter the **credit limit**. Enter the credit limit in both currencies for USD customers.

This is the amount that the customer can purchase on account before payments are required. If the customer goes beyond the credit limit, the program will issue a warning before posting an invoice.

The balance owing will be included automatically once you have provided the outstanding invoice information. If the customer has outstanding transactions, proceed to the next section on historical information. Otherwise,

Click **Create Another** [Create Another] to save the information and advance to the next new Receivables Ledger input screen.

Click the **Address tab**.

Entering Historical Customer Information

The chart on page 622 provides the information you need to complete this stage.

Enter the customer's **name**, **address**, **options**, **taxes** and **credit limit**.

Click the **Historical Transactions tab**. **Click Save Now**.

Click **Invoices**.

Enter the **invoice number**, **date** and **amount** for the first invoice. The default terms should be correct.

Press (tab) to advance to the next field after entering each piece of information.

When all the information is entered correctly, you must save the customer invoice.

Click **Record** to save the information and to display another blank invoice for this customer.

Repeat these procedures to **enter** the **remaining invoices** for the customer, if there are any.

When you have recorded all outstanding invoices for a customer,

Click **Close** to return to the Historical Transactions window for the customer.

The invoices you entered have been added to the Balance field. Continue by entering payments received from this customer, if there are any, or proceed to enter the next customer.

Click **Payments**.

Click the **Number field**.

Enter the **cheque number** for the first payment.

Press (tab) and **enter** the **payment date** for the first payment. Again, discounts apply only to full payments made before the due dates, so you should skip the Discount fields.

Click the **Amount Paid column** (on the line for the invoice being paid).

Enter the **payment amount**.

Press (tab) to advance to the next amount if other invoices are being paid. Delete any amounts or discounts that are not included in the payment.

Click **Record** to save the information and to display an updated statement for this customer.

Repeat these procedures to **enter** the **remaining payments** from the customer.

When you have recorded all outstanding receipts from a customer,

Click **Close** to return to the Receivables Ledger window for the customer.

The payments you entered have been added to the customer's Balance field.

Click **Create tool** 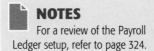 to open another new Receivables Ledger input screen.

Click the **Address tab** to prepare for entering other customers. After entering all customer records and historical data,

Click **Save And Close** 🖫 Save and Close (or ☒) after adding the last customer. **Close** the **Customers window** to return to the Home window.

Display or **print** the **Customer List** and the **Customer Aged Detail Report**, including terms and historical differences, to check your work.

Preparing the Payroll Ledger

NOTES
For a review of the Payroll Ledger setup, refer to page 324.

Use the Flabuless Fitness Employee Information Sheet, Employee Profiles and Additional Payroll Information on pages 622–624 to create the employee records and add historical information.

We will enter the information for Flabuless Fitness employee George Schwinn.

Click **Employees & Payroll** in the Modules pane list.

Click the **Employees icon** Employees ▾ in the Home window.

Click the **Create button** 🗎 Create or **choose** the **File menu** and **click Create**.

Entering Personal Details for Employees

The Payroll Ledger new employee information form will open at the Personal information tab screen so you can begin to enter the employee record.

The Payroll Ledger has a large number of tabs for the different kinds of payroll information. The cursor is in the Employee field. By entering the surname first, your employee lists will be in correct alphabetic order.

Type Schwinn, George **Press** (tab).

Type 55 Carter St. to enter the Street address.

The default city and province, those for the store, are correct.

Click the **Postal Code field**.

Type l8b2v7 **Press** (tab).

The program corrects the postal code format and advances the cursor to the Phone 1 field.

> **Type**   9054261817

The default **Language Preference** is correctly set as English.

> **Click**   the **Social Insurance Number (SIN) field**. You must use a valid SIN. The program has corrected the telephone number format.
>
> **Type**   532548625   **Press** ⌨tab.

The cursor advances to the Birth Date field. Enter the month, day and year using any accepted date format. Birth Date is a required field.

> **Type**   9-18-69   **Press** ⌨tab **twice**.

The cursor moves to the Hire Date field, which should contain the date when the employee began working for Flabuless Fitness.

> **Type**   1-6-03

The next two fields will be used when the employee leaves the job — the date of termination and the reason for leaving that you can select from the drop-down list. The final option designates employees as active or inactive. All employees at Flabuless Fitness are active, so the default selection is correct.

We have not yet created Job Categories to identify salespersons, so we will assign employees to them later. The Date Last Paid will be entered automatically by the program.

Entering Employee Tax Information

> **Click**   the **Taxes tab** to advance to the next set of employee details.

This screen allows you to enter income tax–related information for an employee, including the historical amounts for the year to date. Tax Table is a required field.

> **Click**   the **Tax Table list arrow** to see the list of provinces and territories.
>
> **Click**   **Ontario**, the province of taxation for Flabuless Fitness employees.
>
> **Press**   ⌨tab to advance to the **Federal Claim** field.
>
> **Type**   9600   **Press** ⌨tab to advance to the **Federal Claim Subject To Indexing**. This is the amount of personal claim minus pension and tuition/education exemption amounts.
>
> **Type**   9600   **Press** ⌨tab to advance to the Provincial Claim field.

Since 2001, provincial personal income taxes have not been linked to the rates for federal income taxes, so separate **provincial claim** amounts are needed.

> **Type**   8681   **Press** ⌨tab.
>
> **Type**   8681   **Press** ⌨tab to enter the Provincial Claim Amount Subject To Indexing.

The cursor advances to the **Additional Federal Tax** field. Prekor is the only employee with other income who chooses to have additional taxes withheld.

> For **Prekor**, click the **Additional Fed. Tax** field and type **50**.

If an employee is insurable by EI, you must leave the box for **Deduct EI** checked. The default EI contribution factor, 1.4, for Flabuless Fitness is correct. We entered it in the Payroll Taxes Settings window (page 655).

NOTES
The program will allow you to omit the Social Insurance Number but you must enter the employee's birth date.

NOTES
For all Flabuless Fitness employees, the total federal and provincial claim amounts are subject to indexing. Governments raise these claim amounts based on inflation and budget decisions.

All employees at Flabuless make CPP contributions so this check box should remain selected.

We will enter the historical income tax amounts next.

Click the **Historical Amount field** for **Income Tax**.

Type 1562.21 **Press** (tab) to advance to the EI Premiums Historical Amount field. Enter the amount of EI paid to date.

Type 217.54 **Press** (tab) to move to the CPP Contributions Historical Amount field.

Type 375.20

Entering Income Amounts for Employees

We defined all the types of income for Flabuless Fitness in the Names, Incomes & Deductions setup (page 652). All employees use the following types of income, although not all will have regular amounts and not all will be used on all paycheques:

- Advances
- Benefits
- No. Clients
- Bonus
- Tuition
- Travel Exp.

For Schwinn the following incomes are also used: Vacation (Vac.) Owed, Vacation (Vac.) Paid, Regular and Overtime 1.

For Kisangel and Prekor the following incomes are used: Salary and Commission. Because Quebec is not selected as the province of taxation, Benefits (Que) is not preselected. Advance, Benefits and Vacation checkmarks cannot be removed.

All the details you need to complete the Income tab chart are on page 623.

Click the **Income tab**.

On the Income chart you can indicate the types of income that each employee receives (the **Use** column), the usual rate of pay for that type of income (**Amount Per Unit**), the usual number of hours worked (**Hours Per Period**), the usual number of pieces for a piece rate pay base (**Pieces Per Period**) and the amounts received this year before the earliest transaction date or the date used for the first paycheque (**Historical Amount**). The **Year-To-Date (YTD) Amount** is added automatically by the program based on the historical amounts you enter and the paycheques entered in the program.

Checkmarks should be entered in the Use column so that the fields will be available in the payroll journals, even if they will not be used on all paycheques.

Click **Regular** in the Income column to select the line.

Press (tab) to advance to the Amount Per Unit field where we need to enter the regular hourly wage rate.

Type 16

Press (tab) to advance the Hours Per Period field.

The usual number of work hours in the bi-weekly pay period is 80. You can change the default amount in the Payroll journals. Salaried workers normally work 150 hours each month.

Type 80 **Press** (tab) to advance to the Historical Amount field.

WARNING!
Enter employee historical payroll details carefully. You will be unable to edit these fields after finishing the history or after making Payroll Journal entries for the employee.
They must also be correct because they are used to create T4s for tax reporting.

NOTES
The program skips the Quebec tax fields because you selected Ontario as the province of taxation.

NOTES
In the chart on page 623, the incomes that are used by an employee have a ✔ or an amount in the employee's column.

NOTES
Checkmarks are added by default for all incomes, deductions and expenses that have linked accounts.

WARNING!
Do not click the Use column beside Regular as that will remove the checkmark.

Historical income and deduction amounts for the year to date are necessary so that taxes and deductions can be calculated correctly and T4 statements will be accurate.

> **Type**   8960   **Press** (tab).

The amount is entered automatically in the YTD column and the cursor advances to the Use column for Overtime 1.

> **Press**   (tab) so you can enter the overtime hourly rate.
>
> **Type**   24
>
> **Press**   (tab) **twice** to advance to the Historical Amount field. There is no regular number of overtime hours.
>
> **Type**   336

The next three income types do not apply to Schwinn, so they should not be checked. The next income that applies is No. Clients, the piece rate method of pay. There is no historical amount, but we need to enter the rate or amount per unit (survey). The remaining incomes (No. Clients, Bonus and Travel Exp.) are correctly checked. There is no fixed amount per unit or period and there are no historical amounts.

> Pressing the space bar when you are in the Use column will also add a ✓ or remove one if it is there. Pressing ⊕ will move you to the next line in the same column.
>
> **Click**   the **Use column beside Salary** to remove the ✓.
>
> **Click**   the **Use column beside Commission** to remove the ✓.
>
> **Click**   **No. Clients** in the Income column to select the line. **Press** (tab).
>
> **Type**   10   to enter the amount received for each completed survey.

If employees have received vacation pay, enter this amount in the **Vac. Paid** field. Vacation pay not yet received is entered in the **Vac. Owed** field. Any advances paid to the employees and not yet repaid are recorded in the **Advances Paid** field. There is no record of advance amounts recovered.

We need to add the historical advances, benefits and vacation amounts for Schwinn. Schwinn has $100 in advances not yet repaid, and he has not used all the vacation pay he has earned this year.

> **Scroll**   **to the top** of the list so that the information for Advance is available.
>
> **Click**   the **Historical Amount column beside Advance** to move the cursor.
>
> **Type**   100
>
> **Press**   (tab) to move to the Amount Per Period column for Benefits. The group insurance premiums paid by the employer are employee benefits.
>
> **Type**   5 **Press** (tab) to move to the Historical Amount for Benefits.
>
> **Type**   35 **Press** (tab) to advance to the Historical Amount for Vac. Owed.
>
> **Type**   371.84 **Press** (tab) to advance to the Historical Vac. Paid Amount.
>
> **Type**   385.92

For **Prekor**, click the Use column for Regular, Overtime 1 and Commission to remove the ✓. Enter the monthly salary and press (tab). Enter 150 as the number of hours worked in the pay period. Press (tab) and enter the historical amount. For No. Clients, enter 10 as the amount per unit. For Travel Exp., enter 120 as the historical amount. You cannot remove the ✓ for Vac. Owed and Vac. Paid, even if they are not used.

For **Kisangel**, repeat these steps but leave Commission checked and enter the historical amount. For Tuition, enter 440 as the historical amount.

Pay Periods Per Year, another required field, refers to the number of times the employee is paid, or the pay cycle. Schwinn is paid every two weeks, 26 times per year.

Click   the **list arrow** beside the field **for Pay Periods Per Year**.

Click   **26**.

Retaining Vacation pay is normal for full-time hourly paid employees. Part-time and casual workers often receive their vacation pay with each paycheque because their work schedule is irregular. You will turn the option to retain vacation off when an employee receives the vacation pay, either when taking a vacation or when leaving the company (see page 282). If the employee is salaried and does not receive vacation pay, the option should also be turned off. For Schwinn, or any employee who receives vacation pay, leave the option to Retain Vacation checked and type the vacation pay rate in the % field.

Double click   the **% field beside Retain Vacation**.

Type   6

For **Prekor** and **Kisangel**, click Retain Vacation to remove the ✓.

Employee wages may be linked to the default expense account or to another account. Wage expenses for all Flabuless Fitness employees are linked to the default accounts entered on page 656.

Entering Default Payroll Deduction Amounts

Click   the **Deductions tab** to open the screen for payroll deductions.

On this screen, you can indicate which deductions apply to the employee, the amount normally deducted and the historical amount — the amount deducted to date this year. All deductions are selected in the Use column. These are the deductions you entered previously (page 654).

By entering deduction amounts here, they will be included automatically on the Payroll Journal input forms. Otherwise, you must enter them manually in the Journal for each pay period. Since all three employees participate in the RRSP and CSB plans, you can enter the information here so that the deductions are made automatically. You should make permanent changes by editing the employee ledger record.

If you choose to calculate deductions as a percentage of gross pay in the Payroll Settings, the Percentage Per Pay Period fields will be available.

Click   **RRSP** in the Deduction column to select the line.

Press   (tab). You should enter the amount that is withheld in each pay period.

Type   50   **Press** (tab) to advance the cursor to the Historical Amount field.

Type   350   **Press** (tab) to advance the cursor to the Use column for CSB Plan.

Press   (tab). Enter the amount that is to be withheld in each pay period.

Type   50   **Press** (tab) to advance the cursor to the Historical Amount field.

Type   350   **Press** (tab) to update the YTD Amount and advance to the Use column for Garnishee.

NOTES
Employees may be paid yearly (1), semi-annually (2), monthly for 10 months (10), monthly (12), every four weeks (13), every two weeks for a 10-month year (22), twice a month (24), every two weeks (26) or weekly (52).

NOTES
When you select a specific account, all payroll expenses for that employee will be linked to the same account — the one you identify in this field. If you want to use different accounts for different wage expenses, you must use the linked accounts.

NOTES
For one-time changes, you can edit deduction amounts in the Payroll journals on the Deductions tab or the Deductions Details screen.

Click   the **Use column for Garnishee** to remove the ✓. Schwinn does not have wages withheld.

For **Prekor**, enter 200 as the Amount and 400 as the YTD amount for Garnishee.

The remaining deductions are not used by Flabuless Fitness. The names were deleted (page 651) so they do not appear on the chart.

Entering WSIB and Other Expenses

Click   the **WSIB & Other Expenses tab**.

The user-defined expenses we created in the Additional Payroll Names screen (page 651) and the default WSIB rate (page 655) are entered on this screen.

In Ontario, WSIB (Workplace Safety and Insurance Board) is the name for Workers' Compensation Board, so the tab is labelled WSIB. In other provinces, the tab label will be WCB & Other Expenses.

The default WSIB rate is entered from our setup information, but you can enter a different rate for an individual employee in this field. The rate is correct for Schwinn.

For **Kisangel**, enter 1.02 as the WSIB rate.

Other user-defined expenses are also added on this screen. Flabuless Fitness has only group insurance as a user-defined expense.

Click   the **Gp Insurance Amt. Per Period**. Enter the amount that the employer contributes in each pay period.

Type   5   **Press** (tab) to advance to the Historical Amount field.

Type   35

The remaining expenses are not used by Flabuless Fitness.

NOTES
The Ontario name was changed to emphasize safety rather than compensation for accidents. WSIB (or WCB) pays workers when they have been injured on the job and are unable to work.

Entering Employee Entitlements

We entered the default rates and amounts for entitlements as Payroll Settings (page 655), but they can be modified in the ledger records for individual employees.

We must also enter the historical information for entitlements. This historical number will include any days carried forward from the previous periods. The number of days accrued cannot be greater than the maximum number of days defined for the entitlement for an employee. The number of Net Days Accrued, the amount unused and available for carrying forward, is updated automatically from the historical information and current payroll journal entries.

Click   the **Entitlements tab**.

You cannot enter information directly in the Net Days Accrued fields on the Entitlements tab screen.

Schwinn receives vacation pay instead of paid time off so the vacation entitlements details should be removed. The defaults for sick leave and personal days are correct.

Click   **8.00** in the **Track Using % Hours Worked field for Vacation**.

Press   (del) to remove the entry.

Press   (tab) to advance to the Maximum Days field.

Press   (del) to remove the entry.

Click   the **Historical Days field for Sick Leave**.

Type   12

NOTES
If employees take days before the sufficient number of hours worked have been accrued, the program will warn you. Then you can allow the entry for entitlements or not. This entry is similar to allowing customers to exceed their credit limits.

Press ⬇ to advance to the Historical Days field for PersonalDays. The number of days is added to the Net Days Accrued.

Type   4 **Press** (tab) to enter the amount.

For **Kisangel** and **Prekor**, the default entries for tracking and maximum days are correct, but you must enter the Historical Days for each entitlement.

Entering Direct Deposit Information

Click   the **Direct Deposit tab**.

All three employees have elected to have their paycheques deposited directly to their bank accounts. On this screen, we need to enter the bank account details. For each employee who has elected the Direct Deposit option, you must turn on the selection in the Direct Deposit Paycheques For This Employee check box. Then you must add the three-digit **Bank Number**, five-digit **Transit Number**, the bank Account Number and finally the amount that is deposited, or the percentage of the cheque.

Click   the **Direct Deposit Paycheques For This Employee check box** to add a ✓.

Click   the **Bank Number field**.

Type   102 **Press** (tab) to advance to the Transit Number field.

Type   89008 **Press** (tab) to advance to the Account Number field.

Type   2998187 **Press** (tab) **twice** to advance to the Percentage field.

Type   100

The Memo tab will not be used at this time. You could enter a note with a reminder date to appear in the Daily Business Manager, for example, a reminder to issue vacation paycheques on a specific date or to recover advances.

Entering Additional Information

Flabuless Fitness has chosen to enter the name and phone number of the person to be contacted in case of an emergency involving the employee at work. We added the names for these fields in the Payroll Settings (page 651).

Click   the **Additional Info tab** to access the fields we added for the ledger when we entered Names.

You can indicate whether you want to display any of the additional information when the employee is selected in a transaction. We do not need to display the contact information in the Payroll Journal.

Click   the **Emergency Contact field**.

Type   Adrian Ingles

Press (tab) **twice** to move to the Contact Number field.

Type   (905) 722-0301

Entering T4 and RL-1 Reporting Amounts

The next information screen allows you to enter the year-to-date EI insurable and pensionable earnings. By adding the historical amounts, the T4 slips prepared for income taxes at the end of the year and the record of employment termination reports will also be correct.

NOTES
All banks in Canada are assigned a three-digit bank number and each branch has a unique five-digit transit number. Account numbers may range from five to twelve digits.

NOTES
The paycheque deposit may be split among multiple bank accounts by entering different percentages for the accounts.
To delete bank account details, change the status to Inactive and then delete the bank information.

NOTES
Additional information for other ledgers may also be displayed or hidden in journal transactions.

WARNING!
The Contact Number field is not predefined as a telephone number, so its format will not be corrected automatically by the program.

Because there are yearly maximum amounts for CPP and EI contributions, these historical details are also needed. Totals for optional deductions are also retained in the employee record.

> **Click** the **T4 and RL-1 Reporting tab** to open the next screen we need to complete.

In the **Historical EI Ins. Earnings** field, you should enter the total earned income received to date that is EI insurable. The program will update this total every time you make payroll entries until the maximum salary on which EI is calculated has been reached. At that time, no further EI premiums will be deducted.

Pensionable Earnings are also tracked by the program. This amount determines the total income that is eligible for Canada Pension Plan. The Pension Adjustment amount is used when the employee has a workplace pension program that will affect the allowable contributions for personal registered pension plans and will be linked with the Canada Pension Plan. Workplace pension income is reduced when the employee also has income from the Canada Pension Plan. Since Flabuless Fitness has no company pension plan, the Pension Adjustment amount is zero.

The T4 Employee Code applies to a small number of job types that have special income tax rules.

> **Click** the **Historical Amounts field for EI Ins. Earnings**.
>
> **Type** 9681.92
>
> **Click** the **Historical Amounts field for Pensionable Earnings**.
>
> **Type** 9716.92
>
> **Correct** any employee information **errors** by returning to the field with the error. **Highlight** the **error** and **enter** the **correct information**. **Click each tab** in turn so that you can check all the information.

When all the information is entered correctly, you must save the employee record.

> **Click** **Create Another** ![Create Another] to save the record and to open a new blank employee information form.
>
> **Click** the **Personal tab** so that you can enter address information.
>
> **Repeat** these procedures to **enter** other employee **records**.
>
> **Click** **Save And Close** ![Save and Close] after entering the last record to save the record and close the Payroll Ledger.
>
> **Display** or **print** the **Employee List** and the **Employee Summary Report** to check the accuracy of your work.
>
> **Close** the **Employees window** to return to the Home window.

Entering Job Categories

Now that we have entered all the employees, we can set up job categories and indicate which employees are in each category.

> **Click** the **Settings icon** ![Settings]. Then **click Payroll** and **Job Categories**.

On the Job Categories screen, you enter the names of the categories and indicate whether the employees in each category submit time slips and whether they are salespersons. Categories may be active or inactive. We need a new category called Sales.

NOTES
The EI Insurable amount is the total of gross wages, including overtime wages and vacation pay, but not benefits.
Pensionable earnings include these same incomes plus benefits.

NOTES
We will not use the remaining tax information fields for Flabuless Fitness. Flabuless Fitness does not have a company pension plan with regular payroll deductions, so there is no plan registration number. The Pension Adjustment amount is used when an employee contributes to a company pension plan and these payments reduce the amount the employee can contribute to a private registered pension plan. The company pension plan payments also affect the CPP amount received at retirement, but not CPP premiums.

NOTES
You can print these reports from the Reports menu in the Employees window.

NOTES
Refer to page 336 if you want to review the setup for job categories.

Notice that if you do not create categories, the employees in the default selection <None> are salespersons so they can be selected in the Sales Journal.

Click   the **Job Category field below <None>**.

Type   Sales **Press** ⌕tab⌕ to add checkmarks to the next two columns and set the status to Active.

Click   **Assign Job Categories** to change the screen.

The Sales category is selected and the screen is updated with employee names. Initially, all are Employees Not In This Job Category.

You can add employee names to the category by choosing an employee and clicking **Select** or by choosing **Select All**. Once employees are in a category (the column on the right), you can remove them by selecting an employee and clicking **Remove** or clicking **Remove All** to move all names at the same time.

Click   **Select All** to place all employees in the Sales category.

Click   **OK** to save the information and return to the Home window.

Setting Up Payroll Remittances

Because we have entered all payroll settings and all suppliers, we can set up the payroll remittances information. This process has three steps: identifying the suppliers who receive payroll remittance amounts, linking the suppliers to the taxes or deductions they receive, and entering opening dates and balances. First we should designate the payroll authorities. Refer to the chart on page 617 for the Payroll remittance settings.

The suppliers to which we remit payroll taxes or other deductions are Ancaster Insurance, Minister of Finance, Mt. Hope Investment Corp., Receiver General for Canada and Workplace Safety & Insurance Board.

Click   the **Search field**.

Type   Ancaster **Click** ⟶ to open the Search Results screen.

The results show two entries: one for the supplier we want and one supplier address entry for the city of Ancaster.

Double click   **Ancaster Insurance** to open the supplier's record.

Click   **Payroll Authority** to add the ✓ and change the supplier's payroll status.

Click   the **Next Supplier tool** ▶ **repeatedly** to access the record for the **Minister of Finance**, the next payroll authority.

Click   **Payroll Authority** to add the ✓ and change the supplier's payroll status.

Repeat   these **steps** for the remaining payroll authorities: **Mt. Hope Investment Corp.**, **Receiver General for Canada** and **Workplace Safety & Insurance Board**.

Close   the **Payables Ledger window**. **Close** the **Search Results window**.

Click   the **Settings icon** . Then **click Payroll** and **Remittance**.

All the payroll items that are linked to liability (remittance) accounts are listed: taxes, deductions and user-defined expenses. For each liability, we can select a supplier and enter the balance forward date and amount.

NOTES
Refer to page 335 if you want to review payroll remittance setup.

NOTES
Refer to the Company Information on page 617 and the Trial Balance on page 620 to complete the remittance setup.

NOTES
You can also click the Search tool 🔍 to open the Search window. Click Suppliers from the drop-down list for Select A Record Or Transaction Type To Find.
Click Ancaster Insurance and then click OK to open the supplier's record.
To open the next supplier record, you can also click the Select list arrow and click Minister of Finance.

> **Click** the **List icon** in the Payroll Authority column on the line for EI to see the list of suppliers we marked as Payroll Authorities.
>
> **Click** **Receiver General for Canada**.
>
> **Click** **Select** or **press** ⟨enter⟩ to return to the Remittance Settings screen.

The Receiver General for Canada appears beside EI. The cursor advances to the Balance Forward Date field for EI. We need to enter the balances owing at the time we are converting the data to Simply Accounting and the pay period covered by those amounts. These balances are in the Trial Balance on page 620. The effective date is April 1 for all liabilities.

> **Type** Apr 1 **Press** ⟨tab⟩ to advance to the Balance Forward field.
>
> **Type** 563.28 **Press** ⟨tab⟩ to advance to the Payroll Authority field for CPP.
>
> **Enter** the remaining **Payroll Authorities**, **dates** and **balances**.
>
> **Click** **OK** to save the settings.

Preparing the Inventory Ledger

Use the Flabuless Fitness Inventory Information and chart on pages 624–625 to record details about the inventory items on hand.

Entering Inventory Records

The following keystrokes will enter the information for Flabuless Fitness's first inventory item, Body Fat Scale.

> **Click** **Inventory & Services** in the Modules pane list.
>
> **Click** the **Inventory & Services icon** . Again, with no inventory items on file, the icon window is empty.
>
> **Click** the **Create button** or **choose** the **File menu** and **click** **Create**:

The cursor is in the Item Number field. Use this field for the code or number for the first item. When you sort inventory by description, the two item fields shown here will be reversed — the Description field will appear first. Item Number is a required field.

> **Type** A010 **Press** ⟨tab⟩ to advance to the Item Description field, the field for the name of the inventory item.
>
> **Type** Body Fat Scale

SIMPLY VERSION

There isn't a Build tab in the Simply version, and only two show icons will be included in the tool bar. The Show Activities tool applies only to Premium features, and the Refresh tool is used in the multi-user option in Premium.

NOTES

If you skip the Inventory icon window (Setup menu, User Preferences, View), you will see this Inventory Ledger immediately when you click the Inventory icon.

The Type is set correctly for this item as Inventory rather than Service.

The Show Quantities In field allows you to select the units displayed in the ledger. If you have entered different units for stocking, selling and buying, these will be available from the drop-down list. The Quantity On Hand and Value fields are updated by the program as are the Purchase Orders and Sales Orders Pending.

Click   the **Minimum Level field**. Here you should enter the minimum stock level or re-order point for this inventory item.

Type   2

Click   the **Units tab** to see the next information screen:

You can enter different units for items when the units for buying, stocking and selling differ. Flabuless Fitness uses the same units for stocking and selling but some buying units are different. For example, if items are purchased in dozens and stocked individually, the relationship is 12 to 1. The Stocking Unit must be changed. Body Fat Scales are purchased in cartons of 12 scales and stocked and sold individually (unit).

Double click   the default entry **Each** for the Stocking Unit Of Measure.

Type   Unit

Click   **Same As Stocking Unit** for the **Buying Units** section to remove the ✓.

The relationship fields open so that you can indicate how many stocking units are in each buying unit.

Press   ⌈tab⌋ to advance to the Unit Of Measure field.

Type   Carton **Press** ⌈tab⌋ **twice** to advance to the Relationship field.

Type   12 **Press** ⌈tab⌋.

Check that the entry is 12 Unit Per Carton. If it is not, click the drop-down list and choose this relationship.

Click   the **Pricing tab** to open the next group of inventory record fields:

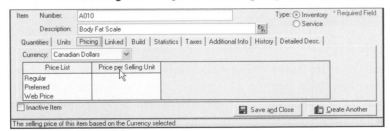

The Currency field and foreign price fields are available only if you indicated that inventory prices should be taken from the Inventory Ledger and not calculated using the exchange rate. The pricing option appears on the Inventory Settings screen only after you enter foreign currency information. Therefore, you must add and save currency information first. Taking prices from the Ledger is the default setting.

⚠ WARNING!

Enter inventory details very carefully. You cannot remove an inventory record or change the Type if there is a quantity on hand. You must edit the History fields to reduce the quantity and value to zero. Then remove the item and re-enter all the details correctly.

To change the Type, close the ledger to save the changes in the history. When you open the ledger again, you may edit the Type.

⚠ WARNING!

You must enter the unit relationship information before entering the history for inventory so that purchase prices and average costs will be calculated correctly.

📄 NOTES

To see the Inventory Ledger Settings, refer to page 657. You cannot change these settings while the Inventory Ledger is open.

📄 NOTES

By working from the Inventory Ledger Settings, Price Lists screen, you can create new price lists and update all prices from one screen. In Chapter 18, we update inventory prices using this approach.

On the Pricing tab screen, you can enter regular, preferred and Web prices in the currencies that you have set up. If you created additional price lists, their names will also appear on this screen. The home currency (Canadian Dollars) is selected first.

Click   the **Regular Price Per Selling Unit field**. Here you should enter the selling price for this inventory item.

Type   100 **Press** (tab) to advance to the Preferred Selling Price field.

The regular price is also entered as the default Preferred and Web Price. We do not have Web sales so we can accept the default entry for Web prices. Preferred selling prices are shown in brackets in the Inventory Information chart on pages 624–625.

Type   90 to replace the default entry.

Choose United States Dollars from the Currency list to open USD price fields:

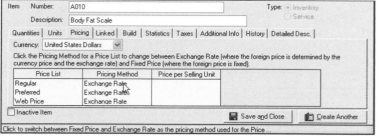

The pricing method is entered separately for each price. You can choose either Exchange Rate or Fixed Price for Regular and Preferred prices.

Click   **Exchange Rate** beside Regular to change the entry to Fixed Price.

Press   (tab) to advance to the Regular Price Per Selling Unit field.

Type   100 **Press** (tab) to advance to the Pricing Method field.

Click   **Exchange Rate** to change the entry to Fixed Price.

Press   (tab) to advance to the Preferred Price Per Selling Unit field.

Type   90 **Press** (tab).

Click   the **Linked tab** to open the linked accounts screen for the item:

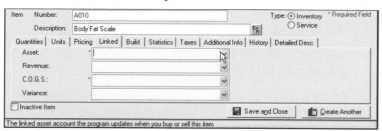

Click   the **Asset field list arrow**.

Here you must enter the **asset** account associated with the sale or purchase of this inventory item. The Inventory chart on pages 624–625 shows that all accessories use account *1520*. All fitness equipment items use *1540* as the asset account. All available asset accounts are in the displayed list. Asset account is a required field.

Enter the account by clicking the list arrow and choosing from the drop-down account list, or

Type   1520 **Press** (tab).

The program asks you to confirm the account class change for account 1520:

Click **Yes** to accept the change.

The cursor advances to the **Revenue** field. Here you must enter the revenue account that will be credited with the sale of this inventory item. Again, you can display the list of revenue accounts by clicking the list arrow. Or,

Type 4020 **Press** (tab).

The cursor advances to the **C.O.G.S.** field. Here you must enter the expense account to be debited with the sale of this inventory item, normally the *Cost of Goods Sold* account. Flabuless Fitness keeps track of each inventory category separately and has different expense accounts for each category. The appropriate expense account is updated automatically when an inventory item is sold. The C.O.G.S. account is another required field.

Click the list arrow beside the field to display the list of available expense accounts. Or,

Type 5050 **Press** (tab) to advance to the Variance field.

Click **Yes** to accept the account class change.

Simply Accounting uses the **Variance** linked account when sales are made of items that are not in stock. If there is a difference between the historical average cost of goods remaining in stock and the actual cost when the new merchandise is received, the price difference is charged to the variance expense account at the time of the purchase. If you have not indicated a variance account, the program will ask you to identify one when you are entering the purchase.

Type 5070 or click the list arrow and choose the account.

Click the **Build tab**.

Click **Yes** to accept the account class change and access the Build screen:

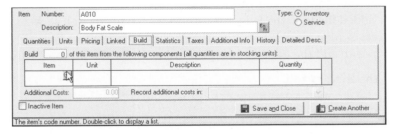

The Build feature is available in Premium but not in the Simply version. On this screen you define how this item is made or built from other inventory items. Then, in the journal, you can build the item by choosing it from the available list and entering the number of units you want to build. This screen holds the components portion of the Item Assembly Journal.

NOTES
If you did not change the account class for expense accounts, you will not see the message about account class changes for 5050 and 5070. However, if all expense accounts are designated as Cost of Goods Sold accounts, you cannot produce an accurate Gross Margin Income Statement.

NOTES
As soon as you click the next tab, you will be prompted to change the account class for the variance linked account.

SIMPLY VERSION
The Build tab screen is not included in the Simply version. Click the Statistics tab as the next step.

Click   the **Statistics tab** to open the next tab information screen:

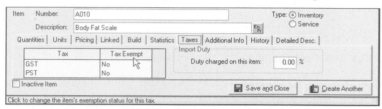

On this screen, you can enter historical information about the sale of the product. It would then be added to the inventory tracking information for reports.

The first activity field, the Date Of Last Sale, refers to the last date on which the item was sold. The next two sections contain information for the Year To Date and the previous year. Since Flabuless Fitness has not kept this information, you can skip these fields. Refer to page 377 in the Adrienne Aesthetics application (Chapter 10) for a more detailed description of these historical Statistics fields.

Click   the **Taxes tab** to input the sales taxes relating to the inventory item:

You can indicate whether the item is taxable for all the taxes you set up, provincial and federal sales taxes in this case. Both PST and GST are charged on sales of all inventory items, so the default entry No for **Tax Exempt** is correct.

> For service items, you must change the PST entry to Yes because PST is not charged on services offered by Flabuless Fitness.

Duty is also entered on this screen. You must activate the duty tracking option before the duty rate field becomes available. Since no duty is charged on the imported inventory, you can leave the duty rate at 0%.

We have not added fields to the ledger record as we did for Payroll so we can skip the **Additional Info** screen.

The next step is to add the opening historical balances for the inventory items.

Click   the **History tab**:

This screen has information about the starting quantities for the item at the time of conversion to Simply Accounting. The opening quantities and values are added to the quantity on hand and value on the Quantities tab screen. History is entered in stocking unit quantities (the same as selling units for Flabuless Fitness).

Click   the **Opening Quantity field** to enter the opening level of inventory — the actual number of items available for sale.

Type   10   **Press** `tab` .

The cursor advances to the Opening Value field, where you should enter the actual total cost of the inventory on hand.

Type   400

The remaining tab allows you to enter further descriptive information.

Click   the **Detailed Desc. tab**:

This optional information provides a detailed description of the inventory item (about 500 characters) as well as a picture in image file format.

Type the detailed item description in the Long Description text box.

Click   **Browse** beside Picture. **Click C:** in the Look In field drop-down list. **Double click SimData**, **Setup**, **Logos** and **scale.bmp** to add the file name and picture.

Correct any **errors** by returning to the field with the mistake. **Highlight** the **error** and **enter** the **correct information**. **Click** the different **tabs** to see all the information that you entered.

When all the information is entered correctly, you must save your inventory record.

Click   **Create Another** [🗐 Create Another] to save the record and advance to a new input screen.

Click   the **Quantities tab** to prepare for entering the next item.

Repeat these procedures to **enter** other inventory **records**.

Entering Inventory Services

The final items on the inventory chart are services that Flabuless Fitness provides. Entering service items is similar to entering inventory, but there are fewer details.

You should have a blank Inventory & Services Ledger window open at the Quantities tab screen.

Click   **Service** to change the Type in the upper-right section of the screen:

There are fewer tabs and fields for services because some item details do not apply. The Unit Of Measure and Selling Price have the same meaning for services as they do for inventory items. Because service items are not kept in stock or purchased, only the selling unit is applicable, there is no minimum quantity and the History tab and fields are

NOTES
A picture file for the Body Fat Scale has been added to the SimData\Setup\Logos folder with your other data files. We have not provided picture files for the remaining inventory items.

NOTES
If you add a .bmp format picture file, you will see the picture in the box beside the Long Description field. Other file formats may be used, but the pictures will not be displayed.

Simply **SIMPLY VERSION**
The Time & Billing tab screen is used to set up Time & Billing, a feature that is not available in the Simply version. The Activity setting and Internal Customer also apply to the Time & Billing feature, so they do not appear on the Simply version screen.

removed. Flabuless Fitness' services are not exported, so you do not need to enter foreign prices. Only expense and revenue accounts are linked for services. The other two linked account fields do not apply and are removed for services. Remember to use *Revenue from Services* and *Cost of Services* as the linked accounts for inventory services.

Enter   the **Item Number** and **Description** and the **Unit Of Measure**.

Click   the **Pricing tab** and add **Regular** and **Preferred prices** in Canadian dollars. Select Canadian Dollars as the currency if necessary.

Click   the **Linked tab**. **Enter** the linked accounts for **Revenue (4040)** and **Expense (5065)**. Accept the account class change.

Most services in Canada are subject to GST. Some services are subject to Provincial Sales Taxes but others are not. These rules also vary from one province to another. Therefore, you should indicate in the Ledger record whether the service is exempt from the tax. By indicating in the Ledger that the service is exempt, PST will not be calculated on sales of the services. All services offered by Flabuless Fitness are exempt from PST, so you should change the Tax Exempt setting in the Taxes tab screen to Yes for PST.

Click   the **Taxes tab**.

Click   **PST**. **Press** $\boxed{tab}$ to advance to the Tax Exempt column.

Click   **No** to change the entry to Yes.

Click   **Create Another** [Create Another].

Click   the **Units tab**. **Repeat** these procedures to **enter other service records**.

Click   **Save And Close** [Save and Close] after entering the last service record.

Close   **Inventory & Services window** to return to the Home window.

Display or **print** the **Inventory List**, **Summary**, **Quantity** and **Price Lists** reports to check them for accuracy.

Finishing the History

The last stage in setting up the accounting system involves finishing the history for each ledger. Before proceeding, you should check the data integrity (Home window, Maintenance menu) to see whether there are any out-of-balance ledgers that will prevent you from proceeding. Correct these errors and then make a backup copy of the files.

Making a Backup of the Company Files

With the Flabuless Fitness files open, use the File menu Backup command to create a backup. You may also want to create a complete working copy of the not-finished files.

Choose   the **File menu** and **click Backup** or **click** the **Backup tool** [🗐].

Click   **Browse** and **choose** the **data folder you want** for the not-finished backup of the data file.

Double click   the **File name field** in the Backup wizard screen.

Type   `nf-flab`

Click   **OK** to create a backup copy of all the files for Flabuless Fitness.

The "NF" designates files as not finished to distinguish them from the ones you will work with to enter journal transactions. You will return to your working copy of the file so you can finish the history.

Changing the History Status of Ledgers to Finished

Refer to page 92 and page 249 for assistance with finishing the history and correcting history errors.

Choose the **History menu** and **click Finish Entering History**.

If your amounts, account types and linked accounts are correct, you will see the warning about this step not being reversible and advising you to back up the file first.

Click **Proceed** when there are no errors and you have backed up your files.

If you have made errors, you will not see the warning message. Instead you will see a list of errors.

Click **Print** so that you can refer to the list for making corrections.

Click **OK** to return to the Home window. **Make** the **corrections**, and then **try again**.

Click **Proceed**.

The Flabuless Fitness files are now ready for you to enter transactions. The ledger icons in all module windows now appear without the open history icons. All the ledgers are ready for transactions.

Congratulations on reaching this stage! This is a good time to take a break.

Finish your **session**. This will give you an opportunity to read the next section and the instructions before starting the source document transactions.

Exporting Reports

Simply Accounting allows you to export reports to a specified drive and path. The files created by the program may then be used by spreadsheet or wordprocessing programs.

Exporting files will allow you to perform additional calculations and interpret data for reporting purposes. This process of integrating Simply Accounting files with other software is an important step in making the accounting process meaningful.

The following keystrokes will export the opening Balance Sheet for Flabuless Fitness to a spreadsheet.

Display the **Balance Sheet** or the report you want to export.

Click the **Export Report tool** 📑 or **choose** the **File menu** and **click Export** to display the following screen:

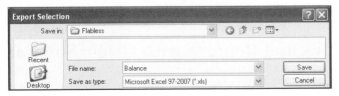

NOTES
If modules are hidden and then later unhidden, they will appear with the open history quill pen icon, as we saw when we added the Payroll Ledger for Lime Light Laundry in Chapter 9. When you later view these modules and choose the History menu, open or unfinished modules will be listed individually so you can set them as finished one at a time.

Project and Time and Billing do not have not-finished (open history) symbols.

NOTES
Integration with other software is described further in Appendix I on the Student CD-ROM.

NOTES
Depending on your previous export selection, your default format and folder may be different from the ones we show here.

Logos may be entered in the Save In field if you did not change folder selections after adding the picture file.

Click   the **Save As Type list arrow** to see the types of files you can create:

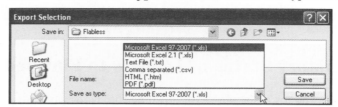

File formats available for export purposes include HTML for Web pages, Text for a wordprocessing format file, Microsoft Excel Versions 97–2007 and 2.1, Comma separated and PDF.

Click   **Microsoft Excel 97-2007** as the type for the Balance Sheet in the Save As Type field. Use the field list arrow to display the file type options if needed.

Choose   the **location** for your exported file. By default your working folder is selected, or the folder you used for the previous exported report.

Click   the **list arrow** for the **Save In field** to access the drive and folder you want.

Accept   the default **file name**, or **type** the **name** you want for your file. The program assigns an extension to the file name so that Microsoft Excel will recognize the new file as an Excel file.

Click   **Save**. You will return to your displayed report.

To create a text file, click Text File. To generate a file that you can view with Acrobat Reader, but not modify, click PDF.

Any Simply Accounting report that you have on display can be also be opened directly as a Microsoft Excel spreadsheet. Formulas for totals, and so on, are retained and you can then use the spreadsheet file immediately.

Display   the **Simply Accounting report** you want to use in Excel.

Click   the **Open In Excel tool** or **choose** the **File menu** and **click Open In Microsoft Excel** to see the file name window:

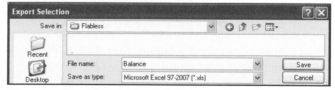

Choose a **location** for your spreadsheet data file.

Click   **Save** to open the spreadsheet. Your Simply Accounting data file will remain open.

Close   the **Excel file** when finished.

You can now work with a report that you have exported.

Using Simply Files and Reports with Other Software

Finish the session using Simply Accounting. Start the software program you want to use with the exported file, referring to the program manuals if necessary. When the blank document or spreadsheet screen appears,

Choose the File menu and click Open if this is a Windows program. Change folders if necessary to locate and then select the exported file. Be sure that the selected file type also matches the format of your exported file (e.g., .txt for a text file, or .xls for Excel).

Some spreadsheet programs can open and convert a file that was saved in the format of a different program. For example, Microsoft Excel can open (or save) text files or Comma Separated Files. Simply choose the alternative file type in your Open File (or Save File) window. Click OK. Your exported file should replace the blank document screen.

Once you have exported a financial statement as a text file, you can include it in a written report prepared with any wordprocessing program. You can then use the features of the wordprocessing software to enhance the appearance of the statement using format styles that are consistent with the remainder of the report. If you have exported a spreadsheet file, you can use the spreadsheet program to perform additional calculations. Then you can save the modified report as a text file or copy the cells you want to be incorporated in a wordprocessing report. We used exported spreadsheets to create the bank statements for this text.

When working with a spreadsheet program, you can use the calculation capabilities of the spreadsheet program to make comparisons between statements from different financial periods. You might also want to use the charting or graphing features to prepare presentation materials.

Exporting reports offers advantages over re-creating the statements. Not only do you save the time of retyping, but you also ensure greater accuracy by avoiding errors made while retyping the numbers and accounts.

NOTES
The bank statements for Chapter 15 and for Chapter 16 — Case 6 in Appendix E on the Student CD-ROM — were created by exporting the General Ledger reports to a spreadsheet, modifying the data and then copying the results to a wordprocessing file.

SOURCE DOCUMENT INSTRUCTIONS

Instructions for April

1. **Enter** the **transactions** for April using all the information provided.

2. **Print** the following **reports**:
   a. Journal Entries (All Journals) for April, including foreign amounts, corrections and additional transaction details
   b. Customer Aged Detail Report for all customers for April
   c. General Ledger account reports for
      - Bank: Hamilton Trust Chequing
      - Revenue from Sales
      - Sales Returns and Allowances
   d. Supplier Purchases Summary for Footlink Corporation, all categories, for April

3. **Export** the **Balance Sheet** as at April 30, 2010, to a spreadsheet application. **Calculate** the following **key ratios** in your spreadsheet and compare them with the ratios in the Daily Business Manager Business Performance indicators:

   a. current ratio   b. quick ratio

4. **Set up** a **budget** for use in May and June and **enter amounts** based on expenses and revenues for April and for the first quarter.

NOTES
You can restore the backup SimData\Setup\flab-apr1 to complete the transactions for April.

Instructions for May

1. **Enter** the **transactions** for May using all the information provided.

NOTES
You can restore the backup SimData\Setup\flab-may1 to complete the transactions for May. This file does not include budget amounts.

2. **Print** the following **reports**:
   a. Journal Entries (All Journals) for May, including foreign amounts, corrections and additional transaction details
   b. Supplier Aged Detail Report for all suppliers for May
   c. Employee Summary Report for all employees for the pay period ending May 31, 2010
   d. Inventory Summary Report (observe and report items that have not sold well over the two-month period)
   e. Customer Sales Summary (all customers, items and categories) for May

3. **Export** the **Comparative Balance Sheet** for April 30 and May 31, 2010, to a spreadsheet application. You will use these at the end of the quarter for three-month comparisons.

4. **Compare** May's **performance against** April's budget **forecast**.

Instructions for June

1. **Enter** the **transactions** for June using all the information provided.

2. **Print** the following **reports**:
   a. Journal Entries (All Journals) for June, including foreign amounts, corrections and additional transaction details
   b. Trial Balance, Balance Sheet and Income Statement on June 30
   c. Inventory Activity Report for Fitness Equipment (All Journals) for June
   d. Bank Transaction Report for all bank accounts from April 1 to June 30

3. **Export** the **Balance Sheet** and **Income Statement** to a spreadsheet application. Combine the Balance Sheet with the comparative one for April and May. **Compare** first- and second-quarter figures, item by item, to assess the performance of Flabuless Fitness. You may want to use Multi-period reports for this comparison.

4. **Make** a **backup copy** of your data files. **Advance** the **session date** to July 1, 2010.

5. **Print** the **Trial Balance**, **Balance Sheet** and **Income Statement** for July 1. **Compare** the end of June and the first of July **statements** and note the changes that result from Simply Accounting closing the books for the new fiscal period.

SOURCE DOCUMENTS

SESSION DATE – APRIL 15, 2010

☐ **Purchase Order #25**   **Dated April 1, 2010**

Shipping date April 8, 2010
From Footlink Corporation

2	E190	Treadmill: Basic T-800B	$ 960.00
2	E200	Treadmill: Basic Plus T-910P	1 280.00
		Freight	40.00
		GST	114.00
		Total	$2 394.00

Terms: 1/15, n/30.

☐ **Cash Receipt #39**   **Dated April 1, 2010**

From Stoney Creek Sports Arena, cheque #147 for $4 429.60 in payment on account including $90.40 discount for early payment. Reference invoice #2191.

☐ **Sales Order #41-DRC**   **Dated April 2, 2010**

Shipping date April 6, 2010
To Dundas Recreation Centre

2	A080	Heart Rate Monitor	$ 75/ unit	
40	A130	Weight Plates	1.20/ kg	
1	E020	Elliptical Exerciser: AE-200	1 700/ unit	
1	E040	Elliptical Exerciser: LE-400	2 200/ unit	
2	E140	Ski Exerciser: Skitrek SE-680	400/ unit	
1	E190	Treadmill: Basic T-800B	1 200/ unit	
5	S010	Personal Trainer: 1 hour	75/ hour	
2	S040	Yoga Instructor: 1 hour	100/ hour	
		Freight (tax code G)	50	
		GST	5%	
		PST	8%	

Terms: 2/10, n/30.
Received cheque #96 for $1 000 as down payment (deposit #15) to confirm
sales order.

> **NOTES**
> Remember that PST is not charged on Freight in Ontario so you need to change the tax code for Freight to G.

☐ **Cheque Copy #101**   **Dated April 3, 2010**

To Footlink Corporation, $8 280 in payment of account including $100 discount
for early payment. Reference invoice #FC-618.

☐ **Cash Receipt #40**   **Dated April 4, 2010**

From Mohawk College, cheque #73 for $5 537 in payment of account including
$113 discount for early payment. Reference invoice #2194.

☐ **Cheque Copy #346**   **Dated April 5, 2010**

To Redux Home Gym Wholesalers, $7 107 USD in payment of account including
$138 discount for early payment. Reference invoice #R-914. The exchange rate
is 1.018.

☐ **Sales Invoice #3000**   **Dated April 5, 2010**

To Dundas Recreational Centre, to fill sales order #41-DRC

2	A080	Heart Rate Monitor	$ 75/ unit	
40	A130	Weight Plates	1.20/ kg	
1	E020	Elliptical Exerciser: AE-200	1 700/ unit	
1	E040	Elliptical Exerciser: LE-400	2 200/ unit	
2	E140	Ski Exerciser: Skitrek SE-680	400/ unit	
1	E190	Treadmill: Basic T-800B	1 200/ unit	
5	S010	Personal Trainer: 1 hour	75/ hour	
2	S040	Yoga Instructor: 1 hour	100/ hour	
		Freight	50	
		GST	5%	
		PST	8%	

Terms: 2/10, n/30.

> **NOTES**
> Remember to change the payment method to Pay Later for the sales invoice that fills the order.
> If you want, you can enter Kisangel as the salesperson for all sales that include service revenue. Then you can use the Sales By Salesperson Report to determine her commission.

☐ **Credit Card Purchase Invoice #HS-114**   **Dated April 6, 2010**

From Hamilton Spectator, $500 plus $25 GST and $40 PST for prepaid
advertisement to run over the next 12 weeks. Purchase invoice total $565 paid
in full by Visa.

☐ **Credit Card Purchase Invoice #W-1149**   **Dated April 6, 2010**

From Westdale Office Supplies, $150 plus $7.50 GST and $12.00 PST for
stationery and other office supplies for store. Purchase invoice total $169.50 paid
in full by Visa.

☐ **Purchase Invoice #FC-691** **Dated April 6, 2010**

From Footlink Corporation, to fill purchase order #25

2	E190	Treadmill: Basic T-800B	$ 960.00
2	E200	Treadmill: Basic Plus T-910P	1 280.00
		Freight	40.00
		GST	114.00
		Total	$2 394.00

Terms: 1/15, n/30.

NOTES

All deposits are made to Bank: Hamilton Trust Chequing from Undeposited Cheques and Cash.

☐ **Deposit Slip #14** **Dated April 7, 2010**

Prepare deposit slip for all receipts for April 1 to April 7 to deposit the funds to Bank: Hamilton Trust Chequing from Undeposited Cash and Cheques. The total deposit for the three cheques is $10 966.60.

☐ **Memo #4-1** **Dated April 8, 2010**

Re: Damaged Inventory
Two (2) stability balls, item A110, were torn and damaged beyond repair. Adjust the inventory to recognize the loss.

☐ **Cheque Copy #102** **Dated April 9, 2010**

To Feelyte Gym Accessories, $1 030 in payment of account including $20 discount for early payment. Reference invoice #FG-1611.

☐ **Memo #4-2** **Dated April 9, 2010**

From Visa, received monthly credit card statement for $240 including $220 for purchases up to and including April 3 and $20 annual renewal fee. Submitted cheque #103 for $240 in full payment of the balance owing.

☐ **Cash Receipt #41** **Dated April 9, 2010**

From Chedoke Health Care, cheque #472 for $6 759.20 in payment of account including $180.80 discount for early payment. Reference invoice #2199.

☐ **Sales Invoice #3001** **Dated April 12, 2010**

To Hamilton District Bd of Education

8	A070	Glide Slidetrak	$ 50 each
5	A110	Stability Balls	10 each
1	E030	Elliptical Exerciser: DE-300	2 000/ unit
1	E060	Bicycle: Dual Action DA-70	600/ unit
2	E070	Bicycle: Recumbent R-80	750/ unit
		Freight	50
		GST	5%
		PST	8%

Terms: 2/10, n/30.

☐ **Credit Card Purchase Invoice #WS-6112** **Dated April 14, 2010**

From Waterdown Sunoco, $92 including GST and PST for gasoline purchase for delivery vehicle. Invoice paid in full by Visa. (Use tax code IN.)

Memo #4-3 **Dated April 14, 2010**

☐ Record payment for GST for March to the Receiver General for Canada. Issue cheque #104 in full payment.

☐ Record payment for PST Payable for March to the Minister of Finance. Remember to collect 5% of the amount owing as the sales tax compensation. Issue cheque #105 in full payment.

NOTES

Use Memo 4-3A and Memo 4-3B as the invoice numbers for the sales tax remittances.

Memo #4-4   **Dated April 14, 2010**

Payroll Remittances: Use April 1 as the End of Remitting Period date to make the following payroll remittances in the Payments Journal.

☐ Record payment for EI, CPP and Income Tax Payable up to April 1 to the Receiver General for Canada. Issue cheque #106 in full payment.

☐ Record payment for Garnisheed Wages Payable up to April 1 to the Receiver General for Canada. Issue cheque #107 in full payment.

☐ Record payment for EHT Payable up to April 1 to the Minister of Finance. Issue cheque #108 in full payment.

☐ Record payment for RRSP Payable up to April 1 to Ancaster Insurance. Issue cheque #109 in full payment.

☐ Record payment for CSB Payable up to April 1 to Mt. Hope Investment Corporation. Issue cheque #110 in full payment.

☐ Record payment for Group Insurance Payable up to April 1 to Ancaster Insurance. Issue cheque #111 in full payment.

☐ Record payment for WSIB Payable up to April 1 to Workplace Safety and Insurance Board. Issue cheque #112 in full payment.

☐ **Purchase Order #26**   **Dated April 14, 2010**

Shipping date April 23, 2010
From Prolife Exercisers Inc.

1	E020	Elliptical Exerciser: AE-200	$	670.00	USD
1	E030	Elliptical Exerciser: DE-300		790.00	USD
1	E040	Elliptical Exerciser: LE-400		870.00	USD
		Freight		110.00	USD
		GST		122.00	USD
		Total	$2	562.00	USD

Terms: 2/10, n/30. The exchange rate is 1.007.

☐ **Credit Card Sales Invoice #3002**   **Dated April 14, 2010**

To Visa customers (sales summary)

2	A010	Body Fat Scale	$ 100/ unit	$	200.00
8	A040	Dumbbells: 5kg set	15/ set		120.00
2	A100	Power Blocks up to 200 kg	300/ set		600.00
8	A110	Stability Balls	10 each		80.00
80	A130	Weight Plates	1.20/ kg		96.00
2	A160	Weights: Olympic 125 kg	250/ set		500.00
6	A180	Workout Gloves: all sizes	10/ pair		60.00
2	E130	Rowing Machine: RM-1000	480/ unit		960.00
1	E210	Treadmill: Deluxe T-1100D	2 400/ unit	2	400.00
3	S020	Personal Trainer: 1/2 day	200/ 1/2 day		600.00
2	S030	Personal Trainer: full day	400/ day		800.00
4	S050	Yoga Instructor: 1/2 day	200/ 1/2 day		800.00
		GST	5%		360.80
		PST	8%		401.28
		Total paid by Visa		$7	978.08

☐ **Employee Time Summary Sheet #14**   **Dated April 14, 2010**

For the Pay Period ending April 14, 2010
George Schwinn worked 80 regular hours and 2 hours of overtime in the period. Recover $50 advance. Issue payroll deposit slip DD19.

☐ **Deposit Slip #15**   **Dated April 14, 2010**

Prepare deposit slip for all receipts for April 8 to April 14 to deposit the funds. One cheque for $6 759.20 is being deposited.

NOTES
Enter Memo 4-4A, Memo 4-4B, and so on, in the Additional Information field as the reference numbers for the payroll remittances.
You cannot enter a date earlier than April 1 in the Pay Ending date field.

NOTES
Edit the default purchase cost entered in the Amount field.

WARNING!
You must use the Paycheques Journal because the pay period and cheque dates are different from the session date.

☐ **Cash Receipt #42**   **Dated April 15, 2010**

From Dundas Recreational Centre, cheque #195 for $6 396.05 in payment of account including $150.94 discount for early payment. Reference invoice #3000 and deposit #15.

SESSION DATE – APRIL 30, 2010

☐ **Cash Purchase Invoice #ES-64329**   **Dated April 21, 2010**

From Energy Source, $120 plus $6 GST paid for hydro service. Purchase invoice total $126. Terms: cash on receipt of invoice. Issue cheque #113 in full payment.

☐ **Cheque Copy #114**   **Dated April 21, 2010**

To Footlink Corporation, $2 371.20 in payment of account including $22.80 discount for early payment. Reference invoice #FC-691.

☐ **Deposit Slip #16**   **Dated April 22, 2010**

Prepare deposit slip for all receipts for April 15 to April 22 to deposit the funds. The total deposit for the single cheque is $6 396.05.

☐ **Sales Invoice #3003**   **Dated April 22, 2010**

To Stelco Health Club (preferred customer)

1	A140	Weights: Olympic 75 kg	$ 135/ set
1	E030	Elliptical Exerciser: DE-300	1 875/ unit
1	E070	Bicycle: Recumbent R-80	680/ unit
2	E140	Ski Exerciser: Skitrek SE-680	360/ unit
2	E190	Treadmill: Basic T-800B	1 100/ unit
		GST	5%
		PST	8%

Terms: 2/10, n/30.

☐ **Cash Purchase Invoice #BC-59113**   **Dated April 22, 2010**

From Bell Canada, $80 plus $4.00 GST paid and $6.40 PST for phone service. Purchase invoice total $90.40. Terms: cash on receipt of invoice. Issue cheque #115 in full payment.

☐ **Cash Purchase Invoice #H-2010-1**   **Dated April 23, 2010**

From City of Hamilton Treasurer, $900 in full payment of first instalment of quarterly property tax assessment. Terms: EOM. Issued cheque #116 in full payment. Store as monthly recurring entry. Recall the stored transaction to issue cheques #117 and #118 as postdated cheques for the next two instalments, dated May 23 and June 23.

☐ **Purchase Invoice #PE-364**   **Dated April 23, 2010**

From Prolife Exercisers Inc. to fill purchase order #26

1	E020	Elliptical Exerciser: AE-200	$ 670.00	USD
1	E030	Elliptical Exerciser: DE-300	790.00	USD
1	E040	Elliptical Exerciser: LE-400	870.00	USD
		Freight	110.00	USD
		GST	122.00	USD
		Total	$2 562.00	USD

Terms: 2/10, n/30. The exchange rate is 0.995.

NOTES
Use H-2010-2 and H-2010-3 as the Invoice numbers for the postdated payments for property taxes.

Credit Card Sales Invoice #3004   Dated April 28, 2010

To Visa customers (sales summary)

5	A020	Yoga Mats	$ 30/ unit	$	150.00
20	A030	Dumbbells: pair	1.50/ kg		30.00
2	A080	Heart Rate Monitor	75 each		150.00
3	A090	Power Blocks up to 100 kg	160/ set		480.00
1	A100	Power Blocks up to 200 kg	300/ set		300.00
2	A180	Workout Gloves: all sizes	10/ pair		20.00
2	E060	Bicycle: Dual Action DA-70	600/ unit		1 200.00
2	E190	Treadmill: Basic T-800B	1 200/ unit		2 400.00
1	E220	Treadmill: Deluxe Plus T-1200P	2 800/ unit		2 800.00
6	S020	Personal Trainer: 1/2 day	200/ 1/2 day		1 200.00
6	S050	Yoga Instructor: 1/2 day	200/ 1/2 day		1 200.00
		GST	5%		496.50
		PST	8%		602.40
		Total paid by Visa		$11 028.90	

Employee Time Summary Sheet #15   Dated April 28, 2010

For the Pay Period ending April 28, 2010
George Schwinn worked 80 regular hours and 4 hours of overtime. Recover $50 advance. Issue payroll deposit slip DD20.

WARNING!
Remember that you must use the Paycheques Journal.

Sales Invoice #3005   Dated April 28, 2010

To Stoney Creek Sports Arena

1	A120	Wavemaster	$ 150/ unit
40	A130	Weight Plates	1.20/ kg
1	E110	Rider: Airwalker RA-900	300/ unit
1	E200	Treadmill: Basic Plus T-910P	1 600/ unit
		Freight	30
		GST	5%
		PST	8%

Terms: 2/10, n/30.

Memo #4-5   Dated April 28, 2010

Transfer $15 000 CAD to Savings account from 1120 Bank: Visa and Interac.

Cash Purchase Invoice #DMC-55   Dated April 28, 2010

From Dundurn Maintenance Co. (use Full Add), $300 plus $15 GST paid for cleaning and maintenance of premises. Terms: cash on receipt. Issue cheque #119 for $315 in full payment. The company bills monthly for their services so store the entry as a monthly recurring transaction.

Credit Invoice #8   Dated April 28, 2010

To Stelco Health Club, $50 allowance for scratched treadmill unit. Reference invoice #3003. There is no tax on the allowance. Enter a negative amount. Create new Subgroup Account 4070 Returns and Allowances. Change the customer terms to net 60; there is no discount. Delete or change the comment.

Credit Card Purchase Invoice #WS-6533   Dated April 28, 2010

From Waterdown Sunoco, $69 including GST and PST for gasoline (tax code IN) and $40 plus $2.00 GST and $3.20 PST for oil change (tax code GP). Purchase invoice total $114.20 charged to Visa account.

Cheque Copy #347   Dated April 30, 2010

To Prolife Exercisers Inc., $2 513.20 USD in payment of account including $48.00 discount taken for early payment. Reference invoice #PE-364. The exchange rate is 1.001.

NOTES
Dundurn Maintenance Co.
(contact Vak Kume)
890 Dundurn St. N.
Hamilton, ON L8G 2P9
Tel: (905) 529-4187
Fax: (905) 529-3116
Terms: net 1
Tax code: G
Expense account: 5240

NOTES
Enter the two items purchased from Waterdown Sunoco on separate lines because you need different tax codes for them.

☐ **Memo #4-6**   **Dated April 30, 2010**

Transfer $7 000 USD to cover the cheque to Prolife Exercisers. Transfer money to Bank: USD Chequing from 1120 Bank: Visa and Interac.

☐ **Bank Debit Memo #91431**   **Dated April 30, 2010**

From Hamilton Trust, authorized withdrawals were made from the chequing account on our behalf for the following:

Bank service charges	$ 35
Mortgage interest payment	1 880
Mortgage principal reduction	120
Bank loan interest payment	420
Bank loan principal reduction	480

☐ **Memo #4-7**   **Dated April 30, 2010**

Prepare the payroll for the two salaried employees, Nieve Prekor and Assumpta Kisangel. Add 2 percent of revenue from services for April as a commission to Kisangel's salary. Issue payroll deposit slips DD21 and DD22.

SESSION DATE – MAY 15, 2010

☐ **Cash Receipt #43**   **Dated May 1, 2010**

From Stelco Health Club, cheque #434 for $6 162.51 in payment of account including $126.79 discount for early payment. Reference sales invoice #3003 and credit invoice #8.

☐ **Purchase Order #27**   **Dated May 1, 2010**

Delivery date May 7, 2010
From Prolife Exercisers

2	E020	Elliptical Exerciser: AE-200	$1 340.00	USD
2	E030	Elliptical Exerciser: DE-300	1 580.00	USD
2	E040	Elliptical Exerciser: LE-400	1 740.00	USD
		Freight	180.00	USD
		GST	242.00	USD
		Invoice total	$5 082.00	USD

Terms: 2/10, n/30. The exchange rate is 1.02.

☐ **Memo #5-1**   **Dated May 1, 2010**

Create new tax code P for purchases that charge only PST at 8%. The status is taxable and PST is not included and not refundable.

☐ **Sales Invoice #3006**   **Dated May 1, 2010**

To McMaster University (preferred customer)

1	E030	Elliptical Exerciser: DE-300	$1 875/ unit
1	E070	Bicycle: Recumbent R-80	680/ unit
1	E080	Home Gym: Basic HG-1400	900/ set
1	E190	Treadmill: Basic T-800B	1 100/ unit
1	E210	Treadmill: Deluxe T-1100D	2 200/ unit
		Freight	40
		GST	5%
		PST	8%

Terms: 2/10, n/30.

☐ **Cash Purchase Invoice #AI-6921**   **Dated May 2, 2010**

From Ancaster Insurance, $2 400 plus $192 PST for six months of insurance coverage. Invoice total $2 592. Issued cheque #120 in payment.

NOTES
You must calculate the amount of the commission manually and then enter the amount in the journal.
    Use the Revenue from Services amount in the Income Statement for the month of April to calculate the commission.

NOTES
Remember to check the prices and edit them when they have changed.

NOTES
Refer to pages 639–641 for assistance with adding tax codes.

NOTES
Use Prepaid Insurance account and tax code P for the insurance purchase.
    If the Tax Exempt setting for PST is set at Yes in the Supplier's Ledger, you will be unable to add PST to the purchase invoice.

Purchase Order #28   Dated May 2, 2010

Delivery date May 10, 2010
From Footlink Corporation

2	E190	Treadmill: Basic T-800B	$ 960.00	
2	E200	Treadmill: Basic Plus T-910P	1 280.00	
2	E210	Treadmill: Deluxe T-1100D	1 920.00	
2	E220	Treadmill: Deluxe Plus T-1200P	2 240.00	
		Freight	50.00	
		GST	332.50	
		Invoice total	$6 772.50	

Terms: 1/15, n/30.

Purchase Order #29   Dated May 4, 2010

Delivery date May 14, 2010
From Redux Home Gym Wholesalers

2	E080	Home Gym: Basic HG-1400	$920.00	USD
		GST	46.00	USD
		Invoice total	$966.00	USD

Terms: 2/10, n/30. Free delivery. The exchange rate is 1.025.

NOTES
The price for E080 has increased.

Purchase Order #30   Dated May 4, 2010

Delivery date May 12, 2010
From Feelyte Gym Accessories

1	A020	Yoga Mats (1 box of 10 mats)	$ 120.00
10	A040	Dumbbells: 5kg set	60.00
10	A070	Glide Slidetrak	250.00
5	A090	Power Blocks up to 100 kg	400.00
15	A110	Stability Balls	60.00
		GST	44.50
		Invoice total	$934.50

Terms: 2/10, n/30.

Cash Receipt #44   Dated May 5, 2010

From Stoney Creek Sports Arena, cheque #198 for $2 354.20 in payment of account, including $48.04 discount for early payment. Reference invoice #3005.

Deposit Slip #17   Dated May 5, 2010

Prepare deposit slip for all receipts for April 29 to May 5 to deposit the funds. The total deposit for the two cheques is $8 516.71.

Memo #5-2   Dated May 5, 2010

Adjust the selling prices for item E080 (Home Gym: Basic HG-1400) to reflect the cost increase for the next delivery. Change the prices in the Inventory Ledger. The new selling prices are

Regular Canadian dollar price	$1 100 CAD
Preferred Canadian dollar price	1 000 CAD
Regular United States dollar price	1 100 USD
Preferred United States dollar price	1 000 USD

Cash Receipt #45   Dated May 7, 2010

From McMaster University, cheque #1257 for $7 521.65 in payment of account, including $153.50 discount for early payment. Reference invoice #3006.

Credit Card Purchase Invoice #WS-6914   Dated May 8, 2010

From Waterdown Sunoco, $69 including GST and PST for gasoline. Purchase invoice total $69 charged to Visa account.

☐ **Purchase Invoice #PE-2014**   **Dated May 9, 2010**

From Prolife Exercisers, to fill purchase order #27

2	E020	Elliptical Exerciser: AE-200	$1 340.00	USD
2	E030	Elliptical Exerciser: DE-300	1 580.00	USD
2	E040	Elliptical Exerciser: LE-400	1 740.00	USD
		Freight	180.00	USD
		GST	242.00	USD
		Invoice total	$5 082.00	USD

Terms: 2/10, n/30. The exchange rate is 1.005.

☐ **Purchase Invoice #FC-768**   **Dated May 10, 2010**

From Footlink Corporation, to fill purchase order #28

2	E190	Treadmill: Basic T-800B	$ 960.00
2	E200	Treadmill: Basic Plus T-910P	1 280.00
2	E210	Treadmill: Deluxe T-1100D	1 920.00
2	E220	Treadmill: Deluxe Plus T-1200P	2 240.00
		Freight	50.00
		GST	332.50
		Invoice total	$6 772.50

Terms: 1/15, n/30.

☐ **Purchase Invoice #FG-1804**   **Dated May 12, 2010**

From Feelyte Gym Accessories, to fill purchase order #30

1	A020	Yoga Mats (1 box of 10 mats)	$ 120.00
10	A040	Dumbbells: 5kg set	60.00
10	A070	Glide Slidetrak	250.00
5	A090	Power Blocks up to 100 kg	400.00
15	A110	Stability Balls	60.00
		GST	44.50
		Invoice total	$934.50

Terms: 2/10, n/30.

☐ **Memo #5-3**   **Dated May 12, 2010**

From Visa, received monthly credit card statement for $940.70 for purchases up to and including May 3. Submitted cheque #121 for $940.70 in full payment.

☐ **Sales Order #5-1-MC**   **Dated May 12, 2010**

Delivery date May 14, 2010
From Mohawk College (preferred customer)

40	A130	Weight Plates	$ 1.10/ kg
1	A170	Weights: Olympic 150 kg	270/ set
1	E050	Bicycle: Calorie Counter CC-60	360/ unit
1	E060	Bicycle: Dual Action DA-70	540/ unit
1	E090	Home Gym: Deluxe HG-1401	1 400/ set
1	E110	Rider: Airwalker RA-900	270/ unit
1	E120	Rider: Powerglider RP-1500	315/ unit
		Freight	30
		GST	5%
		PST	8%

Terms: 2/10, n/30.

☐ **Employee Time Summary Sheet #16**   **Dated May 12, 2010**

For the Pay Period ending May 12, 2010
George Schwinn worked 80 regular hours in the period. He will receive $200 as an advance and have $50 recovered from each of the following four paycheques. Issue payroll deposit slip DD23.

☐ **Deposit Slip #18**   **Dated May 12, 2010**

Prepare deposit slip for all receipts for May 6 to May 12 to deposit the funds. The total deposit for the single cheque is $7 521.65.

☐ **Credit Card Sales Invoice #3007**   **Dated May 12, 2010**

To Visa customers (sales summary)

11	A020	Yoga Mats	$ 30/ unit	$ 330.00
6	A040	Dumbbells: 5kg set	15/ set	90.00
2	A060	Dumbbells: 15kg set	40/ set	80.00
4	A070	Glide Slidetrak	50 each	200.00
2	A080	Heart Rate Monitor	75/ unit	150.00
1	A090	Power Blocks up to 100 kg	160/ set	160.00
1	A100	Power Blocks up to 200 kg	300/ set	300.00
1	A150	Weights: Olympic 100 kg	200/ set	200.00
1	E180	Stair Climber: Unlinked SC-U75	2 100/ unit	2 100.00
1	E220	Treadmill: Deluxe Plus T-1200P	2 800/ unit	2 800.00
4	S020	Personal Trainer: 1/2 day	200/ 1/2 day	800.00
		GST	5%	360.50
		PST	8%	512.80
		Total paid by Visa		$8 083.30

☐ **Purchase Invoice #R-1031**   **Dated May 13, 2010**

From Redux Home Gym Wholesalers, to fill purchase order #29

2	E080	Home Gym: Basic HG-1400	$920.00	USD
		GST	46.00	USD
		Invoice total	$966.00	USD

Terms: 2/10, n/30. Free delivery. The exchange rate is 1.009.

☐ **Cash Receipt #46**   **Dated May 13, 2010**

From Mohawk College, cheque #284 for $1 000 as down payment (deposit #16) in acceptance of sales order #5-1-MC.

Memo #5-4   **Dated May 14, 2010**

☐ Record payment for GST for April to the Receiver General for Canada. Issue cheque #122 in full payment. Clear the GST Report up to April 30.

☐ Record payment for PST Payable for April to the Minister of Finance. Remember to collect 5% of the amount owing as the sales tax compensation. Issue cheque #123 in full payment. Clear the PST Report up to April 30.

Memo #5-5   **Dated May 14, 2010**

Payroll Remittances: Make the following remittances for the period ending April 30. Choose Pay Remittance for payroll remittances.

☐ Record payment for EI, CPP and Income Tax Payable for April to the Receiver General for Canada. Issue cheque #124 in full payment.

☐ Record payment for Garnisheed Wages Payable for April to the Receiver General for Canada. Issue cheque #125 in full payment.

☐ Record payment for RRSP Payable to Ancaster Insurance. Issue cheque #126 in full payment.

☐ Record payment for CSB Payable to Mt. Hope Investment Corporation. Issue cheque #127 in full payment.

☐ Record payment for Group Insurance Payable for April to Ancaster Insurance. Issue cheque #128 in full payment.

☐ **Cheque Copy #348**   **Dated May 15, 2010**

To Prolife Exercisers, $4 985.20 USD in payment of account including $96.80 early payment discount. Reference invoice #PE-2014. The exchange rate is 1.019.

> **NOTES**
> Enter Memo 5-4A and Memo 5-4B as the reference numbers for the tax remittances.

> **NOTES**
> Enter Memo 5-5A, Memo 5-5B, and so on, in the Additional Information field as the reference numbers for the payroll remittances.

☐   **Memo #5-6**   **Dated May 15, 2010**

Create new inventory item:
Item: E105 Home Gym: Free Weight HG-1403
Selling price: $2 200 /set Regular ($2 000 Preferred) CAD
Foreign currency price: $2 200 Regular ($2 000 Preferred) USD
Minimum level: 1
Linked accounts:
  Asset   1540 Fitness Equipment
  Revenue   4020 Revenue from Sales
  Expense   5060 Cost of Goods Sold: Equipment
  Variance   5070 Cost Variance

☐   **Purchase Invoice #R-1047**   **Dated May 15, 2010**

From Redux Home Gym Wholesalers, new inventory item purchase
    2   E105   Home Gym: Free Weight HG-1403 $2 600.00 USD
            GST   130.00 USD
            Invoice total $2 730.00 USD
Terms: 2/10, n/30. Free delivery. The exchange rate is 1.019.

☐   **Sales Invoice #3008**   **Dated May 15, 2010**

To Mohawk College, to fill sales order #5-1-MC
    40 A130   Weight Plates $ 1.10/ kg
     1 A170   Weights: Olympic 150 kg   270/ set
     1 E050   Bicycle: Calorie Counter CC-60   360/ unit
     1 E060   Bicycle: Dual Action DA-70   540/ unit
     1 E090   Home Gym: Deluxe HG-1401   1 400/ set
     1 E110   Rider: Airwalker RA-900   270/ unit
     1 E120   Rider: Powerglider RP-1500   315/ unit
            Freight   30
            GST   5%
            PST   8%
Terms: 2/10, n/30.

SESSION DATE – MAY 31, 2010

☐   **Cheque Copy #129**   **Dated May 18, 2010**

To Footlink Corporation, $6 708 in payment of account including $64.50 discount
for early payment. Reference invoice #FC-768.

☐   **Deposit Slip #19**   **Dated May 19, 2010**

Prepare deposit slip for the single cheque for $1 000 for May 13 to May 19.

☐   **Cash Purchase Invoice #ES-79123**   **Dated May 20, 2010**

From Energy Source, $125 plus $6.25 GST paid for hydro service. Purchase invoice
total $131.25. Terms: cash on receipt of invoice. Issue cheque #130 in full payment.

☐   **Cash Purchase Invoice #BC-71222**   **Dated May 20, 2010**

From Bell Canada, $80 plus $4.00 GST paid and $6.40 PST for phone service.
Purchase invoice total $90.40. Terms: cash on receipt of invoice. Issue cheque
#131 in full payment.

☐   **Credit Card Purchase Invoice #M-1034**   **Dated May 21, 2010**

From Mountview Delivery (use Quick Add for the new supplier), $80 plus $4
GST paid for delivery services. Invoice total $84. Full amount paid by Visa. Enter
tax code G in the Purchases Journal.

Cheque Copy #132   **Dated May 21, 2010**

To Feelyte Gym Accessories, $916.70 in payment of account including $17.80 discount for early payment. Reference invoice #FG-1804.

Cheque Copy #349   **Dated May 22, 2010**

To Redux Home Gym Wholesalers, $3 625.60 USD in payment of account including $70.40 discount for early payment. Reference invoices #R-1031 and #R-1047. The exchange rate is 1.028.

Memo #5-7   **Dated May 22, 2010**

Transfer $4 000 USD to cover the cheque to Redux. Transfer money to Bank: USD Chequing from 1120 Bank: Visa and Interac.

Sales Invoice #3009   **Dated May 22, 2010**

To Chedoke Health Care (preferred customer)

1	E010	Elliptical Exerciser: ME-100	$1 000/ unit
1	E130	Rowing Machine: RM-1000	435/ unit
1	E150	Ski Exerciser: Linked SE-780	410/ unit
3	S040	Yoga Instructor: 1 hour	95/ hour
2	S050	Yoga Instructor: 1/2 day	190/ 1/2 day
		Freight	30
		GST	5%
		PST	8%

Terms: 2/10, n/30.

Cash Receipt #47   **Dated May 22, 2010**

From Mohawk College, cheque #391 for $2 573.44 in payment of account including $72.93 discount for early payment. Reference invoice #3008 and deposit #16.

Cash Receipt #48   **Dated May 24, 2010**

From Chedoke Health Care, cheque #532 for $2 758.31 in payment of account including $56.29 discount for early payment. Reference invoice #3009.

Memo #5-8   **Dated May 24, 2010**

Add Charitable Donations as a payroll deduction. Since Flabuless Fitness will match employee donations, a user-defined expense is also needed.
Create new Group accounts
    2440 Charitable Donations - Employee
    2450 Charitable Donations - Employer
    5390 Charitable Donations Expense
Add Donations as new name (Setup, Settings, Payroll, Names)
    for Deduction 4 on Names, Incomes & Deductions screen
    for User-Defined Expense 2 on Names, Additional Payroll screen
Change Deduction Settings (Payroll, Deductions)
    Deduct Donations by Amount After Tax, EI, CPP, EHT And Vacation Pay
Add new payroll linked accounts (under Payroll Settings)
    2440 for Donations (Linked Accounts, Deductions)
    2450 for Donations (Linked Accounts, User-Defined Expenses, Payables)
    5390 for Donations (Linked Accounts, User-Defined Expenses, Expenses)
Enter amounts in Payroll Ledger for Deductions and WSIB & Other Expenses
    Kisangel: Check Use for the deduction; enter $20 as the deduction and the expense amount per period
    Prekor: Check Use for the deduction; enter $25 as the deduction and the expense amount per period

NOTES
To add deductions, refer to
page 651 for names
page 654 for payroll
    deductions settings
page 656 for linked accounts
page 669 for entering the employee deduction and page 670 for WSIB & other expense amounts.

☐ **Deposit Slip #20**   **Dated May 26, 2010**

Prepare deposit slip for all receipts for May 20 to May 26 to deposit the funds. The total deposit for two cheques is $5 331.75.

☐ **Employee Time Summary Sheet #17**   **Dated May 26, 2010**

For the Pay Period ending May 26, 2010
George Schwinn worked 80 regular hours in the period and 2 hours of overtime. Recover $50 advanced and issue payroll deposit slip DD24.

☐ **Credit Card Sales Invoice #3010**   **Dated May 26, 2010**

To Visa customers (sales summary)

2	A050	Dumbbells: 10kg set	$ 25/ set	$ 50.00
4	A060	Dumbbells: 15kg set	40/ set	160.00
4	A070	Glide Slidetrak	50 each	200.00
1	A080	Heart Rate Monitor	75/ unit	75.00
2	A090	Power Blocks up to 100 kg	160/ set	320.00
1	A100	Power Blocks up to 200 kg	300/ set	300.00
1	A150	Weights: Olympic 100 kg	200/ set	200.00
6	A180	Workout Gloves: all sizes	10/ pair	60.00
1	E040	Elliptical Exerciser: LE-400	2 200/ unit	2 200.00
1	E060	Bicycle: Dual Action DA-70	600/ unit	600.00
1	E080	Home Gym: Basic HG-1400	1 100/ set	1 100.00
1	E100	Home Gym: Multi HG-1402	2 000/ set	2 000.00
1	E110	Rider: Airwalker RA-900	300/ unit	300.00
1	E200	Treadmill: Basic Plus T-910P	1 600/ unit	1 600.00
4	S020	Personal Trainer: 1/2 day	200/ 1/2 day	800.00
8	S050	Yoga Instructor: 1/2 day	200/ 1/2 day	1 600.00
		GST	5%	578.25
		PST	8%	733.20
		Total paid by Visa		$12 876.45

☐ **Cash Purchase Invoice #DMC-68**   **Dated May 28, 2010**

From Dundurn Maintenance Co., $300 plus $15 GST paid for cleaning and maintenance of premises. Terms: cash on receipt. Issue cheque #133 for $315 in full payment. Recall stored transaction.

☐ **Debit Card Sales Invoice #3011**   **Dated May 28, 2010**

To Bruno Scinto (cash and Interac customer)

1	A020	Yoga Mats		$ 30.00
1	A080	Heart Rate Monitor		75.00
1	E170	Stair Climber: Adjustable SC-A60		1 500.00
1	E220	Treadmill: Deluxe Plus T-1200P		2 800.00
		GST	5%	220.25
		PST	8%	352.40
		Invoice total paid in full		$4 977.65

Debit Card #5919 7599 7543 7777. Amount deposited to Visa and Interac account.

☐ **Credit Card Purchase Invoice #WS-7823**   **Dated May 30, 2010**

From Waterdown Sunoco, $115, including GST and PST, for gasoline and $40 plus $2.00 GST and $3.20 PST for tire repairs. Purchase invoice total $160.20 paid in full by Visa. (Remember to change the tax code for the tire repairs.)

☐ **Memo #5-10**   **Dated May 31, 2010**

Print customer statements. Prepare invoice #3012 to charge Hamilton District Bd of Education $77.91 interest — 1.5% of the overdue amount. Terms: net 15.

NOTES
Remember that if you want to preview the customer statement, you must choose Custom Simply Form as the Form Type in the Reports and Forms settings on the screen for Statements.

☐ **Memo #5-9**   **Dated May 31, 2010**

Prepare the payroll for Nieve Prekor and Assumpta Kisangel, the salaried employees. Kisangel took one day personal leave. Add 2 percent of service revenue for May as a commission to Kisangel's salary. Issue payroll deposit slips DD25 and DD26.

☐ **Bank Debit Memo #96241**   **Dated May 31, 2010**

From Hamilton Trust, authorized withdrawals were made from the chequing account on our behalf for the following:

Bank service charges	$ 35
Mortgage interest payment	1 870
Mortgage principal reduction	130
Bank loan interest payment	400
Bank loan principal reduction	500

SESSION DATE – JUNE 15, 2010

☐ **Purchase Order #31**   **Dated June 2, 2010**

Delivery date June 7, 2010
From Footlink Corporation

2	E190	Treadmill: Basic T-800B	$ 960.00
		Freight	30.00
		GST	49.50
		Invoice total	$1 039.50

Terms: 1/15, n/30.

☐ **Purchase Order #32**   **Dated June 3, 2010**

Delivery date June 8, 2010
From Prolife Exercisers

2	E020	Elliptical Exerciser: AE-200	$1 340.00	USD
2	E030	Elliptical Exerciser: DE-300	1 580.00	USD
		Freight	120.00	USD
		GST	152.00	USD
		Invoice total	$3 192.00	USD

Terms: 2/10, n/30. The exchange rate is 1.021.

☐ **Purchase Order #33**   **Dated June 3, 2010**

Delivery date June 15, 2010
From Feelyte Gym Accessories

1	A080	Heart Rate Monitor (1 carton of 12)	$360.00
20	A110	Stability Balls	80.00
2	A180	Workout Gloves: all sizes (2 boxes of 10)	80.00
		GST	26.00
		Invoice total	$546.00

Terms: 2/10, n/30.

☐ **Purchase Invoice #TD-1127**   **Dated June 5, 2010**

From Trufit Depot

2	E110	Rider: Airwalker RA-900	$240.00
2	E130	Rowing Machine: RM-1000	384.00
		GST	31.20
		Invoice total	$655.20

Terms: 2/5, n/30. Free delivery.

☐ **Sales Invoice #3013**   **Dated June 5, 2010**

To Hamilton District Bd of Education

60	A130	Weight Plates	$ 1.20/ kg
1	E020	Elliptical Exerciser: AE-200	1 700/ unit
1	E030	Elliptical Exerciser: DE-300	2 000/ unit
1	E050	Bicycle: Calorie Counter CC-60	400/ unit
1	E130	Rowing Machine: RM-1000	480/ unit
1	E150	Ski Exerciser: Linked SE-780	450/ unit
		Freight	30
		GST	5%
		PST	8%

Terms: 2/10, n/30.

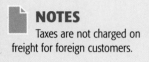

NOTES

Taxes are not charged on freight for foreign customers.

☐ **Sales Invoice #3014**   **Dated June 5, 2010**

To Buffalo Health Clinic, New York (preferred USD customer)

1	E210	Treadmill: Deluxe T-1100D	$2 200/ unit USD
1	E220	Treadmill: Deluxe Plus T-1200P	2 600/ unit USD
		Freight	60 USD

Terms: 2/10, n/30. The exchange rate is 1.021.

☐ **Purchase Invoice #FC-861**   **Dated June 7, 2010**

From Footlink Corporation, to fill purchase order #31

2	E190	Treadmill: Basic T-800B	$ 960.00
		Freight	30.00
		GST	49.50
		Invoice total	$1 039.50

Terms: 1/15, n/30.

☐ **Purchase Invoice #PE-2079**   **Dated June 8, 2010**

From Prolife Exercisers, to fill purchase order #32

2	E020	Elliptical Exerciser: AE-200	$1 340.00	USD
2	E030	Elliptical Exerciser: DE-300	1 580.00	USD
		Freight	120.00	USD
		GST	152.00	USD
		Invoice total	$3 192.00	USD

Terms: 2/10, n/30. The exchange rate is 1.011.

☐ **Employee Time Summary Sheet #18**   **Dated June 9, 2010**

For the Pay Period ending June 9, 2010
George Schwinn worked 80 regular hours in the period (no overtime) and took one day of sick leave. Recover $50 advanced and issue payroll deposit slip DD27.

☐ **Cheque Copy #134**   **Dated June 9, 2010**

To Trufit Depot, $642.72 in payment of account including $12.48 discount for early payment. Reference invoice #TD-1127.

☐ **Cash Receipt #49**   **Dated June 9, 2010**

From Hamilton District Bd of Education, cheque #1431 for $10 952.73 in payment of account including $115.94 discount for early payment. Reference invoices #3001, #3012 and #3013.

☐ **Memo #6-1**   **Dated June 9, 2010**

From Visa, received monthly credit card statement for $313.20 for purchases made before June 3, 2010. Submitted cheque #135 for $313.20 in full payment of the balance owing.

☐ **Deposit Slip #21**   **Dated June 9, 2010**

Prepare deposit slip for the single cheque for $10 952.73 being deposited.

☐ **Credit Card Sales Invoice #3015**   **Dated June 9, 2010**

To Visa customers (sales summary)

10	A030	Dumbbells: pair	$1.50/ kg	$	15.00
4	A040	Dumbbells: 5kg set	15/ set		60.00
2	A080	Heart Rate Monitor	75/ unit		150.00
2	A090	Power Blocks up to 100 kg	160/ set		320.00
1	A100	Power Blocks up to 200 kg	300/ set		300.00
2	A120	Wavemaster	150/ unit		300.00
1	A140	Weights: Olympic 75 kg	150/ set		150.00
1	A170	Weights: Olympic 150 kg	300/ set		300.00
1	E110	Rider: Airwalker RA-900	300/ unit		300.00
1	E120	Rider: Powerglider RP-1500	350/ unit		350.00
1	E170	Stair Climber: Adjustable SC-A60	1 500/ unit		1 500.00
2	E190	Treadmill: Basic T-800B	1 200/ unit		2 400.00
8	S010	Personal Trainer: 1 hour	75/ hour		600.00
4	S020	Personal Trainer: 1/2 day	200/ 1/2 day		800.00
6	S040	Yoga Instructor: 1 hour	100/ hour		600.00
2	S050	Yoga Instructor: 1/2 day	200/ 1/2 day		400.00
		GST	5%		427.25
		PST	8%		491.60
		Total paid by Visa			$9 463.85

☐ **Memo #6-2**   **Dated June 14, 2010**

Record payment for GST for May to the Receiver General for Canada. Issue cheque #136 in full payment. Clear the GST Report up to May 31.

☐ Record payment for PST Payable for May to the Minister of Finance. Remember to collect 5% of the amount owing as the sales tax compensation. Issue cheque #137 in full payment. Clear the PST Report up to May 31.

☐ **Memo #6-3**   **Dated June 14, 2010**

Payroll Remittances: Make the following payroll remittances for the pay period ending May 31 in the Payments Journal.

☐ Record payment for EI, CPP and Income Tax Payable for May to the Receiver General for Canada. Issue cheque #138 in full payment.

☐ Record payment for Garnisheed Wages Payable for May to the Receiver General for Canada. Issue cheque #139 in full payment.

☐ Record payment for RRSP Payable to Ancaster Insurance. Issue cheque #140 in full payment.

☐ Record payment for CSB Payable to Mt. Hope Investment Corporation. Issue cheque #141 in full payment.

☐ Record payment for Group Insurance Payable for May to Ancaster Insurance. Issue cheque #142 in full payment.

☐ Record payment for Charitable Donations Payable for May to Canadian Cancer Society. Create a new supplier record and select Payroll Authority for the supplier. Choose the new supplier in the Payroll Remittance Settings screen for both Donations entries. Include employee and employer contributions in remittance. Issue cheque #143 in full payment.

☐ **Cheque Copy #350**   **Dated June 15, 2010**

To Prolife Exercisers, $3 131.20 USD in payment of account including $60.80 discount for early payment. Reference invoice #PE-2079. The exchange rate is 1.018.

NOTES
Enter Memo 6-2A and Memo 6-2B as the reference numbers for the tax remittances.

NOTES
Enter Memo 6-3A, Memo 6-3B, and so on, in the Additional Information field as the reference numbers for the payroll remittances.

NOTES
You cannot create the new supplier from the Pay Remittance form in the Payments Journal — you must close the Remittance Journal.
Refer to page 673 for setting up payroll authorities and remittances.

NOTES
The next deposit, from Buffalo Health Clinic, will cover the bank overdraft.

☐   **Purchase Invoice #FG-2187**   **Dated June 15, 2010**

From Feelyte Gym Accessories to fill purchase order #33

1	A080	Heart Rate Monitor (1 carton of 12)	$360.00
20	A110	Stability Balls	80.00
2	A180	Workout Gloves: all sizes (2 boxes of 10)	80.00
		GST	26.00
		Invoice total	$546.00

Terms: 2/10, n/30.

SESSION DATE – JUNE 30, 2010

☐   **Cash Receipt #50**   **Dated June 16, 2010**

From Buffalo Health Clinic, cheque #638 for $4 860 USD in payment of account.
Reference invoice #3013. The exchange rate is 1.02.

☐   **Sales Invoice #3016**   **Dated June 16, 2010**

To Stelco Health Club (preferred customer)

40	A130	Weight Plates	$ 1.10/ kg
1	E080	Home Gym: Basic HG-1400	1 000/ set
1	E100	Home Gym: Multi HG-1402	1 875/ set
1	E105	Home Gym: Free Weight HG-1403	2 000/ set
		Freight	30
		GST	5%
		PST	8%

Terms: 2/10, n/30.

☐   **Memo #6-4**   **Dated June 16, 2010**

Transfer $30 000 from the Visa bank account to the savings account.

☐   **Memo #6-5**   **Dated June 18, 2010**

Pay $8 000 to the Receiver General for Canada for quarterly instalment of
business income tax. Issue cheque #144. Create new Group account 5550
Business Income Tax Expense. (Hint: Remember Business Income Tax Payable.)

☐   **Memo #6-6**   **Dated June 18, 2010**

Create appropriate new Heading and Total accounts around the new Group
account 5550 to restore the logical order of accounts.

☐   **Cash Purchase Invoice #BC-86344**   **Dated June 19, 2010**

From Bell Canada, $100 plus $5 GST paid and $8 PST for monthly phone service.
Purchase invoice total $113. Terms: cash on receipt of invoice. Issue cheque #145
in full payment.

☐   **Cash Purchase Invoice #ES-89886**   **Dated June 19, 2010**

From Energy Source, $120 plus $6 GST paid for hydro service. Purchase invoice
total $126. Terms: cash on receipt of invoice. Issue cheque #146 in full payment.

☐   **Cash Sales Invoice #3017**   **Dated June 20, 2010**

To Jim Ratter (choose Continue)

1	A010	Body Fat Scale		$100.00
		GST	5%	5.00
		PST	8%	8.00
		Invoice total		$113.00

Received cheque #16 in full payment.

☐ **Cheque Copy #147**   **Dated June 20, 2010**

To Footlink Corporation, $1 029.60 in payment of account including $9.90 discount for early payment. Reference invoice #FC-861.

☐ **Cheque Copy #148**   **Dated June 23, 2010**

To Feelyte Gym Accessories, $535.60 in payment of account including $10.40 discount for early payment. Reference invoice #FG-2187.

☐ **Cash Receipt #51**   **Dated June 23, 2010**

From Stelco Health Club, cheque #499 for $5 478.17 in payment of account including $111.80 discount for early payment. Reference invoice #3016.

☐ **Deposit Slip #22**   **Dated June 23, 2010**

Prepare deposit slip for two cheques totalling $5 591.17 to deposit funds.

☐ **Credit Card Sales Invoice #3018**   **Dated June 23, 2010**

To Visa customers (sales summary)

Qty	Code	Item	Price	Amount
10	A020	Yoga Mats	$ 30/ each	$ 300.00
40	A030	Dumbbells: pair	1.50/ kg	60.00
2	A050	Dumbbells: 10kg set	25/ set	50.00
2	A060	Dumbbells: 15kg set	40/ set	80.00
2	A100	Power Blocks up to 200 kg	300/ set	600.00
10	A110	Stability Balls	10 each	100.00
2	A150	Weights: Olympic 100 kg	200/ set	400.00
1	E070	Bicycle: Recumbent R-80	750/ unit	750.00
1	E090	Home Gym: Deluxe HG-1401	1 500/ set	1 500.00
1	E110	Rider: Airwalker RA-900	300/ unit	300.00
1	E140	Ski Exerciser: Skitrek SE-680	400/ unit	400.00
1	E170	Stair Climber: Adjustable SC-A60	1 500/ unit	1 500.00
4	S020	Personal Trainer: 1/2 day	200/ 1/2 day	800.00
8	S040	Yoga Instructor: 1 hour	100/ hour	800.00
4	S050	Yoga Instructor: 1/2 day	200/ 1/2 day	800.00
	GST		5%	422.00
	PST		8%	483.20
	Total paid by Visa			$9 345.20

☐ **Employee Time Summary Sheet #19**   **Dated June 23, 2010**

For the Pay Period ending June 23, 2010
George Schwinn worked 80 regular and 2 overtime hours in the period and took 1 day of sick leave. Recover $50 advanced and issue payroll deposit slip DD28.

☐ **Memo #6-7**   **Dated June 24, 2010**

Issue a cheque to George Schwinn for vacation pay. George wants to pay for his upcoming vacation. A contract has been arranged with a local delivery company to complete deliveries during his absence. Issue cheque #149.

☐ **Sales Invoice #3019**   **Dated June 25, 2010**

To Lockport Gymnasium, New York

Qty	Code	Item	Price
1	E010	Elliptical Exerciser: ME-100	$1 100/ unit USD
1	E040	Elliptical Exerciser: LE-400	2 200/ unit USD
1	E180	Stair Climber: Unlinked SC-U75	2 100/ unit USD
1	E190	Treadmill: Basic T-800B	1 200/ unit USD
	Freight		60 USD

Terms: 2/10, n/30. The exchange rate is 1.005.

 WARNING!
Remember to remove all wage amounts, deductions and user-defined expense amounts for the vacation paycheque.
    Remember to turn on the Retain option after creating the vacation paycheque.

NOTES
You cannot reverse this NSF cheque or enter a negative receipt for it because it was a cash sale. You cannot adjust the invoice by changing the method of payment.

Entering the Bank Account in the Sales Invoice for the amount of the NSF cheque will reverse the bank deposit and restore the accounts payable.

Use Quick Add to create a new partial record for Jim Ratter. For the Ratter invoice, credit chequing account for $113, credit Other Revenue for $20, debit Accounts Receivable for $133. Refer to Accounting Procedures, page 628.

NOTES
Use tax code IN for $113, the sale portion of the bad debt. Use No Tax as the code for the $20 handling charge. Remember to "pay" the account. Refer to Accounting Procedures, page 628.

NOTES
Use the Paycheques Journal to enter the piece rate pay and bonuses.
- Click Enter Taxes Manually so that you can edit the income tax amounts.
- On the Income tab screen, remove all hours, wage, salary and benefit amounts. Do not remove Vacation Accrued for Schwinn.
- On the remaining tab screens, remove entitlement hours and deduction and user-defined expense amounts.
- Click the Taxes tab.
- Click Recalculate Taxes.
- Enter the income tax amount. Do not change the EI or CPP amounts.
- Click Enter Taxes Automatically after creating the bonus cheques.

Memo #6-7   **Dated June 25, 2010**

Received Bank Debit Memo #99142 from Hamilton Trust. Cheque #16 from Jim Ratter for $113 was returned as NSF. Prepare a sales invoice to charge Ratter for the sales amount and add $20 in service charges for the cost of processing the cheque. Create new Group account 4220 Other Revenue. Terms: net 30.

Purchase Order #34   **Dated June 25, 2010**

Delivery date July 1, 2010
From Scandia Weights Co.

1	A130	Weight Plates (1 order of 100 kg)	$	60.00
3	A140	Weights: Olympic 75 kg		225.00
3	A150	Weights: Olympic 100 kg		300.00
3	A160	Weights: Olympic 125 kg		375.00
3	A170	Weights: Olympic 150 kg		450.00
	GST			70.50
	Purchase invoice total			$1 480.50

Terms: net 30.

Cash Purchase Invoice #DMC-89   **Dated June 28, 2010**

From Dundurn Maintenance Co., $300 plus $15 GST paid for cleaning and maintenance of premises. Terms: cash on receipt. Issue cheque #150 for $315 in full payment. Recall stored transaction.

Memo #6-8   **Dated June 29, 2010**

Write off Jim Ratter's account because attempts to locate him were unsuccessful. The outstanding amount is considered a bad debt. Improved screening of customers who pay by cheque will be implemented immediately.

Credit Card Purchase Invoice #WS-9855   **Dated June 30, 2010**

From Waterdown Sunoco, $98 including GST and PST paid for gasoline. Purchase invoice total $98 paid in full by Visa.

Credit Card Sales Invoice #3020   **Dated June 30, 2010**

To Visa customers (sales summary)

2	A070	Glide Slidetrak	$ 50 each		$	100.00
20	A130	Weight Plates	1.20/ kg			24.00
1	E060	Bicycle: Dual Action DA-70	600/ unit			600.00
8	S010	Personal Trainer: 1 hour	75/ hour			600.00
2	S030	Personal Trainer: full day	400/ day			800.00
3	S050	Yoga Instructor: 1/2 day	200/ 1/2 day			600.00
	GST		5%			136.20
	PST		8%			57.92
	Total paid by Visa					$2 918.12

Memo #6-9   **Dated June 30, 2010**

Prepare the payroll for Nieve Prekor and Assumpta Kisangel, the salaried employees. Add 2 percent of service revenue for June as a commission to Kisangel's salary. Issue payroll deposit slips DD29 and DD30.

Prepare separate payroll cheques to pay all employees for completed surveys and quarterly bonuses. Withhold 10 percent income tax. (See margin notes.)

Kisangel $300 bonus, 20 completed client surveys, $50 income tax
Prekor $250 bonus, 28 completed client surveys, $53 income tax
Schwinn $250 bonus, 26 completed client surveys, $51 income tax

Issue cheques #151, #152 and #153.

☐ **Bank Credit Memo #7642**   **Dated June 30, 2010**

From Hamilton Trust, semi-annual interest was deposited to bank accounts. $155 was deposited to chequing account and $815 to the savings account. Remember interest receivable balance $420.

☐ **Bank Debit Memo #143661**   **Dated June 30, 2010**

From Hamilton Trust, authorized withdrawals were made from the chequing account on our behalf for the following:

Bank service charges	$ 35
Mortgage interest payment	1 850
Mortgage principal reduction	150
Bank loan interest payment	380
Bank loan principal reduction	520

☐ **Memo #6-10**   **Dated June 30, 2010**

Prepare quarterly adjusting entries for depreciation on fixed assets using the following amounts:

Cash Registers	$ 300
Computer Equipment	150
Furniture & Fixtures	80
Retail Premises	2 450
Van	1 875

☐ **Memo #6-11**   **Dated June 30, 2010**

Increase the allowance for doubtful accounts by $500 in preparation for the next fiscal period.

☐ **Memo #6-12**   **Dated June 30, 2010**

Prepare adjusting entries for the following:

Office Supplies used	$ 290
Linen Supplies used	120
Prepaid Insurance expired	2 016
Prepaid Advertising expired	620
Payroll Liabilities accrued for Schwinn	680

Create a new Group liability account Accrued Payroll 2260.

R E V I E W

The Student CD-ROM with Data Files includes Review Questions and Supplementary Cases for this chapter that encourage group work and report analysis. The cases also include bank reconciliation and online banking.

CHAPTER SEVENTEEN

Stratford Country Inn

OBJECTIVES

After completing this chapter, you should be able to

- **plan** and **design** an accounting system for a small business
- **prepare** a conversion procedure from manual records
- **understand** the objectives of a computerized accounting system
- **create** company files
- **set up** company accounts
- **assign** appropriate account numbers and account classes
- **choose** and **enter** appropriate settings for all ledgers
- **create** supplier, guest and employee records
- **enter** historical data and account balances in all ledgers
- **finish** entering historical data to prepare for journal entries
- **enter** accounting transactions from realistic source documents

COMPANY INFORMATION

Company Profile

NOTES
Stratford Country Inn
100 Festival Road
Stratford, Ontario
N5A 3G2
Tel 1: (519) 222-6066
Tel 2: (888) 272-6000
Fax: (519) 272-7960
Business No.: 767 698 321

Stratford Country Inn is situated in Ontario just outside the Stratford city limits, close to Stratford Festival Theatres. The Inn has room for approximately 50 guests, with additional cots available for families who want to share rooms. In addition to the theatre, which attracts most of the guests, the Inn has facilities for rowing and canoeing on the small lake area near the Thames River, and a forested area nearby is used for lovely summer walks or cross-country skiing in winter. Boxed lunches and dinners are provided for picnics on the waterfront before theatre events or for afternoons in the woods or on the lake. Many guests stay for several days at a time, and weekly rates are offered.

For an additional cost, a private consultant will pamper the guests with aromatherapy sessions. The consultant pays a rental fee to the Inn for use of her studio.

NOTES
For the accommodation business, the terms Guest and Supplier replace Customer and Vendor.

Guests come from near and far, and even a few American theatre groups have become regular visitors. The Inn prepares invoices and accepts payments in United States dollars for US accounts. For the American groups, an agency books group tours for a fixed price that includes theatre tickets and accommodation. Most individual guests pay by Visa or MasterCard. All guests pay GST and PST on the services provided by the Inn. The PST rate for accommodation is 5 percent instead of the standard 8 percent. Regular guests, corporations such as colleges, universities and schools, or agencies that reserve blocks of theatre tickets and accommodation have credit accounts. Groups place a deposit to confirm their accommodation. In the event of overbooking, guests who cannot be placed at the Inn are put up at a nearby bed & breakfast at the Inn's expense.

The grounds of the Inn include conference rooms for discussions and debates about theatre performances and related topics. Buses take guests to the theatre and return them to the Inn on a scheduled basis. Meals can be included for those who want an all-inclusive package. The Inn's dining room serves all full accommodation guests and also caters to the public and to guests who choose not to take a full meal package.

The owner, manager and desk attendant look after the front office. Five additional staff cater to all the other needs of the guests.

Accounts Payables have been set up for food supplies, a maintenance contract (a cleaning crew vacuums the Inn), maintenance and repairs (electrical and carpentry work), linen supplies for kitchen and guest rooms and laundry services for towels and bedding.

By June 30, the Inn was ready to convert its accounting records to Simply Accounting and had gathered the following reports to make the conversion:

- Chart of Accounts
- Post-Closing Trial Balance
- Supplier Information
- Guest Information
- Employee Information and Profiles

Simply SIMPLY VERSION
The terms Customer and Vendor will replace the terms Guest and Supplier.

CHART OF ACCOUNTS

STRATFORD COUNTRY INN

ASSETS
Bank: Stratford Trust CAD Chequing
Bank: Stratford Trust USD Chequing
Bank: Credit Card
Accounts Receivable
Advances Receivable
Purchase Prepayments
Prepaid Advertising
Prepaid Insurance
Food Inventory
Linens & Towels
Blankets & Bedding
Supplies: Computer
Supplies: Office
Supplies: Dining Room
Supplies: Washroom
Computer Equipment
Accum Deprec: Computers
Furniture & Fixtures ▶

▶Accum Deprec: Furn & Fix
Vehicle
Accum Deprec: Vehicle
Country Inn & Dining Room
Accum Deprec: Inn & Dining Room
Grounds & Property

LIABILITIES
Bank Loan
Accounts Payable
Prepaid Sales and Deposits
Credit Card Payable
Vacation Payable
EI Payable
CPP Payable
Income Tax Payable
EHT Payable
Group Insurance Payable
Tuition Fees Payable
WSIB Payable ▶

▶PST Payable
GST Charged on Services
GST Paid on Purchases
Mortgage Payable

EQUITY
E. Prospero, Capital
Current Earnings

REVENUE
Revenue from Inn
Revenue from Dining Room
Rental Fees
Sales Tax Compensation
Other Revenue
Exchange Rate Differences

EXPENSE
Advertising & Promotion
Bank Charges and Card Fees
COGS: Food ▶

▶Depreciation: Computers
Depreciation: Furn & Fix
Depreciation: Vehicle
Depreciation: Inn & Dining Room
Purchase Discounts
Interest Expense: Loan
Interest Expense: Mortgage
Hydro Expenses
Maintenance & Repairs
Overflow Accommodation
Telephone Expense
Vehicle Expenses
Wages: Management
Wages: General
Wages: Dining Room
EI Expense
CPP Expense
WSIB Expense
EHT Expense
Tuition Fees Expense

NOTES: Use appropriate account numbers and add subgroup totals, headings and totals to organize your Chart of Accounts as necessary. Remember to add a test balance account for the setup.

POST-CLOSING TRIAL BALANCE

STRATFORD COUNTRY INN

June 30, 2010	Debits	Credits		Debits	Credits
Bank: Stratford Trust CAD Chequing	$33 964		▶ Accum Deprec: Vehicle		10 000
Bank: Stratford Trust USD Chequing			Country Inn & Dining Room	400 000	
(2 985 USD)	3 000		Accum Deprec: Inn & Dining Room		20 000
Bank: Credit Card	12 000		Grounds & Property	200 000	
Accounts Receivable (deposit)		$ 1 000	Bank Loan		25 000
Advances Receivable	250		Accounts Payable		7 780
Prepaid Advertising	50		Credit Card Payable		395
Prepaid Insurance	400		Vacation Payable		4 946
Food Inventory	1 650		EI Payable		1 092
Linens & Towels	2 000		CPP Payable		1 759
Blankets & Bedding	3 000		Income Tax Payable		3 109
Supplies: Computer	400		EHT Payable		577
Supplies: Office	500		Group Insurance Payable		330
Supplies: Dining Room	800		WSIB Payable		1 310
Supplies: Washroom	250		PST Payable		3 200
Computer Equipment	4 000		GST Charged on Services		3 080
Accum Deprec: Computers		1 200	GST Paid on Purchases	700	
Furniture & Fixtures	38 000		Mortgage Payable		300 000
Accum Deprec: Furn & Fix		4 200	E. Prospero, Capital		361 986
Vehicle	50 000 ▶			$750 964	$750 964

SUPPLIER INFORMATION

STRATFORD COUNTRY INN

Supplier Name (Contact)	Address	Phone No. Fax No.	E-mail Web Site	Terms Tax ID
Avon Maintenance Services (Ken Sparkles)	66 Kleen Road Stratford, Ontario N5A 3C3	Tel: (519) 272-4611 Fax: (519) 272-4813	www.avonservices.com	net 30 631 393 461
Bard's Linen & Towels (Jason Bard)	21 Venice Street Stratford, Ontario N5A 4L2	Tel: (519) 271-2273 Fax: (519) 271-9333	bard@bards.com www.bards.com	2/10, n/30 after tax 763 271 673
Bell Canada (Bea Heard)	30 Whisper Road Stratford, Ontario N5A 4N3	Tel: (519) 273-2355	bheard@bell.ca www.bell.ca	net 1 634 345 373
Minister of Finance	PO Box 3000, Stn A Toronto, Ontario M5C 1M2		www.gov.on.ca/fin	net 1
Perth County Hydro (Wynd Mills)	66 Power Road Stratford, Ontario N5A 4P4	Tel: (519) 272-6121	www.perthenergy.com	net 1 721 431 214
Receiver General for Canada	PO Box 20002, Stn A Sudbury, Ontario P3A 5C3	Tel: (800) 959-5525	www.cra-arc.gc.ca	net 1
Stratford Service Centre (A.L.L. Ledfree)	33 MacBeth Avenue Stratford, Ontario N5A 4T2	Tel: (519) 271-6679 Fax: (519) 276-8822	ledfree@ssc.com www.ssc.com	net 1 634 214 211
Tavistock Laundry Services (Martin Tavistock)	19 Merchant Road Stratford, Ontario N5A 4C3	Tel: (519) 271-7479 Fax: (519) 271-7888	www.tavistock.com	net 30 639 271 343
Tempest Food Wholesalers (Vita Minns)	35 Henry Avenue Stratford, Ontario N5A 3N6	Tel: (519) 272-4464 Fax: (519) 272-4600	vita@tempest.com www.tempest.com	net 30 673 421 936
Travellers' Life				
Workplace Safety & Insurance Board				
Zephyr Advertising Services (Tom DeZiner)	32 Portia Blvd. Stratford, Ontario N5A 4T2	Tel: (519) 271-6066 Fax: (519) 271-6067	tom@westwinds.com www.westwinds.com	net 1 391 213 919

LIST OF PAYROLL AUTHORITIES

STRATFORD COUNTRY INN

Supplier Name	Payroll Remittance
Receiver General for Canada	EI, CPP and Income Tax
Workplace Safety & Insurance Board	WSIB
Minister of Finance	EHT
Travellers' Life	group insurance

OUTSTANDING SUPPLIER INVOICES

STRATFORD COUNTRY INN

Supplier Name	Terms	Date	Inv/Chq No.	Amount	Total
Avon Maintenance Services	net 30	June 7/10	AM-68	$525	
	net 30	June 14/10	AM-85	525	
	net 30	June 21/10	AM-101	525	
	net 30	June 28/10	AM-127	525	
			Balance owing		$2 100
Tavistock Laundry Services	net 30	June 8/10	TL-693	$840	
	net 30	June 22/10	TL-742	840	
			Balance owing		$1 680
Tempest Food Wholesalers	net 30	June 23/10	TF-113	$2 000	
	net 30	June 30/10	TF-183	2 000	
			Balance owing		$4 000
			Grand Total		$7 780

GUEST INFORMATION

STRATFORD COUNTRY INN

Guest Name (Contact)	Address	Phone No. / Fax No.	E-mail / Web Site	Terms / Credit Limit
Festival Club of Rosedale (Jane Birken)	3 Rosedale Valley Rd. Toronto, Ontario M5G 3T4	Tel: (416) 482-6343	janebir@conundrum.com	net 5 $6 000
Hamlet Holiday Agency (Ron Doleman)	60 Tibault Avenue Stratford, Ontario N5A 3K3	Tel 1: (519) 272-6461 Tel 2: (800) 777-7777	rdoleman@hamlet.com www.hamlet.com	net 5 $6 000
Metro Arts Appreciation Group (R. Downey)	4400 Yonge St. North York, Ontario M6L 3T4	Tel: (416) 923-8142	RDowney@artnet.com www.artnet.com	net 5 $6 000
NY Friends of Shakespeare (J. Monte)	33, 16th Avenue Buffalo, NY 13002	Tel 1: (716) 755-4992 Tel 2: (888) 755-5000	monte@aol.com	net 5 $4 000 (USD)
Waterloo University Literary Club (T. Fornello)	88 College Rd. Waterloo, Ontario N2A 3F6	Tel: (519) 431-6343	fornello4@uwo.ca	net 5 $6 000

OUTSTANDING GUEST INVOICES

STRATFORD COUNTRY INN

Guest Name	Terms	Date	Inv/Chq No.	Total
Hamlet Holiday Agency	net 30	June 30/10	Deposit #40 (Chq 317; enter a negative invoice)	$1 000

EMPLOYEE INFORMATION SHEET

STRATFORD COUNTRY INN

	Owen Othello	Clara Claudius	Mary MacBeth	Hedy Horatio	Juliet Jones	Shelley Shylock	Bud Romeo
Position	Manager	Clerk	Cook	Waiter	Concierge	Waiter	Service
Social Insurance No.	691 113 724	873 863 211	284 682 556	294 654 421	177 162 930	891 263 634	254 685 829
Address	38 Falstaff St. Stratford, ON N5A 3T3	147 King Henry St. Mary's, ON N4X 1B2	3 Bard Cr. Stratford, ON N5A 6Z8	17 Elizabeth St. Stratford, ON N5A 4Z1	5 Capella Cres. Stratford, ON N5A 5M1	29 Avon St. Stratford, ON N5A 5N5	42 Hosteller St. New Hamburg, ON N0B 2G0
Telephone	(519) 272-2191	(519) 373-6495	(519) 277-1338	(519) 278-5343	(519) 273-9122	(519) 273-5335	(519) 381-3738
Date of Birth (mm-dd-yy)	6-29-71	4-21-64	8-3-69	12-3-76	1-25-70	3-12-80	5-27-69
Date of Hire (mm-dd-yy)	3-1-98	5-2-91	6-1-01	6-1-03	1-1-02	1-1-06	12-16-00
Federal (Ontario) Tax Exemption - TD1							
Basic Personal	$9 600 (8 681)	$9 600 (8 681)	$9 600 (8 681)	$9 600 (8 681)	$9 600 (8 681)	$9 600 (8 681)	$9 600 (8 681)
Other	$4 480 (4 480)	–	$9 600 (7 371)	$2 570 (2 570)	$17 619 (15 402)	$9 660 (9 684)	$9 600 (7 371)
Total Exemptions	$14 080 (13 161)	$9 600 (8 681)	$19 200 (16 052)	$12 170 (11 251)	$27 219 (24 083)	$19 260 (18 365)	$19 200 (16 052)
Indexed Amounts	$9 600 (8 681)	$9 600 (8 681)	$19 200 (16 052)	$9 600 (8 681)	$27 219 (24 083)	$9 600 (8 681)	$19 200 (16 052)
Additional Federal Tax	–	–	–	$50.00	–	$50.00	–
Employee Taxes							
Historical Income tax	$4 110.12	$2 796.42	$3 029.01	$2 655.52	$3 345.44	$1 013.86	$1 499.66
Historical EI	$501.60	$376.20	$513.51	$329.55	$468.16	$176.36	$325.85
Historical CPP	$989.34	$721.44	$1 014.83	$621.80	$917.87	$294.49	$613.90
Employee Income							
Advances: Historical	–	–	–	$100.00	–	–	$150.00
Benefits: Historical	$2 800.00	–	–	–	–	$2 470.00	–
Vacation Pay Owed	–	–	$1 400.57	$898.85	$1 276.85	$480.96	$888.77
Regular Wage Rate	–	–	$22.00/hr.	$14.00/hr.	$20.00/hr.	$12.00/hr.	$14.00/hr.
No. Hours Per Period	160	160	80	80	80	80	80
Wages: Historical	–	–	$22 880.00	$14 560.00	$20 800.00	$7 872.00	$14 560.00
Overtime 1 Wage Rate	–	–	$33.00/hr	$21.00/hr	$30.00/hr	$18.00/hr	$21.00/hr
Overtime 1: Historical	–	–	$462.00	$420.00	$480.00	$144.00	$252.00
Regular Salary	$3 800/mo.	$2 850/mo.	–	–	–	–	–
Salary: Historical	$22 800.00	$17 100.00	–	–	–	–	–
Commission	1% (Sales–Returns)	–	–	–	–	–	–
Pay Periods	12	12	26	26	26	26	26
Vacation Rate	4 weeks	4 weeks	6% retained	6% retained	6% retained	6% retained	6% retained
Wage Account	Management	General	Dining Room	Dining Room	General	Dining Room	General
Deductions							
Group Insurance	$30.00	$60.00	$30.00	$15.00	$30.00	$15.00	$30.00
Insurance: Historical	$180.00	$360.00	$390.00	$195.00	$390.00	$195.00	$390.00
WSIB and User-Defined Expenses							
WSIB Rate	2.55	2.55	1.70	1.70	2.55	1.70	2.55
Tuition: Historical	$2 800.00	–	–	$1 450.00	–	$2 470.00	–
Entitlements (Rate, Maximum Days, Clear, Days Accrued)							
Vacation	8%, 30, No, 20	8%, 30, No, 20	–	–	–	–	–
Sick Leave	5%, 15, No, 9	5%, 15, No, 7	5%, 15, No, 8	5%, 15, No, 9	5%, 15, No, 10	5%, 15, No, 3	5%, 15, No, 8
T4 and RL-1 Reporting							
EI Insurable Earnings	$22 800.00	$17 100.00	$23 342.00	$14 980.00	$21 280.00	$8 016.00	$14 812.00
Pensionable Earnings	$22 800.00	$17 100.00	$23 342.00	$14 980.00	$21 280.00	$8 016.00	$14 812.00
Withheld	$5 781.06	$4 254.06	$4 947.35	$3 801.87	$5 121.47	$1 679.71	$2 829.41
Net Pay	$17 018.94	$12 845.94	$18 394.65	$11 278.13	$16 158.53	$6 336.29	$12 132.59

Payroll Information

General Payroll Information   E. Prospero, the owner, has arranged group insurance for his employees, and all employees have elected to join the plan. As entitlements, all staff may take 10 days' sick leave per year, and the vacation allowances are quite generous for the industry — four weeks of paid vacation for salaried staff after three years of service and 6 percent for all hourly paid employees. As an additional benefit, employees are reimbursed for their tuition fees on completion of eligible courses. Salaried employees are paid monthly, and hourly employees are paid every two weeks. All employees are eligible for EI and pay CPP; the EI factor is 1.4. The Inn pays 0.98 percent of payroll for EHT, the provincial health tax. WSIB rates vary for different types of work performed by the employees of the Inn.

Wage expenses for the manager, the dining room staff and the remaining general employees are tracked separately in three different payroll expense accounts.

Employee Profiles and TD1 Information

E. Prospero   owns the Inn and oversees all activities. Together with family members, he fills in where needed. He does not collect a salary and is not recorded as an employee.

Owen Othello   is the salaried manager for the Inn. He welcomes guests, instructs other employees and discusses issues, problems and plans with the owner. He is single and studies part time in an MBA program. One night a week he commutes to Toronto. An education allowance — $140 per month federal and $140 provincial — and $2 800 for tuition increase his basic tax claim amounts. Othello is the salesperson for all sales, and beginning in July, he will receive a commission of 1 percent of sales.

Clara Claudius   has been with the Inn the longest and works as the desk attendant. Although her primary job is reservations clerk, she also performs the accounting for the Inn. She too is salaried. Because her husband is also fully employed, she uses only the basic single tax claim amounts. They have two young children as dependants.

Mary MacBeth   works as the cook in the dining room. As a single parent with dependent children, she is allowed to use the eligible dependant claim as the spousal equivalent for tax purposes. She is paid at an hourly rate of $22 per hour for the first 40 hours each week and $33 per hour after that.

Hedy Horatio   divides her time between waiting tables and helping the cook for her pay at the rate of $14 per hour plus $21 per hour for overtime hours. She studies part time at Conestoga College in the chef training program. The $1 450 tuition fee and the education tax claims — $140 per month federal and $140 provincial — supplement her basic single claim.

Juliet Jones   deals with requests from guests, working as the concierge and arranging for room service. She lives with and cares for her father and therefore has the eligible dependant claim plus a caregiver claim. She also has additional deductions transferred from her father ($4 000 federal and provincial) to supplement her basic single claim. Her hourly wage rate is $20 for the first 40 hours in the week and $30 for additional hours.

Shelley Shylock   waits tables in the dining room at the Inn. During the summer and festival months, she works full time for the Inn at the rate of $12 per hour and $18 for hours beyond the first 40 each week. She works part time until summer while she is a full-time student at the University of Waterloo. The education deduction of $465 ($468 provincial) per month plus tuition fees at $5 940 supplement her tax claim amounts.

NOTES
Enter entitlements as Payroll Settings and edit records for each employee as needed.
Tuition is a user-defined payroll expense and taxable benefit. The benefits for Othello, Horatio and Shylock have already been paid, so only historical amounts are entered.
Remember that WSIB is the name for WCB in Ontario.

NOTES
The claim amounts subject to indexing do not include education and tuition amounts. The amount subject to indexing is used by the program to update claim amounts when a new tax table is introduced, based on the government indexing rate.

NOTES
Federal education amounts include the monthly allowance for textbooks.

Bud Romeo   takes care of room service requests and also handles the baggage for the guests. He is married with two dependent children, so he has the spousal claim amount in addition to the basic single amount. He too is paid hourly at the rate of $14 per hour and $21 per hour for the time beyond 40 hours per week.

INSTRUCTIONS

1. Use all the information presented in this application to set up the company accounts for Stratford Country Inn in Simply Accounting using the following steps:
    a. Create company files in a new data folder for storing the company records.
    b. Enter the company information. Start a new fiscal period on July 1, 2010, and finish the period on September 30, 2010. Choose Accommodation as the industry.
    c. Enter names and printer information.
    d. Prepare the settings by changing the default settings as necessary.
    e. Organize the Balance Sheet and Income Statement accounts.
    f. Create accounts to correspond to your Balance Sheet and Income Statement. Add appropriate account numbers and types.
    g. Set up currency information for the USD transactions. The exchange rate on June 30 is 1.005.
    h. Change the account class for bank and credit card accounts and set up the cheque sequence.
    i. Enter linked accounts for the ledgers and credit cards. The fee is 2.75 percent.
    j. Enter sales tax information and create tax codes for GST @ 5%, refundable; PST @ 8% for regular transactions and PST @ 5% for accommodation. On some items, GST alone is charged and on others PST is charged alone. GST is also sometimes charged with PST at 5 percent and sometimes with PST at 8 percent.
    k. Enter guest, supplier and employee information.
    l. Enter historical balances in all ledgers.
    m. Create two Job Categories: Sales (employees are salespersons) and Other (employees in this category are not salespersons). Assign Othello to Sales and all other employees to the Other category.
    n. Set up Payroll Authorities and Payroll Remittances. Add the balance forward amounts from the Trial Balance as at July 1, 2010.
    o. Back up your files.
    p. Finish entering the history for all ledgers and finish your session.

2. Using the information provided, enter the source documents for July using Simply Accounting.

3. After you have completed your entries, print the following reports:
    a. Journal Entries (All Journals) from July 1 to July 31, 2010
    b. Supplier Aged Detail Report for all suppliers on July 31, 2010
    c. Guest Aged Detail Report for all guests on July 31, 2010
    d. Employee Summary (all employees) for the pay period ending July 31, 2010
    e. Income Statement for the period ending July 31, 2010

WARNING!
Save your work and make backups frequently.

WARNING!
Remember to use a test balance account to check the trial balance before finishing the history for the General Ledger. Print the appropriate reports to check your work as you enter the company data.

NOTES
Set up two taxes, GST and PST. GST is refundable and PST is not refundable.
Then create tax codes for:
GST only
PST only at 8%
GST with PST at 5%
GST with PST at 8%

SIMPLY VERSION
Remember that the term Vendors and Customers will replace Suppliers and Guests.

SOURCE DOCUMENTS

Create new accounts or supplier and guest records as needed for the source documents that follow.

NOTES
PST is paid on purchases at the rate of 8 percent.

Telephone:
(519) 271-BARD (2273)
Fax:
(519) 271-9333

Website:
www.bards.com
E-mail:
bard@bards.com

Invoice:	BLT-64

Sold to: Stratford Country Inn
100 Festival Road
Stratford, ON
N5A 3G2

Date: July 1, 2010

STOCK NO.	QTY.	DESCRIPTION	PRICE	AMOUNT
1601	20	Satin Sheets	35.00	700.00
1801	100	Bath Towels	10.00	1000.00
2802	100	Face Cloths	3.00	300.00

CUSTOMER COPY	Terms on Account: 2/10, N/30			GROSS	2000.00
Method of payment:	On Account	C.O.D.	Credit Card	GST 5%	100.00
GST #763 271 673	✓			PST 8%	160.00
				TOTAL	2260.00

---

66 Kleen Road, Stratford, ON N5A 3C3
Telephone (519) 272-4611
Fax: (519) 272-4813
www.avonservices.com

Invoice:	AM-148
Date:	July 5, 2010
Sold to:	Stratford Country Inn
100 Festival Road
Stratford, ON
N5A 3G2
Phone:	(519) 222-6066

Code	Service Description	Price
KX-55	Vacuum Premises
Floor Polishing
Washroom Cleaning
Maintenance and repairs

Recurring bi-weekly billing | 1000.00 |

Signature:	*E Prosper*	Terms: Net 30 days	GST	50.00
		GST #631 393 461	Amount owing	1050.00

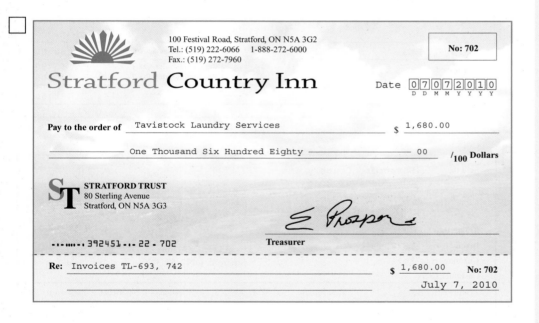

Waterloo University Literary Club
88 College Road
Waterloo, ON N2A 3F6

No: 413

Date 0 6 0 7 2 0 1 0
     D D M M Y Y Y Y

Pay to the order of Stratford Country Inn $ 1,000.00

——————————— One Thousand ——————————————————— 00/100 **Dollars**

WT **Waterloo Trust**
550 King Street
Waterloo, ON N2A 3F8

T. Fornells

Chair

� 60431 ⑅ 105 ⑅ 413

- -

Re: Deposit #55 — booking rooms in Inn   **No: 413**

————————————————————— $1,000.00   July 6, 2010

---

100 Festival Road, Stratford, ON N5A 3G2
Tel.: (519) 222-6066   1-888-272-6000
Fax.: (519) 272-7960

No: 702

Stratford **Country Inn**   Date 0 7 0 7 2 0 1 0
                                          D D M M Y Y Y Y

Pay to the order of Tavistock Laundry Services $ 1,680.00

——————— One Thousand Six Hundred Eighty ——————— 00   /100 **Dollars**

ST **STRATFORD TRUST**
80 Sterling Avenue
Stratford, ON N5A 3G3

E. Prosper

Treasurer

⑅ 392451 ⑅ 22 - 702

- -

Re: Invoices TL-693, 742 $ 1,680.00   **No: 702**

——————————————————————   July 7, 2010

100 Festival Road, Stratford, ON N5A 3G2
Tel.: (519) 222-6066   1-888-272-6000
Fax.: (519) 272-7960
prospero@stratfordinns.com

Stratford Country Inn

The comfort of Home   www.stratfordinns.com

VISA   No: 27 V

SALES SUMMARY
STATEMENT

Week _____ July 7, 2010 _____

Accommodation ☑

Restaurant ☑

Transaction	Amount	
Accommodation and Room Services	5,250	00
Restaurant Services	1,750	00

GST # 767 698 321	**Goods and Services Tax**	350	00
Approved:	**Provincial Sales Tax 1**	262	50
E Prospero	**Provincial Sales Tax 2**	140	00
	VISA Receipts	7,752	50

Sold to: Stratford Country Inn
100 Festival Road
Stratford, ON
N5A 3G2

Billing Date: July 8, 2010

Invoice No: TF-284

Customer No.:   3423

Customer Copy

TEMPEST
Food Wholesalers

35 Henry Avenue
Stratford, ON N5A 3N6

Telephone:
(519) 272-4464
Fax:
(519) 272-4600
Website:
www.tempest.com

Date	Description	Charges	Payments	Amount
July 8/10	Fish and Meats	1000.00		1000.00
	Fresh Fruits	200.00		200.00
	Fresh Vegetables	200.00		200.00
	Dry Goods	200.00		200.00
	Dairy Products	200.00		200.00
	Baking Goods	200.00		200.00
	Recurring bi-weekly billing			

Terms: Net 30 days	**Subtotal**	2000.00
GST #673 421 936	**GST 5%**	exempt
Signature: *E Prospero*	**PST 8%**	exempt
Overdue accounts are subject to 16% interest per year	**Owing**	2000.00

Invoice No: TL-798

Date: July 8, 2010

Customer: Stratford Country Inn
100 Festival Road
Stratford, ON
N5A 3G2

Phone: (519) 222-6066

TAVISTOCK
LAUNDRY
Services

19 Merchant Road   Phone: (519) 271-7479
Stratford, ON   Fax: (519) 271-7888
N5A 4C3   www.tavistock.com

GST #639 271 343

Code	Description	Price	Amount
C-11	10 Loads Sheets	40.00	400.00
C-14	5 Loads Pillow Covers	20.00	100.00
C-20	15 Loads Towels	20.00	300.00
	Recurring bi-weekly billing		

Overdue accounts are subject to a 2% interest penalty per month		**Sub-total**	800.00
Terms: Net 30 days		**GST**	40.00
Signature: *E Prosper*		**Total**	840.00

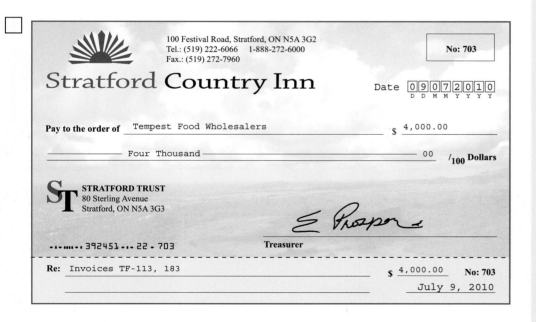

100 Festival Road, Stratford, ON N5A 3G2
Tel.: (519) 222-6066   1-888-272-6000
Fax.: (519) 272-7960

No: 703

Stratford Country Inn

Date | 0 | 9 | 0 | 7 | 2 | 0 | 1 | 0 |
D D   M M   Y Y Y Y

Pay to the order of   Tempest Food Wholesalers $ 4,000.00

———— Four Thousand ———————————————— 00 /100 **Dollars**

ST   STRATFORD TRUST
80 Sterling Avenue
Stratford, ON N5A 3G3

E Prosper

⑈392451⑈⑈ 22 ⑊ 703   **Treasurer**

- -

Re: Invoices TF-113, 183 $ 4,000.00   **No: 703**
                                      July 9, 2010

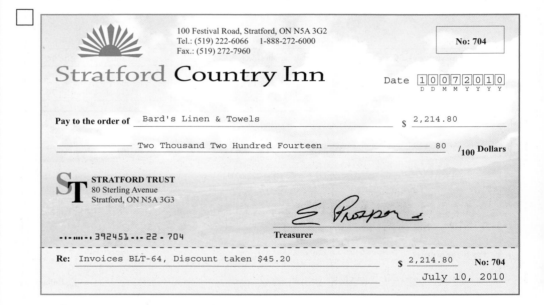

Hamlet Holiday Agency
60 Tibault Avenue,
STRATFORD, ON N5A 3K3

No: 349

Date 1 0 0 7 2 0 1 0
D D M M Y Y Y Y

Pay to the order of   Stratford Country Inn $ 2,312.00

——————— Two thousand, three hundred & twelve ——————— 00 /100 **Dollars**

SB **Scotia Bank**
44 Welland Avenue
STRATFORD, ON N5A 3F6

Treasurer

⑆⑈⑆ 64299 ⑆⑆ 168 ⑆⑆ 349

Re: Deposit #56 (Cheque #317)   **No: 349**

Invoice #701 $2,312.00   July 10, 2010

---

100 Festival Road, Stratford, ON N5A 3G2
Tel.: (519) 222-6066   1-888-272-6000
Fax.: (519) 272-7960

No: 704

Stratford **Country Inn**

Date 1 0 0 7 2 0 1 0
D D M M Y Y Y Y

Pay to the order of   Bard's Linen & Towels $ 2,214.80

——————— Two Thousand Two Hundred Fourteen ——————— 80 /100 **Dollars**

ST **STRATFORD TRUST**
80 Sterling Avenue
Stratford, ON N5A 3G3

Treasurer

⑆⑈⑆ 392451 ⑆⑆ 22 ⑆ 704

Re: Invoices BLT-64, Discount taken $45.20 $ 2,214.80   **No: 704**

July 10, 2010

33 MacBeth Avenue
Stratford, ON N5A 4T2
Tel: (519) 271-6679
Fax: (519) 276-8822
www.ssc.com

Date: July 11, 2010   **Invoice:** 1143

Customer: Stratford Country Inn
                100 Festival Road
                Stratford, ON
                N5A 3G2

Phone: (519) 222-6066

GST #634 214 211

Code	Description	Price	Amount
M-114	Lube, Oil and Filter	40.00	40.00
XF-1	Fuel	120.00	120.00
		Sub-total	160.00

APPROVAL	CUSTOMER COPY			GST	8.00
EP	Cash	VISA	On Account	PST	12.80
		✓		**Owing**	180.80

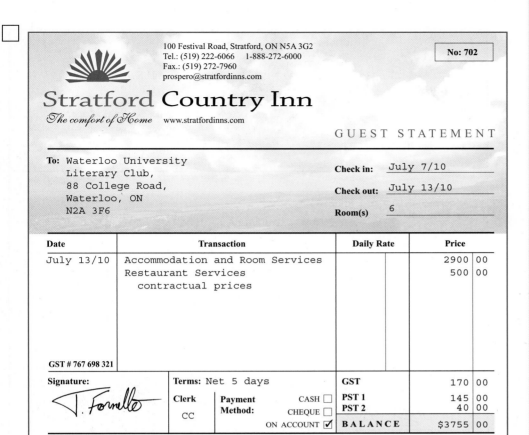

100 Festival Road, Stratford, ON N5A 3G2
Tel.: (519) 222-6066   1-888-272-6000
Fax.: (519) 272-7960
prospero@stratfordinns.com

No: 702

Stratford Country Inn

The comfort of Home   www.stratfordinns.com

GUEST STATEMENT

To: Waterloo University
Literary Club,
88 College Road,
Waterloo, ON
N2A 3F6

Check in:	July 7/10
Check out:	July 13/10
Room(s)	6

Date	Transaction	Daily Rate	Price	
July 13/10	Accommodation and Room Services		2900	00
	Restaurant Services		500	00
	contractual prices			

GST # 767 698 321

Signature: *J. Fornello*

Terms: Net 5 days

Clerk
CC

Payment Method:
CASH ☐
CHEQUE ☐
ON ACCOUNT ☑

GST	170	00
PST 1	145	00
PST 2	40	00
BALANCE	$3755	00

NY Friends of Shakespeare
33, 16th Avenue,
Buffalo, NY 13002

No: 137

Date 13 07 2010
D D M M Y Y Y Y

Pay to the order of   Stratford Country Inn $ 1,000.00 (USD)

———————— One thousand ——————————————— 00/100 Dollars

CB **Chase Bank**
4, 12th Avenue
Buffalo, NY 13002

J. Monte

⑆⑆⑉⑈ 93937 ⑆ 301 ⑆ 137

- -

Re: Deposit #57 — booking rooms in Inn. United   **No: 137**
States Currency. Currency Exchange 0.9815 $1,000.00 (USD)   July 13, 2010

100 Festival Road, Stratford, ON N5A 3G2
Tel.: (519) 222-6066   1-888-272-6000
Fax.: (519) 272-7960
prospero@stratfordinns.com

Stratford Country Inn

The comfort of Home   www.stratfordinns.com

VISA

No: 28 V

SALES SUMMARY
STATEMENT

Week _____ July 14, 2010 _____

Accommodation ☑

Restaurant ☑

Transaction	Amount	
Accommodation and Room Services	4,900	00
Restaurant Services	2,100	00

GST # 767 698 321

Approved:

E Prospero

Goods and Services Tax	350	00
Provincial Sales Tax 1	245	00
Provincial Sales Tax 2	168	00
V I S A Receipts	7,763	00

---

100 Festival Road, Stratford, ON N5A 3G2
Tel.: (519) 222-6066   1-888-272-6000
Fax.: (519) 272-7960
prospero@stratford.com

Stratford Country Inn

The comfort of Home   www.stratfordinns.com

ET27

EMPLOYEE TIME
SUMMARY SHEET

Pay period ending: July 14, 2010

Name of Employee	Regular hours	Overtime hours	Sick days
☐ Horatio, Hedy	80	0	0
☐ Jones, Juliet	80	0	1
☐ MacBeth, Mary	80	2	0
☐ Romeo, Bud	80	2	0
☐ Shylock, Shelley	80	2	0

Memo: Issue cheques #708 to #712
        Recover $100 advance from Horatio and Romeo

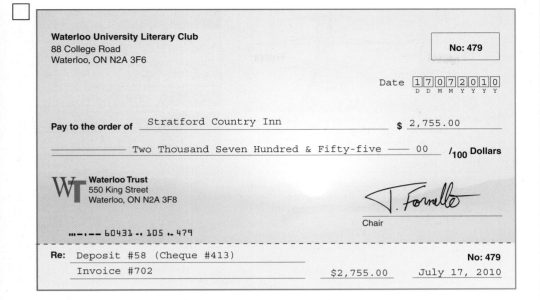

Waterloo University Literary Club
88 College Road
Waterloo, ON N2A 3F6

No: 479

Date 1 7 0 7 2 0 1 0
D D M M Y Y Y Y

Pay to the order of   Stratford Country Inn $ 2,755.00

——————— Two Thousand Seven Hundred & Fifty-five ——— 00   /100 **Dollars**

Waterloo Trust
550 King Street
Waterloo, ON N2A 3F8

Chair

⑈⑉⑉–⑈⑉–– ᑗ0431 –⑉ 105 ⑉– 479

Re: Deposit #58 (Cheque #413)   **No: 479**

      Invoice #702 $2,755.00   July 17, 2010

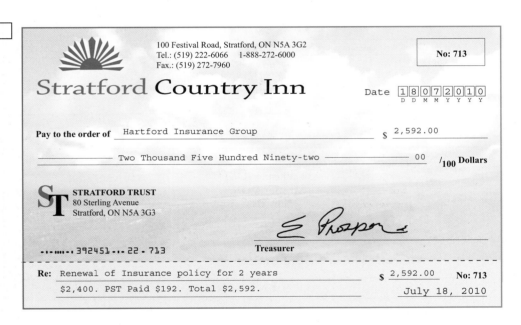

100 Festival Road, Stratford, ON N5A 3G2
Tel.: (519) 222-6066   1-888-272-6000
Fax.: (519) 272-7960

No: 713

Stratford Country Inn   Date 1 8 0 7 2 0 1 0
D D M M Y Y Y Y

Pay to the order of Hartford Insurance Group $ 2,592.00

——————— Two Thousand Five Hundred Ninety-two ——————— 00   /100 **Dollars**

STRATFORD TRUST
80 Sterling Avenue
Stratford, ON N5A 3G3

Treasurer

⑈⑉⑉⑈⑈⑈⑉⑈ 392451 ⑉⑈⑉ 22 ⑉ 713

Re: Renewal of Insurance policy for 2 years $ 2,592.00   **No: 713**

      $2,400. PST Paid $192. Total $2,592.   July 18, 2010

PERTH COUNTY HYDRO
66 Power Road, Stratford,
Ontario N5A 4P4
www.perthenergy.com

**Customer
Care:**
272-6121

CUSTOMER NAME / SERVICE ADDRESS
Stratford Country Inn
100 Festival Road
Stratford, ON
N5A 3G2

Date:	July 18, 2010
Account No:	3921 462 513
Invoice No:	37232

Months	Reading	Description	Net Amount
1	86527	Commercial Consumption	300.00
1		Flat Rate Charge — Water Heaters	60.00
1		Rental of Equipment	40.00
		Total Current Charges	400.00
		Previous Charges 385.20	
		Total Payments, Thank You 385.20	
		Balance Forward	0.00
		Adjustments	0.00

*Paid in Full with
cheque #714 for $420
07/18/10   E Prosper*

Average Daily KWh Consumption		GST #721 431 214	Due Date	GST 5%	20.00
Same Period Last Year	**This Bill**	After due date, a 1.5% monthly late payment interest charge will apply.	July 25/10		
269	258		**Pay This Amount**	**TOTAL**	420.00

**30 Whisper Road
Stratford, ON
N5A 4N3**

www.bell.ca

Account Inquiries: 273-BELL (2355)

Account Number
519-222-6066

Account Address

Stratford Country Inn
100 Festival Road
Stratford, ON
N5A 3G2

July 18, 2010

ACCOUNT SUMMARY

Current Charges	
Monthly Services (June 12 to July 12)	240.00
Equipment Rentals	50.00
Chargeable Messages	30.00
GST 634 345 373	16.00
PST	25.60
Total Current Charges	361.60
Previous Charges	
Amount of Last Bill	323.00
Payment Received June 19 — Thank You	323.00
Adjustments	0.00
Balance Forward	0.00

*Paid in Full — chq
#715 — 07/18/10
E Prosper*

| Invoice:
BC-66431	PLEASE PAY THIS AMOUNT UPON RECEIPT ➡	$361.60

Invoice No: AM-184

Date: July 19, 2010

Sold to: Stratford Country Inn
100 Festival Road
Stratford, ON
N5A 3G2

Phone: (519) 222-6066

66 Kleen Road, Stratford, ON N5A 3C3
Telephone (519) 272-4611
Fax: (519) 272-4813
www.avonservices.com

Code	Service Description		Price
KX-55	Vacuum Premises Floor Polishing Washroom Cleaning Maintenance and repairs Recurring bi-weekly billing * new price as described in our previous notice	*	1100.00

Signature: E Prospero

Terms: Net 30 days	**GST**	55.00
GST #631 393 461	**Amount owing**	1155.00

---

100 Festival Road, Stratford, ON N5A 3G2
Tel.: (519) 222-6066   1-888-272-6000
Fax.: (519) 272-7960
prospero@stratfordinns.com

No: 703

Stratford Country Inn
The comfort of Home   www.stratfordinns.com

GUEST STATEMENT

To: NY Friends of Shakespeare,
33, 16th Avenue,
Buffalo, NY
13002

Check in: July 14/10

Check out: July 20/10

Room(s): 8

Date	Transaction	Daily Rate	Price	
July 20/10	Accommodation and Room Services		2600	00
	Restaurant Services		400	00
	contractual prices			
	All amounts billed in			
	United States currency			
	Exchange rate: 1.0195 CAD			
GST # 767 698 321				

Signature: J. Monte

Terms: Net 5 days		**GST**	150	00
Clerk CC	**Payment Method:** CASH ☐ CHEQUE ☐ ON ACCOUNT ☑	**PST 1**	130	00
		PST 2	32	00
		BALANCE	$3312	00

Festival Club of Rosedale
3 Rosedale Valley Rd.
Toronto, Ontario
M5G 3T4

No: 61

Date 2 0 0 7 2 0 1 0
    D D M M Y Y Y Y

Pay to the order of   Stratford Country Inn $ 1,000.00

───────── One Thousand ─────────── 00 /100 **Dollars**

R **Royal Bank**
B 56 Bloor Street
    Toronto, ON M5N 3G7

Jane Birker

Chairperson

⑈─── 34298 ⑈021⑈ 061

Re: Deposit #59 — booking rooms in Inn   No: 61

─────────────────────── $1,000.00   July 20, 2010

Metro Arts Appreciation Group
4400 Yonge Street,
North York, ON
M6L 3T4

No: 79

Date 2 0 0 7 2 0 1 0
    D D M M Y Y Y Y

Pay to the order of   Stratford Country Inn $ 1,000.00

───────── One Thousand ─────────── 00 /100 **Dollars**

CIBC **CIBC**
      4800 Yonge Street
      North York, ON M6L 3T4

R. Downes

⑈─── 396421⑈214⑈079

Re: Deposit #60 — booking rooms in Inn   No: 79

─────────────────────── $1,000.00   July 20, 2010

STRATFORD TRUST
80 Sterling Avenue
Stratford, ON N5A 3G3

VISA

Statement Period M D Y	Account Number	Account Enquiries	Daily Interest Rate	Annual Interest Rate
From 06/15/10	4512 6221 1384 6201	1-800-272-VISA	.05068%	18.5%
To 07/15/10				

Trans. Date	Post Date	Particulars	Amount	Bus. Exp.
06 13	06 16	Stratford Service Centre, Stratford, ON	85.00	*EP*
06 18	06 21	Office Supplies Unlimited, Stratford, ON	88.00	*EP*
06 25	06 27	Stratford Service Centre, Stratford, ON	133.00	*EP*
06 28	06 30	Bullrich Dept. Store #32, Stratford, ON	113.00	*EP*
06 28	06 30	Bullrich Dept. Store #32, Stratford, ON	-24.00	*EP*
07 11	07 13	Stratford Service Centre, Stratford, ON	180.80	*EP*
06 20	06 20	Payment — Thank You	-422.00	*EP*

*Balance $575.80 paid in Full
by cheque # 716
E Prospero
July 21/10*

Credit Limit	Opening Balance	Total Credits	Total Debits	Your New Balance
8500.00	422.00	446.00	599.80	575.80

Available Credit	Payment Due Date Month Day Year	Overlimit or Past Due	Current Due	Minimum Payment	Payment Amount
7924.20	07/24/10		57.00	57.00	575.80

Stratford Country Inn
The comfort of Home   www.stratfordinns.com

100 Festival Road, Stratford, ON N5A 3G2
Tel.: (519) 222-6066   1-888-272-6000
Fax.: (519) 272-7960
prospero@stratfordinns.com

VISA   No: 29 V

SALES SUMMARY
STATEMENT

Week   July 21, 2010

Accommodation ☑
Restaurant ☑

Transaction	Amount	
Accommodation and Room Services	5,000	00
Restaurant Services	1,950	00

GST # 767 698 321

Approved: *E Prospero*

Goods and Services Tax	347	50
Provincial Sales Tax 1	250	00
Provincial Sales Tax 2	156	00
VISA Receipts	7,703	50

Sold to: Stratford Country Inn
100 Festival Road
Stratford, ON
N5A 3G2

TEMPEST
Food Wholesalers

Telephone:
(519) 272-4464
Fax:
(519) 272-4600
Website:
www.tempest.com

Billing Date: July 22, 2010
Invoice No: TF-344
Customer No.: 3423
Customer Copy

35 Henry Avenue
Stratford, ON N5A 3N6

Date	Description	Charges	Payments	Amount
July 22 /10	Fish and Meats	1000.00		1000.00
	Fresh Fruits	200.00		200.00
	Fresh Vegetables	200.00		200.00
	Dry Goods	200.00		200.00
	Dairy Products	200.00		200.00
	Baking Goods	200.00		200.00
	Recurring bi-weekly billing			

Terms: Net 30 days	Subtotal	2000.00
GST #673 421 936	GST 5%	exempt
Signature: *E. Proper*	PST 8%	exempt
Overdue accounts are subject to 16% interest per year	Owing	2000.00

Invoice No: TL-841

Date: July 22, 2010

Customer: Stratford Country Inn
100 Festival Road
Stratford, ON
N5A 3G2

Phone: (519) 222-6066

TAVISTOCK
LAUNDRY
Services

19 Merchant Road
Stratford, ON
N5A 4C3

Phone: (519) 271-7479
Fax: (519) 271-7888
www.tavistock.com

GST #639 271 343

Code	Description		Price	Amount
C-11	10 Loads Sheets	*	45.00	450.00
C-14	5 Loads Pillow Covers		20.00	100.00
C-20	15 Loads Towels		20.00	300.00
	Recurring bi-weekly billing			
	* new prices			

Overdue accounts are subject to a 2% interest penalty per month	Sub-total	850.00
Terms: Net 30 days	GST	42.50
Signature: *E. Proper*	Total	892.50

Zephyr Advertising Services
32 Portia Blvd.,
Stratford, ON
N5A 4T2

Telephone (519) 271-6066
Fax (519) 271-6067
www.westwinds.com
orders: contact tom@westwinds.com

Stratford Country Inn
100 Festival Road
Stratford, ON
N5A 3G2

ZA - 6998

Date	Description	Charges	Amount
July 23, 2010	Brochures & Flyers	100.00	100.00
		GST	5.00
		PST	8.00

Paid in full
cheque # 717
July 23/10
E. Prospero

GST # 391 213 919	**Terms:** Cash on Receipt	Total	113.00

NY Friends of Shakespeare
33, 16th Avenue,
Buffalo, NY 13002

No: 181

Date 2 4 0 7 2 0 1 0
      D D M M Y Y Y Y

Pay to the order of Stratford Country Inn $ 2,312.00 (USD)

———— Two Thousand, three hundred twelve ———— 00 /100 **Dollars**

CB Chase Bank
4, 12th Avenue
Buffalo, NY 13002

J Monte

⑈⑆⑈ 93937 ⑈ 301 ⑈⑈ 181

Re: Deposit #61 — (Cheque #137) Invoice #703.   **No: 181**
U.S. Currency. Currency Exchange 1.021 Cdn. $2,312.00 (USD)   July 24, 2010

STRATFORD SERVICE CENTRE

33 MacBeth Avenue
Stratford, ON N5A 4T2
Tel: (519) 271-6679
Fax: (519) 276-8822
www.ssc.com

Date: July 25, 2010		**Invoice:** 1207

Customer: Stratford Country Inn
100 Festival Road
Stratford, ON
N5A 3G2

Phone: (519) 222-6066

GST #634 214 211

Code	Description	Price	Amount
R-69	Transmission—overhaul	500.00	500.00
XF-1	Fuel	100.00	100.00
		Sub-total	600.00

APPROVAL	CUSTOMER COPY			GST	30.00
EP	Cash	VISA	On Account	PST	48.00
		✔		**Owing**	678.00

---

100 Festival Road, Stratford, ON N5A 3G2
Tel.: (519) 222-6066   1-888-272-6000
Fax.: (519) 272-7960
prospero@stratfordinns.com

No: 704

Stratford Country Inn
The comfort of Home   www.stratfordinns.com

GUEST STATEMENT

To: Metro Arts Appreciation Group,
4400 Yonge Street,
North York, ON
M6L 3T4

Check in:	July 21/10
Check out:	July 26/10
Room(s)	5

Date	Transaction	Daily Rate	Price	
July 26/10	Accommodation and Room Services		2200	00
	Restaurant Services		200	00
	contractual prices			
GST # 767 698 321				

Signature:	Terms: Net 5 days		GST	120	00
R. Downes	Clerk	Payment Method:	PST 1	110	00
	CC	CASH ☐ CHEQUE ☐	PST 2	16	00
		ON ACCOUNT ☑	**BALANCE**	$2646	00

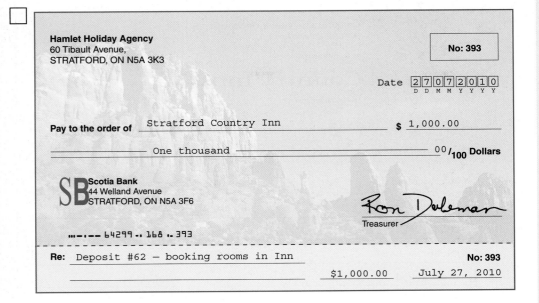

Hamlet Holiday Agency
60 Tibault Avenue,
STRATFORD, ON N5A 3K3

No: 393

Date 2 7 0 7 2 0 1 0
      D D M M Y Y Y Y

Pay to the order of   Stratford Country Inn $ 1,000.00

———————— One thousand ————————————— 00/100 Dollars

SB Scotia Bank
44 Welland Avenue
STRATFORD, ON N5A 3F6

Ron Deleman
Treasurer

⑈⑈⑈⑈⑈⑈ 64299 ⑈ 168 ⑈ 393

Re: Deposit #62 — booking rooms in Inn

$1,000.00   July 27, 2010   No: 393

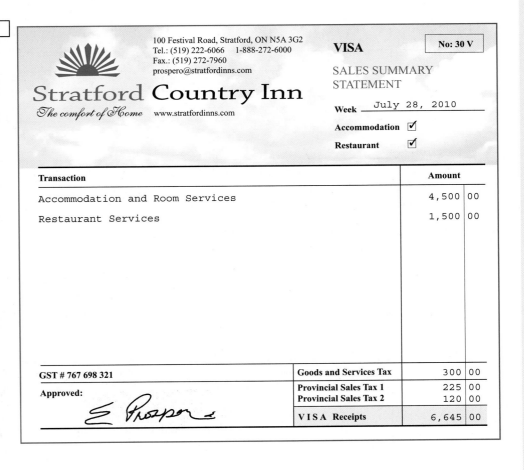

100 Festival Road, Stratford, ON N5A 3G2
Tel.: (519) 222-6066   1-888-272-6000
Fax.: (519) 272-7960
prospero@stratfordinns.com

Stratford Country Inn
The comfort of Home   www.stratfordinns.com

VISA   No: 30 V

SALES SUMMARY
STATEMENT

Week July 28, 2010

Accommodation ☑
Restaurant ☑

Transaction	Amount	
Accommodation and Room Services	4,500	00
Restaurant Services	1,500	00

GST # 767 698 321

Approved:
E Prospero

Goods and Services Tax	300	00
Provincial Sales Tax 1	225	00
Provincial Sales Tax 2	120	00
VISA Receipts	6,645	00

100 Festival Road, Stratford, ON N5A 3G2
Tel.: (519) 222-6066   1-888-272-6000
Fax.: (519) 272-7960
prospero@stratford.com

| ET28 |

Stratford Country Inn

The comfort of Home   www.stratfordinns.com

EMPLOYEE TIME
SUMMARY SHEET

Pay period ending: July 28, 2010

Name of Employee	Regular hours	Overtime hours	Sick days
☐ Horatio, Hedy	80	2	0
☐ Jones, Juliet	76	4	0
☐ MacBeth, Mary	80	0	0
☐ Romeo, Bud	80	0	1
☐ Shylock, Shelley	80	2	0

Memo: Issue cheques #718 to #722
Recover $50 advance from Romeo

---

100 Festival Road, Stratford, ON N5A 3G2
Tel.: (519) 222-6066   1-888-272-6000
Fax.: (519) 272-7960
prospero@stratfordinns.com

| No: 705 |

Stratford Country Inn

The comfort of Home   www.stratfordinns.com

GUEST STATEMENT

To: Festival Club of Rosedale,
3 Rosedale Valley Road,
Toronto, ON
M5G 3T4

Check in: July 26/10

Check out: July 30/10

Room(s) 6

Date	Transaction	Daily Rate	Price	
July 30/10	Accommodation and Room Services		1800	00
	Restaurant Services		200	00
	contractual prices			

GST # 767 698 321

Signature: *Jane Birker*

Terms:			
Clerk CC	Payment Method:	CASH ☐ CHEQUE ☐ ON ACCOUNT ☑	

GST	100	00
PST 1	90	00
PST 2	16	00
BALANCE	$2206	00

100 Festival Road, Stratford, ON N5A 3G2
Tel.: (519) 222-6066   1-888-272-6000
Fax.: (519) 272-7960
prospero@stratfordinns.com

Stratford Country Inn

The comfort of Home   www.stratfordinns.com

MEMO

From: the owner's desk
To: Clara Claudius
July 31, 2010

1. a) Pay Owen Othello, manager, salary and sales commission for
      one month. Issue cheque #723.
   b) Pay Clara Claudius, desk attendant, salary for one month. Issue
      cheque #724.
2. Transfer $35,000 from Credit Card Bank account to Chequing account.
3. Prepare adjusting entries for the following:
   a) Food Inventory on hand $1395
   b) Write off $200 of Prepaid Insurance
   c) Write off $50 of Prepaid Advertising
   d) Depreciation on assets:
      Country Inn & Dining Rooom $600
      Computers $100
      Furniture & Fixtures $600
      Vehicles $800
4. Pay quarterly balances owing as at July 1
   a) To Minister of Finance (EHT)
   b) Workplace Safety and Insurance Board (WSIB)
   c) Travellers' Life (Group Insurance)
   Issue cheques # 725, 726, 727

R E V I E W

The Student CD-ROM with Data Files includes a
comprehensive supplementary case for this chapter.

Part 3
Advanced Premium Features

CHAPTER EIGHTEEN

Flabuless Fitness

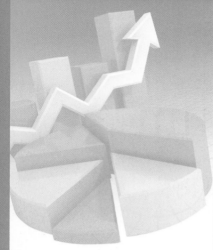

OBJECTIVES

After completing this chapter, you should be able to

- **set up** inventory service activities for time and billing
- **update** prices from Inventory Settings
- **enter** employee time slips
- **import** activity summaries to prepare employee paycheques
- **import** activity summaries to prepare customer invoices
- **display** and **print** time and billing reports
- **set up** additional currencies
- **build** new inventory from Inventory Ledger record details
- **set up** multiple inventory locations
- **add** inventory locations to journal entries
- **transfer** inventory between locations
- **show** related accounts for multiple fiscal periods
- **display** and **print** multi-period financial reports

COMPANY INFORMATION

Time and Billing Profile

Flabuless Fitness will modify its service inventory to invoice customers according to the time spent on various activities. The Time and Billing module of the Premium version is designed for this purpose. After modifying the service records to price the services according to the time spent providing them, the company can track the work performed by each employee for each customer.

Additionally, new suppliers in countries outside of North America will sell inventory to the company. Even with the extra shipping charges, the new prices are very competitive. No duty is charged on imported gym and exercise equipment.

In July, Flabuless Fitness will provide repair service for the equipment it sells. Repair work is billed in three ways: regular repairs are billed at an hourly rate; equipment that is under warranty is repaired at no charge; and repairs for customers with service contracts are charged at a flat rate for each service call regardless of the time required to complete the repairs. Repair work will be managed from a second location that Reeves is preparing to open nearby in Burlington, Ontario. The Burlington store will also sell the complete range of fitness accessories. Other inventory items can be shipped to that location if requested by customers. Two inventory locations will be set up for the two stores so that Reeves can track the inventory at each location.

Reeves hired two new employees, Yvonne Tinker and Moishe Alee. Tinker will assist Schwinn with the repairs and maintenance of exercise equipment. Tinker is also trained as a yoga instructor and can provide service as a personal trainer. Alee will work as the primary sales associate in the new store.

The company's fiscal period will be reduced to one month and customer invoice summaries will be used to reduce the number of source documents that you enter in this application.

SOURCE DOCUMENTS

SESSION DATE – JULY 1, 2010

☐ **Memo #7-1**   **Dated July 1, 2010**

Prepare an adjusting entry to reverse the year-end adjustment for $680 for accrued payroll. (Debit Accrued Payroll and credit Wages.)

☑ **Memo #7-2**   **Dated July 1, 2010**
743   Change the company fiscal dates. The new fiscal end is July 31, 2010.
Change account number for 1150 Net Bank to 1190 to accommodate the new bank account for foreign currency transactions.

☑ **Memo #7-3**   **Dated July 1, 2010**
744   Add euro as a foreign currency to prepare for purchases from a new supplier in Germany. The linked account for exchange rate differences is 4120 and the exchange rate on July 1 is 1.5805.
Create new Subgroup account 1150 Bank: Euro Chequing. 1150 is a Bank class account and the next cheque number is 101.
Add 1150, the new bank account, as the linked account for Payables and Receivables bank transactions in euros.

☑ **Memo #7-4**   **Dated July 1, 2010**
746   Set up inventory locations for the two stores: Hamilton and Burlington. The Hamilton store is the primary location for inventory and the Burlington store is the secondary location for accessories and repair work.

☑ **Memo #7-5**   **Dated July 1, 2010**
747   Create new inventory service records to add services and include Time & Billing information:

Item	Description	Selling Price Reg	(Pref)	Unit	Related to Time?	Billable?	Billing Basis	Rate
S060	Repair Service	$ 80	($75)	Hour	Yes	billable	billable time	
S070	Contract Repairs	100	(90)	Service Call	No	billable	flat fee	1 call × price
S100	Warranty Repairs	0	(0)	Service Call	No	non-billable		

Linked accounts: Revenue: 4050 Revenue from Repairs (new Subgroup account)
              Expense: 5065 Cost of Services
Taxes: Charge GST and PST on repair service work.

✓ · **Memo #7-6**   **Dated July 1, 2010**

751   Edit the remaining service inventory records to add Time & Billing information and change the Canadian dollar prices.

Item	Selling Price Reg	(Pref)	Unit	Related to Time?	Relation	Billable?	Billing Basis
S010	$ 75	($ 70)	hour	yes		billable	billable time
S020	210	(195)	1/2 day	yes	3 hours/ 1/2 day	billable	billable time
S030	420	(385)	day	yes	7 hours/ day	billable	billable time
S040	100	(95)	hour	yes		billable	billable time
S050	210	(195)	1/2 day	yes	3 hours/ 1/2 day	billable	billable time

NOTES
The full TD1 claim amounts are subject to indexing.
Refer to pages 324–335 if you need assistance with entering the new employees. There is no historical information for the new employees.
Tinker and Alee will not receive the group insurance benefit or the piece rate pay (No. Clients) or Bonus initially. Those benefits will apply after they finish the probationary work period.

Memo #7-7   **Dated July 1, 2010**

Create two new employee records for Yvonne Tinker and Moishe Alee. Tinker will work exclusively on customer jobs (activities) billed on the basis of time. She will be paid for the hours worked, but her minimum pay will be for 20 hours per week. Alee will be paid a monthly salary as a sales assistant in the Burlington store.

	Tinker, Yvonne	Alee, Moishe
Address:	499 Toolkit Dr.	551 Staefit Dr.
	Hamilton, ON L7F 2P9	Burlington, ON L5T 8H3
Telephone	(905) 458-7192	(905) 688-9101
SIN	420 011 009	128 663 887
Birthdate	06-23-79	08-31-81
Date of Hire	07-01-10	07-01-10
Job Category	Sales	Sales
Tax Table	Ontario	Ontario
Fed Claim	$9 600	$9 600
Prov Claim	($8 681)	($8 681)
Regular Wage	$16/hour	NA
# hours:	20 hours	150 hours
	(min hours in paycheque)	
Overtime Wage	$24/hour	NA
Salary	NA	$2 950 /month
Do not use	Salary, Commission	Regular, Overtime
Pay Period:	Weekly (52 per year)	Monthly (12 per year)
Vacation:	4% Retained	4% Retained
Record Wage	Expenses in: Payroll linked accounts	
WSIB Rate:	1.29	1.29
Sick leave	5%, 15 days max	5%, 15 days max
Personaldays	2.5%, 5 days max	2.5%, 5 days max
Vacation	delete entry	delete entry
Direct deposit	100% of paycheque to	100% of paycheque to
	bank #102	bank #102
	transit #89008,	transit #67752,
	account #341002	account #198823

Cash Receipt #53   **Dated July 1, 2010**

From Lockport Gymnasium, cheque #1628 for $6 526.80 USD in full payment of account including $133.20 discount for early payment. Reference sales invoice #3019. The exchange rate is 1.011.

Memo #7-8   **Dated July 1, 2010**

From Visa, received monthly credit card statement for $98 for purchases made before July 1, 2010. Submitted cheque #154 for $98 in full payment of the balance owing.

SESSION DATE – JULY 14, 2010

☑ **TIME SLIP #1**   **DATED JULY 7, 2010**

756   For George Schwinn

Customer	Item	Actual Time	Billable Time	Billable Amount	Payroll Time
McMaster University	S010	2 hours	1.5 hours	$105.00	2 hours
McMaster University	S070	2 hours	2 hours	90.00	2 hours
Mohawk College	S020	4 hours	4 hours	260.00	4 hours
Mohawk College	S060	2 hours	2 hours	150.00	2 hours
Mohawk College	S100	2 hours	–	–	2 hours

☐ **TIME SLIP #2**   **DATED JULY 7, 2010**

For Yvonne Tinker

Customer	Item	Actual Time	Billable Time	Billable Amount	Payroll Time
McMaster University	S050	7 hours	6 hours	$390.00	7 hours
McMaster University	S060	4 hours	3.5 hours	262.50	4 hours
Chedoke Health Care	S020	4 hours	3 hours	195.00	4 hours
Chedoke Health Care	S060	6 hours	5 hours	375.00	6 hours
Chedoke Health Care	S100	2 hours	–	–	2 hours

NOTES
Remember to enter 330 for 3.5 hours. You cannot enter decimals in the Time Slips Journal.

☑ **Employee Time Summary Sheet #20**   **Dated July 7, 2010**

760   For the Pay Period ending July 7, 2010
Use time slips to prepare the paycheque for Yvonne Tinker. Issue deposit slip #31. Pay George Schwinn for 80 regular hours in the period and 2 hours of overtime. Recover $50 advanced and issue deposit slip #32.

☑ **Sales Invoice #3021**   **Dated July 7, 2010**

762   To McMaster University: Complete sales invoice for $847.50 plus GST and PST from time slip activities. Include all activities to date. Sales invoice total $918.08. Terms: 2/10, n/30.

☐ **Sales Invoice #3022**   **Dated July 7, 2010**

To Mohawk College: Complete sales invoice for $410 plus GST and PST from time slip activities. Include all activities to date. Sales invoice total $442.50. Terms: 2/10, n/30.

☐ **Sales Invoice #3023**   **Dated July 7, 2010**

To Chedoke Health Care: Complete sales invoice for $570 plus GST and PST from time slip activities. Include all activities to date. Sales invoice total $628.50. Terms: 2/10, n/30.

☑ **Memo #7-9**   **Dated July 7, 2010**

764   Create a new inventory record for a promotional fitness package that bundles together several popular fitness accessories. Create new Asset account: 1510 Promotions when prompted.
Item: AP100 Promotional Fitness Package
Unit: package
Minimum: 0
Linked accounts: Asset 1510 Promotions   Revenue 4020   COGS 5050

Currency	Regular Selling Price	Preferred Selling Price
CAD	$210	$200
USD	$210	$200
EUR	€135	€125

Tax exempt: GST No   PST No

Build Components: use 1 of each　A010 Body Fat Scale
A020 Yoga Mats
A040 Dumbbells: 5kg set
A080 Heart Rate Monitor
A110 Stability Balls
A180 Workout Gloves: all sizes

☑ **Memo #7-10**　　　　　　　　　　　　　　**Dated July 7, 2010**

766　Build two packages of the new item Promotional Fitness Package (AP100).

☑ **Memo #7-11**　　　　　　　　　　　　　　**Dated July 7, 2010**

768　The Burlington store is preparing for its official opening. Transfer the following inventory items from the Hamilton store to the Burlington store:

2	AP100	Promotional Fitness Packages
20	A030	Dumbbells: pair
5	A040	Dumbbells: 5kg set
2	A050	Dumbbells: 10kg set
1	A060	Dumbbells: 15kg set

☑ **Purchase Invoice #SW-1775**　　　　　　　**Dated July 10, 2010**

770　From Scandia Weights Inc. to fill purchase order #34
All items shipped to Burlington store

1	A130	Weight Plates (1 order of 100 kg)	$	60.00
3	A140	Weights: Olympic 75 kg		225.00
3	A150	Weights: Olympic 100 kg		300.00
3	A160	Weights: Olympic 125 kg		375.00
3	A170	Weights: Olympic 150 kg		450.00
		GST		70.50
		Purchase invoice total		$1 480.50

Terms: net 30.

☐ **Purchase Invoice #FG-3877**　　　　　　　**Dated July 10, 2010**

From Feelyte Gym Accessories to fill purchase order #35
All items shipped to Burlington store

1	A010	Body Fat Scale (carton of 12)	$	480.00
2	A020	Yoga Mats (boxes of 10)		240.00
1	A080	Heart Rate Monitor (carton of 12)		360.00
2	A070	Glide Slidetraks		50.00
20	A110	Stability Balls		80.00
2	A120	Wavemaster		150.00
2	A180	Workout Gloves: all sizes (boxes of 10)		80.00
		GST		72.00
		Purchase invoice total		$1 512.00

Terms: 2/10, n/30.

NOTES

ABS International
(contact Steele Bunns)
Schumacher Str. 96
55123 Mainz, Germany
Tel: (49-6131) 468 913
Fax: (49-6131) 468 248
Currency: EUR
Terms: net 30
Tax code: G

☐ **Purchase Invoice #ABS-7597**　　　　　　　**Dated July 10, 2010**

From ABS International (use Full Add for new foreign supplier)

5	E050	Bicycle: Calorie Counter CC-60	€	560.00
5	E060	Bicycle: Dual Action DA-70		860.00
5	E070	Bicycle: Recumbent R-80		1 080.00
		Freight		100.00
		GST		130.00
		Purchase invoice total		€2 730.00

The duty rate for these items is 0%.
Terms: net 30.
The exchange rate is 1.583.
Change the default amounts.

✓ **Sales Invoice #3024**   **Dated July 10, 2010**

772   To Stoney Creek Sports Arena (from Hamilton store)

50	A030	Dumbbells: pair	$	1.50/ kg
2	E160	Ski Exerciser: Independent SE-880		600/ unit
2	E210	Treadmill: Deluxe T-1100D		2 400/ unit
		Freight (tax code G)		75
		GST		5%
		PST		8%

Terms: 2/10, n/30.

Memo #7-12   **Dated July 14, 2010**

Remittances: Use the June 30 balances to make the following remittances in the Payments Journal. (See margin notes.)

☐ Record payment for GST for June to the Receiver General for Canada. Issue cheque #155 in payment.

☐ Record payment for PST Payable for June to the Minister of Finance. Collect 5% of the amount owing as sales tax compensation. Issue cheque #156 in payment.

☐ Record payment for garnisheed wages payable for June to the Receiver General for Canada. Issue cheque #157 in full payment.

☐ Record payment for EI, CPP and Income Tax Payable for June to the Receiver General for Canada. Issue cheque #158 in full payment.

☐ Record payment for EHT Payable for the quarter to the Minister of Finance. Issue cheque #159 in payment.

☐ Record payment for RRSP Payable to Ancaster Insurance. Issue cheque #160 in payment.

☐ Record payment for CSB Payable to Mt. Hope Investment Corporation. Issue cheque #161 in payment.

☐ Record payment for Group Insurance Payable for June to Ancaster Insurance. Issue cheque #162 in payment.

☐ Record payment for Charitable Donations Payable for June to Canadian Cancer Society (employer and employee contributions). Issue cheque #163 in payment.

☐ **Sales Order #7-1 DRC & Deposit #17**   **Dated July 14, 2010**

Delivery date July 24, 2010 (from Hamilton store)

From Dundas Recreational Centre, to replace old gym equipment

3	E020	Elliptical Exerciser: AE-200	$1 700/ unit
3	E030	Elliptical Exerciser: DE-300	2 000/ unit
3	E040	Elliptical Exerciser: LE-400	2 200/ unit
5	E050	Bicycle: Calorie Counter CC-60	400/ unit
5	E060	Bicycle: Dual Action DA-70	600/ unit
5	E070	Bicycle: Recumbent R-80	750/ unit
2	E080	Home Gym: Basic HG-1400	1 100/ set
		GST	5%
		PST	8%

Terms: 2/10, n/30.

Deposit cheque #438 for $6 000 received with order.

SESSION DATE – JULY 31, 2010

☐ **Cash Receipt #54**   **Dated July 16, 2010**

From Stoney Creek Sports Arena, cheque #314 for $6 804.63 in payment of account including $138.87 discount for early payment. Reference sales invoice #3024.

NOTES
Choose Previous Year in the report options window to make the June 30 balances available for sales tax amounts.
Choose Make Other Payment to remit the sales taxes.
Choose Pay Remittance to remit payroll taxes and deductions.
You must use July 1 as the End Of Remitting Period Date for the payroll remittances or, if you change the System Settings to allow transactions before July 1, you can enter June 30.
Clear the GST and PST reports for June 30.

☐ **Cash Purchase Invoice #BC-00124**   **Dated July 20, 2010**

From Bell Canada, $110 plus GST and PST for one month of phone service. Purchase invoice total $124.30. Terms: cash on receipt of invoice. Issue cheque #164 in full payment.

☐ **Cash Purchase Invoice #ES-93215**   **Dated July 20, 2010**

From Energy Source, $130 plus GST for hydro service. Purchase invoice total $136.50. Terms: cash on receipt of invoice. Issue cheque #165 in full payment.

☐ **TIME SLIP #3**   **DATED JULY 21, 2010**

For George Schwinn

Customer	Item	Actual Time	Billable Time	Billable Amount	Payroll Time
Dundas Recreational Centre	S020	4 hours	3 hours	$210.00	4 hours
Dundas Recreational Centre	S070	1 hour	1 hour	100.00	1 hour
McMaster University	S060	3 hours	3 hours	225.00	3 hours
McMaster University	S100	2 hours	–	–	2 hours
Stoney Creek Sports Arena	S020	4.5 hours	4 hours	280.00	4.5 hours
Stoney Creek Sports Arena	S060	2 hours	2 hours	160.00	2 hours
Stoney Creek Sports Arena	S100	2 hours	–	–	2 hours

☐ **TIME SLIP #4**   **DATED JULY 21, 2010**

For Yvonne Tinker

Customer	Item	Actual Time	Billable Time	Billable Amount	Payroll Time
Mohawk College	S030	16 hours	14 hours	$770.00	16 hours
Mohawk College	S050	6 hours	6 hours	390.00	6 hours
Mohawk College	S060	3 hours	3 hours	225.00	3 hours
Mohawk College	S100	6 hours	–	–	6 hours
Stelco Health Club	S020	6 hours	6 hours	390.00	6 hours
Stelco Health Club	S060	8 hours	7.5 hours	562.50	8 hours

NOTES
Remember to enter 430 for 4.5 hours.

☐ **Employee Time Summary Sheet #21**   **Dated July 21, 2010**

For the Pay Period ending July 21, 2010

Edit the employee record for Yvonne Tinker. Tinker will be paid every two weeks (26 pay periods per year) and her minimum number of hours will be 40. If her contract hours from time slips are less than 40 hours, she will be paid for 40 hours. Use time slips to prepare the bi-weekly paycheque for Yvonne Tinker for the actual number of hours worked. Issue deposit slip #33.

NOTES
Pay Periods are entered on the Income tab of the Employee Ledger record.
Use the Paycheques Journal for the payroll transactions so that you can enter the correct cheque and period ending dates. You cannot change the cheque date in the Payroll Cheque Run Journal.

George Schwinn worked 80 regular hours in the period and 4 hours of overtime. Issue deposit slip #34 in payment. (Add time from time slips but choose Yes to use regular hours when prompted.)

☐ **Deposit Slip #23**   **Dated July 21, 2010**

Prepare deposit slip for $12 804.63 for two cheques received in previous week.

☐ **Sales Invoice #3025**   **Dated July 21, 2010**

To Dundas Recreational Centre: Complete sales invoice for $310 plus GST and PST from time slip activities. Include all activities to date. Sales invoice total $333.50. Terms: 2/10, n/30.

☐ **Sales Invoice #3026**   **Dated July 21, 2010**

To McMaster University: Complete sales invoice for $225 plus GST and PST from time slip activities. Include all activities to date. Sales invoice total $254.25 Terms: 2/10, n/30.

Sales Invoice #3027   **Dated July 21, 2010**

To Stoney Creek Sports Arena: Complete sales invoice for $440 plus GST and PST from time slip activities. Include all activities to date. Sales invoice total $474.80. Terms: 2/10, n/30.

Sales Invoice #3028   **Dated July 21, 2010**

To Mohawk College: Complete sales invoice for $1 385 plus GST and PST from time slip activities. Include all activities to date. Sales invoice total $1 472.25. Terms: 2/10, n/30.

Sales Invoice #3029   **Dated July 21, 2010**

To Stelco Health Club: Complete sales invoice for $952.50 plus GST and PST from time slip activities. Include all activities to date. Sales invoice total $1 045.13. Terms: 2/10, n/30.

Credit Card Purchase Invoice #WS-12331   **Dated July 24, 2010**

From Waterdown Sunoco, $125 including GST and PST paid for gasoline and $380 plus GST and PST for vehicle repairs. Purchase invoice total $554.40 paid in full by Visa. Use Tax code IN for the gasoline purchase and tax code GP for the repairs.

Sales Invoice #3030   **Dated July 28, 2010**

To Dundas Recreational Centre to fill sales order #7-1 DRC (Hamilton store)

3	E020	Elliptical Exerciser: AE-200	$1 700/ unit
3	E030	Elliptical Exerciser: DE-300	2 000/ unit
3	E040	Elliptical Exerciser: LE-400	2 200/ unit
5	E050	Bicycle: Calorie Counter CC-60	400/ unit
5	E060	Bicycle: Dual Action DA-70	600/ unit
5	E070	Bicycle: Recumbent R-80	750/ unit
2	E080	Home Gym: Basic HG-1400	1 100/ set
	GST		5%
	PST		8%

Terms: 2/10, n/30. Allow customer to exceed credit limit.

TIME SLIP #5   **DATED JULY 31, 2010**

For George Schwinn

Customer	Item	Actual Time	Billable Time	Billable Amount	Payroll Time
McMaster University	S010	4 hours	4 hours	$280.00	4 hours
McMaster University	S070	2 hours	2 hours	90.00	2 hours
Stelco Health Club	S020	4 hours	4 hours	260.00	4 hours
Stelco Health Club	S060	2.5 hours	2.5 hours	187.50	2.5 hours
Mohawk College	S060	3.5 hours	3.5 hours	262.50	3.5 hours
Mohawk College	S100	2 hours	–	–	2 hours

TIME SLIP #6   **DATED JULY 31, 2010**

For Yvonne Tinker

Customer	Item	Actual Time	Billable Time	Billable Amount	Payroll Time
Dundas Recreational Centre	S010	14 hours	13 hours	$975.00	14 hours
Dundas Recreational Centre	S070	2 hours	2 hours	100.00	2 hours
Mohawk College	S020	10 hours	9 hours	585.00	10 hours
Stelco Health Club	S040	9 hours	8 hours	760.00	9 hours
Stelco Health Club	S100	6 hours	–	–	6 hours

NOTES

Remember to enter 230 for 2.5 hours and 330 for 3.5 hours.

☐ **Sales Invoice #3031**   **Dated July 31, 2010**

To McMaster University: Complete sales invoice for $370 plus GST and PST from time slip activities. Include all activities to date. Sales invoice total $395.70. Terms: 2/10, n/30.

☐ **Sales Invoice #3032**   **Dated July 31, 2010**

To Mohawk College: Complete sales invoice for $847.50 plus GST and PST from time slip activities. Include all activities to date. Sales invoice total $910.88. Terms: 2/10, n/30.

☐ **Sales Invoice #3033**   **Dated July 31, 2010**

To Stelco Health Club: Complete sales invoice for $1 207.50 plus GST and PST from time slip activities. Include all activities to date. Sales invoice total $1 282.88. Terms: 2/10, n/30.

☐ **Sales Invoice #3034**   **Dated July 31, 2010**

To Dundas Recreational Centre: Complete sales invoice for $1 075 plus GST and PST from time slip activities. Include all activities to date. Sales invoice total $1 136.75. Terms: 2/10, n/30.

☐ **Bank Debit Memo #143661**   **Dated July 31, 2010**

From Hamilton Trust, authorized withdrawals were made from the chequing account on our behalf for the following:

Bank service charges	$ 35
Mortgage interest payment	1 850
Mortgage principal reduction	150
Bank loan interest payment	380
Bank loan principal reduction	520

☐ **Credit Card Sales Invoice #3035**   **Dated July 31, 2010**

To Visa customers (sales summary). Sold from Hamilton store.

1	A010	Body Fat Scale	$ 100/ unit	$ 100.00
2	A180	Workout Gloves: all sizes	10/ pair	20.00
1	E110	Rider: Airwalker RA-900	300/ unit	300.00
1	E220	Treadmill: Deluxe Plus T-1200P	2 800/ unit	2 800.00
2	S010	Personal Trainer: 1 hour	75/ hour	150.00
2	S030	Personal Trainer: full day	420/ day	840.00
6	S040	Yoga Instructor: 1 hour	100/ hour	600.00
1	S050	Yoga Instructor: 1/2 day	210/ 1/2 day	210.00
4	S060	Repair Service	80/ hour	320.00
	GST		5%	267.00
	PST		8%	283.20
	Total paid by Visa			$5 890.20

☐ **Debit Card Sales Invoice #3036**   **Dated July 31, 2010**

To Interac customers (sales summary). Sold from Burlington store.

1	A010	Body Fat Scale	$100/ unit	$100.00
1	A020	Yoga Mats	30/ unit	30.00
6	A110	Stability Balls	10 each	60.00
2	A180	Workout Gloves: all sizes	10/ pair	20.00
2	S010	Personal Trainer: 1 hour	75/ hour	150.00
1	S040	Yoga Instructor: 1 hour	100/ hour	100.00
1	S050	Yoga Instructor: 1/2 day	210/ 1/2 day	210.00
	GST		5%	33.50
	PST		8%	16.80
	Total paid by Interac			$720.30

☐ **Memo #7-13**   **Dated July 31, 2010**

Prepare the payroll for Nieve Prekor, Assumpta Kisangel and Moishe Alee, the salaried employees. Add 2 percent of service revenue for July as a commission to Kisangel's salary. Issue deposit slips #35, #36 and #37.

☐ **Memo #7-14**   **Dated July 31, 2010**

Interest earned but not yet received for bank accounts for July is $295.

☐ **Memo #7-15**   **Dated July 31, 2010**

Prepare month-end adjusting entries for depreciation on fixed assets using the following amounts:

Cash registers	$100
Computer equipment	50
Furniture & fixtures	25
Retail premises	810
Van	625

☐ **Memo #7-16**   **Dated July 31, 2010**

Prepare end-of-period adjusting entries for the following:

Office Supplies used	$ 100
Linen Supplies used	60
Prepaid Insurance expired	812
Prepaid Advertising expired	100
Payroll Liabilities accrued	1 540

☑ **Memo #7-17**   **Dated July 31, 2010**

772   With two stores open and increased expenses, the prices for all inventory items will be raised. All Regular prices (Canadian and US) will increase by 10 percent. All preferred prices (Canadian and US) will increase by 5 percent. Round all prices to the nearest dollar amount.

☑ **Memo #7-18**   **Dated July 31, 2010**

779   Print all financial reports for the fiscal period.
Back up the data files.
Start a new fiscal year. Do not clear old data.
Change the fiscal end to August 31, 2010.

KEYSTROKES

Modifying Company Information

Changing Fiscal Dates

Restore SimData\flab-time1.CAB to SimData\Time\time.

Accept July 1, 2010 as the session date.

Click Company in the Modules pane list to open the Company window.

Enter Memo 7-1 to reverse the year-end payroll adjusting entry.

Click the Settings icon [Settings], then **click Information**, or **choose** the Setup menu and **click Settings**, **Company** and **Information**.

This will access the fields for fiscal dates:

Most fiscal dates cannot be changed. Only the fiscal end can be edited. After starting a new fiscal period, the fiscal end is updated to one year past the new fiscal start because this period is most commonly used. Flabuless, however, will use a one-month fiscal period to allow for more frequent performance review.

Drag through Jun 30, 2011 in the Fiscal End field.

Type   07-31-2010

Leave the Settings window open so you can add the currency.

Adding a Foreign Currency

The Premium version of Simply Accounting allows more than one foreign currency. Setting up additional currencies is similar to adding the first one. We will add euro as the second foreign currency because a new supplier in Germany will provide some inventory items.

Click   **Currency** to open the Currency Information window:

The currency added previously and its linked account are entered. You can select a different linked account, but you must use the same linked account for all currencies.

Click   the **Foreign Currency column** below United States Dollars. **Click** the **List icon** to see the currency selection list.

Click   **Euro** and then **click Select** to return to the Currency window.

Click   the **Exchange Rate button**:

NOTES

If you choose United States Dollars from the Select A Foreign Currency list, you will see a list of all the dates and exchange rates you have already used.

Euro is selected as the currency because the cursor was on this line in the previous screen. All other currencies you entered will be available from the Select A Foreign Currency drop-down list. You can add exchange rates for any of them.

Click   the **Date column**.

Type   Jul 1 **Press** (tab) to move to the Exchange Rate column.

Type   1.5805

Click   **Display A Reminder If The Exchange Rate Is**.

Click   **OK** to return to the Settings window. **Click OK** to return to the Home window.

Adding a Foreign Bank Account

Before using the currency in transactions, we need to create a new bank account for euro transactions.

Click   the **Chart of Accounts icon** [Chart of Accounts] to open the Accounts window.

Change   the account **number for 1150 Net Bank**, the bank Subtotal account, to 1190 if you have not already done so.

Click   the **Create tool** [icon] to open a new ledger window and **add** the new account **1150 Bank: Euro Chequing**.

Click   **Subgroup Account** to change the Type if necessary.

Click   the **Class Options tab**.

Choose **Bank** from the Account Class drop-down list.

Click   the **Currency list arrow** to see the options:

Click   **EUR**. We must save the account before adding the cheque number.

Click   the **Save tool** [icon].

Click   **Change The Next Cheque Number** to open the Reports & Forms settings.

Click   the **Next Cheque Number field**.

Type   101 **Click OK** to save the number and return to the ledger window.

Close   the **Ledger window** and then **close** the **Accounts windows**.

Adding Linked Bank Accounts

We need to identify the new account as the linked account for euro transactions.

Choose the **Setup menu**. Then **choose** **Settings, Payables** and **Linked Accounts**:

Click   the **Bank Account To Use column** beside Euro.

Click   the **List icon** . Notice that only the Canadian and Euro bank accounts can be selected as the Euro currency bank account.

Double click **1150**.

Click   **Receivables** and **Linked Accounts**.

Click   the **Bank Account To Use column** beside Euro.

Type   1150 **Press** tab . Leave the Settings window open.

Entering Inventory Locations

Before leaving the Settings window, we will add the two stores as the locations for the business and for inventory. Items can be purchased for and sold from either store. Adjustments can also be made for the separate locations. The number of items in each store can, therefore, be monitored. If needed, items can be transferred from one location to another.

Click   **Inventory & Services** in the Settings modules list.

Click   **Locations** in the Inventory settings list:

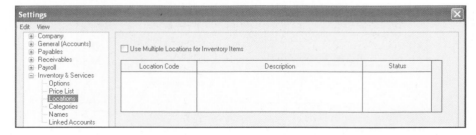

Click   **Use Multiple Locations For Inventory Items** to activate the option:

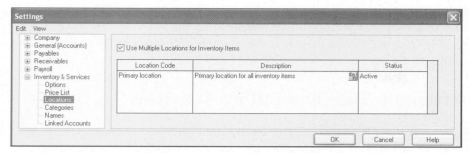

The Code and Description fields are now available; we can enter the two stores. We will accept the default description for the first location.

Press (tab) **twice** to select Primary Location to replace this name.

Type Hamilton

Click the next line of the **Location Code field** for the next store.

Type Burlington **Press** (tab).

Type Burlington Store for accessories

Click **OK** to return to the Home window.

Click **Inventory & Services** in the Modules pane list.

Click **A010 Body Fat Scale** in the Home window Inventory Item list.

The Quantity tab screen includes a Location field.

Click the **Locations field list arrow** to see the two locations you entered:

Select a location from the For Location drop-down list to display the quantity at that location.

Initially, all the stock is at the primary location, the Hamilton store. The quantity at the Hamilton store is the same as the quantity for the All Locations selection. The quantity at the Burlington store is zero.

Close the **Ledger window** to return to the Inventory & Services module window.

Time and Billing

Many businesses that provide services use time as the basis for billing customers. Law firms, consulting businesses and service businesses that complete maintenance and repair work are just a few examples. In addition, these businesses may keep track of how much time each employee spends on a particular job and then compare this with the standard number of hours expected for that type of work. Some jobs can be billed at a flat rate and some, such as warranty repairs or work performed for other departments of the same company, may be provided at no charge. In each of these cases, it is still important to know how much time was spent on the job.

The Time and Billing module in Simply Accounting tracks these kinds of activities by integrating the Payroll, Inventory and Sales ledgers.

Setting Up Time and Billing Activities

Before recording the services provided by employees to customers, that is, filling in time slips, we must modify the inventory records so that we can apply time and billing. First we will create the new services. We will work from the Inventory module.

Choose   **Add Inventory & Services** from the Inventory & Services icon drop-down shortcuts list to open a new record for inventory.

Type   S060 **Press** ⟨tab⟩.

Type   Repair Service

Click   **Service** as the Type of item to modify the form for service items:

The Units tab window appears and Activity is available as an option under Service.

Click   **Activity (Time & Billing)** to add a ✓.

This selection will open the fields related to time and billing on the Time & Billing tab. The Units information is now dimmed. We will enter units on the Time & Billing tab screen, as instructed by the message on the screen. The Internal Service Activity option becomes available because this also applies to the Time & Billing module.

Click   the **Pricing tab** to open the Canadian dollar (home currency) price list.

Click   the **Regular Price Per Selling Unit field**.

Type   80 **Press** ⟨tab⟩ to advance to the Preferred Selling Price field.

Type   75

Click   the **Linked tab**.

Click   the **Revenue account field**. We will add the new account.

Type   4050 **Press** ⟨tab⟩ and **click Add** to start the Add An Account wizard.

Press   ⟨tab⟩ to advance to the account Name field.

Type   Revenue from Repairs

Click   **Next three times** to accept the defaults until you see the **Subgroup And Group Accounts** screen.

Click   **Yes** because this account is a Subgroup account.

Accept   the **remaining defaults** to finish creating the account.

Click   the **Expense field** and **type** 5065

NOTES

Businesses often track the number of hours of service provided internally to other departments in the company as a way of monitoring internal efficiency or tracking departmental costs. They may monitor the time even if there is no charge for the service to the other department.

NOTES

Foreign prices do not apply to services because they are not exported.

⚠ WARNING!

If you do not change the account type to Subgroup Account, the accounts will not be in logical order, and you will be unable to display some reports.

You can make the correction later from the General Ledger to restore the logical account order.

Click   the **Time & Billing tab** to see the next group of fields to be set up:

This screen has all the details that relate to the Time & Billing module. On this screen we must define the unit that the price is based on, indicate whether the unit is based on time and then add the relationship between the time and the unit of measure.

Click   the **list arrow beside Each** in the Unit Of Measure field.

Click   **Hour**.

This Unit is automatically recognized as related to time, and the Relationship fields are now dimmed because we have already indicated a time unit. The next group of fields defines the billing options. Billable is selected as the default for the service activity and this is correct. The other options are that an activity is Non-Billable or that there is No Charge for the activity. Charges for the service can be based on a Flat Fee or on Billable Time. Repair work is based on billable time.

Click   **Flat Fee** in the Charges Are Based On field or its list arrow.

Click   **Billable Time** to change the entry.

The next option allows the time worked on the activity to be credited directly to an employee's paycheque. You can choose whether the time should be charged to the default payroll income account or to overtime. The non-payroll option may be selected if the work is completed by salaried employees. All services offered by Flabuless Fitness are provided by the regular employees at the regular hourly wage rate.

Click   **Non-Payroll** in the Default Payroll Income field or its list arrow.

Click   **Regular** to complete the Time & Billing tab screen as shown here:

Click   the **Taxes tab**. The defaults are correct. Both GST and PST are charged, so the service is not tax exempt for either tax.

Click   **Create Another**   [Create Another]   to save the record.

You are now ready to enter the next service. Service and Activity (Time & Billing) remain selected from the previous entry and are correct.

Enter   **S070** as the Number and **Contract Repairs** as the Description.

Click   the **Pricing tab** and **enter 100** as the Regular Price Per Selling Unit and **90** as the Preferred Price.

Click   the **Linked tab** and **enter 4050** as the Revenue account and **5065** as the Expense account.

Click   the **Time & Billing tab**.

Enter   **Service Call** as the Unit Of Measure.

The service is priced at a flat rate, so the unit is not related to time. Service Call is not recognized as a unit of time so the ✓ is not added. Billable is also the correct choice but we need to enter the rate. Notice that Flat Fee = ___ Service Call x Price is entered as the field label. This means that we must enter a number, not a price. The price will be calculated as the number of completed service calls multiplied by the price that is taken from the Pricing tab fields.

The flat rate for this service is one times the price; each service call is priced at $100 ($90 for preferred customers).

Click   the **field beside Flat Fee =**.

Type   1

Choose   **Regular** as the Default Payroll Income category.

The default tax information is correct. Both GST and PST apply, so the record is complete. Your Time & Billing screen should look like the one shown here:

Click   **Create Another** [Create Another] to save the record.

The final service is provided at no charge to customers, but it is entered as an inventory item so that the time spent on warranty repairs can be monitored. The price will be entered as zero.

Enter   **S100** as the Number and **Warranty Repairs** as the Description.

Click   the **Pricing tab**. Do not enter any prices for the warranty service so that the prices will remain at zero.

Click   the **Linked tab** and **enter 4050** as the Revenue account and **5065** as the Expense account.

Click   the **Time & Billing tab**.

Enter   **Service Call** as the Unit Of Measure.

The service call for warranty work is not related to time because there is no charge for this service. We must indicate that the work is not billable. In addition, employees are paid at their usual wage rate for completing warranty work, even though the customer does not pay, so we must change the payroll category.

Click   the **list arrow beside Billable**. **Click Non-Billable** to change the entry.

Choose `Regular` as the Default Payroll Income category to complete the record:

Another option for services that are normally not billed is to **sometimes charge**. When you choose the No Charge or Non-Billable options, this category becomes available. The pricing options are the same as for billable activities. You can relate the unit to time and enter the number of hours or minutes per unit, or enter a flat fee for the exceptional price. Prices are taken from Price fields on the Pricing tab screen.

Click **Save And Close** to save the record and return to the Inventory & Services module window.

Adding Time and Billing Information to Services

You are now ready to edit the remaining service records to apply time and billing.

Scroll down the Inventory Item list in the Inventory & Services module window.

Click **S010 Personal Trainer: 1 hour** in the Home window list of items and services to open the record.

Click the **Time & Billing tab** to open the Time & Billing screen.

All the fields are dimmed because we still need to mark the service as an Activity for time and billing.

Click **Activity (Time & Billing)** to open the extra fields.

Hour is selected as the Unit. Most of the selections are correct because this unit is automatically recognized as a unit related to time. The service is Billable and charges are based on Billable Time. We need to select the payroll income.

Choose `Regular` as the Default Payroll Income category.

The next service, **S020 Personal Trainer: 1/2 day**, requires additional information to indicate how many hours are in the 1/2 day. The service will still be billed at an hourly rate, but the rate is lower when a longer time period is purchased.

Click the **Next Item tool** to open the record for **S020**.

Click **Activity (Time & Billing)**.

Click **Unit Is Related To Time** to add a ✓ and open the relationship fields.

Each one-half day is based on three billable hours of activity, so the relationship is entered as 3 hours per 1/2 day. The relationship field is a required field when the unit is not Hour or Minute and you indicate that it is related to time.

Click the **first Relationship field**.

Type 3

Click   the **list arrow beside the second Relationship field** to see the list:

The relationship can be based on the number of hours or minutes per unit, or the number of units per hour or minute.

> **Click**   **Hours Per 1/2 Day**.

The next option is correct — the activity is Billable. However, it is charged on the basis of time, not at a flat rate. We need to change the entry for Charges Are Based On.

> **Click**   **Flat Fee** in the Charges Are Based On field or its list arrow.

> **Click**   **Billable Time** and then **choose Regular** as the Default Payroll Income category to complete the record changes.

> **Click**   the **Next Item tool** 🔳 to open the record for **S030**.

> **Click**   **Activity (Time & Billing)**.

> **Click**   **Unit Is Related To Time** to add a ✓ and open the relationship fields.

Each full day is based on seven billable hours of activity, so the relationship is entered as seven hours per day.

> **Enter**   **7** in the first Relationship field.

> **Choose**   **Hours Per Day** from the second Relationship field list.

> **Click**   **Flat Fee** in the Charges Are Based On field or its list arrow.

> **Click**   **Billable Time** and **choose Regular** as the Default Payroll Income category to complete the record changes.

> **Click**   the **Next Item tool** 🔳 to open the record for **S040**.

> **Click**   **Activity (Time & Billing)**.

Again, because Hour is the unit, most of the default details are correct.

> **Choose**   **Regular** as the Default Payroll Income category.

> **Click**   the **Next Item tool** 🔳 to open the record for **S050**.

> **Click**   **Activity (Time & Billing)**.

> **Click**   **Unit Is Related To Time**.

Each 1/2 day is based on three billable hours of activity, so the relationship is entered as 3 hours per 1/2 day.

> **Click**   the **first Relationship field**.

> **Type**   3

> **Click**   the **list arrow beside the second Relationship field**.

> **Click**   **Hours Per 1/2 Day**.

Click   **Flat Fee** in the Charges Are Based On field or its list arrow.

Click   **Billable Time** and **choose Regular** as the Default Payroll Income category to complete the record changes.

Click   **Save And Close** to save the record and return to the Inventory & Services module window.

We will now edit the prices for these services using the Update Price Lists feature in the Inventory Settings.

Updating Inventory Price Lists

The Premium version allows you to define additional price lists and to update prices in a single step on one screen. This feature is available as one of the settings for the Inventory Ledger. If prices are raised by a fixed percentage for one or more items or services, you can make the price changes globally. You can also set the prices in one list relative to the prices in another list by indicating the percentage increase or decrease.

Click   the **Settings icon** and then **click Price List** to see the Price List Settings:

At this stage, you can define new price lists. You cannot remove or modify the predefined price list names. If you want to create a new price list, you can type the new price list names below Web Price in the Description column and click Update Price Lists to open the item list. We need to update Regular and Preferred prices.

Click   the **Update Price Lists button**:

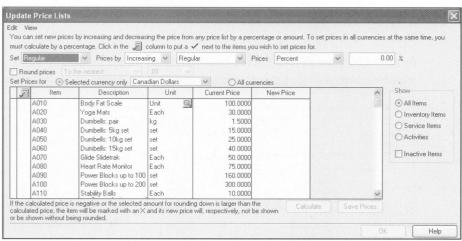

The inventory list opens. You can display the list of all items, only inventory items, only service items or only activities.

You can select the items whose prices you want to update globally. You can set the prices in one list relative to another list by increasing or decreasing the reference prices by a fixed percentage or amount. Then you can round off the prices to the nearest unit — ranging from 0.0001 dollar to 1 000 dollars. You can make the price changes for one currency or for all currencies at the same time. You can also enter or edit individual prices in the new price column, so you can also use this list to enter price changes manually for several inventory items on a single screen, without opening each ledger record separately. If you have different units for stocking and selling, you can select the unit as well.

You can also Round Prices if you want to work with even amounts. Choose the direction for rounding off the price — up to the nearest, down to the nearest or to the nearest unit. Choose the nearest unit you want to round to from the drop-down list.

We will work from the smaller list of Activities. When you are changing a large number of prices, it is more efficient to work from the Price List screen.

> **Click**   **Activities** in the Show list on the right-hand side of the screen:

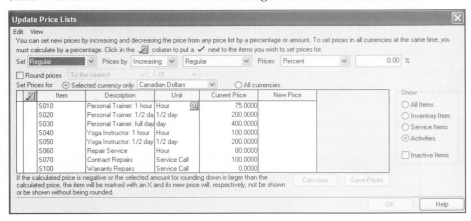

The Regular prices are shown. We will edit these first. We will change the prices directly by entering the revised price in the New Price column. The prices for S010 and S040 are correct.

> **Click**   **S020** and **press** (tab) until the cursor is in the New Price column.
>
> **Type**   210
>
> **Press**   ⬇ to place the cursor in the New Price column for activity S030.
>
> **Type**   420
>
> **Press**   ⬇ **twice** to place the cursor in the New Price column for activity S050.
>
> **Type**   210
>
> **Click**   the **Save Prices button** to save this set of prices and update the list:

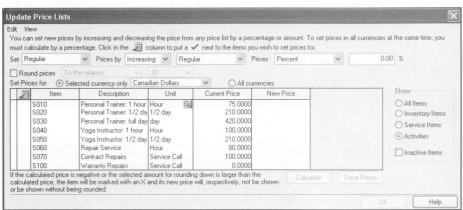

The new prices have become the current prices.

We will update the preferred prices using the global update method. The price for each of the three items is increasing by the fixed amount of $5, relative to the old preferred prices. The current settings would set the **Regular** prices by **Increasing** the

Regular prices by a **percentage**, so we must change these settings. First, we must select the price list we want to change — the preferred prices.

> **Click**   **Regular** in the Set field and **select Preferred** to place this price list on the screen.

The next setting is correct — we are increasing prices, but increasing them relative to the old preferred prices. We must change the reference point in the Prices field.

> **Click**   **Regular** in the Prices field (to the right of Increasing). You can choose any price list as the reference list.

> **Click**   **Preferred** to change the reference price list.

> **Click**   **Percent**. You can choose Percent or Amount as the method.

> **Click**   **Amount**. Now you can enter the amount of the increase.

> **Click**   the **Amount field** (beside Amount) and **type** 5

Now we must select the three items we are changing.

> **Click**   the **Select Item column** 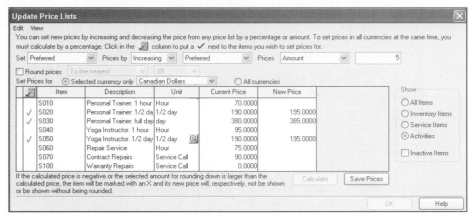 **beside S020** to add a ✓ and choose the item for global updating.

> **Press**   ⊥ to place the cursor in the Select column for activity S030.

> **Click**   to add a ✓ beside S030.

> **Press**   ⊥ **twice** to place the cursor in the Select column for activity S050.

> **Click**   to add a ✓ beside S050.

> **Click**   **Calculate** to apply the formula we entered and update the list as shown:

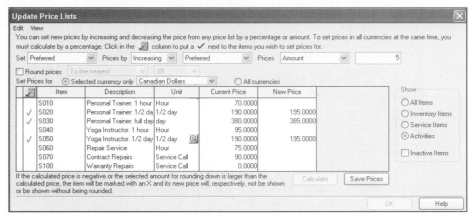

If the new prices are correct, you can save them. If not, you can edit individual prices, apply a different formula or round the prices.

> **Click**   **Save Prices**. The new prices move to the Current Price column.

> **Click**   **OK** to return to the Settings window.

> **Click**   **OK** to save all the changes and return to the Home window.

> **Click**   **Employees & Payroll** in the Modules pane list.

> **Create**   the **two new employee records**.

> **Click**   **Receivables** in the Modules pane list.

> **Enter**   the next **two transactions** (the cash receipt and the Visa payment).

> **Change**   the **session date to July 14**.

Preparing Time Slips

After setting up the service records to mark the activities and enter the billing information, you can track the amount of time that each employee works for each customer at each activity by completing Time Slips.

Time slips for employees may be entered from the Receivables module window or from the Employees and Payroll module window.

These alternatives are illustrated in the two partial Home windows below:

The Receivables module window is already open. We will continue to work in it.

Click the **Create A Time Slip icon** in the Related Tasks pane:

The Time Slips Journal opens. All the tool icons in this window are the same as those found in other journals. Also, as in other journals, employees can be selected from a drop-down list and List icons are available for many of the fields.

Many features in other journals are also available for time slips. You can access these options from the tool buttons as you do in other journals or from the Time Slip menu. For example,

- Click the Store tool ⬇ and enter a name and frequency to store the time slip as a recurring transaction.
- Click the Look Up Time Slip tool 🔍 to look up a time slip just as you look up purchases or sales invoices.
- Click the Adjust Time Slip tool 📋 to adjust a time slip after recording. You cannot adjust a time slip for selecting the wrong employee.

The Time Slips number is updated automatically by the program. Its starting number is taken from the Forms Settings, just like the next number for other forms. If the Time & Billing module is not hidden, the Next Number field for Time Slips is included in the Forms tab Settings screen. The number is correct.

The first time slip is for Schwinn. His first job was completed for McMaster University, a preferred customer.

Click   the **Employee list arrow** and **choose George Schwinn**.

Enter   **July 7** in the Date field for the Time Slip.

Click   the **Customer field List icon** and **select McMaster University**.

Click   the **Item field List icon** to see the Select Activity list:

All services for which you selected Activity as the type of Service and added time and billing details will be on this list. Other services and inventory will not be included.

Double click S010 Personal Trainer: 1 hour to add it to the journal.

The Item and Description fields are the usual ones for inventory and service transactions. The next field is completed from the Time & Billing tab details in the ledger record. Usually the defaults are correct. The **Billing Status** field has a List icon and a selection list. Activities may be Billable, Non-Billable or provided at No Charge. You can change the default entry if needed.

If an activity is billable, you can use the **Timer** in this window to track the time worked on the activity. A checkmark in the **Stopwatch column** indicates that you can use the timer. Some businesses track all time spent for a customer. For example, if a customer phoned for advice, and telephone advice was a billable activity, you could start the timer at the beginning of the phone call and then stop at the end to have an accurate measure of the duration of the call.

To use the timer, click the Stopwatch column for the customer and activity if the ✓ is not already there. Click the Start button. The counter will keep time in seconds until you click Stop. You can use this measurement as the actual time for the activity by clicking Apply Time.

Time is entered as the number of hours, minutes and seconds. The simplest way to explain the format for entering time is with a few examples. The following charts summarize the examples and outline some of the rules:

EXAMPLES OF TIME ENTRIES IN THE TIME SLIPS JOURNAL	
Entering This Number	Records This Time
1 or 01 or 100 or 10000	1 hour
001 or 0001 or 000100	1 minute
00001 or 000001	1 second
130 or 0130 or 013000	1.5 hours (1 hour and 30 minutes)
0110 or 110 or 11000	1 hour and 10 minutes
1030 or 103000	10 hours and 30 minutes
11515 or 011515	1 hour, 15 minutes and 15 seconds
995959	99 hours, 59 minutes and 59 seconds

RULES FOR ENTERING TIME IN THE TIME SLIPS JOURNAL

- A one- or two-digit number is always interpreted as the number of hours (zero minutes, zero seconds).
- For a three-digit entry, the first number represents hours and the next two represent the minutes.
- For a four-digit number, the first two numbers represent hours and the next two represent minutes.
- For a five-digit number, the first number represents the number of hours, the next two, minutes and the final two, seconds.
- For a six-digit entry, the first two numbers represent hours, the next two, minutes, and the last two, seconds.
- You can omit seconds and minutes if they are zero. Leading zeros are not needed for hours.
- The times allowed on a line for one activity range from the shortest time of 1 second, entered as 000001 or 00001, to the longest, 99 hours, 59 minutes and 59 seconds, entered as 995959.

NOTES

An employee may be paid for the actual number of hours, the billable number of hours or some other time agreed on between the employee and the employer. For example, the pay may be limited to a maximum number of hours for a specific job to encourage efficient work habits.

There are three columns for time: the **Actual Time** spent at the activity; the **Billable Time** or amount of time that the customer pays for; and the **Payroll Time** or hours the employee is paid for. Sometimes the customer is billed for fewer hours than the job actually required. For example, if an estimate has been given and the work is much more complex than anticipated, a business will usually not bill the customer for the full amount in the interest of good customer relations. At other times, the customer may be charged for more time than the activity requires. For example, a job may have a minimum time component, such as one hour of labour. Most companies will want to keep track of all times so that they can revise their prices to reflect their true costs.

Schwinn spent two hours completing the first job (actual time); the customer will pay for 1.5 hours of work (billable time); and Schwinn will be paid for two hours of work for this job (payroll time).

> **Click**   the **Actual Time field**.
>
> **Type**   2   **Press** (tab). Your journal now looks like the one below:

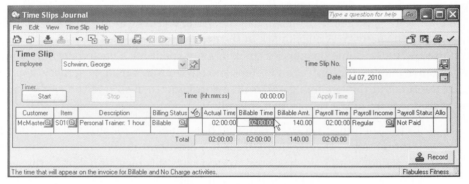

The program enters the actual time as the billable time and the payroll time. The price (**Billable Amt.**) is the billable time multiplied by the price from the ledger for that time unit, 2 hours multiplied by the preferred hourly rate of $70. Notice that the **Payroll Status** is Not Paid. You can edit the billable time, the billable amount, the payroll time and payroll income category for individual activities. We need to change the billable time to 1.5 hours, 1 hour and 30 minutes. The billable time is already selected.

> **Type**   130   **Press** (tab) to update the billable amount to $105.
>
> **Click**   the **Customer list icon** and **select McMaster University** for the second activity.
>
> **Click**   the **Item list icon** and **select S070 Contract Repairs**.
>
> **Click**   the **Actual Time column**.
>
> **Type**   2   **Press** (tab).

This time the flat rate is entered and you cannot edit the billable time. However, you can edit the billable amount. The next activity is for another customer.

Click the **Customer list icon** 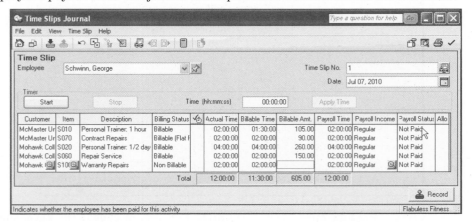. **Select Mohawk College**.

Click the **Item list icon** and **select S020 Personal Trainer: 1/2 day**.

Click the **Actual Time column**.

Type 4 **Press** ⎡tab⎤.

For this ledger record, recall that we entered 3 hours as the usual number of hours in the 1/2 day of activity. The hourly rate was determined as the Preferred Selling Price divided by the usual number of hours — $195 divided by 3 or $65. Thus the amount for 4 hours is 4 x $65 or $260.

Click the **Customer list icon** and **select Mohawk College** for the fourth activity.

Click the **Item list icon** and **select S060 Repair Service**.

Click the **Actual Time column**.

Type 2 **Press** ⎡tab⎤.

Repair service work is billed at a straight hourly rate so the amount is the billable time multiplied by the hourly rate for the preferred customer.

Click the **Customer list icon** and **select Mohawk College** for the final activity.

Click the **Item list icon** and **select S100 Warranty Repairs**.

Click the **Actual Time column**.

Type 2 **Press** ⎡tab⎤.

No amount is entered because the activity is non-billable, but the hours are added to the employee's payroll time. The journal is complete and should look like the one below:

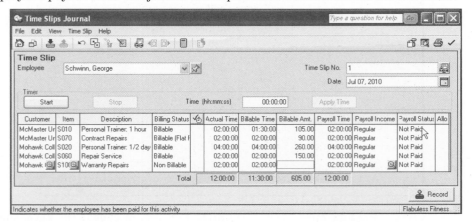

Check the **time slip** carefully before recording and **correct** mistakes.

You can also allocate time slips details to projects or divisions, either on the basis of percent or time.

> ⚠ **WARNING!**
> There is no journal entry to review the time slip, so check it carefully.
>   You can adjust the time slip if you find an error after you record it.
>   You cannot reverse time slips automatically. If you selected the wrong employee, edit the time slip by deleting all time entries. The program will remove the time slip from the system, but the time slip number cannot be used again.

Click the Allo column for the activity line to open the Allocation screen:

Choose the division and the amount of time for that activity that is allocated to the division. Click OK to return to the journal when finished.

Click the **Record button** to save the entry.

Complete **Time Slip #2** and then **close** the **Time Slips Journal**.

Add a **shortcut** for the **Time Slips Journal**. **Choose Create Time Slip** under the Time & Billing heading.

Paying Employees from Time Slips

When activities are set up in the Inventory and Services Ledger, and time slips are entered for employees, Simply Accounting tracks the hours worked so you can use the summary of these time slips to prepare paycheques.

We will use this method to prepare the paycheque for the new employee, Yvonne Tinker, because these activities are her primary responsibility.

Open the **Paycheques Journal**.

Enter **July 7** as the Date and the Period Ending date.

> **NOTES**
> You can also add time slips information in the Payroll Cheque Run Journal by selecting the employee and clicking the Add Time tool button or by choosing Add Time From Time Slips from the Payroll menu. However, the cheque date in the Payroll Cheque Run cannot be changed. It must match the session date.

Choose **Tinker** from the Employee list and **press** tab to enter her information:

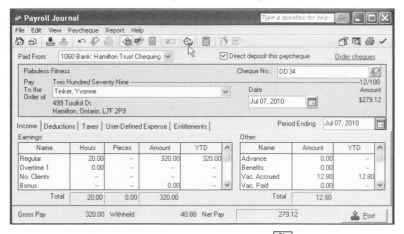

Click the **Add Time From Time Slips tool** or **choose** the **Paycheque** menu and **click Add Time From Time Slips**.

The Payroll Hour Selection screen opens:

> **NOTES**
> The Time Slip tool remains unavailable until you select an employee.

You should enter the dates for the time slips that apply to this pay period. Tinker has worked for one week; therefore, you should include the time slips up to July 7.

These dates are entered as the defaults because we already entered July 7 as the period ending date and July 1 is the date Tinker was hired.

Click **OK** to return to the journal.

The number of hours is updated as shown in the following completed journal entry:

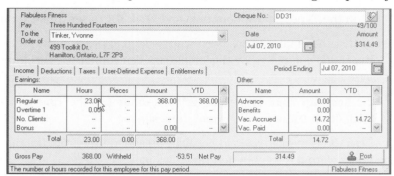

You can edit the number of hours as usual if necessary, and you can add advances or other deductions if they are appropriate.

Review the **journal entry** and, when you are certain that it is correct,

Click **Post** to save the transaction. **Click Yes** to continue.

Choose **Schwinn** from the Employee list and press ⌐tab⌐ to enter his default payroll information.

Click the **Add Time From Time Slips tool** or **choose** the **Paycheque menu** and **click Add Time From Time Slips**:

Again, the time slip period matches the pay period for the employee.

Click **OK** to see the warning:

For Schwinn, the hours worked exceed the hours on his time slip for the various customer jobs because he also performs other duties at the store. You have the option of accepting the Time Slip information or increasing the hours to match the default in the employee records. For Schwinn, the Payroll Ledger entry is the correct one.

Click **Yes** to increase the number of hours and return to the journal. The number of Regular hours remains unchanged at 80 hours.

Click the **Overtime 1 field** and add the overtime hours by **typing** 2.

Click the **Advance field** and **accept** the **default** because only $50 remains to be repaid.

Review the **journal entry** and make corrections if necessary.

Click **Post**. **Click Yes** to continue and save the transaction.

Close the **Payroll Journal**.

⚠ WARNING!
You must complete the step of adding time from the time slips. If you do not, the payroll status for these activities will continue to show as Not Paid and the employee could be incorrectly paid a second time for the same work.

The program will update the Payroll Hours Selection dates for the next paycheque, and the Payroll Status on these Time Slips.

Click　the **Create Time Slip shortcut** to open the Time Slips Journal.

Click　the **Look Up Time Slips tool** .

Type　2　in the Time Slip Number field and **click OK** to see Tinker's time slip.

You should see that the employee has been paid — Paid appears in the Payroll Status column for each job completed by this employee. You cannot use this time slip information for payroll again.

Click　the **Look Up Time Slips tool** and **enter 1** in the Time Slip Number field. **Click OK** to see Schwinn's time slip.

His payroll status too is marked as Paid because we added time from the time slips, even though the hours were not used to determine his pay.

Close　the **Time Slips Journal**.

Preparing Sales Invoices from Time Slips

When sales invoices are prepared for mailing to customers, the activities from the time slips can be added directly to the invoices without re-entering each activity.

Click　**Receivables** in the Modules pane list, if necessary.

Click　the **Sales Invoices icon** to open the Sales Journal.

Choose　**McMaster University** as the customer. Invoice and Pay Later are correct.

Enter　**July 7** as the invoice date.

Time slip activities may be entered using the tool shown below or the Sales menu option:

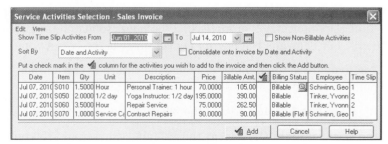

Click　the **Add Time Slip Activities tool** or **choose** the **Sales menu** and **click Add Time Slip Activities** to open the activities list for this customer:

Date	Item	Qty	Unit	Description	Price	Billable Amt.	✓	Billing Status	Employee	Time Slip
Jul 07, 2010	S010	1.5000	Hour	Personal Trainer: 1 hour	70.0000	105.00		Billable	Schwinn, Geo	1
Jul 07, 2010	S050	2.0000	1/2 day	Yoga Instructor: 1/2 day	195.0000	390.00		Billable	Tinker, Yvonn	2
Jul 07, 2010	S060	3.5000	Hour	Repair Service	75.0000	262.50		Billable	Tinker, Yvonn	2
Jul 07, 2010	S070	1.0000	Service Ca	Contract Repairs	90.0000	90.00		Billable (Flat F	Schwinn, Geo	1

Services provided to the customer by all employees will be listed, and you can also include Non-Billable Activities by clicking its check box. You may need to scroll to see the information in all columns. You can Sort the list By Date And Activity, the default, By Employee And Activity or By Activity. You can also Consolidate the list By Date And Activity, combining the amounts for each activity on the same date. You can select all the activities for the invoice, or omit some if they are incomplete or come after the billing date. All activities should be included in the invoice for McMaster University.

Enter   July 1 and July 7 as the date range in the Show Time Slip Activities From and To date fields.

Click   the **Add Activity column** 📋 for the first activity, S010. Only activities with a ✓ in this column are added to the sales invoice.

Click   the **Add Activity column** 📋 for the remaining activities.

Click   the **Add button** 📋 Add to return to the completed Sales Journal:

The activities are now added to the journal. Notice that the Quantity refers to the units in the ledger — for S050, the customer pays for two one-half day units of three hours each. For S070, the flat-rate service call, the quantity is one. You can add other regular services or inventory to the sales invoice if they were sold to the same customer; you do not need to create a separate invoice for them.

You should review the journal entry before posting it.

Choose the **Report menu** and **click Display Sales Journal Entry**:

Flabuless Fitness		Debits	Credits	Division
07/07/10 (J6)				
1200	Accounts Receivable	918.08	-	
2640	PST Payable	-	28.20	
2650	GST Charged on Sales	-	42.38	
4040	Revenue from Services	-	495.00	
4050	Revenue from Repairs	-	352.50	
		918.08	918.08	

The journal entry is the same as any other sales journal entry. The tax amounts are correct because the Service Ledger records include tax information. PST is charged on repairs but not on the other services. GST is charged on all services provided by Flabuless Fitness.

Close   the **report** when you have finished viewing it.

Make   **corrections** if necessary.

To correct the activities, click 📋 to return to the Service Activities Selection list. Previously selected activities are shown as Invoiced in the Billing Status column. Clicking the Add Activity column 📋 will remove the ✓ and restore the status to billable so you can select a different group of activities.

Click   Post 📋 Post to save the journal entry.

Enter   the next **two sales invoices** by adding items from the time slips and then close the Sales Journal.

Building New Inventory

Instead of assembling inventory using the Item Assembly method, you can set up the inventory assembly components as part of the ledger record and then use this information to build an item using the Bill of Materials method. We will create the new inventory Promotional Fitness Package, including the items or materials that make up the package.

Choose **Inventory & Services** from the Modules pane list.

Choose **Add Inventory & Service** from the Inventory & Services icon shortcuts list to open the Inventory Ledger for new Service Activity items. The cursor is in the Item Number field.

Type AP100 **Press** ⌨tab.

Type Promotional Fitness Package

Click **Inventory** as the Type to modify the form for the inventory item.

The Units tab screen is displayed. All units are the same for this package.

Double click **Each** and **type** Package

Click the **Quantities tab**. The Minimum level is correct at 0.

Click the **Pricing tab** to access the price fields.

On the Pricing tab screen, you can enter regular and preferred prices in all the currencies that you have set up. Canadian prices are shown initially.

Click the **Regular Price Per Selling Unit field**.

Type 210 **Press** ⌨tab to advance to the Preferred Price field.

Type 200

Choose **United States Dollars** from the Currency list.

Foreign prices for Flabuless Fitness are fixed, so we need to change the default setting. Clicking the entry will change the setting.

Click **Exchange Rate** beside Regular to change the setting to Fixed Price.

Press ⌨tab to advance to the Regular Selling Price for United States Dollars.

Type 210 **Press** ⌨tab to advance to the Preferred Pricing Method.

Click **Exchange Rate** to change the setting to Fixed Price. **Press** ⌨tab.

Type 200

Choose **Euro** from the currency list.

Click **Exchange Rate** beside Regular to change the setting to Fixed Price.

Press ⌨tab to advance to the Regular Price for Euro.

Type 135 **Press** ⌨tab to advance to the Preferred Pricing Method.

Click **Exchange Rate** to change the setting. **Press** ⌨tab.

Type 125

Click the **Linked tab** to open the linked accounts screen.

Click the **Asset field**.

Type   1510 **Press** ⟨tab⟩. We need to add the account.

Click   **Add** and **press** ⟨tab⟩ to advance to the account field.

Type   Promotions

Accept the remaining **defaults** for the account and the account class change.

Press   ⟨tab⟩ to advance to the Revenue account field.

Type   4020 **Press** ⟨tab⟩ to advance to the COGS account field.

Type   5050

The variance linked account is not needed for this item.

Click   the **Taxes tab** to see the sales taxes relating to the inventory.

The default entry No for Tax Exempt is correct — both PST and GST are charged on the sale of this item. Duty is not charged on this item because it is not purchased.

Click   the **Build tab** to see the information screen that we need for entering the assembly or building components for inventory items:

NOTES

This screen is similar to the upper Components section of the Item Assembly Journal (page 380), but you cannot enter unit costs for the components.

On this screen, we enter the relationship between the new inventory and its components, that is, how many new items we are building and how many of each input item this number of units requires. This is very similar to the Item Assembly Journal, except that we are only defining the building process at this stage. The actual building or assembly still takes place in the journal. One package is created from the set of accessories and one unit of each accessory is used — we build one package at a time.

The components are listed here again for reference:

A010 Body Fat Scale
A020 Yoga Mats
A040 Dumbbells: 5kg set
A080 Heart Rate Monitor
A110 Stability Balls
A180 Workout Gloves: all sizes

Click   the **Build field** to enter the default number of packages being assembled from the set of components.

Type   1 **Press** ⟨tab⟩ to advance to the Item No. field.

Click   the **List icon** and **select A010 Body Fat Scale** to enter the first item.

The cursor advances to the Quantity field after entering the unit and description. Here you need to enter the number of Body Fat Scales included in each Promotional Fitness Package. We are defining the unit relationship between the assembled item and its components. One of each component item is used to make the package.

Type   1 **Press** ⟨tab⟩ to advance to the second Item No. line.

WARNING!
You cannot leave a blank line between the component items.

Enter the **remaining components** and **enter 1** as the quantity for each.

The Additional Costs and its linked account field (Record Additional Costs In) became available once we entered the number of units to build. These fields have the same meaning as they do in the Item Assembly Journal. However, in the Premium version, costs are entered in the ledger record and separate assembly linked accounts can be defined for each item. There are no additional costs associated with creating the package so we should leave these fields blank.

Click the **Quantities tab**. The quantity on hand remains at zero until we build the item in the journal.

Correct any **errors** by returning to the field with the mistake. **Highlight** the **error** and **enter** the **correct information**. **Click** the different **tabs** to see all the information that you entered.

When all the information is entered correctly, you must save the record.

Click **Save And Close** to save the record.

Building an Inventory Item in the Journal

The quantity of Promotional Fitness Packages is still zero. In order to create stock of the package for sale, we must build the item in the Bill of Materials & Item Assembly Journal.

The Build From Bill Of Materials Journal is shown by the hand pointer below:

Build from Bill of Materials

Click the **Build From Bill Of Materials icon** to open the journal:

In the Premium version, you can assemble new inventory items either by using the Item Assembly method that we used in previous applications, or the Bill of Materials method that follows.

The journal resembles the lower half of the Build From Item Assembly Journal screen, but without components and costs (see page 380). The default location is Hamilton.

Click the **Source field**.

Type Memo 7-10 **Press** ⟨tab⟩ to advance to the Date field.

Type 7-7 **Press** ⟨tab⟩ **twice** to advance to the Comment field.

SIMPLY VERSION
In the Simply version, there is one linked Item Assembly Costs account for the ledger, and it is entered on the Inventory Linked Accounts screen. In the Premium version, you can enter a different linked assembly costs account for each item you build.

CLASSIC VIEW
Click the Bill of Materials & Item Assembly icon to open the journal. Choose Build From Bill Of Materials from the Build drop-down transactions list if necessary.

NOTES
Remember that you can choose Build From Item Assembly or Build From Bill Of Materials from the transactions drop-down list once the journal is open.

NOTES
The additional costs and the components information are taken from the ledger record — the Build tab screen details. Item cost, as usual, is the average cost for each component.

Type   Create promotional packages **Press** (tab). The cursor moves to the Item field.

Click   the **List icon** to open the selection list:

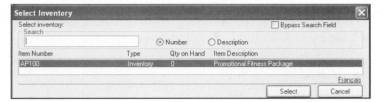

All the items for which you have added build information will be listed on this screen. Because we have entered these details only for the Promotional Fitness Package, it is the only one listed.

Double click AP100 to add it to the journal.

The unit and description are added for the package and the default quantity is 1. The quantity is selected so we can change it. We are creating two packages.

Type   2 to complete the journal entry as shown:

If you have other items to build, you can continue by choosing the items and entering a quantity for each of them.

Review your **work** before posting the transaction.

Choose the **Report menu** and **click Display Bill Of Materials & Item Assembly Journal**.

You will display the journal transaction:

Flabuless Fitness				
07/07/10 (J9)		Debits	Credits	Division
1510	Promotions	192.00	-	
1520	Accessories	-	192.00	
		192.00	192.00	

The asset account balances have been updated by the transaction, just as they are in an Item Assembly transaction. Compare this journal entry with the one on page 382. The inventory quantities are also updated from the transaction — the quantity of packages increases and the quantities for the other items decrease. Any additional costs would be credited to the linked cost account and debited to the assembled item asset account.

Close   the **journal display** and **make corrections** if necessary.

If there is not enough inventory of any item in stock to complete the build, you will see an error message asking you to reduce the quantity to build:

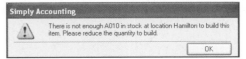

Click OK and reduce the number of units you are building.

NOTES
You cannot change the unit cost using the Build method. The Cost fields are not available in the journal or in the ledger record.

NOTES
The default quantity is taken from the ledger record's Build tab screen, where we entered the rule for building one item at a time.

NOTES
When you link the same asset account to the assembled item and its components, you will see the message that no journal entry results from the transaction. However, all inventory quantities are updated by the transaction.

Click   **Post** to save the entry.

Click the Item list icon to see that the number of promotional packages has been changed to two. Click Cancel to close this screen without making a selection.

You can now sell the package just like any other inventory item.

Multiple Levels of Build

You can use a built item just like any other single inventory item. The process is the same when you are selling the item or using it as a component to build other inventory. We created an additional built item to illustrate this process.

Nested building components are common in construction work. When you use a built item as a component for a second-stage build, you select it on the Build tab screen just like other inventory. When you are building the new second-stage item in the Bill of Materials Journal, the built component may be out of stock. In this case, Simply Accounting provides the following message:

You can now build the primary item, the built component, as part of the same journal transaction.

Click Yes to continue with the additional build:

Simply Accounting will add the out-of-stock item to the Bill of Materials Journal as the first item to build. The number of units built will be those required to complete the secondary build.

Close   the **journal**. Leave the Inventory & Services window open.

Transferring Inventory between Locations

Sometimes the item a customer wants is not located at the store the customer is visiting. When this occurs, items can be transferred from another location where the stock is available. In Simply Accounting, the option to transfer items is available in the Inventory Adjustments & Transfers Journal, accessed from the Transfer Inventory icon in the Inventory & Services module window:

NOTES

If there are further layers of building nested in a transaction, Simply Accounting will offer the chance to build the necessary components at each stage in the same way to complete the initial transaction.

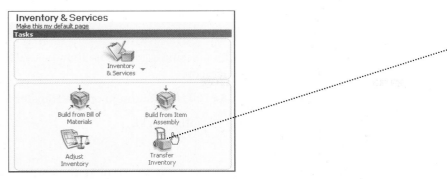

Click the **Transfer Inventory icon** to open the journal with Transfer Between Locations, the type of transaction we need, already selected:

CLASSIC VIEW
Click the Inventory Adjustments & Transfers icon to open the journal. Choose Transfer Between Locations from the drop-down transactions list if necessary.

This is the same journal we used for other inventory adjustments in previous chapters, but there is no field for account numbers. When multiple locations are used, the transfers between locations are made in this journal as well. You can select the type of transaction from the transactions drop-down list as shown:

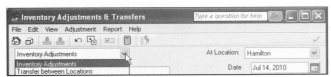

We need to indicate the direction of the transfer, in this case from the Hamilton store to the Burlington store. Hamilton is the default location for both fields because it is the primary location.

Click the **From** drop-down list to see both locations:

Click **Hamilton** in the From list.

Choose Burlington from the To drop-down list.

As for other types of transactions, we need to enter the date, the source and a comment. Then we will enter the items that are being moved.

Click the **Source field**.

Type Memo 7-11 **Press** (tab) to move to the Date field.

Enter **July 7** as the date of the inventory move.

Click the **Comment field**.

Type Move inventory to Burlington store

Press   [tab] to advance to the Item code field. A list of items is available, as it is for inventory fields in other journals.

You can access the inventory list by pressing [enter] in the Item field, double clicking the field or clicking the List icon.

Click   the **List icon** and **select AP100**, the first item on the transfer list.

Press   [tab] to move to the Qty (quantity) field.

Type   2

Enter   the **remaining items** in the same way to complete the entry as shown:

NOTES
The successful recording message for the transfer does not include a journal entry number.

When you record (post) the transfer, the inventory at the two locations will be updated — the quantity at the Hamilton store is reduced and the quantity at the Burlington store is increased. You can see the changes that you made by accessing the ledger records for the items and choosing the locations on the Quantity tab screen. However, no journal entry results from this transaction and you cannot look up or adjust the entry, so check it carefully before posting. When you are certain that the transaction is correct, you must save it.

Click   **Post** [Post] to save the entry. **Close** the **journal** to return to the Inventory Home window.

Adding Location Information for Purchases

Now that we have multiple locations for inventory, we must indicate which location the inventory is taken from or sent to when we make purchases, sales and adjustments. By choosing the correct location, we can accurately keep track of the quantity on hand at each store.

The purchase order from Scandia Weights should be delivered to the Burlington store.

Open   the **Purchases Journal** (click the Create Purchase Invoice shortcut).

Choose PO #34 in the order number field and **press** [tab] to place the order on screen as an invoice:

When the order was entered, locations were not set up. The location field (Store Items At) is dimmed and unavailable. Hamilton, the primary location, is entered, and this is not correct. We need to edit the order to change the location before filling it.

Choose **Purchase Order** from the Transaction drop-down list to restore the purchase order. **Click Yes** to confirm that you are discarding the invoice.

Choose **PO #34** in the Quote/Order field list. **Press** (tab) to place the order on the screen. The fields are still dimmed and cannot be edited.

Click the **Adjust Purchase Order tool** 🖺 , or **choose** the **Purchase menu** and **click Adjust Purchase Order** or **press** (ctrl) **+ A**. We can now modify the order.

Click the **Store Items At drop-down list arrow** and **click Burlington**:

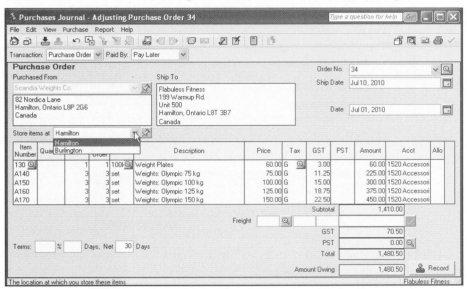

We can now fill the order.

Choose Invoice from the Transaction drop-down list.

Simply Accounting shows you the following confirmation message:

Click **Yes** to confirm that you are changing the order to an invoice and that the changes to the order have been saved.

Enter **July 10** as the purchase invoice date and add the invoice number to complete the transaction.

Click the **Fill Backordered Quantities tool** 🖺 , or **choose** the **Purchase menu** and **click Fill Backordered Quantities**.

Review your **journal entry**. Location details are not included in the journal entry, but the inventory records will be correctly updated.

Close the **display** when finished.

Click **Post** 🖺 Post to save the entry when you are certain that it is correct.

Click **OK** to confirm that the order has been filled and **click Yes** to confirm successful posting.

> **Adjust** purchase order **#35** by **adding** the **location**. **Fill** the order.
>
> **Enter** the **purchase from ABS International**, after using Full Add to enter the new European vendor.
>
> **Close** the **Purchases Journal**.
>
> **Enter** the **remaining transactions** for July.

Entering Locations in Other Journals

All journals that use inventory items also have a location field. In the Sales Journal, you choose the location from the Items Stored At drop-down list as shown:

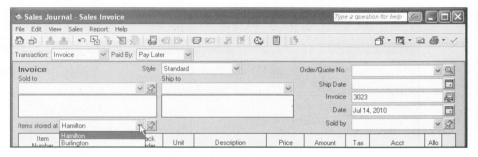

For inventory adjustments, that is, losses or movement of inventory stock for in-store use, choose the location from the At Location drop-down list as shown:

For building items from item assembly or from a bill of materials, enter the location in the At Location field as shown:

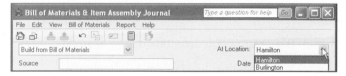

If the location you chose does not have sufficient stock of any items needed to complete the build, you will see the following message:

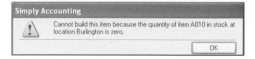

You can transfer inventory to the required location or choose a smaller quantity.

Updating Inventory Prices

At the end of the month, all inventory prices must be increased. Rather than changing each record for regular and preferred prices in both Canadian and US dollars, we will use the Update Price List method that we used earlier to edit the activity prices. This method is more efficient when many prices must be changed or when they are changed by a fixed amount or percentage. In this case, we are increasing prices by 10 percent. The feature also allows us to round off the prices automatically.

> **Click** the **Settings icon** [Settings].

Click   **Inventory & Services** and then **click Price List**.

Click   **Update Price Lists**.

Click   **Inventory Items** to restrict the list to the ones we need.

Click   the **select item column heading** 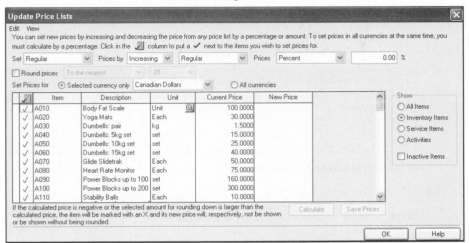 to select all items as shown:

The upper part of the screen has the rules for the change. We are increasing Canadian Regular prices by a fixed percentage, so these entries are already correct. The entry shows that we are setting prices for the selected currency only (Canadian dollars). We need to enter a percentage and the rule for rounding prices.

Click   **0.00** in the % field.

Type   10

Press   tab to move to the check box for rounding.

Click   the **rounding check box** to add a ✓ and open the next field we need.

You can round up, round down or round to the nearest amount. We want to round to the nearest dollar, so we just need to add the unit. One cent (.01) is the default entry. The units range from one ten-thousandth of a dollar (.0001) to one thousand dollars (1 000.00).

Click   the list arrow beside the unit with .01 (one cent) as the default entry.

Choose   1.00 (one dollar) as the unit. Your settings should match the following:

Click   **Calculate** to update the prices and add them to the New Price column.

You can edit individual prices if you want. They have not yet been saved. The price of A130 (weight plates) has actually decreased because of the rounding factor. We will edit this price individually.

Click   **1.00** in the New Price column for A130.

Type   1.50

Click   **Save Prices** to transfer the new prices to the Current Price column.

Now we need to update the preferred Canadian prices and the US dollar prices. We will set Preferred Canadian prices by increasing preferred Canadian prices by 5 percent and rounding to the nearest dollar. The increase, 10 percent, and the rounding rules are still entered from the previous update. All items remain selected.

> **Click**   the **Set drop-down list arrow** and **select Preferred**.
>
> **Press**   (tab) **twice** to move to the second price list field — the reference list.
>
> **Click**   the **drop-down list arrow** and **select Preferred**.
>
> **Click**   **10** in the % field and **type** 5   Your settings should be like the ones shown in the following screen:

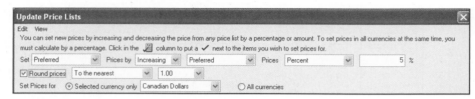

> **Click**   **Calculate** to update all prices.

We will edit the price for A130.

> **Click**   **1.00** in the New Price column for A130.
>
> **Type**   1.20
>
> **Click**   **Save Prices** to transfer the new prices to the Current Price column.

We will update the preferred US dollar prices next because most of the settings are already correct. We will set Preferred US dollar prices by increasing preferred US dollar prices by 5 percent and rounding to the nearest dollar. We need to change the selected currency.

> **Click**   **Canadian** in the Selected Currency Only field to display the list.
>
> **Choose**   **United States Dollars** to change the selection as shown:

> **Click**   **Calculate** to update all prices.
>
> **Click**   **1.00** in the New Price column for A130 so you can change this price.
>
> **Type**   1.20 **Click Save Prices**.

The final change is for Regular US dollar prices. These prices should be set by increasing regular US dollar prices by 10 percent and rounding to the nearest dollar.

> **Choose**   **Regular** in the Set price field.
>
> **Choose**   **Regular** in the next price reference field.
>
> **Click**   **5** in the % field and **type** 10

Your settings should match the ones we show here:

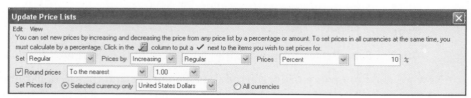

Click	**Calculate** to update all prices.
Click	**1.00** in the New Price column for A130 so you can change this price.
Type	1.50 **Click Save Prices**.
Click	**OK** to return to the Settings screen and **click OK** again to return to the Home window.

Displaying Time and Billing Reports

The various Time and Billing reports provide different ways of organizing the same information. You can view the reports by customer, by employee and by activity.

Customer Time & Billing Report

Click	the **Report Centre icon** in the Home window. **Click Time & Billing**. **Click** the ⊞ beside **Billing** and beside **Payroll** to expand the list of available reports:

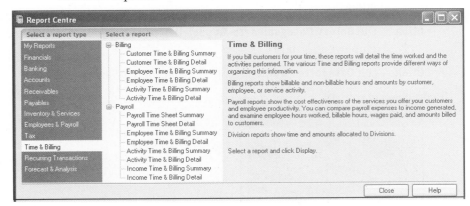

Click	**Customer Time & Billing Summary** under **Billing**. **Click Modify This Report**:

Time and Billing reports by customer show the time and billed amounts organized by customer. Summary and Detail reports are available. **Detail** reports include a report line for each activity or employee on each time slip while the **Summary** reports show only the totals for each selected category (activity or employee). You can select one or more customers for inclusion in the report. The reports will include columns for several billing details — actual time spent on activities, non-billable time, no-charge time, billable time, billable percentage (the proportion of the total time worked for which the customer was charged) and billable amounts. In addition, if you changed the prices for

NOTES
Sorting and filtering are not available for Time & Billing reports, but you can choose the columns to include in the report.

NOTES
From the Home window, choose the Reports menu, then choose Time & Billing. Click Billing and click Time By Customer to see the report options.

NOTES
Time & Billing reports can include a large amount of information. A good way to understand these reports is to prepare a very complete report. For example, select the Detail Report, choose all employees, click all Details and Activities and choose Activities and Customers as the categories for the report. Then choose all service activities from the next list. Print the report. Click the Modify tool or choose Modify Report from the Options menu in the report. Compare this report with the Summary Report for the same details and categories.

any of the services, the report will show these changes as amounts written down or up and as percentages of the billable amounts. In the report, the invoiced amounts will then be different from the billable amounts. The effective billable percentage shows the relation between the invoiced amount and the billable amount. You can customize the report by selecting the columns to include. The report details can also be grouped — by date, by activity or by employee.

You can include **invoiced activities** (bills have been sent) or **uninvoiced activities** (bills have not been created and sent) or both.

The next decision for the report relates to the **categories** you want to include. You can report on the time spent according to the **activities** performed for the customer, or according to the **employee** who completed the work or both. In all cases, the categories are shown for each customer you selected.

Enter   **Start** and **Finish dates** for the report.

Choose   the **customers** for the report. **Press** and **hold** ⌨ctrl and **click** the **customer names** to begin a new selection. Then **click Select All** to include all customers.

Choose   the **invoicing details** for the report. **Click** a **detail** to remove a ✓ or to add it.

Click   the **Select Categories To Report list arrow** to select activities or employees or both.

Click   the **Categories button** to open the secondary selection list.

If you choose Activity, you will see the list of activities:

If you choose Employees as the category, you must select from the employee list. If you choose both Activity and Employees, you must choose from lists for both.

Initially, all activities are selected and clicking will change the selection. The selection acts like a toggle switch. To begin a new selection of activities,

Click   **Select All** to clear all selections.

Press   and **hold** ⌨ctrl and **click** the **activities** you want in the report to begin a new selection. Then **click Select All** to include all activities.

Click   **OK** to return to the report options screen.

Click   **OK** to see the report.

The report shows the amount of time worked for each customer according to the activity, employee or both, depending on the category you selected.

Close   the **report** when you have finished.

Employee and Activity Time & Billing Report

The other two Time and Billing reports are similar to the Time By Customer Report, except that they organize the amounts by employee or by activity. The first options screen for the **Employee Time & Billing Report** (Summary or Detail) will show the

Employee list, and the second selection screen will list the customers, the activities or both, depending on the category you choose. The Time by Employee Report shows the time and billed amounts for each employee for each customer, each activity or both, depending on the categories you choose.

Similarly, the first options screen for the **Activity Time & Billing Report** (Summary or Detail) will show the Activity list, and the second selection screen will list the customers, the employees or both, depending on the category you choose. The Time by Activity Report shows the time and the billed amounts for each activity for each customer or by each employee or both, depending on the category you choose.

Other report options are the same as they are for the Time by Customer Report, and both reports are available as a Summary or a Detail report.

Payroll Time Sheet Reports

The Time Sheet Report provides a summary of the hours of each income category that is on the time sheets. The number of hours of non-payroll, regular payroll and overtime for each employee can be included.

> **Click**   **Payroll Time Sheet Summary** under **Payroll. Click** **Modify This Report**:

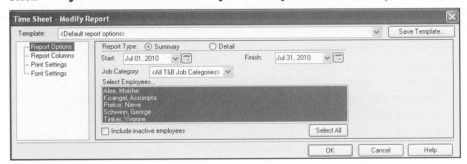

NOTES
From the Home window, choose the Reports menu, then choose Time & Billing. Click Payroll and click Time Sheet to see the report options.

The **Summary** Report will provide the total number of hours in each payroll category for each employee selected for each time period during the report interval. The **Detail** Report will show the number of hours in each payroll category for each time sheet.

You can customize the report by selecting columns for the payroll category. Non-payroll, Regular and Overtime 1 columns — the payroll category in the ledger record for the activity — may be selected.

> **Enter**   **Start** and **Finish dates** for the report.
>
> **Choose**   the **employees** for the report. **Press** and **hold** $\boxed{ctrl}$ and **click** the **employee names** to begin a new selection. Then **click Select All** to include all employees.
>
> **Click**   **OK** to display the report.
>
> **Close**   the **report** when you have finished.

Employee Time & Billing Payroll Reports

The remaining Payroll Time reports provide information about the cost effectiveness of the service activities by comparing the labour costs with the income generated — the amount billed to the customer. Employee productivity is also measured by examining the actual hours, billable hours, wages paid and invoiced amounts.

> **Click**   **Employee Time & Billing Summary** under **Payroll**.

NOTES
From the Home window, choose the Reports menu, then choose Time & Billing. Click Payroll and click Time By Employee to see the report options.

Click   Modify This Report:

Summary and Detail reports are available. **Detail** reports include a report line for each time sheet entry while the **Summary** reports show only the totals for each selected category. You can select one or more employees for inclusion in the report. The reports will include several time and billing **details** — actual time spent on activities, payroll time, payroll percentage (payroll time as a proportion of actual time), billable time, billable percentage (the proportion of the total time worked for which the customer was charged), billable amounts, the actual payroll expense and the productivity ratio (the billable amount compared to the payroll expense) can be included. The effective productivity ratio percentage shows the relation between the invoiced amount and the payroll expense amount. You can customize the report by selecting from these time and billing details (report columns).

The report can include **activities** for which you have **paid** the employees, activities that have **not yet been paid**, activities that are **non-payroll** or all three payroll details.

The next decision for the report relates to the **categories** you want to include. You can report on the time spent according to the **activity** performed by the employee, according to the **customer** for whom the work was completed, or according to the **income** (that is, regular, non-payroll or overtime) or any two of these three categories. In all cases, the categories are shown for each employee you selected.

You can also group report details — select from date, activity, customer or income.

Enter   **Start** and **Finish dates** for the report.

Choose   the **employees** for the report. **Press** and **hold** ⌈ctrl⌉ and **click** the **employee names** to begin a new selection. Then **click Select All** to include all employees.

Choose   the **payroll details**. **Click** a **detail** to add or to remove a ✓.

Choose   the **categories** for the report from the drop-down list.

Click   the **Categories button** to open the secondary selection list.

If you select the Activities category, you will see the complete list of all services defined as activities in the ledger.

Choose   the **activities** for the report. **Press** and **hold** ⌈ctrl⌉ and **click** the **activity names** to begin a new selection. Then **click Select All** to include all activities.

Click   **OK** to return to the report options screen.

Click   **OK** to see the report. By default the report will print in landscape orientation (sideways on the page) so that all details can fit on a line.

Close   the **report** when you have finished.

NOTES

If you select Customers or Income as the category, you will see selection lists for each category. If you selected two categories, you can choose from selection lists for both categories.

Activity and Income Time & Billing Payroll Reports

These two reports are similar to the Time by Employee Report except that they organize amounts by activity or by income category. The three reports provide essentially the same information but organize the details in different ways.

The first options screen for the **Time by Activity Report** will show the Activity list, and the second selection screen will list the customers, employees, incomes or any two of these that you select, depending on the category you choose. The Time by Activity Report shows the same details as the Time by Employee Report but lists them for each activity for each customer, each employee, each income or any two of these, depending on the categories you choose.

Similarly, the first options screen for the **Time by Income Report** will show the income list, and the second selection screen will list the customers, the employees, activities or any two of these three, depending on the category you choose. The Time by Income Report shows the same details as the Time by Employee Report but lists them for each activity for each customer, by each employee, each activity or any two of these, depending on the categories you choose.

Other report options are the same as they are for the Time by Employee Report, and both reports are available as a Summary or a Detail report.

Multiple Fiscal Periods and Reports

After you have accumulated two fiscal periods of financial data, you can produce historical reports for these additional periods. Data for the current and previous years are always available, unless you have cleared the information.

Print the **financial reports** for July (Income Statement, Balance Sheet, Trial Balance, Supplier and Customer Aged reports, Employee Summary Report and Inventory Summary and Quantity reports).

Prepare a **list** of inventory items that should be ordered.

Choose the **Maintenance menu** and **click Start New Year** to begin a new fiscal year.

Choose Yes when asked if you want to Back Up Your Data Files Before Beginning The New Fiscal Year and follow the backup instructions.

Choose No when asked if you want to clear the old data.

The Update Locking Date screen opens.

Enter **08/01/10** as the new date. **Click OK** to update the earliest transaction.

Choose the **Setup menu**, then **click Settings**, **Company** and **Information**:

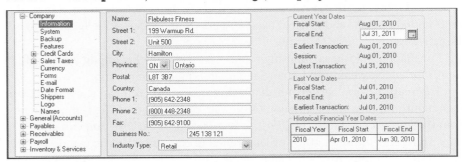

Notice that the first fiscal period, April 1 to June 30, 2010, is now listed in the section for Historical Financial Year Dates.

Drag through the **Fiscal End date**.

Type   08-31-10   **Click OK** to save the date and return to the Home window.

Multi-period Financial Reports

Multiple-period reports are available for the Balance Sheet, Income Statement and Trial Balance. All are accessed from the Financials list of reports.

Click   the **Report Centre icon**.

Click   **Financials** to expand this list of reports.

Click   the ⊞ beside **Balance Sheet**, **Income Statement** and **Trial Balance** to expand the Select A Report list as shown:

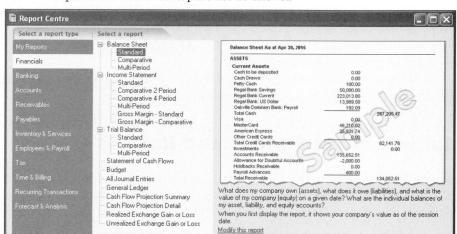

Click   **Multi-Period** under **Balance Sheet**. **Click Modify This Report**:

From the Home window, choose the Reports menu, then choose Financials and Multi-Period Reports and click Balance Sheet to see the report options.

The regular financial reports available in comparative form compare two fiscal periods or dates. Reports for the previous fiscal period are also available in regular reports. The Multi-period Reports show more than two periods and can include fiscal periods before the previous one.

For Flabuless Fitness, monthly reports are available beginning with April, the first month for which we entered financial data in Simply Accounting.

There are several options for displaying the report. You can show the balances for each month for any interval ranging from one to 12 months. The report can be ordered from the earliest period to the latest or from latest to earliest. You can show Amounts Only, Difference In Percentage or Difference In Amounts, just as you do for regular comparative reports. And you can compare the first period with each subsequent period, or you can compare each period with subsequent periods.

After choosing the options for the report,

Click   **OK** to see the report.

Close   the **report** when you have finished.

The **Income Statement** and **Trial Balance** are available for the same periods as the Balance Sheet. They have the same report options. To see these reports,

Click   **Multi-Period under Income Statement** (or **Trial Balance**) and then **click Modify This Report**.

Choose the **report options** and **click OK**.

Close   the **report** when you have finished. **Close** the **Report Centre**.

Related Historical Accounts

Because we have advanced to the next (third) fiscal period, we can see the list of related accounts. You can see and edit the related historical accounts in the General Ledger record for the account in the Related Historical Accounts tab screen.

Click   the **Accounts icon**.

Double click the **account** you want to open its General Ledger record.

Click   the **Related Historical Accounts tab** to see the accounts used in previous periods.

If an account currently being used has a different name and number than the account used for the same purpose in a previous period, you can link them.

Each account shows itself as the related historical account if it has been used for more than two fiscal periods. Each account can be related to only one account. Therefore, if the account is already related to itself, you cannot select it again. Instead, you can link a new account to the old one.

Open the record for the previously used account. Then select the new account from the account selection list in the Related Historical Accounts tab.

Close   the **Ledger window** and then **close** the **Accounts window**.

If you have used different accounts for the same purpose over the periods and you have related them, you can add the related accounts to the Account List. To see the report of related account numbers,

Choose the **Reports menu**, then **choose** **Lists** and **click Accounts**.

Click   **Related Historical Accounts** and then **click OK** to see the report.

The report will list all General Ledger accounts with the current information and the accounts that were used for those same purposes in previous fiscal periods — the information that is stored in the General Ledger Related Historical Accounts tab fields.

Close   the **report** when you have finished.

Close   the **Home window** to exit the Simply Accounting program.

R E V I E W

The Student CD-ROM with Data Files includes Review Questions and Supplementary Cases for this chapter.

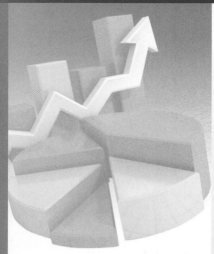

CHAPTER NINETEEN

Able & Associates

OBJECTIVES

- **activate** departmental accounting
- **create** departments
- **add** departments to accounts, vendors and clients
- **add** departments in journal entries
- **apply** line discounts in sales journal entries
- **display** and **print** department reports

After completing this chapter, you should be able to

COMPANY INFORMATION

Company Profile

NOTES
Able & Associates Inc.
88 Practice Blvd.
Huntsville, Ontario P1H 1T2
Tel: (705) 463-2145
Fax: (705) 465-1110
Business No.: 167 344 577

Able & Associates Inc. is a partnership of two chartered accountants, Count and Memor Able. They began their practice in Huntsville, Ontario, two years ago, shortly after receiving their C.A. designations. They each invested capital to start up the office. By relying extensively on electronic communications, remote access to client computers and frequent phone calls, they are able to serve clients throughout a large geographic area. Only occasional on-site meetings are required and local clients often come to their office. Most of their revenue comes from auditing and preparing regular financial statements and income tax returns for small business clients. They share office space and office expenses, including a full-time office assistant. Count works in the office full time, but Memor is there only four days a week, spending the other day working in a small family business. Thus, they allocate their joint expenses using a 60/40 percent division.

Most of the clients have contracts with Able & Associates and pay fees on a monthly basis. These clients are entitled to a discount of 2 percent of their fees if they pay within 10 days of the invoice date. Full payment is requested within 30 days. One-time clients do not receive discounts. Some regular vendors also offer discounts for early payment.

On March 31, at the end of the fiscal period, they decided to use the departmental accounting feature in Simply Accounting to track their financial performance. Payroll taxes were remitted at year-end. To prepare for allocating opening account balances to departments, all opening account balances were transferred to unallocated accounts in the corresponding financial statement section. The following business information was used to set up the accounts:

- Chart of Accounts
- Post-Closing Trial Balance and Statement of Opening Account Balances
- Vendor Information
- Client Information
- Employee Information
- Accounting Procedures

NOTES
For this professional service business, the terms Client and Vendor are used.

CHART OF POSTABLE ACCOUNTS

ABLE & ASSOCIATES INC.

ASSETS
10800 Bank: Chequing
11000 Investments
11200 Prepaid Association Dues
11400 Prepaid Subscriptions
11600 Prepaid Insurance
12000 Accounts Receivable
13400 Office Supplies
14400 Office Equipment
14800 Office Furniture
15000 Library ▶

▶LIABILITIES
21000 Bank Loan
22000 Accounts Payable
22500 Visa Payable
23000 EI Payable
23100 CPP Payable
23200 Income Tax Payable
24200 WSIB Payable
26500 GST Charged on Services
26700 GST Paid on Purchases

EQUITY
34500 Invested Capital: C. Able ▶

▶34800 Invested Capital: M. Able
35500 Retained Earnings
36000 Current Earnings

REVENUE
41000 Revenue from Services
41500 Revenue from Interest
41800 Other Revenue
42000 Sales Discounts

EXPENSE
51200 Association Dues
51300 Bank and Card Fees ▶

▶51400 Interest Expense
51500 Insurance Expense
51600 Publicity and Promotion
51800 Purchase Discounts
52000 Subscriptions
52200 Telephone Expense
52400 Rent
54000 Salaries
54100 EI Expense
54200 CPP Expense
54300 WSIB Expense

NOTES: The Chart of Accounts includes only postable accounts and the Current Earnings account. Able & Associates use five-digit account numbers for the General Ledger accounts.

POST-CLOSING TRIAL BALANCE

ABLE & ASSOCIATES INC.

April 1, 2010	Debits	Credits			Debits	Credits
10800 Bank: Chequing	$ 21 300		▶	21000 Bank Loan		$ 15 000
11000 Investments	44 000			22000 Accounts Payable		2 260
11200 Prepaid Association Dues	2 800			22500 Visa Payable		1 400
11400 Prepaid Subscriptions	1 500			26500 GST Charged on Services		1 200
11600 Prepaid Insurance	4 500			26700 GST Paid on Purchases	640	
12000 Accounts Receivable	2 100			34500 Invested Capital: C. Able		33 000
13400 Office Supplies	1 800			34800 Invested Capital: M. Able		22 000
14400 Office Equipment	12 000			35500 Retained Earnings		28 580
14800 Office Furniture	8 000				$103 440	$103 440
15000 Library	4 800	▶				

STATEMENT OF ACCOUNT OPENING BALANCES

ABLE & ASSOCIATES INC.

April 1, 2010	Debits	Credits			Debits	Credits
19500 Unassigned Assets	$102 800	▶		29500 Unassigned Liabilities		$ 19 220
				39500 Unassigned Capital		83 580
					$102 800	$102 800

Note: The true account balances are shown for the regular postable accounts in the Trial Balance. The three unassigned accounts in the Statement of Opening Balances are temporary holding accounts. The temporary balance in these accounts is the sum of all balances for that section of the Balance Sheet. These balances will be transferred back to the regular accounts to set up the departmental opening balances.

VENDOR INFORMATION

ABLE & ASSOCIATES INC.

Vendor Name (Contact)	Address	Phone No. Fax No.	E-mail Web Site	Terms Tax ID
Bell Canada (Yap Long)	500 Central Line. Huntsville Ontario P1F 2C2	Tel: (705) 466-2355	yap.l@bell.ca www.bell.ca	net 1
Muskoka Maintenance (M. Handimann)	72 Spoiler St. Huntsville Ontario P1P 2B8	Tel: (705) 469-0808 Fax: (705) 469-6222	handimann@yahoo.com	2/10, n/30 295 416 822
Northlands Office Mgt. (Hi Bilding)	59 Condor St. Huntsville Ontario P1D 4F4	Tel: (705) 283-9210 Fax: (705) 283-2310	bilding@northlands.com	net 1
Office Plus (B. Laser)	4 Paper Corners Huntsville Ontario P1E 1G1	Tel: (705) 466-3335	www.officeplus.ca	1/15, n/30 822 101 500
Receiver General for Canada	Sudbury Tax Services Office PO Box 20004 Sudbury, ON P3A 6B4	Tel 1: (800) 561-7761 Tel 2: (800) 959-2221	www.cra-arc.gc.ca	net 1

OUTSTANDING VENDOR INVOICES

ABLE & ASSOCIATES INC.

Vendor Name	Terms	Date	Invoice No.	Amount	Total
Office Plus	1/15, n/30	Mar. 21/10	OP-2339	$2 260	$2 260

CLIENT INFORMATION

ABLE & ASSOCIATES INC.

Client Name (Contact)	Address	Phone No. Fax No.	E-mail Web Site	Terms Credit Limit
Adrienne Aesthetics (Adrienne Kosh)	65 Bytown Ave. Ottawa, Ontario K2C 4R1	Tel 1: (613) 722-9876 Tel 2: (613) 722-8701 Fax: (613) 722-8000	a.kosh@adrienneaesthetics.com www.adrienneaesthetics.com	2/10, n/30 $10 000
Flabuless Fitness (Stephen Reeves)	199 Warmup Rd., Unit 500 Hamilton, Ontario L8T 3B7	Tel: (905) 642-2348 Fax: (905) 642-9100	sreeves@flabfit.com www.flabfit.com	2/10, n/30 $10 000
Gorgeous Gifts (Gitte Gurlosi)	600 First St. Huntsville Ontario P1L 2W4	Tel: (705) 462-1203 Fax: (705) 462-3394	gg@ggifts.com www.ggifts.com	2/10, n/30 $10 000
Truman Tires (Tyrone Truman)	600 Westminster St. London, Ontario N6P 3B1	Tel: (519) 729-3733 Fax: (519) 729-7301	tt@trumantires.com www.trumantires.com	2/10, n/30 $10 000

OUTSTANDING CLIENT INVOICES

ABLE & ASSOCIATES INC.

Client Name	Terms	Date	Invoice No.	Amount	Total
Adrienne Aesthetics	2/10, n/30	Mar. 25/10	843	$2 100	$2 100

EMPLOYEE INFORMATION SHEET

ABLE & ASSOCIATES INC.

Tryin, Reelie (Office Assistant)

Social Insurance No.	429 535 644	Total Federal (Ontario) Tax Exemption - TD1 $9 600 (8 681)
Address	200 Water St. #301 Huntsville, Ontario P1H 2L8	Employee Incomes (Reg. hours) Salary $3 500 /month (150 hours)
Telephone	(705) 446-2190	
Date of Birth (mm-dd-yy)	04-04-77	WSIB Rate 0.89
EI, CPP & Income Tax	Calculations built into Simply Accounting program	

Accounting Procedures

Taxes (GST and PST)

Able & Associates Inc. is a professional service business using the regular method of calculating GST. GST, at the rate of 5 percent, is charged on all services and paid on purchases. The difference between the GST charged and GST paid is remitted to the Receiver General for Canada quarterly.

Accounting services are exempt for PST, but the business pays PST on purchases.

Departments

Able & Associates has two departments, one for each partner. The division of most assets is 60 percent and 40 percent, to be consistent with their initial investments in the partnership and their time in the office.

Discounts for Early Payments

Able & Associates offers discounts to regular clients if they pay their accounts within 10 days. Full payment is expected in 30 days. No discounts are allowed on partial payments. Different discounts are applied occasionally for clients in special circumstances. These are entered as line discounts for the sales.

Some vendors with whom Able & Associates has accounts set up also offer discounts for early payments.

INSTRUCTIONS

1. **Record entries for the source documents** in Simply Accounting. Transactions indicated with a ✓ in the completion box beside the source document have step-by-step keystroke instructions on the pages indicated.

2. **Print** the following **reports and graphs** after you have finished making your entries. Instructions for departmental reports begin on page 801.

   a. Comparative Balance Sheet with Departments for April 1 and April 30.
   b. Income Statement with Departments for April 1 to April 30.
   c. Departmental Income Statement.
   d. Journal Report for April 1 to April 30 for all journals.

SOURCE DOCUMENTS

SESSION DATE — APRIL 30, 2010

☑ **Memo #1**   **Dated April 1/10**

788   Create two departments for Able & Associates:
        1001: C. Able   2001: M. Able

☑ **Memo #2**   **Dated April 1/10**

790   Assign accounts to departments. Invested Capital accounts are used by the department named in account. All accounts are used by both departments.

☑ **Memo #3**   **Dated April 1/10**

791   Assign departmental opening account balances by transferring the unassigned balances from the chart below. Add linked accounts and then finish the history.

Department		1001: C. Able	2001: M. Able	Source
10800	Bank: Chequing	$ 12 780	$ 8 520	Debit from Unassigned Assets
11000	Investments	26 500	17 500	Debit from Unassigned Assets
11200	Prepaid Association Dues	1 680	1 120	Debit from Unassigned Assets
11400	Prepaid Subscriptions	900	600	Debit from Unassigned Assets
11600	Prepaid Insurance	2 700	1 800	Debit from Unassigned Assets
12000	Accounts Receivable	2 100		Debit from Unassigned Assets
13400	Office Supplies	1 080	720	Debit from Unassigned Assets
14400	Office Equipment	7 200	4 800	Debit from Unassigned Assets
14800	Office Furniture	4 000	4 000	Debit from Unassigned Assets
15000	Library	2 400	2 400	Debit from Unassigned Assets
21000	Bank Loan	9 000	6 000	Credit from Unassigned Liabilities
22000	Accounts Payable	1 356	904	Credit from Unassigned Liabilities
22500	Visa Payable	840	560	Credit from Unassigned Liabilities
26500	GST Charged on Services	720	480	Credit from Unassigned Liabilities
26700	GST Paid on Purchases	384	256	Debit from Unassigned Liabilities
34500	Invested Capital: C. Able	33 000		Credit from Unassigned Capital
34800	Invested Capital: M. Able		22 000	Credit from Unassigned Capital
35500	Retained Earnings	17 150	11 430	Credit from Unassigned Capital

☑ **Memo #4**   **Dated April 1/10**

793   Clients: Assign C. Able to Adrienne Aesthetics and M. Able to Flabuless Fitness. The remaining clients are associated with both departments.

☑ **Cash Purchase Invoice #NO-2010-4**   **Dated April 3/10**

795   From Northlands Office Mgt., $1 400 plus $70 GST for rental of office suite. Invoice total, $1 470 paid by cheque #3011. $840 (60 percent) of the expense should be assigned to C. Able and $560 (40 percent) to M. Able.

☑ **Cash Receipt #48**   **Dated April 4/10**

796   From Adrienne Aesthetics, cheque #8101 for $2 058, including $42 discount in full payment of invoice #843. Assign all amounts to C. Able.

☑ **Sales Invoice #851**   **Dated April 5/10**

797   To Adrienne Aesthetics, $5 800 plus $290 GST for auditing financial statements and $900 plus $45 GST for monthly accounting fee. Invoice total $6 730.50. Terms: 2/10, n/30. Additional 5 percent discount applies to the fee for auditing, by special arrangement with client. Adrienne Aesthetics is C. Able's client.

☐ **Cheque Copy #3012**   **Dated April 5/10**

To Office Plus, $2 237.40, including $22.60 discount in full payment of invoice #OP-2339. (You cannot assign these amounts — see margin notes.)

☐ **Cash Sales Invoice #852**   **Dated April 10/10**

To Truman Tires, $1 000 plus $50 GST for monthly fee for accounting assistance. Assign $600 (60%) of the fee to C. Able and $400 (40%) to M. Able. Received cheque #2900 for $1 029 in full payment, including 2% discount for early payment. (See margin notes.)

☐ **Sales Invoice #853**   **Dated April 14/10**

To Flabuless Fitness, $5 000 plus GST for preparing special financial reports for potential investors and $700 plus GST for monthly accounting fee. Invoice total $5 460 (with discount). Terms: 2/10, n/30. Additional 10 percent discount applies to the fee for preparing financial reports. Assign 100% of all amounts to M. Able.

☐ **Sales Invoice #854**   **Dated April 20/10**

To Gorgeous Gifts, $3 000 plus $150 GST for assistance with response to Canada Revenue Agency audit and $500 plus $25 GST for monthly accounting fee. Invoice total $3 675. Terms: 2/10, n/30. Assign $1 800 plus $300 (60%) of revenue amounts to C. Able and $1 200 and $200 (40%) to M. Able.

☐ **Cash Purchase Invoice #BC-233008**   **Dated April 22/10**

From Bell Canada, $400 plus $20 GST and $32 PST for monthly telephone and Internet service for one multi-line office telephone, two mobile phones and networked Internet service. Invoice total, $452 paid by cheque #3013. Assign $240 (60%) of expense amount to C. Able and $160 (40%) to M. Able.

☐ **Purchase Invoice #OP-5102**   **Dated April 25/10**

From Office Plus, $3 000 plus $150 GST and $240 PST for new boardroom table and chairs (Office Furniture account). Invoice total $3 390. Terms: 1/15, n/30. Assign $1 800 (60%) of the asset account amount to C. Able and $1 200 (40%) to M. Able. (See margin notes.)

☐ **Memo #5**   **Dated April 25/10**

Remit the GST owing to the Receiver General as at March 31. Issue cheque #3014. Assign $720 for GST Charged on Services and $384 for GST Paid (60% of GST amounts) to C. Able and $480 for GST Charged on Services and $256 for GST Paid (40%) to M. Able.

☐ **Cash Sales Invoice #855**   **Dated April 30/10**

To various one-time clients, $6 000 plus $300 GST for personal income tax preparation. Total cash received $6 300 deposited to bank account. Assign $3 600 (60%) of revenue amount to C. Able and $2 400 (40%) to M. Able.

✓ **Memo #6**   **Dated April 30/10**

798 Prepare payroll for Tryin, office assistant. Issue cheque #3015. Assign 60% of all amounts to C. Able and 40% to M. Able.

☐ **Memo #7**   **Dated April 30/10**

The following transactions appeared on the monthly bank statement for the bank chequing account. Assign 60% of all amounts to C. Able and 40% to M. Able.

	Amounts for C. Able	Amounts for M. Able
Bank charges $60	$ 36	$ 24
Bank Loan principal $300	180	120
Bank Loan interest $200	120	80
Interest on Chequing account $60	36	24
Interest from Investments $180	108	72
Bank net withdrawal $320	192	128

NOTES
For the sale to Truman Tires, enter 600 as the amount for account 41000 - 1001, and on the second line, enter 400 as the amount for account 41000 - 2001. The amounts for Bank: Chequing, Sales Discounts and GST will remain unallocated.

NOTES
For the purchase from Office Plus, enter 1800 as the amount for account 14800 - 1001, and on the second line, enter 1200 as the amount for account 14800 - 2001. PST will be added to these allocated amounts automatically. The amounts for Accounts Payable and GST will remain unallocated.

☐   **Memo #8**   **Dated April 30/10**

Enter the adjustments for supplies used and prepaid expenses expired in April. Assign 60% of all amounts to C. Able and 40% to M. Able. Create new Group Expense account 52600 Supplies Used.

	Amounts for C. Able	Amounts for M. Able
Office Supplies $100	$ 60	$ 40
Prepaid Insurance $500	300	200
Prepaid Association Dues $400	240	160
Prepaid Subscriptions $250	150	100

KEYSTROKES

Departmental Accounting

Most companies are divided into departments such as sales, marketing, service, finance, human resources and manufacturing. And most companies want to track the costs and performance of these departments separately. The departmental accounting feature in Simply Accounting permits more detailed company reporting and analysis.

Unlike projects that work only through journal entries, departments are connected to all ledgers and journals. Departments can be associated with individual accounts, vendors and clients, and you can choose departments for accounts in journal entries.

Each account may be used by only one department or by more than one department. For example, automotive parts in a car dealership will be used by the service department but not by the human resources or sales departments. Other accounts, such as a bank account, may be connected to all departments. Similarly, individual vendors, such as a car-parts vendor, may be linked to a specific department while others, such as utility providers, are linked to all departments. Clients, too, may be connected to specific departments. When you set up these connections, the departmental links are added to journal entries automatically, and you can generate detailed reports with departmental information.

Departmental account balances are generated when you add departmental information to journal entries, but they cannot be added as opening account balances in the ledgers. Therefore, ideally, you will add departmental information when you create company files so that you can have departmental information for all accounts. You can also choose to use departments only for income statement accounts and start using departments at the beginning of a fiscal period when these accounts have zero balances.

Setting Up Departments

Restore `SimData\able1.CAB` to `SimData\Able\able`. Enter April 30 as the session date.

The history for the company files is not finished. Some linked accounts are missing and the ledgers are not balanced. (See margin notes.)

Creating Departments

Before using departmental accounting, you must activate the feature and create the departments. The feature is not turned on by default, and you can add departments to an existing Simply Accounting data file.

📄 **NOTES**
We cannot finish the history yet. Accounts Receivable and Accounts Payable accounts are needed in journal entries (to add opening department balances — see page 791), so they have not yet been entered as linked accounts. In addition, Accounts Receivable and Accounts Payable begin with zero balances. As a result, these opening balances do not match the totals of the historical client and vendor invoices.

Click the **Settings icon** , and then **click General (Accounts)** and **Departments**:

Click **Use Departmental Accounting** to see the warning:

Adding departments is not a reversible step, unless the departments have not yet been used.

Click Cancel if you are not working with a separate copy of the data file. Make a backup first.

Click **OK** to return to the Departments Settings screen.

For each department you want, you must assign a four-digit code and a name.

Click the **Code field**.

Type 1001 **Press** `tab` to advance to the Description field. The Status is automatically set as Active.

Type C. Able

Unused departments can have their status set to Inactive by clicking Active.

Click the **Code field** on the next line.

Type 2001 **Press** `tab` to advance to the Description field.

Type M. Able

Click the **Assign Accounts button** to open the next screen:

From this screen, you can indicate which accounts use the departments. The cursor was on M. Able in the previous screen, so this department is selected. You can select departments from the drop-down list in the Department field.

Initially, all accounts use all departments. You can select accounts that are to be removed for a department.

NOTES
The Department Code must be a four-digit number. No letters or other characters are allowed.

NOTES
Able & Associates uses five-digit account numbers.

The two investment accounts are separated according to the partner, so we should assign each one only to its correct department. That is, we can remove *34500 Capital Investments: C. Able* for M. Able and remove *34800 Capital Investments: M. Able* for C. Able. We are working with the M. Able department first.

Scroll down   the list of Accounts That Use This Department.

Click   **34500 Invested Capital: C. Able** to select the account.

Click   **Remove**. The account moves to the list of Accounts That Do Not Use This Department on the left side of the screen.

Choose   **1001 C. Able** from the Department drop-down list.

Click   **34800 Invested Capital: M. Able** to select the account.

Click   **Remove**.

To move an account back to the "Use" list, click it again and then click Select.

Click an account that you want to change and then press and hold ⸢ctrl⸥. Click the next account until all the accounts you want are included.

Click the Remove button to shift the selected accounts to the other column.

Click Remove All to shift all the accounts to the "Do Not Use" column.

If only a few accounts use a department, it is easier to place them all on the "Do Not Use" side and then move the few to the "Use" side.

Reverse this procedure to move an account from the "Do Not Use" to the "Use" side. Click the account on the "Do Not Use" side and then click the Select button.

Click   **OK** to return to the Settings window. **Click OK** to return to the Home window.

Adding Departments to Accounts

Instead of adding department information to accounts from the Department Information window, you can modify the account ledger record from the Accounts window.

Click   **Company** in the Modules Pane list. **Click** the **Chart of Accounts icon**.

Double click 34500 Invested Capital: C. Able in the list of accounts to open the General Ledger.

A new tab, Departments, has been added to the ledger record.

Click   the **Departments tab** to open the new screen:

Notice that 2001 M. Able is located on the left side under Departments Not Used With This Account because we moved it earlier on the Settings screen. 1001 C. Able is in the Departments Used With This Account column.

On this screen, you can designate the departments that the account uses. You can modify these selections at any time. You can see that this screen is the same as the one for Department Information, except that now we are "moving" the department instead of the account. However, in the General Ledger, you change the information for only one account at a time.

Click a department to select it or press ⌨ctrl and click more than one department if you want to select additional departments. Clicking Select will add the department to the account. Clicking Remove will remove a selected department from the account and place it on the "Not Used" side. Remove All and Select All will move all departments at once to the other side.

Close   the **Ledger window**. **Close** the **Accounts window**.

Adding Opening Departmental Balances

When you create a new company data file and add general ledger accounts, you must enter the opening account balances as well, but you cannot split these balances among the departments. However, when you are entering transactions and have set up departments, you can choose a department from any Account field that allows you to select an account. We will use this approach to enter the opening departmental balances for all accounts. Initially we placed the total for all Balance Sheet accounts in the "unassigned" placeholder accounts for each section. When we transfer these amounts back to their appropriate accounts through General Journal entries, we can also assign departments.

After entering the transfers, the three unassigned accounts should all have zero balances and your Trial Balance should match the one on page 783.

Click   the **General Journal icon**.

Enter   **Memo 3A** as the Source, and **enter April 1** as the date.

Click   the **Comment field** and **type** `Transfer opening asset account balances to departments`

Click   the **Account field List icon** to see the modified Select Account list.

Each account has a ⊞ icon added to it to indicate additional information is available. When you click the ⊞, all departments used by that account will be listed, so you can select a department for the transaction.

Click   the ⊞ **icon** beside **10800 Bank: Chequing**:

The modified list now shows the departments connected with the account.

Bank: Chequing has both departments available for a journal transaction. If you click the ⊞ beside *34500 Capital Investments: C. Able*, you will see that you can select only the one department that we assigned to it.

NOTES
You can enter all the debit asset accounts first and then enter a single total for 19500 Unassigned Assets. We have chosen to transfer the balances for one account at at time so we can check our work more easily. For each transfer, the amount from 19500 Unassigned Assets should match the amount in the Trial Balance on page 783.

NOTES
Typing the account number may be faster because the Select Account list appears without the department sub accounts expanded. You must click the ⊞ each time.

Click   **10800 - 1001 Bank: Chequing - C. Able**.

Click   **Select** to return to the journal with the cursor in the Asset field.

Type   **12780** to enter the portion of the asset for this department.

Click   the **Account field list icon** again.

Double click   **10800 - 2001 Bank: Chequing - M. Able**. The cursor advances to the Credits field.

Type   **-8520** (add a minus sign to the amount). **Press** (tab). The amount moves to the Debits column because we typed the minus sign.

Click   the **Account field** and **type** 19500

Press   (tab) to enter the total balance for the asset as a credit entry.

Notice that the accounts with departments all use the same format: account number, space, hyphen, space, department number. We can use this format to enter account numbers directly in a journal without using the Select Account list. You can omit the spaces when typing these numbers. Simply Accounting will add them.

Click   the **Account field** on the next blank line.

Type   11000-1001

Press   (tab) to enter the account and advance to the Debits field.

Type   26500

Click   the **Account field** and **type** 11000-2001

Press   (tab) and **type** -17500 to move the amount to the Debits field.

Click   the **Account field** and **type** 19500 **Press** (tab) to enter the credit amount. At this stage, your journal entry should look like the one below:

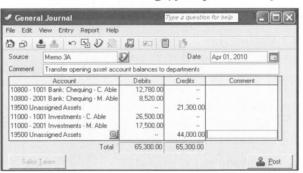

Before continuing, we will review the journal entry.

Press   (ctrl) + **J** to open the journal display:

Able & Associates Inc.			
04/01/2010 (J1)	Debits	Credits	Project
10800 - 1001 Bank: Chequing - C. Able	12,780.00	-	
10800 - 2001 Bank: Chequing - M. Able	8,520.00	-	
19500 Unassigned Assets		21,300.00	
11000 - 1001 Investments - C. Able	26,500.00	-	
11000 - 2001 Investments - M. Able	17,500.00	-	
19500 Unassigned Assets	-	44,000.00	
	65,300.00	65,300.00	

The journal entry is different from the usual one in one significant way — we were able to divide the balance in each asset account between the two departments. These separate amounts can be added to the standard financial reports and will enable us to produce separate reports for each department.

Close   the **journal display**.

Enter   the **remaining asset account balance transfers**.

Review   the **journal entry** again to verify that the total debits and credits match the initial account balance for *Unassigned Assets*.

Post   the **journal entry** after entering all the asset account balances.

Enter   the **liability account balance transfers** as the second journal entry.

Review   the **transaction** and then **post** it when the amounts are correct.

Enter   the **capital account balance transfers** as the third journal entry.

Review   the **transaction** and then **post** it when the amounts are correct.

Close   the **General Journal** to return to the Company module window.

Compare   your **Trial Balance** with the one on page 783 and make corrections if needed.

We are now ready to finish the history for the company files. If you entered the amounts correctly, the account balances for *Accounts Receivable* and *Accounts Payable* should match the historical invoice balances. However, we must still add the missing essential linked accounts.

Finishing the History

To access *Accounts Receivable* and *Accounts Payable* as postable accounts in the General Journal, we did not enter them as linked accounts. To finish the history, you must add these essential linked accounts.

Click   the **Settings icon** . **Click Payables** in the left panel of the Settings window and then **click Linked Accounts**.

Enter   **22000 Accounts Payable** as the linked account for Accounts Payable.

Enter   **22000 Accounts Payable** as the linked account for Prepayments and Prepaid Orders.

Click   **Receivables** in the left panel of the Settings window and then **click Linked Accounts**.

Enter   **12000 Accounts Receivable** as the linked account for Accounts Receivable.

Enter   **12000 Accounts Receivable** as the linked account for Deposits and Prepaid Orders.

Click   **OK** to save the settings.

Choose   the **History menu** and **click Finish Entering History**.

Click   **Backup** and continue to back up the not-finished file. **Click OK** when the backup is complete.

Click   **Proceed** to finish the history.

Adding Departments to Client Records

If some clients or vendors deal with only one department, you can add this information to the ledger record. C. Able has Adrienne Aesthetics as an exclusive client, and Flabuless Fitness deals only with M. Able.

NOTES

Do not enter sales tax information when prompted for the GST accounts.

NOTES

Remember you can adjust General Journal entries after posting. Refer to page 43.

WARNING!

If you try to finish the history now, you will see the error message that the essential linked accounts are missing.

WARNING!

Make a backup copy of the not-finished file so you can correct opening balance amounts later if necessary.

NOTES
If a client or vendor is used by more than one department, you should not add a department to the record.

Click   **Receivables** in the Modules pane list. **Click Adrienne Aesthetics** in the Clients List pane to open the record at the Address tab screen.

A Department field is added to the Address tab screen.

Click   the **Department list arrow** to see the drop-down list of departments:

Click   **1001 C. Able** to select the department.

Next we need to select the departmental revenue account as the client's default.

Click   the **Options tab** so you can change the default revenue account.

Click   the **Revenue Account field list arrow** to see the expanded account list:

NOTES
Notice that another field is added to the ledger record – the Standard Discount field. Entering a rate in this field will add it to the Sales Journal automatically as the line discount rate (see page 797). You can still change the line discount rate in the journal.

By selecting the departmental account in the ledger record, department information will be added as the default when you sell to this client.

Choose   **41000 - 1001 Revenue from Services - C. Able** from the account list.

Click   the **Next Client tool** ▶ to open the record for Flabuless Fitness.

Choose   **41000 - 2001 Revenue from Services - M. Able** from the Revenue Account list.

Click   the **Address tab** and **enter 2001 M. Able** in the Department field.

Click   **Save And Close** 🖫 Save and Close .

The remaining clients work with both departments so we cannot add one department exclusively for them.

Adding Departments to Vendor Records

If a vendor is connected exclusively with one department, you can add the department to the vendor record, just as you do for clients. At this time, all vendors are used by both departments so we will not add departments to the records.

If you want to add departments to vendor records, open the Payables module window and then open the vendor record. The Department field has been added to the Address tab screen.

Click the Department field list arrow to see the departments and click the one you want.

On the Options tab screen, choose the departmental account as the default for expenses.

Repeat this procedure for other vendors. Close the last vendor record.

Adding Departments to Journal Transactions

Entering Departments for Purchases

Adding departmental details to purchases involves selecting the appropriate departmental General Ledger subaccount instead of the main one.

Before proceeding, you should create shortcuts for the journals in other modules.

Create **shortcuts** to create and pay vendor invoices, to create paycheques and to create General Journal entries.

Click the **Pay Vendor Invoices shortcut** to open the journal.

Choose **Make Other Payment** from the transaction (Pay) list.

Choose **Northlands Office Mgt.** as the vendor. **Press** (tab). The default general Rent account and tax code are added from the vendor's record.

Enter **April 3** as the payment date.

Click the **List icon** 🔍 beside *Rent* to open the Select Account screen. **Click** the ⊞ **icon** beside **52400 Rent**:

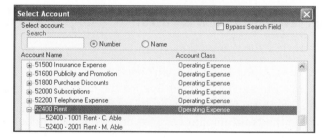

Department subaccounts are added, just as they were in the General Journal.

Click **52400 - 1001 Rent - C. Able**. **Press** (enter) to add the account for C. Able's share.

Click the **Amount field**. **Type** 840

Click the second journal line **account field List icon**.

Choose **52400 - 2001 Rent - M. Able**. **Press** (enter) to add the account for M. Able's share.

Click the **Amount field**. **Type** 560

Enter line **Descriptions**, **Source** and **Comment** to complete the entry.

Choose the **Report menu** and **click Display Payments Journal entry**:

Able & Associates Inc.				
04/03/2010 (J4)		Debits	Credits	Project
26700	GST Paid on Purchases	70.00	-	
52400 - 1001	Rent - C. Able	840.00	-	
52400 - 2001	Rent - M. Able	560.00	-	
10800	Bank: Chequing	-	1,470.00	
		1,470.00	1,470.00	

The rental expense amount has been shared between the two departments, but the other amounts have not. Because no single department is linked to the vendor, and the other accounts for the transaction are not accessible, they remain unallocated.

Close   the **journal display** to return to the journal.

Click   the **From bank account list arrow**:

You can change the default bank account for this payment, but you can choose only one account for the single cheque. A complete allocation requires access to both bank department subaccounts. Therefore, you cannot allocate the bank amount.

Make   **corrections** if necessary and **post** the **transaction**.

Close   the **Payments Journal**.

Entering Departments for Receipts

Restore the **Receivables module** as the Home window if necessary.

Click   the **Receipts Journal icon** [Receipts ▼] to open the journal.

Choose   **Adrienne Aesthetics**. **Press** (tab) to add the outstanding invoice.

Enter   **April 4** as the date.

Enter   **8101** as the client's cheque number.

Accept   the **discount taken** and **amount received**.

Press   (ctrl) **+ J** to review the transaction.

All amounts are allocated to C. Able except the bank account amount. The accounts are allocated because we set up a unique department link for the client in the ledger record. The allocated amounts are those for the default linked accounts for the journal. In this case, we can also allocate the bank amount because only one department is involved and we can access the account.

Close   the **display** to return to the journal.

Click   the **Deposit To bank account list arrow**:

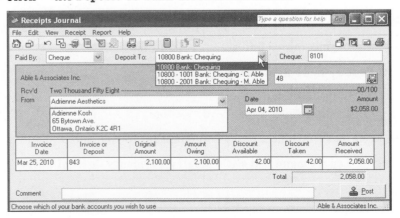

Click   **10800 - 1001 Bank Chequing - C. Able** to update the journal entry.

Press   (ctrl) **+ J** to review the transaction:

Able & Associates Inc.				
04/04/2010 (J5)	Debits	Credits		Project
10800 - 1001 Bank: Chequing - C. Able	2,058.00	-		
42000 - 1001 Sales Discounts - C. Able	42.00	-		
12000 - 1001 Accounts Receivable - C. Able	-	2,100.00		
	2,100.00	2,100.00		

The entry is now completely allocated and it is correct. All amounts, including the discount, are attributed to C. Able's department.

Close   the **display** to return to the journal.

Make   **corrections** if necessary and **post** the **transaction**.

Close   the **Receipts Journal**.

Entering Departments for Sales

Click   the **Client Invoices icon** 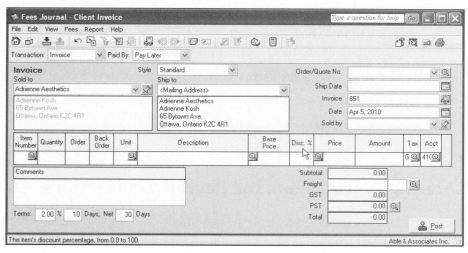 to open the Fees journal.

Choose   **Adrienne Aesthetics**. **Press** (tab) to add the client's default record details.

Enter   **April 5** as the date. This time the default revenue account is correct:

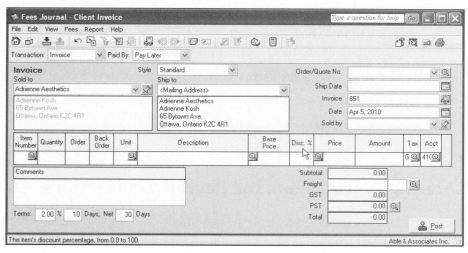

The account is taken from the record because a single department is linked to the client and we added this as the default revenue account.

Two columns — **Base Price** and **Disc. %** — have been added to the journal. These fields allow us to add discounts that apply only to a single invoice line, so you can enter different discount rates for each invoice line. Able & Associates offer discounts for special circumstances. For part of this invoice, a 5 percent discount applies.

Entering Line Discounts

Click   the **Description field**.

Type   prepare audited financial statements

Press   (tab) to advance to the Base Price field.

Type   5800

Press   (tab) to advance to the Disc. % (Discount percent) field.

Type   5

Press   (tab) to apply the amount of the discount — $290.00 — and add $5 510, the new discounted unit price, to the Price field.

To have the amount entered automatically, you can enter the quantity for the line.

> **Click**   the **Quantity field**. **Type** 1 **Press** (tab) to update the line.

The discounted amount, $5 510, is now entered as the amount.

> **Press**   (ctrl) + **J** to review the transaction as we have entered it so far:

Able & Associates Inc.				
04/05/2010 (J6)		Debits	Credits	Project
12000 - 1001	Accounts Receivable - C. Able	5,785.50	-	
26500 - 1001	GST Charged on Services - C. Able	-	275.50	
41000 - 1001	Revenue from Services - C. Able	-	5,510.00	
		5,785.50	5,785.50	

Again, all amounts are allocated correctly because we have a single department linked to the record. Notice that the discount is taken directly to reduce revenue; it is not linked to the sales discount account used for early payments.

> **Close**   the **display** to return to the journal and complete the entry.
>
> **Click**   the **Description field**. **Type** monthly fee
>
> **Click**   the **Amount field**. No discount applies to this service.
>
> **Type**   900
>
> **Press**   (tab) **twice** to add the tax code and advance to the Account field.
>
> **Choose**   **41000 - 1001 Revenue from Service - C. Able**. The default account appears only for the first invoice line, so we must add it here.
>
> **Review**   the **entry**, **make corrections** and then **post** the **transaction**.
>
> **Close**   the **Sales Journal**.
>
> **Enter**   the **payment** to Office Plus.
>
> **Enter**   the **next group of transactions** up to the payroll entry on April 30.

Entering Departments for Payroll Transactions

Payroll amounts are allocated to departments differently from amounts in other journals. If an employee works only with one department, you can add the department to the employee's ledger record.

> **Click**   the **Create Paycheque shortcut** to open the journal.
>
> **Choose** **Tryin, Reelie**. **Press** (tab) to add the employee's default record details.

All Payroll Journal accounts are linked accounts, so you cannot choose the department subaccounts to enter allocations. Instead, you can open the Department Allocation screens from the Paycheque menu as shown:

NOTES
Allocate to Departments is also available in the Payroll Cheque Run Journal from the Payroll menu. You can allocate for each employee separately.

Choose the **Paycheque menu** and **click Allocate To Departments** or **click** the **Allocate Amounts To Departments tool** to open the Allocation screen:

All accounts used in the journal entry are listed, and you can allocate one or more of them, or all, in the same way, or you can use different percentages or amounts.

Click   the **Department Detail button** (in the Dept. column) for Salaries:

This screen is similar to the one we use to enter division allocations. You can select one or more departments for each journal entry amount. And you can apply the same allocation to all accounts, just as we did for divisions in Chapter 13. Payroll amounts for the Ables are allocated by percentage, but you can allocate by amount if you prefer. You do not need to allocate the entire amount for an account. We want the same breakdown to apply to all amounts.

Click   the **Department List icon** 🔍 to see the list of departments:

Click   **1001 C. Able**. **Click Select** to add the department.

Press   `tab` **twice** to advance to the % (percentage) field.

Type   60 **Press** `tab` to advance to the Department field again.

Press   `enter` and **enter M. Able** for the rest of the allocation.

Press   `tab` and **accept** the **default entry** — 40 percent.

Click   **Apply This Allocation To All Accounts By Percentage**.

Click   **OK** to return to the account list screen. A ✓ has been added to each account in the Dept. column.

Click   **10800 Bank Chequing** to select the account line.

Click   the **Dept. Detail button** for this account:

You can see that the same 60–40 allocation is applied. But in this window, you have the option to change the allocation for the single account without affecting the others.

Click   **OK** to accept the amounts already entered (or Cancel).

Click   **OK** again to return to the journal and review the entry.

Press   (ctrl) + **J** to view the journal entry:

Able & Associates Inc.		Debits	Credits	Project
04/30/2010 (J15)				
54000 - 1001	Salaries - C. Able	2,100.00	-	
54000 - 2001	Salaries - M. Able	1,400.00	-	
54100 - 1001	EI Expense - C. Able	50.86	-	
54100 - 2001	EI Expense - M. Able	33.91	-	
54200 - 1001	CPP Expense - C. Able	95.29	-	
54200 - 2001	CPP Expense - M. Able	63.52	-	
54300 - 1001	WSIB Expense - C. Able	18.69	-	
54300 - 2001	WSIB Expense - M. Able	12.46	-	
10800 - 1001	Bank: Chequing - C. Able	-	1,613.63	
10800 - 2001	Bank: Chequing - M. Able	-	1,075.75	
23000 - 1001	EI Payable - C. Able	-	87.19	
23000 - 2001	EI Payable - M. Able	-	58.13	
23100 - 1001	CPP Payable - C. Able	-	190.57	
23100 - 2001	CPP Payable - M. Able	-	127.05	
23200 - 1001	Income Tax Payable - C. Able	-	354.76	
23200 - 2001	Income Tax Payable - M. Able	-	236.50	
24200 - 1001	WSIB Payable - C. Able	-	18.69	
24200 - 2001	WSIB Payable - M. Able	-	12.46	
		3,774.73	3,774.73	

You can see that all amounts are split 60 to 40 between the two departments.

Close   the **display** to return to the journal.

Make   **corrections** if necessary and **post** the **transaction**.

Close   the **Paycheques Journal**.

Enter   the next **two General Journal entries** with allocations for all accounts.

Handling Unallocated Amounts

We saw that some accounts in the journals were not allocated. Most of the affected accounts are Balance Sheet accounts and many users prefer to apply departmental accounting only to Income Statement accounts to avoid these incomplete entries. Unallocated amounts can also leave Departmental Balance Sheets out of balance as some amounts will not be included. For example, in a purchase of assets, the asset account was allocated but the GST account was not.

   To prepare complete Departmental reports without unallocated amounts, you can enter General Journal adjusting entries to transfer the balances from the main account to the correct departmental subaccount. You can see that this could be a time-consuming exercise as you would have to first determine all the appropriate amounts. Furthermore, the linked *Accounts Receivable* and *Accounts Payable* accounts are not accessible as postable accounts. You would still be unable to allocate these amounts. For this exercise, we will not enter the adjustments for unallocated amounts.

NOTES
In the Accountants' Edition of Simply Accounting, all accounts are available for posting. Your accountant would be able to make these adjustments for you by working with an accountant's copy of your data file. Refer to Chapter 12.

Department Reports

Many of the standard Simply Accounting reports can have department information added to them. In addition, the primary financial statements, the Balance Sheet, Income Statement and Trial Balance are available as departmental reports. As before, we will work from the Report Centre.

Click the **Report Centre icon** in the Home window.

Click **Financials** to open the list of financial reports.

Click the ⊞ **beside Balance Sheets** to expand this list.

Click the ⊞ **beside Income Statement** to expand this list.

Click the ⊞ **beside Trial Balance** to expand this list:

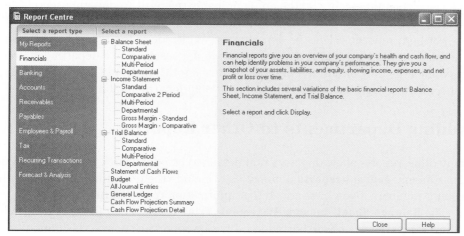

You can prepare a Departmental version of each of these reports.

Displaying Departmental Balance Sheets

If you want Balance Sheet information for each department, you should prepare the Departmental Balance Sheet.

Click **Departmental** under **Balance Sheet**. **Click** **Modify This Report**:

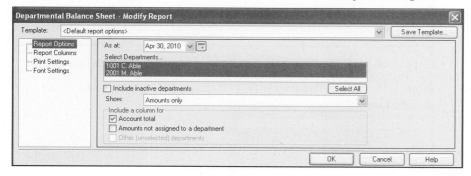

From the Home window, choose the Reports menu, then choose Financials and Departmental Reports and click Balance Sheet to see the report options.

You can report on one or more departments or all departments. The departments are shown as column headings, so you have a complete Balance Sheet for each department you selected. Remember that the Balance Sheet for each department separately may not balance if some amounts were not allocated.

Reports can include **Amounts** only or each amount as a **Percentage Of The Total**. You can also add **extra columns** for the total amount for each account, for amounts not assigned to any department and for the total amount for other departments not included in the report.

Choose the **departments** you want to include.

Choose the **Amounts** or **Percentage** option.

Choose the **additional columns** you want and **click OK**.

Close the **display** when you have finished.

Departmental Income Statement and Trial Balance Reports

Departmental Income Statements and Departmental Trial Balances are also available. The Departmental Income Statement is probably the most frequently used of these reports.

For both reports, select the departments to include in the report and choose whether you want to include amounts that are not assigned to a department. You can show amounts only or add the percentage of the total amount in your reports. In other respects, these reports are like the standard non-departmental reports.

Adding Departments to Other Reports

Many other reports allow departmental details to be added after you set up and use departments. **Journal reports** automatically include the department number with the account numbers if you have added that information to the journal transaction.

The **Balance Sheet**, **Income Statement**, **Trial Balance** and **General Ledger** all have a **Show Departments** check box added. Division reports also have this option.

Access the **report options** in the usual way from the Report Centre or from the Reports menu.

The Show Departments option is shown in the Balance Sheet Options window:

Click **Show Departments** to have the details added to the report.

Click the **Select Departments button** to open the department list:

Select the **departments** you want to add to the report.

Click **OK** to return to the initial Balance Sheet Options window.

Choose other **report options** in the usual way and **click OK** to see the report.

Close the **display** when you have finished.

Department information can also be added to client and vendor reports. The Vendor Aged and Aged Overdue reports and the Pending Purchase Order Report allow you to group the vendors by department for the report. The Client Aged and Aged Overdue reports and the Pending Sales Order Report have the same option for grouping clients by department.

The following Vendor Aged Report Options screen shows this option:

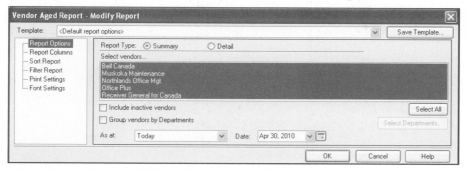

Click   **Group Vendors By Departments** to select the option.

Click   the **Select Departments button** to open the department list.

Select   the **departments** you want to add to the report.

You can include or omit vendors that do not have an assigned department.

Click   **OK** to return to the Vendor Aged Report Options screen.

Choose other **report options** in the usual way.

Click   **OK** to see the report.

Close   the **display** when you have finished.

Close   the **Report Centre** if it is open.

R E V I E W

The Student CD-ROM with Data Files includes Review Questions and Supplementary Cases for this chapter.

Part 4
Appendices

Installing Simply Accounting

The main instructions for installation refer to the regular Premium version of the program. Margin notes outline the differences for the Simply version and for the Student version that accompanies this text.

NOTES
From the My Computer window, you can right-click D: and click Autoplay to start the autorun feature and show the Installation screens on this page.

Start your **computer** and the **Windows program**.

Close any **other programs** that you have running before beginning.

Insert the **program CD** in the CD-ROM drive.

Installation from the CD-ROM drive should begin immediately.

Many computers have drive D: as the CD-ROM drive, so we will use that in the keystrokes that follow.

First you must choose the language you want for the installation instructions:

Accept English or **choose French** from the drop-down list.

Click OK. The following options screen appears to begin the installation:

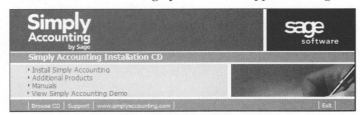

If you have any other programs running, click (Exit), close the other programs and start again.

Click Install Simply Accounting.

If installation does not begin immediately, follow the instructions in the box on page A-3.

Wait for the Setup Language selection screen to appear:

IF INSTALLATION DOES NOT BEGIN IMMEDIATELY

You can install the program from the Windows opening screen or from the desktop. Many computers have drive D: as the CD-ROM drive, so we will use that drive in the keystrokes that follow.

Double click the **My Computer icon** ⊞ My Computer. **Double click** the **Control Panel icon** Control Panel or **name** ⊞ Control Panel to see the components that are installed on your computer.

If you are using the icon view for the My Computer window, you will see the Control Panel icon. If you are viewing by list or by detail, you will see the name with a small icon.

Or, **click Start** on the task bar, **choose Settings** and **click Control Panel.**

Double click the **Add Or Remove Programs icon** ⊞ Add or Remov....

Click the **Add New Programs icon** ⊞ Add New Programs on the left side of the window.

The installation may begin immediately at this stage. If it does not,

Click the **CD Or Floppy button** to proceed. Insert the CD if you have not already done so.

Click Next to continue. Windows will search for the installation program.

Click Browse. The CD drive window should open with the Simply Accounting installation CD and the setup program shown. If it does not, locate the CD from the Browse window.

Double click the Simply folder to open it. The installation may begin at this stage. If not,

Click Setup (or **Setup.exe**).

Click Open to open the Run Installation Program window.

Click Finish to begin the installation with the Setup Language screen.

Or, you can start from the Run menu. **Choose Start** and then **click Run. Type d:\Simply\setup** in the Open field and **click OK**. (For drive D:, substitute the drive letter for your CD-ROM drive.)

NOTES
   The Windows XP instructions in the shaded box beside this note will begin the installation of the Simply Accounting Program directly and bypass the CD installation screens on the previous page.
   The instructions may be different for Windows Vista.

Click   your **language preference** and **click Next**.

When the InstallShield setup window closes, the Welcome screen appears. You can now choose to install the full regular or the trial version of the program:

Click   Next to accept the default **Full Version option**:

You must enter the serial number exactly as it appears on the program package or CD case before you can continue.

The cursor is in the Serial Number field ready for you to enter the number.

Type   your **Serial Number** in the space provided.

WARNING!
   Do not install the Trial Version.

STUDENT VERSION
   The serial number is printed on the Simply Accounting program CD. The serial number for all copies of the Student version is
      242P2U2-1000000

WARNING!
   The serial number is case sensitive. You must type it exactly as it appears on the program case.

Click   **Next** to advance to the license agreement:

Read   the **agreement**, and if you accept the agreement, **click I Accept** to begin installing the program.

You will now see the screen that allows you to learn more about installing Simply Accounting in a network environment:

SIMPLY VERSION

You will not see this screen when you install the Simply version.

Click   **Installation Guide** to learn more. **Close** the **Help window**.

Click   **Next**.

The screen you see next will depend on which firewall program you are using. Simply Accounting uses the Connection Manager program to access data files. If you have a firewall installed on your computer, you must allow this program to access your data. If you do not allow access through your firewall, you cannot open your data files.

If you are using the Microsoft Windows firewall, you will see this screen:

Click   **Yes** so that the firewall setup will continue. **Click Next**.

You may see a list of files. If a firewall prompt does not appear automatically, you may need to configure your firewall manually to allow access to all the listed programs:

NOTES

If you see a run-time error message about the Connection Manager when you attempt to open a Simply Accounting data file, you may need to start the Connection Manager program and/or configure your firewall settings manually to allow access for all the programs listed on this screen.

Click   **Learn More** for help with firewall settings. **Close** the **Help window**.

Click   **Next**.

The next screen prompts you to enter your name and your company name:

STUDENT VERSION
In the Student version, enter the name of your school as the company name.

Enter the **required information**. **Press** ⟮tab⟯ to advance to the next field.

Click **Next**. Your next decision concerns the type of installation you need:

NOTES
You will not see this screen for single-user versions or for the Student version.

SIMPLY VERSION
You will not see this screen when you install the Simply version because it applies to multi-user setups.

Workstation Installation applies when you are working on a network that has the program already installed. If the server also has your data installed, choose Data Only Installation. Clicking **Learn More** will explain these options in detail. If you are working on a stand-alone computer, or you are installing the program to a network server, you would choose **Install Full Version**.

Make the **selection** for your system setup. **Click Next**.

Now you must choose the location of your program files:

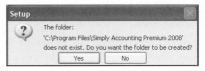

SIMPLY VERSION
The default destination folder will be Simply Accounting 2008.

Click **Next** to accept the default location, C:\Program Files\Simply Accounting Premium 2008.

To choose another folder, click Browse and choose an existing folder from the pop-up window, or type an alternative location in the Browse window. Click OK.

You will be asked if you want the program to create this folder:

Click **Yes** to continue and select the program components to install:

STUDENT VERSION
You will not see the screen for component selection.

Accept the **Typical** installation option to include all the program elements.

Click   Next.

The next screen asks you to enter a name for Simply Accounting in your Programs folder:

The name you enter here will be the name that appears on the Programs list. You can accept the default name, Simply Accounting Premium 2008, or type a different name such as Simply 2008.

Click   Next to see the screen about participating in the feedback program:

To provide feedback about the program, choose Yes. Otherwise choose No.

Click   Next to proceed to the screen confirming your choice of components:

To omit any of these components, click Back to return to the previous screens and choose the Custom installation option.

By default, all components are selected for installation as follows:
- **Simply Accounting Program**: the Simply Accounting program that you will need to perform the accounting transactions for your company. It will be placed in the main Simply Accounting Premium 2008 folder under the Program Files folder or the folder location you selected.
- **Sample Data**: complete records for a sample company — Universal Construction. They will be placed under Documents and Settings, inside a folder named Simply\Samdata.

- **Templates**: predefined charts of accounts and settings for a large number of business types. These files will be stored in a folder under Simply Accounting Premium 2008 called Template. Two starter files with only charts of accounts also appear in this folder.
- **Crystal Reports Print Engine**, **Customizable Forms** and **Management Reports**: a variety of commonly used business forms and reports that you can customize to suit your own business needs and the program to access and print them. The reports and forms will be placed in a folder under Simply Accounting Premium 2008 called Forms.
- **Microsoft Office Documents**: a variety of MS Office documents designed for integrated use with Simply Accounting. They are placed in a Reports folder under Simply Accounting Premium 2008
- **New Business Guide**: a number of checklists showing the steps to follow in setting up a new business, customized for a variety of business types in different provinces. These guides include addresses, phone numbers and Web addresses that you can contact for further information. You can access the guides from the Simply Accounting Business Assistant menu or from the Programs list.
- **Manuals**: documentation that will help you learn the program.
- **Add-in for Microsoft Outlook**: a program link that connects your data with MS Outlook.

> **Click**   **Next**.
>
> **Wait**   until the program prompts you with the Microsoft Outlook message:

Simply Accounting will coordinate with your Microsoft Outlook program database.

> **Click**   **OK** to continue.

You can choose to place a shortcut on your desktop to open the program:

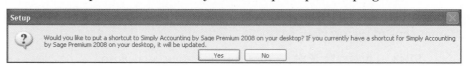

> **Click**   **Yes** when prompted to add the desktop shortcut.

The Install program creates the folders for all the components described above.

In addition, the installation procedure adds names in the Programs list for the Simply Accounting program, Microsoft Office documents, Help, data repair utilities and the New Business Guide.

The next option is to view the ReadMe file, or start the program or both:

We will start the program immediately so we can register and activate the program.

> **Click**   **Yes, I Want To Start Simply Accounting**.
>
> **Click**   **Finish** to complete the installation and open the ReadMe screen.
>
> You may be prompted to restart your computer. If so, click OK to restart.

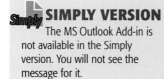
SIMPLY VERSION
The MS Outlook Add-in is not available in the Simply version. You will not see the message for it.

WARNING!
Wait for the Setup window to close after you close the ReadMe window. This may take some time.

Registering and Activating Simply Accounting

Read   the **information** about recent changes to the program that may not yet be documented elsewhere.

Close   the **ReadMe screen** to see the Registration message:

If you choose Remind Me Later, choose the Help menu and click Enter Key Code to see the screen shown above. This reminder message will also appear each time you start the program.

Until you register and activate the program, you will be allowed to use the program for a limited number of days. If you have already registered and have the activation codes, skip the next step.

Have your product serial number ready for the registration. You can register online or by telephone. The telephone number is provided. To register online, start your Internet connection. Enter the Web address given on the registration information screen or double click the Web address on this screen. Follow the instructions provided. Print a copy of the codes screen for reference.

When you register, you will provide the Serial Number from the program package or CD and receive a Client ID number, a Key Code number and a payroll ID number. These numbers will be linked to the serial number you provided and cannot be used for a different copy of the program.

Click   **Activate Now** to start the activation procedure:

Enter   your **Company Name** and the **Client ID** and **Key Code** provided by Sage Software for the program you have registered.

Enter all names and numbers exactly as they are given to you, including spaces and punctuation. The Key Code is also case sensitive, so be sure to type upper-case letters when required.

If you make a mistake, the program will warn you and you can re-enter the information.

Click   **OK** to continue to Simply Accounting's Welcome screen:

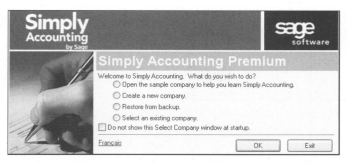

Click   Open The Sample Company.... Click OK to continue to the Session
Date window:

Click   OK to accept the default session date.

You can now view a short video to learn more or access this video later from the
help menu.

Close   the **information screen** about the new Home window.

Another information screen about payroll services opens. **Close** this **window**.

If you see a message about automatic updates, refer to page A–10. Do not turn
on the update feature (remove the ✓).

Unlocking the Payroll Features

We will unlock and activate the payroll module before proceeding. You will not need to
unlock payroll in the Student version of the program.

Choose the **Help menu** and **click Unlock Auto Payroll** as shown:

An information screen about payroll services for Simply Accounting opens:

This screen advises you that you need a Payroll ID and subscription to the Simply
Accounting Payroll Plan — a fee-based service — to use the payroll features in the
program. To learn more about the payroll plan or to subscribe, click Tell Me More.

SIMPLY VERSION
You will see an additional screen about upgrading to the Premium version of Simply Accounting. Close this screen to continue.

NOTES
If you have not activated the program yet, you can activate the program from the Help menu. Choose Enter Key Code from the Help menu to open the You Have XX Days Remaining screen shown on page A-8.

Click   Enter Payroll ID:

Your client ID number will be entered from the activation procedure. You must enter the Payroll ID number provided when you registered the program.

Click   the **Payroll ID field** and **type** the **number** provided, exactly as it is given to you.

If the activation is successful, you will see the following message:

Click   OK to continue.

You can now use all features of the program.

Click   ☒ to close the Simply Accounting Home window.

Click   Exit to close the Simply Accounting installation screen unless you want to install other programs or documents.

Click   ☒ to close the Control Panel window if it is open.

Turning Off Automatic Updates

The next time you start Simply Accounting, you may see a message about automatic program updates:

You can download updates automatically or periodically when needed. If you are working with the data files in this text, you should not update the program beyond the version we use, which is Release B. Therefore, you should turn off the automatic update option. You can get updates later from the Help menu, Check For Updates.

Click   Always Check For Product Updates At Startup to remove the ✓ and turn off the automatic update option.

Click   OK to continue accessing your data files.

Windows Basics, Shortcuts & Terms

WINDOWS BASICS

This section explains the Windows terms and procedures commonly used in the text.

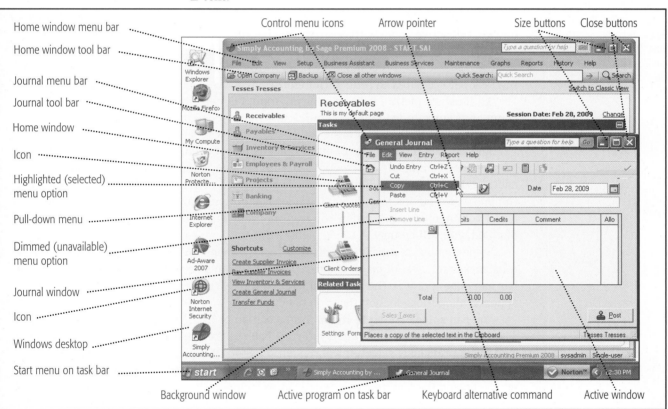

The illustration above shows the Simply Accounting program on the Windows XP desktop. The General Journal is open and active with the Home window in the background. The Journal's Edit menu is pulled down and Copy is selected.

The **mouse** is used to move the cursor. When you move the mouse, an **arrow** or **pointer** moves to indicate the cursor placement. If you **click** (press) the left mouse button, the cursor will move to the location of the arrow (if this is a legitimate place for the cursor to be at the time). That is, you use the mouse to **click** (point to and click) a screen location, item on a list, command or icon.

The arrow or pointer changes shape depending on what actions you may perform. When you are moving the mouse, it appears as an arrow or hand pointer.

When you are in a field that can accept text, it appears as a long **I-shaped bar**. Clicking will change it to an insertion point — a flashing vertical line in a text field. When the computer is processing information and you are unable to perform any action, you will see an **hourglass**. This is your signal to wait.

Dragging refers to the method of moving the mouse while holding the left button down. As you drag through the options in a menu, each one will be successively highlighted or darkened. Dragging through text will highlight it. Point to the beginning of the text to be highlighted. Then click and hold the mouse button down while moving through the entire area that you want to highlight. Release the mouse button at the end of the area you want to highlight. You can highlight a single character or the entire contents of a field. The text will remain highlighted and can be edited by typing new text. Delete text by pressing the Backspace key or ⟨del⟩. Clicking a different location will remove the highlighting.

To **double click** means to press the left mouse button twice quickly. This action can be used as a shortcut for opening and closing windows. Double clicking an icon or file name will open it. Double clicking the Control icon will close the window. The Simply Accounting files are set up to open journals and windows with a single click instead of a double click.

The **active window** is the one that you are currently working in. If you click an area outside the active window that is part of a background window, that window will move to the foreground. To return to a previous window, click any part of it that is showing. If the window you need is completely hidden, you can restore it by clicking its button on the task bar. Click ⊟ to reduce (minimize) an active window to a task bar button.

An **icon** is a picture form of your program, file name or item. **Buttons** are icons or commands surrounded by a box frame. In Simply Accounting, clicking the Home window tool button 🏠 will bring the Home window to the front and make it active.

The **menu bar** is the line of options at the top of each window. Each menu contains one or more commands or selections (the **pull-down menu**) and can be accessed by clicking the menu name. Each window has different menu selections, and the options in the pull-down menus may differ. To choose an option from the menu, click the menu name and then click the option you want in order to **select** (**highlight**) it. If an option is dimmed, you will be unable to highlight or select it.

Some menus are **cascading menus**. When the menu option you want has an arrow, ▶, it has a second level of menu choices. To select from a cascading menu, click the menu bar name and point to the first-level menu option. When the next level of the menu appears, click the selection that you need.

You can **select multiple items** from a screen or list. Click the first item to select it. Then press and hold ⟨ctrl⟩ while you click each of the other items you want to select. The items previously selected will remain selected. If the items are in a list and you want to select several items in a row, click the first item and then press and hold ⟨shift⟩ while clicking the last item that you want to include. All the items between the two will also be selected. To change your selection, click somewhere else.

The **Control Menu icon** is situated in the upper left-hand corner of each window. The icon looks different for different programs and windows. It has its own pull-down menu, including the Close and Size commands. To close windows, you can double click this icon, choose Close from its pull-down menu or click the **Close button** ⊠ in the upper right-hand corner of the window.

Size buttons are located in the upper right-hand corner of the window. Use them to make a window larger ⧠ (**Maximize** to full screen size) or to reduce the window to a task bar button ⊟ (**Minimize**). If the window is full screen size or smaller than usual, restore it to its normal size with the ⧉ (**Restore**) button.

You can also change the size of a window by dragging. Point to a side. When the pointer changes to a two-sided arrow ⬌ or ⬍, drag the window frame to its new size.

NOTES

Often a program will include dialogue boxes that look like windows but do not have menu bars. Usually they require you to make a choice, such as answering a question, before you can proceed. You cannot make a dialogue box into a background window; you must click one of the options such as Yes, No, OK, Proceed, Cancel and so on to continue. Closing the dialogue box without making a choice is like choosing Cancel.

When a window contains more information than can fit on the screen at one time, the window will contain **scroll arrows** (⌄, ›, ⌃, or ‹) in any corner or direction next to the hidden information (bottom or right sides of the window). Click the arrow and hold the mouse button down to scroll the screen in the direction of the arrow you are on.

Input fields containing data may have a **drop-down** or **pop-up list** from which to select. A **list arrow** beside the field ⌄ indicates that a list is available. When you click the arrow, the list appears. Click an item on the list to add it to the input field directly.

SHORTCUTS

Using the Keyboard Instead of a Mouse

All Windows software applications are designed to be used with a mouse. However, there may be times when you prefer to use keyboard commands to work with a program because it is faster. There are also times when you need to know the alternatives to using a mouse, as when the mouse itself is inoperative. It is not necessary to memorize all the keyboard commands. A few basic principles will help you to understand how they work, and over time you will use the ones that help you to work most efficiently. Some commands are common to more than one Windows software program. For example, `ctrl` + C (press and hold the Control key while you press C) is commonly used as the copy command and `ctrl` + V as the paste command. Any selected text or image will be copied or pasted when you use these commands.

The menu bar and the menu choices can be accessed by pressing `alt`. The first menu bar item will be highlighted. Use arrow keys, ↑ and ↓, to move up and down through the pull-down menu choices of a highlighted menu item or ← and → to go back and forth to other menu items. Some menu choices have direct keyboard alternatives or shortcuts. If the menu item has an underlined letter, pressing `alt` together with the underlined letter will access that option directly. For example, `alt` + F (press `alt`, and while holding down `alt`, press F) accesses the File pull-down menu. Then pressing O (the underlined letter for Open) will give you the dialogue box for opening a new file. Some tool buttons in Simply Accounting have a direct keyboard command, and some menu choices also have a shortcut keyboard command. When available, these direct keystrokes are given with the tool button name or to the right of a menu choice. For example, `alt` + `f4` is the shortcut for closing the active window or exiting from the Simply Accounting program when the Home window is the active window.

To cancel the menu display, press `esc`.

In the Simply Accounting Home window, you can use the arrow keys to move among the ledger and journal icons. Press `alt`, `alt` and → to highlight the first icon, and then use the arrow keys to change selections. Each icon is highlighted or selected as you reach it and deselected as you move to another icon.

To choose or open a highlighted or selected item, press `enter`.

When input fields are displayed in a Simply Accounting window, you can move to the next field by pressing `tab` or to a previous field by pressing `shift` and `tab` together. The `tab` key is used frequently in this workbook as a quick way to accept input, advance the cursor to the next field and highlight field contents to prepare for immediate editing. Using the mouse while you input information requires you to remove your hands from the keyboard, while the `tab` key does not.

A summary of keyboard shortcuts used in Simply Accounting is included on page A-14.

SUMMARY OF KEYBOARD SHORTCUTS

Shortcut	Resulting Action
ctrl + A	Adjust, begin the Adjust a Posted Entry function.
ctrl + B	Bring the Home window to the front.
ctrl + C	Copy the selected text.
ctrl + E	Look up the Previously Posted Invoice (from a journal lookup window).
ctrl + F	Search, begin the search function.
ctrl + J	Display the journal entry report.
ctrl + K	Track shipment from a previously posted invoice lookup screen.
ctrl + L	Look up a previously posted transaction (from the journal window).
ctrl + N	Look up the next posted Invoice (from a journal lookup window).
ctrl + N	Open a new record window (from a ledger icon or ledger record window).
ctrl + P	Print, open the print dialogue box.
ctrl + R	Recall a stored journal entry (from a journal window when an entry is stored).
ctrl + R	Remove the account record, or remove the quote or order (from ledger, quote or order window).
ctrl + S	Access the Save As function from the Home window (Home window, File menu) to save the data file under a new name. Keep the new file open.
ctrl + S	Save changes to a record; keep the ledger window open (from any ledger window).
ctrl + T	Store the current journal entry (open the Store dialogue box).
ctrl + V	Paste the selected text at the cursor position.
ctrl + X	Cut (delete) the selected text.
ctrl + Z	Undo the most recent change.
alt + C	Create another record; saves the record you are creating and opens a new record form to create another new record.
alt + N	Save and close; save the new record and close the ledger.
alt + P	Post the journal entry or record the order or quote.
alt + f4	Close the active window (if it has a close button). Closes the program if the Home window is active.
alt + the underlined character on a button	Select the button's action. An alternative to clicking the button and/or pressing enter.
alt	Access the first item on the menu bar.
alt + alt	Select the first icon in the Home window.
tab	Advance the cursor to the next field.
shift + tab	Move the cursor to the previous field.
Click	Move the cursor or select an item or entry.
shift + Click	Select all the items between the first item clicked and the last one.
ctrl + Click	Select this item in addition to ones previously selected.
enter	Choose the selected item or action.
Double click	Select an entire word or field contents. In fields with lists, open the selection list.
→	Move right to the next icon to select it or to the next character in text.
←	Move left to the next icon to select it or to the next character in text.
↓	Move down to the next icon or entry in a list to select it.
↑	Move up to the previous icon or entry in a list to select it.

ACCOUNTING VS. NON-ACCOUNTING TERMS

We have used accounting terms in this workbook because they are familiar to students of accounting, and because we needed to provide a consistent language for the book. The most frequently used non-accounting terms are included here for reference and comparison, in case you want to leave the non-accounting terms selected (Home window, Setup menu, User Preferences, Options screen).

The chart shows the terms used for the Simply version and for the Premium version when the Other Industry type is selected. For other industries in the Premium version, the terms in the chart on the following page — Terminology Used for Different Types of Industries — will replace the Non-accounting Terms for Payables and Receivables. For example, you may see Providers and Expenses or Supporters and Revenues. The term Suppliers generally replaces Vendors.

SUMMARY OF EQUIVALENT TERMS

MAJOR TERMS	ACCOUNTING TERMS	NON-ACCOUNTING TERMS
	Journal Entries	Transaction Details
	Payables	Vendors & Purchases
	Receivables	Customers & Sales
	Post	Process

DETAILED LIST: LOCATION	ACCOUNTING TERMS	NON-ACCOUNTING TERMS
Setup menu – Settings screen	Payables	Vendors & Purchases
	Receivables	Customers & Sales
Setup menu, User Preferences, View screen – Modules/Pages	Payables	Vendors & Purchases
	Receivables	Customers & Sales
Graphs menu	Payables	Unpaid Purchases
	Receivables	Unpaid Sales
Reports menu and Report Centre – Financials	General Ledger	Transactions by Account
Report Centre – Financials	All Journal Entries	All Transactions
Reports menu and Report Centre	Payables	Vendors & Purchases
	Receivables	Customers & Sales
Reports menu	Journal Entries	Transaction Details
Reports menu – Management Reports	Payables	Vendors & Purchases
	Receivables	Customers & Sales
All Icon window menus	Journal	Transactions
Accounts ledger window	General Ledger	Chart of Accounts Records
Vendors ledger window	Payables Ledger	Vendor Records
Customers ledger window	Receivables Ledger	Customer Records
All journals (button and menu)	Post	Process

TERMS AND INDUSTRY TYPES

In the Premium version, the terms and labels change when you select different types of industries (Setup menu, Settings, Company, Information screen). The chart on the following page summarizes the terms you will see when you apply different industry types.

TERMINOLOGY USED FOR DIFFERENT TYPES OF INDUSTRIES

INDUSTRY — TERMS OR LABELS USED IN RECEIVABLES LEDGER

INDUSTRY	Customers	Sales Invoices	Sales Quotes	Sales Orders	Sales Journal – Sales Invoice
Simply Version (all)	Customers	Sales Invoices	Sales Quotes	Sales Orders	Sales Journal – Sales Invoice
Premium Version					
Accommodation	Guest	Charges	Sales Quotes	Sales Orders	Sales Journal – Charge
Agriculture	Customers	Customer Invoices	Customer Quotes	Customer Orders	Revenues Journal – Customer Invoice
Construction/ Contractor	Customers	Bills	Estimates	Contracts	Sales Journal – Contracts
Educational Service	Clients	Statements	Client Quotes	Client Orders	Sales Journal – Bill
Entertainment	Customers	Sales Invoices	Sales Quotes	Sales Orders	Sales Journal – Sales Invoice
Food & Beverage	Guest	Charges	Sales Quotes	Sales Orders	Sales Journal – Charge
Manufacturing/ Industrial	Customers	Sales Invoices	Sales Quotes	Sales Orders	Sales Journal – Sales Invoice
Medical Dental	Patients	Statements	Patient Quotes	Patient Orders	Fees Journal – Statement
Non–profit	Supporters	Statements	Supporter Quotes	Supporter Orders	Revenues Journal – Statement
Other	Customers	Sales Invoices	Sales Quotes	Sales Orders	Sales Journal – Sales Invoice
Personal Service	Clients	Client Invoices	Client Quotes	Client Orders	Revenues Journal – Client Invoice
Professional Service	Clients	Client Invoices	Client Quotes	Client Orders	Fees Journal – Client Invoice
Real Estate/ Property	Clients	Statements	Client Quotes	Client Orders	Revenues Journal – Statement
Retail	Customers	Sales Invoices	Sales Quotes	Sales Orders	Sales Journal – Sales Invoice
Service	Clients	Client Invoices	Client Quotes	Client Orders	Revenues Journal – Client Invoice
Transportation	Customers	Sales Invoices	Sales Quotes	Sales Orders	Sales Journal – Sales Invoice

INDUSTRY — TERMS OR LABELS USED IN PAYABLES LEDGER

INDUSTRY	Vendors	Purchase Invoices	Purchase Quotes	Purchase Orders	Purchases Journal – Purchase Invoice
Simply Version (all)	Vendors	Purchase Invoices	Purchase Quotes	Purchase Orders	Purchases Journal – Purchase Invoice
Premium Version					
Accommodation	Suppliers	Invoices	Purchase Quotes	Purchase Orders	Purchases Journal – Invoice
Agriculture	Suppliers	Purchase Invoices	Purchase Quotes	Supplier Orders	Purchases Journal – Purchase Invoice
Construction/ Contractor	Suppliers	Invoices	Quotes	Orders	Purchases Journal – Invoice
Educational Service	Suppliers	Invoices	Purchase Quotes	Purchase Orders	Purchases Journal – Invoice
Entertainment	Suppliers	Supplier Invoices	Supplier Quotes	Supplier Orders	Expenses Journal – Supplier Invoice
Food & Beverage	Suppliers	Invoices	Purchase Quotes	Purchase Orders	Purchases Journal – Invoice
Manufacturing/ Industrial	Suppliers	Purchase Invoices	Purchase Quotes	Purchase Orders	Purchases Journal – Invoice
Medical Dental	Suppliers	Invoices	Supplier Quotes	Supplier Orders	Expenses Journal – Invoice
Non–profit	Providers	Invoices	Provider Quotes	Provider Orders	Expenses Journal – Invoice
Other	Vendors	Purchase Invoices	Purchase Quotes	Purchase Orders	Purchases Journal – Purchase Invoice
Personal Service	Suppliers	Supplier Invoices	Supplier Quotes	Supplier Orders	Expenses Journal – Supplier Invoice
Professional Service	Vendors	Vendor Invoices	Vendor Quotes	Vendor Orders	Expenses Journal – Vendor Invoice
Real Estate/ Property	Suppliers	Invoices	Supplier Quotes	Supplier Orders	Expenses Journal – Invoice
Retail	Suppliers	Purchase Invoices	Purchase Quotes	Purchase Orders	Purchases Journal – Purchase Invoice
Service	Suppliers	Supplier Invoices	Supplier Quotes	Supplier Orders	Expenses Journal – Supplier Invoice
Transportation	Vendors	Purchase Invoices	Purchase Quotes	Purchase Orders	Purchases Journal – Purchase Invoice

Terms for Project   Project (for Other, Service, Personal Service, Professional Service, Transportation and all industries in Simply version),
Division (for Accommodation, Education, Entertainment, Food, Manufacturing and Retail),
Crops (for Agriculture), Job Site (for Construction), Partner (for Medical), Fund (for Non-profit), Property (for Real Estate)

Correcting Errors after Posting

We all make mistakes. This appendix outlines briefly the procedures you need to follow for those rare occasions when you have posted a journal entry incorrectly and you need to reverse it manually. In most cases, you can use the Adjust Journal Entry or Reverse Entry procedures to make corrections.

Obviously, you should try to detect errors before posting. Reviewing journal entries should become routine practice. The software also has built-in safeguards that help you avoid mistakes. For example, outstanding invoices cannot be overpaid and employee wages and payroll deductions are calculated automatically. Furthermore, names of accounts, customers, vendors, employees and inventory items appear in full, so that you may check your journal information easily.

Before making a reversing entry, consider the consequences of not correcting the error. For example, misspelled customer names may not be desirable, but they will not influence the financial statements. After making the correction in the ledger, the newly printed statement will be correct (the journal will retain the original spelling). Sometimes, however, the mistake is more serious. Financial statements will be incorrect if amounts or accounts are wrong. Payroll tax deductions will be incorrect if the wage amount is incorrect. GST and PST remittances may be incorrect as a result of incorrect tax codes or sales or purchase amounts. Discounts will be incorrectly calculated if an invoice or payment date is incorrect. Some errors also originate from outside sources. For example, purchase items may be incorrectly priced by the vendor.

For audit purposes, prepare a memo explaining the error and the correction procedure. A complete reversing entry is often the simplest way to make the corrections for a straightforward audit trail. With Simply Accounting's one-step reversing entry feature from the Adjust Entry window, the reversing entry is made automatically. This feature is available for General Journal entries, paycheques, sales, purchases, receipts, and for most payments. Choose Adjust Invoice from the pull-down menu under the corresponding transaction menu, or click the Adjust Invoice tool in the journal. Then make the corrections if possible, or choose Reverse Entry from the pull-down menu under the corresponding transaction menu or click the Reverse tool. Under all circumstances, you should follow Generally Accepted Accounting Principles. Simply Accounting will create the reversing entry automatically and then include the correct entries if you save the changes to a journal entry.

However, this feature is not available for all journals. And when the journal entry deposit account for a receipt is not the bank account (because the deposit was made later) you need to reverse a receipt to record an NSF cheque. Therefore, we will illustrate the procedure for reversing entries in all journals.

Reversing entries in all journals have several common elements. In each case, you should use an appropriate source number that identifies the entry as reversing

NOTES
Adjusting entry procedures are shown on:
page 43 – General Journal
page 129 – Purchases
page 131 – Other Payments
page 139 – Payments
page 184 – Sales
page 279 – Payroll
Reversing entry procedures are explained on:
page 45 – General Journal
page 140 – Purchases
page 179 – Receipts
page 282 – Payroll

(e.g., add ADJ or REV to the original source number). You should use the original posting date and add a comment. Make the reversing entry as illustrated on the following pages. Display the journal entry, review it carefully and, when you are certain it is correct, post it. Next, you must enter the correct version of the transaction as a new journal entry with an appropriate identifying source number (e.g., add COR to the original source number).

Reversing entries are presented for each journal. Only the transaction portion of each screen is shown because the remaining parts of the journal screen do not change. The original and the reversing entry screens and most of the corresponding journal displays are included. Explanatory notes appear beside each set of entries.

GENERAL JOURNAL

Use the same accounts and amounts in the reversing entry as in the original entry.

Accounts that were debited should be credited and accounts that were credited originally should be debited.

Click the Sales Taxes button if you used this screen. Choose the tax code and, if necessary, enter the Amount Subject To Tax with a minus sign.

Repeat the allocation using the original percentages.

The General Journal display is not shown because it basically looks the same as the journal input form.

You can use the Adjust Entry or Reverse Entry features instead. See page 43 and page 45.

GENERAL JOURNAL: Original Entry

Account	Debits	Credits	Comment	Allo
1360 Marble Inventory	400.00	--	inventory for contracts	
2670 GST Paid on Purchases	20.00	--	GST paid @ 5%	
2120 A/P - Marblehead Suppliers	--	420.00	terms: net 20	
Total	420.00	420.00		

Reversing Entry

Account	Debits	Credits	Comment	Allo
2120 A/P - Marblehead Suppliers	420.00	--	reversing A/P amount	
1360 Marble Inventory	--	400.00	reversing inventory amount	
2670 GST Paid on Purchases	--	20.00	reversing GST paid amount	
Total	420.00	420.00		

PURCHASES JOURNAL

The only change you must make is that positive amounts in the original entry become negative amounts in the reversing entry (place a minus sign before the amount in the Amount field).

Similarly, negative amounts, such as for GST Paid in GST remittances, must be changed to positive amounts (remove the minus sign).

If freight was charged, enter the amount of freight with a minus sign.

Use the same accounts and amounts in the reversing entry as in the original entry. Tax amounts change automatically.

Repeat the allocation with the original percentages.

You can use the Adjust Invoice and Reverse Invoice options instead (page 129 and page 140). Reversing a paid invoice will generate a credit note.

Remember to "pay" the incorrect and reversing invoices to remove them from the Payments Journal and later clear them.

PURCHASES JOURNAL (NON-INVENTORY): Original Entry

Item Number	Quantity	Order	Back Order	Unit	Description	Price	Tax	GST	PST	Amount	Acct	Allo
					equipment rentals		GP	30.00	48.00	600.00	5110 Tool Rentals	√

Invoice Received ☑

Freight: GP

Terms: ___ % ___ Days, Net 20 Days

Subtotal	600.00
GST	30.00
PST	48.00
Total	678.00

12/14/10 (J21)	Debits	Credits	Division
2670 GST Paid on Purchases	30.00	-	
5110 Tool Rentals	648.00	-	
- Service Division			518.40
- Sales Division			129.60
2200 Accounts Payable	-	678.00	
	678.00	678.00	

Reversing Entry

Item Number	Quantity	Order	Back Order	Unit	Description	Price	Tax	GST	PST	Amount	Acct	Allo
					reverse equipment rental fee		GP	-30.00	-48.00	-600.00	5110 Tool Rentals	√

Invoice Received ☑

Freight:

Terms: ___ % ___ Days, Net 20 Days

Subtotal	-600.00
GST	-30.00
PST	-48.00
Total	-678.00

12/14/10 (J22)	Debits	Credits	Division
2200 Accounts Payable	678.00	-	
2670 GST Paid on Purchases	-	30.00	
5110 Tool Rentals	-	648.00	
- Service Division			-518.40
- Sales Division			-129.60
	678.00	678.00	

PAYMENTS JOURNAL – OTHER PAYMENTS: Original Entry

Acct	Description	Amount	Tax	GST	PST	Allo
5150 Tele	telephone expenses	300.00	GP	15.00	24.00	√

Subtotal	300.00
Tax	39.00
Total	339.00

12/12/10 (J24)	Debits	Credits	Division
2670 GST Paid on Purchases	15.00	-	
5150 Telephone Expense	324.00	-	
- Sales Division			97.20
- Service Division			226.80
1050 Bank: Chequing CAD	-	339.00	
	339.00	339.00	

Reversing Entry

Acct	Description	Amount	Tax	GST	PST	Allo
5150 Telephor	reversing telephone expense entry	-300.00	GP	-15.00	-24.00	√

Subtotal	-300.00
Tax	-39.00
Total	-339.00

12/12/10 (J26)	Debits	Credits	Division
1050 Bank: Chequing CAD	339.00	-	
2670 GST Paid on Purchases	-	15.00	
5150 Telephone Expense	-	324.00	
- Sales Division			-97.20
- Service Division			-226.80
	339.00	339.00	

PAYROLL REMITTANCES

Simply Accounting - Confirmation

Adjustment amounts will adjust the amount owing for remittances and create a transaction that will affect the account balances in linked payroll accounts.

If your payroll accounts prior to this adjustment already have the correct balances, you will need to reverse the transaction created by the adjustment by making a miscellaneous transaction (general journal) entry.

Do you want to continue?

[Yes]   [No]

OTHER PAYMENTS

The only change you must make is that positive amounts in the original entry become negative amounts in the reversing entry (place a minus sign before the amount in the Amount field).

Similarly, negative amounts, such as for GST Paid in GST remittances, must be changed to positive amounts (remove the minus sign).

Use the same accounts and amounts in the reversing entry as in the original entry. Tax amounts change automatically.

Repeat the allocation with the original percentages.

You can use the Adjust Invoice and Reverse Invoice options instead (page 131).

PAYROLL REMITTANCES

Payroll remittance entries cannot be reversed. You must make corrections in the Adjustments column of the Remittance Journal if incorrect amounts were remitted. When you enter an amount in the Adjustments column, the program warns you with the message shown here.

Positive remittance adjustment amounts create expense account entries – they do not affect the payable amounts in the ledger. You must make additional General Journal adjusting entries so that the final ledger amounts are correct.

PAYMENTS

Click the Include Fully Paid Invoices tool button.

The change you must make is that positive amounts in the original entry become negative amounts in the reversing entry.

If a discount was taken, click the invoice line for the payment being reversed in the Discount Taken field. Type the discount amount with a minus sign. Press `tab` to enter the payment amount. The minus sign will be added.

If no discount was taken, click the invoice line for the payment being reversed in the Payment Amount field. Type a minus sign and the amount.

Click Yes to continue if you see the warning about posting a negative cheque amount.

This will restore the original balance owing for the invoice.

If you have already cleared the paid invoice, prepare a new Purchases Journal entry for the amount of the payment (non-taxable) to restore the balance owing. Enter a positive amount in the Amount field for the amount of the cheque and the Bank account in the Account field. On the next line, enter the discount amount (positive) with the Purchase Discounts account in the Account field. This will debit the Bank and Purchase Discounts accounts and credit Accounts Payable.

You can also use the Adjust Payment tool or the Reverse Payment feature. (See page 139 and page 179.)

CREDIT CARD PAYMENTS

Enter the same amounts as in the original entry.

Add a minus sign to the Additional Fees And Interest amount and to the Payment Amount in the reversing entry.

PAYMENTS: Original Entry

Due Date	Invoice or Prepayment	Original Amount	Amount Owing	Discount Available	Discount Taken	Payment Amount
Dec 31, 2010	L-4441	565.00	565.00	11.30	11.30	553.70

| Prepayment Reference No. 205 | | | | | Prepayment Amount | 0.00 |
| | | | | | Total | 553.70 |

12/10/10 (J28)		Debits	Credits	Division
2200	Accounts Payable	565.00	-	
1050	Bank: Chequing CAD	-	553.70	
5130	Purchase Discounts	-	11.30	
		565.00	565.00	

Reversing Entry

Due Date	Invoice or Prepayment	Original Amount	Amount Owing	Discount Available	Discount Taken	Payment Amount
Dec 31, 2010	L-4441	565.00	0.00	0.00	-11.30	-553.70
Dec 31, 2010	LTR-100	226.00	0.00	0.00		

| Prepayment Reference No. 205 | | | | | Prepayment Amount | 0.00 |
| | | | | | Total | -553.70 |

12/14/10 (J33)	Debits	Credits	Division
1050 Bank: Chequing CAD	553.70	-	
5130 Purchase Discounts	11.30	-	
2200 Accounts Payable	-	565.00	
	565.00	565.00	

Simply Accounting - Confirmation

This cheque does not have a positive amount and is using a cheque number. Do you want to continue anyway?

[Yes]   [No]

CREDIT CARD PAYMENTS: Original Entry

Credit Card Payable Account Balance:	235.00
Additional Fees and Interest:	20.00
Payment Amount:	150.00

12/13/10 (J34)	Debits	Credits	Division
2250 Credit Card Payable	130.00	-	
5040 Credit Card Fees	20.00	-	
1050 Bank: Chequing CAD	-	150.00	
	150.00	150.00	

Reversing Entry

Credit Card Payable Account Balance:	105.00
Additional Fees and Interest:	-20.00
Payment Amount:	-150.00

12/14/10 (J35)	Debits	Credits	Division
1050 Bank: Chequing CAD	150.00	-	
2250 Credit Card Payable	-	130.00	
5040 Credit Card Fees	-	20.00	
	150.00	150.00	

INVENTORY PURCHASES: Original Entry

Item Number	Quantity	Order	Back Order	Unit	Description	Price	Tax	GST	PST	Amount	Acct	Allo
W101	8			Each	Aluminum R14 Wheels	72.00	G	28.80		576.00	1360 Wheels	
W102	8			Each	Aluminum R15 Wheels	78.00	G	31.20		624.00	1360 Wheels	

☑ Invoice Received

	Subtotal	1,200.00	
Freight G 🔍 5.00		100.00	✔
	GST	65.00	
	PST	0.00	🔍
Terms: 2.00 % 15 Days, Net 30 Days	Total	1,365.00	

12/14/10 (J36)	Debits	Credits	Division
1360 Wheels	1,200.00	-	
2670 GST Paid on Purchases	65.00	-	
5065 Freight Expense	100.00		
- Sales Division			100.00
2200 Accounts Payable	-	1,365.00	
	1,365.00	1,365.00	

Reversing Entry

Item Number	Quantity	Order	Back Order	Unit	Description	Price	Tax	GST	PST	Amount	Acct	Allo
W101	-8			Each	Aluminum R14 Wheels	72.00	G	-28.80		-576.00	1360 Wheels	
W102	-8			Each	Aluminum R15 Wheels	78.00	G	-31.20		-624.00	1360 Wheels	

☑ Invoice Received

	Subtotal	-1,200.00	
Freight G 🔍 -5.00		-100.00	✔
	GST	-65.00	
	PST	0.00	🔍
Terms: 2.00 % 15 Days, Net 30 Days	Total	-1,365.00	
	Amount Owing	-1,365.00	

12/15/10 (J38)	Debits	Credits	Division
2200 Accounts Payable	1,365.00	-	
1360 Wheels	-	1,200.00	
2670 GST Paid on Purchases	-	65.00	
5065 Freight Expense	-	100.00	
- Sales Division			-100.00
	1,365.00	1,365.00	

SALES JOURNAL (INVENTORY AND NON-INVENTORY): Original Entry

Item Number	Quantity	Order	Back Order	Unit	Description	Price	Amount	Tax	Acct	Allo
T101	12			Each	P155/80R14 Tires	65.00	780.00	GP	4020 Revenue from Sales	√
					repairs		200.00	GP	4040 Revenue from Services	√

Comments

	Subtotal	980.00	
	Freight	50.00	G 🔍 ✔
	GST	51.50	
	PST	78.40	🔍
Terms: 2.00 % 10 Days, Net 30 Days	Total	1,159.90	

12/13/10 (J39)	Debits	Credits	Division
1200 Accounts Receivable	1,159.90	-	
5050 Cost of Goods Sold	359.24	-	
- Sales Division			359.24
1400 Winter Tires	-	359.24	
2640 PST Payable	-	78.40	
2650 GST Charged on Sales	-	51.50	
4020 Revenue from Sales	-	780.00	
- Sales Division			780.00
4040 Revenue from Services	-	200.00	
- Service Division			200.00
4190 Freight Revenue	-	50.00	
- Sales Division			50.00
	1,519.14	1,519.14	

INVENTORY PURCHASES

Change positive quantities in the original entry to negative ones in the reversing entry (place a minus sign before the quantity in the Quantity field).

Similarly, change negative quantities, such as for returns, to positive ones (remove the minus sign).

Add a minus sign to the freight amount if freight is charged.

Use the same accounts and amounts in the reversing entry as in the original entry. Tax amounts are corrected automatically.

Repeat the allocation using the original percentages.

You can use the Adjust Invoice and Reverse Invoice options instead (page 129 and page 140).

Remember to "pay" the incorrect and reversing invoices to remove them from the Payments Journal and later clear them.

SALES JOURNAL

For inventory sales, change positive quantities in the original entry to negative ones in the reversing entry (place a minus sign before the quantity in the Quantity field). Similarly, change negative quantities, such as for returns, to positive ones (remove the minus sign).

For non-inventory sales, change positive amounts in the original entry to negative amounts in the reversing entry (place a minus sign before the amount in the Amount column).

Add a minus sign to the freight amount if freight is charged. Add the salesperson.

Use the same accounts and amounts in the reversing entry as in the original entry, and the same method of payment.

Repeat the allocation using the original percentages.

You can use the Adjust Invoice and Reverse Invoice options instead (page 184). Reversing a paid invoice will generate a credit note.

Remember to "pay" the incorrect and reversing invoices to remove them from the Receipts Journal and later clear them.

Reversing Entry

Item Number	Quantity	Order	Back Order	Unit	Description	Price	Amount	Tax	Acct	Allo
T101	-12			Each	P155/80R14 Tires	65.00	-780.00	GP	4020 Revenue from Sales	√
					repairs		-200.00	GP	4040 Revenue from Services	√

Comments	Subtotal -980.00
	Freight -50.00 G
	GST -51.50
	PST -78.40
Terms: 2.00 % 10 Days, Net 30 Days	Total -1,159.90
	Amount Owing -1,159.90

12/15/10 (J41)	Debits	Credits	Division
1400 Winter Tires	359.24	-	
2640 PST Payable	78.40	-	
2650 GST Charged on Sales	51.50	-	
4020 Revenue from Sales	780.00	-	
- Sales Division			-780.00
4040 Revenue from Services	200.00	-	
- Service Division			-200.00
4190 Freight Revenue	50.00	-	
- Sales Division			-50.00
1200 Accounts Receivable	-	1,159.90	
5050 Cost of Goods Sold	-	359.24	
- Sales Division			-359.24
	1,519.14	1,519.14	

DEPOSITS

You cannot enter a negative amount in the Deposit field so you must "pay" the deposit.

Click the Payment Amount field for the Deposit line and press ⌈tab⌋. Deposit amounts are shown in red under the heading Deposits.

DEPOSITS or PREPAYMENTS: Original Entry

Invoice Date	Invoice or Deposit	Original Amount	Amount Owing	Discount Available	Discount Taken	Amount Received
Dec 15, 2010	130	866.10	866.10	17.32		

Deposit Reference No. 14	Deposit Amount 500.00
	Total 500.00

12/19/10 (J42)	Debits	Credits	Division
1050 Bank: Chequing CAD	500.00	-	
2150 Prepaid Sales and Deposits	-	500.00	
	500.00	500.00	

Reversing Entry

Invoice Date	Invoice or Deposit	Original Amount	Amount Owing	Discount Available	Discount Taken	Amount Received
Dec 15, 2010	130	866.10	866.10	17.32		
	Deposits					
	14	500.00	500.00			500.00

Deposit Reference No. 15	Deposit Amount 0.00
	Total -500.00

12/19/10 (J43)	Debits	Credits	Division
2150 Prepaid Sales and Deposits	500.00	-	
1050 Bank: Chequing CAD	-	500.00	
	500.00	500.00	

NOTES

When you post the transaction, you will be asked to confirm that you want to make the payment to the customer.

Click Yes to continue.

Simply Accounting - Confirmation

The total of the deposits being used is more than the total of the invoices being paid. This means that you are about to give the difference back to the customer in cash. Do you want to continue?

[Yes]   [No]

RECEIPTS WITH DEPOSITS: Original Entry

Invoice Date	Invoice or Deposit	Original Amount	Amount Owing	Discount Available	Discount Taken	Amount Received
Dec 15, 2010	130	866.10	866.10	17.32	17.32	848.78
	Deposits					
	14	500.00	500.00			500.00

Deposit Reference No. 15				Deposit Amount		0.00
				Total		348.78

12/22/10 (J43)	Debits	Credits	Division
1050 Bank: Chequing CAD	348.78	-	
2150 Prepaid Sales and Deposits	500.00	-	
4150 Sales Discounts	17.32	-	
1200 Accounts Receivable	-	866.10	
	866.10	866.10	

Reversing Entry

Invoice Date	Invoice or Deposit	Original Amount	Amount Owing	Discount Available	Discount Taken	Amount Received
Nov 29, 2010	124	1,017.00	0.00	0.00		
Dec 15, 2010	130	866.10	0.00	0.00	-17.32	-848.78
	Deposits					
	14	500.00	0.00			-500.00

Deposit Reference No. 15				Deposit Amount		0.00
				Total		-348.78

12/23/10 (J44)	Debits	Credits	Division
1200 Accounts Receivable	866.10	-	
1050 Bank: Chequing CAD	-	348.78	
2150 Prepaid Sales and Deposits	-	500.00	
4150 Sales Discounts	-	17.32	
	866.10	866.10	

PAYROLL JOURNAL: Original Entry

Income | Deductions | Taxes | User-Defined Expense | Entitlements   Period Ending Dec 24, 2010

Earnings:

Name	Hours	Pieces	Amount	YTD
Regular	80.00	--	1,280.00	31,360.00
Overtime 1	5.00	--	120.00	936.00
Piece Rate	--	10.00	50.00	50.00
Bonus	--	--	100.00	100.00
Total	85.00	10.00	1,550.00	

Other:

Name	Amount	YTD
Advance	200.00	200.00
Benefits	35.00	35.00
Vac. Accrued	58.00	1,911.00
Vac. Paid	0.00	--
Total	293.00	

Gross Pay	1,585.00	Withheld	-422.01	Net Pay	1,327.99	Post

Income | Deductions | Taxes | User-Defined Expense | Entitlements

Deductions:

Name	Amount	YTD
CSB	50.00	50.00
Union Dues	15.85	324.81
Total	65.85	

Income | Deductions | Taxes | User-Defined Expense | Entitlements

EI	25.09	QPIP
CPP/QPP	71.79	
Tax	259.28	
Tax (Que)		

Income | Deductions | Taxes | User-Defined Expense | Entitlements

	Amount per pay period
Medical prem	30.00

Income | Deductions | Taxes | User-Defined Expense | Entitlements

The number of hours worked in this pay period: 80.00

	Days Earned	Days Released
Vacation		
Sick Leave	0.50	1.00
Personal Day	0.25	

RECEIPTS

Click the Include Fully Paid Invoices tool.

Change positive amounts in the original entry to negative amounts in the reversing entry.

If a discount was taken, click the invoice line for the payment being reversed in the Discount Taken field. Type the discount amount with a minus sign. Press (tab) to enter the payment amount. The minus sign will be added. Type a minus sign and enter the amount for the deposit.

If no discount was taken, click the invoice line for the payment being reversed in the Payment Amount field. Type a minus sign and the amount for invoices and deposits.

This will restore the original balance owing for the invoice.

If you have already cleared the invoice, make a new Sales Journal entry for the payment amount (non-taxable) to restore the balance owing. Enter both the cheque and discount amounts as positive amounts to credit Bank and Sales Discounts.

You can use the Adjust Receipt and Reverse Receipt options instead (page 179).

If the NSF cheque uses a different bank account from the deposit entry, you must reverse the receipt manually. Choose the Bank account in the Deposit To field.

PAYROLL JOURNAL

Redo the original incorrect entry but DO NOT POST IT!

Click the Enter Taxes Manually tool to open all the deduction fields for editing.

Type a minus sign in front of the number of hours (regular and overtime) or in front of the Salary and Commission amounts. Press (tab) to update the amounts, including vacation pay (i.e., change them to negative amounts).

For the Advance field, change the sign for the amount. Advances should have a minus sign in the reversing entry and advances recovered should be positive amounts. ▶

PAYROLL JOURNAL CONTINUED

▶ Click the Deductions tab and edit each deduction amount by typing a minus sign in front of it.

Click the Taxes tab. Check the amounts for CPP, EI and Tax with the original journal entry because these amounts may be incorrect (the employee may have reached the maximum contribution since the original entry, or may have entered a different tax bracket). Change the amounts to match the original entry if necessary. The Employee Detail Report will provide the amounts entered for each paycheque.

Click the User-Defined Expenses tab. Change the original positive amounts to negative by adding a minus sign.

Click the Entitlements tab. You cannot enter a negative number for days released so you must edit the number of days earned. Click the number in the Days Earned field for the entitlements taken. Add back the number of days released from the original entry. For example, change 0.5 to 1.5 if 1 day was taken.

Repeat the allocation with the original percentages.

Remember to click the Calculate Taxes Automatically button before you make the correct payroll entry.

The year-to-date balances will be restored.

You can use the Adjust Cheque option or Reverse Cheque instead to reverse and correct the Payroll Journal entry (see page 279 and page 282). Using the reverse cheque approach may be safer, as payroll transactions are complex.

12/24/10 (J45)		Debits	Credits	Division
1210	Advances Payable	200.00	-	
5310	General Wages	1,458.00	-	
5320	Piece Rate Wage Expense	50.00	-	
5330	Commissions and Bonuses	100.00	-	
5375	Medical Premium Expense	30.00	-	
5410	EI Expense	35.13	-	
5420	CPP Expense	71.79	-	
5430	WSIB Expense	53.89	-	
5460	EHT Expense	15.53	-	
1050	Bank: Chequing CAD	-	1,327.99	
2300	Vacation Payable	-	58.00	
2310	EI Payable	-	60.22	
2320	CPP Payable	-	143.58	
2330	Income Tax Payable	-	259.28	
2390	EHT Payable	-	15.53	
2400	CSB Payable	-	50.00	
2410	Union Dues Payable	-	15.85	
2460	WSIB Payable	-	53.89	
2465	Medical Payable	-	30.00	
		2,014.34	2,014.34	

Reversing Entry

| Income | Deductions | Taxes | User-Defined Expense | Entitlements | | Period Ending | Dec 24, 2010 |

Earnings:

Name	Hours	Pieces	Amount	YTD
Regular	-80.00	--	-1,280.00	28,800.00
Overtime 1	-5.00	--	-120.00	696.00
Piece Rate	--	-10.00	-50.00	-50.00
Bonus	--	--	-100.00	-100.00
Total	-85.00	-10.00	-1,550.00	

Other:

Name	Amount	YTD
Advance	-200.00	-200.00
Benefits	-35.00	-35.00
Vac. Accrued	-58.00	1,795.00
Vac. Paid	0.00	--
Total	-293.00	

Gross Pay -1,585.00 Withheld   422.01 Net Pay   -1,327.99   👤 Post

| Income | Deductions | Taxes | User-Defined Expense | Entitlements |

Deductions:

Name	Amount	YTD
CSB	-50.00	-50.00
Union Dues	-15.85	293.11
Total	-65.85	

| Income | Deductions | Taxes | User-Defined Expense | Entitlements |

EI	-25.09	QPIP
CPP/QPP	-71.79	
Tax	-259.28	
Tax (Que)		

| Income | Deductions | Taxes | User-Defined Expense | Entitlements |

Amount per pay period

Medical prem	-30.00

| Income | Deductions | Taxes | User-Defined Expense | Entitlements |

The number of hours worked in this pay period: -80.00

	Days Earned	Days Released
Vacation		
Sick Leave	1.50	
Personal Day		

12/24/10 (J46)		Debits	Credits	Division
1050	Bank: Chequing CAD	1,327.99	-	
2300	Vacation Payable	58.00	-	
2310	EI Payable	60.22	-	
2320	CPP Payable	143.58	-	
2330	Income Tax Payable	259.28	-	
2390	EHT Payable	15.53	-	
2400	CSB Payable	50.00	-	
2410	Union Dues Payable	15.85	-	
2460	WSIB Payable	53.89	-	
2465	Medical Payable	30.00	-	
1210	Advances Payable	-	200.00	
5310	General Wages	-	1,458.00	
5320	Piece Rate Wage Expense	-	50.00	
5330	Commissions and Bonuses	-	100.00	
5375	Medical Premium Expense	-	30.00	
5410	EI Expense	-	35.13	
5420	CPP Expense	-	71.79	
5430	WSIB Expense	-	53.89	
5460	EHT Expense	-	15.53	
		2,014.34	2,014.34	

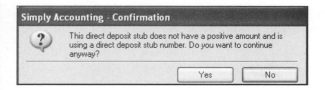

NOTES
When you are reversing a direct deposit entry, you must confirm that a negative amount is entered as the net deposit.
Click Yes to continue.

ITEM ASSEMBLY JOURNAL: Original Entry

Assembly Components

Item	Qty	Unit	Description	Unit Cost	Amount
T104	20	Each	P205/75R15 Tires	40.00	800.00
W101	20	Each	Aluminum R14 Wheels	72.00	1,440.00
			Additional Costs		200.00
			Total		2,440.00

Assembled Items

Item	Qty	Unit	Description	Unit Cost	Amount
WHP1	5	pkg	Tires/Wheels/Winter Pkg	488.00	2,440.00
			Total		2,440.00

12/24/10 (J47)		Debits	Credits	Division
1420	Winter-Holiday Tire Packages	2,440.00	-	
1360	Wheels	-	1,440.00	
1400	Winter Tires	-	800.00	
5045	Assembly Costs	-	200.00	
		2,440.00	2,440.00	

ITEM ASSEMBLY JOURNAL
Re-enter the assembly as you did originally.
Type a minus sign in front of each quantity in the Qty field in both the Assembly Components and Assembled Items sections.
Also type a minus sign in front of the amount for Additional Costs.

Reversing Entry

Assembly Components

Item	Qty	Unit	Description	Unit Cost	Amount
T104	-20	Each	P205/75R15 Tires	40.00	-800.00
W101	-20	Each	Aluminum R14 Wheels	72.00	-1,440.00
			Additional Costs		-200.00
			Total		-2,440.00

Assembled Items

Item	Qty	Unit	Description	Unit Cost	Amount
WHP1	-5	pkg	Tires/Wheels/Winter Pkg	488.00	-2,440.00
			Total		-2,440.00

12/24/10 (J48)		Debits	Credits	Division
1360	Wheels	1,440.00	-	
1400	Winter Tires	800.00	-	
5045	Assembly Costs	200.00	-	
1420	Winter-Holiday Tire Packages	-	2,440.00	
		2,440.00	2,440.00	

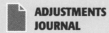

ADJUSTMENTS JOURNAL

Change the sign for the quantity in the Qty field (positive to negative or negative to positive).

Repeat the allocation using the original percentages.

ADJUSTMENTS JOURNAL: Original Entry

Item	Qty	Unit	Description	Unit Cost	Amount	Acct	Allo
T108	-2	Each	P185/60R15 Tires	48.00	-96.00	5100 Invenl	✓
				Total	-96.00		

12/25/10 (J49)	Debits	Credits	Division
5100 Inventory Adjustment	96.00	-	
- Sales Division			96.00
1400 Winter Tires	-	96.00	
	96.00	96.00	

Reversing Entry

Item	Qty	Unit	Description	Unit Cost	Amount	Acct	Allo
T108	2	Each	P185/60R15 Tires	48.00	96.00	5100 Invenl	✓
				Total	96.00		

12/25/10 (J50)	Debits	Credits	Division
1400 Winter Tires	96.00	-	
5100 Inventory Adjustment	-	96.00	
- Sales Division			-96.00
	96.00	96.00	

TRANSFER FUNDS JOURNAL: Original Entry

Currency:	JPY ▾ Exchange Rate: 0.0100000 $
Transfer from:	1050 Bank: Chequing CAD ▾
Transfer to:	1060 Bank: Foreign Currency ▾
Amount:	200,000 **JPY**
Comment:	Transfer to cover cheque

TRANSFER FUNDS JOURNAL

The easiest way to reverse the transfer is to enter the same amounts but switch the bank accounts. Enter the original Transfer From account in the Deposit To field. Enter the original Deposit To account in the Deposit From field.

There is no journal entry to review. You can see the reversal in the General Journal Report. The two related General Journal Report entries are shown here.

You can also use the Adjust Entry or Reverse Entry procedure for the transfer in the General Journal. When you look up transactions, the transfer entry is included. You can select it and then adjust it or reverse it like any other General Journal transaction (page 43 and page 45).

Reversing Entry

Currency:	JPY ▾ Exchange Rate: 0.0100000 $
Transfer from:	1060 Bank: Foreign Currency ▾
Transfer to:	1050 Bank: Chequing CAD ▾
Amount:	200,000 **JPY**
Comment:	reversing funds transfer

			Account Number	Account Description	Debits	Credits	Foreign A...
12/24/10	J51		FundsTransfer, Transfer to cover cheque				
			1060	Bank: Foreign Currency	2,000.00	-	¥200,000
			1050	Bank: Chequing CAD	-	2,000.00	¥200,000
1 Japanese Yen equals 0.0100000 Canadian Dollars							
12/24/10	J52		FundsTransfer, reversing funds transfer				
			1050	Bank: Chequing CAD	2,000.00	-	¥200,000
			1060	Bank: Foreign Currency	-	2,000.00	¥200,000
1 Japanese Yen equals 0.0100000 Canadian Dollars							

BILL OF MATERIALS JOURNAL: Original Entry

Items to Build

Item	Unit	Description	Quantity to build
AP100	Package	Promotional Fitness Package	2

07/31/10 (J5)	Debits	Credits	Division
1510 Promotions	192.00	-	
1520 Accessories	-	192.00	
	192.00	192.00	

Reversing Entry

Items to Build

Item	Unit	Description	Quantity to build
AP100 🔍	Package	Promotional Fitness Package	-2

07/31/10 (J6)	Debits	Credits	Division
1520 Accessories	192.00	-	
1510 Promotions	-	192.00	
	192.00	192.00	

TRANSFER INVENTORY JOURNAL: Original Entry

Transfer between Locations ▾	From	Hamilton ▾	to	Burlington ▾
Source	Memo 48		Date	Jul 16, 2010 🖩
Comment	Inventory transfer to new store			

Item	Qty	Unit	Description	Unit Cost	Amount
A030 🔍	100	kg 🔍	Dumbells: pair	0.75	75.00

Reversing Entry

Transfer between Locations ▾	From	Burlington ▾	to	Hamilton ▾
Source	Memo 49		Date	Jul 16, 2010 🖩
Comment	Reverse inventory transfer			

Item	Qty	Unit	Description	Unit Cost	Amount
A030 🔍	100	kg 🔍	Dumbells: pair	0.75	75.00

BILL OF MATERIALS JOURNAL

Change the sign for the quantity in the Quantity To Build field (positive to negative or negative to positive).

Notice that the journal entries are exactly the same as those for the Item Assembly Journal transactions.

TRANSFER INVENTORY JOURNAL

Enter the transaction in the same way as the original one with one change — add a minus sign to the quantity in the Qty field.

No journal entry results from this transaction. However, the inventory ledger records will be updated for both locations.

Working in Multi-User Mode

WORKING IN MULTI-USER MODE

The Premium version is available in multi- and single-user versions. The Student Premium and Simply versions are both single-user versions of the program.

In multi-user mode, several people can access and work with a data file at the same time. Some features and functions are not available in multi-user mode. These restrictions are described in the text whenever they apply. Access to some aspects of the program may be restricted to the system administrator (sysadmin).

Accessing Data Files

The Premium version allows several users to access the data files at the same time, with or without passwords. When no users and passwords are set up for a data file, access to the file is the same for multi- and single-user mode. The data file opens in single-user mode. Once the data file is open, you can switch to multi-user mode from the File menu.

If you try to open a data file that is currently used by another user in single-user mode, you will see the following error message:

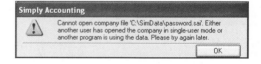

Click   OK to close the message.

Only one person at a time can work with a data file in single-user mode, so you must switch the status of the open file to multi-user.

Choose the **File menu** and **click Switch To Multi-User Mode**.

If you have not entered users, the Add Users wizard will begin (see the instructions in Appendix H, page A-90 on the Student CD-ROM). Otherwise, you will see the following warning:

WARNING!
Be sure to finish working with the open journals and ledgers before closing all the open windows.

Click   Yes to proceed.

No changes are apparent in the Home window, but some menu options are dimmed because they are not available in multi-user mode. All Refresh tools in the ledger and journal windows will be available and no longer dimmed.

If users and passwords have been set up for the program, you will see the following screen when you open the data file:

Enter your user name and password; choose whether you want to work in single-user or multi-user mode and then click OK. Passwords are case sensitive. That is, you must type the password in upper- or lower-case letters, exactly as the password was created initially. For more information on passwords, refer to Appendix H on the Student CD-ROM.

If another user is already working with the data file when you try to access it in single-user mode, you will see the following warning:

You must open the data file in multi-user mode, wait until the other users have finished or, if only one person is using the file, switch that user's file to multi-user mode.

Click   **OK** to return to the Select Company window.

To switch to single-user mode at any time:

Choose the **File menu** and **click Switch To Single-User Mode**.

If other users are currently using the file, you will see the following warning:

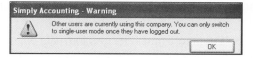

Click   **OK** to return to the Home window.

If you are working in multi-user mode, your user name and "Multi-user" will appear in the status bar in the Classic view as shown:

When you close a data file in multi-user mode, you will see the following closing message about backups:

Before making a backup, you must switch to single-user mode. If other users are still working with the data file, close the file without making a backup.

Click   **Yes** to close the file.

Refreshing Data in Multi-User Mode

In multi-user mode, different users can work with and modify the same data file at the same time. Therefore, the program allows you to automatically refresh the data set with changes made by other users or to refresh the data set only when the Refresh option is selected. All ledger, journal and report windows include Refresh tools that allow you to update the data periodically. If you want the program to update the data continually, you can change this preference setting for individual users.

Choose the **Setup menu**, then **choose User Preferences** and **click Options**:

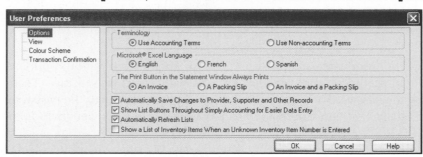

Click   **Automatically Refresh Lists** to change the setting.

Click   **OK** to save the change.

Refresh Tools

All journals have the **Refresh Lists** tool in the tool bar 🖼. This tool applies to the multi-user mode — different users use, access and modify the company data files simultaneously. Clicking the Refresh Lists tool ensures that you use the most recent version of the data set — the one that exists after all changes from all users have been applied.

All report windows include the **Refresh Report** tool icon 🔲. In multi-user mode, the journal entry number is omitted from the journal display (different users may be creating journal entries at the same time so the number is not known for certain until after posting).

The **Refresh Invoices** tool 🖼 in the Payments and Receipts journals ensures that the list of outstanding invoices for a vendor or customer is the current one, after applying the changes made by other users.

The **Refresh Data** tool 🔲 in the icon windows looks the same as the Refresh Report icon and serves the same purpose, updating accounts (vendors, customers, employees or inventory) with changes made by other users. It appears just before the Select A Report tool in all ledger icon windows. The icon is dimmed in single-user mode and when you are creating a new ledger record.

In ledger windows, the **Refresh Record tool** 🔲 updates the ledger record with changes made by other users. The tool is located on the Select account line in the ledger and looks the same as the Refresh Report tool.

A

abbreviations, 2–3
access rights, A–87, A–88
accessing
  see also opening
  data files, 6–7, 112
  data files, in multi-user mode, A–28–A–29
  Purchases Journal, 113
  Report Centre, 142
  saved reports, A–73–A–74
  supplier's Web site, 472–474
account class
  available account classes, 219
  Bank class, 218, 470
  credit card accounts, 220, 419
  default classes, 90
  default selection, 43
  described, 218
  entering, 218–220
  expense accounts, 220
  Gross Margin Income Statement, 395
  payroll and inventory setup, 637–638
Account List, 55–56
account reconciliation
  see also Reconciliation & Deposits Journal
  Add Prior Outstanding, 595
  adding account statement journal entries, 599–602
  bank statement reconciliation, 591–602
  clearing data, 608
  comparison of bank statement and transaction report, 591–593
  credit card bank account, 602
  described, 588
  displaying banking reports, 602–605
  group deposits, 596–597
  linked accounts, 589–591
  marking journal entries as cleared, 596–599
  naming reconciliation accounts, 589–591
  NSF cheques, 598–599
  online reconciliation, 582, 588
  reconciling the account, 593–596
  show corrections, 596
  showing deposit slip details, 597–598
  turning on account reconciliation feature, 588–589
Account Reconciliation Journal. *see* Reconciliation & Deposits Journal
Account Reconciliation Report, 604
account type, 42, 83

accountant's copy, 489–490, 492
accountant's journal entries, importing, 492–494
accounting basics
  accrual-basis accounting, A–124–A–125
  assets, A–115
  audit trail, A–121
  Balance Sheet, A–115–A–117
  basic accounting equation, A–117
  cash-basis accounting, A–124–A–125
  contra-accounts, A–120–A–121
  debits and credits, A–118, A–126
  equity, A–116
  expenses, A–117
  Generally Accepted Accounting Principles (GAAP), A–122–A–124
  Income Statement, A–117
  journal entries, A–118
  ledgers, A–118–A–120
  liabilities, A–116
  net income (loss), A–117
  revenues, A–117
  summary of account changes, A–120
  trial balance, A–120
accounting equation, A–117
accounting terms, A–15, 78
accounting transactions summary, A–126
accounts
  see also specific accounts
  account class. *See* account class
  account type, 42, 83
  Add An Account wizard, 248
  adding departments, 790–791
  asset accounts, 174, 222
  changing account numbers, 92
  deleting accounts, 58
  editing accounts in General Ledger, 87–88
  expense accounts. *See* expense accounts
  group accounts, 84
  input fields, 78
  inventory asset account, 370
  linked accounts. *See* linked accounts
  list of accounts, 37
  new accounts. *See* new accounts
  number of digits, 77
  numbering of, 37, 77
  organization of, 37, 83, 84
  postable account, 84
  revenue accounts, 366
  subgroup accounts, 84
  subgroup total account, 84–85
  subtotal, 42
accounts payable
  adjustment of posted invoice, 129–131
  adjustment of posted payment, 139–140
  automatic update, 116
  cash purchases, 121–123, 128–129
  changing a stored entry, 141–142
  Continue feature, 133–134
  discounts for early payments, 131–134

  displaying supplier reports, 142–148
  editing supplier record, 138–139
  graphing supplier reports, 149–150
  new supplier records, adding, 124–129
  open-invoice accounting, 106, 204–205
  opening data files, 112
  payments, accounting for, 118–121
  printing supplier reports, 148–149
  purchases, accounting for, 113–117
  recall of stored entry, 137–138
  recurring journal entry, 117–118
  reversal of posted purchase entry, 140–141
  sales taxes in General Journal, 134–137
  setup. *See* receivables and payables setup
  terminology, 228
accounts receivable
  adding new customer, 174–179
  adjustment of posted Sales Journal entry, 184–186
  cash sales, 172–174
  credit card sales, 182–184
  customization of sales invoice, 166–168
  discounts for early payments, 154, 168, 171
  displaying cash flow reports, 192–194
  displaying customer reports, 187–191
  displaying tax reports, 191–192
  editing customer record, 181–182
  graphing customer reports, 195–198
  NSF cheques, 154, 179–181
  open-invoice accounting, 154, 204–205
  opening data files, 162
  printing customer reports, 194–195
  receipts, accounting for, 168–172
  recurring sales entry, 184
  reversing a receipt, 179–181
  sales, accounting for, 162–168
  setup. *See* receivables and payables setup
  shortcuts for other transactions, 186–187
Accounts window, 88–92
accrual-basis accounting, 74, A–124–A–125
activity reports, 775
Activity Time and Billing Report, 777
Add An Account wizard, 248, 676
Add Users wizard, A–90–A–92
Additional Date and Field, 40
Additional Information tool, 419–420
adjustments
  see also corrections; editing; errors; reversing entries
  for bad debts, 628–629
  closing adjusting entries, 98–99
  date of adjusting entry, 45
  and deposit slips, 581
  General Journal entry, 43–45
  inventory adjustments, 371–373
  opening balances, 92
  payments, 121

customer statements, 194–195
Customer Time & Billing Report, 775–776
customers
see also Sales Journal
adding departments to records, 793–794
adding new customer, 174–179
clearing paid client transactions, 607–608
clearing paid supplier transactions, 607
Credit Limit field, 178
customer reports. *See* customer reports
default comments, 231–232
default revenue account, 164
deposits, 424–426
editing customer record, 181–182
entering in Receivables Ledger, 241–244, 663–664
foreign customers, 457, 477–480
Full Add, 175
historical client information, 244–247
historical customer information, 664–665
inactive, 611
Internal Customer option, 175, 176
language for conducting business, 177–178
multiple customer addresses, 176, 242–243
one-time customer, 183
Options tab screen, 177–178
payment terms, 177
preferred customers, 383–384
Quick Add, 175
removal of records, 611–612
salespersons, adding to client records, 340
saving a new customer account, 179
saving the client record, 247
session date, 176
Ship-To Address screen, 242–243
shipping address, 176, 177
tax options, 178
customization
accessing saved reports, A–73–A–74
all or individual journals, 81
customer statements, 194–195
deposit slip and reconciliation transaction reports, 605
Expenses Journal, 414–415
filtering reports, A–69–A–70
generally, A–65–A–66
Microsoft Office reports, A–98–A–103

orders and quotes, 167
print options, A–74–A–75
removal of customization details, A–76
report columns, A–66–A–67
report groups, A–71–A–73
sales invoices, A–77–A–82, 166–168
saving new report template, A–70–A–71
sorting reports, A–67–A–68
terminology, 228, 232

D

Daily Business Manager
business performance, 448
discounts, using, 627
fees (sales) due, 443–444
Memo tab screen, 237
opening, 439–440
payments due, 440–441
posting from, 446–448
purchase orders due, 445
recurring transactions due, 442–443
reminders, 79
removing recurring transactions, 445–446
sales order due, 444
tab screens, 440
damaged items, 372, 658
data files
accessing, 6–7
accessing, in multi-user mode, A–28–A–29
described, 2–3
importing and exporting data. *See* integration with other software
installation, 5–6
opening a working copy, 20–21
opening data files, 34–36, 112, 162, 413, 466
opening from backup, 7–10
supplementary files, 5–6
date formats, 18–19, 35, 73, 76, 163, 208, 214, 634
date settings, 18–19
debit card transactions, 222, 403, 433–435
debits, A–118, A–126
deductions, 274, 316, 319–320, 330, 654–655, 669–670
Deductions and Expenses reports, 304
default comments, 231–232, 649
default expense account, 126
default Home window, 70
default revenue account, 164, 366
default settings
backup options, 75, 212–213, 633
company features, 75–76, 213, 633
company information, changing, 212, 633
company logo, 76–77, 215, 634
company settings, 71–74, 638–641
credit cards, 638
date formats, 76, 214, 634
default names, 635
e-mail defaults, 214

forms, 213–214, 633–634
general defaults, 77
general ledger setup, changing in, 71–77
payables default settings, 227
payroll and inventory setup, changing in, 633–635
printer defaults, 81–82, 215, 644–645
receivables and payables setup, changing in, 212–215
receivables default settings, 229–231
sales taxes, 638–641
system defaults, 74–75, 212, 633
transaction confirmation, 80
View menu settings, 80–82
view settings, 78–79
deleting accounts, 58
department reports, 801–803
departmental accounting
accounts, adding departments to, 790–791
client records, adding departments to, 793–794
creating departments, 788–790
department code, 789
department reports, 801–803
finishing the history, 793
journal transactions, adding departments to, 795–800
opening departmental balances, 791–795
payroll transactions, 798–800
purchases, 795–796
receipts, 796–797
sales, 797–798
setting up departments, 788–791
shortcuts for journals, 795
and Simply Accounting 2008 (Release B), 77
standard discount field, 794
unallocated amounts, 800
vendor records, adding departments to, 794–795
departmental balance sheets, 801–802
departmental income statement, 802
departmental trial balance, 802
Deposit Slip Report, 605
deposit slips
see also Reconciliation & Deposits Journal
corrections, 588
entering deposit slips, 581–588
group deposits, 596–597
lookup data, clearing, 610
posting the entry, 588
previewing, 587
reviewing the entry, 587–588
sequencing, 219
showing details, 597–598
deposits
see also prepayments
customer deposits, 424–426
entering receipts, 431–432
initial liability, 432